TOURISM
PRINCIPLES AND PRACTICE

Visit the *Tourism: Principles and Practice*, fourth edition Companion Website with Grade Tracker at **www.pearsoned.co.uk/cooper** to find valuable **student** learning material including:

- Multiple choice questions to test your learning before and after reading each chapter
- Annotated links to relevant sites on the web
- Flashcards to test your understanding of key terms
- An online glossary to explain key terms
- Interactive media resources, including video cases, flash animations and extra cases
- A full compendium of chapter bibliographies for you to print out and take with you to the library

"This is a remarkable book on tourism. Tourism is essentially a 'normal' economic sector of great importance, although it often prompts feelings of imagination and fascination. This book offers a sound analysis of the tourism sector and provides many original and solid insights to both students and teachers."

Peter Nijkamp, Free University Amsterdam

"A great part of this book is devoted to tables, pictures and graphs which I find really useful to describe the issues of Tourism. Case studies spread throughout the text are very useful too and help to understand the topics by providing a different, empirical, point of view. The authors have made a great effort in the book and as a result the title '*Principles and Practice*' is not just a title – it is instead something which strictly addresses the issues."

Mara Thiene, University of Padova

"This is an outstanding textbook for undergraduate students interested in understanding the fundamental issues of tourism. The authors provide in a single volume a comprehensive coverage of all the major aspects of this subject for those starting out in this field. By combining a sound theoretical explanation of tourism demand and a comprehensive description of the structure of the tourism sector and its impacts with actual case studies this work keeps the reader in touch with the real world of this fast growing industry. The vast experience of the writers in teaching and research enable them to make complex issues accessible and interesting to a wide international audience."

Aliza Fleischer, Hebrew University of Jerusalem

"The new edition of *Tourism Principles and Practice* by Cooper *et al.* continues to be a must-have for all the students of tourism worldwide. Not only does it offer the basic outline of how the tourism system operates but it also provides a comprehensive understanding of the constant changes in the environment in which tourism operates. Special attention has been paid to the challenges of the cutting edge of tourism development.

It is a challenging read which attracts the reader to find out more about all the controversies in this field and offers an unbiased insight into both sides of the coin – leaving the students to draw their own conclusions and preparing them to rise to the challenges in their future positions. Instead of ready-made answers it fosters opportunities for re-examining the multifaceted issues of this complex and highly important sector of the world economy.

The new edition of this coursebook surprises the students with even more of the myths and realities about tourism in the 21st century. The book has been enhanced by a series of fresh, carefully selected, case studies provoking the students to scrutinise the realities of tourism practice.

Chapter 10 is a valuable asset to the book discussing the reality of today's tourism – Crises. It analyses destination risks generated by natural and man-made disasters including impacts of climate change on tourism. The benefits of addressing these issues are paramount to understanding the perception of risks involved in this business.

The offered teaching methodologies and philosophies are an important feature of this book that can only serve to enhance the classroom interaction that will occur later in real life."

Professor Nevenka Čavlek, University of Zagreb

Chris Cooper, John Fletcher, Alan Fyall, David Gilbert and Stephen Wanhill

TOURISM

Fourth Edition

PRINCIPLES AND PRACTICE

FT **Prentice Hall**
FINANCIAL TIMES

An imprint of **Pearson Education**
Harlow, England • London • New York • Boston • San Francisco • Toronto
Sydney • Tokyo • Singapore • Hong Kong • Seoul • Taipei • New Delhi
Cape Town • Madrid • Mexico City • Amsterdam • Munich • Paris • Milan

Pearson Education Limited
Edinburgh Gate
Harlow
Essex CM20 2JE
England

and Associated Companies throughout the world

Visit us on the World Wide Web at:
www.pearsoned.co.uk

First published 1993
Second edition 1998
Third edition 2005
Fourth edition published 2008

ISBN: 978-0-273-71126-1

British Library Cataloguing-in-Publication Data
A catalogue record for this book is available from the British Library

Library of Congress Cataloging-in-Publication Data
Tourism : principles and practices / Chris Cooper . . . [et al.]. — 4th ed.
      p. cm.
   Includes bibliographical references and index.
   ISBN 978-0-273-71126-1 (alk. paper)
   1. Tourism.   I. Cooper, Chris, 1952–
G155.A1T5892 2008
338.4'791–dc22

                                         2008001813

10 9 8 7 6 5 4 3 2 1
12 11 10 09 08

Typeset in 10/12pt Minion by 35
Printed and bound in Italy by Rotolito Lombarda, Milan

The publisher's policy is to use paper manufactured from sustainable forests.

BRIEF CONTENTS

CONTENTS

Photograph: Fruit market, Chennai, India © Katherine Harding

Supporting resources

Visit **www.pearsoned.co.uk/cooper** to find valuable online resources

Companion Website for students
- Multiple choice questions to test your learning before and after reading each chapter
- Annotated links to relevant sites on the web
- Flashcards to test your understanding of key terms
- An online glossary to explain key terms
- Interactive media resources, including video cases, flash animations and extra cases
- A full compendium of chapter bibliographies for you to print out and take with you to the library

For instructors
- Customisable PowerPoint slides, including key figures and tables from the main text
- A fully updated Instructor's Manual, including sample answers for all question material in the book
- A video case study of tourism in Mumbai
- Testbank of question material

Also: The Companion Website provides the following features:

- Search tool to help locate specific items of content
- E-mail results and profile tools to send results of quizzes to instructors
- Online help and support to assist with website usage and troubleshooting

For more information please contact your local Pearson Education sales representative or visit **www.pearsoned.co.uk/cooper**

GUIDED TOUR

CHAPTER 4
Tourism Demand Determinants and Forecasting

LEARNING OUTCOMES

The purpose of this chapter is to introduce and discuss determinants of demand and forecasting approaches. We then draw together the chapter by reviewing the major trends in the patterns of demand for tourism from historic and regional perspectives in the major case study. This chapter is designed to provide you with:

- familiarity with the determinants of demand which, at an individual level, are likely to affect propensity to travel;
- an understanding of social, technological, economic and political influences on tourism demand;
- an awareness of the reasons for forecasting demand for tourism;
- an understanding of the major approaches to forecasting demand for tourism; and
- an appreciation and explanation of the key historic and regional patterns of demand for tourism.

Photograph: Beach at Ko Wua Taleb, Ang Thong National Plan, Thailand © Kelly Mina

---

Stunning **colour photography** introduces each chapter and theme, bringing to life a variety of key tourist destinations

Learning outcomes enable you to focus on what you should achieve by reading the chapter

Chapter **introductions** concisely describe the themes and issues explored in each chapter, helping you to assess the importance of the chapter to each specific stage of your studies

Key terms are highlighted throughout the text: definitions are listed in a full Glossary at the end of the book, creating a particularly useful revision tool

Mini case studies concentrate on specific destinations and organisations to illustrate theory, practice, issues and controversies in the tourism industry

Each chapter ends with **self-check questions** for you to test your understanding and track your progress

If you want to explore topics further, **essay questions** encourage stimulating debates and class exercises

Annotated **further reading** sections support the chapter, directing you towards other valuable sources of information

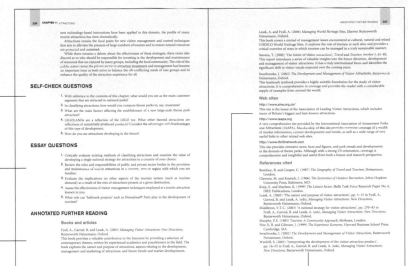

A list of **web sites** relevant to the topics discussed in each chapter provides links to current tourism practice in the real world

References cited within each chapter are listed, encouraging you to read more widely in the subjects that interest you

Long, colourfully illustrated and up-to-date **Case studies** at the end of chapters consolidate the major themes by applying the principles to real-life tourism situations

Log on to **www.pearsoned.co.uk/cooper** to find a wealth of interactive exercises, FT articles on the latest developments in tourism and video cases featuring companies such as Marriott, Air France and the Easy Group. There are also useful revision aids such as flashcards and multiple choice questions to help you build up your knowledge

CASE MATRIX

AUTHORS AND CONTRIBUTORS

AUTHORS

Professor Chris Cooper is Director of the Christel deHaan Tourism and Travel Research Institute at the University of Nottingham, UK. He has a PhD from University College London and worked in market planning and research for the tourism industry before entering higher education. He has authored a number of leading tourism texts and is co-editor of *Current Issues in Tourism*, with C. Michael Hall. Chris Cooper has worked closely with the UN World Tourism Organization helping raise the profile and standards of tourism education globally. He was chair of the UNWTO's Education Council from 2005 to 2007. He has acted as a consultant and researcher in every region of the world.

Professor John Fletcher is Professor of Tourism and Head of Bournemouth University Graduate School, as well as Director of the International Centre for Tourism and Hospitality Research and Editor-in-Chief of the *International Journal of Tourism Research*. John has undertaken tourism development and impact studies throughout the Caribbean, the South Pacific, the Indian Ocean and across Europe on behalf of national governments, local authorities and international agencies. He has led research on projects funded by the EU, USAID, UNWTO, WTTC and international development banks. In his efforts to improve the accessibility of tourism impact research, he has pioneered the development of interactive economic and environmental impact models and has written more than 130 articles, official reports and book chapters on the topic of tourism impacts. He has also written on the place of tourism in national accounts and presented to the British Association for the Advancement of Science. John is a member of the International Academy for the Study of Tourism and a Fellow of the Tourism Society.

Alan Fyall is Deputy Dean (Research & Enterprise) in the School of Services Management, Bournemouth University, UK. He has published widely, with his particular areas of expertise spanning the management of attractions, heritage tourism and destination management. In addition to the previous edition of this text, Alan has co-edited *Managing Visitor Attractions: New Directions* and *Managing World Heritage Sites* published by Elsevier Butterworth Heinemann, while he has also co-authored *Tourism Marketing: A Collaborative Approach* published by Channel View. Alan has managed a number of projects for major clients with particular expertise spanning the determination of suitable structures for emerging Destination Management Organisations. Alan has recently conducted work in the Caribbean and Southern Africa for the Commonwealth Secretariat, and has been involved with projects in the Middle East, Europe, and Central and South East Asia. Alan is currently serving as an adviser to the Commonwealth Tourism Centre, based in Kuala Lumpur, where guidance is being given on the undertaking of a pan-Commonwealth destination audit, and is a Board Member of the Bournemouth Tourism Management Board. Finally, Alan is an Editorial Board Member of *Annals of Tourism Research*, the *International Journal of Tourism Research*, *Journal of Heritage Tourism* and *Anatolia*.

Dr David Gilbert is Professor of Marketing at the School of Management, Surrey University. He has 24 years' academic experience in higher education and over 8 years' operational marketing experience for the private sector, having worked as a Product Manager and as a Marketing Manager for Rank Leisure. He specialises in the teaching of marketing related to: Relationship Marketing, Consumer Behaviour, Market Research, Research Methods and the functions of Marketing Management and was the founder of the MSc in Tourism Marketing at Surrey. His research is in the field of services marketing and his publications are mainly related to the tourism and retail industries. Alongside his academic duties, he has worked with several government and private organisations and consultancies on tourism or marketing project work, as well as having planned and provided training in 19 overseas countries. He was research director of the Thomas Cook Research Centre at the University of Surrey and has in-depth knowledge of marketing in relation to the service industry.

Professor Stephen Wanhill is Professor of Tourism Economics, University of Limerick and Emeritus

Professor of Tourism Research, Bournemouth University and a Visiting Professor at the universities of Nottingham and Swansea. He is a Director of Global Tourism Solutions (UK) and his principal research interests are in the field of tourism destination development. To this extent he has acted as a tourism consultant to a number of UK planning and management consulting firms, and has undertaken a wide range of tourism development strategies, tourism impact assessments, lecture programmes and project studies from airports to attractions, both in the UK and worldwide, covering some 50 countries. He has acted as tourism policy adviser to the Select Committee on Welsh Affairs for a period of five years in the House of Commons and has been a Board Member of the Wales Tourist Board with responsibilities for the development and research divisions.

He is the Editor of *Tourism Economics* and an Editorial Board Member of *Acta Touristica*, the *Service Industries Journal*, *Tourism Management*, the *European Journal of Tourism Research*, the *International Journal of Tourism Research*, and the *Journal of Travel Research*.

CONTRIBUTORS

Dr Bas Amelung is deputy director of ICIS at Maastricht University. Having studied environmental economics at the Free University in Amsterdam, he started his research on tourism at ICIS in 1999. In March 2006, Bas received his PhD for a thesis about the links between global (environmental) change and tourism. His main research interests are Antarctic tourism, the relationships between tourism and climate change, and sustainable development. Bas has been a member of the Steering Group on Scientific Assessment and Policy Analysis for Climate Change (SG-WAB) since March 2004 and he is a co-founder and an executive committee member of the research network e-CLAT: experts in climate change and tourism, e-clat.org.

Paul Barron is Reader in Hospitality Management in the School of Marketing and Tourism at Napier University, Edinburgh. After eight years in management positions in the hospitality industry, Paul commenced his academic career at Glasgow Caledonian University, during which time he completed an MSc in Personnel Management at the University of Strathclyde. Thereafter, Paul spent 11 years at The University of Queensland, Australia during which time he completed his PhD which examined international students' educational experiences when studying hospitality and tourism management at university in Australia. The student educational experience and the increasing internationalisation of the student cohort continue to be research interests. He has authored over 40 articles in the fields of hospitality and tourism and is currently on the editorial board of three international journals.

Tom Baum is Professor of International Tourism and Hospitality Management in the University of Strathclyde, Glasgow, Scotland. He is a specialist in the area of people and work in the tourism sector and has researched, taught and consulted in this area throughout the world. He has supervised over 20 doctoral candidates to completion and has examined PhDs in over 20 universities in eight countries. Tom has written widely on people-related and other tourism areas, including hotel front office, and has published 8 books and refereed over 100 journal and conference papers. He is author of *Human Resource Management for Tourism, Hospitality and Leisure. An International Perspective*, published by International Thomson in 2006. Tom is on the editorial board of a number of journals and has been invited as a keynote speaker at conferences in Asia, Australia, the Caribbean and Europe. Tom was educated in the University of Wales, Aberystwyth for his BA and MA degrees and obtained his PhD from the University of Strathclyde. He is a Fellow of the International Academy for the Study of Tourism.

Dr Dimitrios Buhalis joined the School of Services Management at Bournemouth University in September 2007 as Established Chair in Tourism. He is responsible for e-tourism research and for incorporating e-tourism in all aspects of tourism teaching and research. Dr Dimitrios Buhalis was previously Programme Leader MSc in Tourism Marketing, Leader of E-tourism Research, Reader in Business Information Management at the School of Management, University of Surrey and elected member of the University Senate (2003–7). He has been teaching tourism-related subjects in more than 30 universities around the world. He is regarded as an expert on the impacts of ICTs in the tourism industry and e-tourism, the management of tourism distribution channels as well as strategic tourism marketing and management.

Derek Robbins trained as a transport planner and is currently Senior Lecturer in Transport and Tourism in the School of Services Management at Bournemouth University where he has held a variety of management posts. He has developed specialised undergraduate and postgraduate units in transport on tourism degrees and published widely on the relationship between transport and tourism. Specific research interests include cruise shipping, deregulation of the bus and coach industry, transport impacts of tourists in destination areas, cycle tourism and sustainable transport policies. He is an active member of the Institute of Logistics and Transport and has undertaken consultancy for a number of bodies including the EU and the Lulworth Estate.

Dr Yeganeh Morakabati is Senior Research Associate within the International Centre for Tourism & Hospitality Research at Bouremouth University. Having studied mathematics and computing she went on to study a Masters degree in tourism marketing, Yeganeh received her PhD for a thesis on the effects of natural and manmade disasters on the perceptions of risk held by tourists. She is currently building a database of tourism indicators for the Commonwealth Tourism Centre and writing on international tourism flows, risk and impacts.

John Westlake is Professor of Tourism Management in the School of Services Management at Bournemouth University. He is involved in teaching of masters students and supervising doctoral students. He is active in undertaking research and publishing in academic journals and is on the Editorial Board of the journals *Tourism Economics* and the *International Journal of Tourism Research*. His interests are in the planning for tourism, transport for tourism and tourism and hospitality education where he has been active in publishing and undertaking project work in these areas. John has undertaken work for the UN World Tourism Organization and has been involved in EU funded projects. He is widely travelled, especially in the Asia Pacific region, and maintains close contact with institutions and academic practitioners in many parts of the world.

PREFACE

Welcome to the fourth edition of *Tourism: Principles and Practice*. This edition builds upon the successful restructuring of the third edition and includes a range of new features and content to ensure that the book keeps pace with the changing world of tourism. We have completely revised this edition to provide the reader with up-to-date content, extensive case studies, discussion and essay questions, clear learning objectives and a colourful and user-friendly format. This edition, and the continued success of *Tourism: Principles and Practice*, is a reflection of the growing maturity of tourism as a subject area in higher education.

THE FEATURES OF THIS BOOK

This new edition retains many of the key philosophies that made the earlier editions so successful. In a changing and turbulent environment for tourism, we offer readers the fundamental and underlying principles with which to approach the study of tourism, contributing a complete framework that effectively integrates theory and practice, and which, we feel, stands the test of changing times. Of course, we have updated the text to take into account developments such as the growing concern for climate change events and the maturing response of tourism to the safety and security of tourists.

While the basic structure of this book follows the third edition, we have updated, refined and improved all subject areas, added a new chapter on tourism under crises, substantially revised the tourism marketing material and added new case studies and examples throughout the book. This edition retains the features that we added in the third edition to enhance the use of the book in the classroom. These include:

- The introduction of **Chapter Learning Outcomes** at the beginning of every chapter to orientate the reader and to focus his or her mind in respect of the key concepts that underpin each chapter in the book.

- The inclusion of **Self-check Questions and Essay Questions** at the end of each chapter. These are designed to help the reader consolidate his or her knowledge as they work through the book and to draw out key contemporary issues and apply the theoretical content of the chapter to industry practice.

- The use of a **Major Case Study** at the end of each chapter to allow the reader to link the theory of the chapter to contemporary issues and practice. Each of these case studies with accompanying questions has been specially selected for this book.

- The use of two **Mini Case Studies** embedded within the chapters, again to draw out examples of how the material relates to the real world and to current issues. Discussion questions are provided at the end of each case study.

- The identification of key texts and web-based material in a section of **Annotated Further Reading** at the end of each chapter. Here we have provided a short description of the key sources to guide the reader through the increasingly complex maze of tourism literature. In addition, each section of the book has a bibliography which will act as the first port of call for assignments and presentations and provides an opportunity for guided specialised investigation where core concepts are reviewed in more detail and from which the user may derive a deeper understanding.

- The introduction of **photographs** to bring the material to life and the use of colour in the presentation of the text to make the book more attractive and easier to use.
- The addition of a **Glossary of Key Terms** to guide the reader through the specialist terminology in the chapters.

THE STRUCTURE OF THIS BOOK

Leiper's model of the tourism system, presented in the opening chapter entitled 'An Introduction to Tourism', provides the basic format for the book. In this introductory chapter we clearly define the elements of the system and our approach, and provide a case study analysing the issues surrounding one of the most important innovations in tourism – the use of tourism to alleviate poverty. The main body of the book is then structured around five key headings:

- Part 1 Tourism Demand
- Part 2 The Tourism Destination
- Part 3 The Tourism Sector
- Part 4 Marketing for Tourism
- Part 5 Tourism Futures

Part 1

Part 1 of the book examines all aspects of tourism demand in detail. We review the various concepts of demand, critically examine models of consumer behaviour and the decision-making process as it relates to tourism, look at factors that will influence demand for tourism at individual and global levels and analyse the techniques and approaches used to measure and forecast demand. We have written major case studies for this section that include new ideas of knowledge management for tourism data, the impact of the 2004 Indian Ocean Boxing Day Tsunami upon travel behaviour and an analysis of patterns of tourism demand across the globe.

Part 2

Part 2 of the book is focused upon the destination and how tourism interacts with the economy, the environment and the people. The impacts of tourism are explored along with the various techniques that have been used to measure them. Case studies have been selected to illustrate the diverse issues relating to tourism and its development in a wide range of circumstances. Comparisons and contrasts are also made between the different impact tools available to tourism researchers. Having put down the foundations for the study of tourism's impacts, the concept of sustainability is examined in some detail concluding with a chapter that sets out the parameters of planning and development. An additional chapter has been added to this part of the book examining tourism under crises and including a new and substantial section on tourism and climate change.

Part 3

In Part 3, we turn our attention to the tourism sector and those public sector organisations that influence and support tourism demand and supply. We have adopted an analytical and evaluative approach to this section, identifying the main sub-sectors that, when combined, constitute the tourism sector. We have focused generally on providing insights into the operating characteristics, trends and issues that dominate tourism and, specifically, upon attractions, accommodation, intermediaries, transportation, public sector organisations and destinations. Each chapter aims to show the principles governing the behaviour of the relevant suppliers and to provide examples of good practice that can be adopted elsewhere.

Part 4

Part 4 offers an understanding of the process and application of marketing to the unique characteristics of tourism. In this part, we provide a comprehensive overview of the management of tourism marketing including the strategies and tools that may be applied to deliver the tourism product effectively and efficiently to satisfy the tourism consumer. The chapters will anchor the concepts of marketing in the historical roots of its development and establish why services' marketing is different. Tourism as a service process is covered with major exposure of services and quality concepts. Marketing planning has its own designated chapter covering both tactical and strategic marketing planning procedures in respect of the tourism product. We review the benefits and purposes of marketing planning, consider the structure of a marketing plan and explore the implications of neglecting tourism marketing planning. We then go on to review the marketing mix as a key strategic tool, integral to achieving marketing planning objectives. The final chapter in this part analyses the role of technology and e-business in transforming the way that tourism marketing operates.

Part 5

Part 5 highlights issues that will influence the future of tourism. This section comprises a substantial chapter on the future of tourism. Part Five is instrumental in consolidating the strands and themes discussed throughout the book and presents them in a format that demonstrates the likely future development of all aspects of the tourism system. A wide range of influences are reviewed and assessed, together with an evaluation of impacts on both tourism products and tourists. In this section we have resisted the hype of futurologists and instead provide a disciplined framework within which to analyse tourism futures, including a major case on the tourism space race.

OVERVIEW

The philosophy behind this book remains the same as earlier editions: namely to provide a comprehensive, user-friendly contemporary text which can be used for both teaching and learning about tourism. We have many people to thank for the fact that this book has been produced; Paul Barron and Tom Baum, Dimitrios Buhalis, Derek Robbins and John Westlake each contributed chapters reflecting their own expertise; and David Cox at Pearson Education has been a professional and highly supportive editor.

PUBLISHER'S ACKNOWLEDGEMENTS

The publishers would like to thank the following for their kind permission to reproduce their photographs:

Advertising Archives: 377; Advertising Archives 591; **Alamy Images:** Ace Stock Ltd 87; Adrian Arbib 166; Bruce Percy 488; Bubbles Photolibrary 48; Chuck Eckert 566; Image Broker 251; Oote Boe Photography 557b; Vario Images GmbH & Co. KG 557t; **Britain on View:** Derek Croucher 502; **Corbis:** Antoine Serra/In Visu 452; Arctic-Images 583; Jon Feingersh 94; Paul Hackett/Reuters 122; Reuters 665; Ron Sachs 6; **Mary Evans Picture Library:** Mary Evans Picture Library 512; **Getty Images:** AFP 531; **PA Photos:** 200, 281, 295; PA Photos 68; **Rex Features:** Edward Webb 40; Lehtikuva Oy 179; Tim Rooke 204

Picture Research by: Alison Prior

We are grateful to the Financial Times Limited for permission to reprint the following material:

Chapter 17 Mini Case Study 17.2 Tourism Chiefs face guilt trip on green issues, © *Financial Times*, 14 May 2007; Chapter 18 Madeira: Quality of service is key to region's niche appeal, © *Financial Times*, 10 May 2006; Chapter 19 Is this journey's end for the travel agent?, © *Financial Times*, 14 November 2005; Chapter 19 Run aground: How the climate turned competitive for online travel companies, © *Financial Times*, 16 August 2004; Chapter 19 Sitting pretty (airline lounges), © *FT.com*, 24 October 2006.

We are grateful to the following for permission to reproduce copyright material:

Copyright Clearance Centre for the extracts from "2 psychographic types" from *Cornell Hotel & Restaurant Administration Quarterly* 14(4) Feb 1974 by Plog copyright © Sage Publications Inc. Journals; "The natural environment" published in *Annals of Tourism Research* 17 by Green, Hunter & Moore 1990, pg 270–9 copyright © Elsevier Science & Technology Journals; "Travel agent benefits" from *Service Industries Journal* 10(4) 1990a, by Gilbert copyright © Taylor & Francis Informa UK Ltd – Journals; "Savonlinna Opera Festival" published in *Tourism, Culture & Communication* 6(2) 2006 adapted by Wanhill copyright © Cognizant Communication Corporation; and the following figures "Study of tourism and choice of discipline and approach" published in *Annals of Tourism Research* 8(1) by Jafari & Ritchie 1981, pg 13–34 copyright © Elsevier Science & Technology Journals; "7 elements to motivation" published in *Annals of Tourism Research* 8(2) by Dann 1981, pg 187–219 copyright © Elsevier Science & Technology Journals; "Service quality model" from *Journal of Marketing* 49(4) 1985 by Parasuraman, Zeithaml and Berry copyright © American Marketing Association; "Consumer decision-making framework" from *Journal of Travel Research* 27 by Woodside & Lysonski 1989 copyright © Sage Publications Inc. Journals; "A basic tourism system" published in *Annals of Tourism Research* 6(4) by Leiper 1979, updated 1990 pg 390–407 copyright © Elsevier Science & Technology Journals; World Tourism Organization for extracts from World Tourism Organisation 1980, 1984, 1994; 'Global Code of Ethics for Tourism'; 'Image definition'; 'The UNWTO crisis definition'; 'The Djerba Declaration on Tourism and Climate Change 2003b'; 'Tsunami: One Year On' World Tourism Organisation 2005a; and 'The Evolution of tsunami-affected destinations', 2005b; the tables 'Tourism & Employment: Enhancing the Status of Tourism Professions' 1980; UNWTO data annual; WTO Yearbook of Tourism Statistics WTO Madrid 1989, 1992, 1997, 2003; WTO & UNSTAT 1994; 'Crisis Guidelines for the Tourism Industry' 2003a; UNWTO 2005 and 'Post Tsunami Reassessment' 2005c; and figures from 'Classification of International Visitors 2000' and 'Accor corporate structure' from *Tourism in the age of Alliances, Merges and acquisitions* 2002 copyright © World Tourism Organization; WTTC World Travel & Tourism Council London for details and quotes from *World Travel & Tourism. Climbing to new heights*, 2006; *The Impact of travel and tourism on jobs and the economy* 2006, WTTC Namibia; *Tax Guidelines*, *Blueprint for new tourism* 2003 and *Security Approach Principles* copyright © World Travel & Tourism Council; Pearson Education Limited for figures from *Tourism: Economic Physical and social impacts* by Mathieson & Wall

1982; *Tourism Analysis: A handbook* by Smith 1989; *Tourism Marketing & Management Handbook* 2/e edited by Witt & Martin 1989; and *eTourism: Information Technology for Strategic Tourism Management* by Buhalis 2002 copyright © Pearson Education; Professor Antonios Vitalis on behalf of Massey University for the figure "Geographical elements in a tourism system with two destinations" from *Tourism Systems* by Leiper 1990, Massey University Department of Management Systems Occasional Paper 2, Auckland copyright © Massey University; John Wiley & Sons for the figure "Study of tourism and choice of discipline and approach" from *Tourism: Principles, Practices, Philosophies* by McIntosh & Goddner copyright © 1990 John Wiley & Sons, USA reproduced with permission; Sage Publications Ltd for the figure "An activities-based model of destination choice" by Moscado et al published in *Journal of Vacation Marketing* 2(2) 1996, pg 109–22, an extract from "Destination Branding – New Zealand case study" by Morgan, Pritchard & Piggott published in *Journal of Vacation Marketing* 9(3) 2003, pg 285–299 and an extract from "Scottish tourism: scenarios & vision case study" by Ian Yeoman & Peter Lederer published in *Journal of Vacation Marketing* 2005 copyright © Sage Publications Ltd, reprinted by permission of Sage Publications Ltd; Elsevier for a table and 3 figures from *The Geography of Travel & Tourism* by Brian Boniface 1987; 4 figures, 1 table and an extract from *Managing Visitor Attractions: New Directions* by Alan Fyall 2002 copyright © Elsevier 1987, 2002 reproduced with permission; Pearson Education Inc for a table from *Consumer Behaviour* 3/e by Soloman 1996 copyright © Pearson Education, Inc; Taylor and Francis Books for a table from *The Economic Geography of the Tourist Industry* by Ioannides and Debbage, 1998 copyright © Cengage Learning Services Ltd; Cambridge University Press for a table adapted from *The Stages of Economic Growth* by Walt Whitman Rostow 1959 copyright © Cambridge University Press; Tourism Research Australia for a case study from The Australian Tourism Forecasting Committee from the Tourism Research Australia website as at February 2008 www.tra.australia.com copyright © 2008 Tourism Australia reproduced by permission; John Wiley & Sons Ltd for tables from *Demand Forecasting in Tourism & Recreation* by Witt & Martin,1989 and *Progress in Tourism, Recreation and Hospitality Management* by C Cooper, 1991 copyright © 1989, 1991 John Wiley & Sons Limited, reproduced with permission; The Stationery Office for extracts from "Air Traffic Forecasts for the United Kingdom" 2000; "The Future of Air Transport" 2003; "Transport Statistics Great Britain" 2006; "A New deal for transport: better for everyone" 1998; and "Transport and the Environment" 1994 by Royal Commission on Environmental Pollution www.dft.co.uk © Crown copyright; Euromonitor International for a table from *Euromonitor International Monetary Fund, International Financial Statistics*, 2004 copyright © Euromonitor International, reproduced with permission; Australian Government for an advertisement announcement for the new Sydney Airport published by the *Sun Herald Public* 6th July 1997 copyright © Commonwealth of Australia, reproduced by permission; United Nations, Secretariat, Publications Board and Exhibits Committee for details and extracts from *United Nations Conference on the Environment & Development*, Rio Conference, Agenda 21, 1992, used with permission; UNEP DTIE – *United Nations Environment Programme, Division of Technology, Industry & Economics, Sustainable Consumption and Production Branch* for an extract from "Environmental Impacts of Tourism" http://www.unep.fr/pc/tourism/ copyright © UNEP; Paul Ward, Cool Antarctica for the case study "The environmental impact of tourism in Antarctica" published on www. coolantarctica.com copyright © Paul Ward, reprinted with permission; IAATO for text, 2 tables and 2 pie charts from "The environmental impact of tourism in Antarctica" www.iaato.org copyright © IAATO; University of Pennsylvania Press for a table from *Hosts and Guests* 2nd edition by Smith, 1989 © copyright University of Pennsylvania Press; Guardian News & Media Ltd for extracts adapted from "Tourist drought hits Disneyland Paris: Iraq fallout, strikes & forest fires have kept Americans and Europeans away" by Amelia Gentleman published in *The Guardian* 9th August 2003 and "Tourism is a human rights issue" by Polly Pattullo published in *The Guardian* 31st March 2006 © Guardian 2003, 2006; American Association for the Advancement of Science for an extract adapted from "The Sun. The Sand. The Sex" by Jon Cohen published in *Science Magazine* 28 July 2006, http://www. sciencemag.org copyright © AAAS, reprinted with permission; The Swaraj Foundation for an extract from *Annexure B – Tourism Development Mission* by Rajiv Gandhi Tourism Development Mission for Rajasthan; Foreign & Commonwealth Office for the case study 'Make a difference when you travel' copyright © www.fco.gov.uk/travel; Dr Stanley Plog for the figure 'Why destination areas rise and fall in popularity' by Dr Stanley Plog, 1977 copyright © Dr Stanley Plog; BuaNews for the case study "South Africa: SA Tourism Must Meet World Standards" by Themba Gadebe published by *BuaNews* 10th September 2007 copyright © BuaNews; Planet 21 (www.peopleandplanet.net) and

Centre for Science and the Environment (CSE), Delhi, India for the case study "Encouraging Sustainable Tourism: Chanting the Eco-tourism mantra in India" by Rustam Vania, 30th September 2002 © People & the Planet 2000 – 2007; The BBC for the articles "Calling all tourists to Bamiyan" by Charles Haviland published on www.news.bbc.co.uk 1st September 2007 and 'Tourism revival key for Maldives' published on http://news.bbc.co.uk 7th February 2005 copyright © www.BBC.co.uk; Ecumenical Coalition On Tourism Foundation for the case study 'Tourism: A challenge for the 21st century' 2005 copyright © ECOT www.ecotonline.org/Redingroom; Adrian Lillywhite MD of Cape Verde Property Ltd for the Case Study 'Cape Verde a 21st Century Nation' copyright © Adrian Lillywhite, Cape Verde Property Ltd; Bali Government Tourism Office for the table 'Average Hotel Occupancy Rates' 2004–2005 © copyright Bali Government Tourism Office, reprinted with permission; Department for Education and Skills Publications for an extract from "The Leisure Sector, Skills Task Force" Research paper no 6 by Keep & Mayhew, 1999 © Crown copyright; University of Strathclyde for the case study "Scotland's Commended Hotels" by Dr Alison Morrison copyright © University of Strathclyde, Department of Hospitality and Tourism Management; Office for Official Publications of the European Communities for an extract from European Union Package Travel Directive – EC Council Directive 90/314 © European Communities, 1998–2007 'Only European Union legislation printed in the paper edition of the Official Journal of the European Union is deemed authentic'; Mintel Group for the case study "Inclusive Tours and Travel Agents" copyright © Mintel Group; HMSO for extracts from "Foreign Package Holidays" by MMC, 1998 and "UK 1969 Development of Tourism Act" © Crown copyright; ABTA – The Travel Association for a case study about ABTA copyright © ABTA; Thomas Cook UK Limited for details from MyTravel Group PLC Annual Report & Accounts 2003 and Thomas Cook Group details within 'Merger Mania – Thomas Cook Group plc' copyright © Thomas Cook UK Limited; Cengage Learning Services Ltd for the figure "Conceptual model of the process and factors influencing agents' destinations recommendations" from Tourism Distribution Channels: Practices, Issues & Transformations by Buhalis & Laws, edited by Hudson, Snaith & Miller 2001 copyright © Cengage Learning; Seatrade Communications Ltd for material from The Future of Cruising – Boom or Bust? A Worldwide Analysis to 2015 – a Seatrade Research Report copyright © Seatrade Communications Ltd; Welsh Assembly Government for VisitWales policy objectives published on www.visitwales.co.uk copyright © Welsh Assembly Government 2008; Cruise Lines International Association Inc for the case study 'Cruise Industry Overview' copyright © 2007 Cruise Lines International Association Inc; Pacific Asia Travel Association (PATA) for an extract from the 'Travellers Code' published on www.PATA.org/sustainability copyright © Pacific Asia Travel Association'; United Kingdom Parliament for an extract about Trade & Industry Committee of House of Commons published on www.parliament.uk © Parliamentary copyright; CAB International for a figure from The Competitive Destination: A Sustainable Tourism Perspective by J.R. Brent Ritchie & Geoffrey I Crouch, 2003 published by CABI Publishing and used with permission; Northwest Regional Development Agency for extracts from Managing Destinations in England's Northwest 16th March 2004 copyright © Northwest Regional Development Agency; Paul Whitelaw and Associate Professor Barry O'Mahony for the case study 'London tourism: Devolution, Disaster and Diversification' from Australian Tourism and Hospitality Research Conference, Victoria University, Melbourne, Australia, copyright © CAUTHE 2006 Proceedings; Travel Agent, Home-Based Travel Agent Magazines for the report "New Orleans Report on Tourism Recovery Progress" by Anastasia Mills, Travel Agent published 3rd April 2007 copyright © Travel Agent, Home-Based Travel Agent Magazines; Hanken, Swedish School of Economic and Business Administration for a figure from Strategic Management and Marketing in the Service Sector by Gronroos 1982 copyright © Hanken, reprinted with permission; Dr Peter Tarlow for an extract abridged from e-Review of Tourism Research, Vol 1, No 2, 2003 by Dr Peter Tarlow copyright © Dr Peter E. Tarlow, reprinted with permission; The Free Press, a Division of Simon & Schuster, Inc for 2 figures from COMPETITIVE STRATEGY: Techniques for Analyzing Industries and Competitors by Michael E. Porter copyright © 1980, 1998 by The Free Press and 2 figures from MANAGING BRAND EQUITY: Capitalizing on the Value of a Brand Name by David A. Aaker copyright © 1991 by David A. Aaker. All rights reserved; Madigan Pratt & Associates Inc for the case study "Nisbet Plantation Hotel and Relationship Marketing" copyright © www.MadiganPratt.com; American Marketing Association for the figure 'The marketing mix for services' from Marketing Services edited by Donnelly & George, Booms & Bitner, 1981 copyright © American Marketing Association; Carl Henrik Marcussen and CRT for a figure from "Regional & Tourism Research Trends in the European Online Travel Market, by country/region 06/09/04" by Marcussen & Swedish Centre and a table from "Internet Distribution of European Travel & Tourism Services" by Marcussen 2006 copyright © CRT; eTravel for the table "Consolidation – 5 Global Groups" published by eTravel copyright © eTravel.org Limited. All rights reserved; SITA & Airline Business for the table "Airline IT Trends Survey 2007" copyright © SITA & Airline Business, reprinted with permission; O'Reilly Media, Inc for Web 2.0 chart taken from the article entitled *What is Web 2.0*, copyright © 2005 O'Reilly Media, Inc. This chart is published by permission of O'Reilly Media, Inc., the owner of all rights to publish and sell the same; lastminute.com for a case study about lastminute.com copyright © lastminute.com; BDL Media Ltd for an extract from "Ctrip.com Posts Impressive Results" published on www.chinatechnews. com copyright © BDL Media Ltd, reprinted with permission; Tiscover AG for a screenshot from www.tiscover.com copyright © Tiscover AG; European Travel Commission for a screenshot from www.visiteurope.com/world copyright © Europe – A never-ending journey; Harvard Business School for a table from *The Experience Economy* by Joseph Pine and James Gilmore, 1999 copyright © Harvard Business School Publishing; and Space Adventures Ltd for material about Space Adventures space travel www.spaceadventures.com copyright © Space Adventures Ltd.

In some instances we have been unable to trace the owners of copyright material and we would appreciate any information that would enable us to do so.

ABBREVIATIONS

AA Automobile Association
AAA American Automobile Association
ABTA Association of British Travel Agents
APEX Advanced purchase excursion fare
APT Advanced Passenger Train
ARC Airlines Reporting Corporation
ASEAN Association of South East Asian Nations
ASP Application service provider
ASTA American Society of Travel Agents
ATC Air traffic control
ATMs Air traffic movements
ATOL Air Travel Organisers' Licence
AWES Automatic web-site evaluation system

B2B Business-to-business
B2C Business-to-consumer
BA British Airways
BCG Boston Consulting Group matrix

CGE Computable general equilibrium
CLIA Cruise Line International Association
CPGI Country potential generation index
CPI Consumer Price Index
CRO Central reservations office
CRS Computerised reservation system
CSF Community support framework
CSR Corporate social responsibility
CTO Caribbean Tourism Organisation
CVB Convention and visitor bureau

DAGMAR Defining Advertising Goods for Measured Advertising Results
DICIRMS Destination integrated computer information reservation management system
DMO Destination management/marketing organisation
DMS Destination management system
DPUK Destination Performance UK

EAFRD European Agricultural Fund for Rural Development
EAP Environmental action programme
EAP East Asia and the Pacific
EBRD European Bank for Reconstruction and Development
EC European Community
ECSC European Coal and Steel Community

ECTAA European Travel Agents & Tour Operators Association
EEB European Environmental Bureau
EIA Environmental impact assessment
EIB European Investment Bank
EIS Environmental impact statement
EMS Environmental management system
EPA Environmental Protection Agency
EPS model Extended problem-solving model
ERDF European Regional Development Fund
ESF European Social Fund
ETC European Travel Commission
EU European Union

FBP Family brand performance
FIT Fully-inclusive tour
FLC Family life cycle
FTE Full-time equivalent

GATS General Agreement on Trade in Services
GATT General Agreement on Tariffs and Trade
GDP Gross domestic product
GDS Global distribution system
GNI Gross national income
GNP Gross national product
gwt Gross weight tonnage

IAAPA International Association of Amusement Parks and Attractions
IAATO International Association of Antarctic Tour Operators
IATA International Air Transport Association
IBRD International Bank for Reconstruction and Development
ICAO International Civil Aviation Organisation
ICT Information communication technology
IDD International direct dial
IFC International Finance Corporation
IIPT International Institute for Peace through Tourism
IIT Independent inclusive tour
ILO International Labour Organization
IMC Integrated marketing communications
IMF International Monetary Fund
IPCC Intergovernmental Panel on Climate Change
IPEX Instant purchase fares
IPS International passenger survey
ISIC International Standard Industrial Classification

KM Knowledge management

LAC Limits of acceptable change
LCCs Low-cost carriers
LDC Less developed countries
LPS models Limited problem-solving models
LTV Lifetime value

MA Moving average
MDGs Millennium Development Goals

NAFTA North American Free Trade Association
NATS National Air Traffic Services
NGO Non-governmental organisation
NSRF National Strategic Reference Framework
NTO National tourist organisation

OAS Organization of American States
OECD Organization for Economic Co-operation and Development
OECS Organization of East Caribbean States
OPEC Organization of Petroleum Exporting Countries
OPs Operational Programmes

PATA Pacific Asia Travel Association
PBP Product brand performance
PMS Property management system
PNR Passenger name record
PPC Pay per click
PPT Pro poor tourism
PR Public relations
PRC People's Republic of China

RM Relationship marketing
ROI Return on investment
RTB Regional tourism board

SARS Severe acute respiratory syndrome
SAS Scandinavian Airline System
SBU Strategic business unit
SCH Scotland's Commended Hotels
SDNs Sustainable development networks
SEO search engine optimisation
SIC Standard industrial classification
SIDS Small Island Developing States
SMART Specific, measurable, achievable, realistic, time limits
SME Small and medium-sized enterprise
SPD Single programming document

STB Scottish Tourist Board
STEP Social, technological, economic and political factors
ST–EP Sustainable tourism–eliminating poverty
SWOT Strengths, weaknesses, opportunities and threats

TA Travel agency
TALC Tourist area life cycle
TAT Tourist Authority of Thailand
TCSP Tourism Council for the South Pacific
TDC Tourist Development Corporation
TERN Tourism Emergency Response Network
TGV Train de Grande Vitesse
TIC Tourist information centre
TIP Tourist information point
TO Tour operator
TOP Thomson Open-Line Programme
TPI Tourism Penetration Index
TQM Total quality management
TSA Tourism satellite account

UFTAA United Federation of Travel Agents' Associations
UKTS United Kingdom Tourism Survey
UN United Nations
UNCTAD United Nations Conference on Trade and Development
UNDP United Nations Development Programme
UNEP United Nations Environment Programme
UNESCO United Nations Educational, Scientific and Cultural Organization
UNSTAT United Nations Statistical Commission
UNWTO United Nations World Tourism Organization

VAT Value Added Tax
VFR Visiting friends and relatives
VR Virtual reality

WCS Wildlife Conservation Strategy
WHO World Health Organization
WTO World Tourism Organization
WTTC World Travel and Tourism Council
WWW World Wide Web

YHA Youth Hostel Association
YM/WCA Young Men's/Women's Christian Association

AN INTRODUCTION TO TOURISM

LEARNING OUTCOMES

In this chapter we focus on the concepts, terminology and definitions that underpin the study of tourism to provide you with:

- a basic understanding of the nature of the tourism system and a knowledge of the myths that surround tourism today;
- a comprehension of the issues associated with the academic and practical study of tourism;
- an appreciation of the individual elements which, when combined, comprise the tourism system; and
- a knowledge of basic supply-side and demand-side definitions of tourism and the associated difficulties and issues.

Photograph: Masai Warriors, Masai Mara, Kenya © Hannah Cox

INTRODUCTION

In this chapter we introduce the concept of a tourism system and outline its role in offering a way of thinking about tourism and providing a framework of knowledge for students approaching the subject of tourism. This framework is particularly important in the twenty-first century when the world is experiencing rapid and unexpected change caused by both human and natural agents. In addition, tourism has now become a major economic sector in its own right and we use this chapter to demonstrate the scale and significance of tourism.

At the same time, we outline some of the commonly held myths that surround tourism and identify some of the issues that are inherent both in the subject area and in the study of tourism. In particular, we emphasise the variety and scope of tourism as an activity and highlight the fact that all elements of the tourism system are interlinked, despite the fact that they have to be artificially isolated for teaching and learning purposes. Finally, we consider the difficulties involved in attempting to define tourism and provide some ideas as to how definitions are evolving.

TOURISM – MYTHS AND REALITIES

In a world of change, one constant since 1950 has been the sustained growth and resilience of tourism both as an activity and an economic sector. This has been demonstrated despite the 'shocks' of 11 September, 2001 (9/11), the dual bombings of a major Asian tourism destination – Bali, SARS (severe acute respiratory syndrome) and the threat of bird flu, the second Iraq war, bombings of both the London and Madrid railway systems and the 2004 Boxing Day Tsunami. Despite more recent crises, it was the events of 9/11 that triggered changes in consumer behaviour, changes which have made an impact on travel patterns and operations around the world. Yet, even with these challenges, in 2006 the World Travel and Tourism Council (WTTC) demonstrated the tremendous scale of the world's tourism sector (WTTC, 2006):

1. The travel and tourism industry's percentage of world gross domestic product was 10.3%;
2. The world travel and tourism industry had a turnover of US$6,477.2 billion; and
3. The world travel and tourism industry supported 234 million jobs (8.7% of total world employment).

It is therefore clear that tourism is a major force in the economy of the world, an activity of global importance and significance. It is also a sector that has the capacity to impact negatively upon host environments and cultures, the raw materials of many tourism products. As a result, increased prominence has been given to tourism in the United Nations' world summits such as the 1992 Rio Earth Summit and the World Summit on Sustainable Development in Johannesburg in 2003. A combination of the 'youth' of tourism as an activity – international mass tourism is at best only 40 years old – with the pace of growth in demand has given tourism a Cinderella-like existence, we know it is important, but it is not taken seriously. This has created a variety of issues for the sector. First, as well as demonstrating sustained growth, tourism has been remarkable in its resistance to adverse economic and political conditions. Events such as 9/11, terrorist bombings and the 2004 Boxing Day Tsunami clearly demonstrate the sector's ability to regroup and place emphasis on a new vocabulary including words such as 'safety', 'security', 'risk management', 'crisis' and 'recovery'. Inevitably though, growth is slowing as the market matures and, as the nature of the tourist and his or her demands change, the sector will need to be creative in supplying products to satisfy the 'new tourist'.

Secondly, international organisations support tourism for its contribution to world peace, its ability to delver on the Millennium Development Goals and in particular poverty alleviation, the benefits of the intermingling of peoples and cultures, the economic advantages that can ensue, and the fact that tourism is a relatively 'clean' industry. But an important issue is the stubbornly negative image of tourism as a despoiler of destinations and a harbinger of climate change; even the employment and monetary gains of tourism are seen to be illusory in many destinations. The International Labour Organization (ILO), for example, clearly views tourism jobs as of low quality, arguing that they are concerned with decent work, not just the creation of jobs but the creation of jobs of acceptable quality. A critical issue for the successful future of tourism will therefore be for all involved to demonstrate that the sector is responsible and worthy of acceptance as a global activity. The WTTC has been an influential lobbyist in this regard. As the representative body of the major companies in the tourism sector, it has led an active campaign to promote the need for the industry to take responsibility for its actions and for close public and private sector coalitions.

Thirdly, technology increasingly pervades the tourism sector. Tourism is ideally placed to take advantage of developments in information technology, from the use of the Internet to book travel and seek information about destinations, through the use of mobile telephone technology to revolutionise the way that tourism information can be delivered direct to the user *in situ* at the destination, to the innovative role technology plays in interpreting and displaying destinations. But this has all come at the price of restructuring the distribution channel in tourism and in changing the nature of jobs in the sector.

Finally, in many respects general perceptions of tourism are misplaced. Tourism is surrounded by a number of myths which have contributed unrealistically to its glamorous image. These are demonstrated in Table 0.1.

Table 0.1	Tourism – myths and realities
Myth	The majority of tourism in the world is **international**.
Reality	Tourism in the world is predominantly domestic (people travelling in their own country). **Domestic tourism** accounts for about 80% of tourist trips.
Myth	Most tourism journeys in the world are by air as tourists jet-set from country to country.
Reality	The majority of trips are by surface transport (mainly the car).
Myth	Tourism is only about leisure holidays.
Reality	Tourism includes all types of purpose of visit, including business, conference and education.
Myth	Employment in tourism means substantial travel and the chance to learn languages.
Reality	Most employment in tourism is in the hospitality sector and involves little travel.
Myth	Large multinational companies such as hotel chains and airlines dominate tourism.
Reality	The vast majority of tourism enterprises in every destination are SMEs.
Myth	Tourism is a straightforward sector demanding little research or planning.
Reality	Tourism is a complex multi-sectoral industry demanding high-level planning underpinned by research to succeed.

THE SUBJECT OF TOURISM

In historical terms, tourism activity is a relatively new development and only recently has it been considered worthy of serious business endeavour or academic study. However, the tourism sector is of sufficient economic importance and its impact upon economies, environments and societies is significant enough for the subject of tourism to deserve academic consideration. There is no doubt in our minds that tourism is a subject area or domain of study but that at the moment it lacks the level of theoretical underpinning that would allow it to become a discipline. Nevertheless, the popularity of tourism as a subject, and the recognition of its importance by governments, has accelerated the study of tourism. Tourism as a subject is showing signs of maturity with a growing academic community, increasing numbers of both journals and textbooks which are becoming specialised rather than all-embracing, and a number of professional societies both internationally and within individual countries. We are also seeing a greater confidence in the approaches used to research tourism as the positivist and scientific approaches are augmented with qualitative and more experimental methods. All of these indicators point to the increasing professionalism of the tourism sector.

As an area of study, tourism is still relatively young and this creates a range of issues for all of us involved in teaching, researching and studying the subject:

- The subject area itself remains bedevilled by conceptual weakness and fuzziness. We are therefore faced with many questions that would be taken as common ground in other subjects (such as finding a way through the maze of terminology related to the type of tourism which is less destructive – green, alternative, responsible, sustainable, eco!). This results in a basic lack of rigour and focus leaving tourism as a subject area open to criticism by others. Franklin and Crang for example are unrelenting: 'The rapid growth of tourism has led researchers to simply record and document tourism in a series of case studies, examples and industry-sponsored projects' (2001: 6). This highlights the apparent conflict between 'academic' and 'applied' approaches which is also an unresolved issue.

- The subject encompasses a number of diverse industrial sectors and academic subjects, raising the question for those studying tourism as to whether or not tourism is, in fact, too diverse and chaotic to merit separate consideration as a subject or economic sector. According to Gilbert (1990) what makes tourism difficult to define is the very broad nature of the concept as well as the need for so many service inputs. Tourism also envelops other sectors and industries (Gilbert, 1990: 7) and therefore has no clear boundary due to the expansive spread of activities it covers. We would argue, of course, that it should warrant a subject and sector in its own right, but that there is a need for a disciplined approach to help alleviate potential sources of confusion for students. It is therefore important in this respect to provide a framework within which to locate these subject approaches and industries. In reality the tourism industry consists of a mass of organisations operating in different sectors each of which supplies those activities which are termed tourism.

- As if these problems were not sufficient, tourism also suffers from a particularly weak set of data sources – in terms of both comparability and quality, although the UN World Tourism Organization (UNWTO) has made significant progress in this regard.

- Traditional approaches have tended to operationalise and reduce tourism to a set of activities or economic transactions while more recent authors have been critical of this 'reductionism', stressing instead postmodern frameworks which analyse the significance and meaning of tourism to individuals.

- Finally, tourism does suffer from an image problem in academic circles. Indeed, many are attracted to it as an exciting, vibrant subject and an applied area of economic activity – which we believe that it is. But to be successful, tourism demands very high standards of professionalism, knowledge and application from everyone involved. This is sometimes felt to be in contrast to the image of jet-setting, palm-fringed beaches and a leisure activity.

Photograph 0.1	Tourism has become an increasingly important element of study for many students as the subject gains acceptability in the academic community.

Source: Corbis/Ron Sachs

But there is light at the end of this tunnel. To quote Coles *et al.* (2006), tourism suffers from the difficulties of location 'in a sea of competing academic territoriality and competing constituencies' (p. 294). They suggest that our approach to tourism should be more flexible and fluid, recognising the inputs and value of differing subjects and disciplines to explanation in tourism. This is termed a 'post-disciplinary' approach, and it differs from the earlier ideas of multi- or inter-disciplinary approaches to tourism by being a flexible and creative approach that breaks through the parochial boundaries of disciplines (Coles *et al.* 2006).

A TOURISM SYSTEM

In response to the issues identified above, we feel that is important at the outset to provide an organising framework for the study of tourism. There are many ways to do this. Individual disciplines, for example, view the activity of tourism as an application of their own ideas and concepts, and an approach from say, geography or economics could be adopted. An alternative is to take a post-disciplinary approach as noted above. Figure 0.1 shows one such attempt to integrate a variety of subjects and disciplines and to focus upon tourism.

However, in a book of this nature it is impossible to cover the complete range of approaches to tourism. Instead, as an organising framework, we have adopted the model suggested by Leiper in 1979 and updated in 1990 (Figure 0.2). As Figure 0.2 shows, Leiper's model neatly takes into account many of the issues identified above by considering the activity of tourists, allowing industry sectors to be located and providing the geographical element which is inherent to all travel. It also places tourism in the context of a range of external environments such as society, politics and economies. There are three basic elements of Leiper's model:

1. **Tourists**. The tourist is the actor in this system. Tourism, after all, is a very human experience, enjoyed, anticipated and remembered by many as some of the most important times of their lives. Defining the tourist and attempting to produce classifications of tourists form the latter section of this chapter.

2. **Geographical elements**. Leiper outlines three geographical elements in his model:
   1. traveller-generating region;
   2. tourist destination region; and
   3. transit route region.

   The traveller-generating region represents the generating market for tourism and, in a sense, provides the 'push' to stimulate and motivate travel. It is from here that the tourist searches for information, makes the booking and departs.

   In many respects, the tourist destination region represents the 'sharp end' of tourism. At the destination, the full impact of tourism is felt and planning and management strategies are implemented. The destination, too, is the *raison d'être* for tourism, with a range of special places distinguished from the everyday by their cultural, historic or natural significance (Rojek and Urry, 1997). The 'pull' to visit destinations energises the whole **tourism system** and creates demand for travel in the generating region. It is therefore at the destination where the innovations in tourism take place – new products are developed and 'experiences' delivered making the destination the place 'where the most noticeable and dramatic consequences of the system occur' (Leiper, 1990: 23).

   The transit route region does not simply represent the short period of travel to reach the destination, but also includes the intermediate places which may be visited en route: 'There is always an interval in a trip when the traveller feels they have left their home region but have not yet arrived . . . [where] they choose to visit' (Leiper, 1990: 22).

3. **The tourism sector**. The third element of Leiper's model is the tourism sector, which we can think of as the range of businesses and organisations involved in delivering the

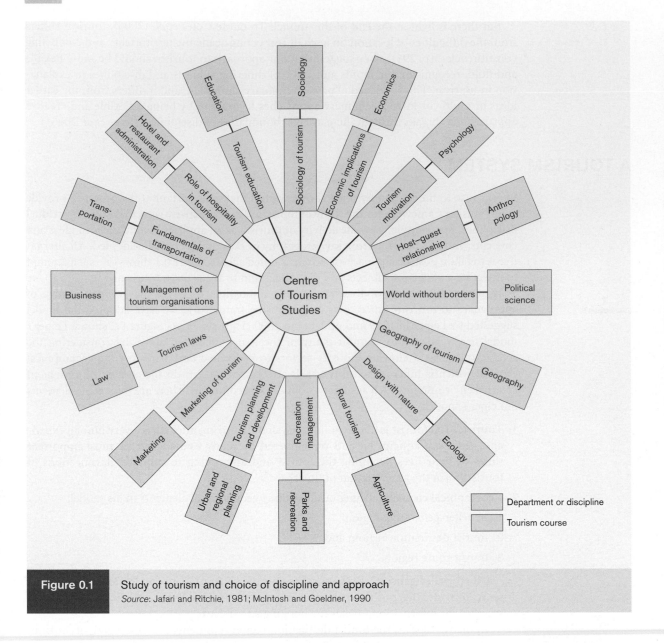

Figure 0.1   Study of tourism and choice of discipline and approach
Source: Jafari and Ritchie, 1981; McIntosh and Goeldner, 1990

tourism product. The model allows the location of the various industrial sectors to be identified. For example, travel agents and tour operators are mostly found in the traveller-generating region, attractions and the hospitality industry are found in the destination region, and the transport industry is largely represented in the transit route region.

Each of the elements of Leiper's tourism system interacts, not only to deliver the tourism product, but also in terms of transactions and impacts and, of course, the differing contexts within which tourism occurs (Figure 0.3). The fact that tourism is also a sector of contrasts is illustrated by examining two major elements of Leiper's model. Demand for tourism in the generating region is inherently volatile, seasonal and irrational. Yet this demand is satisfied by a destination region where supply is fragmented, inflexible and dominated by fixed investment costs – surely a possible recipe for the financial instability of tourism!

The major advantages of Leiper's model are its general applicability and simplicity, which provide a useful 'way of thinking' about tourism. Indeed, each of the alternative models that we have considered tend to reveal Leiper's basic elements when they are dissected.

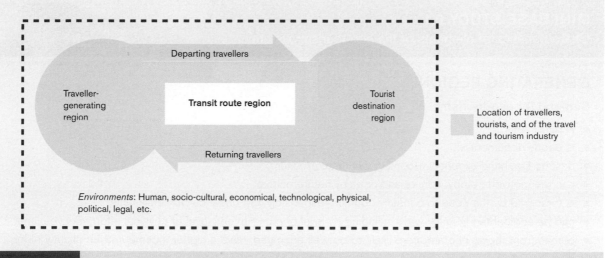

Location of travellers, tourists, and of the travel and tourism industry

Figure 0.2 A basic tourism system
Source: Leiper, 1990

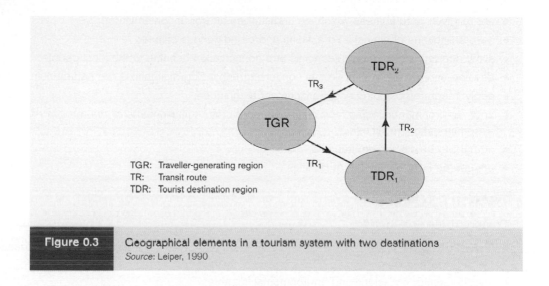

TGR: Traveller-generating region
TR: Transit route
TDR: Tourist destination region

Figure 0.3 Geographical elements in a tourism system with two destinations
Source: Leiper, 1990

There are also other advantages of this approach:

- It has the ability to incorporate interdisciplinary approaches to tourism because it is not rooted in any particular subject or discipline but instead provides a framework within which disciplinary approaches can be located.

- It is possible to use the model at any scale or level of generalisation – from a local resort to the international industry.

- The model is infinitely flexible and allows the incorporation of different forms of tourism, while at the same time demonstrating their common elements. For example, heritage or eco-tourism can be analysed using the model (see Mini Case Study 0.1). Here we can see that eco-tourism does not require a completely new approach, but simply an analysis of each of the particular characteristics of each of the elements of the eco-tourism system.

- Finally, the model demonstrates the highly important principle of tourism studies that all the elements of tourism are related and interact – in essence we are studying a system of customers and suppliers who demand and supply the tourism product and services.

MINI CASE STUDY 0.1
Characteristics of elements of the eco-tourism system

GENERATING REGION

Demand for eco-tourism:

- is purposeful;
- is poorly documented;
- desires first-hand experience/contact with nature/culture;
- has the motive to study, admire and/or enjoy nature/culture;
- is tempered by the need to consume tourism responsibly and offset carbon emissions;
- can be segmented in many ways including by level of commitment, level of physical effort, motives; and
- comes from those who are more likely to be well educated, have a higher income and be slightly older than the average tourist.

DESTINATION REGION

Destinations for eco-tourism:

- are relatively natural areas which are undisturbed and/or uncontaminated;
- have attractions of scenery, flora, fauna and/or indigenous culture;
- allow eco-tourism to deliver economic and conservation benefits to the local people;
- develop eco-tourism with a view to conserving/enhancing/maintaining the natural/cultural system;
- apply integrated planning and management techniques;
- apply environmental impact and auditing procedures to all elements of the tourism destination (such as accommodation, facilities);
- attempt to be carbon neutral; and
- encourage local ownership of facilities.

TRANSIT ZONE

Transport for eco-tourism:

- should be of low impact to the environment in terms of noise, carbon emissions, congestion, fuel consumption and waste;
- should monitor emissions and environmental impacts;
- should promote the conservation ethic;
- should be used as a management tool;
- should encourage use of public transport;
- should encourage the use of locally owned transport companies; but
- reaching a long-haul eco-tourism destination may consume large amounts of aircraft fuel and be more damaging to the environment than the tourist realises, and thus defeat the purpose of the trip itself.

DISCUSSION QUESTIONS

1. Do the principles of eco-tourism apply equally to each of the elements of the eco-tourism system?
2. Should eco-tourists be true to their beliefs and offset their carbon emissions?
3. There is a view that eco-tourism is used by developers as a 'soft' medium to access valued natural resources to pave the way for more aggressive tourism development – do you agree with this view?

- Naturally, in any textbook or course the elements of tourism have to be separated and examined individually, but in reality all are linked and the realisation of their inter-relationships provides a true understanding of tourism.

DEFINITIONS OF TOURISM

We can see from Leiper's model that tourism can be thought of as a whole range of individuals, businesses, organisations and places which combine in some way to deliver a travel experience. Tourism is a multidimensional, multifaceted activity, which touches many lives and many different economic activities. Not surprisingly, tourism has therefore proved difficult to define – the word 'tourist' first appeared in the English language in the early 1800s, yet more than two centuries later we still cannot agree on a definition. In some senses this is a reflection of the complexity of tourism, but it is also indicative of its youth as a field of study. It is difficult to find an underpinning coherence of approach in defining tourism, aside from the need to characterise the 'otherness' of tourism from similar activities such as migration. Yet even this approach is under criticism as both geographers and sociologists increasingly believe that tourism is but one form of 'mobility' and should not be separated out (we examine this in more detail in the second Mini Case Study in this chapter). As might be expected, definitions have been created to cater for particular needs and situations. Yet it is vital to attempt definitions of tourism, not only to provide a sense of credibility and ownership for those involved, but also for the practical considerations of both measurement and legislation.

Definitions of tourism can be thought of as either:

1. demand-side definitions; or

2. supply-side definitions.

Tourism definitions are unusual in that, until the 1990s, they were being driven more by demand-side than supply-side considerations. Some writers find this surprising: 'Defining tourism in terms of the motivations or other characteristics of travellers would be like trying to define the healthcare professions by describing a sick person' (Smith, 1989: 33). The 1990s saw considerable progress in the development and consensus of both demand- and supply-side definitions. This was stimulated by two key initiatives:

- **Demand-side definitions** – the UN World Tourism Organization's 1991 International Conference on Travel and Tourism Statistics – a conference called to tidy up definitions, terminology and measurement issues. The recommendations of this conference were adopted by the United Nations Statistical Commission (UNSTAT) and published as *Recommendations on Tourism Statistics* (WTO and UNSTAT, 1994).
- **Supply-side definitions** – in March 2000 UNSTAT approved the adoption of tourism satellite accounts as the method of measuring the economic sector of tourism.

Demand-side definitions of tourism

Demand-side definitions have evolved, first, by attempting to encapsulate the idea of tourism into 'conceptual' definitions and, second, through the development of 'technical' definitions for measurement and legal purposes.

From a conceptual point of view we can think of tourism as: 'The activities of persons travelling to and staying in places outside their usual environment for not more than one consecutive year for leisure, business and other purposes' (WTO and UNSTAT, 1994). While this is not a strict technical definition, it does convey the essential nature of tourism, i.e.:

- Tourism arises out of a movement of people to, and their stay in, various places, or destinations.

- There are two elements in tourism – the journey to the destination and the stay (including activities) at the destination.

- The journey and stay take place outside the usual environment or normal place of residence and work so that tourism gives rise to activities that are distinct from the resident and working populations of the places through which they travel and stay.

- The movement to destinations is temporary and short term in character – the intention is to return within a few days, weeks or months.

- Destinations are visited for purposes other than taking up permanent residence or employment in the places visited.

From a technical point of view, attempts to define tourism have been led by the need to isolate tourism trips from other forms of travel for statistical purposes. These technical definitions demand that an activity has to pass certain 'tests' before it counts as tourism. Such tests include the following:

- Minimum length of stay – one night (visitors who do not stay overnight are termed **same-day visitors** or excursionists).

- Maximum length of stay – one year.

- Strict purpose of visit categories.

- A distance consideration is sometimes included on the grounds of delineating the term 'usual environment' – the UNWTO recommendation is 160 km.

MINI CASE STUDY 0.2
Tourism and mobilities

A NEW WAY OF THINKING ABOUT TOURISM

The social sciences – in particular geography and sociology – are rediscovering tourism as an area for research, case studies and examples. The approach that these subject areas have adopted, however, is different from the more traditional approach taken by academics in the tourism area. In a new way of thinking about tourism, geographers and sociologists see it as one form of 'mobility', locating tourism within a spectrum ranging from permanent migration to daily shopping.

In other words, geographers and sociologists see tourism as one dimension of our 'connections' with the world ranging across many different localities. No longer are people's activities disconnected and within distinct spaces, rather everyone is networked and connected. Larsen *et al.* (2007) argue that the world in the twenty-first century is a highly mobile one and because tourism is relatively inexpensive and convenient, it blends with other forms of mobility and connections. The key message from the idea of tourism 'as a form of mobility' is that tourism is no longer treated as a distinct and special activity, but simply one that is a part of a range of other activities in society.

The reason that this way of thinking has emerged is partly due to 'space–time compression' – the fact that with transport and communication technology it is possible to visit distant places for a day. In Europe, for example, it is perfectly possible to visit Paris for lunch from the UK. This means that we can think of the idea of tourism being part of a 'leisure mobility spectrum' ranging from daily leisure around the home through to tourism where an overnight stay is taken. Here we can see that what may initially be a tourism-related mobility – travelling to and from a second home, for example – may eventually become retirement migration. In this way, the concept of mobility does provide valuable insights into travel behaviour. In fact, Larsen *et al.* (2007) take this a step further and argue that tourism involves 'travelling, visiting and hosting [that] are necessary to much social life conducted at-a-distance . . . [involving] connections with, rather than escape from, social relations and the multiple obligations of everyday social life' (p. 245). They see tourism as part of 'stretched' social networks, as opposed to a distinct and separate activity, divorced from everyday life. In part this is made possible by technology, communications, advances in transport and the space-compressing nature of globalisation.

THE ISSUES

The approach does create two major issues relating to this chapter:

1. Effectively, it blurs the distinction between home, work and tourist destinations; and between differing types of traveller – whether they are commuters, shoppers or migrants. This makes reconciling the 'mobilities' approach with the drawing up of 'definitions' of tourism problematic – particularly when we go back to the definitions of tourism designed by the UN World Tourism Organization. The UNWTO's definitions see tourism as a distinct activity, taking place away from home and for a period of more than 24 hours. Of course, the formal definitions do now recognise the day trip as an activity, but there is no recognition of the 'spectrum of mobilities' that tourism may embrace, and there is a rigid exclusion of certain types of mobile populations such as migrants, refugees and travellers.

2. It also begs the question as to whether tourism as a subject of study should be a separate and 'exotic' area of study and research (Franklin and Crang, 2001). Instead, there is a case for some elements of tourism explanation to be more closely linked to geography and sociology in the spirit of 'post-disciplinarity' mentioned above.

REFERENCES

Franklin, A. and Crang, M. (2001) 'The trouble with tourism and travel theory', *Tourism Studies* **1**(1), 5–22.
Larsen, J., Urry, J. and Axhausen, K.W. (2007) 'Networks and tourism: Mobile social life', *Annals of Tourism Research* **34**(1), 244–62.

DISCUSSION QUESTIONS

1. Is tourism still a 'special' activity or has it become part of everyday life and expectations?

2. Thinking of your own 'mobility' over the last week, how many trips could be seen as 'leisure related'?

3. Thinking of the world, and the idea of 'space–time compression', there are many places which are highly accessible due to improved transport access. Has this had any impact on your own travel patterns over the last few years?

Supply-side definitions of tourism

The very nature of tourism as a fragmented, diverse product, spread over many industries and comprising both intangible and tangible elements, means that it is a difficult sector to define. As with demand-side definitions, there are two basic approaches to defining the tourism sector – the conceptual, or descriptive, and the technical. From a conceptual point of view, Leiper suggests: 'The tourist industry consists of all those firms, organisations and facilities which are intended to serve the specific needs and wants of tourists' (1979: 400).

A major problem concerning technical supply-side definitions is the fact that there is a spectrum of tourism businesses and organisations, from those which are wholly serving tourists to those who also serve local residents and other markets. The tourism satellite account (TSA) is the agreed approach to defining the tourism sector as it measures the goods and services purchased by visitors to estimate the size of the tourism economic sector (WTO, 2001) (see also Table 0.2). The TSA:

Table 0.2		UNWTO supply-side definition of tourism (International Standard Industrial Classification, ISIC)

ISIC divisions	Business activity[a]	Example
Construction	T	Hotels, recreational facilities, transport facilities, resort residence.
Wholesale and retail	P	Motor vehicles sales, sales of motor vehicle fuels, retail food sales, retail sales of textiles.
	T	Retail sales of travel accessories, souvenir sales, etc.
Hotels and restaurants	P	Fast food restaurants, food.
	T	Hotels, camping sites.
Transport, storage and communications	P	Transport via railways, chauffeured vehicles, inland water transport.
	T	Inter-urban rail, airlines, special rail tour service, long-distance bus services, cruise ships.
Financial intermediation	P	Exchange of currencies, life insurance, credit cards.
	T	Travel insurance.
Real estate, renting and business activities	P	Buying or selling of leased property, letting or owning of leased property.
	T	Rental of ski equipment, letting of owned tourism property.
Public administration	P	Translation services, customs administration, fishing regulation, foreign affairs, border guards.
	T	Tourism administration, information bureaux, visa issuance, regulation of private transport.
Education	P	Adult education, driving schools, flying schools, boating instruction.
	T	Hotel schools, tourism education programmes, recreation and park service schools, tourist instruction.
Other community	P	Swimming, scuba instruction, flying instruction, boating instruction, motion picture entertainment.
	T	Visitor bureaux, travel clubs, travel unions.
Extra-territorial organisations	P	OECD, World Bank, IMF, ASEAN.
	T	International tourism bodies.

[a] P = part involvement with tourism; T = totally dedicated to tourism.
Source: WTO and UNSTAT, 1994

- provides information on the economic impact of tourism, including contribution to gross domestic product, investment, tax revenues, tourism consumption and the impact on a nation's balance of payments;
- provides information on tourism employment and its characteristics; and, importantly
- allows tourism to be compared with other economic sectors.

It is clear from this section that the tourism sector has been late in recognising the importance of supply-side definitions. However, the benefits are clear, as the TSA allows tourism to be compared with other economic sectors and delivers important data for planning and policy, as well as providing an important conceptual framework for studying and researching tourism.

INTERRELATIONSHIPS AND CLASSIFICATIONS

Not only are the elements of tourism all interlinked, but also we can see that tourism has close relationships with other activities and concepts. It is therefore a mistake to consider tourism in isolation from these other related activities. For example, most tourism throughout the world is a leisure activity and it is important to locate tourism in the spectrum of leisure activities.

Although the Latin translation of leisure literally means 'to be free', defining leisure is, if anything, more problematic than defining tourism. In essence, leisure can be thought of as a combined measure of time and attitude of mind to create periods of time when other obligations are at a minimum. Recreation can be thought of as the pursuits engaged in during leisure time, and an activity spectrum can be identified with, at one end of the scale, recreation around the home, through to tourism where an overnight stay is involved (Figure 0.4).

Although same-day visits or excursions are a common recreational activity, for tourism to occur, leisure time has to be blocked together to allow a stay away from home. Traditionally, these blocks of leisure time were taken as paid holiday entitlement, though innovations such as flexitime and three-day weekends have also facilitated tourism.

Tourists

While all-embracing definitions of tourism and a tourist are desirable, in practice tourists represent a heterogeneous, not a homogeneous, group with different personalities, demographics and experiences. We can classify tourists in two basic ways which relate to the nature of their trip:

- A basic distinction can be made between domestic and international tourists, although this distinction is blurring in many parts of the world (for example, in the European Union). Domestic tourism refers to travel by residents within their country of residence. There are rarely currency, language or visa implications, and domestic tourism is more difficult to measure than international tourism. As a consequence, domestic tourism has received little attention (see Chapter 3). In contrast, international tourism involves travel outside the country of residence and there may well be currency, language and visa implications.

- Tourists can also be classified by 'purpose of visit category'. Conventionally, three categories are used:

  1. leisure and recreation – including holiday, sports and cultural tourism and **visiting friends and relatives (VFR)**;
  2. other tourism purposes – including study and health tourism;
  3. business and professional – including meetings, conferences, missions, incentive and business tourism.

Not only are these categories used for statistical purposes, they are also useful for the marketing of tourism. Consider, for example, Figure 0.5 where we demonstrate the flexibility of travel for each of the categories from the point of view of airline fare pricing and validity.

There are many other ways to classify tourists. These range from simple demographic and trip classifications (see, for example, Table 0.3) through their lifestyles and personalities, to

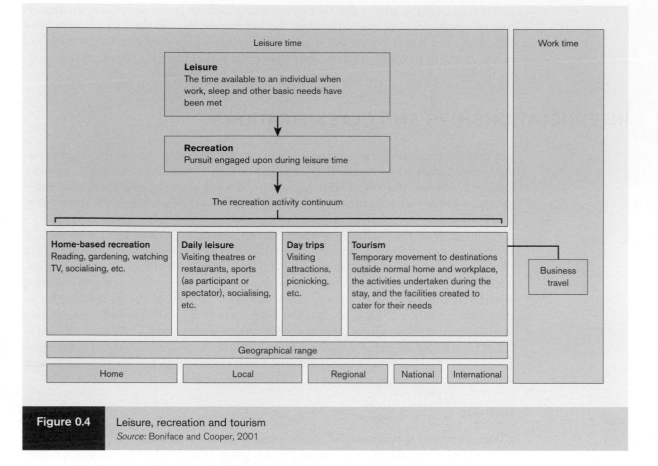

Figure 0.4   Leisure, recreation and tourism
Source: Boniface and Cooper, 2001

their perception of risk and familiarity and postmodern interpretations of consumers and commodities. However, one approach with increasing relevance to contemporary tourism is to classify tourists according to their level and type of interaction with the destination. Classifications of tourists that adopt this approach commonly place mass tourism at one extreme and some form of alternative, small-scale tourism at the other with a variety of classes in between. It is then argued that mass tourism has a major impact upon the destination because of the sheer scale of the industry and the nature of the consumer. On the other hand, small-scale, alternative types of tourism are said to have a much reduced impact upon the destination, not only because of the type of consumer involved but also because they will shun the travel trade and stay in local pensions or with families. In this case, it is argued, the impact of tourism is less disruptive than for mass tourism.

Some commentators have oversimplified the complex relationship between the consumption and development of tourism resources. This is particularly true of the so-called 'alternative' tourism movement, which is lauded by some as a solution to the ills of mass tourism. Indeed, the tenor of much of the writing about alternative tourism is that any alternative tourism scheme is good whilst all mass tourism is bad. There is, of course, a case for alternative tourism, but only as another form of tourism in the spectrum. It can never be an alternative to mass tourism, nor can it solve all the problems of tourism (Archer *et al.* 2004).

These issues, and the fallacy of lauding 'alternative' tourism as a literal alternative to mass tourism, come into clear focus when examined against the frameworks of analysis developed in this book. For example, only by matching appropriate types of visitor to particular types of destination will truly sustainable development be achieved.

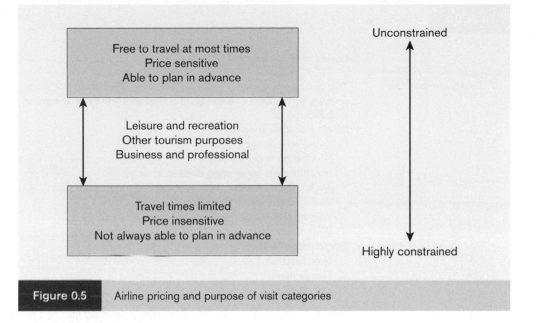

Figure 0.5   Airline pricing and purpose of visit categories

Table 0.3   Suggested socio-economic characteristics for tourism analysis

	Levels of measurement
Socio-economic variable	
1 Age	Collect by single years. It may be convenient to summarise by age cohorts.
2 Sex	Male/female. Age–sex cohorts may also be useful.
3 Education	Given the diversity of educational systems in North America, a basic four-part classification may be most useful: elementary, secondary, post-secondary, non university and university. It may be useful in other circumstances to distinguish between completion of secondary or post-secondary programmes and partial work (drop-out before completion).
4 Occupational status	Categories can include employed full-time, employed part-time, retired (some reference to former occupation may be desired), homemaker, student, unemployed. If employed, refer the respondent to the next question, 'occupation'.
5 Occupation	This is best determined through an open-ended question. Responses can be summarised according to the *Occupation Classification Manual* or other comparable national statistical coding system such as the *Canadian Classification and Dictionary of Occupations*. These codes refer to the type of industry in which the traveller is employed.
6 Annual income	This is an especially sensitive subject; some of the concern over reporting income can be reduced by using income categories. The specific categories should be based on those used in the most recent national census. Household income is often the most relevant measure of income, although the respondent's income may be useful in special circumstances.

Table 0.3	(continued)

Levels of measurement

7 Family composition

This can be an especially important variable if the purpose of study includes some analysis of the effect of travel party composition on travel behaviour. One possible classification is:
Single individual living alone
Husband–wife family
    No children under 18 years
    No children at home or no children at all
    Adult children or other adult relatives living at home
    With children under 18 years
    With no other adult relatives
    With other relatives
Single-parent families
    Male head
    Female head
All other families

8 Party composition

This is closely related to the previous variable for many travelling parties. Levels include:
One person alone
One family with children
Two families with children
Organised group
One couple
Two or more couples
Group of friends (unorganised group)
Other

Trip variable

1 Season or trip period

Calendar quarters:
    January to March
    April to June
    July to September
    October to December
If the trip overlaps two or more quarters, the following convention is often used: for household surveys, use the quarter in which the trip ends; for exits or re-entry surveys, use the date of the survey.
It is sometimes desirable to distinguish weekend trips from other trips.

2 Trip duration

Both days and nights are used as the unit of measurement. The number of nights is usually one less than the number of days; a three-day weekend lasts 'two nights'. The actual number of days or nights up to one week is often collected. Periods longer than one week are often measured as ranges, e.g. 8–15 days (or 7–13 nights).

3 Trip distance

This should be based, in part, on the threshold distance required for definition of a trip. Narrow ranges for lowest levels are desirable to permit aggregating or exclusion of data so that comparisons can be made between surveys using different distance thresholds. A possible classification would be:
    25–49 miles
    50–99 miles
    100–499 miles
    500–999 miles
    1000–1499 miles
    More than 1500 miles (2400 km)
Metric conversion is usually necessary for international comparisons; however, international travel is normally not measured by distance.

Table 0.3	*(continued)*

Levels of measurement

4 Purpose of trip	Very simple classifications are used, such as business versus pleasure. This dichotomy is normally inadequate for analytical purposes and is too simplistic to represent the purposes of many trips. More precise classifications would include:

Conventions or other business meetings
Buying, selling, installation, or other business
Recreation/vacation
Touring/sightseeing
Attending cultural/sporting events
Participating in cultural/sporting events
Visiting friends or relatives
Other family or personal matters
Shopping
Study tour
Health/rest

Many trips involve more than one purpose, so it may be useful to specify 'primary' purpose.

5 Mode of transportation	Private automobile

Rental automobile
Bus/motor coach
Train
Scheduled airline
Chartered airline
Private aeroplane
Boat/ship (additional categories for ferries, cruise ships, private boats may be added as necessary)

Some trips involve multiple modes, such as a combination of scheduled airline and rental car. These combinations may be specified or a primary mode may be requested.

6 Expenditures	Transportation (broken down by mode, if desired)

Accommodation (including camping fees, but not park entrance fees)
Food and beverages (restaurant meals may be separated from food purchased at a store)
Convention or registration fees
Admission fees and other entertainment, including park admissions, licence fees for hunting and fishing
Souvenirs
Other purchases

7 Type of accommodation	Hotels and inns

Motels and motor inns
Resorts
Campgrounds
Hostels
Commercial cottages
Institutional camps
Private cottages
Bed and breakfast/tourist home
Homes of friends or relatives
Other

Additional classifications could be based on size of accommodation, price, public versus private ownership, function (e.g. fishing camp, ski resort), type of location (e.g. airport strip; downtown), availability of liquor and so on.

Source: Tourism Research Planning Committee, 1975; and from *Tourism Analysis: A Handbook*, Harlow, Longman with permission of Pearson Education Limited (Smith, S.L. 1989)

CONCLUSION

Mass tourism, as an activity, remains relatively youthful and, while it has experienced unprecedented growth rates in the past four decades, the study of tourism inevitably lacks the maturity of other subject areas and disciplines. This lack of maturity is manifested in many ways, not least the lack of agreement as to what actually constitutes tourism activity on both the demand and supply side. Nevertheless, the economic importance of tourism has guaranteed increased governmental and international attention and accompanying this has not only been a growing recognition of the significance and importance of tourism and the need to be able to define and measure all aspects of it, but also a need for the sustainable development and management of tourism.

This introduction provides the basic underpinning framework for the remainder of this book, offering contemporary views on important tourism-related definitions, acquainting the reader with the fundamentals of the dynamics of the tourism system, and pointing out the impact of a changing world on the way that tourism does business.

SELF-CHECK QUESTIONS

1. Identify five ways that tourism can contribute to the Millennium Development Goals.
2. Draft a checklist of the security threats posed by tourists when travelling internationally.
3. Review the major methods used to classify tourists – which one do you prefer?
4. Which of the following can be counted as tourists in the official definitions?
   - invading armies
   - space shuttle pilots
   - international conference delegates
   - travelling diplomats
   - nomads
   - immigrants
5. Review the major elements of the tourism system – how do they relate to each other?

ESSAY QUESTIONS

1. Draft a justification for the introduction of a new tourism programme at your educational institution.
2. It has been suggested that tourism is a fragmented sector in search of an industry. Discuss this assertion.
3. Summarise the impacts of London's underground train bombings on tourism to London.
4. Evaluate the barriers to the potential of tourism to be an agent of poverty alleviation.
5. Discuss the view that responsible tourism can never be a replacment for mass tourism.

ANNOTATED FURTHER READING

Books

Goeldner, C.R. and Ritchie, B. (2006) *Tourism: Principles, Practices, Philosophies*, 10th edn, Wiley, New York.
A comprehensive textbook with a strong North American flavour.

Jafari, J. (2001) *The Encyclopedia of Tourism*, Routledge, London.
A comprehensive volume with definitive statements on every tourism term written by the leading expert in each field.

Urry, J. (2000) *Sociology Beyond Societies. Mobilities for the Twenty-First Century*, Routledge, London.
A refreshingly different approach, focusing on the concept of mobilities and tourism.

Web sites

http://www.world-tourism.org
An all-embracing web site providing the official United Nations' view on tourism issues such as pro-poor tourism and providing definitions, definitive statistics and approaches to tourism.

http://www.wttc.org
A comprehensive web site from the private sector's representative body for tourism with up-to-date statistics and reports on the tourism industry and its contribution to economies.

References cited

Archer, B.H., Cooper, C.P. and Ruhanen, L. (2004) 'The positive and negative aspects of tourism', pp. 79–102 in Theobold, W.F. (ed.), *Global Tourism*, Elsevier Butterworth Heinemann, Oxford.

Boniface, B. and Cooper, C. (2001) *Worldwide Destinations: The Geography of Travel and Tourism*, Heinemann, London.

Coles, T., Hall, C.M. and Duval, D.T. (2006) 'Tourism and post-disciplinary enquiry', *Current Issues in Tourism* 9(4–5), 293–319.

Franklin, A. and Crang, M. (2001) 'The trouble with tourism and travel theory', *Tourism Studies* 1(1), 5–22.

Gilbert, D. (1990) 'Conceptual issues in the meaning of tourism', pp. 4–27 in Cooper, C. (ed.), *Progress in Tourism, Recreation and Hospitality Management*, Belhaven Press, London.

Jafari, J. and Ritchie, J.R.B. (1981) 'Towards a framework for tourism education', *Annals of Tourism Research* 8(1), 13–34.

Leiper, N. (1979) 'The framework of tourism', *Annals of Tourism Research* 6(4), 390–407.

Leiper, N. (1990) 'Tourism systems', Massey University Department of Management Systems Occasional Paper 2, Auckland.

McIntosh, R.W. and Goeldner, C.R. (1990) *Tourism: Principles, Practices, Philosophies*, Wiley, New York.

Rojek, C. and Urry, J. (1997) *Touring Cultures – Transformations of Travel Theory*, Routledge, London.

Smith, S.L.J. (1989) *Tourism Analysis: A Handbook*, Longman, Harlow.

Tourism Research Planning Committee (1975) *Standard Definitions and Classifications for Travel Survey*, Federal–Provincial Conference on Tourism, Ottawa.

WTO (2001) *Basic Concepts of the Tourism Satellite Account (TSA)*, WTO, Madrid.

WTO and UNSTAT (1994) *Recommendations on Tourism Statistics*, WTO, Madrid and United Nations, New York.

WTTC (2006) *World Travel and Tourism. Climbing to New Heights*, World Travel and Tourism Council, London.

MAJOR CASE STUDY 0.1
Pro-poor tourism

INTRODUCTION

The World Travel and Tourism Council's vision for a new tourism in the twenty-first century states:

> New Tourism is a force capable of dramatically improving economic and social well-being right across the globe, waiting to be unleashed.
>
> **(WTTC, 2003: 5)**

Indeed, one of the key issues in the twenty-first century will be the development of strategies to tackle poverty. Poverty is an unacceptable human situation. It is also a situation from which people want to escape. Yet tourism has demonstrated a fragmented and ineffective stance towards utilising tourism as an agent of poverty reduction. It is the aim of this case study to explore the potential of tourism to help reduce poverty in the world.

DEFINING POVERTY

Poverty reduction tends to focus on income-based measures of poverty. However, development agencies have increasingly realised that poverty is multidimensional and can be thought of as depriving individuals of capability – in other words, a person is poor if they lack both income and basic capabilities (UNDP, 2006). The World Bank, for example, states that poverty can be thought of as hunger, lack of shelter, sickness and above all powerlessness – in other words, there are many dimensions to poverty. We can look at a range of ways to measure poverty, including not only income measures but also non-income dimensions of poverty such as health, education or housing. Nonetheless, the most obvious approach to measuring poverty is by using income: in other words, a person is considered to be poor, or 'below the poverty line', if their income falls below a level necessary to meet basic needs. Here, for example, the World Bank's definition of poverty is 'anyone living on less than one US dollar per day', although the measure of US$2 is also commonly used. The UN estimates that 2.5 billion people came under the definition of living on less than US$2 per day, with the majority living in Asia, although the most extreme poverty rates are in Sub-Saharan Africa.

REDUCING POVERTY

In the twenty-first century, poverty reduction is a key objective of the world's development agencies. There have been two drivers of the poverty reduction agenda in the twenty-first century. First, the 2002 World Summit on Sustainable Development placed poverty reduction as a development imperative. Secondly, in 2000, the lead international agencies in the world distilled key development goals and targets from the previous decade into a 'Millennium Declaration' comprising Millennium Development Goals (MDGs). The first MDG is to 'eradicate extreme poverty and hunger', calling for a halving of those living on less than US$1 per day by 2015.

Three key strategies to reduce poverty emerge from these initiatives:

1. Accelerate economic growth.
2. Improve the distribution of income and wealth.
3. Accelerate social development.

The World Bank states that to be successful these strategies must be:

- country driven, with broad-based participation by the public and private sector;
- results-orientated, focusing on positive outcomes for the poor;
- comprehensive in their recognition of the multi-dimensional nature of poverty;
- partnerships-based; and
- based on a long-term perspective.

International agencies and charities around the world are working to this agenda, but tourism has been slow to recognise its potential to alleviate poverty. In part this is because it is difficult for tourism to operate in isolation. To be successful as a tool of poverty reduction, tourism must be seen as one dimension of a destination's economy and society. For broader-based approaches such as changing systems of land tenure, planning procedures, training and education, and infrastructure improvements, tourism can play a role but has to work within national and regional policy frameworks.

THE PRO-POOR TOURISM AGENDA

The use of tourism to reduce poverty is sometimes termed **pro-poor tourism** (PPT). PPT has been embraced by the developing world and international agencies (including the UNWTO, UNCTAD, the Asian Development Bank and the World Bank). In 2002, the UNWTO launched an ambitious programme in this area known as 'sustainable tourism–eliminating poverty' (ST–EP) (WTO, 2002) and this was endorsed with considerable funding by the government of Korea. To quote the former Secretary-General of the United Nations Kofi Annan in 2006:

> ST-EP will promote socially, economically and ecologically sustainable tourism, aimed at alleviating poverty and bringing jobs to people in developing countries... These objectives are fully consistent with the goals set out in the 'Millennium Declaration'.

PPT is an approach to tourism development aimed at poverty reduction rather than being a specific product. It aims to 'tilt' tourism towards benefiting the poor and can be defined as 'tourism that results in increased net benefits for poor people'. It is an approach to developing tourism focused on the key question: How can tourism reduce poverty at the local level, and therefore what policies, strategies and plans can be put into place to enhance poverty alleviation?

There are three groups of stakeholders involved in PPT:

1. Governments, who must develop visionary strategies, policies and inclusive approaches;
2. The private sector, who must act as partner, enabler, customer, marketing channel and financial analyst; and
3. The poor as producers, suppliers, workers, participants and above all, decision makers.

But, as mentioned above, tourism is a newcomer to the arena of poverty reduction and, while there is much potential and hope for the approach, there is little real experience of operating pro-poor tourism at tourism destinations. Nonetheless, tourism brings a number of benefits as a sector for pro-poor development:

- Tourism is produced where it is consumed – the tourist has to visit the destination, allowing opportunities for economic gain.
- Tourism is labour intensive and employs a high percentage of women.
- Tourism is naturally attracted to remote, peripheral areas where other economic options are limited.

- Eighty per cent of the world's poor live in 12 countries in all of which but one tourism is significant and growing.
- Tourism conserves natural and heritage resources.
- Tourism is a significant and a leading source of income and employment in the developing and least-developed countries (LDCs). Effectively, tourism is often the only source of comparative advantage.

And of course, there are real benefits to the tourism sector in tackling the issue of poverty. For example:

- reducing poverty at the tourism destination will help to make that destination safer and reduce possible hostile attitudes from the local community;
- poverty reduction will also make the destination more attractive by reducing the numbers of shanty towns and beggars and enhancing the environmental quality of the destination; and
- tourism needs to find ways to enhance its own acceptability in the wider community and poverty reduction is one medium for doing this.

STRATEGIES FOR PRO-POOR TOURISM

One of the key lessons that tourism can learn from international agencies and charities involved in poverty reduction is the imperative to ensure that pro-poor tourism strategies can be implemented at the local level. Ashley, Boyd and Goodwin (2000) identify three types of pro-poor tourism strategies:

1. Strategies focused on economic benefits, including:
   - local job creation to deliver a measure of security in household income;
   - gap filling between other forms of income, for example in non-harvest times;
   - small business opportunities in the tourism market directly and indirectly supplying tourists with goods such as handicrafts and food;
   - local cooperative development; and
   - increasing the economic benefits for the whole community – by renting communal land for camping, for example.
2. Strategies focused on improving living conditions and capacity building. Strategies here include training and education, reducing the environmental impacts of tourism, reducing competition for natural resources, and improved access to services such as schooling, healthcare, communications and infrastructure improvements.

Photograph 0.2   Tourism brings a number of benefits as a sector for pro-poor development. Here local tribes sell crafts to tourists.

3. Strategies focused on participation, partnerships and involvement. Here strategies are designed to change the policy and planning framework to allow participation by local communities in tourism, decision-making and partnerships with the private sector.

The success of tourism as a tool of poverty reduction will then depend upon implementing the most appropriate of these strategies for particular situations and communities. The principles of pro-poor tourism are the same everywhere, but their implementation will vary according to the type of tourism product from, say, small-scale eco-tourism to mass tourism. Destination-based strategies, for example, are appropriate for particular groups, encouraging economic linkages between tourism businesses and local community groups such as farmers. At the destination it is important to reduce leakage through imports, boost partnerships, develop local enterprises and increase community pride. In Asia, a particular group that is being targeted for pro-poor tourism projects is the urban poor. In Asian cities tourism is labour intensive,

has low barriers to entry for workers, and women can be major beneficiaries.

Already, pro-poor tourism initiatives around the world have come up with some valuable lessons for successful implementation. These include the importance of local ownership and control and the need to develop partnerships with the private sector on an equitable footing. Pro-poor tourism must also recognise the basic principles of tourism development and realise that it will only succeed if there is access to transport, accommodation and the wider range of support services and products. Here, location is critical and successful schemes have tended to be in accessible tourism destinations. Of course, the impact may be greater in remote destinations but the scale of the impact may be less. Finally it has to be recognised that success is long term and that pro-poor tourism will not deliver short-term gain.

Despite the growing momentum for the development of pro-poor tourism, there are some issues which make the concept controversial. For example, there is a perception by aid agencies that tourism is for the wealthy and they do not support the concept. In part this stems from a lack of education, training and understanding about pro-poor tourism. There are also some real practical barriers including:

- Significant economic leakages out of the local community, reducing the net benefits of tourism.
- Lack of investment and low interest loans to allow local tourism enterprises to get under way.
- The fact that not all the poor will benefit equally (particularly the very poorest in a society will struggle to benefit) and this can lead to conflict.
- A lack of infrastructure and basic services in very poor areas.
- The fact that the poor often cannot access market and resources to enable successful pro-poor tourism strategies.
- Local land use and other policies that do not favour collaborative pro-poor strategies.

But, however difficult the practical adoption of pro-poor tourism may be, there is no doubt that the philosophy of tourism as a tool for poverty reduction must be embraced by the public and private sectors in tourism. Tourism has a real contribution to make in this area.

WEB SITES

http://www.adb.org/Poverty/default.asp
http://www.propoortourism.org.uk
http://www.worldbank.org/poverty

REFERENCES

Ashley, C., Boyd, C. and Goodwin, H. (2000) 'Pro-poor tourism: putting poverty at the heart of the tourism agenda', *Natural Resource Perspectives* **51** (March) 1–12.

UNDP (2006) *What is Poverty?* UNDP International Poverty Centre One Pager 22, UNDP IPC, Brasilia.

WTO (2002) *Sustainable Tourism – Eliminating Poverty*, WTO, Madrid.

WTTC (2003) *Blueprint for New Tourism*, WTTC, London.

DISCUSSION QUESTIONS

1. Can tourism be a real force for the alleviation of poverty or is the debate simply rhetoric?

2. Do you think that the role of tourism in poverty alleviation should be confined to governments and aid agencies, or is there a role for the tourist in this strategy? How can tourists 'do their bit' to alleviate poverty at the destination?

3. Should the future tourism development agenda also focus on alleviating other problems in society in addition to poverty?

PART 1

TOURISM DEMAND

Phtograph: Coastline at Tulum, Mexico © Graham Meyer

INTRODUCTION

This part of the book provides you with a comprehensive introduction to tourism demand. It aims to provide you with five key knowledge areas:

1. The concepts, definitions and indicators of tourism demand.
2. Tourism consumer behaviour.
3. How tourism demand is measured and reported.
4. The determinants of tourism demand.
5. Tourism demand forecasting.

The part is organised into four chapters, with each covering one or more of the key knowledge areas above. Each chapter explores the area of knowledge in depth and is structured to meet a set of learning outcomes which are provided at the beginning of the chapter. In addition, we identify and annotate selected reading, not an easy task for tourism demand, which has not received the attention that it deserves. A range of case studies brings to life the concepts and theoretical issues in the chapters and a series of self-check, discussion and essay questions throughout the text allows you to review and test your understanding of the material.

In the introduction to this book we identified Leiper's tourism system as an effective organising concept for tourism. Tourism demand originating from Leiper's generating region is effectively the subject of this section of four chapters. In Chapter 1 – Managing Tourism Demand – we introduce the key approaches to tourism demand. There are two key themes running through this chapter. The first is the way that the views of tourism managers have changed as demand has grown since the Second World War. There is no doubt that managing tourism demand is one of the challenges for tourism in the twenty-first century as the volume of tourists grows. We chart how the perceptions of demand have changed over the years, with early pronouncements such as the UN's Universal Declaration of Human Rights in 1948 encouraging everyone to travel as a 'right', to the present day when the tourist is urged to travel 'responsibly'. On this point we provide a mini case study demonstrating how different sectors of the tourism industry have approached the 'education' of tourists to behave 'responsibly'. The second theme of the chapter is the recognition that, in order to manage tourism demand, it is important to understand the nature of demand in terms of definitions, the various components of demand and simple indicators.

Chapter 2 – Tourism Consumer Behaviour – probes more deeply into demand by providing an overview of the consumer decision-making process in tourism. The themes of this chapter focus around, first, understanding the components of the tourism consumer decision process, and, secondly, assessing models of the process. We show that there is a range of factors that influence travel decisions; factors such as motivation, attitudes, perceptions and images. The chapter provides you with a thorough overview of these ideas and the major literature debates. The second theme shows how these factors have been drawn together and structured in the form of models of consumer decision-making. For tourism, these models have been adapted from more general approaches in the consumer marketing literature. Perhaps one of the key lessons from this chapter is to question whether these models are purely academic exercises or have a practical use for tourism managers in a changing world. Finally, the chapter draws these threads together in a major case study showing how consumer behaviour responded to the 2004 Boxing Day Indian Ocean Tsunami.

In Chapter 3 – Measuring Demand for Tourism – we turn to approaches to measuring patterns of consumer demand. This chapter has two distinct sections. First, we provide detail of the approaches used to measure demand for both international and domestic tourism and assess their effectiveness. We go on to consider why tourism demand is measured, what definitions are used and which statistics are normally compiled. Secondly, we describe in detail approaches to collecting market intelligence and managing information, ending the chapter with a major case study on the need for the tourism sector to develop a knowledge management approach. The key lesson from this chapter is the need to be cautious in interpreting and using tourism statistics.

In Chapter 4 – Tourism Demand Determinants and Forecasting – we focus on two key areas of knowledge. First, we provide a detailed assessment of the major determinants of demand for tourism. We consider specific determinants of demand at the individual level and go on to demonstrate how they can be aggregated to explain patterns and rhythms of tourism demand globally. In this way we can show that those countries with a high level of economic development and a stable, urbanised population are major generators of tourism demand – the chapter ends with a major case study analysing global patterns of tourism demand. The second area of knowledge relates to tourism forecasting. We show that an understanding of demand determinants is fundamental to forecasting future demand. Accurate forecasts in tourism are essential to inform decision-making in both governments and the industry, and we examine the different approaches available to forecast tourism demand and the reasons why we should maintain forecasts. This is an important issue given that tourism is a perishable industry and its assets such as beds or aircraft seats cannot be stored. The lesson of this chapter is that, despite the fact that tourism is a volatile industry operating in a world of rapid and unexpected change, tourism forecasts are necessary for informed management decision-making.

CHAPTER 1
Managing Tourism Demand

LEARNING OUTCOMES

In this chapter we focus on the basic concepts, definitions and indicators of tourism demand to provide you with:

- an awareness of how approaches to the management of demand have changed since 1945;
- a thorough understanding of the concept and definitions of tourism demand;
- an awareness of the components of tourism demand;
- a grasp of the importance of indicators of demand such as propensity to travel; and
- a comprehension of the purpose of demand schedules and an understanding of how to interpret them.

Photograph: Courchevel, France © Jason Dusting

INTRODUCTION

In this chapter we introduce the key approaches to tourism demand that underpin its management. There is no doubt that managing tourism demand is one of the challenges for tourism in the twenty-first century as the volume of tourists grows and the remotest corners of the world are visited. In fact, we can chart how the perceptions of demand have changed over the years with early pronouncements such as the UN's Universal Declaration of Human Rights encouraging everyone to travel as a 'right', to the present day when the tourist is urged to travel 'responsibly' and to offset his or her carbon emissions generated from flying.

In order to manage tourism demand it is important to understand the nature of demand in terms of definitions, the various components of demand and simple indicators. In particular, we must recognise the fact that demand comprises much more than just those who are active as tourists. There are large sections of society who would like to travel but who experience barriers to travel. From a management and marketing point of view it is important to understand these barriers and to devise strategies to remove them. Finally, this chapter provides you with a number of techniques that allow you to estimate the demand for tourism, in particular populations.

MANAGING TOURISM DEMAND

Considering Leiper's overall system for tourism that we described in the introductory chapter, demand for tourism is the result of activities and decisions made in the generating region (see Figure 0.2). As such, demand for tourism is a fundamental element in the tourism system. Yet, while the history of tourism may be traced back many thousands of years to the Ancient Greeks and Romans, it is only relatively recently, with the advent of demand for mass tourism, that international tourism activity has become so prevalent in the developed world. Indeed, the rapid expansion of leisure travel from the 1960s onwards continues to influence all aspects of the tourism system today. The level of demand for tourism is predicted to reach unprecedented levels during this century, providing the tourism industry and all those involved in its production and consumption with major challenges.

It is for these reasons that an analytical approach to demand is important. Uysal (1998), for example, provides three compelling reasons for analysing tourism demand:

1. It is an essential underpinning for policy and forecasting.

2. It provides critical information to allow the balancing of provision of supply and demand at destinations.

3. It allows the tourism industry to better understand consumer behaviour and the tourism marketplace.

In this respect we can identify how perceptions and approaches to the management of tourism demand have changed as volumes have increased and the integrity of destinations, and indeed the globe, has been threatened. For example, just after the Second World War, the United Nations (UN) stated in its Universal Declaration of Human Rights that: 'everyone has the right to rest and leisure including . . . periodic holidays with pay' (1948).

By 1980 the Manila Declaration on World Tourism declared the ultimate aim of tourism to be: 'the improvement of the quality of life and the creation of better living conditions for all peoples' (WTO, 1980). With this statement we can see the emphasis changing from the earlier 'right' of everyone to demand tourism to statements stressing the 'quality of demand' and the 'form' of demand and/or experience. This observation is further supported by declarations in the 1990s which state that if individuals demand tourism they must take responsibility for the environment and host societies at the destination: 'tourists share responsibility for conservation of the environment and cultural heritage' (WTO, 1994). This shift in thinking culminated in 1999 with the UN World Tourism Organization's *Global Code of Ethics for Tourism*. In other words, as society increasingly demands travel, it is important to manage tourist behaviour through codes of ethics, visitor guidelines, and education about responsible conduct at destinations. In the twenty-first century this thinking has been taken a step further with calls for tourism to take the responsibility to be carbon neutral in order to reduce climate change. Here tourists are expected to offset carbon emissions generated from flying, as we discuss in Chapter 21 of this book.

Clearly then there is pressure for the management of tourist behaviour through encouraging tourists to exercise their 'right' to travel in a responsible or ethical manner. Since the 1980s, this pressure has come from the media and consumer groups such as Tourism Concern, rather than from the tourism industry itself; indeed it could be argued that the industry entered the movement for responsible tourism rather later than might have been expected. Nonetheless, there is now considerable support for the responsible consumption of tourism with a number of guidebooks for the consumer (see, for example, Mann, 1999). The first Mini Case Study in this chapter examines contrasting examples of initiatives for responsible travel from the public sector, pressure groups and the tourism industry itself and asks you to reflect on their relative effectiveness.

MINI CASE STUDY 1.1
Contrasting approaches to the responsible consumption of tourism

THE PUBLIC SECTOR

The most influential public sector initiative for the responsible consumption of tourism is the UN World Tourism Organization's 'Global Code of Ethics for Tourism'. This initiative sets the framework for the responsible and sustainable development of world tourism (www.worldtourism.org/projects/ethics). The code was developed between 1997 and 1999 and has 10 principles, a number of which relate to responsible tourism behaviour. However, the wording is both diplomatic and non-specific. For example, in article 1, tourism's contribution to mutual understanding and respect between peoples and societies, the code states:

> Tourists themselves should observe the social and cultural traditions and practices of all peoples . . . and tourism activities should be conducted in harmony with the attributes and traditions of the host regions and countries and in respect for their laws, practices and customs.

PRESSURE GROUPS AND CHARITIES

Pressure groups for responsible tourism issue consumer guidelines for behaviour at destinations, while charities such as Oxfam now offer tours to Asia, Cuba and Australia. These tours put the people, their culture and the environment of the destination first and introduce the tourist to the host communities (www.caa.org.au/travel). A San Francisco-based group – Partners in Sustainable Tourism – has put together a comprehensive code for travelling responsibly covering cultural understanding and social and environmental impacts (www2.pirt.org/travelcode.html). The code contrasts with the UNWTO's code of ethics in its specific and useful advice. For example:

> Support the local economy by using locally owned restaurants and hotels, buying local products, made by local people with renewable resources.

THE TOURISM INDUSTRY

The response of the tourism industry to the call for responsible consumption of tourism has been mixed. However, where the industry has embraced the concept, the results have been impressive. For example, the Dutch tour operator TUI has developed an environmental awareness campaign for its dive tourism operation in the Caribbean islands of the Netherlands Antilles (Tour Operators Initiative, 2001). The project began in 1999 and aims to 'provide customers with information on responsible travel and sustainable products at various stages of their holiday'. Their approach is also very practical, providing actionable information and advice to customers from the brochure through to their time on the islands:

- information on responsible travel is provided in the TUI brochure;
- information tips on environmentally sound practice is provided in a booklet with the client's tickets;
- a video on sustainable activities and excursions is shown on the flight;
- hostesses meet clients on arrival and brief them;
- the TUI resource book on sustainable excursions, activities and attractions is available in hotel lobbies; and
- partner companies, such as dive operators, who comply with the programme are actively promoted to clients.

DISCUSSION QUESTIONS

1. Of the three approaches, discuss the relative effectiveness of the communication approaches used.
2. Why has the tourism industry been slow to adopt responsible tourism principles?
3. Considering the examples above, which do you feel will be the most effective in changing tourists' behaviour?

DEFINITIONS OF TOURISM DEMAND

Definitions of demand vary according to the subject perspective of the author and indeed we need the various subject and discipline perspectives in order to understand fully tourism demand. For example, economists consider demand to be the schedule of the amount of any product or service that people are willing and able to buy at each specific price in a set of possible prices during a specified period of time. In contrast, psychologists view demand from the perspective of motivation and behaviour. Geographers, on the other hand, define tourist demand as 'the total number of persons who travel, or wish to travel, to use tourist facilities and services at places away from their places of work and residence' (Mathieson and Wall, 1982).

Each approach is useful. The economic approach introduces the idea of elasticity – which describes the relationship between demand and price, or other variables. The geographer's definition implies a wide range of influences, in addition to price, as determinants of demand and includes not only those who actually participate in tourism but also those who wish to but for some reason do not. On the other hand, the psychologist scratches underneath the skin of the tourist to examine the interaction of personality, environment and demand for tourism.

CONCEPTS OF TOURISM DEMAND

The notion that some individuals may harbour a demand for tourism but are unable to realise that demand suggests that demand for tourism consists of a number of components. We can identify three basic components that make up the total demand for tourism:

1. **Effective** or **actual demand** is the actual number of participants in tourism or those who are travelling, i.e. de facto tourists. This is the component of demand most commonly and easily measured and the bulk of tourism statistics refer to effective demand.

2. **Suppressed demand** is made up of that section of the population who do not travel for some reason. Despite burgeoning demand for tourism across the world, even in the twenty-first century it is still true that only a very small percentage of the world's total population engages in international tourism. Of course, a considerably greater number participate in domestic travel, but in many parts of the world tourism remains an unobtainable luxury.

   Two elements of suppressed demand can be distinguished. First, *potential demand* refers to those who will travel at some future date if they experience a change in their circumstances. For example, their purchasing power may increase, or they may receive more paid holiday entitlement, and they therefore have the potential to move into the effective demand category. Secondly, *deferred demand* is a demand postponed because of a problem in the supply environment, such as a lack of capacity in accommodation, weather conditions or, perhaps, a natural disaster such as the 2004 Boxing Day Tsunami. Again this implies that when the supply conditions are more favourable, those in the deferred demand category will convert to effective demand at some future date.

3. Finally, there will always be those who simply do not wish to travel or are unable to travel, constituting a category of **no demand**. Increasingly people are in this category because they choose to spend their discretionary income on goods other than tourism.

We can also consider other ways in which demand for tourism may be viewed and influenced. For example, *substitution of demand* refers to the case when demand for one activity (say a self-catering holiday) is substituted by another (staying in serviced accommodation). A similar concept is *redirection of demand*, where the geographical location of demand is changed – say a trip to Spain is redirected to Greece because of over-booking of accommodation. Finally, the opening of new tourism supply – say a resort, attraction or accommodation – will:

- redirect demand from similar facilities in the area;
- substitute demand from other facilities; and
- generate new demand.

Economists refer to the first two of these as the 'displacement effect' – in other words, demand from other facilities is displaced to the new one and no extra demand is generated. This can be a problem in tourism and is an important consideration when appraising the worth of new tourism projects.

Finally, given Leiper's model of tourism described in the introductory chapter, it is clear that tourism demand results in flows between the generating region and the destination region. One of the key considerations of tourism demand is understanding the flows of tourism between different generating markets and tourism destinations. These flows are complex and determined by a wide variety of factors including geographical proximity, historical trade and cultural ties, and, of course, the notion of contrasting environments, exemplified by the flow of tourists from northern Europe to the warmer countries of the Mediterranean. These factors can be thought of as either *push* factors (generally determined by the nature of the generating regions – such as affluence) or *pull* factors (destination features such as attractiveness, accessibility and relative price). We look at one approach to explaining these flows in the second Mini Case Study.

A second approach to understanding tourism flows is through the concept of **travel propensity**. In order to manage tourism demand we need to be able to measure and estimate the demand behaviour of different groups in society. One of the most useful indicators of effective demand in any particular population is travel propensity. This measure simply

MINI CASE STUDY 1.2
The gravity model

One approach to explaining the flow of tourism between generating markets and destinations is the gravity model. The gravity model is based upon Newton's law of gravitation and takes into account the push and pull factors that influence tourism demand. Its success and virtually universal use is due to its very simplicity and its adoption by the US Department of Transportation. Effectively, the greater the 'mass' of the generating region or destination, the greater will be the flow of tourists. But the gravity model also adds a constraining factor, that of distance and intervening opportunities. The greater the time and cost involved in reaching a destination from an origin point, the smaller will be the flow.

In effect, the gravity model can be used as a simple tourism demand forecasting tool based upon the size of a generating market (mass or 'push'), the attractiveness of a destination ('pull'), and the distance between them. Finally, it is also possible to construct resorts to act as 'an intervening opportunity' and divert flows from a key market – Cancun in Mexico, for example, was created to capture North Americans travelling to the Caribbean.

The following examples show the effectiveness of the gravity model approach:

- As a destination, Australia has a strong 'pull' factor, with stunning destinations, exotic wildlife and a climate suited to tourism. Yet the other variables of the gravity model conspire to mean that international demand for Australia's tourism will never be on the scale of, say, Spain or the Caribbean. This is due to the constraining factor of the 'tyranny of distance' of Australia from the world's generating markets; and the fact that there are no significant tourism-generating countries to provide the 'push' near Australia.

- Spain's tourism has benefited from its proximity to the large generating markets of Western Europe, providing both the 'push' of the market and minimising the friction of distance. While the 'pull' of Spain is strong – particularly in terms of climate and lifestyle – criticism of some of the early coastal development is easily outweighed by the other two variables.

There are a number of challenges in using the model in practice:

1. First, it is difficult to find surrogate measures for the key variables. For example, 'attractiveness' is difficult to measure so 'population' is often supplemented by using other indicators such as car ownership, education or gross domestic product. Equally, 'physical distance' may be supplemented by measures of 'functional distance' such as time or cost of travel. Also, as transit routes have become busier, it becomes necessary to factor in a measure of 'congestion'.

2. Secondly, the model is 'unconstrained', meaning that there is no upper limit on the number of trips that it can predict. In practice, however, there are ceilings on trip numbers from any origin and this is now factored into the model (Smith, 1996).

REFERENCE

Smith, S.L.J. (1996) *Tourism Analysis*, 2nd edn, Longman, Harlow.

DISCUSSION QUESTIONS

1. Make a list of the quantifiable elements of a destination that might be used as a surrogate measure of attractiveness.

2. Identify six countries in the world that might be expected to receive a large volume of tourists according to the gravity model.

3. Identify a list of 'intervening opportunities' in tourism – either resorts or countries.

considers the penetration of tourism trips in a population. Once we know the levels of travel propensity of a population, we can then begin to explain the reasons why different groups in society have different levels of travel propensity. This is considered in detail in the Major Case Study later in this chapter.

DEMAND SCHEDULES

In economic terms, a demand schedule refers to the quantities of a product that an individual wishes to purchase at different prices at a given point in time. Generally, the form of this relationship between price and quantity purchased is an inverse one, i.e. the higher the price of the product, the lower is the demand; the lower the price, the greater is the demand. This is shown in Figure 1.1.

It is normal to characterise the demand curve DD in Figure 1.1 by an appropriate measure which expresses the responsiveness of quantity to changes in price. Such a measure is termed the 'elasticity of demand' for product X with respect to its own price P_x. The own-price elasticity of demand (ei) measures the ratio of the percentage change in quantity to the percentage change in price, i.e.:

$$ei = \frac{\% \text{ change in quantity}}{\% \text{ change in price}}$$

It is conventional to consider ei in its absolute or positive value, thus we refer to an own price elasticity of demand as 1.0, 2.0, 3.0, etc., and not −1.0, −2.0 or −3.0. The critical value of ei is 1.0; for goods that have an own-price elasticity greater than 1, demand is said to be elastic. Products exhibiting this property are goods that are normally viewed as luxury items – overseas holidays or dining out. When a good has an own-price elasticity of demand of less than 1 it is classed as a necessity. For necessities, quantity adjustments respond sluggishly to price changes – food is classed as a necessity.

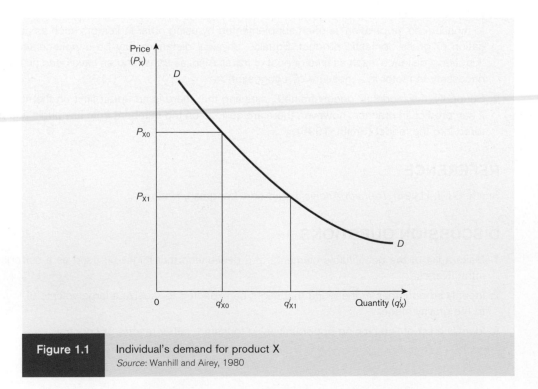

Figure 1.1	Individual's demand for product X

Source: Wanhill and Airey, 1980

So far we have examined both individual consumer demand for a product and also single variables such as price. However, in truth the world is more complex than this and we need to extend the concept of demand schedules in two ways:

- First, there are several factors other than price that affect a consumer's demand for a tourism product. These include prices of other goods, an individual's income and social tastes and habits. In other words, we must ensure that these 'economic' decisions are made within a social context. Economists find that it is not practical to consider variations in all the components at one time so they assume all components are constant except the one in question.

- Secondly, tourism is not only concerned with individuals but also responses of the market to variations in the factors affecting demand. Since individual tourists make up the market, it is reasonable to suppose that market demand curves respond in a similar fashion to individual curves, hence a first approach is to sum the individual demand schedules to arrive at the market schedule. This is illustrated in Figure 1.2, which supposes that there are only two individuals in the market. The market demand schedule is derived from the horizontal summation of the two individual curves. We can see that the market curve has a distinct 'kink' where the two individual curves join: this arises because the market is assumed to consist of only two persons. As the number in the market increases so any kinks are ironed out and a more or less smooth curve results.

Photograph 1.1   Price is a real constraint on demand for tourism, particularly for expensive holidays such as winter sports.

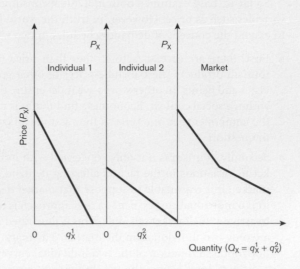

Figure 1.2	Derivation of a market demand curve
	Source: Wanhill and Airey, 1980

CONCLUSION

The generating region of Leiper's tourism system is influential in shaping the nature and scope of tourism flows around the world. As the tourism sector becomes more professional and knowledge-based, the techniques and approaches outlined in this chapter will be increasingly applied to the management of tourism demand. Approaches to the responsible consumption of demand, in other words, tourists exercising their 'right' to travel but doing so in a 'responsible' way, will become increasingly important if the integrity of destinations, and societies and the globe itself is to be preserved.

Definitions of tourism demand tend to be specific to particular viewpoints – for example, economists view demand in terms of schedules as described in this chapter. It is also important to understand that tourism demand is much more than just those who are travelling at any one point in time; indeed an understanding of the barriers preventing people from travelling is important. This is not just from the point of view of increasing society's access to travel, but also from a commercial point of view in increasing the viability of enterprises. Finally, this chapter has outlined some simple estimating techniques which allow you to calculate the potential of particular populations to travel.

SELF-CHECK QUESTIONS

1. Make a list of the reasons why an individual may be in the 'no tourism demand' category.

2. Draft a press release urging conference delegates to ensure that their travel to your conference is carbon neutral.

3. List the reasons why an individual may fall into the 'potential tourism demand' category.

4. Identify 10 reasons why demand for international tourism has grown since 1945.

5. Review the concepts of demand substitution and demand redirection and provide two examples of each.

ESSAY QUESTIONS

1. How might the market and individual demand curves for tourism differ from other commodities, such as, say, food?

2. Critique the concept of 'responsible tourism consumption'.

3. 'The UNWTO's Global Code of Ethics for Tourism is impossible to police.' Discuss this statement.

4. Why is it difficult to come up with a universally agreed definition of tourism demand?

5. Identify and discuss the key barriers to tourism demand that an individual might experience.

ANNOTATED FURTHER READING

Books

Jafari, J. (2001) *The Encyclopedia of Tourism*, Routledge, London.
A number of entries providing a definitive view of elements of tourism demand, the gravity model and other concepts written by the leading expert in each field.

Ryan, C. (2003) *Recreational Tourism Demand and Impacts*, Channel View, Clevedon.
An excellent, thorough overview of tourism demand.

Smith, S.L. (1996) *Tourism Analysis*, 2nd edn, Longman, Harlow.
A comprehensive handbook of analytical approaches, including demand estimation, various indices of demand and models such as the gravity model.

Web sites

http://www.tourismconcern.org.uk
One of the first and most comprehensive pressure groups for the responsible consumption of tourism and a comprehensive resource.

http://www.world-tourism.org
The UNWTO's site is an excellent source for new initiatives in responsible tourism and the Global Code of Ethics.

References cited

Mann, M. (1999) *The Good Alternative Travel Guide*, Earthscan, London.
Mathieson, A. and Wall, G. (1982) *Tourism: Economic Physical and Social Impacts*, Longman, London.
Tour Operators Initiative (2001) *Sustainable Tourism: The Tour Operators Initiative*, TOI, London.
Uysal, M. (1998) 'The determinants of tourism demand: A theoretical perspective', pp. 79–95, in Ioannides, D. and Debbage, K.G. (eds) *The Economic Geography of the Tourist Industry: A Supply Side Analysis*, Routledge, London.
Wanhill, S.R.C. and Airey, D.W. (1980) 'Demand for accommodation', pp. 23–44, in Kotas, R. (ed.), *Managerial Economics for Hotel Operation*, Surrey University Press, Guildford.
WTO (1980) *The Manila Declaration on World Tourism*, WTO, Madrid.
WTO (1994) *The Osaka Declaration*, WTO, Madrid.

MAJOR CASE STUDY 1.1
Indicators of tourism demand: travel propensity

In order to manage tourism demand we need to be able to measure and estimate the demand behaviour ofdifferent groups in society. One of the most useful indicators of effective demand in any particular population is travel propensity. This measure simply considers the penetration of tourism trips in a population. By examining 'propensity' to travel we can begin to understand how markets are changing. For example, in global terms in 1950, 1 international trip was generated per 100 population, a figure that rose to 11 in 2000 and is forecast to increase to 21 trips per 100 population in 2020 (Cooper *et al.*, 2006).

There are two forms of travel propensity:

1. **Net travel propensity** refers to the percentage of the population that takes at least one tourism trip in a given period of time. In other words, it is a measure of the penetration of travel among 'individuals' in the population. The suppressed and no demand components will therefore ensure that net travel propensity never approaches 100% and a figure of 70% or 80% is likely to be the maximum for developed Western economies.

2. **Gross travel propensity** gives the total number of tourism trips taken as a percentage of the population. This is a measure of the penetration of 'trips', not individual 'travellers'. Clearly, then, as second and third holidays increase in importance, so gross travel propensity becomes more relevant. Gross travel propensity can exceed 100% and often approaches 200% in some Western European countries where those participating in tourism may take more than one trip away from home per annum.

Simply dividing gross travel propensity by net will give the *travel frequency*, in other words, the average number of trips taken by those participating in tourism during the period in question.

So, a worked example of travel propensity is as follows:

Out of a population of 10 million inhabitants:

3.0 million inhabitants take one trip of one night or more

i.e. 3 × 1 = 3.0 million trips

1.5 million inhabitants take two trips of one night or more

Photograph 1.2 Propensities for travel in the developing world tend to be higher for those living in the cities than for rural areas.
Source: Rex Features/Edward Webb

i.e. 1.5 × 2 = 3.0 million trips

0.4 million inhabitants take three trips of one night or more

i.e. 0.4 × 3 = 1.2 million trips

0.2 million inhabitants take four trips of one night or more

i.e. 0.2 × 4 = 0.8 million trips

In total 5.1 million inhabitants take at least one trip and there is a total of 8.0 million trips.

Therefore:

$$\text{Net travel propensity} = \frac{\text{Number of population taking at least one trip}}{\text{Total population}} \times 100$$

$$= \frac{5.1}{10} \times 100 = 51\%$$

$$\text{Gross travel propensity} = \frac{\text{Number of total trips}}{\text{Total population}} \times 100$$

$$= \frac{8}{10} \times 100 = 80\%$$

$$\text{Travel frequency} = \frac{\text{Gross travel propensity}}{\text{Net travel propensity}} = \frac{80\%}{51\%}$$

$$= 1.57$$

A further refinement to these calculations can be made to allow us to assess the capability of a country to generate trips, an important activity when seeking new markets. This involves three stages:

- First, the number of trips originating in the country is divided by the total number of trips taken in the world. This gives an index of the ability of each country to generate travellers.
- Secondly, the population of the country is divided by the total population of the world, thus ranking each country by relative importance in relation to world population.
- Finally, by dividing the result of the first stage by the result of the second the 'country potential generation index' (CPGI) is produced.

$$\text{CPGI} = \frac{N_e/N_w}{P_e/P_w}$$

where N_e = number of trips generated by the country
N_w = number of trips generated in the world
P_e = population of the country
P_w = population of the world

An index of 1.0 indicates an average generation capability. Countries with an index greater than unity are generating more tourists than expected by their population. Countries with an index below 1.0 generate fewer trips than average.

An example will demonstrate the usefulness of this approach in understanding tourism demand, as follows.

Mexico is the world's eleventh most populous country with 108.7 million inhabitants in 2005. In the same year Mexico generated 3.6 million outbound tourism trips, a very small number when compared to the potential of the population to travel.

In contrast, in the same year the UK's population stood at 60 million and generated 66 million outbound trips. Why is there such a difference in outbound travel propensity between the two countries?

1. Economic factors – Mexico's economy is less stable than the UK.
2. Social factors such as levels of education, living standards and population growth.
3. Locational factors – there are many destinations close to the UK and travelling within Europe is reasonably priced. In addition, the European tourism industry is mature and well developed, encouraging travel.

Source: Boniface and Cooper (1987), adapted from Burkart and Medlik (1975), pp. 53–60

REFERENCES

Boniface, B. and Cooper, C. (1987) *The Geography of Travel and Tourism*, Heinemann, London.

Burkart, J. and Medlik, S. (eds) (1975) *The Management of Tourism*, Heinemann, London.

Cooper, C., Scott, N. and Kester, J. (2006) 'New and emerging markets', pp. 19–29, in Buhalis, D. and Costa, C. *Tourism Business Frontiers*, Elsevier Butterworth Heinemann, Oxford.

DISCUSSION QUESTIONS

1. The notion of net travel propensity is important when estimating demand from populations with an above average travel frequency. Identify market segments in your country which might be expected to have a high travel frequency and explain why this is so.

2. Take a country of your choice and, using the Internet or other sources, calculate the 'country potential generation index' (CPGI). Compare your result with others in the class and explain the differences.

3. What factors in a country will lead to a high CPGI?

CHAPTER 2
Tourism Consumer Behaviour

LEARNING OUTCOMES

This chapter deals with the factors and influences which, when combined, will influence a consumer's demand for tourism. By reading this chapter you will:

- have a knowledge of the factors influencing the buyer decision process in tourism;

- in particular have an understanding of the theory of motivation;

- have an appreciation of the way that the roles and psychographics of tourists are linked to specific forms of tourism and tourist needs;

- have a knowledge of the key models that seek to explain the decision-making process for the purchase of tourism products; and

- be able to critique models of consumer decision-making in tourism.

Photograph: Venetian masks, Venice, Italy © Graham Meyer

INTRODUCTION

In the previous chapter we outlined basic definitions and concepts of demand and showed how the management of demand has changed since 1945. This chapter probes more deeply into demand by providing an overview of the consumer decision-making process in tourism. There is no doubt that a grasp of consumer decision processes is essential if we are to understand and predict demand for tourism. Demand for tourism at the individual level can be treated as a consumption process that is influenced by a number of factors. These may be a combination of needs and desires, availability of time and money, or images, perceptions and attitude. In this chapter we review the major literature debates surrounding these concepts in order to explain how these factors influence individual behaviour in tourism.

Influences on consumer behaviour can be summarised as attitudes, perceptions, image, roles, motivations and determinants. A number of researchers have attempted to draw together these influences and to structure them in the form of models of consumer decision-making. For tourism, these models have been adapted from more general approaches in the consumer marketing literature. As we will see, this creates some issues in terms of the practical use of these models and their ability to capture the particular nature of the tourism purchasing decision.

THE INDIVIDUAL DECISION-MAKING PROCESS

At the personal level it is clear that the factors influencing demand for tourism are closely linked to models of consumer behaviour. No two individuals are alike and differences in attitudes, perceptions, images and motivation have an important influence on travel decisions. It is important to note that:

- **attitudes** depend on an individual's perception of the world;
- **perceptions** are mental impressions of, say, a destination or travel company and are determined by many factors, which include childhood, family, work experiences, education, books, television programmes and films and promotional images. Perception involves the encoding of information by individuals and influences attitudes and behaviour towards products but does not explain by itself, or when combined with attitudes, why people want to travel;
- **travel motivators** do explain why people want to travel and they are the inner urges that initiate travel demand; and
- **images** are sets of beliefs, ideas and impressions relating to products and destinations.

THE FUNDAMENTALS OF CONSUMER BEHAVIOUR AND TOURISM

Our understanding of the factors that shape tourism consumer behaviour are critical, not only as a key area of tourism research but also to assist tourism managers to understand the way in which tourism consumers make decisions and act in relation to the consumption of tourism products. While the term 'consumer' would seem to indicate a single concept of demand, the reality is that there is a whole diversity of consumer behaviour, with decisions being made for a range of reasons. We need to study the consumer behaviour of tourists to be aware of:

- the needs, purchase motives and decision process associated with the consumption of tourism;

- the impact of the different effects of various promotional tactics, including the Internet;
- the possible perception of risk for tourism purchases, including the impact of terrorist incidents;
- the different market segments based upon purchase behaviour; and
- how managers can improve their chance of marketing success.

Many variables will influence the way consumption patterns differ. Patterns will change based upon the different products available and the way individuals have learnt to purchase tourism products. The variations are complex and therefore it is more practical to deal with general behavioural principles. These are often dealt with in a framework that includes the disciplines of psychology, sociology and economics. Figure 2.1 provides a simplification of some of the main influences affecting the consumer as decision maker. These are discussed within this chapter.

We can view the tourism consumer decision process as a system made up of four basic elements:

1. **Energisers of demand.** These are the forces of motivation that lead a tourist to decide to visit an attraction or go on a holiday.

2. **Effectors of demand.** The consumer will have developed ideas of a destination, product or organisation by a process of learning, attitudes and associations from promotional messages and information. This will affect the consumer's image and knowledge of a tourism product thus serving to heighten or dampen the various energisers that lead to consumer action.

3. **Roles and the decision-making process.** Here, the important role is that of the family member who is normally involved in the different stages of the purchase process and the final resolution of decisions about when, where and how the group will consume the tourism product.

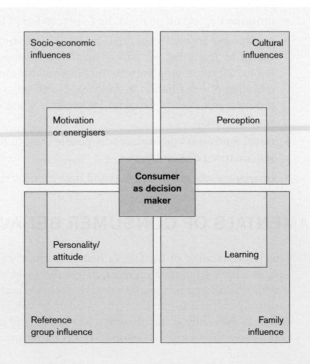

| Figure 2.1 | Consumer decision-making framework |

4. **Determinants of demand.** In addition, the consumer decision-making process for tourism is underpinned by the determinants of demand. Even though motivation may exist, demand is filtered, constrained or channelled due to economic (e.g. discretionary income), sociological (reference groups, cultural values) or psychological (perception of risk, personality, attitudes) factors. We look at determinants of demand in detail in Chapter 4.

ENERGISERS AND EFFECTORS OF DEMAND

Motivation

An understanding of motivation is the key to understanding tourist behaviour, answering the question of why people travel. The classic dictionary definition of motivation is derived from the word 'motivate', which is to cause a person to act in a certain way or to stimulate interest. We can also refer to the word 'motive', which is concerned with initiating movement or inducing a person to act. As would be expected, many texts associated with tourism utilise the concept of motivation as a major influence upon consumer behaviour, taking general theories, such as that by Maslow, discussed below, and applying them to tourists' consumer behaviour.

Maslow's hierarchy model

Maslow's hierarchy of needs (Figure 2.2) is probably the best-known theory of motivation, perhaps because of its simplicity and intuitive attraction. The theory of motivation proposed by Maslow (1970) is in the form of a ranking, or hierarchy, of the arrangements of individual needs. The early humanistic values of Maslow seem to have led him to create a model where self-actualisation is valued as the level 'man' should aspire to. He argued that if none of the needs in the hierarchy was satisfied, then the lowest needs, the physiological ones, would dominate behaviour. If these were satisfied, however, they would no longer motivate and the individual would be motivated by the next level in the hierarchy.

Maslow identified two motivational types, which can be greatly simplified as:

1. deficiency or tension-reducing motives; and

2. inductive or arousal-seeking motives.

Maslow maintained that his theory of motivation is holistic and dynamic and can be applied to both work and non-work spheres of life. He treats his levels of need as universal and innate, yet of such instinctual weakness that they can be modified, accelerated or

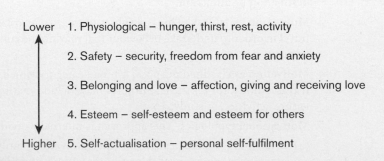

Lower   1. Physiological – hunger, thirst, rest, activity

2. Safety – security, freedom from fear and anxiety

3. Belonging and love – affection, giving and receiving love

4. Esteem – self-esteem and esteem for others

Higher   5. Self-actualisation – personal self-fulfilment

Figure 2.2   Maslow's hierarchy of needs

inhibited by the environment. He also stated that while all the needs are innate, only those behaviours that satisfy physiological needs are unlearned. Although a great deal of tourism demand theory has been built upon Maslow's approach, there are a number of questions that Maslow does not answer:

- It is not clear from his work why he selected five basic needs.
- Why are the needs ranked as they are?
- How could he justify his model when he did not carry out clinical observation or experiment?
- Why did he never try to expand the original set of motives?

Tourism authors have borrowed extensively from Maslow, simply because he has provided a convenient set of containers that can be relatively easily labelled. The notion that a comprehensive coverage of human needs can be organised into an understandable hierarchical framework is of obvious benefit to tourism theorists.

Within Maslow's model, human activity is wired into predetermined, understandable and predictable aspects of action. This is very much in the behaviourist tradition of psychology as opposed to the cognitive approach, which stresses the concepts of irrationality and unpredictability of behaviour. However, Maslow's theory does allow for humans to transcend the mere embodiment of biological needs that sets them apart from other species.

To some extent the popularity of Maslow's theory can be understood in moral terms. It suggests that, given the right circumstances, people will grow out of their concern for the materialistic aspects of life and become more interested in 'higher' things.

The study of motivation in tourism

The study of motivation has been derived from a range of disciplinary areas, which has led to a diversity of approach in tourism – an observation that holds true for many aspects of tourism studied in this book. This diversity is reflected in the approaches of various authors' discussions of how motivation influences tourists' consumer behaviour. The key approaches are outlined below.

Dann

Dann (1981) has pointed out that there are seven elements within the overall approach to motivation:

1. **Travel as a response to what is lacking yet desired.** This approach suggests that tourists are motivated by the desire to experience phenomena that are different from those available in their home environment.
2. **Destination pull in response to motivational push.** This distinguishes between the motivation of the individual tourist in terms of the level of desire (push) and the pull of the destination or attraction.
3. **Motivation as fantasy.** This is a subset of the first two factors and suggests that tourists travel in order to undertake behaviour that may not be culturally sanctioned in their home setting.
4. **Motivation as classified purpose.** A broad category which invokes the main purposes of a trip as a motivator for travel. Purposes may include visiting friends and relatives, enjoying leisure activities, or study.
5. **Motivational typologies.** This approach is internally divided into:
   (a) behavioural typologies such as the motivators 'sunlust' (search for a better set of amenities than are available at home) and 'wanderlust' (curiosity to experience the strange and unfamiliar) as proposed by Gray (1970); and
   (b) typologies that focus on dimensions of the tourist role.

6. **Motivation and tourist experiences.** This approach is characterised by the debate regarding the authenticity of tourist experiences and depends upon beliefs about types of tourist experience.

7. **Motivation as auto-definition and meaning.** This suggests that the way in which tourists define their situations will provide a greater understanding of tourist motivation than simply observing their behaviour.

Dann suggests that these seven identified approaches demonstrate a 'definitional fuzziness' which, if not clarified, may make it difficult to discover 'whether or not individual tourism researchers are studying the same phenomenon'.

McIntosh, Goeldner and Ritchie

McIntosh, Goeldner and Ritchie (1995) utilise four categories of motivation:

1. **Physical motivators:** those related to refreshment of body and mind, health purposes, sport and pleasure. This group of motivators are seen to be linked to those activities which will reduce tension.

2. **Cultural motivators:** those identified by the desire to see and know more about other cultures, to find out about the natives of a country, their lifestyle, music, art, folklore, dance, etc.

3. **Interpersonal motivators:** this group includes a desire to meet new people, visit friends or relatives, and to seek new and different experiences. Travel is an escape from routine relationships with friends or neighbours or the home environment, or it is used for spiritual reasons.

4. **Status and prestige motivators:** these include a desire for continuation of education (i.e. personal development, ego enhancement and sensual indulgence). Such motivators are seen to be concerned with the desire for recognition and attention from others, in order to boost the personal ego. This category also includes personal development in relation to the pursuit of hobbies and education.

Plog

In 1974, Stanley Plog developed a theory which allowed the US population to be classified into a series of interrelated psychographic types. These types range from two extremes:

1. The 'psychocentric' type is derived from 'psyche' or 'self-centred' where an individual centres thoughts or concerns on the small problem areas of life. These individuals tend to be conservative in their travel patterns, preferring 'safe' destinations and often taking many return trips. For this latter reason, market research in the tour-operating sector labels this group as 'repeaters'.

2. The 'allocentric' type derives from the root 'allo' meaning 'varied in form'. These individuals are adventurous and motivated to travel/discover new destinations. They rarely return to the same place twice, hence their market research label 'wanderers'.

The majority of the population fall in between these extremes in an area which Plog termed 'midcentric'. Plog also found that those who were at the lower end of income scales were more likely to be psychocentric types whereas at the upper income band there was more of a likelihood of being allocentric. In a later study it was observed that middle-income groups exhibited only a small positive correlation with psychographic types. This created problems because there were a number of psychographic types who could not, through income constraint, choose the type of holiday they preferred even if they were motivated towards it; after all, to be a wanderer around the globe can be expensive.

Plog's theory closely associates travel motivation to types of destination. Allocentrics, for example, will prefer destinations at the frontier of tourism, unspoilt and undiscovered by the

Photograph 2.1 Motivations for tourism have changed over the years: in the new millennium motivations to see heritage sites and curiosity about the destinations have become dominant.

Source: Alamy Images/Bubbles Photolibrary

travel trade. Psychocentrics, on the other hand, desire the comfort of a well-developed and 'safe' destination. While this is a useful way of thinking about tourists and destinations, it is more difficult to apply it. For example, tourists will travel with different motivations on different occasions. A second holiday or short-break weekend may be in a nearby psychocentric-type destination, whereas the main holiday may be in an allocentric-type destination.

Smith (1990) tested Plog's model, utilising evidence from seven different countries. He concluded that his own results did not support Plog's original model of an association between personality types and destination preferences. Smith questioned the applicability of the model to countries other than the USA. In answer to Smith, Plog (1990) questioned the validity of Smith's methodology. Regardless of this defence, further controlled empirical studies will be required in order to ensure Plog's theory can be justified as a central pillar within tourism theory.

As we have shown, the concept of motivation as a major determinant of tourism behaviour is widely used by tourism authors. Yet most authors fail to provide a scientific basis for their motivation categories, nor is any indication given of the proportion of tourists who would exhibit one type of motivation rather than another. An exception to this is shown in

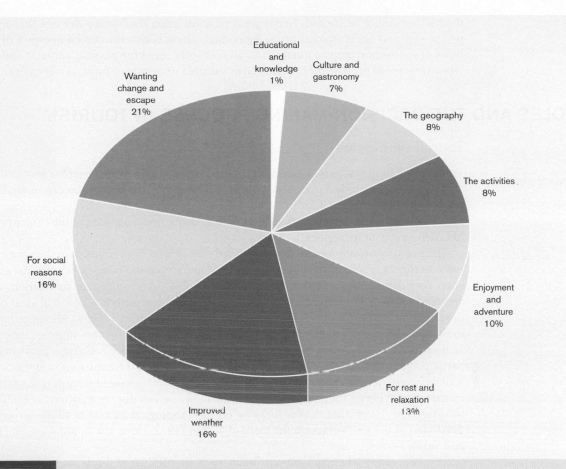

The range of motivators for overseas travel from the UK
Source: Gilbert, 1992

Figure 2.3. Here motivators were identified by research of a sample based upon a quota sample matched to the British Tourist Authority profile for overseas travel from the UK. The response involved individuals providing evidence of a cluster of motives, each of which is important as a determinant of demand.

A summary of the concept of motivation

We can see that the dimensions of the concept of motivation in the context of travel are difficult to map. In summary they can be seen to include:

- the idea that travel is initially need-related and that this manifests itself in terms of wants and the strength of motivation or 'push' as the energiser of action;

- motivation is grounded in sociological and psychological aspects of acquired norms, attitudes, culture, perceptions, etc., leading to person-specific forms of motivation; and

- the image of a destination created through various communication channels will influence motivation and subsequently affect the type of travel undertaken.

Although the motivation literature is still immature in tourism, there is no doubt that motivation is an essential concept in the explanation of tourist demand and almost all the theories are based on the motivation to escape. However, we should remember that while motivation can be stimulated and activated in relation to the 'want' to travel, 'needs' themselves cannot be created. Needs are dependent upon the human element through the psychology and circumstances of the individual. There is also the crucial question of what types of motivation may be innate in us all (curiosity, need for physical contact) and what types are learned because they are judged as valuable or positive (status, achievement).

ROLES AND THE DECISION-MAKING PROCESS IN TOURISM

Tourist typologies

Tourists can be characterised into different typologies or roles which exercise motivation as an energising force linked to personal needs. Utilising this approach, roles can be studied in relation to goal-orientated forms of behaviour or holiday choice activity. Therefore some understanding of tourist roles provides us with a deeper understanding of the choice process of different consumer segments.

The majority of authors who have identified tourist roles have concentrated on the assessment of the social and environmental impact of tourism or the nature of the tourist experience. Any definition or interpretation of tourist roles, such as those of motivation, varies according to the analytical framework used by the individual author. The initial ideas of role developed from the work of sociological theorists such as Goffman (1959). He suggested that individuals behave differently in different situations in order to sustain impressions associated with those situations. As actors have different front and backstage performances, participants in any activity vary their behaviour according to the nature and context of that activity. Consequently individual roles can be identified and managed according to social circumstances. Whereas tourists may vary considerably, we can discern a pattern of roles from the literature. Theoretical studies focusing on the sociological aspects of tourism role were developed in the 1970s through the work of Cohen (1972, 1974, 1984), MacCannell (1976) and Smith (1990).

The interaction of personality attributes such as attitude, perceptions and motivation allow different types of tourist role to be identified. One classification by Cohen is particularly useful and this is presented in Figure 2.4. He uses a classification based on the theory that tourism combines the curiosity to seek out new experiences with the need for the security of familiar reminders of home, reflecting Plog's ideas. Cohen proposes a continuum of possible combinations of novelty and familiarity and, by breaking up the continuum into typical combinations of these two ingredients, a fourfold classification of tourists is produced.

While destinations may be enjoyed as novel, most tourists prefer to explore them from a familiar base. The degree of familiarity of this base underlies Cohen's typology in which the author identifies four tourist roles: organised mass tourist, individual mass tourist, explorer and drifter (see Figure 2.4). Cohen described the first two roles as institutionalised and the latter types as non-institutionalised. Cohen was interested in classifying groups in order to understand not only demand, but the effects or impact of institutionalised forms of tourism. He found these to be authenticity issues, standardisation of destinations, festivals and the development of facilities. He also identified the impact of non-institutionalised forms of tourism upon the destination, which he found acts as a 'spearhead for mass tourism' as well as having a 'demonstration effect' on the lower socio-economic groups of the host community.

Cohen's typology assists in formulating operational approaches to tourism research and forms a framework for management practice. Although it is not complete and cannot be applied to all tourists at all times, it does afford a way of organising and understanding tourist activity.

Role and family influence

As the fundamental social unit of group formation in society, the influence of a family on tourism demand is extremely important. A family often acts as the purchasing unit which

The organised mass tourist
Low on adventurousness he/she is anxious to maintain his/her 'environmental bubble' on the trip. Typically purchasing a ready-made package tour off-the-shelf, he/she is guided through the destination having little contact with local culture or people.

The individual mass tourist
Similar to the above but more flexibility and scope for personal choice is built in. However, the tour is still organised by the tourism industry and the environmental bubble shields him/her from the real experience of the destination.

The explorer
The trip is organised independently and is looking to get off the beaten track. However, comfortable accommodation and reliable transport are sought and, while the environmental bubble is abandoned on occasion, it is there to step into if things get tough.

The drifter
All connections with the tourism industry are spurned and the trip attempts to get as far from home and familiarity as possible. With no fixed itinerary, the drifter lives with the local people, paying his/her way and immersing him/herself in their culture.

Familiarity

Institutionalised tourism
Dealt with routinely by the tourism industry – tour operators, travel agents, hoteliers and transport operators.

Non-institutionalised tourism
Individual travel, shunning contact with the tourism industry except where absolutely necessary.

Novelty

Figure 2.4	Cohen's classification of tourists

Source: Boniface and Cooper, 1987, adapted from Cohen, 1972

may be supplying the needs of perhaps two or more generations. In addition, it socialises children to adopt particular forms of purchasing and acts as a wider reference group. Given the importance of family behaviour in the purchase of leisure products, we may want to question the preponderance of literature which treats consumer behaviour as an individual model of action. For example, the concept of motivation has been presented as essentially an individual one, yet the idea of 'shared motivators' takes into account that family and friends often influence holiday decisions.

Each member of a family fulfils a special role within the group. He or she may act as husband/father, wife/mother, son/brother and daughter/sister. Family decision-making assigns roles to specific members of the family and decision-making may be shared, or conducted by one person. One member of the family may be the facilitator, while information may be gathered by another. The family acts as a composite buying unit with the different role patterns leading to particular forms of tourism product purchasing. We can also see the influence of younger family members on travel behaviour and, in particular, the different generations as they mature, as the following Mini Case Study shows.

The importance of image

An individual's awareness of the world is made up of experiences, learning, emotions and perceptions, or, more accurately, the cognitive evaluation of such experiences, learning, emotions and perceptions. Such awareness can be described as knowledge producing a specific image of the world. This image is critically important to an individual's preference, motivation and behaviour towards tourist products and destinations, as it will provide a 'pull' effect resulting in different demand schedules.

MINI CASE STUDY 2.1
Generations X and Y

INTRODUCTION

Both generations X and Y represent the future of tourism demand for the next 50 years, and yet little in-depth research has been done about their attitudes to travel, or their travel consumer behaviour. Instead, the research has been focused on the current active travel generation – the baby boomers. However, Generation X will soon take their place, with Generation Y following quickly behind. For example, the fore-cast boom in outbound travel from China and India will be led in part by generations X and Y but operators do not understand how they will behave, the intermediaries that they will use, or their tourism product pre-ferences. This case study examines the characteristics of generations X and Y and the implications for tourism behaviour.

DO GENERATIONS IMPACT UPON CONSUMER BEHAVIOUR?

In terms of tourism consumer behaviour, there are divided opinions as to whether there are generational differences:

- Some support the fact that generations X and Y will have differing travel behaviour from, say, their par-ents. This is because each generation grows up within a particular environmental and social system, where the media, culture and world events shape their behaviour, including tourism demand. Effectively, we can define a generation socially as well as demographically.

- Others, however, argue that generations are too large a group to be helpful in explaining different con-sumer behaviour. This is made worse by the fact that with changing social trends people are marrying and having children later in life, extending generational spans: while in the past the traditional definition of a generation as the years between the birth of parents and the birth of their children tended to aver-age around 20 years, it is now nearer 30 years. Within this time span, of course, there will be significant changes in technology and social values.

THE CONSUMER BEHAVIOUR OF GENERATIONS X AND Y

The two generations are very different. Generation Y, for example, are sometimes known as the 'millennial generation', 'connexivity kids', or the 'dot-com generation', suggesting a techno and connected generation. In contrast, Generation X was raised in less secure economic times and tend to be more mobile than their younger generation. They have married and had children later in life than their parents, and are traditional in their family values and behaviour, while careful in their financial management.

Generation Y was born into a period dominated by technology and the ability to be permanently con-nected to friends and peers. Media are important to this generation, particularly broadband Internet and tele-vision, in terms of reality television and the spontaneous availability of programming. They tire of well-known brands quickly and they enjoy finding adverts in other media, such as the Internet, rather than in the usual press and television placement. For tourism, this means that successful tourism products and destinations must 'connect' with these consumers. It is less important to build products *for* them, but to build products *with* them.

Generation X, in contrast, are less concerned with the idea of having products built for them and are more interested in being able to afford new authentic experiences. These are preferably in fresh destinations and will satisfy their curiosity for other countries and cultures in a memorable way. While they are less tech-nologically savvy than Generation Y, they are good at processing and understanding information, and they are catching up with their younger counterparts in their use of the Internet for searching and booking travel. This makes them a challenge for marketers as their demand behaviour demonstrates a lack of brand loyalty – they are more footloose than Generation Y. At the same time their strong family values and financial conservatism means that they seek value for money travel – using low cost carriers for example – and holiday with the family.

Both these generations will be mature, adventurous and active travellers. They represent the demand patterns and consumers of the future and their behaviour will be distinctive, driven by technology and underpinned by their considerable formal education levels which make them aware of opportunities, world geography and tourism destinations.

DISCUSSION QUESTIONS

1. Draft a table summarising 10 characteristics of each generation. How will these characteristics impact upon tourism behaviour?

2. Make a list of the advantages and disadvantages of taking a generational approach to tourism consumer behaviour.

3. Given their technological orientation, will generations X and Y be more inclined to experiment with technologically-based tourism products such as virtual reality or space tourism?

There are various kinds of definition adopted to describe the word 'image' in different fields. For example, the UNWTO defines image as follows:

- the artificial imitation of the apparent form of an object;
- form resemblance, identity (e.g. art and design); and
- ideas, conceptions held individually or collectively of the destination.

Following the work of Gunn (1972), the UNWTO suggests that the tourist image is only one aspect of a destination's general image, with the two being closely interrelated. Nobody is likely to visit a destination for tourism if for one reason or another he or she dislikes it. Conversely, a tourist discovery may lead to a knowledge of other aspects of an economic, political or cultural nature of that destination. The UNWTO further adds that the presentation of a **destination image** must allow for the fact that it is generally a matter not of creating an image from nothing but of transforming an existing image.

Tourist behaviour both of individuals and groups depends upon their image of immediate situations and the world. The notion of image is closely related to behaviour and attitudes. Attitudes and behaviour become established on the basis of a person's derived image and are not easily changed unless new information or experience is gained.

The holiday image

Mayo (1973) examined regional images and regional travel behaviour. Among other things he indicated that the image of a destination area is a critical factor when choosing a destination. Mayo further concluded that, whether or not an image is in fact a true representation of what any given region has to offer the tourist, what is important is the image that exists in the mind of the vacationer.

The tourist may possess a variety of images in connection with travel. These include the image he or she has formed of the destination, of the term 'holiday' itself, of the mode of transport he or she wishes to utilise, of the tour operator/wholesaler or travel agency and of his or her own self-image. For example, it is probable that the term 'holiday' evokes different images for different people. However, it is likely that similar images of a particular holiday experience are held by people within the same segment of society and who have experienced a similar lifestyle or education.

Gunn (1972) identifies two levels of image. Viewed in terms of a country or destination, the 'organic' image is the sum of all information that has not been deliberately directed by advertising or promotion of a country or destination; this information comes from television coverage, radio reports, geography books, history books, what other people have said about the area, newspapers and magazines or the Internet. An imaginary picture is built up which is the result of all this information. The individual, following Gestalt psychology, attempts to make sense of it by forming a pattern or a picture of what he or she imagines the area to be like.

The second level of image is the 'induced' image. This is formed by deliberate portrayal and promotion by various organisations involved with tourism.

It is important to distinguish between these two levels since the induced image is controllable while it is more difficult to influence the organic image. Equally, the source of information is a significant influence upon a consumer's perception of its value. We can identify four stages in the development and establishment of a holiday image:

1. The first is a vague, fantasy type of image created from advertising, education and word of mouth and is formed before the subject has thought seriously about taking a holiday. This belief may be that people engage in taking holidays as a desirable activity.

2. The second stage is when a decision is made to take a holiday and then choices must be made regarding time, destination and type of holiday. This is when the holiday image is modified, clarified and extended. On completion of the holiday plans, the anticipatory image is crystallised.

3. The third stage is the holiday experience itself, which modifies, corrects or removes elements of the image that prove to be invalid and reinforces those that are found to be correct.

4. The fourth stage is the after-image, the recollection of the holiday which may induce feelings of nostalgia, regret or fantasy. This is the stage that will mould an individual's holiday concepts and attitudes and will promote a new sequence of holiday images influencing future holiday decisions.

MODELS OF CONSUMER BEHAVIOUR IN TOURISM

One approach to understanding tourism demand is to identify and evaluate the broader theories and models of consumer behaviour linked to purchasing behaviour. This is far from simplistic for we are faced with a proliferation of research within a subject area that has displayed significant growth and diversity. Perhaps the major utility of these models is to demonstrate the interrelationships of the key factors influencing consumer behaviour in tourism. We also have to understand the particular characteristics of a tourism purchasing decision as opposed to other products, and this includes the implications of tourism as a service activity. We can identify three phases that characterise the development of consumer behaviour theory:

1. **The early empiricist phase** covered the years between 1930 and the late 1940s and was dominated by empirical commercial research. This research was characterised by attempts in industry to identify the effects of distribution, advertising and promotion decisions. The basis for these models came mainly from economic theories relating to the company.

2. **The motivational research phase** in the 1950s was an age where stress was placed on Freudian and drive-related concepts. There was a greater emphasis placed upon in-depth interviews, focus groups, thematic apperception tests and other projective techniques. Activity was directed at uncovering 'real' motives for action which were perceived to lie in the deeper recesses of the consumer's mind. Much of the theory was based around the idea of there being instinctual needs which reside in the 'id' and are governed by the 'ego' which acts to balance unrestrained instincts and social constraints. The 'super ego' in turn

was seen to embody values but to limit action on the basis of moral constraint. The major problem was the focus on unconscious needs which are by definition extremely difficult to prove empirically. Furthermore, they do not always translate into effective marketing strategies.

3. **The formative phase** of the 1960s can be seen as the formative years of consumer behaviour modelling. The first general consumer behaviour textbook became available in 1968 (Engel, Kollat and Blackwell) and other influential books such as Howard and Sheth (1969) followed soon after. The Howard–Sheth model of buyer behaviour is perhaps the most influential one, as it identifies the inputs to the consumer's decision-making process. During the formative phase, models of behaviour proved useful as a means of organising disparate knowledge of social action. The major theorists developed 'grand models' of consumer behaviour which have been subsequently utilised or transformed by authors interested in the tourism choice process.

These grand models can be found to share several commonalities:

- They all exhibit consumer behaviour as a decision process. This is integral to the model.
- They provide a comprehensive model focusing mainly on the behaviour of the individual consumer.
- They share the belief that behaviour is rational and hence can, in principle, be explained.
- They view buying behaviour as purposive, with the consumer as an active information seeker, both of information stored internally and of information available in the external environment. Thus, the search and evaluation of information is a key component of the decision process.
- They believe that consumers limit the amount of information taken in, and move over time from general notions to more specific criteria and preference for alternatives.
- All the 'grand models' include a notion of feedback, that is, outcomes from purchases will affect future purchases.
- The models envisage consumer behaviour as multi-stage triggered by the individual's expectation that a product will satisfy their needs.

THE BUYING DECISION PROCESS IN TOURISM

Figure 2.5 demonstrates that consumer behaviour is normally conceived as a process of stages. As part of this approach the decision to travel is the involvement of some or all of the following stages. The starting point is where a need is recognised and the individual is energised into becoming a potential customer. The stages can be thought of as:

- need arousal;
- recognition of the need – the prerequisite stage;
- level of involvement – amount of time and effort invested in the decision process, e.g. degree of search for information;
- identification of alternatives – brands that initially come to mind when considering a purchase are referred to as the evoked set. However, friends, shop assistants, merchandise, leaflets, advertisements, etc. may provide a consideration step;
- evaluation of alternatives – comparisons are made of the salient attributes based upon criteria of the potential purchaser;
- decision choice made;
- purchase action; and
- post-purchase behaviour – the feelings an individual experiences after the purchase.

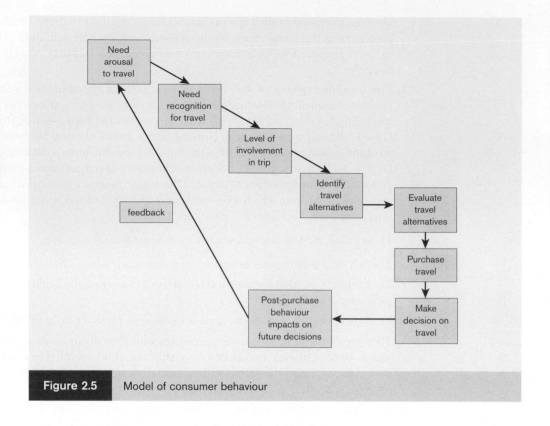

| **Figure 2.5** | Model of consumer behaviour |

Quite often with important purchases, such as travel, the purchaser will doubt the wisdom of their choice and have a need for reassurance to what is known as dissonance or disequilibrium. This psychological state is reduced by the means of guarantees or telephone help lines to deal with queries. It is also reduced by the welcome back of someone on their return from their trip or experience.

Consumer behaviour models are designed to attempt to provide an overall representation of the consumer behaviour process and to identify the key elements of the process and their interrelationships. Engel, Blackwell and Miniard (1986) classified models according to the degree of search or problem-solving behaviour by the consumer:

1. **Limited problem-solving models** (LPS models) are applicable to repeat or mundane purchases with a low level of consumer involvement. Apart from short trips near to home these are not applicable to tourism.

2. **Extended problem-solving models** (EPS models) apply to purchases associated with high levels of perceived risk and involvement, and where the information search and evaluation of alternatives plays an important part in the purchasing decision. Models of tourist behaviour fall into this category.

Given the high cost, risk factor and involvement of a tourism purchase, a number of models of consumer behaviour which seek to explain low involvement purchase behaviour are less relevant and therefore not considered here. The following models are all examples of EPS models.

Wahab, Crampon and Rothfield

One of the first attempts to provide some understanding of tourism purchase behaviour is to be found in the work of Wahab, Crampon and Rothfield (1976). These authors presented the

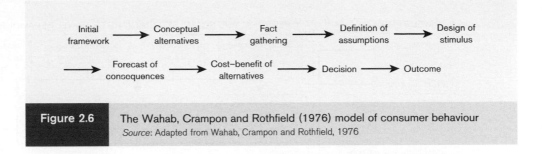

Figure 2.6 The Wahab, Crampon and Rothfield (1976) model of consumer behaviour
Source: Adapted from Wahab, Crampon and Rothfield, 1976

consumer as purposeful and conceptualised his or her buying behaviour in terms of the uniqueness of the buying decision:

- no tangible return on investment;
- considerable expenditure in relation to earned income;
- purchase is not spontaneous or capricious; and
- expenditure involves saving and pre-planning.

They presented a model of the decision-making process based upon the preceding 'grand models' of consumer behaviour and having the stages outlined in Figure 2.6.

Schmoll

Schmoll (1977) argued that creating a model of the travel decision process was not just a theoretical exercise, for its value could be found in its aid to travel decision-making. His model was based on the Howard–Sheth (1969) and Nicosia (1966) models of consumer behaviour – see Figure 2.7.

Schmoll's model is built upon motivations, desires, needs and expectations as personal and social determinants of travel behaviour. These are influenced by travel stimuli, the traveller's confidence, destination image, previous experience and cost and time constraints. The model has four fields, each of which exerts some influence over the final decision – according to Schmoll (1977): 'The eventual decision (choice of a destination, travel time, type of accommodation, type of travel arrangements, etc.), is in fact the result of a distinct process involving several successive stages or fields.'

- **Field 1: Travel stimuli.** These comprise external stimuli in the form of promotional communication, personal and trade recommendations.
- **Field 2: Personal and social determinants.** These determine customer goals in the form of travel needs and desires, expectations and the objective and subjective risks thought to be connected with travel.
- **Field 3: External variables.** These involve the prospective traveller's confidence in the service provider, destination image, learnt experience and cost and time constraints.
- **Field 4: Destination characteristics.** These consist of related characteristics of the destination or service that have a bearing on the decision and its outcome.

The model (with the exception of some changes which incorporate the word travel in the headings and the location of previous experience in Field 3) has been borrowed directly from the 'grand models' already discussed. In Schmoll's model there is no feedback loop and no input to attitude and values, and therefore it is difficult for us to regard the model as dynamic. However, Schmoll does highlight many of the attributes of travel decision-making which, while not unique in themselves, do influence tourism demand. We can include here

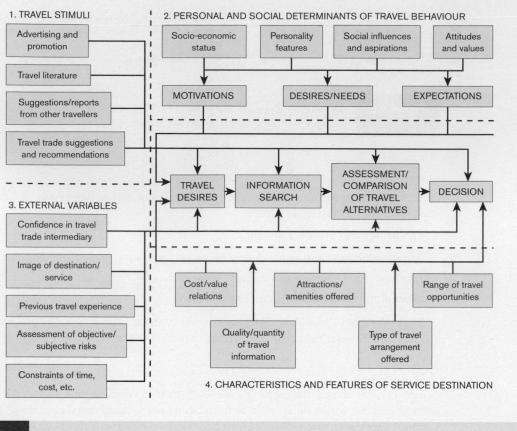

Figure 2.7	The Schmoll model
	Source: Adapted from Schmoll, 1977

decisions regarding choice of a mix of services which make up the product: high financial outlay, destination image, the level of risk and uncertainty, necessity to plan ahead and difficulty of acquiring completeness of information.

Schmoll, while highlighting some of the characteristics associated with the problem-solving activity of travel, simply reiterates the determinants of cognitive decision-making processes. Within Schmoll's work we are introduced again to the importance of image, which plays a significant part in the demand process.

Mayo and Jarvis

Mayo and Jarvis (1981) have also borrowed from the grand theorist models. They have taken the basic Howard–Sheth three-level decision-making approach where problem-solving is seen as extensive, limited or routinised.

Mayo and Jarvis follow the earlier theories by describing extensive decision-making (destination purchase for them) as being characterised as having a perceived need for an information search phase and needing a longer decision-making period. The search for, and evaluation of, information is presented as a main component of the decision-making process whereby the consumer moves from general notions to more specific criteria and preferences for alternatives.

Mayo and Jarvis argue that travel is a special form of consumption behaviour involving an intangible, heterogeneous purchase of an experiential product, yet they then fail to develop an activity-based theory.

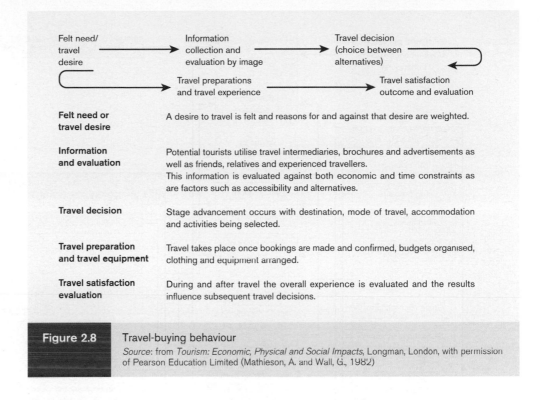

Felt need or travel desire	A desire to travel is felt and reasons for and against that desire are weighted.
Information and evaluation	Potential tourists utilise travel intermediaries, brochures and advertisements as well as friends, relatives and experienced travellers. This information is evaluated against both economic and time constraints as are factors such as accessibility and alternatives.
Travel decision	Stage advancement occurs with destination, mode of travel, accommodation and activities being selected.
Travel preparation and travel equipment	Travel takes place once bookings are made and confirmed, budgets organised, clothing and equipment arranged.
Travel satisfaction evaluation	During and after travel the overall experience is evaluated and the results influence subsequent travel decisions.

Figure 2.8 Travel-buying behaviour

Source: from *Tourism: Economic, Physical and Social Impacts*, Longman, London, with permission of Pearson Education Limited (Mathieson, A. and Wall, G., 1982)

Mathieson and Wall

Mathieson and Wall (1982) offer a five-stage process of travel-buying behaviour (see Figure 2.8). Their framework (as shown in Figure 2.9) is influenced by four interrelated factors:

1. Tourist profile (age, education, income attitudes, previous experience and motivations).
2. Travel awareness (image of a destination's facilities and services which are based upon the credibility of the source).
3. Destination resources and characteristics (attractions and features of a destination).
4. Trip features (distance, trip duration and perceived risk of the area visited).

In addition, Mathieson and Wall recognise that a holiday is a service product with the characteristics of intangibility, perishability and heterogeneity, which in one way or another affect the consumer's decision-making. However, apart from pointing out that consumption and evaluation will occur simultaneously, the basis of their model relies on the previously reviewed grand models. This is not to say that the model reflects the depth of insight of these models; on the contrary, it only incorporates the idea of the consumer being purposive in actively seeking information and the importance of external factors. The model omits important aspects of perception, memory, personality and information processing, which is the basis of the traditional models. The model they provide focuses more on a product-based perspective rather than that of a consumer behaviourist.

Woodside and Lysonski

Woodside and Lysonski's (1989) model considers two types of inputs:

1. the marketing inputs of product, promotion, place and price as the key external inputs; and
2. the tourist's internal variables, including experience, socio-demographic variables, lifestyle and values.

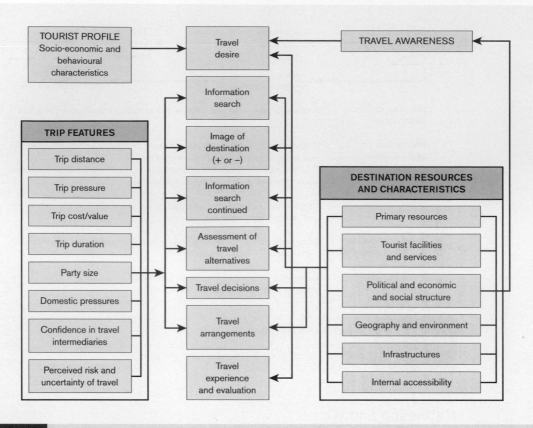

Figure 2.9	The Mathieson and Wall model

Source: from *Tourism: Economic, Physical and Social Impacts*, Longman, London, with permission of Pearson Education Limited (Mathieson, A. and Wall, G., 1982)

The model traces the tourist's unfolding awareness of the destination or product from initial awareness to choice and purchase (Figure 2.10). Woodside and Lysonski's contribution lies in factoring into the model the emotions associated with destination or product choice, the fact that tourists may rank the options, and the perceived likelihood of purchase and situational variables such as the environment. Tourists' ranking of options is seen in Figure 2.10. The categories are:

1. Consideration set – destinations or products considered likely to puchase. Woodside and Lysonski suggest this set ranges from 3 to 5 options.

2. Unavailable set – destinations or products not considered for purchase. This includes 'inept destinations', rejected on the grounds of, say, lack of relevant attractions.

Moscardo *et al.*

Moscardo *et al.* (1996) have provided a different approach to consumer behaviour by stressing the importance of activities as a critical link between travel and destination choice. They argue that motives provide travellers with expectations for activities, and destinations are seen as offering these activities. Figure 2.11 demonstrates this approach as an activities model of destination choice. In this model, Moscardo *et al.* have provided a useful practical outlet for the use of these models by marketers. They argue that activity-based traveller segments can be linked to destination activities through product development and communication strategies.

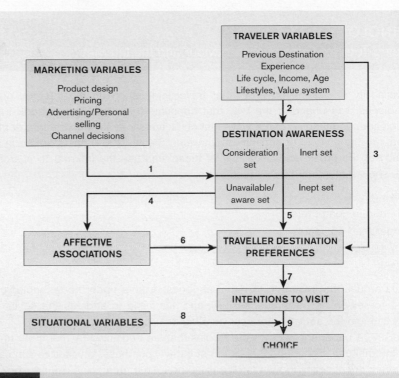

Figure 2.10 The Woodside and Lysonski model
Source: from Woodside, A. and Lysonski, S. (1989) 'A general model of traveler destination choice', *Journal of Travel Research* **27**, 8–14

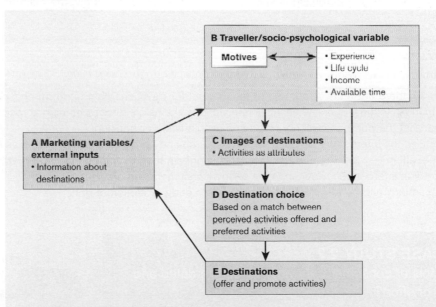

Box A: Contextual or social influence process providing information on the activities available at destinations.
Box B: Travel motives are connected to other socio-demographic variables including life cycle and travel experience.
Box C: How the travel motive groups perceived destinations.
Box D: How the travel motive groups related activity-based images to destination choice.
Box E: Activities available at destinations.

Figure 2.11 An activities-based model of destination choice
Source: Moscado *et al*, 1996

TECHNOLOGY BOX 2.1
Changing Tourism Consumer Behaviour and the Internet

The availability of destination and other travel information on the Internet, coupled with the rise of e-intermediaries, has changed the way that consumers search for and book travel. However, we do not have a clear understanding of the ways that consumers interact with the Internet for travel nor has this been factored into the models of consumer behaviour. Sigala (2004) has stepped in to fill this gap in an extensive study of the profile and behaviour of those who use the Internet to search for and book travel. Her findings show that Internet users tend to be:

- male;
- interested in computers;
- younger than 45 years;
- well educated to college degree level; and
- affluent.

Sigala argues that research to date has focused more upon the technological and e-business models required to sell online travel successfully, and has failed to address the social factors of the adoption of Internet use and the social factors surrounding its use.

In her 2004 paper she reviews the studies that are beginning to inform our understanding of this dimension of Internet use. She found that in terms of travel purchase, key factors such as level of involvement with the product, price, ability to standardise the product and perceived risk are important variables, particularly for complex products such as packages as opposed to single elements of travel. Here, a good example is the purchase of airline tickets from low-cost carriers (LCCs) where there is a price advantage in purchasing from the Internet, the web sites are designed to be user-friendly as Internet purchase is part of the LCCs' business model, and the purchase is simple and risk free. Not surprisingly, the main travel products purchased online are:

- airline tickets;
- accommodation; and
- car rental.

Of course, there are fears about use of the Internet for travel searching and purchase. These concerns range from the insecurity of online financial transactions, the risk of families coming across unsuitable material and fear that the purchase will not result in a usable ticket or booking.

In summary, the Internet will be used for travel search and purchase when it is seen as simple and enjoyable to use, effective, cheaper and risk free. This suggests that contemporary consumer behaviour models should factor in Internet behaviour, in terms of how consumers perceive benefits from using the Internet, the barriers to its use, and factors such as demographics and perception of price.

MINI CASE STUDY 2.2
Are models of consumer behaviour in tourism dated and a waste of effort?

The tourism sector of a country can be crippled overnight by a terrorist incident, the outbreak of war, or a natural disaster. Yet if we cannot predict the response of the consumer to these types of incidents, should we be reassessing the role of consumer behaviour models? Equally, do consumer behaviour models effectively factor in the Internet as a medium of information search and purchase as discussed above, and finally, do the models adequately explain barriers to travel? Of course, there is no doubt that models of consumer behaviour help us to understand the complexity of decisions taken to purchase travel and they assist in the understanding of how the various factors are related. However, models of consumer decision-making in tourism have been criticised on a number of grounds (Swarbrooke and Horner, 1999):

- They are too theoretical and not grounded in any empirical testing – how, for example, would we test them against the observed change in behaviour in travel since the introduction of LCCs across Europe?
- They are beginning to date and no new models have been developed since the mid-1990s, yet the travel sector has changed considerably – what, for example, is the impact of Internet bookings and information sources on such models?
- They do not help in the understanding of how the market would react to different 'shocks' to the system such as 9/11 in contrast to the 2004 Indian Ocean Tsunami. As we show in the major case study at the end of this chapter, the responses have been quite different.
- They view tourism from a Western developed-country perspective, yet we know that China and India will be the main generators of international travel in years to come – do these models help us to understand the psyche and behaviour of the Chinese and Indian consumer?
- They fail to recognise the increasingly diverse types of tourist, or tourism being purchased – market sectors are more varied and less stable than they were in the early to mid-1990s. Effectively, these models are generalised and generic and do not apply to specific market sectors.
- They fail to predict or identify the behaviour of tourists or markets and do not assist the manager in when to intervene in the buying process to secure a purchase.

It is this last point that is critical. If models of consumer behaviour in tourism cannot be used by marketers to fit products to particular market segments, then we have to question their use. How, for example, would a company use these models to develop and launch an adventure tourism product, how do these models help to understand the adoption of an adventure product by the consumer, how should the product be promoted and priced and how do they help managers understand non-users of their product? On this last point there is little research on non-use or non-purchase, partly because it is difficult and expensive to perform. Nonetheless, understanding the non-user is critical to innovation and competitiveness in tourism. Solomon (1996) argues that we should make more overt the link of consumer decision models with marketing to ensure that their continued development will be of use to marketers (Table 2.1).

To summarise, Decrop (2000) has listed the failings of tourism consumer behaviour models:

- they assume a rational tourist;
- they overplay information search;
- they do not distinguish between intervening variables (values) and situational variables (the external environment);
- they do not adequately factor in the emotional elements of tourist decision-making;
- destination is less important than the models suggest; and
- the models do not consider the family life cycle in decision taking.

REFERENCES

Decrop, A. (2000) 'Tourists' Decision-Making and Behaviour Processes', pp. 103–33 in Pizam, A. and Mansfield, Y. (eds) *Consumer Behaviour in Travel and Tourism*, Haworth, New York.

Swarbrooke, J. and Horner, S. (1999) *Consumer Behaviour in Tourism*, Butterworth Heinemann, Oxford.

DISCUSSION QUESTIONS

1. Taking a particular model of travel decision-making outlined in this chapter, how would you adapt it to take into account consumer response to terrorist activity?
2. Draft a checklist of new developments in tourism that are not taken into account by current models of travel decision-making.
3. Make a list of the classic features of a service product – do the current models of travel decision-making adequately take these factors into account?

Table 2.1	Linking consumer decision models with marketing	
Issues at particular purchase stages	**Consumer considerations**	**Marketing considerations**
Pre-purchase stage	How does a consumer decide that he/she needs a travel product? What is the level of involvement/ commitment on the part of the purchaser of a travel product? What are the best sources of information to learn more about alternative choices, and, given the intangible nature of the travel product, which sources have more authority and influence?	How are consumer attitudes towards travel products formed and/or changed? For example, why is the mass tourism experience, so popular in the 1970s, now less popular? What cues does the consumer use to infer which products are superior to others – a critical piece of information for promotion and positioning of travel products.
Purchase stage	Is acquiring a product a stressful or pleasant experience and does this influence the nature of intermediary used – or indeed whether an intermediary is bypassed? What does the destination and type of holiday arrangement purchased say about the consumer?	How do situational factors such as time pressure, family pressure or travel agent displays affect the consumer's purchase decision?
Post-purchase stage	Does the travel product provide pleasure or perform its intended function? How is the travel product consumed and are there environmental or social consequences to the travelling activity?	What determines whether a consumer will be satisfied with the travel experience or whether he/she will buy it again? Does this person tell others about his/her travel experiences and therefore affect their purchase decisions?

Source: Adapted from Swarbrooke and Horner, 1999; Solomon, 1996

THE WAY FORWARD

Consumer decision-making models have tended to be based on a view that tourist consumer behaviour is rational and sequenced. The generic 'grand models' are also designed for the purchase of tangible goods rather than services, and assume individual rather than group purchase, making them less than ideal to explain tourism behaviour. There is also a danger that these models are too generalised and simplified to explain, first, the richness of tourism behaviour and, secondly, the changed tourism marketplace of the twenty-first century. Decrop (2000) argues that what is needed is models that capture both the situational and experiential nature of tourist behaviour, effectively including the complexity of everyday life. This will demand deep and meaningful research into behaviour, utilising qualitative approaches to deliver insights as to how decisions are made and how influences such as experiences, interaction with other members of the travel party and prior experience of the destination or product influence behaviour.

CONCLUSION

Tourism marketing will become more effective if it develops a fuller understanding of what influences the tourist's consumer behaviour. This need has been highlighted since 2001 with the realisation that we could not predict travel demand response to shocks to the system. To do this we require an appreciation of the way consumers behave and the way they recognise specific needs for travel, search for and evaluate information, make purchases and then evaluate what has been consumed as part of the tourism experience. This involves the need to understand some of the approaches to how motivation may function, the roles we adopt as tourists and how sociological changes will affect demand.

The understanding of the consumer is enhanced by the incorporation of these different variables into simplified models. Although these need improvement, they act as a guide to current thinking of how tourism demand may function. Nonetheless, these models of consumer behaviour in tourism remain at a relatively early stage of their development and significant levels of research are still required to clarify what are, effectively, subjective psychological influences upon buying processes in tourism. Indeed, they have been criticised on the grounds that they are too theoretical and offer little assistance to the tourism marketer. This said, they do perform a useful role in clarifying our thinking about the tourist decision-making process and in particular help us to understand the interrelationships of a range of complex variables.

SELF-CHECK QUESTIONS

1. Draft a list of motivations for travel and, thinking of your last holiday, which one was dominant in your mind?
2. Consider tourist typologies that predominate at a tourist destination with which you are familiar.
3. Review the process you went through in the purchase decision process for the last holiday you took.
4. What factors differentiate a high-involvement purchase, such as tourism, from a low-involvement purchase, such as grocery shopping?
5. Consider a tourism product such as a tour operator's brochure – what cues are there to suggest the market targeted by the company?

ESSAY QUESTIONS

1. Consider the factors that might motivate a tourist to travel to a range of different destinations.
2. Does the tourism industry take full advantage of what is known about the buying decision process in tourism in respect of marketing?
3. How might the motivational 'push' of the tourist (e.g. sunlust versus wanderlust) affect the buying decision process for tourism? Identify the elements of the process which are likely to predominate for those motivated by sunlust and wanderlust.
4. 'Designing consumer behaviour models for tourism is purely an academic exercise.' Discuss this statement.
5. Identify and discuss the relative importance of the major influences on a tourist's purchasing decision.

ANNOTATED FURTHER READING

Books

Decrop, A. (2006) *Vacation Decision Making*, CABI Publishing, Wallingford.
A thorough overview of leisure and vacation decision-making processes.

Pearce, P. (2005) *Tourist Behaviour: Theories and Conceptual Schemes*, Channel View, Clevedon.
An excellent research-based text reviewing the major theories and concepts of tourist behaviour.

Pizam, A. and Mansfield, Y. (eds) (2000) *Consumer Behaviour in Travel and Tourism*, Haworth, New York.
A useful edited volume covering all the main elements of consumer behaviour.

Swarbrooke, J. and Horner, S. (2006) *Consumer Behaviour in Tourism*, Elsevier Butterworth Heinemann, Oxford.
A thorough textbook reviewing all aspects of consumer behaviour and broader elements of tourism demand.

References cited

Boniface, B. and Cooper, C. (1987) *The Geography of Travel and Tourism*, Heinemann, London.

Cohen, E. (1972) 'Towards a sociology of international tourism', *Social Research* **39**(1), 164–82.

Cohen, E. (1974) 'Who is a tourist? A conceptual clarification', *Sociological Review* **22**(4), 527–55.

Cohen, E. (1984) 'The sociology of tourism: approaches, issues, findings', *Annual Review of Sociology*, 1984, 373–92.

Dann, G.M.S. (1981) 'Tourist motivation: an appraisal', *Annals of Tourism Research* **8**(2), 187–219.

Decrop, A. (2000) 'Tourists' Decision-Making and Behaviour Processes', pp. 103–33, in Pizam, A. and Mansfield, Y. (eds) *Consumer Behaviour in Travel and Tourism*, Haworth, New York.

Engel, J.F., Blackwell, R.D. and Miniard, P. (1986) *Consumer Behaviour*, Dryden Press, New York.

Engel, J.F., Kollat, D.J. and Blackwell, R.P. (1968) *Consumer Behaviour*, Holt, Reinhardt & Winston, New York.

Gilbert, D.C. (1992) A Study of Factors of Consumer Behaviour Related to Overseas Holidays from the UK, Unpublished PhD Thesis, University of Surrey, Guildford.

Goffman, E. (1959) *The Presentation of Self in Everyday Life*, Pelican, London.

Gray, H.P. (1970) *International Travel – International Trade*, Heath Lexington Books, Lexington, KY.

Gunn, C. (1972) *Vacationscape – Designing Tourist Regions*, University of Texas Press, Austin.

Howard, J.A. and Sheth, J.N. (1969) *The Theory of Buyer Behaviour*, Wiley, New York.

MacCannell, D. (1976) *The Tourist: A New Theory of the Leisure Class*, Macmillan, London.

Maslow, A.H. (1970) *Motivation and Personality*, 2nd edn, Harper & Row, New York.

Mathieson, A. and Wall, G. (1982) *Tourism: Economic, Physical and Social Impacts*, Longman, London.

Mayo, E. (1973) 'Regional images and regional travel consumer behaviour', pp. 211–18, in *TTRA Conference Proceedings*, Idaho.

Mayo, E. and Jarvis, L. (1981) *The Psychology of Leisure Travel*, CBI Publishing, Boston.

McIntosh, R.W., Goeldner, C.R. and Ritchie, J.R.B. (1995) *Tourism Principles, Practices, Philosophies*, Wiley, New York.

Moscardo, G., Morrison, A.M., Pearce, P.L., Lang, C.T. and O'Leary, J. (1996) 'Understanding vacation destination choice through travel motivation and activities', *Journal of Vacation Marketing* 2(2), 109–22.

Nicosia, F.M. (1966) *Consumer Decision Processes: Marketing and Advertising Implications*, Prentice Hall, Englewood Cliffs, NJ.

Plog, S.C. (1974) 'Why destination areas rise and fall in popularity', *Cornell Hotel and Restaurant Quarterly* 14(4) (Feb.), 55–8.

Plog, S.C. (1990) 'A carpenter's tools: an answer to Stephen L.J. Smith's review of psychocentrism/allocentrism', *Journal of Travel Research* 28(4), Spring, 43–5.

Schmoll, G.A. (1977) *Tourism Promotion*, Tourism International Press, London.

Sigala, M. (2004) 'Reviewing the profile and behaviour of Internet users: Research directions and opportunities in tourism and hospitality', *Journal of Travel and Tourism Marketing* 17(2/3), 93–102.

Smith, S.L.J. (1990) 'A test of Plog's allocentric/psychocentric model: evidence from seven nations', *Journal of Travel Research* 28(4), Spring, 40–3.

Solomon M.R. (1996) *Consumer Behaviour*, 3rd edn, Prentice Hall, Englewood Cliffs, NJ.

Swarbrooke, J. and Horner, S. (1999) *Consumer Behaviour in Tourism*, Butterworth Heinemann, Oxford.

Wahab, S., Crampon, L.J. and Rothfield, L.M. (1976) *Tourism Marketing*, Tourism International Press, London.

Woodside, A. and Lysonski, S. (1989) 'A general model of traveler destination choice', *Journal of Travel Research*, 27, 8–14.

MAJOR CASE STUDY 2.1
The impact of the 2004 Boxing Day Indian Ocean Tsunami on tourism consumer behaviour

INTRODUCTION

Bierman (2002) states that 'the marketability of individual destinations and global tourism is vulnerable to sudden changes in market perceptions' (p. 3). This implies that, as tourism is a discretionary activity, the majority of the market will change their behaviour in response to threats and danger. Here the relevance of consumer behaviour becomes clear and poses a new challenge for the twenty-first century – we must be able to understand how tourists' decision-making changes in response to threats such as the 2004 Boxing Day Indian Ocean Tsunami. This is particularly the case given that an important part of a decision to travel and visit a destination is the perception of safety and security. If these perceptions are changed to being negative, then travel will not occur.

Bierman (2002) has devised a rating scale for tourism crises ranging from DESTCON 5 where there is a minimal threat to the marketability of a destination to DESTCON 1 where the marketability of not just one destination is threatened but there is also widespread or regional implications. The 2004 Boxing Day Indian Ocean Tsunami rates as DESTCON 1, killing many thousands of people and classified by the UNWTO as:

> the worst disaster in the history of world tourism, claiming the biggest loss of lives of tourists and workers in the tourism industry.
>
> (WTO, 2005a)

BOXING DAY 2004

Early in the morning of Boxing Day, 2004, an earthquake off the coast of Indonesia triggered a tidal wave, or tsunami, which travelled thousands of kilometres across the Indian Ocean and devastated the coastlines of 12 countries. Not only was the tsunami a major humanitarian disaster, but it also impacted upon coastal tourism destinations in four countries, sweeping away beaches, infrastructure and superstructure,

| Photograph 2.2 | The 2004 Boxing Day Indian Ocean Tsunami was the greatest disaster to hit tourism. |

Source: PA Photos

disrupting the services that tourism demands upon and severely depressing demand for the affected resorts.

THE IMPACT OF THE TSUNAMI ON TOURISM

The major impact on tourism occurred in three countries, the Maldives, Sri Lanka and Thailand. Although the tsunami was at its most devastating in the Aceh province of Indonesia, this is not a tourism area.

In the tourism destinations, not only was the front line of the supply chain – the hotels on the beachfronts – severely damaged, but also the supply chain itself was disrupted as food supplies and infrastructure were swept away. Despite this generalisation, in each country the scale and nature of the impact of the tsunami differed. For example:

- Small island economies such as Sri Lanka and the Maldives are highly dependent upon earnings from tourism. In the Maldives, two-thirds of foreign exchange, 40% of gross domestic product and 20% of employment is dependent upon tourism. In both Sri Lanka and the Maldives, the tsunami devastated coastal areas, destroying accommodation and other superstructure, and severely disrupting the support services for tourism such as water, power, communications and food supply.

- In southern Thailand, the tsunami hit in high season in the popular resort areas around Phuket, killing many tourists. The tsunami had its greatest impact in the resort area of Khao Lak. Ironically, this destination, away from the high-rise accommodation blocks of Phuket, was developed as a low-rise resort and in the event most of the resort superstructure was little higher then the 11-metre wave which swept through the resort, destroying the majority of the rooms.

The response to the tsunami was swift, with international and national humanitarian aid securing health, sanitation, shelter and food supplies. The second wave of aid came in the form of various task forces to repair the damage to tourism resorts, retrain human resources and advise on marketing and communications in order to get tourism back on line (WTO, 2005a). Nonetheless, the task was a mammoth one and continues with initiatives for a tsunami warning system and encouragement for individual properties to put in place warning and evacuation strategies.

The recovery process has, however, also been controversial. For example, in Sri Lanka 350 small businesses employing 5,000 people were affected by the tsunami. Here, schemes to provide credit and loans have run into red tape, many businesses were not insured and so ran into debt, disqualifying them for loans, and many businesses were reluctant to take on more debt. Elsewhere there has been criticism that the recovery strategies failed to include poor workers such as street vendors, taxi and rickshaw drivers and fishing boats (Ashley, 2005). Many countries, in fact, came to the conclusion that the priority was to get the tourists back to their resorts rather than rely upon international aid. This is where our understanding of consumer behaviour in the face of such a disaster is important. While we now have market intelligence on responses to disasters such as terrorist attacks, this natural disaster created a different response from the tourism market.

THE IMPACT ON CONSUMER BEHAVIOUR

Inevitably, tourism demand was depressed for the destinations impacted by the tsunami, and this was particularly the case as all destinations were experiencing growth in 2004 until the tsunami hit. Estimates suggest that, by the end of 2005, air and bed capacity was about 20% lower than before the tsunami. Initially consumer demand was depressed. In the first six months of 2005 for example, the Phuket area received around one-third of the number of visitors compared to 2004 and occupancy was severely reduced (see Table 2.2). This was because:

1. much of the bed stock was destroyed and infrastructure was not repaired; and
2. there was a consumer perception that Phuket resorts were not ready to receive tourists and were still unsafe.

Despite the inevitable reduction in visitors, the impact of the Boxing Day Tsunami upon tourism

| Table 2.2 | Comparisons of international arrivals 2004/2005 for tsunami-affected destinations |

International tourist arrivals (000s)	January	February	March	April	May	June	Six-month total
Thailand							
2005	849.9	892.8	930.9	801.5	808.7	883.7	5167.7
2004	1218.7	897.5	860.4	864.3	806.9	866.2	5511.2
% change	−30.2	−0.5	+8.2	−7.3	+0.2	+2.1	−6.2
Phuket							
2005	12.4	35.6	49.8	30.6	28.1	32.2	188.9
2004	160.0	94.0	82.0	78.2	73.0	76.3	563.8
% change	−92.1	−62.1	−39.3	−60.9	−61.5	−57.8	−66.4
Sri Lanka							
2005	38.1	36.6	50.4	42.2	40.8	45.6	254.1
2004	49.9	43.5	38.4	30.6	30.1	32.1	224.9
% change	−23.5	−15.9	+31.2	+37.8	+35.5	+42.3	+11.5
Maldives							
2005	18.7	29.3	35.7	29.7	25.3	22.5	161.5
2004	61.8	59.6	63.8	55.3	42.1	33.8	316.8
% change	−69.7	−50.8	−44.0	−46.4	−40.0	−33.2	−49.0

Source: WTO, 2005c

consumer behaviour was very different from the other catastrophic events such as 9/11 and certainly did not have the global impact on tourism demand that was triggered by 9/11. Simply, the tourism market is maturing and increasingly sophisticated in its response to such disasters. The market (i) recognised that this was a one-off event, (ii) were sympathetic to the destinations affected, and (iii) became more aware of, and favourable to, the destinations due to media coverage. The WTO's (2005b) report on the tsunami-affected destinations summarises the impact upon consumers in more detail:

- Travellers understood that the tsunami was a one-off event and was unlikely to reccur. This meant that there was no overall uncertainty or concerns in the marketplace.

- The tsunami generated much sympathy and concern for the regions, as well as raising awareness of the destinations and what they have to offer through extensive media coverage.

- Marketing and communications efforts internationally and nationally stressed the message that the best way to help the destinations and their people was to visit them as a tourist. Following the tsunami, celebrities made a point of visiting affected areas.

- The travel trade did not take the destinations off their books and this allowed for a more rapid recovery for the resorts. Charter air services and tour operators, for example, initially cancelled or reduced capacity but from 2005 onwards began to reinstate capacity. Nonetheless, while the capacity was available it was still dependent upon demand from the marketplace to realise visitation to the destinations.

- There was a temporary relocation of demand away from the affected destinations to others that are easily substitutable.

- Generating markets changed as a result of the tsunami. In Sri Lanka and the Maldives, for example, Western European visitors were slow to return but were replaced by visitors from other parts of Asia. In Thailand, a strong marketing campaign successfully encouraged domestic tourism to the tsunami-affected destinations.

CONCLUSION

In summary, the 2004 Boxing Day Indian Ocean Tsunami has demonstrated that tourism consumer behaviour has matured in its response to disasters and shocks to the tourism system. In the case of the tsunami, growing international experience in dealing with the recovery of destinations assisted in creating sympathy for the resorts and a realisation that it was returning visitors that they needed.

REFERENCES

Ashley, C. (2005) 'The Indian Ocean Tsunami and Tourism', *Opinions* **33**, Overseas Development Institute, London.

Bierman, D. (2002) *Restoring Tourism Destinations in Crisis*, CABI, Wallingford.

WTO (2005a) *Tsunami: One Year On*, WTO, Madrid.

WTO (2005b) *The Evolution of Tsunami-affected Destinations*, WTO, Madrid.

WTO (2005c) *Post Tsunami Reassessment,* WTO, Madrid.

DISCUSSION QUESTIONS

1. Examining Table 2.2, explain why each of the destinations, and particularly Phuket, show differing reductions of visitors in the first six months of 2005.

2. The short-term imperative to win visitors back to the resorts means that most resorts have been rebuilt as they were. From a consumer point of view, discuss whether this is a strategic error and, in fact, consideration should have been given to a repositioning of the product away from beach tourism and to a diversification of current markets.

3. Draft a press release to win visitors back to Phuket in 2005, taking into account your knowledge of tourism consumer behaviour.

CHAPTER 3
Measuring Demand for Tourism

LEARNING OUTCOMES

In this chapter, we review the key issues associated with the measurement of tourism demand and the management of tourism information, to provide you with:

- an understanding of the reasons why we measure both international and domestic demand for tourism;

- a knowledge of the main methods used to measure tourism demand;

- a review of what is measured in respect of tourism activity;

- an appreciation of the difficulties of researching tourism markets and why tourism statistics must be interpreted with caution; and

- an awareness of the research process and knowledge management and their applications to tourism.

Photograph: Camel resting at the Pyramids, Egypt

INTRODUCTION

Following on from the last chapter that outlined consumer behaviour in tourism, we now turn to approaches to measuring patterns of consumer demand. In this chapter we describe and critically appraise the measurement of demand for both international and domestic tourism. We treat these separately for convenience, although it is recognised that international and domestic movements may be considered essentially the same activity. Certainly they have much in common. We consider why tourism demand is measured, what definitions are used and which statistics are normally compiled. We include a description of methods commonly used and an indication of their strengths and weaknesses.

Closely linked to the measurement of demand is the concept of collecting market intelligence and managing information. In tourism, this often means using secondary data (for example, data produced by national or regional government bodies), combined with primary data through market surveys. In the latter part of this chapter we provide a practical guide to market research for the tourism industry and, in particular, market surveys. The various stages of research are also explained, from the agreement of research purpose and objectives, through research design, data collection and analysis, to the reporting of the research. We also give emphasis to the importance of a manager making use of findings and feeding them into the decision-making process, as well as the emerging science of knowledge management and how it can be applied to tourism.

DEMAND FOR INTERNATIONAL TOURISM

Why measure international tourism?

National governments are generally extremely keen to monitor and attach measures to the movement of people into and out of their countries. This is for a variety of reasons, many of which have nothing whatsoever to do with tourism, such as security, health and immigration control. The measurement of tourism movement, however, has increasingly been seen as important because of the effects of tourism activity on a country's balance of payments.

The balance of payments is a country's financial accounts. There are movements of monies into and out of these accounts. Any standard economics text will provide a detailed and proper explanation of the various components. An obvious way in which tourism has an impact on the balance of payments is through the spending of international tourists. We can identify two aspects here.

1. Residents of country X, who travel abroad, spend money abroad. This has a negative effect on the balance of payments of country X (and positive effects on the balance of payments of countries visited). With regard to the movement of money, this can be thought of as an import as far as X is concerned. It is referred to as an invisible import since there is no associated tangible good (such as a car or refrigerator); instead it is the 'invisible' tourism experience that has been purchased.

2. Residents of a foreign country, who are incoming tourists to country X, spend money in X. This has a positive effect on the balance of payments of X (and corresponding negative effects on the balance of payments of the country of origin of the tourist). As far as X is concerned, the direction of the spending is such that it is considered to be an invisible export – in other words the spending is on something that cannot be touched or seen.

The two components described above combine to form what is known as the travel account for a country. A positive travel account means that spending by incoming tourists exceeds spending abroad by outgoing tourists, and the combined effect will be of benefit to the balance of payments. Many commentators argue that any comparison of the two types of spending is unfair, since they reflect different activities.

The above analysis does not take into account fares paid to international passenger transport carriers and the various secondary effects of tourist spending. Later in this book we consider the impacts of tourism in detail, including a comprehensive review of the economic impacts.

We can see, then, that governments are keen to measure the movement of international tourism, but particularly incoming tourism because of its economic benefits. There are, however, a number of other important reasons:

- Official records can be built up and trends in movements can be monitored over a period of time. This means, for example, that the effectiveness of a tourist board such as VisitLondon can be monitored, or that any particular promotional campaign, which attempts to attract visitors from a particular country, can be assessed.

- In general, information about the origins of visitors, their trip and attitudes can be used for a variety of purposes in marketing or planning. This is true also for tourism organisations at regional and local levels, provided that data collected at international level can be further broken down and still be reliable.

In addition, some commercial organisations, although a minority, can and do make use of international tourism statistics. An incoming tour operator or wholesaler, for example, needs to be aware of current trends in order that programmes can be adjusted accordingly. Similarly, international and national hotel chains monitor changes in demand as part of their intelligence activity as do airlines such as Singapore Airlines outlined in the case study at the end of this chapter.

Some definitions

In collecting any information on the movement of travellers, it is essential to decide who is to be included. Everyone would agree that a family on holiday should count in the figures, but what about a businessperson, or the crew of a passenger liner, or even a member of the armed forces on duty in a foreign land? See Figure 3.1 for the answers! We can identify a number of principles that should govern the formation of a terminology:

- Definitions should be unambiguous and easy to understand.
- Definitions should normally be consistent with established usage of the words concerned.
- Definitions should, as far as is reasonably possible, facilitate measurement.

There is a major difficulty concerning the word 'tourism' itself. The normal and everyday use of the word relates to pleasure travel, but it would certainly exclude business travel. This is unfortunately not in line with what has become accepted as standard in the tourism literature. It is standard practice to include, as tourists, not only people who travel for pleasure but also those who travel for the purposes of business, visiting friends and relatives, or even shopping as we noted in the introduction to this book. The reasons concern the use that is made of tourism statistics. After all, passenger transport carriers would wish for such a broad range of travellers to be included; a large number of hoteliers are interested in business travel because of the business it generates for them, and so on.

The definitions we give here are those that have become accepted. Figure 3.1 shows the breakdown of all travellers who cross international frontiers into those who are to be included in tourism statistics (to be called 'visitors') and those who are not. The decision as to who to include is based on the purpose of visit. Visitors are divided according to whether or not there is an overnight stay in the country: if there is, then the visitor is deemed to be a tourist; otherwise he or she is a same-day visitor (previously called an excursionist). In summary, for the purposes of classifying international travellers:

- A visitor is a traveller who is included in tourism statistics, based on his or her purpose of visit, which includes holidays, visiting friends and relatives, and business. A fuller list is shown in Figure 3.1.

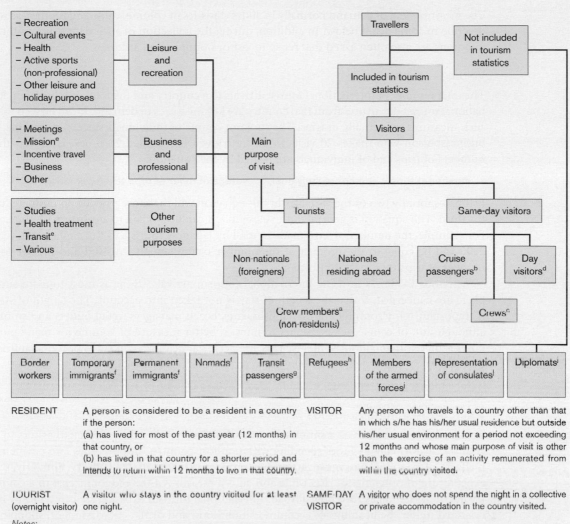

Figure 3.1   Classification of international visitors
Source: WTO, 2000

- A tourist is a visitor who spends at least one night in the country visited.
- A same-day visitor is a visitor who does not spend the night in a collective or private accommodation in the country visited. So, for example, those returning to ship or train to sleep are considered as same-day visitors.

What is measured?

The measurement of demand normally includes statistics of volume, value and profiles, as we describe in some detail below. In addition, during the collection of such data from visitors, questions are also often asked that relate to visitor opinions and attitudes.

Volume statistics

The total number of international tourist arrivals to a country and the total number of international tourist departures from that country are key measures of demand. It can be seen that such measures are actually of trips. They are not counts of individuals since, for example, a businessperson who makes 20 visits to a country will be counted 20 times. However, the numbers of trips and of individuals are related by the equation:

number of trips = number of individuals × average number of trips taken per individual

Estimates for any two of the variables in this equation will therefore provide an estimate for the third. The equation is general in the sense that it can be applied to any group of tourists. For example, the number of trips made in total by Japanese tourists to Ruritania in the year 2006 will be equal to the product of the number of individuals involved and the average number of trips they make to Ruritania.

A serious weakness in using international tourism arrivals, as far as most tourism suppliers are concerned, is that the length of stay is not taken into account. The length of stay is important for accommodation establishments, beach managers, retail outlets and so on, although not, of course, for passenger termini. A better measure of volume for many purposes is therefore total tourist nights. This also acts as a measure of likely impact on a tourist destination. It can be defined as follows:

total tourist nights = number of tourist trips × average length of stay (nights stayed)

Value (expenditure) statistics

Total visitor expenditure is a simple measure of the economic value of foreign visitors to a country. It normally includes spending within a host country, and excludes fare payments made to international passenger carriers for travel into and out of that country. Similarly, the expenditure of outgoing tourists while abroad is a measure of the economic cost to a country due to its nationals travelling abroad. International tourism expenditure can typically be classified under the headings of accommodation, food and drink, entertainment, shopping and travel within the host country. For the purposes of comparison between countries, value statistics are often converted to US dollars.

Visitor profile statistics

Profile statistics are made up of statistics relating to the visitor and those of the visit. Table 3.1 shows information typically collected.

Measurement methods used

Tourism statistics relating to international tourism are normally estimates rather than exact values. The reasons for this mainly centre on the fact that monitoring and measuring what are at times complex movements of people are not easy and are subject to error. We can most easily understand this when contemplating how to obtain detailed profile or expenditure information about tourists. Even the controls at international boundaries and currency controls do not normally work to provide accurate tourism information as they are designed for security or immigration purposes.

Volume statistics are often obtained using counting procedures at entry and exit points to a country, or (for inbound tourism) sometimes through the use of registration forms at accommodation establishments. They can be supplemented by summaries of records kept by international passenger carriers, and by surveys of households, such as a national travel survey which will elicit information on foreign (outgoing) as well as domestic tourism. Research

Table 3.1	Visitor profile statistics
The visitor	**The visit**
Age	Origin and destination
Sex	Mode of transport
Group type (e.g. alone, family)	Purpose of visit
Nationality or country of residence	Length of stay
Occupation	Accommodation used
Income	Activities engaged in Places visited Tour or independently organised

at tourist destinations also provides some information on the movement of international visitors to a country.

Procedures used at entry and exit points have normally been determined on the basis of administrative control and other reasons not specifically related to tourism. Tourism statistics are thus a by-product of the process rather than its main aim. Nevertheless, there are many countries that do make counts and collect information at frontiers for tourism-related purposes. Clearly, islands (such as Great Britain or those of the West Indies) have an advantage in this respect, since there are likely to be fewer entry/exit points anyway. A major problem with counting using accommodation establishments alone is that they give only partial coverage. No estimates would be possible for those staying with friends or relatives, for example.

Expenditure statistics are notoriously difficult to collect. We can derive them using foreign currency estimates from banks, or from suppliers of tourism services and facilities such as hotels or attractions. These methods are cumbersome and normally not satisfactory as they require the cooperation of these organisations and often are only provided as estimates. Increasingly, therefore, information is collected directly from the tourists themselves, through sample surveys of foreign tourists as they leave the country, and from nationals as they return from a foreign trip, either on entry to the country or through household surveys.

DEMAND FOR DOMESTIC TOURISM

Why measure domestic tourism?

Worldwide, relatively few people enjoy the opportunity to travel to and within countries other than their own. By far the most common form of travel is that by residents of a country within that country. International travel, although given high priority by segments of the populations of industrialised nations, is still very much a minority activity. As a very rough guide, we estimate that expenditure worldwide on domestic tourism may be worth up to 10 times that on international tourism.

The UNWTO reported in 1984 that 'there are relatively few countries that collect domestic travel and tourism statistics', and the situation has not changed significantly since then. Much more information is available on international tourism. Why is this?

First of all, international travel involves, by definition, the crossing of a frontier. It is therefore easier to observe and monitor. Domestic tourism involves movement internally and is therefore more difficult to research. Countries that make use solely of registration forms at hotels miss out all aspects of domestic tourism that involve staying at supplementary accommodation establishments or with friends or relatives. A number of countries do not even try to measure domestic demand because it is considered unimportant owing to the nature of their own domestic tourism. For example, in many developing countries very little domestic movement involves staying in serviced accommodation, and so it does not compete with demand from international visitors. The benefits of collecting information always has to be set against its costs, particularly in a developing country where resources may be severely limited.

On the other hand, within the major international tourism-receiving countries of North America and Western Europe, domestic demand and international demand often compete with and complement each other. We can see this clearly in places such as hotel lobbies, on beaches, in restaurants and at attractions. So in countries such as the USA, Canada and the UK, the measurement of domestic tourism is important.

Use is made of domestic tourism statistics in a variety of ways:

- To measure the contribution of tourism to the overall economy. Although it is impossible to assess accurately, estimates can be produced that measure the effect of tourism on a country's gross domestic product.

- For promotion and marketing policies. Many countries promote themselves strongly as destinations to their own residents – in this sense, they compete with foreign destinations for their own tourists' spending.

- To assist area development policies. This can involve inputs into the tourism planning process to ensure that visitor preferences are taken into account.

- To aid social policies. A statistical knowledge of holiday-taking habits by nationals is required in order to deliver social tourism aid to the underprivileged.

In addition to the above, local and regional tourism organisations and individual businesses make use of domestic tourism statistics as an aid to decision-making.

Definitions of visitors vary country by country. When detailed accuracy is important it is advisable to check against the original source. Figure 3.2 gives definitions and classifications of internal (domestic) visitors as recommended by the UNWTO.

What is measured?

The measurement of domestic tourism demand covers similar areas to that of international demand: volume, value and visitor profile statistics. These can be presented for the country as a whole, but they are often more useful if they can be broken down to provide reliable information for specific destination areas. It is common for individual destinations to conduct their own research, and to complement their findings with the general data of a national study.

Measurement methods used

Statistics of domestic tourism are just like those of international tourism in that they are estimates, normally representing informed guesses and subject to different levels of error. Although some countries base them on returns from accommodation establishments, this does not provide proper coverage. It is increasingly common to collect information from the visitors themselves. This is normally done through sample surveys, and can take different forms, as follows.

Household surveys

Household surveys are based on understanding an area's resident population's domestic tourism for pleasure or business purposes. A structured sample of households is constructed and interviewers are employed to collect information using a questionnaire. Questions normally relate to past behaviour, covering trips already made, although studies of intentions are sometimes undertaken. Domestic tourism surveys, national travel surveys and holiday travel surveys (the latter excluding business travel) can all be based on household surveys, as shown in the Mini Case Study 3.1 below. They also provide, as a matter of course, information on foreign travel by residents and also information on those who do not travel.

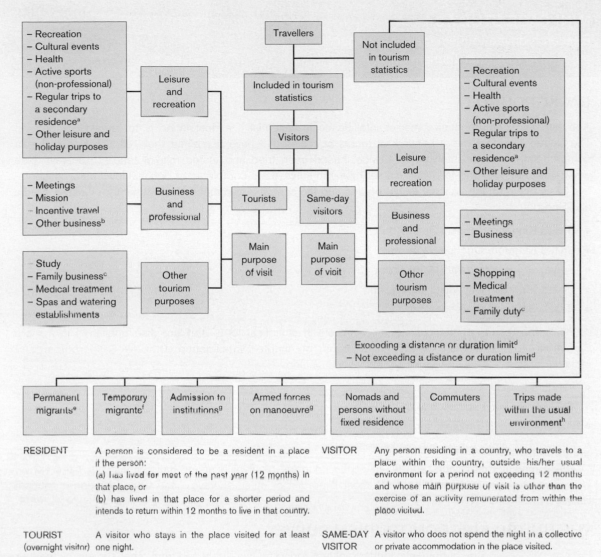

Figure 3.2 Classification of internal visitors
Source: WTO, 2000

RESIDENT A person is considered to be a resident in a place if the person:
(a) has lived for most of the past year (12 months) in that place, or
(b) has lived in that place for a shorter period and intends to return within 12 months to live in that country.

VISITOR Any person residing in a country, who travels to a place within the country, outside his/her usual environment for a period not exceeding 12 months and whose main purpose of visit is other than the exercise of an activity remunerated from within the place visited.

TOURIST (overnight visitor) A visitor who stays in the place visited for at least one night.

SAME-DAY VISITOR A visitor who does not spend the night in a collective or private accommodation in the place visited.

Notes:

[a] Weekly trips to the place of second residence (whether owned, inhabited free of charge or rented) should be classified separately under leisure and recreation.

[b] Persons undertaking frequent trips within the country, e.g. crew members, drivers, tourist guides, salespeople, itinerant sellers, inspectors, artists, sportspeople.

[c] Attending funerals, visiting sick relatives, etc.

[d] Minimum distance and duration of minimum absence and duration of journey may be required for a person to qualify as a same-day visitor.

[e] For a period of less then 6 months, or the minimum time necessary to establish a new residence, including dependants.

[f] For a period of less than 12 months with the purpose of exercising an activity remunerated from within the place of destination, including dependants.

[g] Admission to a hospital, prison and other institutions.

[h] Trips of a routine character, part of a regular business schedule or frequent visits to a place for whatever reason.

MINI CASE STUDY 3.1
Research-driven tourism market intelligence:
the United Kingdom Tourism Survey

BACKGROUND

Accurate and comprehensive market intelligence is essential if a destination is to remain competitive. The United Kingdom has a network of tourist agencies that have combined their resources to deliver a comprehensive market intelligence service, based upon tried and tested market research surveys (see www.staruk.org.uk). The following market research surveys are completed at national level on a collaborative basis between the national tourist boards and the central government's Department for Culture, Media and Sport:

- United Kingdom Tourism Survey;
- United Kingdom Occupancy Survey;
- Survey of Visits to Visitor Attractions;
- United Kingdom Day Visits Survey; and
- British Conference Venues Survey.

While the results of the surveys are available in statistical form, they are also published in a more digestible format to the industry in terms of market intelligence (http://tourismtrade.org.uk/ MarketIntelligenceResearch/). Here, publications include:

- trends and forecasts;
- domestic tourism statistics and research;
- market and trade profiles; and
- foresight, monthly topics and market focus.

These market intelligence reports are based upon the technically sound national surveys listed above. This case study focuses on one of the most important of these surveys – the United Kingdom Tourism Survey.

THE UNITED KINGDOM TOURISM SURVEY

Prior to 1989 estimates of domestic tourism volume and value were obtained from other surveys by the four UK national tourist boards (England, Scotland, Wales and Northern Ireland). The United Kingdom Tourism Survey (UKTS) came about, following reviews of statistical needs by and among the boards, as a result of a requirement for better data: better in the sense of being compatible over the UK as a whole, of covering aspects of tourism not covered by the earlier surveys, and of deriving from larger, and hence more statistically robust, samples (www.staruk.org.uk).

OBJECTIVES

The objective of UKTS is, first, to provide measurements of tourism by residents of the UK, in terms of both volume (trips taken, nights spent away from home) and value (expenditure on those trips and nights). Secondly, it is to collect details of the trips taken and of the people taking them. These objectives extend to:

- tourism by residents of any age;
- tourism for any purpose;
- tourism in the sense of trips away from home which last for one night or more up to a maximum of 60 nights; and
- tourism to any destination in any country of the world, using any accommodation type.

METHOD

The UKTS is a good example of how survey methodology changes to address both financial and technological change. The survey method for the 10 years from 1989 to 1999 was a household interview. Each month, continuously, interviews were conducted face to face in the homes of a fresh representative sample of UK adults aged 15 or more. The sample used was a stratified random sample from the UK's electoral register, leading to named persons for interview. Up to four recalls were made at different times and on different days of the week: no substitutes were used in the sample. By this method, approximately 70,000 interviews were conducted each year in the course of fieldwork.

Between 2000 and 2004 the method changed to telephone interviewing and the sample was reduced to 50,000 adults. The sampling was achieved through random digital dialling with the interviewing spread evenly throughout the year. A particular change was that a longer time period was allowed to recall a respondent who was unavailable at the first time of calling. This is an important aspect when researching a market such as the UK where there is a large number of frequent travellers.

However, this methodology was abandoned in 2005 when it delivered significantly lower estimates for domestic tourism, contradicting both industry experience and other survey results. As a result, the face-to-face methodology was reinstated in 2005. However, this is at the cost of being able to compare year-on-year trends as the change in methodology means that the 2005 results are not comparable to previous years.

INFORMATION COLLECTED

The following information is collected by the UKTS:

- purpose of trip;
- number of nights away;
- accommodation used;
- transport used;
- activities undertaken;
- type of location;
- month trip started;
- booking method;
- demographics (age, gender etc.).

PUBLICATION OF FINDINGS

Findings are published quarterly.

Source: Adapted from *The UK Tourist*, published jointly by the English Tourist Board, Northern Ireland Tourist Board, Scottish Tourist Board and Wales Tourist Board.

REFERENCES

http://www.staruk.org.uk
http://tourismtrade.org.uk/MarketIntelligenceResearch/

DISCUSSION QUESTIONS

1. Recalling past events is a critical element of this type of survey – can you remember your last three tourism trips in sufficient detail to answer the checklist of questions asked by the UKTS above?
2. Tourism demand surveys are very expensive and compromises have to be made in their design to meet budgets. Do you think the public or the private sector should fund such surveys?
3. Draft a checklist of the differences between face-to-face and telephone interviewing.

En route surveys

En route surveys are surveys of travellers during the course of their journey. Strategic points are selected on key surface transport routes to stop or approach people, who are then either interviewed or given a questionnaire or other documentation to complete in their own time for return by post. A major problem with this type of work is that the representativeness of the sample can be in doubt because of incomplete knowledge of traffic movement within a country.

Destination surveys

Surveys are often conducted at popular tourist destinations or in areas where there are high levels of tourist activity. They typically take the form of personal interviews by teams of interviewers. The information provided leads to estimates of the volume and value of tourism to the destination, and profiles of both the visitors and their visits. Questions are also asked to elicit opinions about the destination and associated attitudes. It is difficult in this type of work to ensure that the sample of visitors is representative, though efforts are made to ensure a spread across appropriate days and weeks, and that interviews are conducted at a wide range of sites.

Surveys of suppliers

Surveys of the suppliers of tourism services are sometimes undertaken in order to gain information on occupancy rates, visitor numbers, etc. Accommodation occupancy surveys are, in fact, common worldwide. In North America, airlines have been required through the Civil Aeronautics Board (in the USA) and the Canadian Transport Commission to produce origin and destination data.

USING TOURISM STATISTICS

Some words of caution

According to the UNWTO, international tourist arrivals in 2006 numbered 842 million. It is not so much the size of this figure that is so impressive, but the fact that anybody should know the level of tourism demand or be able to work the figure out. In this chapter, we have detailed methods for measuring tourism demand and it is important to bear them in mind when interpreting the results.

Collecting tourism statistics is time-consuming and complex. In some countries it is taken very seriously, to the extent that attempts are made to assess the size of potential errors. It is then possible not merely to provide a point estimate (that is, a single value) of, say, tourist numbers, but to give lower and upper bounds within which the true value is thought to lie. Some countries review their data collection procedures with a view to minimising errors subject to an acceptable cost. However, not all countries attach the same importance to tourism statistics in general, and to certain measures in particular. For example, the expenditure of incoming tourists normally has high priority attached to it, because of its positive contribution to the balance of payments. On the other hand, the number and spending of tourists who are visiting friends and relatives may be underestimated in countries in which measurement is through serviced accommodation establishments.

It is not surprising, then, that the interpretation of tourism data is fraught with danger. Key points to bear in mind are the following:

- Tourism statistics are normally estimates, often derived from sample surveys. As such, they are liable to various forms of error, many of which are impossible to quantify.
- For measurements which result from sample surveys, in general the smaller the sample size, the greater is the probable error.
- Even though the sample size for data relating to a region or country may give rise to acceptable levels of error, analysis of a subset of the data pertaining to a smaller area or region may not be feasible owing to the much reduced sample size. This is the case, for

example, if the Australian state of Queensland is attempting to gain an accurate measurement of international tourists from a national Australian survey.

- Sample size is not everything! The true random sampling of tourists who are, by their very nature, on the move is not normally possible. A sample has to be formally and carefully constructed.

- Where methodology in collecting data changes (even when it is for the better), it is dangerous to compare results.

- There are serious problems involved in attempting either to compare or to combine figures collected by different countries or organisations.

The final point arises because there is not only considerable variation in the methods employed by different countries, but also variation in the measures adopted. A notable example is that some countries count tourist arrivals (at least one night spent in the country visited), whereas others prefer to count visitor arrivals (this includes excursionists, i.e. those who do not stay overnight).

Interpreting tourism statistics

What then are we to make of the fact that we are told that international tourist arrivals in 2006 worldwide numbered 842 million? This total is certainly arrived at by grossing figures submitted to the UNWTO by governments or national bodies throughout the world. Each component value is subject to different levels of error, arising from different methodologies. It is clear, therefore, that the quoted figure is an estimate, and it is difficult to say how accurate it might be.

The points made above apply more generally than to total international tourist arrivals worldwide. They apply equally to many other situations in which data relating to tourists are collected: at resorts, attractions, passenger termini and so on. However, exact values are normally not what is important and, bearing in mind the shortcomings, we can see that tourism statistics often represent the best estimates available and also provide a guide as to true magnitudes. As a result, they have the following broad benefits:

- They often provide valuable trend data, where information is produced over a number of time periods.

- They contribute towards a database which may influence decision-making, particularly in the areas of marketing, and planning and development.

- They enable the effects of decisions or changes to be monitored.

- They enable current data to be viewed in context.

- They provide a means of making forecasts.

RESEARCH-DRIVEN TOURISM MARKET INTELLIGENCE

Many managers and organisations in the tourism industry attach great value to research and the knowledge that it delivers, using it to place themselves in a strong competitive position. Sound market intelligence is gained from a variety of formal and informal methods, and bridges the gap between the provider of the product or service and the consumer. Deep and meaningful research is the key to understanding the tourism consumer and their needs. Decisions such as those concerning product development and marketing activity can be based on research findings. Moreover, research can be used to highlight specific problems, and even to demonstrate to customers a caring attitude towards them.

We can see that marketing intelligence and marketing research in tourism can therefore:

- provide information for decision-making;
- keep an organisation in touch with its market;

- identify new markets;
- monitor the performance of certain aspects of a business;
- draw attention to specific problems;
- monitor customer reaction to a service or facility;
- reduce waste; and
- demonstrate a caring attitude to the customer.

However, others view research with suspicion, often questioning the accuracy of the results. It can be seen as an unnecessary cost, taking up valuable resources that could be used in a better way. There may just not be the time for it, given the high level of pressure under which many people work. Others may see research as an essentially academic activity with no real value for the business. In any case, some organisations are able to 'feed off' the research conducted and published by others with greater market share, or to make use of the findings and advice of national and regional tourist offices. These issues are further discussed in the major case study at the end of this chapter. There are also problems in researching the activity of tourism itself:

- tourism takes place for a short period of time;
- the decision process is highly emotional and involved and difficult to articulate in survey answers;
- the venue for data collection can be in crowded and busy places; and
- domestic tourism and day trips are challenging to sample as, normally, no international border is crossed.

The potential benefits of research vary considerably by type of organisation and by size. Major airlines and international hotel chains, for example, collect and analyse data as an aid to making decisions and managing their business. Individual hotels and attractions often conduct surveys of guests and visitors to gain profile information, opinions and satisfaction ratings. A small restaurant owner or retailer is unlikely to engage in formal research. All businesses monitor sales, however, and all good managers have an instinct for changes in the marketplace.

THE RESEARCH PROCESS

There is no standard way of approaching research. However, it is instructive to model the research process using the flow diagram shown in Figure 3.3, bearing in mind that stages shown often overlap in time rather than following the precise sequence implied. Some organisations generate research through a planning or marketing department that is able to identify research needs. The reporting of the outcomes can then be fed back into the department concerned for action, and an information base built up. Most organisations, however, generate ad hoc projects if and when the need arises.

Research can be undertaken in house by an organisation using its own resources, or an external agency may be employed. In either case, the same principles apply and the process is essentially the same. There are numerous reputable organisations – such as advertising agencies, market research agencies, consultants, academic institutions – that offer their services, and that either specialise in research or are experienced in research as part of their activity. Normally, when commissioning research, the sponsor will issue a detailed brief. Following discussions, external agencies usually submit research proposals, often in competition, the successful one gaining a contract to undertake the research.

The principles we cover in the rest of this chapter are valid not only for research within the tourism industry, but also for students of tourism in academic settings. Research projects at all levels of study will benefit from the structure imposed by Figure 3.3.

Identify the need for research

↓

Agree on research purpose

↓

Establish research objectives

↓

Develop a research design

↓

Implement the chosen approach

↓

Analyse the data

↓

Report findings

↓

Use the research!

Figure 3.3	The research process

Source: Cooper and Latham, 1990

Agreeing the purpose and setting objectives

Research based on a clear picture of its purpose is likely to lead to findings that will be of benefit. The overall purpose should be agreed by the major parties concerned. This is particularly important for the many public-sector projects in tourism that have to satisfy or are steered by representatives from a wide range of interested organisations. An example here would be an economic impact study of a major sporting event such as a Formula 1 Grand Prix or an Olympic Games where there will be many interested parties.

The purpose is satisfied through the attainment of the research objectives set. The objectives should always be formally stated, and again agreed. This not only avoids later misunderstanding, but also gives a focus to the research. It is possible to match findings later with the objectives set in order to assess the success of the research. For example, the following research objectives are taken from a survey of educational visits to the National Maritime Museum:

- To elicit the profile of educational groups visiting the museum in terms of age, geographical location, sector of school and size of school group.
- To elicit the profile of visits by educational groups in terms of number of visits made, whether schools were on a day trip or staying in London, any publicity or event prompting the visit, and the mode of travel.
- A final objective related to the schools' use and opinions of the museum as an educational resource. The survey aimed to discover the level of use of the educational service and also to obtain schools' opinions of the service and the museum and to identify areas in which the service may be improved.

Research design

A research design is a detailed description or plan; it can be used to guide the implementation of the research. The most significant decision involved in design concerns the approach to be taken. For example:

- What reliance is to be placed on secondary sources?
- Should a sample survey or group discussions be used?
- Which survey technique should be used – personal interviews, telephone interviews, web-based survey or postal survey?

Primary or secondary data?

Secondary data are those that have already been collected, possibly by some other individual or organisation and for some other purpose. In any country the most prolific source is government. Although its data are normally too general in nature to be of practical benefit, they often provide good background information. The same applies to data provided by other national and local bodies such as tourist offices. Before engaging in what may prove to be expensive primary data collection (that is, your own), it is worth a researcher identifying and assessing possible sources of information that could supplement primary data or even remove the need for it. There is little point in collecting information that already exists in an accessible form.

In particular, a tourism enterprise's own records are particularly valuable. Data can be taken from sales invoices, booking forms, general accounts, operating data, internal reports and so on. Many organisations have built up databases over a period of time, and these can form the basis of research data. Nevertheless, there are times when it is necessary to collect primary data, even though it is normal to supplement this with secondary data.

Methods of collecting primary data

In tourism, the most common method by far is the sample survey, either of visitors themselves or of businesses. The four main types of survey are personal interview, telephone interview, web-based survey and postal survey. The choice as to which to use depends on the nature of the research concerned, and takes account of the advantages and disadvantages of each method as demonstrated in the second Mini Case Study in this chapter.

Visitor surveys at attractions are often based on personal interviews using questionnaires at or near exit points. Telephone interviewing has become increasingly popular. It can be used in its own right or as part of an overall strategy. For example, an occupancy survey may involve contact by telephone, followed by a personal visit and the delivery of self-administered questionnaires. Postal questionnaires are often used when the manager does not have direct access to the user, or as a follow-up such as when a holiday is sold, using customer addresses. It is also possible to hand out questionnaires for self-completion: for example, on a return holiday flight or return coach journey. Web-based surveys using email or online survey forms associated with web sites, are growing in popularity and are particularly useful for more in-depth information, such as that required by the Delphi forecasting technique (which is also discussed on page 115). There is also scope in tourism for the use of observation methods – in monitoring the popularity of displays or exhibits, or the movement of visitors at open-air sites.

It is possible to make use of modern computer technology in the collection of primary data. This can lead not only to improvements in accuracy, but also removes the need for data input at a later stage.

In a detailed study of attitudes or perceptions, it is probable that a qualitative approach will be taken in order to achieve greater insight and understanding. This might involve in-depth interviews or discussions with individuals, say with successful managers to analyse their decision-making processes. It can also involve the formation of discussion groups of between six and ten people, led by an experienced facilitator. In this case the interaction between people can stimulate and encourage ideas, or draw out factors such as those that affect holiday choice.

Photograph 3.1 An experienced facilitator leads a small group discussion to draw out detailed information on a key tourism issue.
Source: Alamy Images/Ace Stock Ltd

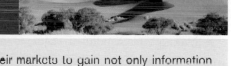

MINI CASE STUDY 3.2
Comparing data collection procedures

Major tourist attractions such as theme parks routinely research their markets to gain not only information on their market profile but also the opinions and satisfaction levels of their visitors. These attractions utilise different data collection procedures in their surveys but, of course, each procedure has its own strengths and weaknesses. Below we consider four of the most commonly used approaches for the collection of data at attractions.

PERSONAL INTERVIEW

Advantages:

- Initial interest can be aroused and visitors may then spend longer at the attraction.
- Complex questioning is possible on, say, visitors' likes and dislikes at the attraction.
- Visual aids and showcards can be used.
- Flexibility allows scheduling to be varied according to, say, the weather.
- It shows a caring attitude to the visitors at the attraction.
- Visitors are usually happy to cooperate.

Disadvantages:

- Time-consuming for interviewer and visitor.
- Administratively difficult scheduling interviewers etc.
- It can be an expensive way to collect data as interviewers can be costly.

TELEPHONE INTERVIEW

Advantages:

- Close supervision and control is possible.
- Access is easy, call-backs are possible if the person who visited the attraction is not available.
- Response rates are usually good.
- Many interviews are possible in a given time period.

Disadvantages:

- Visual aids and complex tasks are not possible.
- Only verbal communication is possible.
- Interview is short (people hang up).
- For attraction surveys it relies on recall and the immediacy of the visit is lost.
- People are tiring of 'cold' calls.

POSTAL SURVEY

Advantages:

- Low cost.
- No intermediary, so answers are reliable and visitors would not answer in a certain way to 'please' the interviewer.
- Superior for sensitive questions (confidentiality must be stressed) on, say, satisfaction levels with the visit.

Disadvantages:

- Many variables are not controlled, since there is no interviewer.
- Mailing list is needed of visitors to the attraction.
- Response rates are low.
- Bias due to non-response.
- Detailed or long questionnaires reduce response.

INTERNET SURVEY

Advantages:

- Substantial cost savings over other survey methods.
- No cost to the respondent in replying.
- Response tends to be very quick.
- Instant feedback of undeliverable mail is useful in replacing respondents.
- Useful as a supplement to other survey methods – say, a follow-up on an interview at the attraction.
- Good for surveying specific populations such as teachers who have taken groups to the attraction.
- Off-the-shelf survey packages are available.

Disadvantages:

- Sample bias due to the type of respondent – random sampling is virtually impossible.
- Evidence on response rates is contradictory.
- Needs high level of expertise to construct the survey.
- Ethical issues of sending unsolicited email.

Source: Adapted from Cooper and Latham, 1990; Tasci and Knutson, 2003

DISCUSSION QUESTIONS

1. For a survey of visitor satisfaction for a holiday island such as Majorca, draft a checklist of the main pros and cons for using each of the four methods outlined in the case study.
2. What are the main sources of tourism market information that lend themselves to collection by an Internet survey?
3. Of the methods in the case study, which is the most cost-effective for a market survey of booking intentions?

Designing questionnaires

Questionnaires are by far the most common type of form used for primary data collection in tourism. They are difficult to construct, though much easier to criticise, and it is certainly sensible for a researcher to pass round his or her attempts to colleagues for suggested changes. Final versions are usually very different from early drafts. It is important to bear in mind the objectives of the research when constructing a questionnaire, as they give focus to it. The temptation to include questions not relevant to the study, but for interest's sake, should normally be resisted. Their inclusion can lead to a respondent tiring or losing interest, and so put at risk answers to more important questions. The steps involved in the design of a questionnaire are as follows:

- Plan what to measure, based on the objectives of the research.
- Formulate the questions.
- Decide on the layout and order of questions.
- Pilot test the questionnaire.
- Correct problems that arise and retest if necessary.

Here are some general guidelines for constructing or assessing the likely effectiveness of a questionnaire:

- Questions should follow a logical order; the questionnaire should flow.
- There should be a simple introduction and early questions should be straightforward.
- Language used should be appropriate to the respondent.
- Questions should be unambiguous.
- Avoid bias within a question, i.e. a question that suggests that a particular answer is acceptable.
- Do not tax the memory of the respondent.
- Instructions on the form (to interviewer or, in the case of self-completion, the respondent) should be highlighted.

- The questionnaire should be as short as possible.
- The form should be attractive, well laid out and easy to follow.

Sampling

Normally research in tourism seeks to gain information on a large number of people (or sometimes businesses). The term 'population', or 'universe', is used to describe all those under consideration. Examples of populations are all holidaymakers at a resort, all business-people using hotels in a city, all users of a leisure complex, or all visitors to an attraction.

For populations that are relatively small, say, the 17 coach operators who use a particular stop, it is possible to undertake a census. However, populations are usually large and it is not practical or cost-effective to contact every single member. Instead, a sample survey is undertaken. The way in which a sample is constructed is a key element in the research process, since the sample must mirror the population from which it is taken. Then findings based on the sample will be valid for the population as a whole. The technicalities of sampling and the validity of making inferences about populations are complex, and are covered in texts on statistics and research methods (see annotated readings at the end of this chapter).

There are a variety of sampling methods in use. The most common is what might be considered a 'loose' approach, where interviewers are given target numbers of interviews to achieve and are asked to contact a representative spread of people by age and sex. This almost certainly leads to a biased sample. At attractions and passenger termini, it is possible to take the selection of respondent away from the interviewer through the use of 'tighter' procedures such as systematic sampling (say, every twentieth person to pass an exit point).

It is difficult to construct with confidence a representative sample of visitors at a tourist destination such as a resort or within large recreation areas. This is because visitors are scattered over large areas and their movement is complex. It is normal to take account of the time of year (sample more heavily in the peak months) and to conduct interviews at venues tourists are likely to frequent (attractions, accommodation establishments, shopping centres, places of interest for destinations, popular sites for recreation areas).

Data analysis

Data from questionnaire returns or other data sheets can be input into computer files for analysis. The use of an appropriate software package speeds up the process and ensures accuracy within the analysis. For quantitative data, for example, the Statistical Package for the Social Sciences (SPSS) is often used, whereas for qualitative data programs such as NVivo is used. The scope of analysis is also increased, because the relationships between variables can be examined in depth.

The first stage is often merely establishing counts or frequencies of response. These are often best expressed as percentages. Thus, 40% of visitors are in family groups, 80% arrive by car and so on. This is followed by the 'cross-tabulation' of variables, in which responses to one question are matched with responses to another. An example of output from this form of analysis is: 30% of holiday visitors to the hotel were dissatisfied with the leisure facilities, compared with only 5% of business visitors.

The use of counts and cross-tabulations is sufficient for the majority of studies. More detailed forms of analysis make use of higher-level statistics, and are common in project work undertaken by students registered for higher degrees.

Reporting research

An essential part of the research process is the final report. This is often accompanied by a formal presentation of findings. The level, method and timing of the reporting should be discussed and agreed at an early stage. Research results may well confirm what the manager already believed, and thus provide him or her with hard evidence to make his or her case to others. They can also lead to some surprises and to changes that were not anticipated. Effective reports should have a number of elements (Cooper and Latham, 1990), such as those listed under the following headings.

Presentation

- Reports should be actionable.
- Findings and recommendations should be linked to objectives set.
- There should be a clear summary of findings and recommendations – it is normal for these to appear at the beginning.
- Language should be appropriate and clearly expressed. The main body of the report should be able to be understood by a non-technical manager. Appendices of technical detail should be included if relevant.

Content

- Background information may be included.
- Research methodology should be included.
- Copies of forms (e.g. blank questionnaire) and letters used in the research should be included, normally as appendices.
- Details of analysis and tables should be clear and easy to understand.
- Diagrams may be used in addition to or instead of tables in order to enhance interpretation.
- Information should be full and complete.
- Appendices should be used for technical or other information that would otherwise detract from the reading of the report.

It is a waste of resources to commission research and then not consider the findings. Provided that the research purpose is clear from the beginning and that the objectives set were appropriate to it, the relevance to decision-making should be clear. The research report then represents an objective view, relevant to the needs of the organisation.

CONCLUSION

The activity generated by tourism demand is prolific – in terms of both volume and revenue generated – and yet its measurement remains problematic at best and wholly inadequate at worst. Since many countries continue to derive their tourism statistics as a by-product of data gained for other, non-tourism-related, research, statistics for international and domestic tourism must be interpreted and utilised with caution and sensitivity.

Despite the difficulties, however, the measurement of incoming and outgoing tourism is crucial for economic and commercial reasons. In addition, the measurement of tourism activity, and an associated understanding of tourist motivations and profiles, provides a wealth of information for the planning, management and marketing of tourism at the destination and an appreciation of consumer behaviour in tourism.

SELF-CHECK QUESTIONS

1. Consider how you might approach the researching of tourism activity at a specific destination of your choice, reviewing the types of information you need to elicit from tourists and the methodology you might employ.

2. What might be some of the key problems in comparing tourism statistics from different areas and regions of the world?

3. Consider who should finance the collection of tourism information in your country.

4. Review the main stages of research and provide a tourism example of each.

5. Do you think there is a role for key international bodies such as the UNWTO to be more involved in the collection of tourism statistics? How might this involvement be manifested and where might the emphasis lie?

ESSAY QUESTIONS

1. Why should tourism statistics be interpreted with caution?

2. Identify the major methods used to measure tourism demand and review the advantages and disadvantages of each.

3. Design a brief for a market survey for a tourist attraction to elicit both the current profile of visitors and their opinions of the attraction.

4. Why is domestic tourism demand difficult to measure?

5. What do you understand by the term knowledge management and how might it be used in tourism?

ANNOTATED FURTHER READING

Books

Brent Ritchie, J.R. and Goeldner, C.R. (1994) *Travel Tourism and Hospitality Research. A Handbook for Managers and Researchers*, 2nd edn, John Wiley, Chichester.
A thorough handbook with authoritative entries on all of the main methods of collecting tourism information as well as guidance on research design, reporting and analysis.

Jennings, G. (2001) *Tourism Research*, John Wiley, Brisbane.
A comprehensive text covering all aspects of tourism research including research design, sampling, data collection, analysis and report writing.

Lennon, J. (ed.) (2003) *Tourism Statistics: International Perspectives and Current Issues*, Continuum, London.
A thorough and excellent international overview of the many issues associated with tourism statistics.

Veal, A.J. (2005) *Research Methods for Leisure and Tourism: A Practical Guide*, Pearson Education, Harlow.
Comprehensive and non-technical guide to researching tourism.

World Tourism Organization (2000) *Data Collection and Analysis for Tourism Management, Marketing and Planning*, WTO, Madrid.
A comprehensive practical guide to collecting and analysing tourism information within a disciplined and coherent framework of statistics.

Web site

www.world-tourism.org
A comprehensive site with the definitive approaches to collecting tourism statistics, definitions and technical handbooks.

References cited

Cooper, C.P. and Latham, J. (1990) 'A layman's guide to market research for the tourist industry', *Insights*, English Tourist Board, London.

Tasci, A.D.A. and Knutson, B.J. (2003) 'Online research modes: waiting for leisure, tourism and hospitality researchers', *Journal of Hospitality and Leisure Marketing* 10(3/4), 57–83.

WTO (1984) *Collection of Domestic Tourism Statistics*, WTO, Madrid.

WTO (2000) *Data Collection and Analysis for Tourism Management, Marketing and Planning*, WTO, Madrid.

MAJOR CASE STUDY 3.1
From market information to knowledge

Researchers, consultants, the industry and government all generate tourism data and information from many surveys and reports. However, the tourism industry has been slow to use that research to improve their competitiveness. Indeed, it could be argued that the effective *transfer* of knowledge to tourism businesses has been slow to develop. Where tourism has been slow to adopt new innovations is in the area of knowledge management and many businesses are less competitive as a result (Cooper, 2006).

Knowledge management is a relatively new approach that addresses the critical issue of competitiveness in a world of constant change. At the same time tourism has been slow to recognise the transition to a *knowledge-based economy* where knowledge is viewed as more than information but also as a resource to be valued and managed. The knowledge economy can therefore be thought of as an economy directly based upon the production, distribution and use of knowledge. The knowledge-based economy has a number of important features that demand a rethinking of our approach to market intelligence; for example, it is helpful in distinguishing between different types of knowledge.

TYPES OF KNOWLEDGE

Knowledge can be thought of as the use of skills and experience to add intelligence to information in order to make decisions or provide reliable grounds for action. Knowledge management classifies knowledge according to its ability to be *codified* and therefore communicated. For tourism this distinction is fundamental and goes a long way to explaining the failure of businesses to adequately capitalise on and manage knowledge. Polanyi's (1966) classification of two knowledge types is clear and has fundamental lessons for tourism:

1. **Tacit knowledge** Tacit knowledge is difficult to codify, difficult to communicate to others as information, and it is difficult to digitise. A good example of tacit knowledge would be the knowledge that is passed from a small tour operator to their assistant through example and conversation. Most knowledge in the tourism sector is tacit (for example, in almost all tourism businesses) yet is often ignored. Estimates suggest that over 90% of any organisation's knowledge assets are tacit.

2. **Explicit knowledge** In contrast to tacit knowledge, explicit knowledge is transferable and easy to codify and communicate. It is therefore usually the focus of an organisation's interest and is found in the form of documents, databases, files, customer directories etc., and other media. Explicit knowledge can be easily transferred and communicated to those that need it in the organisation.

The conversion of tacit to explicit knowledge is critical for tourism, as there is so much tacit knowledge in the sector that could benefit other businesses – and destinations and governments. It is here that the knowledge management approach provides a significant benefit for tourism as it focuses upon the management of tacit and explicit knowledge to create organisational learning, innovation and sustainable competitive advantage.

Photograph 3.2   Co-workers share knowledge around the water cooler.
Source: Corbis / John Feingersh

THE BENEFITS OF MANAGING TOURISM KNOWLEDGE

Managing tourism knowledge delivers a range of significant benefits to tourism businesses:

- Managed access to knowledge reduces search time and shortens learning curves, facilitating new product development and innovation.

- Within the organisation, a knowledge management approach encourages and facilitates enhanced and smarter problem-solving techniques.

- Managed access to knowledge provides an organisation with the ability to respond rapidly to customers, technology and markets.

- Across the organisation, knowledge management systems contribute to more efficient business processes.

- Within the organisation, knowledge management enhances staff performance by encouraging knowledge sharing and mutual trust, and contributes to reducing staff turnover.

- A knowledge management system allows an organisation to leverage and use its intellectual assets; indeed there are exponential benefits from knowledge as more people use it within the organisation.

- Knowledge management encourages partnering and the sharing of core competencies with suppliers, vendors, customers and other external stakeholders.

KNOWLEDGE MANAGEMENT AND SINGAPORE AIRLINES

Singapore Airlines is an award winning international carrier. The airline has adopted the principles of a knowledge management framework in their business operations and particularly to deliver service excellence. Their approach is based upon an outsourced information technology facility run by IBM. This allows the company to focus upon core knowledge needs of service delivery, cost control and customers rather than upon IT.

Their knowledge management approach has the following characteristics (Ahmed *et al.*, 2002):

- Managing booking information – technology is an enabling tool for knowledge management. Singapore Airlines have developed a sophisticated yield management and demand forecasting tool that allows them to sell seats on the same flight to different market segments (such as the business or the leisure segments), closely matching supply and demand. The tool models historic booking and travel data to forecast demand.

- Sourcing information – knowledge management identifies a range of sources of information for an organisation, including employees, customers and external sources (such as monitoring competitors using the 'mystery shopper' approach, where a researcher poses as a customer and evaluates competitors' performance):

  - The company sources ideas and information from its employees by newsletters, networking meetings and a 'staff ideas action scheme' which is used to capture front-line customer contact data and feed it back into service improvement.

  - Singapore Airlines has used market research to gauge customer attitudes to service levels. This information is then factored into the operation of the company. In addition, market research is carried out with 'knowledgeable customers', such as frequent flyers, as well as the more traditional approaches of feedback forms and in-flight surveys.

  - Finally, Singapore Airlines regularly benchmarks against other service organisations – not just airlines, but also banks and other service delivery groups.

Singapore Airlines is a good example of how knowledge management takes raw data and converts it to knowledge upon which the company can make both operational and management decisions. The company uses knowledge management to combine service excellence with cost control and profitability and a 'whole of business' approach to service (Wirtz and Johnston, 2003).

REFERENCES

Ahmed, P.K., Lim, K.K. and Loh, A.Y.E. (2002) *Learning Through Knowledge Management*, Butterworth Heinemann, Oxford.

Cooper, C. (2006) 'Knowledge management and tourism', *Annals of Tourism Research* **33**(1), 47–64.

Polanyi, M. (1966) *The Tacit Dimension*, Doubleday, New York.

Wirtz, J. and Johnston, R. (2003) 'Singapore Airlines: What it takes to sustain service excellence – a senior management perspective', *Managing Service Quality* **13**(1), 10–19.

DISCUSSION QUESTIONS

1. Why do you think that it has taken tourism longer than other economic sectors to realise the value of a knowledge management approach?

2. From Singapore Airlines' point of view, what is the difference between data, information and knowledge?

3. What approaches could you take to collect the tacit knowledge from senior managers in a tourism organisation such as a large company or tourist board?

CHAPTER 4

Tourism Demand Determinants and Forecasting

LEARNING OUTCOMES

The purpose of this chapter is to introduce and discuss determinants of demand and forecasting approaches. We then draw together the chapter by reviewing the major trends in the patterns of demand for tourism from historic and regional perspectives in the major case study. This chapter is designed to provide you with:

- familiarity with the determinants of demand which, at an individual level, are likely to affect propensity to travel;

- an understanding of social, technological, economic and political influences on tourism demand;

- an awareness of the reasons for forecasting demand for tourism;

- an understanding of the major approaches to forecasting demand for tourism; and

- an appreciation and explanation of the key historic and regional patterns of demand for tourism.

Photograph: Beach at Ko Wua Taleb, Ang Thong National Park, Thailand © Kelly Miller

INTRODUCTION

This chapter focuses upon the key determinants of demand for tourism and goes on to show how an understanding of these underlying influences allows us to forecast tourism demand. It is difficult to generalise about the determinants of demand. There is, for example, a particular problem in terms of linking different levels of generalisation. At one level (in Chapter 2) we have already considered the individual's consumer behaviour with reference to tourism and analysed the various influences upon behaviour. In this chapter we consider specific determinants of demand at the individual level and go on to demonstrate how they can be aggregated to explain patterns and rhythms of tourism demand globally. In this way we can show that those countries with a high level of economic development and a stable, urbanised population are major generators of tourism demand.

An understanding of demand determinants is fundamental to forecasting future demand. For example, we can predict that effective demand for tourism will be highly concentrated among the affluent, industrialised nations. This information is important for managers and accurate forecasts in tourism are essential to inform decision-making in both governments and the industry. The final section of the chapter examines the different approaches available to forecast tourism demand and the reasons why we should maintain forecasts, particularly the fact that tourism is a perishable industry and its assets such as beds or aircraft seats cannot be stored. There is no doubt that forecasts are necessary, despite the fact that some argue that as tourism is a volatile industry operating in a world of rapid and unexpected change forecasts are increasingly irrelevant.

DETERMINANTS OF DEMAND FOR TOURISM

Determinants at the individual scale

Although an individual may be motivated to travel, the ability to do so will depend on a number of factors related to both the individual and the supply environment. These factors can be termed determinants of demand (demand determinants) and represent the 'parameters of possibility' for the individual – even within the developed world many are unable to participate in tourism for some reason. For example, a certain level of discretionary income is required to allow participation in tourism, and this income, and indeed the type of participation, will be influenced by such factors as job type, life-cycle stage, mobility, level of educational attainment and personality.

Once a decision to travel has been taken, the ability to undertake the trip, and the nature of that trip will be determined by a wide range of interrelated factors. These can be broadly divided into two groups:

1. The first group of factors can be termed lifestyle, and includes income, employment, holiday entitlement, educational attainment and mobility.
2. The second group can be termed life cycle where the age and domestic circumstances of an individual affect both the amount and type of tourism demanded.

Naturally, these factors are interrelated and complementary. In a Western society, a high-status job is normally associated with an individual in middle age with a high income, above average holiday entitlement, education and mobility.

Lifestyle determinants of demand for tourism

Income and employment

Income and employment are closely linked and exert important influences upon both the level and the nature of tourism demanded by an individual. Tourism is an expensive activity that demands a certain threshold of income before participation is possible. Gross income gives little indication of the money available to spend on tourism – rather, it is discretionary income that provides the best indicator: that is, the income left over when tax, housing and the basics of life have been accounted for. Clearly, two households with the same gross incomes may have very different discretionary incomes, although discretionary income is difficult to measure.

The relationship between income and tourism is a complex one. For example, certain tourism activities are highly sensitive to income – additional holidays and expensive pursuits such as skiing holidays are a particular case in point. The relationship is also characterised by the fact that, at the extremes of the income spectrum, tourism demand is strongly affected, whereas in the middle of the spectrum it is much more difficult to discern a clear relationship. For example, a very low discretionary income markedly depresses travel propensity. As discretionary income rises, the ability to partake of tourism is associated with the purchase of leisure-orientated goods, until, with a high discretionary income, travel may reach a peak and then level off as the demands of a high-status job, and possibly frequent business trips, reduce the ability and desire to travel for pleasure.

A fundamental distinction is between those in employment and those unemployed. The impact of unemployment on the volume of tourism demand is obvious, but the nature of demand is also changed by employment uncertainty. This encourages later booking of trips, more domestic holidays and shorter lengths of stay, and switches demand away from commercial accommodation to Visiting Friends and Relatives (VFR), therefore leading to lower spending levels.

The nature of employment not only influences travel propensity by determining income and holiday entitlement, but it also has an effect upon the type of holiday demanded, as the mechanism of peer and reference group pressure is felt.

Paid holiday entitlement

The increase in leisure time experienced by most individuals in the developed world since 1950 is well documented. However, the relationship between an individual's total time budget, leisure time and **paid holiday entitlement** is complex. A number of surveys suggest that, in a developed Western economy, individuals have anything from 35 to 50 hours' free time a week at their disposal. This free time is greater for males, the young and single adults. Of this free time some two-thirds is spent around the home. However, to enable tourism, leisure time has to be blocked into two or more days to allow a stay away from home. While this obviously is the case with paid holiday entitlement, patterns of leisure time have changed over the past 20 years to allow three-day weekends, flexitime and longer periods of absence for those in employment.

A variety of holiday arrangements now exists worldwide, with most nations having a number of one-day national holidays, as well as annual paid holiday entitlement by law or collective agreements. Individual levels of paid holiday entitlement would seem to be an obvious determinant of travel propensity, but in fact the relationship is not straightforward and, rather like the income variable, it is clearer at the extremes. For example, low levels of entitlement do act as a real constraint upon the ability to travel, while a high entitlement encourages travel. This is in part due to the interrelationship between entitlement and factors such as job status, income and mobility. As levels of entitlement increase, the cost of tourism may mean that more of this entitlement will be spent at home.

Paid holiday entitlement tends to be more generous in developed economies and less so in the developing world. The pattern of entitlement is also responsible in part for the seasonality of tourism in some destinations simply because some of the entitlement has to be taken in the summer months. To an extent, this is historical and is rooted in the holiday patterns of manufacturing industries. It does, however, have an impact upon the nature of demand for tourism. In some countries, notably France, staggering of holiday entitlement has been attempted to alleviate seasonality.

Education and mobility

Level of educational attainment is an important determinant of travel propensity as education broadens horizons and stimulates the desire to travel. Also, the better educated the individual, the higher the awareness of travel opportunities, and susceptibility to information, media, advertising and sales promotion, as we saw in the case study of generations X and Y in Chapter 2.

Personal mobility also has an important influence on travel propensity, especially with regard to domestic holidays. The car is the dominant recreational tool for both international and domestic tourism. It provides door-to-door freedom, can carry tourism equipment (such as tents or boats) and has all-round vision for viewing. Ownership of a car stimulates travel for pleasure in all but recessionary times.

Race and gender

Race and gender are two critical determinants of tourism demand, but the relationships are not clearly understood. Most surveys of participation in tourism suggest that it is whites and males who have the highest levels of effective demand for tourism. However, changes in society are acting to complicate this rather simplistic view. For example, in Japan, 'office ladies' are important consumers of travel.

Clearly, for the purposes of analysing each variable we have to separate them, but it must be remembered that they all are complementary and interrelated. Indeed, this is such that some writers have attempted to analyse tourism or leisure lifestyles by performing multivariate analysis on the determinants of tourism demand and then trying to group individuals into particular categories. To date these analyses have met with limited success. Even where they have been commercially adopted as market segments it is difficult to correlate them with other variables such as media habits.

However, leisure or tourism lifestyles are considerations when viewing the important role of fashion and style in holiday choice. Tourism demand has always been susceptible to fashion and can be influenced perhaps more readily than demand for some other goods by marketing and promotional activity.

Life-cycle determinants of demand for tourism

The propensity to travel, and indeed the type of tourism experience demanded, is closely related to an individual's age. Although the conventional measurement is chronological age, 'domestic age' better discriminates between types of tourist demand and levels of travel propensity. Domestic age refers to the stage in the family life cycle reached by an individual, and different stages are characterised by distinctive holiday demand and levels of travel propensity, as demonstrated in the first Mini Case Study for this chapter.

MINI CASE STUDY 4.1
Domestic age and tourism demand

Considering an individual's domestic age – or position on the 'family life cycle' (childhood, young adult, married, etc.) is an effective explanatory variable of travel behaviour. Here, we can see that there is a distinctive pattern of demand found at each stage in the family life cycle (FLC). This is because at each stage in the FLC individuals can be thought of as having:

- **preoccupations** – which are the mental absorptions arising from motivations;
- **interests** – which are feelings of what an individual would like to do, or represent the awareness of an idea or opportunity; and
- **activities** – which are the actions of an individual.

→

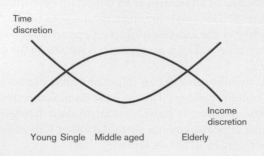

| Figure 4.1 | Traditional leisure paradox |

Each stage in the life cycle is characterised by particular combinations of these three factors. For example, in adolescence the preoccupation is with socialising and finding independence while in married adulthood the preoccupations are more with establishment and social institutions. As an individual progresses through life the combinations of the factors, and the nature of the factors themselves, change. At certain 'crisis' points the whole combination is 'unfrozen' and completely reformed. An example here would be having children. At this point in an individual's life, previous constraints and influences upon holiday-taking are totally changed as holidays become more organisational and less geographical. The FLC framework can also be linked to lifestyle variables to provide a multidimensional analysis. In married middle age, for example, holiday entitlement, income and mobility are often at a maximum and this is reflected in the level of holiday-taking (see Figure 4.1). Equally, companies such as Disney and McDonald's utilise the concept to win children as customers at an early age in order to retain them into later life. With the decline in birth rates in the developed world it is important to create hotel, activity and restaurant products that will socialise children to want to take certain types of activity holidays so as to encourage demand at a later stage in their life.

The FLC has a number of stages, as shown in Figure 4.1.

CHILDHOOD

At this stage decisions are taken for the individual in terms of holiday-taking. However, children do have a significant influence upon both their parents' decisions and their satisfaction levels at the destination and as a result children are becoming of interest to tourism researchers (see for example Pearce, 2005). By the age of 10 or 11 years some children take organised holidays with school or youth groups and day trips are common. These are usually domestic with self-catering arrangements.

ADOLESCENCE/YOUNG ADULT

At this stage, sometimes known as the bachelor stage, young single people not living at home have a preoccupation for independence, socialising and a search for identity. Typically, holidays independent of parents begin at around 15 years, constrained by lack of finance but compensated by having few other commitments, no shortage of free time, and a curiosity for new places and experiences. This group has a high propensity to travel, mainly on budget holidays using surface transport and self-catering accommodation. Here the preoccupation is simply to 'get away' – the destination is unimportant, and is often associated with rites of passage such as the American 'Spring Break'. In the twenty-first century, however, we are seeing this group living at home longer.

MARRIAGE

Marriage represents the first 'crisis' in terms of unscrambling the preoccupations, interests and activities of an individual. Preoccupations turn to establishment and lifetime investments. This FLC stage can have a

| Photograph 4.1 | At certain stages of the domestic life cycle the needs and demands of children determine the family's holiday decisions. |

number of options. For example, nowly married couples who are young and with no children may have few constraints on travel. Before the arrival of children young couples often have a high income and few other ties, giving them a high travel propensity, frequently overseas. The arrival of children represents the second 'crisis' which, coupled with the responsibility of a home, may mean that constraints of time and finance depress travel propensity. Holiday preferences switch to domestic destinations, self-catering accommodation, and visiting friends and relatives. This is known as the full nest stage and constraints on travel will depend on the age of the children.

EMPTY NEST STAGE

As children grow up, reach the adolescence stage and begin to travel independently, constraints of time and finance are lifted from parents and their travel propensity increases. This is often a time for long-haul travel – the cruise market typically comprises this group.

OLD AGE

The emergence of early retirement at 50 or 55 years is creating an active and mobile group in the population of many countries who will demand both domestic and international travel. However, it is too simplistic to view senior travellers as homogeneous and there are many different categories – partly defined by the tension between physical health and financial resources. In later retirement, lack of finance, infirmity and often the loss of a partner act to offset the increase in free time experienced by this group. Holidays become more hotel-based and travel propensity decreases.

→

The explanatory framework provided by the FLC approach is a powerful one. It has implications for the supply of facilities, for the analysis of market needs of particular population groups (for example, the growing numbers of elderly people in some Western countries) and has clearly been used as a basis for market segmentation by tour operators and wholesalers. However, the FLC as outlined in this chapter is only appropriate for developed Western economies and even here it is a generalisation as it does not consider, for example, one-parent families, divorcees or other ethnic groups living within Western economies.

Nonetheless, the FLC concept helps us to understand how situation-specific life-stage conditions exert a great influence on consumer behaviour. For example, the majority of recreational tourism in the USA is made up from the family market. The cycle is not just a progression by phase or age but represents likely fluctuations in discretionary income and changes in social responsibilities. For example, the bachelor stage represents an individual living away from home with few responsibilities but with the need for affiliation with others and the likelihood of purchases of leisure and entertainment, personal care items and clothes. It is also useful in explaining many barriers to travel – energy and social ties tend to decline with age, while women with young children demonstrate lower levels of travel.

REFERENCES

Pearce, P.L. (2005) *Tourist Behaviour*, Channel View, Clevedon.

DISCUSSION QUESTIONS

1. Draft a checklist of typical holidays at each of the main stages of the FLC.
2. How do tour operators use the FLC to segment their products?
3. Draft a checklist of the barriers to tourism that might be experienced at each stage of the FLC.

SUPPRESSED DEMAND FOR TOURISM

So far in this chapter the concern has been to identify factors that influence effective tourist demand. Yet tourism is still an unobtainable luxury for the majority of the world's population, not just in undeveloped and developing countries, but also for many in the developed world. There are a variety of reasons why people do not travel:

- Travel is expensive and demands a certain threshold of income before people can enter the market. It competes with other products for available funds.
- Lack of time is a problem for some individuals who cannot allocate sufficient blocks of time to stay away from home. This may be for business or family reasons.
- Physical limitations (such as ill health) are a significant reason for many people not travelling. In particular, heart disease and mental/physical handicap act as a major constraint on travel.
- Family circumstances, such as single parenthood or having to care for elderly relatives, may prevent travel.
- Government restrictions such as currency controls and visas may act as a real barrier to travel (both inbound and outbound) for some countries.
- Lack of interest/fear are real barriers for some individuals.

It is not uncommon for people to experience a combination of two or more of these barriers. For example, a one-parent family may find lack of income and time will combine with family circumstances to prevent tourism travel. Obviously, it is just these groups who would most benefit from a holiday and tourism planners are increasingly concerned to identify these barriers and devise programmes to encourage non-participants to travel. Perhaps the best-known example of this is the 'social tourism movement' which is concerned with facilitating the participation in travel by people with some form of handicap or disadvantage, and the measures used to encourage this participation.

MACRO DETERMINANTS OF TOURISM DEMAND

In the previous sections we identified a range of key determinants on tourism demand that operate at the individual level. In order to begin to understand patterns of tourism demand at a broader scale, it is necessary to find aggregate measures of these determinants. For example, taking the concept of travel propensity that we introduced in Chapter 1, we might expect travel propensity for a particular population to increase with such aggregate characteristics as:

- income;
- level of urbanisation;
- education levels; and
- mobility levels (such as car ownership).

However, it will decrease with characteristics such as:

- large household size; and
- increasing age.

At the aggregate level the relationship between travel propensity and the characteristics of a population is not straightforward. In particular, we must remember that the variables identified above are all related. A high travel propensity would be expected for a developed Western economy with a high degree of urbanisation, high incomes, small household sizes and high levels of mobility. Conversely, low travel propensities would be expected for rural societies with large family sizes and low incomes.

There are also a number of factors that will determine the propensity of a population to travel to particular destinations. We have already examined in detail the importance of destination 'image' in Chapter 2, and here the difficult issue of measuring promotional spend by a destination in creating the image needs to be considered. In addition, other relevant factors include economic distance, cultural distance and the relative cost of living at the destination. Economic distance, for example, relates to the time and cost of reaching a destination and is a key element of the gravity model discussed in Chapter 1. Although the idea of 'friction of distance' can be used here, in practice distance alone is not the only consideration. For example, it is ironic that international destinations are often closer in economic distance terms than many domestic destinations. (It is easier, and often cheaper, for a traveller to reach the Spanish Costas from London, than it is to reach the Scottish island of Skye.) Cultural distance refers to the difference in culture between the origin area and the destination. For more adventurous travellers this acts to attract rather than to deter a visit. Costs at a destination are not an absolute quantity but have to be considered relative to the value of the traveller's own currency. This is graphically demonstrated by the ebb and flow of traffic across the Atlantic dependent upon whether the dollar or the euro is the stronger. Perception of price is also an important consideration – Switzerland is perceived by many as an expensive destination but in fact prices have fallen in recent years vis-à-vis many European currencies. However, measurement of such variables can be problematic. Clearly, there are many influences upon demand that can be labelled as determinants, as shown in Table 4.1.

Table 4.1	The major determinants of tourism demand	
Economic determinants	**Social-psychological determinants**	**Exogenous determinants (business environment)**
Disposable income	Demographic factors	Availability of supply resources
GNP per capita income	Motivations	Economic growth and stability
Private consumption	Travel preferences	Political and social environment
Cost of living (CPI)	Benefits sought	Recession
Tourism prices	Images of destinations	Technological advancements
Transportation costs	Perceptions of destinations	Accessibility
Cost of living in relation to destinations	Awareness of opportunities	Levels of development, infrastructure and superstructure
Exchange rate differentials	Cognitive distance	Natural disaster
Relative pricing among competing destinations	Attitudes about destinations	Epidemics
	Amount of leisure time	War, terrorism
Promotional expenditures	Amount of travel time	Social and cultural attractions
Marketing effectiveness	Paid vacations	Degree of urbanisation
Physical distance	Past experience	Special factors/Olympic Games, mega events
	Life span	Barriers and obstacles
	Physical capacity, health and wellness	Restrictions, rules and laws
	Cultural similarities	
	Affiliations	

Source: Uysal, 1998

STEP ANALYSIS

When individual purchasing patterns and the influences upon them are aggregated to the national level it is possible to gain a clearer view as to the influences upon global patterns of demand for tourism. This is known as performing a **STEP analysis** – analysing the impact of:

S   social factors;

T   technological factors;

E   economic factors; and

P   political factors.

Social factors

Levels of population growth, its development, distribution and density affect travel propensity. Population growth and development can be closely linked to the stages of economic growth of a society by considering the demographic transition where population growth and development are seen in terms of four connected phases.

1. **The high stationary phase.** This corresponds to many undeveloped countries with high birth and death rates, keeping the population at a fluctuating, but low level. An example here would be Ethiopia, where social and health conditions conspire to retain the country in this phase and render many forms of tourism impossible.

2. **The early expanding phase.** Here high birth rates continue, but there is a fall in death rates due to improved health, sanitation and social stability. This leads to a population expansion characterised by young, large families. India is a good example of a country in this phase; it is unable to provide for its growing population and is gradually becoming poorer. Clearly, tourism is a luxury that cannot be afforded for many, although in India there is a growing gap between a wealthy middle class and the poor. As a result, India has developed an inbound tourism industry to earn foreign exchange and the growing middle class are travelling internationally.

3. **The late expanding phase.** Argentina demonstrates the classic features of this phase, having experienced a fall in the birth rate rooted in the growth of an industrial society and birth control technology. Most developing countries fit into the early expanding and late expanding phases with a transition to the late expanding phase paralleling the economic stage known as the 'drive to maturity' (see Table 4.2).

4. **The low stationary phase.** This phase corresponds to the high mass consumption stage of economic development exemplified by the UK or Sweden (see Table 4.2). Here, birth and death rates have stabilised at a low level and some countries are not replacing their population, but for many European countries there are fluctuations as seen by the 'baby boom' of the late 1940s and early 1950s.

Population density has a less important influence on travel propensity than has the distribution of population between urban and rural areas. Densely populated rural nations may have low travel propensities owing to the level of economic development and the simple fact that the population is mainly dependent upon subsistence agriculture and has neither the time nor the income to devote to tourism. In contrast, densely populated urban areas normally indicate a developed economy with consumer purchasing power, giving rise to high travel propensity and the urge to escape from the urban environment.

The distribution of population within a nation also affects patterns, rather than strict levels, of tourist demand. Where population is concentrated into one part of the country, tourism demand is distorted. This asymmetrical distribution of population is well illustrated by the USA where two-thirds of the population live in the eastern third of the country. The consequent east to west pattern of tourist flows (and permanent migrants) has placed pressure on the recreation and tourist resources of the Western states.

Social changes since the Second World War in the developed world have changed travel demand patterns. Most of these countries are experiencing a slowing of the birth rate, with some having projections of population decline. This, combined with extensions in life expectancy, has created an ageing population. In the past, the older generation in the 'third age' or 'grey panther' group is often made up of those who did not pay into pension schemes and consequently whose pension and benefits barely keep up with inflation. These groups and the unemployed are likely to adapt their lifestyle to basic activities and seek cheap travel activities. However, the post-war 'baby boomers' are now reaching retirement age and are demonstrating a significant demand for more 'upmarket' products.

Technological factors

There is no doubt that technology has been a major enabling factor in terms of converting suppressed demand into effective demand. This is particularly the case in terms of transport technology where the development of the jet engine in the late 1950s gave aircraft both speed and range and stimulated the variety of tourism products available in the international market to meet pent-up demand for international travel. Developments in aircraft technology have continued but so has the level of refinement and access to the motor car. Similarly, the development of information technology, and, in particular, the Internet and mobile technology, is a critical enabling factor in terms of tourism demand. Generally, technology acts to increase access to tourism by lowering the cost or by making the product more accessible. Examples here include access to travel information and booking on the Internet, and developments in 'recreational technology' such as windsurfing, durable outdoor clothing, heli-skiing and heli-hiking, and off-road recreational vehicles.

Economic factors

A society's level of economic development is a major determinant of the magnitude of tourist demand because the economy influences so many critical, and interrelated, factors. One approach is to consider a simple division of world economies into the affluent 'north', where the countries are major generators and recipients of both international and domestic tourism, and the poorer 'south'. In the latter, some countries are becoming generators of international tourism but mostly tourism is domestic, often supplemented by an inbound international flow of tourists. In fact, the economic development of nations can be divided into a number of stages, as outlined in Table 4.2.

As a society moves towards the high mass consumption stage in Table 4.2, a number of important processes occur. The balance of employment changes from work in the primary sector (agriculture, fishing, forestry) to work in the secondary sector (manufacturing goods) and the tertiary sector (services such as tourism). As this process unfolds, an affluent society usually emerges and the percentage of the population who are economically active increases from less than a third in the developing world to half or more in the high mass consumption stage. With progression to the drive to maturity, discretionary incomes increase and create demand for consumer goods and leisure pursuits such as tourism.

Table 4.2	Economic development and tourism	
Economic stage	**Some characteristics**	**Examples**
Traditional society Long-established land-owning aristocracy, traditional customs, majority employed in agriculture. Very low output per capita, impossible to improve without changing system. Poor health levels, high poverty levels.	**The undeveloped world** Economic and social conditions deny most forms of tourism except perhaps domestic VFR.	Parts of Africa, parts of Southern Asia.
Preconditions for take-off Innovation of ideas from outside the system. Leaders recognise the desirability of change.	**The developing world** From the take-off stage, economic and social conditions allow increasing amounts of domestic tourism (mainly VFR). International tourism is also possible in the drive to maturity. Inbound tourism is often encouraged as a foreign exchange earner.	Parts of South and Central America;[a] parts of the Middle East,[a] Asia and Africa.
Take-off Leaders in favour of change gain power and alter production methods and economic structure. Manufacturing and services expand.		
Drive to maturity[b] Industrialisation continues in all economic sectors with a switch from heavy manufacturing to sophisticated and diversified products.		Mexico; parts of South America.
High mass consumption Economy now at full potential, producing large numbers of consumer goods and services. New emphasis on satisfying cultural needs.	**The developed world** Major generators of international and domestic tourism.	North America; Western Europe; Japan; Australia; New Zealand.

[a] Countries that are members of the Organization of Petroleum Exporting Countries (OPEC) are a notable exception in these regions.
[b] Centrally planned economies merit a special classification, although most are at the drive to maturity stage.
Source: Boniface and Cooper 1987, adapted from Rostow, 1959

Other developments are closely linked to the changing nature of employment. The population is healthier and has time for recreation and tourism (and has paid holiday entitlement). Improving educational standards and media channels boost awareness of tourism opportunities, and transportation and mobility rise in line with these changes. Institutions respond to this increased demand by developing a range of leisure products and services. These developments occur in conjunction with each other until, at the high mass consumption stage, all the economic indicators encourage high levels of travel propensity. Clearly, tourism is a result of industrialisation and, quite simply, the more highly developed an economy, the greater the levels of tourist demand.

As more countries reach the drive to maturity or high mass consumption stage, so the volume of trade and foreign investment increases and business travel develops. Business travel is sensitive to economic activity, and although it could be argued that increasingly sophisticated communication systems may render business travel unnecessary, there is no evidence of this to date. Indeed, the very development of global markets and the constant need for face-to-face contact should ensure a continuing demand for business travel.

Political factors

Politics affects travel propensities in a variety of ways. For example, the degree of government involvement in promoting and providing facilities for tourism depends upon the political complexion of the government. Governments that support the free market try to create an environment in which the tourism industries can flourish, rather than the administration being directly involved in tourism itself. Socialist administrations, on the other hand, encourage the involvement of the government in tourism and, through 'social tourism', often provide opportunities for the 'disadvantaged' to participate in tourism. Governments in times of economic problems may control levels of propensity for travel overseas by limiting the amount of foreign currency that can be taken out of a country or demanding a monetary bond to be left in the country while the resident is overseas. Government restrictions on travel also include visa and passport controls as well as taxes on travel. Generally, however, these controls are not totally effective and, of course, they can be evaded.

We can also identify inadvertent political influences – for example, a government with an economy suffering high inflation may find that inbound travel is discouraged. In a more general sense, unstable political regimes (where civil disorder or war is prevalent) may forbid non-essential travel, and inbound tourism will be adversely affected.

FORECASTING TOURISM DEMAND

In an industry as volatile as tourism and in times as uncertain as today, it is important for both governments and the tourism industry to have reliable and accurate forecasts to allow them to plan and make decisions for the future. The accuracy of a forecast is an essential consideration in any tourism management or investment decision – too high a forecast and beds will lie empty, theme park rides will be unused and staff will be laid off; too low a forecast and opportunities will be missed, too few beds will be provided and theme parks will be congested. Essentially, these problems arise from the nature of tourism as a 'perishable' service industry – beds, rides and restaurants cannot be stored and this underlines the need for accurate forecasts of tourism demand. Frechtling (2001) identifies three further reasons why tourism demand forecasting is important:

1. the inseparability of the production and consumption of tourism means that enterprises have to be aware in advance of the level of demand for their product;
2. the tourism product comprises a range of complementary providers – forecasts ensure that these are available when they are needed; and

3. the tourism product needs large investment in fixed costs meaning that accurate forecasts of demand are essential.

Of course, failure to forecast tourism demand accurately can have devastating consequences for both business and destinations as supply and demand will be unbalanced. Indeed, forecasting is difficult in tourism due not only to the lack of good statistical information from the past, but also to the complex and volatile nature of tourism demand.

Forecasting methods

There is a wide variety of methods available for forecasting tourism demand. Archer (1994) lists the factors that determine the choice of method to use:

- purpose of the forecast – this relates to the level of detail required and the scope of the forecast;
- the time period required;
- level of accuracy required;
- availability of information – there is no point in recommending a complex quantitative approach if the information is not available to support it; and
- the cost of the forecast and the available budget.

Managers can choose from two basic methods for forecasting tourism demand:

1. quantitative approaches; and
2. qualitative approaches.

However, in practice, the most successful forecasts are those that use a combination of these two methods, utilising the strengths or relative strengths of each. The Australian government is acutely aware of the need for accurate forecasts and has established the Tourism Forecasting Committee for this purpose, as outlined in the second Mini Case Study in this chapter.

MINI CASE STUDY 4.2
The Australian Tourism Forecasting Committee

BACKGROUND

Australia's Tourism Forecasting Committee was established to provide the Australian tourism sector with accurate forecasts of tourism. These forecasts are for domestic, inbound and outbound tourism and are provided in particular for tourism investors, Australian government tourism agencies, Tourism Australia – the country's national tourist agency, and the tourism industry itself. The committee delivers 'consensus forecast': in other words, the various members of the committee have agreed them. The committee is independent but funded by Tourism Research Australia, which is a business unit of Tourism Australia.

The Tourism Forecasting Committee was previously known as the Tourism Forecasting Council (established in 1993). It draws upon a wide range of expertise to formulate its forecasts. The committee is wide-ranging in its make-up to ensure representation across relevant tourism stakeholders in both the public and private sectors. It comprises the following members:

- Tourism Australia – the national tourist board;
- Australian Standing Committee on Tourism – government representatives;
- Department of Industry, Tourism and Resources – the Australian government department with responsibility for tourism.
- Australian Tourism Export Council – investors;
- Australia Bankers Association;

- Tourism and Transport Forum Australia – industry representatives;
- Property Council of Australia – investors;
- Qantas; and
- Queensland Tourism Industry Council – industry representatives.

KEY OBJECTIVES

The three key objectives of the Tourism Forecasting Committee are to:

1. improve private and public sector investment and marketing decision-making;
2. provide an understanding of changing industry dynamics, including in times of increasing uncertainty; and
3. assist in the formulation of public policy at national and regional levels within the Australian tourism sector.

In order to achieve these objectives, the Committee is assisted by a technical committee and a forecasting and analysis section within Tourism Research Australia. Working with these three groups the Committee is charged with:

- developing and enhancing forecasting techniques on both the demand and the supply side;
- recommending dissemination strategies and products to improve the tourism sector's use of forecasts; and
- engaging with other tourism research providers to assist in achieving the committee's objectives.

THE FORECASTS

The Committee's forecasts are based upon two key sources. First, assumptions of future economic activity which utilise data relating to currencies, micro- and macro-economic data and demographics. Secondly, the forecasts build upon Australia's key tourism surveys – the International Visitor Survey and the National Visitor Survey.

The forecasting approach is to undertake three iterative rounds of consultation as follows:

1. An initial forecast is produced by Tourism Research Australia based on econometric modelling.
2. The technical committee then reviews this forecast and adjustments are made using qualitative judgements.
3. Finally the forecast is reviewed by the Tourism Forecasting Committee itself and a consensus view is reached.

The Committee takes the view that this approach delivers forecasts that are the most likely outcome, given historic data, current trends, and the impact of policy and industry events.

A key objective of the Committee is to ensure that its forecasts are both disseminated to and used by the Australian tourism sector. This is done by ensuring that monthly and annual forecasts are available online and as hard copy, while the committee also publishes a monthly bulletin *Forecast* which summarises the most recent forecasts.

DISCUSSION

The Tourism Forecasting Committee delivers forecasts which use a mixed method approach as noted above. They are confident that their forecasts represent the best available estimates of future activity at the time. Of course, there is a danger that the forecasts are treated as targets, and they are subject to all the caveats of data limitations and assumptions. These limitations and assumptions are in terms of both events and the stability of past relationships between the economy and tourism. Finally, the forecasts are not able to take into account 'wild card' events such as the Bali bombing.

WEB SITE

http://www.tra.australia.com/forecasts.asp?sub=0084

→

DISCUSSION QUESTIONS

1. Access one of the Committee's forecasts online. How industry-friendly is this forecast and the language used?

2. The composition of the Committee and its advisers is wide ranging. In your country, which agencies would you like to see on a committee of this kind?

3. Make a list of the ways that these types of forecasts can be used by a tourism business.

Quantitative forecasting approaches

There are numerous quantitative approaches to forecasting demand, ranging from the simplistic to the highly technical.

Causative models

At the complex end of the spectrum are causative models. These models attempt to predict changes in the variables that cause tourism demand and to analyse the relationship between those variables and the demand for tourism. The most well known of these approaches is econometric modelling, commonly using multiple regression. A mathematical relationship is sought that establishes demand as a function of influencing variables (such as the volume of populations, income of populations in the generating markets, price of the tourism product, promotional spending and time). The advantage of this approach is that it allows us to understand the underlying causes of tourism demand and to forecast how these will change in the future. It also allows us to ask 'what if' questions to see how demand will change under a certain set of circumstances.

However, for most managers who work within tourism such an approach is neither possible nor beneficial. It is far more important to be able to undertake relatively simple analyses in order to interpret demand data, and to highlight trends. These approaches are known as non-causal models and usually depend upon the extrapolation of past trends into the future.

Non-causative models

These models are often known as time series models. Essentially they rely on extrapolating future trends from the past and use techniques such as moving average, exponential smoothing and trend curve analysis. While these models can be criticised as inappropriate for a volatile industry such as tourism, where past situations may not carry forward into the future, they do deliver surprisingly accurate forecasts. The worked example below shows how this approach can be used effectively by managers in tourism to provide estimates of future tourism demand.

Worked example

Table 4.3 shows the (artificial) quarterly demand for trips on the Smithson ferry over a five-year period. It is required to construct a model for this demand, and to produce forecasts for the following year. Even a cursory glance at the data shows us that demand is highly seasonal. Quarter 3 is the peak season of the year. By considering any of the four quarters over the five-year period, there is clear evidence of upward movement, so at this stage it is expected that the analysis will identify an increasing trend. It can be noted even at this stage that demand in year 5 quarter 1 is not in line with the previous values for the same quarter, and hence is unusual.

The aim is to construct a multiplicative model for the demand *D*; that is

$$D = T*S*R$$

Table 4.3	Demand (thousands of passengers)			
	Quarter			
Year	Q1	Q2	Q3	Q4
1	63	103	331	74
2	75	118	355	75
3	83	118	410	83
4	92	130	444	99
5	79	135	477	103

where T is the trend value for that quarter, S is the seasonal index for that quarter, and R is the random or unpredictable element.

The first stage is to compute a four-quarter moving average. For each four consecutive values in the series, their average is calculated and is set against the middle of that time period. For example, take the four consecutive values starting with year 4 quarter 2; these values are 130, 444, 99, 79. Their average is 188 and this is set against the middle of the time period. Note that since the four values taken cover all quarters of the year, their average is 'de-seasonalised' (Table 4.3).

The four-quarter moving averages are now centred as shown in Table 4.4, so as to correspond with the given quarterly time periods. For example, the first two four-quarter moving averages 142.75 and 145.75 are averaged to give 144 (to the nearest whole number). In this way each consecutive pair is converted to a centred moving average.

Table 4.4	Demand (thousands of passengers)			
	Quarter			
Year	Q1	Q2	Q3	Q4
1 Original series	63	103	331	74
4-quarter m.a.		142.75	145.75	149.5
Centred m.a.			144	148
2 Original series	75	118	355	75
4-quarter m.a.	155.5	155.75	157.75	157.75
Centred m.a.	153	156	157	158
3 Original series	83	118	410	83
4-quarter m.a.	171.5	173.5	175.75	178.75
Centred m.a.	165	173	175	177
4 Original series	92	130	444	99
4-quarter m.a.	187.25	191.25	188	189.25
Centred m.a.	183	189	190	189
5 Original series	79	135	477	103
4-quarter m.a.	197.5	198.5		
Centred m.a.	194	198		

m.a. = moving average.

Table 4.5	Seasonal index of demand			
			Quarter	
Year	Q1	Q2	Q3	Q4
1			230	50
2	49	76	226	47
3	50	68	234	47
4	50	69	234	52
5	41	68		
Average (seasonal index)	48	70	231	49

A table showing seasonal indexes can now be produced. The centred moving averages, having been constructed using all seasons of the year, are divided (one by one) by the demand figures of Table 4.3 to produce a seasonality factor for each period of time. The answers are normally multiplied by 100 to give a percentage. So, for example, using Tables 4.3 and 4.4, the seasonality factor for year 1 quarter 3 is equal to:

$$\frac{331}{144} \times 100 = 230\%$$

The average of the seasonal factors for each quarter is calculated and shown at the foot of Table 4.5. These four values are the seasonal indexes of demand.

Using standard simple regression analysis based on the centred moving averages of Table 4.4, trend values can be calculated for any time period. The regression line has the equation:

$$\text{trend} = 133.3 + 3.67 \text{*} t$$

where $t = 1, 2, 3, \ldots$ is time starting with the value 1 at year 1 quarter 1, the value 2 at year 1 quarter 2, and so on. Incidentally, regression output gives a correlation coefficient of 0.99 indicating an excellent straight line fit to the centred moving averages. Substituting $t = 1, 2, \ldots, 20$ into the equation for the regression line, and taking trend values to the nearest whole number, leads to Table 4.6.

Since the original demand data are to be modelled by the product $T \text{*} S \text{*} R$, dividing the values by the corresponding trend value and then by the appropriate seasonal index from the base of Table 4.5 produces for each period of time the random element R. For example, for year 1, quarter 1, it is calculated as:

$$\frac{63/48\%}{137} = 95.8$$

Table 4.6	Trend (thousands of passengers)			
			Quarter	
Year	Q1	Q2	Q3	Q4
1	137	140	144	148
2	152	155	159	163
3	166	170	174	177
4	181	185	188	192
5	196	199	203	207

Table 4.7	Residual index of demand (%)			
	Quarter			
Year	Q1	Q2	Q3	Q4
1	96	105	100	102
2	103	109	97	94
3	104	99	102	96
4	106	100	102	105
5	84	97	102	102

Table 4.8	Forecasts of demand for year 6
Quarter 1	101 000
Quarter 2	150 000
Quarter 3	504 000
Quarter 4	108 000

Table 4.7 represents a complete table of values of R, given to the nearest whole number. These values represent the extent to which demand is made up of the trend identified, combined with the seasonal index. Where the value of R is close to 100%, the random or unpredictable element is negligible in its effect. Only in the case of year 5 quarter 1 is there a sizeable effect on demand due to R. Demand in this quarter could not have been predicted (by this model) because of some random event (which would in practice probably be known).

In order to use the model of demand established to forecast future demand, it is simply a matter of forming for any particular future time period the product of the trend value for that period (found using the regression line equation), and the appropriate seasonal index from the base of Table 4.5. This method is only suitable for short-term forecasting.

Taking into account that passenger numbers throughout have been in thousands, the forecasts of demand for year 6 are as shown in Table 4.8.

Analysing patterns of demand over time

An analysis of tourism demand in the long term requires an examination of trends. A recommended first step in the search for a trend within demand data is to sketch a graph showing demand over time. It may be possible to describe the movement simply. The four diagrams in Figure 4.2 provide simple illustrations of patterns of demand over a period of time. The continuous lines drawn are suggested models which 'fit' the given demand values and which may then be used to describe the demand and, if required, to project future demand by extrapolation.

The process of formally fitting a line or curve to data to produce a model of demand is called trend curve analysis. In many cases, this can be done 'by eye', without employing statistical methods. Should the importance of the analysis require a more formal and rigorous approach, then standard regression analysis can be employed to find a curve of best fit. Sophisticated calculators and software packages, such as spreadsheets or statistics, will perform these calculations. In this way, and using transformations of variables, a wide range of demand patterns can be analysed.

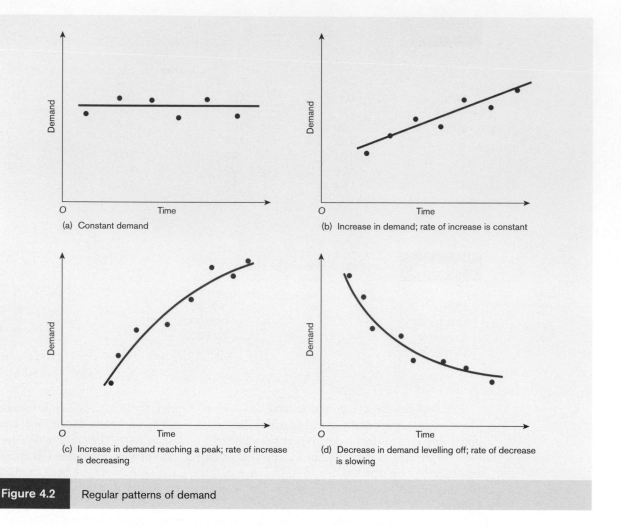

| **Figure 4.2** | Regular patterns of demand |

Seasonality

We know that within most patterns of demand in tourism, there are regular fluctuations due solely to the time of year. This phenomenon is called **seasonality**. It is often the result of changes in climate over the calendar year. Thus a destination that is essentially attractive because of its beaches and hot summers is likely to have a highly seasonal demand. The same applies to demand for holidays at a ski resort that has snow for only part of the year. There are, though, other influencing factors, such as the timing of school and work holidays, or regular special events held at a destination.

As tourism is a service industry, it is not possible to stockpile the product – a hotel room that is unsold on a particular night, an unsold seat on a flight or an unsold theatre ticket all have an economic value of zero. Seasonality of demand therefore causes major problems for the tourist industry. It can result in only seasonal employment for employees, and the underuse or even closing down of facilities at certain times of the year. It can also result in an overstretching by some destinations and businesses at times of peak activity, to compensate for low demand off-season. This leads to overcrowding, overbookings, high prices and ultimately to customer dissatisfaction and a worsening reputation.

Responses to seasonality in order to reduce it vary. Typically they involve attempts to create or shift demand to the shoulder or trough months, either through setting price differentials or through the introduction or enhancement of all-year facilities. Marketing may be targeted at groups that have the time and resources to travel at any time of the year, notably the elderly.

In an analysis of monthly demand data, note is often taken of the number of days in the month. Even with identical daily demand in January and February, one would expect their monthly demand figures to differ by about 10%. There can be substantially different levels in demand for the tourism product on different days of the same week, depending on the precise business or activity involved. Hotels often experience differences in room bookings at weekends compared with weekdays. This is particularly the case where a hotel is able to fill with businesspeople during the week at high rates, and achieves at best only reasonable occupancy at weekends through special offers. In some parts of the world, Sundays are often 'dead' nights for large, city-centre hotels. Attractions or recreation sites often attract more visitors at weekends than on weekdays.

Certain destinations receive tourists on certain days of a month as determined by passenger transport schedules. This can affect tourism businesses and needs to be taken into account when comparing sales in the same month of successive years – there may, for example, be four Saturdays in August one year, and five the next.

Our normal calendar can also affect the way demand data are analysed. This is particularly the case for Easter, which occurs in different weeks of successive years and can be in March or April. Thus comparing monthly figures year on year for these two months can be misleading, particularly if Easter is a period of high demand. Other national holidays may cause problems for the business analyst, since demand is affected considerably. The comparison of a week's business with that of the corresponding week of the previous year would take account of the dates of bank holidays, etc.

Like any business activity, tourism is subject to and part of general economic cycles. Also regular events such as festivals, games or exhibitions cause cycles in tourism movement. As shown in the above section, tourism demand can be developed into formal and often complex models. However, it has to be recognised that even the most complete of analyses of a pattern of tourism demand provides a model that will vary from the true demand by some degree. All series contain elements of the irregular, random or unpredictable. These can take the form of sudden price changes, epidemics, floods, unseasonal weather or even wars.

Qualitative forecasting approaches

Qualitative approaches to forecasting demand are mainly used to predict long-term trends, or to examine specific scenarios in the future such as environmental or technological influences, or the likely impact of a new product. While there are a number of techniques available, the most common ones are the Delphi technique and scenario writing.

The Delphi technique

The Delphi technique relies upon a panel of experts to deliver a consensus view of the future. The panel is selected according to their expertise and a questionnaire is compiled relating to the particular future trend or forecast required. Once the panel members have completed the questionnaire, results are combined and circulated to the panel to give them a chance to change their views, once they see the forecasts of other panel members. This process then goes through a number of iterations, often three or four, before a consensus forecast is reached (Figure 4.3).

There are significant advantages to this approach, as it does not rely on one individual view and can be tailored to particular needs. However, the Delphi technique can be expensive to implement and may be subject to the influence of a strong panel member; and its effectiveness depends on both the choice of questions and the selection of panel members (see Taylor and Judd (1989) for a good account of the use of the Delphi technique in tourism).

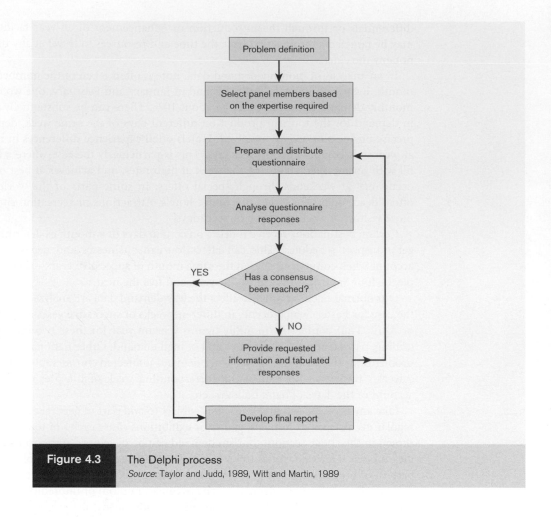

Figure 4.3	The Delphi process
	Source: Taylor and Judd, 1989, Witt and Martin, 1989

Scenario writing

Scenario writing is not only a technique to forecast future tourism demand, but also an approach that clarifies the issues involved. It relies upon creating alternative hypothetical futures relating to particular 'states' or sets of circumstances that will impact upon demand in the future (Witt and Martin, 1989). It involves assessing the variables that we examined in the section on STEP analysis and then creating long-term scenarios of how they may change, based upon the current situation as a baseline. The steps in scenario writing are as follows:

1. Baseline analysis – this describes a current situation – for example, the market for a theme park.

2. A future scenario – a description of a potential situation in the future. Usually at least one such scenario is designed – for example, a terrorist attack on a theme park.

3. A future path for the future scenario – where more than one future scenario is designed, a path for each is written – for example, the implementation of the various stages of a crisis management plan for the theme park.

Such an approach is ideal for examining the impact of climate change on tourism demand and it also focuses attention on the decisions that need to made as the scenario unfolds. We deal with this in more detail in Chapter 21.

Issues in forecasting tourism demand

In a world of rapid and unexpected change, it could be argued that forecasts are irrelevant. However, the changing nature of the environment within which tourism occurs makes it all the more important to forecast the future in order to manage it. Nonetheless, there are some problems related to forecasts (Archer, 1994). These include:

- levels of accuracy – the importance of this issue depends on what is being forecast, the time horizon used and the purpose of the forecast;

- availability of good quality data;

- the influence of variables and events external to tourism – the 2005 London bombings are a good example here;

- the need to monitor forecasts after they have been done; and identification and quantification of the variables – it is often difficult to quantify variables we use in forecasting – for example, how do you accurately measure promotional spend?

CONCLUSION

This chapter has outlined a comprehensive range of determinants upon tourism demand at both the individual and aggregate level. Of course, it is important to recognise that, while we separate out these determinants for descriptive purposes, in fact they are all related – a person with a high income, access to cars, a good education and generous holiday entitlement is likely to travel more frequently than someone who has a low income, limited education and no access to a car. These determinants can be aggregated for different populations to allow us to predict and describe patterns of demand around the world. The case study at the end of this chapter shows that globally, demand remains – and is anticipated to remain – concentrated in the affluent, industrialised nations of the world where the determinants of demand at an individual level, such as income and paid holiday entitlement, predominate. This is what we would expect from the analysis of demand determinants. However, emergent nations in the East Asia and Pacific region, where economic power is becoming increasingly focused, are becoming major generators and receivers of tourism.

As a service industry, the assets of tourism are perishable as they cannot be stored. Add to this a volatile sector and a changing world and it is important that tourism managers have the techniques to forecast the future and thus control it. Here, both qualitative and quantitative approaches are critical in predicting flows and patterns of demand, in addition to numerical estimations of probable future tourism activity.

Difficulties associated with forecasting and the models utilised are exacerbated by the fact that demand for tourism at the aggregated world level is characterised by uncertainty and a vulnerability to events that are uncontrollable. However, it is important for the tourism sector that we are able to forecast and manage the future and perhaps the best approach is to use a combination of both quantitative and qualitative approaches.

SELF-CHECK QUESTIONS

1. Review the major determinants of demand at an individual level and assess their relative importance.

2. Draft a checklist of the reasons why access to a car is such an important determinant of tourism.

3. Review the key determinants of demand at an aggregate level and rank their importance for international tourism.

4. List three advantages of quantitative approaches to demand forecasting and three advantages of qualitative approaches.

5. Identify the top 10 international tourism-generating countries in the world and plot them on a world map – what does this tell you?

ESSAY QUESTIONS

1. Taking a country or region of your choice, look at the patterns of demand for tourism and explain them in respect of social, technological, economic and political factors.

2. Identify the main determinants of demand for tourism and assess their relative importance.

3. Compare the advantages and disadvantages of each of the main approaches to forecasting tourism demand.

4. 'In a world of unexpected and rapid change, forecasting tourism demand is a waste of time.' Discuss this statement.

5. Review the relevance of the life cycle and lifestyle demand determinants for the developing world.

ANNOTATED FURTHER READING

Books

Brent Ritchie, J.R. and Goeldner, C.R. (1994) *Travel Tourism and Hospitality Research. A Handbook for Managers and Researchers*, 2nd edn, John Wiley, Chichester.
A thorough handbook with authoritative entries relating to tourism demand determinants and forecasting.

Frechtling, D. (2001) *Forecasting Tourism Demand. Methods and Strategies*, Butterworth Heinemann, Oxford.
A very user-friendly account of the techniques and issues of tourism demand forecasting.

Song, H. and Witt, S.F. (2000) *Modeling and Forecasting Demand in Tourism*, Academic Press, New York.
A thorough and technical review of tourism demand forecasting.

Witt, S.F. and Moutinho, L. (eds) (1989) *Tourism Marketing and Management Handbook*, 2nd edn, Prentice Hall, Hemel Hempstead.
An excellent handbook with key reviews of tourism demand determinants, and approaches to forecasting.

WTO (2001) *Tourism 2020 Vision – Global Forecasts and Profiles of Market Segments*, WTO, Madrid.
An excellent and comprehensive review of future patterns of tourism demand and the key changes in determinants across the world.

References cited

Archer, B.H. (1994) 'Demand forecasting and estimation', pp. 86–92, in Ritchie, J.R.B. and Goeldner, C.R. (eds), *Handbook of Travel, Tourism and Hospitality Research*, Wiley, New York.

Boniface, B. and Cooper, C. (1987) *The Geography of Travel and Tourism*, Heinemann, London.

Frechtling, D. (2001) *Forecasting Tourism Demand. Methods and Strategies*, Butterworth Heinemann, Oxford.

Rostow, W.W. (1959) *The Stages of Economic Growth*, Cambridge University Press, Cambridge.

Taylor, R.E. and Judd, L.L. (1989) 'Delphi Forecasting', pp. 535–9, in Witt, S.F. and Moutinho, L. (eds) (1989) *Tourism Marketing and Management Handbook*, 2nd edn, Prentice Hall, Hemel Hempstead.

Uysal, M. (1998) 'The determinants of tourism demand: a theoretical perspective', pp. 79–98 in Ioannides, D. and Debbage, K. (eds) *The Economic Geography of the Tourist Industry*, Routledge, London.

Witt, S.F. and Martin, C.A. (1989) 'Demand forecasting in tourism and recreation', pp. 4–32 in Cooper, C.P. (ed.), *Progress in Tourism, Recreation and Hospitality Management*, Vol. 1, Belhaven, London.

MAJOR CASE STUDY 4.1
World patterns of demand for tourism

PATTERNS OF DEMAND: THE HISTORIC TREND

Since the Second World War, there has been rapid growth worldwide in international tourism (see Table 4.9). After the war increasing proportions of the populations of the industrialised nations were in possession of both the time (in the form of paid leave from employment) and the money (owing to increased disposable incomes) to engage in international travel. Supply to meet this increased demand for leisure tourism in particular was developed mainly in the form of the standard, mass package tour. This was made possible by the arrival of the jet aircraft in 1958, and by cheap oil. Further, international travel was boosted by a substantial increase in business travel.

Over this period, international tourism has shown itself on a worldwide scale to be robust, showing resilience against such factors as terrorism and political unrest in many parts of the world, worldwide economic recession and fluctuating exchange rates. Even 9/11 and subsequent shocks to the system had a lesser impact on this momentum than was at first feared, as discussed in Chapter 2. Generally, at times of economic growth, demand for travel has increased; on the other hand, during times of recession, demand has either remained constant or has soon recovered, in both cases due to new travellers entering the market and existing travellers taking more frequent trips. In addition to growth, we also see that the market has diversified as it has matured, with a huge growth in the array of destinations available. This global experience of

Table 4.9	International tourism trends: arrivals and receipts worldwide, 1950–2005	
	Arrivals (thousands)	Receipts[a] (US$ million)
1950	25 282	2 100
1960	69 296	6 867
1970	159 690	17 900
1980	284 841	102 372
1990	455 900	264 100
2000	687 300	473 400
2005	806 000	680 000

[a] Excludes international fare receipts.
Source: UNWTO, annual

almost uninterrupted growth is not, though, equally shared by all destinations. For example, tourists tend to stay away from destinations that they rightly or wrongly perceived to be unsafe – this has clearly affected tourism to the Middle East and North Africa, and following 9/11 other Muslim countries have also been affected. Other destinations might suffer because they are simply no longer fashionable.

THE 1980S

As the market has matured, the average annual growth rate has tended to decrease. During the period up to 1980, international arrivals doubled every ten years or so. In contrast, the 1980s experienced a slowing of average annual growth rates to a little over 4%. Growth in the latter half of the decade was, in fact, more in line with that of the previous two decades and followed the slow growth of the early 1980s.

We can explain such unevenness of tourism demand by a number of major factors and events. The decade opened with economic recession which acted to dampen international travel, and volume did not really recover until 1984. The years 1984 and 1985 were record years with European destinations doing particularly well. However, the accident at the nuclear power plant in Chernobyl, in the then Soviet Union, combined with terrorist activity, the Libyan bombing incident and the weakening of the US dollar against other major currencies, all conspired to contribute to the depressing of demand for tourism. As a result, international travel was severely affected. The effect was not so much in terms of total numbers, which were up on the previous year anyway, but in terms of tourism flows and changes in types of trip taken. Many destinations suffered badly, whereas others gained. The second half of the decade saw a return to some sort of normality, both in terms of growth rates and in terms of types of trip taken.

THE 1990S

The 1990s opened with the Gulf War and further economic recession, leading to great uncertainty for international tourism. In the short term, the build-up to the Gulf War, the war itself and the aftermath led initially to the virtual cessation of travel to the Gulf, the Eastern Mediterranean and North Africa. It not only depressed international tourism further afield, but also the economic recession experienced by the majority of industrialised countries was aggravated by it. The lessons of earlier years were that international tourism would recover and develop with new products, destinations and generating markets and indeed this has been the case, with tourism responding well to the growth in

economic and social conditions and little or no slow-down was seen in international tourism flows in the 1990s. In particular the decade was characterised by the growth of overseas travel by residents of developing countries and the acceleration of multiple, but short-haul, trips from travellers in industrialised countries.

THE NEW MILLENNIUM

Tourism in the early years of the new millennium has been characterised by contrast. The millennium opened with optimism and the success of the Sydney Olympic Games, considerably boosting arrivals to Australia. However, the subsequent terrorism activities of 11 September 2001, the Bali bombings of 2002, wars in Afghanistan and Iraq, the SARS outbreak in Asia, the tsunami of 2004 and the terrorist attacks on surface transport in both Spain and the UK severely affected the pattern of tourism demand. In addition, uncertainty, recessions in generating countries and tightened security at both borders and in the airline industry prompted consumers to holiday at home rather than internationally.

The terrorism incidents of 2001 saw international tourism arrivals decline by 0.5% over 2000. However, they recovered to grow by 2.7% in 2002, although, as the industry struggled to attract the market, price competition depressed receipts from tourism in 2002. However, tourism demand has shown itself to be robust and arrivals and receipts recovered by 2005.

PATTERNS OF DEMAND: THE REGIONAL DIMENSION

Table 4.10 shows the changes in the share of international tourism worldwide of the different regions over the period 1950 to 2005. Regional shares have to be viewed in the context of a greatly changing total, and so even a constant share represents substantial growth.

Europe and, to a lesser extent, the Americas have for some time dominated the international travel scene in terms of numbers of arrivals and receipts. More specifically, it is Western Europe and North America that have given rise to a high level of geographical concentration of movement.

In 2005, Europe accounted for just over half of all international tourist arrivals. We can identify a number of factors that explain the leading position held by Europe:

- Large segments of the population receive relatively high incomes, resulting in high levels of disposable income.

- Paid leave from work and a supportive social security system is normal in European countries.

Table 4.10	Regional share of international tourism, 1950–2005						
	1950 (%)	1960 (%)	1970 (%)	1980 (%)	1990 (%)	2000 (%)	2005 (%)
(a) Share of arrivals							
Europe	66.5	72.5	70.5	68.4	63.5	57.8	51.3
Americas	29.6	24.1	23.0	18.9	18.8	18.4	16.6
East Asia/Pacific	0.8	1.0	3.0	7.0	11.4	15.7	18.3
Africa	2.1	1.1	1.5	2.5	3.4	3.9	4.5
Middle East	0.9	1.0	1.4	2.4	2.1	3.3	4.8
South Asia	0.2	0.3	0.6	0.8	0.7	0.9	0.9
(b) Share of receipts							
Europe	41.3	56.8	62.0	59.3	54.4	49.1	51.2
Americas	50.5	35.7	26.8	24.9	26.1	27.8	21.2
East Asia/Pacific	1.4	2.8	6.2	7.3	14.4	17.2	19.0
Africa	4.2	2.6	2.2	2.7	1.9	2.3	3.2
Middle East	2.3	1.5	2.3	4.3	2.5	2.5	4.0
South Asia	0.3	0.5	0.6	1.5	0.8	1.0	1.4

Columns do not necessarily add up to 100% because of rounding.
Source: Based on UNWTO data, annual

- High proportions of the populations of, for example, Germany, France and the UK attach very high priority to the annual foreign holiday and are reluctant to let it go even in times of recession.
- There is a wealth of both artificial and natural attractions.
- Demand for foreign travel is satisfied by a large tourist industry and the necessary infrastructure.
- Adoption of the euro in many countries and the expansion of the European Union has facilitated travel.
- International travel need not involve great distances, owing to the number of relatively small countries.

A number of these factors are equally applicable to North America. However, the sheer size of the USA and Canada means that the majority of their populations prefer to take domestic trips. Nevertheless, there are substantial numbers of North Americans who do engage in foreign travel each year, not merely within their own continent but also in long-haul trips.

The shares of Europe and the Americas have fluctuated somewhat over the years, with some evidence of a decline in terms of both numbers of arrivals and tourism receipts. The clearest trend though has been the emergence of countries of the East Asia and the Pacific (EAP) region as both receivers and generators of international tourism. The EAP share of arrivals worldwide was only 1% in 1960, but grew to 3% in 1970, 11% in 1990 and 18% in 2005. The increasing share is of an expanding market. This represents remarkable growth in a highly competitive environment.

We can see that the shares of international tourism of Africa, the Middle East and South Asia have throughout the period 1950 to 2005 been small, though with a high level of fluctuation. As regions, they are not able to compete with Europe, the Americas and the EAP either in terms of generating or receiving large numbers of international tourists. The reasons for this are mainly economic. Destination countries within these regions can compete for specific markets from the major generating countries. Many, though, have been vulnerable to the effects of unrest and war, not necessarily in their own countries but near enough for them to be perceived as dangerous places to visit. In general, their incoming international tourism has suffered when business conditions have been depressed in the traditional tourism generating countries.

PATTERNS OF DEMAND: CHARACTERISTICS OF GENERATING MARKETS

It is essential for destinations to understand the origins of their tourists. Here, there are some generalisations

Photograph 4.2	Asia is becoming a significant generator of international tourism.

Source: Corbis/Paul Hackett/Reuters

that we can make as a specific country's market normally has the following features:

- It includes at least one of the four top generators of international tourism worldwide.
- It includes neighbouring states, since the distance and cost involved are relatively small.
- It includes countries further afield if, as is the case between the USA and Western Europe, air travel is available and at a cost within the reach of large segments of the population.
- It depends on the size of the population of generating states and their propensity to travel.
- It depends on ease of movement across borders.
- It depends on the real and perceived price of trips to the destination.
- It depends on the attractiveness of the destination.
- It depends on the social, cultural and historic links between countries.
- It depends on marketing activity and an appropriate supply in terms of sectors such as transport and accommodation.

WEB SITE

www.world-tourism.org

REFERENCE

UNWTO (annual), *Tourism Highlights*, WTO, Madrid.

DISCUSSION QUESTIONS

1. Why is the East Asia and the Pacific region set to become a major destination in the world?
2. Describe the impact of 11 September 2001 on international tourism demand patterns.
3. International tourism growth was phenomenal during the twentieth century. Identify some constraints to tourism in the twenty-first century that might slow this growth.

PART 2

THE TOURISM DESTINATION

Photograph: Yellowstone National Park, Wyoming, USA © Hannah Cox

INTRODUCTION

Part 2 of this book examines the relationship between tourism and the destination. Because of the simultaneous nature of production and consumption within the tourism sector there are far more wide-reaching implications for this form of development than there are with many other development options. The chapters in this part take on an analytical flavour as they focus upon the multitude of models and approaches that have been used to investigate the various implications of tourism and its development. Each chapter examines the relevant models that have been used and compares and contrasts their efficacy.

The presence of tourists brings with it environmental and socio-cultural impacts as well as the economic impacts. Therefore the choice to pursue tourism as a development option needs to be made after considering all of the factors relating to its impacts and the resources upon which tourism will draw. Impact models if they are to be of use to tourism planners and policy makers must consider all of the effects of tourism (positive and negative) across all of the planes of influence (economic, environmental and socio-cultural) within a single analytical framework. An overarching aim of this part of the book is to put this fact into context and show how this can be achieved.

The main driving force that explains the relentless growth of the tourism industry over the past century is the economic benefits associated with it. Chapter 5 examines both the economic significance of tourism to various destinations and how it can be measured and then goes on to look at the methodologies that have found favour in measuring its economic impact. To understand the economic significance of tourism it is necessary to look at the structure of the local economy and the level of dependence that exists upon the income, employment and foreign exchange earned from tourism. Where high levels of dependence are apparent there is concern that the destination becomes vulnerable because of tourism's sensitivity to factors outside of the control of the destination. This is particularly important as we start the twenty-first century in a world interrupted by terrorist activity. The ability to measure the economic significance of tourism using accounting practices such as tourism satellite accounts provides governments with the facility to understand the importance of the sector but offers little opportunity for specific policy decisions. In order to understand the economic policy relevance of tourism to a destination it is necessary to turn attention to the economic impacts of tourism and their associated multiplier values.

The economic impact of tourism can be measured using a number of techniques of which ad hoc and input–output multiplier models have been the most important over the past 30 years or so. More recently there has been a growth in the adoption of computable general equilibrium models that provide the results that one normally expects from input–output models but with the added power of being able to simulate economic changes. Finally, this chapter looks at the often overlooked economic costs associated with tourism and its development and stresses the need for policy makers to focus on the net economic benefits.

Chapter 6 examines the importance of the environment as a resource for tourism and the difficulties created by its use as a 'free' input to the tourism product. Attention is brought to the fact that tourism tends to suffer from a negative environmental image whereas in fact it has both negative and positive attributes. A range of environmental issues is discussed in order to demonstrate the scope of the topic and its importance. The importance of not being simply focused on the direct environmental effects is stressed together with ways of looking at the indirect and induced environmental consequences associated with production in general and tourism production in particular. Distinctions are drawn between environmental impact assessments (EIAs) and environmental auditing and the relative roles played by each.

The socio-cultural impacts of tourism are examined in Chapter 7. This chapter begins with a review of the various approaches used to study tourism development and its implications for socio-cultural impacts. The major models that have been used to explain the development of tourism are combined to provide an overview that demonstrates the commonality of the models but highlights the inadequacy of the framework to produce solutions within a dynamic world. Fundamental issues regarding the cultural impact of tourism on host populations are put forward and questioned. Caution is expressed regarding the tendency to adopt biased views because of the focus of studies upon negative impacts. Positive contributions to socio-cultural aspects are discussed together with more specific negative issues such as crime, sex tourism and displacement. The chapter concludes by looking at some of the data sources available for the study of the socio-cultural impacts.

Much has been said in the literature over the past quarter of a century about the need to achieve sustainable tourism development. The definition and concepts are examined in Chapter 8 before an attempt to define sustainable tourism is made. The different types of sustainability are considered and the existence of any form of production that can be truly sustainable is questioned. Those factors working in favour of sustainable tourism and those working against are reviewed before attention is focused upon the two main ways forward in moving towards a more sustainable sector, limiting activity through thresholds and modifying the delivery and nature of the sector. The limits to development are discussed under the headings of carrying capacity and a great deal of discussion looks at the strengths and weaknesses of this approach. Concern is expressed about the use of the term sustainability as a marketing ploy rather than one with any real grounding and then some different types of tourism products are examined, including eco-tourism, drawing attention to their strengths and weaknesses.

There is a variety of models that have been put forward to explain general economic development and the role that can be played by tourism within such models is an important consideration. Chapter 9 starts by briefly looking at each of the main models and determining whether or not there is a role for tourism within general economic development. Once it is established that most of these models do provide a key role for tourism the chapter moves on to look at the characteristics of tourism that make it an attractive development option. Tourism planning takes place at different levels from international levels (such as the Caribbean or Europe) through to national and then to local planning levels. Each of these levels is discussed prior to looking at the key stages of the process of tourism development planning. The importance of each stage is considered followed by a brief look at the specialisms needed to construct tourism development plans. The chapter concludes by looking at what can go wrong and the reasons for plan failure.

Finally, tourism operates in a dynamic world and, whereas there are many forces that drive tourism forward to higher volume and deeper penetration, there are also forces that deter people from tourism or at least tourism in specific areas. Therefore tourism development strategies must also consider how best to deal with the negative forces that work against tourism growth. Two major deterrents are travel-related risks and climatic change. These two factors are examined in Chapter 10 where, in the first half, the chapter's focus is on travel related risks, such as terrorism and political unrest. The latter half of the chapter examines the impact of climate change and the ability of destinations to adapt to such changes.

CHAPTER 5
The Economic Impact of Tourism

LEARNING OUTCOMES

This chapter focuses on the economic impacts of tourism and aims to provide you with:

- an understanding of the economic contribution of tourism locally, nationally and internationally;

- an understanding of the methods used to estimate tourist expenditure and the way in which the significance of tourism can be measured;

- an appreciation of the positive and negative economic impacts of tourism activity; and

- a general knowledge of the approaches that may be used to measure the economic impacts of tourism and the strengths and weaknesses associated with each approach.

Photograph: Christmas market, Pondicherri, India © Maggie Wells

INTRODUCTION

This chapter examines the economic significance of tourism as well as the economic impacts associated with the industry. In the same way that the literature tends to exaggerate the negative impacts of tourism upon host societies and environments, so the positive impact of tourism upon economies is often overstated. Therefore the positive and negative economic impacts of tourism will be discussed. An integral part of this chapter is a critical assessment of the methods of measuring economic impact drawing, particularly, on the application of multiplier analysis, **tourism satellite accounts** (TSAs) and computable generalised equilibrium models. All the multiplier models that are outlined in this chapter generate information that is valuable to policy makers and planners. It should also be noted that, within known limitations, **multiplier analyses** provide powerful and valuable tools for estimating and analysing the economic impact of tourism and comparing the performance of tourism with that of alternative industries.

OVERVIEW

In spite of the many altruistic and well-meaning reasons sometimes put forward to support the case for tourism development, such as those originally proposed in the Manila Declaration (WTO, 1980a), it is the economic benefits that provide the main driving force for tourism development. Foreign exchange earnings, income and employment generation are the major motivations for including tourism as part of a development strategy. Tourist expenditure is as 'real' as any other form of consumption and international tourist expenditure can be seen as an **invisible export** from the host country, whereas domestic tourism can be seen as an 'export' from the hosting region to the other local regions. Domestic tourism can also, in some instances, be seen as an import substitute for the national economy. Tourism activity can be seen as import substitution when tourists choose to take their vacation within the national economy rather than travel abroad.

International tourism activity is often easier to measure than domestic tourism activity because it involves custom/immigration procedures and currency exchange. Many countries collect information from visitor arrivals at the frontier providing a good source of data relating to the volume of arrivals, country of origin and purpose of visit. Currency exchange information is collected and monitored by central banks and this provides some useful information, but is by no means ideal, relating to tourist spending. Tourist expenditure can only be estimated with some degree of accuracy by undertaking specific visitor expenditure surveys, normally at exit points. Such surveys tend to be time-consuming and costly. Some countries attempt to estimate the level and patterns of tourist spending from central bank statistics, while others try to economise by collecting tourist expenditure data at infrequent intervals (say, every five years). In order to use economic impact analyses for the purpose of tourism planning and development strategies it is important to have reliable flows of expenditure data. Therefore, visitor expenditure data should be collected by exit surveys each year, or at least every other year. This information can be collected along with demographic data and other variables that will help underscore other important surveys for, say, the market research referred to in Chapter 18.

During the past few decades many economies have experienced growth in their service sectors, even when the more traditional agricultural and manufacturing sectors have been subject to **stagnation** or decline. The global importance of the service sectors can be identified by the introduction of the General Agreement on Trade in Services (GATS) following the Uruguay Round of negotiations. Tourism is the largest service-based industry and, as such, has been partly responsible for this service sector growth. In **developing**

countries the service sector is responsible for around 40% of **GDP**, while in developed or industrialised economies it is responsible for more than 65% of GDP. In spite of its economic importance, the service sector has not been given adequate prominence in economic text-books, which have tended to concentrate on the more traditional manufacturing industries. The dearth of material on service-based industries in the major textbooks can be, in part, explained (if not excused) by the lack of available and comparable statistics for service-based sectors. This shortfall in data is improving but, in general, it is tradition that has dictated the content of such books rather than pragmatism. The latter half of the 1980s saw a growing interest in the operation and performance of service industries. In 1985, it was observed that, because of the strength of **intersectoral linkages**, the service sector generally performs a more important function in the process of development than that suggested merely by looking at the service sector's contribution to a country's GDP. From the mid-1990s, the international world has been dominated by the service industries and they have also been responsible for the accelerated drive towards **globalisation**. International tourism activity enjoyed strong growth throughout the 1990s, often growing faster than other commercial services and at a rate that was almost twice as fast as international trade. Although the number of international tourist arrivals experienced a slight dip of just 0.5% in the period 2000 to the end of 2001 (following the events of 11 September 2001) it recovered much of its growth impetus with the following year growing at 2.7% for 2001 to 2002. However, hidden within these overall growth figures is the fact that the number of international tourist arrivals to the

Photograph 5.1	International tourism increases foreign exchange flows.
	Source: Travelex PLC

Americas declined in 2001 (−6.1%) and 2002 (−4.4%). Each of the other regions showed a significant turnaround in 2002 and all recorded positive growth trends.

Recognition of the importance of the service sector to the world economy came in the form of the establishment of the General Agreement on Trade in Services (GATS). GATS grew out of the World Trade Organization's Uruguay Round of the General Agreement on Tariffs and Trade (GATT). The main declared purpose of GATS is the liberalisation of services. However, a brief examination of the slowdown in the growth of trade might suggest that GATS was introduced because the strong growth in service industries would accelerate the World Trade Organization's processes and influence.

Along with the movement towards the liberalisation of international trade has been the growth of *globalisation*. Globalisation refers to the result of a collection of forces that tend to change the way that the economic, political and cultural worlds operate. As the world becomes economically smaller, the concept of globalisation has taken on a more central position on the stage of global politics. From the earliest days when the world economy first started to transform from subsistence farming and fishing towards a market-based economy there has been a sustained growth in the geographical reach of businesses. However, this process of globalisation accelerated throughout the latter half of the last century. It has been referred to as a process in which the geographical distance between economic factors, producers and consumers becomes a factor of diminishing significance.

Tourism, as a major element of the service economy, has for some time been applauded for its sustained and rapid growth. However, not even its most ardent supporters would have forecast just how well it has been able to stand up to the pressures of global economic recession, even recessions that have severely damaged many of the world's major industries. The world has staggered from recession to recession over the past two decades and even the mighty giants of industry (such as IBM and Ford) have been forced to rationalise their activities. Although the purpose of this chapter is to examine the economic impact of tourism, it is useful to examine the economic significance of tourism to a number of countries, most notably the prime generators and/or recipients of international tourists. The economic significance of tourism is determined not only by the level of tourism activity that is taking place, but also by the type and nature of the economy being considered. For instance, the economic significance of tourism activity to a developing country may well be measured in terms of its ability to generate an inflow of foreign exchange or to provide a means for creating greater price flexibility in its export industries, whereas, for a developed or industrialised economy, the researcher may be looking at tourism's ability to assist diversification strategies and to combat regional imbalances.

The significance of tourism may be assessed in terms of the proportion of total global visitors attributable to individual countries, for here one can assess the relative importance of single countries in determining the volume of world travel. On the other hand, the significance of tourism may be examined with respect to the importance of tourist activity to the economy of each destination. This chapter examines both aspects in order to establish how some countries are extremely important as tourist generators and how other countries are highly dependent upon such tourism activity.

International tourism in selected countries

Events that have happened throughout the 1990s and early 2000s have had a profound effect on the pattern of international tourism. How long-term these effects will be depends, to a large extent, on the future political and economic stability of the world. The financial crises that hit the **tiger economies** affected not only the flow of tourism activity but also the geographical patterns. The events of 11 September 2001 and the subsequent conflicts in the Middle East have brought a significant change to the nature of tourism flows. Therefore, although the global figures for international tourist arrivals and spending indicate a recovery path from the crisis period of 2001, the anatomy of that recovery portrays a different picture.

Table 5.1	Principal tourist-generating countries, 1990–2004: expenditure (US$bn)			
Country	**1990**	**1995**	**2000**	**2004**
Germany	38.9	60.2	53.0	71.0
United States	37.4	44.9	64.7	65.6
Japan	28.7	36.8	31.9	38.2
United Kingdom	18.2	24.9	38.4	56.5
France	12.4	16.4	17.9	28.6
Top 5 countries	135.5	183.1	205.9	259.9
Rest of world	133.7	227.7	273.5	374.8
World total	269.2	410.8	479.4	634.7
Top 5 as % of world total	50.3	44.5	42.9	40.9

Source: Derived from WTO, 1988; 1992; 1997: UNWTO, 2007

For instance, within Europe, international tourist arrivals to Spain increased by 4.6% in 2001 even though international tourist arrivals to Europe as a whole fell by 0.5%. Destinations such as the UK (−9.4%), France (−2.6%), Germany (−5.9%) and Italy (−3.9%) all recorded declines in the number of arrivals for that period. The following year (2001/2) showed a growth in international tourist arrivals to Europe as a whole of 2.3% with all countries except Switzerland, Poland and Portugal showing a positive growth over the previous year. As commonly occurs, tourist spending over these two years was more volatile than arrivals, with Europe showing an overall decline of 1.7% in 2000/1 and a growth of 6.5% in 2001/2. The selection of countries for inclusion in tables of top generating and top recipient countries is at best difficult and at worst arbitrary. However, the countries selected in Tables 5.1 and 5.2 (France, Germany, Italy, Japan, Spain, the UK and the USA) have been included because they are among either the top five tourist-generating countries with respect to tourist expenditure and/or the top five countries with respect to tourism receipts.

Table 5.1 shows the principal tourist-generating countries, with respect to the level of their international tourist expenditure, over the time period from 1990 to 2004. It can be seen that, over the years covered by the table, the proportion of the world's total tourist expenditure attributable to the top five generating countries has declined from the 50% level recorded in 1990 (which it held throughout the late 1980s to the latter half of the 1990s, with a peak of just over 54% in 1988) to just under 41% in 2004. It can also be seen that the United States overtook Germany as the prime tourism generating country (in terms of expenditure) in 2000 only to relinquish that gain by 2004 whereby the United States suffered as a result of 9/11. The UK has continued to grow strongly, tripling the amount of tourist spending generated over the 1990–2004 period. Japan, following its economic crises, had witnessed a 27% fall in the amount of tourist spending generated between 1986 and 2001 only to bounce back again by 2004 showing an increase of about one-third over the 1990 to 2004 period.

Table 5.2 shows the top five countries in terms of tourism receipts. The proportion of total global tourist receipts attributable to the top five countries has fluctuated around the lower half of the 40% range during the 1990s but had dropped below 40% by 2000 and to less than 35% by 2005. This drop in dominance of the top five can be partly explained by the political events since 9/11 and the subsequent bombings in London and Madrid, and partly by the more rapid growth of tourism in other regions of the world. The USA improved its position relative to the other top recipient countries by 2000 but then its growth stuttered following 2001 and its total receipts in 2005 were still less than its receipts in 2000. In 1986 the USA was responsible for 14.8% of the world total tourism receipts; in 1996 this figure had risen to 15.3% but by 2005 they were responsible for less than 12% of the world total.

Table 5.2	Principal destinations in terms of tourism receipts, 1990–2005: tourism receipts (US$bn)			
Country	**1990**	**1995**	**2000**	**2005**
United States	43.0	63.4	82.4	81.7
Spain	18.5	25.3	30.0	47.9
France	20.2	27.6	30.8	42.3
UK	15.4	20.5	21.9	30.7
Italy	16.6	28.7	27.5	35.4
Top 5 countries	113.6	165.5	192.5	237.9
Rest of world	156.6	245.2	289.1	444.8
World total	270.2	410.7	481.6	682.7
Top 5 as % of world total	42.0	40.2	39.9	34.8

Source: Derived from WTO, 1988; 1992; 1997: UNWTO, 2007

A fact that becomes clear when examining the top tourist expenditure generating and receiving countries is the high degree of correlation between the listings. Tourism does not perform well as a global redistributor of income and wealth in the same way as it does for regional redistribution. This is particularly true if the relationship between developed and developing countries is considered. It is the developed and industrialised countries that tend to populate the lists in both the top generators of tourist expenditure and the top recipients.

The division between the performance of developed and developing countries is of additional significance when it is considered that, on average, the industrialised countries are responsible for 70% of total world exports and yet receive over 70% of all tourism receipts, which contrasts with developing countries that are responsible for less than 30% of all world exports and received less than 30% of all tourist receipts.

Dependence upon tourism

Table 5.3 provides another way of examining the economic significance of tourism for countries by looking at dependence on tourism receipts (**economic dependence**) relative to total export earnings and gross national income (GNI) for 2004. It can be seen that among these developed economies, tourism receipts as a percentage of total export earnings ranges from

Table 5.3	Tourism receipts expressed as a percentage of total export earning and gross national income, 2004				
Country	**Tourism receipts (US$m) (1)**	**Export earnings (US$m) (2)**	**(1) as a % (2)**	**GNI[1] (US$bn) (3)**	**(1) as a % of (3)**
Spain	47 891	279 912	17.1	1 100	4.4
France	42 276	575 112	7.4	2 200	1.9
Italy	35 398	456 020	7.8	1 800	2.0
United Kingdom	30 669	582 215	5.3	2 300	1.3
United States	81 680	1 258 403	6.5	12 900	0.6
Germany	29 204	1 118 398	2.6	2 900	1.0
Japan	12 439	702 781	1.8	5 000	0.2

[1] Gross national income (GNI) calculated using World Bank Atlas Method.
Source: Derived from Euromonitor, International Monetary Fund (IMF), International Financial Statistics

Table 5.4	Tourism balance sheets for the top ten tourist spenders, 2004		
Country	International tourism receipts (US$bn)	International tourism expenditure (US$bn)	Balance (US$bn)
Germany	27.6	71.0	−43.4
United States	74.5	65.6	8.9
United Kingdom	28.2	56.5	−28.3
Japan	11.2	38.2	−27.0
France	40.8	28.6	12.2
Italy	35.6	20.5	15.1
China	25.7	19.1	6.6
Netherlands	10.3	16.4	−6.1
Canada	12.8	16.0	−3.2
Russian Federation	5.2	15.7	−10.5

Note: A minus balance indicates where the country spends more than it receives through tourism activity.
Source: Derived from UNWTO, 2005

the relatively unimportant 1.8% for Japan to the quite significant 17.1% experienced by Spain. Confirming this dependency level, the table also shows the percentage of GNI attributable to tourism receipts which indicate that only 0.2% of Japan's GNI is attributable to tourist receipts but this figure rises to 4.4% for Spain.

Two major problems that exist when making international comparisons of tourism expenditure and receipts are that the data are generally expressed in current prices and are standardised in US dollars. The problems created by this form of presentation is that (1) it does not take into account the effects of **inflation**, and (2) movements in the value of the dollar exchange rate (which have been both frequent and dramatic over the past decade or so) will appear to be changes in the local value of tourist receipts and expenditure. The twenty-first century has started with very low levels of inflation but more recently there are signs that this benign economic climate is starting to experience higher rates of inflation, the US dollar has suffered as a result of its massive **trade deficit** and its involvement in the conflicts in Afghanistan and Iraq, and finally, the sharp increases in demand for oil and mineral resources that have accompanied the rapid development of the economies of China and India are putting enormous pressures on world resources and hence price inflation.

Table 5.4 takes the analysis one step further and examines the relationship between tourism receipts and expenditures in order to establish the net effect of travel on selected countries of the world. In 2004 the USA, France, Italy and China all had positive tourism balance sheets. That is, they earned more from international tourism receipts than their national residents spent as tourists outside of the country. However, Germany, the UK, Japan, the Netherlands, Canada and the Russian Federation were all subject to a negative tourism balance sheet. That is, the residents of those countries spent more abroad on international tourism than the countries received from international tourism receipts.

There have been various attempts at finding consistent ways to measure the level of demand or the significance of tourism activity to any individual country. The most universally accepted approach is through the construction of tourism satellite accounts.

Tourism satellite accounts

One approach to determining the economic significance of tourism to an economy is to construct tourism satellite accounts. This methodology has been approved and adopted by the United Nations and the World Tourism Organization in 2000. Tourism satellite accounts (TSAs) perform a different role from economic impact models that attempt to estimate the net economic benefits associated with tourism activity. To be of use TSAs must be built around an **input–output model** and they take a demand-orientated approach rather than the supply-orientated approach associated with input–output models. As the TSA name suggests they are a set of accounts that can be used to determine the size or significance of tourism within an economy, but not the impact of tourism. They are based on the national accounts data but this information is rearranged so that particular emphasis can be placed on tourism activities. Like input–output models, they also provide a means whereby tourism can be viewed in parallel with other industries and across international boundaries. The underpinning philosophy of TSAs is to add credibility to tourism, which suffers because it does not fit into a single industry and its socio-economic impact is often difficult to measure.

In terms of the discussions in this chapter, the multiplier models are used to determine the economic impact of changes in tourist spending on the income, employment, government revenue and foreign exchange of any economy. They can also be used to identify **opportunity costs** by examining the effects of comparable changes in other industries. TSAs, on the other hand, offer a way of improving the estimation of the significance of tourism to an economy.

The concept of tourism satellite accounts is based on the need for a framework that will provide consistency over time and between countries and comparability between industries when calculating the significance of tourism to an economy. Providing the extensive data needs can be met with timely and accurate data the accounts should do much to promote the importance of tourism globally and within countries. There have been some serious concerns, however, that tourism satellite accounts require more data than are often available

MINI CASE STUDY 5.1
Tourism as a redistribution mechanism of wealth

Tourism has been lauded as an excellent vehicle for redistributing income from rich areas with abundant employment opportunities to poorer areas where employment opportunities are scarce. Consider domestic tourism in an economy such as France. The tendency is for people from the relatively affluent urbanised areas of, say, Paris to travel to less populated, poorer and more scenic rural areas. This results in a transfer of demand from the wealthier urban areas to the sparsely populated rural areas. Such transfers can stimulate investment and act as a catalyst for general economic development.

The same redistributive qualities of tourism have not been so apparent at the international level where the vast majority of tourism activity takes place between the wealthy industrialised economies. Tourism has done little to bridge the north–south divide. Indeed, it has been argued quite convincingly that tourism can exacerbate the income inequalities between rich countries such as the USA and less rich countries such as Kenya. The drive towards globalisation by some of the key elements of the tourism industry adds further substance to this belief.

The existence of economies of large-scale production, **comparative advantage** and the global nature of communications might suggest that any attempt to redress the imbalances will result in a misallocation of resources.

DISCUSSION QUESTIONS

1. Explain why tourism may act as an effective means of redistributing wealth at national level but often fails to do so at regional levels within an economy.

2. If the natural market forces are left to their own devices will tourism result in income redistribution that works in favour of the poorer segments of the population (nationally and internationally)?

3. What actions could be taken to encourage tourism to assist in redressing income inequalities without damaging the development of the industry?

resulting in data being estimated or 'imported' from other economies to be used as a proxy for the TSA. Thus, TSAs may be constructed using data that are less than accurate and this will serve only to undermine the confidence that can be attached to these accounts and harm the reliability of the estimates derived from them.

THE GENERATION OF ECONOMIC IMPACTS BY TOURIST SPENDING

Tourists spend their money on a wide variety of goods and services provided by a wide range of businesses. For example, tourists purchase accommodation, food and beverage, transport, communications, entertainment services, goods from retail outlets and tour/travel services. This money may be seen as an injection of demand into the host economy, i.e. demand that is created by people from outside the area of the local economy. In the case of international tourism, the tourist expenditure is a result of non-nationals spending within the national economy. In the case of domestic tourism, the tourist expenditure is a result of spending by people that do not live within the local area in which the money is spent. However, the total value of international and domestic tourist expenditure represents only a partial and sometimes misleading picture of the economic impact. The full assessment of economic impact must take into account other aspects such as:

- **leakages** of expenditure out of the local economy;
- indirect and induced effects; and
- **displacement** and opportunity costs.

LEAKAGES OF EXPENDITURE OUT OF THE LOCAL ECONOMY

When tourists make expenditures within an economy the amount of money that stays within that economy depends upon the extent of leakages that occur. For instance, if a tourist purchases a carved wooden souvenir from a gift shop in Beijing, the extent of leakages will depend upon whether the carving was imported or made locally. If the carving was imported the tourist is really only buying the **value added** that was created within the local economy, i.e. the value of local transport, import, wholesale and retail margins, government taxes and duties, etc. The extent of leakages can result from demand-side factors such as the fact that different types of tourist and different types of tourist activity tend to be associated with differences in propensities to purchase imported goods. The leakages can also be associated with supply-side factors, particularly in developing economies where the local capacity to supply the needs of tourists may be small and there is consequently a high proportion of demand met through imported goods and services. Wherever money flows out of circulation, either by being spent on goods and services from outside or simply being withdrawn through savings, this constitutes a *leakage*.

THE MEASUREMENT OF ECONOMIC IMPACT

The measurement of the economic impact of tourism is far more involved than simply calculating the level of tourist expenditure. Indeed, estimates of the economic impact of tourism based on tourist expenditure or receipts can be not only inaccurate, but also very misleading. Before examining how the economic impact is measured, it is necessary to look at the different aspects of the economy that are affected by tourism expenditure.

To begin with, a difference can be drawn between the economic impact associated with tourist expenditure and that associated with the development of tourism. The former refers to the ongoing effects of, and changes in, tourist expenditure, whereas the latter is concerned with the one-off impact of the construction and finance of tourism-related facilities. The difference between these two aspects of impact is important because they require different methodological approaches. The calculation of the economic impact of tourist expenditure is achieved by using multiplier analysis and the estimation of the economic impact of tourism development projects is often achieved by resorting to **project appraisal** techniques such as **cost–benefit analysis.**

The measurement of the economic impact of tourist expenditure, if it is to be meaningful, must encompass the various effects of tourist spending as it impacts throughout the economy. That is, the direct, indirect and induced effects associated with tourist expenditure need to be calculated.

Direct, indirect and induced economic effects

Tourist expenditure has a 'cascading' effect throughout the host economy. It begins with tourists spending money in 'front-line' tourist establishments, such as hotels, restaurants and taxis, and then permeates throughout the rest of the economy. It can be examined by assessing the impact at three different levels – the direct, indirect and induced levels.

Direct effects

The direct level of impact is the value of tourist expenditure *less* the value of imports necessary to supply those 'front-line' goods and services. Thus, the direct impact is likely to be less than the value of tourist expenditure except in the rare case where a local economy can provide all of the tourist's wants from its own productive sectors.

Indirect effects

The establishments that directly receive the tourist expenditure also need to purchase goods and services from other sectors within the local economy, for example hotels will purchase the services of builders, accountants, banks, food and beverage suppliers, electricity and water, etc. Furthermore, the suppliers to these 'front-line' establishments will also need to purchase goods and services from other establishments within the local economy and so the process continues. The generation of economic activity brought about by these subsequent rounds of expenditure is known as the indirect effect. The indirect effect will not involve all of the monies spent by tourists during the direct effect since some of that money will leak out of circulation through imports, savings and taxation.

Induced effects

Finally, during the direct and indirect rounds of expenditure, income will accrue to local residents in the form of wages, salaries, distributed profit, rent and interest. This addition to local income will, in part, be re-spent in the local economy on goods and services and this will generate yet further rounds of economic activity.

It is only when all three levels of impact (direct *plus* indirect *plus* induced) are estimated that the full positive economic impact of tourism expenditure is fully assessed. However, there can be negative aspects to the economic impact of tourist expenditure.

Measuring the economic impact of tourist expenditure

At a national level, the UNWTO publishes annual tourist statistics for countries throughout the world. These statistics include figures relating to tourist expenditure, but it would not be correct to assume that these figures reflect the economic impact of tourist expenditure. These figures relate to how much tourists spend in a destination. They take no account of how much of that sum leaks straight out of the economy (paying for imported goods and services to satisfy tourist needs) or how much additional impact is experienced through the 'knock-on' effects of this tourist spending.

At a sub-national level the availability of tourist expenditure data is far more sparse. Some countries, such as the UK, undertake visitor expenditure surveys (for example, International Passenger Survey (IPS) and United Kingdom Tourist Survey (UKTS)) which allow expenditure estimates to be made at the regional level. However, it is often necessary to undertake specific tourist expenditure surveys to establish the tourist spend in particular areas.

In order to translate tourist expenditure data into economic impact information the appropriate multiplier values have to be calculated. The term *multiplier* is one of the most quoted economic concepts in the study of tourism. Multiplier values may be used for a variety of purposes and are often used as the basis for public sector decision-making.

THE MULTIPLIER CONCEPT

The concept of the multiplier is based upon the recognition that sales for one firm require purchases from other firms within the local economy, i.e. the industrial sectors of an economy are interdependent. This means that firms purchase not only primary inputs such as labour and imports, but also intermediate goods and services produced by other establishments within the local economy. Therefore, a change in the level of final demand for one sector's output will affect not only the industry that produces that final good/service but also other sectors that supply goods/services to that sector and the sectors that act as suppliers to those sectors as well.

Because firms in the local economy are dependent upon other firms for their supplies, any change in tourist expenditure will bring about a change in the economy's level of production, household income, employment, government revenue and foreign exchange flows (where applicable). These changes may be greater than, equal to or less than the value of the change in tourist expenditure that brought them about. The term 'tourist multiplier' refers to the ratio of two changes – the change in one of the key economic variables such as output (income, employment or government revenue) to the change in tourist expenditure.

Therefore, there will be some value by which the initial change in tourist expenditure must be multiplied in order to estimate the total change in output – this is known as the *output multiplier*. In the same way, there will be a value that, when multiplied by the change in tourist expenditure, will estimate the total change in household income – this is known as the *income multiplier*. The reason why the initial change in tourist spending must be subject to a multiplier effect can be seen from Figure 5.1.

Figure 5.1 shows that the tourist expenditure goes, initially, to the front-line tourist establishments that provide the tourists with their goods and services. This money will be re-spent by the firms that receive it. A proportion of the money will leak directly out of the economy in the form of imports and savings (the tan boxes in the diagram). These imports may be in the form of food and beverage that the tourist consumes but are not provided locally, or in respect of services provided to the establishment by individuals or firms located outside the economy being analysed. Where the tourist consumes a product that has been imported into the local economy, they are only consuming the value added (**distributive trade**, importation, transport, local taxes, etc.) rather than the full cost of the product. The money paid to persons outside the economy cannot have any further role in generating economic activity within the local economy and, thus, the value of tourist expenditure that actually circulates in the local economy is immediately reduced. The remaining sum of money will be used to purchase locally produced goods and services, labour and entrepreneurial skills (wages, salaries and profits) and to meet government taxes, licences and fees. These effects are all known as the direct effects.

We can see from Figure 5.1 that money will flow from the tourism-related establishments to other local businesses. This money will also be re-spent, some of it leaking out as imports, some of it leaking out of circulation through savings and some going to the government. The remainder will be spent on labour and entrepreneurial skills and purchases from other

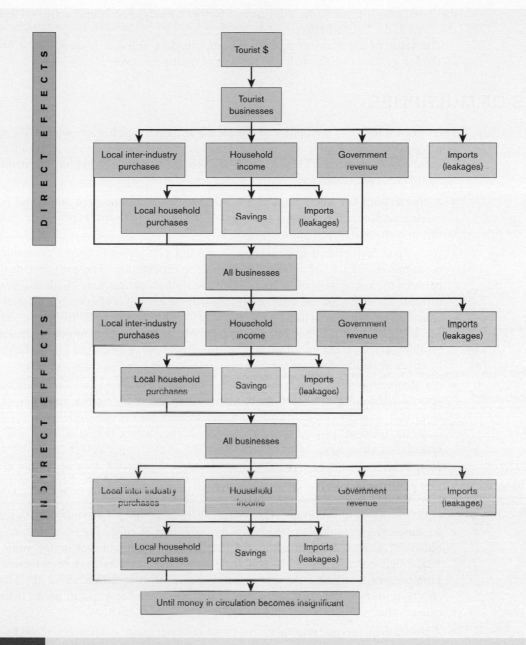

| **Figure 5.1** | The multiplier process |

businesses for goods and services. The businesses that receive money in payment for their goods/services will also make purchases locally, import goods and services and pay government taxes. These effects are known as the indirect effects.

During each round of expenditure, some proportion of money accrues to local residents in the form of income (wages, salaries and profits). Some of this money will be saved (by either households or businesses) and will cease to circulate in the economy, i.e. a leakage. The income that accrues to local households and is not saved will be re-spent. Some of it will leak out of the system as imports and some of it will go to the government as tax. The remainder will be re-spent as household consumption. This spending of income accrued as a result of the initial tourist expenditure will generate further rounds of economic activity – this effect is known as the induced effect.

The value of any tourism multiplier is meaningless unless it is qualified by both the methodology used to estimate it and the type of multiplier involved.

TYPES OF MULTIPLIER

There are a number of multipliers in regular use and each type has its own specific application. However, considerable confusion and misleading conclusions can be derived if they are misused or misinterpreted. This issue will be discussed later in this chapter. The major types of multipliers are as follows:

- A **transactions (or sales) multiplier** that measures the amount of additional business revenue created in an economy as a result of an increase in tourist expenditure. Similar to this in concept is the output multiplier.

- An **output multiplier** that measures the amount of additional output generated in an economy as a result of an increase in tourist expenditure. The principal distinction between the two multipliers is that output multipliers are concerned with changes in the actual levels of production and not with the volume and value of sales. Not all sales will be related to current production (some sales may have been made from inventories and some productive output may not be sold within the time-frame of the model and, therefore, result in an increase in inventories). Therefore, the value of an output multiplier may well be larger or smaller than the value of the corresponding transactions multiplier.

- An **income multiplier** which measures the additional income (wages and salaries, rent, interest and profits) created in the economy as a result of an increase in tourist expenditure. Such income can be measured either as *national income* (*regional* in the case of domestic tourism) or as *disposable income*, i.e. the income that is actually available to households either to spend or to save. However, as mentioned earlier, the income which accrues to non-nationals who have been 'imported' into the area should be excluded because the incomes that they receive cannot be considered to be benefits to the area. On the other hand, the secondary economic effects created by the re-spending of non-nationals' incomes within the area *must* be included within the calculations.

- An **employment multiplier** which is a measurement of either the total amount of employment generated by an additional unit of tourist expenditure or the ratio of the total employment generated by this same expenditure to the direct employment alone. Employment multipliers provide a useful source of information about the secondary effects of tourism, but their measurement involves more heroic assumptions than in the case of other multipliers and care is needed in their interpretation.

- A **government revenue multiplier** that measures the impact on government revenue, from all sources, associated with an increase of tourist expenditure. This multiplier may be expressed in gross terms, that is, the gross increase in government revenue as a result of an increase in tourist spending, or in net terms when the increase in government revenue is reduced by the increase in government expenditures associated with the increase in tourist activity.

Since the different types of multiplier are calculated using the same database they are closely interrelated. However, the concepts involved in each of the above multipliers are very different as are the magnitudes of each of the different multipliers calculated for the same economy. Some examples of these multiplier values are shown later in this chapter. Given the number of different multiplier concepts that are available it is not surprising to find that there has been some confusion over their interpretation. This confusion has been compounded by the fact that there are also a variety of methods that may be used to calculate each of the above multipliers.

METHODOLOGICAL APPROACHES

There are five major techniques that have been employed to measure the economic impact of tourism. Although they are often viewed as alternative approaches by many authors, with the exception of the base theory approach, each of the other methodologies plots out the natural evolution of a single concept as it struggles to overcome the inherent weaknesses and limitations. The five approaches are:

- base theory models;
- Keynesian multiplier models;
- ad hoc models;
- input–output analysis; and
- computable general equilibrium (CGE) models.

Base theory models

The basic assumption underlying base theory models is that there exists a stable relationship between each of the export sectors and the local sectors of an economy, so that changes in the level of tourist expenditure will create predictable and measurable changes in the level of activity in local sectors. An example of this approach is given under the following subheading. Base theory multipliers are normally oversimplified formulations and are now rarely used.

Multiplier analysis using base theory

One early and interesting application of the technique by R.R. Nathan and Associates (1966) was used to calculate the short-run employment effects created by tourism expenditure in each of 375 counties and independent cities of Appalachia. The final model used took the form:

$$\frac{E}{E_{rx2}} = \frac{1}{1 - E_{rc}/E_r} \tag{5.1}$$

where E_r is total local employment, E_{rc} is local employment servicing local consumer demand and E_{rx2} is the direct change in employment created by a change in tourism expenditure.

Nathan Associates developed the multiplier model further, to measure long-term effects, by incorporating investment activity. This model took the form:

$$\frac{E_r}{E_{ix2}} = \frac{1 + i_2}{1 - E_{rc}/E_r} \tag{5.2}$$

where i_2 is a statistically estimated parameter (the value of which lies between 0 and 1) which relates the change in investment to the change in tourism activity.

This model is far too simplistic to be accurate in calculating tourism multiplier values.

Keynesian multiplier models

These multipliers are designed to measure the income created in an economy by an additional unit of tourist expenditure. The Keynesian multipliers were the first rigorous attempt at measuring the economic impact of an **exogenous change in demand**. The simplest formulation of the multiplier (k) is shown in equation (5.3):

$$k = \frac{1}{1 - c + m} \tag{5.3}$$

where 1 is the additional unit of tourism expenditure and leakages are the proportion of this expenditure which goes into savings $(1 - c)$ and imports (m), i.e.:

$$k = \frac{1}{\text{leakages}}$$

To develop this model into a long-term formulation, which takes investment into account, is shown in equation (5.4):

$$k = \frac{1}{1 - c + m - i} \qquad (5.4)$$

where i is the marginal propensity to invest.

Similarly the effects of the re-spending of money accruing to the public sector can be built into the model, and this is shown in equation (5.5):

$$k = \frac{1}{1 - c + m - i - g} \qquad (5.5)$$

where g is the marginal propensity of the public sector to spend.

A typical Keynesian short-term multiplier model is shown in equation (5.6). The derivation of this model is given in Archer (1976):

$$k = \frac{1 - L}{1 - c(1 - t_i)(1 - t_d - b) + m} \qquad (5.6)$$

where L = first round leakages out of the economy, t_i = the marginal rate of indirect taxation, t_d = the marginal rate of taxation and other deductions and b = the marginal rate of transfer payments.

The difference in the value of the multiplier created by applying exactly the same data to the short-term models shown in equations (5.3) and (5.6) highlight the dangers of relying on a model whose structure is too simplistic. For example, if we let $L = 0.5$, $c = 0.9$, $m = 0.7$, $t_i = 0.16$, $t_d = 0.2$ and $b = 0.2$ and calculate the income multipliers using, first, the model shown in equation (5.1) and then, again, using the more developed model shown in equation (5.6), the results are:

$$\frac{1}{1 - c + m} = \frac{1}{1 - 0.9 + 0.7} = 1.25$$

and

$$\frac{1 - L}{1 - c(1 - t_i)(1 - t_d - b) + m} = \frac{1 - 0.5}{1 - 0.9(1 - 0.16)(1 - 0.2 - 0.2) + 0.7} = 0.40$$

The two multiplier values derived from the same database are very different and would result in very different policy implications. However, even the more developed model shown in equation (5.6) is far too simplistic and is unable to measure variations in the form and magnitude of **sectoral linkages** and leakages out of the destination's economy during each round of transactions. Even the most complex and comprehensive Keynesian models developed for some studies are unable to provide the level of detail that is required for policy-making and planning. One practical solution is to use ad hoc models.

Ad hoc *models*

The next step in the evolution of the multiplier approach was intended to overcome the 'broad brush' approach adopted by the Keynesian model wherein each sector was treated in an identical manner. The ad hoc models, although similar in principle to their Keynesian counterparts, are constructed specifically for each particular study. The simplest form of ad hoc model, using matrix algebra, is shown in equation (5.7):

$$A * \frac{1}{1 - BC} \qquad (5.7)$$

where A = the proportion of additional tourist expenditure remaining in the economy after first round leakages, i.e. A equals the $(1 - L)$ expression in the Keynesian model, B = the propensity of local people to consume in the local economy and C = the proportion of expenditure by local people that accrues as income in the local economy.

The ad hoc model shown in equation (5.7) is too simplistic for serious application but more advanced models have been developed and used widely to calculate tourist multipliers to estimate the effect of tourist expenditure on income, public sector revenue, employment and imports. One such model, developed in the early 1970s (Archer and Owen, 1971) is:

$$\sum_{j=1}^{N} \sum_{i=1}^{n} Q_j K_{ij} V_i \frac{1}{1 - c \sum_{i=1}^{n} X_i Z_i V_i} \tag{5.8}$$

where j = each category of tourist j = 1 to N, i = each type of business establishment i = 1 to n, Q_j = the proportion of total tourist expenditure spent by the jth type of tourist, K_{ij} = the proportion of expenditure by the ith type of tourist in the jth category of business, V_i = the direct and indirect income generated by unit of expenditure by the ith type of business, X_i = the pattern of consumption, i.e. the proportion of total consumer expenditure by the residents of the area in the ith type of business, Z_i = the proportion of X_i which takes place within the study area and c = the **marginal propensity to consume**.

The multiplicand equation (5.8) measures the direct and indirect effects of tourist expenditure while the multiplier measures the induced effects. In order to trace the flows of expenditure through successive rounds, separate equations are estimated for a range of V_i values. Examples of these are provided in the literature (see, for example, Archer and Owen, 1971).

Multiplier studies using ad hoc models are commonly used and examples can be found in the USA, the UK, South Pacific islands, Caribbean and elsewhere. More recent models have achieved even greater levels of **disaggregation**, even down to the levels of individual establishments.

Although models of this type can produce a large quantity of detailed and accurate information for policy-making and planning purposes, they are unable to provide the wealth of data yielded by the final methodological approach to be discussed, input–output analysis.

Input–output analysis

In order to overcome the subjectivity inherent in the ad hoc multiplier approach and to provide a more encompassing estimate of economic impact, the multiplier models commonly being used adopted the input–output framework. The input–output model approach presents a general equilibrium, rather than the partial equilibrium approach used in ad hoc models, to studying economic impacts. Input–output analysis begins with the construction of a table, similar to a table of national/regional accounts, which shows the economy of the destination in matrix form. Each sector of the economy is shown in each column as a purchaser of goods and services from other sectors in the economy, and in each row as a seller of output to each of the other sectors. The structure of an input–output table is shown in Figure 5.2. The table may be subdivided into three major quadrants. First, the inter-industry matrix (located in the top left-hand quadrant) details the sales and purchases that take place among the various sectors of the economy (for example, X_{11}, X_{12}, X_{13}, etc. are the sales of sector 1 to all other sectors within the economy, whereas $X_{11}, X_{21}, X_{31}, X_{41}$, etc., represent the purchases of sector 1 from all other sectors within the economy). Secondly, the bottom left-hand quadrant shows each sector's purchases of primary inputs (such as payments to labour, W, profits, P, taxes, T and imported goods and services, M). Thirdly, the right-hand quadrant shows the sales made by each sector to each source of final demand.

The simplest formulation is shown in equations (5.9) and (5.10) where, for ease of explanation, all forms of final demand are represented by a column vector ($\mathbf{Y}$).

SALES TO	INTERMEDIATE DEMAND Productive sectors						FINAL DEMAND Final demand sectors				TOTAL OUTPUT
PURCHASES FROM	Industry						H	I	G	E	
	1	2	3	4	...	m					
Industry 1	X_{11}	X_{12}	X_{13}	X_{14}	...	X_{1m}	C_1	I_1	G_1	E_1	X_1
Industry 2	X_{21}	X_{22}	X_{23}	X_{24}	...	X_{2m}	C_2	I_2	G_2	E_2	X_2
Industry 3	X_{31}	X_{32}	X_{33}	X_{34}	...	X_{3m}	C_3	I_3	G_3	E_3	X_3
Industry 4	X_{41}	X_{42}	X_{43}	X_{44}	...	X_{4m}	C_4	I_4	G_4	E_4	X_4
...	.	.	.	.	...	.	.	.	.	.	.
Industry m	X_{m1}	X_{m2}	X_{m3}	X_{m4}	...	X_{mm}	C_m	I_m	G_m	E_m	X_m
Wages and salaries	W_1	W_2	W_3	W_4	...	W_m	W_C	W_I	W_G	W_E	W
Profits/ dividends	P_1	P_2	P_3	P_4	...	P_m	P_C	P_I	P_G	P_E	P
Taxes	T_1	T_2	T_3	T_4	...	T_m	T_C	T_I	T_G	T_E	T
Imports	M_1	M_2	M_3	M_4	...	M_m	M_C	M_I	M_G	M_E	M
Total inputs	X_1	X_2	X_3	X_4	...	X_m	C	I	G	E	X

where:
X = Output
C = Consumption (households)
I = Investment (private)
G = Government expenditure

E = Exports
M = Imports
W = Wages and salaries
P = Profits and dividends
I = Taxes

Final demand sectors:
H = Household consumption sector
I = Investment expenditure sector
G = Government expenditure sector
E = Exports sectors

Figure 5.2 Basic input–output transactions table

$$X = AX + Y \tag{5.9}$$
$$X - AX = Y$$
$$(I - A)X = Y$$

$$X = (I - A)^{-1}Y$$
$$\Delta X = (I - A)^{-1}\Delta Y \tag{5.10}$$

where X = a vector of the total sales of each sector of the economy, i.e. $[x_1 + x_2 + x_3 + x_4]$, A = a matrix of the inter-industry transactions within the economy, Y = a vector of final demand sales, I = an identity matrix (equivalent to 1 in simple algebra) and Δ = a change in a variable.

A change in the level of final demand (Y) will create an increase in the level of activity within the economy which manifests itself as changes in the output and sales of each sector. Further sub-models are required to calculate the effects on business revenue, public sector revenue, imports, employment and income. The model shown in equation (5.10) is still too simplistic for practical application and must be developed further.

For instance, in the simplified model discussed above, the imports of the economy are shown as a single row vector. However, the robust and flexible framework of input–output models allows the researcher to incorporate a matrix of import functions in order to draw distinctions between competitive and non-competitive imports. This is an extremely useful distinction because competitive imports are, by their very nature, far less predictable than non-competitive imports.

Incorporating an import function matrix which examines the trade-off between domestic production and competitive imports results in equation (5.10) being revised as follows:

$$\Delta X = (I - K^*A)^{-1}\Delta Y \tag{5.11}$$

where K^* = a matrix where the diagonal values reflects the level of competitive imports associated with each sector which, when applied to the A matrix, reduces the domestic component of output by the required amount.

In this manner, changes in primary inputs (ΔP) created by a change in tourist expenditure (ΔT) will be given by:

$$\Delta P = B(I - K^*A)^{-1}\Delta T \tag{5.12}$$

where B = an $m \times n$ matrix of primary inputs.

Furthermore, the input–output model can be developed in order to provide information with respect to changes in employment levels brought about by changes in tourism expenditure. Let ΔL represent the change in employment and E be an $m \times n$ matrix of employment coefficients. The model will now take the form shown in equation (5.13):

$$\Delta L = E(I - K^*A)^{-1}\Delta T \tag{5.13}$$

Using this procedure, the labour usages of each productive sector can be incorporated on either a skill or educational requirement basis and this will allow the multiplier model to provide human resource planning information. Thus, multiplier models can provide information which will inform the future training needs for the destination.

In general, the input–output model can be as comprehensive as data, time and resources allow. Notwithstanding the fact that input–output analysis has been subject to criticism because of its general approach and the aggregation of firms into 'whole industries', the sectors of the model can be disaggregated to achieve the highest level of detail – even down to the level of individual establishments.

There are several weaknesses and limitations apparent with input–output models and most of them are the result of the restrictive assumptions upon which the model is based. For instance, the input–output model as discussed so far implicitly assumes that there are no such things as **supply constraints**. Supply constraints can inhibit the ability of an economy to supply the quantity and quality of goods and services needed to accommodate an increase in tourism expenditure. If capacity is inadequate to meet the additional demand and if insufficient factors of production, especially labour, are available, then additional tourism expenditure creates inflation and additional goods and services may have to be imported. Thus the size of the multiplier, if measured by an appropriate model, will fall. Within the input–output model framework the existence of supply constraints can be incorporated by building in a restrictions matrix that will channel unsupportable supply requirements into the import matrix. Such a way of working around this problem has the disadvantage that it tends to act as a switch in the sense that it will either be 'on' or 'off'. The reality of supply constraints is that there are likely to be some inflationary pressures that build as supply capacity is approached and such inflationary pressures may bring about other undesirable effects on the production function of many sectors within the economy. This is always a problem when the model that is being used is static rather than dynamic.

Most multiplier models are static in nature but can be made dynamic. Static models assume:

- that production and consumption functions are linear and that the intersectoral expenditure patterns are stable;
- that all sectors are able to meet any additional demands for their output; and
- that relative prices remain constant.

The first of these assumptions is that any additional tourism expenditure occurring will generate the same impact on the economy as an equivalent amount of previous tourism expenditure. Thus, any additional production in the economy is assumed to require the purchase of inputs in the same proportions and from the same sources as previously required. Similarly, any consequential increase in consumer demand is assumed to have exactly the same effect upon the economy as previous consumer expenditure. These anomalies arise because of the use of average rather than marginal production coefficients. The difference between the two often comes down to the existence or otherwise of economies of large-scale production and the stability of the production functions themselves.

With respect to the stability of the production functions, tourism, being a labour-intensive personal service, tends to be associated with fairly stable production functions. Thus, the use of average technical coefficients and the assumption of linear homogeneity in production tends not to be a serious drawback when using input–output analysis to study service-based economies. However, the problems of not being able to handle price changes are a major drawback of static systems.

Computable general equilibrium (CGE) models have been developed to overcome some of these limitations.

Computable general equilibrium (CGE) models

Computable general equilibrium models are constructed from a series of relationship equations that are compiled into social accounting matrices. Therefore, if constructed properly, CGE models allow for the effects of interaction between all elements of the economy unlike the input–output models that focus upon the supply side through output changes. For instance, CGEs can allow prices to vary and for resources in an economy to be reallocated from one sector to others. This adds further to the flexibility afforded by input–output analyses. Furthermore, the CGE approach, because it is based upon a series of equations that explain the behaviour of individual sectors that are then simultaneously solved for the economy, means that changes from a wide range of sources (such as tax, price inflation, interest rate, exchange rate changes, etc.) can be analysed. In contrast, the input–output approach is based on looking at the effect of an exogenous change in final demand on each of the different sectors of the economy. Although the addition of the dynamic aspects to the input–output framework are clearly welcome, there is much work to be done before such models can make significant improvements to the accuracy of impact estimates. Inter-regional input–output models have been constructed for many areas, such as that for the United Kingdom in the 1970s. These models incorporate trade flows (goods and services) between the regions and allow the researcher to estimate effects created in one region as a result of changes in another. However, to create realistic models the data requirements are enormous and at the end of the day there has to be some trade-off between accuracy and cost.

WEAKNESSES AND LIMITATIONS OF MULTIPLIER MODELS

Each of the multiplier model approaches outlined above contains several inherent problems that need to be overcome if they are to produce meaningful results. The majority of these problems stem from two distinct areas: the assumptions necessary to apply the models and the data needs.

Restrictive assumptions

Every economic model is founded upon a series of assumptions. The realism of those assumptions is clearly crucial to the model's performance – unrealistic assumptions will provide unrealistic results. During the early attempts at multiplier analysis the assumptions used were very restrictive. Sectors were all assumed to have the same propensities to import, employ labour, pay taxes and they were all assumed to be producing homogeneous output. As the models have become more sophisticated, one by one these assumptions have been replaced with more realistic ones. The homogeneity of output can be overcome by the sectoral disaggregation, the differential needs for imports, tax liabilities and labour requirements can all be catered for within the post-Keynesian model structures. However, the greatest obstacles to improving the accuracy of estimates are found in the dynamics of the model. Most impact models are static in nature, providing a snapshot of an economy at one point in time. If the model is static it will not be able to reflect the effects of changes in relative prices, changes in production and consumption functions as a result of changes in relative prices and/or supply constraints. To build these bridges and enhance the accuracy of the estimates, it is necessary to calculate price and income elasticities of demand and supply, relative returns on investment within dynamic capital markets and the effects of changes in interest and foreign exchange rates. In order to achieve this, it is necessary to know whether each sector is operating close to operational capacity because, as they move towards full capacity, pressure will be placed on the prices of some resources and this will affect other sectors as they compete for resources, and so on. This leads to the second category of problems, that is, those associated with data deficiencies.

Recent attempts to build in such enhanced assumptions by using CGE models have not been too successful in overcoming these weaknesses and limitations. For instance, it is not uncommon for CGE models to assume that economies are always in full equilibrium at all times. This is clearly unrealistic for most economies. Many economies have some unemployment and are not populated by sectors that are all running at full capacity. Therefore models using such an assumption are likely to underestimate the true economic impact of an increase in tourism activities. Furthermore, CGE models tend to be based on assumptions that reflect developed market systems with relative prices constantly adjusting to reflect demand and supply circumstances. This is not always the case and can lead to inaccurate estimates. Finally, as pointed out by authors such as Miller (2002) and Cooper and Wilson (2002), most CGE models are heavily constrained by theory in the way that the dynamics are included and they typically do not perform well when subjected to statistical tests.

Data deficiencies

Secondary data (published and unpublished data) are rarely adequate to meet the requirements of the more demanding and advanced models. This means that researchers need to spend considerable time, effort and money collecting data for multiplier purposes.

Other data difficulties arise out of the nature of tourism itself as a multi-product industry directly affecting a large number of sectors in an economy. Tourist expenditure is spread across several sectors of an economy and accurate surveys of visitor expenditure are required in order to obtain an acceptable breakdown of this expenditure into its various components, e.g. accommodation, meals, beverage, transportation and shopping.

Furthermore, problems often arise when attempting to integrate this visitor expenditure into the categories disaggregated in the input–output table. Rarely are pre-existing input–output tables produced in a form sufficiently disaggregated to accept the detailed data derived from visitor expenditure surveys. In such cases, either the tourist expenditure data have to be compressed to fit the sectors already identified in the input–output table, with a consequent loss in the accuracy of the results, or else much time and effort has to be expended on disaggregating the existing input–output table.

If, however, an input–output (or alternative) model is constructed especially for the study, then the matrix can be arranged in a form which fits the tourist expenditure pattern and the data can be fed directly into the model. The development of the CGE models demonstrates the need to enhance the dynamic nature of the models but adds considerable pressures to the data needs of the models. Rarely do we have sufficient information to calculate the effects of relative price changes on the allocation of resources within an economy. The movement of people from region to region as the relative prosperity of regions changes is, itself, a dynamic event and is determined by a host of economic, social and environmental factors. Foreign exchange rate data need to be considered on a global basis because international tourism is a global industry. Therefore, the data demands associated with making the models dynamic and sensitive to economic interactions between sectors and regions are formidable.

As economic impact models become more sophisticated and are able to reflect some of the dynamic processes it will be possible to estimate the 'net' economic benefits of tourism in a more meaningful way. As with any change in economic output, there is likely to be positive as well as negative economic impacts. To date the negative economic impacts have been sadly neglected by most model structures.

These negative economic impacts can manifest in a number of ways ranging from the misallocation of resources, an increase in the demand for public goods and infrastructure as a result of urbanisation, through to the displacement of existing business.

Negative economic impacts

The production of tourist goods and services requires the commitment of resources that could otherwise be used for alternative purposes. For instance, the development of a tourism resort in Spain may involve the migration of labour from rural to urban areas which brings with it economic implications for both the rural and urban areas – the former losing a productive unit of labour whereas the latter implying additional infrastructure pressure for health, education and other public services. If labour is not in abundance then meeting the tourists' demands may involve the transfer of labour from one industry (such as agriculture or fishing) to tourism industries, involving an opportunity cost that is often ignored in the estimation of tourism's economic impact. Furthermore, if there is a shortage of skilled labour then there may be a need to import labour from other countries such as Morocco and this will result in additional economic leakages as income earned from this imported labour may, in part, be repatriated (**repatriated income**).

Similarly, the use of capital resources (which are often scarce) in the development of tourism-related establishments precludes their use for other forms of economic development. To gain a true picture of the economic impact of tourism it is necessary to take into account the opportunity costs of using scarce resources for tourism development as opposed to alternative uses.

Where tourism development substitutes one form of expenditure and economic activity for another, this is known as the displacement effect. The displacement effect should be taken into account when the economic impact of tourism is being estimated. Displacement can take place when tourism development is undertaken at the expense of another industry and is generally referred to as the opportunity cost of the development. However, it is more commonly referred to when a new tourism project is seen to take away custom from an existing facility. For instance, if a destination such as St Lucia finds that its all-inclusive hotels are running at high occupancy levels and returning a reasonable yield on the investment, the construction of an additional all-inclusive hotel may simply reduce the occupancy levels of the existing establishments. This means that the destination may find that its overall tourism activity has not increased by as much as the new business from the development. This is displacement.

The size of multiplier values

The size of multiplier values will vary under different circumstances because it is dependent upon the patterns of tourist expenditure, the nature of an area's economy and the extent to which the various sectors of the economy are linked in their trading patterns.

A large number of tourism multiplier studies have been carried out since the 1960s. Table 5.5 shows the range of values of tourism output multipliers for a selection of industrialised countries, US states, cities and rural areas. The figures are provided only to give an indicative

Table 5.5	The range value of tourism output multipliers for selected destinations

Country or region	Tourism output multiplier
Medium to large industrialised economies	2.00–3.40
Selection of US states	1.57–2.20
City/urban economies	1.24–1.51
Rural area economies	1.12–1.35

Source: Compiled by the author from published articles and unpublished reports to governments

view of the relative size of output multipliers. Of course, the values will also depend upon the methodology used to calculate them and the following multiplier values were derived from the average of studies that used the unorthodox multiplier (output change as a result of a change in tourist expenditure) at the direct, indirect and induced level, using input–output analysis.

For policy-making and planning purposes, income multipliers are often seen to be the most useful because they provide information about national or local income rather than merely business output or turnover. Table 5.6 shows the range of income multiplier values for a variety of types of destinations. Care must be taken when comparing multiplier values between countries. First, the analyses may be undertaken over different time periods and, even though multiplier values tend not to be subject to drastic changes even over two decades, they do tend to increase as economies develop and improve their sectoral linkages. Secondly, and more importantly, using the different methodologies can make a significant difference to the values. For instance, input–output models, because they are based upon a general equilibrium approach, tend to yield significantly higher multiplier values than ad hoc models and, depending upon the level of comprehensiveness and detail achieved in the ad hoc models, this difference may be as high as 30%. It has been suggested that input–output based multipliers often return higher multiplier values than their CGE counterparts (Dwyer et al., 2003) because they may not pick up the negative effects created by relative price changes or demand displacement. However, there is a tendency for CGE models to underestimate the economic impact of tourism when they are based on assumptions of full capacity and market equilibrium.

It is also noticeable from Table 5.6 that the size of the income multiplier values tends to be correlated with the size of the economy. In general, the larger the economy, the higher will be the multiplier value, although there will obviously be some exceptions to this. The reason for this correlation is that larger economies tend to have a more developed economic structure which means that they have stronger intersectoral linkages and lower propensities to import in order to meet the demands of tourists, the tourist industry, non-tourist industries

Table 5.6	The range of tourism income multipliers for selected types of destinations

Country or region	Income multiplier
National economies	1.23–1.98
Small island economies	0.39–1.59
US states and counties	0.44–1.30
UK regions and counties	0.29–0.47
UK cities and towns	0.19–0.40

Source: Compiled by the author from published articles and unpublished government reports

and the local population. The higher the propensity to import in order to meet local and tourist demand, the lower the income multiplier.

In addition to calculating the levels of output, income, employment and government revenue generated by additional units of tourist expenditure, multiplier analysis provides valuable information concerning its impact on a country's net foreign exchange flows. The impact model can be used to determine not only the direct import requirements necessary to meet the tourists' demands but also the indirect and induced imports required or generated as a result of the initial tourist expenditure. When all import requirements are summed and deducted from the international tourist expenditure the result will be the net foreign exchange flow. This can be further explored by examining the expenditure of local people when travelling abroad and a travel and tourism trade balance can be calculated.

The multipliers most vulnerable to criticism (and inaccuracies) are the employment multipliers. Therefore great care must be exercised in their interpretation. The data used for their measurement and the assumptions underlying the model constructions are more heroic for employment than for any other type of effect. The two major problems relate to the fact that:

- in the majority of studies employment is assumed to have a linear relationship with either income or output, whereas the available evidence suggests that this relationship is non-linear; and
- multiplier models assume that employment in each sector is working at full capacity, so that to meet any increase in demand will require additional employment. In practice, this is unlikely to be true and increases (or decreases) in the level of tourist expenditure will not generate a corresponding increase (or decrease) in the number of people employed.

In consequence, tourism employment multipliers should be interpreted as only an *indication* of the number of full-time equivalent (FTE) job opportunities supported by changes in tourist expenditure. Whether or not these job opportunities will materialise depends upon a number of factors, most notably the extent to which the existing labour force in each sector is fully utilised, and the degree to which labour is able to transfer between different occupations and between different sectors of the economy.

Table 5.7 shows the employment multipliers for several countries and regions. We can see that these employment multipliers are of a different magnitude from those relating to either output or income. This reflects the need for considerably larger amounts of tourist spending to generate one new full-time equivalent job opportunity.

Unlike the income and output multipliers, it is not possible to compare employment multipliers between different destinations when they are presented in this form. This is because the table figures show the number of full-time equivalent job opportunities created by 10,000 units of tourist expenditure where that unit is expressed in the local currency. Thus, differences in the unit value of local currencies will provide employment multipliers of different

Table 5.7	Tourism employment multipliers for selected destinations per 10,000 units of tourist expenditure (i.e. dollars, pounds or lira)

Country/city	Employment multiplier
Bermuda	0.44
Fiji	0.79
Jamaica	1.28
Malta	1.59
UK (Edinburgh)	0.37

Table 5.8	Standardised employment multipliers for selected destinations

Country	Employment multiplier
Jamaica	4.61
Mauritius	3.76
Bermuda	3.02
Gibraltar	2.62
Solomon Islands	2.58
Malta	1.99
Western Samoa	1.96
Republic of Palau	1.67

magnitudes. A more sensible way of making international comparisons of employment multipliers is to express them as a ratio of total employment generated to direct employment. Examples of this latter type of employment multiplier are shown in Table 5.8.

Table 5.8 shows that in Jamaica, for every new full-time employee directly employed as a result of an increase in tourist expenditure, a further 4.61 full-time equivalent job opportunities are created throughout the Jamaican economy. Again, we can see that the more developed the tourism economy, the larger the employment multiplier.

THE POLICY IMPLICATIONS OF MULTIPLIER ANALYSIS

Tourism multipliers measure the present economic performance of the tourism industry and the short term economic effects of a change in the level or pattern of tourism expenditure. They are particularly suitable for studying the impact of tourist expenditure on business turnover, incomes, employment, public sector revenue and the balance of payments.

In the 1970s some economists argued strongly in favour of rejecting multiplier analysis as an appropriate technique for studying impact on the grounds that these models yield 'no useful guideline to policy-makers as regards the merits of tourism compared with alternatives' (Bryden, 1973: 217), yet a number of writers have shown that this is precisely the type of information which multiplier analysis can provide in a short term context. For example, Diamond (1976) used an input–output model of the Turkish economy to measure sectoral output multipliers (for tourism and other sectors) in relation to four policy objectives that reflected Turkish planning priorities. His work demonstrated that multiplier analysis deals effectively with problems associated with short-term resource allocation.

Resource allocation is not the primary use of multiplier analysis. The technique is most frequently used to examine short-term economic impacts where policy objectives other than the efficiency of resource allocation are considered important. A detailed input–output or CGE model, for example, can yield valuable information about the structure of an economy, the degree to which sectors within the economy are dependent upon each other, the existence of possible supply constraints and the relative capital and labour intensities of each sector.

Detailed multiplier models are suitable for:

- analysing the national or regional effects of public or private sector investment in tourism projects;
- simulating the economic impact, sector by sector, of any proposed tourism developments and hence determining the future requirements of factors of production, such as labour needs;

MINI CASE STUDY 5.2
Tourism satellite accounts for Namibia 2004–6

| Table 5.9 | Tourism satellite accounts for Namibia 2004–6 |

Travel and Tourism	N$m and (% of National Accounts)		
	2004	2005 (estimated)	2006 (estimated)
Personal travel and tourism	2 137.09 (11.11%)	2 299.11 (11.33%)	2 529.17 (11.41%)
Business travel and tourism	501.68	515.41	561.59
Corporate	371.30	392.81	430.94
Government	130.38	122.60	130.65
Government expenditure – individual	10.55	12.06	13.23
Visitor exports	2 915.23	3 584.51	4 192.26
Travel and tourism consumption	5 564.56	6 411.10	7 296.26
Government expenditure collective	246.32 (2.84%)	259.70 (2.85%)	284.91 (2.86%)
Capital investment	955.43 (10.29%)	1 174.47 (11.99%)	1 311.97 (12.26%)
Exports (non-visitor)	195.67 (17.90%)	206.70 (20.03%)	225.81 (21.04%)
Travel and tourism demand	6 961.98	8 051.96	9 118.94
Travel and tourism direct impact only Employment ('000) and (% of total)	17.96 (4.66%)	18.34 (4.66%)	18.84 (4.69%)
Gross Domestic Product (direct impact only)	**1 240.06** **(3.36%)**	**1 372.41** **(3.52%)**	**1 584.23** **(3.72%)**

Source: WTTC, *Namibia, The Impact of Travel and Tourism on Jobs and the Economy*, 2006

DISCUSSION QUESTIONS

1. Why do we need to measure the significance of tourism economic activity?

2. If the individual components that make up the data required to create a set of tourism satellite accounts are examined it can be seen that, even with a standardised system in place (and adhered to) there are many problems in achieving consistency. What are these flaws and how can they be addressed?

3. The data that are used to construct the satellite accounts are, in practice, variable from destination to destination and sometimes foreign data and relationships are 'imported' to fill information gaps. Is this a valid way of filling information gaps and what are the dangers of adopting this approach?

- examining the relative magnitudes of the impacts made by different types of tourism and by tourism compared with other sectors of the economy; and
- identifying the optimal tourism mix (those associated with relatively high net benefits).

For instance, a tourism input–output study of Jamaica examined the economic impact of tourism expenditure by purpose of visit, winter or summer visit, first and repeat visit in order to determine which tourists generated the highest level of income, employment and government revenue per unit of expenditure. This type of information can be used to target future marketing in order to maximise the desired benefits derived from tourism activity.

CONCLUSION

The economic impact of tourism on a host economy is generally positive but also carries with it some negative aspects. The literature is biased towards the positive aspects of economic impacts. It is important to establish how significant tourism spending is to an economy because this allows policy makers and planners to determine dependency and to develop strategies for the future. Of particular note is the fact that tourism spending tends to take place between the richer, industrialised countries rather than between industrialised and non-industrialised countries.

Tourism satellite accounts have been derived in order to present a clearer picture of the economic significance of tourism to a given destination. Built along similar lines to national accounts, such tables provide insight into the contribution that tourism makes towards gross national product and the proportion of demand that is attributable to tourism activity. Such tables tend to be based around input–output models in order to provide an accurate picture. However, they are not impact models and further analyses are required in order to determine optimal policy decisions.

There have been a variety of attempts to develop models that will estimate the economic impact of tourism but only the ad hoc, input–output and CGE models are of sufficient accuracy and of policy use. The input–output and CGE methods provide the most comprehensive picture of tourism's economic impacts and also information that is useful to the tourism development planners. However, these models are also the most expensive type of impact model. The input–output methodology provides income, employment and government revenue multipliers as well as demonstrating the import requirements per unit of tourist spending. All of these different forms of economic impacts can be estimated at the direct, direct plus indirect and direct plus indirect plus induced levels of impact. This information has been successfully used to target market segments in order to enhance the economic benefits associated with tourist spending. Recent developments in the estimation of tourism impact analyses includes the combining of economic, environmental and social impact models with forecasting techniques in order to provide a comprehensive planning tool. There are weaknesses associated with economic impact models but most of these can be alleviated by the adoption of various procedures.

SELF-CHECK QUESTIONS

1. Identify two policy areas that can be informed by knowing the (a) economic significance and (b) the economic impact of tourism.
2. Identify five different methods used to measure the economic impact of tourism.
3. Identify five different multipliers that can be derived from economic impact models.
4. What are the three different levels of economic impact in an economy?
5. What are the major areas of weaknesses in economic impact models?

ESSAY QUESTIONS

1. Can tourism satellite accounts provide meaningful information for policy makers that cannot be provided by economic impact models?

2. Examine the relative advantages and disadvantages of each of the major types of tourism economic impact models.

3. What are the limitations and weaknesses of existing tourism economic impact models and how may some of them be overcome?

4. Given the reliability of tourism-related statistics, is it realistic to believe that the adoption of tourism satellite accounts will achieve the consistency and comparability that is the prime objective underlying their implementation?

5. What is the relationship between tourism satellite accounts and tourism economic impact models?

ANNOTATED FURTHER READING

Books

Bull, A. (1998) *The Economics of Travel and Tourism*, Longman, Sydney.
An introductory text that covers many aspects relating to the economics of tourism.

Jafari, J. (2001) *The Encyclopedia of Tourism*, Routledge, London.
A comprehensive volume with definitive statements on every tourism term written by the leading expert in each field.

Sinclair, T. and Stabler, M. (1997) *The Economics of Tourism*, Routledge, London.
A text that covers a broad range of economic aspects relating to tourism.

Articles

Dwyer, L., Forsyth, P., Spurr, R. and VanHo, T. (2003) 'Tourism's contribution to a state economy: a multi-regional general equilibrium analysis', *Tourism Economics* 9(4), 431–48.
An examination of a recent multiplier application.

Frechtling, D. (1999) 'The tourism satellite account: foundations, progress and issues', *Tourism Management* 20(1), 163–70.
This article outlines the concepts and coverage of TSA and how it expands the scope of traditional tourism analysis. It outlines how the results may be employed in these analyses and explores the major issues of developing the TSA concepts and measurement techniques.

Jones, C., Munday, M. and Roberts, A. (2003) 'Regional tourism satellite accounts: a useful policy tool?', *Urban Studies* 40(13), 2777–94.
The authors examine some of the methodological difficulties in constructing a TSA at the regional level and the implications for deriving an effective tourism policy from such models.

Web sites

http://www.euromonitor.com
Euromonitor International (2007)

http://www.imfstatistics.org/imf
International Monetary Fund data and statistics

www.oecd.org

The OECD web site provides information covering the economic indicators relating to OECD members; it also provides information on a variety of economic policies.

http://www.world-tourism.org

The UN World Tourism Organization provides an overview of the current state of international tourism through its tourism highlights as well as a catalogue of its publications and online data. In addition it provides viewpoints and summaries on a variety of tourism issues.

http://www.world-tourism.org/sustainable/concepts.htm

WTO Manila Declaration, 1980.

References cited and bibliography

Archer, B.H. (1976) 'The anatomy of a multiplier', *Regional Studies* 10, 71–7.

Archer, B.H. (1982) 'The value of multipliers and their policy implications', *Tourism Management* 3(2), 236–41.

Archer, B.H. and Fletcher, J.E. (1990) *Multiplier Analysis*, Les Cahiers du Tourisme, Series C, No. 130, April.

Archer, B.H. and Owen, C. (1971) 'Towards a tourist regional multiplier', *Regional Studies* 5, 289–94.

Bryden, J.M. (1973) *Tourism and Development: A Case Study in the Commonwealth Caribbean*, Cambridge University Press, Cambridge.

Cooper, A. and Wilson, A. (2002) 'Extending the relevance of TSA research for the UK: general equilibrium and spillover analysis', *Tourism Economics* 8(1), 5–38.

Diamond, J. (1976) 'Tourism and development policy: a quantitative appraisal', *Bulletin of Economic Research* 28(1), 36–50.

Dwyer, L., Forsyth, P., Spurr, R. and VanHo, T. (2003) 'Tourism's contribution to a state economy: a multi-regional general equilibrium analysis', *Tourism Economics* 9(4), 431–48.

Fletcher, J.E. (1989) 'Input–output analysis and tourism impact studies', *Annals of Tourism Research* 16(4), 541–56.

Fletcher, J.E. and Archer, B.H. (1991) 'The development and application of multiplier analysis', pp. 28–47, in Cooper, C. (ed.), *Progress in Tourism, Recreation and Hospitality Management*, Vol. 3, Belhaven, London.

Fletcher, J.E. and Snee, H.R. (1985) 'The need for output measurements in the service industries: a comment', *Services Industries Journal*, 5(1), 73–8.

Fletcher, J.E. and Snee, H.R. (1985) 'The service industries and input–output analysis', *Service Industries Review* 2(1), 51–79.

Leontief, W. (1966) *Input–Output Economics*, Oxford University Press, New York.

Miller, R. (2002) Preface to Cooper, A. and Wilson, A., *Tourism Economics* 8(1), 5–38.

Milne, S.S. (1987) 'Differential multipliers', *Annals of Tourism Research* 14(4), 499–515.

OECD (2001) *National Accounts*, OECD, Paris.

Sinclair, M.T. and Sutcliffe, C.M.S. (1982) 'Keynesian income multipliers with first and second round effects: an application to tourist expenditure', *Oxford Bulletin of Economics and Statistics* 44(4), 321–38.

TCSP (1992) *The Economic Impact of International Tourism on the National Economy of Fiji*, a report published by the Tourism Council for the South Pacific, Suva, Fiji.

UNWTO (2007) *Yearbook of Tourism Statistics*, UNWTO, Madrid.

Wanhill, S.R.C. (1988) 'Tourism multipliers under capacity constraints', *Service Industries Journal* 8(1), 136–42.

WTO (1980a) *Manila Declaration on World Tourism*, WTO, Madrid.

WTO (1980b) *Tourism and Employment: Enhancing the Status of Tourism Professions*, WTO, Madrid.

WTO (1988) *Yearbook of Tourism Statistics*, WTO, Madrid.

WTO (1992, 1997, 2002a) *Yearbook of Tourism Statistics*, WTO, Madrid.

WTO (2000b) *The Tourism Satellite Account (TSA): A Strategic Project for the World Tourism Organization*, Report by the Secretary-General, Madrid, November 2000.

WTO (2003) *Yearbook of Tourism Statistics*, WTO, Madrid.

WTTC (2006) 'The impact of travel and tourism on jobs and economy', available from http://www.oxfordeconomics.com/OE_Tourism.asp#

MAJOR CASE STUDY 5.1
Tourism and day visitors to Gibraltar

Tourist and day visitor activity in Gibraltar includes staying visitors, cruise ship passengers and daytrippers across the land frontier. Gibraltar has become a shopping destination and the vast majority of visitors (arriving at the land frontier) do so to make purchases from retail outlets. In the year 2006 the total tourist expenditure was £210.5 million of which more than £160 million was on various forms of shopping.

The average party size of people visiting Gibraltar was 2.0 for those arriving by air and 2.5 for excursionists arriving from Spain. Although those arriving by air tended to stay on average for 4 days, the average length of stay for visitors to Gibraltar overall is very low because of the dominance of excursionists from Spain. The day visitor content is also reflected in the fact that the two largest spending categories are shopping and duty free.

Staying visitors (the more traditional form of tourist activity) were responsible for just over £34.05 million expenditure. Day visitors from across the land frontier were responsible for more than £167.15 million and the remaining expenditure was split between cruise ship visitors (£8.07 million), yacht visitors (£470,000) and transit visitors (£760,000).

Tourist expenditure by port of entry provides a similar picture with the tourist expenditure by each entry point being:

Air	£34.810	million
Sea	£8.540	million
Land	£167.150	million

Total tourist expenditure (£210.5 million) is associated with the following effects:

Direct income = £54.600 million
Direct plus indirect income = £88.032 million
Direct plus indirect plus induced = £197.331 million

Direct employment = 1,799 FTEs
Direct plus indirect employment = 2,674 FTEs
Direct plus indirect plus induced employment = 3,383 FTEs

(Note: The job and income effects are distributed across all of the sectors of the Gibraltar economy as the effects of tourist expenditure impact on virtually every area of productivity (directly and indirectly).)

Direct government revenue = £17.677 million
Direct plus indirect government revenue = £26.364 million
Direct plus indirect plus induced government revenue = £53.191 million

Direct import requirements = £93.892 million
Direct plus indirect import requirements = £116.417 million
Direct plus indirect plus induced import requirements = £155.907 million

The largest single component of tourist expenditure was attributable to those visitors arriving by land, where 7.815 million visitors spent £167.2 million. A major proportion of their total expenditure was on retail shopping. This is clearly a major export for Gibraltar and the direct level of income generated by day visitor spending amounts to £38.025 million, which increases to £63.151 million when the indirect effect is taken into consideration. This level of economic activity directly supports 1,143 FTE job opportunities and this together with the economic activity stimulated by it supports a total of 2,300 FTE job opportunities.

The government revenue derived from day visitor spending amounted to £14.579 million at the direct level and when the indirect and induced effects are taken into account this figure rises to £40.044. The amount of imports required to meet the demands of this

Photograph 5.2   Tourism on the Rock of Gibraltar.
Source: Courtesy of Government of Gibraltar

activity are £83.257 million directly; this goes up to £127.387 million when the indirect and induced effects are included.

THE VALUE OF TOURISM TO THE ECONOMY

Tourism has always been an important source of exports for Gibraltar. However, since the land frontier with Spain has been opened the economy's tourism industry has flourished. Visitors not only come to stay in Gibraltar but they also come as excursionists to explore the sights and heritage and also to shop.

Tourism in Gibraltar has changed beyond recognition compared with its performance in the 1970s and 1980s. The opening of the frontier with Spain has considerably altered both the volume and pattern of tourist spending.

The number of visitors to Gibraltar arriving by air in 1974 was 53,399 (38% of total arrivals). This figure was relatively stable through to the mid-1980s whereafter it grew rapidly, to a peak of 162,438 in 1989 and then fell, just as rapidly, down to a low of 66,219 in

1996 after which it has been growing steadily to the current level of visitors (143,914) in 2006 (just 1.76% of total arrivals). In contrast, the number of visitors arriving by sea was relatively stable through the period 1970 (92,943 – 78.7% of total arrivals) to the mid-1990s, but has shown a relatively steady increase from 1997 onwards accounting for 225,567 in 2006. The major impact has been the change in the volume of visitors arriving by land. In 1970 this was zero as the frontier was closed between Gibraltar and Spain. In 1982 with limited access across the border the figure was 46,595 and this figure grew rapidly with the relaxation of border restrictions, to a stable base of 2,260,039 in 1985. Cross-frontier traffic has grown steadily since that time and the 2006 figure was 7,815,661 or 95.5% of total arrivals.

Clearly such a major change in the shift away from the proportion of staying visitors arriving by air and sea in favour of day visitors crossing the frontier has changed the pattern of spend associated with visitors to Gibraltar. The volume and value of day visitors across the land frontier dominates the tourism statistics. This can be seen from the various tables shown

Table 5.10	Total tourist expenditure by category of spend, 2006

	% of total
Accommodation, food and beverage	16.6
Shopping	71.4
Transport etc.	4.7
Other	7.4
Total	**100.0**

Table 5.12	Tourist expenditure, day visitors to Gibraltar, 2006

	% of total
Accommodation, food and beverage	5.5
Shopping	86.5
Transport etc.	4.4
Other	3.6
Total	**100.0**

where items such as purchases of food and beverage, petrol, other shopping and duty free are significant elements of total expenditure. On the other hand, accommodation costs have become a minor part of the total tourist expenditure pattern.

The breakdown of tourist expenditure by type is shown in Table 5.10: it can be seen that shopping in total accounts for 79% of the total expenditure if the duty free and fuel sales are included under this heading and this further increases to more than 80.0% if the food and beverages bought in shops is included.

Table 5.10 shows how the £210.5 million total tourist expenditure in 2006 was distributed across the various categories. The importance of shopping and shopping-related activities is clear from this breakdown and once the different types of tourists are examined it can be seen that this influence is from the large number of land-based day visitors.

STAYING VISITORS

Staying visitors in general spend around half of their total expenditure on accommodation and meals. Gibraltar is not an exception to this rule and some 52.2% of total spending was attributable to these two categories (see Table 5.11).

Table 5.11	Staying visitors, 2006

	% of total
Accommodation, food and beverage	52.2
Shopping	25.2
Transport etc.	5.5
Other	17.1
Total	**100.0**

DAY VISITORS

The dominance of the day visitor to Gibraltar means that the total expenditure pattern of all tourists to Gibraltar reflects the day visitor pattern. It is a quite distinct pattern, with shopping accounting for more than 86.5% of total spend. Given the volume of day trip visitors to Gibraltar this represents a significant amount of trade (see Table 5.12).

MULTIPLIER VALUES

The multiplier values associated with each form of economic activity within the Gibraltar economy are set out in Table 5.13. These are partial multiplier values in that they reflect the ability of each sector to generate output, income and government revenue. These values should not be viewed judgementally. Variations between the direct, indirect and induced levels of income, government revenue or import impacts associated with one unit of output can be a result of many factors including the nature of the production function. For instance, the construction industry has a relatively high propensity to import because it imports the majority of its material inputs and these account for a large proportion of its total inputs. However, other sectors may import through wholesalers and this is reflected in the high import value of the wholesale sector. Labour-intensive sectors are likely to have higher than average income effects and those sectors that attract particular taxes and excise duties may be associated with high government revenue multipliers.

Table 5.13 shows the direct plus indirect plus induced multiplier values, by sector within Gibraltar in 2000. As production functions and spending patterns tend to change slowly over time the values shown may be considered to be valid for up to a decade (assuming no drastic changes are made to the economic structure). The multiplier values associated with external

Table 5.13	Direct plus indirect plus induced multiplier values (partial)			
Sector	Output	Income	Government revenue	Imports
Manufacturing	1.5259	0.8048	0.2343	0.6328
Electricity and water	2.1047	0.9495	0.3257	0.6478
Construction	1.5403	0.4925	0.2317	0.8375
Wholesale	1.4430	0.4976	0.2740	0.7186
Retail	1.6683	0.5639	0.2429	0.7019
Hotels	2.1224	0.9761	0.3167	0.4873
Restaurants	2.0259	1.0158	0.3057	0.4491
Transport	1.3677	0.5113	0.1446	0.6854
Communications	1.7403	0.8690	0.3711	0.5726
Financial services	1.3179	0.6697	0.1001	0.5001
Real estate and business services	1.7782	1.1678	0.3065	0.3551
Government and welfare services	2.1806	1.2953	0.5606	0.4835
Other services	1.7425	0.9588	0.3090	0.5532

Table 5.14	Direct plus indirect plus induced multiplier values (complete)			
Sector	Output	Income	Government revenue	Imports
Tourism	1.7013	0.6294	0.2492	0.6678
Financial services	1.3179	0.6697	0.1001	0.5001
Other exports	1.4430	0.4976	0.2740	0.7186
Total	1.4657	0.5869	0.2105	0.6341

trade may be considered to be complete multipliers and will differ from those shown in Table 5.13.

The income multiplier for tourism expenditure, at 0.6294, places Gibraltar in the lower half of the small island economies (0.39 to 1.59) range of income multipliers shown in Table 5.6. This is not surprising given the very small size of Gibraltar (see Table 5.14).

DISCUSSION QUESTIONS

1. 'The fact that some sectors have higher income and employment multipliers than others means that governments should only encourage investment in those sectors that have high multiplier values.' Discuss.

2. Why do the complete multipliers differ from the partial multipliers?

3. How can you use this type of multiplier information for future tourism planning?

4. What limitations and words of caution should be applied to the results shown above?

5. What other information do you need to make the above more useful for the policy makers?

CHAPTER 6
The Environmental Impact of Tourism

LEARNING OUTCOMES

The objective of this chapter is to provide you with:

- an understanding of the physical impacts of tourism on the environment, both direct and indirect, positive and negative;

- a review of strategies and techniques that may be implemented to measure and quantify the impacts of tourism on the environment such as environmental impacts assessment;

- an appreciation of the difficulties of assessing environmental impacts; and

- real-life examples to encourage the application of theory to practice.

Photograph: Serengeti National Park, Tanzania/Kenya © Hannah Cox

INTRODUCTION

Any form of industrial development will bring with it impacts upon the physical environment in which it takes place. In view of the fact that tourists must visit the place of production in order to consume the output, it is inevitable that tourism activity will be associated with environmental impacts. The identification of the need to follow an environmentally compatible pattern of tourism development is now well into its third decade but in spite of the fact that environmental issues are high profile, little has been achieved to ensure that future developments are environmentally sound.

ENVIRONMENTAL IMPACT

At the end of the 1970s the OECD set out a framework for the study of environmental stress created by tourism activities. This framework highlighted four main categories of stressor activities including permanent environmental restructuring (major construction works such as highways, airports and resorts); waste product generation (biological and non-biological waste which can damage fish production, create health hazards and detract from the attractiveness of a destination); direct environmental stress caused by tourist activities (destruction of coral reefs, vegetation, dunes, etc. by the presence and activities of tourists); effects on the population dynamics (migration, increased urban densities accompanied by declining populations in other rural areas).

In 1992, the United Nations Conference on the Environment and Development, held in Rio de Janeiro, added further impetus to a debate that was growing stale and a new maxim emerged where 'Only whatever can be sustained by nature and society in the long term is permissible'. This new impetus was given the title Agenda 21 to reflect the fact that it was a policy statement aimed at taking the world into the twenty-first century. What made Agenda 21 significant was the fact that it represented the first occasion when a comprehensive programme of environmental actions was agreed to be adopted by 182 governments. The Agenda was based around a framework of themes that were aimed at providing an overall strategy to transform global activity onto a more sustainable course. The matters addressed within Agenda 21 were not solely environmental because they included aspects such as human development and the redressing of the imbalance between rich and poor nations. However, many of the matters discussed and the strategies recommended were environmentally based.

Now, in the twenty-first century and in spite of the programme's elegance and simplicity, the adoption of this maxim requires enforcement that is still far beyond the reach of most legislative frameworks and none of the recommendations made in Agenda 21 were legally binding to the 182 nations that approved its adoption. Furthermore, the implementation of this maxim requires that those charged with the construction of the necessary legislative framework be fully informed of the environmental repercussions of productive and consumptive activities. To date this is not the case. The literature on the environmental impacts of tourism is often biased, painting highly negative pictures of tourism with respect to its associated environmental impacts. In this chapter we examine the nature of environmental impacts, how they can be identified and measured and how this information can be integrated into the tourism planning process.

Tourism and the environment

The environment, whether it is natural or artificial, is the most fundamental ingredient of the tourism product. However, as soon as tourism activity takes place, the environment is

inevitably changed or modified either to facilitate tourism or through the tourism production process. Environmental preservation and improvement programmes are now an integral part of many **development strategies** and such considerations are treated with much
greater respect than they were during the first two-thirds of the last century. Relatively little
research has been undertaken within a standardised framework to analyse tourism's impact
on the environment. The **empirical studies** that have taken place have been very specific case
studies – such as the impact of tourism on the wildlife of Africa, the pollution of water in the
Mediterranean or studies of particular coastal areas and mountains. But the diverse areas
studied, the varying methods used to undertake those studies and the wide range of tourism
activities involved makes it difficult to bring these findings together in order to assemble a
comprehensive standardised framework within which to work.

In order to study the physical impact of tourism it is necessary to establish:

- the physical impacts created by tourism activity as opposed to other activities;
- what conditions were like before tourism activity took place in order to derive a baseline
  from which comparisons can be made;
- an inventory of flora and fauna, together with some unambiguous index of tolerance
  levels to the types of impact created by different sorts of tourism activity; and
- the secondary levels of environmental impact that are associated with tourism activity.

The environmental impacts associated with tourism development, just like the economic
impacts, can be considered in terms of their direct, indirect and induced effects. Again some
of the impacts can be positive and some negative. It is not possible to develop tourism without incurring environmental impacts, but it is possible, with correct planning, to manage
tourism development in order to minimise the negative impacts while at the same time
encouraging the positive impacts.

Positive environmental impacts

On the positive side, the direct environmental impacts associated with tourism include:

- the preservation/restoration of ancient monuments, sites and historic buildings, such as
  the Great Wall of China (PRC), the Pyramids (Egypt), the Taj Mahal (India), Stonehenge
  and Warwick Castle (UK);
- the creation of national parks and wildlife parks, such as Yellowstone Park (USA), the
  Amboseli National Park and the Maasai Mara National Reserve (Kenya), Las Canadas
  (Tenerife), the Pittier National Park (Venezuela), Fjord Land National Park (New Zealand);
- protection of reefs and beaches, such as the Great Barrier Reef (Australia), Grand Anse
  (Grenada); and
- the maintenance of forests, such as the New Forest (UK), Colo I Suva (Fiji).

Conservation and **preservation** may be rated highly from the point of view of researchers,
or even the tourists. However, if such actions are not considered to be of importance from
the hosts' point of view, it may be questionable as to whether they can be considered to be
positive environmental impacts. When evaluating the net worth of preservation and conservation activities the opportunity costs associated with such activities must also be taken into
account. African wildlife parks, such as Etosha National Park in Namibia, may result in the
grazing lands of nomadic tribes being limited and hence constrain food production capability.

Negative environmental impacts

On the negative side, tourism may have direct environmental impacts on the quality of water,
air and noise levels. Sewage disposal into water will add to pollution problems, as will the use
of powered boats on inland waterways and sheltered seas. Increased usage of the internal

combustion engine for tourist transport, oil burning to provide the power for hotels' air conditioning and refrigeration units all add to the diminution of air quality. Noise levels may be dramatically increased in urban areas through nightclubs and other forms of entertainment as well as by increased road, rail and air traffic.

Physical deterioration of both natural and built environments can have serious consequences:

- hunting and fishing have obvious impacts on the wildlife environment;
- sand dunes can be damaged and eroded by over-use;
- vegetation can be destroyed by walkers;
- camp fires may destroy forests;
- ancient monuments may be disfigured and damaged by graffiti, eroded or literally taken away by tourists (the Byzantine Fort in Paphos, Cyprus, for instance, is a World Heritage Site subject to pilfering);
- the construction of a tourism superstructure utilises real estate and may detract from the aesthetics; and
- the improper disposal of litter can detract from the aesthetic quality of the environment and harm wildlife.

Examples of direct negative environmental impacts include:

- the erosion of paths to the Pyramids at Giza, Egypt by the camels used to transport tourists;
- the dynamiting of Balaclava Bay (Mauritius) to provide a beach for tourist use; and
- the littering of Base Camp on Mount Everest, Nepal by tourists and the erosion of the pathway to this site.

The building of high-rise hotels on beach frontages is an environmental impact of tourism that achieves headline status. This kind of obvious environmental rape is now less common than it was during the rapid growth periods of the 1960s and 1970s. In a number of countries, particularly island economies, the issue of land usage is often high on the agenda of planning meetings. Regulations have been introduced to restrict beachfront developments to a height no greater than that of the palm trees (as for example in Mauritius), or restrict development to a certain distance back from the beach (as in some parts of India).

Tourism activities can put scarce natural resources, such as water, under severe pressure. Tourists tend to be far more extravagant with their use of water than they are at home with estimates of up to 440 litres per person per day being made for areas around the Mediterranean. To put this into context, this is up to twice the normal usage of residents in urban areas of Spain or Italy. Some activities, such as swimming pools and golf courses, require intensive use of these scarce resources and the latter can add further to the environmental impacts if fertilisers and weeding chemicals are used. Tourism Concern have estimated that the average golf course in tropical countries like Thailand requires 1,500 kg of fertilisers, pesticides and other treatments per annum and uses the same amount of water that would be consumed by approximately 60,000 village residents. Similar physical depletion can be witnessed in terms of deforestation as trees are cleared for land use and fuel.

Tourism is responsible for high levels of air and noise pollution through the transportation networks and leisure activities. Air transport is claimed to be a significant factor in global warming and tourism is responsible for the vast majority of international air transport. At the local level air transport near urban areas can cause severe pollution problems along with ground transport systems such as tour buses that use up resources in an attempt to maintain climate control for their passengers. Other forms of transport, such as jet skis, quad bikes and snowmobiles, can create excessive noise pollution in coastal areas, national parks and areas of outstanding natural beauty. The noise from snowmobiles (particularly the older models) can be really intrusive when the area is a place of natural beauty. For instance, at the Yellowstone National Park the *Idaho News* reported in 2006 that a survey showed that snowmobile noise could be heard for 70% of the time available at 11 out of 13 sampling sites. This noise and the pollution from snowmobiles adds further pressure on the wildlife and vegetation. Furthermore, the construction of additional roads and car parking facilities encroaches

MINI CASE STUDY 6.1
Environmental impacts of tourism

EFFECTS OF OTHER INDUSTRIES ON TOURISM

Impacts from other industries often have a more dramatic effect on the environment and can seriously affect tourism.

- Oil spills, like the oil tanker disaster that occurred off the Galapagos Islands (Ecuador) in January 2001, can cause severe short-term damage to tourist attractions. In that case, a freight ship loaded with 160,000 gallons of diesel fuel and 80,000 gallons of other petroleum products ran aground on the coast of San Cristóbal and spilled nearly all of its load. Unique local marine and land species and the tourism potential of the area were badly affected.

- Agricultural run-off or industrial discharges can cause water pollution and may cause algae blooms like those that occurred in the Adriatic Sea in the early 1990s. In spite of improved control of sewage from tourism developments, the Mediterranean sea floor is increasingly carpeted with these quick-growing invaders, many rising 30 inches or more above anchoring runners. They appear equally adept at colonising rock, mud and sand in a virtually continuous swath that can extend from the beach out to a depth of about 150 feet, smothering coral reefs, fish and other sea flora and fauna in the process.

- Destructive practices such as blast fishing, fishing with poisonous chemicals like cyanide, and muro-ami netting (pounding reefs with weighted bags to scare fish out of crevices) directly destroy corals. They can also destroy a major draw for tourists.

Cyanide fishing was formerly used only to gather tropical fish for aquariums. Now the demand for live fish in restaurants in Hong Kong and other Asian centers is also driving this devastating practice. The market for live fish is now estimated at more than $200 million annually. Each year, an estimated 330,000 pounds of cyanide is sprayed on Philippine coral reefs alone. Cyanide fishing operations are moving from the over-harvested and devastated reefs of the Philippines to destroy remote and pristine coral reefs in eastern Indonesia, Papua New Guinea, Palau, Tuvalu, the Federated States of Micronesia, and other nations in the Western Pacific.

Source: United Nations Environment Programme, Division of Technology, Industry & Economics, Sustainable Consumption and Production Branch. http://www.uneptie.org/pc/tourism/sust-tourism/env-industry.htm

DISCUSSION QUESTIONS

1. 'The tourism industry is a relatively "clean" industry and just gets a bad press.' Discuss this statement with respect to the environmental impact of tourism.

2. 'Environmental damage is simply a part of the twenty-first century and there is no point in trying to clean up the tourism industry unless all industries are brought into line.' Discuss.

3. Should a percentage of profits from tourism businesses be earmarked for environmental conservation/development that will benefit the local population?

4. Are certification schemes likely to succeed in 'greening' the tourism industry?

on wildlife habitats and the pollution from vehicles can be so severe that at times areas such as Yosemite Valley are enshrouded in smog and not visible from the air. The smog is harmful to all species of animal and vegetable (UNEP, 2004). The problems associated with littering (such as the high profile given to the littering by tourists at Base Camp on Mount Everest) present significant danger to wildlife as well as being unsightly and expensive to clear. Similarly, solid waste disposal, if not undertaken properly, can be a major despoiler of the environment in coastal areas, rivers, lakes and roadsides. Such pollution can also give rise to serious health risks to humans as well as wildlife. *Our Planet* magazine reported that the wider Caribbean region received 63,000 port calls from ships on an annual basis and that this activity alone resulted in 82,000 tons of rubbish. Given that cruise ships are responsible for 77% of the total waste generated this represents a major pollution problem for the islands where the cruise ship passengers create four times more daily rubbish than their local resident counterparts (*Our Planet* (UNEP), 2006, volume 10, no. 3).

It is also important to note that many environmental factors are interdependent – often in ways that are not yet fully understood. Damage to coral reefs by divers, cruise ship anchors, or through the construction of coastal developments will reduce the local diversity and population of fish and other creatures that may feed off the coral. This, in turn, may reduce the numbers of birds that feed on the fish and so on. In order to determine the full impact of environmental changes accurately, the ecological system and the way in which it responds to environmental stress must be understood.

The effect of any loss to biological diversity is an increased threat to the food chain, can imbalance species and soil formation, and result in less ability to absorb greenhouse gases. A loss of biodiversity also hinders nature's ability to withstand the natural shocks caused by droughts, earthquakes, floods and hurricanes. Finally, it reduces the enjoyment that tourists experience when visiting areas by reducing the variety and wealth of flora and fauna available.

ENVIRONMENTAL IMPACT ASSESSMENT

There are no generally accepted models for environmental impact assessment (EIA). In many environmentally sensitive tourism destinations the need for EIAs has become more frequent and expected when considering tourism development and its relationship with the environment. Many countries have now incorporated the need for EIAs within their planning legislation but even the absence of legislation to support environmental planning should not deter tourism planners from undertaking their own environmental impact assessments on proposed developments. Environmental protection is so much easier and less costly than environmental correction even when such remedial action is possible.

It is important to understand the motivation that underlies a particular environmental impact assessment before an appropriate methodology is selected. For instance, an EIA may be undertaken in order to determine a development's impact upon a specific ecology or even upon a single 'rare' species. This type of assessment may not require the evaluation of the environmental impacts in monetary terms. However, other EIAs may be instigated for the express purpose of determining the financial implications of environmental correction in order to reflect accurately the net economic returns of tourism activity or in an attempt to retrieve some of these costs from the industry. Furthermore, EIAs may be required in order to compare alternative developments so as to allocate resources in a manner that maximises the economic benefits of development while minimising the negative environmental impacts. In this case there is a need to take a general equilibrium approach which enables the researcher to compare and contrast development options not only between various tourism strategies but also between different industrial structures.

Finally, EIAs may be required simply to raise the profile of environmental issues. That is, future developments should not be evaluated solely in economic terms but in a more holistic

Photograph 6.1	Oilspills can be disastrous for the local tourism industry as well as for the environment.
	Source: Alamy Images/Adrian Arbib

manner that includes the effects upon the local environment. This approach allows the democratic processes of development choice to be fully informed. It also highlights the fact that environmental impacts and environmental audits should become a way of life for business organisations as well as governments and individuals.

Once the environmental consequences of our actions are recognised this information can be incorporated at every decision-making level to ensure the effective use of the planet's finite resources. Environmental awareness during the production and consumption processes may also bring long-term economic and social benefits. For instance, the effective use of scarce resources, particularly energy-related resources, can result in lower marginal costs of production. On the other hand, the careless or reckless use of resources during either the production or consumption processes can add to social resentment of tourism development. This may hinder future development and will certainly detract from the effective use of resources.

In spite of the fact that there is no single accepted framework for conducting EIAs, the true scope of environmental impacts should not be underestimated. Most forms of industrial development impact upon land use, energy consumption and other direct forms of physical impacts. However, to assess the overall environmental impact it is necessary to take into account the consequential impacts occasioned by the direct productive activity. In the same way that the economic impacts associated with tourism development can be direct and indirect, the same must be said for environmental impacts. If tourism activity requires the production of output from a diverse range of industries, including those that do not supply tourist goods and services directly, then the environmental impact associated with the output and production processes of these supporting industries should also be included in the overall evaluation. For example, if the level of tourism increases, and this causes hotels to increase their purchases from the building and construction industry, then the environmental damage created by that increased building and construction must also be included. This is also true with respect to the effects of the quarries that supply the builders and the transport system that facilitates it.

In some areas attempts have been made to construct tourism/environment balance sheets to assess the net effect of tourism development with respect to the environment. One such approach for Scotland concluded that tourism is an important sector of the Scottish economy and that, although there are widespread environmental impacts associated with tourism activity, they were only regarded as being serious in a few specific locations and that careful management could overcome these problems. In 1991 the UK Department of Employment set up a task force to examine the relationship between tourism and the environment in England and the report published under this same title supported the major views expressed by the Scottish Tourism Coordinating Group. However, this suggests that in places where the environmental impacts are serious over a wider range of areas then careful management may not be able to overcome these problems. In this latter case it may be questionable as to whether tourism development should be considered at all.

THE EIA PROCESS

It is important to identify environmental impacts associated with tourism development at an early stage because:

- it is easier to avoid environmental damage by either modifying or rejecting developments than it is to rectify environmental damage once a project has been implemented; and
- projects that rely heavily upon areas of outstanding beauty may become non-viable if such developments degrade the environment.

There is a variety of methods that may be used for EIA including checklists and network systems, but generally the EIA is a process that enables researchers to predict the environmental consequences associated with any proposed development project. To draw up a checklist of environmental impacts it is necessary to establish what potential impacts can occur as a result of tourism activity and Green's checklist is a fine example of the scope of what is involved.

Green's checklist of the environmental impacts caused by tourism

THE NATURAL ENVIRONMENT

(a) Changes in floral and faunal species composition

- Disruption of breeding habits
- Killing of animals through hunting
- Killing of animals in order to supply goods for the souvenir trade
- Inward or outward migration of animals
- Destruction of vegetation through the gathering of wood or plants
- Change in extent and/or nature of vegetation cover through clearance or planting to accommodate tourism facilities
- Creation of a wildlife reserve/sanctuary

(b) Pollution

- Water pollution through discharges of sewage, spillage of oil/petrol
- Air pollution from vehicle emissions
- Noise pollution from tourist transportation and activities

→

(c) Erosion

- Compaction of soils causing increased surface run-off and erosion
- Change in risk of occurrence of land slips/slides
- Change in risk of avalanche occurrence
- Damage to geological features (e.g. tors, caves)
- Damage to river banks

(d) Natural resources

- Depletion of ground and surface water supplies
- Depletion of fossil fuels to generate energy for tourist activity
- Change in risk of occurrence of fire

(e) Visual impact

- Facilities (e.g. buildings, chairlifts, car parks)
- Litter

THE BUILT ENVIRONMENT

(a) Urban environment

- Land taken out of primary production
- Change of hydrological patterns

(b) Visual impact

- Growth of the built-up area
- New architectural styles
- People and belongings

(c) Infrastructure

- Overload of infrastructure (roads, railways, car parking, electricity grid, communications systems, waste disposal, and water supply)
- Provision of new infrastructure
- Environmental management to adapt areas for tourist use (e.g. sea walls, land reclamation)

(d) Urban form

- Changes in residential, retail or industrial land uses (move from houses to hotels/boarding houses)
- Changes to the urban fabric (e.g. roads, pavements)
- Emergence of contrasts between urban areas developed for the tourist population and those for the host population

(e) Restoration

- Reuse of disused buildings
- Restoration and preservation of historic buildings and sites
- Restoration of derelict buildings as second homes

(f) Competition

- Possible decline of tourist attractions or regions because of the opening of other attractions or a change in tourist habits and preferences

Source: Green *et al.*, 1990 (with permission from Elsevier Science)

In spite of the apparent comprehensiveness of this checklist it is evident that the listed aspects focus primarily on direct tourism activities and development. This is an inadequate approach because the indirect consequences must also be assessed. It is also important that environmental resources should be utilised efficiently. This means not only that they should be effectively used within the tourism industry but that this effectiveness should also be evaluated in relative terms in comparison with alternative economic development strategies. Only then can fully informed and sound rational planning decisions be made.

Once the potential impacts have been considered a checklist consisting of the fundamental elements at risk can be assembled. This checklist can then be used to form the basis of an evaluation matrix which will assess the impact of proposed developments on each of the fundamental elements according to whether the development will have no impact, minor impacts, moderate impacts or major impacts.

An EIA will examine:

- environmental auditing procedures;
- limitations to natural resources;
- environmental problems and conflicts that may affect project viability; and
- possible detrimental effects to people, flora and fauna, soil, water, air, peace and quiet, landscapes, cultural sites, etc. that are either within the proposed project area or will be affected by it.

Figure 6.1 sets out a typical process which an environmental impact assessment would adopt. A proposed development is put forward by a developer and this is initially assessed using the destination's environmental policy document as a performance indicator. Following this initial evaluation the proposal moves forward to site selection and undergoes a preliminary environmental impact assessment. This assessment can then be compared in more detail with the environmental performance indicators identified in the policy legislation/regulations in order to investigate potential conflicts.

Environmental indicators

There is a wide range of environmental indicators that can be used. However, few countries have instigated data collection procedures to monitor these environmental variables. The OECD (2004) provides an ongoing programme that highlights core environmental indicators. The development of harmonised environmental indicators with its member countries is pursued under the belief that there is no one universal set of environmental indicators but rather several sets intended to meet the needs of different purposes and audiences. More emphasis is now given to the conceptual framework of environmental indicators. The framework should include indicators that meet the criteria initially set out by the OECD in 1994 when it subdivided indicators into the following categories:

- climate change and ozone layer depletion;
- eutrophication;
- acidification;
- toxic contamination;
- urban environmental quality;
- biodiversity;
- cultural landscapes;
- waste;
- water resources;
- forest resources;
- fish resources;

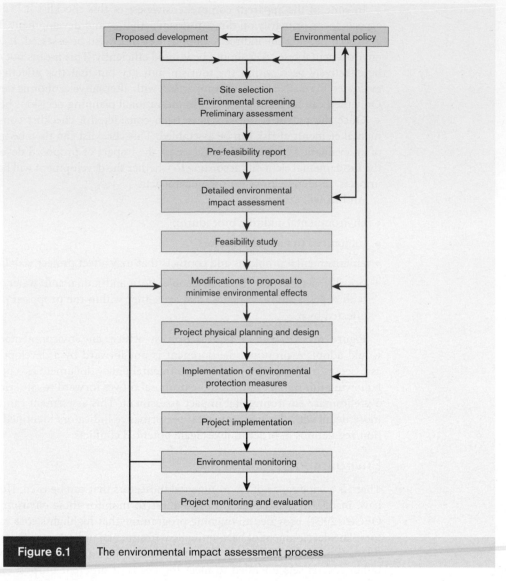

Figure 6.1   The environmental impact assessment process

- soil degradation;
- material resources; and
- socio-economic, sectoral and general indicators.

    The criteria for indicator selection are that they should:

- provide a representative picture of conditions or society's response;
- bc simple, easy to interpret and able to show trends over time;
- be responsive to changes in the environment and related human activities;
- provide a basis for international comparisons;
- be either national in scope or applicable to regional environmental issues of national significance; and
- have a threshold or reference value against which to compare it.

    These criteria should be expanded further to allow for intersectoral comparisons if they are to facilitate future development planning and the optimum use of resources.

Environmental indicators should not be confined to a role of simply measuring what we do, they should also provide information as to what we *should* do.

Once the preliminary assessment has been completed, a pre-feasibility study is undertaken followed by a detailed EIA that attempts to evaluate specific environmental costs and benefits. Again the results of the impact assessment are compared with the environmental policy and, if no serious conflicts arise, the proposal can move forward to a full feasibility study and modifications can be introduced to minimise any negative environmental impacts and bring the project in line with policy.

The physical planning and design of the project can then take place together with the introduction of measures designed to protect the environment in line with environmental policy. At this stage the project can be implemented and the project's development can then be monitored in terms of its future environmental impact.

However, if the EIA is undertaken in order to estimate the economic costs of correcting for the environmental impacts, or to compare the environmental performance of various industries, the above approach requires some modification. To examine impacts within a cohesive framework it is important that economic and environmental indicators are combined within a single model. This approach to EIA has been undertaken by researchers from Bournemouth University (UK) in studies for the government of Mauritius (1994) and the Wales Tourist Board (2002). The integration of economic, environmental and social impacts is essential if tourism strategies and choices are to be well informed and steps taken to prevent tourism development exceeding the carrying capacity of the destination. The Mauritius and Welsh models utilise the economic linkage information acquired during the input–output analysis (see Chapter 5) to provide the framework for estimating the indirect and induced environmental impacts associated with an industry's output level. The model relies only upon quantifiable environmental indicators in order to maintain objectivity. By constructing a set of environmental indicator coefficients that relate output by sector to environmental effects, planners are able to identify the environmental impact of any given change in the pattern or volume of production. The direct, indirect and induced environmental consequences of production in each industry can be assessed in exactly the same way that economic effects are measured. By utilising the economic linkage information to trace the consequential environmental effects of production, the model can provide a uniform framework for comparing not only the different types of tourism activity but also tourism with other forms of industrial activity. The confinement to measurable environmental indicators provides a platform for at least regional and national comparisons, and at best international comparisons. Because of the reliance on quantifiable variables the financial implications of production and consumption can also be estimated. Finally, because such models are constructed as interactive computer-based models, they are ideal for facilitating the **environmental auditing** process required of developments into the future.

ENVIRONMENTAL AUDITING

Unlike EIAs which focus on the effects of any given change in demand, environmental auditing represents a modus operandi, an ongoing process of monitoring and evaluation. The major differences between EIAs and environmental auditing are:

- environmental audits are generally voluntary in nature while EIAs tend to be written into the legislation and required as part of the planning approval process;

- environmental audits are part of an ongoing process – even a sense of attitude – rather than the one-off EIA studies; and

- environmental audits are concerned with performance and focus on how well a process is functioning. In this sense the environmental audit should become part of the organisational structure of private and public sector bodies alike.

However, one of these distinguishing features, the voluntary nature of environmental auditing, is also its Achilles heel. Without the necessary legislation and regulation required to enforce the implementation and quality of environmental auditing, it is unlikely to be an effective environmental protector. Also, because tourism is a fragmented industry with no clear boundaries, the environmental auditing needs to be economy-wide rather than solely aimed at tourism establishments. There is also an argument that common standards of environmental audits and performance indicators should be adopted on a universal basis because of the dangers of conflict if different industries pursue different environmental goals. All of these factors point to a single conclusion, namely, that environmental auditing is a macro rather than micro issue and that the distinction between EIAs and environmental auditing is becoming narrower. A more satisfactory solution is to adopt the general equilibrium EIA approach which encompasses all industrial output and consumption and facilitates the identification of consequential as well as direct impacts. In this way the EIA model can be a subset of the environmental audit process and be used to generate relative performance indicators that will act as benchmarks for each of the productive sectors within the economy. Legislation could then be drafted in such a way as to reward businesses that perform better than their industry average, thereby rewarding best practice.

Where environmental legislation and regulations are in force, then environmental auditing should be used to ensure that these legal and planning requirements are fulfilled. Where there are no legal or regulatory requirements, then environmental auditing should still be implemented in order to secure the long-term benefits associated with the effectiveness of appropriate development.

The environmental auditing process involves three distinct aspects:

1. An assessment of the system, how it functions and the implications of its operation.
2. A rigorous testing of the system to see how its performance compares with some optimal ideal or benchmark performance.
3. The certification of the results from the above comparisons.

Environmental auditing can take place at establishment and corporate levels for national and multinational businesses. However, with the recognition by many countries that the public sector has a vested interest in the development of tourism, environmental auditing should not only be incorporated into the legislation for private sector businesses, it should also be part of the operational remit of public sector divisions and departments. The adoption of environmental auditing can effect good use of resources as well as help create a good marketing image.

Finally, neither the public nor the private sector owns the environment. It is important that all of the stakeholders should be consulted when there are any proposals to implement development policies that will impinge or detract from the environmental store. These consultations can take many forms but should be undertaken well in advance of any implementation to allow proper time to consider and evaluate opposition and alternative strategies. The public announcement shown in Figure 6.2 demonstrates how such consultative procedures can be organised. In this example, the proposal for a second airport in Sydney, Australia, was under consideration and the public was being informed of the preparation of an EIA. It is commendable to note that the public were invited to attend preliminary information seminars prior to the release of the draft environmental impact assessment report. The airport development has not gone ahead but the consultation process did open up the forum for debate.

Having progressed through the 'cautionary platform' of tourism research, the major thrust of experienced researchers is now one of acceptance. That is, there is an acceptance that destinations should not have the ideological stances of 'puritan' researchers imposed upon them. Indeed, destinations should have sovereignty over their own economic and environmental destiny providing that destiny does not impinge upon the destiny of others.

Second Sydney Airport
p r o p o s a l

The Commonwealth Government is assessing Badgerys Creek and the Holsworthy Military Area as potential sites for the Second Sydney Airport. An Environmental Impact Statement is being prepared to consider the impact of these proposals. Preliminary information is available on:

- **Flight Paths** information prepared by Airplan
  - **Master Plans**
    - **Road and Rail Access to the Sites**
    - **Assessing the Impact of Noise**
      - **Air Traffic Forecasts** Information prepared by
         Commonwealth Department of Transport and Regional Development;

to assist you to understand these proposals. When the Draft EIS has been completed it will be released for public comment.

Come to a preliminary information session prior to the release of the Draft EIS

Helensburgh
Helensburgh Community Centre
Walker Street, Helensburgh
Tuesday 22 July, 6.00 pm – 9.30 pm

Penrith
Penrith Civic Centre
High Street, Penrith
Saturday 26 July, 10.00 am – 2.30 pm

Telephone Information Line: 1800 818 017

HOW TO FIND OUT MORE

- Fax the Community Access Centre on (02) 9600 9741
- Look up the internet at http://www.magnet.com.au/2sydair and e-mail us at 2sydair@magnet.com.au

Figure 6.2	Public announcement for the new Sydney Airport

Source: Advertisement from the *Sun Herald*, 6 July 1997, p. 9 © Commonwealth Department of Transport and Regional Development

Thus, if it is decided that tourism is an appropriate catalyst for economic development, it should not be suffocated under a barrage of concern for environmental conservation. Where tourism researchers can best help these destinations is to provide the framework for environmental auditing so that development may move forward in an optimal manner.

ENVIRONMENTAL ACTION PROGRAMMES

In addition to the development of viable and acceptable environmental impact assessment models, there has been a wide range of environmental initiatives undertaken in order to enhance the net effects of tourist activities and move towards some consideration of environmental sustainability. There are environmental protection agencies located at regional (for example, EU) and national levels throughout the world and further tiers of agencies at sub-national levels. Within Europe, the European Commission produces policy directives and guidelines in the form of environmental action programmes (EAPs) as well as commissioning wide-ranging research projects into the specifics of environmental issues. The latest

EAP is the sixth such plan and will direct environmental policy throughout the first decade of this century. The European EAP targets four priority areas for urgent action with seven thematic strategies. These four areas include: climatic change; environment, health and quality of life; natural resources and issues relating to waste; nature and biodiversity. These are very broad areas and are impacted on by tourism in all of its forms. The European Environmental Bureau (EEB) sees the sixth plan as being particularly important in view of the fact that it will oversee the period of enlargement of the EU. These projects range from the sewage and waste disposal problems created by youth tourism in the eastern cantons of Belgium, through the more widely applicable case studies relating to coastal zone management and transport systems to the more specialised analysis of golf tourism and its ecological implications.

Within the USA the Environmental Protection Agency (EPA) provides national environmental policies while state EPAs provide local directives. The US EPA's declared role is to protect human health and to safeguard the natural environment. The national agency works to develop regulations and enforce their implementation as well as commissioning research into environmental issues and providing support (policy and financial) to state EPAs.

In spite of the proliferation of environmental protection agencies since the 1980s there is still no consensus on the way that the environment should be protected from the activities of tourism. This in part may be the result of the fact that tourism's environmental impacts tend to be most obvious in specific areas rather than across nations. Unlike its position with respect to agriculture, energy and transport, the EU has so far failed to produce a comprehensive environmental policy with respect to tourism and much of the policy has been left to individual member countries.

Environmental impact assessments (EIAs) and environmental impacts statements (EISs) are studies that estimate the potential or expected environmental impacts of proposed actions or developments. In many countries EIAs or EISs are required (by legislation) for developments that exceed some minimum threshold level. For instance, in Mauritius an EIA is required on any tourism real estate development where there are more than nine tourism bungalows to be built. In Ghana EIAs are required if a planned hotel construction involves more than 40 rooms or if it is to be located within a national park, reserve, hilltop or island. However, the criteria for determining whether or not an EIA or EIS is required vary from always to only when there are significant environmental implications. The vagueness of the latter approach often renders environmental legislation impotent and even when there are detailed criteria there are quite often ways of circumventing the requirement, such as developing multiple adjacent sites where each site may be below the prescribed threshold and yet the development as a whole may vastly exceed that criteria.

To be effective environmental legislation must be enforceable, rigorous and given the same serious consideration as the financial aspects of the proposed development. The UNWTO produced a tourism and environmental publication in 1992 that illustrated 'an integrated approach to resort development' (Inskeep and Kallenberger, 1992) by referring to six case studies. These case studies covered a wide variety of resorts in Indonesia, the Republic of Korea, Mexico, the Dominican Republic, Turkey and the Canary Islands of Spain.

In spite of the range of countries included in the case studies some general conclusions and recommendations could be noted. One major conclusion was that serious environmental problems can be prevented by the adoption of sound planning and development. The recommendations made by the authors encompassed not only the physical needs of integrated planning such as adequate infrastructure, the implementation of appropriate design standards and the need to integrate the resort planning exercise into the local or regional planning process, but also the organisational structures and training of human resources.

However, EIAs and EISs tend to apply to new developments. What can be done to mitigate the damage that is being done by the operation of existing sites? A survey undertaken by the United Nations Environment Programme (UNEP) revealed that more than 100 codes of conduct exist for national tourism organisations, the industry and tourists. For instance, environmental codes of conduct have been adopted by the Tourism Industry Association of Canada and the American Society of Travel Agents as well as by national bodies and individual companies that are targeting the environmentally aware tourists and/or operating in particularly fragile areas. International organisations such as the World Tourism Organization and the World Travel and Tourism Council also promote environmental codes of conduct to the tourism industry.

While some countries have attempted to create an economic framework that will encourage best practice from an environmental point of view, and examples of these can be found in the national parklands of New Zealand, Africa and the Great Barrier Reef Marine Park of Australia, others have attempted to produce comprehensive environmental guidelines for developers. The UNWTO, UNEP and the EU have all published guidelines for the development of tourism in protected areas such as national parks.

Some players within the private sector have been notable in their attempts to drive home greater environmental awareness and the pursuit of best practice. Large private sector businesses have adopted environmental management systems which contain four distinct elements:

1. An environmental review – baseline impact studies that produce environmental inventories of the businesses activities and functions.
2. An environmental policy – a publicly stated set of identifiable and achievable objectives.
3. The design of an implementation and environmental system – setting out the mechanisms by which the objectives will be pursued.
4. An environmental audit – which can be used to measure the business's actual performance against its declared objectives.

Airlines such as KLM Royal Dutch Airlines and British Airways have been active in a number of ways. The former has been trying to increase the use of public transport by its employees and its customers and the latter has developed a series of environmental awareness events for managers, the creation of the Tourism for Tomorrow Awards programme and the adoption of energy-saving technology for its own activities. American Airlines developed a programme to standardise the approval procedures for chemical products in an attempt to reduce its purchases of environmentally harmful products, and ferry companies, such as P&O European Ferries, developed a cost-effective and environmentally friendly means of disposing of hazardous wastes.

Disney has been effective in forming a committee to evaluate the ways in which freshwater conservation measures can be combined with wastewater reuse and it has also provided its employees with the means to dispose of their personal hazardous wastes such as oils and other household chemicals safely. The European operations of CenterParcs are noted for their car-free resorts which provide a more healthy environment for guests and, while the Maya Mountain Tours Company of Belize provides teaching facilities for students and researchers into environmental ethics, the Grecotel hotel chain ensures that all of its staff are trained in environmental issues. The Greek National Tourist Office uses policies of spatial zoning, visitor management plans, financial incentives and awareness campaigns in an attempt to drive home the need for better environmental management.

There are also dangers embodied in the growing awareness of environmental issues. With imperfect information the tourist can easily be misled into believing that specific tourist products are environmentally sound. This may encourage tourists to purchase tour operators' packages that are anything but environmentally friendly.

It is only the largest of private sector businesses that normally have the expertise and resources to implement their own environmental management systems. Given the fact that the tourism industry is dominated by SMEs, the full impact of environmental management systems will be relatively minor.

MINI CASE STUDY 6.2
Eco-tourism in Thailand: the thin end of the wedge?

ECO-TOURISM

Close-to-nature jungle safaris, scuba diving on pristine coral reefs, wilderness trekking to hilltribe villages . . . With no system of regulation in place, anyone can call themselves an 'eco-tourism' business and the money comes rolling in. But many tour operators have a strange idea of what being green means.

A boat run by a self-proclaimed 'eco-tourism' company is heading toward a pristine coral reef in the Andaman Sea. Once at the destination, the boat drops anchor in the open sea, instantly destroying myriad rich coral and the homes of many marine animals.

So much for Thai-style eco-tourism. To counter environmentally destructive mass tourism, the Tourism Authority of Thailand (TAT) launched the concept of eco-tourism here three years ago, but tour companies seem to have their own idea of what being green is.

Targeting the young and adventurous, companies advertise their jungle treks, diving trips and other 'close-to-nature' expeditions as eco-tourism. With no real concern for the environment, the surging popularity of nature tourism means an accelerated invasion of pristine areas and, as a result, more ecological degradation.

Ideally, eco-tourism is environmentally friendly and sustainable tourism which also benefits the local communities. But in fact, many eco-tourism ventures all over the country are destroying the very eco-systems they claim to protect. With poor planning and no benefits for the locals, eco-tourism often ends up providing little beside social tension and environmental degradation while leaving tourists feeling dissatisfied and cheated. Such problems have led to the fledgling eco-tourism industry coming under heavy fire as mere hype and sheer hypocrisy.

Pradech Phayakvichien, TAT's deputy governor of planning and development, said eco-tourism in Thailand needs time to mature.

'We're in the transition period. We need more networking and cooperation between concerned agencies such as government, non-government organisations, business operators, tourists and local communities in order to fulfil the objectives of ecotourism,' he said.

One of the main factors in eco-tourism's failure, he said, is the lack of participation by local communities due to poor management skills and weak bargaining power against the tourism industry.

'They also lack information, expertise and money to manage the tourism business in their areas,' he said, adding that the government must intervene by giving financial assistance and expert advice to community eco-tourism operations.

At present, many communities are struggling with drastic social and environmental change resulting from the reckless behaviour of tourists and tour companies.

A case in point is the Umphang Wildlife Sanctuary where TAT launched its pilot eco-tourism project a few years ago despite the fact that the sanctuary, by law, does not allow human intrusion.

The project encouraged a large influx of trekkers and tourists far beyond the area's capacity. The sanctuary is now facing severe degradation. Like mass tourism, mass jungle trekking fattens the wallets of tour operators while hurting the eco-system and the hilltribe people's source of livelihood. The eco-tourism plague has spread far and wide to most other pristine areas in the country.

'No matter what you call it, mass or eco-tourism, it makes no difference to us local villagers because we never benefit from it anyway,' said Meeya Hawa, a villager in Jao Mai, a small Muslim fishing village in Trang province.

'Some of us may be hired as cheap labour in resorts or restaurants. But nothing more,' she said, adding that the environmental damage far outweighs the economic gains.

This quiet Muslim fishing village is located on beautiful Hat Yao beach and is a gateway to many virgin islands. Although the villagers see a large number of tourists passing through every year, they have no stake in tourism money.

'When the tourists come, they stay at comfortable resort hotels and ignore our small huts. They go to the islands by the resort's boat and eat at the resort's restaurant. And they throw garbage into the sea which we have worked so hard to preserve,' she said.

Only a handful of tourists stay in the villagers' homes, travel in their boats, or eat the indigenous food they cook.

What she wants, she said, is the kind of tourism which is run and managed by the community for the community.

Instead of letting individual villagers provide tourism services with the money going into personal pockets, Meeya said the environment will be more effectively protected if tourism is a community effort.

Many villagers are selfish and are doing their business without concern for the environment. Such tourism is short-lived and hurts the community as a whole.

Meeya Hawa, a Jao Mai villager and conservation activist

'Community effort,' she said, 'will also give the villagers more bargaining power against tour companies.'

While TAT still has no concrete measures in place to support community-run eco-tourism, it acknowledges the role of non-governmental organisations (NGOs) in strengthening local community groups, a crucial condition for eco-tourism success.

For instance, the Thai Volunteers Service is working with the villagers at Jao Mai in Trang to develop community tourism which is environmentally friendly.

'They are on the right track although they lack marketing experience, which we have. If TAT and NGOs and the communities can work together, we can create tourism which benefits both the villagers and nature,' commented TAT's Pradech.

Kiriwong, a strong and tightly knit community at the foot of Khao Luang Mountain in Nakhon Si Thammarat, is a good example of community-based eco-tourism.

Apart from being the gateway to Khao Luang, the highest mountain in the south, the village's century-old forest orchards also attract a large number of visitors.

While rural Thailand lacks social security schemes, Kiriwong has a long history of community welfare funds and committed village groups. This community consciousness comes in handy when the village decides to regulate tourism activities in the wake of increasing numbers of tourists and environmental threats.

They set up Kiriwong Eco-tourism Club under its Tambon Administrative Council to draw up rules and regulations for tourists to prevent environmental degradation.

Nipat Boonpet, the club secretary, said Kiriwong has limited the number of mountain trekkers to only 30 a month. Each trekker pays about 3,000 baht for a four-day trek which covers food, accommodation, luggage carriers, sightseeing, contact fees, and a donation to the community.

'The Khao Luang mountain is like the roof of our houses. We have to safeguard it, otherwise it might collapse which would mean big trouble for us,' he said.

All profits go back to Kiriwong's community welfare funds.

Kiriwong's income from its eco-tourism business is secondary since the community lives primarily on their forest orchards.

'We keep our tourism business small because we want to avoid the mistakes of other tourist spots,' said Nipat. 'We're often tempted though, because tourism is easy money. But we have to constantly ask ourselves if we want to lose our roots or have our families break down by opening up our community too much and too soon.'

Not all tourists are happy with Kiriwong's arrangement though. The fee, they say, is too high, thus making nature trips to Khao Luang unaffordable to students with no income.

The mountain, they add, belongs to everyone and the Kiriwong villagers have no right to claim ownership and to charge people.

Flooded by complaints, Kanittha Ponoum, director of TAT's Nakhon Si Thammarat office, said Kiriwong 'misinterprets its role' and should lower the fee and give preferential treatment to students as a compromise.

Although Kiriwong is considering a new fee structure, it insists that the charges are essential to limit the number of tourists to a level within nature's carrying capacity.

→

'Tourists only think of costs in terms of what they pay for food, travelling and accommodation. Nature for them is free. It is not,' said Nipat of Kiriwong.

According to Pradech, tourists also must change their behaviour for eco-tourism to succeed. Although TAT is stepping up its domestic eco-tourism campaign, Pradech said Thai tourists in general lack environmental concern for the places they visit.

The number of tourists has increased every year. This means more pressure on nature and local communities.

Short of a real revolution in environmental awareness among tour operators and tourists alike, eco-tourism will remain just another hyped-up marketing strategy while short-sighted tourist businesses continue to erode the natural environment on which they depend.

Source: Article taken from the *Bangkok Post*, Saturday 10 May 1997

DISCUSSION QUESTIONS

1. By developing eco-tourism is there a danger that we encourage tourism to develop in areas that are too sensitive to sustain tourism activity?

2. Once tourism development has started is it only a matter of time before the level of activity increases beyond its environmental capacity?

3. What policies and systems could be used to try and control the nature and type of tourism development in such cases?

There are some areas of the planet that are extremely fragile where even very small numbers of tourists can have a very high environmental impact. Such areas are, typically, deserts, mountains, polar regions and savannas. In such areas one could question the environmental viability of any amount of tourism irrespective of how low key or what activities they undertake when in these areas. Tourism in such areas is often characterised by very marked seasonality patterns. Although where these areas have an indigenous population tourism can bring much needed revenue and employment opportunities, it can also damage the fragile stability of the economy driving them to become dependent upon ever increasing levels of tourist activity, with the environmental and socio-cultural damage that comes with this growth. Where the areas do not have indigenous human populations the presence of tourists and their associated activities can have serious repercussions on the flora and fauna and the impacts of tourists can bring about permanent and irrecoverable damage to the environment.

Tourism in the Arctic and Antarctic regions has grown dramatically over the past few decades and poses serious threats to the local populations and the integrity of the environment. It has grown to sufficient proportions to attract the larger tourism businesses and this increase in the level of tourism brings new hazards to tourists and to the environments they visit. Small aircraft have been known to run into problems when taking sightseeing tourists in the Antarctic and the debris of crashed vehicles is sometimes left behind as it is not economically viable to recover the remnants. The pollution caused by increased vehicular activity in the region adds to the pressures being imposed on the environment. Major Case Study 6.1 at the end of the chapter highlights the scale of tourist numbers and activities in Antarctica in order to provide some insight into the growing problems involved in conserving the polar regions.

Photograph 6.2 Wildllife hunting?
Source: Rex Features/Lehtikuva Oy

CONCLUSION

Environmental impacts are not unique to tourism and tourism receives a disproportional share of criticism for its negative environmental impacts. Environmental impacts manifest themselves at the direct, indirect and induced levels and all three levels of impact should be taken into account during the process of assessment. The methods of assessment available to researchers have been developed in a piecemeal fashion, limiting their usefulness for generalisations. However, the adoption of a matrix approach, utilising input–output modelling structures, provides the most promising outlook for a universally acceptable framework for the study of such impacts. International agencies, through statements such as Agenda 21, have declared their intentions to develop an environment-friendly approach to policy-making. Similarly, national governments are responding to the pressures from these international bodies as well as from their own populations, to move towards a more environmentally friendly development path. Finally, the private sector (at least as represented by the larger businesses) is responding to pressures by implementing environmental management systems.

There is an overwhelming need to bring some credibility to the study of environmental impacts and this can be achieved by focusing upon the objective environmental indicators, such as those listed by the OECD, rather than subjective data sets that may only have local relevance.

SELF-CHECK QUESTIONS

1. With respect to the environmental impacts associated with tourism activity, list three positive and negative impact examples at the (a) direct (b) indirect, and (c) induced levels of impact.

2. What made Agenda 21 so unique?

3. Explain briefly the difference between environmental impact assessments (EIAs) and environmental audits.

4. What are the major difficulties associated with trying to identify the environmental impacts caused by tourism activity?

5. How would you define eco-tourism?

ESSAY QUESTIONS

1. 'The environment is often an unpriced element of the tourism product which distorts the workings of the market system. This prevents the market from achieving an optimal level of tourism activity.' Discuss.

2. Environmental resolutions have been made on the international stage for more than 20 years. Why have they had so little impact on the environmental performance of the tourism industry?

3. 'When assessing the environmental impact of any sector of production, all environmental consequences of that production should be examined not simply the direct effects.' Discuss.

4. What general conclusions can be drawn from the analysis of tourism's environmental impacts?

5. What are the processes involved in implementing an environmental management system and what are the weaknesses involved from such an implementation?

ANNOTATED FURTHER READING

Books

Gunn, C.A. and Var, T. (2002) *Tourism Planning*, 4th edn, Routledge, London and New York.
Provides a comprehensive overview of tourism development.

Hall, M.C. and Page, S.J. (2002) *The Geography of Tourism and Recreation: Environment, Place and Space*, 2nd edn, Routledge, London and New York.
This book provides a broad overview of tourism development in terms of demand, supply and impacts.

Middleton, V.T.C. with Hawkins, R. (1998) *Sustainable Tourism, A Marketing Perspective*, Butterworth Heinemann, Oxford.
A book rich with case studies that examines the feasibility of sustainable tourism and the role of marketing in driving the industry in that direction.

Articles

Buckley, R. (2003) 'Ecological indicators of tourist impacts in parks', *Journal of Ecotourism* 2(1), 54–66.

The author discusses the importance of indicators which are discriminating, quantifiable, actionable, sensitive, ecologically significant, integrated, and feasible in practice. Emphasis is given to the need for indicators that reflect the priority conservation values of the protected areas concerned, and the types of use, and not merely for management processes.

Garcia, C. and Servera, J. (2003) 'Impacts of tourism development on water demand and beach degradation on the island of Mallorca (Spain)', *Geografiska Annaler Series A. Physical Geography* **85**(3–4), 287–300.
Paper includes a focus on over-reliance on tourism and includes economic impacts and benefits. Also states poor planning development has led to strain on resources and resulted in the dwelling capacity being exceeded. Mallorca demonstrates an unsustainable situation.

Gossling, S. (2002) 'Global environmental consequences of tourism', *Global Environmental Change* **12**(4), 283–302.
In 2000, almost 700 million international tourist arrivals were counted worldwide. Even though a global activity of this scale can be assumed to have a substantial impact on the environment, its consequences have never been assessed and quantified. In this contribution, five major aspects of the leisure-related alteration of the environment are investigated: (1) the change of land cover and land use, (2) the use of energy and its associated impacts, (3) the exchange of biota over geographical barriers and the extinction of wild species, (4) the exchange and dispersion of diseases, and (5) a psychological consequence of travel, the changes in the perception and the understanding of the environment initiated by travel.

Web sites

http://www.earthsummit2002.org/es/2002/bergen/energy_summary.html
The Earth Summit web site sketches out the major issues discussed at the Earth Summits including the latest discussions relating to environmental sustainability

http://www.environment.gov.au/
The Australian Environmental portal provides information relating to the Australian environment.

http://www.epa.gov/
This is the USA's Environmental Protection Agency web site and includes material on US policies on environmental issues relating to tourism.

http://www.greentourism.org.uk/
The tourism and environment web site demonstrates how Scotland is working towards creating a framework for environmentally sustainable tourism.

http://eea.europa.eu/themes/tourism
The European Environmental Agency acts as a portal for information relating to environmental aspects in Europe including tourism.

http://www.uneptie.org/pc/tourism/sust-tourism/env-3main.htm
The United Nations Environmental Programme covers a wide range of environmental topics including this section which looks at sustainable tourism.

References cited and bibliography

Burnett, G.W. and Conover, R. (1989) 'The efficacy of Africa's national parks: an evaluation of Julius Nyerere's Arusha Manifesto of 1961', *Society and Natural Resources* **2**, 251–60.
Cohen, E. (1978) 'The impact of tourism on the physical environment', *Annals of Tourism Research* **5**(2), 215–37.

De Kadt, E. (ed.) (1979) *Tourism: Passport to Development?*, Oxford University Press, New York.

Getz, D. (1986) 'Models in tourism planning', *Tourism Management* 7(1), 21–32.

Green, D.H., Hunter, C.J. and Moore, B. (1990) 'Applications of the Delphi technique in tourism', *Annals of Tourism Research*, 17, 270–9.

Inskeep, E. (1991) *Tourism Planning: An Integrated and Sustainable Development Approach*, Van Nostrand Reinhold, New York.

Inskeep, E. and Kallenberger, M. (1992) *An Integrated Approach to Resort Development: Six Case Studies*, WTO, Madrid.

Lorch, J. and Bausch, T. (1995) 'Sustainable tourism in Europe', in *Tourism and the Environment in Europe*, EU, Brussels.

Mathieson, A. and Wall, G. (1982) *Tourism: Economic, Physical and Social Impacts*, Longman, Harlow.

OECD (1994) *Environmental Indicators*, OECD core set and Paris.

OECD (2004) http://www.oecd.org/searchResult/0,2665,en_2649_34283_1_1_1_1_1,00.html

UNEP (2004) http://www.uneptie.org/pc/tourism/sust-tourism/env-3main.htm

Welford, R. and Gouldson, A. (1993) *Environmental Management and Business Strategy*, Pitman, London.

MAJOR CASE STUDY 6.1
The environmental impact of tourism in Antarctica

THE IMPACT OF VISITORS

Antarctica doesn't have any 'residents' in that everyone who goes is a visitor for a short time. There are two groups of visitors who can have an impact on Antarctica, tourists and those who go as part of a national Antarctic programme. In terms of numbers, tourists greatly outnumber national programme personnel: 37,000 as against 4,000 in the 2006/07 season for instance (tourist numbers were up 14% on the previous year leading to calls to limit the number of tourists allowed to go). The national programme personnel clock up far more person-days however, and impacts are difficult to compare directly.

While tourists may spend only a relatively small time on landings, they will naturally want to visit the most picturesque and wildlife-rich areas of Antarctica, and they tend to do so in numbers far greater than the entire complement of many Antarctic bases. There is also the fact that those national programmes that are supplied by ship (as the majority are) have relatively few visits of those ships, whereas in the season, the great majority of all shipping activity in Antarctica is of tour ships. There have been accidents with ships being grounded

on uncharted rocks and there have been oilspills. With the best safeguards in the world, the more ships there are, the more accidents there are likely to be.

Tourism in Antarctica is at present self-regulated by the International Association of Antarctic Tour Operators (IAATO). This is an organisation that applies strict guidelines to its member tour operators and ships. Such guidelines limit the size of the ships that can cruise Antarctic waters and also how many people can be landed at sites around Antarctica. So far IAATO is perceived as being successful in its aims and in regulation for Antarctic protection – though there are always those who would have no tourism at all. The real potential threat from tourists is from non-IAATO member ships and tour operators who run cruises with larger ships and greater numbers of people landing. This has not happened yet but, if it does, there is at present little or nothing that could be done. Another threat comes from smaller expeditions that are becoming increasingly common by individuals and small parties.

Antarctica requires careful planning and a series of fail-safe rescue procedures if anyone gets into difficulty. These smaller expeditions can sometimes fail to do this adequately and resort to 'humanitarian' requests for aid from shipping or nearby national bases when they get into difficulty. In recent years, for example, a small helicopter crashed into the sea off the Antarctic peninsula requiring rescue, and an attempt to fly across Antarctica via the Pole in a small aircraft ended in the aircraft crashing and the pilot being rescued by nearby base personnel. There is no guarantee that derelict or crashed vehicles left by private expeditioners will be removed from Antarctica as they should be.

Table 6.1 analyses the number of tourists visiting Antarctica in 2005–6 according to their country of origin (shown graphically in Figure 6.3), and Table 6.2 shows the activities engaged in while there (see also Figure 6.4).

Source: Tourist Data from IAATO. See http://www.iaato.org/; http://www.coolantarctica.com/Antarctica%20fact%20file/science/threats_tourism.htm

Table 6.1	Antarctica tourist numbers 2006–7, seaborne, airborne, landed and cruise	
Country of Origin	**Numbers**	**Percentage**
United States	13 319	35.5
United Kingdom	5 052	13.5
Germany	4 590	12.2
Australia	2 966	7.9
Unknown	1 750	4.7
Canada	2 026	5.4
Netherlands	1 017	2.9
Switzerland	1 026	2.9
Others	5 716	15.2
Totals	**37 552**	**100.0**

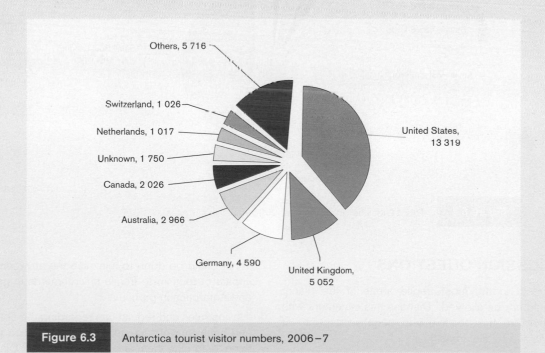

Figure 6.3	Antarctica tourist visitor numbers, 2006–7

Table 6.2	Antarctica tourist activities 2005–6	
Activity	**Numbers**	**Percentage**
Small Boat Landing	187 144	45.9
Ship Cruise	75 604	18.5
Small Boat Cruising	71 267	17.5
Station Visit	34 296	8.4
Kayaking	16 775	4.1
Walk	8 116	2.0
Scuba Diving	5 869	1.4
Helicopter Flight	2 934	0.7
Remote Underwater Vehicle	1 572	0.4
Camping	1 445	0.4
Aircraft Flight	836	0.2
Other	675	0.2
Climbing	606	0.1
Ice Landing	525	0.1
Skiing	8	0.002
Totals	**407 672**	**100**

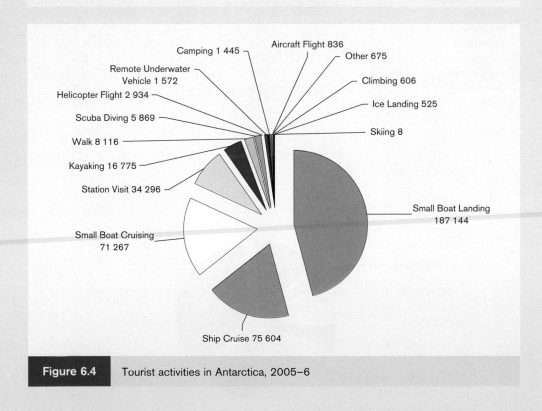

Figure 6.4	Tourist activities in Antarctica, 2005–6

DISCUSSION QUESTIONS

1. 'Tourism in the most fragile areas of the planet should not be allowed.' Discuss this statement with respect to the positive and negative aspects of tourism in fragile areas.

2. What could be done to minimise the environmental impact of tourism to fragile environments in general and Antarctica in particular?

3. 'Having rules and regulations regarding the activities and behaviour of tourists while in Antarctica is one thing, enforcing them is a different matter.' Discuss.

CHAPTER 7
The Socio-cultural Impact of Tourism

LEARNING OUTCOMES

The learning outcomes of this chapter may be defined as:

- identifying those aspects of socio-cultural behaviour that are most susceptible to tourism activity and most likely to be influenced and changed as a result of it;

- understanding the various approaches to studying the socio-cultural aspects of tourism and the relationship between them;

- providing a framework for the study of the relationship between tourism development and socio-cultural impacts; and

- encouraging the reader to understand key concepts.

Photograph: Hong Kong skyline at night © Hannah Cox

INTRODUCTION

Tourism is a product that is based upon simultaneous production and consumption. For tourism output to have occurred the tourists must visit a destination and consume the product of the sector *in situ*. There is a wide range of **service industries** in the world, but there is often no need for the consumer to visit the place of production in order to consume the product. However, tourism is a personal service and, as such, can only be consumed by the tourist visiting the destination. The implications of this for the destination's population is that not only will it be subject to the changes created by the stimulation and change in direction of the local economy, it will also come into contact with an alien population during the production process. Changes in economic growth and development will always be associated with changes in the socio-cultural characteristics of an area. As the population becomes wealthier and healthier, their wants and needs change and this influences their spending choice and lifestyles. However, because tourism brings visitors into contact with the local population it adds further dimensions to the socio-cultural change.

The contact between visitors and local residents can be beneficial or detrimental to the host population depending upon the difference in cultures and the nature of the contact. Much of the literature on social impacts is biased in that it focuses attention upon the detrimental impact of tourism on the host population. Similarly, little attention has been paid to the fact that there can also be socio-cultural impacts on the tourist population, which can again be either positive or negative. In reality socio-cultural impacts tend to contain a mixture of both positive and negative strands and these impacts affect both hosts and guests.

THE NATURE OF SOCIO-CULTURAL IMPACTS OF TOURISM

The aim of this chapter is to outline the nature of socio-cultural impacts, to examine those contacts that are positive and those that may be deemed to be negative. In order to do this it is important to include an examination of the process of tourism development because the speed and nature of development can be a major influence on the magnitude and direction of socio-cultural changes. The chapter will also investigate the causal factors for socio-cultural impacts, suggest possible methods for measurement and outline some policy implications.

The socio-cultural impact of tourism is manifested through an enormous range of aspects from the arts and crafts through to the fundamental behaviour of individuals and collective groups. The impacts can be positive, such as the case where tourism preserves or even resurrects the craft skills of the population or the enhancement of cultural exchange between two distinct populations. The impacts can also be negative, such as the **commercialisation and bastardisation** of arts, crafts and ceremonies/rituals of the host population. The impacts can also detract from cultural exchange by presenting a limited and distorted view of one of the populations.

A factor often overlooked by researchers is the socio-cultural impact of tourism on the visitor population. For instance, the growth of UK tourists visiting Spain throughout the 1960s and 1970s resulted in culinary and beverage changes in the UK (paella and Rioja wine being two Spanish products that benefited from this exchange). Visitors to Australia would often find it hard to resist adopting the beach-based lifestyle and the barbecue when they returned home. There is evidence of socio-cultural impacts, ranging from the clothes we wear, the food we eat and our general lifestyles and attitudes, which can all be influenced by places we visit.

There is a tradition of viewing the socio-cultural impacts as a combined effect because of the difficulty in distinguishing between sociological and cultural impacts. This distinction is also somewhat artificial given the fact that sociological and cultural effects overlap to a large extent. There is also a tradition of examining the socio-cultural impacts of tourism purely in terms of the contact that takes place between the host and visiting populations: this is a very limited approach. The true socio-cultural impact of tourism is far-reaching and encompasses direct and indirect effects in a manner similar to the economic impacts. Again, some of these consequential impacts may be beneficial while others may be seen as detrimental. These matters will be explored in greater detail below.

APPROACHES TO THE STUDY OF SOCIO-CULTURAL IMPACTS OF TOURISM

There is a variety of ways in which we can examine the relationships between tourism development and socio-cultural and socio-economic changes. Authors such as Cohen (1984) looked at the study of socio-cultural impacts from four different but overlapping viewpoints:

1. Tourism impact studies.

2. Host–guest interaction.

3. Tourist systems.

4. Tourists and their behaviour.

The studies that have taken place have ranged from those that have attempted to provide formal models to explain tourism development and the host–guest interaction (such as those by Butler (1980), Doxey (1975) and Smith (1989)). Although none of these models has met with a great deal of success, they have created frameworks within which researchers can examine appropriate issues. Many of the other studies relating to the socio-cultural impact of tourism have been specific case study approaches which have lacked the universal rigour that allows the development of an overarching theoretical understanding.

The development of the tourist product is inextricably linked to the contribution that tourism development can make to general economic development. In fact, the relationship between tourism development and general economic development can be studied under the heading of dependency or core–periphery theory, which relates to the enrichment of metropolitan areas at the expense of underdeveloped peripheral areas. Studies of dependency theory often cite examples of the Caribbean and the South Pacific to highlight not only the economic and political dependence resulting from tourism activity, but also the socio-cultural dependence. However, the issues are more far-reaching than the effects upon small island developing states (SIDS) and we find that all countries that are in the tourism business experience socio-cultural changes as a result of tourism activity. In some countries, such as Spain, the dynamics of socio-cultural change have been found to be surprisingly rapid as the effects of tourism development in Costa Brava demonstrated in the late 1960s and early 1970s.

The development of the tourism product will, to some extent, be determined by the type of tourism activity that takes place. This, in turn, will be partly determined by the nature of the destination and the socio-economic characteristics of the tourists. Similarly, the magnitude and direction of the economic and sociological impact of tourism on the host population will be partly determined by the type of tourism product.

The impact brought about by the interaction of hosts and tourists is a well-documented phenomenon, and the findings of researchers, such as Smith (1989) in her book on the anthropology of tourism, have rapidly gained acceptance in the academic world. The categorisation of tourists into typologies is now accepted as an orthodox tool in the study of socio-cultural impacts. Authors such as Doxey (1975) have explored the changing relationship between guests and hosts through his construction of his Index where that relationship travels from a state of euphoria, through apathy to annoyance, and ends up with a state of open antagonism as the visitor presence becomes more and more pronounced. Plog (1977) and Butler (1980) both used the dynamics of change as part of their explanatory models, but here they were looking at the changing fortunes of the destination as the visitors revised their perceptions.

The typology of tourists

Typology is a method of sociological investigation that seeks, in this instance, to classify tourists according to a particular phenomenon, usually motivations or behaviour. A simple example of a typology which has implications for the development of the tourism product is shown in Table 7.1.

- Package tourists – usually demand Western amenities, are associated with rapid growth rates and often lead to the restructuring of the local economy.

- Independent tourists – usually fit in better with the local environment and social structure, are associated with relatively slow growth rates and often lead to local ownership.

A more detailed typology, such as the one devised by Valene Smith, relates the type of tourist to volume and adaptation levels.

Before examining the different approaches that can be used to study the socio-cultural impacts of tourism it is important to consider some fundamental matters relating to these impacts that are often ignored by researchers. In spite of the fact that some researchers regard socio-cultural change as one of the evils of tourism development, any form of economic development will, by definition, carry with it implications for the social structure and cultural aspects of the host population. This is true for both international and domestic tourism development. To condemn tourism development because it will inevitably bring with it socio-economic change is tantamount to consigning a destination to a cultural museum. This choice can only come from the host population and not from external researchers who become too embroiled in the sociological resources that are used in the tourist transactions. Furthermore, to criticise researchers for forecasting future growth levels of tourism and human resource requirements on the grounds that such forecasts ignore the fact that these employees are members of families is to deny the whole essence of sound tourism planning. Successful tourism development can only be achieved by undertaking rigorous quantitative and qualitative research.

The speed and concentration of tourism development are also important influences on the magnitude and direction of social impacts and must be taken into account when attempting to attribute the cause of socio-cultural impacts. The nature of the tourism development process and its impact on the host population can be categorised into a variety of subsets and the analyses of each of these subsets can shed additional light on the type and source of impacts attributable to tourism development.

Table 7.1	Typology of tourism: frequency of types of tourist and their adaptations to local norms		
Types of tourist	**Number of tourists**	**Adaptation to local norms**	
Explorer	Very limited	Accepts fully	
Elite	Rarely seen	Adapts fully	
Off-beat	Uncommon but seen	Adapts well	
Unusual	Occasional	Adapts somewhat	
Incipient mass	Steady flow	Seeks Western amenities	
Mass	Continuous flow	Expects Western amenities	
Charter	Massive arrivals	Demands Western amenities	

Source: Smith, 1989. Reprinted by permission of the University of Pennsylvania Press

With respect to the speed of development a broad analytical approach would suggest that if tourism develops rapidly, the accompanying change to the economy would create a new power structure. In contrast, slow tourism development tends to be associated with small, locally owned developments with less change to the power structure.

THE TOURISM DEVELOPMENT PROCESS

Studies that look at the socio-cultural impact of tourism on specific types of destinations according to their resource base are quite common (see for example, Gill and Williams (1994), Price (1992), Stokowski (1996)). Although tourism development can take place in a wide variety of forms, a typical development scenario considers the tourism product as it grows from infancy to maturity and looks something like this:

- A few tourists 'discover' an area or destination.
- In response to this discovery, local entrepreneurs provide new or special facilities to accommodate the growing number of visitors and service their needs. More importantly, they provide the means to attract more visitors in the future.
- The public sector provides new or improved infrastructure to cater for the inflow of visitors.
- Finally, **institutionalised or mass tourism** is developed, which is commonly resort based and sold as a package. It is based upon large-volume production techniques in order to exploit economies of large-scale production in marketing, accommodation and transport, such as high payload factors for aircraft.

Many regional and national tourism development plans have attempted to shortcut the above tourism evolution cycle by aiming for the final stage of mass tourism straightaway, but few destinations can make this leap without first securing outside capital and expertise and incurring severe social stress.

Unfortunately, there is no single coherent body of knowledge or theory which comprehensively explains tourism development. Evidence, such as it is, is rather piecemeal and comes from a number of disparate case studies. Furthermore, the situation is compounded by the fact that different disciplines approach the subject matter in different ways, and although many aspects of the studies may overlap, it is difficult to tie the different conclusions together into a single body of thought.

The different approaches may be categorised under the following headings:

- psychological;
- sociological;
- socio-economic.

THE PSYCHOLOGICAL BASIS OF TOURISM DEVELOPMENT

In Chapter 2 we introduced Stanley Plog's (1977) approach to a typology of tourists and in this chapter we have reiterated how useful such typologies can be in the study of socio-cultural impacts. Plog devised his classification in terms of **psychographic analysis**, and in this way attempted to explain why resort destinations appear to follow a pattern that causes them to rise through a period of development and then fall into a period of decline. He saw a continuum of market segments with two diametrically opposed groups occupying either pole (see Figure 7.1). In 2004, Stanley Plog revisited his earlier work and modified the categories of tourists, replacing the allocentrics with venturers and the psychocentrics with dependables (Plog, 2004). Plog also updated his chart in 2003.

Plog's theory suggests that the tourist segments can be divided into different psychographic traits, i.e. allocentrics, near allocentrics, midcentrics, near psychocentrics and

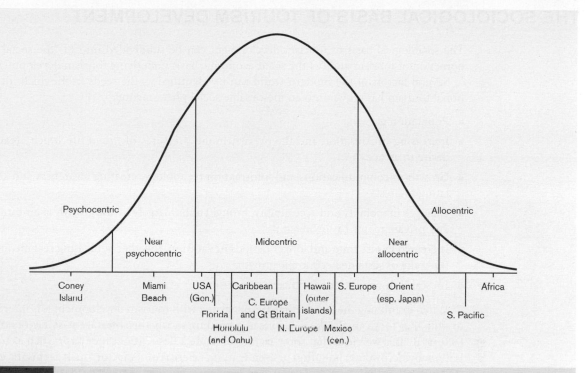

Figure 7.1	Psychographic positions of destinations
	Source: Plog, 1977

psychocentrics. The polar extremes of these groups can be described as exhibiting the following characteristics:

- **Allocentrics** seek cultural and environmental differences from their norm, belong to the higher income groups, are adventurous and require very little in the way of tourism plant.
- **Psychocentrics** seek familiar surroundings, belong to the lower income groups, are unadventurous and demand a high level of tourism plant.

According to Plog's framework, a resort may typically begin by attracting a small number of allocentrics (trendsetters), similar to Smith's explorers, but will soon develop in order to attract larger numbers of visitors. Using Plog's terminology this development will move the resort into and through the near allocentrics and then into the midcentrics. During this process the allocentrics will be alienated and they will move on to look for new destinations to 'discover'.

Resorts that have a strong competitive advantage, in terms of climate, location or top-quality tourism plant, such as DisneyLand in Florida, USA, may continue to thrive in the midcentric market. However, many resorts will tend to lose favour (perhaps because they are considered by tourists to be too commercialised) and continue their drift towards the psychocentric markets by offering lower tariffs, more comprehensive packaging and more scheduling of activities – the complete 'no-surprise vacation'.

Contrary to original thoughts concerning Plog's theory, this process of rise and decline is not immutable. Such a process may have seemed inevitable for many resorts in the past but, once decision makers realise that limited tourism development can be an attractive means of growth, they may develop tourism plant that is compatible with the environment and the indigenous characteristics of a region, and target them at the 'desired' market segments. Alternatively, recognition of the importance of quality tourism plant can allow destinations to maintain a midcentric position in the market continuum.

THE SOCIOLOGICAL BASIS OF TOURISM DEVELOPMENT

The sociological basis of tourism development can be subdivided into (a) the social phenomenon of tourism and (b) the socio-economic basis underlying tourism development.

Several factors of the modern world can be identified as the seeds from which international tourism has grown into an inescapable social phenomenon:

- Population growth.
- Increasing urbanisation and the overwhelming pressures of urban life which create the desire to escape.
- Growth in communications and information technology, creating awareness and stimulating interest.
- Changes in mobility and accessibility, brought about largely by the growth of air transport and private motor car ownership.
- Increased leisure time and longer periods of vacation, together with rising real incomes in the wake of sustained economic growth.
- Increases in world trade for business tourism.

When examining the factors that are associated with tourism development it is interesting to note that they can also be categorised according to whether they are *push* factors or *pull* factors. By this we mean that some factors generate a desire to escape (*push*) such as urbanisation, overcrowding, pollution or even tedium, whereas other factors such as specific events (Olympics) or climate and natural phenomena generate a magnetism that attracts tourists (*pull*). There are a number of factors that will influence the attitude of people towards tourism at both domestic and international levels. These include the following:

- **Age.** The age of the tourist will, within certain boundaries, influence the type of tourism activity pursued. For instance, there is likely to be less demand from the elderly for trekking and mountaineering vacations than from other age groups. Similarly, the greatest demand for tourist destinations with a hectic nightlife is likely to be from the 18–35-year-old age group. Of course there are always exceptions to these rules.
- **Education.** There is a tendency to associate the more adventurous and independent vacations with the more educated portion of the population. These would include Plog's allocentrics as well as Smith's explorers and elite travellers.
- **Income levels.** Income levels have an obvious influence on the decision of people to travel, the location to which they travel, the nature of the activities undertaken while away and the mode(s) of transport utilised.
- **Socio-economic background.** The previous experiences of people will play an important role in determining the type of holiday they will consume in future time periods. For instance, children from the higher **socio-economic groups**, who are accustomed to frequent trips abroad, are likely to continue this pattern throughout adulthood.

In addition to the socio-economic characteristics of the tourists, the tourism development process, together with its implications for socio-cultural impacts, should be examined. This approach encompasses all three approaches discussed so far – the psychological basis, the sociological basis and the socio-economic basis for tourism development. In general there is a *direct* socio-cultural impact which occurs as a result of the contact between the host population and the visitors. De Kadt (1979) suggests that there are three broad categories of such contact:

1. When the tourists buy goods and services from the hosts.
2. When the hosts and tourists share a facility such as the beach, a train or bus, a restaurant or bar, etc.
3. When tourists and hosts come together for the prime purpose of cultural exchange.

The first two of these types of contact are associated with the majority of the negative aspects of social contact, whereas the third type of contact is generally considered to be positive in nature. To draw comparisons between this work of de Kadt and the typology-based research of Smith, it is evident that the explorer/adventurer tourist is most likely to take part in the latter, positive type of interaction – providing a favourable association between this type of tourist and their socio-cultural impacts. However, the mass and charter tourist is more likely to be predominantly concerned with the first two types of contact, thereby making their presence generally unfavourable from a socio-cultural impact point of view. A crude conclusion can be drawn from this somewhat simplistic approach – the negative types of interaction are by far the most common and the positive types of contact are relatively rare.

The demonstration effect is also an aspect of the *direct* socio-cultural impact of tourism. Tourists influence the behaviour of the host population by their example. This is an area where tourism development is at a distinct disadvantage when compared with the use of alternative industries as a means to economic development. Tourism is a product that requires simultaneous production and consumption. Although international tourism may be seen as an export industry, in the same way as, say, oil or automobiles, it has the disadvantage that the consumer must visit the place of production (the factory) in order to consume it. This means that tourism will bring with it the physical presence of tourists and this will stimulate changes in the behaviour and dress style of the host population.

It is not even necessary for tourists to come into direct contact with members of the host population for the demonstration effect to take place. Those members of the host population who are influenced by the behaviour of the tourists are likely to influence other members of their community by their changed attitudes and behaviour. This can be classified as an *indirect* socio-cultural impact. Moreover, if tourism development is successful, new employment opportunities created by the increased activity will be the harbinger of social change in the same way that any form of economic development will change the consumption habits, the location and the behaviour of the local population. These changes will be stimulated further by the introduction of new or enhanced forms of communications, transport and infrastructure primarily provided for tourism development. These latter factors may also be considered to be *indirect* socio-cultural impacts but this time they are associated with many types of economic development, not just tourism. However, the diversity of productive sectors associated directly and indirectly with the tourism industry is such that these types of socio-cultural impacts will probably be more widely spread as a result of tourism development than any other industry.

As an economy grows and develops there will probably be an increase in income levels and the proportion of the population involved in the monetised sector. This will alter the consumption patterns of the local population. Such changes, if they include consumer durables such as television, videos and radio, will expose the local population to a greater range of wants and, in so doing, speed up the process of social change. These effects, because they are a result of increased income levels and consumer spending, may be seen as being *induced* socio-cultural impacts. This latter type of socio-cultural impact will also be evident irrespective of the type of economic catalyst that generated the development and is not uniquely attributable to tourism development.

The magnitude of the direct socio-cultural impact associated with tourism development will also be determined by the extent of the difference in socio-cultural characteristics between hosts and guests. Inskeep (1991) suggests that these differences include:

- basic value and logic system;
- religious beliefs;
- traditions;
- customs;
- lifestyles;
- behavioural patterns;

- dress codes;
- sense of time budgeting; and
- attitudes towards strangers.

To add further complexity to our understanding of the problems, the speed of development and change will have an important role in determining the magnitude of the socio-cultural changes because time allows for the process of adaptation. Compounding the issue further is the fact that the tourists' cultures when abroad (it is probable that the tourists will represent several different cultures) are different from the tourists' cultures at home. In other words, tourists often take on different attitudes and adopt different codes of behaviour when they are on vacation and away from their normal environment.

As discussed earlier, the socio-cultural impacts associated with tourism can be either positive or negative. One of the positive impacts highlighted by de Kadt was the exchange of cultural information, ideas and beliefs. But tourism can also be used to help stimulate interest in, and conserve aspects of, the host's cultural heritage such as in Petra, Jordan, York in the UK and Machu Picchu (the lost city of the Incas) in Peru. This is a significant positive socio-cultural impact and extends over ancient monuments, historic sites, arts, crafts and cultural ceremonies and rituals. If tourists appreciate the cultural heritage of a destination, that appreciation can stimulate the hosts' pride in their heritage and foster local crafts, traditions and customs.

The negative socio-cultural impacts are sometimes the result of *direct* contact and the demonstration effect and these can distort the traditional crafts and customs into shorter, commercialised events that offer the host community little in the way of rich cultural experience. Negative socio-cultural impacts can also be generated if the tourism development is not managed properly and the full economic potential of that development is not realised. For instance, foreign employment in tourism-related jobs and foreign investment in tourism projects both add to the local resentment of tourism development. The exclusion of hosts from certain tourist facilities (such as private beaches, casinos and transport services such as the Sky Train in Bangkok where locals have been excluded by high prices and limited flexibility off the tourism route) will further increase the pressure of resentment and may create conflict between the host population and the tourists.

As with any form of economic development, the new income-earning opportunities created by tourism development are unlikely to be evenly distributed across the destination. This may give rise to some members of the host community feeling resentful and antagonistic towards tourism development. Tourism destinations such as Jamaica in the Caribbean have experienced social problems because tourism development was confined to the north and western coast, although more recently attempts have been made to redress this imbalance. In tourism's favour, it is generally developed in areas where there is little in the way of competing industries (particularly manufacturing); therefore it helps provide employment opportunities in areas where they may be most needed. The creation of job opportunities with higher wage rates than those paid by the more traditional industries of fishing and agriculture can create social pressures between hosts who occupy these posts and their families and peers who do not.

A major problem can also occur because of a real (and sometimes only apparent) difference in wealth between the tourists and their hosts. It is true that there are occasions when the tourists are generally much wealthier than the hosts with whom they come into contact. However, this difference may be exacerbated by the fact that tourists exhibit spending patterns and behaviour that is very different from their norm, simply because they are on vacation. The normal spending habits of tourists is not information readily available to the average host. Furthermore, the difference in wealth between tourist and host may not be as severe a problem as initially perceived given the fact that the vast majority of international tourism takes place between industrialised countries and not between industrialised and developing countries.

When attempting to measure the level of irritation generated by tourist–host contact, Doxey (1975) drew up the following Index:

1. **The level of euphoria** – the initial thrill and enthusiasm that comes along with tourism development results in the fact that the tourist is made welcome.

2. **The level of apathy** – once tourism development is under way and the consequential expansion has taken place, the tourist is taken for granted and is now seen only as a source of profit-taking. What contact is made between host and guest is done on a commercial and formal footing.

3. **The level of irritation** – as the industry approaches saturation point, the hosts can no longer cope with the number of tourists without the provision of additional facilities.

4. **The level of antagonism** – the tourist is now seen as the harbinger of all ills, hosts are openly antagonistic towards tourists and tourists are regarded as being there to be exploited.

5. **The final level** – during the above process of 'development' the host population has forgotten that all they once regarded as being special was exactly the same thing that attracted the tourist, but in the rush to develop tourism circumstances have changed. The social impact has been comprehensive and complete and the tourists will move to different destinations.

Although we have discussed a wide range of approaches to the study of the socio-cultural impact of tourism, there are some very strong common strands. If the typology used by Valene Smith is linked to the host–guest interaction suggested by Doxey, within the framework proposed by Butler and Plog then the commonality can be seen. Figure 7.2 shows each of these theories combined within a two-dimensional frame.

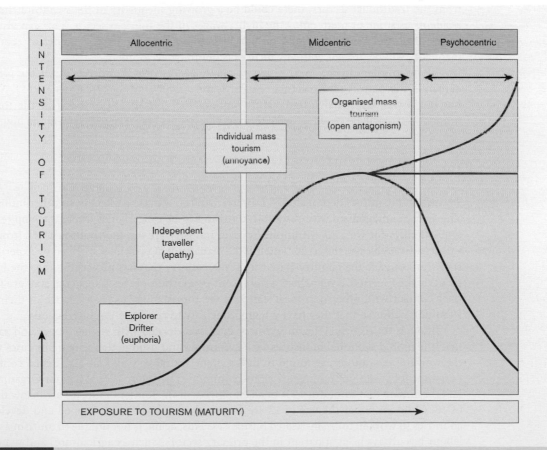

| **Figure 7.2** | The approaches to studying the socio-cultural impact of tourism |

Although Figure 7.2 presents the various approaches within a single framework, the framework is a static one. This means that it is still hampered by the fact that the dynamics of the process are not reflected and thus its practical applicability is severely limited.

SOME GENERAL NEGATIVE SOCIO-CULTURAL IMPACTS OF TOURISM

There is a wide variety of ways in which the development and operation of tourism can create social tensions and impact on the integrity of the local culture. The most obvious and direct effect is the bringing together of two different cultures and this is an issue that threads its way throughout this chapter. However, the socio-cultural impact of tourism may arise from some general but less obvious factors.

Economic factors

The majority of tourism activity takes place between the industrialised economies of the world. However, where tourism takes place between the industrialised and the less developed destinations or regions, there can be an enormous imbalance of economic power between the tourists and the hosts. Where tourists are much wealthier than the people with whom they come into contact there is likely to be some attempt at emulation as well as some resentment. This may be reflected in behaviour, dress and spending patterns. Furthermore, where tourism results in the migration of labour from rural to urban areas and attracts workers from the traditional sectors, there could be a growing inequality in the wealth of the local residents as some of them enjoy the higher wages of the tourism sector. This can also lead to social tensions. But it should be borne in mind that the latter channel of economic inequality will be present with any form of economic development.

The tax burden on the local residents may be increased in order to meet the growing demands for better infrastructure (roads, water supply, sewage treatment, etc.). Where tourism drives improved infrastructure without the costs being reflected in the tourism product, there will be growing social tension as residents may struggle to meet the higher tax demands.

Labour factors

The economic factors demonstrated how tourism can attract workers from other industries. The level of antagonism with respect to tourism can be exacerbated where the employment opportunities for workers within the tourism industry are limited to lower level, front-line workers. In such cases the senior and middle management positions are filled by experienced staff from outside the country (often from the country that has provided either the investment or the tourists). Even where a significant proportion of the managerial staff are locals, their contact with other non-local staff and the tourists may cause a change in their consumption habits so that they have a high propensity to consume imported goods.

Although tourism may be an industry that is associated with higher wages and salaries than the more traditional industries such as farming and fishing, there are many cases where the working conditions are found to be less than desirable. Child labour, casual contracts, part-time jobs with no training are all too common. The International Labour Organization (ILO) estimate that some 10–15% of all employees in the tourism industry are below the age of 18. Children under the age of 12 are frequently employed in developed and developing countries to work in tourism-related businesses. This, again, is not unique to tourism as child labour has always been apparent in the primary sectors (such as agriculture) and manufacturing sectors (such as textiles).

MINI CASE STUDY 7.1
Income inequality in Taman Negara National Park, Malaysia

In western Malaysia, the Taman Negara National Park is a privately owned park and resort which can house 260 visitors at a time. The park employs 270 people and 60% of the staff in the administrative headquarters are locals. In 1999 these local staff earned about US$120 a month; for comparison, Malaysians living off the land at that time were earning on average about US$40 a month.

Despite the positive effects of increased park employment, the difference in income between the two local groups has led to social tension and driven up boat fares and the cost of everyday goods. Little of the tourism money generated by the park stays in Malaysia, and park employees spend almost 90% of their income outside the region or on imported goods. Thus local inhabitants, whose culture has been marketed to attract tourists, benefit only to a very limited extent. Indeed, many have taken to illegal hunting and fishing in the park, contrary to its protective regulations.

Source: ILO report on human resources development, employment and globalisation in the hotel, catering and tourism sector, 2001 from http://www.ilo.org/public/english/dialogue/sector/techmeet/tmhct01/tmhctr2.htm; report for discussion at the Tripartite Meeting on Human Resources Development, Employment and Globalization in the Hotel, Catering and Tourism Sector, Geneva, 2–6 April 2001, International Labour Office, Geneva

DISCUSSION QUESTIONS

1. 'The income and employment inequalities experienced by any country or region as their economy develops may lead to social tensions and a change in the lifestyles and behaviour of the population. This is not a condition unique to tourism development and should be accepted rather than seen as a criticism of the tourism industry.' Discuss.

2. Would it be better, from a socio-cultural point of view, to isolate tourists from the local population by putting them into private resorts or to integrate them by developing tourism into existing sites?

3. What policies could be implemented to mitigate some of the tension that has been experienced at Taman Negara National Park?

Behavioural and demonstration factors

If the tourists are not aware of, or care for, the local customs they may behave in a way that creates severe social friction between tourists and residents and, ultimately between the residents themselves. The planet is rich in customs and every custom gives the tourist an opportunity to adapt to the local norms or to insult their hosts, often without ever knowing that they have done so. Slurping of soup may be seen as the result of poor table manners in the UK but is an expression of appreciation in China; putting your chopsticks vertically into the bowl of rice in Japan is a symbol of death and is usually only seen in funeral ceremonies; showing the soles of your shoes is considered offensive in a number of countries including Thailand and Iran; inappropriate dress in Muslim countries can cause offence, so too can inappropriate consumption (such as alcohol) or nude sunbathing in countries that may be conservative in this respect.

There are many destinations in the Middle East, the Far East, the Caribbean and the South Pacific that would find the lack of adherence to local social behaviour codes difficult to tolerate. Those that are exposed to such inappropriate behaviour or dress codes may find that, over time, they come to accept them and even emulate such behaviour, causing tension between the residents.

MINI CASE STUDY 7.2
Tourism is a human rights issue

By Polly Pattullo

There's no stopping us now. We are no longer content with a modest holiday in our own back yards; we want to explore every nook and cranny of the world. And at the same time we have become aware of the damage we can do to the planet when millions of us from the rich north take our holiday in the poor south, *writes Polly Pattullo*.

Tourism has become a human rights issue – it impacts on the environment, the survival of indigenous people, the wellbeing of other cultures; it also means that our dollars often never reach the host countries. The inequalities and exploitation of the poor by the rich is intrinsic to the worst sort of tourism practices.

We are aware that tourism can have these negative impacts, though it's sometimes hard to know what to do about it. But now consumers are on the warpath: we're buying more fair-trade produce than ever before and we're beginning to recognise that we can extend this to tourism. Fairly-traded ethical tourism means an end to the manufactured smile of the weary waiter or the desperate flirtation of the prostitute on the tropical beach. The result is an economic exchange that benefits our hosts as well as us holidaymakers.

However, with tourism it seems it's hard to act ethically; our intentions may be good but perhaps day-dreaming in a hammock is preferable.

One of the problems about ethical tourism is that we're not sure how to do it. We are still left largely in the dark when it comes to making ethical decisions about holidays. The reason is that until recently, the very powerful tourism industry has been happy to leave us ignorant and powerless. So how would we know that our carefully chosen hotel was built over a sacred site or that local communities were displaced to build it; or that the chambermaids work for a pittance and never get a holiday?

We can't know this unless we can trust the tour operators to care about these things. In the past, they did not. Sustainable tourism was, to a great extent, seen as a niche issue, something that only mattered to a hardcore minority; it was argued that it was not the industry's responsibility to review their own behaviour.

But globalisation has brought about a new mindset, and not just among the radical few. More and more consumers are looking to take responsible holidays and the industry is just beginning to respond.

However, the patchwork of accreditation schemes that exist are often more concerned with a nod to environmental good practice, often at the expense of social and economic relationships. That's the sort of greenwashing that gives eco-tourism a bad name.

So it is up to us punters to search out our own ethical holidays. There are pockets of good practice initiatives linked mainly to the small specialist operators. Look for prominent mission statements that talk of partnership. Go for holidays that are controlled by local people. In this way you will put your money into the pockets of local people and ensure sustainable development.

Tourism is a tricky business to get right to satisfy the needs of guests and hosts. Grassroots partnerships can guarantee more equitable tourism that will lead to fair-trade tourism becoming a cool way to holiday. It may be glib but ethical tourism means happy hosts as well as happy tourists. And the smile of the waiter, perhaps no longer so weary, may just be genuine.

Source: http://blogs.guardian.co.uk/travelog/2006/03/ethical_dilemma.html

DISCUSSION QUESTIONS

1. 'Although tourism can effectively redistribute income from urban to rural areas within an economy, it has not been successful as a vehicle to redistribute income from the wealthy industrialised countries to the poorer less developed countries.' Discuss.

2. Is it possible to have such a product as ethical tourism? Analyse and discuss the issues raised by Polly Pattullo in the above blog and comment on the limitations and constraints created by the global structure and organisation of the tourism industry.

Resource use factors

Tourism is about real estate development and thus will place high demands on land use. These demands will compete with alternative local use and may result in land price inflation. Where land price inflation occurs it can create social tension as local residents are competed out of their properties.

Environmental and cultural damage resulting from tourism can lead to social tension. This is a common problem in areas where there are heritage sites and examples can be found in places like Paphos, where there was open pilfering by the tourists and residents from the site of the Byzantium Fort. It is not only the man-made heritage that is being stolen; precious and irreplaceable fossils in areas such as the Petrified Forest of Arizona are also subject to looting by smugglers and tourists. Similarly, where the social tensions increase there can be vandalism and wilful damage to heritage sites.

Competition between locals and tourist businesses for local resources is commonplace, such as the use of a beach or mountain area. The economics of the situation gives the tourist businesses the upper hand in such competitions and the locals often find that their use of the facilities are removed or downgraded.

SOME SPECIFIC NEGATIVE SOCIO-CULTURAL IMPACTS OF TOURISM

Sex

The fact that tourists will travel abroad to enjoy uninhibited casual sexual encounters is not a new phenomenon. Sexual exploitation has grown as rapidly as tourism in many destinations. The early European tourists were to some extent motivated by the liberal attitude towards sex in some of the Third World countries they visited. More recently, a major tourism market has grown up around sex tourism and destinations such as Thailand, Gambia and some of the Central European countries have actively marketed the sexual content of their products. The proliferation of AIDS has done much to dampen the rapid growth of this element of the tourism industry but it is still a significant part of the market. It is questionable whether tourism created the social disruption associated with the sex trade or whether the sex trade has stimulated the tourism market. But, as with all forms of prostitution, it is impossible to be conclusive as to the rights and wrongs of either party. Certainly the growth of paedophile activity is one element of the tourist industry that is outlawed in many of the tourist-generating countries and can only be pursued under the guise of international tourism. The United Nations defines sex tourism relating to children to be 'tourism organised with the primary purpose of facilitating the effecting of a commercial sexual relationship with a child'. The growth of such activities is often supported by a network of facilitators ranging from pimps and brothels through to the seemingly more respectable taxi drivers and hotel workers. The Internet has only added to the problem by creating an international communication network that can market these services on an international scale. So prolific is this problem that agencies such as ECPAT have been set up to campaign against child prostitution. The acronym stands for 'End Child Prostitution, Child Pornography and Trafficking of Children for Sexual Purposes'.

The future development of tourism using specific sexual activities as its main catalyst may be in doubt in the current world of AIDS and other sexually transmitted diseases. However, many tourists from industrialised countries may expect to relax their sexual morals during a vacation and this can lead to a thin line being drawn between destinations that are primarily trading on sex and those that offer an environment wherein tourists can relax their sexual morals.

MINI CASE STUDY 7.3
Dominican Republic: the sun, the sand, the sex

Jon Cohen

Boca Chica, Dominican Republic – At the Plaza Isla Bonita bar that stretches from the main downtown street to the beach, the cocktail waitresses dress in campy 'Ship's Ahoy' outfits with sailor hats and midriff tops. When not serving high-octane rum drinks, they dance suggestively to the blaring merengue, bachata, and reggaeton music. Tables and bar stools fill with young Dominican women, who flirt aggressively with American, Dutch, German, and Italian men twice if not three times their age. Sanky Pankies – local young men who favor dreadlocks, bling bling, and tank tops – cruise the perimeter looking for foreign women or men.

The waitresses sing along when a popular song comes on by the band Mambo Violento: *Sin gorrito, no hay cumpleaño* – without a little hat, there is no birthday party. But in this case, a little hat is a condom, and the birthday party doesn't involve cake.

Sex tourism is booming in several of the resorts here, says Antonio de Moya, an epidemiologist and anthropologist who has long studied the subculture and works with the presidential AIDS program COPRESIDA. In the past 15 years, the Dominican Republic has become a tourist magnet, attracting 3.4 million vacationers in 2004, more than double the number who visited in 1991, according to the Caribbean Tourist Organization. And the Caribbean as a whole entertained more than 21 million tourists in 2004. Today, sex tourism and HIV/AIDS have become hot topics in Jamaica, Cuba, Barbados, the Bahamas, St Lucia, St Marteens, and Curaçao.

| Photograph 7.1 | Tourism nightlife. |

Source: PA Photos

Deanna Kerrigan, an international health specialist at the Johns Hopkins Bloomberg School of Public Health in Baltimore, Maryland, studies sex work in the Dominican Republic. She stresses that outside resorts such as Boca Chica, tourists are not the main clients. 'There is a very large local sex-work industry,' says Kerrigan. Sex is sold everywhere, from brothels and rendezvous homes called *casas de citas* to discos and car washes. HIV prevalence in the country's estimated 100,000 female sex workers ranges from 2.5% to 12.4%, depending on the locale. Kerrigan says the places with lower prevalence reflect 'intensive interventions' by nongovernmental organizations such as the one she collaborates with called the Centro de Orientación e Investigación Integral.

Sex workers of course could have both local and foreign clients, but three women working the main street here this warm winter evening insist that they avoid Dominicans. 'A Dominican will pay 300 pesos and be on top of you for 2 hours,' says Aracelis, as the other women laugh and nod their heads. 'And they don't want to use condoms.' Aracelis and her friends insist that *sin gorrito, no hay cumpleaño*, and all say they are HIV-negative. But they still worry. 'The first thing I say when I leave the house in the morning is "Please, God, take care of me,"' says Aracelis. Then, as though her prayers were answered, she notices an elderly German man. 'He's my boyfriend, not a client,' she says, prancing over to him. 'He sends me money every month.'

Source: http://www.sciencemag.org/cgi/content/full/313/5786/474

DISCUSSION QUESTIONS

1. 'The strong growth of sex tourism in some destinations may mean that these destinations are faced with the choice of either having tourism based on the sex trade or not having tourism at all.' Discuss the issues involved in this statement.

2. In some destinations commercial sexual exploitation has developed in parallel with the growth in tourism. Tourism based upon the sex trade involves complex issues and may have serious implications for the long-term future of the industry. Is the control of the sex industry simply a local legislative and enforcement matter or is it an issue that should have international intervention?

3. Discuss the socio-cultural and ethical issues of the tourist sex industry and any actions that may be undertaken to control it.

Crime

The link between tourism and crime is hard to establish. Many writers, such as Mathieson and Wall (1982), have suggested the link but find it hard to establish whether crime increases simply because of the increased population density (urbanisation) or whether it is more specifically associated with tourism. Clearly the presence of large numbers of tourists carrying relatively large sums of money and valuables with them provides a source for illegal activities including drugs trafficking, robbery and violence. Brazil, Florida, and Jamaica are just three of the many destinations that have been the subject of international press coverage because of acts of violent crimes against tourists. Tourists are sometimes obvious victims of crime where they are clearly identifiable by language or colour and can be expected to be carrying significant sums of money with them.

Tourism is often the catalyst for the growth of gaming activities and a number of destinations have used casino developments as a means of attracting tourist spending. Unless properly monitored and controlled, such developments can induce social behaviour that is detrimental to social cohesion.

Where hotels attempt to protect their guests by the use of armed agents this can often inflame the social tension between tourists and local residents.

Health

The problem of AIDS has already been mentioned. However, there are other less newsworthy diseases that can be transmitted when people from different communities interact, such as the recording of more than 8,500 cases of malaria in the UK largely through tourists and VFR traffic. Although often not fatal, these illnesses can cause social and economic stress to the host population who may have less immunity to the diseases than the tourist population. Where tourism growth is rapid and unplanned there can be infrastructure failures that lead to health hazards.

Other aspects

Following the lead of Cohen (1988), it is possible to categorise the key themes that characterise the interface between culture and tourism. There are a variety of ways in which such categories can be constructed but the following issues reflect the major concerns that are currently being debated:

- **Commodification** – where the demands of tourism lead to the mutation and sometimes destruction of the meaning of cultural performances and events. Tourists are likely to have different time-frames and expectations from local residents and this may result in religious rituals and traditional ethnic customs and rites being changed to suit the needs and wishes of tourists. This process is sometimes referred to as reconstructed ethnicity.
- **Staged authenticity** – where 'pseudo-events' are presented to satisfy tourists' needs for new (simulated) experiences, such as the Fijian firewalkers (see below).
- **Standardisation** – where the tourists' search for the familiar leads to a loss of cultural diversity.
- **Alien cultural experiences of tourists** – which examines the apparent inability to enjoy meaningful cultural experiences without travelling to different environments.

Commodification

Commodification is a long-standing criticism relating to tourism's effect on culture and art. Crafts, ceremonies and rituals are often driven into an exploitation stance, abbreviated, made more colourful, more dramatic and spectacular in order to capture the attention and imagination of an audience that often does not possess the underlying knowledge/experience that would make the unadapted version appealing. Countless examples can and have been cited, from the sale of concrete paving slabs with carvings of Bob Marley on them in Jamaica, the *Bula Fiji* carved wooden knives and clubs, to the Polynesian dances of Western Samoa and the limbo dancers of the Caribbean. Where culture becomes a commodity for financial transactions it is difficult to be objective. Although it is true that the demands of people from alien cultures who are operating on a very tight and sometimes fixed time budget are very different from the local demands, it is sometimes this foreign demand that enriches and/or preserves decaying and dying skills and performances.

Staged authenticity

With growing public awareness regarding cultural and ethnic differences there has been increasing demand for tourism products that offer cultural authenticity, that is, environments where the tourists can 'get behind the scenes' to meet and observe the real people. Although, in the Plog sense, this may be considered a great leap forward in perception and understanding by volume tourists and a movement back from the psychocentric scale of the tourist market, it can also be regarded as being a signal for impending cultural devastation for some destinations. This represents the social impact dilemma of post-1980 tourism development.

In order to differentiate their product from other tourism products on the market destinations have highlighted environmental, climatic and cultural differences. In this last instance, they are using their cultural heritage as a promotional device to attract increasing numbers of tourists. Although this may be considered to be a positive step in achieving greater awareness concerning cultural differences and, perhaps, a greater empathy between tourist and host, it also exposes a deeper layer of the sociological structure and thereby risks further 'contamination'.

However, there are ways of differentiating the tourism product, providing tourists with sufficient cultural exposure to satisfy their demands while preserving the true cultural identity of the host population. One such way is the use of staged authenticity whereby the host population provides a more realistic performance of cultural heritage than existed before, but still ensures that the tourists do not manage to penetrate behind the stage curtains. Figure 7.3 demonstrates the concept and dangers of staged authenticity.

In Figure 7.3 the arena is divided into three distinct areas:

A – the previous level of tourist penetration into the host culture;

B – the new level of cultural penetration that is considered to be authentic by the tourist but is, in fact, staged authenticity; and

C – the true cultural heritage of the host society that maintains its integrity by keeping tourists on the other side of the firewall curtain.

Although effective in the short term, this approach to cultural impact containment can lead to increasing levels of penetration when the firewall curtains are continually retreating in order to provide greater tourist experiences and diversity within a competitive market. Even if the social firewall does not retreat there is a danger that some of the tourists will manage to penetrate beyond the curtain. Eventually there will be nowhere for the host population to maintain the integrity of their culture. There is an additional danger in the form of a *gradual* cultural impact. The very act of staging the authenticity of the culture can blur the

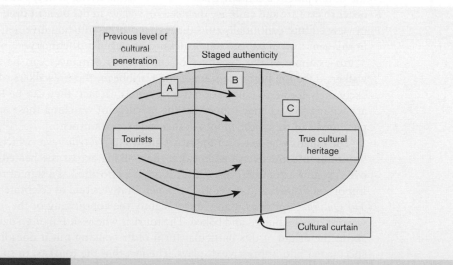

Figure 7.3   Levels of cultural penetration

Photograph 7.2	Firewalking for tourists.
	Source: Rex Features/Tim Rooke

true boundaries of the local heritage and, in so doing, distort the cultural heritage that is being maintained behind the firewall curtain.

It has also been argued that the so-called authenticity of culture is a fleeting moment in the development calendar. Culture is a dynamic living concept and changes continually in order to capture and embrace the needs of society in the present time period. From this point of view culture continually runs through a process of being invented and reinvented and so, in this sense, all of culture can be defined as staged authenticity.

An example of the dynamics of cultural performances can be seen in the Fijian firewalkers. Like the limbo dancers of the Caribbean, the firewalkers of Fiji are, today, almost exclusively found in cultural centres or hotels. In fact, they can be found wherever tourists are willing to exchange money for the privilege of watching these ancient customs that are packaged and transformed into dinner-side entertainment.

The Fijians who perform the ritual known as *Vilavilairevo* (which translates literally into 'jumping into the oven') accept that the walking across the heated stones of a *lovo* (earth oven) is now a commercial event. It is rarely performed as a sign of respect for powerful and important visitors and never as a commemorative ritual to celebrate (and test the legend of) *Tui Qualita*. Nor does it any longer signify the conquering of the *lovo* in which a defeated warrior may be buried and baked. The tourists who visit Fiji often have no prior information about the origin of this particular form of firewalking but it does little to detract from the spectacular and impressive displays. The fact that the tourists, in spite of any narrative that may accompany the firewalking events, are unaware of the true meaning and significance of the ritual does not mean that tourism's mutation of the custom has created a gulf between host and visitor. That gulf existed prior to the performance and may well be one of the reasons why the tourist chose that destination. The commercialisation of the event in itself is also not wholly bad in that it generates much-needed currency for communities and, given its redundancy as part of modern-day Fijian culture, preserves a custom and instils pride in the history and culture of the Fiji people.

Standardisation

Tourists, although they may search for unfamiliar environments and cultures, often search for familiar facilities. Examples such as McDonald's demonstrate this effect quite clearly. This introduces a number of factors into the development scenario. First, there is the development of superstructure that might be quite different from that normally found in the local environment. Secondly, the operation of those facilities may introduce work practices and systems that are different from those normally found in the local economy, particularly their employment structures and conditions as well as their purchasing strategies. Finally, by building familiar structures within unfamiliar environments there is a loss of diversity that is as real to the socio-cultural environment as the loss of a species may be to biodiversity. This issue becomes more problematic as you move into the high volume tourist markets where destinations must not appear too strange if they wish to capture large segments of the market.

Alien cultural experiences of tourists

This issue revolves around the apparent inability of tourists to take part in or enjoy meaningful cultural experiences within their home environment. As with many of the aspects that underlie the motivation of tourists, it is not so much the inability of tourists to enjoy meaningful cultural experiences within their home environment, indeed many do so without even recognising the fact, it is more the reflection that tourists search for different – *or alien* – experiences. The desire to experience different climatic conditions (sun, rain or snow) and different environmental surroundings (deserts, rainforests, cities or rolling green fields) is willingly accepted. Therefore, it is not an absurd proposition to suggest that tourists may actively seek out cultural experiences that are deliberately different from their norm – indeed such motivation is becoming an increasingly important aspect of twenty-first-century tourism.

SOME GENERAL POSITIVE SOCIO-CULTURAL IMPACTS ASSOCIATED WITH TOURISM

Tourism fosters local pride

Tourism can inspire pride in a destination's heritage. Often we forget the value of the things that surround us and only when seen through the eyes of tourists do we revalue our culture. Ceremonies and rituals become jaded over time and can lose their appeal to local residents. Tourism can put new life into such ceremonies and make them come alive once more. The same is true regarding old skills and crafts that, without tourism, may have ceased to exist in a modern world where they lose relevance. Of course, it can be argued that if these skills or crafts were past their sell-by date and would have ceased to exist then they should be allowed to have a peaceful natural death and not be preserved as something that is 'quaint' for the sake of tourism.

Tourism for socio-cultural awareness and peace

Tourism takes people to new places and broadens their understanding and knowledge of other cultures and environments. This is an educational process and is an important part of the industry. If channelled properly this education can lead to a greater awareness, sympathy and admiration for other societies. This cultural exchange that takes place between tourists and local residents can help foster peace between communities. So strong is the belief in the relationship between tourism and peace that in 1986 the International Institute for Peace through Tourism (IIPT) was set up. The IIPT has organised several conferences since its inception and in November 2000 made the Amman Declaration that set out the fundamental objectives of the IIPT and those that were aligned to the movement. This was ratified by more than 450 delegates from 60 countries and included the chief executive officers of 22 major international tourism corporations. The Amman Declaration was a far-reaching document that attempts to incorporate socio-cultural, environmental and economic objectives under a single banner.

Tourism provides shared infrastructure

When tourism is developed in a destination the local infrastructure is often enhanced to meet the needs of this development. The local community can find that the quality of their life is significantly enhanced through being able to enjoy this improved infrastructure. This can be as simple as the increased health afforded by improved water supply and sewage treatment to the more complex issues surrounding the provision of an airport and access to regular international flights. New sporting venues, entertainment facilities, restaurants and a better range of food and beverage available for consumption are just some of the many positive side-effects that tourism can create for the local population.

Tourism can provide direct socio-cultural support

The tourism industry can provide much-needed funds to help restore heritage sites or conserve natural and cultural sites. Examples of such good practice can be found on the Tour Operators Initiative web site http://www.toinitiative.org/index.php?id=48. They include examples such as the Travel Walji's case, where the company is not only providing direct financial support to conservation in the Karakorum region of South Asia but is also providing indirect support to the area through its tourism development aid.

Tourism can yield enormous socio-cultural benefits as well as devastating costs. The net effect depends upon the responsibility exercised by the various stakeholders of the industry, including the public and private sectors as well as the tourists and residents. To be able to evaluate the net socio-cultural benefits of tourism it is necessary to be able to measure the benefits and costs in an objective and acceptable framework.

METHODS OF MEASURING THE SOCIO-CULTURAL IMPACT OF TOURISM

Data collection

The socio-cultural factors influenced by tourist activities are, in general, the most difficult ones to measure and quantify. Whereas the economic and many of the environmental indicators do lend themselves to objective measurement, the socio-cultural impacts are often highly qualitative and subjective in nature. The nature of socio-cultural impacts can range from those impacts that are obvious and measurable, such as the outbreak of particular types of disease and/or infection, to those that are hard to identify and measure such as changes in customs and codes of conduct. On the other hand, there are those impacts that may be identifiable, such as increased crime rates, drug abuse and prostitution, but are difficult to attribute to tourism rather than to other factors of influence (such as media intrusion).

There is a wide range of data sources that may be utilised in order to examine the social impact of tourism. It is important to recognise that some of these data may not be exclusively related to tourism activity. Where causes of variable changes are multivariate then deeper analysis must be undertaken in order to filter out other influences. Complete filtering is unlikely to be possible.

Data collection sources can be categorised into primary and secondary. Primary data can be collected by undertaking household and visitor surveys. This method of data collection is time-consuming and costly. It is also sometimes difficult to maintain the appropriate level of objectivity and the resident awareness questionnaires require very careful construction if they are to provide data that are both unbiased and in a form that is user-friendly. Other forms of primary data collection include the interviewing of **focus groups, key informants, Delphi analyses** and participant observation. Table 7.2 distinguishes between interview/questionnaire/Delphi approaches and those that use observation techniques.

There are a variety of secondary sources for gathering information with respect to socio-cultural impacts. These include criminal activity statistics, notification of infectious diseases statistics, employment and unemployment data, newspaper reports/articles and other media coverage. Some of these data are quantitative in nature whereas others are quite subjective and care must be taken in the interpretation. Table 7.2 distinguishes between those data that are collected, assimilated and tabulated for other purposes, and information (largely qualitative) that can be gleaned from scanning past and present newspaper cuttings, television and radio news and documentary programmes and other media forms of covering current affairs.

The two fundamental means of assessing socio-cultural impacts in a destination are by surveying both tourists and local residents. There are several factors that should be taken into account when undertaking a local resident survey.

Table 7.2	Data from different sources			
	Primary data		Secondary data	
Indicators (changes in)	Survey	Observe	Data	Media
Crime rates/levels	X		X	X
Prostitution		X	X	X
Drug abuse	X		X	X
Promiscuity	X	X	X	X
Gambling	X		X	X
Family relationships	X		X	X
Social values	X	X	X	X
Creative expressions	X	X		X
Traditional ceremonies	X	X		X
Safety levels	X		X	
Health	X		X	
Community organisations	X		X	X
Infrastructure	X	X	X	X
Collective lifestyles	X	X		X
Economic independence	X		X	X
Population dispersion	X		X	
Cultural commercialisation	X	X	X	X
Host/tourist hostility	X		X	X
Demonstration effects	X	X		
Economic and social dualism	X		X	X
Psychological stress	X		X	X
Living standards	X		X	X

First, it is important, as with all sampling procedures, to obtain a representative sample of the population. This may seem obvious, but several social impact studies have relied entirely upon random sampling of the immediate population (those directly in the vicinity of the tourist facilities). In order to gauge the true impact and its level of penetration it is important that the survey population is seen as being wider than this. Secondly, it is important to establish whether or not the respondent correctly identifies who is a tourist. The misperception as to what constitutes a tourist can render local resident surveys misleading. Thirdly, in areas subject to seasonality, it is also important to undertake the survey at different times of the year. Quite often a good indicator of the magnitude of the social impact of tourism is how quickly the levels of awareness, resentment and other characteristics decline once the peak season recedes. Where there is a significant level of decline shortly after the peak season one can assume that the impacts, although severe during the peak period, are not too deeply embedded in the local population. Where remedial action is required in visitor management flows or **infrastructural investment**, there is every chance that these actions will be successful. If the levels of resentment continue to run high during the off-peak periods then there is a distinct possibility that any remedial action will need to be fundamental, even to the point of reducing the peak levels of tourism flows.

In order to complement the work that has already been undertaken in the field of economic and environmental impacts and to provide a common framework for the analysis of socio-cultural impacts, researchers at Bournemouth University have attempted to embed the process of socio-cultural impacts within the economic and environmental model structure. The inclusion of socio-cultural impacts within such a model allows for the direct, indirect and induced impacts to be considered as well as providing a vehicle for the study of social and cultural changes as a result of other (non-tourism-related) factors.

At this point in time the number of socio-cultural variables that can be included at such a detailed and quantifiable level are limited but include indicators such as:

- the ratio of tourists to host population;
- the number of contacts between hosts and guests for transactions;
- the number of contacts between hosts and guests while sharing facilities;
- the number of contacts between hosts and guests for socio-cultural purposes;
- differences between host and guest age distributions;
- percentage of local population coming into contact with tourists;
- percentage of population working in tourism-related industries weighted by indirect and induced employment;
- tourist/host clustering; and
- the nature of tourism.

The above data should be collected and analysed at relatively frequent intervals. Some of these data are readily available in most countries and systems can be put into place to show those ratios on a weekly or monthly basis. Others are more difficult to acquire and may only be available at discrete time intervals.

CONCLUSION

This chapter has examined the nature and determinants of the socio-cultural impacts associated with tourism development. In so doing, the nature of the tourism development process has been explored together with the influence of socio-economic factors in driving the development of tourism. The typological studies undertaken by researchers such as Smith and Plog have provided a framework which facilitates the further development of socio-cultural impact methodologies and that framework can be used to show the commonalities of the models suggested by Butler and Doxey. But, it was noted, this framework is static and is severely limited by the nature of the variables used. The development of tourism can have specific implications for incidents of crime and health, as well as influencing the individual and collective lifestyles of the local population. It was also noted that there are positive aspects to tourism's socio-cultural impacts and that these should not be neglected when evaluating the performance of tourism in a given destination. It is also important to recognise the fact that tourists can also transmit socio-cultural impacts back to the populations of the originating countries.

The problems associated with measuring either the desirability of preserving the cultural heritage of a destination or determining how this is influenced by the presence of tourists make it a difficult area of research. The staged authenticity approach to tourism development can provide a firewall in order to maintain the integrity of the local cultural heritage. However, staged authenticity can also act as a catalyst for further cultural penetration and act as the 'thin end of the wedge' for further intrusion.

There are data available that can be used to analyse the magnitude and direction of socio-cultural impacts and these were examined in order to suggest a framework for an integrated tourism impact model.

SELF-CHECK QUESTIONS

1. What are the major approaches to studying the socio-cultural impacts of tourism?

2. What models have been put forward to explain the development of tourism and its impact on the local population?

3. Identify three direct positive socio-cultural impacts of tourism and three indirect positive socio-cultural impacts of tourism.

4. Identify three direct negative socio-cultural impacts of tourism and three indirect negative socio-cultural impacts of tourism.

5. What are the major difficulties involved in measuring the socio-cultural impacts of tourism and what sources of data are available?

ESSAY QUESTIONS

1. 'It is not the *absolute* characteristics of the tourists that determine the degree of socio-cultural impact on a destination, it is the *relative* difference between the profiles of the tourists and those of the local population that is important.' Discuss.

2. Examine the commonalities and differences between the tourism typology studies, the life-cycle theories and the work of Doxey as a means of studying the determination of socio-cultural impacts.

3. 'The lack of a baseline from which to measure tourism's socio-cultural impacts and the inability to isolate changes from other sources such as television and films makes it impossible to determine the impacts of tourism.' Discuss.

4. Are the socio-cultural impacts associated with tourism development necessarily negative?

5. What key variables can be used to measure the magnitude, scope and direction of socio-cultural impacts? Outline the weaknesses and strengths of these variables.

ANNOTATED FURTHER READING

Books

Duval, D.T. (2004) *Tourism in the Caribbean: Trends, Development, Prospects*, Routledge, London.
A book that examines a wide range of tourism issues in the Caribbean, including the cultural implications and tourism impacts at historic sites.

Gartner, W.C. and Lime, D.W. (eds) (2000) *Trends in Outdoor Recreation, Leisure and Tourism*, CABI, Wallingford, Oxford.
A comprehensive collection of papers examining the implications of tourism for development, the economy, society and on the environment.

Krippendorf, J. (1987) *The Holiday Makers – Understanding the Impact of Leisure and Travel*, Heinemann, London.
The author places his arguments in favour of responsible tourism in the context of Maslow's pyramid of needs and looks at the demands and effects of the tourists once they have satisfied their basic demands.

Mathieson, A. and Wall, G. (1982) *Tourism: Economic, Physical and Social Impacts*, Longman, Harlow.
Although somewhat dated it still provides a very readable journey into the impacts of tourism upon society and culture.

Smith, V.L. and Eadington, W.R. (eds) (1995) *Tourism Alternatives: Potential Problems in the Development of Tourism*, University of Pennsylvania Press, Philadelphia.
A reflection on the socio-cultural impacts of alternative forms of tourism development.

Articles

Berno, T. (1999) 'When a guest is a guest: Cook Islanders view tourism', *Annals of Tourism Research* **26**(3), 656–75.
This article reports the findings of cross-cultural psychological research undertaken in the Cook Islands. It is argued that differences in the ways that hosts and guests conceptualise tourism in the Cook Islands are related to the socio-cultural and psychological impacts of the industry.

Brunt, P. and Courtney, P. (1999) 'Host perceptions of socio-cultural impacts', *Annals of Tourism Research* **26**(3), 493–515.
This paper investigates community perceptions of the socio-cultural impacts of tourism and examines the extent to which they coincide with their classifications made by academic writers.

Graburn N.H.H. and Barthel-Bouchier, D. (2001) 'Relocating the Tourist', *International Sociology* **16**(2), 147–58.
This article traces the arrival and the subsequent debates about the place of the tourist in sociology. The sociology of tourists focused first on their economic and then their physical and socio-cultural impacts, in the stereotypical case of mass tourists of the metropolis visiting historical and peripheral locations. More recently, Graburn and Smith differentiated tourists by class, gender and lifestyle, and then by national origin.

Web site

http://www.theepicentre.com/Destinations/customs.html
The Epicentre web site provides a rich tapestry of different customs and culinary traditions adopted by a wide range of countries.

References cited and bibliography

Butler, R.W. (1980) 'The concept of a tourist area cycle of evolution: implications for management of resources', *Canadian Geographer* 24(1), 5–12.

Cohen, E. (1984) 'The sociology of tourism: approaches, issues and findings, *Annual Review of Sociology* 10, 373–92.

Cohen, E. (1988) 'Authenticity and commoditization in tourism', *Annals of Tourism Research* 15, 371–86.

De Kadt, E. (ed.) (1979) *Tourism: Passport to Development?*, Oxford University Press, New York.

Doxey, G.V. (1975) 'When enough's enough: the natives are restless in Old Niagara', *Heritage Canada* 2(2), 26–7.

Gill, A. and Williams, P. (1994) 'Managing growth in mountain tourism communities', *Tourism Management* 15(3), 212–20.

Inskeep, E. (1991) *Tourism Planning: An Integrated and Sustainable Development Approach*, Van Nostrand Reinhold, New York.

Jafari, J. (1987) 'Tourism models: the sociocultural aspects', *Tourism Management*, 8(2), 151–9.

Mathieson, A. and Wall, G. (1982) *Tourism: Economic, Physical and Social Impacts*, Longman, Harlow.

Murphy, P.E. (1985) *Tourism: A Community Approach*, Methuen, New York.

Plog, S.C. (1977) 'Why destination areas rise and fall in popularity', in Kelly, E.M. (ed.) *Domestic and International Tourism*, Institute of Certified Travel Agents, Wellesley, MA.

Plog, S.C. (2004) *Leisure Travel: A Marketing Handbook*, Pearson Prentice Hall, Upper Saddle River, NJ, p. 59.

Price, M.F. (1992) 'Patterns of the development of tourism in mountain environments', *Geojournal* 27(1), 87–96.

Smith, V.L. (1989) *Hosts and Guests: The Anthropology of Tourism*, 2nd edn, University of Pennsylvania Press, Philadelphia.

Stokowski, P.A. (1996) *Riches and Regrets: Betting on Gambling in Two Colorado Mountain Towns*, University Press of Colorado, Niwot.

Stokowski, P.A. (2000) 'Assessing social impacts of resource-based recreation and tourism', pp. 265–74, in Gartner, W.C. and Lime, D.W. (eds), *Trends in Outdoor Recreation, Leisure and Tourism*, CABI, Wallingford.

Stymeist, D.H. (1996) 'Transformation of Vilavilairevo in tourism', *Annals of Tourism Research* 23(1), pp. 1–18.

MAJOR CASE STUDY 7.1
Udaipur as a learning city

BACKGROUND FOR STUDY ON TOURISM IN UDAIPUR, WINTER 2001

Tourism has been highly touted as a route to the development of a city or environment. It professes to bring much-needed revenue and employment to the inhabitants of the place, while simultaneously claiming to preserve its cultural, historical, or natural 'attractions'. These arguments are currently being used by the Rajasthan government in its mission to expand tourism in the state (an estimated expenditure of nearly Rs 1,200 crore (27.7 million US$)). Because Udaipur and its surrounding villages are targets within this development plan, it is relevant and pressing to consider the influence these new policies/plans will have on the people of Udaipur, their economy, environment, culture and social relationships.

The following background paper seeks to bring out critical points from the *Rajiv Gandhi Tourism Development Mission for Rajasthan* (the most current proposal on tourism development in Rajasthan), as well as to highlight pertinent information about tourism. This article can be used as a starting point from which to generate critical and creative ideas for the further exploration of tourism.

THE PLANS OF THE RAJASTHAN GOVERNMENT

Annexure B in the *Tourism Development Mission* lists eight areas for which the growth of tourism in Rajasthan is important:

1. Employment generation
2. Poverty alleviation
3. Empowerment of women
4. Survival of rural artists
5. Upliftment of rural artists
6. Improvement in urban and rural infrastructure
7. Better image, quality of life and attitude of people
8. Revival of traditions and heritage conservation and management

These points form the comprehensive plan to uplift and empower the people of Rajasthan through an economy based in tourism – the largest growing industry in the world. This plan seeks to include urban and rural areas, as well as women, in increasing incomes, improving infrastructure, and encouraging full-spectrum participation.

From this list, we can roughly draw four categories by which to understand tourism:

1. tourism as an economic industry;
2. the environmental implications of tourism;
3. the effects of tourism on social relationships; and
4. the impact of tourism on culture, arts and language.

These categories are not mutually exclusive; they overlap and interact in a variety of ways. However, for the purpose of this case study the focus will be on the fourth aspect: the impact of tourism on culture, arts and language.

THE IMPACT OF TOURISM ON CULTURE, ARTS AND LANGUAGE

[W]hen we travel, we buy a product, a product that includes people. Travel offers an exciting chance (for those who can afford it) to buy or become, if only for a little while, a part of another culture.

Deborah McLaren

Tourism in Udaipur, as in the whole of Rajasthan, largely highlights its traditional crafts and cultural and historical monuments. By creating more access to rural areas and artisans, the government sees two levels of benefits. One, tourists have increased interest in rural regions; and two, rural economies are uplifted as artisans and other members of the community have the ability to capitalise on their traditional skills (with possibilities even for world travel, the *Tourism Development Mission* suggests). Further, by making historical and cultural sites attractive for corporate investment, more funds can enter the state. For example, the *Tourism Development Mission* suggests an 'Adopt-a-Monument Scheme' for corporate and institutional donors. It also seeks to lease out premier heritage sites to internationally acclaimed hotel chains. By functioning on a competitive bid system, the government hopes to bring in a hefty sum of money, while simultaneously attracting big names to develop the heritage and culture of Rajasthan.

There are several questions to be asked here. First, can rural life serve as a tourist attraction? By turning traditional ways of living and the production of crafts into tourism products, people compromise their cultures and common functions of their lives. The 'products' that sell best become the focus of work and life. This not only distorts traditional meanings and uses, but it also contributes to the disappearance of those crafts that do not sell. In addition to crafts, there is concern that innovations and knowledges are being pirated and patented as 'intellectual property'. Tourists enter forests, farmlands and sacred places and walk away with local plants or wildlife, healing treatments, grains, spices, etc. This 'bio-piracy' results not only in economic loss, but also in the loss of living systems.

In considering the cultural and historical impacts of tourism in Udaipur, the major touristed sites in the *Tourism Development Mission* include Jag Niwas, City Palace and Saheliyonki-Bari. If these sites are turned solely into sources for corporate income generation (they are not far from there), how will they lose meaning for the community? A cultural or historical site represents different qualities and values to a community – whether through use, religious significance, location, etc. When the 'ownership' of such a site shifts to a single party for economic benefit, the community associations to that site – largely cultural – also change. This may be reflected in a loss of perceived responsibility to a site, loss of traditional access and use, and resentment when cultural or historical significance is perverted.

Author's note: Udaipur, known as the City of Dawn, or the Jewel of Mewar, is set at the edge of seven lakes.

It is a place of beauty and has significant heritage resources including gardens, museums, palaces and temples.

Source: http://www.swaraj.org/shikshantar/ulcrtourism.htm

DISCUSSION QUESTIONS

1. Can rural life be sustainable if it is used as a tourism product?

2. If income generation becomes dependent upon the 'sale' of culture and heritage, how is this likely to distort the future development of those resources?

3. If crafts and skills only survive because of their value to tourism should we be concerned if some crafts and skills disappear?

CHAPTER 8
Sustainable Tourism

LEARNING OUTCOMES

This chapter focuses on the sustainability issues relating to the development and operation of tourism activities and is intended to provide you with:

- an understanding of the concept of sustainability and an appreciation of the difficulties associated with trying to derive a universally acceptable definition;

- an appreciation of how the sustainability issue pervades all aspects of the tourism process and applies to all of the **stakeholders** involved in the tourism process;

- a recognition of the different ways that tourism can pursue sustainability objectives and the limitations likely to be experienced;

- an understanding of the concept of carrying capacity and the difficulties involved in applying that concept in the real world; and

- an insight into alternative forms of tourism, including eco-tourism products and how they attempt to improve the sustainability of tourism and what their limitations may be.

Photograph: Torres del Paine National Park, Chile

INTRODUCTION

This chapter investigates the concept, definition and practical applications of sustainable tourism. Sustainability has become a fashionable term with respect to tourism development and operation. However, there is a significant amount of confusion relating to the meaning of sustainability and whether or not such a thing is achievable with respect to the tourism sector. The chapter looks at the historical background of sustainability and how it applies to tourism activity. Following a debate about the origin of the term and its definition in general, the implications of the concept for tourism are considered. The threshold levels of destinations are examined under the heading of carrying capacity, a fundamental aspect of sustainability. Carrying capacity is associated with economic, environmental and social impacts as well as the ability of the tourism product to withstand degradation as flows increase. Finally, no discussion on sustainability would be complete without looking at the alternative tourism products that have been put forward in the name of sustainability.

HISTORICAL BACKGROUND

Sustainability is now one of the most common concepts used in tourism development discussions. At the same time it is also one of the least understood concepts and both academics and practitioners are still a very long way from reaching a consensus regarding its definition. The analytical framework of sustainability is broad, encompassing economics, environmental and socio-cultural issues while using ethics and the platforms of intra- and inter-generational equity as the instruments of the debate. Type 'sustainable development' into an Internet search engine and you will find 4.5 million listings with more than 1.5 million relevant references. Sustainable tourism produces 1.5 million listings with more than 250,000 relevant references. There are literally hundreds of definitions of sustainability. The movement towards today's environmental sustainability platform can be traced back to the late nineteenth century when the first formal signs of concern about the planet upon which we live manifested themselves in the formation of protection societies and national parks (Yellowstone National Park, USA, 1872; Royal Society for the Protection of Birds, UK, 1889; National Trust, UK, 1894). National Parks were formed in many Commonwealth countries (Australia, Canada and New Zealand) towards the later stages of the nineteenth century and within the UK at the start of the twentieth century. Economics has never been far away from the issues of sustainability because of its focus upon the optimum use of scarce resources, and sustainability issues have been explored for the best part of a century. The 1960s were a catalytic decade that saw the first major movements towards mass concern for the planet, perhaps in response to the post-war period of rapid economic development and special changes together with the realisation of the planet's fragility fuelled by the first images of Earth from space. The early 1970s witnessed the first United Nations (UNEP) Conference on the Human Environment (Stockholm, 1972) which produced an action plan for the environment based on:

1. the global environmental assessment programme (Earthwatch);

2. environmental management activities; and

3. international measures to support the national and international actions of assessment and management.

The Stockholm Conference resulted in the commissioning of the World Conservation Strategy (WCS) (1980), which can be seen as the implementation arm of the human environmental action plan in that its focus was on explaining how development and conservation could work together. The next landmark in the pathway to sustainability was the Bruntland Report (1987) which stated (p. ix) that one of its primary goals was to:

> help define shared perceptions of long-term environmental issues and the appropriate efforts needed to deal successfully with the problems of protecting and enhancing the environment, a long-term agenda for action during the coming decades, and aspirational goals of the world community.

The Bruntland Report has been criticised on the grounds that many of its predictions and concerns did not materialise but it provided an invaluable platform for the debate on the north–south poverty divide as well as underscoring the global concerns that had been the outcome of the Stockholm Conference. Within five years of the Bruntland Report the Earth Summit was held in Rio de Janeiro (1992) putting down a landmark for sustainability in the form of a broad action strategy that is known as Agenda 21. The good intentions that came out of the 1992 Summit still apply today; what has been lacking has been any significant action to implement the resolutions that came out of the Summit. This was the main focus of the Johannesburg Summit of 2002. The next decade or so will be the test to see if there is a genuine will among governments to implement the global strategies and actions that were set out more than a decade ago.

Any form of production and consumption will have sustainability implications and therefore the debate on sustainable development should rightly encompass all forms of activity. Tourism in particular comes under the sustainability spotlight because (a) production and consumption tends to take place in areas where the natural or man-made resources are fragile (for example, areas of natural beauty, coastal areas, heritage buildings, etc.) and (b) the environment and culture are often used as a major component of the product without being subject to the price mechanisms that apply to many natural resources.

DEFINITIONS OF SUSTAINABILITY

The Bruntland Report (1987) defined sustainability to be 'meeting the needs of the present generation without compromising the ability of future generations to meet their own needs' and it went on to identify some basic principles of sustainability. These identified needs were to:

- take a holistic approach to planning and strategy;
- protect the environment (biodiversity) and man-made heritage;
- preserve the essential ecological processes;
- facilitate and engage public participation;
- ensure that productivity can be sustained into the long-term future; and
- provide for a better level of fairness and opportunity between different countries.

The last identified need in the above list could be in direct conflict with the overall definition of sustainability that the Bruntland Report used. This is the debate between intra-generational equity and inter-generational equity. If the latter objective is pursued without concern for the former than there is an implicit assumption that the distribution of wealth and opportunity in the present day is somehow optimal and this is not a point that many would be able to defend.

Murcott (1996) lists 57 definitions of sustainability that range from the early definitions proposed by Coomer (1979), which suggested that a sustainable society is not a no-growth society but one that lives within the self-perpetuating limits of its own environment, through the WCS (IUCN, 1980) definition that focused its attention on maintaining the essential ecological processes, to the more recent suggestion by Choucri (1997), who argues that it is the process of managing social demands without eroding life support properties or mechanisms of social cohesion or resilience.

The vagueness of the definitions and, according to Butcher (1997), the hypocrisy that often accompanies the international organisations that have flaunted sustainable development on the global stage, have tended to undermine the principles of sustainable development and have done little to enhance the implementation of sustainable practices around the world. To be effective any objective must possess certain characteristics. They should be clear, unambiguous, non-conflicting, measurable and achievable. The reality of sustainable development as it has been defined to date is that it fails on nearly all of these counts. On that basis alone sustainable development cannot be considered to be achievable.

The term 'sustainable development' could be replaced by terms such as 'wise use' or 'sound planning' as they have in the past, but even here it is too vague and still begs any mechanism by which it could be measured or achieved. Economists could argue that all resources should be properly costed and included within the market process so that rational decisions can be made on the basis of complete information. But the issue is much wider than the economics of the environment; the planet's heritage and culture are also part of the system and these too should be included within the decision-making processes.

The responsibility of pursuing sustainability is also a matter of some importance because it is not simply the responsibility of the international organisations or the governments that support them. Industry has a key role to play in recognising the importance of social responsibility and long-term objectives. Consumers are also an important stakeholder in the quest for sustainability, yet both industry and consumers are driven by short-term needs and objectives that work counter to the long-term goals of sound planning and sustainability.

The proponents of sustainability can be subdivided into two schools of thought: those that may be classified as strong or full sustainable supporters and those that may be deemed to be weak or partial sustainable supporters. In order to examine the two schools it is necessary to define the different types of resource that are subject to depletion or degradation. Simplistically we can categorise them into four types of capital stock:

1. Human – the population, welfare, health, workforce, educational and skill base.
2. Physical – productive capital such as machinery, equipment, buildings.
3. Environmental – man-made and natural resources, biodiversity.
4. Socio-cultural – well-being, social cohesion, empowerment, equity, cultural heritage.

These four categories of capital stock are shown in Figure 8.1. In reality there are significant overlaps between these categories. However, they do serve to explain the differences between the two schools of thought and the concept of sustainability.

At any point in time there is a given stock of each form of capital. These capital stocks can be used for production that will be either consumed or invested back into the capital stock. The strong sustainability proponents would argue that sustainability meant that the level of each of these individual capital stocks must be maintained for future generations. The weak sustainability proponents would argue that the total capital stock (i.e. the sum of all four categories) must be maintained but that it is possible to deplete one stock in order to increase another. Clearly some of the capital stocks are responsive to investment. Education and health services are two ways of improving the quality of the population and workforce and this stock can be increased over time by such investment. In the long term there are likely to be diminishing returns to such investments. The physical capital stock is that capital used for productive purposes and this can and is being invested in all the time both for replacement purposes and for new investment to increase productive capacity. Some aspects of the environmental capital can respond to investment, the creation of national parks, cleaning up rivers, preventing air and noise pollution being examples on the natural environment side, and, with respect to the built environment, the construction of new homes, shopping malls, hotels, etc. However, there is clearly a trade-off between these two elements of the environmental stock. Bridging the environmental capital stock with the socio-cultural stock there is also scope for investment in temples and monuments. Finally, with respect to the socio-cultural

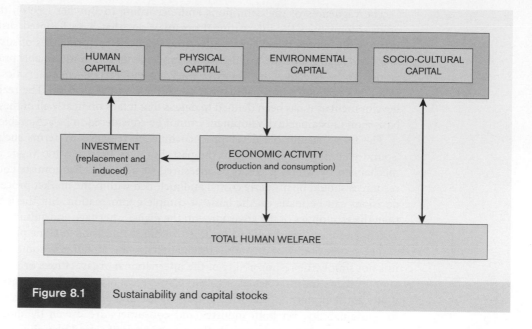

| Figure 8.1 | Sustainability and capital stocks |

capital stock it is possible to invest in customs and traditions by training and raising the profiles of them within the local population and to visitors to ensure their continuity.

If the strong sustainability approach is adopted there is a serious question mark over any form of production because, although it is possible to invest in some of the capital stocks and to restore their levels, it is not possible to increase the level of others without adopting a no-growth stance. For instance, new physical capital cannot be created without depleting some of the environmental capital stocks. Wherever land or raw materials are used then this represents a depletion of that capital stock and unless alternative land or raw materials can be recovered from elsewhere such a process will have a finite future and cannot be sustained.

DEFINITIONS OF SUSTAINABLE TOURISM

With respect to tourism the definition of sustainability has not achieved any better success. Using the Bruntland definition as its starting point the World Tourism Organization defines sustainable tourism thus:

> **Sustainable tourism development** meets the needs of present tourists and host regions while protecting and enhancing opportunity for the future. It is envisaged as leading to management of all resources in such a way that economic, social, and aesthetic needs can be fulfilled while maintaining cultural integrity, essential ecological processes, and biological diversity, and life support systems.

There have been many variations of this definition used by regions and countries around the world. For instance, the Organization of East Caribbean States (OECS) provides the following definition:

> The optimal use of natural and cultural resources for national development on an equitable and self-sustaining basis to provide a unique visitor experience and an improved quality of life through partnership among government, the private sector and communities.

Whichever definition of the hundreds that have been published seems most relevant, the key factors that come out of the debate on definitions of sustainability are that sustainability requires appropriate consideration of the long-term economic, environmental, socio-cultural and political well-being of all stakeholders, and that to achieve such long-term goals requires the engagement of all of the stakeholders involved in the production and consumption process.

SUSTAINABILITY OF TOURISM

Tourism is not an industry that sits easily within the concept of sustainability. International tourism, for instance, involves major transport components, cultural mixes and fierce resource competition. Examining each aspect of sustainability with respect to tourism activity and development paints a depressing picture.

Economic aspects working against sustainable tourism

To work within the parameters of 'wise use' or 'sustainability' it is important that the net long-term economic benefits are optimal. The economic impact of tourism, discussed in Chapter 5, means that tourism competes with other industries for the use of factors of production, and as such it can stimulate price inflation by driving up the cost of land and labour. It attracts workers from rural areas who may have been employed in the traditional industries causing the output levels in those industries to fall. Scarce investment funds may be attracted to the tourism industry on the promise of rapid returns and foreign exchange inflows. This can distort the allocation of resources in the longer term and lead to structural unemployment. Where tourism development takes place in industrialised urban areas the above may not present severe obstacles, but to less developed countries or sparsely populated regions the effects associated with the development of tourism can be economically traumatic.

Environmental aspects working against sustainable tourism

Airlines are responsible for a major aspect of air pollution and the vast majority of air transport is for tourism purposes. Tourism is about real estate development and so it competes for land use and depletes the natural environmental stock as it does so. Tourism activities can be severely disruptive to biodiversity from the extreme activities of hunting and fishing to the less obvious disruptions through wildlife observing and hill walking. The spectacular is often headline material, such as the effects of boats, anchors and pollution on the coral reefs in the Caribbean. The unusual also captures headlines, such as visitors to the Antarctic, the degradation of the environment at Everest Base Camp, and the erosion of ancient monuments. The increased presence of tourists in the tombs of the Valley of the Kings, Egypt can raise the humidity levels by several percentage points and this increases the erosion from pollutants. The less spectacular is no less devastating, such as the increased use of fossil fuels for energy consumption and water desalination, and the construction of roads, airports and sea ports to cater for the travel of tourists. The introduction of large numbers of visitors to environmentally fragile areas will always be accompanied by tension between the natural environment and tourism.

Socio-cultural aspects working against sustainable tourism

Tourists, whether they come from the explorers that Valene Smith suggests adapt to local norms or the mass tourists who do not adapt at all, will always have socio-cultural impacts on the local community. They may be through natural curiosity where the empathetic visitor is intrigued by local customs and traditions so they go to observe and that observation can set in motion a commercialisation process that will sooner or later change the events. Or it could be the psychocentric visitor who wishes no surprises, does not wish to get involved but, through the demonstration effect of their behaviour, dress and customs alters the corresponding behaviour, dress and customs of the local residents. Because tourism requires the tourists to visit the destination these negative impacts are bound to be a threat.

Irrespective of the difficulties encountered when trying to define sustainable tourism in a usable and acceptable manner, there are approaches that can be taken to mitigate some of the threats to the long-term viability of the industry. One approach is to set limits on the future growth of tourism in each destination. This would not necessarily improve the net benefits derived from tourism for any destination and in a destination where tourism was already creating problems it would not secure its long-term viability. Another approach is to change the behaviour of the stakeholders in the tourism industry to make the products currently provided more sustainable. This could involve better socio-cultural and environmental management within businesses together with better awareness and behaviour from tourists towards the destination's environment and culture. It would also probably require some changes to the economic structure and power balance between the businesses involved in the supply chain of tourism products so that local factors were fully and equitably included within the market processes. The third approach is to replace the current (unsustainable) tourism products with new products that are sustainable.

To be successful it is likely that a combination of all three approaches will be necessary. That is, there will need to be a change in the behaviour of stakeholders with businesses, tourists and local residents behaving more responsibly, with limits or thresholds being placed on developments and activities (carrying capacity) and with new products being introduced that have greater empathy with the local environment and culture. The following discussion examines the issues surrounding the identification of carrying capacity for a destination.

Photograph 8.1	Eco-lodges take tourism to a higher level.

Source: ECOCLUB.com – International Ecotourism Club

Thresholds and carrying capacity

The fact that tourism activity impacts on the social, cultural, environmental and economic aspects of a destination brings with it certain implications for sustainability. Even with a more aware tourism industry or more environmentally friendly types of tourism activity there will be thresholds beyond which the negative impacts easily outweigh the economic advantages. It would be unrealistic to assume that these impacts could be eliminated altogether and, therefore, the volume of tourists and the type of activity they pursue will have a direct implication for sustainability. If it is assumed that there are both positive and negative impacts associated with tourism and that the net effects are likely to diminish as the volume of tourism increases there will be certain thresholds beyond which additional tourists will create unacceptable net impacts (economically, environmentally or socially). Exceeding these thresholds is likely to affect every facet of tourism development. For instance, exceeding:

- physical thresholds will limit the volume of tourist flows and expose tourists to safety hazards;
- environmental thresholds will also limit the tourist flows by creating secondary problems, such as health hazards, or detract from the attractiveness of a destination;
- social and cultural thresholds will generate resentment and antagonism towards tourists from the host population;
- tourist flow thresholds will affect the satisfaction levels of tourists and cause them to search elsewhere for a better product; and
- economic thresholds will result in misallocation of resources and factors of production.

The main difficulty with which we are faced is finding the level of the thresholds beyond which tourism should not venture. As with the definitions of sustainability, defining these thresholds and the carrying capacity implied by them is a difficult task. Scientists from a wide range of specialist fields have attempted, with varying degrees of success, to provide a working definition of carrying capacity. For instance, ecologists might define carrying capacity as 'the population of an identified species which can be supported throughout the foreseeable future, within a defined habitat, without causing permanent damage to the ecosystem upon which it is ultimately dependent'. If this type of definition is transferred to the human species some modifications must be made unless the 'defined habitat' is taken to be the planet as a whole. That is, the territorial boundaries are not unique or limiting in terms of the ability of the species' population to survive. What happens within one territorial boundary may well influence the long-term viability of the species in others.

With respect to tourism, one approach is to adopt Hardin's (1991) formulation of human impact and simply transfer it to tourism such as that set out below:

tourism's impact = tourist population × tourist impact, per capita

However, this is not sufficient and such a definition fails to reflect the variety of influences relating to the nature of the tourist activity, the vulnerability of the destination, technological change and so on.

Carrying capacity has been defined as 'the maximum number of people who can use a site without an unacceptable alteration in the physical environment and without an unacceptable decline in the quality of experience gained by visitors' (Mathieson and Wall, 1982). Note that the use of words like 'acceptable' means that there will be alterations and decline and this means that sustainability in its purest sense will not be achieved. Note also that the term 'tourist presence' is used as opposed to the more simple notion of tourist numbers. This is because it is necessary, when attempting to identify the levels of carrying capacity, to weight the absolute numbers of tourist arrivals to take account of a number of factors as follows:

- the average length of stay;
- the characteristics of the tourists and hosts;

- the geographical concentration of tourists;
- the degree of seasonality;
- the types of tourism activity;
- the accessibility of specific sites;
- the level of infrastructure use and its spare capacity;
- the extent of spare capacity among the various productive sectors of the economy.

Another aspect rarely touched upon in the literature is the fact that different tourists interact with each other in different ways. For example, destinations in the Caribbean, such as St Lucia, draw their tourists from a variety of countries, but the majority of tourists come from the US market and a significant number come from European countries. The problem here is the fact that the Caribbean is a relatively inexpensive destination for the American market, which is close by, whereas it is a relatively expensive destination for the European market, because of the high cost of transport involved in the package. This means that European tourists are more likely to be of a higher socio-economic grouping than their American counterparts. This problematic mix can shorten the **tourist satisfaction** ratings quite significantly, suggesting that, from the tourists' point of view, carrying capacity may be as much influenced by the mix of tourists as by the volume of tourists.

When attempting to determine or identify carrying capacity, it is essential that tourism presence is measured in some unambiguous manner. One possibility is to discuss carrying capacity in terms of *tourism units*, where a tourism unit is a standardised concept based upon tourist numbers weighted by some composite factor derived from the above influencing elements. In this way each destination is likely to have different carrying capacity levels. However, the derivation of some standardised unit is difficult. For example, there are problems to be encountered if the number of day visitors is to be incorporated into the overall tourist numbers. This is because day visitors tend to be associated with different levels of impact per hour per tourist from those of their staying counterparts. The shorter the stay of tourists the more pressing will be the sense of time budgeting and the higher will be the level of expenditure per unit of time.

Composite indicators can be constructed to provide some insight into the threshold levels of tourism activity. For instance, McElroy (2004) discusses the strengths and limitation of a Tourism Penetration Index (TPI) for selected Caribbean islands where the index is based on per capita visitor spend, average daily density of visitors (in aggregate) and hotel rooms per square kilometre. The use of such indices is highly questionable given that they do not take into account temporal variations (seasonality), the spatial spread and size of the island (which influences the density indicator) and the retention of revenue from tourism. Many other factors could also be included such as the geographical spread of economic activity, the nature of visitor host interactions, etc. but these data are expensive and time-consuming.

An issue already raised above is that the carrying capacity definitions tend to include the term 'acceptable'. However, the question that needs to be asked is to whom should a change be acceptable or unacceptable? If, as in the case of social impacts, the host population is the body that should consider the acceptability of developments, how is this reflected in policies? In a perfectly democratic political system then we could argue that the residents would be able to register their views on proposed developments. However, such perfect democracy may be hard to find. Furthermore, much tourism development is driven by the private sector who may take a much narrower perspective on the issues surrounding development.

The issue becomes even more complex with respect to any environmental carrying capacity. Who should consider and vote on the acceptability or otherwise of a project that brings environmental impacts? The environment itself may signify changes and species of flora and fauna may suffer from development but they do not have a vote. How will environmental acceptability be considered and voiced within the planning framework?

The above issues relate to all aspects of carrying capacity, perhaps with the exception of the acceptability of developments to tourists. Visitor satisfaction surveys are frequently undertaken by many destinations to monitor acceptability. Furthermore, if the carrying capacity in this respect is exceeded, tourists will vote with their feet and go elsewhere.

In spite of the problems involved in converting this theoretical definition of carrying capacity into an operational tool, it does fit in well with modern development strategies that increasingly incorporate attempts to impose some constraint on the ultimate level of development to prevent damaging impacts on the environment and society or to avoid the risk of over-dependence.

The dynamics of carrying capacity

The literature on carrying capacity, rather like the literature on tourism development planning, gives the impression that it is in some way static or absolute. The very word capacity makes one think of a specific level like filling the seats on a boat or an aircraft, but nothing could be further from the truth. Carrying capacity is an extremely fluid and dynamic concept. As with many human traits, exposure to stimuli brings with it acceptability. Socio-cultural tolerance levels change over time with gradual exposure to tourists. If, for example, a small island destination goes from 100 to 1 million tourists in the space of a year it is likely that the socio-cultural, economic and environmental impacts will be devastating. Take the same destination and increase the volume of tourists by the same amount over a 50-year period and the discernible impact is likely to be far less. People become accustomed to change – it does not make the change any less but it does make it more acceptable. Economies too are better at adjusting to structural change that takes place over a long time period, rather than dealing with rapid changes. Sufficient time will allow for the necessary linkages and support services to be brought into place and, in consequence, allow the destination to optimise its benefits from tourism. Even the environment, or at least the local population's concern for it, may be better able to cope if change comes slowly and proper visitor management systems can be implemented to mitigate negative impacts.

In effect the carrying capacity of today will not be the carrying capacity of tomorrow. In the 1950s few of the top tourist destinations in the world could have imagined the volume of tourists that they are playing host to today. This dynamic characteristic of carrying capacity, together with the difficulty in finding a universally acceptable definition, has resulted in some bodies, such as the United States National Park Service, choosing to adopt an alternative terminology, that of limits of acceptable change (LAC), as their planning indicator.

Therefore, carrying capacity is a dynamic concept in the sense that the threshold levels that determine carrying capacity are likely to grow over time, providing that the development of tourism is sound. Unplanned rapid development could easily result in low tolerance levels and carrying capacities of much lower values.

Other factors influencing carrying capacity

In addition to the characteristics of the tourists and their hosts, there are a number of other factors that will influence the carrying capacity of a destination. It has already been noted that the speed of change is an important factor. The difference between the tourists and hosts is also an important consideration. It is not the absolute characteristics of either population group that is important, but the relative difference. This is one reason why domestic tourism is often, but not always, more acceptable than international tourism in terms of the socio-cultural impacts.

If the demographic profiles of tourists are similar to those of the host population, particularly in relation to age distribution, socio-economic grouping and religion, then the socio-cultural impact of increasing tourist numbers is likely to be relatively low. On the other hand, major differences in any of these factors can result in significant socio-cultural impacts even though the number of tourists in both scenarios is the same.

The fact that there are four broad groups of capacity indicators, economic, environmental, socio-cultural and tourist satisfaction levels, gives rise to some difficulty in establishing exactly what the carrying capacity of a specific destination may be. It is likely that, for any given destination, the carrying capacity will be reached in just one of these areas before it is reached in the rest. Thus, a destination may find that tourism activity brings pressure to, say, the local ecosystem before it creates any significant threats to the social structure, the culture or the economy. This means that, regardless of the threshold limits in these latter areas, the carrying capacity for this destination is dictated by the vulnerability of the ecosystem. In order to move away from the qualitative to the quantitative approach for determining carrying capacity it is necessary to delineate the different areas of study (outlined below) and examine the processes by which carrying capacity is determined and how it may change over time.

The process of determining carrying capacity

Figure 8.2 outlines the process by which carrying capacity is influenced and can be measured. The diagram shows the broad groups of factors that determine carrying capacity along with the different stages that can influence the magnitude and direction of the impacts and hence the carrying capacity. The different areas of the flow diagram are set out under the following subheadings.

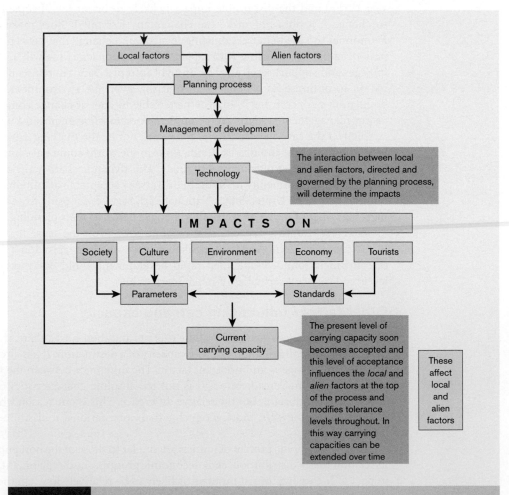

| **Figure 8.2** | The determinants and influences of carrying capacity |

Local factors

There are many local factors that will influence the magnitude and direction of impacts but what is important, besides the nature of the local factors, is the relative difference between the local factors and the tourist counterparts and the speed of change. Looking at individual factors we can see how complex the issues are.

Social structure

The social structure of the destination is vital in determining the scale and nature of any impacts. For example, taking two extreme views, the social structures of London, New York and Sydney are more able to absorb and tolerate the presence of tourists than cities such as Apia in Western Samoa or Port Louis in Mauritius. The former can tolerate the presence of tourists without incurring any significant changes to their social structures because those changes have already occurred. They are larger in population and cosmopolitan in structure, making them more adaptable to change. The latter have relatively small populations, the extended family system is still largely intact (particularly in Apia) and they are not as cosmopolitan in structure. Therefore, some societies can accept large-volume tourism with little obvious effect while others cannot. In general, the smaller the local population, the more dramatic will be the social impact of tourism, particularly if that tourism is based upon large-volume tourist flows.

Cultural heritage

The cultural heritage of a destination is very important when attempting to determine the impact and carrying capacity. The more unusual the cultural background, the more attractive a destination may become to potential tourists. Ironically, the more unusual the cultural background, the more likely it is to be adversely affected by the presence of tourists. The end result is either the destruction of the cultural heritage or, more probably, the distortion of the local culture through staged authenticity and the over-commercialisation of cultural features and traditions, such as dances and costumes, religious ceremonies, arts and crafts. The destination can soon be in danger of becoming a caricature of itself.

Environment

The environment *will* be changed by the presence of tourists no matter how sympathetic they may be or how careful the tourism activity is planned. The environment can be either artificial or natural. In general the former is more resilient to tourism impacts than the latter. Environmental change is inevitable and will be more obvious and pronounced in those areas that are sparsely populated and not subject to frequent high volume tourist visits. The more fragile and unique an environment, the more vulnerable it is to change from the presence of humans. It is important to remember that the environment is also changed by many factors, not just tourism, and it is often difficult to isolate those effects created by tourists from those created by other factors.

Economic structure

The economic structure will determine the benefits and costs associated with tourism activity. In general, the more developed and industrialised the economy, the more robust and adaptable it will be. As economies grow and diversify, so too do the skills of the workforce. This, together with a more refined capital system, allows such economies to respond and adapt to the changes brought by tourism. These countries will be able to secure the greatest benefits from tourism activity while incurring the minimum costs. In contrast, economies that are not sophisticated may find that rapid developments in tourism can distort the allocation of resources quite drastically and set up importation habits that may be difficult to break in the future.

Tourism development, particularly rapid development, tends to be resort-based and this may bring with it the economic problems associated with:

- migration from rural to urban areas; and
- the transfer of labour from traditional industries to tourism and its related industries.

Economies have to be mature to be able to adjust to these pressures.

Political structure

The political structure can affect the impacts of tourism and its carrying capacity in a number of ways. To begin with, political instability will deter tourists and therefore hinder tourism development. Some groups of tourists are more sensitive to political instability than others but few tourists are unaffected by the prospect of political instability. The political structure may also have direct influences upon tourism development if, in reflecting the ideals and beliefs of the population, it is decided that tourism development should be constrained or even discouraged. Some countries limit tourism development by restricting the number of visas issued within any given year (Bhutan, for example), whereas others may increase the costs of obtaining visas or make the acquisition of visas difficult, thereby restricting them to only the most determined. The political openness may well reflect the willingness of society to welcome tourism development and this may either raise or lower the carrying capacity thresholds.

Resources

The availability of local resources (labour, capital, land, etc.) is likely to have a major influence on the acceptability and desirability of tourism development, and even on the form that development takes. Where resources are scarce, competition for them will be high and the opportunity cost of using these resources for tourism will also be high. The local infrastructure is also part of the resource base. If tourism development means that the local infrastructure will be over-utilised then this will create a capacity constraint (at least in the short term) that may well become operative before any of the other carrying capacity constraints are approached. If the infrastructure is over-utilised because of tourism development then this may well breed resentment and hostility among the local population and then the social impact of tourism will create a carrying capacity constraint.

On a more positive note, tourism development may well result in an improved infrastructure, which will also be available to hosts as well as tourists, and this may increase the carrying capacity level by enhancing the lives of the local community.

Alien factors

Tourist characteristics

Clearly, the characteristics of the tourists who visit any given destination are an important factor in determining the social and cultural impact of tourism on the host community. For instance, tourists who belong to the mass or charter groups are more likely to have a greater social and cultural impact than those who belong to the explorer, adventurer and ethnic tourist categories. The former tends to demand Western amenities and bring their culture with them without adapting to the local norms and customs. The latter tend to be far more sympathetic towards local customs and traditions and actively seek them out as part of their vacation experience. This, however, is not always the case. The important factor is the relative difference between tourists and hosts. The greater the difference between the host's and the tourist's social and cultural backgrounds, the greater the impact and consequent change. Tourist characteristics also include visitor expenditure patterns, mode of transport, structure and size of party, age, educational background, income and purpose of visit. All of these factors will influence the nature and magnitude of the impacts on the host community.

Carrying capacity is centred around tolerance levels:

- how tolerant the ecological system is to tourist intrusion and activity, as well as those activities created as a result of tourism activity;

- how tolerant the socio-cultural structure is to the introduction of foreign cultures, ideals and beliefs; and
- how much tolerance there is within the economic structure.

However, carrying capacity is also about the tolerance levels of the tourists. A destination that is considered to be overcrowded by the tourists has exceeded its carrying capacity and, in consequence, will find its tourist arrivals diminishing or the composition of tourists changing. The composition of tourists may change as the destination lowers prices in an attempt to shore up falling numbers. The tolerance level of tourists introduces a further complication into the issue of determining carrying capacity. Different categories of tourists will display different levels of tolerance with respect to deviations from their expected experience.

Figure 8.3 demonstrates how tolerance levels associated with different types of tourist and within different types of resort may change. The figure represents two planes. The horizontal plane depicts the nature and characteristics of the destination with a range moving from the fragile and vulnerable, such as Antarctica, through the vulnerable but less fragile areas, such as the Galapagos Islands, to the more organised and controlled but nevertheless vulnerable game parks, such as those found in Kenya, right through to the full-blown totally dedicated destinations such as Hawaii and Benidorm in Spain.

The vertical plane represents the type of tourist and ranges from the explorer to the mass tourist as you move down the plane. The diagonal line running from the top left-hand corner through to the bottom right-hand corner demonstrates the 'fit' between tourist and destination. Thus, starting in the top right-hand corner we find that the explorer will seek out the fragile but exclusive destinations such as Antarctica. At the bottom left-hand corner, reading across the horizontal plane and down the vertical plane we find that the mass tourist will seek out the no-surprise destinations such as Benidorm. The range along the line between these two polar extremes also shows the 'fit' between the characteristics of the tourist and the destination. The dotted lines that run alongside the central diagonal line represent the tolerance levels. By this we mean that each type of tourist will be associated with an average given level of tolerance with respect to how close a destination may match her or his

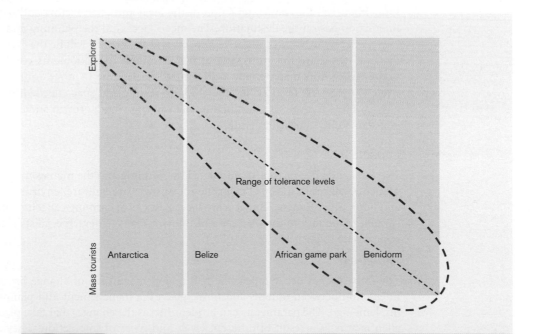

| **Figure 8.3** | The relationship between tourists, destinations and tolerance levels |

expectations. Thus, the explorer may generally be regarded as being fairly intolerant of significant deviations from her or his expectations. If the destination does not live up to expectations he or she will quickly seek alternative destinations. At the other extreme, the mass tourist is generally more tolerant of deviations from the expected. Thus, the corridor of tolerance increases in size as we move away from the top left-hand corner. The tolerance levels of destinations can also be seen in this diagram in the sense that the central diagonal line still shows the 'fit' between tourist and destination, but the corridor of tolerance may also relate to the destination's tolerance to changes in tourism. Fragile destinations are unable to cope with significant changes in the volume of tourism whereas the more commercial purpose-built destinations are more able to absorb such deviations.

Types of tourist activity

The types of tourist activity pursued will be closely linked to the characteristics of the tourists who take part in them. However, the presence of certain activities, such as gambling, can bring specific social problems and stresses that are far greater in magnitude than those associated with the same number of tourists undertaking different activities. Gambling can bring with it increased risks to the host community (and to other tourists) in terms of exposure to prostitution, drugs and crime. All of these factors will help create much lower carrying capacities than might normally be associated with tourism. It need not be just the emotive cases of gambling and prostitution that can limit the carrying capacity. Destinations with very fragile ecosystems or with, say, rare bird species, may suffer more severely at the hands of the special interest groups who would actively seek out and disturb the habitats, albeit unintentionally.

Planning, management and technology

Planning is concerned with the organisation of factors in order to manipulate future events. The management of tourism is the process by which plans are put into practice. Changes in technology will have direct and indirect effects on the difficulties associated with the planning and management tasks. Given the interaction between local and alien factors within the host environment, the planning and management process should aim to secure the maximum positive benefits (as dictated by the planning objectives) while incurring the minimum costs. Figure 8.2 shows that the planning, management and technology factors act as a funnel between the 'raw' interaction of the local and alien factors and the impact that this interaction has on the destination. The more successful the planning and management, the lower will be the levels of negative impacts and the greater will be the carrying capacity. The dynamic nature of this process is such that suitable developments combined with appropriate visitor flow management will 'naturally' select the required tourist market segments, while allowing the local factors the amount of time and space needed to adapt to the alien factors. The end result is a destination that can enjoy both growth and sustainability (growth + sustainability = development).

Impacts

The local and alien factors, manipulated by planning and the management of tourism development, will result in impacts on the social structure, culture, environment and economy, and upon other tourists. Impacts are the yardsticks of carrying capacity, but they are derived variables. The task to the planner and tourism management specialists is to ensure that the appropriate impacts occur.

Parameters

The impacts that occur reflect the nature and magnitude of change brought about by the interaction between tourists and hosts, given the management and planning that has been implemented. The parameters can be identified as the changes that take place to the local and alien factors as a result of different levels and types of interaction. They are *factual* in the sense that they are devoid of value judgements and simply relate tourist host interaction and tourist presence to changes in the social, cultural, environmental and economic factors.

MINI CASE STUDY 8.1
Sustainable development networks (SDNs) for Grenada

BACKGROUND

The report of the Rio Conference, Agenda 21, identified a number of important aspects of information technology and electronic networks for sustainable development. These included:

- The wide range of users and providers of information.
- The need to develop the capacity to provide and use information.
- The need for appropriate information.
- The widening gap between the information rich and poor.
- The potential of electronic networks.

The sustainable development network programme initiated by the UNDP in 1989 has established some twenty SDNs that are viewed by many governments as an indispensable tool for implementing national Agenda 21s.

In a review of Chapter 40 of Agenda 21, Roberto Bissio (Director of the Third World Institute [IteM]) wrote:

> The large proportion of the analysis and recommendations devoted to electronic networking clearly demonstrates an unprecedented understanding by the Earth Summit that we are not dealing here with just another technology (no other heads of State conference ever praised the virtues of fax, phone or telegraph) but with a substantial reformulation in the way people deal with each other on a global scale. The Earth Summit itself was an impressive demonstration of the potential of electronically assisted networking.

The importance of information for small island developing states (SIDS) is unquestionable. Information represents market power and can lead to economic success. Yet many small island states are not able to enjoy levels of information similar to their large national competitors. This suggests a role for collaboration in the process and dissemination of information.

The information required for decision-making in the context of sustainable development poses far greater challenges, including the following:

- The collection of different types of data to determine the status and trends of the planet's ecosystem (e.g. biodiversity, global warming).
- The setting and acceptance of global standards relating to the categories and the quality of the data collected.
- The identification and adoption of acceptable indicators of sustainable development.
- The integration of information from many different disciplines.
- The need to disseminate information among departments and organisations.

THE CHALLENGES FACING GRENADA

In 2002 the United Nations called for a thorough review of the Barbados Program of Action that was adopted in 1994. As of January 2004 there are 41 nations that are recognised as SIDS by the UN. The limited resources and the many other associated problems such as transport difficulties and the isolation of small island developing states, typified by islands such as Grenada, in the Caribbean, makes these challenges even greater. It is essential to provide assistance with the establishment of access to the global electronic networks and, without in any way limiting that access, provide guides to the information that is particularly relevant to the needs of small island developing states. SIDSNET is not a duplication of other networks; it is a guide to the world of networks for people and information relevant to the sustainable

→

development of small island developing states. Decision and policy makers in the governments of small island developing states clearly need access to the most up-to-date information about the latest technological innovations and policies which are best able to deal with threats to the fragile ecosystems for which they are responsible.

Source: Adapted from http://www.upei.ca/~meincke/barbpap.htm

DISCUSSION QUESTIONS

1. Consider the above with respect to tourism development and identify the type of data that could be shared between governments that would benefit tourism planning.

2. Identify the ways in which technology could assist governments in creating such a network.

3. Where data are available across national boundaries who should be responsible for collecting and maintaining such data banks?

Standards

The standards may be seen as acceptable limits applied to the parameters. They refer to the value judgements imposed by the host and tourist populations with respect to how much a variable may change without incurring irreversible or undesirable damage to the nature of tourism and the environment in which it takes place.

Carrying capacity determination

Carrying capacity is the dependent variable. It is not possible to overemphasise the word variable because it is not a fixed value based on tourist presence. The dynamic nature of carrying capacity is based upon the changing tolerance levels of each of the determining factors as a result of both exposure and management.

The feedback over time, between carrying capacity and the local and alien factors, will be responsible for increasing/decreasing the magnitude of acceptable tourist presence. The carrying capacity will also feed back into the planning and management stages in order to inform and enhance the processes of visitor and destination management.

If the carrying capacity is exceeded, with respect to any of the impact areas, the tourism development process will be hindered and the development may be considered unsustainable. The damage created by exceeding the carrying capacity may be related to any of the impact areas or in terms of tourist satisfaction, but the end result will be the same. Either the destination will experience diminishing numbers as its tourism industry declines – tourists pursuing alternative destinations – or the mix of tourist arrivals may change, making it increasingly difficult for the destination to achieve its declared planning objectives.

The vulnerability of different destinations to tourist presence will be a major factor in setting the acceptable standards to be maintained during the management process. To illustrate this point the plight of World Heritage Sites can be examined. The very nature of World Heritage Sites means that they are not only finite but also irreplaceable and the successful management of such sites is vital. The World Heritage Convention requires that the international community cooperates to ensure that measures taken to protect and conserve these sites are effective. The management of these sites is almost always translated into access control. The management of Keoladeo National Park in India relies upon the access provided by the restricted number of trained guides or by bicycles and specified trails set out for the tourists. In other areas more arbitrary, but still restrictive, limits are set, such as the 11,800 visitors per annum allowed to view the resident gorilla families. Alternative strategies can also be used, such as the spacing of tourist visits, or restrictions based on a specific aspect of a destination in order to manage its overall tourism development.

Measurement criteria

Carrying capacity is subject to multiple determination and, as such, each of the separate components must be investigated. Tables 8.1 and 8.2 are provided to give some guidance to the variables that may be measured, the thresholds that may be encountered and the effects of over-exploitation.

Clearly, understanding the implications for each of the indicators is an important aspect of being able to determine the thresholds of successful tourism development. As mentioned earlier in this chapter, setting limits on tourism activity is only one aspect of striving towards successful tourism development. Destinations can also work towards changing the behaviour of the stakeholders involved in the tourism process either by creating an appropriate economic framework or by investing in awareness campaigns. They can also encourage the development of more sustainable forms of tourism activity. Given that both of these strategies work towards meeting tourism demand in a way that minimises the net negative impacts they can be considered within the same framework.

Table 8.1	Variables and thresholds	
Impact on	**Variable**	**Threshold(s)**
Economy		
Dependency	Contribution to GNP	Diversity/imports
Finance	Level of investment	Availability of funds
Labour	Employment	Shortages/training
Price inflation	Consumer price index	Social costs/distribution
Wealth	Income growth/distribution	Wage inflation/imports
Environment		
Changes	Species/populations	Extinction/balance of population
Hazards	Fires, erosion, pollution	Costs/risks
Viability of wildlife	Urbanisation	Land usage/species count
Physical resources		
Access	Cost/time/volume	Congestion/hazards
Accommodation	Number/size/quality	Occupancy
Attractions	Number/size/type	Access/available land
Land	Proportion of land usage	Land price inflation
Transportation	Cost/capacity	Congestion/hazards
Infrastructure	Investment/quality	Capacity/health risks
Political framework		
Strategies	Goals range/scope	Conflicts, goals missed
Resources	Expenditure/revenue	Budgetary deficits
Cooperation	Partnerships	Lack of participation/funds
Society/culture		
Population	Migration	Distribution/infrastructure
Living standards	Real income/wealth	Inflation
Values	Crime/drugs/health	Social disruption/costs
Traditions	Participation/quality	Occurrence/characteristics

Table 8.2	Scale of development and its effect on impacts and carrying capacity	
Effect on	**Small-scale dispersed**	**Large-scale concentrated**
Accommodation		
Range of products	Highly limited	Diverse
Range of prices	Low/medium	Low/medium/expensive
Seasonality	Peaked	Wider but more problematic
Size of business	SME	SME to international
Ownership	Local	Non-local
Characteristics of facilities		
Range	Highly limited	Diverse
Finance	Local	Mixed local/foreign
Usage	Peaked	High volume
Need for support	Low	High
Labour market		
Demand/supply	Learning by doing	Demand for high skills
	Local labour	Mixed local/migrant labour
	Constrained by local supply	Increased migration
Transport		
Infrastructure	Limited	High but congestion during peaks
Supplier	Private sector	Greater public supply
Stimulating supply	Low-level effect	High-level effect

Sustainable tourism products

Terms such as eco-tourism and alternative tourism have taken a prominent position in tourism literature (academic and marketing) since they were introduced in the mid-1980s. Eco-tourism has been misused as a term both intentionally, as a marketing ploy, and unintentionally due to a lack of understanding and, in common with the term sustainability, there has been considerable debate about an acceptable definition. Wight (2001) points out that the World Tourism Organization estimated that some 10%–15% of global tourism could be classified as eco-tourism in 1997. However, within that same year the WTO revised this estimate to 20%. It is hard to find any credibility in these proportions given the dominance of mass tourism in total global tourism activities. Eco-tourism is unequivocally linked to natural tourism attractions rather than their man-made counterparts and environmental sustainability is often found to be a core component of such a product's definition. However, it is also accepted that many definitions of eco-tourism include some reference to indigenous cultural sustainability. According to Weaver (2004), a further factor that is associated with definitions of eco-tourism relates to their educational or learning opportunity components. Once all of these aspects are incorporated into a single tourism product it can be seen that eco-tourism will not appeal to the masses at present. The masses seek sand, sea, sun vacations within a wide variety of areas that may or may not also be areas of outstanding natural beauty. Eco-tourism demands a high level of interpretation whereas the mass tourism product does not. This is not to say that mass tourism products would not benefit from greater interpretation.

Both eco-tourism and alternative tourism imply small-scale, indigenous low-key activities. Where the former holds the preservation of the natural environment at its core, the latter may not necessarily do so. Indeed, the latter may simply be at the beginning of the tourism development process for a destination soon to be enveloped in a more commercial package as the product develops. Eco-tourism suggests that it has in place constraints that will prevent or inhibit uncontrolled development. However, both forms of tourism activity can provide a temporary runway for the take-off of the destination as it moves towards mass tourism. There is no product currently on the market that could come close to being classified as mass sustainable tourism. The presence of large numbers of tourists in high densities with the necessary infrastructure for transportation and public health and safety defies the laws of sustainability.

The 1980s also saw the emergence of the 'Three Rs' being applied to sustainability in the corporate world. The fact that the corporate world was even thinking about sustainability was a huge leap forward, although the cynics would argue that they were paying lip-service to a concept that would pay dividends in terms of increased sales. Tour operators such as Thomsons did not find sustainable tourism products to be the 'hot' products that this line of thinking promised. The three Rs were:

- Reduce
- Reuse
- Recycle

The very fact that these words were being used in corporate circles represents a major shift in attitudes towards the environment and social responsibility. Middleton (1998) expanded this list to 10 Rs which included:

- Recognise
- Refuse
- Replace
- Reduce
- Reuse
- Recycle
- Re-engineer
- Retrain
- Reward
- Re-educate

Although some of the additional Rs may be considered to be contrived and there is considerable overlap between several of them, the list does serve to show just how far away the three Rs were from presenting a significant step towards sustainability. Furthermore, a major R in the form of 'Responsibility' was not included in the Middleton list. Middleton's marketing approach provides some good examples of the issues relating to sustainable tourism.

MINI CASE STUDY 8.2
The Foreign & Commonwealth Office encourages tourists towards more sustainable activities

MAKE A DIFFERENCE WHEN YOU TRAVEL – AND GET MORE OUT OF YOUR HOLIDAY

You've just booked your dream holiday – a round-the-world adventure or a relaxing fortnight on a sun-kissed beach. But how will your travels affect the people and the places you visit? Will your plane generate huge amounts of greenhouse gases getting you there? Will your off-the-beaten-track excursions harm indigenous cultures? It doesn't have to be like this – there are ways to minimise the negative effects of your dream holiday and even have a positive impact on the country you visit.

Tourism can be a source of economic growth. Travel and tourism have become major world industries. According to the World Travel and Tourism Council, there are over 700 million international travellers a year, including 19 million from the UK. That figure is expected to double by 2020. Tourism generates over 10% of global Gross Domestic Product and employs over 250 million people. It is the main money earner for a third of developing nations and the primary source of foreign exchange earnings for most of the 49 least developed countries.

But what about its impacts on local communities and the environment? A sustainable approach to tourism aims to ensure that communities in destination countries are able to benefit from the business tourism brings, while minimising the negative impacts on local cultures, the environment and wildlife. It's about taking responsibility for your travels and making sure your visit has a positive social, environmental and economic impact.

Can you make a difference? Just simple things can make an enormous difference when you travel. The following tips are based on guidelines produced by the Rough Guide, Lonely Planet and the Travel Foundation. Think how you can have a positive impact on the people and places you visit, and help ensure that they inspire future generations of travellers.

If you think you are too small to make a difference, try sleeping with a mosquito.

Before you go

- Think about where your money goes when booking your holiday. For example staying in locally owned accommodation will benefit local families – ask your tour operator.

- When you've finished with your holiday brochures, pass them on to a friend or recycle them.

- Plan a sustainable holiday – ask to see your tour operator's sustainable tourism policy, whether your hotel operates sustainably, and about activities you do while away. For example, can you book excursions that will contribute to the local economy and protect indigenous cultures and wildlife?

- Pack appropriately – waste disposal is a major expense in poorer countries. Recycle packaging from new clothes and toiletries before you go.

- Small gifts from home can be a great way to say thank you to your hosts – think about what might be of most use to the local community.

On the flight

- The amount of carbon burnt fuelling your flight will do more damage to the environment than any other aspect of your travels. Organisations like Climate Care and Carbon Neutral can help you offset your carbon emissions by investing in projects that prevent or remove an equivalent amount from the atmosphere.

- Read up on the countries you plan to visit – make sure you've got a good guidebook. The welcome will be warmer if you take an interest and speak even a few words of the local language.

- But use your guidebook as a starting point rather than as a bible – following it slavishly will close you off to new or unknown experiences or attractions.

Shop responsibly

- Help the local economy by buying local produce – shop at markets or local grocers and buy local crafts and products.

- Haggling can be fun, but don't be obsessed with getting the lowest price – remember how wealthy you are compared to local people in some countries.

- Don't buy products made from endangered species, hardwoods, shells, or ancient artefacts. If in doubt – please don't buy. For more information on endangered species and to report a concern, visit the WWF-UK Souvenir Alert Campaign for tourists.

Respect the local culture

- Respect local cultures, traditions and holy places. For example, ask permission before you photograph local people and dress appropriately at all times.
- Speaking at least a few words of the local language can make a big impression.
- Realise that the people in the country you are visiting often have different time concepts and thought patterns from your own. Remember that you're on holiday – don't expect people to be the same as back at home.
- Ask questions rather than assume you have all the answers beforehand.
- Displaying expensive jewellery or cameras, particularly in very poor communities, may distance you from the culture you've come to experience.

Use natural resources sparingly

- In many destinations natural resources such as water, wood and fuel are precious – local people may not have enough for their own needs. Help conserve resources in your hotel, lodge or camp by turning off (or down) heating, air conditioning, lights and the TV when not required. Let staff know if you are happy to reuse towels and bed linen rather than having them replaced daily.
- Use public transport, hire a bike or walk where possible – you'll meet local people and get to know the place better.
- Don't discard litter. Waste disposal is a major expense in poorer countries. Use biodegradable products, reuse bottles, plastic bags and other containers and take used batteries home with you.

Help preserve the environment and wildlife

- Help preserve the natural environment for others to enjoy. Please don't pick flowers and plants or collect pebbles and seashells. Coral is extremely fragile and takes decades to grow. Don't step on or remove any coral when swimming or diving.
- Don't support activities which exploit wild animals. Swimming with dolphins, watching dancing bear performances and having your photo taken with lion and tiger cubs, monkeys or snakes can condone and encourage animal cruelty. For more information on animal exploitation and to report a concern, visit the Born Free Foundation travellers' alert.

Your holiday shouldn't unnecessarily disturb or damage wildlife or their habitats. When on an excursion, if you feel there is unnecessary disturbance, make a complaint to the local operator and your holiday representative.

Source: Details correct at the time of printing. http://www.fco.gov.uk/servlet/Front?pagename= OpenMarket/Xcelerate/ShowPage&c=Page&cid=1100182468244

DISCUSSION QUESTION

The above information is an example of governments attempting to encourage travellers in their countries of origin to take a more 'sustainable' approach to their vacations. How effective do you think such campaigns can be and what are the advantages of tackling the tourists in the normal country of residence?

SUSTAINABILITY AS A STRATEGY

In spite of the difficulties involved in trying to find an acceptable definition for sustainability that will have practical value and the enormous problems in trying to measure crucial factors such as a destination's carrying capacity, there is a way forward. Sustainability more than anything else involves a process of recognition and responsibility. Recognition that the resources which are used to produce the tourism products are expendable and vulnerable. Responsibility for the wise use of these resources rests across all stakeholders from the governments and planners, through the industry that delivers the product to the tourists and their hosts who temporarily coexist within the destination. A sustainable strategy must engage all of the stakeholders in the planning of tourism. The involvement of local resident participation is as difficult to achieve in practice as trying to get the industry to behave in a more environmentally and socially sympathetic manner.

From an environmental point of view there have been numerous attempts at trying to 'green' the industry. These attempts have been in the form of awareness campaigns through to certification schemes but none of them has been successful to date. The major problem has been the failure of the companies and organisations that have touted their certification programmes to demonstrate to the industry that certification truly saves them money or generates additional demand. Tourists are still largely driven by the pleasure factors of the product rather than their social and environmental conscience. Therefore consumers must share their responsibility because without a demonstrable demand for certified green products the certification process will not be embraced by the industry without some form of supporting legislation. The certification companies have by and large failed to put credible programmes into the marketplace because the enforcement that must accompany certification is expensive and time-consuming making it an unwelcome burden on the industry. The only effective way of providing such certification schemes would be through a non-profit public sector body in the same way that health and safety standards are enforced.

The only practical way forward from a planning point of view is to develop integrated impact-modelling tools. One such tool was developed by staff at the International Centre for Tourism and Hospitality, Bournemouth University. It demonstrates the use of fully integrated impact software and provides a valuable planning tool that demonstrates the interrelatedness between each of the different types of impact, analyses them within a unified framework and allows these impacts to be examined from either forecasted future impacts or from those drawn as hypothetical case studies.

Economic sustainability for tourism requires holistic planning across all industrial sectors. It must also reach beyond the destination to make sure that intermediaries such as tour operators are not able to circumvent or put undue pressure on the planning processes. The formation of partnership chains throughout the industry would be one way to achieve this but is unlikely ever to happen given the competitiveness of the tourism industry and the predominance of SMEs. The quality of the tourism product demands staff training that is universally acceptable and the economic environment must make environmentally and socio-culturally sound behaviour the best economic choice.

Environmental sustainability in tourism requires greater awareness and knowledge about the impacts and ways of translating those impacts into the economic marketplace. The responsibility of tourists and businesses must be made clear and there needs to be a legislative system that penalises failure to abide by those systems. The indirect and induced environmental consequences of activities must be included in the calculation of their market prices but it must also be recognised that environmental and social systems change over time as a natural consequence of development and such changes need to be accommodated.

MINI CASE STUDY 8.3
South Africa: SA tourism must meet world standards

Themba Gadebe *BuaNews* (Tshwane), 10 September 2007

BRITS

South Africa's tourist destinations must meet international standards to be well received by visitors during the 2010 FIFA World Cup, says Madibeng Local Municipality Mayor, Fande Molokoane.

'It is of great importance to keep our tourism destinations in high standards,' Ms Molokoane said at the recent launch of the Madibeng Tourism Month.

'With the great soccer spectacle of the 2010 FIFA World Cup gaining momentum by the day, we have a responsibility as Madibeng to play a role in the success of the event.'

She called on the stakeholders in the industry to stand ready for the world's greatest soccer event, adding that her municipality is ready to give any assistance.

'We would also like the members of the media to start making awareness about our destinations as we prepare ourselves for the arrival of hosts of tourists for the 2010 FIFA World Cup,' she said.

The Madibeng municipal area has 24 lodges, 21 guest houses, ten art galleries, nine nature reserves, nine holiday resorts, nine camping sites as well seven caravan parks.

This includes a heritage site in Mmakau which was recently awarded a national status. Mayor Molokoane said it would be injustice to mention tourism destinations in Madibeng and not talk of the Hartebeespoortdam which is 'one tourism destination that attracts scores of tourists locally and internationally'. She indicated that government had developed a plan for the dam to maintain international standards.

'A Remediation Plan is currently under way at the dam which is a joint initiative by the Department of Water Affairs and Forestry as well several municipalities surrounding the dam,' she said. On Friday, Madibeng will be joining its sister municipality, Rustenburg, in marking the 1000-days' countdown to the beginning of the 2010 FIFA World Cup. On Saturday, all nine host cities will be staging celebratory events, with the main one being hosted at the Union Buildings in Tshwane.

President Thabo Mboki is expected to speak at the event with other major role-players, including the 2010 Local Organising Committee chairperson Danny Jordaan and chairperson Irvin Khoza, Minister of Sport and Recreation Makhenkisi Stofile, Minister in the Presidency Essop Pahad and Deputy Minister of Finance Jabu Moleketi.

The countdown event is seen as an opportunity to update South Africans and the international community about the progress made in the quest to deliver a successful world cup. Rustenburg is an official 2010 host city, and will showcase matches at the Royal Bafokeng Stadium. The city will also host the Confederations Cup in 2009.

Madibeng and Rustenburg fall under the Bojanala Platinum District with three other local municipalities. The area is in close proximity to Tshwane, yet another host, which will see matches played at Loftus Stadium.

Source: http://allafrica.com/stories/200709101092.html (10 September 2007)

DISCUSSION QUESTION

'Specific events, such as the 2010 FIFA World Cup can act as a tremendous driving force to bring tourism development issues to the forefront of people's minds. In so doing they can act as a catalyst for tourism planning and development. However, events such as these can drive tourism development in a direction that conflicts with sustainable tourism.' Discuss the issues raised by this statement.

CONCLUSION

Sustainability is a difficult concept. It is complex and hard to define and, if taken literally, the pot of gold at the end of the sustainability rainbow may be considered to be unattainable. However, this should not detract from the ambition of trying to achieve sound tourism planning and for the stakeholders in tourism to find ways of making the most efficient use of the resources and ensuring that tourism has a long-term future. To do this there will come a time (already reached in many destinations) when there is need to limit development to some predetermined threshold. This brings into play the notion of carrying capacity. Carrying capacity can only be examined in a case-by-case situation because it is sensitive to location, the type of tourist activity, the difference in cultures between tourists and guests, the speed of tourism growth and the temporal dimension of development. Time is a great healer and it allows destinations to adapt and adjust to the presence of tourists and their associated impacts. Thus, carrying capacity is a dynamic rather than static concept.

Carrying capacity thresholds may manifest themselves in economic, environmental, socio-cultural and political structures. The determination of carrying capacity at any one point in time will be the type of impact with the greatest change relative to its impact threshold. Once the carrying capacity threshold has been reached in one of these variables it will limit or change the tourism development process if that process is not to suffer long-term damage. The major influences on the level of carrying capacity are the differences between the nature of the tourists and their activities and those of the local population, weighted by the speed of change.

In addition to limiting the nature and volume of tourism activity there is a need to modify the behaviour of the stakeholders in tourism. The behaviour of the industry and tourists should reflect the needs of the local destination. Eco-tourism and alternative tourism products have been around since the 1980s but many of them owed their title to a marketing approach rather than any real attributes of the product. The eco-tourism product is essentially natural resource-based and is dependent upon low-volume tourist activity. This is useful for the sustainability of tourism in a specific area but offers little scope for the sustainability of global tourism which is largely made up of the mass sand, sea and sun tourism products. It is important to examine the relationship between the impacts of tourism and the scale and dispersion of tourism activity. In general, small-scale dispersed tourism activity is likely to have a lower impact level than large-scale concentrated tourism development. However, small-scale dispersed tourism activity is unlikely to be able to cater for the major tourist market segments. The only hope of making this latter type of activity 'green' is through the recognition and adoption of appropriate corporate responsibility by the private sector combined with a fully engaged public participation in the planning of tourism.

SELF-CHECK QUESTIONS

1. Define sustainability.
2. What are the major obstacles to achieving sustainable development?
3. What methods can be used to make tourism more sustainable than it is at present?
4. What is meant by the term 'carrying capacity'?
5. How sustainable are sustainable tourism products?

ESSAY QUESTIONS

1. Critically appraise the attempts that have been made to find a universally acceptable definition of sustainability. What are the major stumbling blocks and how might they be resolved?

2. What do you understand by the term 'carrying capacity' and what are the problems encountered when trying to define it?

3. 'Carrying capacity is a dynamic concept.' Discuss.

4. 'The carrying capacity of any given destination is influenced more by the speed of tourism development and the *relative* differences between tourists and hosts than it is by their *absolute* characteristics.' Discuss.

5. In what ways should the behaviour of the stakeholders in tourism be modified to move the industry towards a more sustainable future?

ANNOTATED FURTHER READING

Books

Gartner, W. and Lime, D. (eds) (2000) *Trends in Outdoor Recreation, Leisure and Tourism*, CABI Publishing, London.
A collection of edited papers that deals with a wide range of planning and policy issues related to tourism. The book provides in-depth analyses for the more advanced student.

Gunn, C.A. and Var, T. (2002) *Tourism Planning*, 4th edn, Routledge, London and New York.
Provides a comprehensive overview of tourism development.

Inskeep, E. and Kallenberger, M. (1992) An *Integrated Approach to Resort Development: Six Case Studies*, WTO, Madrid.
A collection of case studies that explores the issues relating to planning in the real world. The cases would have provided greater insight if they had been more varied but nevertheless the book provides good insight into many of the issues involved in tourism planning.

Middleton, V.T.C. with Hawkins, R. (1998) *Sustainable Tourism, A Marketing Perspective*, Butterworth Heinemann, Oxford.
A book rich with case studies that examines the feasibility of sustainable tourism and the role of marketing in driving the industry in that direction.

Shaw, G. and Williams, A. (2002) *Critical Issues in Tourism: A Geographical Perspective*, Routledge, London.
This text examines the relationships and complexities of tourism and the mobility of people temporally and geographically. By examining the process of tourism and the systems of mobility it highlights the impact of tourism throughout the whole process of the activity rather than simply at the destination.

Articles

Luiz, A. (2003) 'Sustainable tourism development: a critique', *Journal of Sustainable Tourism* 11(6), 459–75.
The author provides a brief critique of some of the many weaknesses in the sustainable tourism literature. It explores six issues that are often overlooked but which must be addressed in research: the role of tourism demand, the nature of tourism resources, the imperative of intra-generational equity, the role of tourism in promoting socio-cultural

progress, the measurement of sustainability, and forms of sustainable development. Finally, it is argued that in order to transform research on sustainable tourism to a more scientific level, a systems perspective and an interdisciplinary approach are essential.

Stem, C.J., Lassoie, J.P., Lee, D.R. and Deshler, D.J. (2003) 'How "eco" is ecotourism? A comparative case study of ecotourism in Costa Rica', *Journal of Sustainable Tourism* 11(4), 322–47.
The authors question the contribution of eco-tourism to conservation and community development, citing negative impacts, such as solid waste generation, habitat destruction, and socio-cultural ills.

Van Fossen, A. and Lafferty, G. (2001) 'Contrasting models of land use regulation: community, government and tourism development', *Community Development Journal* 36(3), 198–211.
In this paper the authors assesses the capacity of local communities and sub-national governments to influence patterns of tourism development, within the context of a globalising economy. Through a comparison of the contrasting examples of Hawaii and Queensland, the paper indicates the consequences of different approaches to land-use regulation. It points to the importance of planning and policy processes that integrate community interests, in order to achieve long-term, sustainable tourism development.

Web sites

http://www.gdrc.org/uem/eco-tour/eco-tour.html
A useful site listing codes of practice, definitions, tools and strategies for sustainability and links to the accreditation companies and organisations.

http://www.waksberg.com/research.htm
René Waksberg's site is an invaluable research tool for all those interested in tourism in general and contains a large section of links relevant to sustainable development.

www.unesco.org/whc/nwhc/pages/sites/srf9.htm
This UNESCO site contains a list of cultural and heritage sites and discusses the management of protected areas and sustainable tourism in general.

References cited and bibliography

Bruntland, G. (ed.) (1987) *Our Common Future: World Commission on Environment and Development*, Oxford University Press, Oxford.

Butcher, J. (1997) 'Sustainable development or development', pp. 27–38 in Stabler, M.J. (ed.) *Tourism Sustainability – Principles to Practice*, CAB International, Wallingford.

Butler, R.W. (1997) 'The concept of carrying capacity for tourism destinations', pp. 11–22 in Cooper, C.P. and Wanhill, S.R.C. (eds), *Tourism Development: Environmental and Community Issues*, Wiley, Chichester.

Choucri, N. (1997) 'Global system for sustainable development research TDP-MIT', Unpublished notes, MIT, Cambridge, MA, January.

Coomer, J. (1979) 'The nature of the quest for a sustainable society', in Coomer, J. (ed.) *Quest for a Sustainable Society*, Pergamon Press, Oxford.

Duval, D. (ed.) (2004) *Tourism in the Caribbean: Trends, Development, Prospects*, in the series edited by M. Hall, Contemporary Geographies of Leisure, Tourism and Mobility, Routledge, London.

Gartner, W. and Lime, D. (eds) (2000) *Trends in Outdoor Recreation, Leisure and Tourism*, CABI, New York.

Hardin, G. (1991) 'The tragedy of the unmanaged commons: population and the disguises of providence', in Andelson, R.V. (ed.) *Commons Without Tragedy: Protecting the Environment from Overpopulation – A New Approach*, Barnes and Noble Books, Savage, MD.

IUCN, UNEP and WWF (1980) 'World conservation strategy: Living resource conservation for sustainable development', IUCN, Gland, Switzerland.

Johnson, P. and Thomas, B. (1994) 'The notion of capacity in tourism: a review of the issues', pp. 297–308 in Cooper, C.P. and Lockwood, A. (eds), *Progress in Tourism, Recreation and Hospitality Management*, Wiley, Chichester.

Mathieson, A. and Wall, G. (1982) *Tourism: Economic, Physical and Social Impacts*, Longman, Harlow.

McElroy, J. (2004) 'Global perspectives of Caribbean Tourism', pp. 39–56 in Duval, D.T. (ed.) *Tourism in the Caribbean*, Routledge, London.

Middleton, V.T.C. with Hawkins, R. (1998) *Sustainable Tourism: A Marketing Perspective*, Butterworth Heinemann, Oxford.

Murcott, S. (1996) http://www.sustainableliving.org/seminar96/murcott.htm

Weaver, D.B. (2004) 'Manifestations of ecotourism', pp. 172–86 in Duval, D.T. (ed.) *Tourism in the Caribbean*, Routledge, London.

Wight, P. (2001) 'Ecotourists: not a homogenous market segment', in Weaver, D. (ed.) *The Encyclopaedia of Ecotourism*, CABI, Wallingford.

MAJOR CASE STUDY 8.1
Encouraging sustainable tourism: chanting the eco-tourism mantra in India

If there is an ideal eco-tourism destination in India, it is Sikkim. This Eastern Himalayan state of India with its pristine mountains, crystal-clear lakes and rich cultural and natural diversity is fast gaining popularity. Attracting some 200,000 tourists a year, of which 12,000 are foreigners, it has witnessed a 15% growth in the past three years. Rustam Vania reports on the country's potential for eco-tourism development.

Recognising the opportunities this sector offers to Sikkim, the Chief Minister Pawan Chamling says, 'The enormous biodiversity of Sikkim is for the people. Sikkim cannot afford to have large polluting industries. Along with education, computers and agro-based industries, eco-tourism is a way towards sustainable development for us.' The state has had a record of taking tough decisions to protect the environment.

Tree felling has been severely restricted, grazing has been banned in the reserved forests and attempts are being made to make Sikkim a plastic-free state. Eco-tourism is seen as the developmental option for the future. Inaugurating the South Asian meeting on eco-tourism in the state capital Gangtok in January (2002), Union tourism minister Jagmohan grandly announced, 'We want to make Sikkim a model of eco-tourism for India and the world.'

The state government now has a tourism plan, which includes orchid tourism – over 454 species of orchids are found in the region – and butterfly parks – 50% of the butterflies of the Indian subcontinent are found in Sikkim. 'We should target this high-value market. Last year, ten groups came from rhododendron societies across the world, spending over Rs 80 lakh,' says K.C. Pradhan, retired chief secretary of Sikkim and a keen promoter of rhododendron tourism.

Pema Gyaltsen, from Yuksom in Western Sikkim understands the gap between rhetoric and reality. 'We don't want the government to dole out tin sheets to spruce up our houses for tourists . . . We want to know about guest management skills, a greater share in tourism benefits,' he demands.

Worried that with the rush to the pristine corner of the Eastern Himalayas will come garbage, deforestation and immigration – and no economic benefit to the local people – Gyaltsen and a group of young people have formed the Kanchenjunga Conservation Committee (KCC) to start a conservation education programme for tourists and porters.

OLD WINE IN A NEW BOTTLE?

The Indian government has also discovered the eco-tourism mantra. The National Tourism Policy 2002, is keen to promote nature and cultural destinations. It plans to market just about everything – from coastal resorts, cruise destinations, to traditional cuisines, to 'village tourism', to adventure tours in the Himalayas, to wildlife. It chants the right words about sustainability and community involvement, saying that eco-tourism 'should be made a grassroots, community-based movement through awareness, education and training of local community as guides and interpreters'.

But plans are easy to make, difficult to undertake. India's track record in tourism, leaving aside nature tourism, is abysmal. According to government documents, a majority of tourists visiting India rate facilities – from roads to accommodation – as average or poor. No wonder the country gets less than 0.38% of the share of tourists of the world – fewer visitors than tiny Singapore. In nature tourism too – the 'tiger tourist' kind – policy is equally disjointed. The National Action Plan 2002, prepared by the Ministry of Environment and Forests, plans to 'use increased tourism revenue entirely to augment available resources for conservation'.

Yet, on the ground, the handling of the increasing number of tourists in national parks tells an entirely different story. Park management is ill prepared to deal with tourists and, without this, tourism is creating new problems – increasing pressures on the carrying capacity of these protected areas on one hand, and sharpening tensions between the park and the local community, which is not benefiting from the visitor's economy, on the other.

TIGER TOURISTS

Take Ranthambore – a prized tiger reserve in the Aravalli Hills. Tourism has boomed here. Big hotel chains, from the Tata-owned Taj hotels to the luxurious Oberois have set up shop here. Many say, this is former US president Bill Clinton's legacy. His visit to Ranthambore has made it a popular destination, attracting – according to some estimates – over 60,000 tourists last year. Tourists pay phenomenal rates – from Rs 10,000 to Rs 30,000 a night – in some of these hotels, which promise a ride into the park for a near certain view of the tiger.

So what does the tiger reserve itself gain from this increased tourist traffic? The economics are simple. Indian visitors pay Rs 25 per visit and foreigners Rs 200 as park fees. In addition, Rs 200 for a video camera and Rs 125 for a jeep come to the park. The rest – from hotel rooms, to guides, to jeeps and canters (a small bus) – stays with the industry. G.V. Reddy the park director concurs, 'We only earn from the park

Photograph 8.2   Indian tigers attract the tourists.

entrance fee. I feel a 10% fee should be paid per tourist by hotels to the park.' In the absence of a policy, tourism is adding to the pressures working against conservation. Reddy says they have no legal control over where hotels are erected. Hotels are mushrooming in the buffer zone around the park.

The only control Reddy and his colleagues have is to restrict entry. They have done this by limiting the number of jeeps into the park. The park management signs a contract with the operators, binding them to the rules. But as may be imagined, this has led to a virtual goldmine for the jeep operators and their jeeps are booked months in advance. The money for hiring jeeps and guides is not shared with the tiger they market.

Contrast this with the National Wildlife Action Plan 2002–2016, which says that all tourism receipts and the penalties collected in a protected area should go to a local trust fund headed by the park manager. It should be used in the proportion of 70% for community benefit works and 30% for park management and development activity, not covered by the protected area's budget.

And what of the local people? The wildlife action plan says, 'preference in regular or occasional employment has to be given to local people'. Yet, opportunities for employment generated by tourism in Ranthambore, as in most parks, are unevenly shared. Ran Singh, a guide in the park, grumbles, 'Hotels employ trained staff from outside and the forest department rarely hires locals for development work or as forest guards within the park. On the other hand local villagers often lose crops to animals from the park.'

Now, with the entry of the big 'outside' hotels, local jeep operators, who ferry tourists within the park, are an unhappy lot too. These hotels are buying their own fleets of jeeps so that they can milk the benefits directly.

To conserve the park, local people are faced with severe restrictions on grazing and fuelwood collection, but no benefits. It is not surprising that villagers living near the park feel it is for foreigners only. Their alienation and desperation makes for annual 'battles' between desperate graziers with slingshots and helmet-wearing park officials.

More hopefully, managers of the Periyar National Park in the Western Ghats of Southern India are creating tourism products that they hope will not only benefit the local communities but also help the short-staffed and poorly funded forest department to achieve their conservation goals. With funding from the Global Environment Facility's (GEF), park authorities working on an eco-development project have created committees to work with villagers on creating alternative livelihood options and enhanced agricultural productivity.

Members of one such eco-development committee have set up the Periyar Tiger Trail project, which includes 23 former poachers, who previously made a living by trading forest goods illegally. This eco-tourism project is a joint collaboration between the Kerala Forest Department and the ex-vanaya bark collectors' eco-development committee.

The ex-cinnamon bark poachers turned tourist guides' intimate knowledge about plants and animals and their survival instincts make them ideal guides for eco-tourism activities. Besides taking small groups of tourists on foot into the forest, they also assist forest guards in patrolling. The intelligence network of the park authorities has improved tremendously. Poachers have been caught redhanded. A fast regeneration of cinnamon trees is seen in Periyar forests and an unprecedented 89 cases of sandalwood poaching were reported since the scheme was launched.

The idea of eco tourism is still at a nascent stage in India and the country is beginning to see the first steps towards guidelines and policies.

This is a shortened version of an article, originally titled, *Eco-tourism: Scrambling for Paradise*, which first appeared in *Down to Earth* (31 July 2002), published by the Centre for Science and Environment in Delhi, India. (The photograph did not appear in the article.) © People & the Planet 2000–2004 (excluding photograph)

Source: http://www.peopleandplanet.net/ doc.php?id=1759 (30 September 2002)

DISCUSSION QUESTIONS

1. With such nature-based tourism products as these in India how should the authorities attempt to balance the economic, environmental and socio-cultural costs and benefits of tourism? In particular, who should pay for paradise and who should benefit?

2. Comment on the control strategies referred to above such as that of product diversity (such as the orchid tourism) to that of controlling tourist entry and consider what other types of strategies might be implemented to work towards sustainability.

3. Is there scope for accreditation schemes in such an environment; if so what sort of scheme would you recommend and why?

CHAPTER 9
Tourism and Development Planning

LEARNING OUTCOMES

The objectives of this chapter are to ensure that you:

- understand how tourism fits into the general theories of economic development;

- understand the importance of integrated tourism planning and development, development planning layers and the role of the community in this respect;

- are able to identify characteristics of the tourism product that have implications for tourism planning and development; and

- can outline the major steps involved in the tourism planning and development process.

INTRODUCTION

Any form of economic development requires careful planning if it is to be successful in achieving the implicit or explicit objectives that underlie the development. In this chapter we show that tourism development, because it is a multi-sector activity and because it brings with it the environmental, social and economic impacts discussed in Chapters 6–8, requires considerable planning if it is to be successful and sustainable. The role of tourism within the major general economic development theories is examined. We also show that the development of tourism will not be optimal if it is not undertaken as a partnership that engages all of the stakeholders rather than being left entirely in the hands of the private sector. The private sector tends to be associated with a myopic view that is focused upon short-term profits whereas the public sector is often associated with a conservative approach towards development. We therefore identify in this chapter that tourism development planning requires careful cooperation and coordination of both the public and private sectors together with the engagement of the local community. This chapter also demonstrates that the emphasis of tourism development planning has moved away from the rigid 'grand design' master plan in favour of more flexible and reactive development plans. This change in approach is due, in no small way, to the recognition that development is not a finite concept. Development is infinite and takes place in an ever-changing environment. Therefore development plans should attempt to facilitate the desired objectives while taking into account the changing factors that influence not only the objectives but also the means of achieving them.

TOURISM AND ECONOMIC DEVELOPMENT THEORIES

There have been a number of theories put forward to explain the process of economic development (see Nafziger, 1997). A few of the more influential economic development theories in their time include:

- The English classical theory of economic stagnation.
- Marx's historical approach.
- Rostow's identification of stages of economic growth.
- Vicious circles of demand/supply and investment.
- Balanced and unbalanced growth theories.
- Theories of dependence.

It is possible to examine the main threads of these theories in order to identify whether or not there is a role for tourism within the more general theories of economic development, although it should be noted that since the 1970s there has been a tendency to move away from the grand theoretical notions of economic development and instead use a more specific, case-by-case, approach. Nevertheless, it can be helpful to look at the characteristics of tourism development within a framework of general economic development.

English classical theory of economic stagnation

This theory grew out of the classical writings of early economists Malthus, Mill and Ricardo. To understand the concept of the theory it needs to be noted that such writers were very much influenced by Newtonian physics with its belief that life was never random and was ordered by some 'grand design'. Of the various assumptions employed by the classical economists, the operation of this theory can best be seen by focusing upon just two of them: that in the event of no technological progress, output was constrained by the scarcity of land, and the law of diminishing returns.

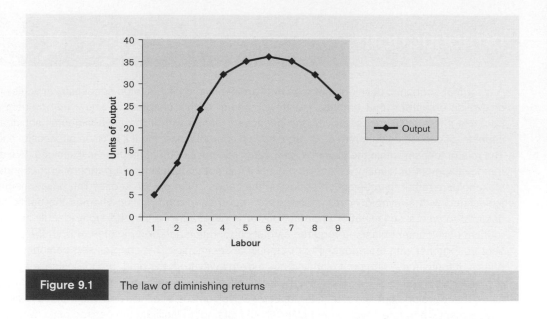

| **Figure 9.1** | The law of diminishing returns |

In Figure 9.1 it can be seen that additional units of labour with a fixed amount of land increase output per unit of labour significantly when the labour is increased from 1 to 3. However, when a fourth unit of labour is added the increase in output, although positive, is not as great as the previous increase. The increase in output achieved when the fifth and sixth units of labour are added becomes progressively less. If more than six units of labour are added the output starts to decline as diseconomies of large scale are experienced.

The theory also suggests that the long-term wage rate, the natural wage rate, was at the subsistence level. Therefore, in spite of short-term deviations from the natural wage rate, it would always tend to return to the natural level.

Under this theory, if food production increases, wages rise and the extra food available means that the population becomes healthier and grows. As the population increases there are more mouths to feed and more units of labour with the fixed supply of land. As the labour force is increased the average wage rate falls and continues to do so until the subsistence wage rate is reached. If the wage rate falls below subsistence level then the population declines and the scarcity of labour forces the average wage rate back up to its natural level. Given the lack of any technological progress, the only way to mitigate the diminishing returns is to increase the capital accumulation per worker. But even here, the classical economists had tied themselves into an economic straitjacket. The need to acquire profits and interest payments in return for increased capital stocks requires the existence of increased availability of surplus value (output less the cost of labour) but the diminishing returns assumption means that the surplus diminishes and hence the return on capital. With diminishing returns on capital there is reduced incentive to increase the capital per worker and the route to economic stagnation and decline is set. There are good grounds for viewing the English classical theory as a theory of doom and gloom.

The flaws in the theory are many and include the neglect of technological progress that can multiply the output per worker manifold. Also, the assumption that population growth was uniquely determined by prosperity is found to be wanting, particularly in industrialised countries where voluntary birth control has stabilised population levels. The ownership of capital and land is not necessarily the prerogative of the private capital owners. State owner-ship of capital and land may result in a different set of objectives that may allow continued growth.

Marx's historical approach to development

Marx's historical materialism approach to development is framed within a dynamic world rather than based on the static scenario used by the classical economists. Within this dynamic view of development, changing technology, enhanced organisation of production and the development of human skills all work together to provide lubricant for the engine of change. The world, as seen by Marx and Engels, moved naturally from **feudalism** to **capitalism** to **socialism** and then to **Communism**. The economic consequences of the rise to capitalism include demand expanding more slowly than productive capacity and an increase in monopolistic power that forces out small businesses creating a segment of the population of workers who are without property. The dynamics of this results in what Marx referred to as a reserve army of unemployed that acts as a buffer to absorb the shocks as the economy expands and contracts during business cycles. The result is a series of crises where the ownership of productive capacity is repeatedly challenged by the educated proletariat until Communism is established and socialism through the state becomes redundant.

There are a number of flaws in Marx's view of economic development, including the observed facts, that revolution when the proletariat took the state, happened in Russia rather than the West at a time when Russia was one of the least developed capitalistic countries in Europe. The theory relies upon there being a conflict of the objectives held by capitalists and those held by the proletariat. If there is no conflict and both sides realise that they can prosper if they both decide to share a fast-growing output then the dynamism of Marx's theory takes a serious blow. In spite of this, Marx's theory still finds a great deal of support from those either discontented with the distribution of wealth in their country or worried about the threats of the recent trends towards globalisation and the dominance of multinational corporations.

Rostow's theory of growth and development

The processes of change identified within Marx's dynamic world were not evenly distributed. If a historical view is taken, the existence of the pre-capitalist societies was spread over long periods of time with little evidence of significant changes to economic life. It was the recognition that there were five distinct stages through which economies pass as they develop that led to Rostow identifying the stages in his influential work (Rostow, 1990). The five stages were:

1. The (pre-industrial) traditional society.
2. The preconditions for economic take-off.
3. Economic take-off.
4. Self-sustained drive towards maturity.
5. The age of mass consumption.

Rostow's work was more a collection of identified sequential trends rather than a theory. The tenet of Rostow's paper is that there is a natural inertia that needs to be overcome before self-sustained development takes place. This inertia is overcome by a build-up of transport investment; enhanced organisation and production in agriculture; and increased imports – particularly capital. These three factors Rostow refers to as the preconditions for take-off. The preconditions were deemed to have been met when countries experience a rapid increase in net investment, have a major leading economic sector with strong linkages to other sectors and have in place the necessary infrastructure to support the development of modern industries.

Once the preconditions for take-off have been met and take-off has started, the economy is deemed to be on a route of self-sustained consistent growth. This stage is associated with migration from rural to urban areas, a developed labour force and a state system that provides stability. This process of self-sustained growth will continue until it matures into a stage of mass consumption where the ownership of durable goods such as automobiles, white goods and other equipment is considered to be the norm.

Rostow's view of economic development was more influential within government circles, where it presumably struck some familiar chords in US government offices, than it has within academic circles. Rostow's academic peers received his theory with mixed views and it was severely criticised by some as being too vague, overly-simple and impossible to test. His theory was also criticised on the basis that it lumped together a wide range of countries under the category of traditional economies irrespective of their resources, history or structure. The theory relating to the role played by net investment in breaking down the natural inertia of economies is not supported by empirical evidence and there is no demonstrable reason as to why the components of each stage should not occur at any time in the development process rather than only in the stage to which Rostow refers. A fundamental criticism of Rostow's theory is that it implicitly assumes that development today will mirror the development process that was experienced by today's developed countries. This ignores the effects of international linkages and trade as well as assuming that today's developing countries all have the same objectives for development as were pursued by the industrialised countries of today.

Vicious circles of demand/supply and investment

This theoretical approach suggests that countries are poor because they always have been. The poverty leading to poverty premise can be examined from either the demand side or the supply side in order to arrive at the same conclusion. From the demand side it is suggested that if a country is poor then the levels of income will be low. This means that the level of demand for goods and services will also be low and therefore there is no incentive for entrepreneurs to invest in additional productive capacity. This means that the amount of capital per worker remains low, productivity remains low, and this sustains the link between low income and low demand. From a supply side there is a suggestion that low income levels present few opportunities for saving and this means that there is little in the way of capital availability to invest in productive capacity. With low investment there is low capital per worker and this maintains the low productivity which leads to low income and savings.

These mechanisms are appealing from the point of view of simplicity but it is their simplicity that gives most cause for concern. The link between income levels and savings at national level is not as obvious as this theory suggests. Corporate saving is an important element of total savings and in many cases the marginal propensity to consume may not be significantly higher than in industrialised countries where there are constant forces trying to induce consumers to spend more. The simplicity of the theories also suggests a level of volatility that is not apparent in national economies. For instance, a small injection of additional demand would lead to the opportunity to invest in additional capital per worker, leading to additional productivity, higher income levels and higher demand. This would expand the economy out of its poverty trap.

Balanced and unbalanced growth approaches

These theories are variants of a theme and relate to whether development occurs across all sectors or whether there is development in a few leading sectors that will act as a catalyst for development across the economy as a whole. The balanced growth theory suggests that it is not possible to overcome the natural inertia in a stagnant economy by investing in and developing only a few export sectors. There is indivisibility in infrastructure that requires a broader development platform if it is to be successful and investment decisions often have linkages with other investment decisions without which they would not be viable. As an alternative there is the suggestion that unbalanced growth, where investment occurs in just a few leading sectors, is far more achievable with resources of developing countries and that these leading sectors will drag the other sectors up in their wake.

Dependency theory of development

The dependency theory of economic development suggests that the ability of an economy to achieve autonomous development is determined by its dependency upon other capitalist countries. The greater the dependency upon other capitalist economies the lower the ability to achieve economic development. Proponents of this theory cite the colonial periods as evidence of foreign powers exploiting less developed countries in order to grow richer as a result of their relationship – even to the point of de-industrialising them. There are many instances where colonialism can be seen to have had such a negative impact on a colony's economic development, although it is often difficult to determine how much development would have taken place without colonialism. Furthermore, there are many countries that were never colonised and that have remained underdeveloped, such as Afghanistan and Ethiopia. Nevertheless, there are few people who would argue that colonialism and dependency did not lead to the suffocating of indigenous development forces through:

- migration of workers from rural to colonial organised urban areas;
- 'cropping' the best workforce members to work in colonial offices;
- foreign trade on unfair terms; and
- opening of local markets to foreign companies.

The development theories and tourism's role

Within the English classical theory of development there is no clear role for any industry beyond the limits imposed by the scarcity of land. Tourism development is a form of real estate development and as such it will add to the pressures on the use of land without providing a way of breaking down the constraining factors associated with diminishing returns.

As a vehicle or catalyst of change, there is a clear role for tourism within Marx's theory of development. Tourism can speed up the process of change because it has product characteristics (see below) that enable it to develop quickly and help the transfer process perhaps from capitalism through to socialism and eventual Communism. However, there are elements of the industry that thrive on exploiting economies of large-scale production (natural monopolies such as airlines) that would resist the movement from capitalism to more egalitarian-based systems. But, overall, tourism can be seen as an excellent driving force for economic, social and political change.

If the role of tourism is examined with respect to Rostow's stages of economic development there is clearly a strong role that can be played by tourism. The development of the transport and infrastructure, together with the import of capital, that is seen as a precondition for take-off is a fundamental part of most tourism development. Thus tourism can be used as a catalyst to overcome the inertia of developing countries. The organisation of agricultural production is also often associated with the injection of the additional demand presented by tourism development.

Tourism could play a significant role within the vicious circle theory of development simply by either injecting additional demand into an economy or providing a stimulus to investment. The introduction of tourism under this theory of development would result in an expanding economy when viewed from either a demand or a supply side.

In either the balanced or unbalanced growth theory approaches there is a clear role for tourism within the theories, either as part of the overall broad balanced approach to development or as one of the leading sectors in an unbalanced approach. Why tourism would be chosen as a lead sector within the unbalanced approach to development can be found in the extent of linkages that tourism has with other industries within an economy. Often they are far more widely spread and of deeper significance than those traditionally found with primary goods markets such as agriculture or fishing.

It is not difficult to relate modern-day tourism traits to the dependency theory of development. There are often fears about dependency on tourism as an industry and as a

Table 9.1	The role for tourism in major development theories

Theories	A role for tourism
English classical theory	✗
Marx's theory	✓
Rostow's theory of growth	✓
Vicious circle theory	✓
Balanced/unbalanced	✓
Dependency theory	✓

dependency upon foreign suppliers (particularly tour operators and transport companies) as they are the lifeline of tourism development. As such the dependency theory is more an explanation of underdevelopment rather than one that tries to explain development. There is a role for tourism but it can be either a stimulant or an inhibitor of development depending upon ownership of the tourism establishment.

In summary, of the major theories that have attempted to enhance our understanding of the economic development of countries, there is a major role that can be played by tourism except in the case of the English classical theory where there is little scope for any industrial sector other than the latitude offered by the availability of land and its relationship with population (see Table 9.1). Tourism leads the global economy as an engine of development as we enter the twenty-first century. Its growth performance has been nothing short of astonishing over the last half of the twentieth century. The result of this is that tourism is a development option that most governments fondly embrace.

When the discussion turns to 'sustainable' development the key economic development theories discussed above are all found to be lacking as they do not encompass the environmental and socio-cultural aspects that must be considered if sustainability is to be explored. Nor does the market system fully reflect the true cost of resources upon which so much of tourism depends. This is a topic that is explored in Chapters 6 and 8.

INTEGRATED PLANNING AND DEVELOPMENT

There are a variety of approaches that may be adopted when planning for the development of any industry or any economy. One can take a proactive stance and develop strategies to secure the desired development path. This approach requires deep and thorough understanding of not only the local economy and its structure, limitations and strengths, but also the probable effects of external factors, how they may impinge on the local development process and what form these external effects are likely to take. Alternatively, one can adopt the reactive stance of chaos theory. This approach is based upon the premise that there are too many variables, internally and externally, to be able to plan. These variables cannot be controlled nor can they be predicted with sufficient levels of accuracy. Therefore, it is better to develop reactive schemes so as to be in good order to meet the unexpected rather than to attempt a proactive but indeterminable development path. This latter approach has been likened to training policy makers on flight simulators so that their reactions develop in positive and enlightened ways. However, both proactive and reactive approaches can use such an analogy. Pilots are trained to fly to predetermined paths and schedules while, at the same time, they are trained to be able to react sensibly to unexpected events. The same may be said about tourism development planning. To rely purely on reactive policy solutions is to forsake the prospect of optimising tourism development.

Photograph 9.1 | Intensive tourism development.
Source: Alamy Images/Image Broker

A second issue that has given rise to much academic debate since the 1990s is the notion of sustainable development (see Chapter 8). Although much that has been said about sustainable development is sound from an academic viewpoint, it is neither innovative nor radical. The notion that we must look forward to future generations when we are planning to consume finite resources is commendable and such notions should also be transferred to all other production and consumption activities, not just tourism. Furthermore, the term 'sustainable development' is a misnomer and has led to much confusion. Development has sometimes been confused with the concept of growth and it is *this* misunderstanding that has caused the increased volume of literature to be published proclaiming the call for sustainable development. In reality, development has to be sustainable to be classified as development at all, otherwise it is short-term growth. Most textbooks that attempt a definition of development include some statement about self-sustained growth. However, the allocation of finite resources to productive activities is not sustainable unless technological inventions and innovations can find alternative resources in the future. There is a danger in inhibiting specific forms of tourism activities in order to reduce the immediate impacts of tourism in the short term because such remedial actions may unleash far more devastating and less sustainable impacts in the future. Clearly, there is no simple answer to the sustainability debate, only to state that development planning has *always* been concerned with sustainability issues and it is only 'bad' planning that has given so much impetus to these recent debates.

Tourism and development

If tourism is to be incorporated into a country's development plan it must be organised and developed according to a strategy constructed on sound foundations. These foundations should take account of the coordination of the tourism-related sectors, and the supply and demand for the tourism product. The process of development planning involves a wide cross-section of participants who may bring with them goals that are conflicting. Furthermore, different stakeholders may well bring with them incompatible perceptions about the industry and the development process itself. Before looking at the process of tourism development planning it is worth considering some of the advantages and disadvantages associated with selecting tourism as a catalyst for general development.

MINI CASE STUDY 9.1
Calling all tourists to Bamiyan

By Charles Haviland, BBC News, Bamiyan, central Afghanistan

Breakfast is being prepared at the Abdul Hamid Hotel. The proprietor, Abdul Hamid, is rushing around with his helpers preparing a meal of unleavened Afghan bread and a thick white butter, and omelettes.

This is a popular breakfast stop, about two hours up from Bamiyan town into the hills on the way to the popular Band-e Amir lakes.

It is a modest establishment – perhaps not the type of hotel or restaurant that well-heeled travellers would want. But business is buzzing.

In the dining area, 15 young men are already devouring their feast. Others, including us, take their food to the rise across the road and eat al fresco.

There, we unexpectedly find ourselves eating next to the burnt-out shell of a tank – a reminder that Afghanistan is still an abnormal tourist destination.

The dirt road on which the hotel sits is perhaps the spine along which Afghan tourism will develop.

RELATIVE SECURITY

Afghanistan has mountains galore, sweeping valleys, rushing rivers and deserts. And a culture thousands of years old.

And, in Bamiyan province, it now has relative security.

Two hours' bumpy ride further on, we reach Band-e Amir – long ago declared Afghanistan's first national park but only now being implemented as such.

These are six lakes with extraordinarily blue water, sitting under towering pink cliffs. Each lake is held up by a natural 'dam' of limestone, and has a string of waterfalls tumbling out of it.

Today, on a Friday, there are several hundred tourists, nearly all of them Afghan. Some come from other parts of Bamiyan, others from further afield.

The brave plunge into the water, which is chilly here at 3,000 metres up.

Mohammed Ayub and his large family are spending the day here in their big tent.

They, like many others, have come because they believe the lakes have religious importance – an association with Hazrat Ali, an important descendant of the Prophet Muhammad.

'We can buy bread here, and hire boats,' he says. But they bring all the rest of their food and a stove. He is happy.

MORE ORGANISATION

Others, on the busier side of the lake where simple cafés serve meat and rice, are less content with the facilities.

They include almost the only foreigners to be seen, Ivana Stipic Lah from Croatia and her husband Samo Lah from Slovenia. They work in Kabul and have left the city as tourists for the first time.

'Someone has to build a road here,' says Samo. 'And, let's say, toilets. When we asked someone where we can find a toilet, he said "all around"!'

'It needs a little more organisation,' Ivana agrees. She reflects that in parts of Bamiyan town they had been told they needed tickets but there was nowhere to buy them.

'If you want to be a tourist in Afghanistan you have to be ready for a huge adventure,' she adds, laughing.

Zahir, an Afghan usually resident in Belgium, is staying a few days here with his family and relatives. They have had a great time and caught a lot of fish. But he says things could be better.

'The accommodation is just a small house, no showers no lights, so it's very poor,' he says.

'Of course, I would like to have proper toilets and proper kitchens, proper beds and a proper home.'

BLUNT TALK

Asked where else he goes as a tourist in Afghanistan, he mentions the Blue Mosque in the northern city of Mazar-e Sharif, describing it as 'fantastic'.

He would like to see Kandahar and the south, but says it's probably not secure enough now.

Once back in Bamiyan town, I climbed a steep fortress – part of an old ruined Muslim city with fantastic views over the valley, including the remains of the 6th-century Buddhist statues destroyed by the Taliban.

My companion on the walk, Amir Fuladi, is a local development expert drawing up a tourism blueprint for the government to consider.

He speaks bluntly about Bamiyan as it is today, saying the roads are not good, there are few good hotels and people simply do not know how to receive tourists.

'The quality of services is really bad,' he says. 'There is no information centre. There is no guide.'

Mr Fuladi says local people need to develop a more commercial attitude – more focused on making a profit.

He is recommending that these pitfalls be gradually rectified, and tourism developed with social care.

'The majority of the benefits should go to the poor families or the local people,' he says.

He is recommending that any newly-built hotel should have a fixed quota of local employees and use local materials and foods.

'And then, people who want to invest, they can come.'

But he is also concerned that the environment be protected.

On a recent visit to Band-e Amir he was shocked to see cars driving onto the fragile limestone rocks, a vehicle being washed in the lake, and a lot of rubbish. This, he says, must change.

Bamiyan Province has all the natural and cultural potential for tourism. Now, hotels must be built and more roads constructed, as people learn to use local products and resources to increase its attractions.

What would be best of all to bring in the tourists would be for security to take a grip around the country, not just in Bamiyan.

Source: http://news.bbc.co.uk/1/hi/world/south_asia/6969984.stm

DISCUSSION QUESTION

Comment on the difficulties of using tourism as a catalyst for development under such harsh conditions with limited infrastructure, facilities and trained human resources. What key areas would you recommend a tourism strategic plan should address and how would you implement it?

Tourism product characteristics

The tourism product is unique in terms of the range and diversity of activities encompassed. Few products can compete with the wide variety of activities included under the heading of tourism. Tourists can add to this uniqueness by bringing their own extra dimension to the product. Furthermore, the tourism product must be consumed within the geographical boundaries of the destination in which it is offered. The producers of the tourism product, however, are not always confined to the local economy and in this growing age of globalisation tourism may include transport businesses, accommodation owners, tour operators, travel agents and information providers that are based outside of the destination. As with any personal service, production and consumption occur simultaneously and, in the case of tourism, such production affects most other sectors (directly and indirectly) of the economy. As seen elsewhere in this book, this **simultaneity of production** and consumption also creates specific social (and to some extent, environmental) impacts not normally associated with the production of other goods and services.

Tourism as a means of wealth redistribution

Tourism is widely recognised as one of the fastest earners of foreign exchange and one of the most effective income redistribution factors in many countries. Although able to provide strong redistribution effects within an economy when residents of urban areas spend some of their income in the less populated poorer regions of their country, it has been disappointing as a vehicle to redress the global economic imbalance between north and south. Nevertheless, it has provided a valuable source of foreign exchange to the smaller developing countries that find it difficult to compete in the tangible goods markets.

Domestic tourism is a very effective means of redistributing income between different areas within a national economy. This is because tourism tends to take place in the more sparsely populated scenic areas where there is little in the way of manufacturing industry. Therefore tourism provides the opportunity to create employment and income in areas with limited alternative sources. Thus, English residents head for Cornwall, the Peak District, Scotland and Wales for the domestic trips, the French leave Paris en masse in August and generally head south. The mass exodus of people out of the cities throughout Europe, the Americas and Australia during the main vacation periods is evidence of this domestic redistribution at work.

The literature on international tourism as a means of income redistribution is somewhat deceptive. Many of the articles written about tourism development tend to focus upon economically, environmentally and/or socially vulnerable destinations. This is because they provide a more visible stage on which to examine each of the consequences of tourism development. However, in reality, the vast bulk of international tourist movement takes place between industrialised countries. To support this viewpoint it can be noted that in 2002 more than 88% of total international tourist arrivals in Europe came from other European countries and that globally more than 80% of international tourist arrivals tend to be residents within the region where they arrive. In terms of the north–south debate, tourists escape the industrialised countries to visit other industrialised countries and the south enjoys little in the way of a significant share of the wealth created by tourism. This is a fact that should be borne in mind when examining the global consequences of tourism development.

Tourism as a labour-intensive industry

Tourism, in common with most personal service industries, is labour intensive. For developing countries with surplus labour and for industrialised countries with high levels of unemployment, tourism provides an effective means of generating employment opportunities. In general, at a time when the labour:capital ratio is moving strongly against labour in most production industries, the importance of the labour-absorbing qualities of tourism cannot be overlooked. However, in many countries there are labour shortages and it is not uncommon to find these countries importing labour to work in their tourism industries. Under such circumstances one might question whether these countries have a comparative advantage in tourism and whether or not their factors of production would be better employed in alternative industries.

Even in those situations where there is an abundance of labour it may be the case that there are other factors of production that provide arguments in favour of development routes other than through tourism. Where there are clear indications that the local destination would benefit from the employment created by tourism, this view should be tempered by the characteristics of the labour force generally associated with tourism-related

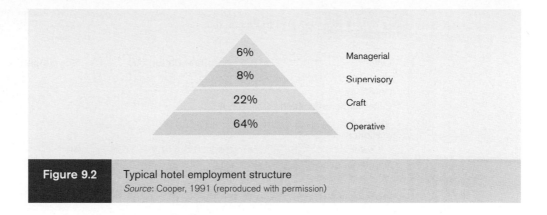

Figure 9.2	Typical hotel employment structure
	Source: Cooper, 1991 (reproduced with permission)

establishments. The employment profile of large hotels, for example, tends to yield a relatively flat occupational pyramid such as that shown in Figure 9.2. This means that middle and senior management posts are relatively scarce compared with the high number of low-skill employees. Such an occupational pyramid results in a lack of career development and, consequently, a lack of staff motivation. A point also worthy of consideration is the predominance of females and young people employed in tourism-related establishments.

Attempts have been made to increase the height of the occupational pyramid by, for example, the introduction of departments and layers of middle management posts in luxury hotels. This, it was hoped, would provide a much-needed impetus to career prospects and motivation. However, recent experience suggests that there has been a reversal of this trend with 'de-layering' and the career development prospects in large hotels is not significantly different from that exhibited three decades ago. Thus, although tourism may provide a quick and ready means of increasing the number of employed people in the local economy, its contribution to long-term development may be questionable. To expand this argument further it is necessary to consider the secondary employment effects associated with tourism development and here one can find a much broader range of skill requirements and career development paths. Therefore, although the direct employment effects of tourism may be subject to some limiting characteristics, the indirect effects do not suffer in the same way.

Tourism and on-the-job training

The development of travel and hospitality skills in the local labour market is unlikely to make large demands on educational resources. The educational qualifications of those employed in the accommodation sector are heavily weighted in favour of those with only a rudimentary education. This is undesirable both from the point of view of the future of the industry and in terms of the overall development of the destination. There is often an urgent need for training and education at all levels in both the private and public sectors. However, industry often chooses to ignore this need and to enjoy the benefits of a cheap and plentiful labour market, and the public sector is often more concerned with the short-term goal of achieving employment opportunities rather than the development of a well-educated and qualified labour force. There is an unquestionable need for education and training in the tourism and hospitality industries and the reliance upon untrained labour with on-the-job training is responsible for many poor-quality tourism products. These destinations fail to compete with high-quality tourism destinations that, in consequence, are able to charge higher prices and enjoy more buoyant demand for their products.

The poor quality and inadequate education and training related to the tourism and hospitality industries is an aspect that has been known for almost two decades, as Table 9.2 demonstrates. From a short-term growth point of view rather than as a development option, this educational profile has both positive and negative implications. On the positive side it

Table 9.2	Level of training in tourism	
Level	**Accommodation (%)**	**Supplementary activities (%)**
University	1	3
Other higher education	4	5
Secondary		
Higher	30	45
Lower	34	40
No qualifications	31	7

Source: WTO, 1980

means that the labour force for tourism growth can be mobilised relatively quickly. The training can be undertaken on the job, which means that units of labour can be brought in quickly from either the unemployed or, as is often the case in developing countries, from agriculture and fishing industries. On the negative side, the lack of educational qualifications found in tourism-related businesses means that the growth of tourism does not necessarily result in a more educated labour force – one of the factors perceived to be an important ingredient in the economic development process.

The structure of the tourism industry

One of the more notable features of the tourism industry is the proportion of the total businesses that are classified as small and medium-sized enterprises (SMEs). The nature of tourism as a personal service industry tends to make it attractive to individual and family entrepreneurs. The proliferation of small businesses brings with it both advantages and disadvantages. In the first instance it facilitates quick start-ups and flexible supply sources that can respond rapidly to fluctuations in demand. It is also an industry that, from the outside, does not appear technically daunting and thus encourages budding entrepreneurs to enter the industry. There are few barriers to entry in the sense that businesses can be started with small amounts of investment and there is room for product differentiation to provide some monopolistic power to the smallest businesses. However, these advantages can also be the source of the industry's worst problems in terms of:

- inadequate staff training (unstructured informal training);
- too high a debt/equity ratio leading to business failure (borrowing on the goodwill of the business); and
- inefficiency problems because of a failure to capitalise on economies of large-scale production.

Although the vast majority of business establishments in tourism may be considered to be SMEs, a significant proportion of the total output of the industry is attributable to the larger national and multinational corporations. Nevertheless, there is certainly scope for a wide range of business structures within tourism, from bed and breakfast units through to international hotel chains, from independent sightseeing flight operators to national airline giants. Each type of business has its own operating characteristics with a tendency for the smaller firms to be more labour intensive and dependent upon local suppliers, to the larger companies that make extensive use of capital and bulk purchase from a global warehouse.

Protectionism

The simultaneity of production and consumption of tourism means that the tourist must travel to the destination to enjoy the product. This makes tourism unique as an export industry. The consumers of international tourism (the importing country) often fail to recognise their tourist spending overseas as an import and hence do not see it as a serious threat to the level of employment in their own countries. Thus, tourism tends to escape the danger of being singled out for protectionism or trade retaliation, except as part of a general macro-economic policy which restricts foreign exchange allowances to correct balance of payment problems. Having said that, it is often the existence of foreign exchange restrictions in many of the developing regions of the world that explains the relatively slow rates of growth in interregional tourism (as, for example, in South-East Asia). Similarly, when countries are faced with currency crises (such as the UK in the 1960s and 1970s, and Malaysia in the 1990s) the government of the day imposes restrictions on the amount of currency that outbound tourists can convert.

Multitude of industries

Tourism is a composite industry product. That is, it is composed of the output of the travel, accommodation and food and beverage, retail, entertainment sectors plus many others. This means that its economic and development impacts are felt quite widely from the initial impact onwards. It also tends to suggest that tourism has strong linkages with many other sectors of the economy and it is the strength of these linkages that determines the value of the output, income and employment multipliers associated with tourist expenditure.

The variety of industries included under the umbrella of tourism means that there are a variety of employment opportunities generated by tourism activity. This may stimulate the labour market and the delivery of vocational training.

Price flexibility

Many developing countries are dependent upon the world market prices for primary agricultural produce for their foreign exchange receipts. That is, the prices of, say, cocoa, sugar, rice, etc., are determined in world commodity markets where individual countries have very little say in determining the final price of the goods. Tourism, on the other hand, provides a source of foreign exchange that is subject to some degree of control by the host country. Product differentiation, either through natural endowments or man-made resources, can provide some price-setting power. The greater the product differentiation that is either innate or can be engineered, the greater the monopolistic power and hence the greater freedom a destination has in setting its own price. Product differentiation can be based on natural factors, ranging from broad aspects such as climate (Florida, Bermuda and Iceland as examples) to specific natural attractions (such as Victoria Falls, Great Barrier Reef and Grand Canyon). Differentiation can also be achieved through socio-cultural aspects, heritage (such as the Pyramids of Egypt, the Great Wall of China and Stonehenge in the UK) and even in terms of the quality of the tourism product itself. Basically, it does not matter what aspect is used to differentiate the product providing there is sufficient demand for it. However, tourism is also highly price competitive.

Price competitive

The bulk of the tourism market, which is resort tourism, is extremely price sensitive and, consequently, internationally competitive. The effects of currency fluctuations on the number of international arrivals and the volume of tourist expenditure adequately demonstrate this fact. Although most mass tourism destinations claim a high degree of product differentiation, a brief examination of the major tour operators' brochures selling sun, sand and sea products will show that the major battleground is fought not on hotels, the quality of beaches or the sea, but the price of the package. Price competition is a fundamental feature of the budget tourism market for both destinations and operators.

Seasonality

A striking feature of tourism in many countries is the way in which the level of activity fluctuates throughout the year. This is not a characteristic unique to tourism – agriculture is also an industry used to seasonal fluctuations in activity – but the majority of industries are not subject to the degree of seasonality experienced by tourism establishments. Seasonality in tourism can be caused by either supply factors, such as those mentioned above, or demand factors such as the availability of tourists to travel at different times of the year. For instance, international holiday packages aimed at attracting family groups from Europe or the USA would need to bear in mind that the availability of most families will be determined by the school holidays. The effect of this can be seen by searching for flight costs during school term periods and those during school holiday periods. The latter tend to be associated with a premium price tag. Therefore the forces of seasonality attack the consumption of the product from both sides of the market, demand and supply.

Irrespective of the cause of the seasonality in the tourism industry, it tends to be reflected in:

- employment (casual/seasonal staff);
- investment (low annual returns on capital);
- pricing policies (discounted off-season prices).

From an economics point of view, any business subject to seasonal fluctuations in demand for its output is faced with a dilemma. If it purchases sufficient resources to meet the peak load demand, then it will have to carry spare productive capacity for the remainder of the year. If it gauges its resources according to the average level of demand it will spend part of the year carrying spare capacity and be unable to meet the peak-load demand level. Alternatively, it can take on variable resources (staff) to meet the peak-load demand and then shed these variable factors of resources during the off-season. Although attractive from the point of view of the profit and loss account, this widely practised solution does nothing to improve employer/employee relations. Also, there is an inherent waste in taking on staff each year on a temporary basis, investing in human resources (by training) and then losing that investment at the end of the main season.

In order to offset some of the costs associated with seasonality many hotels and operators offer holidays for off-season periods with heavily discounted prices. By offering lower prices it is possible to induce visitors to a destination at a time when they would otherwise not visit. However, there are limits to such discounting. First, the revenue that establishments receive during the off-season must *at least* cover the variable costs of production. If this is the case then, by opening in the off-season, they will be able to maintain their staff and, perhaps, make some contribution to their **fixed costs**. Secondly, the discounting of off-season packages should not be so great as to damage the desirability of the main season product.

There are also destinations that do not suffer much from seasonal variations and this provides them with a competitive advantage by allowing them to operate at a higher throughput of tourist activity across the year without suffering from as much socio-cultural and environmental impacts as their seasonal competitors.

High operating leverage/fixed costs

Many of the tourism-related industries are subject to high levels of fixed costs. That is, there is a large capital element that must be committed before any output is produced. In industries subject to this type of cost structure (e.g. airlines and hotels) the volume of sales becomes the all-important factor. This aspect is shown in Figure 9.3, where the vertical axis measures revenue and costs, and the horizontal axis depicts the quantity of output produced during the time period under consideration. The break-even output for the non-tourism industry is represented by Q1 whereas Q2 shows the break-even output for the tourism industry. The cost curve C_1 relates to the cost function of a non-tourism industry and C_2 relates to the cost function of a typical tourism-related industry. We can see that both industries are subject to the same variable-cost structures (that is why the two cost functions run parallel to each other) but the tourism-related industry is subject to a higher fixed-cost

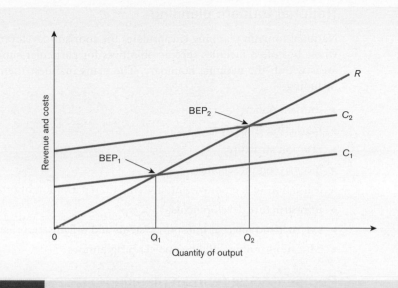

| **Figure 9.3** | The effect of fixed costs on the break-even point of production |

element. The end result is that the break-even point for the tourism-related industry (BEP_2) is much higher than that for the non-tourism industry, thus the volume of output becomes all important for high fixed-cost industries. The break-even point refers to that level of revenue and output that will just cover the costs involved in producing the output.

The preoccupation with volume displayed by industries that have high operating leverages can also influence the mindset of the national tourist organisations. Many tourist destinations base their tourism development plans on volume figures. Countries the world over tend to celebrate the fact that visitor numbers exceed some *magical* annual threshold and many countries still express the targets/objectives of their development plans in terms of bed spaces and tourist nights. However, the presence of tourists in itself is not the main objective of any of these destinations. The primary aims are economic and the indicators of performance and targets should be expressed in economic rather than volume figures and/or constrained by environmental or social indicator values.

Clearly, there is overwhelming evidence to support the view that there are a number of factors related to the tourism industry which make it an attractive development option. But some of these factors may make it less attractive if they are not controlled or alleviated by proper planning.

DEVELOPMENT PLANNING LAYERS

Tourism development planning can take place at international, national and sub-national levels.

International tourism planning

At the international level organisations such as the WTO, EU, OECD, Caribbean Tourism Organisation (CTO) and the Tourism Council for the South Pacific (TCSP) all undertake, albeit limited, forms of tourism planning. This level of planning is often weak in structure, detail and enforcement. It is generally provided in guideline form in order to assist the member states.

National tourism planning

National tourism planning encapsulates the tourism development plans for a country as a whole but often includes specific objectives for particular sub-national regions or types of areas within the national boundary. The plans manifest themselves in a variety of forms including:

- tourism policy;
- marketing strategies;
- taxation structure;
- incentive/grant schemes;
- legislation (e.g. employment, investment, repatriation of profits);
- infrastructure developments;
- external and internal transport systems and organisations; and
- education/training and manpower programmes.

Regional/local tourism planning

Regional and local tourism planning deals with specific issues that affect a sub-national area. It tends to be much more detailed and specific than its national counterpart and can vary quite significantly from area to area. For instance, there may be areas where tourism development is to be encouraged and others where specific types of tourism facilities, such as a casino, are actively discouraged. Such plans may relate to a state within a country, to a county, a city or even a local resort area.

However, there are constraints on how different regional plans can be from other regional plans or from the national plan. Certainly they should not detract from the overall aims and objectives of the national plan or those of another region. Ideally, the sub-national plans should work in harmony with the national plan as far as local conditions will allow.

Plans at all levels should include consideration of how information is transferred to the consumer – the tourist. It should also be borne in mind that what you *do not* tell the tourist is often as vital as what you *do* tell them. This is particularly true from the point of view of visitor management when attempts are made to direct the tourists towards some specific regions but away from others. Such information can be disseminated through a variety of media including the Internet, which is becoming increasingly important as a tool for tourism development and marketing. However, traditionally the following media have been used:

- visitor orientation centres;
- tourist information centres;
- advertising brochures, maps, magazine articles and broadcasting;
- self-guided tours and trails;
- official guides;
- posters and displays.

The above can all be seen as a means to visitor awareness and can be used to support more formal programmes run by tourism officials.

THE TOURISM DEVELOPMENT PLANNING PROCESS

The concept of planning is concerned with organising some future events in order to achieve pre-specified objectives. Integrated planning and development is a form of comprehensive planning: comprehensive because it integrates all forms of planning – economic, physical,

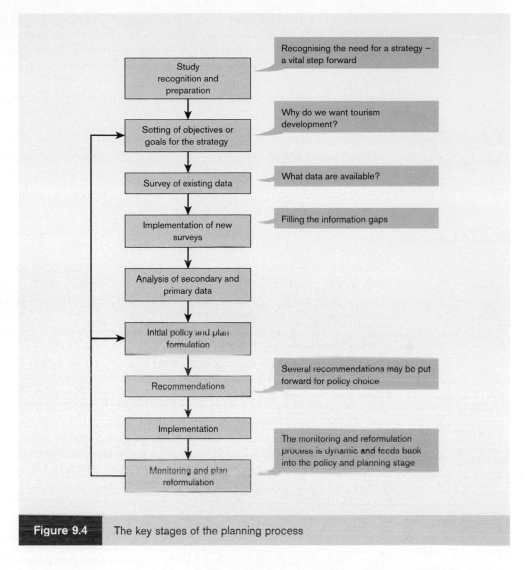

Figure 9.4   The key stages of the planning process

social and cultural. Planning should not be seen as a static concept, rather it attempts to deploy the best strategy in a world of changing internal and external influences. Although planning as a dynamic concept can take a variety of forms, there is a consistent structure that can be applied to the process of planning. That structure is set out in Figure 9.4.

Study recognition and preparation

The study recognition and preparation are really concerned with the recognition by the planning authorities (normally the government), private industry and the local community that tourism is a desirable development option, together with some awareness of the constraints within which it must develop. The fact that it is recognised that a strategy is required is an important indication that the government and people are aware of the complexity of the tourism industry and its need for coordination.

Setting of objectives or goals for the strategy

In order to design a development plan successfully it is necessary to have a clear understanding of the objectives that are to be achieved by the development of tourism. A common mistake in tourism development planning is to lose sight of the reasons why tourism has been selected as a development option. If it is the case that tourism is seen as the most appropriate vehicle for generating foreign exchange and employment opportunities, these goals should be embedded in the development plan from the start. This helps to avoid the problems encountered when the objectives are set down in terms of visitor numbers or annual guest nights.

Some major objectives, commonly found in tourism development plans, are set out below:

- To develop a tourism sector that, in all respects and at all levels, is of high quality, though not necessarily of high cost.
- To encourage the use of tourism for both cultural and economic exchange.
- To distribute the economic benefits of tourism, both direct and indirect, as widely and to as many of the host community as feasible.
- To preserve cultural and natural resources as part of tourism development and facilitate this through architectural and landscape design which reflect local traditions.
- To appeal to a broad cross-section of international (and domestic) tourists through policies and programmes of site and facility development.
- To maximise foreign exchange earnings to ensure a sound balance of payments.
- To attract high-spending 'upmarket' tourists.
- To increase employment opportunities.
- To aid peripheral regions by raising incomes and employment, thus slowing down or halting emigration.

It is important that the objectives set out in the development plan are *clear*, *unambiguous*, *non-conflicting* and *achievable*. We can see from the above list of objectives that these examples are not specific in nature, thus it would be difficult to assess whether or not the objective had indeed been achieved. Also, some of the objectives may be conflicting, particularly those relating to the type of tourist to be attracted and their desired impact. Where the objectives are vague and/or conflicting, the tourism development plan is doomed to failure from the start.

Survey of existing data

Before setting out on the data collection stage it is vital to undertake an existing data search. Although this may sound obvious, there are many instances where data that are crucial to tourism development planning are collected and held by government agencies not expressly concerned with the planning process. Thus, when researchers go out into the field to collect **primary data** they are told that businesses have already supplied this information. The authors have come across incidences where no fewer than five hotel surveys were being conducted concurrently. This is not only wasteful in terms of time and resources, it also depletes the goodwill of the business community.

Implementation of new surveys

Once the existing data are known and the scope of the planning objectives have been set, the information gap can be filled by undertaking primary data collection. The data requirements for development planning are quite comprehensive and include:

- tourist characteristics/travel patterns;
- tourist attractions;
- accommodation facilities;
- other tourist facilities;

- land availability and use;
- economic structure – all sectors;
- education and training needs and provisions;
- environmental indicators;
- socio-cultural characteristics;
- investment and available capital – all sectors;
- public and private sector organisations; and
- relevant legislation and regulation.

All of the above factors are considered with respect to both their existing states and their projected states within the development plan's timescale.

The survey of existing data and primary data collection should generate an awareness of the importance of good-quality data for planning, management and monitoring purposes. The authorities should implement a long-term strategy of data enhancement by setting up a management information system that is flexible enough to accommodate the collection of new data when they become available and to encompass issues not necessarily identified within the current strategy.

Analyses

Once the objectives have been formulated, the analytical framework chosen will determine the precise sets of data to be collected. Once collected, the data are analysed by considering a wide range of issues. The major issues to be considered generally fall into four subject areas:

1. **Asset evaluation.** This area of analysis examines the existing and potential stock of assets, the ways in which they can be developed and the probable constraints on that development. The asset evaluation should also include an appraisal of the infrastructure in order to determine whether or not further investment is required. The asset evaluation should begin with a broad approach, looking at assets across a wide range of sectors and their alternative uses. The evaluation could then be focused to concentrate on the tourism-related assets and how they should be best employed within that framework.

2. **Market analysis.** The market analysis is clearly a crucial component of a sound development plan. The market analysis undertaken during tourism development planning is sometimes too narrow in scope to be of optimum use. Initial issues that need to be addressed concern global, regional and country market trends by type of tourism activity. Another fundamental question is 'Why do tourists come to this destination?' Too many development plans of the past have relied upon the assumption of constant market share and this is not a valid assumption. To appraise the development plans, attempts must be made to determine whether or not the proposed developments are appropriate, the markets that are likely to be attracted by these developments and the price level or **tariff structure** that should be adopted. The market analysis must also incorporate a study of developments in competitive markets and/or in competitive modes of transport. Generally these issues will be tackled within a competitive and comparative advantage study that incorporates a SWOT analysis.

3. **Development planning.** A major issue to be studied under this heading is the time phasing of the development plan in order to ensure successful implementation. The possible sources of funding of the development are examined and the appropriate level of foreign funding (if any) is calculated. The analysis section encompasses all issues, such as the number of foreign employees, the marketing strategy to be adopted, investment incentives, organisational structures and training programmes.

4. **Impact analyses.** The impact analyses should be all-embracing, covering issues such as the probable effects that the development will have on the host community and the

environment, the economic implications in terms of key indicators (employment, income, government revenue and foreign exchange flows) and the probable economic rates of return. Analyses should also examine the risks involved and the sensitivity of the results to changing assumptions. The integration of economic, environmental and socio-cultural impact analyses is a vital advancement to tourism planning tools which took place in the closing years of the twentieth century. The incorporation of a forecasting model, so that future economic, environmental and social impacts can be assessed, is equally crucial. Tourism researchers are constantly striving to develop enhanced planning tools for use in tourism development and models, such as those developed within the International Centre for Tourism and Hospitality Research, Bournemouth University, will play a major part in providing the framework for future tourism planning exercises.

The analyses set out above are of both a quantitative and qualitative nature and most of these issues must be faced before a move can be made towards formulating policy recommendations.

Policy and plan formulation

The results from the analyses of the survey data are unlikely to yield a unique solution and, instead, will tend to suggest a number of possibilities for development strategies. The process from here is one of formulating draft plans on the basis of each policy option derived from the analyses. The alternative plans are then evaluated in terms of their potential economic, physical and socio-cultural costs and benefits, together with any possible problem areas that may result from the implementation of each plan. The plans that achieve the most objectives while not exposing the destination to potentially serious problems are then selected and drawn up in full. Finally, a 'preferred' plan is drafted for policy consideration.

Recommendations

The preferred plan that has been selected on the basis of the analyses, having now been completed in detail, is submitted to the authorities by the planning team. This submission is sent to the authorities, together with recommendations concerning the optimum methods of developing tourism in the destination and, in so doing, achieving the plan's objectives. It is more than likely that the planning team will present the authorities with a selection of recommendations that all fulfil the requirements of the preferred plan. It is at this stage that feedback between the authorities and the development plan team is essential in order to focus attention on issues where attention is needed and to play down areas where it is not. During the process of these discussions the final development plan is formulated. Therefore, the recommendations stage should really be regarded as a period of dialogue between the planning team and the policy makers.

Implementation of the plan

The methods of implementing the development plan will have been considered throughout most stages of its construction. Thus, during the secondary data survey stage attention will have been paid to many aspects that relate to implementation – such as the existing legislative and regulatory frameworks. By the time that the implementation stage is reached, all of the necessary legislation and regulation controls will have been brought into effect. Furthermore, the methods used to facilitate public debate and discussions relating to the development will have been devised and enquiry and appeal mechanisms will be in place. During the implementation stage particular attention will need to be paid to the phasing of the plan and the critical path analyses will have highlighted areas that may be the cause of concern.

Photograph 9.2 Low-intensity tourism development.
Source: Beachcomber Hotels (Dinarobin Hotel Golf & Spa)

Monitoring and reformulation

Once the development plan has been implemented it must be closely monitored in order to detect any deviations that may occur from the projected path of development. Any such deviations, and there will probably be some, must be analysed in order to assess how they will affect the development plan and its objectives. Once this secondary analysis has been completed, the research team can report back to the authorities with recommendations as to how the plan and its policy recommendations should be modified in order to stay on target. External and internal factors may influence the performance of the strategy and it is important that the monitoring systems enable the research team to be fully informed about all relevant changes. Furthermore, even with the best-laid plans, unexpected events do occur and it is here that the reactive policy skills of the research team and policy makers come into play. For instance, there could be outbreaks of disease that are of international headline importance (the outbreak of the plague in India, the foot-and-mouth crisis in the UK), terrorist activities (Bali, Cairo, London, Madrid and New York) or a destination may be deemed to be unsafe by governments (such as – at various times – Cyprus, Indonesia, Saudi Arabia and Sri Lanka) that cause the international flows of tourists to deviate from their expected path. Even positive developments in competing countries, such as the liberalisation of South Africa, can have unforeseen effects on other destinations. It is important that the research team is aware of how sensitive the strategy is to each of the conceivable variables and how best to react to such events. Even then the tourism plan is likely to face inconceivable events where the research team and policy makers will have to rely upon intuition.

MINI CASE STUDY 9.2
Tourism: a challenge for the 21st century

By Ranjan Solomon

Those who shape tourism policy today argue that tourism can be a key factor for accelerated development, education, employment and dignity for the world's poorest countries. They even argue that tourism can help reduce poverty with fair and progressive liberalization. The World Tourism Organization, in fact, made this affirmation recently. The World Tourism Organization is calling for 'Liberalization with a Human Face' – a progressive asymmetrical loosening of restraints with special benefits for the poorest, with safety nets and real regard for sustainability. Increasing foreign exchange, promoting entrepreneurship, stimulating infrastructure investment and creating millions of skilled jobs in tourism, they claim, can make a significant contribution to the Millennium Development Goals. Almost in contrast, United Nations Secretary-General, Kofi Annan, argues: 'We will have time to reach the Millennium Development Goals – worldwide and in most, or even all, individual countries – but only if we break with business as usual. . . . And we must more than double global development assistance over the next few years. Nothing less will help to achieve the Goals.'

WTO CLAIMS

Francesco Frangialli, Secretary General of the World Tourism Organization, underscoring the size of the world's largest industry, said last year 763 million trips were taken with tourists spending US$622 billion.

There are varying statistics about how much of this actually reaches the destinations and gets into the hands of the communities that have been the hosts. Quite conveniently, tourism bureaucrats and policy makers do as much as they can to conceal the massive amounts that stay back in the countries of tourist's origins in the form of 'leakages' – often meaning that the host countries must count themselves lucky if they get even 30 percent at the end of the transactions. The harshest thing about this is that there are subtle, and not so subtle, attempts to organize global trade in tourism in a manner that is deliberately designed to guarantee profits to the rich. Meanwhile, the poor countries will provide most, if not all, the 'raw materials' needed to make tourism profitable. That includes land in prime locations, water sources for entertainment and consumption (always excessive), and amusement facilities as in golf courses/amusement parks after evicting farmers, roads that the local populations will never see or get to ride on, special transportation, hotels with overworked and underpaid staff. This does not take into account the huge trafficking in girls, boys, young women whose role it is entertain the 'sex tourists' – on holiday away from home, family, ethics, and moral responsibility. Nor does it account for the violation of the cultural rights and dignity of the people who have to virtually commodify and sell their culture in forms and patterns that satisfy the 'tourist-customer' for a 'few dollars more' as the tour-package agent would say.

ASYMMETRY AND LIBERALIZATION ARE INCOMPATIBLE

In the face of these horrific ground realities, Frangialli continues to insist that tourism trade can be one of the most decisive factors in achieving the goals of development and sustainability in the global trading system particularly in the world's poorest countries. He argues that now is the moment to carry forward what he refers to as 'tourism liberalization with a human face' – prioritizing poverty alleviation along with fair trade and triple bottom line sustainable development.'

Tourism is one of the oldest areas of economic activity covered under the WTO's General Agreement on Trade in Services (GATS). Tourism and travel-related services account for about 11 percent of World GDP and employ about 200 million people worldwide. Even though many countries such as the Caribbean nations, Tanzania and Kenya have a long history of involvement in the global tourist trade they still are relatively weak in their ability to hold and retain the gains from tourism. This is mostly because receiving countries can hardly manage to negotiate fair trade arrangements largely stemming from the fact that they are over-reliant on tourism exports and foreign investments.

POOR ARE THE LOSERS

With control no more in their hands, it is hard to see how there can be a 'human face' to tourism liberalization. It is a contradiction in terms. Under the GATS regime, tourism spaces in the developing world are under the control of multinationals and their interests. Governments, in their anxiety to earn the crumbs of foreign exchange from investors and the arriving tourist, will, meanwhile, offer what they have at terms dictated to by the investor. In the end tourism will weigh heavily in favour of the rich countries and the rich in the poorer ones. The poor have been, and always will be, the losers.

For as long as the rich and powerful are going to draw up the parameters and architecture of tourism policy, nothing will change – not much in any case. How can it? For after all, the investor is there to make profits. Social responsibilities do not factor – evidence of this is too thin to be counted or weighed in. The occasional burst of charity is not what we are talking about and asking for. Tourism is, virtually, for all intents and purposes, one with a purely economic function in so far as the industry is concerned. It does not seek to respond to the higher callings of a human pilgrimage into the unknown – seeking knowledge, truth, knowing and understanding the depth and variety of human cultural experience, the enormously bountiful qualities of nature, the waters, the birds, and animals. These remain the theatre where tourism happens. And, as in theatre, it is too often reduced to a performance and handed no more than commodity value.

CHALLENGE

Despite the fact of a power packed industry backed, as it is, by the muscle of national and local governments and international agencies like the World Bank, IMF, and the World Trade Organization, there has been resistance that has been successful in many instances. Civil society groups, faith-based communities from the major religions of the world, progressive minded academics, intellectuals, and lawyers, can join hands with tourism activists in organizing people who are being compelled to negotiate away their community interests to resist blueprints drawn up by external factors with no reference to the host communities and countries.

A process by which people become the planners of tourism in their environs is the right way forward. This must include their right to say NO and to set the parameters of what a tourism plan is likely to be. External interventions must also be invited in by the local communities – not imposed under any pretext.

The World Tourism Organization has set as its theme for this year 'Travel and transport from the imaginary of Jules Verne to 21st century reality'. 21st century reality compels us to think otherwise. 2005, in particular, is sadly the year that follows the devastating tsunami, the year of tragedy in Iraq, the continued occupation of Palestine with no solution in sight, the year when more people went hungry to bed, more children died of malnutrition, hunger, and disease, more young people were unemployed, and millions denied justice. Tourism cannot maintain the status quo of seeing the privileged few continue to scout around the world, enjoying leisure and recreation under exploitative and excruciating conditions for people in the developing world. It is to these questions and challenges that tourism must turn its center of attention.

In the context of the tsunami (just ten months ago), Katrina (barely a few weeks now), and the continuing threat especially to coastal/small island communities because of the arrival of mega-tourism ventures (the recent rampage in Biminis, The Bahamas) are but examples of a tourism industry gone awry and drunk with the power of capital/investment capacities to the detriment of people and environments. With this letter we also bring to your attention the appeal of the Global Tourism Interventions Forum (GTIF). Please look under www.ecotonline.org under campaigns. We encourage those who find themselves in agreement with the appeal to sign in their organizational and/or individual capacities.

Instead, tourism must busy itself with initiating encounters of solidarity – people-to-people, culture-to-culture, people-to-nature, religion-to-nature, between those who seek justice and those who are denied it. Tourism could be a precursor to the notion of 'one-world', in contrast to what it is today. Tourism is largely an avenue and instrument for the rich and affluent whose wealth has been accumulated in the context of unjust structures and systems of society. Incremental changes in policy with slogans like 'liberalization with a human face' will stop far short of what is needed – an overhauling of tourism practice to guarantee it is just, participatory, and geared to authentic human advancement.

→

ECOT Statement for the World Tourism Day (27 September 2005), published on 16 September by ECOT, written by Ranjan Solomon. Ranjan Solomon was the Executive Director of Ecumenical Coalition on Tourism (ECOT) from 2005–2007. Since 2008 the Executive Director is Caesar D'Mello.

Source: www.ecotonline.org

DISCUSSION QUESTIONS

1. 'There are so many issues to be addressed and so many tiers of planning and policy-making with respect to tourism that it is not possible to find a planning process that will deliver.' Discuss this statement in the light of the comments made above.

2. Critically appraise the comments made about tourism policy, the tourism industry and the characteristics of tourism used in the above case study.

The development plan team

The development plan team will need considerable expertise and experience in the formulation of such plans. In general, the team will consist of four groups of specialists, falling into the broad categories of technical services, marketing specialists, planners and economists. In more detail, the likely spread of specialist skills will include:

- market analysts;
- physical planners;
- economists;
- environmental scientists;
- infrastructure engineers;
- transport engineers;
- social scientists;
- draughtsmen and designers; and
- legal experts.

The plan will be constructed over a period of time and this time can be broken down into five distinct phases.

1. **Identification and inventory of the existing situation.** This phase includes:
    (a) characteristics and structure of current consumer demand;
    (b) study of consumer choice;
    (c) current land use, land tenure and land-use control;
    (d) existing natural and artificial attractions;
    (e) ecosystem factors – particularly those considered to be vulnerable;
    (f) economic structures and the capacity thresholds of industries;
    (g) labour force skill mix and educational base, together with availability;
    (h) accommodation facilities;
    (i) tourist services facilities;
    (j) infrastructure facilities and their capacities;
    (k) transport facilities and their capacities;
    (l) graphic presentation of physical inventory.

The above data will be used to establish the adequacy of existing structures and facilities, the classification and cost organisation of existing facilities (together with an index of standards currently achieved), and the economic impact of present tourism activity. This then leads on to the second phase.

2. **Forecasts for the future.** This phase will include forecasts of future demand and probable tourist movements and needs. This will be complemented by an analysis of the implications of these forecasts for future production levels of each relevant service and good, together with the infrastructural requirements. Anticipated standards of service will be examined and the economic forecasts of local repercussions will be estimated.

3. **Plan formulation.** The formulation of the plan will include proposed programmes of market organisation and promotion, comprehensive land-use and control planning, detailed infrastructural plans and the economic, environmental and social evaluations associated with the proposed development plan. Again it is likely to include a graphic presentation of land use and infrastructure, together with a mapping of social impacts and the constraints imposed by the environmental considerations.

4. **Specific project development.** This phase will include an analysis of specific policies and projects for marketing and tourism management. The physical planners and architects will draw up selections of alternative layouts relating to specific projects and alternative solutions to infrastructural development problems will be developed. Costs of the alternative projects and infrastructural schemes will be assessed, along with the economic analysis of the various possible investment projects. Once the specific projects have been selected from the various alternatives these will, again, be subject to graphic presentations. The local environmental issues will be assessed and methods of alleviating problems will be set out. Examples of environmental planning actions could be broadly-based, such as the treatment of raw sewage and the maintenance of water quality, or highly specific, such as the planned periodic movements of footpaths to prevent serious erosion. Matters relating to visitor orientation programmes, visitor management and interpretation will all be considered and set out within this phase.

5. **Implementation.** The implementation programme will be set into motion with construction and supervision, technical and managerial assistance in tourism development projects, and financial analysis, and the recommended infrastructure investment programme will commence. The implementation stage will include the setting up of the continuing monitoring and re-evaluation activities to ensure that the strategy is performing optimally and so that adjustments can be made swiftly if the circumstances (internally or externally) change.

TOURISM DEVELOPMENT PLANNING: WHEN IT GOES WRONG

Even the best-laid plans can be knocked off course or fail because of unexpected events. Disaster management is an important element of modern-day planning and tourism is subject to a wide range of disasters, including earthquakes, hurricanes, outbreaks of infectious diseases and acts of terrorism. A large number of tourism development plans are, to varying degrees, unsuccessful. Given the fact that such plans operate in an environment that is constantly changing because of forces acting outside the control of the authorities, often outside the geographical area of the destination, perhaps this is not surprising. For instance, the terrorist attacks on the USA on 11 September 2001 have changed tourism flows in ways that have severely damaged the tourism development plans of many Caribbean states. However, many plans fail as a result of inadequacies in the development plans themselves. Discussions about this latter type of failure can be broken down into two categories: failure at the design stage and failure at the implementation stage.

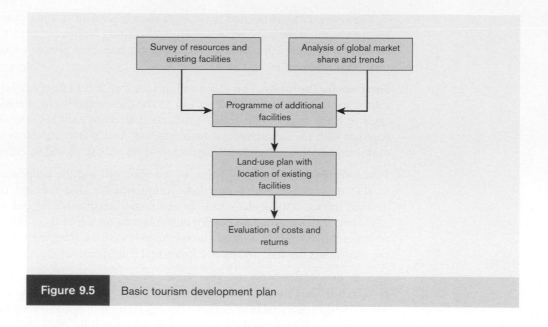

| Figure 9.5 | Basic tourism development plan |

Design stage plan failure

Many of the tourism development plans that fail do so because, at the design stage, they follow no more than the basic formulation of tourism development. Consider the basic tourism development plan in Figure 9.5. A plan of this structure will provide a general framework for state and municipal/local investments and will help to guide and evaluate the proposals of private developers. However, this type of plan structure lacks the analytical detail and scope necessary for a successful tourism development plan. Quite often this absence of analytical components is a reflection of the planning bodies who carry out the construction of the plan, bodies lacking in planning expertise and experience.

More importantly, the plan does not give a clear statement with respect to its objectives – objectives must be achievable, unambiguous and non-conflicting. The plan also fails to take into account the wider issues relating to environmental and social impacts because it is driven uniquely by its financial returns. One of the dangers of drawing up development plans in order to seek external funding is that the myopic view of financial profit and loss accounts may cause the planners to overlook some of the fundamental issues involved. This may well result in a plan that will fail financially as well as structurally.

The development plan takes no consideration of the impact of tourism on the host community, the environment and the economy. The projects are only evaluated on a financial basis (profit and loss accounts) and take no account of social costs and benefits.

Too much emphasis is placed upon physical development, i.e. supply-led tourism development, without proper consideration of returns to capital investments and effects on the market. The plan structure fails to make adequate market assessment. The global approach of examining tourist flows from the tourist-generating countries and projecting forward to future time periods under the assumption that all destinations will receive their fair share, fails to address the fundamental issue of *why people want to come to this particular destination*. Unless this issue is addressed future projections can be wildly off target.

Taking the above points into account, the basic development plan structure can be modified as in Figure 9.6.

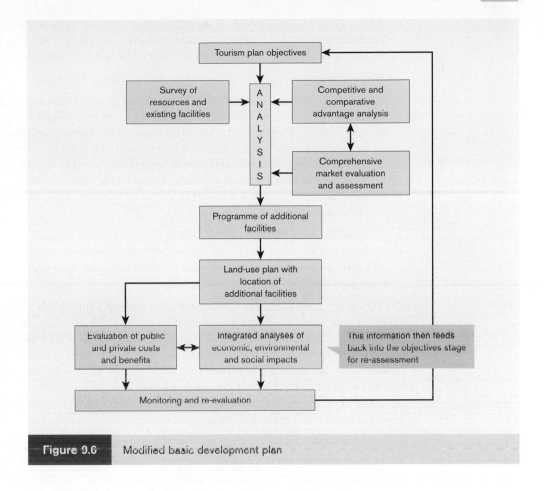

Figure 9.6   Modified basic development plan

Implementation stage plan failure

Problems encountered at the implementation stage are largely, but not exclusively, concerned with miscalculations regarding the use of land and the control of land usage. Tourism is, after all, an activity largely involved in real estate development. The type of land difficulties encountered during the implementation stage include the following:

- Those that actually undertake the development are sometimes more concerned with real estate speculation rather than the operation of tourist facilities. Thus, the motivation for development (particularly when incentives are on offer) may be more to do with capital gain than the tourism product. Such speculative development can lead to poorly designed facilities which are inefficient to operate, or facilities situated in poor locations.

- Development often takes place on the basis of a high debt/equity ratio using land values as security for the loans. This may lead to financial failure when property sales and operating profits do not materialise.

- The planning authorities often underestimate the difficulties that can be encountered when attempting to control the use of land. The only certain way of controlling land usage is by ownership.

- Failure to introduce the required planning legislation quickly enough to implement the development plan, or the lack of ability to enforce such legislation.

- If the specific sites earmarked for development are 'leaked' prior to the implementation of the development plan, land speculation and price inflation is likely to follow. This will alter the economic evaluations and may turn a viable project into a certain failure.

Other problems that may be encountered include the following:

- Failure to coordinate intermediaries in the travel trade, private sector development and public sector provision. Tour operators are an extremely influential component of the tourism process. If left to market forces then oligopolist behaviour can put severe pressure on the economic profitability and local benefits derived from tourism will suffer. Lack of coordination between public and private sectors can result in supply bottlenecks, affecting most aspects of the tourism product, damaging the economic benefits associated with the tourism activity, adversely affecting visitor satisfaction, and consequently causing the plan to miss its targets.
- Poor communications and infrastructure.
- Inadequate procedures to deal with public opposition and representations concerning the proposed development. A lack of such a mechanism can slow the development process down considerably and result in plan failure.

One of the most common scenarios from unsound tourism planning policies is over-exploitation – when the carrying capacity thresholds of a destination are exceeded such as in Aya Napa in Cyprus where the local population was displaced by tourism development or Benidorm in Spain during the rapid growth stages that created pressures on infrastructure, water supply, health and safety. Such excesses tend to lead to a decline in the quality of the tourism product and, ultimately, to a decline in the 'quality' of tourists, i.e. tourists associated with greater undesirable impacts and lower spend. Under such circumstances the destination may find some or all of the following indicators:

- ecological imbalance through overuse of resources;
- outbreaks of diseases through infrastructural failure;
- congestion, queues and economic inefficiencies;
- deterioration of natural and artificial environment through overuse;
- resentment towards tourists;
- increases in criminal activities; and
- destruction of host community's values.

Although some of the above problems can be alleviated, such as improving the infrastructure to reduce the health risks of water and sewage treatment failure, some of them cannot. The effects of over-exploitation can be minimised, however, by diverting pressures. For instance, ecological imbalances can be tackled by:

- appropriate visitor flow management;
- fencing-off areas subject to overuse;
- providing alternative routes and facilities for tourists to relieve others;
- dispersing tourists over wider or to different areas;
- zoning tourism-related activities;
- educating tourists and hosts to limit socio-cultural damage; and
- encouraging more positive local involvement in tourism activities.

One of the most well-tried techniques is that of access control – the volume or flow of tourists can be controlled economically, through prices, or physically, through closures, limiting parking facilities, transport or issuing quotas.

There are, of course, dangers associated with these remedial actions. For instance, dispersing tourists to other areas or to a wider area can sow the seeds for greater long-term problems if the source of the over-exploitation is not harnessed. Dispersing tourists temporally by extending the tourist season can reduce the time that some destinations need to recover from the industry's activities. Redirecting tourism flows may alleviate damaged areas in the short term, but only to replace them with newly damaged areas in the longer term. Such dispersion can also conflict with the prime objectives of the tourism plan. Zoning brings with it many limitations and problems, particularly in border areas. Therefore, when the remedial actions are implemented they should be seen as short-term alleviation methods until the true source of the problems can be tackled.

Finally, the issue of quality should be embedded in all aspects of tourism development planning. The issue of quality is vital for successful tourism development and should manifest itself in the structure and nature of the plans, the educational institutions that train the management and labour force and the monitoring and evaluation of the tourism development process. There are destinations, such as Mauritius and some Indonesian resorts, that owe their competitive advantage to the 'quality' of their tourism product and use 'quality' as a means of product differentiation. Quality should not be confused with high price or up-market tourism. It is just as important to strive for quality in a bed and breakfast or one-star hotel as it is in a five-star hotel or resort. However, when quality is the only factor leading to a competitive edge, then the development of the destination is vulnerable because quality is replicable by other destinations. This means that quality should be considered as a vital part of any tourism development strategy if the strategy is to achieve long-term success.

CONCLUSION

Tourism, as an industry, fits well into the various economic development theories that have been put forward over the past couple of centuries. The only theory that does not provide a positive role for tourism in achieving general economic development is the English classical theory which provides little hope for any industry. The remaining theories all suggest that tourism would be a useful component of general economic development.

The successful development of tourism requires the construction of a development plan or strategy that is flexible and thorough. Flexibility is required in order to adjust and reformulate in response to internal and external changes. Thoroughness is required because of the complexity of the tourism industry and the economic, environmental and social consequences of its development. The issue of 'sustainability' is no more than sound planning because development requires that the path chosen is one that is in some way sustainable. Although the process of tourism development planning will be specific from destination to destination there are processes that need to be followed at national and sub-national levels and these processes provide the framework for tourism development planning.

Tourism development plan failure, when it occurs, is likely to be attributable to failures at either the design stage (inadequate planning structure) or the implementation stage. Both forms of failure are common but in many instances there are remedial actions that may be taken to alleviate some of the problems encountered by failure. Finally, it is important that authorities have contingency plans in place to deal with unexpected events that may knock the tourism strategy off course.

SELF-CHECK QUESTIONS

1. Which theories of economic development provide the best basis for tourism as a catalyst for economic development?

2. What are the major steps, and their sequence, that need to be undertaken as part of the planning process?

3. What reasons can be cited to explain tourism development plan failure at the design stage?

4. Why do tourism master plans/strategies fail at the implementation stage?

5. List the characteristics of the tourism product that influence its attractiveness as a development option. In so doing identify whether the characteristic provides a positive or negative influence when considering tourism as a development option.

ESSAY QUESTIONS

1. What indicators can be used to measure economic development and what are their weaknesses or limitations?

2. Tourism development is a complex issue that requires a complex solution. What factors make tourism planning complex and how can they be catered for within the planning process?

3. 'It is better to plan tourism development and fail than it is to allow tourism to develop in an unplanned manner.' Discuss this statement, incorporating the various forms of plan failure that can occur.

4. What characteristics make tourism an attractive industry for economic development?

5. What are the characteristics of the tourism product that make planning such an important aspect of successful development?

ANNOTATED FURTHER READING

Books

Gartner, W. and Lime, D. (eds) (2000) *Trends in Outdoor Recreation, Leisure and Tourism*, CABI Publishing, London.
A collection of edited papers that deals with a wide range of planning and policy issues related to tourism. The book provides in-depth analyses for the more advanced student.

Gunn, C.A. and Var, T. (2002) *Tourism Planning*, 4th edn, Routledge, London and New York.
Provides a comprehensive overview of tourism development.

Inskeep, E. and Kallenberger, M. (1992) *An Integrated Approach to Resort Development: Six Case Studies*, WTO, Madrid.
A collection of case studies that explores the issues relating to planning in the real world. The cases would have provided greater insight if they had been more varied but nevertheless the book provides good insight into many of the issues involved in tourism planning.

Nafziger, E.W. (1997) *The Economics of Developing Countries*, 3rd edn, Prentice Hall, Upper Saddle River, NJ.
An excellent book on theories of economic development and the issues relating to the development process.

Swarbrooke, J. (1999) *Sustainable Tourism Management*, CABI Publishing, London.
This book examines the definition of sustainable tourism and looks at tourism management in practice from around the world.

Articles

Ceron, J-P. and Dubois, G. (2003) 'Tourism and sustainable development indicators: the gap between theoretical demands and practical achievements', *Current Issues in Tourism* 6(1), 54–75.

This paper outlines the historical context in which indicators appeared, and links this to the need for improving information systems.

Ghina, F. (2003) 'Sustainable development in small island developing states', *Environment, Development and Sustainability* **5**(1–2), 139–65.
This paper explores the status of sustainable development in small island developing states (SIDS). It is the position of this paper that issues related to environmental vulnerability are of the greatest concern. A healthy environment is the basis of all life-support systems, including that of human well-being and socio-economic development.

Lino Grima, Ä.P., Horton, S. and Kant, S. (2003) 'Introduction: natural capital, poverty and development', *Environment, Development and Sustainability* **5**(3–4), 297–314.
Can development occur without running down natural resources in an unsustainable way? The concept of natural capital offers a way for those with divergent views (ecologists and economists for example) to discuss this difficult question. Four aspects are examined:

1. The role of institutions in facilitating sustainable development.
2. Examples from (eco)tourism illustrate the potential – and limits – of applicability of the concept.
3. Measurement issues for natural capital are then considered.
4. The concept is applied to agricultural strategy in fragile lands, where the trade-off between the environment and development is likely to be most severe.

Some implications for future research and policy are developed.

Poirier, R.A. (1995) 'Tourism and development in Tunisia', *Annals of Tourism Research* **22**(1), 157–71.
Economic liberalisation policies, externally imposed structural requirements, and Tunisia's comparative advantage have led the government to pursue tourism on a large scale. The growth of this sector has been phenomenal, as evidenced by large-scale hotel resort enclaves for Europeans and supportive infrastructural commitments by government and the private sector.

References cited and bibliography

Ashworth, G. and Dietvorst, A. (1995) *Tourism and Spatial Transformations: Implications for Policy and Planning,* CAB, Oxford.

Bodlender, J. and Gerty, M. (1992) *Guidelines on Tourism Investment,* WTO, Madrid.

Chopra, S. (1991) *Tourism and Development in India,* Ashish, New York.

Cooper, C. (1991) *Progress in Tourism, Recreation and Hospitality Management,* Wiley, Chichester.

De Kadt, E. (1979) *Tourism, Passport to Development,* Oxford University Press, Oxford.

Edgell, D. (1990) *International Tourism Policy,* Van Nostrand Reinhold, New York.

Hall, C.M. and Jenkins, J.M. (1994) *Tourism and Public Policy,* Routledge, London.

Inskeep, E. (1993) *National and Regional Planning, Methodologies and Case Studies,* WTO/Routledge, Madrid/London.

Inskeep, E. and Kallenberger, M. (1992) *An Integrated Approach to Resort Development,* WTO, Madrid.

Jansen-Verbeke, M. (1998) *Leisure, Recreation and Tourism in Inner Cities,* Routledge, London.

Johnson, P. and Thomas, B. (eds) (1992) *Perspectives on Tourism Policy,* Mansell, London.

Kinniard, V.H. and Hall, D.R. (eds) (1994) *Tourism Development: The Gender Dimension,* Belhaven, London.

Lawson, F. (1995) *Hotels and Resorts: Planning, Design and Refurbishment,* Butterworth Heinemann, Oxford.

Murphy, P. (1997) *Quality Management in Urban Tourism*, Wiley, New York.

Nafziger, E.W. (1997) *The Economics of Developing Countries*, 3rd edn, Prentice Hall, Upper Saddle River, NJ.

Rostow, W.W. (1990) *Stages of Economic Growth: A Non-Communist Manifesto*, 3rd edn, Cambridge University Press, Cambridge.

WTO (1980) *Tourism and Employment: Enhancing the Status of Tourism Professions*, WTO, Madrid.

MAJOR CASE STUDY 9.1
Cape Verde: a '21st Century Nation'

On the 5th July 2007, the Republic of Cape Verde will celebrate 32 years of independence...

The uninhabited islands 400 miles west of Senegal, West Africa, were discovered and colonized by the Portuguese in the 15th century; 500 years later the Republic gained independence in 1975. As the Cape Verdeans celebrate their national holiday, Adrian Lillywhite, MD of Cape Verde Property Ltd, the first UK agent operating in the market, looks at how this archipelago is fast becoming a 21st century nation.

Cape Verde's economy is primarily service-based due to its lack of natural resources and tourism has come to play a key role. Since 1991, the government has pursued market-oriented economic policies, including an open welcome to foreign investors and a far-reaching privatization program.

From 1994 to 2000 there was a total of about $407 million in foreign investments made or planned, of which 58% were in tourism (US Department of State).

Retaining economic relations with its past colonial rulers, Portugal, has meant that Cape Verde has enjoyed strong growth since the 1990s linking its currency with the Portuguese escudo and the euro in 1999. The annual GDP growth rate is around 7% and the Minister of the Economy, Growth and Competitiveness has announced that Cape Verde intends to join the World Trade Organization (WTO) in 2008.

VAST MODERNIZATION AND DEVELOPMENT

In tandem with economic growth, Cape Verde has been undergoing vast modernization and development of its infrastructure including new roads, ports and airports. Minister of Infrastructures, Transportation and the Sea, Manuel Inocncio Sousa, commented, 'This

(economic) growth is being induced by tourism, by real estate and hotel investments, by the rapid increase in the flow of tourists to Cape Verde and by related activities. We need to respond to this growth with the same rhythm of development and modernization in the country's entire infrastructure.' US$ 450 million is to be spent on modernizing ports with the aim of making Cape Verde a platform in the Atlantic for air and sea transportation.

Already Cape Verde is a popular stop for Atlantic cruise liners and provides much needed tourism revenue for the surrounding areas. The number of cruise ships stopping in Cape Verde is expected to increase from 20–30 in 2006 to 60 or 70 in 2007, over a 100% increase according to the President of the Leewards Islands Chamber of Commerce, Industry and Services, Orlando Mascarenhas.

This coupled with the regular direct flights from the UK (Gatwick and Manchester) to the main island of Sal and the expected direct flight from Gatwick to the island of Boa Vista will result in ever increasing visitor numbers.

TOURISM 'PIVOTAL'

According to the Cape Verdean National Statistics Institute (INE) Cape Verde's hotels welcomed 233,000 tourists in 2006, 26.4% more than 2005, and this figure is set to rise again in 2007. The Cape Verdean Government is acutely aware of the pivotal role which tourism plays in the Republic's future and with that in mind a Tourism Master Plan is being formulated which will include a Development Agenda and a Strategic Action Plan for Tourism.

Adrian Lillywhite comments, 'The tourist appeal of Cape Verde is far reaching. The islands have become popular with not only the Portuguese and Italians but the British, Irish and increasingly the Asian population.

China for example has named Cape Verde as an approved tourist destination which will no doubt raise the Republic's profile globally.'

As tourism has grown so too has the demand for real estate on the untouched islands. 2006 saw capital growth rates of between 15 and 20% on Sal, the island of primary development, and this rate is predicted to be maintained over the next couple of years.

Property prices are very much dependent on location with the more easily accessible islands and beachfront sites demanding higher premiums. Adrian comments, 'The property market consists primarily of off-plan and new build properties with prices to suit every budget. 1 bedroom apartments in Santa Maria town on Sal for example average at €50,000 rising to €249,000 for a frontline 1 bedroom apartment and €600,000 for a frontline 4 bedroom villa in a popular resort area.'

ATTRACTIVE RENTAL YIELDS

In addition to capital growth, rental yields of up to 15% per annum in some areas are a strong attraction for investors. 'A 2 bedroom apartment in a quality development will fetch 800 euros per week inclusive of water and electricity and some developments are offering 5% rental guarantees,' comments Adrian.

It is worth noting also that the Cape Verdean diaspora (the vast majority of which live in Portugal and the eastern USA) are increasingly buying property back in their motherland. Impressed by the rapid improvement in the infrastructure, resource provision and economic stability, many are purchasing second homes and properties for their retirement.

The Cape Verdean government is supporting this activity by the Instituto das Comunidades (IC) preparing a guide for emigrant Cape Verdeans to help explain the process of purchasing land or a home.

The 5th July will not only be a celebration of independence but of achievement by Cape Verde and its people. In 1975 there were many question marks over the new Republic; however, it seems that hard work and a progressive, inclusive attitude have put Cape Verde in good stead to be a real success story for Africa in the 21st century.

Source: http://www.pattinson.co.uk/public/content/articles/Cape_Verde_a_21st_Century_Nation.htm

DISCUSSION QUESTIONS

1. Outline the major steps you would take to ensure that tourism in Cape Verde achieves its potential and provides a sustainable industry for the local population.

2. What are the key strengths, weaknesses, opportunities and threats to tourism development in Cape Verde and how would you exploit the opportunities and mitigate the threats?

CHAPTER 10
Tourism under Crises

LEARNING OUTCOMES

This chapter will provide you with:

- an understanding of travel risk and travel risk perceptions;

- an understanding of how travel risk perceptions can affect travel decisions;

- an insight into how terrorist attacks may impact on destinations and the length of time needed to recover from such attacks;

- an understanding of the impact of climate change;

- an insight into the simulation models used to predict climate change and its effects on tourism;

- an understanding of how destinations may adapt to climate change.

Photograph: Great Wall of China, China © Ryan and Lynette Sauvé

Photograph 10.1   Terrorism impacts directly on residents and tourists.
Source: PA Photos

40% in most hotels since the October 2002 bombings and has been as low as 10% in some areas such as Nusa Dua. Overall occupancies on the island stood at an average of 18% on 26 October 2002, down from a level of just over 70% in the days prior to the tragedy. The first post-bombing signs of recovery were not evident until October 2003, when the number of arrivals exceeded the level that was recorded in 2001, a year before the attack took place. This, however, only represents the benchmark of a stagnant destination. If tourism in Bali was increasing throughout the first part of this century then one would need to factor in the potential growth of arrivals lost as a result of the incidents. By 2004 the situation had improved markedly with foreign arrivals returning, and even exceeding, the pre-bombing figures. However, Bali was not to be given the time to recover because in December 2004 the tsunami hit the region, causing widespread damage and loss of life, although not in Bali itself.

The December 2004 Indian Ocean earthquake triggered a series of tsunamis that ripped through the Indian Ocean, affecting most countries in the region from Indonesia to Africa. The immediate effect was a loss of life of just under 230,000 people and the destruction of coastal areas, many of them tourist resorts that were located on the shores of the Indian Ocean. There were some distinct differences between different locations, with many tourist resorts being devastated by the tsunami and many tourist lives lost, while in others the effects were slight. In Indonesia, where the epicentre of the earthquake was located, the impact of the earthquake and resulting tsunami on the tourism industry was relatively minor. This was because the damage and death toll was largely confined to Banda Aceh, which is not a main tourism destination and is located 1,000 km away from Bali (the main tourism resort accounting for more than 40% of the total inbound tourism to Indonesia, see Figure 10.1). The major tourism effects experienced by Indonesia were from the secondary effects of the tsunami as tourists chose to stay away from the entire country during the six weeks clean up period following the tsunami.

The tourist arrivals and expenditure in 2005 were only 5% down on the 2004 figures, which suggest that the total tourist revenue from international tourists fell from US$4.8 billion to US$4.5 billion (see Figure 10.2). This US$277 million shortfall in revenue was equivalent to just 2.2% of the country's total

→

Figure 10.1   Map of Indonesia
Source: Based on CIA COM

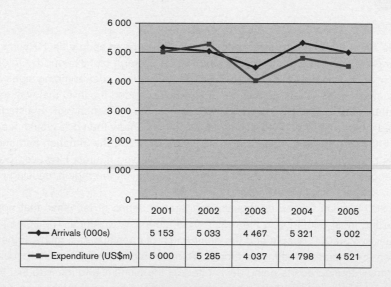

	2001	2002	2003	2004	2005
Arrivals (000s)	5 153	5 033	4 467	5 321	5 002
Expenditure (US$m)	5 000	5 285	4 037	4 798	4 521

Figure 10.2   Indonesia: international arrivals and expenditure, 2001–5

exports of commercial services in 2005. The tourist-generating countries for Indonesia also showed stability, the only exceptions being China and Singapore where there is a cultural aversion to visiting a country where so many people have lost their lives.

The duration of the impact of the tsunami on Bali tourism was incredibly brief, taking only six weeks to restore the number of arrivals to the pre-disaster level. Figure 10.2, which shows the levels of tourist arrivals and expenditure from 2001 to 2005, clearly shows the impacts of the Bali bombings and the tsunami on

| Table 10.1 | Average hotel occupancy rates, Bali 2004–5 |

Average hotel occupancy rates (January–September)

	Jan	Feb	Mar	Apr	May	Jun	Jul	Aug	Sep	Annual average
2005	44.6	41.0	44.8	50.3	47.4	51.3	57.9	55.8	55.4	49.83
2004	44.6	40.5	38.9	45.2	46.2	51.3	52.8	53.8	57.6	47.88

Source: Bali Government Tourist Office

tourism activity in Indonesia. The World Bank suggested that the rapid recovery from the tsunami was partly because Bali has such a strong identity that travellers often do not recognise it as being one of the 17,000 islands that make up Indonesia, as well as the fact that it was shielded from the worst of the tsunami.

Table 10.1 also shows that the hotel occupancy rates bounced back quickly to their pre-disaster levels with six of the first nine months showing greater occupancy levels than those experienced in 2004. However, the resilience of tourism in Bali was soon to be tested yet again when terrorists detonated bombs targeted at the tourism industry in October of that year (although not on the same scale as the 2002 attack).

Figure 10.3 shows the impact at resort rather than national level. It can be seen that following the October 2002 attacks Bali was well on the road to recovery in 2004, some 18 months after the attack, but the December tsunami and the terrorist strike in October 2005 sent the number of tourists into decline for 2005 and 2006. However, there is every indication mid-2007 that the volume of tourist activity in Bali has recovered and is now greater than it was in the previous record period of 1999.

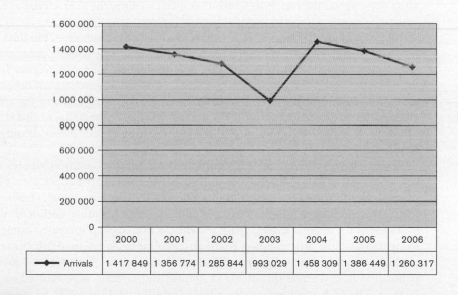

| Figure 10.3 | Bali: international tourist arrivals, 2000–6 |

DISCUSSION QUESTION

What actions can the government and tourism industry take to minimise the damage and improve the recovery following such natural and terrorist disasters? Is there a difference in the actions needed when it is a natural disaster as opposed to a terrorist attack?

TOURISM AND TERRORISM

As we have already seen, tourism is not only susceptible to natural disasters it is also affected by man-made disasters, such as the outbreak of war, political unrest and terrorism (e.g. Tiananmen Square in 1989, the Balkan Wars of the 1990s, the Gulf War in 1991, Luxor attacks 1997). Perhaps more importantly, in terms of the impact on tourism, tourists have recently become a frequent target of terrorist acts in order to provide the perpetrators with a higher profile in the media. Most of the violence has played on the tourists' decision-making, generating fear and insecurity to travellers and creating a major barrier to travel and thus a limitation to the growth of the industry. In addition to the openly stated fear of personal harm, there can be a lack of interest in travel, which masks this underlying fear.

Tourists may well perceive acts of terrorism to be a higher risk than natural disasters when travelling to specific destinations. Natural disasters are relatively rare and, unlike many acts of terrorism, are not specifically centred on tourists. Therefore, when tourists are considering a trip to the more politically volatile areas, such as some countries in the Middle East, they are likely to be far more concerned about man-made disasters than they are about natural disasters. Conversely, when travelling to the Caribbean during hurricane season tourists may be more aware of the risks relating to natural disasters than they are about acts of terrorism.

The perception of travel-related risk associated with terrorism has changed in recent times as a result of the change in the magnitude and frequency of the attacks. Where attacks in the past have been relatively small scale, the events of 9/11 (2001), the Bali bombings (2002, 2005), the Madrid bombings (2004), incidents in Turkey and Egypt (2005) and the attacks on the London transport network (2005) have all made the risk of terrorism a part of the international travel scene. The extent to which tourists perceive the risk from terrorist acts often depends on the region to which they are travelling, the characteristics of the traveller and how recently a terrorist incident has taken place.

While disasters of one form or another can strike any destination, the time period necessary for recovery varies significantly from destination to destination. There are a number of factors that can explain why it may take one destination longer to recover from a disaster than another destination, including the timing of the attack, the stage of development of the tourism industry, the scale of the attack, the frequency of attacks and the responses made after an attack. Figure 10.4 shows the impact of various terrorist attacks aimed at the tourism industries in six selected countries by looking at tourist arrivals before, during and after the terrorist attack.

Figure 10.4 shows an index of tourist arrivals for six countries where −1 is the year before a terrorist attack, 0 is the year during which the terrorist attack took place and +1 is the year after the terrorist attack. It is interesting to see that the countries fall into two groups, with Egypt, Indonesia and the USA all ending up with a similar decline in the number of tourist arrivals, whereas Kenya, Spain and the UK end up with increased numbers of arrivals compared with the situation prior to the attacks. One explanation of this clustering of results could be the fact that in Egypt and Indonesia the attacks were focused mainly on international visitors whereas the attacks in Madrid and London were centred on the transport systems. The USA attack was unprecedented and shocked the world whereas the victims of the Kenya attack were predominantly Israeli visitors. In isolation it is difficult to attribute these differences to specific factors and, of course, they are not unrelated in that the 9/11 event was followed by the Bali bombings and then Egypt, Madrid and the UK a few years later. Questions to be asked include: do tourists come to accept the risk of terrorism as more and more events take place, or are they more confident with the tighter security that follows? Also, it should be borne in mind that all of these countries invested heavily in enhanced marketing campaigns following the events and it may be more helpful to examine tourist expenditure as well as the number of arrivals.

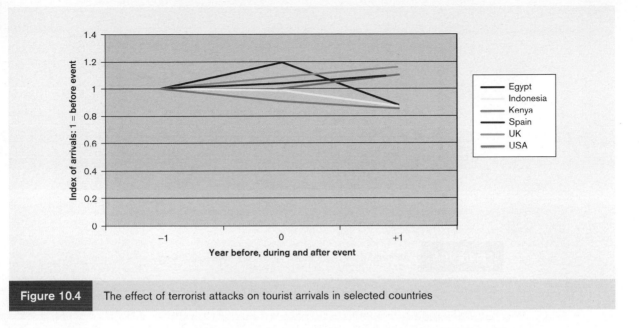

| **Figure 10.4** | The effect of terrorist attacks on tourist arrivals in selected countries |

When the tourism industry is under pressure and trying to recover from a negative shock it is not surprising to find tour operators and destinations reducing prices to make the destination more competitive and attract a wider range of visitors. Therefore one would expect to see that the fall in the volume of tourist expenditure is greater than the fall in the number of tourist arrivals. Figure 10.5 shows the patterns of change in tourist expenditure for the same countries that were shown in Figure 10.4. Figure 10.5 confirms this, showing that the three countries that suffered the greatest impact in terms of the drop in tourist arrivals suffered a slightly greater proportional drop in tourist expenditure, whereas those countries that

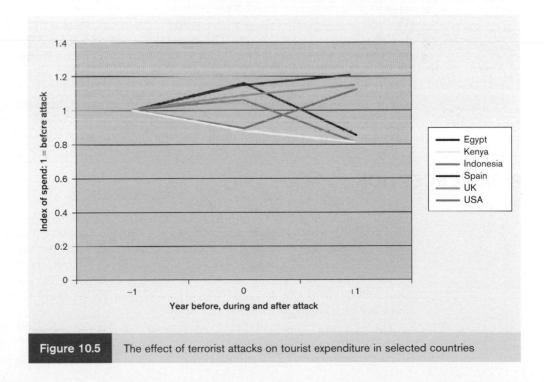

| **Figure 10.5** | The effect of terrorist attacks on tourist expenditure in selected countries |

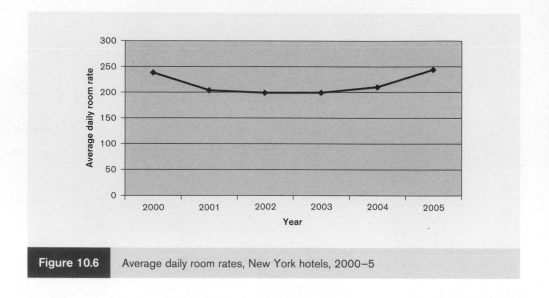

| Figure 10.6 | Average daily room rates, New York hotels, 2000–5 |

were able to maintain or increase the number of tourist arrivals also enjoyed an increase in the level of tourist spend.

The fall in tourist expenditure can be observed by looking at some of the component prices of travel such as the cost of airline tickets and hotel rates. As an example, air fares fell dramatically after 9/11 in order to try and coax travellers back on to aircraft amid fears of further attacks. Further, the growth of the low-cost airlines only helped underscore the fall in the cost of travel at a time when oil prices were rapidly rising. Hotel prices were also being offered at bargain basement prices. For instance, if the average daily room rates for New York hotels are examined it can be seen that there is a marked effect following the event of 9/11. In 2000 the average daily room rate in New York was US$237. Even though the terrorist attack on the Twin Towers did not occur until September, the average daily room rate fell for that year to just US$204 and the true underlying rate was revealed the following year when the average rate was only US$198. The room rates were kept low for 2003 (US$199) to maintain occupancy levels and the pre-attack levels of room rates were not restored until 2005 (see Figure 10.6).

Of course, the frequency of terrorist attacks affects the perceptions that travellers have about the risk associated with travel. Indonesia, for example, has been subjected to two significant terrorist attacks, the first in 2002 and the second in 2005, not to mention the 2004 tsunami. Does this make Indonesia a risky place in the minds of potential tourists?

RISK PERCEPTION

Generally speaking, the perception of travel-related risk experienced by an individual will be determined by a variety of factors, including the individual's aversion to risk, their consideration of what may occur as a result of their decisions or behaviour, the potential scale of a threat, the probability of incidence and, often more importantly, the media's coverage of earlier events or threats. If the individual or a close friend/relative has been exposed to risky situations prior to the decision-making process then this is likely to have a significant influence on an individual's perception of risk.

There are many aspects of the tourism product that give rise to risk and upon which travellers' perceptions will be formed. For instance, even the product itself is an unknown to the first-time visitor and therefore holds an element of risk in that it may not live up to the

Table 10.2	Examples of divergence between actual and perceived risk	
Type of risk	**Perception[1]**	**Actual[2]**
Health risks	India China Thailand	Thailand Egypt Caribbean
Crime risks (theft, fraud, etc)	USA Italy Spain	Thailand South Africa Caribbean

Source: [1] Morakabati (2007); [2] Norwich Union Insurance Report (2006)

tourist's expectations. Travel is fraught with risks in terms of accidents, getting lost, disruptions through industrial action, the effect of the weather on the transport system and acts of terrorism. Even the destination may hold risks in terms of health, crime, being an unfriendly environment or finding that an onward flight or the hotel is over-booked. Some of these risks may not figure strongly in some people's minds whereas they may be the central focus for some travellers.

Risk during the tourism decision and consumption process is the uncertainty as to whether there will be a difference between the expected and the actual outcomes of decisions or actions. If the level of perceived risk is greater than some personal threshold limit, the tourist may try to reduce exposure to this risk by, say, not travelling or travelling elsewhere. Normally, this threshold value is reached more quickly for a discretionary tourism product than, say, for business tourism. Risk perceptions are often formed in ways that do not reflect reality, but it is the perceptions that are important because they will guide the decision. Thus, it does not matter how incorrect or wrong a perception of risk may be, it will still influence the behaviour of the potential tourist in exactly the same way that decisions would be affected by changes in the level of actual risk.

In a recent study of travel risk perceptions it was found that there was little correlation between the perceptions of travellers and the frequency and magnitude of claims experienced by a major insurance company. Table 10.2 shows the top three countries for travel risk as perceived by travellers (based on a survey of 730 travellers from a wide range of countries of origin) and the top three countries/regions in terms of travel insurance claims from a leading travel insurance company.

CLIMATE CHANGE AND TOURISM

The earth's climate has demonstrably changed since pre-industrial times (before 1750) and is anticipated to continue changing for centuries to come. The Intergovernmental Panel on Climate Change (IPCC) has recently declared that 'Warming of the climate system is unequivocal, as is now evident from observations of increases in global average air and ocean temperatures, widespread melting of snow and ice, and rising global average sea level' (IPCC, 2007a). The global mean temperature has increased approximately 0.76 °C between the end of the nineteenth century and the beginning of the twenty-first. Most of the temperature change observed since the middle of the twentieth century can very likely be attributed to human activities that are increasing greenhouse gas concentrations in the atmosphere. Tourism is one of the human activities that contributes directly to climate change (Peeters, 2007). It is responsible for an estimated 5% of total emissions, 40% of which are caused by aviation, and 35% by other modes of transport. Air travel needs to be seen as the most problematic global environmental impact of tourism (Gössling *et al.*, 2005). The increasing trend for short breaks adds to this problem, with flights getting shorter but far more frequent.

Tourism is a highly climate-sensitive economic sector, as a result of its close connections to the environment and climate itself. Indeed, the impacts of a changing climate are already becoming evident at destinations around the world, making clear that climate change is not a remote issue for tourism. The capacity of the tourism sector to adapt to climate change is relatively high because of tourism's dynamic nature. Therefore there will be important opportunities for tourism to reduce the vulnerability of communities to climate change through sustainable development.

The following section provides an overview of the main types of impacts of climate change on tourism and the regions that are most vulnerable. It also presents some of the main avenues for adaptation that are open to tourism stakeholders. The primary source of information is the comprehensive report on climate change and tourism (Scott *et al.*, 2007), commissioned by the UN World Tourism Organization (UNWTO) and the United Nations Environment Programme (UNEP).

Climate change impacts on tourism

Tourism businesses and the destinations in which they operate are clearly sensitive to climate variability and change. Climate defines the length and quality of tourism seasons and plays a major role in destination choice. In addition, climate affects a wide range of environmental resources that are critical to tourism, such as snow depth, biodiversity and stocks of fresh water. It also influences various facets of tourism operations, including heating, cooling and snowmaking. All in all, there are three broad categories of climate change impacts that could affect the competitiveness and sustainability of tourism destinations: direct climatic impacts; indirect environmental change impacts; and indirect societal change impacts.

Direct climatic impacts

Direct impacts include changes in the frequencies and patterns of extreme weather events, and changes in climate-related push and pull factors. In addition, costs for heating and cooling, as well as snowmaking, are directly linked to thermal conditions, which are changing. Adequate climatic conditions are key for all types of tourism activities, ranging from conventional beach tourism to special interest segments. As a result, the redistribution of climatic assets among tourism regions will be one of the most prominent impacts of projected climate change. Changes in the length and quality of climate-dependent tourism seasons (i.e. sun-and-sea or ski holidays) could have considerable implications for competitive relationships between destinations and, therefore, the profitability of tourism enterprises.

Substantial shifts in the world's climate suitability patterns have been projected (Amelung *et al.*, 2007). In Europe, towards the end of the century, the Mediterranean region is expected to become much less attractive for tourism in summer and more attractive in the shoulder seasons of spring and autumn. At the same time, northern Europe, the traditional source regions of the majority of tourists to the Mediterranean, is projected to become more suitable for tourist activities year round, particularly in the summer (Amelung and Viner, 2006). As a result, more of these tourists might opt to stay within their own region, and more people from the south might decide to escape hot summer temperatures in the Mediterranean by travelling to northern Europe during the summer months. In North America, the number of cities in the USA with excellent conditions in the winter months is likely to increase, so that southern Florida and Arizona could face increasing competition for winter sun holiday travellers (Scott *et al.*, 2004). Other world regions may have the potential for an even more substantive redistribution of climate resources for tourism than North America and Europe. In particular, the tropics may be vulnerable, although no detailed analyses for these regions have been performed so far.

Indirect impacts from environmental change

Climate change also has an impact on tourism in more subtle and indirect ways, through changes in the environment and through changes in society. Environmental and climatic conditions are such critical resources for tourism that any changes will have an inevitable effect on the industry. Changes in water availability and snow cover, biodiversity loss, degradation of the aesthetics of destination landscapes, coastal impacts, damage to infrastructure and the increasing incidence of vector-borne diseases all impact on tourism in various ways.

A significant share of tourism takes place in warm, dry and sunny places, where water availability already acts a constraint for tourism development. Climate change is likely to intensify this problem, as for major tourism regions such as the Caribbean and the Mediterranean rainfall levels are projected to decrease further. Competition for water will intensify between different uses, including drinking water (residential population), irrigation (agriculture) and swimming pools and golf courses (tourism). The tourism industry is generally considered to be wasteful with regard to water. Specific segments such as golf tourism can have an enormous impact on water withdrawals. According to Mastny (2002), an 18-hole golf course can consume more than 2.3 million litres a day.

Ironically, climate change is also projected to increase the likelihood of heavy precipitation and other extreme weather events. As a result, the tourism sector is likely to be affected not only by water shortages, but also by water excesses such as floods, which will impact on both natural and cultural heritage attractions in many regions. The higher frequency and higher intensity of natural hazards such as flooding, coastal erosion, and more frequent hurricanes and tropical storms will also damage tourism facilities and infrastructure.

Nature and biodiversity constitute important resources for tourism that will be strongly affected by climate change. The existence of certain endemic animal populations, birdsong, the flowering of plants, coral reefs, the type and cover of forests and other facets of biodiverisity will be impacted by climate change. Between 20 and 30% of plant and animal species assessed are likely to be at risk of extinction if increases in global average temperature exceed 1.5–2.5 °C (IPCC, 2007b). Among other things, this will alter landscape aesthetics, a factor that greatly influences destination choice.

The health of millions of people will also be put at risk by projected climate change, particularly in those regions that have a low adaptive capacity. Countries identified as having the lowest adaptive capacity are predominantly in Sub-Saharan Africa and developing countries in Asia. The greatest impacts are likely to be caused by proportionally small increases in diseases that currently have major impacts already and will become even more widely prevalent. Examples include diarrhoea, malnutrition, and malaria and other so-called vector-borne diseases transmitted by mosquitoes, flies and other vectors. These health impacts will compromise some destinations' ability to cater adequately for tourism, and will also affect tourists themselves, who will be exposed to new health risks when travelling.

Indirect impacts from societal change

Climate change is thought to pose a risk to future economic growth and to the political stability of some nations. According to the influential Stern Review (2006), there could be an eventual permanent reduction in consumption per capita of 20% later in the twenty-first century or early twenty-second century, if we do nothing to slow down climate change. Any reductions of global GDP due to climate change would be likely to have negative implications for anticipated future growth in tourism spending.

Tourism, as we have seen from the earlier part of this chapter, is known to be sensitive to security issues. Regional climate change can bring about the degradation of fresh water resources, declining food production, increased storm-related disasters, and trans-boundary environmental migration. All of these impacts could overwhelm local capacities to respond to them and result in violence and the destabilisation of fragile governments. Climate change-associated security risks have been identified in a number of regions where tourism is highly important to the local economies, such as the Caribbean and Central America, Mediterranean and North Africa and China.

The Stern Review notes that tackling climate change is a pro-growth strategy for the longer term, with the benefits of strong, early action considerably outweighing the costs of doing nothing. Taking action, however, also has its price. National or international mitigation policies – that is, policies that seek to reduce greenhouse gas emissions – have an impact on tourist behaviour in a number of ways: by increasing the costs of travel and perhaps real income through inflation, and by fostering environmental attitudes and changes in travel behaviour.

Climate change policy initiatives such as carbon trading are likely to increase transport costs enough to outweigh economic savings achieved through efficiency gains. Leisure travellers and short-haul travellers appear to be more sensitive to such price increases than business travellers and those on long-haul trips. One reason for this may be that there are more choices and possibilities for substitution for shorter trips compared with longer ones. In addition, tourists who can afford long-distance holidays are likely to be wealthier than average. An increase in air fares may not have an immediate effect (i.e. tourists cannot or do not want to change their plans quickly), but over time tourists will learn to avoid the more expensive option of air travel and become more aware of alternative transport options, such as buses and trains.

In common with the role played by the perception of tourists towards travel risk, their perception with respect to transport, particularly air travel and its carbon footprint, is possibly more important than tourists' responses to price changes. Again, as with terrorist attacks, there is a key role played by the media that influences tourists' behaviour in response to climate change. Examples of this can be found in the concerns about the impact of 'anti-travel' sentiments in Europe, and concerns about the costs of carbon taxes or other mitigation policies have been expressed in Australia, New Zealand and Asian long-haul destinations.

Impacts on vulnerable destination types

The positive and negative impacts of climate change on the tourism sector will vary substantially by market segment and geographic region. There will be 'winners and losers' at the business, destination and nation level. In order to minimise associated risks and capitalise upon new opportunities, all tourism businesses and destinations will need to adapt to climate change in a sustainable manner. The vulnerability of tourism is of particular concern to those areas where tourism constitutes the major livelihood of local communities (dependency). The following section looks at the potential impacts of climate change on three major destination types with established vulnerabilities: mountains, islands and coastal zones, and natural and cultural heritage areas.

Mountain and winter sports destinations

Mountain regions are important destinations for global tourism, and snow cover and pristine mountain landscapes are their principal attractions. These features are also very vulnerable to climate change. Sensitive mountain environments will be altered by climate change, with implications for their attractiveness for nature-based tourism, as well as for the frequency and magnitude of natural hazards.

The impact of climate change on the snow-based sports tourism industry is potentially severe. The industry has been repeatedly identified as being at risk regarding global climate change, because of the close linkage between economic performance and climate. The key climate change impacts of interest to the winter sports industry relate to natural snow reliability and also technical snow reliability (i.e. cold temperatures to make snow). The latter is important in areas where snowmaking is almost universal among ski areas and covers a high proportion of terrain suitable for skiing.

Known vulnerabilities exist in a range of European and North American countries, but the projected impacts on destinations in these nations vary in magnitude and relate to different time horizons. The Australian and Scottish ski industries could disappear completely if some of the projections relating to moderate or high warming scenarios over the next 50 years materialise. Within most regional markets, however, the probable consequence of climate change will be limited to a contraction in the number of ski operators and destinations.

A recent study conducted for the Organization for Economic Cooperation and Development (Abegg *et al.*, 2007) suggests that the number of ski areas in the European Alps that are considered 'naturally snow reliable' will drop from 609 (91%) to 404 (61%) under a +2 °C warming scenario and would further decline to 202 (30%) under a +4 °C warming scenario. By comparison, climate change scenarios for the European Alps project an annual warming of 2.3 to 3.3 °C by mid-century and 2.9 to 5.3 °C by the end of the twenty-first century (Agrawala, 2007). Warming is even more pronounced in the winter months.

Developments in natural snow reliability do not tell the whole story, however. Evidence from North America suggests that advanced snowmaking systems substantially lower the vulnerability of ski areas. Such systems may be beneficial for a ski area as a whole, but require investments that may be too large for individual actors. This may partly explain why advanced snowmaking systems are less common in Europe than in North America, where ski resorts tend to be more integrated. Snowmaking is no solution for snowmobiling, which is another major snow-based winter sport in North America. Snowmobiling is completely reliant on natural snowfall, which makes this industry much more vulnerable to climate change than the ski industry. Under the rapid climate change scenarios, a reliable snowmobile season will disappear from most regions of eastern North America within 50 years.

Impacts on islands and in coastal zones

Islands and coastal zones are among the most vulnerable types of tourist destinations with respect to climate change. They are likely to experience an increased intensity and frequency of extreme events, sea-level rise, increased climate variability, changes in ocean circulation and changes in natural ecosystems. It is very likely that the most immediate and significant of these will be changes in the nature of extreme events (e.g. flooding, tropical cyclones, storm surges, heatwaves) and climatic variability (e.g. droughts, and prevailing winds accelerating coastal erosion). Coastal areas are particularly vulnerable to extreme wind events. Major wind-storm disasters and the losses generated by them have increased drastically in recent decades. Extreme events can destroy ecosystems, such as mangrove forests, tropical forests and coral reefs. Coral reefs especially are a crucial resource for tourism and other sectors. In many destinations, reefs are the key pull factor for tourists as a visitor attraction and can be considered a major economic asset. The increase in sea surface temperature and increasing acidity of the water will impact marine life and coral reefs and erode these assets.

Given that most tourism activities take place in coastal zones, sea-level rise is of major importance to tourism. It aggravates coastal erosion and leads to the loss of beaches. Sea-level rise is primarily a consequence of the expansion of sea water (warmer water takes up more space); the continued melting of mountain glaciers and small ice caps add to this. Further global sea-level rise could range from 20 to 60 cm by 2100.

Even small rises in sea level will result in significant erosion, increased flood hazard, contamination of freshwater aquifers, loss of protective coral reefs, mangrove areas and sand beaches. In small island regions especially, much of the biological diversity and most of the population, agricultural land and capital assets are located in these areas and are, therefore, at risk. Among these vulnerable islands are major tourism destinations. In the Indian Ocean, the Maldives average only 1.5 m above sea level and projected rates of sea level rise are likely to inundate large areas of the different islands and atolls. Other low lying islands, such as the Bahamas and Kiribati, face similar problems.

MINI CASE STUDY 10.2
Tourism revival key for Maldives

It is often promoted as the last paradise on Earth, but the Maldives and its precious tourism industry were devastated by December's tsunami. Kirsten Magasdi visited the archipelago for BBC World's *Fast Track* programme.

The island nation's economy relies more heavily on tourism than any other tsunami-affected country.

Nowhere else is more aware of the threat posed by rising seas than the Maldives.

About 99% of its territory is sea – and on the 1,200 low-lying coral islands that straddle the equator, nowhere is more than one-and-a-half metres above sea level.

FLOODED

The country campaigns against the effects of climate change to protect its very survival, but the tsunami made it face its worst fears.

A total of 49 inhabited islands were flooded and one-quarter of the 87 resort islands were put out of operation and are now undergoing repairs.

The tsunami cost 82 lives, with another 20 locals still missing.

The death toll may sound small when compared with other affected countries – but this is a nation of only 300,000 people.

Many here rely on tourism. It provides two-thirds of employment and the largest proportion of GDP.

It may seem at odds staying at a luxury resort while local communities struggle to get back on their feet, but with bookings down 50%, the Maldivians want tourists back.

'The tourist dollars do help in the recovery and rehabilitation of people and this is our lifeline, so if it's disrupted it aggravates the situation,' says Hassan Sobir, the Maldives High Commissioner in Britain.

'Fortunately, because of the geography – maybe sheer luck – many islands have been spared in terms of damage.'

Scientists say the archipelago was spared the full force because the huge coral reefs that encircle the islands absorbed much of the impact – as did breakwaters built around the capital, Male, after previous flooding.

NEW DEVELOPMENT

The set-up in the Maldives is an unusual one.

A one-resort-per-island policy separates guests from locals and from other tourists, giving a sense of isolation that is one of the Maldives' main selling points.

Central to this strategy is that each island is self-sufficient, generating power, waste management and water supply.

It means the usual risk of water contamination and disease that often follow disasters has largely been avoided.

It also means repairs will be localised.

However, rebuilding these remote islands, accessible only by seaplane or boat, will take months and cost an estimated $1.5 bn.

Despite the crisis, the government still plans to develop 11 new island resorts over the next two years.

Hoteliers like François Huet, the general manager of the Banyan Tree Hotel, welcome the move.

'It's an opportunity to develop different kinds of competition to stimulate the market,' he says.

GREEN FUNDS

The Maldives does not have a long history as a tourist destination – just three decades – during which it has moved to the top of the luxury holiday lists, is a favourite for honeymooners and a premier dive location.

When the first hotel, Kurumba, opened in 1972 it was very basic.

Its founder is often credited with kick-starting the tourism industry.

Back then there were only 1,000 tourists a year. Last year, there were more than 500,000.

Mohamed Umar Maniku built Kurumba and is now chairman of the resort development company, Universal Enterprises.

'When we started there were already three big destinations in Asia – Sri Lanka, Thailand and the Seychelles.

'We never had anything and so we thought if they can be successful, why not us?'

Developing tourism has also helped raise environmental concerns.

Some hotels like the Banyan Tree and Angsana have green funds where they match guest donations of one dollar a night for conservation projects.

Those contributions have now been doubled and are going towards tsunami recovery.

Staff are also donating part of their salary.

And on the island of Fen Fushi, children learn about protecting marine life while their parents all work at the nearby resort Sun Island.

Bringing tourism and nature together is not only their future, but also that of the Maldives.

Source: http://news.bbc.co.uk/1/hi/world/south_asia/4237389.stm

DISCUSSION QUESTION

Discuss the actions that vulnerable destinations such as the Maldives can take to sustain their tourism industry in a world of climatic change.

Impacts on natural and cultural heritage

The natural environment is often a very important determinant of tourism demand. Landscape ranks among the most important factors in destination choice, and tourists are attracted to national parks because they represent an aesthetically pleasing and healthy environment with interesting flora and fauna. The impact of climate change on biodiversity and natural landscapes may have a negative influence on their amenity value and hence on visitor numbers.

Cultural heritage includes considerations of built heritage (historic and architectural), archaeological heritage and socio-cultural heritage. The most obvious impact of climate change on cultural heritage is the direct effect of rising sea level on structures near coasts that may be flooded or damaged by coastal erosion. Increased rainfall resulting in rising water tables will also have an effect on the foundations or the fabric of buildings. Saving vulnerable sites from climate change, including world famous destinations such as Venice, will in many cases be very costly.

Implications for tourism demand patterns

The response of tourists to the complexity of destination impacts will determine how tourism demand patterns will be affected by climate change. Climate, the natural environment and personal safety are three primary factors in destination choice, and climate change is anticipated to have significant impacts on all three of these factors. Climate is also a principal driver of seasonality in demand, which has been described as one of the most problematic features of the tourism industry.

Weather and climate are of universal importance in defining destination attractiveness and central motivators in the selection of holiday destination and the timing of discretionary travel. Temperature and sunshine have been found to influence travel patterns and tourism expenditures. In addition, the weather conditions experienced at the destination are believed to influence holiday satisfaction. As climate is an important resource for tourists, projected changes in the distribution of climate resources are forecast to have important consequences for tourism.

Simulation models have been used to explore the potential impact of climate change on the level of aggregated international tourism demand (e.g. Hamilton *et al.*, 2005). Anticipated impacts include a gradual shift in preferred destinations to higher latitudes and to higher elevations in mountainous areas. Tourists from temperate nations that currently dominate international travel (e.g. northern Europe) are expected to spend more holidays in their home country or nearby, adapting their travel patterns to take advantage of new climatic opportunities closer to home. This shift in travel patterns would have three important implications: proportionally more tourism spending in temperate nations, proportionally less spending in warmer nations now frequented by tourists from temperate regions, and a modest net reduction in total international tourist numbers.

The above studies assume the existence of certain temperature thresholds, above which further temperature increases lead to deterioration in the level of attraction of specific destinations. Little is known about such thresholds, however; for instance, about what tourists perceive to be 'too hot' for any particular tourism destination. Equally little is known about the role of tourist perceptions of the environmental impacts of global climate change at destinations. Perceptions of coral bleaching, glacier losses or reduced wildlife prevalence may be more important for tourism demand than the actual changes that occur. Information on tourist climate preferences and key thresholds, and tourist perceptions are important knowledge gaps that need to be addressed if potential long-range shifts in tourist demand are to be more accurately forecast (Gössling and Hall, 2005).

Adaptation to climate change

Regardless of the level of success of efforts to reduce emissions, a certain amount of climate change is unavoidable. Even if emissions were reduced to zero today, the global average temperature would still increase by another 0.6 °C. The IPCC has therefore indicated that there is a need for societies around the world, and economic sectors like tourism, to adapt to climate change in the decades ahead. Adaptation to climate change refers to an adjustment in natural or human systems in response to actual or expected climatic stimuli or their effects, which moderates harm or exploits beneficial opportunities.

The tourism industry is known to be remarkably resilient to shocks. Recent disasters from which tourism has quickly recovered include SARS, terrorist attacks and the Asian tsunami. The resilience and dynamic nature of the tourism industry suggests a relatively high climate change adaptive capacity within the sector as a whole. This capacity, however, is thought to vary between the sub-sectors of the tourism industry. Tourists have the greatest adaptive capacity, with relative freedom to avoid destinations impacted by climate change or to shift the timing of travel to avoid unfavourable climate conditions. Large tour operators, who do not own the infrastructure, are also in a good position to adapt to changes at the destination level because they can respond to clients' demands and provide information to influence clients' travel choices. Destination communities and tourism operators with large investments in immobile capital assets (e.g. hotel, resort complex, marina or casino) have the lowest adaptive capacity.

The new risks introduced by climate change pose additional challenges to the design of new tourism infrastructures. Similarly, existing infrastructure may have to be modified if current performance standards are inconsistent with the changed climatic conditions. For example, tourist accommodation in tropical areas should be built or retro-fitted to be cyclone-proof, withstanding both high average wind speeds and extreme conditions (Becken, 2005). Early-warning systems can help to reduce risks further.

Some climate-related risks cannot be avoided by any adaptation measures. In such cases, insurance is critical. It enables the industry to spread the burdens of such risks. In time, some

Photograph 10.2   Climate change may be happening much faster than experts predicted.
Source: PA Photos

risks may become uninsurable, however, as the insurance industry faces the prospect of a growth in the number and size of claims as a consequence of climate change. In fact, the insurance industry is already implementing risk-reduction strategies. A number of insurers in the USA recently decided to reduce coverage in Florida and the Gulf of Mexico. Such changes in insurability will have major implications for future tourism reinvestment in and development of disaster-prone regions such as the Caribbean.

Adaptation is not limited to technical or behavioural measures; it can also include management of tourism's natural resource base. Conservation of biodiversity and maintenance of ecosystem structure and function are important climate change adaptation strategies. Establishing and enforcing protected areas is generally considered to be one of the most appropriate strategies for ensuring that terrestrial, freshwater and marine ecosystems are resilient to the additional pressures arising from climate change.

Protecting the natural environment can also help to reduce the risk of avalanches and rock slides in mountain destinations. These destinations also have a wide range of climate change adaptation options available to cope with reduced natural snowfall and to take advantage of longer warm-weather tourism seasons. The importance of snowmaking as an adaptation to climate variability and change cannot be overstated. In eastern North America and Australia, snowmaking is almost universal among ski operators. In other ski regions such as Western Europe, western North America, East Asia and South America, snowmaking is not as extensively used, but is continuing to grow.

The sustainability of some adaptation strategies has been questioned. Glacier preservation and expansion of ski areas into higher elevations have been criticised for harming fragile ecosystems and reducing landscape amenities. Communities and environmental organisations have expressed concern about the extensive water and energy use associated with snowmaking, and about the chemical additives involved in the process. For some ski operators, snow-making may be uneconomic altogether, because of the elevated costs of energy, infrastructure and water.

Product and market diversification are common adaptation strategies to cope with the business challenges of pronounced tourism seasonality. Many ski resorts have made sub-stantial investments to provide alternative activities for non-skiing visitors (e.g. snowmobiling, indoor pools, health and wellness spas, retail stores). A number of former ski resorts have further diversified their business operations to become 'four season resorts', offering non-winter activities such as golf, boating and white-water rafting, mountain biking, paragliding, horseback riding and indoor skiing. Product diversification is also a key adaptation option for island and coastal destinations. Many of them seek to become less dependent on beach tourism and other climate-sensitive activities by adding golf courses, cultural heritage sites and shoping malls to their portfolio.

Climate change risk management should be integrated into business practices relating to revenue and cost, assets and liabilities, and the wider supply chain. As the above sections show, tourism businesses, entrepreneurs and investors can improve their management of cli-mate change risks, independent from the adaptation policies undertaken at an institutional level (e.g. international organisations, national governments or communities). This includes managing vulnerabilities to direct impacts from climate change, and those to changes in the resource or customer bases. For example, business planning might benefit from an under-standing of which markets might react most strongly to temperature increases or to the negative perception of air travel.

CONCLUSION

Travel, particularly discretionary travel, is to some extent determined by tourists' perceptions of travel-related risks. Some of these risks can be mitigated by choosing destinations that minimise the perceived level of natural or man-made risks, others such as accident risks can influence the mode of travel which may, in effect, influence the destination choice. Perceived travel-related risks do not always, in fact may rarely, coincide with actual levels of risk and are often influenced more by the way in which the media report incidents such as terrorist attacks or hurricanes than they are by the actual risk. The management of the way that media report incidents could help align the differences between perceived and actual risks but there is no obvious vehicle to bring such management into play. The response of destinations to disasters post-event or as a precaution may help to allay some tourists' concerns about travel to specific destinations. However, a too obvious security response may generate greater levels of anxiety in tourists than would be the case without lower profile security measures.

Climatic change adds to the factors that influence perceived travel risk and major envir-onmental events such as tsunamis, earthquakes and hurricanes attract a great deal of media attention. Destinations can adapt to climatic change within limits by building infrastructure and superstructure designed to withstand extreme weather conditions, developing tourism facilities on land with higher elevations or away from areas that are known to be more at risk of temperature or rainfall levels that exceed the threshold of acceptability exhibited by tourists, but this is a slow and very expensive process. Some businesses, such as inter-mediaries, are better able to adapt to climatic change whereas others have no room at all for adaptation. The only certain thing is that travel-related risk has always been a part of the industry, it has become more important over the past couple of decades and is likely to continue to influence tourists' decision-making in an increasingly significant way.

SELF-CHECK QUESTIONS

1. What are the different factors that influence travel risk and travel-risk perceptions?
2. What factors are likely to determine the impact of terrorist attacks on tourism destinations?
3. How can regional tourism suffer when only one or two countries within that region are in conflict?
4. What are the major direct and indirect impacts of climate change on tourism destinations?
5. How might tourism destinations adapt to climate change and what are the limitations to such adaptations?

ESSAY QUESTIONS

1. There are significant differences between man-made and natural travel-related risks in terms of their nature and characteristics. What are the implications of these differences for tourists and the tourist industry?
2. There would seem to be significant differences between the perceived and actual level of travel-related risks. What factors can cause such differences and what are the implications for future discretionary travel choices?
3. What are the likely implications of climatic change for the future patterns of tourist arrivals and expenditure?
4. The evidence of terrorist activity or political unrest in one or two countries can influence the level of tourism demand across an entire global region. Consider the validity of this statement with respect to travel to the Middle East region.

References cited and bibliography

Abegg, B., Agrawala, S., Crick, F. and de Montfalcon, A. (2007) 'Climate change impacts and adaptation in winter tourism', pp. 25–60 in S. Agrawala (ed.), *Climate Change in the European Alps: Adapting Winter Tourism and Natural Hazards Management*, OECD, Paris.

Agrawala, S. (ed.) (2007) *Climate Change in the European Alps: Adapting Winter Tourism and Natural Hazards Management*, OECD, Paris.

Amelung, B. and Viner, D. (2006) 'Mediterranean tourism: exploring the future with the tourism climatic index', *Journal of Sustainable Tourism* 14(4), 349–66.

Amelung, B., Nicholls, S. and Viner, D. (2007) 'Implications of global climate change for tourism flows and seasonality', *Journal of Travel Research* 45(3), 285–96.

Becken, S. (2005) 'Harmonizing climate change adaptation and mitigation. The case of tourist resorts in Fiji', *Global Environmental Change – Part A* 15(4), 381–93.

Becken, S. and Hay, J. (2007) *Tourism and Climate Change – Risks and Opportunities*, Channel View, Cleveland.

Dubois, G. and Ceron, J.-P. (2006) 'Tourism/leisure greenhouse gas emissions forecasts for 2050: factors for change in France', *Journal of Sustainable Tourism* 14(2), 172–91.

Gössling, S. and Hall, C.M. (2005) 'Uncertainties in predicting tourist flows under scenarios of climate change', *Climatic Change* 79(3–4), 163–73.

Gössling, S., Peeters, P., Ceron, J.-P., Dubois, G., Patterson, T. and Richardson, R.B. (2005) 'The eco-efficiency of tourism', *Ecological Economics* 54(4), 417–34.

Hamilton, J.M., Maddison, D. and Tol, R.S.J. (2005) 'Climate change and international tourism: A simulation study', *Global Environmental Change* 15(3), 253–66.

IPCC (2007a) *Climate Change 2007: The Physical Science Basis*. Contribution of Working Group I to the Fourth Assessment Report of the Intergovernmental Panel on Climate Change (Solomon, S., Qin, D., Manning, M., Chen, Z., Marquis, M., Averyt, K.B.,

Tignor, M. and Miller, H.L. (eds)), Cambridge University Press, Cambridge and New York.

IPCC (2007b) 'Sumary for Policymakers', in Parry, M.L., Canziani, O.F., Palutikof, J.P., van der Linden, P.J. and Hanson, C.E. (eds), *Climate Change 2007: Impacts, Adaptation and Vulnerability*. Contribution of Working Group II to the Fourth Assessment Report of the Intergovernmental Panel on Climate Change, Cambridge University Press, Cambridge and New York.

Journal of Sustainable Tourism 14(4), 2006. Special issue: Tourism and its Interactions with Climate Change. Guest Editor: David Viner.

Mastny, L. (2002) 'Travelling Light: New Paths for International Tourism'. Worldwatch Paper 159, Washington DC.

Morakabati, Y. (2007) 'Tourism, Travel Risk and Travel Risk Perceptions', PhD Thesis, Bournemouth University, 2007.

Norwich Union Insurance Report (2006) *Daily Telegraph*, 11 July 2006.

OECD (2006) *Climate Change and Winter Tourism. Report on Adaptation*. http://www.oecd.org/dataoecd/58/4/37776193.pdf

Peeters, P. (2007) *Tourism and Climate Change Mitigation – Methods, Greenhouse Gas Reductions and Policies*, NHTV Academics Studies No. 6, NHTV, Breda.

Scott, D., Amelung, B., Becken, S., Ceron, J.-P., Dubois, G., Gössling, S., Peeters, P. and Simpson, M. (2007) *Climate Change and Tourism: Responding to Global Challenges*, WTO, Madrid and UNEP, Paris.

Scott, D., McBoyle, G. and Schwartzentruber, M. (2004) 'Climate change and the distribution of climatic resources for tourism in North America', *Climate Research* 27(2), 105–17.

Stern, N. (2006) *The Economics of Climate Change: The Stern Review*, Cambridge University Press, Cambridge.

MAJOR CASE STUDY 10.1
The Egyptian bombings, 2005

DAY AFTER EGYPT BOMBINGS, ON VACATION, WITH RESOLVE

SHARM EL SHEIK, Egypt, July 24 – A day after one of the worst terrorist attacks in Egyptian history, tourists at this sun-baked resort woke up Sunday determined, for the most part, to stick to the languid rhythms of a beach holiday.

The beaches were crowded with sunbathers, except in front of one hotel that had been all but obliterated by the attack.

On Vacation, With Resolve Sailboats and wind-surfers skittered across the waves, and scuba divers bobbed up and down in the tide as they prospected the Red Sea's coral reefs. The beaches were crowded with sunbathers, except in front of the Ghazala Gardens hotel, which had been all but obliterated early Saturday by one of the three bombs. By the hotel, the empty blue-and-white chairs spoke eloquently about the carnage that had taken place.

Officials said Sunday that 64 people were killed, substantially fewer than the 90 reported Saturday night. Among the dead, at least 7 were European tourists.

Certainly, some vacationers packed up and dashed for the airport, and the flights arriving were emptier than normal. But most visitors reacted to the attacks with a mix of stoicism, defiance and even nonchalance.

'We decided to take a walk today, just to make the point that it wouldn't make us change our routine,' said Sheila Atalla, who is here from Scotland with her husband and son. They ventured to the Ghazala Gardens, which became a macabre tourist attraction until the police obscured the view with canvas.

But with a drumbeat of attacks in London, Madrid, Bali, Istanbul and New York, people here suggested that yet another act of terror – as tragic as it was – had lost some of its power to inspire dread.

Mieke Frowein, a 35-year-old psychotherapist from the Netherlands, was jolted awake by the first explosion, which shook her room so violently that she thought it was an earthquake. She ran to her window and saw people running in the street and screaming.

'My first reaction was, "let's get out of here",' Ms. Frowein recalled. 'But after I had a night's sleep, I decided, no, we should stay. It's the wrong thing to run away.'

In calculating risk these days, tourists said, it makes little difference whether you stay home or travel to an exotic resort. The disasters that can befall travelers are both manmade and natural, as demonstrated by last year's tsunami, which killed thousands of European tourists.

Then, too, some here noted that the largest group of people killed in this attack were Egyptians. Among the seven foreigners who have been identified were, according to Egyptian officials and news reports, tourists from Britain, Germany, Italy and the Czech Republic.

Alexei Antipov, a 20-year-old Russian, was walking to the Hilton Dreams, his hotel, when he saw a green truck roar across his path and crash into the lobby of the Ghazala Gardens. He sensed it was a car bomb, he said, and moments later was thrown to the ground by the force of the blast.

Recovering in a hospital with wounds to his right arm, left leg and stomach, Mr Antipov said the attack could just as easily have happened in Moscow. 'There's no safe place in the world anymore,' he said.

Andre Gibhard, 36, a banker from Pretoria, South Africa, spent part of Sunday afternoon sipping a beer at the poolside bar at the sister hotel of the Ghazala Gardens, doing his best to ignore the devastation behind him.

'It's in the back of your mind all the time,' said Mr Gibhard, who arrived Saturday after the bombings. 'But you can't let terrorists intimidate you. We're going to be out shopping tonight at 10 o'clock.' Besides, he added, 'We already live in one of the world's most dangerous places.'

Ms Frowein said she did not think much about security before coming here. 'I figured this was probably a safe place, but terrorism is so erratic,' she said, noting that even the Netherlands had been scarred by Islamic militant violence.

(From The Official Tour Egypt Voice in Sharm el-Sheikh, Egypt, 25 July 2005)

MORE THEN 1,000 TOURISM EMPLOYEES PROTEST BOMBINGS IN SHARM

SHARM EL-SHEIKH – More than 1,000 Egyptian hotel workers, Bedouin sheikhs and foreign dive school instructors marched through Sharm el-Sheikh on Sunday to condemn bombs which killed 88 in the Red Sea resort.

'There is no God but God and terrorism is the enemy of God,' chanted the Egyptian protesters, including hotel chefs, technicians and road sweepers, as they marched along the main road of Sharm el-Sheikh, hit by three bombs on Saturday.

'The feeling is very sad and very angry. We are not going to be scared by the bombers,' said Sherif Saba, an Egyptian investor in the diving and beach resort.

Protesters marched into the night, waving Egyptian flags and holding aloft signs in Arabic, English, Spanish, Italian and Russian.

'We will not be terrorised,' read one banner. Hotel chefs marched with 'Stop terrorism' written on their hats. Dive schools employees had the same slogan printed on their T-shirts.

The protesters said funeral prayers for the dead at the car park where one of the bombs exploded. Several placed flowers on a car splattered with blood of the victims, who were mostly Egyptian.

'People are against those who did this. They have no religion and not from us, neither as Bedouin or Egyptians. It's a cowardly act,' said Saleh Mohamed, a south Sinai Bedouin wearing flowing robes and a lilac headscarf.

Egyptians come from all over the country to work in Sharm el-Sheikh. Resort workers are worried the attacks will scare off tourists, who provide employment for more than a million people.

Visitor numbers to the Red Sea resort and the rest of Egypt dipped after militants killed 58 tourists in Luxor in 1997. The industry was also hit by the September 11, 2001, attacks on the United States.

A militant Islamist group has claimed responsibility for the Sharm el Sheikh attacks in an internet statement but analysts doubt its credibility.

'We don't want them here. No country accepts them,' said Hajja Nasra, a fully covered Bedouin woman dressed in black.

(South Sinai Travel, 24 July 2005)

RUSSIANS IN NO HURRY TO END VACATIONS IN EGYPT (24 JULY 2005)

As European countries evacuated hundreds of tourists after three explosions killed at least 88 people in Sharm el-Sheikh, undeterred Russian vacationers continued arriving at and leaving the Egyptian Red Sea resort as usual over the weekend.

No Russians have asked to cut their vacations short, and the 800 people who left on four charter planes

Saturday had been booked on those flights well in advance, Irina Tyurina, a spokeswoman for the Russian Tourism Union, said Sunday.

Some 3,500 to 4,000 Russian tourists were in Sharm el-Sheikh at the time of the Friday night attacks, Tyurina said.

Only one was wounded – Alexei Antipov, 20, of Moscow – and he was hospitalized with injuries that were not life-threatening, Foreign Ministry spokesman Alexander Yakovenko said, Interfax reported.

President Vladimir Putin on Saturday sent a telegram to Egyptian President Hosni Mubarak offering his condolences regarding the blasts, according to the presidential web site, www.kremlin.ru.

The Egyptian resorts of Sharm el-Sheikh and Hurghada, along with Turkey, are the most popular destinations for Russian vacationers throughout the year.

However, June and July are the off-season for Egypt, with the number of Russian tourists dropping to a third of the usual level. Russian air carriers offer 18 weekly flights to the resort during those months.

Moreover, Russians were largely unaffected by the explosions because few stay in hotels in Naama Bay, which was targeted by the bombers, Tyurina said. 'Naama Bay has lost its attractiveness to Russian tourists because it is too crowded and noisy and its hotels are among the most expensive,' she said.

Usually, Russian tourists stay in hotels by smaller bays and come to Naama Bay in the evening to visit bars, discos and restaurants, Tyurina said.

Tyurina said it was too early to predict the impact of the attacks on Egyptian tourism but suggested that prices for package tours might drop if travelers were to start avoiding the country.

She said some Russians who had bought tours for the upcoming months contacted travel agencies Saturday afternoon and Sunday in hope of exchanging their tickets for trips to Turkey or Tunisia. Only a few have flatly refused to go to Egypt, she said.

WHAT MUSLIMS LEADERS THINK OF THE VIOLENCE (24 JULY 2005)

IAMS (International Association of Muslim Scholars) Condemns Sharm El-Sheikh, London Attacks.

A LOOK AT SOME OF THE LATEST NEWS (24 JULY 2005)

And here, from the BBC, is an overview of the Egyptian press' reaction to the bombings.

We are also told that Thomas Cook has suspended all flights to Sharm.

Currently, the number of arrests are up to 70, while hitting the news just now are many reports on what appears to be a much less serious explosion in Cairo (the bomber himself was the only casualty).

Currently, the police believe they are specifically looking for three bombers who left Sharm after the attacks. A fourth one is believed to have blown himself up.

Security officials suspect four terrorists used two pickup trucks loaded with 880 pounds of explosives, possibly hidden under piles of vegetables. They drove into Sharm along desert tracks from the north.

Two of the men left a green Isuzu pickup packed with explosives in the Old Market area, which later blew up after apparently being set off by a timing device, the officials said. The bomb blew a 16-foot-wide crater into the middle of the road, which police have cordoned off with yellow tape.

The two other militants drove a white pickup truck to Naama Bay. One got out along the way in a parking lot where he planted a small bomb rigged with a timer in a suitcase. The other slammed the truck into the Ghazala hotel in a suicide bombing. As frantic people fled the scene, the bomb exploded in the parking lot 150 yards away from the hotel, killing at least seven Westerners, the officials said.

Local investigators are examining the possibility that foreigners carried out the blasts.

Egyptian health officials say at least 34 of the victims have yet to be identified. Those killed were mostly Egyptians, but among the dead were two Britons, two Germans, an Italian and a Czech, according to health officials here.

SOME PERSPECTIVE ON SHARM (24 JULY 2005)

Of course, right now much of the news is about the mass exodus of tourists from Egypt, not just from Sharm but from other areas as well. They seem to be leaving in droves.

However, to put some perspective on all of this, the Sharm bombing seems to be in a pattern of large scale attacks that have been going on lately in other places of the world. Egypt is probably about as safe as anywhere else just at this moment, and may be safer. Who knows where terrorists might strike next, but if the pattern holds, it will almost certainly be somewhere else. Furthermore, it is very likely that most militants are pretty much laying low at this point, with the Egyptian security forces sweeping the land.

Terrorism has become a problem for the world, not just Egypt, and we have learned from London, New

York, Spain and elsewhere that they can happen anywhere.

Our hearts go out to those who have suffered in Sharm, but they also go out to those in London and elsewhere. Tourists will likely avoid Egypt for a while, as they are probably avoiding London just now, but it is perhaps more likely to expect these criminals to move on to other locations next. Its a sad world at the moment, but somewhere we hope that there is light at the end of the tunnel. I think everyone of every nation is sick and tired of this sort of action.

Source: Adapted from http://touregypt.net/teblog/sharmnews/index.php?paged=16

DISCUSSION QUESTIONS

1. 'The more frequent terrorist attacks become, the less impact they will have on the volume and receipts of destinations.' Discuss this statement in terms of destinations that have suffered multiple terrorist incidents such as Egypt and Indonesia. Has terrorism become an acceptable part of tourism and if not what are the implications of continuing violence aimed at tourists?

2. Terrorism has changed the way the tourist industry operates. In what ways has terrorism changed each of the key sectors of the tourism industry?

3. The time period of recovery necessary to restore tourism to its previous level following an incident is determined by a variety of factors. Examine what those factors are and in so doing discuss what may be done to improve the speed of recovery.

PART 3

THE TOURISM SECTOR

Photograph: Machu Picchu, Peru

INTRODUCTION

In Part 3 we turn our attention to the tourism sector and public sector organisations that influence and support tourism demand and supply. We have adopted an analytical and evaluative approach to this section, identifying the main subsectors that, when combined, constitute the tourism sector. We have focused generally on providing insights into the operating characteristics, trends and issues that dominate tourism and, specifically, upon attractions, accommodation, intermediaries, transportation, public sector organisations, and destinations. Although these do not represent an exhaustive range of enterprises, they do illustrate the dominant characteristics of the tourism sector and demonstrate key operational practices.

Leiper defined the tourism 'industry' as 'the range of businesses and organisations involved in delivering the tourism product' and, in the light of his model of the tourism system (as discussed in detail in the opening chapter 'An Introduction to Tourism'), these businesses and organisations represent a key element. However, despite the unique nature of tourism and the differing attributes of the individual sectors, there are common characteristics, trends and issues that are evident across the board:

- The low level of *concentration* in a sector where small businesses dominate despite the fact that a relatively few, large corporations have market prominence.
- The high ratio of *fixed costs* to *variable costs* which has considerable implications for financial stability and which dominates tactical and strategic operation.
- The high levels of customer contact, demanding staff to be highly trained in both operational aspects and customer care.
- The low levels of technological adoption across much of the sector.
- The general lack of marketing and human resource management expertise remains a constraint in all sectors of tourism, albeit to varying degrees.
- The importance of location vis-à-vis access to markets.
- The **perishable** nature of the product for all tourism sectors demands continued investment in reservation and yield management systems.
- The prevalence of seasonal and irrational demand patterns, involving enterprises in the use of promotional and pricing strategies.
- The inconsistent adoption of the principles of sustainability, environmental auditing and EIA techniques.
- The increasing degree of **vertical**, **horizontal** and **diagonal integration** throughout the sector.
- The increasing adoption of *collaboration* within and across the various segments of the tourism sector.
- The traditional outlook of service industries and, arguably, the so-called 'under-management' of the tourism sector which means that the sector as a whole is vulnerable to ideas and takeovers from other industrial sectors.
- Conversely, the increasing professionalism of the sector.

These are issues and difficulties that dominate tourism as a whole, irrespective of subsector. Nevertheless, it is also possible to isolate the key sectors and attribute more detailed and precise characteristics to each; thus, we have divided this section into six chapters. This said, it is important that the reader should understand the complex linkages and interrelationships that exist between the various individual tourism sectors and the mutual dependency of one sector on the next. It is the objective of this section, therefore, to highlight these complex relationships and to explore the implications of these on tourism as a whole.

In Chapter 11, the focus of attention is on the attractions segment of the tourism sector, incorporating natural and artificial attractions. Attractions are integral to the tourism product, often providing the primary motivation for tourist visits, yet they continue to receive a patchy and undisciplined coverage in the literature. We use this chapter to explore many of the issues associated with the development and management of attractions as well as consider some of the possible visitor management techniques that may be implemented to address the adverse social, cultural and environmental impacts of tourism at both natural and artificial sites.

Chapter 12 is concerned with accommodation, perhaps the most visible and ubiquitous of all sectors of tourism. The scope and size of the sector is explored and the relationship between this subsector and the complete tourism product is discussed. We also evaluate many of the key issues that are currently influencing the accommodation sector such as hotel consortia, yield management, the potential of information technology, the new-found emphasis on environmental issues and the role and importance of quality and branding.

Chapter 13 introduces and reviews the role of intermediaries in the packaging and distribution of the tourism product. The distribution of the tourism product is unusual in so far as it is achieved, almost exclusively, by intermediaries, rendering the distribution channel extremely competitive and susceptible to fierce power struggles and damaging price wars. The structure of the distribution channel and the respective roles of intermediaries make the distribution of the tourism product very risky, particularly in light of the precarious economics of tour operation/wholesaling and the intense financial pressures that dominate their operation. The chapter also explores online developments and the increasing consolidation and concentration of tourism intermediaries.

Chapter 14 concentrates on transportation for tourism and offers a thorough review of the issues which dominate this sector. Particular emphasis is placed on the changing competitive framework with a focus on the development of low cost airlines and the continued expansion and popularity of cruising.

In Chapter 15, we concentrate on those public sector organisations that are crucial to tourism and discuss the role of governmental intervention in tourism. We consider the importance of public sector involvement in tourism and review its current, and changing, role: increasingly, the public sector is withdrawing from tourism and private sector organisations are being encouraged to step in. However, it is argued here that, while tourism must involve participation and funding by the private sector, there are many clear and powerful reasons why the public sector must remain involved:

- Many core tourist attractions – such as landscapes, culture and built heritage and architecture – are public goods and, to this end, public sector involvement is at least desirable and at best, crucial.

- Many activities such as planning, research, resource allocation, management and regulation can be undertaken most effectively – and most impartially – by the public sector.

- The lack of expertise in the tourism sector in certain key areas (such as marketing), and the domination of small businesses with inadequate funds to promote themselves sufficiently, provides a compelling argument for continued involvement of the public sector.

We also use this chapter to demonstrate the global and local policy frameworks for tourism and to provide an overview of the likely administrative structure of a national tourist office (NTO). In addition, the impact of the public sector in respect of its demand and revenue management roles (marketing, promotion and information provision) and its supply and cost management roles (planning controls, building regulations, land-use decisions, market regulation, market research, and planning and investment incentives) are also considered in detail.

Finally, Chapter 16 introduces the nature and role of destinations and the variety of forces in the external environment impacting on their future. The chapter explores the means by which destinations are managed and marketed, and pays particular attention to the collaborative nature of destinations and the organisational and governance structures advocated for their effective management.

It is clear that, while the individual sectors of tourism are interlinked and, to some extent, are mutually dependent upon each other, there is a potential for conflict within and between sectors. This may be attributed to the fact that each sector is working to its own agenda with a view to its own profit maximisation. One of the primary objectives of the public sector, therefore, is to temper overambitious individual providers and sectors and to provide a strategic approach to product development, distribution and marketing for the overall benefit of the destination. However, it may be argued that the intermediaries are perhaps the most powerful determinants of the ultimate success or failure of a destination in terms of revenue, market share and visitor numbers, since it is in the hands of the intermediaries that influence is exerted most directly on tourism demand.

In the next six chapters, we explore many of the key issues in respect of the above and provide the reader with a greater understanding and appreciation of the tourism sector, its core business and its operating practices.

CHAPTER 11

Attractions

LEARNING OUTCOMES

Attractions are an integral part of the tourism product and, in this chapter, we focus on providing you with:

- a review of the nature, purpose, and classification of attractions;

- a discussion of the roles and responsibilities of the public and private sectors in respect of the development and management of tourist attractions;

- a consideration of all issues associated with the management of attractions;

- an analysis of environmental issues in respect of attractions; and

- an evaluation of strategies that have been developed with a view to alleviating environmental and visitor impacts of tourism at attractions.

Photograph: The Sagrada Familia, Barcelona, Spain © Andrea Bannuscher

INTRODUCTION

For many tourist destinations around the world, it is their attractions that often serve as the catalyst for tourist visits. Attractions are numerous, diverse, fragmented geographically and often have limited resources at their disposal for purposes of management. In order to shed some light on the management complexity and diversity of development of attractions this chapter is broken down into four main sections. The first section introduces the nature and purpose of attractions, their characteristics, and issues pertinent to both natural and man-made attractions. The second section builds on this foundation by exploring a range of issues relating to their development. The third section concentrates on the management of attractions with issues of ownership, the problems of cost structure, pricing and revenue generation, the employment and training of staff, and attempts to counter seasonality featuring strongly. The final section outlines the variety of visitor management techniques in existence and attempts made by operators of attractions to manage visitor impacts in a more sustainable manner. This leads on to the issue of sustainable tourism development in which the object is to manage tourism growth in a manner that ensures that tourists do not destroy by pressure of numbers the very attractions they come to see. In this discussion, the choice – or balance – between regulation and market solutions is discussed, with a closing discussion on the impact on attraction authenticity of 'modern' attraction management.

THE NATURE AND PURPOSE OF ATTRACTIONS

Attractions provide the single most important reason for leisure tourism to a destination. Many of the components of the tourist trip – for example, transport and accommodation – are demands derived from the consumer's desire to enjoy what a destination has to offer in terms of 'things to see and do'. Thus a tourist attraction is a focus for recreational and, in part, educational activity undertaken by both day and stay visitors that is frequently shared with the domestic resident population. Every region and every town boasts of at least one attraction, adding to its appeal as a destination. Attractions also serve a variety of different purposes, since for many their origins had nothing to do with tourism. For example, attractions often have an explicit educational purpose, are often central to the protection, or in fact creation, of cultural identities, and can contribute to the conservation and protection of many historic sites. This variety of 'sense of purpose' is important in that it helps explain why attractions are often so difficult to manage, especially those that fall within the domain of the public sector, such as museums. They often have to accommodate the numerous wishes of their stakeholders, the various expectations of different visitor groups (often from different countries), meet the needs of owners or trustees, and serve on occasion as **attraction 'icons'** for national governments in international marketing strategies. Examples of the latter are the use of images of the Coliseum when marketing Rome, the use of Table Mountain when marketing South Africa, or those of the London Eye, sponsored by British Airways, when promoting London and the UK overseas.

In addition to the above, there are many examples where attractions have played a catalytic role in the regeneration of an area or destination. The success of the Guggenheim Museum in Bilbao, Spain and the National Museum of New Zealand and its contribution to the development of Wellington as a destination are two examples of 'best practice'. Such iconic or **'flagship'** attractions can be used to pull in visitors, meet needs of local residents, and develop stronger tourism activities within the destination. While a destination rarely survives long term on the basis of one attraction, it can be the key pump-primer in more sustainable development of a destination.

With such diversity present within the attractions' sector, the uniform definition and categorisation of attractions has proved elusive, as has the ability of many attractions to share

Photograph 11.1 British Airways' London Eye, one of London's more recent 'iconic' attractions, which features in much of the UK's international marketing and publicity material.
Source: Newscast

'best practice' both from attractions of a similar kind and from attractions elsewhere around the globe. The fact that tourist attractions may be shared with the host community can give rise to conflict in popular destinations, where tourism is perceived to cause problems of crowding, traffic congestion, environmental damage and litter. There can thus be little doubt that the management of tourist attractions is a challenging activity with so many publics to please.

CHARACTERISTICS OF ATTRACTIONS

There are many different types of attraction, and a number of attempts have been made to classify them. Classification is possible along a number of different dimensions:

- ownership;
- capacity;
- **market or catchment area;**
- permanency;
- type.

Early attempts at classification were according to type, distinguishing between natural resources and artificial 'man-made' features or products. Man-made features were as follows:

- Cultural – religion, modern culture, museums, art galleries, architecture, archaeological sites.

- Traditions – folklore, animated culture, festivals.
- Events – sports activities and cultural events.

Natural resources included national parks, wildlife, viewpoints and outstanding natural phenomena such as Uluru (Ayers Rock) in Australia or the Niagara Falls in Ontario, Canada. Classification by type is the most common way in which countries collect attraction statistics, but here some form of permanency is required so that public access can be controlled and measured, which implies that even some iconic attractions are never listed in official statistics.

An alternative and more complex approach is that designed by Clawson and Knetsch (1966) and shown in Figure 11.1. In one diagram, Clawson and Knetsch linked the classification of attractions in a spatial sense, according to their proximity to markets, to their level of uniqueness and to their intensity of use. Clawson's approach is flexible and best utilised as a way of thinking about attractions. For example, a major historic building is clearly a resource-based attraction, but it may extend its market by adding a user-orientated element, such as a leisure park or garden development, as has occurred with many of the stately homes and palaces in Britain and continental Europe. Parks Canada has adopted a variant of Clawson's ideas to provide functional zones related to use in their parks (Mini Case Study 11.1).

MINI CASE STUDY 11.1
Functional zoning applied by Parks Canada

Parks Canada has developed a classification of its park resources based heavily upon Clawson's ideas. In effect, the zones range from Zone I, a pure resource-based zone, through to Zone V, a pure user-based zone. Between the two extremes, a continuum of zones is maintained through appropriate planning and management strategies:

- **Zone I**   Special preservation areas: small and specific areas designated for a particular reason, such as the presence of endangered species. Entry is strictly controlled and access is by permit.

- **Zone II**   Wilderness: areas with specific natural history and/or environmental value. Activities include dispersed hiking and some camping.

- **Zone III** Natural environments: access is compatible with the environment and this is the first zone where motorised access is allowed. However, this access is to the edge of the zone; entry beyond this is via strategically located trails.

- **Zone IV**   Recreation areas: includes campsites, boating, skiing and motorised access. Interpretative services are designed to explain and protect the environment.

- **Zone V**   Park services: includes centralised visitor support services, park administration offices, etc., which are all located and designed to blend in with the surroundings. In some parks this zone is located outside the park boundary.

Source: Adapted from Murphy, 1985

DISCUSSION QUESTIONS

1. For a destination/country of your choice, allocate its range of attractions according to the ideas advocated by Clawson. What is the overall balance of attractions in your chosen destination/country and what challenges does this 'balance' contribute to the overall management of the attractions' product?

2. What particular management issues may be unique to wilderness-based attractions?

3. Propose your own form of classification of attractions and suggest how this may or may not benefit the future management of attractions.

Photograph 11.2   The Grand Canyon, one of the world's 'iconic' natural attractions.
Source: Grand Canyon National Park

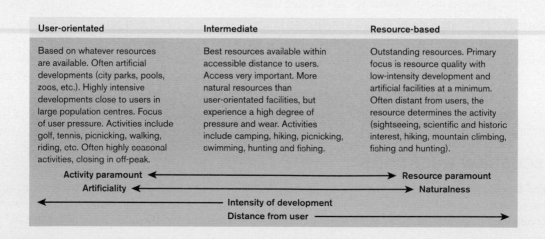

User-orientated

Based on whatever resources are available. Often artificial developments (city parks, pools, zoos, etc.). Highly intensive developments close to users in large population centres. Focus of user pressure. Activities include golf, tennis, picnicking, walking, riding, etc. Often highly seasonal activities, closing in off-peak.

Intermediate

Best resources available within accessible distance to users. Access very important. More natural resources than user-orientated facilities, but experience a high degree of pressure and wear. Activities include camping, hiking, picnicking, swimming, hunting and fishing.

Resource-based

Outstanding resources. Primary focus is resource quality with low-intensity development and artificial facilities at a minimum. Often distant from users, the resource determines the activity (sightseeing, scientific and historic interest, hiking, mountain climbing, fishing and hunting).

Activity paramount ← → Resource paramount
Artificiality ← → Naturalness
← Intensity of development →
← Distance from user →

Figure 11.1   Clawson's classification of recreation resources
Source: Adapted from Clawson and Knetsch, 1966; Boniface and Cooper, 1987

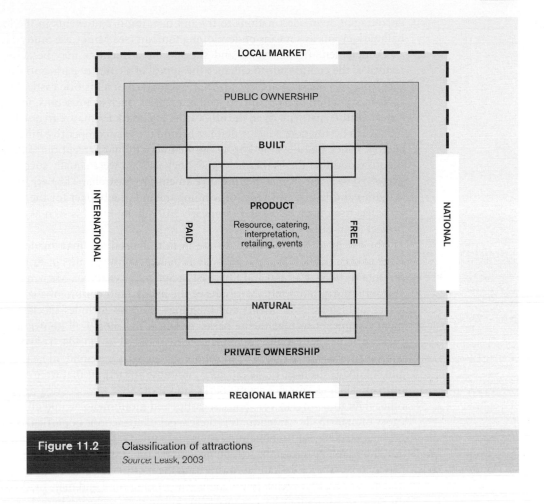

Figure 11.2   Classification of attractions
Source: Leask, 2003

In this chapter, for purposes of analytical convenience, we have adopted the more recent classification shown in Figure 11.2. Although not exhaustive, Figure 11.2 identifies the principal features of classification used in various settings and demonstrates the diversity of the attraction product around the world. At the core of the recent classification rests the core product offered by the attraction, which represents the resource/attributes that attract visitors in the first place. Also within the core are those aspects of the attraction which contribute to its presentation, such as interpretation, and generation of additional income and revenue streams – a facet of most attractions irrespective of their natural or man-made origins. Going further, it will be appreciated that this basic classification may be subdivided again into attractions which are site-specific because of the physical location of facilities and therefore act as a destination, and attractions which are temporary because they are events. International events that are regarded as world class normally stand alone as **hallmark** activities, while others may be used to complement site-specific attractions. It is what is happening at the time that is usually more important for events than their location, so **mega-events**, such as the Olympics, and exhibitions, for example world trade fairs, may move around the globe. However, some hallmark events do evolve in and become specific to their location, so that they become branded by it. Thus several of the most spectacular events in the form of parades or carnivals have become associated with major cities, for example, the Rio Carnival, the Pamplona Bull Run in Spain or the Calgary Stampede in Alberta. This is because cities provide access to a large market and have the economic base to support them. Similarly, important religious festivals are often connected with locations that are considered the foundations of the faith, such as Mecca and Jerusalem. In this respect, the growth in cultural tourism is encouraging many destinations to try and turn important events in the local calendar into hallmark events as a means of developing tourism (see Mini Case Study 11.2).

Complementarity of events and site-specific attractions may be achieved by staging a festival of the countryside to enhance the appeal of a country park, and similarly for the performance of a Shakespeare tragedy in the courtyard of a historic castle. Events are also used to give animation to object-orientated attractions, such as museums, to encourage new and repeat visitors, particularly in the off-season. Hallmark events are frequently used to raise the image of a destination, a factor that lies behind the very competitive bidding for the Olympic Games, which had a lasting impact on the international perception of Barcelona in 1992. It is considered that the Games held in Sydney in 2000 were equally successful and have been perceived as a ten-year marketing investment for Australia. They are, however, very costly activities and within two years of winning the bid, the budget for the London Olympics in 2012 has risen from £2.5 billion to nearly £10 billion, but it is seen as a major regeneration project for East London.

The extent to which attractions are in fact 'natural' or 'man-made' represents the next stage of classification. Natural attractions include country parks in Britain, lakes in Canada, mountains in Switzerland and the coast in Spain, for example. Man-made attractions, however, are more commonly the results of the history and culture of a country which leaves a legacy of historic monuments and buildings, but also includes specially created entertainment complexes such as theme parks, of which the most well known are the Walt Disney parks, originating in California, but now reproduced in Florida, Tokyo, Paris, Hong Kong, with one further park due to open soon in Shanghai. One could, in fact, go one stage further and subdivide the man-made category into those attractions that were created specifically for tourism, such as Disney's theme parks, and those that were created originally for purposes other than tourism. Historic houses, castles and monuments would all come under this category of man-made attraction. It is these types of attractions in particular that often have the greatest challenges in maintaining their authenticity, the addition of cafés, restaurants and gift shops for purposes of income generation often diluting the 'purity' of the attraction product, but they are essential for meeting the requirements of the average visitor.

The varying approaches to the management of natural and man-made attractions and the different pressures they have to face help explain their inclusion here. For example, while the Grand Canyon may have management objectives that focus on conservation issues and the management of visitors, theme parks have at their core objectives of entertainment and income generation. The division between natural resources and artificial attractions, however, is not always clear-cut. Many natural attractions require considerable inputs of infrastructure and management in order to use them for tourism purposes. This is the case of water parks, ski resorts, safari parks, aquaria and many attractions based on nature. This infrastructure may also be put in place to protect the resource from environmental damage. In many countries, it is no longer possible to have open public access to many forests. Specific sites are designated for cars, caravans and camping, and there are colour-coded trails for walkers.

Man-made attractions that are the legacy of history and culture also share with natural resources the fact that they cannot be reproduced without considerable expense and alterations to their authenticity, unlike attractions designed principally for entertainment. They therefore deserve greater protection and management input to guard against excessive use. Such attractions are commonly in the control of the state. A good example is Stonehenge in the UK, which exhibits all the features of being resource-based and non-reproducible, so that for some time too many visitors have threatened it. Measures to resolve this have included the construction of a new visitor centre some distance from the monument and putting a cordon around the stones to prevent them being further defaced by touching and, in some instances, chipping of the stones by capricious visitors. From this it follows that when looking at the development of attractions, we can place them on a scale that has at one end those that have been built or designed for visitor purposes such as family recreation parks, which are in the minority, and at the other, cultural resources and facilities that were neither for visitors nor can be adapted for them. The bulk of attractions would then be spread out between these two poles.

The next basis upon which classification can be attributed is the pricing policy adopted for access to attractions, that is whether or not access is free or an admission charge is required. Many countries around the world offer free access to their national museums, galleries and monuments – such attractions considered by governments to be the national heritage of the population at large (tax concessions are often also connected to such a strategy). This is not always the case, however, with the decline of the public purse sometimes serving as the catalyst for the levy of admission charges at previously 'free' attractions. Understandably, the contrasting objectives between the public and private commercial sector operators of attractions affects the operational and management approaches adopted. More recent studies, however, suggest that the increasingly competitive markets that attractions now find themselves in are leading to greater commonality of management practice, because once paying visitors are introduced to attractions in the public and voluntary sectors, then pressure builds up for the visitor experience, in support of admissions, to become the marketed output, as in the commercial sector. This is something that is often resisted by the curatorial staff of these attractions, who are rightly concerned about the authenticity of the visitor experience. For example, in the 1980s, the Victoria and Albert Museum was heavily criticised for using the marketing strap-line 'Ace caff with rather a nice museum attached!' to stimulate a reappraisal of the museum by the public, a marketing strategy that would be considered quite acceptable today.

The market in which the attraction draws its visitors represents the final classification in Figure 11.2. For example, while Universal Studios' theme parks may have an international audience, since they are based on the global film industry, the Eden Project in England a national audience, and the wineries of Western Australia a regional audience, the majority of attractions have a much smaller local audience. Clearly the nature of the market and the volume of visitors may well determine the nature and management of the product offering, particularly with regard to pricing, visitor spend and interpretation.

NATURAL ATTRACTIONS

In the instance of natural features it is often the quality of the resource that provides the attraction, whereby location becomes secondary. Their appeal is both national and international. Thus tourists come from all over the globe to enjoy the Himalayas in Nepal, the Blue Ridge Mountains of Virginia, or the Ring of Kerry in Southern Ireland. Traditionally, water-based resources, either coastlines or lakes, have always been the most important tourism resource and still are, but with more frequent holiday-taking, the countryside and panoramic scenery have witnessed increasing usage. However, natural amenities are not only confined to the landscape but also include, for example, climate (which accounts for the dominant tourist flows still being north–south to sun resorts), vegetation, forests and wildlife.

The most common aspect of natural resources is that they are generally fixed in supply and are able to provide only a limited amount of services in any given time period. But in many cases, the services provided by this fixed stock of natural amenities can be put to several different uses. Thus if it is proposed to increase the land available for tourism and recreation purposes, it may often be at the expense of other land users, say, industry. There is therefore a trade-off that must take place to ensure that the resource is used to the best advantage of society. This is demonstrated in Figure 11.3, where the vertical axis represents the **social net benefits** (social benefits less social costs) of using a given area of land for tourism or industrial purposes. The schedule TT illustrates how these net benefits decline as more land is made available for tourism, and similarly for the schedule II which applies to industrial use. At Q_1 the social net benefit from the last portion of land devoted to industry

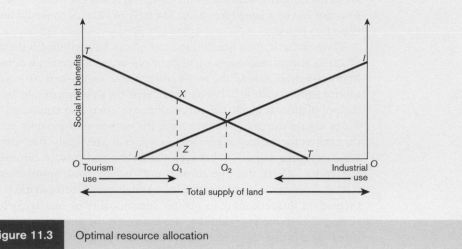

| Figure 11.3 | Optimal resource allocation |

is measured by the distance ZQ_1, while that for tourism use is given by XQ_1. Clearly, the net benefits obtainable from tourism use are much greater than those that can be gained from industrial use and so it will pay society to switch land from industrial designation to tourist use. The optimal point will be at Q_2 where the net social benefits from each use are equalised. By undertaking such a move, society increases social net benefits by the amount XYZ, for the total gain from tourism use is XQ_1Q_2Y but this must be offset by a loss to industry of ZQ_1Q_2Y.

The essence of land-use planning and the legislation that enforces it is to determine some optimal allocation in the manner shown by Figure 11.3. In this way land is zoned for a variety of uses, from tourism and recreation through to urban development, and when disputes occur as to use it is customary to hold some form of public inquiry in which the benefits and costs of alternative choices are evaluated to reach an appropriate decision. Most governments maintain strict planning controls on alternative uses of land, whether it is publicly or privately owned. Thus social considerations via the political process are the main driving force behind land allocation; for example, the planning of the London Olympics involves the relocation of a number of firms away from East London. In the case of privately owned land, social choice may be enforced through compulsory purchase by the state. In some cases the stark choice presented in Figure 11.3 is nullified in practice because multiple land use is possible. National Parks in Britain, such as the Lake District, for example, include residential, farming, forestry, recreational activities and small-scale production within their boundaries.

Market failure and public provision

One of the problems concerning the provision of outdoor areas for leisure purposes on a large scale is that they are rarely commercially viable in terms of the investment costs and operating expenditure necessary to establish and maintain them. The reasons for this lie in their periodic use (weekends and holidays) and the political and administrative difficulties of establishing private markets in what are perceived by the public as gifts of nature. This suggests that, if left to market forces, the result is more likely to be under-provision of natural resources for leisure purposes rather than over-provision. Yet there are considerable social benefits to be enjoyed by the population from the availability of recreational amenities and in the control of land use to prevent unsightly development spoiling the beauty of the landscape.

Economists ascribe the term **market failure** to situations of the kind outlined above and in such circumstances it is common for the state to make the necessary provision. Thus some

85% of outdoor recreation areas in the USA are owned by the Federal Government, with the object of encouraging consumption and protecting the resource for the enjoyment of future generations. Public facilities made available for the purpose of encouraging consumption are termed merit goods, to indicate that the facilities are socially needed even if the willingness to pay for them in the marketplace is somewhat limited. The recognition of this principle in the USA goes back to 1872 with the enactment of the Yellowstone National Park. In Britain, planning and development for tourism purposes is largely a post-1945 phenomenon, commencing with the National Parks and Access to the Countryside Act in 1949, though it was not until the 1960s that positive action in the field of tourism and recreation provision really got going. The worldwide growth of tourism has prompted many other countries to enact similar legislation to manage natural resources in a way that will sustain their use for consumption, while at the same time providing protection against overuse.

There is another aspect of state provision: the so-called **public or collective good**. The principal feature of such goods or services is that it is not realistically possible to exclude individuals from consumption once they have been made available. Private markets for these goods would quickly disintegrate because the optimal strategy for the individual consumer is to wait until someone else pays for the good and then to reap the benefits for nothing. Thus if the good or service is to be provided at all, it may be consumed by everyone without exception and normally without charge at the point of use. The natural environment is a typical example of a public good and the growing pressure of tourist development has created concern for the environment in a number of countries. The point at issue is that public goods form no part of the private costs facing the tourism developer and are therefore open to abuse through overuse. In response the state, in addition to enforcing collective provision out of taxation, regulates individual behaviour through legislation to preserve environmental amenity. For example, in Bermuda tourists are not allowed to hire cars, but only mopeds, while on the Greek island of Rhodes, vehicles are banned from the touristically attractive town of Lindos. Mauritius has a planning law that restricts buildings to a height no greater than the palm trees. In practice, this means hotels of only two storeys and thus permits adequate screening on the seaward side. Where legislation is considered impractical, or overly restrictive, then the approach is to try to change behaviour through educational awareness campaigns. The purpose of such codes is to disseminate information and persuade tourists that on their own volition they should avoid damage to the environment and adverse sociocultural impacts. These codes apply not only to visitors; there are also industry codes to educate staff and the business community in the recycling of materials and respect for the environment, as well as codes for the host community to help in understanding tourism and the benefits it brings, so as to encourage better relationships between hosts and guests.

Managing the attraction resource

Given a fixed amount of natural resources for leisure purposes, it is only possible to alter the supply by adopting different use patterns. Critical to this is the generally accepted premise that tourists should not destroy through excessive use the natural features that they came to enjoy. This view is encapsulated in the concept of sustainable tourism development, which argues that economic growth is only acceptable if it can maintain, at a minimum, the stock of tourist assets intact from one generation to another. Emphasis tends to be placed on the natural environment because it cannot be directly substituted for artificial facilities, and the danger of irreversible damage appears more likely. This danger is also present with man-made attractions such as historic artefacts, but here the concept is more subjective in that it has to do with authenticity; namely, at what point does repair and replacement of stone, say, on a historic monument owing to erosion and visitor damage, mean that it is no longer authentic? This is further complicated by the fact that perception seems to vary according to the nature of the historic artefact under consideration – whether it is glassware, tapestry, a sculpture or features of a building.

It has already been noted that the application of capital, labour and management to the natural environment is often necessary to render them suitable for tourist use, as in the case of a beach resource. This permits more intensive use of the beach provided that the necessary safeguards are put in place to prevent over-exploitation of the free availability of the resource in its role as a public good. One way of achieving this is to restrict accommodation provision to match the desired density of the population on the beach. A high-quality resort would aim at allocating 20 square metres per person, compared with 10 square metres per person for a budget resort. In other situations, the degree of inaccessibility may be used to control visitor numbers. This is illustrated in Figure 11.4, which demonstrates the inverse relationship between visitor numbers and difficulties of access and is also indicated in Clawson's classification (Figure 11.1). This inverse relationship may be due to time, distance or restrictions imposed by the managing authority. For example, with natural attractions that draw visitors both at the national and international level, it is common for the authorities to implement 'park and ride' schemes so as to control the flow of cars in the area. Another popular strategy is the use of **honey pots**, whereby a variety of attractions, shops, restaurants and accommodation is clustered around one or two viewpoints to create a complex capable of absorbing a high population density.

The honey pot concept augments natural attractions with artificial, user-orientated attractions capable of drawing visitors away from the rest of the natural resource area. It is well known, for example, that the demand for domestic tourism and recreation facilities arises, in the main, from urban areas but that pressures on attractions and rural areas generally decrease with distance from city centres. Hence greater opportunities for protection and management of natural sanctuaries for wildlife and vegetation can be found by locating them in areas remote from urban environments. As the city centre is approached so there is a need to provide purpose-built facilities to cope with day excursions and weekend trips. Depending on the climate and country these will include seaside or lakeside resorts, mountain resorts, health centres, spas, and themed and nature parks. Within the city boundary there will be a requirement for town parks, and sport and leisure complexes. Thus as the volume of leisure demand increases so the need to augment natural attractions with artificial facilities arises. In this respect, cities such as Amsterdam, St Petersburg and Istanbul have always been great magnets for tourists because of their historical and cultural resources. For these same reasons, cities everywhere are becoming tourist destinations in their own right rather than just places where people live and work. Today's better-educated traveller is looking for experiences that combine educational interest and entertainment, with the result that cultural

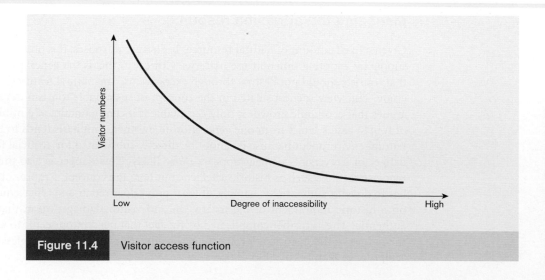

Figure 11.4   Visitor access function

tourism is expanding worldwide and, with it, the growth in urban tourism, so that no major city today can count itself as world class unless it has an acknowledged cultural centre.

MAN-MADE ATTRACTIONS

Many man-made attractions are products of history and culture. The range of museums and art galleries in the world's top tourist destinations is usually extensive and many are subject-specific, for example, the Rijksmuseum in Amsterdam, or Chicago's Museum of Science and Industry. In addition to this are numerous historic buildings, which include castles, palaces, churches, houses and even completely walled medieval towns such as Carcassonne in France, as well as a variety of early industrial sites which are capable of satisfying the public's interest in bygone times.

Where old industrial buildings, disused market halls, railway stations and docks are located close to urban centres, it has been quite common to convert them into tourist zones which serve both visitors and residents alike. Since shopping is an important tourist activity, the focus has been on speciality shopping – as in Faneuil Hall, Boston – intermingled with hotels, leisure attractions and also business facilities – a convention centre, exhibition hall or trade centre. In this way, tourism has replaced manufacturing and distribution industries which have left the inner core for more spacious and cheaper locations on the outskirts of the city, and has proved to be a feasible economic option for urban regeneration, as in the development of Baltimore's Inner Harbor, South Street Seaport, New York, Darling Harbour, Sydney and Birmingham's Gas Street Basin in the UK.

Over and above the attractions left by historical legacy, there are numerous engineered attractions whose principal role is one of entertainment. Such attractions are user-orientated and are capable of handling thousands of visitors per day: they include theme and leisure parks, sporting venues, theatres and all-weather holiday centres. Theme parks will also include an educational function – for example, Futurescope in France – as well as providing exciting 'white knuckle' rides in the form of roller coasters, runaway trains, log flumes and oscillating 'pirate' ships.

One of the most famous theme parks (in the true sense), Colonial Williamsburg in Virginia, USA, is a living museum. It was originated by establishing an old city within a new one and by the staff creating a time capsule of the colonial period of America through role play and using the technology of the day. Its success has drawn in a range of partners to propagate the cultural richness of the state of Virginia. A similar re-creation has taken place at Beamish in the north of England. The museum has been positioned at a time just before the First World War and staff demonstrate the technology and converse with visitors in the way of life of that period. As far as possible the houses, shops, transport system, goods and artefacts are genuine articles of the time that have been brought to the site from all parts of the UK. In this manner, Beamish and Colonial Williamsburg have crossed the boundary between a theme park and a museum. In so doing they have captured the public's imagination by allowing participation. The public is now attuned to experiencing the sights and sounds of the era being witnessed, which gives opportunities for using technology creatively to enhance the visitor experience. We know that ultimately it is the visitor experience that is the marketed output of tourist attractions. The acceptance of the content and style of this experience is determined by fashion, which has its own dynamic that is born out of the spirit of enquiry and competition within society to alter its patterns of consumption and value systems.

To this extent, animals in captivity in the form of zoos or safari parks are no longer acceptable to many people and there is a marked decline of interest in static attractions and object-orientated museums, unless they are national collections or they are best presented in this way, as for example jewellery. The quest for improving the attraction experience forces theme and leisure park operators to install more complicated rides and challenging entertainment as the public seeks to increase the skill content of their consumption. Similarly, historic properties, museums and gardens change their displays and feature special exhibitions/events to maintain interest. Some attractions are fortunate enough to be able to tie themselves to regular events aimed at an enthusiast market, for example automobile rallies, for which demand is more or less continuous.

DEVELOPING ATTRACTIONS

Already it is clear that the range of attractions is extensive and that there are numerous variations in respect of the product concept or creativity of the design and its appeal. This we will term the imagescape to match the use of the word 'imagineers' by the Disney Corporation when describing its designers. The concept is based on the fact that all attractions, in some part, measure their performance by the number of visitors, the quality of the experience they give them, and the memories that they take home to ensure repeat visits or the spread of word-of-mouth recommendation. To enhance the experience, the modern approach is to place tangible objects, say, a thrill ride or a collection of museum artefacts (despite their intrinsic value), within the context of a specific theme or image in a particular setting or environment: hence the word 'imagescape'.

This approach is consistent with the post-industrial societal views espoused by Pine and Gilmore (1999) in their seminal publication, *The Experience Economy*, where it is argued that the production system should be re-engineered to add value through marketing experiences. This implies producing services with attached goods, rather than the traditional mass production process in which commodities are uniformly produced and sold on price. In this way, customers are able to receive a package that relates to their needs. Following this viewpoint, Figure 11.5 offers an abstract perspective of an attraction product where the core element is represented by the 'imagescape' – the idea of which is to communicate the fundamental nature of the visitor experience to the potential target markets. Clearly a variety of 'imagescapes' are possible. Examples may include 'art and media', 'childhood', 'fame and notoriety', the 'human body', 'myths and fantasy', the 'natural world' and 'war and conflict', to name but a few.

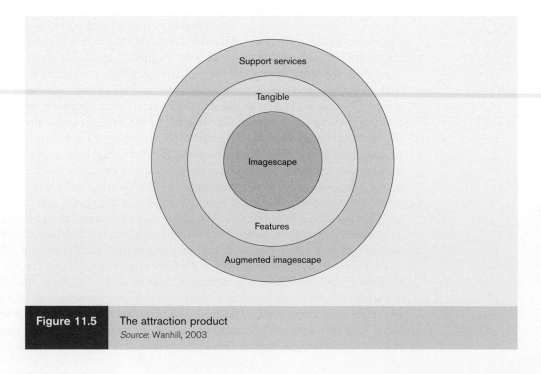

Figure 11.5	The attraction product
	Source: Wanhill, 2003

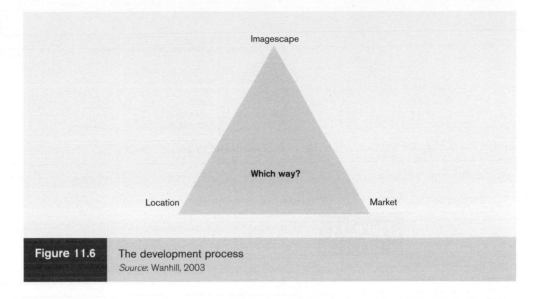

Figure 11.6	The development process
	Source: Wanhill, 2003

The attraction development process

When contemplating attraction development the ideal process from a demand standpoint is one of Market → Imagescape → Location. In reality, however, this demand-led sequential process is seldom implemented, only applying to **'footloose'** attractions that have flexibility across all three aspects in order to generate economic success. Given that most attraction developments are constrained more often than not by their location, type and ownership, a more common process — especially in the instance of regeneration – is one of Location → Imagescape → Market (see Figure 11.6), which raises the danger of 'talking up the market' to justify the development. Several millennium projects sponsored by the Heritage Lottery Fund in the UK have gone this way and some have had to close. This reflects the fact that location, imagescape and market are inextricably bound up with one another. If site selection becomes at most a second choice, this throws greater weight on to the market–imagescape mix in order to achieve visitor numbers commensurate with notions of the economic viability of the attraction. How in reality these three factors are balanced clearly depends upon the overriding objectives of the attraction and the status of its owners.

The market–imagescape mix

What is clear from the above is that both market and imagescape are inextricably linked to each other vis-à-vis the development of attractions, as evidenced in Figure 11.7. The type of attraction which carries the least commercial risk is that identified in the first quadrant (QI), that of **'me too' attraction development**. The fact that parallel attractions already exist in the marketplace ensures that the creators of the attraction are able to benefit from previous market performance and the passage of trends over a specified time period. One of the dangers of 'me too' developments is that assumptions are often made, incorrectly, that if a concept works in one location then it will automatically work elsewhere. It is also a problem in some countries with the overdevelopment of heritage attractions – often perceived as a 'quick win' for politicians, but frequently short of visitors after the initial spurt of interest. Before giving the 'green light' to such attractions it is advisable to evaluate the likely displacement of visitors from other attractions and so anticipate the genuine additionality, if any, to the destination in question.

Success in delivering **'grand inspiration' attractions** in QII is clearly dependent on the imagescape meeting the needs and expectations of the market. Pre-market evaluation of the concept is difficult in that the market is frequently unaware of what the concept will look like.

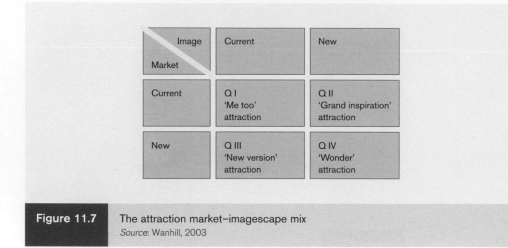

Image — Market	Current	New
Current	Q I 'Me too' attraction	Q II 'Grand inspiration' attraction
New	Q III 'New version' attraction	Q IV 'Wonder' attraction

Figure 11.7   The attraction market–imagescape mix
Source: Wanhill, 2003

In terms of assessment, a common strategy in this area is to try to reverse the project evaluation sequence by estimating the volume of visitors needed to make the project both feasible and viable at a price the market is prepared to pay.

Even if this is successful, however, there still remain the problems of raising finance and finding a suitable location. The fact that most available land is owned by the public sector is a hindrance in that very few local or regional authorities have the vision to foresee the positive impact of such attractions. Equally, many developers have experienced and recognised the ability of local pressure groups to 'kill off' sound project proposals.

'**New version**' attractions in QIII represent on the one hand a reformulation of the attraction product, yet preserving the existing imagescape, because the current public has become too familiar with it and, on the other, expansion to new locations and access to new markets. The expansion of the Disney concept to Japan, Paris and now Hong Kong represents a good example of the latter type of development. Such developments are supply-led, as they are generating demand in spatial terms where it has not been previously and so there is a need for substantial market research and forecasting in order to take account of both short-term conditions and longer-term ones. Yet there is no guarantee of success as realised by the financial difficulties of Disneyland Paris, so that in the case of Hong Kong Disney was careful to lay off the bulk of the investment on the government of Hong Kong. For established attractions, meeting the needs of new and future markets may require a much greater leap forward in terms of imagescape development for the new version to be successful, something that was achieved successfully by the opening of the Guggenheim in Bilbao.

Those attractions that carry with them the highest level of risk are labelled '**wonder**' **attractions**, as identified in QIV. This type of attraction represents projects on a grand scale that deliver significant economic impacts on their location. Because the development of such attractions contains considerable risk and uncertainty, it is fair to say that very few examples of attraction development would sit in this category: Disney's EPCOT (opened in 1982) and Sydney's Opera House (opened in 1973) are two examples of success, though only after a financial struggle, particularly the Opera House, which came in ten years late and fourteen times over budget. London's Millennium Dome is an example of how a part regeneration development can go off course! This can be attributed to political interference and a lack of clarity in the marketplace of what it was supposed to be. It was designed as a celebration for the year 2000, but was judged by the press as a commercial attraction, so that the out-turn of 6.5 million visitors for the year as against a forecast of 12 million was declared a financial 'disaster' in the media and the political arena, and an embarrassment to the British government. With the clear majority of all attraction developments achieving annual attendance levels of

200,000 and below, it is no surprise that investments of the above scale are few and far between. The risks are high and the funding required is such that they tend to proceed with the support of governments and large leisure corporations working in partnership. That said, if the balance is right the potential benefits to accrue from success are considerable. With regard to the innovation process with 'wonder' attractions, the departure from existing imagescapes is common in that the new attraction often sets the standard for others to follow and is an inspiration for subsequent development.

In trying to develop a successful attraction, the discussion above leads to the conclusion that the creativity of the imagescape has to connect to the needs and expectations of the market. In the majority of cases, attractions as a product group tend to defy business logic in that they are frequently supply-driven with many being developed for purposes other than tourism and in other economic sectors. Although this is maybe obvious with regard to many public attractions such as museums, monuments and historic houses, it is also true for many themed attractions such as Disney, in that the Disney characters were established icons long before the development of the theme parks in California and Florida. This, and to a large extent the future of attraction development, appears to lie with new developments that customers recognise by association with known products: the development of corporate brand attractions being a perfect example of this, such as the Guinness Storehouse in Dublin, Ireland and Niketown in the USA. Investments of this kind may be regarded as brand extensions or stretching.

MINI CASE STUDY 11.2
Savonlinna Opera Festival

In many instances festivals and events are designed to augment the tourist product of a destination. Hallmark events are stand-alone products because it is what is happening at the time that is important rather than their location. However, some become branded by their location and in so doing contribute greatly to the image of the destination through becoming an iconic attraction. Such an example is the Savonlinna Opera Festival, which is an annual event that takes place every July in Olavinlinna Castle, which adjoins the town of Savonlinna that is situated in the Etelä-Savo region, a lake area of Eastern Finland, but in this case location choice is highly relevant. What determines the establishment of most opera festivals is the place and the setting and for Savonlinna the setting is the courtyard of a medieval castle, with exceptional acoustics, that juts out into a lake. One can compare this to the Dalhalla Opera Festival in mid Sweden, which is located in an old quarry that has its own natural lake and, again, first class acoustics.

The history of the Savonlinna Opera Festival dates back to 1912 when it was founded by the famous Finnish soprano Aino Ackté (1876–1944). Unfortunately, the Savonlinna Festival was swallowed up in the maelstrom of the First World War and then caught up in the political turmoil between Finland and Russia, so it did not appear again until 1930. In the recessionary period of the 1930s and with war clouds again on the horizon, this revival was short-lived. But memories of the Festival lingered on in the town, and after a period of close on four decades, it was started again in 1967 with the production of Beethoven's *Fidelio*. The artistic revival of the Festival is considered by the management team to date from the production of Mozart's *Magic Flute* during the 1973 season. At that time the Festival lasted only one week, but it has progressed now to a stable formula of three weeks of own productions of four to five operas over 24–26 performances, some concerts and one week when it hosts a guest company (initiated in 1987 with the Estonian Theatre Company from Tallin). To accomplish this task, the Festival has a full-time staff of 12 and three craftsmen in its workshop, with total employment rising to some 660 persons during the season, including its own chorus and orchestra.

Opera is recognised as one of the most expensive of the performing arts, and sums of US$500,000 per performance in the major opera houses are not uncommon. Equally public subsidy per attendance by far outstrips any other performing art. This is because it is 'a 19th century art form that has built into it 19th

➔

century cost assumptions' (Lord Guthrie, English Arts Council, 1995). By this is meant that costs are dictated by a long gone composer and his/her librettist, and there is little the artistic director can do about this without radically changing the experience, which would be self-defeating if it fails to attract audiences. Thus the traditions and conventions in the repertoire lead to high costs and prices in today's market, despite relatively high amounts of public subsidy given to enable the art form to survive.

As a charitable organisation, the underlying philosophy of the Festival is one of service to the public at large through offering a quality experience that is comparable to any other world-class venues. However, the experience is constrained by the requirement to break even 'one year with another' from a variety of revenue sources, of which some 62% comes from ticket sales, the remainder being made up of public subsidy, sponsorship and commercial trading of opera recordings, guest performances and so on. This means that despite the many operas that exist, in order to meet revenue targets, most opera companies position the bulk of their work around a popular few, either in the form of new productions or revivals. These are the operas that are popular with audiences worldwide and can be relied on to fill seats. Audiences tend to fall dramatically for contemporary opera even at reduced ticket prices. These aspects are reflected in the artistic policy of the Festival:

- one new production every year;
- one new opera every three years;
- carrying over some (popular) operas from previous years;
- a guest company performing two (usually popular) operas in the last week.

In this the Festival office is attempting to balance artistic endeavour against prudential financial management. The potential monetary risks from changing the repertoire are high; hence the marketing concentrates on retaining existing customers, bringing in around 70%–75% repeat business every Festival. The management is cautious about experimenting with tradition and new ventures. For example, some years ago the Festival launched a winter season for one week, which proved to be very damaging financially. On the other hand, while repeats of popular operas sell well, venues do not get the same critical acclaim as they would for new productions or totally new operas. It may thus be appreciated that the art of opera management is about maintaining a balance between filling seats, controlling costs and artistic integrity.

The success of the Opera Festival witnessed the establishment of a summer ballet event in 2002 and the opening of a new concert and conference centre and a holiday home fair, all in the same year. From the perspective of the municipality, cultural tourism has become the catalyst for the establishment of arts amenities for the town, as well as drawing in new businesses through building a successful image of the area as a place to live and work. The town has around 28,000 inhabitants, but being a popular tourist resort, the population rises to around 100,000 during the main season when the Festival is running. An indirect measure of the importance of the Festival to the town's tourism sector can be gauged from the expansion of flights between Helsinki and Savonlinna to five flights per day during the period of the Festival, dropping to two flights per day afterwards.

Source: Adapted from Wanhill, 2006

DISCUSSION QUESTIONS

1. The popular view of opera is that it is an elite art form, so to what extent should it be subsidised from the public purse, if at all, given the many other calls on government money, such as health, welfare and education?

2. The pricing process for opera seats is similar to other arts venues. Suggest the various criteria that may be used to set seat prices.

3. Cultural values and economic values do not necessarily go together, yet cultural change is irreversible. Should art forms of the past be preserved when most people do not suffer any great sense of loss if they disappear?

MANAGING ATTRACTIONS

The sheer diversity, geographic fragmentation, varying pattern of ownership and funding, scale and market–imagescape mix are such that the management of visitor attractions can be a very complex and demanding proposition. This applies especially with regard to attempts made to date in developing a cohesive national strategy for visitor attractions, which in turn creates a sound strategic platform for the management of individual attractions. Work by Middleton (2003) outlines those conditions for a national strategy for visitor attractions would be beneficial. Such conditions include:

- the destabilising effects of a sudden massive injection of unanticipated capital into an already saturated market;
- where large, newly-opened projects are putting established attractions at a significant disadvantage;
- instances of major expenditure on other major urban regeneration projects;
- situations where there is a steady decline of local authority annual revenue funding for traditional attractions such as museums and galleries;
- where the industry structure is one in which the great majority of attractions are small businesses, with only a very small percentage of larger attractions capable managerially and financially of marketing themselves professionally and organising their own data collection; and
- where there is a lack of management information and where the attractions sector is populated by more non-commercial 'public' institutions than by commercial 'private' businesses.

If the majority of the above conditions are in place, Middleton identifies seven key components that ought to be considered for action recommendations in any national strategy for visitor attractions. The seven factors are:

- the collection and dissemination of effective research on a comparable basis and which covers both demand- and supply-side perspectives;
- application of expertise to the analysis and communication of trends and their implications in terms that the majority of smaller attractions will be able to understand and respond;
- advice, and perhaps support, on assessing quality of visits and providing customer assurance via benchmarking initiatives;
- collection and dissemination of good practice examples in visitor attraction management and operations;
- coordination and possibly funding for/provision of training and management development;
- influence over funding bodies concerning the criteria they apply to bids from new and existing attractions including advice to government on the way in which taxes in the sector are imposed and collected; and
- influence and advice to public-sector bodies, especially local authorities, that they may consider in relation to their own decisions on planning and funding activities for attractions in their areas.

Moving away from the notion of a national strategy, however, a number of issues are fundamental to the day-to-day management of visitor attractions.

Economic aspects

As with natural resources, a great many man-made tourist attractions, because of their historical legacy, are not commercially owned. They are owned by central government, in the case of national collections, quasi-public bodies which are at an 'arm's length' from the government, local government and voluntary bodies in the form of charitable trusts. Ownership status is in fact one of the key determinants of attraction management. Leask (2003: 11) for example, concludes that ownership proved to be a 'key independent variable with regard to determining the entire approach to attraction management'. This was particularly the case for 'managing revenue and overall yield, visitor management strategies and the management of environmental impacts at attractions'.

Issues of ownership

Public ownership

Publicly owned attractions may receive all or a substantial part of their funds from general taxation, either directly or via grant-in-aid for quasi-public bodies. They are thus provided in the manner of a merit good and as a result impose a degree of coercion on everyone, as individuals are not free to adjust the amounts that are made available. This is shown by Figure 11.8: the schedule SS is the quantity of, say, museum services supplied to each person as a result of public provision. The distance $0t$ represents the amount of income foregone per person in terms of tax and A the demand curve of individual A and similarly for B. At a tax cost $0t$, A demands only Q_A museum services while B demands Q_B. Clearly, the supply of services exceeds A's demand by XY, but falls below B's demand by YZ. It follows therefore that public provision is likely to generate political debate and lobbying as individuals try to alter the amounts produced to suit their own requirements. In market-orientated economies the trend has been towards charging for national museums in order to cut public expenditure, though there is still resistance among certain sections of the community, including museum managers, who feel that museums have a public obligation requirement. As a consequence, only voluntary admission donations have been introduced in some instances, with a recommended minimum contribution, while other museums have simply refused to charge for admission in exchange for tax breaks, and those that are free still make charges for special exhibitions.

It is evident from the above discussion that the classification of goods and services into public and private provision is by no means clear-cut. It is up to society to decide upon the dividing line through the political process. Nevertheless, governments do have to make everyday decisions on which projects to promote. This is particularly true of tourist

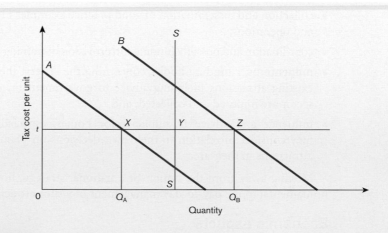

Figure 11.8   Public provision

attractions, because they are frequently sponsored by local authorities and voluntary organisations who look to central government for grant assistance. To aid decision-making, economists have devised the analytical framework of cost–benefit analysis, which takes a wider and longer look at project decisions. The diversity of tourism expenditure is such that the most feasible method of assessing government support is to look at the impact that spending by visitors to the attraction has on local income and employment via the multiplier process. Implicit in this process is the requirement that the normal financial checks will be undertaken to ascertain whether the project is able to sustain itself operationally: if not, then it will need permanent subsidy if it is to proceed.

Voluntary organisations

Many museums and events have arisen out of the collections or interests of a group of enthusiasts who come together to provide for themselves and others collective goods and services which are unlikely to have any widespread commercial appeal (market failure) and are equally unlikely to be of sufficient importance to attract central provision by the state. These organisations are in effect clubs and normally have non-profit aims. But, in contrast to the public sector, they are not able to raise funds from taxation and so in the long run must cover their costs out of income. Yet, unlike the private commercial sector, many find their income source is not made up principally of admission charges and visitor spending inside the attraction, and those that do will have a different pricing policy than commercial operators. Membership fees, gifts and bequests often take on a far greater significance in the income statement. As a consequence, recruiting new members to share the collective visitor experience is a priority task for these organisations.

As these voluntary associations grow in size, there comes a point where it pays them to be incorporated as charitable trusts. By law, this can usually only be for the purposes of education, religion, relief of the poor, or the public good, and allows them to qualify for public funding and tax relief for capital and revenue expenses. One of the most well-known examples of the latter in the UK is the National Trust, which was started in 1895 with the object of protecting places of historic and natural significance for the nation. The Trust maintains a wide range of historic properties, parks and woodlands, and is an institutional model that has been copied elsewhere. Acquisition has normally been via bequests from previous owners together with substantial endowments that provide the economic foundations for the organisation. Given the breadth of its facilities, with the potential of taking on more, it has a policy of expanding membership, since its objective, as with any other club, is to encourage consumption among like-minded persons. However, it is also careful to hedge the demand risk by receiving income from a variety of sources, namely, admission charges from non-members, shops and catering, grants and donations, sponsorship, events and services rendered, for example, lecture programmes. On the cost side, like other voluntary societies, the Trust benefits from some labour inputs and materials being provided free of charge. An events example is the Sealed Knot Society, which undertakes re-enactment battles of the English Civil War (1642–51). Similarly, there are several military history associations in the USA that undertake re-enactments of events that took place in the American Civil War (1861–65).

Commercial sector

For the commercial attractions the rules of market economics apply. They are required to make profits so as to contribute a return on the capital invested. In theory this return, at a minimum, should be equal to the current cost of raising money for investment purposes, and for new or 'venture' projects considerably more. In situations where attractions are owned by multi-product firms or conglomerates, the ability of the facility to contribute to the cash flow of the overall business is often given a higher priority than return on capital. Production industries frequently have long lead times between incurring costs and receiving revenues. In these circumstances, the ownership of subsidiaries capable of generating ready cash inflows into the organisation on a daily and weekly basis can contribute greatly to total financial stability.

The principal economic concerns of most commercial attractions are the same ones that face many other tourist enterprises, namely their cost structure and the seasonal nature of demand. Furthermore, for user-orientated attractions, fashions and tastes also play a considerable part. As noted earlier, theme park owners have to add new rides and replace old ones long before they are physically worn out simply to maintain attendances. Historic properties and museums can fall back on the intrinsic value of their buildings and collections, but even here presentation and interpretation have become more important. The Major Case Study at the end of this chapter provides a very pertinent example of commercial theme park attraction development and identifies many of the contemporary issues and future challenges faced by commercial attraction operators.

Costs

Typically, the cost structure of tourist attractions is made up of a high level of fixed, and therefore unavoidable, costs in relation to the operational or variable costs of running the enterprise. The main component of the fixed costs is the capital investment required to establish the attraction in the first place and capital additions from new development. The economic consequence of having a high level of fixed costs is to raise the break-even point in terms of sales or visitor numbers as shown in Figure 11.9. The revenue line from sales to visitors over a given time period is represented by R. The lines C_1 and C_2 are total cost schedules according to different visitor numbers: the slope of these cost schedules is determined by the variable costs incurred per visitor (marginal costs) and where they cut the revenue and costs axis determines the level of fixed costs. It may easily be seen that with overall fixed costs of F_1 the break-even point (BEP_1), which is at the intersection of R and C_1, is achieved at V_1 level of visitors. If fixed costs are set at F_2, then the number of visitors needed to break-even rises substantially to V_2, which increases the amount of risk in the successful running of the operation. This also has an impact on location, because for user-orientated attractions population catchment areas in terms of ease of access to the site are of prime importance. The greater the visitor numbers required in order for an attraction project to break even, the fewer are the number of acceptable locations. It follows from this that government initiatives

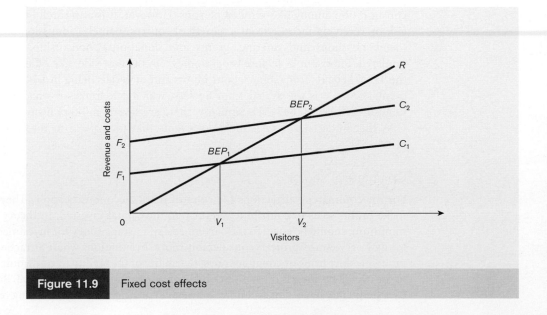

Figure 11.9   Fixed cost effects

to stimulate the development of tourist attractions largely hinge, for their success, on the amount of assistance that can be given to help with the capital costs of starting up the project. This assistance may be in the form of cash grants, subsidised ('soft') loans, shared ownership, the provision of benefits-in-kind such as land, infrastructure and access routes or a combination of any of these. For example, the site for Disneyland Paris was obtained at 1971 agricultural prices, in spite of the fact that it had already been zoned for urban development. As a rule, cash grants are perceived by the commercial sector as the most effective form of financial help.

Pricing policy

The effects of having high fixed costs also spill over into pricing policy. The difference between the price charged for admission to an attraction and the variable or marginal cost of providing the visitor experience for the customer is the contribution margin per customer towards paying the fixed costs and meeting targets on profitability. As shown in Figure 11.10, where the contribution margin desired is low because fixed costs are low, the marginal cost of supplying an additional unit is relatively high and so provides a good guide to setting the price level. This is known as cost-orientated pricing. On the other hand, where there are high fixed costs, the admission charge has to be set considerably above the **marginal cost** of provision, in order to ensure a high contribution margin to meet the financial costs of servicing the investment that has been sunk into the attraction. In this instance, the marginal cost of provision is no longer a good guide to pricing and the enterprise is forced to take a market-orientated stance in its pricing policy. The difference between the admissions price and marginal cost is the range of price discretion that the organisation has, for it must cover its operating costs in the short run but may take a longer-term perspective in terms of how it might cover its fixed costs. By seeking out a range of different market segments with a variety of different prices, including discounts for volume sales and long-term contracts, the commercial attraction operator will try to optimise the yield (the difference between price and marginal cost) on the site's assets. This is termed **yield management** and the operator's ability to improve the yield will be constrained be the economic climate surrounding the firm, which will include the customers' perceptions of value for money ('what the market will bear'), personal income levels, particularly amounts for discretionary (non-essential) spending, and the degree of competition. For performing arts venues, once the repertoire is fixed then the marginal cost per seat falls to zero, so yield management is effectively **revenue management**, hence major cities often have discount ticket booths located in 'theatreland'

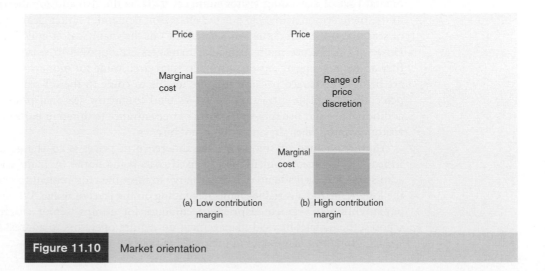

| **Figure 11.10** | Market orientation |

to dispose of surplus tickets for today's performances, since any price greater than zero represents a contribution to fixed expenses.

Managing people

The perception of attractions in recent years vis-à-vis employment has changed in that many jobs in the sector are no longer viewed as low paid and seasonal but represent opportunities that offer real benefits and long-term development. This is reflected in a gradual improvement in good management, recruitment, training, appraisal procedures and the development of career structures. Many of these points were noted by Swarbrooke in 2002 when identifying those issues deemed important for the future success of managing visitor attractions. It was noted also that attractions would have to contend with flatter organisational structures and the empowerment of staff, an increased emphasis on quality and a growth in performance-related pay for valued employees.

Despite recognition of much of the above by many attractions, there still remains across the leisure sector in the UK a considerable skills gap. This was noted by Keep and Mayhew (1999) whereby, in particular, information technology and customer care skills were deemed to be lacking, with little evidence of training for volunteers. These points were also noted by Watson and McCracken (2002; 2003) in their study of attractions in Scotland. A number of key environmental factors were highlighted as significant drivers for future change, notably developments in technology, legislative changes (including requirements on health, safety and employment issues), and external socio-economic trends. Irrespective of one's particular viewpoint, it is clear that attractions need to continue to acquire more professional approaches to the recruitment, development and overall management of people if the sector as a whole is going to sustain growth and popularity in the years to come, and at best catch up with their more 'professional' sector neighbours (such as transportation, intermediaries and the hospitality sector) in managing their workforce.

Managing seasonality

Seasonality becomes an issue in tourist attractions because the product, the visitor experience, cannot be stored. This being the case, it is peak demand that determines capacity and user-orientated attractions are frequently designed to a standard based on a fixed number of days per annum when capacity is likely to be reached or exceeded. This implies that at most times of the year the attraction has too much capacity. The level of investment is therefore more than what would be required if the product was storable. In turn, seasonality can affect pricing policy, as presented in Figure 11.11. SS is the supply schedule representing the incremental cost of expanding visitor numbers. D_2D_2 is the demand for the visitor experience in the main season, while D_1D_1 is the off-season demand. Market clearing requires a policy of seasonal price differentiation, charging P_2 in the main season and P_1 in the off-season. However, in practice many attraction managers are opposed to seasonal pricing because, they argue, it simply reacts on customers' perceived value for money. Visitors feel that they are being overcharged because they are unable to come in the off-season. To counter this perception problem, attraction operators tend to narrow seasonal price ranges and offer additional product benefits, in the form of free entrance to different parts of the site, to those visitors coming when the attraction is not busy.

Another method of smoothing the difference in prices is to charge a two-part tariff. Instead of the major contribution to fixed costs being borne by main season visitors, the admission price is made up of a fixed charge to meet the requirement to cover fixed costs in the long term and a variable charge depending on the level of usage. While most attractions pay attention to segmented pricing techniques for groups, senior citizens, children and schools, the dictates of yield management do require operators to address the seasonal and spatial limitations of demand in their pricing policy.

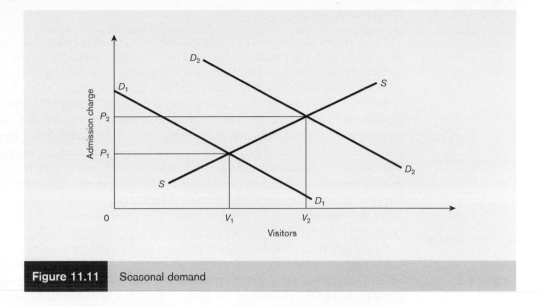

Figure 11.11   Seasonal demand

Managing visitors

Price has often been used as a method of regulating demand and enforcing exclusivity as in luxury resorts such as Malibu and the Maldives, or in luxury hotels, for example the Mandarin and Shangri La hotels in Asia. To be able to use price to limit the number of visitors requires that consumption should be excludable – only those who pay can benefit from the visitor experience. But this is frequently deemed undesirable in the case of natural resources or the historical and cultural artefacts of a country, either because they are public goods, so that it is not practical to exclude consumption, or because they are merit goods whereby it is to the benefit of society that consumption should be encouraged. Even commercial attractions would have difficulty in using price as the sole regulator of visitor numbers. In any one year such attractions have a variety of peaks and troughs, which would therefore entail a whole range of different prices. In Western economies, the public does not respond well to wildly fluctuating prices and so all attractions resort to some non-price methods to manage visitor flows.

A number of possible actions exist to manage visitors at busy times and thereby avoid congestion and improve the visitor experience. These start with marketing and information provision and go through to techniques that can influence the visitor's behaviour on the site. Some attractions have adopted deliberate demarketing at peak times, but where they are nationally or internationally known this is only of limited effectiveness. First-time visitors to capital cities nearly always want to see the principal landmarks: Prague Castle in the Czech Republic, the Grand Palace in Bangkok, and the Empire State Building in New York City. The first step at any site is to deal with car and bus traffic, if only to prevent congestion building up and blocking main roads. Once on site, visitors can be channelled using internal transport systems, for example land trains, where distances involve a considerable amount of walking. For theme parks, queue management is often necessary for popular attractions and rides, so that excessive waiting does not detract from the visitor's enjoyment. This may be achieved by ensuring that the queue line passes through a stimulating environment, with the ability to view the attraction as the latter is approached, by providing entertainers and by using markers to indicate the length of time people will have to wait at different stages of the queue.

Environmental impacts

The concern for the tourism environment, be it natural or artificial, is linked with the notion of sustainable development, as discussed in detail in Chapter 8. Rarely in history has any society willingly absorbed the imposition of a variety of outside cultures upon it, yet, in the interests of generating local economic activity and employment, this is precisely what host communities are expected to do with regard to the development of tourism. The situation is depicted in Figure 11.12. Suppose the local economy is positioned at A and the desire is to increase employment. The adverse consequence is where such a policy can only be accomplished by a move from A to B, which trades off employment against environmental quality. The concept of sustainable tourism development used here argues that economic growth and environmental quality are not mutually exclusive events. By changes in technology to improve the use of resources, compensating for the run down of some resources, controlling waste and managing visitor flows to prevent or repair damage to non-renewable tourism resources, it is possible to reach a position such as C in Figure 11.12.

Going 'green' can build a platform for long-term growth by offering a better tourist product, saving resources and raising the public's perception of the tourism industry. Sustainable development thus offers a way to escape the 'limits to growth' syndrome illustrated by a move from A to B, by searching out a way forward that will maintain community well-being. But care of the environment is more than just preservation or protection: some of the key principles that should govern environmental policy for the implementation of any tourism development plan are:

- recognition of a two-way relationship between tourism and the environment, yielding possibilities of conservation through tourism;
- visitor management to reduce pressure;
- environmental improvement for the benefit of residents and visitors;
- sensitive development that respects and, if possible, enhances the environment;
- responsible operation through ecologically sound practice in tourism businesses and the means of travel.

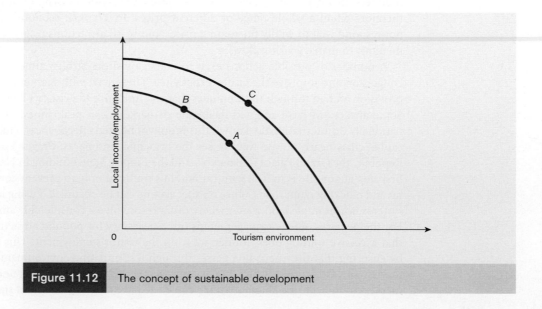

Figure 11.12   The concept of sustainable development

Table 11.1	Tourism in relation to the environment

Tourism to environment	Environment to tourism
Opportunities Commercial returns for preservation of built environment and natural heritage. New use for redundant buildings and land. Increased awareness and support for conservation.	**Opportunities** Fine scenery and heritage as visitor attractions. Eco-tourism based on environmental appreciation.
Threats Intrusive development. Congestion. Disturbance and physical damage. Pollution and resource consumption.	**Threats** Off-putting, drab environments. Pollution hazards on beaches, in water, and in rural and urban areas. Intrusive developments by other industries.

The significant feature that is not always given the coverage it deserves in the media is the existence of this two-way relationship between tourism and the environment, as illustrated in Table 11.1. The tendency in the discussion of the impacts of tourism has been to give weight to the negative aspects of tourism on the environment rather than the positive opportunities that are available.

Regulation or market solutions?

The question posed is how should the mechanism for sustainable development work? In market-orientated economies the policy preference is for solutions based on the principle that the **polluter should pay**, thus prices should reflect not only the economic costs of provision but also the social costs. The different approaches to the impact of visitors on the tourism environment are shown in Figure 11.13. DD is the demand schedule and at low rates of tourist consumption, say, V_1, the social cost per unit (SC) is equal to the economic cost (EC) of usage. Thus up to V_1 current consumption does not interfere with future consumption or damage the resource. If only current demand is considered then the resource would be used to a level V_2 with visitor expenditure settling at point B. This results in resource depletion to the extent that SC is as high as point A. The market solution is to drive consumption back to V_3 by imposing a tourist tax CE on usage to compensate for the renewal cost of the resource.

The difficulty with market solutions is that, as discussed elsewhere, many natural attractions have public good properties whereby consumption is non-excludable and there is an element of public resistance to charging for a nation's heritage which is presumed to belong to all, although some museums and galleries do discriminate between domestic and foreign visitors, through having, say, a local residents' 'privilege' card. In such situations there is little choice other than to control visitor flows by influencing behaviour and/or to follow a programme of continual repair and maintenance. The significant aspect of many environmental matters is that the assets involved do not pass through the marketplace and the sheer number of agents involved in tourism, both public and private, with very different objectives and performance measures, make it virtually impossible to achieve concerted action other than through a regulating agency that has the force of law, which leaves little scope for market economics. The British experience, for example, has been that rarely have visitors or tourist businesses been charged directly for the social and environmental costs generated

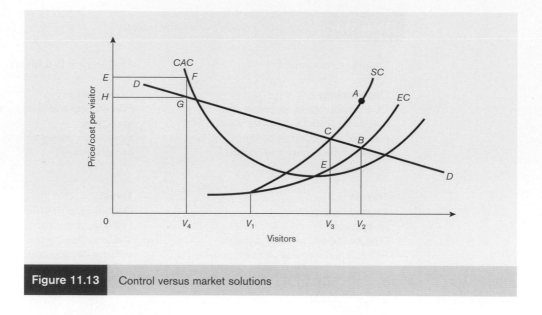

Figure 11.13 Control versus market solutions

by their actions at the destination. The money is paid indirectly through general taxation and most of the burden of coping with congestion, litter and visitor management falls on the public sector, particularly local authorities. To this extent the government tries to take account of the influx of visitors in its support grant for local provision of public services. This is not to say that the 'polluter pays' principle through the application of 'green' taxes may not be appropriate in certain circumstances. Thus the Australian authorities raise a specific charge on visitors to the Great Barrier Reef, a popular destination that is under considerable environmental pressure, and the UK's Air Passenger Duty is claimed to be a tax to compensate for the greenhouse gas emissions caused by air transport.

The pure conservation solution requires that demand is driven back to V_1 by simply limiting the number of visitors, so that no social costs are incurred whatsoever and any social benefits that may be gained by expanding demand to V_3 are ignored. Such a position contrasts strongly with the ideas expressed in Table 11.1 and may be morally repugnant since it may conflict with the desirability of development for the welfare of the local community. A more extreme situation, one in which society becomes over-zealous in its actions, is depicted by V_4 in Figure 11.13. *CAC* represents the combined average cost curve of the tourism plant in the community. If demand is forced back to V_4 it may be seen that this plant is no longer viable, for the average cost of supply (point *F*) is greater than the average visitor spend (point *G*), and so in order to survive in the longer term the tourism enterprises have to be subsidised by an amount *EFGH*. One of the paradoxes of tourism is that those who do not see that their income is directly dependent on the tourism industry are frequently opposed to it, yet closing down the tourism plant reverses the multiplier process. Quite soon local businesses and employment are affected, and the economic rationale for the community may be impaired, which can affect the very jobs of those who are opposed to tourism development.

Regulation and market solutions to manage the tourism environment are not necessarily mutually exclusive. A compromise is to assign quotas at the conservation level V_1 to tourist enterprises, but at the same time allowing market forces to work by levying a graduated environmental charge on those businesses exceeding their quotas, or, in regulatory terms, requirements to undertake compensating environmental projects when businesses apply for planning permission to expand. The object here is to position society as near as possible to point *C* in Figure 11.13. To ensure that allocations are adjusted in an optimal manner, businesses are allowed to buy and sell quotas so as to reach a level appropriate to their own organisation. Currently, it is the excessive production of greenhouse gases that is causing most concern, which is why these principles have been embodied in carbon trading schemes devised by the EU. Destinations such as Canada, Ireland, New Zealand and Scotland, where the landscape is recognised as a major visitor attraction, are looking to innovative carbon off-set projects to maintain their competitive position. The concept of a carbon neutral destination is one that is considered to have significant tourism benefits.

Clearly, the model depicted in Figure 11.13 is not static. In times of growth this is of benefit, for it is politically less painful to refuse planning permission for new projects than it is to regulate existing operators. Over time it is expected that new technologies for mainten-ance and repair, and improved visitor management techniques will enable the SC schedule to be shifted to the right. This should allow a greater number of visitors to be handled at a lower cost to the environment, which is the essence of the sustainable tourism development argument depicted in Figure 11.12.

Attraction authenticity

It is the concern of social researchers that tourists should be given a genuine appreciation of the destination they are visiting. In too many cases, it is argued, tourists are given the impres-sion that the destination is some idyllic fantasy world, and that they are fooled into this by attractions, particularly events, that are staged and may have little relevance to the culture of the country. Thus the tourists do not see the real landscape and way of life of the host com-munity. This implies a loss of authenticity in the visitor experience. However, authenticity from the tourists' perspective is subjective and is of differing importance to different market segments. Some tourists do not want an authentic experience: the purpose of going to leisure or theme parks to participate on the rides is for entertainment and excitement.

The ideal situation is considered to be where both the host community and the visitor see the experience as authentic. However, given mass tourism flows, it is virtually impossible to meet the curiosity of visitors without staging events and certain aspects of historic attrac-tions. Many historic properties in Britain stage period tableaux to give visitors an impression of what living was like at those times. The visitor knows that they are staged, yet at the same time every effort is made by the provider to give the most authentic representation possible, even including the reproduction of smells, as in the Jorvik Centre in York, which places vis-itors in a 'time car' to travel around the re creation of a Viking village. Authenticity becomes questionable when the destination tries to conceal the staging of an event by giving visitors the impression that what they are seeing is real, when in fact it may be an artificially created event or belong to a time gone by and have no place in the current life of the community. Historic and cultural staging presents the visitor with the salient features of a community's heritage and reduces the need for encroaching on the private space of the host population. It may also generate pride and interest among the local community who have previously taken these aspects for granted.

CONCLUSION

Attractions are an integral – and important – component of the tourism product. As we note in early chapters, certain attractions are so alluring in their own right that they provide the sole motivation for a visit. However, for most attractions to survive and flourish, other elements of the tourism product must also be on offer at a destination, at a complementary level, quality and price, to support the attraction and to provide the tourist with the neces-sary supporting infrastructure and superstructure.

As an area of investigation and study, tourist attractions are becoming increasingly important. Their contribution to the overall tourism product has been recognised and, as new technology-based innovations have been applied in this domain, the profile of many tourist attractions has risen dramatically.

Attractions remain the focal point for new visitor management and control techniques that aim to alleviate the pressure of large numbers of tourists and to ensure natural resources are protected and sustained.

While there remains a debate about the effectiveness of these strategies, there exists also discord as to who should be responsible for investing in the development and maintenance of resources that are enjoyed by many groups, including the local community. The role of the public sector versus the private sector in attraction investment and management has become an important issue as both strive to balance the oft-conflicting needs of user groups and to enhance the quality of the attraction experience for all.

SELF-CHECK QUESTIONS

1. With reference to the contents of this chapter, what would you see as the main customer segments that are attracted to national parks?

2. In classifying attractions, how would you compare theme parks to, say, museums?

3. What are the main factors affecting the establishment of a new large-scale theme park attraction?

4. LEGOLANDs are a reflection of the LEGO toy. What other themed attractions are reflections of industrially produced products? Consider the advantages and disadvantages of this type of development.

5. How do you see attractions developing in the future?

ESSAY QUESTIONS

1. Critically evaluate existing methods of classifying attractions and examine the value of developing a single national strategy for attractions in a country of your choice.

2. Review the roles and responsibilities of public and private sector bodies in the provision and maintenance of tourist attractions in a country, area or region with which you are familiar.

3. Evaluate the implications on other aspects of the tourism system (such as tourism demand) as a result of the mix of attractions present at a given destination.

4. Assess the effectiveness of visitor management techniques employed at a tourist attraction known to you.

5. What role can 'hallmark projects' such as Disneyland® Paris play in the development of tourism?

ANNOTATED FURTHER READING

Books and articles

Fyall, A., Garrod, B. and Leask, A. (2003) *Managing Visitor Attractions: New Directions*, Butterworth Heinemann, Oxford.
This book provides a valuable contribution to the literature by providing a selection of contemporary themes, written by experienced academics and practitioners in the field. The book explores the nature and purpose of attractions, aspects relating to the development, management and marketing of attractions, and future trends and market developments.

Leask, A. and Fyall, A. (2006) *Managing World Heritage Sites*, Elsevier Butterworth Heinemann, Oxford.
This book covers a myriad of management issues encountered at cultural, natural and mixed UNESCO World Heritage Sites. It explores the role of tourism at such sites and provides a critical overview of ways in which tourism can be managed in a truly sustainable manner.

Stevens, T. (2000) 'The future of visitor attractions', *Travel and Tourism Analyst* 1, 61–85.
This report introduces a series of valuable insights into the future direction, development and management of visitor attractions. It has a truly international focus and identifies the significant shift in visitor trends expected over the coming years.

Swarbrooke, J. (2002) *The Development and Management of Visitor Attractions*, Butterworth Heinemann, Oxford.
This landmark textbook provides a highly suitable foundation for the study of visitor attractions. It is comprehensive in coverage and provides the reader with a considerable supply of examples from around the world.

Web sites

http://www.alva.org.uk/
This site is the home of the Association of Leading Visitor Attractions, which includes many of Britain's biggest and best-known attractions.

http://www.iaapa.org
A very comprehensive site provided by the International Association of Amusement Parks and Attractions (IAAPA). Membership of this site provides extensive coverage of a wealth of market information, current developments and trends, as well as a wide range of very useful links to other related web sites.

http://www.thrillnetwork.com
This site provides extensive news, facts and figures, and park trends and developments in the domain of theme parks. Although with a strong US orientation, coverage is comprehensive and insightful and useful from both a leisure and research perspective.

References cited

Boniface, B. and Cooper, C. (1987) *The Geography of Travel and Tourism*, Heinemann, London.

Clawson, M. and Knetsch, J. (1966) *The Economics of Outdoor Recreation*, Johns Hopkins University Press, Baltimore, MD.

Keep, E. and Mayhew, K. (1999) *The Leisure Sector*, Skills Task Force Research Paper No. 6, DfEE Publications, London.

Leask, A. (2003) 'The nature and purpose of visitor attractions', pp. 5–15 in Fyall, A., Garrod, B. and Leask, A. (eds), *Managing Visitor Attractions: New Directions*, Butterworth Heinemann, Oxford.

Middleton, V.T.C. (2003) 'A national strategy for visitor attractions', pp. 270–83 in Fyall, A., Garrod, B. and Leask, A. (eds), *Managing Visitor Attractions: New Directions*, Butterworth Heinemann, Oxford.

Murphy, P.E. (1985) *Tourism: A Community Approach*, Methuen, London.

Pine II, B. and Gilmore, J. (1999) *The Experience Economy*, Harvard Business School Press, Cambridge, MA.

Swarbrooke, J. (2002) *The Development and Management of Visitor Attractions*, Butterworth Heinemann, Oxford.

Wanhill, S. (2003) 'Interpreting the development of the visitor attraction product', pp. 16–35 in Fyall, A., Garrod, B. and Leask, A. (eds), *Managing Visitor Attractions: New Directions*, Butterworth Heinemann, Oxford.

Wanhill, S. (2006) 'Some economics of staging festivals: the case of opera festivals', *Tourism, Culture and Communication* 6(2), 137–49.

Watson, S. and McCracken, M. (2002) 'No attraction in strategic thinking: perceptions on current and future skills need for visitor attraction managers', *International Journal of Tourism Research* 4(5), 367–78.

Watson, S. and McCracken, M. (2003) 'Visitor attractions and human resource management', pp. 171–84 in Fyall, A., Garrod, B. and Leask, A. (eds), *Managing Visitor Attractions: New Directions*, Butterworth Heinemann, Oxford.

MAJOR CASE STUDY 11.1
LEGO Theme Parks

BACKGROUND

The growth of LEGOLAND parks came under the Global Family Attractions division of the LEGO Company and, as they are branded parks, their history and development has been, and still is, very much bound up with the core business of the company, which is toy manufacturing. The company is wholly owned by a Danish family, the Kirk Christiansens, which is somewhat unusual for an organisation of this size. Since the early 1960s the company has become truly international: at its largest it had 57 subsidiaries spread around 30 countries, with worldwide sales of its product in over 130 nations, with some 8,400 employees and

Photograph 11.3   The entrance to the LEGOLAND Windsor theme park, a truly global tourism brand.
Source: LEGOLAND, Windsor, The LEGO Company

a turnover well in excess of US$1 billion, prior to the virtual standstill of the toy market in 2003. The basis of the company's growth has been the eight-stud plastic brick that offers creative play to children in the form of a new toy every day. This may be appreciated when it is realised that the mathematics of combinations dictates that six bricks can be combined in 102,981,500 ways.

HISTORY

Understanding some of the history of the company is significant for comprehending the development of the LEGOLAND parks as they are a cross between the usual themed ride park and the 'brand'. The story begins with Ole Kirk Christiansen establishing his joinery and carpentry business in Billund, Jutland, in 1916. But, like most of Denmark, Billund was an agricultural area that suffered greatly during the inter-war depression and in order to find alternative employment, since construction work had come to a halt, Ole started manufacturing wooden products in 1932, both household goods and toys, seeing particularly good prospects for the latter since children will always need playthings. In 1934 he called both his toys and his company LEGO, which is an abbreviation for the Danish words *leg godt*, meaning 'play well'. He also inscribed his aim on a wooden sign in his workshop that read 'Only the best is good enough', which has remained the motto of the company to this day.

The next major step took place in 1949 when, based on the ideas of an English inventor, Hillary Page, the company produced interlocking plastic bricks, but at that time sold only in Denmark. In 1954 Ole's son, Godtfred, realised that the bricks could be worked into countless combinations and developed the 'LEGO System of Play', which was introduced into the Danish market in 1955, using a town plan as the basis for building houses, shops and other buildings with small plastic bricks. But the breakthrough came in 1958, when the company patented a way to improve the clutching strength of the bricks (and therefore structural stability) by placing inner tubes inside the hollow

underneath part. In 1960 the wooden toy workshop burnt down and the company decided to concentrate on a single product idea: the LEGO building bricks. This 'one-brand company' phase was to last until 1979, when Kjeld Kirk Christiansen (Godtfred's son) took over as managing director and developed the product along the following lines: Duplo for the 1–3-year-olds; LEGO System for the 3–9-year-olds; LEGO Technic for the 9–16-year-olds; and LEGO Dacta for use in schools.

THE PARKS

As shown in Table 11.2, there are currently four parks, with the original in Billund being the best performer on average. The accepted thesis in the 'post-Fordist' society is that to retain market position suppliers should no longer sell goods with attached services but rather services with attached goods to create experiences so that each customer receives a bespoke package. It might be thought that the first park, opened at Billund in 1968 and generating around 625,000 admissions in that year, is an early development of this concept, but the reality was somewhat more indirect and personal, as it was born out of Godtfred's frustrations with disruptions caused by visitors to the factory and the desire to halt this and find an alternative solution to cater for the needs of visitors.

Its development came about from three sources of inspiration:

- Godtfred had seen a miniature park in Holland, which gave the idea for the 1-to-20 scale Miniland to be found in every park today;
- Godtfred was impressed with the Louisiana movement in modern art and hired its chief of exhibitions, Arnold Boutrup, to mastermind the development of the park;
- the creative ability of his cousin, Dagny Holm, in using the brick to make outstanding models.

Nevertheless, it has turned out that the Billund park, unlike its replicas Windsor and Carlsbad in California,

Table 11.2	LEGO global family attractions				
LEGOLAND	Opening year	Area (hectares)	Visitors 2000 (millions)	Visitors 2005 (millions)	Design standard (millions)
Billund, Denmark	1968	10	1.56	1.48	Site restricted
Windsor, UK	1996	60	1.49	1.42	1.40
Carlsbad, CA, USA	1999	52	1.40	1.33	1.80
Günzburg, Germany	2002	140	–	1.32	1.50

which principally serve the domestic resident population, has become an iconic international tourist attraction that reaches sacrosanct status among LEGO enthusiasts, since it is regarded as the natural home of LEGO. Replication has only served to elevate the standing of Billund, which does suffer from too many visitors on peak days, but this is difficult to control through 'de-marketing' methods because they are tourists, many being international, who are hard to reach through normal communications channels such as local radio announcements telling listeners that the park is likely to be full early on today.

The gap in park development is also explained along personal lines, arising from the involvement of the company in a consortium to create the Hansa-Park in Germany during the late 1960s. This was not a success and LEGO withdrew from the venture, leaving Godtfred determined neither to cooperate with anyone in the park business nor to undertake any park expansion outside Billund. At the beginning of the 1990s, under Kjeld's stewardship, the latter policy was changed and park development was seen as a way of growing the market for the core business. The planning for the Windsor project was started in 1990 and since opening it has been an undoubted accomplishment. The parks are planned along the following guidelines:

- The overall strategy is that their design and existence is to support the toy sales. Thus, for example, Castle Land/Hill is themed on the LEGO Castle Play System and the Dragon Ride contained within it tends to be the most popular activity. It is probably the most important themed area when it comes to linking the brand, the product and the company.

- Prospective locations are in regions where sales are substantial and there is strong brand awareness.

- They are family parks for children aged between 2 and 13 years and the investment requires a resident catchment area of around 20 million, with about 50% or more being target families.

- They should be located in an established tourist area yielding a steady flow of visitors.

- They should be within attractive rural surroundings with planning permission for leisure development.

- The minimum site requirement is 40 hectares.

- Support services in terms of suppliers and general tourist infrastructure should be locally available.

Designing theme parks revolves around market penetration rates in terms of the defined catchment area, and therefore the number of rides and attractions that would warrant the estimated penetration rates at the proposed admission charges. This requires considerable financial investment and in current terms the LEGOLAND parks cost about US$180–200 million each to build: to date, the company has financed these internally. The latter gives advantages in decision speed and ensuring minimal information leakages to competitors. For this money, taking LEGOLAND Deutschland as an example, there are around 40 rides and attractions covering 12 hectares of land, with a further 20 hectares allocated for parking and the remainder of the site will be used for administration, park expansion, woodlands and other 'green' areas. LEGOLAND Deutschland has a full-year staff of about 120 and a seasonal workforce of around 600 employees. Sponsorship of attractions is accepted but there is no franchising. The company mimics Disney in quality and this it sees as being achievable only through complete control so that every day can be seen as 'fresh as springtime' by the visitors.

Given that LEGO toys have a worldwide distribution, the aim is to develop each park optimally, but in a way that specifically supports the brand. A significant aspect of the development of the park at Carlsbad was to increase the US exposure of the toy and so boost market penetration. It follows therefore that the parks have a high degree of commonality in their imagescapes, save where local cultural adjustments are clearly necessary. Thus Legorado in Billund, which has a Wild West imagescape, is not suitable in California in the light of current American cultural attitudes towards this period of their history. As a counterpoint to the company's strategy, it should be noted that a new line of toys can fail or have a short lifetime, while investment in new rides in the parks is expensive as they have to be written off over four to six years. The risk is therefore that the parks end up with rides that have no reference to the LEGO product portfolio. The hybrid nature of the parks also has consequences for performance measurement: for example, it is customary to measure capacity in theme parks by ride throughput, but the LEGO parks have a great deal of 'soft' capacity in the form of workshops where model makers are on display and give advice to visitors. Similarly, Miniland is a passive visual activity that can absorb a variable number of visitors. Calculating the return on capital employed is also problematic as the role of the parks in uplifting toy sales creates a longer pay-back time.

STRATEGIC CHANGE

Towards the end of the 1990s the company set itself the mission statement of being the strongest global brand among families with children by 2005. But although acclaimed as the toy of the last century and widely admired by developmental psychologists for the scope it offers for children's inventiveness and experimentation, and by parents for creativity and the quiet absorption that results, the brick has been a casualty of the advance of high-tech gadgetry (with instant action and gratification) for older age groups of children against the simpler toys (and in this case a 'make and create' toy) of yesteryear. This has seen sales growth fall back, forcing the company to trim its costs and embark on new developments. The company fought back with the introduction of robotics (LEGO Mindstorms), Bionicle (LEGO Technic) and licensing agreements with the Walt Disney Corporation, Lucas Licensing Ltd (Star Wars) and Warner Bros (Harry Potter) to obtain characters. It will be readily appreciated that, from the perspective of the parks, the LEGO Company has no iconic children's characters as can be found in the theme parks of Disney or Universal Studios. However, these new products are fashion items, matching the achievement of the films as with the Harry Potter figures, and in 2003 with the turbulence in the toy market and no new films coming on stream, the company saw a significant fall in its global sales. Plans were mooted for further parks in Japan and the USA (Florida being an obvious choice), but in 2004 the company decided to focus solely on its core business, which was the LEGO brick. The result was a substantial downsizing (arguably 'rightsizing') of its activities to adjust its costs and assets to a lower revenue base, so as to bring the organisation into profit. As part of this rightsizing the company's direct owner-

ship and operation of the LEGOLAND parks were sold in July 2005 for around US$440 million to the Merlin Entertainments Group (owned by Blackstone Capital Partners) and replaced by a considerably smaller financial investment in the form of an ownership share of 15%. Merlin also operates other leisure attractions, such as the Sea Life centres, the Dungeons, and the Earth Explorer, and with 34 attractions worldwide and over 12 million visitors a year the Group is the second largest operator of leisure attractions in Europe. Apart from expanding existing parks Merlin plans to open a fifth park within the next few years.

Source: Adapted from Wanhill, 2003

REFERENCE

Wanhill, S. (2003) 'Economic aspects of developing theme parks', pp. 39–57 in Fyall, A., Garrod, B. and Leask, A. (eds), *Managing Visitor Attractions: New Directions*, Butterworth Heinemann, Oxford.

DISCUSSION QUESTIONS

1. What criteria would determine where Merlin is likely to develop a fifth park and in which location?

2. Building experiences around the core product by brand stretching has been very successful for many production companies. Has LEGO made the right choice?

3. To what extent does the 'hybrid' nature of the theme parks limit international expansion?

CHAPTER 12

Accommodation

LEARNING OUTCOMES

During this chapter, we will focus on the accommodation sector and some of the issues that currently influence it. The learning objectives for this chapter, therefore, may be defined as:

- identifying and assessing the scope of the accommodation sector of the hospitality industry;

- understanding the structure of the accommodation sector, the role of brands and the different ownership models that predominate;

- assimilating the sector's historical development and the effect of this on today's operation; and

- discussing some of the key issues that dominate the sector today and that will influence its future development.

Photograph: Hotel front, Merida, Mexico © Graham Meyer

INTRODUCTION

Accommodation or lodging is, by a long way, the largest and most ubiquitous sub-sector within the tourism economy. With few exceptions, tourists require a location where they can rest and revive during their travels through, or stay within, a tourism destination. We can therefore see that accommodation is an important support facility in Leiper's destination region and, with few exceptions, commercial accommodation facilities are found wherever tourists venture. Of course, there is great diversity in the size, type and organisation of this accommodation. This diversity ranges from:

- accommodation that provides for one or two guests in simple, home-style facilities, the 'bed and breakfast', to 'bedroom factories', hotels that operate with a capacity to cater for up to 5,000 guests;
- accommodation in a very basic, functional form, or in extreme luxury and opulence;
- ownership which can be private and informal, or accommodation that may be provided within units operated by major multinational organisations; and
- accommodation that meets the needs of guests with varying requirements and motivations for travel – for example, business, conventions, leisure and pilgrimage.

In short, accommodation is characterised by extreme heterogeneity and any attempt to generalise about the sector must take this into account.

In this chapter, we are primarily concerned with those establishments and organisations that provide places of rest and revival on a commercial and organised basis. We therefore give rather less consideration to lodging in the VFR sector where accommodation is, usually, within the family or friend's home of those being visited – this contrasts with what we might describe as the 'commercial home' within which paying guests are taken into a personal home on a business basis (Di Domenico and Lynch, 2007). Although VFR is, in many countries, the most important tourist motivation, its value to the commercial accommodation sector is generally more limited.

This chapter, therefore, is mainly concerned with:

- fully or partially serviced accommodation such as hotels, motels, rhyokan (a Japanese-style lodging house), aparthotels, guest houses, bed and breakfasts, and farmhouses;
- self-catering accommodation such as apartments, country cottages, gites, campus accommodation, camping and static caravan sites, and timeshare;
- accommodation support facilities where provision is made for campers, caravanners and trailer owners who bring their own accommodation with them, in other words mobile sites; and
- accommodation within mobile transportation such as cruise ships, ferries, trains and airliners.

These accommodation types vary in their importance and contribution to both domestic and international tourism. There are also close links between accommodation providers and other sectors within tourism where the cross-sectoral characteristics of tourism organisations are increasing with integration in the tourism industry. For example, hotels have always been major providers of food service but this role has, as we shall see, changed significantly in recent years. Hotels are also, however, major providers of leisure, sporting and entertainment facilities as well as business and conference services. Likewise, accommodation's relationship with transportation is one of long-standing but it is one that is increasing in its sophistication and complexity, as transport providers recognise that accommodation can be an attraction to guests in its own right and not just a necessary service to be provided en route.

ACCOMMODATION AND THE TOURISM PRODUCT

In the context of the tourism sector in general, accommodation rarely has a place or ratio-nale in its own right. It is rare for a tourist to select to stay in a hotel or other form of accom-modation for its own sake. Rather, the choice is made because the accommodation provides a support service for the wider motivation that has brought the visitor to the destination, whether for business or leisure purposes. It is arguable that some resort hotels may fall out-side this generalisation in that guests may choose to stay at Greenbriars or Gleneagles because of the accommodation experience that such hotels provide but, generally, this motivation will be coupled with the desire to avail themselves of a wider tourism product within the resort or locality.

Accommodation is a necessary component in the development of tourism within any des-tination that seeks to serve visitors other than day-trippers. The quality and range of accom-modation available will both reflect and influence the range of visitors to a location. As such, achieving the appropriate balance of accommodation to meet the destination's strategic tourism development objectives can be a challenge. It is arguable, for example, that the inability of traditional destinations such as the Isle of Man to create new market opportu-nities in the wake of the decline of its traditional visitor base (family holidays) was directly linked to its old and inflexible accommodation stock. We can identify situations where accommodation is seen as part of the overall tourism infrastructure without which tourists will not visit the location. It therefore also assists in attracting wider investment in the tourism product at the locality. For example, the province of Newfoundland, in Canada, built four hotels in strategic locations as part of its tourism development strategy in the early 1980s. Accommodation can also feature as an element in wider economic development strategies. Similarly, the town of Akueryi, in Iceland, built and operates a hotel at a deficit because it is seen as an essential support facility for wider economic development, particu-larly in the fisheries sector. Accommodation, therefore, has an integral but varied role as part of the wider tourism product.

Accommodation also plays an important role in the overall economic contribution which tourism makes at a local and national level. It is difficult to generalise about the proportion of total tourist expenditure that is allocated to accommodation because this varies greatly according to the market, accommodation type and nature of product purchased. As a very general rule, perhaps 33% of total trip expenditure is allocated to this sector but this varies greatly between different market segments. It decreases in the case of fully inclusive packages to, for example, the Mediterranean resorts where intermediaries negotiate low-cost bulk pur-chases of apartments or hotel rooms. By contrast, the proportion may be considerably higher in the case of domestic tourism where transportation costs are, generally, lower than is the case with international travel. Accommodation may be sold as a **loss leader** to promote expenditure on other components of the tourism product in casino and other specialist resorts. Off-season offers are frequently promoted whereby hotel rooms are provided 'free' on condition that guests purchase a specified minimum in terms of food and beverage. This strategy recognises important dimensions of the accommodation sector:

- demand is highly volatile and fluctuates on a seasonal and weekly basis; and
- accommodation can act as the catalyst for a range of additional sales opportunities within complex tourism and hospitality businesses – traditionally, casino hotels have discounted accommodation in anticipation of generating considerable profits from customers at the gaming tables, while golfing hotels may seek to generate profits from green fees rather than room revenues.

Indeed, accommodation pricing in general is a complex and, sometimes, controversial area. Rack room rates (those formally published as the price of the room) are rarely achieved and extensive discounting for group bookings, advance reservations and corporate contracts are widespread. Fixed pricing is generally only successful and commonplace within the budget hotel sector. Yield, measured against potential, often runs at little more than 60% in the mid- to upper-market levels of the hotel industry in some countries, although locations such as Hong Kong are very different and see occupancy percentage rates running in the high 80s and above. Yield maximisation systems are in place, within most large companies, in order to ensure that achieved rates are designed to optimise occupancy potential. Managing contracts in order to maximise yield is also an important strategy for accommodation units with the objective of replacing low yield groups or aircrew business with higher yield business or fully inclusive tour (FIT) guests.

DEFINING THE ACCOMMODATION SECTOR

Hotels

Hotels are undoubtedly the most significant and visible sub-sector within accommodation or lodging. Although a highly varied collection of properties in most countries, hotels are the tourism sub-sector that provides the greatest total employment in global terms and probably accounts for the highest level of receipts. The traditional view of a hotel was an establishment providing accommodation as well as food and beverage services to short-stay guests on a paying basis. This view has influenced most attempts to define hotels. But, as we shall see later in this chapter, this is a somewhat inadequate description in view of the growth of ancillary activities commonly associated with the hotel sector (leisure, business, etc.) and the withdrawal of many hotel companies from the operation of food and beverage services entirely.

In many countries of the world, hotel businesses are dominated by small, family-owned operations, which have developed hand in hand with the tourism sector often earlier in the twentieth century and, in particular, since 1945. Thus, the typical hotel business is represented by 30-bedroom seafront establishments in resorts, country house hotels or the wide range of city properties. This small business sector has declined in importance in recent years, faced with the challenge of branded multiple operators offering a range of products from budget to luxury. The cost of reinvestment in order to meet changing consumer demand combined with the marketing and operational challenges posed by technology have forced many hotels of this kind out of business. Those that do survive successfully in the contemporary tourism industry do so because they have recognised the importance of niche marketing by tailoring their products and services to meet the specific niche requirements of identified market groups. An important survival strategy for small, independent hotels is membership of a marketing consortium representing similar operations at a national or international level. Best Western and Golden Tulip are two of the best-known international consortia.

The group or chain component of the hotel sub-sector accounts for upwards of 10% of the property stock in most European countries but this figure is much higher in South-East Asia and in North America. In terms of the bedroom inventory of most countries, the percentage penetration of groups/chains is rather greater:

- up to 40% of the total in the UK; and
- over 60% in the USA.

This reflects the fact that hotels that are part of multiples tend to be considerably larger (and generally more recently built) than independents. The almost universal trend in the hotel sub-sector is for multiples to gain market share from independent operators within expanding markets.

Ownership and management of hotels reflect the growing complexity of business formats within the private sector generally. There are three major operating models with various combinations:

1. Hotel companies may *own and operate* the hotels that are marketed under their name or they may have a part equity stake in the property.

2. Alternatively, the hotel may be operated and owned by a *franchise partner* – this is a rapidly growing business format, especially within the budget market. Franchises may be operated at an individual property level or as part of a master franchise arrangement whereby a company owns or operates a large number of properties, typically at a national or regional level, under the umbrella of an established brand or brands. HFS Hospitality is an American company that operates master franchises on behalf of a number of established brands but manages these franchises, in large part, through individual local franchisees and owners. HFS is, thus, frequently referred to as the world's largest hotel company although its actual ownership is minimal.

3. Finally, the hotel company may *manage the property on behalf of an owner* – this is a common format at the top end of the international market, to be found in the portfolios of major companies such as Hilton, Hyatt, Inter-Continental and Marriott.

A major influence on the publicly quoted hotel sector in recent years has been that of increasingly focused performance demands placed upon operators by stock market investors. In the past, especially in Europe, average return on investment within the hotel sector was considerably below that achieved in other industrial and service sectors. This reflects in part the small business structure of hotel companies as well as perceptions of an operating culture that sets hotels apart from other businesses – one where the focus was on hospitality rather

MINI CASE STUDY 12.1
Thistle Hotels

Thistle Hotels is one of the UK's leading four-star hotel companies with 47 properties and a total of just under 11,000 bedrooms. Thistle Hotels tend to be located in key city centre and countryside locations and with 18 hotels in London alone is the capital's largest hotel group. Indeed Thistle Hotels boast they have:

an unrivalled choice of hotels, strategically placed in prime locations the length and breadth of Britain. Each offers something special for the business or leisure traveller.

BRIEF HISTORY

Mount Charlotte Investments entered the hospitality sector in the early 1960s by buying several hotel, pub and restaurant businesses. Robert Peel became an executive director in 1976; joint Managing Director in 1977 and Chief Executive in 1978. Shortly thereafter Mount Charlotte sold the pubs and restaurants and focused on hotels.

A DECADE OF EXPANSION

Between 1978 and 1988, Mount Charlotte acquired almost 50 hotels throughout the UK, predominantly in small groups. In the latter half of the decade, the strategic focus moved to large London properties with the purchase of 15 central London hotels, including the 690-room Mount Royal overlooking Oxford Street and The Barbican Hotel with 469 bedrooms.

STRATEGIC PURCHASE OF THISTLE

Mount Charlotte's most important strategic acquisition was that of 34 Thistle hotels from Scottish & Newcastle Breweries Plc in 1989, which made it the largest operator of hotels in both London and Scotland.

It also bought the Thistle brand, which since 1990 has been used to champion the upgrading of many of the Mount Charlotte hotels from three-star to four-star, and adopted the name as the parent company.

In 1990, Mount Charlotte was acquired by Brierley Investments Ltd and in 1991 Brierley sold 20% of its investment to the Government of Singapore and 10 per cent to Temasek Holdings.

In 1998, following Robert Peel's departure, Ian Burke, formerly of Bass Plc, was appointed as chief executive. Thistle Hotels announced the sale of approximately 30 provincial hotels, which did not fit in with the portfolio, and embarked on a three-year programme to strengthen the Thistle brand and position itself as a full service four-star hotel group with properties in more popular locations. As a result, the majority of hotels in the Thistle portfolio were renamed to reflect their locations and reinforce the Thistle brand, for example The Mount Royal in London will become the Thistle Marble Arch and The Portland in Manchester became the Thistle Manchester. The renaming of the hotels is only part of the programme as the brand will be further developed to ensure a consistent product and service experience. The company entered a period of continued investment and refurbishment and new brand standards were developed for both the product and hotel services.

In June 2003, Thistle became a 100% owned subsidiary of Brierly International Ltd. Over the last five years Thistle has invested more than £230 million to improve the quality of hotel facilities available throughout the UK. Under new ownership, Thistle plans to carry on with its investment programmes throughout the entire company. Phase 1, which sees capital expenditure within key hotels throughout the group, is already in place.

Recent initiatives have seen a concentration on improving customer service through an analysis of internal and external assessments. The overall strategy is aimed a providing a 'feel at home' environment for all guests and a desire to exceed guests' expectations.

The increased involvement of Briery International Ltd has seen the development of sales and marketing alliances with Affinia Hotels & The Benjamin, First Hotels and Rotana Hotels. These alliances have been developed to provide an international network of hotels within selected key markets.

DEVELOPMENT OF THE PRODUCT AND BRAND

Thistle's goal is to continue to develop a full service hotel chain that operates under a strong and widely recognised brand. The Thistle brand aims to stand for the whole guest experience – not just accommodation but food, drink and leisure. CoMotion is one example of a 'brand within a brand' – a classy, friendly fusion of New York deli and Italian café. Faya and Gengis Restaurants, offering a variety of Asian and Mediterranean dishes, are signature food and beverage outlets in most Thistle hotels, but many hotels also provide individual restaurants that utilise local produce and provide guests with a unique food and beverage experience. Fourteen Thistle hotels offer Otium Leisure Clubs, which provide guests with leisure and spa facilities.

For the business traveller, Thistle offers hotels in most business centres including Aberdeen, Birmingham, Bristol, Cardiff, Edinburgh, Glasgow, Liverpool, Manchester and Newcastle. In addition, there are Thistle hotels in resort areas such as the Thistle Stratford-upon-Avon in Shakespeare country, the Thistle Grasmere in the English Lake District and the Thistle Brighton situated on the sea front of this popular south coast resort.

THE CURRENT STRATEGY FOR ACHIEVING BUSINESS SUCCESS HAS FOUR ELEMENTS

- To establish, maintain and improve brand, product and service standards in all aspects of a full service hotel operation.
- To improve operations management in rooms inventory, food and beverage provision and the meetings business.
- To focus hotel asset management on upgrading the portfolio – by improvement, acquisition or disposal.
- To underpin these profit drivers with business support in information technology and people management.

Source: www.thistlehotels.com

Photograph 12.1	An example of a luxury hotel development in Dubai where the development of the hotel itself contributes to the prestige image of the resort.

Source: Jumeirah International

than profitability. The view was that the two were, in some way, incompatible. This perception lost its primacy in North America some time before influencing the European industry. The success of many Asian companies in combining the two objectives of profitable service and excellence has led to change in Europe as well. Companies such as Accor, Marriott and Premier Travel Inn, each owners and operators of a portfolio of different hotel brands, now operate to profit criteria designed to satisfy City interests as their first priority. In this context, Le Meridien's Welcome Charter (included in Mini Case Study 12.3 discussed later) demonstrates that hospitality and profitability *can* be entirely compatible objectives within the accommodation sector.

Guest houses, bed and breakfasts, farmhouse accommodation, inns

This sub-sector brings together a number of different types of operation with the common characteristics of offering accommodation plus some food and beverage (often just breakfast) in a small, family-style environment. Such properties may provide many similar facilities to smaller hotels, although the category also includes simple and limited operations where guests may share facilities and, indeed, meals with their hosts.

Internationally there are significant contrasts in the operation of this sub-sector:

- In the UK, bed and breakfast and guest house enterprises are not significantly different, although the former require fewer controls in order to operate. Indeed, it is a sub-sector where many operators take guests on a seasonal or sporadic basis and, as a result, can offer a flexible accommodation resource to a city or locality, available for use as and when required, but without large fixed costs, particularly in terms of labour.
- Bed and breakfast enterprises in the USA, however, tend to be rather more sophisticated in their approach and comprehensive in their services. In European terms, they resemble inns or small hotels and are frequently members of national or regional marketing consortia.
- In Canada, inns are similar and can be grouped together on a themed or regional basis for marketing purposes. The Historic Inns of Atlantic Canada is one example and membership depends upon a number of criteria, of which one is age – all properties must have been built before 1930. Some Canadian inns offer very sophisticated facilities. One example is the Spruce Pine Acres Country Inn in Port au Port, Newfoundland, which is a modern, purpose-built facility with just six bedrooms, but its services also include a licensed dining room, a well-equipped meeting room and full electronic business provision.

Farmhouse accommodation is a central component in the growing international agritourism movement. Not only has this become a major feature of tourism development in a number of countries such as Ireland and New Zealand, but it is also a component in the development plans of countries in Eastern Europe and Asia. Accommodation is, generally, similar to that afforded by bed and breakfast operations but the context is different. Provision is usually within a working farm environment and guests may be able to participate in various aspects of the agricultural working routine as part of their stay. Marketing of farmhouse accommodation includes consortia operating at a national and/or international level.

Small, independent operators across this sub-sector face significant challenges from the growing budget hotel sector, especially in Europe. In physical product terms, there may be considerable similarities between the two in terms of their bedrooms – indeed, budget properties may well exceed the competition in this respect. For example, the growth of the budget sector has forced the generally unregulated family-style property in the UK to upgrade their facilities or to cease operating. As a result, many such operations now provide en-suite bathrooms, multi channel television and tea and coffee-making facilities.

Self-catering accommodation – apartments, cottages, gites, etc.

Self-catering accommodation is an important and varied component of the lodging sector within tourism. Essentially, what such properties have in common is a combination of accommodation with additional recreational areas and the facility to prepare food on a personal basis. Apartments form a major element within the accommodation available in many Mediterranean resorts but the sector also includes:

- individual cottages and gites – frequently adapted from normal residential use; and
- purpose-built cottage colonies developed and marketed as a distinct brand – for example, Rent an Irish Cottage, established in 1968 by Shannon Development (a public sector body) but subsequently sold off to private interests in the early 1990s.

Self-catering holiday accommodation may be rented as part of a vacation package, through an agency or independently directly from the owner. Alternatively, holiday accommodation ownership is a major component in the tourism industries of some countries and specific destinations. This is so much so in some places that in the off-season communities can be just a fraction of those at peak periods. In some countries, ownership of a country or beach cottage is commonplace and not confined to the wealthy, as in Scandinavia – for example, Norway with the seaside or mountain *hutte*. Where holiday homes are not purpose-built but purchased within the normal housing environment, they can create considerable distortion to the local property market and resentment within local communities through rising prices that exclude younger residents from the local housing market. North and West Wales and the coastal regions of Cornwall are examples of areas where holiday homes from time to time have become a sensitive political issue. In Denmark, the ownership of second homes is confined to people residing in the country for taxation purposes, which excludes the offshore ownership that can be found in many Mediterranean destinations. The community issues arising from second-home ownership are reviewed and discussed in more detail in Part 2, dealing with the impacts of tourism.

It is quite common for local residents' homes to form the accommodation for self-catering vacations. This may be through a number of mechanisms:

- House-swap schemes, by which a family from, say, Sweden, exchanges homes for a month with counterparts (often in the same professional or work area) from Canada; the exchange may include use of vehicles and responsibility for pets as well as accommodation.

- Major events can also prompt local residents to vacate their homes in favour of visitors on a pay basis – SW19 in London experiences much of this during Wimbledon tennis fortnight as does the village of Silverstone during the British Formula 1 Grand Prix weekend.

Campus accommodation

Campus accommodation includes facilities that are used both within and outside the tourism sector. For much of the time, most campus accommodation is used on a semi-permanent basis by students, as many readers of this book will know. However, increasingly, universities and colleges seek to utilise a resource that is underused during major periods of the year when students are on vacation. Accommodation is, therefore, widely used not only for conference and meetings purposes, but also as a leisure location, especially by campuses close to scenic or vacation areas. In addition, some campuses include permanent hotel-style facilities, designed for short-term visitors such as those attending executive development modules in business schools. Generally, the trend is towards upgrading facilities in campus accommodation so that its use for non-student lets is competitive with other accommodation providers. The marketing of campus facilities is also now professional – in Scotland, an umbrella organisation, the Scottish Universities Accommodation Consortium, is responsible for supporting this aspect.

Time-share

Time-share is a form of period-constrained (i.e. one or two weeks a year) self-catering, holiday home ownership, which provides additional benefits to owners in the form of possible access to similar properties in resorts throughout the world through exchange consortia. Many time-share properties also provide a range of additional services and facilities, including food service and sports/recreation so that they have much in common with resort hotels. Pressure selling of time-share has gained the sector a bad reputation in some countries.

Youth accommodation

Youth travel is an important, growing and little researched sector of the tourism market. The extent of such travel and the specific facilities designed to meet its needs vary greatly between countries. Young people tend to utilise accommodation at the low cost end of the market – bed and breakfasts, youth hostels such as those run by the Youth Hostel Association (YHA), Young Men's Christian Association (YMCA) and Young Women's Christian Association (YWCA) and their local equivalents as well as camp sites. Books such as *Cheap Sleeps Europe* (Wood, 2005) and *Eastern Europe on a Shoestring* (Stanley, 1997) provide information and listings of establishments with quality guidance based on user experience. Such information across the accommodation range is also increasingly available via web blogs which give potential customers a very direct source of information on guest experiences in establishments (see, for example, www.hotelchatter.com).

Specialist accommodation providers to the youth market, such as youth hostels in many countries, YMCA/YWCAs and backpacker hostels in Australia, have moved from offering simple, frequently dormitory-style accommodation, to providing greater comfort, a more sophisticated product and more comprehensive services. In some cases, there is little to distinguish these providers from equivalently priced hotel products – the YMCA in Hong Kong is a good example. These trends reflect changing youth market demand, expectations and travel experience together with the increasing affluence of young people in many countries.

Camping and caravan sites

An important component in the domestic and international tourism of many countries is that where visitors bring their own accommodation to the destination in the form of tents, caravans or trailers. The accommodation levels provided on these sites has improved greatly from the camping experience of earlier generations but is still restricted in terms of space and privacy. An important provider, within tourism, is the sub-sector offering sites for campers or caravanners. Such sites may be basic fields with few if any utilities provided or sophisticated resort locations including a range of comfort services as well as leisure, food service and retail options.

Some sites offer permanently sited tents or caravans and tourists travel to the locations for a one- or two-week stay. Companies, such as Eurocamp, package these site holidays in Mediterranean locations for north European clients on very much the same basis as hotel or apartment-based fully inclusive packages. Permanent caravan sites include vehicles for short-term let, as well as those owned by visitors who may use the accommodation on a regular basis throughout the season.

Medical facility accommodation

This area is not normally seen as part of the tourism industry although facilities in hospitals, especially private institutions, are close to the best available within tourism accommodation. However, some specialist medical facilities also offer quality accommodation to relatives and friends. This may be true of premium children's hospitals, for example.

Nursing homes and other long-stay facilities for the elderly, likewise, are not normally associated with tourism. However, this market has attracted increasing attention from hotel companies such as Accor and Marriott who have developed a long-stay product for the seniors market which is a hybrid of a luxury hotel and a nursing home, offering medical as well as leisure facilities within the one establishment.

In Eastern Europe, countries such as Romania have spa tourism where resorts offer integrated medical treatment and hotel accommodation at all levels from the very basic to the very luxurious.

Cruise liners and ferries

Long-distance passenger liners were, of course, the main form of transport for those wishing for transatlantic or intercontinental travel in the era that preceded the development of wide-bodied jets. Such liners provided functional accommodation to all but first-class passengers, designed as a necessary facility and ancillary to the prime purpose of transport. Likewise, ferries provided functional but limited accommodation services.

The growth of cruising from European and North American ports in the 1960s grew as an alternative use for the now-redundant liners and little attempt was made to alter the form of accommodation or the attendant facilities provided. Accommodation management also retained a marine and functional ethos. The building of dedicated cruise ships has changed the focus of on-board services from one where the main purpose was transport to an environment where the cruise itself became equally important to the destinations visited. The popularity of the 'cruise to nowhere' concept in South-East Asia testifies to this. Modern cruise ships have more in common with all-inclusive resorts than with traditional marine transport. From an accommodation perspective, they are designed to offer comfort, facilities and service comparable to that of equivalent resort hotels. Indeed, the terminology used and the culture is that of hotel services.

Ferries, too, have changed in a similar way, particularly those offering longer services between, for example, the UK and Scandinavia or Spain. Sea transport is explored in more detail in Chapter 14, which covers the different modes of transportation.

Trains and aircraft

Although luxuriously appointed accommodation as part of train travel has a long history, the more common model was that akin to seaborne comfort. The natural constraints of space, which railways impose on sleeping accommodation, are difficult to overcome and, as a result, most overnight sleeper facilities remain basic and functional. However, there has been a revival of luxury, on-train accommodation, spearheaded by companies such as Orient Express in Europe and between Singapore and Bangkok, as well as by a number of operators in India, Australia and South Africa. These trains, either modernised versions of old rolling stock or purpose-built, provide hotel comforts to the maximum permitted by space constraints.

Aircraft are faced with similar space constraints in providing sleeping accommodation for regular fare-paying passengers. A number of first-class products make claims to provide bed-like comfort for long-haul travellers, with similar provision but on a lower scale for business class. However, by comparison with their hotel equivalents, even the best of these products is akin to dormitory-style accommodation with a lack of real space or individual privacy, though the new Airbus 380, which is the world's largest passenger jet and can seat up to 800 passengers, offers considerable variations in configurations to raise the level of comfort. Most customer airlines are planning for 555 seats in a three-cabin layout.

Visiting friends and relatives

While outside the commercial accommodation sector, VFR tourists generally, but not exclusively, utilise facilities within the homes of their family or friends. As a result, their economic contribution to a community or region may be limited but, nonetheless, VFR constitutes a major element within the tourism industries of many countries, especially domestic tourism. In many developed countries, as family ties continue to weaken, it is likely that fewer and fewer people may use the VFR option. Where the return home is to a society that is markedly different from that where the tourists originate (for example, Afro- or Irish-American visitors to their roots), it is quite likely that commercial accommodation providers will be used for VFR trips, although payment may well be by the host family rather than the visitors.

THE DISTINCTIVE NATURE OF ACCOMMODATION

In addition to the heterogeneous nature of the accommodation industry discussed above, the hospitality and accommodation sector is distinct from other industries in three areas.

The first of these areas is the concept that hospitality and accommodation comprise both tangible and intangible factors. The tangible aspects of hospitality and accommodation would include the physical surroundings, the equipment needed to provide hospitality and accommodation, the decor, the location and perhaps the food and beverage that were consumed by the guest. The management of the tangible aspects of hospitality and accommodation are complex and guests will make judgements concerning the appearance and surroundings of a commercial accommodation provider in comparison to their expectations. Similarly, while the provision of food and beverage at its most basic level merely satisfies essential human needs, the dining experience often forms an integral aspect of the overall accommodation experience and the provision of food and beverage is considered important as it will influence a staying guest's lasting memories. In addition, the management of food and beverage is further complicated by the guest's not unreasonable expectation to be provided with food and beverage that has been appropriately and hygienically produced and served.

In comparison, the intangible aspects of hospitality and accommodation are potentially much more complicated than the tangible aspects and would include the atmosphere present in an establishment and, importantly, the service that the consumers of the product experience.

Most hospitality and accommodation products are a combination of both tangible objects and intangible performances or experiences. The tangible/intangible emphasis will depend on both the accommodation provider and the activity. For example, a guest's experience in a hotel restaurant will involve the combined effect of numerous intangible activities – including the acquisition of supplies, the preparation of the meal, and the serving of the meal. The tangible components behind all this – the building, the interior decor, the kitchen equipment, the table, the chairs, the cutlery and of course the food items are obviously necessary for the service, but it is the intangible service activities that make up the key product offering. On the other hand, while there will be greater emphasis on intangible aspects concerning the concierge activity in a hotel, it is the tangible aspects of accommodation provision that will outweigh the intangibles.

The second area concerns the inseparability of the production and consumption of goods and services in the hospitality and accommodation sector. Essentially this means that the guest has to be present during the production and consumption of the accommodation provision – the guest has to be present during the overnight stay. This is in contrast to the provision of a physical good, such as a washing machine that may be manufactured in China but consumed in the UK.

The concept of inseparability in the provision of goods and services in the hospitality and accommodation sector further means that the goods and services consumed by the guest or customer have no lasting value. While it is recognised that the guest will benefit from staying in a hotel overnight, apart from the memory of the stay the guest will experience no lasting physical benefit from the experience. Similarly, eating a meal in a hospitality provider will satisfy the customer's hunger; however, that customer will start to feel hungry again in four or five hours. Compare this to the purchase of a washing machine that will continue performing the task for which it was bought for a number of years.

The third area that distinguishes accommodation from other industries is the fact that it is immediately perishable. Essentially this means that accommodation cannot be stored and if it is not sold for any given night, the opportunity for the sale is lost forever. Even if all subsequent nights are full due to a sudden surge in demand, lost revenue from the previous empty night can never be recovered. Demand, therefore, plays an especially significant role in the production and delivery of accommodation. In certain accommodation situations where demand is steady, for example in public institutions, the concept of perishability does not pose a significant problem. However, the majority of accommodation providers experience seasonal fluctuations in demand, which affect both the management of accommodation provision and the nature of the investment. For example, in high latitude destinations where the main summer season is short, it is very difficult to justify more than basic hotel provision and in peripheral areas only chalet-style or static caravan developments may be justified.

THE MANAGEMENT OF COMMERCIAL ACCOMMODATION

While it is recognised that the management of commercial accommodation provision is a complicated business and it is beyond the scope of this chapter to discuss all aspects of this activity, this section aims to highlight two fairly unique aspects of the management of such businesses.

First, the concept of overbooking is relatively common within commercial accommodation. Overbooking is the act of selling more rooms than are actually available in an attempt to ensure that the accommodation element of the business is full. This activity has increased in popularity due to the number of reservation cancellations and no-shows that are experienced in commercial accommodation provision. For example, according to the reservation system, a hotel might be fully booked; however, guests' plans may change, resulting in their cancelling their reservation, or not informing the hotel and just not turning up. Depending on the time of year, the level of cancellations and no-shows might be as high as 15%, and in order to combat this hotels will regularly overbook by a similar amount.

Overbooking is however a sensitive activity and should a guest with a reservation turn up then, technically, the hotel has breached the contract with that guest. Due to potential legal liability and the substantial damage to the hotel's reputation and goodwill, some hotels have completely eliminated the practice of intentional overbooking. Others continue to take that risk in an effort to ensure that their hotel is completely full, but safeguard themselves by making out-booking arrangements with other properties, usually with an upgrade for the guest to compensate for the inconvenience.

Secondly, and in an effort more closely to manage the reservation system and as a means of ensuring the maximum number of rooms are full at any given time, accommodation providers have increasingly been adopting concepts such as yield or revenue management. Donaghy, McMahon and McDowell (1995) consider that yield management is a revenue maximisation technique which aims to increase the net yield (or revenue) through the predicted allocation of available accommodation capacity to predetermined market segments at optimum price. First developed in the airline industry (which also suffers from acute perishability) yield or, as it is more commonly known today, revenue management (Schwartz, 2003), has been adopted by many commercial accommodation providers. Essentially yield management means that the accommodation provider sells accommodation to the right people at the right price and at the right time. Practically speaking, the accommodation provider might examine historical reservation charts in an effort to identify periods of low demand. Thereafter, rooms that have proved difficult to sell in the past will be subject to marketing, advertising and discounting as a means of stimulating demand. The accommodation provider will adopt a flexible pricing policy based on the number of rooms available and the demand for those rooms. Indeed the cost of accommodation might increase the closer to the date the reservation is made. Thus it is usual for guests to be paying a variety of rates for staying in the same type of room, in the same hotel, on the same night. This activity will also assist accommodation providers in identifying periods of high demand and ensuring that rooms are not sold at a discounted rate, thus maximising yield.

SECTORAL OVERLAP

The accommodation sector may or may not exist in organisational isolation from other sectors of the tourism economy. In other words, there are operations that provide accommodation facilities and nothing else to their customers – some budget hotel products, self-catering cottages and campsites are examples of businesses where there may be minimal horizontal integration with other activities in tourism. By contrast, there are operations where accommodation is just one of a range of integrated tourism services provided by the one organisation. All-inclusive resorts and cruise ships, offering a wide range of entertainment, leisure, retail and food service facilities in addition to accommodation, provide good examples. The problem, from a definitional point of view, is that terms in the accommodation area are used very loosely so that the word 'hotel' may be employed to describe a small, family-owned bed and breakfast establishment, a budget hotel, a luxury country house property or an integrated resort such as Gleneagles in Scotland. As a result, official definitions are rarely of much value and are mainly used in order to regulate or grade the sector.

An important trend, in the hotel sector, is the disaggregation of accommodation from other aspects of hotel services, particularly in the moderate and economy sectors of the market-place. The customer may not always be aware of this disaggregation because it frequently represents a business rather than a service arrangement. Both Hallam and Baum (1996) and Espino *et al.* (2006) discuss the growing trend towards outsourcing food and beverage services within hotels, to either individual operators or to branded chain restaurants, allowing some hotel companies to concentrate on high-yield, low-cost accommodation provision while ensuring that their customers have access to appropriate food service opportunities. Other concepts, such as Embassy All-Suites in the USA, and Travelodge in the budget sector in the UK, have been designed as almost exclusively accommodation providers, encouraging guests to make use of external food service, leisure and entertainment facilities. This disaggregation process appears to represent a growing trend in the tourism industry at one end of the market. At the other end, increasingly sophisticated integrated all-inclusive resort provision points in the opposite direction.

SECTOR ORIGINS AND THE INFLUENCE OF THE USA

Accommodation has been a travel requirement since the first trading, missionary and pilgrimage routes were established in Asia and Europe in pre-Christian times. The basis of such accommodation was, generally, non-paying with travellers provided with a roof and sustenance as part of religious obligation or in the hope that similar hospitality might be offered to the host in the future. Possibly the first reference to commercial accommodation provision in Europe comes from thirteenth-century Florence but an identifiable commercial accommodation sector cannot really be identified until the late eighteenth century when coaching inns in Britain developed in response to organised stagecoach travel and the first large hotels were opened in France and the USA. The dawn of the railway era stimulated hotel development in many countries of Europe and elsewhere and the railway companies were among the main promoters of hotel building, proximate or integral to main termini in cities such as New York, London or Edinburgh. In many respects, these were the first hotel multiples or chains with which we are familiar today.

The latter half of the nineteenth century also saw increased travel stimulate the development of some of the great luxury hotels of the major capital cities of the world, many of which continue to set standards of luxury for the industry today. Hotels such as the Waldorf Astoria in New York, the Savoy, Dorchester and Claridges in London and the Ritz in Paris all date from this era. Raffles in Singapore and the Taj Mahal in Mumbai, while somewhat different in the motivation for their establishment, also date from the same period and represent a tradition of European-style accommodation or hotel-keeping which provided the dominant model until superseded by the American approach in the late 1940s and early 1950s. At the other end of the luxury scale, the growth of popular and accessible tourism options in most industrialised countries stimulated the development of low-cost seaside accommodation in resorts such as Deauville, Douglas, Blackpool and Atlantic City.

The post-1945 period saw the development of the American model of accommodation management and operations. Dominated, in its early days, by concepts of standardisation, risk-avoidance and the application of Fordian principles of mass production, the American model is one that has spawned most of the major hotel corporations which increasingly dominate the international accommodation sector: Hilton, Hyatt, Holiday Inn, Sheraton, InterContinental all have their origins in this concept of the hotel, although not all the companies in question are American-owned today.

The American influence on the contemporary accommodation or lodging sector has been profound and it is arguable that this source continues to dominate new ideas, products and systems. The European concept of professional hospitality has been very important, especially in translating service from the *mine host* environment of the small hospitality business

The purposes of accommodation classification are varied. They include:

- *standardisation* – to establish a system of uniform service and product quality that helps to create an orderly travel market distribution system for buyers and sellers;
- *marketing* – to advise travellers on the range and types of accommodation available within a destination as a means of promoting the destination and encouraging healthy competition in the marketplace;
- *consumer protection* – to ensure that accommodation meets minimum standards of accommodation, facilities and service within classification and grade definitions;
- *revenue generation* – to provide revenue from licensing, the sale of guidebooks and so forth;
- *control* – to provide a system for controlling general industry quality; and
- *investment incentive* – to give operators incentive to upgrade their facilities and services, in order to meet grading/classification criteria.

Accommodation classification, however, is not without problems. One of these relates to the subjectivity of judgement involved in assessing many key aspects of both the tangible and intangible elements of the accommodation experience such as personal service or the quality of products. As a consequence, many classification schemes concentrate, primarily, on the physical and quantifiable attributes of operations, determining level of grade on the basis of features such as

- room size;
- room facilities, especially whether en-suite or not; and
- availability of services – laundry, room service, 24-hour reception.

However, this is commonly done without any attempt to assess the quality of such provision or the consistency of its delivery. Other problems with classification schemes include:

- political pressures to offer classification and grading towards the top end of the spectrum to most hotels, thus creating a top-heavy structure;
- the cost of administering and operating a comprehensive classification assessment scheme, especially where subjective, intangible dimensions are to be included;
- industry objections to state-imposed, compulsory schemes; and
- the tendency of classification schemes to encourage standardisation rather than individual excellence within hotels.

Mini Case Study 12.2 is an extract from the research study undertaken prior to implementing changes to the VisitScotland (formerly the Scottish Tourist Board) scheme. Within this scheme, star grading (one to four stars) is based exclusively upon assessment of quality and will provide the headline information for consumer choice and information. Information on facilities will be provided in directories and similar publications. Thus, a small establishment, excelling in its service but limited in the range of facilities available for guests, could be graded as five star while a large, international property with a full range of product attributes (leisure, business) could be graded as three star on the basis of the quality of its service and products.

Quality and quality assessment are rooted in the culture and context of the country in which they are located. As a result, a five-star or de luxe hotel in South-East Asia will be significantly different from a property that purports equivalence in Turkey or the UK. At best (and even this is debatable), classification can provide a guide to national standards. Even this is not always the case. In Spain, for example, the level of tax that a hotel pays is related to its grade, with five-star properties paying more than twice the amount of four-star hotels. As a consequence, there are few five-star hotels in Spain and a clustering of four-star properties covering a wide range of standards. Hotels such as Sofitel, InterContinental and Crowne Plaza are classified as four star when, elsewhere in Europe, these hotel brands would

MINI CASE STUDY 12.2
Scotland's Commended Hotels

Scotland's Commended Hotels (SCH) is best described as an association of individually owned and managed country and town house hotels, ranging within the four to five star quality range. The hotels pride themselves on the individuality of their products and services, with a particular emphasis on quality ambience and personal attention to guest needs. The consortium came into being in 1990 when the then British Tourist Authority (now VisitBritain) discontinued its development promotion of distinctive regional and product collections.

SCH is a cooperative, organised on a membership basis with a democratic, participative structure, reporting to an elected Board of Directors. The focus of the organisation is on achieving consensus in its strategies and operations and thus ensuring that its members have shared market positions and stated values. The main purpose of SCH is to market the products and services of its membership within the domestic and international marketplace; to promote cooperation and guest referral; and to obtain purchasing advantage, on behalf of members, through volume arrangements.

Membership criteria include the requirement that hotels:

- are independently owned and managed;
- have high standards of food and beverage;
- are graded as a minimum of Four Crown Highly Commended within the scheme;
- have a maximum of 40 bedrooms;
- are individual and original in character; and
- are actively committed to SCH and participate in the activities of the consortium, particularly through brochure display and referral.

The strengths of SCH can be summarised as follows:

- association of top, independently owned hotels all having the same stated values;
- in comparison to the identified competitor organisations, it is a low-cost consortium to join;
- variety of hotel types, which are individual, personally managed and not standardised;
- comprehensive geographic spread, good range of prices, with quality products at each price level;
- strong market proposition of collectively good products;
- members directly involved in selling the products;
- VisitScotland support of the only cohesive consortium that represents the Scottish hotel product.

(With thanks to Dr Alison Morrison, Strathclyde Business School)

DISCUSSION QUESTIONS

1. From an organisational perspective, what effects, both positive and negative, can you identify that would occur as a consequence of an independently owned hotel becoming part of Scotland's Commended Hotels?
2. How would you exploit the characteristics of member hotels when marketing the SCH product?
3. What benefits and opportunities might be provided to staff who are employed in one of SCH's hotels?

attract higher levels. Indeed, neighbouring Sofitel and Novotel properties in Madrid are both classified as four star, making a mockery of parent company Accor's branding intentions where they are clearly differentiated.

Probably the major difficulty faced by hotel classification schemes in Europe and North America is how to include the growing number of budget or economy hotels within schemes without creating unworkable ambiguities. The modern budget or economy hotel room contains a comprehensive range of simple but comfortable furnishings and facilities in a spacious, clean and modern environment. The comfort to be found in such rooms is primarily related to the physical product and is, generally, offered with minimum levels of service. One effect of the growth within this sector has been to create very real problems for hotel classification systems, which find it difficult to accommodate physical comfort with the absence of services available to the guest.

The AA in the UK has created a special category to cater for budget accommodation, called 'lodges', as did VisitScotland as early as 1993. VisitScotland (STB, 1996) states:

> The introduction of this category [lodges] acknowledges the popularity and growing pro-vision of purpose built bedroom accommodation designed primarily to provide convenient overnight accommodation for short stay visitors. Many establishments of this nature do not provide meals or offer lounge facilities and are unlikely to meet the requirements of a normal Crown classification. These establishments will usually have 100% of bedrooms en suite and have restaurant or dining facilities nearby.

Budget hotels in Europe are a response to changing customer needs and expectations and their importance can be dated from the mid-1980s. Prior to their development, the con-sumer in search of low-cost accommodation would have patronised one of the large number of small, independent hotels, guesthouses or bed and breakfast establishments, generally at the unclassified, one- or two-star level, to be found in all Western European countries. Products and services were very varied – just the problem faced by Kemmons Wilson in the USA some 30 years previously. The option of quality, low-cost and modern accommoda-tion in the form of budget hotels, branded under names such as Formule 1, Travelodge, Premier Inn and Campanile, has moved a significant volume of demand away from tradi-tional operators and resulted in both widespread upgrading of facilities and business failure in this sector.

As a consequence, the overall quality of bedroom accommodation in the lower-priced seg-ments of the Western European lodging industry has improved significantly over the past two decades. The quality gap between this sector of the market, measured in physical prod-uct terms, and that provided by mid- to upper-sector hotels (three to five stars) has decreased greatly as a result and, with the growing impact of low-cost technology, this is a gap that is likely to narrow further. It is a reasonable expectation that, just as en-suite facilities, hot beverage equipment, international direct dialling (IDD) telephones and satellite television services are virtually the norm throughout much of the accommodation range, additional benefits (fax, Internet) will become available to properties at all levels and simultaneously.

The challenge for higher priced and graded accommodation providers, therefore, is to ensure clear market differentiation between their offering and that of the budget sector. However, as up to 50% of the custom of budget hotels in the UK is from the business market, this suggests that, at present, they are not particularly successful in doing so. The key differentiation that they are able to offer, given that physical attributes no longer provide such clear water, is that of service in its widest sense. There is considerable evidence that there is an accommodation market that is able and willing to pay considerably more for the benefits that attentive, individualised and problem-solving service provides. Balmer and Baum (1993) provide a theoretical explanation for this, based on the work of Herzberg.

Accommodation organisations place increasing emphasis on their ability to respond posit-ively to the service demands of their customers and companies such as Ritz Carlton and

Marriott have established international reputations for their focus on service. Mini Case Study 12.3 is taken from Le Meridien's Welcome Charter, designed to provide new staff with an induction into the group's service quality standards.

MINI CASE STUDY 12.3
Le Meridien

This case study contains an extract from Le Meridien's *Welcome Charter Manual* which contains guidelines for all departments within the company's hotels. The Charter is the outcome of guest surveys conducted within 20 hotels and 5000 members of the chain's 'Carte Noire' loyalty programme. In this case, we include the section entitled 'Welcome basics', which is applied to all departments of the hotel.

WELCOME BASICS

Mission statement

To be the Number One for quality and consistency in the international up-market hotel business.

Brand positioning

An international brand of hotels of four-star level and above, which serves business and leisure guests, and is European in character, French in origin and integrated with local culture.

We will deliver superior profitability by recognising that our guests are the most important people in our business and our employees are our most important resource. Suppliers will be treated as partners.

Respect for oneself and for guests

Performance Criteria

Appearance

- Uniforms must be impeccable and complete at all times (including polished shoes).
- Badges must be worn at all times.
- A neat appearance is essential:
  - neat, conventional hairstyle
  - tasteful, subtle makeup
  - discreet jewelry
- Immaculate hygiene at all times.

Language

- A warm, but never familiar approach.
- Direct, but not arrogant or vulgar.
- Distinct, precise diction.
- Controlled physical gestures.
- Greet the guest in the local language if appropriate but converse with them in the language that suits them best.

Posture

- Maintain dignified poise in every situation.

→

Caring for guests

Performance Criteria

The smile

- The most universal of all languages.
- Understood by everyone and the starting point for all welcome actions.

Consideration

- Know how to recognise and anticipate the expectations of our guests.
- All times, show courtesy and willingness to please.

Listen

- Know how to listen to a guest in order to assimilate both requests and complaints accurately.
- Never argue with a guest.

Be available

- Know how to stop doing something in order immediately to satisfy a request from a guest.
- Do not let guests repeat the same request to several departments. Do it for them.

Professionalism

Performance Criteria

Responsibility

- Always keep a cool head – whatever the circumstances.
- Know how to reassure guests.
- Remain vigilant to constantly ensure guest safety.

Efficiency

- Respond quickly and ensure that guest requests are always followed through.

Offer a choice

- Always find and propose alternatives to guests to avoid ever being unable to satisfy them.

Reliability

- Always honour a promise made to a guest.

Provide information

- Keep informed in order to be able to keep guests informed.
- Always inform guests if unforeseen circumstances arise which may cause problems.

Nurture a team spirit

- Make a positive contribution to the hotel's overall friendly atmosphere.
- Always support each other since guests notice this.

Source: Le Meridien

DISCUSSION QUESTIONS

1. How might Le Meridien assist employees to achieve the requirements detailed in the case study?
2. How might Le Meridien measure the effectiveness of the charter?
3. What other suggestions can you make that would further enhance working relationships between staff members?

THE ACCOMMODATION SECTOR AND ENVIRONMENTAL ISSUES

The accommodation sector is not one that we generally think of as evoking images of pollution and environmental degradation. However, the structure of the sector, with operational units widely dispersed in some of the most fragile natural environments as well as within ancient and historic cities, means that its environmental impact can be very significant at both macro and micro levels. Indeed, visitors' fascination with the most fragile natural, historic and cultural environments may create demand for accommodation in locations that, otherwise, would be totally off the beaten track.

The accommodation sector's impact, in environmental terms, is varied and complex. The key areas are included under the following subheadings.

Water use

Tourists are high consumers of water and many major tourist destinations are located in areas of potential or actual water shortage. Much of the water that visitors use during their time is within accommodation units – for baths, showers, in the swimming pool, laundry, maintaining green and attractive garden areas and sports facilities such as golf courses. Generally, tourists are less likely to visit destinations or stay in accommodation where there are restrictions on the use of water or where its quality is sub-standard. However, the long-term impact of unregulated water use by tourists can be very significant. In parts of southern Spain, for example, the permanent lowering of the water table affects other economic activities, notably agriculture. Likewise, rice farmers in Phuket, Thailand have had restrictions placed on their cropping seasons in order to preserve water for tourists. Sectors of the accommodation industry have responded to the pressures of a finite water supply and also the increasing tendency to charge businesses for consumption by activating varied water conservation measures. Towel reuse opportunities are in place in many hotels, whereby guests are asked to indicate which of their towels require laundering and which can be reused. Some hotels, such as the Holiday Inn in Phuket, has its own water treatment plant which permits sufficient treatment of waste water to allow for its use in the hotel's gardens and leisure facilities.

Energy use

Reducing energy use, whether for heating in a winter climate or air-conditioning in hot climates, has clear environmental as well as financial savings to the business concerned. The *Hong Kong Guide* identifies practical routes to energy conservation within all departments of hotels. Computer technology permits the more effective control of energy, whether heat, air-conditioning or light, and it is possible, for example, to close down rooms, corridors or whole blocks automatically if vacated by guests.

Recycling

Reuse of paper products from reception and administrative areas, replacement of individual shampoo sachets in bathrooms with dispensers and the avoidance of disposable tableware are examples of how the accommodation sector can recycle items normally bound for disposal.

Waste disposal

Accommodation operations, especially large hotels, create large amounts of liquid and solid waste, which requires sensitive disposal. In some situations, especially small island locations such as the Maldives, disposal is a major problem and solid waste may need to be shipped off island for disposal. In some countries, hotels quite freely dispose of liquid waste directly into the sea or rivers. This can be seriously damaging to health and the environment.

Fragile nature

Hotels and other accommodation units located within fragile natural environments (such as safari lodges) pose major threats to the fauna and flora of such locations. Such environments need to be managed with appropriate sensitivity so that guests are not disappointed in their experience but, at the same time, their presence does not destroy the very resource they have come to experience.

The critical concern here is one of the education of both employees within accommodation units and of their guests in the importance of environmental sensitivity and responsibility. The accommodation sector's role, in environmental and conservation terms, is not entirely negative. The contribution to the conservation and, indeed, enhancement of historic houses and castles in many parts of the world, adapted for hotel use, cannot be ignored for these are properties which may otherwise not have found another suitable use without conversion to accommodation facilities.

INFORMATION TECHNOLOGY AND THE ACCOMMODATION SECTOR

In common with all other areas of services and, indeed, most areas of tourism, the accommodation sector is increasingly influenced by developments in the information and communications technology field (see Chapter 20 for a full review of information technology in the hotel industry). In many respects, technology has permitted the creation of highly labour-efficient and quality product budget or economy units by centralising all non-customer contact functions (reservations, marketing, finance) and allowing the property to concentrate on the delivery of a limited but consistent product. Technology impacts both at the unit level, within accommodation, and in terms of macro marketing and financial aspects:

- **Unit level.** Technology is the key to the efficient management of resources at unit level – energy, stock, human and financial. The training implications for effective use of technology in the small accommodation business, is an issue that is not widely recognised.
- **Macro level.** The significant development at this level is the increasing dominance of global distribution system (GDS) as the lead method of securing market share and marketing advantage for major accommodation brands. At the same time, cost of participation within GDS means that small companies and independent operators have had difficulty from this technology-driven avenue of reaching key customers unless they were able to establish sufficient market presence through participation in an established consortium such as Best Western.
- **The Internet.** This has allowed small operators to bypass the power of the GDS, either directly through their web site, via email or through locally organised reservation bureaux that arrange bookings online. For example, it is rare for small hotels or bed and breakfast establishments to take in passing trade. Most guests arrive from prior bookings, if only by email. From the perspective of consumers, this has opened up a much wider choice of accommodation, allowing the small operator the chance to 'niche' market his or her product.

HUMAN RESOURCES AND THE ACCOMMODATION SECTOR

Service-intensive businesses within accommodation are also labour-intensive and are always likely to remain so. This is despite considerable improvements in:

- productivity through use of technology;
- training;

- systems efficiency; and
- management effectiveness.

There are few significant labour-saving initiatives that can drastically reduce the level of employment in, say, housekeeping. By contrast, the budget or economy sector is able to provide a quality product without significant service levels through minimising the level of staffing employed.

In spite of significant changes to the use and productivity of labour within the sector, accommodation remains an area that provides employment opportunity for a wide range of skills and aptitudes, reflecting not only the diversity of businesses that operate under the accommodation umbrella but also the variety of tasks that working in the sector demands. In many communities, accommodation businesses contribute socially by providing employment opportunities for people who would find it difficult to work in other sectors of the economy. Accommodation also provides relatively easy access to employment for new immigrants (legal and illegal) as well as those entering the labour market for the first time (school leavers, students). These positive dimensions must be counterbalanced by recognition of perceived and actual problems with respect to work conditions, pay and general industry image issues, especially in developed countries. These issues and their wider human resource implications are addressed in detail elsewhere (Baum, 2006).

CONCLUSION

In this chapter, we have addressed the largest and, arguably, the most important sub-sector within tourism at a domestic and international level. The purpose of the chapter has been to demonstrate the position of accommodation within the wider tourism sector and to show how its diversity meets the requirements of virtually all tourism market groups. The origins of the accommodation sector are considered and the dominant influence of the US model of commercial hospitality discussed. Issues such as standardisation, the management of standards and the accommodation sector's environmental responsibilities are addressed.

Accommodation is a rapidly changing sector within tourism and, as a consequence, it is an area where many businesses are casualties in the face of competition from new products and service/product standards. It is unlikely that the pace of change will slow in the foreseeable future.

SELF-CHECK QUESTIONS

1. In what ways has the accommodation sector changed since 1945 and what effect has this had on the wider tourism industry?
2. Account for the diversity in the accommodation sector between different countries and regions.
3. Given its diversity, how can the accommodation sector provide meaningful comparisons of quality?
4. Review and discuss the key issues facing the accommodation sector and their likely impact in the future.
5. What are the benefits, to the small independent hotel, of participation in a marketing consortium such as Scotland's Commended Hotels?
6. What practical problems might occur with the cooperative model used by SCH?
7. What are the unique characteristics of accommodation? Can you think of any other special features that characterise the accommodation industry that are not found in other service businesses?

ESSAY QUESTIONS

1. Critically examine the impacts on the wider accommodation sector of the trend towards greater consolidation and concentration among international hotel groups.

2. Recent years have seen a significant growth in the demand for and supply of budget-style accommodation. To what extent has this trend impacted on the future strategic direction of other 'non-budget' hotels and hotel groups?

3. Evaluate the application of yield management techniques across the full range of accommodation types. What are the benefits and drawbacks of its application in each?

4. Examine the extent to which online developments and Internet bookings may have changed customers' buying behaviour towards their choice of hotel.

5. What factors have underpinned the development of resort-based hotels and to what extent are future tourism trends compatible with such developments?

ANNOTATED FURTHER READING

Books

Kandampully, J. (2002) *Services Management: The New Paradigm in Hospitality*, Pearson Education Australia, New South Wales.
This book adopts a services management approach to the study of hospitality and provides a critical overview of four key aspects for readers. The first part of the book introduces and examines the service paradigm while the second part explores the domain of services quality. Part Three then introduces the area of marketing of services before concluding in the fourth part with an examination of services growth and the pursuit of excellence. A very interesting book which provides some valuable insights for readers.

Olsen, M., West, J. and Tse, E. (1998) *Strategic Management in the Hospitality Industry*, John Wiley & Sons, New York.
This book explores the dynamics of strategy in the context of hospitality. It introduces the various stages of the strategic management process and offers a number of very useful examples which blend the theoretical and practical aspects of strategy. The book closes with valuable coverage of managing service quality and the relationship between leadership and strategy.

Rutherford, D.G. (2002) *Hotel Management and Operations*, John Wiley & Sons, New York.
A very useful book which examines the various management and operational aspects of the hotel sector.

Yu, L. (1999) *The International Hospitality Business: Management and Operations*, Haworth Hospitality Press, New York.
This book provides a comprehensive overview of the international hospitality industry and is primarily designed to cover the complex and difficult issues faced by hospitality managers when they are assigned to work overseas. The book introduces the international business context, the geography of hospitality developments, and provides a very useful overview of the differences in cultural, political and economic systems throughout the world. The book also provides valuable accounts of organisational structures and development strategies, and offers comprehensive coverage of the various hospitality management functions. The book concludes with a look to the future and those issues impacting on the industry in the years to come.

Web sites

http://www.ehotelier.com

A very comprehensive news and features-related web site of the international hotel sector. The site provides a 'one-stop shop' for the hospitality researcher.

http://www.shangri-la.com

The corporate web site of the Shangri-La corporation. In addition to the consumer aspects of the web site, there exists a good supply of material for those wishing to keep abreast of developments within the corporation.

http://www.wiredhotelier.com

Another very comprehensive news and features-related web site with considerable coverage of the international hotel sector. It provides a valuable resource base for practitioners, academics, researchers and students with a wealth of useful information online.

References cited

Balmer, S. and Baum, T. (1993) 'Applying Herzberg's hygiene factors to the changing accommodation environment: the application of motivational theory to the field of guest satisfaction', *International Journal of Contemporary Hospitality Management* 5(2), 32–5.

Baum, T. (2006) *Human Resource Management for Tourism, Hospitality and Leisure. An International Perspective*, International Thomson, London.

Di Domenico, M. and Lynch, P.A. (2007) 'Host/guest encounters in the commercial home', *Leisure Studies*, Vol. 26.

Donaghy, D., McMahon, U. and McDowell, D. (1995) 'Yield management: An overview', *International Journal of Hospitality Management* 14(2), 139–50.

Espino, T., Lai, P. and Baum, T. (2006) 'Make or buy service operations in the hotel businesses. An empirical application in Scotland', Proceedings of Euroma Conference, Glasgow, June.

Gee, C. (1994) *International Hotels. Development and Management*, Educational Institute of the American Hotel and Motel Association, East Lansing, MI.

Hallam, G. and Baum, T. (1996) 'Contracting out food and beverage operations in hotels: a comparative study of practice in North America and the United Kingdom', *International Journal of Hospitality Management* 15(1), 41–50.

Nickson, D. (1997), 'Continuity or change in the international hotel industry', pp. 213–28 in *Hospitality, Tourism and Leisure Management: Issues in Strategy and Culture*, Foley, M., Lennon, J. and Maxwell G. (eds), Cassell, London.

Schwartz, Z. (2003) 'Hotel revenue management with group discount room rates', *Journal of Hospitality and Tourism Research* 27(1), 24–47.

Stanley, D. (1997) *Eastern Europe on a Shoestring*, Lonely Planet, London.

STB (1996) *Quality Assurance*, Scottish Tourist Board, Inverness.

Wood, K. (2005) *Cheap Sleeps Europe: The Definitive Guide to Cheap Accommodation*, Robson Books, London.

MAJOR CASE STUDY 12.1
Shangri-La Hotels

INTRODUCTION

The story of Shangri-La Hotels and Resorts was created in 1971 when a de luxe hotel was founded in the city of Singapore. Today, Hong Kong-based Shangri-La Hotels and Resorts group is the largest Asian-based de luxe hotel group in the region. In addition it is regarded as one of the world's finest hotel management companies, receiving international awards and recognition from prestigious publications and industry partners.

The name Shangri-La was inspired by James Hilton's legendary novel, *Lost Horizon*; a tranquil haven in the mountains of Tibet, Shangri-La cast a spell on all who resided there. Today, Shangri-La stands as a synonym for paradise. Even though mythical in origin, the name perfectly encapsulates the genuine serenity and service for which Shangri-La Hotels and Resorts have come to be recognised.

The Shangri-La brand comprises 52 de luxe hotels and 10 resorts in key cities of Asia and the Middle East and most sought-after leisure destinations. New properties are under development in Europe and North America, with scheduled opening dates between 2009 and 2012. Most of these hotels and resorts bear the Shangri-La logo and represent the majority of establishments within the chain. Located in city and resort destinations, without exception, these hotels operate at the top end of the market and provide five-star luxury. The modern and sophisticated Shangri-La 'S' logo not only resembles uniquely Asian architectural forms, but also reminds the beholder of majestic mountains reflected in the waters of a tranquil lake.

The second main brand within the group is the Traders brand that was established in 1989 and is intended for the cost conscious traveller. Hotels operating under the Traders Hotels brand offer mid-level service and facilities with the Shangri-La service guarantee. Currently there are 12 Traders Hotels operating in China, India, Malaysia, Myanmar, the Philippines, Singapore and Dubai with further operations being developed in China and scheduled to open between 2009 and 2012.

Utilising a chop – the traditional seal of quality used by Chinese traders for 5,000 years – the Traders logo reflects the brand's philosophy of offering the business traveller first-rate quality with the greatest value for money.

GROUP AIM AND OBJECTIVES

The overall aim of the Shangri-La group is to delight customers by providing quality and value through distinctive service and innovative products. In order to achieve this, the company has identified eight guiding principles. These are:

1. ensuring leadership drives for results and with the aim of working together as one team;
2. to make customer loyalty a key driver of the business through consistency in delivery of service, delighting customers in every customer contact and ensuring that executives have a customer contact role;
3. the encouragement of empowerment and therefore demanding decision-making at customer contact point;
4. the commitment to the financial success of individual operating units and the company as a whole in both the short and long term;
5. the creation of an environment where associates may achieve their personal and career goals;
6. the demonstration of honesty, care and integrity in all relationships.
7. ensuring that procedures are customer- and employee-friendly and are suitably enabled by technology; and
8. the guarantee that the organisation will be environmentally conscientious and provide safety and security for customers and associates.

SHANGRI-LA CARE

Shangri-La are committed to highly personalised guest service and therefore recruits for attitude and trains for skills. The acclaimed training programme, Shangri-La Care, is divided into three modules and, in line with the group's strategic plan to be an industry leader, ensures that all members of staff undergo the modules within six months of joining the group.

Shangri-La Care is a living culture within the group, strongly supported by the top management and continuously cascaded through the organisation. All hotels are required to allocate a specific budget for training and development, and the general manager is personally responsible for ensuring that all the allocated funds are appropriately spent.

Module one – Shangri-La hospitality from caring people

Launched in 1996, this module addresses how to make guests feel special and important by focusing on the five core values of Shangri-La Hospitality: Respect, Humility, Courtesy, Helpfulness and Sincerity. It also emphasises the value of 'Pride Without Arrogance' as the service hallmark.

Module two – delighting customers

Launched in 1998, this module focuses on the importance of guest loyalty and how it can only be achieved by delighting guests on a continuous basis. It emphasises that employees must be guest obsessed and willing to 'go the extra mile', be flexible and never say no, and have the ability to anticipate guests' needs and respond appropriately and quickly.

Module three – recover to gain loyalty

Launched in 2003, this module highlights the importance of recovery when a mistake is made. Emphasis is placed on the concept that when recovery is done well, it is often an opportunity to gain further guest commitment and loyalty. However, recognition is placed on the fact that if there is no or poor recovery, the lifetime value of the guest is lost in addition to at least 25 others who may hear of the incident through word of mouth. Therefore, this module teaches the five steps to recovery – Listen, Apologise, Fix the problem, Delight (the Extra Mile) and Follow-up.

AWARDS

Regarded as one of the world's finest hotel companies, Shangri-La is consistently recognised as an industry leader in readers' polls of prestigious publications worldwide. For example, in 2003 and 2004 the company received nine awards, including Preferred Hotel Chain (*TIME, Asia*), Best Asia Pacific Hotel Group (*Travel Weekly*, UK), Best Business Hotel Brand in Asia-Pacific (*Business Traveller, Asia-Pacific*), Best Hotel Chain in Asia (*The Asset*), Best Overseas Hotel Group (*The Guardian* and *The Observer*, UK) and Best Hotel Chain for Business and Vacation in Asia (*Asiamoney*).

In addition, individual hotels consistently receive awards from international publications. For example, in 2003, the Shangri-La Hotel, Sydney received the awards of 'One of the World's Top Hundred Best Hotels' (*Conde Nast Traveller*, UK) and 'One of the Best Foreign Hotels' (*Daily Telegraph*, UK).

PRESERVING NATURE

As a result of Shangri-La's commitment to environmental awareness, 20 hotels have received ISO 14001 certification, the international environmental management system standard.

This certification is only awarded to organisations which are able to show ISO 14001 compliance throughout all operations. These environmentally friendly and cost-efficient practices include installing energy-saving light bulbs, biodegradable cleaning materials, water restrictors, and sewage treatment facilities to prevent water pollution.

All properties follow an environmental management system (EMS) manual which helps to identify and address the immediate and long-term impact of the hotel's operations on its local environment. And every six months, the Lloyd's Register of Quality Assurance sends a representative to inspect the hotels to ensure not only that the system is being maintained but that continual environmental improvement is achieved by setting new environmental objectives and targets.

Amongst efforts to continually improve its contribution to local environments, the organisation has recently transferred from coal to diesel at Shangri-La Golden Flower, Xian; changed to low sulfur diesel at the Island Shangri-La, Hong Kong; and are changing from coal to gas at its Beijing properties.

Shangri-La Hotels and Resorts is a founding member of the Asia Pacific Hotels Environmental Initiative. In accordance with the group's environmental policy, all Shangri-La and Traders hotels have 'Green Programs' to identify ways to reduce wastage, eradicate practices that damage the environment and generally promote environmental awareness.

SHANGRI-LA PEOPLE

The Shangri-La Group endeavours to attract and retain talented people. The reasoning behind this is a belief that motivated staff who share the organisation's goals are key to maintaining and improving upon the standards of excellence by which the company has come to be known. There is a recognition that a commitment to a complete career path and the provision of a working environment where all people are valued and involved is essential to be able to become a preferred employer.

Therefore the company believes that the ideal Shangri-La employee is created by a combination of nature and nurture, thus great emphasis is placed on hiring people with the right attitude and potential. Thereafter the organisation strives to equip its people with the necessary skills through appropriate training and development. Consequently, each year a minimum

2% of payroll expenses is invested in the training and development of employees.

SHANGRI-LA AND CORPORATE SOCIAL RESPONSIBILITY

Overview

Shangri-La's Corporate Social Responsibility (CSR) programme is an all-encompassing approach to our stakeholders, beyond that of revenue, profit and legal obligation.

There is nothing of more value to Shangri-La than our reputation with our customers, employees, the members of the communities in which we operate, and our shareholders and suppliers.

Customers   We will give our customers fair value in the markets in which we serve, and look at each customer as a potential long-term relationship for our group. Thus, we will endeavour to earn their loyalty through providing quality service and experiences.

Employees   We will respect our employees as individuals in the belief that all employees want to do a good job, and it is our responsibility as leaders to provide the environment, processes and motivation to enable them to fulfil their potential.

Honesty and candour will be practiced as we counsel our employees in their performance and job/career expectations.

We will offer career opportunities to qualified internal candidates and employees of other Shangri-La hotels in preference to external candidates.

We will conduct ourselves as an equal opportunity employer and will not discriminate on the basis of race, religion, sex, age, family status or disability.

Suppliers   Underlying our expectations is the principle of integrity, in all of our behaviours and in all of our relationships. We must personally and professionally always act ethically.

We will treat suppliers with respect as business partners who play a vital role in our mission of serving.

We will award business based upon quality and price without personal favouritism.

We will endeavour to create long-term 'win-win' relationships with reputable suppliers that allow us to enjoy excellent quality, price, and supplier involvement in order to continuously improve our product, services and profitability.

Communities   We will be good corporate citizens through leadership and involvement in civic and charitable organisations.

We will take a leadership role in every community with respect to environmental issues and programmes.

We will respect the cultural and religious traditions of the countries in which we operate and make every effort to educate ourselves in the ways of their people.

Source: www.shangri-la.com

DISCUSSION QUESTIONS

1. Why do you think that Shangri-La Hotels and Resorts have created the Traders Hotel brand?

2. What are the key aspects of Shangri-La Hotels and Resorts that differentiate this company from other major hotel organisations?

3. Shangri-La Hotels and Resorts appear to adopt a relatively unique approach to the management of their human resources. How do you consider that this approach assists in achieving their overall aim?

4. What are the benefits to all stakeholders of Shangri-La's commitment to corporate social responsibility?

CHAPTER 13

Intermediaries

LEARNING OUTCOMES

The focus of the chapter is the packaging and distribution of the tourism product. By the end of this chapter, therefore, you will:

- be familiar with the nature and structures of intermediation and the arguments for and against disintermediation of distribution channels in tourism;

- be aware of online developments and the increasing consolidation and concentration of tourism intermediaries;

- be familiar with the operating characteristics, roles and functions of retail travel agents and tour operators;

- have an understanding of the process of distribution; and

- be aware of the financial constraints on the operation of intermediaries and the difficulties these inflict.

Photograph: Niagra Falls, Ontario, Canada © Hannah Cox

INTRODUCTION

In this chapter we show that the principal role of intermediaries is to bring buyers and sellers together. For travel and tourism, intermediation comes about through tour operators or wholesalers assembling the components of the tourist trip into a package and retailing the latter through travel agents, who deal directly with the public. However, as this chapter shows, this is not the only way by which the tourist product reaches the customer and we discuss several other distribution channels. The structure of intermediation is complicated by the fact that some retail agents and some of the principal suppliers, such as airlines, also act as tour wholesalers. Much of this trend has been driven by online developments and the rapid adoption of electronic technologies in facilitating the supply of and demand for tourism products. Online travel trends will be explored in this chapter with their impact on the traditional industry examined.

In this context, the chapter outlines the roles played by the retail travel agent and the tour operator respectively. We point out the differences between the North American and European travel trade systems, although our main emphasis is on the commonality of the underlying principles governing their activity. The conceptual aspects of tour operation are relatively straightforward but the implementation requires considerable organisation and planning, particularly in view of the time lags involved. We therefore discuss the main stages of tour operation in some detail. Finally, the factors making for market dominance are analysed.

THE NATURE OF INTERMEDIATION

In all industries the task of intermediaries is to transform goods and services from a form that consumers do not want into a product that they do want. For everyday household requirements, this is performed mainly through holding bulk supplies and breaking these down into amounts required by individuals, as well as bringing the goods to the marketplace. In tourism the situation is somewhat different, for it is quite possible to buy the components of the tourism trip (accommodation, transport, excursions and entertainment) directly from producers. This dispenses with the need for an intermediary. Traditionally, this has not happened to any great degree because the linkages (termed distribution channels) between the suppliers of tourism products and their potential customers are imperfect, and so the output of the travel intermediary is what is termed a *search* good, since it offers consumers the opportunity of avoiding the effort and cost of undertaking the production activity. However, as will be mentioned throughout this chapter and dealt with in Chapter 20, the information communications technology (ICT) revolution in recent years has made it easier, through the growth of low-cost airlines and the provision of supplier web sites, for experienced travellers to assemble their own itineraries.

Thus, from the perspective of economics, the role of intermediaries is to improve distribution channels and so make markets by bringing buyers and sellers together. It is argued that distribution channels often both influence consumer behaviour by branding the product and thereby supplying a credence good, as well as determining the ability of the industry to respond to consumers' requests efficiently in terms of the product as a search good. In this manner, distribution channels quite clearly help determine the competitiveness of suppliers and destinations. The bulk of this work falls upon the tour operator or wholesaler who packages the main components of the tourist trip (legally not fewer than two) into a single product and sells this at one price through retail travel agents or, particularly in North America, airline sales offices. This identifies the tour operator as the principal (a trade term) economic entity and not merely as the agent selling on commission. The latter role is that of the retail travel agent, who provides an outlet for the actual sales of tours, tickets and travel services, such as insurance or foreign exchange, to the public.

Benefits

By making markets, travel intermediaries bestow benefits on producers, consumers and the destination. These benefits include the following:

Producers:
- Are able to sell in bulk and so transfer risk to the tour operator, though wholesalers do attempt to cover themselves by a variety of agreements and release clauses. The latter may vary from four or more weeks to seven days.
- Can reduce promotion costs by focusing on the travel trade, rather than consumer promotion, which is much more expensive.

Consumers:
- Can avoid search and transaction costs in both time and money by being able to purchase an inclusive tour.
- Gain from the specialist knowledge of the tour operator and the fact that the uncertainties of travel are minimised. For example, cruising and coach tours are attractive to senior citizens because the holiday starts the moment they board the ship or coach.
- Often gain most from lower prices, notably in the case of resorts dealing with large numbers of visitors as in the Mediterranean, Mexico, Florida and Hawaii. In such destinations wholesalers are able through their buying power to negotiate discounts of up to 60% off the normal tariff.

Destinations:
- Especially in developing countries where budgets are limited, may benefit considerably from the international marketing network of tour operators. However, it is naive to expect, as some countries do, that this should be a responsibility of these companies, particularly as the Internet has made it so much easier for national tourist organisations (NTOs) to promote their tourist areas.

Clearly some disadvantages do exist. For the producer, use of intermediaries will reduce margins, and their degree of marketing control and influence over the process of distribution, although they would hope to make this up in improved business performance. It is also likely that ultimate customer service will be beyond their control with most attention being directed at the channel intermediaries rather than the end consumer. For the consumer, further concentration and consolidation of tourism intermediaries may actually reduce choice and increase prices. For destinations, if they become overly dependent on intermediaries for bookings, they are very much susceptible to the 'whims' and 'vagaries' of the marketplace, and the ability of intermediaries to influence consumer choice by 'switch' selling to more profitable locations.

Structure

A schematic diagram of the structure of distribution channels is shown in Figure 13.1. Independent travellers put their own itinerary together. This they can do by purchasing the key components of accommodation and transport directly from suppliers, from their own outlets or web sites, or via the retail travel agent in the high street or through their web site. It is common in domestic tourism for consumers to purchase their trip requirements directly because they usually have good product knowledge and ready access to a telephone, if not the Internet, to make reservations. However, in order to boost the market for the domestic product in Britain, the national and regional tourist boards have produced travel brochures which they distribute in a number of ways: directly through the mail or 'downloads' in response to enquiries or from a mailing list (termed direct response marketing), through tourist information centres (TICs), or by persuading the travel trade to give commissionable brochures rack space in their shops. These brochures simply give the public a portfolio of

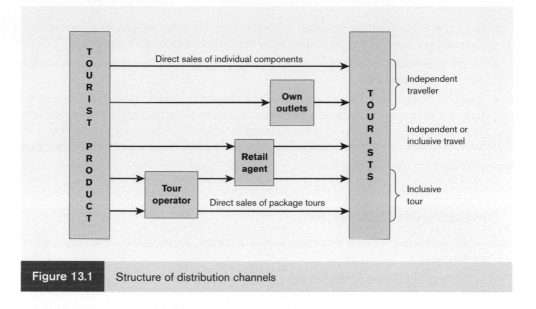

Figure 13.1   Structure of distribution channels

products to choose from, which avoids the tourist boards being classified as 'organisers' according to the 1992 EU Package Travel Directive (see Mini Case Study 13.1) that regulates provision within Europe, protects consumers and adds credence to the product.

MINI CASE STUDY 13.1
European Union Package Travel Directive

The issue of consumer protection in relation to the package holiday contract was first raised in the EU in 1982. Up until the Directive on Package Travel was adopted in 1990, all the then 12 Member States had very different provisions for package holidays. The justification for the Directive was in the completion of the Single Market covering all of the EU at that time, which required the harmonisation of business practices. It naturally applies to all countries subsequently joining the EU and so now covers 27 Member States. However, a European directive, as opposed to a regulation, allows Member States to implement it in the best way they see fit and two years were given for the appropriate legislation on package travel to be enacted in each country. The Directive was in effect minimum harmonisation, as it allowed Member States to adopt or retain more stringent conditions of consumer protection.

The Directive defined a package as a prearranged combination of at least two of the following:

- transport;
- accommodation;
- other significant tourist services.

The package has to be sold at an inclusive price and cover a period of more than 24 hours or include overnight accommodation.

Any tourist business involved in providing combinations of the above services in a prearranged form comes within the terms of the Directive, which, in effect, broadened the range of travel organisers who may be classified as a tour operator. In essence, the Directive required Member States to give the force of law to what was already in the codes of conduct established by trade associations, but with three enhancements:

→

- the travel organiser (tour operator) is contractually liable for the proper performance of the elements of the package, whether provided directly by the organiser or other suppliers;

- bonding of holidays was extended to all travel organisers offering arrangements that came within the definition of a package;

- travel organisers and their agents are legally obliged to provide their customers with additional information on visa requirements, health formalities, transport stops and connections (and accommodation to be provided as necessary), local representation or an emergency telephone number, insurance and similar matters to ensure that the client is fully aware of the circumstances of the holiday purchase.

Source: EC Council Directive 90/314 on Package Travel, Package Holidays and Package Tours.

DISCUSSION QUESTIONS

1. What events might occur that could disrupt a holiday, yet leave the travel organiser not liable for breach of contract?

2. Is the legal protection of the holiday traveller now excessive?

It has been common for airlines, bus and shipping companies to have their own outlets in large cities from which the public may purchase travel products directly, though less so today in the face of ICT developments. Airlines have been particularly keen to secure their presence in the market by locating offices on flagship sites in capital cities. These serve both the trade and the public, and are especially important in cities such as Bangkok, Berlin, London or New York where not only are there large numbers of business travellers, but also many overseas holidaymakers travelling independently. International hotel chains and hotel marketing consortia also use individual establishments for selling rooms in other properties belonging to the group. This has become routine with the advent of modern reservation systems.

The founding companies of today's travel trade, Thomas Cook (see Major Case Study 13.1) and American Express, are both travel agents and wholesalers, and so history is on the side of the retail agent that buys directly from producers. Through agency agreements (which, in the United States, are requirements set by what have been historically termed conferences representing the domestic and international airlines, shipping companies and railways), retailers sell the individual components of the trip, such as transport tickets, accommodation, and excursions, but they may also put together their own brand of tours, over-brand another tour operator's brochure or have a specialist wholesaler put together a brochure for them. Such own branding is a practice that has been traditionally more common in North America than in Europe, as has been the use of travel counsellors in agencies to assemble specially tailored packages for clients.

Traditionally, travel agents have made the bulk of their money from selling **inclusive tours** and airline tickets, though the situation regarding the latter has changed, because the major full-service carriers, in the face of competition from low-cost carriers, have cut their distribution cost by removing commissions to travel agents and global distribution systems (GDSs) in an effort to lower their bottom-line costs. Agents have responded to this by charging a handling fee to customers. In Europe most inclusive tours are associated with foreign travel, whereas in North America domestic trips are the dominant source of inclusive tour sales. The importance of business travel has led to the growth of agencies, usually belonging to a chain, dealing solely with this aspect of tourism, to the extent of providing 'implants', albeit electronically, in major corporations solely for the purpose of covering their corporate travel needs, including arranging meetings, conventions and incentive travel awarded to staff. More recently banks have organised travel departments to serve not only their own needs, but also those of their privileged (high net-wealth) customers.

Photograph 13.1   Thomas Cook, holidaymaking in the 1950s. Although a major player in the business of travel intermediation, Thomas Cook has over 160 years of travel industry experience.
Source: Advertising Archive

MINI CASE STUDY 13.2
Inclusive tours and travel agents – current and future trends

While the volume and value of overseas holidays continues to grow in the UK, the volume of inclusive tours undertaken has remained static at around 20 million visits per year with the total number of holidays being taken exceeding 46 million in 2006. The duration of stay has decreased slightly in recent years with larger numbers of the travelling public taking an increasing number of short breaks. For example, for the period 2001–4 the demand for short breaks rose by 34%; partly fuelled by the exponential growth in low-cost air-lines and the increasing numbers of new destinations available to travellers. This trend has also contributed to the continued growth of the independent sector where the volume of independent holidays first exceeded inclusive tours in 2003. In 2006, it was forecast that independent holidays would account for just over 58% of all holiday trips, this reflecting a rise of 11% since 2001 and with there being no signs of decline. Interestingly, although Spain remains a firm favourite for the inclusive tour, it is also high in demand for independent travellers who are able to benefit from low-cost flights, very often from regional airports, and overall familiarity with the destination. For the future, destinations further afield, like Cape Verde and Brazil, are forecast to grow in popularity while it is anticipated that the overall overseas market will grow by 25%, and spend by 35%, in the period up to and including 2011. That said, the average spend per consumer, although set to increase, is set to do so by a smaller margin of 8%.

Despite the surge in popularity in independent bookings and travel, 19.7 million trips (42% of all over-seas holidays) were still sold by travel agents in 2006, this despite the fact that competition from online providers reduced travel agency sales by 7% between 2001 and 2006. Somewhat predictably, perhaps, travel agencies remain highly popular with older markets, while the provision of high-tech devices and plasma screens and innovative approaches to customer service have done much to retain, in part, younger markets. Interestingly, for longer-stay trips, cruises and the luxury end of the market, travel agencies remain very popular and an integral part of the booking experience.

Source: Mintel Report on Inclusive Tours (August, 2006) and Mintel Report on Travel Agents (October, 2006)

DISCUSSION QUESTIONS

1. Under what circumstances/conditions do you consider the decline in the number of inclusive tours is likely to be reversed and regain popularity?

2. How may travel agencies increase their presence and influence in markets for both domestic and over-seas tourism?

The most common way of distributing foreign holiday travel in Europe is still through inclusive tours packaged by tour operators and sold by travel agents, despite the Internet, digital TV and the proliferation of call centres, which permit holiday packages to be marketed directly to the public by wholesalers. At one stage it was thought that the developments in the marketplace identified in Table 13.1 would soon lead to the demise of the traditional travel agent, as the percentage share of the market held by **direct-sell** holidays rapidly expanded to displace normal high street bookings, especially when there could be cost savings of 10% or more. Major tour operators in Europe do have direct-sell brands within their portfolio, which currently amount to around 20% of their turnover, and the expectation is that this will rise to 50% in the next few years. Within North America, the domestic nature of the product is such that online bookings are already over 50% for the major travel companies.

Table 13.1	Some developments and trends in the marketplace affecting travel agencies

- Tourism principals and suppliers are eager to control costs of distribution, improve their communication function and bypass the use of agencies by developing Internet-based interfaces with consumers.
- Commission capping or termination by a number of international airlines.
- Development of 'no-frills' airlines that perform most of their reservations online.
- Increased computer literacy and confidence among consumers.
- Emergence and rapid development of electronic intermediaries.
- Expansion of customer relationship management systems and their gradual integration with loyalty schemes.
- E-ticketing will eventually enable the entire process of making reservations and purchasing tourism processes paperless.
- Traditional intermediaries (such as Thomas Cook) re-engineering their processes in order to update their offering, improve customer satisfaction and remain competitive.
- Tourism destinations develop regional systems to enhance their representation, boost their image and attract direct bookings.

Source: Based on Buhalis, 2003

Although direct selling of foreign tours has been slow to capture the public's attention and is still behind that of products purchased by more time-honoured means, it has also been put forward that the increasing sophistication of the travelling public, combined with the ease of making reservations, would lead to the demise of the package holiday and **disintermediation** of the tourism distribution system. Principals in this instance may be a tour operator, a hotel or a transport company. While it is true that more people are travelling independently, evidence to date, as noted above, suggests that traditional purchasing patterns will continue in many markets (especially 'grey' markets and those on a low budget), for it still remains the case that operators can negotiate cheaper arrangements through their bulk purchasing power, they are also able to respond to the public's demands by building in more options to their package offers and they are bound by economic regulations that offer quality assurance and security to the customer. It is not so much that we are looking at disintermediation in the wake of the ICT revolution but **reintermediation** as the industry adjusts its strategic positioning and reinvents itself.

Integration, consolidation and concentration

The term **integration** is an economic concept describing formal linking arrangements between one organisation and another. Vertical integration is where the linking occurs along the production process, for example, when an airline establishes its own tour operating company. This would be an example of vertical integration forwards into the marketplace, of which the most common in terms of intermediaries is where a tour wholesaler acquires through merger or purchase a retail travel chain.

Tour operators owning airlines provide an example of vertical integration backwards and this is also common among scheduled airlines, which form alliances with (and even own) multinational hotel chains and surface transport companies to secure trading advantages over their rivals. One of the widest range of integrated activities may be found in the French conglomerate Groupe Accor. Originally known for its hotel operations, Groupe Accor's interests now include all aspects of tourism, as can be seen in Figure 13.2.

Looking at developments over time, it appears that the degree of vertical integration varies with the **product life cycle**. We illustrate this in Figure 13.3. At the early stage of development, as in the case of Thomas Cook, there is a high degree of vertical integration as there

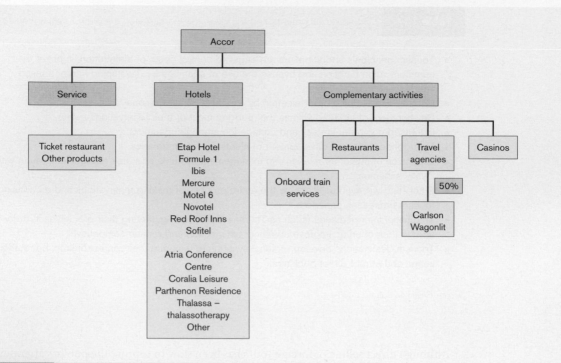

Figure 13.2   Accor corporate structure
Source: WTO, 2002

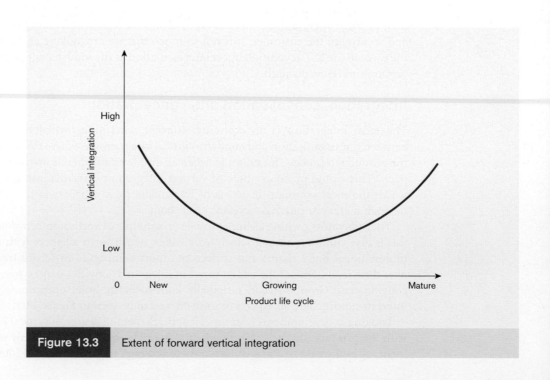

Figure 13.3   Extent of forward vertical integration

are few suppliers. But as demand expands so specialists develop to increase the efficiency of the distribution channel. Operators are bound together by their mutual interest in helping the market to grow. As the market matures, competitive pressures for market share force companies to seek the benefits of forming vertical links. These include:

- economies of scale through the linking of complementary activities, investing in new technologies and improved management expertise in, say, foreign exchange transactions, forecasting and marketing;
- cutting out the intermediary by being able to control costs and quality standards under the umbrella of one organisation;
- securing supplies and increasing buying power; and
- protecting market position by guaranteeing retail outlets on prime high street sites.

It is important to note that vertical integration forwards does not necessarily have to come about through ownership. Control may be exercised by franchising. This is a licensing agreement whereby the parent company grants another, usually smaller, firm the right to sell its products and use its brand name, but in return the firm should not sell the products of its competitors. In Germany, the package holiday business was developed by the major retail groups, such as Karstadt, Neckermann and Quelle in the 1960s. They already had the advantage of retail shops and mail order systems to distribute their products. Owing to stricter cartel laws, further expansion through vertical integration was difficult, so they developed market power through mutual shareholding agreements and a system of tied agency licensing, which gave them exclusive outlets for their products and protected their profit margins.

Another organisational aspect of the travel trade sector that should be considered is *horizontal integration*. This occurs when two tour operators or two travel agents amalgamate, either through merger or takeover. This strategy was very prevalent amongst retail travel chains in Britain during the 1980s and became known as the 'march of the multiples'. The reasons for this are similar to those for vertical integration but also include the spatial dimension of extending the geographical spread of outlets to ensure representation in all regions. Thomas Cook and Lunn Poly in Britain, and American Express and Carlson Wagonlit Travel (which acquired the historically famous Ask Mr. Foster travel agency network that was founded in 1888) in the USA, are examples of major chains that have traditionally increased their geographical representation.

For the retailers, horizontal integration strengthens their buying power with regard to wholesalers. They support this by developing their own corporate identity in the design and style of operation of their branch outlets, so as to raise the public's awareness of the company. Naturally, the march of the multiples has drawn criticism from independent travel agents owing to loss of their market share. In Britain, as in North America, many small travel agencies have formed themselves into consortia to give themselves the same negotiating power as the multiples and the national trade associations, the American Society of Travel Agents (ASTA) and the Association of British Travel Agents (ABTA), have been enthusiastic in their support for independents. Both bodies have a mission to facilitate the business of selling travel through effective representation, shared knowledge and the enhancement of professionalism. They seek a retail travel marketplace that is profitable, growing and a rewarding place to work, invest and do business. Large tour operators have also grown by amalgamation, but instead of enforcing a uniform brand image, as in the case of multiple retailers, they usually maintain a range of products, including acquired brands, to meet the consumer's need for choice.

Criticism of major tour operators and wholesalers usually comes from destinations, particularly those in less-developed countries. The latter have expressed concern over the strength of the economic buying power of large wholesalers, which allows them to obtain prices below those that would occur in markets where competition prevails. It is further argued that their specialist knowledge allows them to influence consumer choice in tourism-generating countries and so gives them the opportunity to switch sales to destinations that are more profitable to the company. Continued integration activity, be it vertical or horizontal, in addition to increasing numbers of mergers and acquisitions has led to further consolidation and concentration of tourism intermediaries, especially in Europe (see Major Case Study 13.1).

The major beneficiaries of consolidation are clearly consumers and shareholders, with consumers in a number of markets benefiting from highly competitive price wars and shareholders in terms of their rising stock values. A note of caution is necessary here, however, as the cost of consolidation for some companies has been excessive and threatens to damage their very existence in the future.

For the independent sector businesses, of which there remain many, the future demands greater differentiation, and an ability to deal with barriers that increase with consolidation, most notably in the form of price wars. Whether it is increased levels of service provision or a focus on niche destinations or travel products, independents are likely to experience more, rather than less competition from an ever more consolidated sector in the future.

Online travel

The significant development and growth of **online travel**, predominantly on the back of the development of information technologies and telecommunications plus phenomenal growth of the Internet and electronic commerce, has been one of the great success stories for tourism generally, and tourism intermediaries in particular, aspects which are discussed again in Chapter 20. The volume of online tourism-related transactions is anticipated to reach over one-third of all e-transactions in the near future with considerable implications for intermediaries and their competitors across the wider tourism industry – and none more so than for the four major GDSs which still dominate the distribution of travel products, notably Sabre and Worldspan, which dominate in the USA, and Galileo and Amadeus, which are market leaders in Europe. Back in 1996, Sabre was the first GDS to venture online with its launch of Travelocity.com, a virtual agency. At the same time, Expedia.com was launched by USA Networks (see Mini Case Study 13.3). This was then followed by Amadeus.net in 1997 by Amadeus Global Travel Distribution and the purchase of TRIP.com by Galileo International in 2000. After just three years in operation, Travelocity.com and Expedia.com were among the 10 largest US distributors of travel products in terms of revenue. In Europe, lastminute.com was launched in 1998 and eBookers.com in 1999, demonstrating that new methods of online communication were able to cross entry barriers to a market previously outside the scope of new players.

One of the biggest contributors to the growth in the purchase of e-tickets has been the rise of discount 'no-frills' airlines, especially across the USA and Europe, and their replication elsewhere in Asia and Australia. The principal catalysts for change were Southwest Airlines in the United States and easyJet and Ryanair in the UK and Ireland respectively, leading to AirAsia in Malaysia and Virgin Blue in Australia. Whereas Southwest Airlines dominates the US online market with sales in excess of US$1.5 billion (over a quarter of its overall sales), online sales for easyJet are well in excess of 90% of its business. For airlines generally, although they are subject to the same rules as travel agencies, they often are able to offer special rates and exclusive deals and so motivate consumers to purchase tickets directly rather than via a travel agent. This incredible growth has been in a remarkably short time period and reflects most dramatically how certain parts of the wider tourism industry have capitalised on changing trends in technology and their greater acceptance by the consumer. In response to the fierce competition from the 'no-frills' carriers and the growth of virtual intermediaries, many international airlines are coming together in order to compete head-on with the new players. For example, in December 2001, the virtual intermediary Opodo was launched by nine European airlines with an initial focus on the German, French, Italian and British markets. Collectively, Air France, British Airways, Lufthansa, Alitalia, Iberia, KLM,

MINI CASE STUDY 13.3
Expedia

Launched in 1996 by Microsoft, Expedia.com was the first e-intermediary to enter the online travel market by a non-travel organisation. With a very broad product offering which encompassed all aspects of the tourism product, Expedia grew very quickly, entering the UK market in 1998 and being voted Europe's primary travel site in August 1999. Expedia grew exponentially to the extent that Expedia Inc., the parent group, was floated on the Nasdaq stock exchange at the end of 1999. A year later, the UK site – Expedia.co.uk – launched web-enabled phone (WAP) and personal digital assistant (PDA)-compatible platforms whereby travellers could access essential travel information en route. At the same time, Expedia held 25% of the major online market for travel products in the USA with reservation income reaching a staggering US$1.8 billion. Expedia was second only to Travelocity in the USA, the e-intermediary developed by the Sabre Holdings Corporation which recorded a market share of 35% in 2000.

The success of Expedia continued apace in that significant revenue gains in 2001 led to the acquisition of a controlling interest in Expedia Inc. by USA Networks (now IAC/InterActiveCorp). Expedia Inc. is now fully owned by IAC with annual gross travel bookings currently in excess of $17 billion. Following a corporate strategy of continued growth IAC and Expedia separated into two publicly-traded companies in 2005. For the future, Expedia Inc. is seeking to keep abreast of changing traveller plans, patterns of purchase behaviour and the experiences desired by travellers via a strategy of constant innovation and brand development.

Source: Expedia.co.uk, 2007 and Horner and Swarbrooke, 2004

DISCUSSION QUESTIONS

1. Identify some of those factors which may still inhibit some individuals from making reservations 'online'.
2. What travel products are most conducive to being purchased 'online'?
3. How may small, independent travel agents and tour operators compete with the proliferation of 'online' specialists such as Expedia?

Aer Lingus, Finnair and Austrian Airlines have used Amadeus technology to develop a serious competitor to existing players. One cautionary note is the move by some airlines to withdraw commissions to online agencies. Although this may represent a temporary initiative it does introduce an element of uncertainty for the future relationship between producers and intermediaries in their efforts to find the most effective and cost-efficient means of reaching the final consumer.

The fact that there remains in some parts of the market much caution with regard to the use of virtual intermediaries explains in part the development of 'click-and-mortar' agencies, whereby a combination of online and offline services – often in the form of a network of traditional travel agencies and/or call centres – is a strategic response to the concerns of many. In addition, many traditional players are now developing the reverse, as part of the reintermediation process, in that they are developing a web presence to complement their traditional business.

In addition to the above, and consistent with traditional intermediaries and the wider tourism industry, consolidation is occurring also in the virtual marketplace. In the USA alone, in 2001, the top five industry leaders controlled nearly 60% of the online travel market. Clearly, the speed with which online travel has developed is remarkable. The speed with which consolidation has begun to impact the structure of the industry is even more remarkable, however, in that in the space of seven to eight years a number of the new players are now rewriting the rules of competition for the established conglomerates.

Photograph 13.2	One of the new e-intermediaries in the global marketplace, Expedia has tapped into the power of the Internet and offered customers considerable choice online. *Source*: Expedia

THE ROLE OF THE RETAIL AGENT

As has begun to become apparent from the above discussion, the primary task of travel agents is to supply the public with travel services. This they do on behalf of their suppliers or principals. An agent may also offer travel-related services such as insurance or foreign exchange. For providing these services, the agent is rewarded by commission from the principals. Traditionally, commission amounts to 10% of the selling price, but this is normally 1% or 2% less for hotel bookings and rail travel, while, as noted earlier, major airlines have moved to a zero commission model, so that agents now charge the customer a booking fee. Insurance will usually generate commission of around 30% and car hire can, on occasions, make considerably more than the basic 10%. Sales of travellers' cheques and currency will yield no more than about 2%. However, by dealing with preferred suppliers and achieving specified sales targets, agents can achieve 'overrides', which are extra commission amounting to about 2.5% of sales. The fast changing nature of this sector in the new arena of e-intermediaries implies that commission rates and what is commissionable in the future, both for traditional and virtual players, is likely to be the subject of continual negotiation and debate.

How a retail travel agency should set about discharging its primary function is a matter for discussion. Where an agent has no wholesaling function and therefore does not share in the risk of tour production by holding stock, it is suggested that the agent's main concern should be the choice of location to ensure ready availability of the principals' products in the marketplace. The agent has access to a principal's stock through the reservation system and here efficiency is important. The customer expects instant confirmation and staff at the agency do not want to waste time with repeated telephone calls. Instant availability on a computer screen permits the staff in the traditional agency to share the booking process with the customer to reinforce the buying decision. This approach to the role of the retailer likens the agent to a 'filling station' for travel: creating demand is the responsibility of the principals. If demand is given, then controlling costs is the best way for the agent to maintain profitability.

An alternative view argues that the acquisition of product knowledge and the assumption of the risks involved in assessing the extent and nature of demand is the job of the agent. The agent should thus take on the role of a travel counsellor to give the public impartial advice and seek to generate business in the local market area. Many countries have national associations for travel agents that also act as regulating bodies that encourage this approach through their respective codes of business practice, such as ABTA (see Mini Case Study 13.4) in Britain and ASTA in the USA. Likewise, these bodies link with the United Federation of Travel Agents' Associations (UFTAA), which acts internationally and liaises closely with the International Air Transport Association (IATA).

It has already been noted that the counselling role has been far more prevalent in North America than in Europe. It appears that in Europe the tour operator's brochure, together with advertising and promotion, and more recently use of the web, has held greater sway in destination choice, thus conforming to the filling station model. However, the process of reintermediation in Europe has seen travel agents changing their ways of operating by harnessing ICT to their own advantage through Sabre's Travelocity and Galileo's range of agency web products. These have allowed agents to have full access to air, rail, hotel and car rental reservations, so as to put together independent inclusive tours (IITs) for their customers, thus moving them firmly in the direction of travel counsellors. Figure 13.4 represents a conceptual model of the process and factors influencing agents' destination recommendations. Concern has been expressed about the impartiality of advice in that while agents want to meet their clients' needs they are also mindful of the different rates of commission on offer and any bonuses. In the case of corporate chains, this is known as 'switch' or 'directional' selling and can be described as a 'sale or attempted sale by a vertically integrated travel agent of the foreign package holidays of its linked tour operator, in preference to the holidays of other operators' (MMC, 1998: 4). This anti-competitive practice is against the 'level playing field'

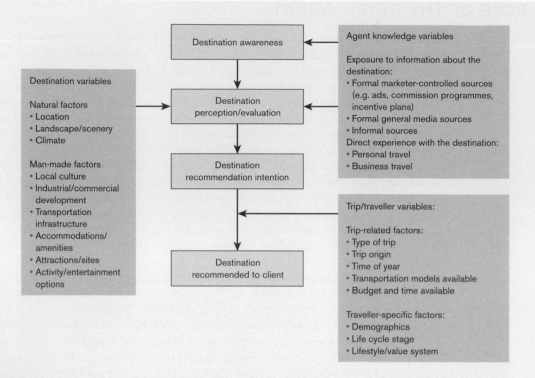

Figure 13.4 Conceptual model of the process and factors influencing agents' destinations recommendations
Source: Hudson *et al.*, 2001

MINI CASE STUDY 13.4
ABTA – The Travel Association

The Travel Association was founded in 1950 to promote the interests of its members and raise their pres-tige. In doing this, it has also come to represent the interests of consumers through developing procedures to safeguard against tour companies that suddenly go out of business and fail to meet their obligations to their customers. It now represents both travel agents and tour operators and, as a trade association, has an agreed Code of Conduct for its members, which, although not legally binding, does give ABTA the power to expel, fine or reprimand those members who fail to comply with its standards. The Travel Association requires that the public should receive the best possible service from its members and that in matters of competition for business between them, the interests of the travelling public should predominate. There are a whole range of standards that members are expected to comply with; these include: advertising; brochures, booking conditions and travel information; web sites and online trading; documentation; altera-tions to an agreed holiday; cancellations by the customer or by the provider; overbooking; surcharges; building works at resorts; resort representation; handling complaints; and arbitration. These are compliant with the European Travel Agents and Tour Operators Association (ECTAA).

ABTA has a continually evolving set of rules and regulations for membership, from the extension of bonding (a financial guarantee from, say, a bank or an insurance company in the event of failure and payment into a reserve fund) to all members in 1972, to the more recent setting of standards for web site provision for direct sales and promotion. However, ABTA's remit is much wider than regulation, since as a trade association it:

1. commissions research into the technological and business environment that is likely to affect its members;

2. provides an information service to members;

3. offers legal advice;

4. undertakes training, validates courses and sets the standards for professional qualifications in travel and tourism;

5. promotes the travel industry through public relations;

6. acts as a spokesperson and lobbying body with respect to the British government and the EU.

To meet the challenge of the ICT revolution and the arrival of low-cost carriers, ABTA has been working with the insurance industry since 2006 to extend the current business model of consumer protection, based as it is on the predominance of the package holiday, to all travellers and is currently lobbying to update the legislation to ensure that the provisions that apply to providers of inclusive tours are extended to all travel providers.

Source: ABTA – The Travel Association

DISCUSSION QUESTIONS

1. Is it not an impossible task for trade associations to represent fairly the rights of consumers, when their obligations are to their members?

2. How important is bonding in the travel industry?

3. To what extent is bonding a restriction on new entry to the industry?

concept required by regulating bodies and the consumer has recourse to complaint procedures, which act as a constraint on such activities. However, one has to accept that agents will give prominence on their shelves to the products of their principals.

Retail agency economics

Traditionally the retail travel trade has been characterised by ease of entry. This is because the retailer carries no stock and so capitalisation is relatively low. All that is required is a suitable shop front and the acquisition of agency agreements from tour operators to sell their products. It is then up to the marketing skill of the agent to establish the business within the locality. If the agent wishes to offer air transport services worldwide, which is essential for dealing with business travel, then it is necessary that the agent holds a licence from IATA. This requires a thorough investigation of the agency by IATA, particularly the qualifications and experience of the staff.

In the USA virtually all retailers are members of both IATA and the Airlines Reporting Corporation (ARC), which allows them to sell both international and domestic air tickets. ARC is an airline-owned company serving the travel industry with financial services, data products and services, ticket distribution, and settlement in the United States, Puerto Rico and the US Virgin Islands. An ARC appointment is essential for retail agents in the USA and normally enables an agent to obtain other licences without difficulty.

A representative breakdown of the operating accounts of a medium to large travel agent is shown in Table 13.2. The example is drawn on European experience and is standardised to 1 million currency units of turnover. Table 13.2 gives an indication of the items that enter the **operating account** and shows that inclusive tours and ticket sales, of which the majority continue to be airline tickets, are by far the most important sales items. Transport tickets, other than for airlines, include sales arising from acting as an agent for rail, shipping and

Table 13.2	Travel agency operating accounts
Item	**Currency units**
Sales	
Independent inclusive and package tours	640 000
Transport tickets	269 000
Insurance	10 000
Car hire	4 000
Miscellaneous	77 000
Total	1 000 000
Revenue	
Commission	69 000
Other income	32 000
Total	101 000
Costs	
Payroll expenses	46 500
Communications	11 000
Advertising	4 000
Energy	2 000
Administration	7 000
Repairs and maintenance	500
Accommodation expenses	12 500
Depreciation	2 500
Total	86 000
Net income	15 000

Source: Trade information

coach companies. Miscellaneous includes independent bookings of accommodation, excursions, ground handling services, theatres, etc., foreign exchange transactions and the sale of travel goods such as luggage, sports items, first aid kits and travel clothes.

The most important item of income to the agent is commission and, since there exists considerable pressure on commissions in some markets, it will be appreciated that the ability of the agent to generate turnover is crucial, particularly for the independent retailer. The latter has been trebly squeezed: first, by fierce competition from the multiples and virtual intermediaries, secondly, from the fact that the relative cost of holidays has fallen in real terms while overheads have been generally increasing and, thirdly, from zero commissioning of airline tickets, but low capitalisation has enabled them to adjust to these changes. The major item of 'Other income' in the revenue statement is charges for ticket provision, but this also includes interest earned on clients' deposit money. For accounting purposes the latter is a profit item, which is only indirectly sales-related. It could be excluded here and added into the net income statement afterwards.

The largest item of cost is remuneration to staff (including payments to directors or owners). The difficulty that independent agents experience in trying to expand turnover has tended to make them cost-orientated in the operation of their businesses. Controlling costs, especially for the smaller agent, has been the short-term recipe for survival and this in turn has served to keep staff salaries low, which creates difficulties in both attracting experienced staff and retaining existing staff when compared to multiples, but with their changing role they can no longer afford not to invest in new technology and staff professionalism. Administration costs include: printing, stationery, insurance, bonding levy, legal and professional fees, bank charges, accounting and record keeping, and any travel that may be incurred. Accommodation expenses refer to charges arising from occupation of the premises.

Although the independent retailer can compete with the multiple and virtual intermediary on the basis of the level of personal service, the argument for raising commission rates has always been a strong one. The difficulty is that in a competitive environment higher commission rates may simply be countered by the multiples and virtual intermediaries offering larger discounts and so independents must look to their own ability for creating personalised packages and stocking exclusive products for their survival. Under pressure from the budget airlines the multiples are already closing down high street branches in favour of increasing direct sales via the Internet.

THE ROLE OF THE TOUR OPERATOR/WHOLESALER

Despite the growth of urban tourism since the 1980s to the world's major cities, the dominant international leisure tourism flows are still short haul to sun resorts, although the falling cost of long-haul travel has made previously considered exotic destinations more accessible. Therefore, it is not surprising that much of the work of tour operators and wholesalers is bound up in providing single destination inclusive or package holidays. Multi-centred holidays are more common on long-haul travel where the period of stay may extend to three weeks. There is still a buoyant market for coach tours, which were the main form of inclusive holiday before the arrival of low-priced air travel in the 1950s, although Vladimir Raitz took the first group of holidaymakers on a tour by air to Corsica in 1949 (their accommodation was in tents). It was operated by Hickie Borman and would be considered today as a tailor-made package and therefore outside the EU 1992 definition of a 'prearranged' inclusive tour (see Mini Case Study 13.1). That same year Raitz founded the British company Horizon Holidays (later acquired by Thomson), which is considered to be the first business to introduce the modern form of package holiday when, in 1950, in order to circumvent exchange controls by paying the whole price in the country of origin, Horizon marketed combined transport and accommodation arrangements to Corsica (Bray and Raitz, 2001).

At its most fundamental, tour operating is a process of combining aircraft seats and beds in hotels (or other forms of accommodation), in a manner that will make the purchase price attractive to potential holidaymakers. As we noted earlier, tour wholesalers achieve this through bulk buying which generates economies of scale that can be passed on to the customer. Despite the increasing popularity in the use of operators' web sites, the most essential link in this process remains the tour operator's brochure, which communicates the holiday product to the customer. The brochure must include within it:

- illustrations which provide a visual description of the destination and the holiday;
- copy, which is a written description of the holiday to help the customer match the type of product to his or her lifestyle; and
- price and departure panels which give the specifications of the holiday for different times of the season, duration of stay and the variety of departure points.

Large tour operators and wholesalers normally sell a wide portfolio of tours and therefore have a range of brochures. For instance, there will be separate brochures for summer sun and winter sun holidays, ski holidays, long-haul travel and short breaks. Popular destinations will have tour operators' brochures dealing solely with holidays to that country or region, and the number has continued to grow. Research has shown that the place to visit is often the first holiday decision made by some travellers. The brochure is designed to encourage customers to buy and may be the only information they might have concerning the resort until they arrive there, though more and more are obtaining information over the Internet even if they are not booking directly by this means. However, the brochure cannot be a comprehensive travel guide. The number of pages is limited by considerations of cost and size, and operators try to put as much detail about accommodation and resorts as they can in the space available, but in so doing they must also conform to the legal requirements of the consumer protection legislation that exists in the country where the brochure is marketed. Clearly, the contents of the brochure must be consistent with the brand image each operator is trying to convey, as they will each be competing for the customer's attention on travel agents' brochure racks.

Principal stages of tour operating/wholesaling

Although the conceptual principles of tour operating are easy to follow – linking transport and accommodation to produce a package that can be offered in a brochure – the practicalities of the tour-operating cycle require careful planning, preparation and coordination. For example, media advertising in support of the brochure must be booked well in advance, particularly if numerous channels are to be used. The process of brochure production is initiated early on in the cycle to ensure that printing deadlines are met. There are myriad tasks to be performed, not only by separate divisions within the tour company, but also by outside contractors. The task of coordinating all these activities usually falls upon the marketing department.

Because of the complexity of organising package trips, there are tour operators and wholesalers who do not put together their own programme. They simply contract the work out to a wholesaler and pass on the bookings as they come in. An example of this are organisations known as *affinity groups*. They range from travel clubs whose members may have ethnic ties with particular countries, to professional associations who may arrange to have their meetings in different parts of the world.

Figure 13.5 presents a stylised layout of an operating cycle for a large-scale summer programme selling 1 million or more holidays. From initial research to the commencement of sales, the period spans some 14 months and, to first departures, 21 months. For winter programmes and short breaks, which are normally smaller in volume, the corresponding preparation periods are somewhat less. The example shown should not be taken as definitive since, by nature of the very many activities that are being performed and the differing objectives of tour companies, there will always be variances on timings; for example, spreading the season into April or curtailing it at the end of September or in mid-October.

Research

Key outcomes of research are the forecasts of overall market size and the changing patterns of holiday-taking. These will assist in the selection of destinations, which in turn will be constrained by conditions of access, the extent of the tourist infrastructure and the political climate of the host country. In terms of destination choice, a specialist tour operator is able to respond far more quickly to changing market conditions than the volume or mass tour operator. The latter usually has long-term commitments to existing destinations which may include capital tied up in resorts. From destination choice, the research process will enable the operator to derive a market strategy, whereby one of four main options is possible. The first, market penetration, suggests that the destination continues to appeal to existing markets with the same product but through more manipulation of the elements of the marketing mix. The second, product development, suggests that the destination develops a new product to appeal to its existing market while, third, market development suggests that the existing destination product is targeted to new segments within the wider market. Finally, destinations could diversify in that they develop totally new products for new markets – a strategy that brings with it slightly higher risk than the preceding three strategy options.

Capacity planning

The market forecasts can be used to plan total capacity, which, together with the market strategy, will set tour specifications by type, destination and volume. Once the tour

ACTIVITY	Year 1					Year 2												Year 3									
	Aug	S	O	N	D	Jan	F	M	A	M	J	J	A	S	O	N	D	Jan	F	M	A	M	J	J	A	S	O
Research																											
• Review market performance	X																										
• Forecast market trends	X	X																									
• Select and compare new and existing destinations			X	X																							
• Determine market strategy				X	X																						
Capacity planning																											
• Tour specifications					X	X																					
• Negotiate with and contract suppliers						X	X	X																			
Financial evaluation																											
• Determine exchange rates							X	X																			
• Estimate future selling prices								X	X																		
• Finalise tour prices									X	X																	
Marketing																											
• Brochure planning and production										X	X	X															
• Brochure distribution and launch												X	X														
• Media advertising and sales promotion														X	X												
• Market stimulation												X									X						
Administration																											
• Recruit reservation staff													X														
• Establish reservation system														X	X	X											
• Receive reservations by telephone and view data															X	X	X	X	X	X	X	X	X	X	X	X	X
• Tour accounting and documentation															X	X	X	X	X	X	X	X	X	X	X	X	X
• Recruit resort staff																			X	X	X						
Tour management																											
• Customer care at resort																					X	X	X	X	X	X	X
• Customer correspondence																					X	X	X	X	X	X	X
• Payment of suppliers																						X	X	X	X	X	X

Figure 13.5   Tour-operating cycle of an abroad summer programme

programme has been planned, negotiations for beds and aircraft or coach seats may take place. Bed contracts may take two forms: an allocation (also referred to as an allotment) or a guarantee (also referred to as a commitment). An allocation operates on a sale-or-return basis with an appropriate release date. This type of contract is usually negotiated with medium-grade hotels and above, where opportunities for resale are generally easier. The risk is thus transferred from the tour operator/wholesaler to the hotelier. In turn the hotelier covers this risk by making contracts with several operators and quoting variable rates. With a guarantee, the wholesaler agrees to pay for the beds whether they are sold or not. Such a commitment naturally brings with it a cheaper rate than an allotment and is commonly applied for traditional destinations that enjoy high demand, or to self-catering properties for the purpose of obtaining exclusive contracts. As a rule, guarantee contracts would be below 20% of a tour operator's portfolio.

Aircraft seats may be contracted in a variety of ways. The largest tour operators and wholesalers are likely to have their own airline and some airlines, particularly in the USA, also have tour wholesaling divisions or companies. In other circumstances, the tour operator may contract an aircraft for the whole season (a 'time charter'), for specified flights (a 'whole plane charter'), or purchase a block of seats on a scheduled service or a chartered airline (a 'part charter'). The use of scheduled services tends to be for specialist tours (which are often escorted) or tailor-made packages for customers. As scheduled flights, even using codesharing, are likely to work on a break-even 'load factor' of 70% or less, airlines are prepared to give good discounts for inclusive tour excursion fares, which they make available through airbrokers, termed 'consolidators', to the advantage of agents putting together IITs.

Where an operator has contracted for a time charter, it is important to maximise the utilisation of the aircraft. The underlying principle is that charters should be operated back to back, namely that the plane should fly out with a new tour group and return with the previous group. Empty flights (known as 'empty legs') will arise at the beginning and end of the season, and these must be allowed for in the costing of seats. In summer the aircraft is likely to be used for three return trips or 'rotations' per day (two in winter) following the flight patterns shown in Figure 13.6. Aircraft may be used to rotate from one point of departure to a range of destinations or from a variety of departure points to one destination, or a combination of the two.

However, in the interests of protecting scheduled airlines from unfair competition through charters taking their normal traffic at peak times, aviation authorities have usually imposed operating restrictions on charter airlines. These may include the following:

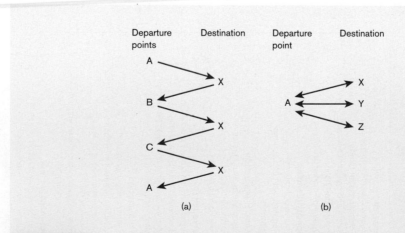

Figure 13.6   Time charter aircraft flight patterns: (a) 'w' pattern; (b) radial pattern

- The trip must be an inclusive tour, which implies the provision of accommodation as well as an airline seat.
- Airport terminals used by passengers must be the same on both the outward and return journeys.
- The air ticket must be for a round trip and is neither transferable nor part-usable in the sense that the holder may not use the return portion without having first travelled on the outbound flight.

Financial evaluation

We can see from Figure 13.5 that tour operators and wholesalers have to finalise prices some eight months or more before the first tour departs. Apart from the usual hazards of forecasting so far in advance, there are several inherent risks that must be accounted for. These are:

- contracts with local suppliers are commonly made in the currency of the destination country;
- the currency for payment of airlines is usually US dollars;
- airlines maintain the right to raise prices in response to increases in aviation fuel costs; and
- alterations in dues, taxes or fees levied by governments.

Tour operators and wholesalers cover these risks (termed hedging) by trying to build in anticipated changes in exchange rates for the purposes of determining tour prices and then buying forward the foreign exchange required at an agreed rate in order to meet contractual obligations, and by bringing in surcharges at the point of final billing of customers. Because the latter have proved unpopular, operators have tried to avoid their negative impact by offering no-surcharge guarantees, limiting the amount of surcharge liability, or offering cancellation options. In this context, it is worth noting that surcharges are often regulated by codes of conduct issued by the trade association and/or consumer protection legislation, as in the EU Package Travel Directive, which requires that latest date for price revisions (about a month before departure) must be included in the contract and that any significant alterations to the contract give the customer the right of cancellation without incurring penalties.

Marketing

Brochure production starts several months prior to the publication date with initial agreements about printing arrangements. It is usual for the layout of the brochure to be undertaken by a specialist design studio following the guidelines laid down by the tour operator's own staff. A variety of styles may be considered before the final choice is made. Particular attention is paid to the front cover to make sure that it conveys the right message to the target market segment and to ensure that it is likely to stand out on the travel agent's brochure racks. The draft final document is scrutinised for errors and corrected, with the pricing panels being left to the last possible moment before full production, to allow for any unforeseen economic changes.

It is important for the brochure to be launched well before the summer season starts because there is a section of the market that likes to book early in order to guarantee the destination and to take advantage of any promotional prices. The pattern of brochure distribution depends on the nature of the tours being offered and a trade-off between the costs of sending to all agents in order to maximise brochure exposure and limiting the number of outlets in the knowledge that the majority of the business will come from a minority of agents. Specialist wholesalers offering high-priced trips will restrict the number of retailers and in so doing convey the message of product exclusiveness to the customer. In any event, they are unlikely to be in a position to support a large network of travel agents. For cost-effective reasons even mass tour operators limit the number of agents they appoint and, as indicated previously, very large wholesalers often have their own retail travel chain to distribute their products.

Monitoring the progress of advertising and sales campaigns is achieved through booking patterns. Typically operators are looking for capacity utilisation factors of 85–90% in order to break even. Past experience enables wholesalers to establish reference booking patterns so as to compare actual with predicted bookings. Tour operators/wholesalers reserve the right to cancel or 'consolidate' holidays, for example, merging flights or combining itineraries and switching accommodation, if the demand take-up is insufficient. This makes it relatively easy for operators to test new products in their brochures. However, on the supply side, merging charter flights is not normally feasible for a summer programme after January because of the cost of airline cancellation charges. Large operators benefit here by having their own airline.

On the demand side, consolidation is a common source of annoyance to customers and leaves the travel agent with the unenviable task of advising his or her clients of the changes. Tour operators defend this practice on the grounds that if they were unable to use cancellation or consolidation to reduce overcapacity, then the average price of a holiday would rise. Underestimating demand is less of a difficulty because there is usually some flexibility in the system for procuring extra flights and accommodation. On the other hand, tour operators protect themselves against cancellation by their clients. Refunds are normally arranged on a sliding scale, so that the cancellation of a holiday six or seven weeks before departure may result only in a lost deposit, but after that the amount of the purchase price returned falls relatively sharply to zero for a cancellation only a day or so before departure.

Owing to the negative effects of consolidation on customers and the wider impacts this may have on public relations, tour operators and wholesalers prefer to use market stimulation techniques to boost sluggish booking patterns. Such tactical marketing (as opposed to strategic) methods will depend upon the time available and may vary from increasing advertising expenditure through special discounts for booking by a certain time, to substantial price cuts some six to four weeks before departure. Critical to obtaining last-minute sales is a network of retailers linked into the operator's own computer reservation system so that price promotions may be quickly communicated to the travelling public via this distribution channel, as well as own web site postings and distribution to e-intermediaries. Consumers, in turn, have recognised the bargains on offer and these have, over the years, encouraged later booking.

Administration

Owing to the seasonal nature of tour operation, the extra staff required to run the reservation system and represent the operator/wholesaler overseas are recruited and trained when needed, with only a core being employed all year. Frequently the same staff come and work for the same operator every year, which reduces the need for training.

The reservation system holds the tour operator's stock of holidays and careful attention is paid to matching the information held by the system to that contained in the brochure. Normally, travel agents make direct bookings through computer terminals in their own offices, but many agents still have to make telephone connections for clarification of the product on offer and to meet additional requests from increasingly knowledgeable clients.

Tour management

Specialist tour operators are most likely to offer escorted tours whereby a tour manager accompanies holidaymakers throughout the whole of their journey in order to oversee arrangements. For the volume package tour market, the function of the operator's resort representative is to host the tour. This involves meeting the tourists when they arrive and ensuring that the transfer procedures to the places of accommodation go smoothly. The representative will be expected to spend some time at the resort before the start of the season checking facilities, noting any variations from the brochure and, with the authority of the company, requesting discrepancies to be put right. During the holiday, the representative is required to be available to guests at the various hotels to give advice and deal with the many problems that may arise, as well as supervising (and sometimes organising) social activities and excursions, where they earn commission on sales.

After the holiday the operator/wholesaler will receive customer correspondence that will include compliments, suggestions and complaints. Most correspondence can be dealt with by a standard letter and justified complaints may receive a small refund. For serious complaints, national travel associations may offer arbitration services which can reconcile disputes before steps are taken to instigate legal proceedings.

Tour operator economics

We have already considered many of the economic aspects of tour operation in our discussion of the benefits of intermediation and the way in which a tour programme is put together. Essentially the mass tour operator or wholesaler relies on the economies of scale generated by bulk purchase and this in turn allows individual packages to be competitively priced to the consumer on the basis of a high take-up rate of offers made.

Once the tour operator/wholesaler is committed to a programme, the financial risks are substantial, irrespective of tactical risk-avoidance strategies such as late release clauses, surcharges and consolidation. This is because most of the costs of running the programme, if it is to run at all, are unavoidable and therefore fixed. The marginal or variable costs of selling an extra holiday are very small, which accounts for the large discounts on offer for 'late-availability' trips that give the customer only a short period of notice (sometimes just a few days) before departure.

Leverage

The financial structure of tour operation is illustrated in Figure 13.7. R is the revenue line which increases with the level of capacity utilisation and C_1 the total cost line attributable to running the tour programme. It may be seen that C_1 cuts the revenue and costs axis some way above the point of origin. The latter is caused by the high level of fixed costs in relation to the variable costs of tour operation. The financial term for this is a 'high operating leverage', which is a characteristic of tour operation. By way of contrast, C_2 is a total cost line, which has a low operating leverage: fixed costs are relatively small when compared to the steeply rising variable costs.

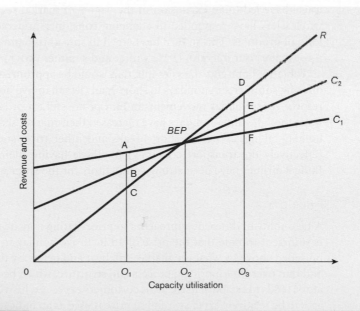

| **Figure 13.7** | Financial structure of tour operation |

Consider a tour operator who is planning a break-even capacity utilisation level of O_2, but demand is such that O_3 holidays are sold. Clearly, O_3 is well above the break-even point (*BEP*) and so the operator makes substantial profits as shown by the difference DF between R and C_1. A firm that has a low operating leverage would not do so well, as can be seen from the difference DE between R and C_2. Conversely, if the tour operator did not manage to achieve targeted break-even sales and the realised utilisation was some way below the required level, say, O_1, the losses AC can be severe and may result in the collapse of the operator. We show in Figure 13.7 that a firm with a low operating leverage would not be so badly affected, for AB is much less than AC.

There is thus considerable financial risk associated with tour operation and this acts as a deterrent to entry. It is important to realise that once a tour programme has been arranged and the day of departure is near, then even costs that were once variable now become fixed, so operators are willing to discount heavily at the last minute in order to make a contribution to their fixed expenses. Specialist operators cover this risk by dealing with niche markets, and using scheduled airline services and high-grade hotels for which reservations may be readily cancelled if the minimum number of confirmed bookings for the tour is not met. The major tour operators address this financial risk by securing their market position through vertically integrating their operation both forwards and backwards. The tied agency scheme in Germany was particularly effective in allowing the large tour operators to profit from their market position. It is in the middle ground, among wholesalers who have neither their own chartered aircraft (and so must purchase a part charter) nor their own retail network, where the financial risk tends to be at its highest. These are the tour operators that are most likely to go out of business when demand falters. To safeguard the public from lost holidays or from being stranded abroad when a tour operator collapses, responsible governments have legislation requiring operating licences, for example, the UK Air Travel Organisers Licence (ATOL), which was initiated in 1972, and bonding arrangements through a bank or an approved insurer, though the fund is not always sufficient to meet the losses or extra expenses incurred.

Sales mix

During the 1950s holiday tourism was largely centred around the traditional summer break at a coastal resort, but rising affluence, longer holiday periods and an increasing desire to travel have led to an expansion in the degree of market segmentation. Tour operators and wholesalers have responded to changing consumer preferences by diversifying their portfolio of products. This in turn has helped to spread risk and generate all-year business. Thus most major tour operators have winter and summer programmes.

Table 13.3 presents the sales mix that would be appropriate for a large European operator offering summer sun holidays to short-haul (less than five hours' flying time) Mediterranean resorts. Most holiday movements in Europe are still towards beach destinations in summertime, though winter holidays have increased their market share in response to more frequent holiday-taking, as well as short breaks and other trips, such as minimum rated packages (effectively the transport cost only) for those having their own holiday accommodation. Budget airlines have been strong competitors for the latter market.

Pricing

A taxonomy of different approaches to price-setting may be found in Chapter 19, but here it is sufficient to note that the price of an inclusive holiday in a wholesaler's brochure will be bounded above by what the market will bear and below by the cost of providing the holiday, and that over time a pricing process and structure, which becomes the model for most operators, tends to establish itself. Thus customers expect exclusive holidays and tailor-made packages to be relatively expensive and so price is used as an indicator of quality, which in turn gives the tour operator the opportunity of securing higher margins. The volume market for inclusive

Table 13.3	Sales structure of a large tour operator	
Sales		**Percentages**
Summer inclusive tours		45
Winter inclusive tours		30
Short breaks and Others		20
Excursions and insurance		4
Interest on deposits		1
Total		**100**

Source: Trade information

tours is sold competitively on price, so costs and capacity utilisation have greater significance. Hence operators will consider a range of offers, taking account of factors such as:

- seasonal effects – the range of variation between low- and peak-season prices is usually around 20 to 30%;
- exchange rate movements;
- competitors' prices and the degree of product differentiation and brand value;
- load factors;
- component costs and their complexity, for example, supplements for extended stay;
- promotional pricing to encourage early booking and late-availability discounts;
- market segmentation pricing, with special offers for senior citizens, young people and families with children below a certain age; and
- discounts for affinity group travel.

The price structure for a typical mass market inclusive tour undertaken within Europe is shown in Table 13.4. Competition keeps profit margins low, and so the emphasis is on volume sales and cost control to sustain net income. In these circumstances, the importance of hedging on foreign exchange is readily appreciated, because uncovered fluctuations in exchange rates may easily erode slender profit margins. This does not entirely remove the risk, for the tour operator/wholesaler still has to predict the amount of business going to each destination.

Air seats

For wholesalers who operate their own airlines or secure whole plane or time charters, an important element in determining the tour price is the costing of an air seat. This is calculated from the following formula:

$$s = \frac{dR}{(d-1)LN} + t$$

where s = unit seat cost per round trip, d = number of aircraft departures, R = aircraft cost per rotation, L = load factor, N = number of seats per flight and t = airport tax.

As an example, consider an aircraft of 350 seats contracted on a time charter for 30 departures. The rotation cost is calculated at 45,000 currency units, the load factor at 90% and airport tax is ascertained to be 20 currency units. By substitution into the above formula, the unit seat cost per return flight is:

$$s = \frac{30 \times 45,000}{29 \times 0.9 \times 350} + 20$$

$$= 168$$

Table 13.4	Price structure of a 14-night inclusive tour	
Item	**Percentages**	
Price	100	
Direct costs		
Accommodation	41	
Air seat (including taxes)	32	
Transfers, excursions, etc.	3	
Agent's commission	10	
Total	86	
Gross margin	14	
Indirect costs		
Payroll expenses	4	
Marketing	3	
Office expenses	2	
Total	9	
Net income		
Trading profit	5	
Interest on deposits	1	
Total	6	

Source: Trade information

Note that the number of departures in the denominator of the equation is reduced by 1 to allow for empty legs.

Strategic positioning

History has shown that while there are no major constraints on entry into travel wholesaling, the mass holiday market in any country tends to be dominated by only a handful of companies. The tour operator/wholesaler has no monopoly over airline seats or hotel beds and product standards are easy to emulate. This being the case, the lessons of success indicate strategic market positions secured by a combination of the following factors:

- economies of scale through bulk purchase and volume distribution;
- low-cost distribution network, particularly IT direct sales, together with national coverage;
- developing new products and markets, and adopting new technologies;
- competitive pricing;
- multi-branding to attract different market segments; and
- product differentiation to avoid competing on price alone.

As with major retail stores and supermarket chains, volume throughput and national presence are critical to the success of a mass tour operator. This being the case, in a European context, it is unlikely that any wholesaler can compete effectively, particularly on price, in the mass market segment with sales of under a million holidays. When account is taken of the organisation structure needed and bonding requirements of around 10% of turnover if belonging to a recognised trade association with its own reserve fund, but as much as 25% otherwise (EU Package Travel Directive), it will be appreciated that the costs of entry into the volume market do act as a considerable deterrent. However, once the volume market has been penetrated, the substantial fixed costs involved are easily transferable to rival operations.

The factors giving rise to a winning strategy are also the cause of a high degree of sales concentration in the tour operation industry, leaving small operators to create their own distinctive market share through specialised holidays. The economics of the industry are such that this situation is one that can only continue: markets are **contestable** and the large operators are prepared to defend their market position by diversifying their products, even into specialist areas, by multi-branding to reach economic sales levels in particular markets quickly, by undertaking price wars and generally enforcing the success criteria outlined above. This of course is subject to legislation on competition policy in their source markets, termed **anti-trust legislation** in the USA.

CONCLUSION

We have used this chapter to review the way in which the individual elements of the tourism product may be packaged together for convenience and then distributed to the market efficiently. There are important variations in the way in which this procedure is executed in different regions of the world but, as a result of the predominant north–south flow in tourism, it is the northern countries of the world that have developed the most sophisticated network of distribution to satisfy the volume of market demand.

However, it is important to remember that the distribution of the tourism product is the aspect of the tourism system that has changed most rapidly over recent years as new technology permeates the marketplace and direct access to the tourism product becomes even more prevalent. The counter to this is the way the travel trade has been able to reshape itself to meet these changes.

SELF-CHECK QUESTIONS

1. Review and discuss the roles of travel agencies and tour operators.
2. Identify the benefits and drawbacks of further consolidation and concentration in the distribution channel in tourism.
3. Compare and contrast differences in the distribution of the tourism product between the USA and Europe.
4. Identify potential threats to the continued dominance of travel agencies and tour operators and assess the likely impact of technological progress in respect of distribution.
5. What are the implications of 'switch selling' for both the tourism intermediary and the consumer?

ESSAY QUESTIONS

1. Critically discuss the arguments for and against disintermediation of the distribution channel in tourism.
2. To what extent is bonding still important in the travel industry?
3. 'It is an impossible task for trade associations to represent fairly the rights of consumers when their obligations are to their members.' Discuss.
4. Critically explore the benefits and drawbacks of the adoption of a multichannel strategy for a tour operator of your choice.
5. Critically discuss the future strategic options for independent intermediaries in light of the trend towards further consolidation and concentration in the tourism industry.

ANNOTATED FURTHER READING

Books

Buhalis, D. (2003) *eTourism: Information Technology for Strategic Tourism Management*, Pearson Education, Harlow.
This book provides an extensive overview of the digitisation of all processes and value chains in the tourism and hospitality industries. It explores in depth the impacts of information communication technology (ICT) across all tourism sectors as well as providing a useful debate as to how the application of ICT is fundamental to the future competitiveness of the tourism industry.

Papatheordorou, A. (2006) *Corporate Rivalry and Market Power: Competition Issues in the Tourism Industry*, I.B. Tauris, London.
This very timely text provides an important and original analysis of competition issues in the tourism industry. Although the book explores corporate rivalry and competition issues across all sectors of the tourism industry, the chapters relating to the impact of technology and travel distribution systems are particularly pertinent to many of the issues raised in this chapter.

WTO (2002) *Tourism in the Age of Alliances, Mergers and Acquisitions*, WTO, Madrid.
A very credible account of the increasing concentration and consolidation of the global tourism industry. Detailed analysis of each sector of tourism is provided with critical discussion relating to current and future issues for each sector, including tourism intermediaries, to encourage future debate.

Web sites

www.abta.com
This very useful web site provided by the Association of British Travel Agents offers a wealth of information for the UK travel trade and consumer. With 85% of the UK's package holidays sold through ABTA members the site is comprehensive in its coverage of all aspects of travel and tourism. ABTA's Code of Conduct is a strong feature of the site as is its coverage of issues relating to arbitration, disability and financial protection.

www.travelmole.com
Travelmole provides an excellent resource base for students, academics and practitioners in travel and tourism. It contains extensive news reports on all sectors of tourism and is comprehensive and contemporary in its coverage.

www.tui-group.com
This corporate web site provides some valuable insights into the TUI AG organisation, its products, markets, and range of business units, and serves as an excellent resource base.

References cited

Bray, R. and Raitz, V. (2001) *Flight to the Sun: the Story of the Holiday Revolution*, Continuum, London.

Buhalis, D. (2003) *eTourism: Information Technology for Strategic Tourism Management*, Pearson Education, Harlow.

Horner, S. and Swarbrooke, J. (2004) *International Cases in Tourism Management*, Elsevier Butterworth Heinemann, Oxford.

Hudson, S., Snaith, T., Miller, G. and Hudson, P. (2001) 'Travel retailing: "switch selling" in the UK', pp. 172–84 in Buhalis, D. and Laws, E. (eds), *Tourism Distribution Channels: Practices, Issues and Transformations*, Continuum, London.

MMC (1998) *Foreign Package Holidays*, HMSO, London.

WTO (2002) *Tourism in the Age of Alliances, Mergers and Acquisitions*, WTO, Madrid.

MAJOR CASE STUDY 13.1
Merger mania – Thomas Cook Group plc

The recent £2.8 billion merger between MyTravel and Thomas Cook, which in turn has created the second biggest travel operator in Europe – the Thomas Cook Group – in part reflects the challenging conditions being faced by the two companies in what is a very competitive, fickle and unstable market environment. It comes as no surprise that one of the principal drivers behind the merger was the need to cut costs substantially, estimated at £75 million a year, as well as maintain a strong market presence in the UK, Germany, Scandinavia, France, Canada and the Benelux countries! Although the planned savings will undoubtedly lead to job losses and the closure of many Thomas Cook shops, the combined pressures of low-cost airlines and online bookings being faced by the 'traditional' players are such that one could argue that there really was no alternative!! Before exploring the actual merger in more depth it is worth introducing the historical context of the two companies.

THOMAS COOK – A HISTORICAL OVERVIEW

With its origins going back as far as the mid-1800s, Thomas Cook grew from a one-man excursion 'organiser' to what is today one half of Europe's second largest travel operator. Thomas Cook's first European tour took place during the summer of 1855 whereupon two significant innovations arose. The first, the hotel coupon, enabled travellers to pay for hotel accommodation and meals instead of using money. The second, the circular note, proved to be the forerunner for the travellers' cheque, which enabled tourists to obtain local currency in exchange for a paper note issued by Thomas Cook. After a turbulent period of development in the early 1900s, Thomas Cook benefited considerably from the post-war holiday boom, which saw 1 million Britons travelling abroad by 1950. Although Thomas Cook remained the largest and most successful company in the industry, the 1960s brought with it ever-increasing competition from numerous new players who sought to undercut Thomas Cook. Acquired by a consortium of the former Midland Bank, Trust House Forte and the Automobile Association in 1972, a number of radical changes were implemented to withstand the competitive threat – including its again highly innovative Money Back Guarantee scheme in 1974.

Thomas Cook later became a wholly owned subsidiary of the Midland Bank Group and began to concentrate on the long-haul, rather than short-haul package tours' market.

After celebrating 150 years of operation in 1991, Thomas Cook was acquired from the Midland Bank by Westdeutsche Landesbank (WestLB), Germany's third largest bank, and LTU Group, Germany's leading charter airline, in 1992. Eventually, Thomas Cook became a wholly owned subsidiary of WestLB before entering a period of rapid growth which saw the acquisition of Sunworld, Time Off and Flying Colours in quick succession. This period of growth for Thomas Cook then culminated in merger with Carlson Leisure Group's UK travel interests and the subsequent formation of JMC in 1999.

The new millennium saw the acquisition of Thomas Cook by C&N Touristik AG, an acquisition which was eventually approved by the European Community in March 2001. Recognising the heritage and respect for the global travel brand that is Thomas Cook, C&N Touristik AG renamed themselves as Thomas Cook AG and are now able to benefit fully from being one of the most recognised and most respected brands in the world.

MYTRAVEL – A HISTORICAL OVERVIEW

MyTravel Group plc began life in 1972 as Airtours when its founder, David Crossland, acquired two travel agency outlets in Lancashire in the UK. Through further acquisitions and the organisation of package holidays Airtours expanded very quickly to the extent that by 1986 it was handling in the region of 290,000 customers per annum. In the same year, Airtours sold its travel agency business which, by then, comprised 21 outlets. The money generated was used to fund further expansion of the tour operating business – via strategies of horizontal and vertical integration – to the extent that it was eventually floated on the London Stock Exchange in 1987 with a market capitalisation of £28 million. Since flotation, a number of significant developments have taken place. For example between 1987 and 1995, Airtours developed Eurosites, a camping operator with sites across Europe, began short (mostly one-day) trips to major European cities, and acquired Pickfords Travel Service Limited, in addition to acquiring Hogg Robinson Leisure Travel Limited, the Aspro Travel Group, and the Tradewinds brand. Once the acquisitions were completed, Airtours launched their 'Going Places' brand which sought to bring together their retail shops under one umbrella. There then followed the introduction of a ski-based programme, followed by the acquisition of the Scandinavian Leisure Group (SLG), and their first entry into the fly/cruise market with the acquisition of the MS *Seawing* and MS *Carousel* cruising ships. After acquisition of further travel agents Airtours diversified by acquiring Late Escapes, a telephone sales business – a move that was in response to the emerging change in travel booking patterns taking place in the market. Toward the end of this period, Airtours also acquired Sunquest Vacations – one of Canada's largest tour operating businesses.

The next seven years saw yet more growth and expansion in a number of sectors. Hence, between 1996 and 2003 a strategy of acquisition continued with established names such as Sun International SA of Belgium, Cresta Holidays Limited and Bridge Travel Services Limited, both weekend break specialists, Direct Holidays Limited (as its name suggests a tour operating business specialising in the direct sell market), the Panorama Holiday Group (a specialist in Tunisia), and Travelworld, a travel agency business with outlets based in the north of England. The years 1999 and 2000 saw yet more acquisitions with a variety of European-based tour operating businesses coming into the Airtours family. Expansion further afield saw the acquisition of DriveAway Holidays Pty Limited – an Australian car-renting and leasing company – and Kemwel, a similar operation in the United States. In May 2000, an ambitious e-commerce strategy was developed, named MyTravel, including the launch of www.mytravelco.com. The wider e-commerce strategy offered a more holistic approach in that appropriate content and product features were integrated with distribution and customer relationship management. The strategy was multichannel in that customers could purchase products and services from a multitude of technology platforms with a high degree of personalisation. For example, in addition to a wide range of holidays, flight-only offers, tailor-made itineraries, charter flight tickets, cruises and numerous holiday extras, Airtours gave customers the facility to create their own personal portfolio of dream destinations. It also includes LateEscapes – a holiday auction site – virtual tours, independent hotel reviews, a magazine and world weather reports.

Perhaps the most significant change for the future was that which occurred in 2002 – the rebranding of the company name Airtours plc to MyTravel plc. This move incorporated the development of a multichannel distribution capability with MyTravel.com in the UK, Scandinavia and America. Thus, the new e-commerce strategy served as the driver for the new group company name – MyTravel Group plc – the e-developments driving organisational change. This period also saw the launch of MyTravel Lite – the group's low-fare airline and the first UK budget airline used by a UK tour operator – and the rebranding of the Airtours international and premier fleets to MyTravel Airways.

However, in 2003 a number of overly optimistic forecasts led to a financial crisis to the extent that the company reported a loss of £358.3 million after making a loss of £20.4 million in 2002. As a consequence of the loss in 2002, a wave of bad publicity emanated from the press and in turn, many people withheld bookings for fear that the company would suffer financial collapse, thus making the summer 2003 period particularly challenging. Thereafter MyTravel undertook a myriad of initiatives to regain momentum but it was not until December 2006 that it finally returned to profit!

THE MERGER

Through a combination of organisational consolidation, cost reductions, economies of scales and operational efficiencies, the merger between MyTravel and Thomas Cook is planned to save at least £75 million a year, although it is not expected that the full benefit of synergies will be realised for about three years. In 2006, the 'value' of the merged group would have been £7,949 million with a combined total of 19.1 million passengers, 2,926 retail outlets, 97 aircraft and just under 33,000 employees. The strategy for the new group is built in four pillars, namely: the need to integrate the businesses and deliver synergies; strengthening of the mainstream tour operating model through continued operational improvements and quality product delivery; growing of its independent travel segment; and, extending the group's financial services and in particular the leveraging of Thomas Cook's recognised strengths in this area. The new company is debt-free and has high financial reserves so is in a strong position to proactively participate in further market consolidation in Europe.

Source: Horner and Swarbrooke, 2004; www.mytravelgroup .com; MyTravel Group PLC Annual Report & Accounts 2003; www.thomascookgroup.com

DISCUSSION QUESTIONS

1. To what extent is this merger likely to serve as a catalyst for other similar mergers, both in Europe and beyond? Discuss.

2. What do you consider the risks to be of undertaking such a merger and what are the 'competitive' consequences for those non-merged companies that exist and smaller, independent operators across Europe?

3. Is there really no alternative to further consolidation and concentration in the sector? Discuss.

CHAPTER 14

Transportation

LEARNING OUTCOMES

The primary objective of this chapter is to demonstrate the importance of transportation to the overall tourism product and to illustrate their interdependence. Transport is responsible not only for physically moving tourists from the main originating areas to the destination, but also for transporting tourists once they arrive at the destination. With this in mind, on completion of this chapter, you will have:

- an understanding of the major modes of transportation for tourism and the competitive advantages and disadvantages of each;

- an appreciation of the influence of political developments on transportation for tourism;

- a knowledge of the purpose and impact of regulation in transportation;

- an awareness of issues and future trends that will have an impact upon transportation for tourism; and

- an understanding of transport as a tourist attraction.

Photograph: The Golden Gate Bridge, San Francisco, USA © Kelly Miller

INTRODUCTION

Tourism is about being elsewhere and, in consequence, the main function of transport in the tourism system is one of transit, carrying tourists between generating regions and the tourist destination regions. The relationship is two sided. Adequate transportation infrastructure offering access from generating markets is one of the most important prerequisites for the development of any destination. In most cases mass tourism has been developed in areas where extensive transportation networks were in place and the potential for additional tourism-related development was available. The fact that in most destinations worldwide the traveller can find adequate hospitality and leisure facilities close to transportation terminals demonstrates the interrelationship between their development.

On the other hand, tourism demand has stimulated the rapid development of transportation. As the number of tourists requiring safe, quick and comfortable transport to their destinations at a reasonable cost increased, the transportation industry has had to adjust in order to accommodate this demand. In response, technology has developed new vehicles with improved speeds, increased capacity and lower operating costs.

In this chapter we provide a framework for the analysis of passenger transportation operations for tourism. We explore the modes and elements of transportation, examine issues such as regulation of transport and its environmental impacts, and perform a competitive analysis for the major modes of transportation. Finally, the chapter illustrates the major future political, environmental and economic challenges for tourist transportation.

TRANSPORT AS A COMPONENT OF THE TOURIST PRODUCT

Transportation is an essential element of the tourist product in three ways:

- the means to reach the destination;
- a necessary means of movement at the destination;
- in a minority of instances it is the actual tourism attraction or activity.

Transport as transit

By far the most important contribution of transport is as a means of transit, which accounts for 90% of tourist use of transport. It is a derived demand, which is not undertaken for its own sake but merely as a means of getting from the tourism generating region to the tourism destination. This can produce significant operational difficulties because the transport operator has little control over the demand for such services. The busiest tourism routes are those which link originating regions, which display high levels of income and leisure time, with popular tourist destinations. For example, there remain large traffic flows between affluent countries of northern Europe and countries with Mediterranean resorts in southern Europe. The future prospects for such routes are more a function of the relative affluence of the former and the relative attractiveness of the latter than they are of any actions taken by the transport operator. Furthermore, tourism is a fragile industry and traffic flows can undergo significant change instantaneously as a result of a natural catastrophe, conflict or instance of political instability such as displayed by the fall in transatlantic air travel in the immediate aftermath of events post-9/11.

Not only is the size of demand outside the control of the transport operator, so too are the patterns of demand. The derived nature of transport demand means that factors such as climate, restrictions to vacation entitlement from work, religious festivals and the dates of school holidays all influence when the demand for tourism transport occurs creating peaks and troughs. For cold climate regions such as northern Europe there are clear periods of peak seasonal demand from June to mid-August, but within this pattern there are more subtle peaks, particularly day of the week peaks. In many destinations such as the UK, Denmark or the ski resorts of the Alpine region of North Tyrol and Salzburg there is a preference to travel on Saturdays for main holidays, heavily influenced by accommodation providers, many of which only accept Saturday to Saturday bookings. The growth of short weekend break holidays has contributed to Friday travelling peaks on some modes of transport.

These peak periods of demand create operational problems because like many service industries transport production cannot be stored, it is consumed at the point of production. Therefore to meet demand at peak periods the transport operator has to provide extra capacity which may then be underutilised during the **off-peak** periods. If one is not careful, serving peak demand can become unprofitable. Transport operators must take care to ensure the revenue earned (which could be over a relatively short peak period) exceeds the full costs of providing the capacity, including all fixed costs, which are incurred over the whole year. The most commonly cited examples of **peak** capacity are related to fleet size. Coach companies, rail operators and airlines all have potential for the fleet size to be determined by the peak season with some vehicles not really required to meet off-peak demand. However, the operational problems extend to other elements of the transport system such as the terminal. For example, Palma airport (Majorca) has four passenger terminals, but only fully utilises them during the peak summer season when it becomes one of the busiest airports in Europe.

Transport operators have powers to generate or increase levels of demand or even influence patterns of demand, although only marginally. Their most powerful tool is price. For instance, very low prices can be used to generate or stimulate extra demand during the off-peak period. Nevertheless, very low fares to Majorca in January may well increase demand for air services during that off-peak month but will not generate passenger numbers to match those of the peak period and, with the low fares, overall yields will also be low. Operators can also charge higher fares for peak days of demand to reduce fluctuations. UK rail operators have used higher leisure fares for travel on Fridays and many charter airlines in Europe have charged higher fares for Saturday travel.

Despite being a derived demand, transport for transit can be viewed as part of the leisure experience with the journey being important for some categories of visitor. The view from the coach or the excitement of flying are examples of potential enjoyment. However, for the business traveller, transport may be seen as a necessary evil, a disutility which must be experienced to reach the destination. The degree to which travel is part of the leisure experience has been analysed as a continuum. It is influenced by:

- the mode of transport. Some modes are intrinsically more enjoyable than others;
- the personality of the tourist;
- the frequency with which the tourist uses that mode;
- the group with whom one travels. Supervising young children will for instance add stress to the journey.

However, increases in traffic result in increased congestion, contributing to unscheduled and unacceptable levels of delay that reduce the pleasure gained from travelling for a range of modes such as driving (still often portrayed as a pleasure activity by motoring manufacturers in their advertising campaigns) and air travel. While still very rare, instances of air rage and road rage are increasing.

Transport at the destination

Once at the destination, visitors make use of taxis, rental cars, scheduled bus and coach services, and rail and, dependent on the destination, even ferries. For longer excursions where the country is seen as the destination area, scheduled domestic air may be used and rail should increase in significance. Travel in the destination area accounts for around 10% of tourist use of transport. This of course involves tourists sharing scheduled local transport services, which were not specifically designed for their use, with the local population. Sometimes this provides an ideal fit with the two markets complementing each other. This is true of tourism to major cities such as Amsterdam, Helsinki, Boston and Brisbane where tourism demand for bus and metro services tends to commence after 9.30–10.00 am when the peak period of local use for commuting to work is over. Therefore tourists provide an opportunity for the transport operator to earn additional revenue at a time when there is spare capacity. Special product developments such as off-peak travelcards allow unlimited travel but only after the morning peak. This can help the operator control and manage this division, although some conflicts between local and tourist use during the early evening peak may be unavoidable.

In other locations there can be conflicts between tourist and local requirements. The vintage bus fleet in Malta is more suited to tourists than the local population whereas ticketing policy does not reflect the needs of tourist users well. Visitor expenditure figures illustrate the importance of transport as an element of the product. Transport at the destination can represent as much as 15% of international visitor expenditure within a large country such as Indonesia.

Some transport operators in destination areas tailor products specifically for tourism such as the half day and whole day coach excursion to attractions in the surrounding region. Sightseeing tours on the top of a double-deck bus with the roof removed are familiar sights in many destination areas, particularly cities. Having first begun in capital cities such as London, the concept has over recent years expanded and in 2001 Guide Friday, the largest operator of such tours, were operating in 30 UK destinations and seven European destinations (Robbins, 2003). A more recent development pioneered in the USA are 'Duck Tours', which undertake a sightseeing tour using a Second World War amphibian landing craft, with a short water-based section included on the tour route. These tours do give the tourist mobility around the destination area and on the bus tours tickets are valid all day so one can hop on and hop off. However, for many the vehicle itself becomes the attraction and perhaps that rightly falls under the next section.

Transport as the tourist attraction

Increasingly, there are instances of transport, both within and between countries, becoming an attractive tourist product in its own right. The largest mass market is the cruise industry (see Major Case Study 14.1). Other examples include:

- railway products – the Palace on Wheels (India), the Blue Train (South Africa), the Orient Express, and the Eastern & Oriental Express;
- sea products – day trips by ferry;
- canal cruises in a narrow boat.

COMPONENTS OF THE TRANSPORTATION SYSTEM

We can identify four basic elements in any transportation system, namely:

- the way;
- the terminal;
- the vehicle; and
- motive power.

These elements vary for each transportation mode but performance is dependent on the interaction of these four elements. Speed, capacity, safety, security and even perceived quality of service for each mode is dictated by the weakest element in the system.

The way

The way is the medium of travel over which the vehicle operates. It may be purely artificial, such as roads or railways, or natural, such as air or water. Railways and inland waterways restrict vehicle movement to very specific patterns, or pathways, while road offers a much greater degree of vehicle flexibility over the route network. At first sight air and sea would appear to allow unlimited flexibility but international regulations and conventions dictate otherwise. Significant areas of airspace over a country are reserved solely for military use and the civil airspace is delineated into air corridors and controlled by **air traffic control** (ATC) systems, such as NATS in the UK, utilising sophisticated computer systems and comprehensive radar coverage. Likewise, although less rigorous, there are designated shipping lanes. In considering transport modes, the availability of the way is very important and requires considerable investment. A shortage in capacity leads to inefficient services, congestion and unscheduled delays. Currently in the UK congestion on the rail network has resulted in reduced numbers of services on some routes in an attempt to improve reliability. In contrast, in mainland Europe, where land is at less of a premium, rail use has been encouraged by expanded rail capacity with the addition of new high speed lines. Capacity overload on the ATC system can result in aircraft having to circle busy airports for significant amounts of time awaiting a landing slot. Traffic congestion on roads is a phenomenon familiar to many in developed and developing countries.

The terminal

Public transport terminals give the passenger access to the vehicle, or act as an interchange between different modes of transport. Not all modes need to have sophisticated terminals; buses and coaches for instance can and do operate from roadside locations although town and city centre terminals are often more substantive. Perhaps the most complex terminal is

Photograph 14.1	Terminal 5 at Heathrow: on time and on budget – to maximise use of Heathrow's two parallel runways.

Source: BAA, Artist's Impression

an airport and the dramatic growth in air transport worldwide has witnessed the development of many new airports in recent years (Hong Kong, Kuala Lumpur and Athens).

In fact, most terminals are becoming integrated transportation points as they can act as interchanges where travellers can transfer between vehicles or modes. Switzerland has examples of integrated rail and air transport with rail termini at the airports of Zurich and Geneva further linked to main rail routes and then the post-bus to the final destination. Airports can be used as transfer points between aircraft, often organised into the well-structured patterns of arrival and departures required for hub airports in the hub-and-spoke route networks initially developed in the deregulated US domestic market, but also must interface with other modes of travelling, such as the car, coach or train.

The design of terminals and the amenities they offer depend heavily upon the type of journey and mode of transportation involved, as does the length of time spent at the terminal. Air will generally require the longest visit, with arrival at the airport required one to two hours (or even longer where security measures dictate) prior to scheduled departure. Travellers will also tend to allow excess time for infrequently undertaken long-distance rail journeys, whereas arrival will be just in time for shorter, frequent and familiar rail journeys such as commuting. The basic requirement is for toilet facilities and light refreshment, although the length of time the passenger is held as a captive customer creates retail opportunities which airport terminals seek to exploit fully, with up to 60% of airport revenue from retail activity. This share appears to be falling in European airports following the abolition of duty free sales for passengers travelling within the EU in June 1999 (Graham, 2003). Main line city centre termini for intercity rail traffic have also sought to exploit retail opportunities (Liverpool Street and Victoria Stations in London).

For private transport such as the car there is still a requirement for the user to access the vehicle and for the vehicle to access the way, although there is no designated terminal where this must happen. The relative importance of the terminal is often and easily overlooked. The comfort and convenience of the journey can be influenced as much by the experience at the terminal as by the experience on the vehicle. Airlines seek to gain a competitive advantage for high yield first and business class passengers with the use of VIP lounges. Airports also demonstrate the importance of the terminal in the capacity of the overall transport network. All terminals need sufficient capacity for both vehicular movements and also for passenger movement. In the case of the airport these activities are separated. The vehicle movements are airside, predominantly measured as air traffic movements (ATMs) and catered for by runways (together with the capacity of ATC). The number of runways, the use and availability of taxiways, the number of parking stands for aircraft and the number of exit points on the runway for smaller aircraft who do not need the full length of the runway, all dictate the number of ATMs an airport can handle each hour. Shortage of capacity to meet forecast demand at London airports in 2015 (DfT, 2000) led to the proposals set out in the aviation White Paper of December 2003 to develop a second runway at London Stansted followed by a possible third runway at London Heathrow (DfT, 2003).

Passenger capacity is a function of the terminal facilities to handle the passengers carried by the ATMs. Essential facilities include check-in, baggage handling and baggage reclaim, passport, immigration and customs controls as well as the shopping and refreshment facilities. Since 1985 virtually all increases in airport capacity in London have been achieved by the development of more terminals. However, squeezing more capacity into airports brings its own problems. Maximum runway throughput can only be achieved with queuing aircraft (on the ground for take off and in stacks for landing) which itself affects reliability (Graham, 2003). Airlines publish longer scheduled flight times to allow for the delays in an attempt to retain punctuality and yet despite this over 25% of flights from many European airports such as Madrid, Rome, Paris (Charles De Gaulle – CDG – and Orly) as well as London are over 15 minutes late. The position in the USA is equally difficult with congestion well documented. Additional runway capacity will be a major requirement in many destinations if growth rates are to be maintained (see Mini Case Study 14.2).

The vehicle

The carrying unit is the actual transportation media: the vehicle that facilitates the movement. The nature of vehicles has been influenced by numerous factors, which include travel demand and technological developments, as well as the other elements of the mode, particularly motive power. In the past few decades developments have occurred in the carrying units which have enabled greater speed, which usually, but not always, resulted in greater efficiency and sometimes improved consumer comfort. Executive style coaches with on-board services, airline-style reclining seats on trains and railway-viewing cars and flat seats in airline business class are all examples of improved comfort.

Motive power

Finally, and perhaps the most important, motive power is the key element in transportation development. Natural power of horse-drawn carriages and sailing vessels provided the initial energy for transportation. The expansion of steam power provided the opportunity for the introduction of steamships and railways which were such a driving force behind the creation of mass tourism in Europe, while the internal combustion engine stimulated the development of road and air transportation. Finally, jet propulsion enabled air transportation to be competitively priced and gave aircraft speed, range and increased vehicle size. The combination of speed (which allowed the vehicle to make more return trips each 24 hours) and increased vehicle size dramatically reduced operating costs per seat km (Doganis, 2002), enabling these savings to be passed on to the consumer in the form of lower fares. Not all technological advances led to increased efficiency. Concorde, which was withdrawn from passenger service in 2003, had relatively poor productivity despite its very high speed, largely as a result of the low vehicle capacity (approximately 100 seats) and was only viable operating predominantly a business service with a premium fare. Likewise the Hovercraft offered high-speed sea crossings but a combination of high fuel consumption and poor reliability in rough weather prevented its development into the mass mode that was predicted in the 1960s.

Speed of travel has largely stabilised in the last decade with no major technological advances. Naturally the speed for any mode is governed by the interaction of the various components. Cars can move faster than 70 mph (100 km per hour) but limitations of the way mean that maximum speed limits are required for the safety of other road users (both car drivers and where there is no segregation pedestrians, cyclists and so forth). The rail industry even more clearly demonstrates the limitations the way imposes on vehicle speeds. Most of the alignment of the UK national rail network dates back to the nineteenth century when they were constructed. While new high-speed rail vehicles have been developed, this technology, pioneered by the **Train à Grande Vitesse** (TGV) network in France, cannot be adopted onto existing track due to track alignment and particularly the angle of bends. The solution of matching the vehicle speed to the way is to build a new high speed rail link as adopted with the development of the TGV in France, and copied in much of Europe including the UK with the opening of the first phase of the high-speed Channel Tunnel rail link in 2003. Attempts to run faster trains over existing track is a much more technologically difficult project, although the development of tilting trains, first attempted by the ill-fated **advanced passenger train** (APT) project in the UK in the early 1980s, is now coming to fruition with Virgin's Pendolino trains. Amtrak's attempts to introduce high-speed trains in the US market, where rail has a significantly lower share than Europe, has run into technical difficulties, although the journey time from New York to Boston has been reduced from 5 hours to 4.

Vehicle size has shown a mixed picture between modes. Economies of scale in both construction and operation has resulted in the introduction of increasingly larger cruise ships (Major Case Study 14.1). There is an imminent significant advance on aircraft size with the delivery of the first Airbus A380 to Singapore Airlines scheduled for late 2007. The A380 has a capacity of 555 passengers in tri-class seating, and is designed to serve heavily-trafficked routes, especially if there are capacity problems at the airports, enabling airlines to reduce unit costs and carry more passengers per ATM. However, this technological advance has not been without its setbacks. The project has been beset by technical problems, delaying production by over a year and forcing a sharp cutback in the schedule of planned deliveries to airlines.

There is a fundamental difference of opinion between the two main manufacturers, Airbus and Boeing. Boeing have dropped their project for a larger aircraft on the grounds that the trend in large deregulated markets such as the US domestic market is for airlines to offer more frequent services with smaller aircraft. Their strategy has been on developing a fuel efficient medium-sized jet, 787, the Dreamliner, which the manufacturer premiered in July 2007. The range of three aircraft will have between 210 and 330 seats, but with some 50% of their primary structure made from composite materials they are of light weight and 20% more fuel-efficient than current competitor models. Airlines will require both types of aircraft, but the two manufacturers clearly disagree as to the type and size of aircraft that will make up the bulk of airline orders over the next 20 years. The major developments in motive power and vehicle technology are illustrated in Table 14.1.

The recent history of transport for tourism is characterised by changes in technology but the emphasis is moving to more environmental considerations. Engine technology has resulted in more fuel-efficient engines helping to reduce emissions including greenhouse gases (CO_2). Car engine efficiency has improved by 1.5% per annum (Royal Commission on Environmental Pollution, 1994) and the rate of technical progress is accelerating (RAC, 2002).

Table 14.1 The historical development of tourism: recent changes in transport

	1930s	1940s–1950s	1960s–1970s	1980s–1990s	2000 on
Air	Civil aviation established. Travel is expensive and limited.	Propeller technology. Travel still limited. Basic terminals. 400–480 km/h.	Jet aircraft. Boeing 707. Cheap fuel. 800–950 km/h. Charters take off.	Wide-bodied jet 747. Extended range. Fuel efficient. No increases in speed except Concorde.	Concorde withdrawn. Megacarriers emerge of 500–800 seats. More fuel efficient carriers – Boeing Dreamliner
Sea	Ocean liners and cruises. Short sea ferry speed less than 40 km/h.	Little competition from air. No increase in speed.	Air overtakes sea on N. Atlantic. Hovercraft and faster craft being developed.	Fly–cruise established. Larger and more comfortable ferries. Fast catamarans developed.	Even larger cruise ships (Project Genesis).
Road	Cars 55 km/h. Coaches develop.	Cars 100 km/h.	Cars used for domestic tourism. Speed 115 km/h.	Speed limits in USA. Rise in car ownership rates. Urban congestion. Green fuel. Improved coaches.	LPG powered and hybrid vehicles.
Rail	Steam era. Speed exceed cars.	Railways at peak.	Electrification. Cuts in rail systems: some resorts isolated.	High-speed networks develop in Europe. Business products offered – memorabilia and steam.	Even faster trains to 300 kph.

Table 14.2 Mode of transport and visitor type with examples of product types

Visitor type	Road		Air			Sea/water		Railways
	Car	Coach	Scheduled	Charter	Low Cost Carriers	Ferry	Cruise	
Holiday – inclusive tour	Car hire Fly–drive	Coach tour	Packages – long haul – city break	Long/medium/short-haul packages		Ferry package	Cruise	Orient Express
– independent	Touring private car	Scheduled coach	Self packaging – internet	Seat only to – villa – second home	Short-haul and city break – accommodation booked by Internet independently – second home	Private car		7- or14-day ticket InterRail
Business and conference	Company car	Executive coach	Fully flexible fare		On frequent short-haul routes (30% of passengers)	High speed catamaran		TGV or Bullet Train
VFR	Private car	Scheduled	Cheapest fare	Group travel	Cheap fares	Private car		Excursion fare Group fare
Other special and common interest, e.g. religion	Car hire Private car	service Coach charter	Cheap or flexible fare					
Same day visitors (excursion)	Private car	Scheduled excursion fare	Scheduled excursion fare	Special flights	Domestic routes	Coach/car excursion	Local day cruise	Day excursion fare

The last two decades have seen quieter engines, particularly in the case of aircraft, where new EU regulations regarding noise emissions are being phased in.

The development of fuel-efficient technology has also been encouraged by the unpredictability of the cost of fuel caused by a number of major incidents:

- In 1973–74, the Arab–Israeli War.
- In 1978–79 the Iranian crisis.
- In 1991 the Gulf War.
- War in Afghanistan in 2001.
- War in Iraq in 2003.

COMPETITOR ANALYSIS

The most obvious way of analysing transport is by mode. There are four major modes:

- road;
- rail;
- water;
- air.

The choice of mode of transport by the visitor is related to purpose of travel. Table 14.2 provides an indicative structure for modal choice. Furthermore, the visitor's choice of mode of transport is affected by:

- distance and time factors;
- status and comfort;
- safety and utility;
    - comparative price of services offered;
    - incentives/promotional marketing;
    - geographical position (choice in peripheral or remote locations);
    - availability;
    - reliability;
- range of services offered;
- level of competition between services;
- frequency of service;
- comfort;
- reliability;
- convenience;
- flexibility.

The relative importance of these major influences upon modal choice will vary from one visitor type to another, although visitor types are no longer as homogeneous as previously assumed: some inclusive tour passengers will elect to travel business class by scheduled air rather than by charter and a significant percentage of passengers using low-cost airlines are business passengers.

Increasingly transport operators are attempting to identify segments of demand for which specific categories of service will appeal. In Europe coaches now offer degrees of comfort and service unheard of in the 1970s while ferry companies have become expert in organising a range of centred, or varied itineraries for motorists holidaying overseas with their own car.

Road transport

The car dominates road transport, which is almost the perfect tool for tourist use offering the following attractions:

- the control of the route and the stops en route;
- the control of departure times;
- door-to-door flexibility;
- the ideal capacity for families;
- the ability to carry baggage and equipment easily;
- the ability to use the vehicle for accommodation in the case of recreational vehicles and caravans;
- privacy;
- the freedom to use the vehicle once the destination is reached; and
- the low perceived cost.

Some nations tend to utilise a car much more than others for recreation and tourism. This is partly dependent on levels of economic development, which itself influences levels of car ownership among the population, but also is dependent upon geography (average distances travelled for tourist trips), climate and the cost, quality and availability of alternatives. Nevertheless, the car share is very high in developed countries. Trips by car account for approximately 90% of the pleasure/personal and business trips taken by Canadian and US residents, for almost 60% of the total holiday trips in Europe and over 70% of all UK domestic holiday trips.

Growth rates of traffic over the last 50 years have been phenomenal. For instance, in the UK the modal share of car for all journey purposes has grown from 35% of all passenger kilometres in 1955 to 85% by 2005 (DfT, 2006). However, over the same period both disposable time and disposable income have increased resulting in far more travel overall so the increase in vehicle kilometres is eight-and-a-half fold. Likewise traffic volume in the USA increased by 76% between 1980 and 2000. The leisure and tourism share of all this traffic is not insubstantial. Around 13% of all passenger kilometres are accounted for by holiday trips but day trip excursions and appropriate VFR traffic would increase the 'tourism' share to nearer 30% of all kilometres. Peeters *et al.* (2007) estimate that tourism accounts for between 15 and 20% of passenger kilometres travelled in Europe by surface modes of transport.

These dramatic growth rates of car use are now considered unsustainable by governments in many developed countries as car users are imposing huge costs on others which they do not directly pay for (termed **externalities**). The contribution of cars to greenhouse gas emissions is high at around 20% of the total UK emissions (RAC, 2002) and growing despite improving engine efficiency. Cars also affect local air quality and produce particulates which are linked to asthma and other respiratory complaints, generate huge costs to society in terms of congestion, road accidents and visual intrusion. Large numbers of vehicles can reduce the attractiveness of tourist destinations, most particularly popular rural locations such as national parks.

Traffic growth rates in developing countries may be even higher if high rates of economic growth are coupled with significant population growth. Ironically, higher levels of car ownership can be seen as proof of economic success by governments and yet the externalities of car use are equally problematic.

The UK government has set out a number of policies at least to reduce the rate of traffic growth if not to see absolute traffic levels fall (DETR, 1998). Recent developments have seen the concept of road pricing, charging the motorist directly for using the most congested parts of the road network at the most congested times, gain ground. The introduction in February

2003 of congestion charging for a central core area of London between 0700 and 1830 on weekdays has attracted international attention. While it is not the first road pricing scheme, schemes such as Singapore's pre-date it, it is the first on this scale. Early results have exceeded expectations, with traffic falls of 18% and congestion reduced by 30% over the first year of operation. Stockholm trialled a similar scheme for six months in 2006 and following a referendum it is scheduled to be implemented on a permanent basis sometime soon.

Other forms of road pricing are aimed at long-distance travel in the form of motorway/autobahn/interstate highway tolls. They have a relatively long history in Europe and the USA and were introduced in the UK for the first time in 2003 (M6 Toll), and again increases in the level of charges can be used as a tool to manage traffic growth. UK policy options include combining both elements into an electronic national road pricing scheme using satellite technology, although such a scheme will take at least 10 years to implement and a strong political will. Over 1.75 million UK residents signed an electronic petition against electronic road pricing. Road pricing has the advantage of narrowing the price advantage of the car over other forms of public transport by placing a greater element of car use costs at the point of use. Currently the point of use cost of a car is very low (petrol costs plus perhaps a little extra for vehicle maintenance) and the price advantage is enhanced for family groups of 3–5 people. However, if the cost of car travel rises too steeply, there are fears that tourism growth rates may slow or even move into decline. Indeed, since 2002 road traffic growth has stagnated both in the UK and also other Western European countries (Germany, Holland and Belgium (Robbins and Dickinson, 2007)), but day visits and domestic tourism trips have also fallen slightly.

The coach

In many developed countries the scheduled bus and coach networks have seen a significant decline in passenger numbers. However, the coach still plays a role in the tourism market, divided into three sectors. First, scheduled long-distance coaches are used as an alternative usually to rail or car to travel to the destination, although long-distance coach services in the USA (for instance Greyhound and Trailways) are in direct competition with air. This mode is particularly useful for short and medium-distance journeys. It has traditionally attracted the elderly and inexpensive markets and the stereotype is of the lower occupational or social groups and the over-50s market. Beyond a certain threshold distance, lack of comfort and the relatively slower speed compared with other modes has to be traded off against cheaper and more attractive pricing structures. The coach network is more dense than the rail network, offering more destinations, and can be quicker than rail in areas where there has been investment in new roads versus an ageing rail system (northern Portugal). For some destinations it may be the only public transport alternative. In the UK the extensive National Express network has seen a significant rise in competition on main routes from MegaBus.com which has in particular targeted a student market with e ticketing and departure points at university campuses.

The second sector is the coach tour. Again the market traditionally attracts an over-50s market, but often from higher socio-economic groups and attracting passengers from car-owning households. The break from driving, the scenic views from the coach and the social interaction with the other coach passengers are all attractions for this type of holiday.

The third sector is the hired coach. This has traditionally been employed at the destination by groups for transfers to and from the terminal, most notably airports on inclusive tour holidays. In addition, sightseeing trips and tours are normally conducted by coaches or minibuses. Safaris in particular use the adapted microbus for sightseeing and game watching, such as in Kenya.

The importance of the coach market can be overlooked. It is estimated coaches carried 860 million US passengers in 2000 with the vast majority (90%) carried on privately hired vehicles.

Railway transport

Overall the rail share of travel for holiday purposes is traditionally not high. However, the rail shares for certain corridors (especially high-speed lines) are higher as is the share for city centre to city centre traffic and for business and conference traffic. Railway termini are often located in city centre locations compared to airports, which are often located 20 or 30 km away from the centre, which increases their attraction for this market. For rail the main competition between modes is often based upon the time and distance comparison, city centre to city centre, compared with air. Beyond a certain distance, some visitors see rail as being too cumbersome and tiring and it is then that notions of adventure and sightseeing take over as the attractions of the rail mode. However, the traditional model demonstrated in Figure 14.1 is beginning to break down, with rail services losing out to low-cost air carriers on many routes at distances significantly below 500 km. One factor contributing to this is price. Rail has very high fixed costs (track, signalling, engineering costs), which either result in high fares (UK) or very high levels of subsidy (France, Germany) or a combination of both.

Trains are a relatively 'green' form of travel both in terms of fuel efficiency and also in terms of emissions, although the performance of ageing diesel trains has been criticised. Electric trains are much more fuel-efficient than cars per passenger km travelled. Rail also has a hugely better safety record than car travel.

The EC has been pressing for increased competition on rail networks throughout Europe (European Commission Directive 91/440/EEC) but the impact of rail privatisation in the UK has not been entirely beneficial to this mode of transport and is now unlikely to be copied by other countries. For further studies on UK rail privatisation see Kain (1998) and Welsby and Nichols (1999).

Although train operators try to emphasise the rest and relaxation of travel by train, rarely do they offer high-quality services throughout the network of a country so journeys involving a change from main high-speed lines to branch lines are more variable. The luxury and comfort attributes are therefore limited to journeys between 200 to 500 km between major cities with airlines currently making inroads.

The most important reasons for travelling by train are:

- safety;
- the ability to look out of the train and see en route;

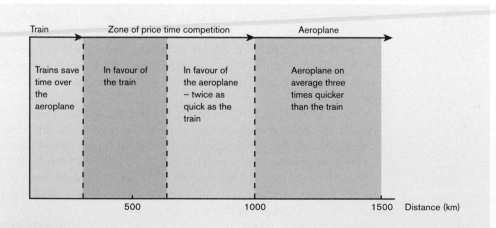

Figure 14.1 Competition between the aeroplane and the high-speed train on international routes in Europe
Source: Adapted from *Business Travel World*, May 1997

- the ability to move around the coach;
- arriving at the destination rested and relaxed;
- personal comfort;
- centrally located termini; and
- environmentally-friendly form of transport.

The traditional market for the train has been regarded as the independent holiday visitor, particularly the VFR category; they may also attract a significant 'fear of flying' market. Although in the USA trains are considered a second-rate means of passenger transportation, in Western Europe trains hold a valuable market share of passenger traffic, primarily because of policies of protectionism and subsidy by the respective governments. However, the introduction of high-speed and intercity services, such as the TGV in France, has improved the level of service and comfort offered. The opening of the Channel Tunnel in 1993 has created rail demand from London to Paris and Brussels. In addition there is an aspiration to change the image and function of trains towards an environmentally-friendly, traditional, stylish, relaxed, reliable and consumer-orientated form of transport.

Sea transport

In broad terms, we can divide water-borne transport into short sea ferry transport and ocean-going cruises. Other categories exist, such as inland waterway craft and small pleasure craft, but assume less significance as a means of transport as they are more destination prod ucts in their own right. Cruising should also be thought of as a holiday product as much as a mode of transport. Ferry services, which include or exclude vehicles, can provide lifeline services to islands as well as a focus for visitors who normally are packaged holidaymakers, independent or same-day visitors. Catamarans tend to be faster than conventional forms of ship technology but, in general (unless for short sea commuting such as between Hong Kong and Macau), business visitors tend to choose other modes of transport. Owing to the vagaries of the sea, visitors either like, accept or dislike this means of transport. Geographical factors tend to determine the provision of ferry transport, leaving some destinations heavily dependent upon such links. Examples include:

- Aegean island-hopping or travel to and from the Greek mainland; or
- channel crossings such as the English Channel, Irish Sea, the Cook Strait between the North and South islands of New Zealand, and the Baltic Sea.

As far as the transportation of vehicles and merchandise is required on short sea crossings, ferries offer inexpensive, reliable and safe services. Ferry transportation is the only possibility in the case of remote and small islands which have no airport. This situation can be found in Greece, where there are only 15 airports to serve 95 inhabited islands, a coastline of 14,854 km and 750 ports and anchorages. In this case, large ferries provide coastal shipping services linking the mainland ports and islands as well as the islands with each other. Piraeus port handles 13 million passengers per annum, and is therefore a very important facility in the provision of tourism transport services. Furthermore, smaller regional ferries undertake transportation between the islands, especially during the summer peak period.

However, in many cases, air can be a viable alternative to sea transportation between larger islands and the mainland. The main advantage of ferry operators when compared with air transportation is price, combined with the fact that passengers can carry their own vehicles and use them at the destination. The popularity of motoring holidays and self-drive packages, as well as the introduction of roll on–roll off facilities, which enables the ports to handle a much greater volume of vehicles, demonstrates the increase of passenger demand for ferry services.

In Europe, the gradual liberalisation of air transportation, the decrease of air fares, the construction of the Channel Tunnel and the development of alternative modes of travel have

Photograph 14.2	*Queen Mary 2*, the world's largest cruise ship.
	Source: Cunard Line

forced the ferry companies to improve the luxury of their vessels considerably, to increase the cruising speed, to increase their size and to install leisure facilities. Routes with longer crossings can enhance the leisure facilities – casinos, cabaret bars, cabins – to offer a consumer-orientated service.

Modern vessels, such as the wave-piercing catamaran and hydrofoils, have been introduced on some routes in recent decades. Their main aim is to offer a shorter crossing time than the traditional ferry service. Their speed is up to three times that of a conventional ferry, while they have a great manoeuvrability, fast turn-around in port and need minimum dock facilities. They therefore attract upmarket tourists who appreciate the importance of their time and desire to reach the destination as soon as possible. However, these vessels are:

- much more expensive than the ferries;
- vulnerable in rough seas and strong winds;
- noisy; and
- environmentally insensitive, with higher CO_2 emissions and wave actions that contribute to coastal erosion.

Air transport

Travelling by air is probably the most important transportation innovation of the twentieth century. It has enabled the transportation of passengers in the shortest time and it has boosted the demand for long-haul trips. In fact no part of the world is now more than 24 hours flying time from any other part.

Air transportation has managed in the past few decades to gain a very significant share of the transportation market, especially for movements over 500 km. As new aircraft, such as the Boeing 747–400 series, have come into operation, the range for air travel has been extended to up to 15,000 km for non-stop flights.

Scheduled airlines offer a safe, convenient, reliable, frequent and relatively consumer-orientated product; airlines attract business travellers, who appreciate the speed and flexibility between the various flights, especially on popular routes, as well as the leisure passengers who enjoy the ability to arrive at the destination quickly, and without spending time and money en route. Normally, ground services and the terminal facilities are much more advanced and sophisticated than for any other mode. Finally, airlines offer a number of incentives for their loyal customers through various 'frequent flyer' programmes. Traditionally, air transportation is the most expensive mode, especially for the short-haul routes, for example, in Europe, where an economic cruising speed cannot be achieved, but this has changed over recent years with the introduction of new business models. Leisure passengers have always been offered lower promotional fares by minimising the opportunities for alterations on the travel arrangements and by securing the passenger as early as possible. These fares, including advanced purchase excursion fare (APEX), previously standby, and other forms of instant purchase fares (IPEX), were experimented with. However, more sophisticated yield management, assisted by Internet booking and e-ticketing, has enabled some airlines to alter their fares in order to achieve maximum yield by taking account of potential demand and supply factors, historical data, time lost before the flight and current load factors. Thus appropriate prices are suggested for the current market environment in order to maximise the airline yield. Following on from developments in the USA, in Europe we have seen the emergence of low-cost, no-frills airlines (see Mini Case Study 14.1).

The term low cost is often associated with budget airlines or no-frills carriers. The concept developed in the USA following deregulation of air services in 1978, pioneered by Southwest Airlines. The concept transferred to Europe in the early 1990s with the emergence of several carriers copying the Southwest approach between 1995 and 1998. Outside Europe and the USA adoption of the low-cost model has been slow. However, since 1999 there has been the emergence of carriers in Australia, Canada (albeit with very low market share), South Africa and Latin America. Southwest Airlines was set up in 1971 to operate services within Texas. Its home base was the subsidiary airport in Dallas (Love Field) which was much closer to downtown Dallas than the main airport Dallas Fort Worth, an irony considering the subsequent criticism levelled at low-cost carriers, particularly in Europe, over the use of airports up to 100 km from town centres. Its strategy from the first was to offer low fares and high point-to-point frequencies on short-haul routes within Texas. Following deregulation of the US domestic market in 1978 it cautiously expanded into services between states, concentrating predominantly on short flights of 2 to 4 hours which it could serve with a single type of Boeing 737 aircraft (Lawton 2002), selecting routes where there was no competition. Today it is America's second largest airline (passengers carried) and in January 2007 announced a profit for the 34th consecutive year in marked contrast to other US airlines. The driving force behind this success are very low costs. Doganis (2006: 176) indicates that low-cost carriers can achieve costs per seat at around 40% of the costs of full service airlines on short to medium haul routes (2–4 hours). There are a number of texts that show how low-cost carriers achieve their low operating costs. Doganis (2006) offers the most detailed analysis, although the strategies summarised below are also covered by Duval (2007), Groß and Schröder (2007), Hanlon (2007), Lawton (2002) and Page (2005) among others. Some differences have emerged between low-cost carriers, but by and large they will feature most of the following:

- Operation from secondary airports at major cities or from regional airports

  This generates two distinct sets of savings:

  - Landing charges and operating costs are lower. Many airports offer discounts, but the volume of traffic that low-cost airlines can bring to small airports is so attractive that some moved beyond discounts to offering subsidies. In Europe, subsidies offered by airports owned by the public sector have been ruled as being anti-competitive and unlawful following judgements on RyanAir's agreements with Charleroi Airport in Belgium and the now discontinued service to Strasbourg.

  - The use of uncongested airports enables very rapid turnaround time (often under 30 minutes) maximising aircraft utilisation productivity.

- Standardised fleet, initially on one aircraft type

  - Reduces maintenance costs and the storage costs of spares.
  - Reduces pilot and crew training costs.
  - As the airline expands and operates routes of varying length and different character-istics, the fleet may diversify to two or three configurations of this aircraft type.

- Maximised aircraft capacity

  - Operating a single class of seating.
  - Adopting a low seat pitch (29' – 31'), which is acceptable to passengers on short flights.
  - Utilising galley space freed up by not providing free food and for additional seating.

- Minimise in-flight costs

  - By not offering free food and beverage on board but charging for these services.
  - By operating with the minimum number of cabin crew allowed by safety regulations.
  - By not offering pre-assigned seating at check-in.
  - Adherence to very strict baggage limits and, more recently, even charging for baggage destined for the hold.
  - By minimising ex-gratia payments to customers in carriage. In the event of delay and cancellation – the airline will, at best, offer a refund of the fare paid or a place on the next available flight which might be some days hence.

- Reduce sales and distribution costs

Mini Case Study 14.1 explores in greater depth the expansion of the low-cost concept across Europe and Australasia, and the possibility of developing the concept to long-haul routes.

Charter flights are utilised widely to facilitate the movement of holidaymakers on pack-age tours, although up to 20% of passengers are carried on 'seat only' arrangements. Most charter airlines are owned by tour operators who attempt to integrate their operations vertically (see Chapter 13), such as Thomsonfly.com and Thomson Holidays in the UK. Charter airlines offer ad hoc transportation services, although in peak seasons they operate to a timetable, which although not formally published is known to tour operators. Services are characterised by:

- minimal flexibility in altering flights;
- flying at inconvenient and therefore not busy hours for the terminal and achieving very high utilisation of the plane over a 24-hour period;

MINI CASE STUDY 14.1
The expansion of the low-cost concept in airlines

EUROPE

In Europe deregulation of air transport came later and in three phases, the third of which became operational in 1997. Essentially, this allowed carriers from one member state to offer services between other member states and to operate as a carrier within another member state, and to fix fares without reference to regulatory authorities.

Ryanair began in 1985 on the route Waterford Ireland to London Gatwick at a time when the regulatory regime between the UK and Ireland was liberal. However, while the fares undercut Aer Lingus the airline made substantial losses and, following a visit to Southwest Airlines in the early 1990s, it decided it had to reduce its cost base along the lines pioneered by them. Although this saw the company move into profit from 1992, it did not expand to non-UK–Irish routes until deregulation in 1997, since when it has displayed phenomenal growth. By 2006 it had 436 routes across 24 countries carrying 42.5 million passengers.

EasyJet, the second largest low-cost airline in the UK, began operations in 1995 based at Luton and in 2006 operated 307 routes from 80 airports carrying 33 million passengers. Debonair commenced operation in 1996 but went into receivership in 1999 to illustrate that not all such ventures were a success. Some argue that Debonair was more of a hybrid and included a business class cabin and some frills which affected its cost base. Another low-cost operator, Virgin Express, based in Brussels (launched in 1996), has also adapted the Southwest model to allow interchange, which again impacts on the cost base.

An interesting development was the establishment of low-cost subsidiaries by established scheduled airlines. Go was set up in 1998 by BA and Buzz (2000) by KLM. These were short-lived experiments: the former is now part of easyJet and the latter Ryanair.

Although the low-cost industry has seen concentration into two main groupings following takeovers and business failures, there have also been new low-cost carriers entering the market. Flybe is the UK's number three low-cost airline and developed from British European Airways. It is based in regional locations in the UK including Birmingham, Southampton and Exeter, carrying around 6 million passengers in 2006. Bmibaby is an offshoot of the scheduled carrier British Midland International and operates mainly from a location in central England; in 2004 it operated 40 routes to 10 countries.

The evidence from both the USA and Europe is that the very low fares of low-cost carriers has meant that although low-cost carriers will attract passengers from the higher cost full service airlines, they also generate significant new traffic. Contrary to popular belief they also carry business passengers, although the number varies significantly from route to route, attracted in part by the high frequency on some routes.

Full service airlines are beginning to copy a number of the operating strategies of the low-cost carriers in an attempt to control costs, most notably e-ticketing, automated check-in and reducing or even eliminating the meals service, particularly on routes from regional airports. While full service carriers will have to retain important short-haul services, particularly into their main hub airports to facilitate passengers **interlining** to their more profitable long-haul services, many commentators have forecast increased withdrawal from other short-haul routes. They find it difficult to compete on cost, not least because of their use of congested primary airports, making quick turn round and high aircraft utilisation difficult. Interestingly, British Airways (BA) have recently sold BA Connect, its regional airline business operating on 159 routes and carrying 10 million passengers, to Flybe.

AUSTRALASIA

As stated earlier, adoption by the rest of the world of the concept of low-cost airlines has been slow. One essential requirement is at least a very liberal if not deregulated operational environment. Two low-cost airlines were launched in Australia in 2000 following the earlier failure of a start-up carrier Compass.

Technically the Australian domestic market has been deregulated since 1990, but following the failure of Compass has operated as a duopoly with Ansett and Quantas. Some commentators suggest that predatory behaviour by the two incumbents significantly contributed to Compass failing (Lawton, 2002).

Virgin Blue is a wholly owned subsidiary of the Virgin Group. Its emergence was dependent on the Australian government removing restrictions on the foreign ownership of domestic airlines. While the company's growth strategy is focused on under-served markets away from the busiest and most crowded airports, where they believe there is route growth potential very much along the lines of the Southwest model, in 2001 they also entered Australia's busiest business route (Sydney–Melbourne). In the opening year of operation Virgin Blue carried around 650,000 passengers at an impressive average load factor of 74%. While early results are considered satisfactory it is envisaged that it would take 3–4 years to achieve profitability, although in February 2007 it announced a small half-yearly profit. In 2003 it operated 37 domestic routes capturing a 30% market share. Its costs were 40% less than Ansett before the latter's collapse.

The second Australian low-cost carrier, Impulse, ceased operations on trunk routes in May 2001. It used Boeing 717–200 jets with a capacity of 117 seats rather than the low-cost airlines' normal choice (Boeing 737s) and as a result incurred higher unit cost. It also chose routes in the Brisbane–Melbourne–Sydney triangle, which meant it was in direct competition with Quantas and Ansett on virtually all routes, rather than trying to develop new markets. Following the demise of Ansett in 2001 the Australian market is a duopoly again, albeit one of the incumbents is a low-cost carrier.

Other low-cost carriers to emerge include WestJet (Canada), Kulula.com (South Africa), Gol Transportes Aerosand (Brazil) and AirAsia (Malaysia). There are two trends to monitor and these are the emergence of low-cost carriers operating between different sovereign territories or countries and scheduled carriers developing their own low-cost operations such as United Airlines with Ted in the United States and Thai Airways with Nok in Thailand. Many scheduled carriers have considered starting up a low-cost carrier and some are doing so (Air Canada and Tango) either to counter the possible competition from others doing so or because it might be profitable.

LONG HAUL

There has been increasing debate as to whether the low-cost no-frills principles of operation can be applied to long-haul services. Following increased competition from new low-cost carriers in the USA, Southwest has extended its operations to routes of over 1,000 km and its longest route is Philadelphia to Oakland (3,626 km). However, the cost savings achievable over full service airlines on long-haul services will be lower, perhaps 20–25% (see Francis *et al.*, 2007 for a fuller analysis). Full service airlines already achieve high vehicle utilisation, there are limits as to the minimum acceptable seat pitch for longer flights and it is unlikely an airline can offer no refreshments. Nevertheless, Zoom has commenced services from the UK to Canada/USA with one-way fares (including taxes) from £129.

REFERENCES

Francis, G., Dennis, N., Ison, S. and Humphreys, I. (2007) 'The transferability of the low-cost model to long-haul airline operations', *Tourism Management* **28**(2), 391–8.

Lawton, T. (2002) *Cleared for Take-off: Structure and Strategy in the Low Fare Airline Business*, Ashgate, Aldershot.

DISCUSSION QUESTIONS

1. Why do low-cost airlines use secondary and regional airports?

2. Why don't low-cost airlines use the main computerised reservation systems used by the world's main airlines?

3. How might so called 'full fare' or scheduled carriers respond to the competition from low-cost airlines?

- reduced seat pitch to fit in as many seats as possible;
- consolidation of flights if not fully booked; and
- reducing the space within the aircraft;

The higher load factor achieved on charter services (of 90% or more) compared with scheduled services (averaging 70%) is the final factor explaining the substantial difference in the unit cost of production and the price at which the product can be sold. For a more detailed analysis of charter airline costs see Doganis (2002).

Charter airlines held a substantial share (almost 50%) of the short-haul intra-European market in the 1980s, with the dominant pattern of demand being the carrying of tourists from north Europe to the resorts and tourist destinations in the south. However, they have lost substantive market share since the mid-1990s as a result of direct competition from the low-cost carriers. Charter airline seat costs per km are probably below those of low-cost airlines and yet it is the latter that have achieved rapid growth over the last 10 years. The trend towards independent holidays, growing second home ownership and direct booking on the Internet have all contributed to the declining appeal of the package holiday and therefore the performance of charter airlines. Charter airlines have developed a number of strategies for their future survival and development. Some, like Thomsonfly.com, have diversified to become hybrid airlines which offer scheduled services using the same low-cost model, although on some routes they still carry predominantly passengers on an inclusive tour. This strategy should also enable them to compete more successfully for the seat-only traveller. Most charter airlines have also diversified into long-haul routes, for which their more varied fleet is well suited and where they compete solely with full service carriers.

People who travel for their economic activities and therefore have their fares paid by their employers require maximum flexibility in order to be able to alter their travelling arrangements at short notice; as a result business travellers tend to prefer scheduled airlines. Services, terminals and aircraft have to be designed to facilitate the function of the busy business traveller. It is estimated that business travellers account for about 30% of all international air traffic.

Leisure travellers' share of air transportation has increased rapidly during the recent decades. Leisure travellers have much more time and they do not necessarily require very high-quality services. They are free to make their holiday arrangements well in advance and thus they do not need flexibility. However, unlike the business traveller they do pay their own fares and, therefore, they are price conscious. The development of specific leisure fares by scheduled airlines as well as the charter airlines in Europe appeared to cater for the needs of this market adequately until the emergence of low-cost carriers demonstrated otherwise. Overall it is estimated that around 15% of international tourism uses air transportation while 86% of Europeans use it for trips outside of Europe.

POLITICAL INFLUENCES ON TRANSPORT FOR TOURISM

International tourist movements have always been affected by the activities of governments and transport for tourism has also been influenced by such factors. Barriers to communication, apart from distance, have been border controls, the need for visas or transit visas and customs controls. For rail and road the boundary between nations is the place of border control, and for sea transport the land/sea interface or the port is the point of control; however, for air transport the airport terminal, wherever located, is the processing point.

The concept of sovereignty of airspace versus the freedom of the high seas has always been a factor limiting and influencing provision of transport for tourism by air. Rail transport across and between nations, apart from gauge differences, has always been relatively smooth compared with quota regulations for coaches in transit or entering other countries. The motorist has been affected by the insurance requirements for a Green Card and international driving licences, but in Europe such barriers and restraints have all but disappeared.

Because of its very nature, transport for tourism by air has developed as a complex political issue and the key factors need to be highlighted. Airlines are important within the national economy for foreign exchange and for fare payments from foreign travellers. Generally, airlines have been owned by the state, have been subsidised by governments and have been seen to be prestige elements flying the colours of the national flag. Scandinavian Airline System (SAS) and Air Afrique are exceptions to the rule that most countries possess their own national airline. Equally, the size of an airline is not necessarily related to the size of traffic potential of that country; the example of KLM illustrates this point.

Transport for tourism operates within a competitive political and economic environment, especially in the international context, because it represents the means to transfer across borders and to cross other territories to reach the intended destination. This competitive environment is illustrated by the extent to which transport for tourism has been regulated and controlled by governments.

REGULATION OF COMPETITION

Since their inception, transport modes have been subject to regulation by governments for safety and technical reasons. In addition, legal and economic forms of regulation have applied to specific transport modes. In many countries transport operation has been subject to legislation to protect so-called 'pioneer operators', who incur costs, set up routes and pick-up points, but are then vulnerable to another operator moving in without those costs to recoup. This was the basis of bus and coach legislation in the UK, which had been heavily regulated from 1930 until deregulation of coaches in 1980, followed by the deregulation of the bus industry in 1985. The US (1982), Scandinavia, Portugal and Greece have all followed. A new period of fierce competition on long-distance coach services in the UK appears imminent with the emergence of Megabus.com. Railways tend to be natural national monopolies and to be state-owned and subsidised, but in Europe there have been attempts to privatise and to introduce competition following the European Commission Directive 91/440/EEC.

Regulation policies

Policies on regulation have tended to focus on air transport to a greater degree than other modes; international air law is a factor that controls the extent to which national airlines may operate. In the United States the so-called anti-trust provisions have always existed to prevent the development of price fixing, cartels and collusion between competitors. In Europe, under the Treaty of Rome, transport has been deemed to be subject to competition rules and the European Commission has outlawed agreements between pairs of national carriers who pool their capacity and revenues, and still judges whether potential mergers of airlines are anti-competitive or not.

The need for regulation of transport has hinged on the relative ease of entry into operation of a service; the barriers to entry are relatively low compared with other industries. Given that the evils of cut-throat competition can lead to both the demise of a regular reliable schedule and social disadvantages to travellers, regulation policies have specified procedures for entry into and exit from operation. The arguments for and against regulation are many, but basically, in the short term, customers benefit from deregulation with increased competition and efficiency through lower fares; but in the long term, they may suffer disadvantages from the lack of an organised and reliable schedule of services as competitors go out of business.

The Airline Deregulation Act 1978 was introduced in President Carter's era in the United States and led to the development of an open skies policy. This Act is often cited as the extreme of what deregulation can do in practice. The Civil Aeronautics Board (CAB) was phased out as a regulatory body devising policy. Its role had been to devise regulations on conditions of service such as frequency and capacity, on exit and entry into operation and on fares and prices. Such matters then became the subject of free competition within the US domestic environment. Up until the late 1970s the International Airline Transport Association (IATA) was the de facto controlling body worldwide, being a trade association for airlines, though in reality it represented governments as well. However, ever since the famous Show Cause Order where IATA had to show good cause why it should be exempt from the provisions of US anti-trust provisions, this body has lost its stature and strength to implement fare structures to protect its high-cost member airlines. IATA's influence varies from continent to continent and it is still strong in parts of Europe, Africa and Latin America.

Following the Chicago Convention of 1944 where a truly multilateral agreement between countries was not reached, a series of bilateral arrangements between governments emerged. National governments approve and license carriers nominated to fly between the home country and an overseas destination; fares are fixed by reference to IATA conference machinery or between respective governments. Even in a truly deregulated environment fares are fixed by mutual agreement between partners or merely filed. The so-called 'five freedoms of movement' giving technical and traffic rights to airlines are still important for international movements. These are outlined in Figure 14.2. Subsequent to the Chicago Convention, sixth and seventh freedoms have been formulated.

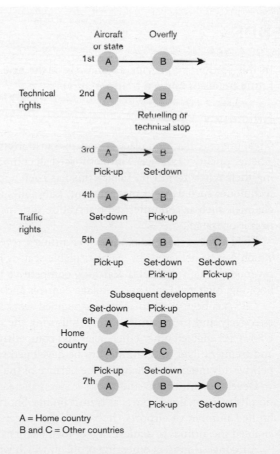

| **Figure 14.2** | The five freedoms of the air as agreed at the Chicago Convention, 1944 |

The extent to which US domestic policies have been translated to overseas situations has been limited. Within the USA, as a result of fierce competition, instability arose when a great number of air carriers entered the market and the fares reached their lowest levels. However, in the following years only a few carriers could survive and most of the small or weak airlines were absorbed or merged with the stronger ones.

European skies were quite reluctant to open up to complete deregulation. This is partly because of the public sector's role in the airline industry as well as the social role of the carriers to maintain uneconomic routes in the peripheral areas purely for national and social reasons. After three directives from the European Commission, the development of true cabotage arrangements for Europe, seen as one domestic territory, finally happened on 1 April 1997. Europe, though, is still dominated by state-controlled and owned airlines, some of which have received substantial subsidies from the European Commission.

There is another issue which involves the agreements made between United States and the UK over air traffic between the two countries and the extent to which the EU has a right to be involved. Historically, bilateral agreements between the US and the UK were the so-called Bermuda I agreement dated 1946 and the Bermuda II agreement that replaced it in 1977. In 2002 the European Court of Justice declared that the 1977 agreement meant that the UK had failed to fulfil its obligations under the European Treaty and in effect the EU has held that it sees itself as having the right to govern and negotiate agreements between the whole EU region with foreign countries such as the USA. A US–EU open skies deal was signed in April 2007 which further deregulates the transatlantic market, although of course no EU airline has access to any part of the large US domestic market.

FUTURE TRENDS

In this section we provide an analysis of the external environment and its impact on the future trends of tourism transportation.

Efficiency

Great pressure has been placed upon all transportation modes to reduce their prices and offer a better quality of service. This has forced all companies to identify new methods of increasing their efficiency; in particular this has been applied in the airline world where modern techniques such as yield management, hub-and-spoke operations and modern distribution channels such as computerised reservation systems (CRSs) have changed the way that business is operated.

Yield management maximises the airline's revenue by suggesting the maximum prices which can be achieved for every available seat. It has been defined as the maximisation of revenue through optimum seat mix, competitive buy-up pricing strategies, accurate overbooking, high yield spill and spoilage controls and demand forecasting.

CRS has been used to control scheduled seats and fares in order to distribute products effectively and to maximise profits following the deregulation of air transportation in the USA. CRS enabled other efficiencies and competitive techniques (such as yield management and frequent flyer programmes) to be developed while becoming a source for strong competitive advantage and changing the balance of the airline world.

Development of hub-and-spoke systems increased the rationalisation of air transportation by using major airports as transit points. Short-haul flights (spokes) connect through a limited number of airports (hubs) and passengers are transferred to long-haul trips. This enabled the airlines to achieve higher load factors and keep prices down.

Air congestion is an emerging problem which will influence the airlines severely since the lack of terminal and air-corridor capacity is now becoming apparent. It is suggested that the growth in intra-Europe traffic by the year 2010 will lead to many of Europe's leading airports reaching their capacity; the result would damage air transportation and stimulate people to switch to alternative modes.

A number of improvements are therefore required at airports and, more specifically, on the control procedures, the design and construction of the terminals and the interconnectivity with other modes of travel. Furthermore, the efficiency of airlines should increase byextending hub operations, reorganising the schedule, utilising larger aircraft and by achieving higher load factors.

Some see the solution being larger aircraft, such as the Airbus A380, offering 555 seats, but there remains uncertainty over passenger acceptance of such large aircraft and the ability of route structures and infrastructure (air traffic control, airports, etc.) to sustain and support such large loads.

Globalisation and integration

Globalisation is one of the major trends in the international tourism industry and involves a convergence in tastes, preferences and products. The global firm is one that capitalises on this trend and produces standardised products contributing to the homogenisation of the world tourism market. Essentially this means an increase in worldwide business between multi-national corporations irrespective of the geographical location and can lead to the virtual firm as a transport operator.

The truly global carrier, as some have predicted, has not really emerged, in part due to wishes by governments and other trading blocs to retain national sovereignty as vested in their national carriers. However, there has been a further consolidation of strategic and marketing alliances and an integration of services and operations.

Airlines, as they expand their services on a global basis, are forging strategic alliances because of:

- the maturity of domestic traffic;
- the competition for terminal space and slots;
- the need for extensive networks worldwide;
- the necessity for economies of scale in airline operation;
- the control of the new distribution channels (CRS); and
- the gradual deregulation in world transportation.

Many examples can illustrate the globalisation of airlines but perhaps the best is British Airways, which:

- has franchise operations such as with British Mediterranean Airways;
- in 1992 bought a stake in US Air, which it decided to sell in 1996 but has plans for a transatlantic alliance with American Airlines;
- has shares in Quantas and plans for closer relationships with carriers such as Iberia;
- is a major player in the Oneworld Alliance and has codeshare agreements with alliance and some non-alliance carriers.

Other schemes include the Star Alliance programme, which at its inception in 1997 comprised the founder members Thai, Air Canada, United, Lufthansa and SAS, and in 2004 had 14 members. Some of its objectives were to:

- integrate products and connecting services;
- offer common check-in and reservation services;
- share airport lounge services; and
- share marketing, communications and rewards services.

As far as vertical integration is concerned, the transportation industry has always acknowledged that travellers need to use a combination of the various modes in order to complete their trip. Therefore, transportation companies are moving towards alternative modes which can be combined and offer integrated services. As a result, chauffeur services are offered by various airlines for their loyal and full-fare customers, while fly–drive programmes are very successful. Finally, the ambition of airlines such as Lufthansa to penetrate into rail transport, by offering private services primarily for their airline clients, demonstrates the point.

The trend towards globalisation has been seen in respect of numerous attempts to merge. To date, few attempts have been successful especially in the European context due to great pride in government ownership and national sovereignty. There have been notable examples of bankruptcy in the early 2000s in the form of Sabena the Belgian flag carrier and Swissair, which later re-emerged as Swiss International Airlines. In 2004 the merger of Air France and KLM was finally approved by the competition regulators in Brussels and Washington.

Environmental policies

The environment will become the biggest challenge to tourism transport over the coming decade. It is not easy to measure tourism's contribution to global warming, although Peeters (2007) estimates it at 4–10% worldwide, with tourism's contribution in the developed world somewhat higher (10–20%). There is a growing body of literature which confirms transport as the dominant contributor to tourism's environmental impacts. Høyer (2000) calculates that travel to and from the Tyrol region in Austria, together with local transport within the destination area, is responsible for between 40 and 60% of tourism's total environmental impact on the region. A case study of Amsterdam, where international tourist arrivals by air form a significant share of the overall market, estimates the transport contribution at a higher figure of 70%, although local transport around the destination accounts for a mere 1%. In contrast the share of accommodation is estimated at 21% and visiting attractions and other leisure facilities account for a relatively small 8% of environmental impacts (Peeters and Schouten, 2005).

Concern has been expressed about the continued growth of both car traffic and air traffic and in particular their contribution to both greenhouse gasses and other noxious emissions. Already policies of restraint on car use are being explored and introduced by various governments and the introduction of congestion charging in London appears to show that policies of constraint can be both successful and, perhaps more importantly, politically popular. There are some concerns that for certain large department stores turnover has been reduced by up to 9%, but there are other factors in play (not least a reduction in North American visitors to the UK post-9/11) and the majority of businesses are reporting increased turnover. Other similar schemes appear inevitable.

The position with regard to air travel is more mixed. Air transport accounts for approximately 3.5% of global CO_2 but the forecast growth of air traffic estimates that CO_2 emissions from aviation will double over the next 15 years, and that calculation allows for continued improvements in aviation technology and more efficient aircraft. Air transport will account for 6–10% of CO_2 emissions by 2050, at a time when many other sectors are actually reducing CO_2 emissions in line with government targets, and yet most governments still retain a 'predict and provide' approach (see Mini Case Study 14.2). Such is the relative economic importance placed on air transport (it is estimated that London Heathrow alone accounts for 1% of the UK's GDP) government is attempting to meet demand for air services where and when it arises, leading to the decision to expand airports. Environmental groups argue that there should be some form of pollution taxation and the view that aviation fuel should not be zero rated for VAT is gaining ground. The impact of air transport on the environment will emerge as a large-scale controversial topic over the coming years. Increases in environmental taxes or airport charges will disproportionately affect the cost structures of fast growing low-cost carriers and fares will have to rise.

MINI CASE STUDY 14.2
Tourism and the environment: mixed signals

POSITIVE SIGNALS

The UK government is committed to reducing greenhouse gas emissions, particularly CO_2 emissions. Following the 1997 World Climate Change Conference in Kyoto, the UK set itself the ambitious target to reduce emissions by 20% over 1990 levels by the year 2010, in excess of the protocol targets. As it happens the UK will not meet this target, but it is on schedule to cut emissions by around 14%.

Despite missing this initial target, the UK government, perhaps given additional urgency by the Stern Review (Stern, 2007), has continued to set itself new targets for CO_2 reductions, and is a keen supporter of a European-wide approach including the EU carbon trading scheme.

Aviation may seem a small player in terms of worldwide CO_2 emissions with a 3.5% global share, but aviation emissions are rising fast when most sectors are reducing CO_2 emissions. By 2050 aviation's share could reach 10%.

Aviation was excluded from the Kyoto protocol, but the UK government seems to be aware of its significance and is pressing for its inclusion in the EU carbon trading scheme.

AVIATION POLICY

The DfT forecasts continued growth in the demand for air transport services. There has been a fivefold increase in air travel over the last 30 years and the government forecasts that it will increase from this very high current figure by a further two or three times over the next 30 years. It is estimated that at least half the population fly once a year.

How should the Government deal with these forecasts? What are the options?

One obvious option is to deflate the demand for aviation growth. Much of the additional air traffic is holiday/leisure traffic and more of it is outbound (UK residents flying abroad) than inbound (overseas visitors to the UK) which produces a negative economic outcome.

Furthermore much of the extra traffic is for short-break additional holidays. Long journeys of a short duration make a disproportionately high contribution to our carbon footprint.

There are news stories, admittedly not yet supported by hard statistical evidence, that as a result of global warming more Germans are opting to take beach holidays on the Baltic Coast in Germany (travelling by train) as an alternative to Mediterranean holidays by air. They are seeking to both benefit from global warming, in the form of higher temperatures and improved climate in the Baltic, while significantly reducing their own carbon footprint. Should more UK residents take more of their holidays in the UK?

An alternative option is to deflate the demand for aviation growth with a range of environmental taxes. Currently there is no Value Added Tax (VAT) on aviation and aviation fuel is not taxed. New 'green' taxes would raise the price of air tickets which is likely to reduce the demand for travel.

Other ideas include increasing efficiency, by charging an additional tax to the airlines for every empty seat on an aircraft that lands or takes off. The logic is that this will result in fuller aircraft, so an increase in passengers does not also have to result in an increase in the number of flights. In reality, load factors are already high and in any event it may encourage some airlines to offer very cheap promotional fares where sales are low.

PREDICT AND PROVIDE

Government's response is to develop additional airport capacity (DfT, 2003). This is most urgently required for airports in the London area. Capacity at London Heathrow is being dramatically increased from the current 65 million passengers per annum to over 90 million passengers per annum with the construction of Terminal 5, scheduled to open in 2008. In practical terms the further increase in capacity means:

→

- a second runway at London Stansted by 2012;
- a third runway at London Heathrow by 2015–20;
- a second runway at London Gatwick is not ruled out, but not before 2019.

This is expansionist policy by any measure. It is an attempt to meet all the forecast demand.

Aviation growth at this level means CO_2 emissions from aviation will rise by 2050, unless there is some form of technological miracle, when overall we are seeking a reduction nationwide. The government appears to be encouraging rather than discouraging our emissions by providing such levels of capacity. Is it right? Clearly aviation is very important to the UK economy, but does this justify this set of policies?

REFERENCES

DfT (2003) *The Future of Air Transport*, Stationery Office, London.

Stern, N. (2007) *The Economics of Climate Change – The Stern Review*, Cambridge University Press, Cambridge.

DISCUSSION QUESTIONS

1. What are the main policy options to reduce CO_2 emissions from aviation?
2. In what ways do you think the aviation industry can make a positive contribution to sustainable development?
3. What actions can we as individuals take to reduce our carbon footprint from international travel?

CONCLUSION

As tourism demand grows, transportation – and indeed transportation infrastructure – will become increasingly important. New technology in respect of every aspect of transportation will be influential, and the transport industry of the future will supply visitors with ticketless travel, smart card technology for payment, and also perhaps for visa and passport purposes in certain country groups.

However, the transport industry for tourism has many issues confronting it as the numbers of visitors worldwide increase. All forms of transport pollute the environment and some will never be able to develop totally green policies. Airlines will still burn kerosene and create noise. Trains can be electrically operated, but ultimately rely on nuclear or fossil fuels. Coaches and cars burn fossil fuels and seaborne craft likewise, except leisure craft that are wind-driven. As other suppliers of the elements of the tourist product develop more environmentally-friendly policies and practices, operators must be seen as natural polluters in the foreseeable future – whether curbs on transport operators that pollute will affect the price or availability of transport for tourism remains to be seen.

SELF-CHECK QUESTIONS

1. What is the purpose of government regulation of transport? Is it desirable?
2. Compare and contrast the environmental impacts of different modes of transport.
3. List the components of a transport system and illustrate how the overall performance of a mode of transport is governed by the relative strengths and weaknesses of each.

4. Explore how transport demand in destination areas brings benefits to public transport operators. Does it also bring conflicts or problems?

5. What do airlines gain from membership of inter-airline alliances?

ESSAY QUESTIONS

1. Critically evaluate the long-term prospects of the cruise industry. Can the growth rates of the last 20 years be sustained?

2. Transport for tourism is a derived demand. Using specific examples outline the operational difficulties this brings transport operators and review potential policies to serve uneven patterns of demand.

3. Examine the case for policies to reduce our dependency on cars for travel purposes. What will be the impact of such policies on the tourism industry?

4. Discuss the viewpoint that transport for tourism is a homogeneous product.

5. Critically assess the impact of deregulation of the aviation industry.

ANNOTATED FURTHER READING

Doganis, R. (2006) *The Airline Busineess*, 2nd edn, Routledge, London.
A key text from an acknowledged leading author on airline economics and planning. The book includes chapters on airline regulation, airline alliances, the emergence, strategies and economics of low-cost no-frills carriers and e-commerce.

Graham, A. (2003) *Managing Airports: An International Perspective*, 2nd edn, Butterworth Heinemann, Oxford.
A detailed text on the operation and management of airports. Very current and includes a chapter analysing the impact of 9/11 as well as detailed data on many aspects of airport operation.

Lumsden, L. and Page, S. (2004) *Tourism and Transport*, Elsevier, Oxford.
An edited volume with contributions from 15 authors exploring the relationship between transport and tourism and their dependence upon each other. Includes chapters on cruise ships, airports, airlines, the role of transport in tourism development with case studies of Zimbabwe and North Queensland, and transport requirements in tourist destinations.

Page, S.J. (2005) *Transport and Tourism: Global Perspectives*, 2nd edn, Pearson, Harlow.
The main textbook that explores the relationship between transport and tourism. Covers all modes and includes a wide range of case studies. Topics include airline alliances, the role of the airport, environmental impacts of tourism transport and case studies of transport provision in the destination (Malta) to name but a few.

Peisley, T. (2006) *The Future of Cruising – Boom or Bust: A Worldwide Analysis to 2015*, Seatrade Communications, Colchester.
The latest in a series of detailed reports on the size, characteristics and profitability of the cruise ship industry. Includes up-to-date statistics on the size of the cruise market, capacity at the main destinations, recent trends, the number and value of new ship orders and an analysis of the main cruise lines. There is also a section on ongoing challenges, which include health (noroviruses), environmental initiatives and security. Comprehensive and current.

Web sites

http://www.cruising.org

The site of the Cruise Line International Association (CLIA) and dubbed 'the official site of the cruise industry'. A good way to keep up to date with current developments in the cruise industry, although it does have a US bias (not a problem given the nature of the industry). The Press room/Research menu gives access to the detailed news items and more detailed industry reports.

http://www.dft.gov.uk

The site of the Department for Transport in the UK and therefore with an obvious UK bias. Nevertheless, one can download detailed policy documents from this site such as the 1998 White Paper on policies to manage road traffic growth or the 2003 White Paper on airport development, which include concepts and ideas that can be applied more widely. Some of the published statistics include international comparisons.

http://europa.eu.int/comm/dgs/energy_transport/index_index_en.html

The site for the Transport Directorate of the EU. Again full EU White Papers can be downloaded from the site and it also offers access to transport statistics for the whole of the EU area. Current policy documents prominent on the site are on rail development and on inter-modal comparisons of the charges for transport infrastructure.

References cited

Bjelicic, B. (2007) 'The Business Model of Low Cost Airline – Past, Present, Future', in Groβ, S. & Schröder, A. (ed.) (2007) *Handbook of Low Cost Airlines: Strategies, Business Processes and Market Environment*, Erich Schmidt Verlag, Berlin, pp. 11–30.

DETR (1998) *A New Deal for Transport: Better for Everyone*, Stationery Office, London.

DfT (2000) *Air Traffic Forecasts for the United Kingdom 2000*, Stationery Office, London.

DfT (2003) *The Future of Air Transport*, Stationery Office, London.

DfT (2006) *Transport Statistics Great Britain*, Stationery Office, London.

Doganis, R. (2002) *Flying Off Course: The Economics of International Airlines*, 3rd edn, Routledge, London.

Doganis, R. (2006) *The Airline Business*, 2nd edn, Routledge, London.

Duval, D.T. (2007) *Tourism and Transport – Modes, Networks and Flows*, Channel View Publications, Clevedon.

Graham, A. (2003) *Managing Airports: An International Perspective*, 2nd edn, Butterworth Heinemann, Oxford.

Groβ, S. & Schröder, A. (ed.) (2007) *Handbook of Low Cost Airlines: Strategies, Business Processes and Market Environment*, Erich Schmidt Verlag, Berlin.

Høyer, K.G. (2000) 'Sustainable tourism or sustainable mobility? The tourism case', *Journal of Sustainable Tourism* 8(2), 147–60.

Hanlon, P. (2007) *Global Airlines – Competition in a transnational industry*, Elsevier Butterworth Heinmann, London.

Kain, P. (1998) 'The reform of rail transport in Great Britain', *Journal of Transport Economics and Policy* 32(2), 247–66.

Lawton, T. (2002) *Cleared for Take-off: Structure and strategy in the low fare airline business*, Ashgate, Aldershot.

Knorr, A. (2007) 'Southwest Airlines: The Low Cost Poineer at 35' in Groβ, S. & Schröder, A. (ed.) (2007) *Handbook of Low Cost Airlines: Strategies, Business Processes and Market Environment*, Erich Schmidt Verlag, Berlin, pp. 77–110.

Page, S.J. (2005) *Transport and Tourism*, Elsevier, Oxford.

Peeters, P. (2007) 'Mitigating Tourism's Contribution to Climate Change – An Introduction', pp. 11–26 in *Tourism and Climate Change Mitigation: Methods, greenhouse gas reductions and policies*, Peeters, P. (ed.), NHTV, Breda.

Peeters, P. and Schouten, F. (2005) 'Reducing the ecological footprint of inbound tourism and transport to Amsterdam', *Journal of Sustainable Transport* 14(2), 157–71.

Peeters, P. Szimba, E. and Duijnisveld, M. (2007) 'European tourism transport and the main environmental impacts', *Journal of Transport Geography* 15(2), 83–93.

RAC Foundation (2002) *Motoring Towards 2050*, RAC Foundation, London.

Robbins, D. (2003) 'Public Transport as a Visitor Attraction', pp. 86–102 in *Managing Visitor Attractions: New Directions*, Fyall, A., Garrod, B. and Leask, A. (eds), Butterworth Heinemann, Oxford.

Robbins, D.K. and Dickinson, J.E. (2007) 'Achieving Domestic Tourism Growth and Simultaneously Reducing Car Dependency: The Illusive Prize', pp. 169–88 in *Tourism and Climate Change Mitigation: Methods, greenhouse gas reductions and policies*, Peeters, P. (ed.), NHTV, Breda.

Royal Commission on Environmental Pollution, 18th Report (1994) *Transport and the Environment*, Stationery Office, London.

Welsby, J. and Nichols, A. (1999) 'The privatisation of British Railways', *Journal of Transport Economics and Policy*, 33(1), 55–76.

MAJOR CASE STUDY 14.1
The cruise ship industry

The cruise ship industry has grown into a genuine form of mass tourism over the last 25 years. The measurement of cruise-taking can be quite misleading, as the usual figure quoted is the number of cruises taken (Table 14.3). However, there is a very significant difference in terms of consumption and economic impact between a passenger on a short cruise of say 3 to 4 days and a passenger cruising for 14 days or longer. A measure of cruise days, as used in Table 14.4, is more illuminating. Nevertheless the growth over the last

20 years by any measure has been staggering with annual growth rates between 1980 and 2005 of 8.2% per annum (CLIA, 2006).

To accommodate the growth there has also been substantial investment in new vessels. Growth rates in cruise capacity have averaged 7.6% between 1981 and 2005 (CLIA, 2006) so overall occupancy levels have been virtually unchanged. This represents huge levels of investment. Between 2006 and 2010 there are confirmed orders for 30 vessels and furthermore

Table 14.3	Total cruise passenger market ('000)				
Year	North America	UK	Rest of Europe	Rest of world	Total
1990	3 640	179	330	345	4 495
1991	3 979	187	354	414	4 980
1992	4 136	219	407	490	5 460
1993	4 480	254	420	467	5 940
1994	4 448	270	502	1 196	6 280
1995	4 378	340	694	1 481	6 440
1996	4 656	416	785	N/A	6 850
1997	5 051	522	928	N/A	7 580
1998	5 428	663	902	850	8 210
1999	5 894	746	994	1 160	9 067
2000	6 882	754	1 096	N/A	10 138
2001	6 906	776	1 130	1 380	10 192
2002	7 470	824	1 296	1 608	11 198
2003	8 195	963	1 709	1 474	12 340
2004	9 107	1 029	1 764	1 463	13 383
2005	9 670	1 071	2 145	N/A	14 400 est.

Source: CLIA (2006); Peisley (2006)

Table 14.4	Cruise capacity for selected destinations (CLIA members)

	Bed Days											
Destination	1989 '000	%	1995 '000	%	2001 '000	%	2002 '000	%	2006 '000	%	% Change 1989–2006
Caribbean	10 982	44.5	15 245	42.8	21 833	36.6	26 741	42.1	31 956	39.2	191.0
Alaska	1 598	6.5	3 008	8.4	4 698	7.9	5 053	8.0	6 356	7.8	297.7
Bahamas			2 761	7.7	4 699	7.9	2 876	4.5	6 073	7.5	
Mexico			1 754	4.9	1 167	1.9	3 386	5.3	5 214	6.4	
Mediterranean	1 879	7.6	3 447	9.7	7 546	12.7	6 497	10.2	10 504	12.9	459.0
North Europe	774	3.1	1 582	4.4	4 837	8.1	6 932	10.9	6 800	8.4	778.5
Total World Bed Days (all Destinations)	**24 699**		**35 661**		**59 581**		**63 595**		**81 454**		**230**

Source: CLIA (2006)

these vessels are getting larger with 18 of them carrying over 3,000 passengers (Peisley, 2006). When Cunard's *Queen Mary 2* (QM2) undertook its maiden voyage in January 2004, it was the largest cruise vessel at 148,528 gwt, although as a luxury vessel it did not carry the most passengers (2,620). However, by May 2006 it had been superseded by Royal Caribbean Cruise's (RCC) *Freedom of the Seas* at 158,000 gwt carrying 3,634 passengers, and in February 2006 the same company ordered what will become the world's largest and most expensive cruise ship (named Project Genesis), at 220,000 gwt and carrying a staggering 5,400 passengers, with delivery expected in 2009. Obviously some older vessels are being withdrawn, for instance Cunard have announced the withdrawal of the iconic QE2 in late 2008, but Peisley (2006) estimates that on current trends worldwide capacity will increase by 75% by 2015.

PATTERNS OF DEMAND

The US market dominates cruise demand (Table 14.3). Around 65% of all cruise passengers are from North America. The 1990s saw very dramatic rates of growth from the UK market, which has seen it emerge as the most significant European market (ahead of Germany), but its significance is dwarfed by North America.

Although there has been diversification of destinations by the cruise companies the Caribbean region still dominates with around 39% of all cruise days. Table 14.4 shows the main cruise destinations in 2006. However, the annual figures of capacity hide a significant pattern. There are many more cruise ships in the Caribbean between October and the following March than there are between April and September

and Cruise Line International Association (CLIA) statistics show that around 62% of annual Caribbean capacity is offered between October and the following March.

The Caribbean therefore takes on huge significance for the future growth and prosperity of the global cruise industry as other important destination markets demonstrate seasonal demand. The Mediterranean has a season stretching from March to September, while other important destinations such as Alaska and North Europe (Baltic, Norwegian Fjords) have even shorter peaks during the same season. Cruise lines have found it increasingly difficult to find alternative destinations to the Caribbean between October and March. There have been some successes such as European cruises to the Atlantic Islands, and a few select vessels embark on a 3-month 'world cruise' commencing in December or January, but overall progress has been slow. Vessels are therefore repositioned from seasonal markets back to the Caribbean to achieve high annual utilisation.

Following a decade of falling market share, cruise capacity in the Caribbean grew significantly in 2002 (Table 14.4) due to a significant repositioning of ships away from the Mediterranean to the Caribbean by US cruise lines as a reaction to 9/11. European destinations are now recovering lost ground following this initial reaction, although demand in the Caribbean remains strong.

TRENDS IN THE INDUSTRY

- Cruise passengers are attracted from an ever increasing range of socio-economic, income and age groups. Penetration in the North American market has been increased by a trend towards shorter

Table 14.5	Market share of North American market by length of cruise, 2005	
Length of cruise	%	% growth 1980–2005
2–5 days	33.9	680.9
6–8 days	52.2	511.2
9–17 days	13.5	505.4
18+ days	0.4	111.8
Total	100	592.5

Source: CLIA (2006)

cruises (Table 14.5). Cruises of between 2 and 5 days were by far the fastest growing segment of the North American market between 1980 and 1991, but since 1991 the average length of cruise has began to rise again and the market share of short cruises has stagnated at about one-third of all North American cruises. The provision of cruises by tour operators, pioneered by Airtours in 1995 and adopted by Saga and Thomson amongst others, widened the appeal and affordability of cruising in the UK market and now accounts for 35% of all UK cruise passengers. The CLIA have reported that over 1 million children now take a cruise worldwide.

- As previously stated, vessels are getting bigger, bringing operational economies of scale to the cruise lines. This is changing the nature of the product, with fewer ports of call as the vessel becomes more of the leisure experience (the experience economy). The vast majority of the mega vessels are deployed in the Caribbean but in a strategy to enable the region to cope with this additional demand as many as six cruise brands own private uninhabited Caribbean islands.

- There has been the creation of an oligopoly following the take over of P&O cruises by Carnival. The three largest cruise companies, Carnival Corporation, Royal Caribbean Cruises and Star Cruise Group, now account for 80% of all cruise capacity, a share which continues to grow driven both by acquisition and by organic growth in the form of new vessels.

FUTURE PROSPECTS FOR GROWTH

The cruise industry is bullish about its future prospects. The CLIA estimates that only 17% of the US population have ever cruised. There are similar figures for the UK market. Mintel (2003) estimate that only 13% of the UK population have ever cruised and for the rest of the world the levels of penetration are even lower. Market research surveys by the CLIA indicate that 51 million North Americans indicate an intention to cruise in the next three years. With such a large untapped market they argue that the growth rates of the last 20 years can be sustained well into the future. They further argue that a high percentage of cruise passengers cruise again. The 'large potential untapped market' argument is convincing given past trends, and clearly cruise companies have confidence in it otherwise they would not be investing in 30 new vessels. However, such surveys do need to be treated with some caution bearing in mind they are asking hypothetical questions about future consumption.

Forecasts of future rates of growth show an expected 20 million cruises by 2010 and 25 million by 2015 (Peisley, 2006).

BARRIERS TO CONTINUED GROWTH

Discounting

There is some evidence that the dramatic growth over recent years has been partially 'supply led' rather than demand led. Industry sources cite heavy discounting in both the North American and European markets. The temptation for cruise lines to discount is obvious. Once substantial investment in new vessels is made, those vessels have to be filled. There is scope for significant on-board spend, the three largest areas being at the bar, on shore based excursions and in the casino areas of vessels. Indeed cruise lines will argue that passenger psychology is such that a low brochure price makes marketing sense. Passengers will put substantial energy into achieving relatively small savings in the brochure price and yet while actually on the cruise itself they are far less conscious of spending levels. However, as new capacity has come on stream discounting by the major cruise lines has been fierce, reducing cruise line yields and affecting cruise line profitability. The concerns of the financial markets over falling profitability and the potential of future overcapacity in the market led to falls in the share price of all the major cruise companies in 2000.

Over recent years yields have begun to recover form their low point of 2003 and, although discounting will continue for the foreseeable future, both revenues and profits for the two largest cruise companies increased in 2005. Carnival reported a $2.2 billion profit based on a revenue of $11bn and RCC returned $716 million profit on a revenue of $4.9bn. Despite this recovery a number of financial and corporate analysts question whether the compound market growth rates of around 8% can be sustained into the longer term, and whether the need for widespread discounting is evidence of a market approaching maturity, if not saturation.

SATURATION OF CRUISE DESTINATION AREAS

Around 24 cruise line brands operate around 70 vessels in the Caribbean over the year. Berth capacity offered by cruise vessels was predicted to exceed the number of hotel beds by 2006 (Wood, 2000) and Caribbean governments are beginning to question the value of cruise activity continuing to grow at this level. The majority of the mega vessels coming on stream are destined for the Caribbean market. The number of ports the largest vessels can call at are reduced but the socio-cultural or environmental impacts of each call on small port destinations are considerable. The cruise call does bring economic benefit for the destination. The ships may require fresh water, sewage disposal facilities, bunkerage and fresh food, all offering the potential for local jobs. Passenger spend can, however, remain relatively low, perhaps $50 per passenger limited to shopping, light refreshments (perhaps lunch) and organised excursions, which if booked on board may see much of this spend retained by the cruise line.

The trend for cruise lines to purchase small uninhabited Caribbean islands may overcome some of these problems but reduces the economic benefit to the region. Cruise lines also argue that the trend to larger vessels is helpful in accommodating growth without a comparable increase in ship calls. Nevertheless, local governments are giving consideration to limiting cruise calls to the region along the lines of the quotas introduced in the number of cruise calls to Bermuda in the mid-1980s. It is difficult to envisage the continued growth of cruising at current levels if the Caribbean does not accommodate a fair share of future growth. The most significant issue is alternative destinations to absorb global cruise growth between October and March.

ENVIRONMENTAL PRESSURES

Continued growth at the current levels may not represent sustainable development. A large cruise ship generates around 210,000 gallons of sewage, millions of gallons of grey water, 25,000 gallons of oily bilge water plus solid waste and hazardous waste every week. The disposal of ship waste and sewage, while more highly regulated than before, undoubtedly causes damage with such a high concentration of vessels in the Caribbean (Lester and Weeden, 2004; Wood, 2004). There is also increased pressure for additional dredging to deepen harbours to enable ports to accept the larger vessels.

CONCLUSION

The cruise industry is confident of future profitable growth. The former CEO of Princess Cruises, Peter Ratcliffe, sums up the industry view:

> Our industry has sustainable long-term growth characteristics despite the impact of recent events on short-term trading. The key indicators of demographics, penetration, high levels of customer satisfaction and trends in leisure spend point to significant growth over the long term and increasing globalisation of the industry.

Time will tell whether this optimistic view for continued growth is right.

Source: http://www.cruising.org

REFERENCES

CLIA (2006) *Cruise Industry Overview: Marketing Edition*, Cruise Line International Association, New York.

Lester, J. and Weeden, C. (2004) 'Stakeholders, the natural environment and the future of Caribbean cruise tourism', *International Journal of Tourism Research*, **6**(1), 39–50.

Mintel (2003) 'Cruises', *Leisure Intelligence*, April 2003.

Peisley, T. (2006) *The Future of Cruising – Boom or Bust: A Worldwide Analysis to 2015*, Seatrade Communications, Colchester.

Wood, R. (2000) 'Caribbean cruise tourism: globalization at sea', *Annals of Tourism Research*, **27**(2), 345–70.

Wood, R. (2004) 'Cruise ships: deterritorialized destinations', pp. 133–45 in *Tourism and Transport*, Lumsdon, L. and Page, S. (eds), Elsevier, Oxford.

FURTHER READING

Dowling, R.K. (ed.) (2006) *Cruise Tourism: Issues, Impacts, Cases*, CABI Publishing, Wallingford.

DISCUSSION QUESTIONS

1. How have cruise lines widened the age and socio-economic profile of passengers?

2. What are the main benefits and disbenefits of cruise calls to the Caribbean region?

3. What are the potential barriers to the continued growth of the cruise shipping industry?

CHAPTER 15
Public Sector and Policy

LEARNING OUTCOMES

The focus of this chapter is on the role of the public sector, in the shape of governmental organisations, in tourism. Specifically, upon completion, the reader will have:

- a knowledge of the key organisations globally with an interest in and influence upon tourism;

- an understanding of the key functions of NTOs and an insight into how such offices might be structured and how responsibilities are divided;

- an overview of the role of the public sector; and

- a knowledge of the instruments available to governments in order to manipulate demand for tourism and control the supply of it.

Photograph: View of the Twelve Apostles, Port Campbell National Park, Australia © Hannah Cox

INTRODUCTION

Governments are involved with tourist organisations at both the international and national level. In the latter case they are normally the instigators for the establishment of a **national tourist organisation** (NTO), while in the former instance they are partners along with other member states in such bodies as the UN World Tourism Organization (UNWTO), the European Travel Commission (ETC), the Pacific Asia Travel Association (PATA) and so on. All these bodies can contribute to the formation of a country's tourism policy. In this chapter we look at the overall policy framework and consider the experience of different governments in order to illustrate the changes that occur in policy, noting the very many organisations that express an interest in tourism at the national level. As national tourist offices are commonly the executive agency for government policy, their administrative structure and functions are considered in some detail. The last part of the chapter examines intervention by the public sector in tourism. Particular consideration is given to the variety of instruments governments have at their disposal to manage the direction of tourism development in the interests of the host community.

PUBLIC POLICY FRAMEWORK

With tourism as one of the main international economic drivers in the twenty-first century, together with increasing demands from the domestic population for leisure and recreation, the industry is a development option that few governments can afford to ignore. A critical difference between tourism and many other agents of development is that of inseparability, in that tourism is consumed at the place of production, thus involving itself with the host community, and requiring some **commodification** and sharing of traditions, value systems and culture. Since the tourist industry does not control all those factors that make up the attractiveness of a destination and the impact on the host population can be considerable, it is necessary for the options concerning the development of tourism to be considered at the highest level of government and the appropriate public administrative framework put in place. As a rule the greater the importance of tourism to a country's economy the greater is the involvement of the public sector, to the point of having a government ministry with sole responsibility for tourism. While tourism can be planned to be more or less sustainable at the destination end through the range of policies analysed in this chapter, it must not be forgotten that there is the continuing issue of the 'carbon footprint' generated by domestic and international travel to the destination, arising particularly from the growth in low-cost air transport (see Chapter 14). The airlines' response has been to increase fuel efficiency and introduce composite materials that are capable of being recycled and lighter in the air.

Beyond the national horizon, governments are involved in supporting a variety of multinational agencies. The official flag carrier for international tourism is the UNWTO (Mini Case Study 15.1), which is vested by the United Nations with a central and decisive role in promoting the development of responsible, sustainable and universally accessible tourism. Elsewhere there are a number of other international bodies whose activities impinge upon tourism: these include the World Bank (whose commercial arm is the International Finance Corporation (IFC), which takes on private sector projects, whereas its other arm, the International Bank for Reconstruction and Development (IBRD), provides government funding for structural adjustment and infrastructure developments), other United Nations' bodies (such as the International Civil Aviation Organization (ICAO), the World Health Organization (WHO) and UNESCO), the International Air Transport Association (IATA), and the Organization for Economic Cooperation and Development (OECD).

MINI CASE STUDY 15.1
The United Nations World Tourism Organization (UNWTO)

The UNWTO can trace its origins back to 1925 to a non-governmental body that after the Second World War became the International Union of Official Travel Organisations (IUOTO). IUOTO was made up of a mixture of private and public sector organisations dealing with the technical aspects of travel and tourism. However, by the 1960s, the growth of tourism, its international dimensions and the increasing activities of national governments in this field, necessitated the transformation of IUOTO into an intergovernmental body, the World Tourism Organization. The latter was ratified in 1974 and was empowered to deal on a world-wide basis with all matters concerning tourism and to cooperate with other competent world agencies that came under the umbrella of United Nations organisation. The prefix UN was added at the end of 2005.

The UNWTO is an operative rather than a deliberative body that pays particular attention to the interests of the developing countries in the field of tourism. Its functions include:

- helping member countries, tourist destinations and businesses maximise the positive economic, social and cultural effects of tourism;

- collecting statistics, identifying and forecasting markets;

- assisting in tourism planning as an executing agency of the United Nations Development Programme (UNDP), with emphasis on its pro-poor strategy;

- advising on the harmonisation of policies and practices;

- sponsoring education and training, and identifying funding sources;

- promoting the broader relationship of visitors to the physical and social environment, by defining sustainability as development which meets the needs of present tourists and host regions while protecting and enhancing opportunities for the future;

- encouraging the implementation of a Global Code of Ethics for Tourism for promoting peace, the observance of human rights and fundamental freedoms.

As an intergovernmental body the UNWTO's membership works largely in terms of political groupings that can bring pressure on the general formulation of tourism policy. In order to benefit from advances in operational practice, the UNWTO has an affiliate membership scheme for organisations working within the tourism sector. While the general assembly of the UNWTO is largely concerned with debates on policy, the meetings of affiliate members usually take up topical issues affecting tourism, for example taxation. A major success of the UNWTO has been the methodological design of the Tourism Satellite Account, which has set the standard for measuring the economic importance of tourism within the framework of the United Nations system of national accounts.

DISCUSSION QUESTIONS

1. Consider the benefits of having a world body that has tourism as its sole sphere of interest.

2. What priorities would you attach to the range of functions covered by the UNWTO?

3. If your country is a member of the UNWTO, what benefits do the tourist authorities perceive they get from membership?

At a lower level, there is a variety of regional bodies such as the Organization of American States (OAS), Pacific Asia Travel Association (PATA) and the European Travel Commission (ETC). Most of their efforts are devoted to promotion and marketing, though they do provide technical assistance and promote codes of conduct to encourage travel that is respectful of other people's lives and places. For example, PATA has adopted the following Traveller's Code:

1. Be Flexible
   Are you prepared to accept cultures and practices different from your own?

2. Choose Responsibly
   Have you elected to support businesses that clearly and actively address the cultural and environmental concerns of the locale you are visiting?

3. Do Your Homework
   Have you done any research about the people and places you plan to visit so you may avoid what may innocently offend them or harm their environment?

4. Be Aware
   Are you informed of the holidays, holy days, and general religious and social customs of the places you visit?

5. Support Local Enterprise
   Have you made a commitment to contribute to the local economy by using businesses that economically support the community you are visiting, eating in local restaurants and buying locally made artisan crafts as remembrances of your trip?

6. Be Respectful and Observant
   Are you willing to respect local laws that may include restrictions of your usage of or access to places and things that may harm or otherwise erode the environment or alter or run counter to the places you visit?

(Source: PATA Sustainable Tourism Committee at its
13 April 2002 meeting in New Delhi, India. www.PATA.org/sustainability)

As an organisation whose membership is made up of the NTOs of Europe, the ETC carries out its objective to promote the region as an attractive destination through its web portal VistEurope.com, consumer advertising and travel trade promotions, public relations, market research and professional development for its members, and liaison with the principal international agencies. Its work is supported by the European Commission, which sees tourism as an activity of great economic and social significance within the European Union (EU), particularly for the peripheral and somewhat poorer regions of Europe. Although a wide variety of regional disparities exist across the EU, from early on it was realised that there is a distinct tendency for the poorest regions to be situated on the outer areas of the Union and, since the late 1980s, greater emphasis has been given to stimulating small tourism firms and indigenous development in areas to take advantage of their natural surroundings.

Apart from the World Bank, funds for developing tourism in low-income countries may be obtained from regional banks such as the European Bank for Reconstruction and Development (EBRD) for Eastern Europe and the Commonwealth of Independent States; the Inter-American Development Bank; African Development Bank; Asian Development Bank; Arab Bank for Economic Development in Africa; East African Development Bank; and the Caribbean Development Bank. Their principles of operation are mainly for the granting of medium- or long-term loans (often with various grace periods and low rates of interest) to specific projects or to national development institutions, and providing technical assistance in project preparation. They are sometimes prepared to take a minority shareholding in investments, provided there is an option for onward selling, preferably to host country nationals.

Looking at the structure in Europe, officially tourism in the EU comes under Directorate General Enterprise, but the development work of Directorate General Regional Policy also involves tourism projects as a means of overcoming regional disparities. With the adoption of the Single European Act (1987), there is a commitment by the EU to promote economic and social cohesion through actions to reduce regional disparities, and the Maastricht Treaty (1992) acknowledged, for the first time, the role of tourism in these actions. The resources for mitigating regional differences are drawn from the structural funds, which are made up of contributions from member states with the express purposes of helping less well off regions (see Major Case Study 15.1). Alongside public monies, commercial funding of tourism projects is obtainable from the European Investment Bank.

The direct role of the EU in tourism is seen as one of simplification, harmonisation and the easing of restrictions on trade. Specifically, strategy is developed around the following objectives:

- improving the quality of European tourism services through both product development and training to upgrade skill levels, taking account of trends in demand;

- stimulating the demand for European tourism outside common borders;

- ensuring the safety and security of travellers;

- improving the business environment in which tourist enterprises operate, particularly through the exchange and dissemination of information via the new technologies;

- encouraging the diversification of tourist activities and products through improving the competitiveness and profitability of the industry; and

- moving forward tourism developments in a sustainable manner by giving due regard to the cultural and environmental dimensions of tourism, in order to guarantee that the activity continues on a regular basis.

It is important that, in developing its strategy for tourism, the European Commission does not duplicate the work of other organisations. Ultimately, the differing nature of the tourist product within Europe leaves the Commission with little option but to assign the primary role of tourism policy to member states and proceed with tourism projects only in close partnership with national and regional bodies. The principle applied is that of subsidiarity, which argues for decisions to be made at the lowest level of authority so as best to meet local needs and be as close as possible to the citizen, which is seen as a requirement to safeguard democratic control of European institutions and to maintain the variety of regional differences and cultural identities. Tourism policy is therefore, to a large degree, the responsibility of member states but the provision of research and statistics, facilitation in terms of easing frontier formalities and improvements to transport infrastructure, together with general image promotion in association with the ETC, appear to be the most favoured policies for the Commission.

All European countries have NTOs: some are part of government as in France or Spain, or in Eastern Europe, while others are established independently of government but are supported by central grants and other income-generating activities, as in the UK. The case for public sector involvement in tourism rests on concepts of market failure, namely that those who argue for the market mechanism as the sole arbiter in the allocation of resources for tourism are ignoring the lessons of history and are grossly oversimplifying the complex and varied nature of the product. In an EU context, research among member states has indicated a number of sources of market failure that the respective governments are seeking to address:

- Developing tourism as a common good that collectively benefits many businesses, with the NTO acting as a broker between suppliers and potential visitors.

- Infant industry development as part of regional policy (including peripheral areas), where commercial viability requires public sector support through the provision of essential infrastructure and financial incentives.

- Improving the tourism product, via the implementation of measures such as benchmarking good practice and training programmes for tourism workers.

- Incorporating the concept of sustainable and balanced growth into tourism by taking account of socio-cultural and environmental issues in tourism planning.

By way of contrast, the US Congress took a much more market-orientated stance and closed down the United States Travel and Tourism Administration (USTTA) in 1996, some 15 years after its establishment. In place of USTTA, a Tourism Industries office was established within the Department of Commerce with the twin objectives of increasing the number of exporters by providing research and technical assistance to communities and businesses interested in tapping international markets, and coordinating tourism-related activities and policies within government itself. The major responsibility for tourism marketing and development rests with the individual states, and the US travel industry, which campaigns vigorously to seek federal involvement in promoting the image of the USA worldwide, arguing that it should not be left to a few strong destination brands, such as Florida, New York or Hawaii, and major companies, such as Disney, Hyatt and Hertz, to 'pull the tourism train'.

Nevertheless, much of the tourist product in the USA is under federal control through the Department of the Interior, whose responsibilities include:

- preserving national scenic and historic areas;
- conserving, developing and utilising fish and wildlife resources;
- coordinating federal and state recreation programmes; and
- operating job corps conservation youth camps.

The Forest Service of the Department of Agriculture also takes an active role in promoting and sustaining the nation's landscape.

The US experience of changes in direction of tourism policy is not uncommon in other countries. In Britain, the Development of Tourism Act 1969 was instigated by the recognition of tourism as an important earner of foreign exchange after the devaluation of 1967. Over the years since the Act's inception, the economic policy emphasis for tourism has shifted back and forth to the extent that there is little doubt that the frequent alterations in direction have been more of a handicap than a benefit to the development of public sector tourist organisations in Britain. There have been continual changes in tourism ministers followed by one tourism review after another, though all falling short of repealing the Act, but rather confining themselves to using funding as a means to curtail or expand the activities of the national boards. The tourism policies of various UK governments were once summed up by the Trade and Industry Committee of the House of Commons in the following manner:

> The truth is that the Government cannot quite decide what its own role is. Along with general policy on industry, the present Government does not want to interfere with the development of the tourism industry in the private sector. Indeed, we were told that 'the Government see their own main role in relation to tourism as promoting a general economic climate favourable to the industry's development'. Given that the Government cannot control the most important climatic factor in this context – the weather – more specific strategies are needed. The Government minimises the appearance of involvement by reducing policy aims to statements of the obvious but maintains the fact of involvement in the tourist boards and the grants provided through them. The trouble is that this actual financial commitment is then left without there being any clear specific strategy to guide its use.
>
> (*Source*: House of Commons Trade and Industry Committee, *Tourism in the UK*, Vol. 1, HMSO, London (paragraph 73).)

On the question of financial commitment, the UNWTO has long used the rule that the minimum of 1% of a country's tourist receipts should be devoted to the NTO, but in Britain this has never been the case and the industry continually laments what it sees as the short-sighted policies of the UK Treasury that cause inadequate representation in source markets due to limitations on VisitBritain funds. With increasing devolution, the responsibilities for VisitScotland and Visit Wales have been transferred to their governing authorities (the Northern Ireland Tourist Board was established by statute in 1948 and has always been separate), which has given them much higher funding allocations, but this it is argued has only served to create a fragmented presence abroad and ineffective impact and waste, due to uncoordinated actions and spending. In summary, the professional view is that the UK's Department of Culture, Media and Sport, which is responsible for tourism, has repeatedly espoused policy targets, but has not created a cohesive strategy for their achievement, nor has it been able to ensure that VisitBritain can act as an adequate catalyst to implement, encourage or fund effective programmes.

For political reasons there is always the temptation for governments to switch policy directions. This gives the impression of the dynamics of change, but can, in practice, generate chaos through conflicting objectives. It takes a long time to create tourist destinations and build up market positions. It is, therefore, rather simplistic to behave as if the factors influencing such developments can be turned on and off as with a tap. One of the principal difficulties is that tourism is a diverse and fragmented industry with many different economic agents acting in their own interests (often on the basis of imperfect information), which may not be to the long-term benefit of tourism as a whole. Uncoordinated market competition can, in these circumstances, produce cyclical growth patterns, with a consequent waste of resources. This places a premium on an overall planning body such as an NTO, which is able to give a sense of direction by marketing the destination and acting as a distribution channel by drawing the attention of potential tourists and the travel trade to the products that the numerous suppliers in a country have to offer.

ADMINISTRATIVE FRAMEWORK

There are considerable variations in the structure of the public administration of tourism, which in turn depend on the size of the tourist industry and the importance the government attaches to the various reasons advanced for public sector involvement in tourism. A generalised hierarchical structure is presented in Figure 15.1: it demonstrates a chain of direction from the governing assembly, which could be a council of ministers, a congress or a parliament, downwards to the destinations, where tourism policy and plans are implemented.

A list of some of the most common arguments put forward for government participation in tourism include:

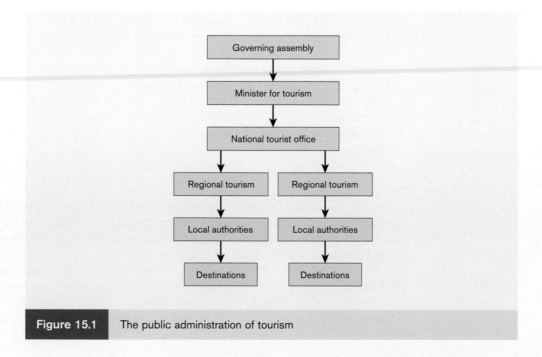

Figure 15.1　The public administration of tourism

- foreign exchange earnings and their importance for the balance of payments;
- employment creation and the need to provide education and training;
- tourism is a large and fragmented industry requiring careful coordination of development and marketing;
- the need to maximise the net benefits to the host community;
- spreading the benefits and costs equitably;
- building the image of the country as a tourist destination;
- market regulation to protect consumers and prevent unfair competition;
- the provision of public goods and infrastructure as part of the tourist product;
- protecting tourism resources and the environment;
- regulating aspects of social behaviour, for example, gambling; and
- the requirement to monitor the level of tourism activity through statistical surveys.

In most cases, where tourism is a significant element of economic activity, so that much weight is attributed to the arguments presented above, it is common practice to have a Ministry of Tourism. This is particularly true of island economies, which frequently form some of the world's most attractive tourist destinations. The position of the NTO within this framework may be inside or outside the ministry. In the latter case, the NTO becomes a government agency or semi-governmental body. It usually has a separate constitution, enacted by law, and a board of directors appointed from outside government which, in theory, gives independence from the political system. However, the link is maintained through the NTO being the executive arm of government policy as agreed by the ministry and public money providing the major source of funds for most NTOs. The reality is that few governments can resist giving specific policy directions for developments that are likely to influence political results in locations where the electoral outcomes are close. This allows local political parties at the destination to usurp tourism plans, either by frustrating developments or having projects inserted into plans that have a high political visibility but are of little economic worth, which results in a trail of poor value for public money that often ends in financial insolvency. Good NTOs are attuned to this and build flexibility into the planning process to deal with barely concealed electoral calculations, ensuring that they receive prior written instructions from the responsible minister before proceeding.

Some NTOs, normally termed a convention and visitor bureau (CVB), are simply private associations whose constitution is determined by their membership, which may include government representation. Income is thus raised from a variety of sources and, similar to other businesses, the existence of these bureaux is dependent on the demand for their services in the marketplace. In times of recession, such associations often have difficulty raising funds from the private sector to maintain their activities and need to have injections of public funds to continue with long-term projects.

Since the 1980s, the upsurge in market economics has seen more and more governments urging their NTOs to generate matching funds from the tourist industry. Methods to achieve this objective have included joint marketing initiatives and charging for a range of services, for example, market research reports and brokerage fees from arranging finance. However, the main obstacles to raising private sector revenue have always been the long-term and non-commercial nature of many of the tasks undertaken by NTOs. Added to this is the fact that when NTOs do embark on commercial activities they may be criticised by the private sector for unfair competition, because they are largely funded from taxation. Some countries, for example many of the island tourist destinations such as Bermuda, have recognised these difficulties and have levied specific tourist taxes on the private sector to pay for the work of the NTO, although where such taxes are not separately set aside for tourism, it can also be argued that the tourist industry is just another source of tax revenue.

Structure of a national tourist organisation

A stylised organisational layout for an NTO, illustrating its principal divisions, is presented in Figure 15.2. This type of NTO is at 'arm's length' from the Ministry of Tourism by virtue of having its own chairman and board of directors. Where an NTO is a division of a ministry, which may have a wider portfolio of activities than just tourism, then it is usual for the director of tourism to report to the senior civil servant in the ministry rather than a board. Many NTOs have only marketing responsibilities and are designated as such, as this is considered to be their primary function, with tourism development being placed in the general portfolio of a national or regional planning authority. In these cases Figure 15.2 should not have a development division and research activity is likely to be included under the marketing division, but the industry view is that it is better served when both marketing and development are under one body, as in Figure 15.2.

Clearly, the exact structure of an NTO will depend upon the objectives laid down for it by government and the tasks the organisation has to undertake in order to meet those same objectives. For example, Visit Wales, the Welsh Assembly Government's tourism department (note that the former Wales Tourist Board was merged into the Assembly Government in April 2006 and that Visit Wales is now part of an Assembly Government Department and not a separate organisation) sees its principal role as providing leadership and strategic direction to the tourism industry in Wales, targeting resources towards priorities that will most benefit the industry as outlined in its objectives:

- to assist in raising the quality of the tourism offer in Wales;
- to stimulate growth in the demand for Wales and to position Wales as a must see travel destination;
- to use effective partnership working to achieve mutual benefits for Wales;
- to encourage, support and reward innovation;

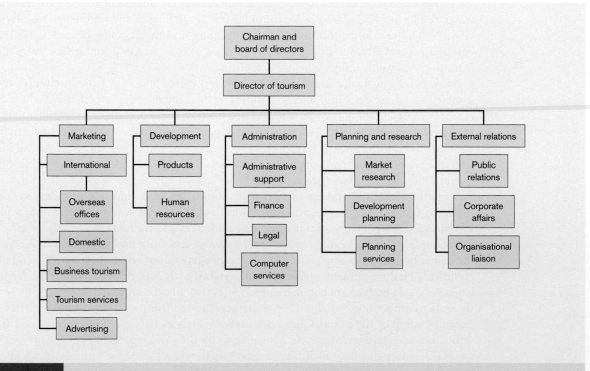

| **Figure 15.2** | Structure of a national tourism organisation |

- to encourage a skilled and professional workforce equipped to deliver a quality Wales experience.

For any organisation maintaining quality in the face of competition is important for retaining value. It is measured indirectly through physical and qualitative evaluation indicators as formalised in classification and grading schemes, discussed for the accommodation sector in Chapter 12. This being the case, quality evaluation will always be an inexact science and one that is resolved through expert judgement and opinion. Since NTOs do not own the tourism product they have to work in partnership with many other businesses to create a positive, distinctive and motivating identity for their country as an attractive destination in target markets. Innovation is commonly associated with new products and this is the basis on which pubic funding in the form of grants and subsidised loans are normally given. However, the concept is broader than this, since it may also encompass new methods of production, new sources of supply, new markets or simply improving the structure of the organisation. In sum innovation is about new ways of doing things that add value to the business.

It is clear that NTOs are generally set multiple objectives by their political masters, which makes it difficult to maximise any one. Thus trying to maximise the economic gain, particularly in the short term, may not be in the long-term interests of the host community and could be at variance with the objective of protecting the natural and built environment. Managers have to become adept at creating optimal policies that satisfy a bundle of objectives, so as to minimise conflict. This makes it important that governments should not set NTOs objectives that may seriously conflict with each other. Too often governments talk of tourism quality yet measure the performance of the NTO in terms of numbers. Common examples of policy objectives that are most likely to be at variance with each other are:

- maximising foreign exchange earnings versus actions to encourage the regional dispersion of overseas visitors;
- attracting the high-spend tourist market versus policies to expand visitor numbers;
- maximising job creation through generating volume tourist flows versus conservation of the environment and heritage; and
- community tourism development versus mass tourism.

Marketing function of NTOs

Marketing is the principal responsibility of an NTO and therefore usually forms the largest functional area, especially when overseas offices are included. The marketing division formulates the NTO's marketing strategy and is given the task of maintaining the web site, producing the advertising campaign and publicity materials, and promoting sales through the media and the travel trade. The latter is achieved through the provision of 'familiarisation' visits to the destination, circulating a regular newsletter and press releases and attending a series of travel trade shows, of which the most significant are the International Travel Exchange, Berlin and the World Travel Market, London. Overseas offices are responsible for exercising the functions of the marketing division in a manner that takes particular account of the preferences of the travel trade and the potential visitors in the countries or areas where they are located. They also act as 'shop windows' where potential visitors may obtain information and brochures about the host country, though ICT developments have reduced the necessity for this. Many governments do not actively promote domestic tourism and so their NTOs have this section absent from their structure.

Business tourism often merits its own section within an NTO because of its importance in terms of tourist expenditure and the different servicing requirements of meetings, exhibitions and incentive travel groups when compared with leisure tourism. Likewise, advertising is such a key activity that it may command its own specialist group to plan campaigns and deal with outside advertising agencies. Tourism services includes a multitude of tasks such as:

- operating a reservation system either directly through the web site or, as is more common, via links to commercial providers;

- licensing and grading of hotels, restaurants and other suppliers (which may include price controls);
- handling tourist complaints, which may be formal procedures attached to licensing;
- programming festivals, events and tours; and
- managing tourist facilities provided either solely or jointly by the NTO, for example, tourist information centres (TICs) or tourist beaches as in Cyprus.

Development function of NTOs

The development division can only have truly operational involvement if it is given funding to engage in projects with the private sector and implement training programmes and activities. If this is not the case then it can only take on a coordinating and strategic role. The former is achieved by acting as a 'one-stop shop' for prospective developers through inter-mediation to obtain planning permission, licences and any financial assistance or incentives from the relevant authorities. In a strategic role the development division will acquire the planning functions that have been allocated to the planning and research division in Figure 15.2. The reason for the separation in Figure 15.2 rests on the fact that an operational development division is likely to be too heavily involved in day-to-day project management to be able to incorporate long-term development planning. The latter is a research activity and therefore best located in the unit equipped for this task. The planning services section is an important addendum to the role of an NTO in that it seeks to capitalise on the expertise of the organisation to provide advice and even undertake studies for the private sector and other public bodies, for example, drawing up tourism plans for local communities.

The remaining divisions shown in Figure 15.2 are, to a large extent, self-explanatory. Administration is responsible for the internal smooth running of the NTO and will normally adjudicate on legal matters in respect of tourism legislation, including, in some countries, carrying out prosecutions. External relations is a functional area of considerable significance because the NTO is frequently the representative of the government, both at home and over-seas, and has to deal with a mass of enquiries from the public, the media and commercial operators, as well as taking an active stance in public relations to support the advertising and sales promotion administered by the marketing division. It is for the latter reason that external relations may be allocated to marketing, although the tasks given to the division are usually much broader than those required by marketing, as is the case of liaison activities with a variety of public bodies and voluntary associations who have an interest in tourism.

Given the complexity of the tourist product, more recent emphasis on the liaison role of the NTO has focused on building partnerships in line with models of community tourism development, so as to bring the various stakeholders together. If the institutional framework is to function in a manner that is socially compatible, then there is a prerequisite for local involvement in the development process to encourage discussion about future directions. Cultural conflicts need to be resolved through, say, staging development and using market-ing communication channels to prepare guests better for their holiday experience. From experience in less developed countries (LDCs), the greater the difference in lifestyles between hosts and guests and the less the former have been exposed to visitors, then the longer should be the period of adaptation.

IMPACT OF THE PUBLIC SECTOR

In the light of public sector involvement with tourism, either directly through a ministry with responsibility for tourism and the NTO, or indirectly through, say, foreign policy, legal controls or the provision of infrastructure, the government has at its disposal a series of instruments that can be used to manage tourism flows to meet its policy objectives. The manner in which actions by governments influence tourism may be classified in two ways:

- demand and revenue management; and
- supply and cost management.

Demand and revenue management

There are primarily five policy instruments used by governments to manage demand:

- marketing and promotion;
- information provision and network development;
- pricing;
- controlling access: and
- security and safety.

Marketing and promotion

As has already been observed, marketing is the principal function of the NTO and its job is to create and protect the 'brand image' of the country/destination. The specific techniques are discussed in Part 4 of this book, so it is sufficient here to point out that the key requirements for effective marketing are clear objectives, a thorough knowledge of markets and products, and the allocation of adequate resources. It would, however, be putting the 'cart before the horse' without the product, which is generally not under the control of the NTO, hence the importance of assigning the NTO some development powers. Typically, with many other calls on the government's budget, finance officials are naturally parsimonious with regard to expenditure on marketing because of difficulties in measuring effectiveness. As a rule, the amounts spent by governments and other public organisations on destination promotion are only a fraction of what is spent in total by the private sector. One of the main reasons for this is that private enterprises are competing for market share *at the destination*, whereas governments are interested in expanding the total market *to the destination*.

The issue of marketing effectiveness is very pertinent to the earlier discussion on conflicting objectives for public sector managers. The latter normally have to satisfy a range of stakeholders, with the result that campaigns are often 'me too' watered down propositions that fail to differentiate from the rest of the 'clutter' in the marketplace and squander resources. Attempts to break though this may generate considerable controversy in the media that has political repercussions, for example, the storm over Australia's 'Where the bloody hell are you?' campaign. Similarly, establishing destination identities is usually conceived as exercises in local pride, which fail as 'promotional hooks' for attracting tourists and in creating a distinctive sense of place.

Information provision and network development

The ability of tourists to express their demands depends upon their awareness of the facilities available, particularly attractions, which are a key component of leisure tourism. For a number of years there has been government interest in creating computer-based national reservation systems. NTOs in Europe have already been operating 'Holiday Hotlines' and out-of-hours telephone information. In many countries, local tourist information centres (TICs) offer a booking service to personal callers, though still very much a manual system requiring TIC staff to telephone accommodation establishments to check availability. For example, in Britain, the TIC network was used to develop the 'Book a Bed Ahead' scheme for the independent traveller touring different parts of the country. However, as more and more bookings are being made electronically, what is ideal is a fully networked computerised reservation system (CRS). The key to penetrating the source markets from the destinations lies in using the CRS to link suitable accommodation to a range of 'things to see and do', so what is being sold is a complete holiday, not just accommodation. Although desirable, this does not necessarily mean complete packaging of other products: it is common just to use complementary suppliers in marketing and to couple this with the provision of good information on site. Others would go further and recommend a complete destination management system (DMS) that acts as a neutral facilitator and reservation system to the tourist industry, which would put small businesses on the same footing as the major corporate suppliers.

Implementation of a complete DMS via the NTO or regional tourist association is no easy task: in the past, proposals at the local level have foundered on the unwillingness of small enterprises to give commission, to make booking allocations available, competitive jealousies concerning the equity of how bookings will be distributed by TIC staff and arguments over classification and grading, an essential ingredient for the inclusion in such a scheme, as in all tourist bureau publications. Such experiences suggest that a complete DMS cannot be implemented or sustained without a great deal of public sector involvement and cooperation, particularly if the ETC's ideal of Europe as a single destination is to be realised. As discussed further in Chapter 20, there is now a variety of such systems available that enable potential visitors to assemble their own itineraries. The usual role of the NTO is to act as a facilitator to bookings through provision of information on its web portal that gives links to agencies providing reservation services, so that end-users and resellers can access the product of the destination. By this means NTOs enable end-users and resellers to search, book and pay in a single application, as well as building networks to connect businesses and consumers to TICs. The reasons why people do not book online are to do with ease of booking, credit card security, trust in the supplier and lack of consistent information, though it is becoming clear that even the smallest accommodation provider is requiring a web site and email facilities because the chances of potential guests walking in without prior notification are becoming fewer and fewer. In this respect, the adoption of ICT is crucial, for by lowering distribution costs for suppliers and reducing search cost for consumers, via the Internet in particular, market potential is widened. Experience has shown that the ICT phenomenon has radically increased the collective market share of niche products and flattened the sales distribution pattern, producing what has been termed by writers in this field as 'the long tail' that allows many more products to sustain themselves in the marketplace.

The evidence suggests that when planning for tourism the creation of trails or tourist circuits will enhance the visitor experience as well as regulating tourist flows. The establishment of a network of TICs and tourist information points (TIPs) at transport terminals and prominent tourist spots will both help the visitor and assist in dispersion. It is not often appreciated that it is the poorly informed visitor who is likely to contribute to crowding and traffic congestion because of a lack of knowledge about where to go and what there is to see at the destination. Normally, visitors will first look for the main attractions and then move on to lesser attractions as their length of stay increases. Giving prominence to the variety of attractions available, restricting advertising and informing excursion operators of times when congestion can be avoided are examples of the way in which information management can be used to try to relieve pressure on sensitive tourist areas.

In some countries, NTOs use the provision of information to influence tourists' behaviour, as in the PATA example noted earlier. This may come about through editing the information in the tour operator's brochure so that it does not generate unrealistic expectations about a destination and presents the tourist with an informed view of the culture of the host community. An alternative approach is a poster and leaflet campaign aimed directly at the tourist to explain the 'dos and don'ts' of acceptable behaviour; for example, several island resorts offering beach holidays produce leaflets on standards of dress and the unacceptability of wearing only swimsuits in shops, banks and so on.

Pricing

There are several ways in which the public sector may affect the price the tourist pays for staying at a destination. The direct influence arises out of state ownership, notably in the case of attractions. Many of the most important attractions at a destination fall within the public domain, an issue that is examined in some detail in Chapter 11, which is specifically about attractions. The trend in market-orientated economies is for governments to introduce charges for publicly owned attractions. Many of the world's airlines are still owned by governments, though the trend is increasingly towards privatisation or, if not, the liberalisation of air policy, particularly in response to the rise of low-cost airlines (see Chapter 14), which, as noted earlier, has raised issues concerning greenhouse gas emissions. It is not uncommon in less developed countries to find state ownership of hotels and souvenir shops. Thus in some countries the key elements making up holiday expenditure are directly affected by the public sector, to the point of total control in the situation that existed in the former centrally planned economies of Eastern Europe.

Indirect influences come from economic directives such as foreign exchange restrictions, differential rates of sales tax, special duty free shops for tourists and price controls. Exchange restrictions are commonly employed in countries where foreign exchange is scarce and the tourist is usually compelled to change money at an overvalued exchange rate which serves to increase the real cost of the trip. Tourists are discouraged from changing money on the black market by threats of legal prosecution and severe penalties if caught. Counterfeit merchandise is also coming under scrutiny as destinations are tightening up the enforcement of copyright and trademark laws, particularly in Europe. Being fined abroad is one thing, but when returning home tourists run the risk of having their bargain priced goods confiscated and destroyed by customs. In the worst instance, the trademark owner can demand a statement of guilt, which comes with high fees.

The case for price controls is advanced in terms of promoting the long-term growth of the tourist industry and preventing monopolistic exploitation of tourists through overcharging, a practice that can be damaging to the reputation of the destination. The argument for price regulation is illustrated in Figure 15.3. Initially the destination is receiving V_1 visitors, paying an average package price of P_1 for their stay, with equilibrium being determined at the intersection of the demand schedule D_1D_1 and the short-run supply curve S_1S_1. Demand expands to D_2D_2, which gives the opportunity for suppliers to raise prices to P_2, at the market equilibrium point B. This arises because significant parts of the tourism sector, such as airlines and hotels, are open to revenue or yield management systems, whereby market adjustment is more likely to be through price than quantity. These systems are designed to improve

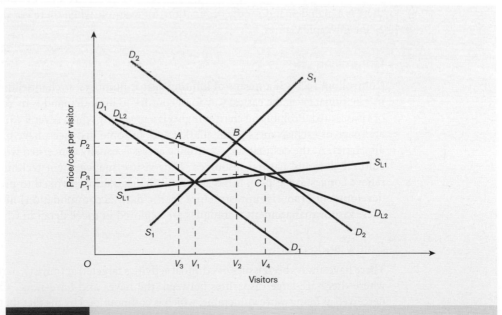

Figure 15.3   Price controls

performance in situations where the product is relatively homogeneous and perishable, demand is seasonal, capacity is fixed in the short run and suppliers have the ability to segment the market. In simple terms this is described as 'making money while you can', which can be counter-productive because demand in the longer term is more sensitive to price than in the short run, as illustrated by the slope of D_{L2}. The reasons for this lie in the number of competing destinations and the holiday price consciousness of travellers. The price control argument says that by keeping price at P_2 existing suppliers will make excess profits, but this could be at the expense of the destination's market share. This is shown on Figure 15.3 as a new market equilibrium position at A, where visitor numbers have fallen back from V_2 to V_3. The destination is perceived as 'pricing itself out of the market'.

There is no doubt that destinations are aware of their price competitiveness and some NTOs compile a tourist price index for their own country as well as others, in order to assess their relative market position. Where governments regulate prices, the objective is to set their level at, say, P_3 which is sufficient to encourage the long-run growth in supply as shown by S_{L1} and commensurate with market expansion to an equilibrium point such as C, giving a growth in visitor numbers to V_4. Producers, on the other hand, are prevented from making short-term excess profits.

Where price controls are enforced, they are normally a further stage in an overall market regulation package, which commences with the registration and licensing of establishments. In the case of hotels this will include classification and possibly a quality grading system. Price regulation can be found in almost all instances where the government manages capacity and therefore restricts competition. Worldwide, the most common example is the licensing and metering of taxis. Where competition exists then the argument put forward in Figure 15.3 hinges upon whether supply adjusts more quickly than demand. There have been many examples of Mediterranean resorts where the growth of bed capacity has outstripped demand and so the problem for the authorities has been more an issue of controlling standards than prices, as well as trying to prevent ruinous competition among hoteliers. In market economics there is a basic ideology that is against regulating prices and, where opportunities for suppliers to make excess profits in the short term do arise, control is often exercised informally through exhortation that it will not be in the long-term best interests of the destination. This has been termed 'maintaining rate integrity' through long-term pricing strategies, so that visitors do not feel that they are being exploited at a time when there is a high demand for the destination, for example when there is a world-class event such as the Olympic Games.

Controlling access

Controlling access is a means of limiting visitor numbers or channelling visitor flows. At an international level, the easiest way for a country to limit demand is by restricting the number of visas issued. Prohibiting **charter flights** is a means by which several countries have conveyed an image of exclusiveness to the market and, in some instances, have protected the **national air carrier**. At the destination, controlling access is usually concerned with protecting popular cultural sites and natural resources. Thus visitor management techniques may be used to relieve congestion at peak times and planning legislation invoked to prohibit or control the development of tourist infrastructure (particularly accommodation) near or around natural sites. Visitor management techniques are explored in more detail in Chapter 11.

Safety and security

There have always been issues of criminal activities targeted at tourists, particularly in countries where there are large disparities between 'the haves and have-nots'. Older age groups are perceived as being more vulnerable, which is compounded by the fact that many tourist environments are designed for open access and some are from the past when the security of guests was not high on the agenda. Increasingly, tourist enterprises have tightened security and visitors have been given advice to make them 'streetwise'. Governments have also instituted special tourist police, as in Egypt and Brazil, and tourism victim support services, for example, in Ireland and Holland.

On the supply side, the cash-rich nature of tourism operations makes them a convenient channel for money laundering from organised criminal gangs, or simply from individuals evading taxes or trying to find a safe haven for their money abroad because they have no confidence in the domestic financial system due to corrupt practices. Casinos, real estate transactions and purchases of luxury items such as jewellery are distinct favourites for money laundering activities.

Unfortunately, terrorism is much more difficult to deal with, because its causes have little to do with tourism. It is associated with political and religious fanaticism, civil wars, and rich–poor income gaps that result in political turbulence in the form of mass protests, for example anti-globalisation movements, and occasional riots and shootings, in which innocent tourists may become targets. What was special about the destruction of the World Trade Center, New York in 2001 (9/11) was that tourist destinations were largely caught unawares, as few had crisis management plans to deal with the consequences for international travel flows, a situation that has now been put right in the principal destinations. On the other hand, dealing with terrorist threats also raises difficulties, in that the stringent entry policies and procedures since the terror attacks of 9/11 have created perceptions of an unwelcoming USA in the minds of prospective tourists, contributing to a decline in America's share of global travel.

Photograph 15.1   Anti-globalisation protests are growing in number throughout the world. As a major global industry, the future development of tourism needs to consider the views of all its stakeholders if it is to be compatible with economic, environmental and wider societal objectives.
Source: Corbis/Antoine Serra/In Visu

Supply and cost management

Government activity on the supply side is concerned with influencing the providers of tourist facilities and services, as opposed to demand management policies aimed at guiding the tourist's choice, controlling the costs of stay or stimulating/regulating visitor numbers. We have already stressed that the development of tourism should be regarded as a partnership between the private and public sectors. The extent of government involvement in this partnership depends upon the prevailing economic, political and social policies of a country. Where the government envisages a particular direction for tourism growth or wishes to speed up the process, it may intervene extensively in the marketplace by setting up a tourist development corporation (TDC) and assigning it the responsibility for building resorts. A well-known example of this process was the building of new resorts in Languedoc–Roussillon, France, but many countries have instituted TDCs at one time or another, for example, Egypt, India, Malaysia, Mexico (see Mini Case Study 15.2), New Zealand and a number of African countries. In theory, once the resort has been built, the development corporation's function ceases and the assets are transferred to the private sector (at a price) and the local authority. This is the general trend in market-orientated economies, but in countries where there is a strong degree of central planning, the TDC often maintains an operational role in running hotels and tours. Beyond this, governments may also establish a development bank with duties to provide special credit facilities for tourist projects and on-lend funds made available by multinational aid agencies. This is common in LDCs where capital funds are short and local capital markets are weak.

The methods that are frequently used by governments to influence the supply side of the tourism industry are:

- land-use planning and environmental control;
- building regulations;
- market regulation;
- market research and planning;
- taxation;
- education and training;
- ownership; and
- investment incentives.

Land-use planning and environmental control

Control over land use is the most basic technique and arguably the one that has the greatest influence on the supply of tourist structures. All governments have a form of town and country planning legislation whereby permission is required to develop, extend or change the use of almost every piece of land. As a rule, the controls are designed to protect areas of high landscape and amenity value: for example, it is now common to restrict the proximity of buildings to the shoreline in coastal developments. The case is that the environment has an intrinsic value, which outweighs its value as a tourism asset. Its enjoyment by future generations and its long-term survival must not be prejudiced by short-term considerations. But, as noted in Chapter 11, it is possible to have conservation through tourism, by recognising the two-way flow between tourism and the environment.

Zoning of land and compulsory purchase are commonly used as a means of promoting tourism development. One of the key aspects of land control is that before any detailed site plans and future land requirements for tourism are published, the appropriate administrative organisation and legislation is in place in order to prevent speculation, land division or parcelling. Dealings or speculation in land prior to legislative control have been a common cause of failure in tourism master plans.

MINI CASE STUDY 15.2
FONATUR, Mexico

Tourism in Mexico began as a totally private sector activity. Its growth was limited in size (largely in the area of Acapulco), the product on offer was generally poor and developments were unplanned. To counteract this, the government of Mexico in 1974 created FONATUR (National Trust Fund for Tourism Development) for the purpose of developing resorts and funded the organisation from oil revenues and World Bank loans. Apart from trying to regulate development, the principal reasons for state involvement were:

- to realise potential demand by increasing the number of resorts;
- to generate foreign exchange;
- to create employment;
- for regional development, in particular moving the jobless from Mexico City to the new resorts and raising regional GDP.

FONATUR has developed five key regional resorts (Cancun, Los Cabos, Ixtapa, Huatulco and Loreto) that have attracted a wide range of international investors and generate over 50% of the country's foreign tourism earnings. The government provided FONATUR with the land it required without charge, the resources to develop a master plan and the money to construct the necessary infrastructure, including hotel building. Once complete, the investment is sold to the private sector. The terms for private sector projects are generous: loans for up to 50% of the capital investment, over a period of 15 years. The 'flagship' project was Cancun on Mexico's Caribbean coast, but this is now mature and issues have arisen about spillover developments outside the original zone and adverse impacts on the environment. These aspects are now being accounted for in FONATUR's current mission statement:

> To be the institution responsible for the planning and development of sustainable tourism projects of national impact – To be an instrument of promotion for investment and training of the tourism sector; thus being the national entity that lends its experience to regions, states, and municipalities, along with small and medium businesses.

The Mexican government's approach here has a long lineage in terms of development policy. Much of regional tourism development planning is underpinned by the 'growth pole' principle, with the aim of raising regional export values through tourism. The focus is the creation of a destination (growth pole) through an investment strategy that provides a balanced range of facilities to meet visitor requirements and at a level that gives the area 'tourism presence' in the marketplace. At a more local level the same principle can be found in the formation of partnerships to promote community tourism development. It is also a dynamic concept in that FONATUR is continually augmenting and upgrading the facilities at the resorts to keep up with tourists' demands, in order to remain competitive and promote Mexico's image abroad.

Source: FONATUR

DISCUSSIONS QUESTIONS

1. Consider the strengths and weaknesses of public ownership of tourism facilities.
2. Is regional intervention an efficient policy in a market economy?
3. Suggest other methods FONATUR might use to stimulate regional development.

Building regulations

Building regulations are used to supplement land-use control and typically cover the size of buildings, height, shape, colour and car-parking arrangements. For example, Mauritius has a rule that restricts coastal developments to two levels, roughly the height of palm trees, which permits adequate screening from the seaward side. Car parking is a matter that is not always given the attention it deserves in some resorts. To private sector operators, car parks are often considered unproductive space and so there is a tendency to avoid having to provide them, leaving visitors little alternative than to park their cars in nearby streets. This may only serve to add to traffic congestion and the annoyance of local residents. In addition to structural regulations, many countries also have protective legislation governing cultural resources such as historic buildings, archaeological remains, religious monuments, conservation areas and even whole towns.

Market regulation

Governments pass legislation to regulate the market conduct of firms in matters of competitive practices and also to limit the degree of ownership in particular sectors of the industry to prevent the abuse of monopoly power. Governments may also regulate markets by imposing on suppliers obligations to consumers. This does not have to be legislation; it could be industry-enforced codes of conduct of the kind laid down as conditions for membership of national travel trade associations, though in Europe such codes have passed into the legislation of member states as a result of the EU Package Travel Directive (see Chapter 13).

One of the economic criteria dictating the optimal workings of markets is that consumers should have complete knowledge of the choices open to them. For if consumers do not have the right to safety, to be informed, to choose or of redress and firms are not behaving according to the accepted rules of conduct, then resources will be wasted, which may be seen to be inefficient. The economic aspects of a consumer policy are shown in Figure 15.4. As the level of protection increases, so wastage or compensation payments decline, while at the same time the costs of protection increase. The optimum amount of protection is where the two schedules intersect at point *A*, which defines level *L* on the axis below. This is the economic rationale: on social or political grounds the state may legislate to ensure nearly 100% protection. But the economic consequences of such an action could be to raise the supply price of

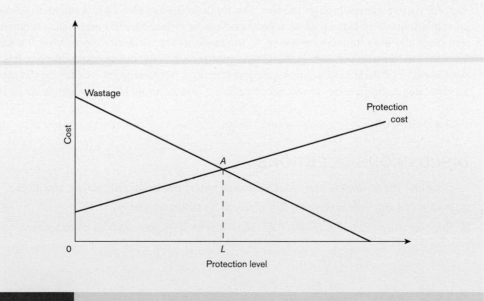

| **Figure 15.4** | Economics of consumer protection |

the good or service to the point where the market is substantially diminished. At the consultation stage of the EU Package Travel Directive amendments were accepted to some of the proposals on the grounds that their compliance would significantly raise holiday prices.

Market research and planning

The tourist industry usually expects the public sector to collect statistical information and carry out market surveys. There have been steps towards the creation of tourism satellite accounts as advocated by UNWTO, but generally not enough is being done, when compared to the traditional statistics collected for the extractive and manufacturing sectors of national economies. Inadequacy means that it is impossible to measure accurately the impact of tourism policy, or monitor trends in the marketplace – and the result is an incalculable loss of unrealised potential. The NTO is naturally concerned with understanding demographic and lifestyle changes in its source markets, for example, the increasing environmental awareness, and how they affect the image of the country. For their own part, governments are interested in monitoring changes in the industry and carry out research to identify the social and environmental benefits and costs of tourism. The emerging research themes that suggest themselves from the new tourism trends discussed in this book are: changes in the demographic structure and lifestyles upon tourism demand; product management and innovations in distribution facing the industry; improving the attractiveness of destinations through product development in a sustainable way by moving towards the idea of being 'carbon neutral'; and the strengthening of public/private sector partnerships.

When dealing with products that belong to the tourism sector, the transformation of invention to innovation cannot be compared to the processes seen in manufacturing. Manufacturing starts with product innovation (invention and introduction of the product), qualitative process innovation (the setting up of the manufacturing systems), and quantitative process innovation (improvements and rationalisation of the production system for mass supply). Tourism products start with the quantitative process innovation by taking established products and using them to increase the efficiency of current service production, which, in turn, leads to qualitative changes in the production system and then wholly transformed or entirely new service experiences, which are the output of the tourism industry. Thus some of the most successful visitor attractions are the result of brand extensions of products that are the output of another industrial process, as, for example, LEGOLAND parks (see Chapter 11).

Taxation

There are two main reasons why governments levy specific taxes on the tourism sector. The first is the classic argument for a tourist tax, namely to allocate to the supply price the external costs imposed on the host community through providing public amenities for tourists. The second is for purposes of raising revenue; tourists are seen as part of the overall tax base and, from a political perspective, they are not voters in the destination country; therefore the welfare burden that taxes impose on consumers, which has to be considered for the domestic population, does not apply to tourists. Where residents and tourists consume goods jointly, then if tourists were less sensitive to price rises, it is possible for the tax revenue raised to more than outweigh the loss of benefit to domestic consumers.

With the growth of tourism worldwide, there has been an escalation in the number of countries levying tourist taxes and in the rates of taxation, drawing the inference that governments principally see such taxes as a source of revenue. It is not unreasonable that the tourist industry should pay taxes as in any other business and the World Travel and Tourism Council (WTTC) has argued that tax payments should be made in accordance with the following guidelines:

- **Equity**: the fair and even-handed treatment of travel and tourism with respect to the other sectors of the economy.

- **Efficiency:** the development of tax policies that have a minimal effect on the demand for travel and tourism, unless specifically imposed for the purpose of regulating tourist flows to, say, environmentally sensitive areas (see Chapter 11).
- **Simplicity:** taxes should be simple to pay and administer, so as not to disrupt the operation of the travel and tourism system.

Being aware of the competitive nature of the leisure tourism product and conscious of market share, the industry is opposed to the increasing number of discriminatory taxes on tourism, the most common forms of which are airport departure taxes, ticket taxes and taxes on hotel occupancy. Their principal argument is they are not normally hypothecated to improvements in travel infrastructure, but submerged in the general tax take (which the industry already pays into via corporation tax, sales taxes, property taxes, and income tax payment made by employees and shareholders), thus raising the price of the tourist product with no noticeable improvement in quality. Moreover, where a country has a large domestic tourism industry, a hotel occupancy tax makes it less costly for domestic tourists to switch demand to destinations abroad, as well as being more expensive for inbound tourists. Opposition can be effective: thus in 2002 the regional government of the Spanish islands of Majorca, Minorca and Ibiza introduced a tourist tax of 1 euro per night on all visitors. This was a way of raising funds for environmental projects, but, after protests from hotel owners about the added cost of vacations on the islands and the burden of collecting the payments from guests, the bed tax was scrapped a year later.

When it comes to raising revenue, casinos can be a very profitable source: governments have been known to take as much as 50% of the 'drop', which is the amount of money taken in from the tables. However, there are clearly many other issues to do with regulation and ethics when it comes to expanding casinos and generating tax revenues in this way.

Although a tourist tax may be paid by the guest at the hotel and collected from the hotelier, the incidence as to who bears the tax will depend on the responsiveness of demand and supply to a price change. In Figure 15.5, the imposition of a tax raises the supply price by moving the supply curve from S_1S_1 to S_2S_2, which in turn reduces the quantity of, say, room sales demanded from Q_1 to Q_2. However, the amount of tax income raised P_2ACD does not all fall on the tourists in the form of a higher price. Price rises from P_1 to P_2 only and the

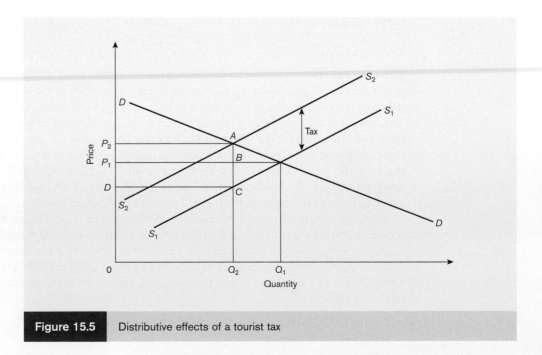

Figure 15.5   Distributive effects of a tourist tax

larger share of the incidence of the tax P_1BCD falls on the supplier in the form of reduced profits. Tourists contribute P_2ABP_1 of the tax revenue. The less sensitive tourists are to price, something that can be reflected in a much steeper demand schedule DD, the greater is the ability of suppliers to pass on the tax in the form of a higher price and, therefore, the larger will be the share of the tax burden falling on the tourists.

Ownership

Mention has already been made of state ownership of attractions, natural amenities and some key revenue-earning activities such as hotels, modes of transport (especially airlines) and souvenir shops. It is possible to add to this list conference centres, exhibition halls, sports and leisure complexes (including casinos), and the provision of general infrastructure. The latter may include banks; hospitals; public utilities (water and energy supplies); telecommunications; road networks; transport terminals; and education and training establishments. The arguments for public ownership of these facilities rest on their importance as essential services for any economic development, the fact that outside investors would expect such provision and economies of scale in production. Traditionally, public infrastructure and transport networks have been regarded as natural monopolies; the minimum scale of production is such as to make it impossible for more than one firm to enjoy all the economies in the market, so that even if they were not publicly owned these organisations would need to be publicly regulated. However, changes in technology are undermining the natural monopoly concept in telecommunications and power generation, reducing further the need for public ownership.

Education and training

The provision of an educated and trained labour force to meet the demands of a modern economy has been a task that has fallen to many governments. In common with other planning activities, this requires an assessment of the current occupational distribution of the tourism workforce, which is then mapped onto the general educational level of each occupational group. Overall forecasts of economic activity for the tourist industry are then turned into workforce needs, which are compared to projections of supply from existing trends in the education system, enabling the estimation of surpluses and deficits. It is then possible to lay down a strategy for the implementation of projects in the education and training sector to bring demand and supply as close together as might be deemed practical, given the somewhat looseness of the linkage between education and the skills base of the labour force. Actions to augment this may be the provision of low-cost housing for key workers in resort areas, as well as immigration policies to add to the quality of the workforce.

Investment incentives

Governments around the world offer a wide range of investment incentives to developers. They may be grouped under three broad headings:

1. **Reduction of capital costs.** This includes capital grants or loans at preferential rates, interest rate relief, a moratorium on loan repayments for, say, x years, provision of infrastructure, provision of land on concessional terms, tariff exemption on construction materials and equity participation.

2. **Reduction of operating costs.** In order to improve operating viability governments may grant tax 'holidays' (5–10 years), give a labour or training subsidy, offer tariff exemption on imported materials and supplies, provide special depreciation allowances and ensure that there is double taxation or unilateral relief. The latter are government-to-government agreements that prevent an investor being taxed twice on the same profits.

3. **Investment security.** The object here is to win investors' confidence in an industry that is very sensitive to the political environment and economic climate. Action here would

include guarantees against nationalisation, free availability of foreign exchange, repatriation of invested capital, profits, dividends and interest, loan guarantees, provision of work permits for 'key' personnel and the availability of technical advice.

The administration of grants or loans may be given to the NTO, a government-sponsored investment bank or the TDC. Tax matters will usually remain the responsibility of the treasury or the ministry in charge of finance. Less-developed countries are often able to attract low-cost investment funds from multinational aid agencies, which they can use to augment their existing resources for the provision of development finance.

It may be taken that policies to ensure investment security are primary requirements for attracting tourism developers. The objective of financial incentives is to improve returns to capital so as to attract developers and investors. Where there is obvious market potential the government may only have to demonstrate its commitment to tourism by providing the necessary climate for investment security. Such a situation occurred in Bermuda during the early 1970s and so, in order to prevent over-exploitation of the tourism resources, the Bermuda government imposed a moratorium on large hotel building.

The impact of financial incentives on the amount of investment is illustrated in Figure 15.6. The schedule SS represents the supply of investable funds while D_1D is the schedule of returns to capital employed. D_1D slopes downwards from left to right as more and more investment opportunities are taken up – the declining marginal efficiency of investment. In the initial situation, equilibrium is at A with the amount of investment being I_1 and the rate of return i_1.

Conditions of market failure imply that the community benefits from tourism investment are not entirely captured in the demand function D_1D. Optimal economic efficiency is where the demand function includes these external effects, as represented by D_2D. The government now implements a range of financial incentives that have the effect of raising the rate of return per unit of capital to i_2, moving the marginal efficiency of investment schedule to D_2D. The new return i_2 equals $(1 + s)i_1$, where s is the effective rate of subsidy. If the amount of investable funds available for tourism is limited at I_1, then the impact of incentives serves

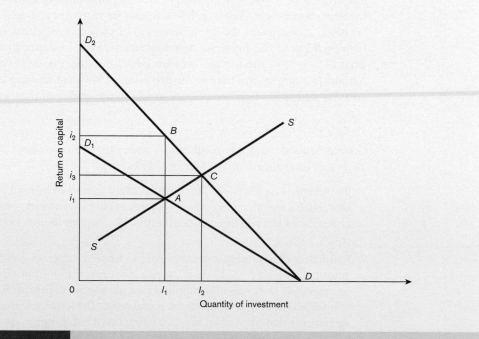

Figure 15.6   Impact of financial incentives

merely to raise the return to investors by raising the equilibrium point to B. The loss to the government treasury is the area $i_1 AB i_2$ which equals the gain to private investors.

There is no doubt that many countries have been forced by competitive pressures for foreign investment into situations that are similar to those above. Countries can become trapped in a bidding process to secure clients and as a result the variety of financial incentives multiplies together with an escalation of the rates of benefit, without evaluating their necessity or their true cost to the economy. Given that the supply of investment funds is responsive or elastic, the net effect of an incentives policy is to expand the amount of tourism projects to I_2 and the rate of return settles at i_3, the equilibrium point being C. The private opportunity cost of the investment funds is the area under the supply curve, $I_1 AC I_2$, while the public willingness to pay for correcting for market failure is the area $I_1 BC I_2$: subtracting the two areas gives a net gain represented by the area ABC.

It is important to note that there are frequent instances where it is gross uncertainty, as in times of recession, rather than limited potential that prevents the private sector investing. In such situations the principal role of government intervention is to act as a catalyst to give confidence to investors. Thus public funds are able to lever in private money by nature of the government's commitment to tourism and enable the market potential of an area to be realised.

In implementing a tourism investment policy the government has to decide to what extent incentives should be legislated as automatic entitlements, as against being discretionary awards. It has already been noted that automatic incentives may give too much money away, when what is required to ensure that the treasury receives maximum benefit from its funds is the application of the concept of 'project additionality'. The latter seeks to provide financial support or the equivalent benefits in kind to the point where the developer will just proceed with the project.

The implication of additionality is an ideal situation where all incentives are discretionary and therefore offered selectively. The legislation would be fairly general, empowering the ministry responsible for tourism to offer loans, grants, tax exemptions and equity investment as it sees fit. As an example, such legislation is embodied in the UK 1969 Development of Tourism Act. Section 4 of the 1969 Act states that:

4. (1) A Tourist Board shall have power—

   (a) in accordance with arrangements approved by the relevant Minister and the Treasury, to give financial assistance for the carrying out of any project which in the opinion of the Board will provide or improve tourist amenities and facilities in the country for which the Board is responsible:

   (b) with the approval of the relevant Minister and the Treasury, to carry out any such project as aforesaid.

   (2) Financial assistance under subsection (1) (a) of this section may be given by way of grant or loan or, if the project is being or is to be carried out by a company incorporated in Great Britain, by subscribing for or otherwise acquiring shares or stock in the company, or by any combination of those methods.

   (3) In making a grant or loan in accordance with arrangements approved under subsection (1) (a) of this section a Tourist Board may, subject to the arrangements, impose such terms and conditions as it thinks fit, including conditions for the repayment of a grant in specified circumstances; and Schedule 2 to this Act shall have effect for securing compliance with conditions subject to which any such grant is made.

   (4) A Tourist Board shall not dispose of any shares or stock acquired by it by virtue of this section except—

      (a) after consultation with the company in which the shares or stock are held; and

      (b) with the approval of the relevant Minister and the Treasury.

The granting of incentives to prospective developers is in accordance with ministerial guidelines, which are regularly reviewed in response to the level of tourism activity.

To have only **discretionary incentives**, however, is a counsel of perfection. Competition for tourism investment frequently requires countries to legislate for automatic financial help in order to attract investors in the first instance. Some countries may legislate for all the incentives discussed here; others for a subset of them. Several countries have been guilty of copying incentive legislation without any real grasp of its meaning.

The appropriateness of the various financial incentives available depends on understanding the nature of the business risk and the probable returns to the tourist industry, as well as the ability of the country to afford them. Thus developing countries may find themselves in no position to offer grants or cheap loans, which highlights the importance of contributions from aid agencies. One of the main sources of business risk in tourist enterprises is the tendency to have a high ratio of capital charges in relation to operating expenses. It is for this reason that incentives to reduce capital costs are the preferred form of assistance when the viability of the business is being considered.

INTERVENTION POLICY

The range of policy instruments available to governments is considerable and enables the public sector to exercise varying degrees of influence over the direction of tourism development. From the perspective of the NTO charged with implementing a national development strategy, it might be thought that once the objectives have been defined then it is simply a matter of packaging the appropriate instruments to achieve the desired results. However, this ignores the political dimension. We have already discussed earlier how outside political influences at the destination level may alter policy at the top, but in any representative political system there are a number of inside influences on the governing authority.

Political parties influence the government of the day through the preparation of the manifesto, which it is the task of the minister to steer through the governing assembly. The pressure groups on the assembly to form policy are many. They range from the governing party itself, various statutory bodies, trade associations, trade unions, individual industries, clubs and ordinary people. Typical activities undertaken include: holding receptions at the assembly; representations to government; meetings with senior civil servants; individual lobbying of elected representatives; and evidence to government committees. The latter are the 'workhorses' of government for policy purposes, as the floor of the assembly is largely a debating chamber where matters under discussion may be secondary to the objective of 'scoring a point' over the opposition.

The membership of a government committee is normally representative of all the major political parties, with a majority in favour of the governing party for voting purposes. A committee will normally conduct its inquiry in three ways:

- invite written memoranda;
- take oral evidence from expert witnesses; and
- undertake fact-finding tours.

All evidence given to a government committee has to be received formally, since it provides the basis on which recommendations are made. The reality is that in making recommendations a committee can act only within its sphere of influence, otherwise it can appear foolish. If a particular project does not appear in the report, it is because no supporting evidence was given. In the taking of oral evidence, the presence of the press can make the questioning combative, and while this may produce headlines for some politicians, it usually serves no useful purpose. With expectations raised, it becomes impossible to have a discussion of the issues without it appearing in the press as a major row.

Generally speaking, to be accepted the recommendations of government committees have to fit into a tourism strategy that is structured around tolerable political criteria rather than tourism needs. It should be remembered that the 'status quo' in politics is a powerful force to be reckoned with. The government is unlikely to accept recommendations that are politically contentious in respect, say, of its manifesto or that require significant legislative changes or are likely to upset the Ministry of Finance. It is not surprising, therefore, that tourism professionals will often be frustrated by the direction of government policy, which may be described as 'the art of the possible' within the context of the various interest groups. At best the outcomes of government committees are improvements to policy and at worst they are a damage limitation exercise, filtering out 'bizarre' ideas.

CONCLUSION

Around the globe governments have intervened to assist and regulate the private sector; this is because the complex nature of the tourist product makes it unlikely that private markets will satisfy all the tourism policy objectives of a country. The role of governmental organisations in the influencing of tourism supply and the manipulation of tourism demand is critical in the shaping of the tourism system. We saw how governmental involvement may influence the demand for tourism in Part 1 of this book and in this part we demonstrate the function of public sector bodies in coordinating and funding the supply aspects of the tourism product. The trend towards pure market-led economics stemming from the 1980s has led to a clawback of state involvement and the questioning of intervention as mechanisms more likely to lead to market distortions than market corrections. This was in total contrast to the concept of sustainable development, which challenges the ability of private markets to improve the distribution of income and protect the environment. The spillover benefits of tourism are well known, and, more than any other industry, tourism deals with the use of natural and cultural resources. The lessons of the past indicate that it is unwise for governments to abandon their ability to influence the direction of tourism development, and many governments have recognised this through their support for tourism as an economic regeneration activity, particularly for cities with the growth in cultural tourism. Tourism is a truly global business that has reduced the power of national governments to shield themselves from outside events, so what is required is a pragmatic approach to intervention and regulation, with an emphasis on collaboration between government agencies through international bodies. It would be convenient if there were a few instruments or levers which could be considered optimal for the implementation of tourism policy. Certainly, the tourist industry responds strongly to legislation and the availability of finance, but the tourist product varies so much around the globe that it is customary for states to adopt a bundle of instruments and adjust them over time, in response to feedback information on their workings.

SELF-CHECK QUESTIONS

1. Why are international tourism organisations important for tourism and tourism development?
2. Suggest some of the areas in a continent of your choice that might be classified as peripheral and the features that would make them attractive for tourism development.
3. Suggest some of the non-governmental organisations in your own country that have a significant influence on tourism policy.

ESSAY QUESTIONS

1. What are the strengths and weaknesses of positioning tourism projects within an overall strategy to guide their use as opposed to opportunistic development?

2. The nature of grant aid from the EU has been described as conditional matching funding. Other forms of grant mechanisms are lump-sum payments, which may be tied to specific projects (conditional) or just given to the overall programme (unconditional). Discuss the relative merits of these different systems.

3. Taking a country of your choice, define the roles and functions of its national tourism office. How might an NTO exercise its responsibilities for marketing a country?

4. Compare and contrast the complementary and conflicting roles of the public and private sector in the coordination and funding of tourism.

5. The new approach in the USA is to treat tourism in the same manner as any other traded good or service and withdraw from direct action – is this correct? What are the principal features of tourism in the USA that seem to dictate a policy that runs counter to that of most governments in the world?

ANNOTATED FURTHER READING

Books

Baud-Bovy, M. and Lawson, F. (1998) *Tourism Recreation Handbook of Planning and Design*, Architectural Press, London.
Manuel Baud-Bovy and Fred Lawson are two of the leading designers in their field and this book is full of practical examples and illustrations of development projects with prescriptions on planning policy and method.

Hall, C.M. (2000) *Tourism Planning: Policies, Processes and Relationships*, Prentice Hall, Harlow.
Michael Hall provides a general text that draws together the various concepts and policies that can be found in the academic literature.

Inskeep, E. (1991) *Tourism Planning: An Integrated and Sustainable Development Approach*, Van Nostrand Reinhold, New York.
A first-class book that has been put together by someone who has worked both as teacher and practitioner. It is rich in experience and carries with it many lessons learnt from years of fieldwork. It is now in need of updating on some issues to reflect more recent thinking.

Mason, P. (2003) *Tourism Impacts, Planning and Management*, Butterworth Heinemann, Oxford.
As with Michael Hall's book, Peter Mason provides a sound overview and synthesis of accepted wisdom in this field, and is a very modern text.

Web sites

http://europa.eu.int/comm/regionalrpolicy
The European Union's principal site for regional policy which encompasses issues pertaining to tourism development.

http://pata.org
A comprehensive web site from the Pacific Asia Travel Association which includes a mass of market data related to the region. PATA is the clear authority on travel and tourism in

the area and this is reflected in its membership which includes nearly 100 government, state and city tourism bodies, over 55 airlines and cruise lines, and hundreds of tourism companies.

http://www.world-tourism.org

An all-embracing web site providing the official view from the United Nations on tourism issues with a definitive set of tourism statistics and approaches to tourism development.

Bibliography

Anderson, C. (2006) *The Long Tail*, R.H. Business Books, Kent.

Baud-Bovy, M. and Lawson, F. (1998) *Tourism Recreation Handbook of Planning and Design*, Architectural Press, London.

Commission of the European Communities (1995) *The Role of the Union in the Field of Tourism*, COM (95), 97 final, Brussels.

Commission of the European Communities (1996) *Structural Funds and Cohesion Fund 1994–99*, Office for Official Publications of the European Communities, Luxembourg.

Dwyer, L., Forsyth, P. and Spurr, R. (2003) 'Inter-industry effects of tourism growth: implications for destination managers', *Tourism Economics* 9(2), 117–32.

Hall, C.M. (2000) *Tourism Planning: Policies, Processes and Relationships*, Harlow, Prentice Hall.

Holloway, J.C. (2002) *The Business of Tourism*, 6th edn, Pearson Education, Harlow.

House of Commons (1969) *Development of Tourism Act 1969*, HMSO, London.

Inskeep, F. (1991) *Tourism Planning: An Integrated and Sustainable Development Approach*, Van Nostrand Reinhold, New York.

Jamal, T.B., Stein, S.M. and Harper, T.L. (2002) 'Beyond labels: pragmatic planning in multistakeholder tourism-environmental conflicts', *Journal of Planning Education and Research* 22(2), 164–77.

Jenkins, J. (2000) 'The dynamics of regional tourism organisations in New South Wales, Australia: history, structures and operations', *Current Issues in Tourism* 3(3), 175–203.

Jensen, T. and Wanhill, S. (2002) 'Tourism's taxing times: VAT in Europe and Denmark', *Tourism Management* 23(1), 67–79.

Mak, J. (2005) 'Tourist Taxes', pp. 441–3 in J. Cordes, R. Ebel and J. Gravelle (eds), *The Encyclopedia of Taxation and Tax Policy*, Urban Institute Press, Washington DC.

Mason, P. (2003) *Tourism Impacts, Planning and Management*, Butterworth Heinemann, Oxford.

Middleton, V.T.C. and Hawkins, R. (1998) *Sustainable Tourism. A Marketing Approach*, Butterworth Heinemann, Oxford.

Myers, J., Forsberg, P. and Holecek, D. (1997) 'A framework for monitoring global travel and tourism taxes: the WTTC Tax Barometer', *Tourism Economics* 3(1), 5–20.

Nilsson, P., Petersen, T. and Wanhill, S. (2005) 'Public support for tourism SMEs in peripheral areas: The Arjeplog project northern Sweden', *Service Industries Journal* 25(4), 579–99.

Pearce, D. (1992) *Tourist Organisations*, Longman, Harlow.

Piga, C.A.G. (2003) 'Territorial planning and tourism development tax', *Annals of Tourism Research* 30(4), 886–905.

Vanhove, N. (2005) *The Economics of Tourist Destinations*, Elsevier, London.

Wanhill, S. (1997) 'Peripheral area tourism: a European perspective', *Progress in Tourism and Hospitality Research* 3(1), 47–70.

Wanhill, S. (2004) 'Government assistance for tourism SMEs: from theory to practice' pp. 53–70 in *Small Firms in Tourism: International Perspectives*, Thomas, R. (ed.), Elsevier, Oxford.

WTO (1993) *Sustainable Tourism Development: Guide for Local Planners*, WTO, Madrid.

MAJOR CASE STUDY 15.1
Tourism project assistance from the European Union

The purpose of this case study is to provide an understanding of the framework for the allocation of structural funds by the European Union; to illustrate the range of criteria against which proposals are judged and funds allocated; to offer an overview of the system in action.

INTRODUCTION

Above the investment help offered separately by the governments of the EU, there is the pan-European programme of regional aid made available to member states through the Union's structural funds. The governing principle is that of *solidarity*, whereby the strong help the weak to improve economic convergence; that is to eliminate major disparities of wealth, and ensure a better spread of economic activities throughout the territories located within the boundaries of the Union. The morality of this principle is generally accepted by member states and therefore acted upon at a political level. In a global world it is argued that it is in the member state's own interest to act internationally.

Regional project assistance is currently given under three general funds and one that is specific to agriculture:

1. The European Regional Development Fund (ERDF), which is focused mainly on productive investment, infrastructure and local business development in less favoured regions, and is the principal vehicle for regional support.

2. The European Social Fund (ESF), which has the task of promoting jobs through investing in educational systems, vocational training and employment assistance.

3. The Cohesion Fund to promote growth-enhancing conditions and factors leading to real convergence for the least-developed member states and regions, such as transport and environmental infrastructure.

4. The European Agricultural Fund for Rural Development (EAFRD), which is targeted at improving agricultural competitiveness, managing the environment, improving the quality of rural life and diversifying the rural economy.

The European Commission recognises that the funds make a major contribution to the development of tourism in the EU and, in so doing, progress the objectives of economic and social cohesion as defined in Article 130a, Treaty of the European Union (the Maastricht Treaty), 1992. In essence, the Commission's policy for using tourism as an instrument of regional economic development is one of taking advantage of the many positive aspects of the industry, namely:

- the continuing growth in tourism worldwide;
- disadvantaged regions often have a comparative advantage in natural tourism resources;
- tourism attracts spending from outside the regions;
- tourism and culture bring people together and help tear down divides;
- tourism has important spillover benefits (multiplier effects) elsewhere in the regional economy; and
- job creation within a relatively short period of time is an important aspect of tourism development.

Tourism, as a part of Europe's wealth that gives identity to its regions and is a source of economic activity and new jobs, has therefore a significant presence in structural interventions. Many programmes have strands specifically devoted to the development of tourist-related infrastructure or projects, protection of heritage, promotion of festivals and so forth.

BACKGROUND

Prior to 1988, there was no coherent system for the disbursement of the structural funds, which resulted in the dissipation of funds over many areas, thus reducing their effectiveness. Therefore, in 1988, a new regulation on the uses of the funds was adopted in preparation for the first planning period 1989–93, with lesser changes for the next interval from 1994–99. The changes were based on three fundamental principles:

1. Transforming structural policy into an instrument with real economic impact by concentration on priority objectives.

2. Using a multi-annual programming approach for expenditure planning to assure member states of the stability and predictability of EU support.

3. Implementing a partnership with all the parties actively participating in structural policy, especially the regional authorities.

Photograph 15.2   The headquarters of the European Union in Brussels, the centre of regional policy decision-making throughout the political union.

Source: European Parliament. ASP: AEL, avenue des Courses 15, 1050 Brussels; PHS: Association des architectes du CIC, rue du Prince royal 19, 1050

From 1989 onwards, member states were required to coordinate, for the first time, the use of the funds and draw together all forms of Union support, including lending by the European Investment Bank (EIB) and the European Coal and Steel Community (ECSC). This also allowed the EU to adopt a greater degree of control on the use of the funds within the sphere of integrated regional development plans put forward by member states.

In general terms, each member state prepares a National Strategic Reference Framework (NSRF) over the course of an ongoing dialogue with the Commission. This prepares the programming of funds, and replaces the previous Community Support Frameworks (CSFs) and the single programming documents (SPDs) that were used to develop a series of Operational Programmes (OPs) up to the last planning period 2000–06. The NSRF comprises the description of the strategy of the state in question and its proposed list of OPs that it hopes to implement.

The NSRF must be sent to the Commission for adoption and appropriate validation, as well as each OP. The OPs present the priorities of the member state (and/or regions) as well as the way in which it will lead its programming. For the 2007–13 period, some 450 OPs have been adopted by the Commission. Economic and social partners as well as civic bodies participate in the programming and management of the OPs.

In contrast to the investment incentives discussed in this chapter, which may be applied in a piecemeal manner, project promoters are only eligible for assistance from the structural funds if their schemes are included within the planning process and meet one of the Community objectives shown in Table 15.1. In the 1994–99 planning period there were six objectives, but at the Berlin Summit, held in March 1999, the Council of Ministers agreed to amalgamate them into three for 2000–06. With the enlargement of the Community from 15 to 25 members in 2004 and the addition of

Table 15.1	Structural funds' objectives, 2000–2006
Objective	**Aim**
Convergence	To promote growth-enhancing conditions and factors leading to real convergence for the least-developed member states and regions (those whose GDP per capita is 75% or less than the EU average).
Regional competitiveness and employment	To strengthen the competitiveness, employment and attractiveness of regions other than those which are the most disadvantaged, by anticipating economic and social changes, promoting innovation, business spirit, protection of the environment, accessibility, adaptability and the development of inclusive labour markets.
Territorial cooperation	To strengthen cross-border, transnational and inter-regional cooperation through promoting common solutions for neighbouring authorities in the fields of urban, rural and coastal development, the development of economic relations and the creation of networks of small and medium-sized enterprises (SMEs).

Bulgaria and Romania in January 2007, the previous Objectives 1, 2 and 3 were replaced by three new Objectives: Convergence, Regional Competitiveness and Employment, and Territorial Cooperation for the planning horizon 2007–13.

The objectives shown in Table 15.1 are used to identify regions and allocate funds. Thus Convergence is supported by ERDF, ESF and the Cohesion Fund, Regional Competitiveness and Employment by ERDF and ESF, while ERDF is the sole fund for Territorial Cooperation.

FUNDING POLICY

The ERDF is the principal instrument for regional intervention and the sums available dwarf the other structural funds. The method of subvention from the funds is grant aid that is conditional to the project and requires matching funding from the project promoter. The limit rate of grant is normally 50% of public expenditure, but has been raised to 85% in the case of projects in the outermost regions. The majority of projects no longer receive support at the limit rate. For tourism investment, grants are unlikely to be in excess of 45% of the investment cost and may usually be less.

Tourism projects tend to be public sector-led and the principal aspects that should be addressed when bidding for European assistance are:

- the use of the project should be 50% non-local;
- the project should result in an increase in overnight stays;
- the project should result in an increase in employment opportunities;

- the economic position of the project within the local area should be examined;
- the project should form part of a tourism strategy for the local area. Thus the project should sit within an NSRF that forms the regional strategy approved by the member state and the Commission; and
- national/regional tourist organisation support will give weight to the application.

EVALUATION

Member states are given considerable flexibility as to how they present a proposal, which is consistent with the principle of *subsidiarity* outlined in this chapter. What follows is therefore representative of the criteria that are employed in evaluating a project proposal, namely:

- the project should be feasible in that the scheme has the capacity to generate revenues above operating costs so that it can support its own running arrangements;
- viability is assured after financial assistance in order that the project can service the capital investment costs out of its operating surplus;
- the need for structural funds support should be proven;
- displacement of visitors from other tourism businesses within the area of the Operational Programme, or from any other European-assisted area, should be minimised; and
- multiplier effects in terms of job creation should be examined.

Impact assessment

A key political objective for public intervention lies in some loosely connected social welfare function that links tourist expenditure to local income generation and thence employment. These are the most significant factors affecting project acceptability, since the primary use of structural funds is to correct for regional imbalances. We may note that tourism and hospitality projects are usually well suited to European funding requirements because they are labour-using and commonly have a high operating leverage; that is, a relatively low level of operating costs but a high level of fixed costs caused by prior capital spending. Once the financing of the capital has been adequately taken care of, the project usually runs into surplus after three years and can maintain itself thereafter.

Tourists come to a destination for many reasons, but if the requirement is to establish the economic worth of an investment that has been assisted through European funds, the first step is to draw up a model to reflect the impact visitors have on tourist expenditure in the area.

Methodology Suppose that there exists a tourist destination with two attractions and a seaside. Visitors are surveyed at both attractions and on the beach to ascertain what motivated them to come to the destination. Total spending at the destination (T) amounts to expenditure at Attraction X (T_x) plus expenditure at Attraction Y (T_y) plus all remaining expenditure (R). Let the pull factor (reason for visit) for Attraction X be a, for Attraction Y, a value b, leaving $c = 1 - a - b$ as the significance of the beach. It follows therefore that attributable tourist expenditure by drawing power is:

Attraction X = aT
Attraction Y = bT
Seaside   = cT
where $T = T_x + T_y + R$

It is proposed that European assistance should be given to Attraction X and so there is a requirement to evaluate its worth in terms of its contribution to tourist spending and employment in the area. The benefits of Attraction X (B) are the difference between with and without the project. The without situation is:

Attraction X = 0
Attraction Y = $b(T_y + R)$
Seaside   = $c(T_y + R)$
$T_w = (b + c)(T_y + R)$

Hence,

$$B = T - T_w$$
$$= T - (b + c)(T_y + R) \qquad (15.1)$$

Expanding T gives,

$$B = T_x + a(T_y + R) \qquad (15.2)$$

Employment effects The benefits shown in equation 15.2 are in two parts. The first term on the right hand side is on-site expenditure and the second, off-site expenditure. The amount of off-site expenditure attributable to the attraction depends on its ability to generate visitors to Attraction Y and the area in general. This is termed the 'visitor additionality' factor. The application of employment multipliers per unit of tourist spending to equation 15.2, either on a full-time equivalent (FTE) or employment headcount basis, will give estimates of the gross employment (E) generated by Attraction X. These multipliers are calculated so as to measure the direct employment effects of the attraction, the indirect effects arising out of intermediate purchases made by the attraction and the induced effects on the local economy as a result of the re-spending of local incomes derived from the attraction, and similarly for off-site expenditure. Thus:

$$E = T_x e_x + aOe_o \qquad (15.3)$$

Where e_x is the employment multiplier appropriate to the attraction, O is the sum of off-site expenditure ($T_y + R$) and e_o the required employment multiplier.

However, equation 15.3 ignores any demand diversion from competitors elsewhere in the area: this is the displacement effect and in this respect it is important to define the boundary of the attraction, since the larger the area the more likely it is that the attraction could divert expenditure and employment from elsewhere. National finance ministries sometimes argue that, in the case of the economy as a whole, all expenditure, and consequently employment, is displacement and there is in effect a zero-sum game being played out in which there are only regional distribution benefits.

At a national level, the above argument assumes that market forces are moving the economy towards full employment equilibrium so that public investment expenditure, whether raised through taxation or borrowing, is simply displacing private funds in the capital market. Similarly, the operation of the attraction is displacing demand in the same or related product markets and likewise in the labour and property markets. In reality, economies do get stuck at a level of Keynesian unemployment disequilibria and one of the major objectives of regional policy is to 'kick-start' a demand deficient economy so as to raise the level of output through the multiplier process. This discussion does not imply that displacement should be neglected so that policy decisions are made in terms of the gross effect only, but merely raises the issue that the logic of the crowding-out effect ends up with a 'do nothing' policy. Modern growth theory places emphasis on the importance of embodied technical progress so that intervention policies designed to help product improvement will affect development through raising efficiency on the supply side.

If d is the proportion of locally diverted demand (or demand diverted from other assisted firms) in equation 15.2, then, from equation 15.3, net employment is:

$$N = E - dE$$
$$= (1 - d)(T_x e_x + aOe_o) \qquad (15.4)$$

Equation (15.4) forms the core of the basic evaluation model that can be used to judge in employment terms the return to public funds given to a business by way of a range of incentives.

Case example In Table 15.2 we present data that have been drawn from case study material on attractions, to show how the employment effects of a tourism project may be measured. The workings of Table 15.2 are along the following lines: using visitor expenditure surveys, the total expected on-site and off-site spending arising from the project is estimated, in euros, at €25,050,000.

It is at this point that the concept of visitor additionality is invoked: clearly, on-site expenditure by visitors is attributable absolutely to the attraction as the customers have demonstrated their preferences through their willingness to pay, but this is not the case with off-site spending. The extent to which off-site spending may be attributed to the attraction depends on the importance of the attraction in the customer's decision to visit the location. This can only be ascertained by surveying visitors and asking about their motivations for coming to the destination. As expected, a much higher percentage is recorded for day visitors and local residents, because they normally make a specific decision to go to a place, an event or an attraction. Using the visitor additionality factors in Table 15.2 to account for attributable off-site expenditure, the gross expenditure benefits (B) from the attraction are:

$$B = €9,350,000 + (0.10 \times €14,212,000)$$
$$+ (0.85 \times €2,420,000) + (1.0 \times €1,573,000)$$
$$= €14,401,100 \qquad (15.5)$$

It is anticipated that the attraction will create 70.5 FTE jobs directly on-site, and so the required additions to this number will be the expected indirect and induced employment generated from on-site spending.

Table 15.2 Assessing the impact of a tourist attraction

Item	On-site expenditure (euros)	Off-site expenditure (euros)
Visitor markets		
Stay	2 431 000	14 212 000
Day	2 711 500	2 420 000
Local residents	4 207 500	1 573 000
Total	9 350 000	18 205 000
Visitor additionality		
Stay	Not applicable	10%
Day	Not applicable	85%
Local residents	Not applicable	100%
Displacement		
Stay	0%	0%
Day	30%	30%
Local residents	100%	100%
FTE multipliers per €10 000		
Direct	0.0695	0.0571
Indirect	0.0375	0.0355
Induced	0.0054	0.0054
Total	**0.1124**	**0.0980**

The direct multiplier is not used here as it refers to the average attraction, so it is better to use the direct estimate of employment in these circumstances. Using the appropriate FTE multipliers shown in Table 15.2 and calculated as a decimal fraction of a given amount of tourist expenditure, this figure comes to $(0.0375 + 0.0054) \times €9,350,000/€10,000 = 40.0$ FTE jobs. Off-site jobs amount to $0.0980 \times €5,051,200/€10,000 = 59.5$ FTE jobs, where €5,051,200 is the total of attributable off-site benefits.

Hence, the gross employment generated (E), in terms of FTEs, is expected to be:

$$E = 70.5 \text{ FTEs} + 40.0 \text{ FTEs} + 49.5 \text{ FTEs}$$
$$= 160.0 \text{ FTEs} \tag{15.6}$$

So far the analysis has only measured gross FTEs likely to be generated by the attraction. The net figures have to account for what is termed displacement, which is factored into Table 15.2. Displacement has to do with the extent to which an attraction may capture tourist spending from competitors in the local area. It is estimated that 0% of staying visitors will be taken from competitors; the attraction is providing more to 'see and do' at the destination and the tourists' budgets have sufficient margin of flexibility. For day visitors, it is probable that 30% will be displaced from other attractions, while for local residents a conservative assumption is made that all expenditure will be displaced from elsewhere in the local economy. The latter assumption is overly pessimistic in practice, for household budgets are not that inflexible.

Weighting the displacement factors in Table 15.2 by the different categories of visitor spending gives an overall displacement expenditure of €7,211,050. Hence the value of d is €7,211,050/€14,401,100, which is equal to 0.5007. Thus, the net employment (N) that can be expected to result from the attraction is:

$$N = 160.0 - 0.5007 \times 160.0$$
$$= 79.9 \text{ FTEs} \tag{15.7}$$

It is this number of FTEs that should be used to evaluate the project's worth in public policy decision-making when applications for European support or comparisons with alternative projects are being made.

PROJECT MANAGEMENT

After the Commission has taken a decision on the OPs, the member state and its regions then have the task of implementing the programmes, i.e. selecting the thousands of projects, and to monitor and assess them. The principle of subsidiarity devolves the monitoring function to the local level through programme management authorities in each country and/or each region. The latter are made up of representatives from central and local government, public agencies and any other interested parties, and they will be responsible for all projects within the OPs. The Commission commits the expenditure to allow the member state to start the programmes.

For every project, targets are set at the approval stage and returns must be submitted quarterly, showing the progress of each scheme against its targets. The member state is required to certify statements of expenditure and payment applications before their transmission to the Commission and to provide an auditing body to ensure the efficient running of the management and monitoring system. The Commission pays the certified expenditure and monitors each OP alongside the member state. Strategic reports are submitted by the Commission and by the member state throughout the given planning period (currently 2007–13). It is a member state's responsibility to make site visits and evaluate project performance: these tasks usually fall to the government department responsible for administering the OP that contains the project. Member states have the responsibility to ensure that European funds are correctly spent and yield good value for money in terms of the project evaluation criteria. This responsibility is regulated by the European Court of Auditors, who have powers of examination and verification to establish that projects are:

- eligible for European funds as specified;
- managed in accordance with European Commission's rules with regard to technical and financial controls; and
- claiming grant against justifiable expenditure.

The above verifications are undertaken by making one or two visits every year and subjecting a group of pre-selected projects to detailed checking.

CONCLUSION

Since about 1975, the entry of the EU into regional policy, in order to create a greater convergence between the economies of the Union, has ended member states' monopoly of regional policy within their borders. Inside the Union, there is a distinct tendency for the poorest regions to be situated on the geographical periphery and the more prosperous regions, with the benefit of market access, to be centrally located. With the adoption of the Single European Act (1987), with the intention to create one market in Europe and a single currency, there is a commitment by the EU to promote economic and social cohesion through actions to reduce regional disparities and the Maastricht Treaty (1992) acknowledged, for the first time, the role of tourism in these actions.

The resources for mitigating regional differences are drawn from the structural funds, which are continually being increased, in real terms, from one planning period to another. The funds have specific objectives, as shown in Table 15.1, and support for tourism development manifests itself in regions that already have an established tourist industry, in cross-border cooperation, rural development and also where tourism has contributed to the diversification of economic activities in areas of industrial decline. Tourism programmes are seen as key activities in reducing regional imbalances. In support of this, the case study discusses the principles of structural assistance and the methodology for project evaluation, with particular emphasis on job creation, though we should be mindful of the clear intention of the European Commission to propagate tourism developments in a sustainable manner, in order to guarantee that the activity continues on a regular basis.

The division of intervention in the tourist industry between member states and the EU is always likely to remain contentious, but given the diversity of the tourist product, the Union has to work in close partnership with national and regional authorities. At the political level, this issue has been technically put to one side by Article 3b of the Maastricht Treaty, which states that

the Community shall take action, in accordance with the principle of subsidiarity, only if and in so far as the objectives of the proposed action cannot be sufficiently achieved by the Member States and can therefore, by reason of the scale or effects of the proposed action, be better achieved by the Community.

DISCUSSION QUESTIONS

1. Why is the EU concerned about regional inequalities?

2. How important is tourism in the EU in respect of its contribution to the GDP of member states and employment in the Union?

3. What are the strengths and weaknesses of positioning tourism projects within an overall strategy to guide their use as opposed to opportunistic development?

4. The nature of grant aid from the EU has been described as conditional matching funding. Other forms of grant mechanisms are lump-sum payments, which may be tied to specific projects (conditional) or just given to the overall programme (unconditional). What are the relative merits of these different systems?

5. How would you go about preparing a local area tourism strategy?

6. With reference to Chapter 5, what are the concepts that lie behind the measurement of direct, indirect and induced income and employment multipliers?

7. The capital investment for the attraction project illustrated in Table 15.2 is €8,360,000. The European Commission decides to grant aid the scheme at 30% of the capital cost. What is the grant cost per direct FTE job created on-site, for the gross employment generated and net jobs created by the project?

8. Suppose the EU introduces a rule limiting grant support to €20,000 per net job created. How much would the project now receive in grant aid as a percentage of the capital cost?

CHAPTER 16

Destinations

LEARNING OUTCOMES

The focus of the chapter is on destinations and their role in the tourism system. By the end of this chapter, therefore, you will:

- be familiar with the nature and roles of destinations in the wider tourism industry;

- be aware of the range of destinations that exist and the context within which they are planned and developed on the one hand, and compete with other destinations on the other;

- be familiar with a number of forces in the external environment impacting on their future;

- be aware of the means by which destinations are managed and marketed; and

- be introduced to the particular collaborative nature of destinations and the organisational and governance structures advocated for their effective management.

Photograph: Rickshaw, Chennai, India © Katherine Harding

INTRODUCTION

In this chapter we show that the destination lies at the core of the travel and tourism system. Destinations come in all shapes and sizes and can be found in a variety of geographical settings such as in urban, rural and coastal environments. Destinations can be countries or a collection of countries, a distinct state, county or province, or in fact represent a local city, town or resort, national park, area of outstanding natural beauty or coastline. As with other parts of the tourism system they can be viewed in both a supply and demand context in that destinations can be seen to represent a mix of products and services that come together to meet the needs of the tourist (supply) or as places where tourists travel to in order to experience particular features or experiences (demand). The geographical location of destinations is, for reasons that will become clearer as you proceed through the chapter, particularly significant as often they do not sit comfortably in convenient political, administrative and/or legislative-bound locations. More often than not, destinations are in fact subject to artificial divides that ignore the more consumer-driven needs and expectations of the tourist. As will become evident throughout this chapter, destinations are traditionally viewed as particularly difficult entities to manage due to the complex relationships of stakeholders that come together to make them work and the multiple objectives that they seek to achieve.

This chapter, therefore, outlines the relationship between the destination and the wider tourism industry before introducing the context within which destination policy, planning and development takes place. The chapter continues by identifying a number of trends impacting on destinations and provides a useful framework which facilitates understanding. The chapter then introduces a range of issues relating to the management and marketing of destinations before concluding with a series of thoughts for the future.

THE NATURE AND ROLE OF DESTINATIONS

The destination really does sit at the core of the wider tourism system in that it represents an amalgam of tourism products that collectively offer a destination 'experience' to visitors. For many consumers (be they day visitors or tourists), particularly in leisure tourism, the destination is the principal motivating factor behind the consumer's decision and expectations. In this context it is, therefore, somewhat surprising to find that even to many experts in the field, the destination remains conceptually difficult to define. One of the principle barriers in neatly defining destinations is the 'inconvenient' nature of boundaries, be they administrative, political or simply geographical, and the means by which they for a variety of reasons do not sit comfortably with the perceptions of the destination to consumers. For example, although London represents an 'iconic' global destination, the wider destination is made up of 33 local authorities which incorporate two cities: the City of London and the City of Westminster. However, for purposes of tourism, especially international visitors, 'tourist' London is essentially the inner core, often referred to as that area within the Circle Line of London's Underground system. Also in the UK, this time in Dorset on the south coast of England, the three destinations of Christchurch, Bournemouth and Poole – although often viewed by visitors as a single 'destination' – represent three different boroughs managed by three different local authorities despite the fact that they 'share' a 12-km beach which to many visitors represents a single destination.

With regard to a neat definition of a destination, it is unavoidable to introduce both supply- and demand-sided viewpoints. So, while supply-sided definitions identify the destination as 'a well-defined geographical area which is understood by its visitors as a unique entity, with a political and legislative framework for tourism marketing and planning' (Buhalis, 2000: 98), demand-sided definitions define destinations as 'places towards which people travel and where they choose to stay for a while in order to experience certain features or characteristics'

(Leiper, 1995: 87 in Buhalis, 2000: 98). In reality, whether one views the destination as a 'tourist place', a 'tourism product', or a 'system of products' does very much depend on the perceptions of the stakeholders either directly and/or indirectly involved with its management. Despite this definitional haze, the UNWTO consider the destination to be the fundamental unit of analysis in tourism (WTO, 2002a). Yes, it is complex and difficult to manage. However, the importance of destinations for the entire tourism system is such that the effective and efficient management of destinations is one of the key priorities for tourism professionals across the world. For this reason alone, it is imperative that a systematic and interdisciplinary approach is adopted for the analysis, planning, management and control of destination development (Manente and Minghetti, 2006: 230). The adoption of a systematic approach to the understanding of destinations has been advocated for some time in that those responsible for destinations are fully aware of the interactions among destination stakeholders and the impact(s) exerted by the competitive environment on the destination 'system'.

Destination types

In view of the above, there are many variations of destinations in existence but the most basic classification is threefold:

- coastal destinations, epitomised in the ever popular seaside resort that has undergone many changes since their modern-day emergence in the mid-eighteenth century with advocacy of inland spas and sea bathing for health cures;
- urban destinations in that major cities have been cultural attractions from ancient times onwards and some, such as Venice, which was popularised in the period of the Grand Tour by Europe's aristocracy, have continued as tourist cities long after their commercial function has diminished;
- rural destinations that range from the ordinary countryside to national parks, wilderness areas, mountains and lakes.

From a planning perspective and noting the definitions attached to the concept of the destination that were given in the previous section, the designation of tourist destination should provide the basis for integrated development to generate the balance of amenities and facilities required by tourists. It also allows for the staging of tourism from one locality to another, opening up new areas as others become saturated. For example, up until recently the concentration of visitors within London's Circle Line put the pressure of tourism almost totally on the City of Westminster and the boroughs of Camden, and Kensington and Chelsea. However, the extension of the Jubilee Line south of the River Thames to Greenwich and the developments along the south bank of the river, have created a new tourist region for London, thus spreading the benefits of tourism and easing the burden on the core boroughs. The next step in this process is the holding of the Olympic Games in 2012, which are planned as a regeneration strategy for the north side of the river, east of the City of London.

It follows from what has been discussed so far that the key features of a tourist destination are:

- logical geographical unit recognised by visitors;
- contains significant visitor attractions;
- access or possible provision of access;
- internal transport network;
- tourist infrastructure and superstructure are present or can be developed;
- administratively possible to plan and manage.

When planning tourist destinations it is often desirable to establish a tourist centre that acts as the hub and gateway to various parts of the area. This allows the public and private sectors to concentrate facilities and obtain economies of development scale.

Coastal

In Britain, as in the rest of Europe, although 'taking the waters' was popularised by the Romans through the building of luxurious *thermae* over hot springs, the foundation of spa towns, the peak periods for seeking cures at spas or at the seaside took place during the Georgian and Victorian eras of the eighteenth and nineteenth centuries. Initially for the wealthy, it was the industrial growth in the north of Europe and on the east coast of the USA, together with the advent of the railways, that popularised coastal resort development. A classic example of this is Brighton, located on the south coast of Britain. The community was formerly a fishing village, known as Brighthelmstone, but the construction between 1784 and 1787 of an Asian-style Royal Pavilion as a residence for the Prince Regent, later King George IV, initiated the transformation of the village into a fashionable resort town. By 1841 Brighton became accessible by rail, and it grew rapidly thereafter.

With the coming of the railways, the growth of the seaside resorts during the latter half of the nineteenth century in Europe and the USA was the result of a partnership between the public and private sectors. The local authorities invested in the promenades, piers, gardens and so on, while the private sector developed the revenue-earning activities, which enhanced the income of the area and in turn increased property tax receipts for the authorities. Pier building was particularly a British phenomenon; 78 were constructed between 1860 and 1910, while very few were built on mainland Europe. The development of seaside resorts is paralleled in the USA with the expansion of the amusement park industry. Although, New York's Coney Island had started up in the 1870s, and their rides and games entertained a countless number of visitors, it was Captain P. Boynton's Sea Lion Park, opened on the Island in 1895, that set the trend and inspired numerous amusement parks throughout the United States, including the three Great Coney Island Parks: Luna Park (1903–47), Dreamland (1904–11) and Steeplechase (1897–1964). In Britain, amusements were developed at the ends of piers, but in 1896 the American 'revolution' crossed the Atlantic with the founding of Blackpool Pleasure Beach.

It was in the 1950s, with the growth of air travel, that the dominance of the seaside resorts of northern Europe over the traditional summer break began to face the challenge of the warm water resorts in southern Europe. This left them facing a different future, to which some have adapted by investing in new markets, for example, the conference trade and the growth in short breaks. The latter are more likely to be taken in the home country, whereas the ideal main holiday today is often considered to be abroad, mainly short haul, but also being made easier by developments in long-haul overseas travel to more exotic destinations. Another major change has been increased settlement in these resorts, simply because they are 'nice places to live'. This has generated local conflict in terms of allocating resources to tourism use versus residential use, and over time has altered the demographic and economic base of the resort, because the priorities of local representatives have changed and they remain not as seaside resorts but as coastal towns. Typical stereotypes of resorts which have become urban settlements are seaside towns that now have a population of above average pensionable age; low economic activity; below average local employment that is seasonal; considerable commuting; a high percentage of second homes; and a high percentage of communal living in apartment blocks and retirement homes. The policy of NTOs in these circumstances is to focus their attention on regenerating a few key resorts that are willing and able to maintain their position in the marketplace.

One of the fundamental lessons to learn from the development of coastal resorts, whether new or old, is the importance of the public–private sector partnership. Embodied in the tourist product are common goods and services, which are either unlikely to be provided in sufficient quantity if left to the market mechanism, or are available without cost, as is the case with natural resources. The principal concern for the environment is that indiscriminate consumption, without market regulation, will cause irreversible damage that cannot be compensated by increasing the stock of other capital. The upshot is that the single-minded pursuit of private profit opportunities within tourism may be self-defeating, as many older resorts have found to their cost. The outcome may not be the integrated tourism development which distils the essence of the country in its design, but a rather crowded, overbuilt and placeless location with polluted beaches – one that is totally out of keeping with the original objectives set by the country's tourism policy. As a number of Mediterranean resorts have discovered, the lack of public involvement in tourism has resulted in overbuilding by the accommodation sector, since this tends to be the major revenue-earning activity where there are substantial short-term profits to be made during the early stages of development. Such building has often been at the expense of the aesthetic quality of the natural landscape and also, when it has been overlaid onto an existing town or village, it may severely disrupt the lifestyle of the local community. For example, the major hotel developments that took place in the resorts of southern Spain during the 1960s and early 1970s were completed under laissez-faire expansionism with little consideration given to planning or control. In general, the public infrastructure was overloaded and, since the second half of the 1980s, there has been a continual programme to correct this imbalance by refurbishing the resort centres to give more 'green' space in the form of parks and gardens, and pull down older hotels, as in the Balearic Islands.

It is evident that the public is becoming more aware of the perceived adverse effects of tourism on the environment and it has become fashionable to 'go green'. Green tourism, eco-tourism or alternative tourism (the words are often used synonymously) is in essence small-scale solutions to what is a large-scale problem, namely the mass movements of people travelling for leisure purposes. Thus, there is a requirement to continue to maintain large 'resortscapes' capable of managing high density flows, such as sun, sea and sand family groups, and it is important that the local economy is sustained, yet in balance with the coastal environment. Local people should be involved in the decision-making, but the 'last settler syndrome' of incoming residents opposing new developments in the seaside economy, which has hampered the regeneration of many older resorts, should be avoided.

Urban

During the last half of the twentieth century, the troubles caused by the move of manufacturing industries from urban areas to cheaper rural locations and the continued flight of the middle classes to the suburbs, severely affected the image of industrialised cities, already dented by issues of congestion and pollution. This has forced local authorities, policy makers and business groups to revive their cities by attracting new industries, residents and visitors through the application of modern city management and marketing systems founded on longer term plans. North American cities, where the revitalisation trend was referred to as 'city boosterism', were the first to practise city marketing strategies with the support of both public and private organisations, for example, Toronto, Baltimore and Boston. Tourism has thrived in the regeneration of run-down industrial and dock areas, at the same time acting as a catalyst to attract new industries, belying the previously held notions that cities are just places where people live and work.

From the early 1980s, major cities have been taking tourism development more seriously and trying to strengthen the sector with strategic plans and tactics hinged upon the existence of quintessential factors for tourism development. While such factors include the social, cultural, economic and environmental endowments of urban areas, their use as tourism assets depends heavily on the success of public and private authorities in integrating tourism development into overall town planning. The characteristics of such tourism derive from both the distinctive nature of urban structures and the manifestation of tourism in such intricate settlements. Some of the common characteristics of city destinations drawn from the empirical and theoretical research available in the literature are:

- Urban destinations are both multi-sold and multi-bought, through offering a range of tourist products and services that create diverse product packages. Shoppers, cultural visitors, visitors on education trips, business visitors, short-break trips, domestic visitors and overseas visitors can all be found in many major city destinations.

- City destinations are often the tourism gateways to their surrounding region. Locations that associate themselves with a major city destination may benefit from the latter's high volumes of visitors, by drawing day trips from tourists basing themselves in the city.

- The sheer scale of heterogeneous products and services sold to visitors and locals in urban areas make each city destination a unique tourism product cluster. Therefore, while there may be some similarities between some urban functions and tourist services, as in accommodation and transport, each city destination is different when it comes to their size, location, heritage, and economic and social functioning.

- Developing and marketing the product clusters of city destinations cannot be directed by a single authority. Residents, private and public tourism stakeholders and other urban authorities need to cooperate to initiate development projects and to effect marketing activities by creating a one-voice strategy. The 'over-fragmentation' of tourism stakeholders in urban areas makes partnerships, alliances and cooperation imperative in the process of developing the tourism economy.

- Despite the fact that tourism-related products and services in cities are manifold, visitors usually concentrate on certain locations and create invisible boundaries that define tourist zones or districts.

- Tourism in urban areas, compared to traditional holiday resorts, is an all-year-round activity with limited seasonality. This is principally due to the diversified demand and supply aspects of city destinations.

- By their very nature, cities embrace more than one economic industry. Hence their economic function depends on the coexistence of various manufacturing and service operations. Whether the economic and social richness of urban areas is tourism-related or not, sustainable tourism development and management can only be fulfilled through the success of local authorities in being able to integrate tourism into the overall urban economic structure. Neither tourism nor other industries should hamper each other's functioning. Opposition to tourism may arise from residents and businesspeople if concentrated tourist flows in certain districts impair the living standards of the city.

Rural

The product strengths of many rural areas lie in their strong natural environments, for example, hills, mountains and lakes, and remoteness, which make them increasingly attractive for tourism development at a time when 'green tourism' is in vogue. The benefits are seen in the rural way of life, physical activity from hill walking to adventure sports, tranquillity, aesthetics of the landscape and so forth. Within Europe, as in many other countries, the promotion of rural tourism by the EU is part of its convergence and cohesion policy. In many rural locations, the outlook for small farmers and therefore the fabric of the landscape, culture and way of life of the rural economy is bleak without the expenditure of substantial sums of public money for little return. Supporting farm tourism is just one of a number of ways in which essential and inevitable subsidies can be paid to farmers, and it seems to be among the more cost-effective measures. Therefore, policies aiming to develop this sector, and in particular, seeking to improve the qualitative characteristics (mainly tourist infrastructure supply in nature, such as transport infrastructure, accommodation facilities, management efficiency, cultural activities in the form of festivals, and food quality, among others), will be able to generate higher tourism revenues, which are beneficial to sustaining local income growth. However, although every location has some tourism potential, it would be naive to suppose that tourism development could be effective in every region. Increasing market segmentation will generate niche markets for some areas, but the cost of supplying these markets could be prohibitive, for in higher latitudes the lack of tourist infrastructure in rural areas is compounded by weather conditions, which limit the length of the season, as in so many of the outlying regions of the world.

On the other hand, there is concern for the social impact of tourism on small, close-knit communities and the environmental threat to undisturbed wilderness. Scenic areas may be protected by zoning landscape for different use patterns, creating intermediate or buffer zones and limiting tourist flows, which is the purpose of creating national parks and designating areas of outstanding natural beauty. This is to protect them from inappropriate developments, so as to preserve the landscape and rural structure.

As a rule, when considering the impact of tourism on the local community, the greater the difference in lifestyles between rural hosts and tourists, and the less the former have been exposed to visitors, then the longer should be the period of adaptation. Phasing development over time and space is the underlying principle here, but any programme for growth is made all the harder when the community lacks the necessary skills, capital, organisation structures and information sources to progress the plan. Solutions for such difficulties could include bringing in 'flagship' projects from outside and inviting the operators to invest long term in the community, forming a development corporation or taking a low-key approach by running a small business extension service backed up by development grants. Although there is always the risk with outside companies that they might, in response to commercial pressures, revert to short-term profit goals, there is no guarantee that local owners will not be even keener to exploit tourism opportunities, particularly when they have the necessary political representation to do so.

Destination policy, planning and development

Prior to the closer examination of those forces in the external environment that are impacting on the future management of destinations, it is advisable to set destinations more broadly, and their management, within the context of tourism policy and planning and the wider context of 'competitiveness'. In essence, all aspects of tourism sit within the broader context of tourism policy. According to Ritchie and Crouch (2003) tourism policy focuses on macro-level policies, is long term in orientation, and concentrates on how critical and limited resources can best respond to perceived needs and opportunities in a changing environment. Tourism policy is significant as it defines the so-called 'rules of the game', sets out the activities and behaviours that are acceptable, and provides common direction and guidance for all tourism stakeholders within a destination. In a strategic sense it facilitates consensus around the specific vision, strategies and objectives for a given destination while it also provides a suitable framework for public and private discussions on the role of the tourism sector and its contributions to the economy and to society in general. In its broadest sense, tourism policy allows tourism to interface with other industrial sectors within the wider economy and link more effectively into other more general strategies such as national and regional economic strategies, spatial strategies and integrated national and regional strategies. Destination management, on the other hand, represents a more micro activity in 'which all the many resident and industry stakeholders carry out their individual and organizational responsibilities on a daily basis in efforts to realize the macro-level vision contained in policy, planning and development' (Ritchie and Crouch, 2003: 147).

Destination competitiveness

Destinations are managed within a broader context of 'competitiveness' and 'stewardship' which relate to the deployment of 'management' resources to both develop and enhance the destination and at the same time protect and conserve its core resources respectively. Hence, the competitiveness of a destination refers to its ability to compete effectively and profitably in the marketplace, while the successful management of a destination involves a balance between traditional economic and business management skills with an increasing need for sensitive environmental management capabilities. The comparative advantage of a destination, meanwhile, refers to a destination's ability to manage its natural and man-made resources effectively over the long term. Fundamental to achieving competitive advantage for its tourism industry, any destination must ensure that 'its overall "appeal", and the tourist experience offered, must be superior to that of the alternative destinations open to potential visitors' (Dwyer and Kim, 2003: 369). One of the particular challenges in defining competitiveness in the context of destinations is that, as already stated, the destination represents an amalgam of many industrial services, such as accommodation, transportation, attractions, entertainment, recreation and food services. This fragmented and highly disparate 'product' clearly does not make the management of the visitor experience an easy task. Despite difficulties of definition, it is sensible for destinations to focus attention on long-term economic prosperity as the yardstick by which they are to be assessed competitively (Ritchie and Crouch, 2003).

In order to remain competitive, destinations need to be aware of both demand and supply factors. With regard to demand, those managing destinations need to take note of the nature, timing and magnitude of demand. At the same, they need to be aware of those products, services, amenities and attractions that are necessary components for a satisfactory destination 'experience'. Ritchie and Crouch (2003: 60) propose a conceptual model of destination competitiveness as a vehicle to facilitate understanding of what is essentially a quite complex issue, the model depicting the 'structure of interrelationships between separate constructs or factors which help to explain a higher-order concept'.

Figure 16.1 demonstrates the open nature of the tourism system in that it is subject to many (micro) influences and pressures arising from the system itself. In addition, numerous (macro) forces exist externally that are profound in their implications for tourism. Although the attractiveness of a destination may remain relatively constant, the means by which competition changes indicate that a constant reassessment of the destination's strengths, weaknesses, opportunities and threats is necessary. The work by Porter (1998) is useful here in that those managing destinations need to understand the contributions of factor conditions, demand conditions, related and supporting industries, and firm strategy, structure, organisation and rivalry in determining destination success. Building on the work of Porter, Figure 16.1 refers to the global (macro) environment; the competitive (micro) environment; core resources and attractors; supporting factors and resources (such as infrastructure, accessibility, and hospitality); destination policy, planning and development; destination management; and qualifying and amplifying determinants. In reality, all destinations, irrespective of size, location and market, need to adapt continually, not simply because they need to modernise but because they need to retain and build on their overall competitiveness over other destinations.

DESTINATION TRENDS

For the next decade, the challenges facing destinations are likely to be significant with a whole host of issues likely to impact on their management and marketing. Both the macro and micro environments are in a constant state of change and evolution and, as such, those managing destinations are encouraged to migrate from their traditional 'inward looking' nature and recognise more fully the true magnitude of events and their impact on how destinations are to be managed in the future. Two studies which set the context well for the future management of destinations are those by Bennett (1999) and King (2002). Future pressures introduced by Bennett (1999) include the need to take due consideration of the needs, wants and expectations of more mature and knowledgeable customers, and the need for more up-to-date and reliable information upon which to base such decision-making. Bennett highlights also the considerable pressures caused by the sustained presence and influence of intermediaries, as well as the parallel imbalance of channel power for destinations in the tourism system. With regard to transportation and technological pressures, developments in useful destination management systems have taken place which now afford them necessity status, while the systematic growth of discount airlines and the surplus of new destinations continues

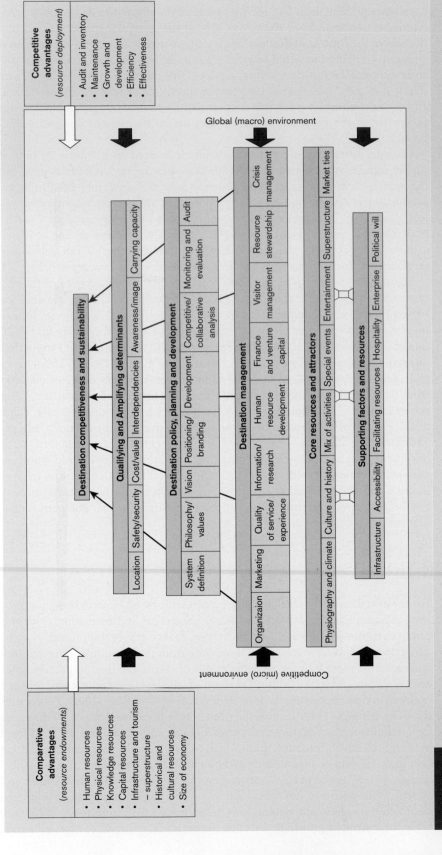

Figure 16.1 Model of destination competitiveness

Source: Ritchie, J.R.B. and Crouch, G. (2005), p. 62, Fig. 3.1 'Conceptual model of destination competitiveness'

to ensure severe competition among destinations for tourist spend. Of all these forces, however, it is, according to Bennett, the long-standing 'dividing line' between the public and private sectors that remains the prime catalyst for change, a dividing line that Bennett considers to have been holding back the potential of destination marketing for far too long.

King (2002) acknowledges the existence of a number of similar pressures. However, he raises also the scenario of traditional distribution channels being increasingly bypassed in the future with more direct contact between the consumer and the supplier likely to take place. King also suggests that a reduction in booking lead times is likely, as is a steady downturn in the demand for mass tourism products leading to a greater pressure for the destination to deliver satisfactions and meet expectations of an increasingly independent tourist. King is very critical of many existing **destination management organisations** (DMOs), in that the majority remain focused on 'what the destination has to offer' and continue to use 'mass marketing techniques more suited to the passive customer' (King, 2002: 106). He develops this theme by alluding to the fact that the customer is now very much an active partner in the marketing process. For destinations to be a success, marketers will therefore need to engage the customer as never before, as well as to be able to provide them with the types of information and experience they are increasingly able to demand.

In the same study, King advances a number of so-called 'new realities' for destination marketers. These include the need for even greater emphasis on a strong brand image, with clearly identified and projected brand values that resonate with key target segments; more direct engagement with the customer to identify their holiday motivations, anticipate their needs and fulfil their aspirations; the establishment of ongoing, direct, two-way and networking consumer communication channels, and for key customer relationship strategies to take place with the eventual development of mass customisation marketing and delivery capabilities; greater emphasis to be given to the creation and promotion of holiday experiences that link key brand values and assets with the holiday aspirations and needs of key customers; and a move away from a relatively passive promotional role to include greater intervention, facilitation and direction in the conversion process.

The 15 Cs Framework

In recognition of the dynamic context within which destinations are being managed now, and are to be managed in the future, Fyall et al. (2006) propose a framework which provides a 'route map' for professionals and researchers working in the field. Although at a developmental phase, and in no way intended to represent a definitive list, Figure 16.2 provides a suitable synthesis of the key challenges facing the domain of destination management and marketing for the next decade. Clearly their degree of importance will vary according to the destination in question. However, the omission of even one of the challenges in the design and implementation of destination management and marketing strategies is likely to hinder the effectiveness of the final plan or strategy in that an inadequate understanding of the wider destination environment is evident. Nevertheless, identifying future issues and strategic challenges is a common practice. The challenge for destinations is to take due notice of the forces at play and to manage destinations accordingly.

Complexity

The complexity of the destination product is not in dispute as all destinations to varying degrees are comprised of multiple stakeholders, multiple components and multiple suppliers, and convey multiple meanings to multiple markets and market segments. Perhaps the issue most pressing in the context of complexity is the pressure for the public sector to increase revenue from private sector sources at a time when considerable pressure is being put on the public purse within the context of emerging destination management structures and the increasing devolution and regionalisation of tourism organisation and funding, most notably in the UK. The complexity of a destination is particularly marked when the

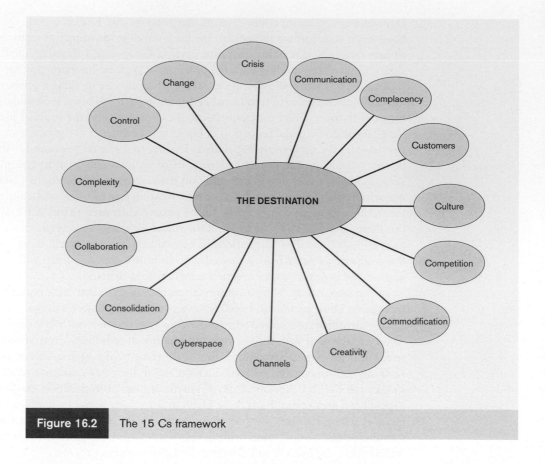

| Figure 16.2 | The 15 Cs framework |

consumer and community dimensions are taken into consideration. For example, consumers will often differ in their perceptions, expectations and desired satisfactions of the 'tourism place'. Only a minority, if at all, will view the destination as a neatly encapsulated bundle of suppliers.

Control

The adoption of a strategic approach to marketing destinations based on destination branding is often undermined due to the inherent difficulties of destination coordination and control. For example, campaigns can be frequently undertaken 'by a variety of tourist businesses with no consultation or coordination on the prevailing message or the destination values being promoted' (Scott *et al.*, 2000: 202). This issue is one that has contributed to London's historical struggle to make a sustained impact in terms of brand positioning. Much has, however, changed with considerable budget increases awarded to Visit London in recent years. In addition, the top down nature of strategy-making and the large sums made available to 'make things happen' have afforded a step change in marketing activity within the capital and a greater ability for the tourism authorities to retain a sense of control over how the destination is positioned and marketed (see Major Case Study 16.1).

One of the consequences of a greater top down orientation is the tendency to ignore the smaller players, many of whom in the past were members of previous forms of destination management structures and tourist boards. This is particularly true in Edinburgh whereby the new network structure is no longer membership based (see Mini Case Study 16.2). That said, tourism businesses do still have the opportunity to participate and are perhaps now freer to do this. The view in Edinburgh is that there is a need to balance the needs of the individual and the destination by establishing the delivery of a total visitor experience, from the point of enquiry to departure, perhaps only possible via a change in attitude and view for all those involved in tourism. For the wider management of destinations, it is recognised that developments are being made in the need to bring tourism's information base up to date as there is considerable evidence to suggest that 'the design and implementation of destination management systems (DMSs) are taking place to the extent that for most destinations, rather than being an aspirational element of their marketing armoury, they are now afforded necessity status and represent a very real opportunity for destination marketers to gain greater control of their product' (Fyall *et al.*, 2006: 77–8).

Change

The migration from the traditional division that has historically existed between the public and private sectors is perhaps that element of change most needed in that it has often been perceived as holding back the potential of destinations. To date, however, most countries around the world retain a strong public bias in their organisational and funding structures. Not only does this result in the retention of a predominantly public 'organisational' mindset but it serves as a barrier to the raising of additional funding and the speed with which DMOs can react to forces in the external environment.

Crisis

The majority of destinations around the world, either directly or indirectly, are to some extent impacted by crises, be they natural or man-made. Crises often impact on established tourism flows and their related spend and accommodation requirements. Unfortunately, the external environment is predictable in its unpredictability. For example, recent terrorist strikes in Egypt, the attacks in London in July 2005, and the Boxing Day Tsunami of 2004, among others, continue to impact negatively on many destinations around the world. It is clear that the future for many destinations is inherently uncertain due to a whole myriad of natural and man-made crises, the one type that is often overlooked being economic crises in the major generating countries, which are economically far more damaging for tourist-receiving countries than more high-profile, media-hungry events such as 9/11. For these reasons alone, any destination management organisation that does not now incorporate some form of crisis management planning into its strategic marketing planning cycle can be accused of grossly ignoring the realities of modern tourism.

Complacency

The crises mentioned above are all significant in that although many destinations clearly suffered from very rapid drops in demand, among other negative impacts, tourists continued to travel, albeit intra-regionally or domestically. For destinations everywhere, irrespective of scale and geographic location, fear of crises ought to be sufficient to prevent complacency among those managing and marketing destinations. For many destinations, however, specific markets have been such reliable sources of custom over many years. However, although in the past destinations could perhaps be excused for being slow to react to forces in the external environment this clearly is no longer the case. Although as a broad phenomenon tourism has proven to be particularly robust, travel and spending patterns do change. Tourism in its broadest sense has consistently proved to be a highly robust phenomenon in that although travel patterns may change the act of travelling remains steadfast and for many markets it is now a necessity rather than a luxury, especially in the developed world.

Customers

It is recognised that the task of managing destinations is never going to be an easy one. Destinations urgently need to develop suitable strategies to accommodate Poon's 'new tourist': that is, tourists that are flexible, segmented, diagonally integrated and environmentally conscious, who seek quality, flexibility and value for money (Poon, 1993). It is thus the case that as every year passes destination marketers need to be more innovative in their adoption of marketing techniques and strategies in meeting the needs of more demanding customers. For example, the highly competitive global market for tourists serves as a catalyst for tourism destinations to seek more innovative 'relationship' marketing strategies so as to engender a degree of loyalty and stimulate lucrative repeat business among their visitor base. That said, in a context of many destinations competing in price-driven, low-margin markets, the costs and benefits to be derived from relationship marketing require significant research before tourism destinations are able to accept the concept as a new paradigm or potential solution to maintain/expand their share of the market for visitors. In view of the inherent imbalance of power, resources and experience between tourism destination 'actors', generating cohesion, mutual trust and respect within the tourism system stand as significant challenges for those marketing tourism destinations in the future.

Culture

Although the cultural division between the public and private sectors within tourism continues to represent a barrier for progress across many countries, on the demand side culture represents one significant opportunity for destinations, especially those that have acquired 'commodity' status in recent years, to differentiate themselves in the future via the development of niche tourism strategies. With regard to aspects of supply, the cultural division between the public and private sectors is considerable by nature of their respective roles in providing for the tourist experience. Although this may be less so across the UK in view of the devolution of tourism and the regionalisation of priorities, destinations are for the most part still reliant on 'public goods' as part of their wider appeal – which in turn raises the issue of who is to pay for their upkeep in the future: the local community or visitors? Despite the pressure in many countries for a greater financial contribution to the costs of developing and managing destinations, the rationale for continued public sector intervention remains strong. For the most part, governments continue to recognise the economic value of tourism (which in turn has contributed to the proliferation of DMOs worldwide) while the 'one-industry' concept of tourism recognises that while businesses have individual goals, the success of the tourism industry relies on effective interrelationships between the public and private sector (Pike, 2004).

Competition

One interesting indirect dimension to competition is the exponential growth in the ownership of second homes, most notably in France and Spain. The phenomenon of second-home ownership is a significant threat in that an increasing percentage of the market now no longer needs variety in their choice of destinations as with their purchase of a second home they have expressed their loyalty, albeit to varying degrees, to a particular destination. Work by Pedro (2006) has explored this phenomenon in greater depth and evaluated the true impact on the management of destinations. Some of the key outcomes include the fact that second-home tourism is labour un-intensive, involves visitors with lower expenditure in general, and represents competition for the traditional hospitality sector. It also involves visitors who do not pay tourism taxes and are not subject to the legislation often associated with tourism accommodation. Finally, the phenomenon inadvertently puts pressure on the price of land and contributes to price inflation in the house and consumer goods markets. One notable fact is that, as evidenced recently, competition is at its most cut-throat post-crisis with evidence from recent disasters suggesting that, although the overall volume of trips taking place remains relatively static, the shift in travel patterns is significant in that domestic and intra-regional travel to more familiar and perceived 'safe' destinations has become the norm.

Commodification

According to Fyall *et al.* (2006: 80), one of the 'outcomes of commodification of the destination product is the continual downward pressure on prices'. The reduction in prices, although beneficial to tourists, reduces the destination-wide yield and poses a considerable challenge for destination marketers in that increasingly more marketing, and marketing spend, is necessary to generate a decreasing yield from tourists. Niche tourism developments are a means to counter such a trend – as best demonstrated by marketing strategies adopted by the Tourism Authority of Thailand and their development of the Amazing Thailand brand and its annual niche-orientated marketing 'straplines'.

Creativity

The considerable challenges that confront those tasked with developing destination brands helps to explain why there is such a paucity of brand innovation in the destination sector as compared to other sectors within the tourism industry. One of the few genuine success stories for destination 'country' branding is that of New Zealand, as highlighted in Mini Case Study 16.1.

MINI CASE STUDY 16.1
Destination branding – New Zealand

Although branding has been used to good effect for many years across most sectors of the wider tourism industry, it is only over the past decade that branding has been adopted by destinations as a means of differentiating their 'product' from competitor destinations. With so many destinations around the world offering similar attractions, accommodation, facilities and even quality of service, the need for destinations to truly differentiate themselves in the marketplace is greater than ever. Where branding is being adopted by destinations there are, however, a number of instances where they are failing to appreciate fully its true potential and are thus merely replicating their 'wallpaper' advertising strategies as 'brand strategies'. Brands ought really to provoke beliefs, induce emotions and trigger behaviour. Branding destinations is a particularly complex task in that they have long histories and numerous and multifaceted associations. According to Morgan *et al.* (2003: 286) countries are 'often (but not always) sovereign states, they are territories governed by competing interests and political agendas and their marketing has to be contextualised in the wider global socio-political system'.

One destination that has gained a very positive reputation for the quality and consistency of its brand presence is New Zealand. Smaller than Japan and marginally bigger than the UK, New Zealand is highly geographically disadvantaged when it comes to international tourism. At the beginning of the 1990s when tourism to the country was in the doldrums, especially when compared to its bigger neighbour, Australia, the development of the New Zealand brand started to take shape. Through the inclusion of many key stakeholders, the pooling of resources, the internal communication of the brand to New Zealanders and the eventual creation of Tourism New Zealand, a realignment of the country's NTO, collectively contributed to the development of a successful brand. With the recognised weakness of limited 'share of voice' the cooperative development of the brand was crucial in developing a true global reach.

In the early stages of brand development it is crucial to establish the core values of the destination and to determine how contemporary the brand is with regard to both consumers and competitors. The next stage is to identify what the country represents and the means by which this should be translated into a 'brand personality'. After much research, New Zealand's new brand was to be built on its four key assets: landscape; people; adventure; and culture. New Zealand was, therefore, repositioned as an adventurous destination on the edge of the Pacific Ocean under the banner of 'New Pacific Freedom' with its key values being identified as contemporary and sophisticated; innovative and creative; and spirited and free. Coupled with the highly effective 'tagline' – 100% Pure New Zealand – the country has been able to develop significantly its global appeal with particular marketing activity in Australia, Japan, the USA, UK, Germany and Singapore. With the added benefit of global media coverage from the Hollywood blockbuster *Lord of the Rings*, New Zealand has been able to benefit significantly from its branding exploits and has over the past decade firmly established itself as a quality differentiated destination.

→

Photograph 16.1	New Zealand has been particularly successful in recent years with the development of its destination brand.
	Source: Alamy Images/Bruce Percy

REFERENCE

Morgan, N.J., Pritchard, A. and Piggott, R. (2003) 'Destination branding and the role of stakeholders: The case of New Zealand', *Journal of Vacation Marketing* **9**(3), 285–99.

Source: Adapted from Morgan *et al*. (2003). For further information on New Zealand visit: http://www.newzealand.com

DISCUSSION QUESTIONS

1. What are some of the principal challenges facing a destination of your choice when determining a suitable destination brand?

2. What are some of the management challenges of implementing a brand internally to resident communities and internal stakeholders?

3. What specific issues are involved when a destination wishes to reposition itself post-crisis?

Communication

In view of the competitive forces at play, there is a strong argument for more varied approaches to the development of communication strategies for destinations. According to King (2002) much greater emphasis needs to be given to the creation and communication of holiday experiences that link key brand values and assets with the holiday aspirations and needs of key customers. In parallel King advocates a move away from a relatively passive promotional role to include greater intervention, facilitation and direction in the conversion process. The migration to an economy based on 'experience' opens the door to the establishment of ongoing, direct, two-way and networking consumer communication channels, and for key customer relationship strategies to take place with the eventual development of mass customisation marketing and delivery capabilities.

Channels

Although there have been significant developments with regard to computer reservation systems and global distribution systems, for the destination it is the growth of destination management and marketing systems that are the principal competitive tools in their quest for gaining greater control over the distribution of the destination product. Irrespective of the location, scale and type of destination in question, the development of a suitable destination management system, whether unilaterally or with other destinations, is a priority that can no longer be ignored.

Cyberspace

The emergence of the Internet and its application in the domains of tourism, travel and hospitality is significant. It has underpinned significant changing patterns of consumption, and has impacted the entire buying processes and the means by which tourism, travel and hospitality products are packaged and sold. The complexity of the destination product and the coordinating role practised by destination marketers clearly makes the development, implementation and management of destination-wide web sites particularly challenging. However, as with the rest of the wider tourism industry, it is a challenge that destinations cannot afford to ignore.

Consolidation

Greater consolidation has impacted significantly on the global tourism industry, most notably in the domains of travel in the form of airlines, hospitality in the form of large international hotel groups, and tourism in the form of intermediaries. For destinations this issue throws open a number of challenges in their attempt to counter the power imbalance that often results from such developments.

Collaboration

Destinations are difficult to organise as there are often numerous stakeholders involved, all with their own aims, goals and motivations, which have to coexist. Whether one is referring to intra-destination networks, inter-destination collaboration, relational brands, or forms of collaboration governance, this move towards the need for greater collaboration is referred to by King (2002) as the 'network economy', in that DMOs will probably enter into strategic relationships with industry partners who can together provide a seamless experience for the customer. This is because it will be the 'relevance of the experience they offer the customer, rather than the destination they promote, which will be the key ingredient for success in the future' (King, 2002: 108). In this context, collaboration is not considered a luxury but a necessity for destinations to survive in the face of considerable competition and environmental challenges. A number of benefits to be derived from cooperative public–private sector tourism organisations are provided by Poetschke (1995: 57–8). These include the reduction in antagonism through representation of all stakeholders; the avoidance of duplication through enhanced communication channels between represented sectors; and the bringing together of expertise. Benefits can also include increased funding potential through the reduction in duplicated efforts as well as industry-based taxes; the creation of a win/win situation through an increase in industry profitability and ensuing increase in government tax revenue; and the provision of infrastructure and investment funds.

MINI CASE STUDY 16.2
Edinburgh

Often described as 'the jewel in Scotland's tourism crown', the success of tourism activity in Edinburgh forms a key part of the city's economic policy. The sector employs 30,000 people, with visitors contributing in the region of £1 billion to the economy per annum. The recent creation of the Edinburgh City Region Brand confirms however that this activity should not be viewed in isolation, rather as a prime target within a broader context. This World Heritage city consistently retains its position as the UK's second most important destination and acts as a gateway for visitors to Scotland. Recent research has shown that those not having visited Edinburgh before consider the city to be on a par with York, Stratford or Chester, while those who have previously visited identify competitor destinations as Barcelona, Amsterdam and Prague. Obviously this creates some interesting challenges for those marketing the city destination and its positioning.

With regard to the management and marketing of Edinburgh, a single national tourism network was established in April 2005 via the integration of the existing national tourism organisation VisitScotland and area tourist boards. The VisitScotland Edinburgh Network Office is one of 15 UK offices which represent VisitScotland's local champions, and represent the organisation in all its activities. They ensure the achievement of local objectives linked to the national vision and strategies through developing strong partnerships with businesses, local authorities and local enterprise companies. One of the consequences of such a development is the tendency to ignore the smaller players, many of whom in the past were members of previous forms of destination management structures and tourist boards. This is particularly true of Edinburgh where the new network structure is no longer membership-based. The view in Edinburgh is that there is a need to balance the needs of the individual and of the destination by establishing the delivery of a total visitor experience, from the point of enquiry to departure, perhaps only possible via a change in attitude and view for all those involved in tourism.

Edinburgh tourism organisations have the benefit of accessing VisitScotland's consumer and market research results alongside those available from the destination's own Network Office. The advantage here is that Scotland as a whole is a relatively small destination, albeit with a vast range of products, with a recently increased marketing budget. This allows the main office to undertake research and activities on which local destinations can act. With regard to changing visitor markets, indications are that younger markets and new markets originating from Western and Eastern Europe are beginning to develop quite strongly. For the future, and to continually develop the appeal of the destination, Edinburgh has participated in national marketing campaigns to develop niche markets based around genealogy, the Freedom of Scotland, activity/outdoor breaks and golf, in addition to more locally-based festival and event developments, such as Eventful Edinburgh. Allied to this, Edinburgh announced its Inspiring Edinburgh campaign in May 2005 and supporting development of the Edinburgh City Region Brand. This aims to build on the legacy of creativity in Edinburgh to develop the destination as a place to live and work (and visit!).

Source: Adapted from Fyall and Leask (2006)

DISCUSSION QUESTIONS

1. What are the principal competitive threats facing Edinburgh and what may be some of the solutions to mitigate their impact?

2. What particular management challenges face historic urban destinations such as Edinburgh which also host many other industrial sectors and . . . residents?

DESTINATION MANAGEMENT AND MARKETING

Destination collaboration

As identified earlier in the chapter, destination management is predominantly a micro-level activity in which 'all the stakeholders carry out their individual and organisational responsibilities on a daily basis in efforts to realise the macro-level vision contained in policy, planning and development' (Ritchie and Crouch, 2003: 111). As pointed out at the beginning of this chapter, however, the fact that destinations are comprised of so many products, stakeholders, and complex management and political relationships, contributes to their being regarded as one of the most difficult 'products' to manage and market. To best manage the complexities and 'imperfections' inherent within destinations it is therefore accepted that destinations need to bring together all parties to collaborate rather than to compete, and to pool resources towards developing an integrated management and delivery system. Referred to by King as the 'network economy' (2002), destination management organisations are, in the future, recommended to enter into strategic relationships with partners who collectively can deliver a seamless visitor experience to customers. It is argued that this will occur due to the fact that it is the significance of the experience they offer the customer, rather than the destination they promote, which will be the key constituent for success in the years to come.

The UNWTO (WTO, 2002b) also recognise that there is a growing need for destinations to develop alliances with a broad range of organisations, even on occasion with potential competitors. Despite this sense of currency and urgency, collaboration among and between destinations is not a new phenomenon. For example, various forms of destination collaboration have taken place in Bali and the Caribbean. In the case of Bali, collaboration was deemed essential in overcoming the island's perceived migration 'downmarket', while in the Caribbean, cooperation among the public and private sectors in tourism was not merely desirable but a necessity in view of the particular characteristics of the tourism industry. Further studies, such as those by Darrow (1995) in the Caribbean, and Henderson (2001) in the Greater Mekong Subregion, explore the means by which destinations can work in partnership with other destinations in improving the inter-regional, inter-state and inter-destination product. Fyall and Garrod (2005: 289–90) highlight a number of advantages that exist with respect to collaboration within and among destinations. These include:

- Reduction in risk through strength in numbers and interconnectedness within and across destinations.
- Efficient and effective exchange of resources for perceived mutual benefit.
- The generation of increased visitor flows and positive economic impacts.
- The potential for collaborative initiatives to counter the threat of channel intermediary powers.
- In peripheral locations, collaboration serving as a significant vehicle to broaden the destination domain.
- The ability to counter greater standardisation in the industry through the use of innovative collaboration marketing campaigns.
- The potential to develop destination-wide reservation systems and two-way dialogue with customers through technological collaboration, whereby the emerging technologies can facilitate relationship building and customer relationship management programmes.
- Further collaboration on the Internet, so affording DMOs the ability to reach large numbers of consumers, to transmit information and offer products at a relatively low cost, to provide complete and more reliable information, to make client reservations quickly and efficiently, and to reduce the costs associated with producing and distributing printed materials.

In addition, it can be argued that such activity may be particularly useful when a country's tourism product is underdeveloped or when existing products are in an advanced stage in the product life cycle. Similarly, it can be argued that collaboration in a promotional sense often starts at the destination level at the 'national' stage of the resort development spectrum. This involves joint campaigns, with state and local government and local businesses taking place alongside campaigns between hotels and major attractions (Prideaux, 2000). Destination collaboration is, however, far from widespread. Indeed, there remain a number of constraints and drawbacks to collaboration both within and between destinations. These include:

- General mistrust and suspicion among collaborating partners due to governance or structures that are inappropriate for moving the shared project forward.

- Inability of various sectors within the destination to work together due to excuses of a political, economic, or even inter-personal nature.

- Instances where particular stakeholders fail to recognise the real value of collaboration and remain closed to the benefits of working together.

- The frequent disinterest in collaboration from 'honey-pot' attractions, where the need to work more closely together is discounted due to their own individual success in the marketplace.

- Competition between municipal authorities that administer separate geographical regions within a recognised destination resulting in inertia (Fyall and Garrod, 2005: 290).

Despite the above shortcomings, inter-organisational collaboration, often in the form of public–private sector partnerships, is a popular strategy for tourism destinations. In their comparative study of the management of tourism on the Gold Coast and Sunshine Coast, both in Queensland, Australia, Prideaux and Cooper (2002: 49) concluded that 'where there is strong co-operation between the private sector and LGAs at representative DMO level and where all key stakeholders in the tourism industry have supported a single brand strategy, the destination can anticipate considerable growth, as demonstrated by the Gold Coast'. Conversely, they concluded that 'where there is a lack of unity or where there are multiple marketing bodies with multiple brands representing the same primary destination there is considerable danger that primary market research will not be undertaken and that marketing strategy will degenerate into unco-ordinated selling campaigns' (Prideaux and Cooper, 2002: 49). Although the situation in the Sunshine Coast appears to have persisted over a long time, Heath and Wall (1992) suggest that problems related to collaboration between local authorities and destination marketing organisations can be overcome, or at least reduced, by establishing greater consensus between stakeholders on the domain 'sense of purpose' as part of a more participative management approach. Greater collaboration is, therefore, viewed as a precondition for effective brand building, which, in turn, becomes a catalyst for further growth of destinations.

Destination management organisations

Destination management organisations (DMOs) represent a recent conceptualisation of the organisation function for the management of destinations, where the 'M' emphasises total management rather than marketing. This refocused philosophy represents a more holistic approach to the management of destinations whereby the DMO is responsible for the well-being of all aspects of the destination. According to Ritchie and Crouch (2003: 73–4) it 'emphasizes the provision of a form of leadership in destination development that makes extensive use of teamwork in all DMO-led initiatives. Destination promotion is no longer the sole purpose of the DMO. While this modified role presents many new challenges, it also provides a much broader range of opportunities for ensuring destination competitiveness.' One can now legitimately argue that the DMO is the most appropriate organisational arrangement to meet fully the experiential needs of visitors. Ritchie and Crouch (2003: 175) argue that a DMO may be either a 'public sector agency or a private sector-driven organization'. Buhalis (2000: 99), meanwhile, suggests that DMOs tend to be 'part of the local, regional or national government and have political and legislative power as well as the financial means to manage resources rationally and to ensure that all stakeholders can benefit in the long term'. Irrespective of their nature, Ritchie and Crouch (2003: 175) advocate that DMOs are constituted in a manner that provides them with the following characteristics. They must:

- Be clearly identifiable as the organization responsible for coordinating and directing the efforts of the many parts of the diverse and complex tourism system.
- Command the support of all important sectors and all major actors in the tourism system.
- Be capable of influencing the decisions and actions of the many public sector agencies/ departments and private firms that directly determine the nature and quality of the tourism experience provided to visitors.
- Possess the tools necessary to stimulate and encourage the type and amount of supply development that is required by the overall tourism megapolicy.
- Be sufficiently independent and flexible to develop innovative strategies that can be implemented in a timely manner in response to rapidly evolving market and environmental conditions.

In addition to the above, South West Tourism, the regional tourism board (RTB) for the South-West of England, confirm that 'working together requires the development of a commitment to a shared agenda; effective leadership; a respect for the needs of the partners; and a plan for the contributions and benefits of all the partners. The dynamic aspect of the process requires specific goals of partnership working to be identified, performance to be evaluated, and the assessment of the continuing fit between partnership activities and community needs and priorities.' With regard to providing an overarching definition, SWT (2005: 10) define a DMO as a:

> structure which enables private and public sector tourism bodies to work together with partners and the local community to achieve better outcomes for the visitor at the destination level, as measured by the needs of the local stakeholders and visitors themselves, and involves bringing together or making better use of resources. It should also assist in improving business performance for the private sector.

Similarly, the North West Regional Development Agency (NWDA, 2004) define a DMO as:

> any organisation, at any level, which is responsible for the management of an identifiable destination. Clearly this could be a local, sub-regional, regional or national body. Due to the complex nature of destinations – where the responsibility of delivering what visitors want is divided between many different organisations and companies – destination management calls for a coalition of many organisations and interests working to a common agenda.

Although the scope of DMOs varies, in most cases they exist to build the destination, to support and bring together the trade, to help minimise business failures, particularly among SMEs, to manage the public realm, to build and develop the destination brand, represent the interests of the trade at national, regional, and subregional organisations, to develop skills and training for the trade, and to deliver an input into the planning process and wider economic development plan. Ultimately, the role of a DMO must be to enhance the long-term competitiveness of the destination.

Roles and structures

Despite the importance and significance of DMOs across the world, it is therefore surprising that no real 'blueprint' exists. That said most DMOs, although varying in their roles and tasks undertaken, demonstrate an effective internal and external focus, especially with regard to marketing. In all reality, DMOs identify and manage stakeholders, manage community relations and develop suitable publication programmes. More importantly, they stress the need to expand the number of roles and tasks to include all that is necessary to manage the

MINI CASE STUDY 16.3
Managing destinations in England's North west

Following a review of tourism in England's Northwest region, new support structures for the industry were put in place in April 2004. The new organisational structure included the closure of the former North West Tourist Board and the establishment of five new tourist boards (or destination management organisations) representing the interests of both the public and private sectors. The Northwest Regional Development Agency (NWDA) maintains overall strategic responsibility for tourism in the region in that the 'executive grouping' has devolved management and operation to the five new tourist boards, namely; Visit Chester and Cheshire, Cumbria Tourism, Lancashire and Blackpool Tourist Board, Marketing Manchester and The Mersey Partnership. Each has responsibility and expertise to lead the development and marketing of their destination, working with the local authorities, tourism businesses and other stakeholders in their area. Interestingly, not only do all five share different titles but all five are at quite different levels of maturity. Within the Northwest, tourist boards are the primary delivery partners for the NWDA when it comes to tourism. Their role is to serve as the centres of expertise and of evidence, and be at the core of subregional thinking and delivery. They have a key coordinating and leadership role, but they can only succeed in this with the active support of tourist board members, local authorities and other stakeholders.

In view of the above, each tourist board is required to lead their destination with the formation of a destination management plan that will direct their activities and those of their partner organisations. The plans are to 'address product development, market opportunities and targets, cluster development, innovation, quality and excellence, skills needs, marketing communications, performance, and regional and national linkages'. The plans also provide linkage to the regional brand strategies vis-à-vis 'attack' and 'slipstream' brands. Although each destination management plan may vary it is expected that the individual tourist boards will lead on the development of the destination; provide a membership offer where appropriate; act as the primary point of engagement with the sector at a subregional level; provide ICT services; provide information through TICs and other means to both visitors and residents; market the destination; provide information to visitors, businesses and others; foster excellence; carry out research; provide advice and support. Clearly engagement between tourist boards and local authorities is essential if this model is to succeed, and there is also the need for a high level of integration vis-à-vis ICT. In effect, local authorities are key partners for the tourist boards.

Although quite prescriptive, the destination management planning approach in general – and the more specific Strategic Marketing Framework for Tourism in England's Northwest – provides clear guidance for all stakeholders and minimises levels of ambiguity and confusion as to who does what, when, for what purpose and with what levels of funding. Within the region there is a strong belief that this approach fosters better coordination, a sharper focus, more resources and stronger partnerships. However, the engagement between local authorities, the five regional tourist boards and other stakeholders will be most productive with the provision of clear, shared objectives and a proper mechanism for ensuring the appropriate management of the region as a series of visitor destinations.

Source: Based on NWDA (2004)

DISCUSSION QUESTIONS

1. What are the benefits of collaborative working in the context of local, regional, national and international destinations?

2. What are the benefits and drawbacks of a centralised 'top-down' and decentralised 'bottom-up' approach to the management of destinations?

destination in its entirety. Ritchie and Crouch (2003: 188) argue that in 'the past, the importance of the marketing and promotion roles of the DMO were of such priority that the DMO label was understood to mean "destination *marketing* organization". It is only in recent years that DMOs have acknowledged how significant their non-marketing roles are in developing, enhancing and maintaining destination competitiveness. Nearly all progressive and effective DMOs in today's world now appreciate the importance of their more broadly based mandate and use DMO to mean "destination *management* organization".'

According to SWT (2005: 10), a DMO can be responsible for the coordination of all those properties that define the destination for visitors through the following functions. Although each will have varying degrees of direct and/or indirect impact, roles could include any mix of the following:

- strategy and planning/policy;
- representation of interest;
- product development;
- marketing;
- skills/training;
- infrastructure development;
- collection and management of information and research;
- sustainability;
- business support and advice;
- coherence, communication and the management of quality; and
- the creation of a strong unified voice for the local industry.

According to SWT (2005: 10), these 'functions', 'represent the key elements that are requirements of a competitive destination'. To achieve these functions clearly requires a large number of stakeholders working towards attaining a structure that delivers them in a mutually beneficial and efficient way.

Despite the above inclusive list of roles/functions, for many DMOs marketing remains a core focus of its activity. In this context, Pike (2004) excludes separate government departments and a number of regional bodies that are responsible for planning and policy. That said, it is difficult to make sweeping generalisations as so many national tourism organisations (NTOs), regional tourism organisations (RTOs) and convention and visitors bureaux (CVBs) vary in the roles undertaken and structures adopted. One of the challenges of comparing and contrasting the roles and structures of DMOs is the significant paucity of information on DMOs generically. Although Pike (2004) provides a worthy historical overview of their development, his text is isolated and represents one of the very few works that explore this phenomenon in any significant depth. Pike is passionate about the role of DMOs, both now and in the future, and, irrespective of their title, argues that while a 'myriad of private and public sector organisations have vested interests in different aspects of society relating to tourism, no other entity has such an active and holistic interest in the quality of the traveller experience, the host community's sense of place, and the profitability of tourism businesses' (2004: 19).

Buhalis (2000) is equally passionate and argues that DMOs should all meet four generic strategies if they are to be a success. He argues that they should:

- enhance the long-term prosperity of local people;
- delight visitors by maximising their satisfaction;
- maximise profitability of local enterprises and maximise multiplier effects; and
- optimise tourism impacts by ensuring a sustainable balance between economic benefits and socio-cultural and environmental assets.

Buhalis (2000: 109) continues by suggesting that DMOs have an overall responsibility 'for the entire destination product and through incentives and policies facilitate the development of products, which is desirable from the demand side, and at the same time does not jeopardise local resources'. In essence, he is arguing that it is the DMO that should serve as the guardian of the image and resources of the destination. One additional area where DMOs will increasingly be looked upon to take the lead is in managing the information and research needs of the destination. Related to this is the need for a suitable framework to analyse/evaluate the effectiveness of the DMO itself, work undertaken in the UK by Destination Performance UK (DPUK), representing a small beginning in what remains an under-researched area.

While the basic roles of a DMO are generally similar at all destination levels, structures put in place will depend on numerous factors, in particular the nature and type of the destination and the level of funding that is forthcoming to meet both operational and strategic targets and ensure ongoing long-term success. Although structures can vary slightly at the national regional/state/provincial level, principal differences in structure can be found at the urban/municipal/city-state level. Some DMOs are membership-based while others tend to represent a loosely connected 'federation' of supporting organisations. It is also the case that the structures of yet others are such that in all reality they merely represent a department or section of local government. With regard to the balance between the public and private sectors in the UK, it is usual for a local authority tourism department to remain in public hands, while convention and visitor bureaux are often privately controlled. Interestingly, very few, if any, countries or regions have experimented with more novel forms of organisation lying somewhere between the public and the private models. For the most part, the public sector remains 'crucial in ensuring optimal use of public tourism resources/services and a balanced sharing of costs and benefits among all the actors involved' (Manente and Minghetti, 2006: 234). For the most part, the involvement of the public sector is critical in order to preserve the local environment, the residents' quality of life, the tourists' quality of experience, and the identity of the destination as a whole. In essence, the public sector serves as an agent for development in that it creates the conditions necessary to succeed. Pike (2004) concludes that ultimately the key goals for DMOs should be to enhance destination image, increase industry profitability, reduce seasonality and ensure suitable long-term funding. To achieve this he advocates that DMOs should be responsible for industry coordination, the monitoring of service and quality standards and the enhancing of community relations.

Governance, funding and effectiveness

In view of the considerable diversity apparent with regard to roles and structures, it perhaps comes as no surprise that governance also varies considerably. That said, Poetschke (1995: 62–3) identifies four critical factors for success with regard to the governance of DMOs of globally competitive destinations:

1. a significant level of private sector control over spending;
2. understanding of the need to incorporate public sector objectives to achieve a balance between marketing and new product development;
3. a dedicated revenue stream that is not subject to annual government control; and
4. a broad, integrated mandate encompassing a function critical to developing a strong tourism industry, such as marketing, education, research and infrastructure development.

Although the orientation of the principal decision-making body, most probably a board, is also important in that orientations will vary quite considerably between an official public board, a private board, or a public–private sector partnership, each body will have to come to terms with considerable diversity, the likelihood of some representatives being unable to grasp the wider 'domain' picture, suspicions of others' sectoral interests, the probability of a cumbersome organisational name to reflect all areas covered, a regional community not fully informed on the advantages of tourism and a paucity of current and reliable statistics.

Irrespective of their structure, the majority of DMOs, at all levels, rely to a large extent on public support, i.e. funding. This proved to be particularly problematical for the former area tourist boards (ATBs) in Scotland where they crossed local political and administrative boundaries and were thus forced to lobby several councils for funding. Sources of funding for DMOs vary considerably, although the gradual reduction in funding from the public sector serves as a principal catalyst for change with greater emphasis on the need to source funds from alternative avenues. One alternative is to increase membership fees for industry members. Although a very logical and laudable rationale, it is frequently unsuccessful due to the propensity for too many stakeholders within the destination benefiting from 'free-rider' activity. One further option is the imposition of a local hotel tax. However, although relatively easy to administer it is arguably one-sided, unfair and in essence not representative of the wider visitor economy. Conceptually logical but impractical to put into practice is a tourism/ recreation tax whereby the cost of implementation often outweighs the benefit to be gained from its imposition. Finally, there is the private sector sponsorship alliance which, although considered successful in the short term, does not represent a sustainable vehicle for the longer-term funding of destinations. In addition, it has been suggested that various types of user fees and more importance placed on partnership and buy-in programmes be advocated.

Related to the above, there are also various means by which a budget, most notably in the public sector, can be determined, for example, by the size of the host population, visitor numbers, as a ratio of visitor spend, by the number of commercial accommodation beds/ rooms, and/or the number of taxpayers/ratepayers. Pike (2004: 51–2) suggests that each of these will be influenced by the local situation vis-à-vis the local political situation, the stage of the destination on the tourism area life cycle (TALC) and the state of maturity of the local industry, the economic importance of tourism relative to other industries, and the overall history of the DMO and its current structure.

One of the perennial problems of destination management has been the extent to which the contribution of DMO efforts to the overall success of the destination can be measured. Pike (2004: 36) argues that the 'lack of suitable data leaves the industry open to attack from politicians and other industries seeking justification for funding from the public purse'. Pike adds that 'isolating and quantifying a DMO's contribution to destination competitiveness is currently an impossible task. Ultimately the success of a destination will be as a result of a combination of factors, many of which will be exogenous to the DMO' (Pike, 2004: 190).

CONCLUSION

Given the foremost position of destinations in the tourism system it is a little surprising that the UNWTO waited so long to conduct an international forum on destination management and that so few academic texts have explored the operations and dynamics of DMOs to date (WTO, 2002a). This is also true of academic research published in journals where there remains a distinct paucity of material that explores the origins, nature, organisational and governance structures, sources of funding and overall performance aspects of DMOs. Further areas lacking research rigour in this domain include strategic planning and implementation, destination competitiveness, destination positioning, human resource management, destination brand management and integrated marketing communications (Pike, 2004).

One of the common themes emerging throughout this chapter is the issue of collaboration. For collaboration to succeed the DMO needs to act as a strong unifying force that is able to bring all component parts of the destination together and develop it in its entirety. Effective collaboration is key while the need to remain cognisant of all those issues and forces impacting on their future direction is vital if destinations are to keep abreast of competitors. In many ways destinations have not changed over the years; they have always been difficult products to manage. What has changed is the quite significant forces for change existing in the macro and micro environments and their long-term impact on the future management of destinations. According to Pike (2004: 2) the vast majority of DMOs, irrespective of where they are in the world, share 'a common range of political and resource-based challenges not faced by private sector tourism businesses'. The most notable challenge is that of year-on-year reductions in contributions from the public purse. This factor alone represents a significant catalyst for change which single-handedly may change how the industry and general public view destinations, especially with regard to boundaries.

DMOs are clearly emerging as the 'glue' that bonds together stakeholders at the destination in their search for increasing competitiveness and long-term sustainability. Costa and Buhalis (2006: 245) add that 'DMOs will play a critical role in ensuring that business opportunities are planned and managed within the context of regional development, and therefore will be contributing to optimization of economic, physical and social impacts' in the years ahead. Nevertheless, evidence suggests that many tourism destinations, whether at a national, regional or local level, still retain a narrow perspective of their process of evolution (Manente and Minghetti, 2006). The same authors continue by asking whether traditional tourism destinations in the mature phase of their life cycle will be able to make an evolutionary leap, or whether in fact competition will be driven by new emerging destinations that see tourism as an important factor of economic development and can learn from other territorial experiences. To conclude, although present across many countries, DMOs are a relatively new phenomenon in many parts of the world where their rationale for establishment, roles and structures, and governance and funding remain unclear. In theory at least, however, they serve as the most appropriate organisational structures for the effective management of destinations.

SELF-CHECK QUESTIONS

1. What are the principal differences in the markets attracted to different types of destinations?

2. What are the differences between 'competitive' and 'comparative' advantage in the context of destinations?

3. Identify five key trends impacting future visitation patterns to urban and coastal destinations.

4. Why is the management of rural destinations particularly challenging?

5. What is the difference between a destination management organisation and a destination management partnership?

ESSAY QUESTIONS

1. A number of commentators argue that destinations are one of the most difficult products to manage. Critically discuss this viewpoint, providing contemporary examples to substantiate your answer.

2. What are the most critical factors in the external environment impacting on the future management of destinations? For a destination of your choice, what strategies do you recommend it adopts to mitigate such impacts?

3. To what extent can urban destinations truly differentiate themselves in the marketplace?

4. What are the benefits and drawbacks of destination branding and why is it that destinations generally lag behind other sectors of the tourism industry in developing suitable branding strategies?

5. What do you consider to be the most appropriate metrics for DMOs to monitor and measure their performance?

ANNOTATED FURTHER READING

Books and articles

Pike, S. (2004) *Destination Marketing Organisations*, Elsevier, Oxford.
This highly readable book is one of very few texts to explore the origins, dynamics and trends of destination management organisations across a whole host of case settings. With a thorough examination of destination image, identity and branding, the book provides a comprehensive overview of the management of destinations.

Ritchie, J.R.B. and Crouch, G. (2003) *The Competitive Destination: A Sustainable Tourism Perspective*, CABI Publishing, Oxford.
This landmark text provides a hugely comprehensive and thorough approach to the study of destinations. It distinguishes clearly between comparative and competitive advantage, introduces a holistic and conceptual model for the study of destinations, and outlines in considerable depth the individual components of the model which include the global macro-environment; the competitive micro environment; core resources and attractors; supporting factors and resources; destination policy, planning and development; destination management; and qualifying and amplifying determinants.

Vanhove, N. (2005) *The Economics of Tourism Destinations*, Elsevier Butterworth Heinemann, Oxford.
This book provides a very useful synthesis of the economic aspects of tourism destinations. It combines theory and practice, emphasises new aspects including the measurement of tourism, supply trends and competition models, and discusses the role of tourism in a development strategy. With a myriad of case examples this is an essential text for both academics and practitioners involved in the management of destinations.

Web sites

http://www.destinationmarketing.org
This site is the home of Destination Marketing Association International (DMAI) and represents a comprehensive resource for official destination marketing organisations. The DMAI is dedicated to improving the effectiveness of over 1,300 professionals from over 600 DMOs in more than 25 countries. For students, the site is a useful hub for educational resources related to destinations and destination management.

http://www.dpuk.org.uk
Destination Performance UK is the membership organisation for local authority tourism services committed to the principles of performance management and best practice. The site serves as a very useful hub for destination performance-related events, activities and publications and although primarily for professional use is mostly accessible to academics interested in this field.

http://www.tmi.org.uk
This site is the home of the Tourism Management Institute, the professional institute for destination management in the UK. The site serves as a very useful point of contact for events, destination management reports, policy documents and academic articles, and a means of engaging with the wider destination and visitor economy community in the UK.

References cited

Bennett, O. (1999) 'Destination marketing into the next century', *Journal of Vacation Marketing* 6(1), 48–54.

Buhalis, D. (2000) 'Marketing: the competitive destination of the future', *Tourism Management* 21(1), 97–116.

Costa, C. and Buhalis, D. (2006) Conclusion: Tourism futures, pp. 241–6 in Buhalis, D. and Costa, C. (eds) *Tourism Business Frontiers: Consumers, Products and Industry*. Elsevier Butterworth Heinemann, Oxford.

Darrow, K. (1995) 'A partnership model for nature tourism in the eastern Caribbean islands', *Journal of Travel Research* **33**(3), 48–51.

Dwyer, L. and Kim, C. (2003) 'Destination competitiveness: Determinants and indicators', *Current Issues in Tourism* **6**(5), 346–69.

Fyall, A. and Garrod, B. (2005) *Tourism Marketing: A Collaborative Approach*, Channel View, Clevedon.

Fyall, A., Garrod, B. and Tosun, C. (2006) Destination marketing: A framework for future research, pp. 75–86 in Kozak, M. and Andreu, L. (eds) *Progress in Tourism Marketing*, Elsevier, Oxford.

Fyall, A. and Leask, A. (2006) Destination marketing: future issues – strategic challenges. *Cutting Edge Research in Tourism: New Directions, Challenges and Applications*. University of Surrey, 6–9 June 2006.

Heath, E. and Wall, G. (1992) *Marketing Tourism Destinations: A Strategic Planning Approach*, Wiley, New York.

Henderson, J. (2001) 'Strategic alliances and destination marketing in the Greater Mekong Subregion', *Pacific Tourism Review* **4**(4), 149–59.

King, J. (2002) 'Destination marketing organisations: Connecting the experience rather than promoting the place', *Journal of Vacation Marketing* **8**(2), 105–8.

Leiper, N. (1995) *Tourism Management*. TAFE Publications, Collingwood, Victoria.

Manente, M. and Minghetti, V. (2006) Destination management organizations and actors, pp. 228–37 in Buhalis, D. and Costa, C. (eds) *Tourism Business Frontiers: Consumers, Products and Industry*. Elsevier Butterworth Heinemann, Oxford.

NWDA (2004) *Great Destinations: A Partnership Approach to Tourism in England's North-west*. North-west Regional Development Agency, Warrington.

Pedro, A. (2006) Urbanization and second-home tourism, pp. 85–93 in Buhalis, D. and Costa, C. (eds) *Tourism Business Frontiers: Consumers, Products and Industry*. Elsevier Butterworth Heinemann, Oxford.

Pike, S. (2004) *Destination Marketing Organisations*. Elsevier, Oxford.

Poetschke, B. (1995) Key success factors for public/private sector partnerships in island tourism planning, in Conlin, M.V. and Baum, T. (eds) *Island Tourism*, Wiley, Chichester.

Poon, A. (1993) *Tourism, Technology and Competitive Strategies*, CABI, Oxford.

Porter, M. (1998) 'Clusters and the new economics of competition', *Harvard Business Review* (Nov–Dec), 77–90.

Prideaux, B. (2000) 'The resort development spectrum: A new approach to modelling resort development', *Tourism Management* **21**(3), 225–40.

Prideaux, B. and Cooper, C. (2002) 'Marketing and destination growth: A symbiotic relationship or simple coincidence?' *Journal of Vacation Marketing* **9**(1), 35–51.

Ritchie, J.R.B. and Crouch, G.I. (2003) *The Competitive Destination: A Sustainable Tourism Perspective*. CABI, Oxford.

Scott, N., Parfitt, N. and Laws, E. (2000) Destination Management: Co-operative marketing, a case study of Port Douglas Brand, pp. 198–221 in Faulkner, B., Moscardo, G. and Laws, E. (eds) *Tourism in the 21st Century*, Continuum, London.

SWT (2005) *South West Tourism: Destination Management Organisation Delivery Plan*. South West Tourism, Exeter.

WTO (2002a) *Thinktank*, WTO, Madrid.

WTO (2002b) *Tourism in the Age of Alliances, Mergers and Acquisitions*, WTO, Madrid.

MAJOR CASE STUDY 16.1
London: Responding to disaster

INTRODUCTION

Tourism represents a key component of the London economy. It accounts for approximately 10% of London's GDP and approximately 8% of the capital's workforce. Total tourism spending amounts to around £15 billion per annum with a 1% sustained increase in overseas visits to London corresponding to a 1.28% increase in jobs (Visit London, 2006a). For domestic visits, the equivalent figure is 0.34%. Overseas visitors also represent major investors in London's cultural landscape in that they purchase approximately 30% of theatre tickets and account for half of all visits to London attractions (Visit London, 2006a). With regard to tourist expenditure per trip, it is estimated that London requires 3.5 domestic visitors and 2 near-European visitors to compensate for the loss of one American visitor (GLA Economics, 2003b). This imbalance is indicative of the structural weakness of London's tourism position and its over-reliance on individual markets. London is thus disproportionately reliant on overseas tourism and is, therefore, particularly vulnerable to unpredictable external events. In addition, London plays an important role in welcoming overseas visitors who then travel to other destinations across the UK. In fact, over half of all overseas visitors spend time in London while 45% come only to London. In addition, approximately 75% of all overseas visitors pass through London as their 'gateway' to the UK (Visit London, 2006b). London is unusual, however, in that although business visitors contribute significantly to the tourist economy, it is largely reliant on high-value overseas leisure markets.

In response to the succession of natural and man-made threats in recent years, many destinations have been forced to re-evaluate their marketing strategies. London is no exception, for in 2001 it was estimated to have lost £1.1 billion in tourist receipts due to the combined effect of foot and mouth disease (FMD) and 9/11 (GLA Economics, 2003a). With the launch of a second war in Iraq early in 2003, initial estimates were that London was to lose a further £0.5 billion. Although considerable, this projection excluded the threat of a direct terrorist attack on London itself. Unfortunately it is now common to hear of 'risk management', 'destination recovery' and 'crisis management' as a matter of course in relation to the management of destinations.

This case study explores London's particular response to a series of crises and explores the specific role played by the Mayor of London in the development of tourism within the city.

LONDON'S DISASTER RESPONSE

To limit the damage caused to London's tourism economy from the succession of negative external threats, the Mayor's Office (MO) instigated the launch of the London Tourism Recovery Group (LTRG) in the first quarter of 2003. The LTRG was a permanent contingency framework designed to support the tourism and hospitality sector in London in times of emergency. Membership of the LTRG included representatives from the London Development Agency (LDA), the Greater London Authority (GLA), MO, Visit Britain (VB), Visit London (VL), the Mayor's Advisory Group, an independent member, and a member from the Tourism Alliance. With the intention of being the principal 'emergency' group of its type, LTRG concluded that the problems facing tourism in London required a market-led response and as such formed a Special Marketing Steering Group early in March 2003. One of its first actions was to identify lessons to be learned from London's previous emergency initiative for the recovery of tourism back in 2001: the London Tourism Action Group (LTAG).

Financed to the value of £4 million, the establishment of LTAG represented a temporary, short-term recovery initiative developed and implemented in an extremely tight timescale. LTAG was not linked specifically to a wider tourism strategy for London and was dominated by discount and value-driven offers. The activities of LTAG were the first significant evidence of cooperation between the key agencies supporting tourism in London, as it was implemented in a strategic vacuum that was predominantly 'bottom up' in nature. A significant outcome of the audit of LTAG was the proposal for a disaster marketing toolkit. The toolkit consisted of a set of guiding principles which to varying degrees underpinned the later recovery initiative. Overall, however, a number of key lessons arose from the LTAG initiative. First, a market-led response was deemed preferable to fragmented, small-scale assistance to suppliers with limited guarantees of success while it was believed that greater effectiveness could

Photograph 16.2   London represents a major iconic 'capital city' destination and is one of the most visited cities in the world.
Source: Britain on View/Derek Croucher

be derived if a single organisation could serve as the delivery vehicle. Significant funds were also deemed necessary for a 'step change' in marketing to take place while there was clearly a need for the establishment of a framework for coordination of key parties in the event of a crisis by consultation with the interested parties. Finally, there was a need to standardise the set-up and procurement for an emergency response team that would expedite and simplify the response as was there a need to establish a dedicated tourism team for the development of tourism within the LDA.

In view of the above lessons, the Special Marketing Steering Group advocated a Tourism Industry Recovery Plan (TIRP) for London in response to the indicators identifying extreme negative impacts on London tourism if no emergency action were to be undertaken. TIRP provided the strategic backbone to emergency action and served as a guiding framework to facilitate the choice of marketing strategies and actions to stabilise London's tourism economy in a

time of considerable unease and market turbulence. TIRP was designed as a fully-integrated marketing programme that adopted five separate but related phases. Phase 1 was a '2-for-1' campaign run by the Association of Train Operating Companies (ATOC) that was already in place whereby the TIRP agreed to an extension to the scheme. The campaign was supported by 15 train operating companies. Phase 2 represented a campaign to encourage Londoners and those living within the M25 area to use the tourism facilities in London by offering discounts on attractions, restaurants and theatres. A number of partners were included from across the hospitality and restaurant, retailing and media sectors. The aim of this phase was to generate more visits to London and support the economic recovery of the important tourism and leisure sector. It was the first ever campaign to be aimed at the local market: targeting Londoners and visitors to London, to encourage them to get out and about and enjoy the best of the capital. After the 'local' nature of

Phases 1 and 2, Phases 3 and 4 represented major image-led campaigns complemented by value offers from commercial partners. These two phases were attempts to combat a continued downturn in forward bookings, visitor arrivals and spend from the domestic, near-Europe and international markets.

The gradual decline in overseas visitors coming to London in the fourth quarter and the limited profile of London as a destination to spend Christmas and the New Year together served as the catalysts for Phase 5 of TIRP. Chronologically following Phases 3 and 4, Phase 5 ran from October 2003 to January 2004, with a particular focus on the period 26 December–4 January. With target markets identified as London and the UK, France, Germany and the Republic of Ireland, the principal objectives were to drive business into the hotels sector, to present London in an interesting and 'surprising' manner, and to help overcome negative perceptions of London's ability to stage large public scale events by generating positive coverage in the UK and internationally. To meet the above, a two-pronged strategy was deemed appropriate. The first aspect was to enhance the quality of information available to prospective travellers throughout this period and to reinforce the reasons to come to London in conjunction with a call to action featuring strong value-led accommodation offers. The second aspect was the organisation of a New Year's Eve event to raise the profile of London as a world-class destination in support of the London 2012 Olympic bid. Although funded and managed separately, the event was a core component of Phase 5.

Phase 5 represented an innovative aspect of TIRP in that it was designed to boost visitors, particularly from overseas, coming to London in the fourth quarter and raise the profile of London as a destination to spend Christmas and the New Year. Through a combination of an events-led package with key travel and accommodation partners, and the organisation of a New Year's Eve event to raise the profile of London as a world-class destination in support of the London 2012 Olympic bid, Phase 5 brought the emergency action to a close.

CONCLUSION

Despite the problems encountered by London in recent years, more visitors are coming to London than ever before. Although not wholly attributable to London's response to disaster it is fair to assume that the speed and confidence of the Mayor and related authorities in developing TIRP was a major factor in maintaining, and in fact growing, London's presence in the marketplace. All acts of terror impact tourism negatively, and the challenge for the future is for the authorities to minimise the negative impacts of such actions in the short, medium and longer term. Most importantly, however, to maintain and build on its position in the world as a leading 'iconic' city destination London needs continually to develop its market and diversify its proposition. The theme of market development represents one of the four pillars of the Mayor of London's Tourism Strategy and has at its core four principal targets: the need to develop markets and reduce dependency on any one market; the need to explore and develop markets that will promote diverse and dispersed tourism business and expand the portfolio of London's offer; to increase the appeal of London as a tourist destination while managing the costs of tourism and spreading the benefits to all London's communities; and to promote, support and actively develop London's role as the principal 'gateway' to the UK. If these four targets can be achieved then London stands an excellent chance of long-term, sustainable growth.

Source: Adapted from Ladkin *et al.* (2006)

REFERENCES

GLA Economics (2003a) *London's Economy Today*, Issue 9: May, GLA Economics, London.

GLA Economics (2003b) *Impact of Gulf War or Terrorist Attack on London's Economy*, GLA Economics, London.

Ladkin, A., Fyall, A., Fletcher, J. and Shipway, R. (2006). London tourism: Devolution, disaster and diversification. CAUTHE *Australian Tourism and Hospitality Research Conference*, Victoria University, Melbourne, Australia, February 2006.

Visit London (2006a) 'The importance of tourism in *London*', http://www.visitlondon.com.

Visit London (2006b) 'Growth in overseas visitors to London to take visitor count to 26.6m', http://www.visitlondon.com.

DISCUSSION QUESTIONS

1. By what means can a destination like London continue to differentiate itself in the international marketplace?

2. What are the benefits and drawbacks to major destinations of implementing price-based promotional campaigns in order to stimulate visitor demand post-crisis?

3. What are the short-, medium- and longer-term challenges for London if it wishes to attract new markets from Eastern Europe, India and China and so reduce its reliance on traditional markets including the United States?

PART 4

MARKETING FOR TOURISM

Photograph: Houses of Parliament, London, England

INTRODUCTION

Marketing is assuming an ever more important role given the lack of stability of world markets. The tourism market will never be the same again given the new realisation that terrorism, weather-induced catastrophes and health-related problems can affect generating countries and tourist demand behaviour. The turn of this century has produced turbulence of an economic, social and increasingly political nature. In turn this has subsequently led to changes in the consumption patterns of travel around the world. Many international tourism companies and destination markets have experienced a softening of demand and reduction in average daily expenditure. The reasons include factors such as over-forecasting and investing in expansion of the tourism supply side which in turn created risk and excessive debt. In addition, other events have compounded the problems of tourism companies whereby the risk of illness, such as SARS in humans or foot and mouth in animals, natural disasters such as tsunamis, ongoing terrorist activity and subsequent conflict have occurred.

All tourism activity is changing from a relaxed thrill and experience of the trip to some apprehension of what may be the downside risk. Given the need for steady demand, the role of marketing will become increasingly important for tourism organisations, operating in both public and private sectors, as they continue to strive to protect and improve their market share.

The process of marketing and its management provides companies and organisations with the many complex tools to affect demand in target markets. It is a complex area that, as this section highlights, requires expertise and experience for success. In this section, we provide a comprehensive evaluation of all aspects of the management of tourism marketing including the strategies and tools that may be applied to deliver the tourism product effectively and efficiently to satisfy the tourism consumer.

In Chapter 17, Managing Marketing for Tourism, we begin by looking at the historical development of marketing in general and how its roots have influenced the application of marketing theory to the tourism product in particular. While marketing in one form or another has been in existence for centuries, the relative recency of sophisticated techniques and an awareness of services marketing requirements have meant that current marketing is evolving rapidly to suit the needs of the tourism industry. We also introduce and discuss the characteristics of the service product such as intangibility, perishability and inseparability which, it is argued, differentiate the tourism product from others. In addition, we outline other characteristics related to the notion of risk which also distinguish the tourism product from manufactured goods. To combat the risk brought about by the characteristics of the product, the concept of quality – and its management – has become a prevailing force in tourism marketing: the lack of control over the service process, which is essentially an unpredictable human encounter, has become a prime target for the application of quality techniques to standardise the delivery of the product. We present key models in respect of the service delivery system appropriate to the tourism industry and outline some of the criticisms that have been levelled at tourism marketing.

Chapter 18, Marketing Planning, is concerned with the introduction of tactical and strategic marketing planning procedures in respect of the tourism product. We define marketing planning and emphasise its role and application to the diverse sectors which, when amalgamated, form the tourism industry. We review the benefits and purposes of marketing planning, consider the structure of a marketing plan and explore the implications of neglecting tourism marketing planning.

Chapter 19, Marketing Mix Applications, relates to the **marketing mix**. This is a key strategic tool which is integral to the effective manipulation of the tourism product and the successful implementation of marketing planning procedures. However, the fundamental starting point for the creation of a successful marketing mix strategy is the definition of target markets since this will dictate the direction of the elements of the marketing mix and provide a focus for all marketing mix decisions and activity.

The final chapter in this part, Chapter 20, provides us with an understanding of how e-tourism has led to a new way of doing business for many small as well as large companies. Tourism is an industry which is characterised by the need for intense levels of exchange of information. It is also a price-sensitive industry where cost control is important. These factors have heralded the use of information technology. As such the tourism industry has undergone both rapid as well as radical change. It is therefore of vital importance that any student of tourism understands the dynamics and applications associated with these changes.

Thus, Part 4 presents a comprehensive approach to the issues and considerations of the marketing of tourism, together with aspects of distribution through information technology. However, the application of marketing management techniques in the tourism industry can be hampered by a number of factors that are inherent in the nature of tourism itself:

- First, it has been suggested that while the tourism product is sufficiently distinctive to demand a unique marketing approach, the result of this has been that marketing strategies, tools and techniques in tourism are less evolved and advanced than in other industries.
- Secondly, the relative immaturity and diversity of the tourism industry has overlooked the need to take into account the unique characteristics of tourism and the complexity of its products.
- Thirdly, the predominant practice in tourism is developing managers from grass roots. The implications of this are that while they may be good generalists few have the marketing training and expertise necessary to maximise marketing potential.
- Fourthly, many enterprises in tourism are small operations which have neither the expertise nor the resources to devote to a fully fledged marketing management approach.
- Finally, the application of technology in tourism has placed a number of pressures on organisations in relation to the requirement to understand how to harness possible applications and improvements for their business.

While some of these criticisms are accurate there have been improvements and changes in the tourism industry. The unique nature of the tourism product is recognised far more by marketers and there is now a body of knowledge and a series of techniques for marketing in the service industries. These are outlined throughout the next chapters. The tourism industry does, however, create its own handicaps to effective marketing:

- Data relating to the market and to the actions of competitors are often weak or scarce.
- A short-term outlook prevails, denying a carefully structured and strategic marketing planning approach.
- Managers in tourism tend to have risen through the ranks and to be generalists. The organisation of the industry thus militates against the development of specialists in tourism marketing.
- In addition, it is important to make the point that the tourism industry is subject to governmental and European regulation of its activities, and consumer protection is well developed in tourism. These factors may be instrumental in restricting the marketing options of a tourism company.

Public sector organisations in tourism are also somewhat handicapped in adopting a true marketing orientation. It is, for example, not uncommon to find visitor and convention bureaux with the following problems:

- They may be hidebound by government personnel operating guidelines in terms of working hours and remuneration of staff.
- They may possess insufficient resources to build a presence in the marketplace, particularly in respect of the international arena and information technology.
- They may lack sufficient marketing expertise.
- They may have little or no control over the quality of the product they are marketing.

This section clearly emphasises the interlinkages that characterise the tourism industry. For example, the nature of tourism demand is inextricably linked to marketing of the product and the manipulation of the marketing mix to attract pre-identified **segments**. Moreover, marketing is also linked to the supply of tourism at the destination being marketed. Therefore, if the destination is to sustain its market share, then the range and quality of the attractions and facilities on offer need to live up to those promises as communicated to target market(s) via the marketing process.

Marketing is, therefore, an important tool in an industry where loyalty in both the distribution chain and to the company is low. Government organisations often find it more cost-effective to market to intermediaries and carriers or enter into joint promotions rather than market directly to potential travellers. Furthermore, due to the pressures of oversupply of capacity in many sectors of the tourism industry marketing is becoming a more important function and we would contend that improving training and education among the tourism workforce, coupled with the realities of increasingly intense competition, are encouraging a new emphasis on marketing management and a greater marketing orientation within the industry.

CHAPTER 17
Managing Marketing for Tourism

LEARNING OUTCOMES

The objective of this chapter is to provide the reader with a comprehensive introduction to marketing as it relates to the tourism industry. By the end of this chapter, therefore, you will:

- understand the concept of marketing, what it is and how it has developed into its current form;
- be able to differentiate between selling and marketing;
- recognise that companies may have different business philosophies and be able to identify the implications of these differences for marketing;
- appreciate the importance of value creation as part of the process of marketing management;
- appreciate the importance of the characteristics of the service product and the implications of these differentiating characteristics for the approach an organisation might adopt for its marketing effort;
- recognise that the purchase of tourism products is associated with the need for quality management and the reduction of perceived risk; and
- be familiar with the key criticisms targeted at tourism marketing and the problems of properly utilising tourism marketing techniques.

Photograph: Sydney Opera House, Australia © Hannah Cox

INTRODUCTION

In this chapter we introduce the evolution and concept of marketing as it applies to tourism. We demonstrate that tourism marketing has emerged as a result of business and social changes which have occurred throughout the past decades as a reaction to the conditions that impinge on business operations. However, while we are able to identify different business philosophies that have influenced the adoption of a marketing orientation and the application of the marketing concept, a fuller understanding of marketing lies in the way marketing management functions in attempting to create and maximise consumer value and satisfactions. In addition, we show that marketing management related to tourism cannot ignore the principal characteristics that set tourism apart from other products. The management of tourism cannot be divorced from the management of service and quality and the tasks related to these are also explored in detail.

WHAT IS MARKETING?

Tourism can be traced back for centuries but because the elements of the product and conditions of the marketplace have changed so enormously in the last few decades there has been a corresponding requirement for a change in business methods. This has led to the adoption and use of tourism marketing. Some believe that marketing is primarily associated with forms of promotion and communication that have been paid for out of marketing budgets. However, this is a very narrow interpretation of the activity of marketing and, as we shall see, marketing is far more than the promotion of a product. This forms only *one* aspect of marketing.

It is often stated that we live in an era of marketing, but what is marketing? One way of attempting to answer the question 'what is marketing?' is to examine accepted definitions. Although it is very easy to describe what the term marketing means, it is far more difficult to describe the practice of marketing. This is because a central tenet of marketing is the body of underlying concepts that form the general guide for organisational and managerial thinking, planning and action. Consequently, for a comprehensive understanding of marketing it is necessary to learn the underlying concepts.

THE EVOLUTION OF MARKETING

Marketing has evolved against a background of economic and business pressures. These pressures have required an increased focus on the adoption of a series of managerial measures based upon satisfying consumer needs. The key to the importance of marketing within tourism has been the level of economic growth in past years which has led to subsequent improvements in living standards, an enlargement of the population and increases in discretionary time. Such early changes led Disney management in 1955 to launch the Disneyland theme park concept and in the same year McDonald's to open its first fast-food restaurant.

Often the need for change has been forced upon the industry because of the changes that have occurred in relation to consumer and market forces. Modern tourism marketing has emerged as a business reaction to changes in the social and economic environment, with the most successful companies or tourist bodies having provided the right organisational structure and product offering for the consumer or visitor. This relies as much upon an approach or attitude to business or the market as it does to specific management expertise. Marketing is therefore initially a philosophy that relies on the art and science of different managerial approaches.

Photograph 17.1	Tourism marketing has been carried out over many years.
	Source: Mary Evans Picture Library

A survey of the literature reveals an account of the history of marketing and modern business practice as having developed in three distinct stages (adapted from Gilbert and Bailey, 1990):

1. **The production era.** This occurred when there was a belief that if products were priced cheaply enough they would be purchased. Therefore, it was important to supply products to the marketplace with the emphasis on consistently reducing costs. The focus of management was on increasing efficiency of production which involved an *inward, product-orientated* emphasis rather than an outward, market-orientated emphasis. The main focus for managers at the time was a concern for improving production capacity, financing expansion, having quality and cost control and meeting the rise in demand. The overriding objective for management was the development of a standardised product which could be offered at the lowest price to the market. The market was characterised by a lack of problems with demand and as such managers focused on process and systems and not the customer. Nowadays, in destinations that have high demand, this approach on process, which ignores the importance of the customer, can be recognised in many aspects of the delivery of the tourism product.

2. **The sales era.** This was an evolutionary phase where companies attempted *to sell the products they had formulated without assessing the acceptability of the product or offer.* The problem is often one of a market with declining demand and surplus capacity, which in turn leads to a search for more effective means of selling. We can recognise this today in declining destinations where hotels or restaurants face greater competition, and there is

often a shift to increase promotional and sales efforts to improve demand. However, there is little analysis as to the reasons for the problems as the belief is that the product is acceptable. In the sales era companies attempted to influence demand and tailor it *to meet their supply* but primarily through simple sales techniques.

3. **The marketing era.** This era is characterised by a reversal of the preceding philosophy as organisations started to provide the products they could sell, *rather* than trying to sell what they had produced or formulated. Organisations adopted a consumer-led approach and concentrated on improving the marketing mix. This era was effectively based upon the recognition that meeting customer needs and providing consumer satisfaction proved the most *effective basis* for planning and that an organisation has to be *outward-looking* to be successful. The philosophy of this era is that tourism business activity has to recognise the customer as the central driving force of an activity that realises survival and prosperity is based upon meeting individual customer needs.

There are continuing arguments as to the dates of the above eras leading up to marketing as we understand it today. Moreover, some question whether they can be treated as discrete periods at all. For our purposes, in the majority of texts, the marketing era is identified to have been established from the 1950s onward. The interesting aspect of living in today's marketing era is that we can still find tourism companies which act as if they are in a preceding era. The important factors that have ushered in marketing during the past half-century are as follows:

- The increases in demand were at a lower rate than the rises in productivity. In tourism, this culminated in an oversupply of accommodation in specific locations, and of aircraft seats on important routes and too many inefficient companies in the marketplace. The increase in competition and the risks associated with the tourism marketplace led to the increased use of marketing. The business system can be viewed as an organism that is concerned with survival and proliferation. Following this argument, when a business system is threatened it will take functional steps to improve the situation. As marketing can provide for tactical change and modification of the system, in times of risk where there is oversupply and market saturation, marketing assumes a much more important role.

- The consumer was becoming more affluent and therefore it was possible to develop products that could be sold using a range of non-price attributes. This required the development of methods designed to create or change consumer attitudes and beliefs.

- The distance between the tourism product provider and tourist has been continually increasing. This led to a need for marketing research related to the gathering of information on market trends, evaluating levels of satisfaction and understanding consumer behaviour.

- New tourism and hospitality products were being launched which required more emphasis on marketing. For example, the large attractions that have been developed in different countries and the setting up of low-cost airlines have required high levels of demand to make them viable.

- As society developed, the mass market splintered into a number of sub-markets, while at the same time the mass market became increasingly difficult to reach. This was due to the increase in specialist media and the potential for a whole range of alternative leisure pursuits. The changes required improved expertise in the segmentation of markets and the provision of different marketing mix strategies which would maximise demand for individual segments.

DEFINITIONS AND CONCEPTS OF MARKETING

Any conceptual definition of a business discipline is, by nature of its condensed form, a limited abstraction of values, techniques and practices which are the focus of its activity. Therefore, no single definition can be comprehensive enough to describe the true essence or complexity of marketing. Various definitions of marketing have been offered based upon the values prevalent at the time. A popular early definition utilised for many years stressed marketing as being a managerial process of providing the right product, in the right place, at the right time and at the right price. This definition is mechanistic and stresses the provision of the product offer without due regard to any of the actors or functions involved in the process.

No definition of marketing can ever disregard the importance of Philip Kotler. He has established himself as the most widely referenced proponent of general marketing theory. Kotler and Keller (2006) define marketing as: 'a societal process by which individuals and groups obtain what they need and want through creating, offering and freely exchanging products and services of value with others'. Kotler argues that the definition has a social basis and is built on the main concepts of wants, needs, demands, satisfactions of marketing and marketers because they are central to the study of marketing. For him, marketing management is the art and science of choosing target markets and getting, keeping, and growing customers through creating, delivering and communicating superior customer value. In 1984 the British Chartered Institute of Marketing defined marketing as: 'the management process responsible for identifying, anticipating and satisfying customers' requirements profitably'.

An examination of both definitions reveals significant core similarities. On comparison it is found that both stress marketing as a process. Such approaches provide a concept as one where the process is established by way of a marketing channel connecting the (tourism) organisation with its market. This is based upon management aiming to convert customer purchasing power into effective demand. In addition the British Chartered Institute clarifies the management responsibility to be one of assessment of consumer demand through the identification and anticipation of customer requirements. This denotes the importance of research and analysis as part of this process.

One important difference is that Kotler's definition is more appropriate to non-profit organisations where there is free entrance or subsidisation towards the cost of a service. It is also more fitting when facilitators of tourism such as tourist boards are considered.

However, the most important aspect, and one that should be at the heart of any definition of marketing, is the emphasis placed on the consumer's needs as the origin of all of the organisation's effort. The **marketing concept** has been expressed in many succinct ways from the: 'Have it your way' from Burger King, to 'You're the boss' of United Airlines. This is the basis of the modern marketing concept whereby the principal means of success is based not only on identifying different consumer needs but also on delivering a tourist product whose experiences provide sets of satisfactions that are preferable to those of the competitors. In addition these satisfactions have to be delivered with attention to their cost-effectiveness, since marketing has to be evaluated on the basis of its efficiency of expenditure.

We have seen how the definitions of marketing lead to the marketing concept, whereby the consumer is the driving force for all business activities. Prior to the introduction and discussion about the notion of the marketing concept we will emphasise the aspects of delivering value prior to differentiating the principles and activities associated with marketing and selling.

The concept of value within tourism

As mentioned above, the aspect of delivering superior value is an important part of the marketing management approach. This means companies have to find ways to ensure they optimise the delivery of value. As such there is a requirement for a way of uncovering the value sought by the customer, the development of that within the company and then the delivery of optimum value to the end customer (see Table 17.1).

The value of a tourism product incorporates a number of different aspects which include the perception of price, quality and image as well as the economic and social aspects of the consumer. Consumers of today have far more information with which to make comparisons

Table 17.1	A system for delivering value		
Approaches	**Uncovering value needs**	**Developing value**	**Delivering value**
Gathering/analytical	Data/feedback of company representatives, surveys, etc.	Operations/customer interfaces and touch points	Logistics/product quality, service
Organisational	Interpretation of customer requirements and resultant expected organisational competencies	Training/motivation of staff and working with suppliers who also add quality	Improved attitudes and behaviour of employee interfaces

between alternative offers. As we are dealing with perceptions these will differ as they are based upon the available time individuals have to carry out comparisons. No one company projects a single image as this is a multi-attribute concept. Also, some individuals have a wide network of acquaintances and may consult alternative information sources in making a decision about what offer delivers more value than another. This means perceptions of value will fluctuate within the population.

Product perceived value is based upon:

- Actual price asked and the relativity to prices for the same or similar product offered elsewhere.
- Perceived quality, service and image associated with the brand/product.
- Convenience of purchasing method or channel, and its congruence to the needs of the customer.
- Consumer difficulty in ability to assess the benefits/relative price of the product.
- Experience associated with the purchase or consumption process.

It will be seen from the last point in the list above that the focus on any judgement of value for money will include intrinsic aspects, so that either the purchase itself as a pre-trip activity or the actual tourism experience can be treated as of value for its own sake. For example, an experiential perspective may include the symbolic, hedonic and aesthetic aspects of the consumption process. This means that practical consumer judgement has to include hedonic criteria, based on an appreciation of the good or service for its own sake. As such, value can be based upon the thinking and feeling dimensions of purchase and consumption behaviour. Consumption by value criteria is based upon a multiplicity of inputs which contribute in varying ways to consumer judgement in different choice situations. In fact, tourism can be thought of as producing a **total tourist experience** that will include everything from the pre-planning, the purchase, the journey, the visit/and perhaps stay, the return journey and overall reflection on the activity. This total tourist experience involves all aspects of the offering and experience which provide sets of satisfaction and dissatisfactions related to the whole episode. Marketing has to consider all these aspects to ensure that value and satisfaction is judged to be above the tourist's expectation. A good overall experience will culminate in the tourist being an advocate for a company or destination and lead to the telling of others of their experience in a positive way.

If we consider the early success of McDonald's, the value is not simply the hamburger or fries, it is the way the service, cleanliness and speed of food production has provided an added value to the food. McDonald's customers are made up of a whole series of segments who value a fast, light and reasonably priced meal. This is all achieved by means of a great deal of planning and understanding. The company sets itself a series of high standards to achieve, which is known internally as 'QSCV'. QSCV is Quality, Service, Cleanliness and Value and provides a defined target area of value delivery for its operations. This is only one aspect that is important in the running of the company. The marketplace is dynamic and therefore McDonald's has had to renew itself on a constant basis by introducing new menu items, which fit with the values of health and nutrition, in order to react to the changing market environment.

In order to deliver value through lower prices the low-cost airlines need to keep operating costs significantly lower than the 'traditional' scheduled airlines in order to be successful in the niche they have selected. This is achieved through specific marketing measures such as direct booking by use of the Internet and lower cost by means of ticketless travel and online check-in rather than use of travel agents; high utilisation of aircraft whereby time on the ground is reduced; use of cheaper secondary airports; and reduction in variable costs by not offering free meals on board.

Understanding the overall experience from a marketing perspective is extremely import-ant. However, the marketing concept – where the consumer is the driving force for all business activities – must not be confused with a sales approach. The next section ensures that differ-ence is understood and then we will introduce you to the notion of marketing orientation.

THE DIFFERENCES BETWEEN MARKETING AND SELLING

By now it should be obvious to the reader that marketing and selling are not the same. This is not just a new account as according to Drucker (1973: 64):

> Selling and marketing are antithetical rather than synonymous or even complementary. There will always, one can assume, be a need for some selling, but the aim of marketing is to make selling superfluous.

The contrast between the sales and marketing approach highlights the importance of mar-keting planning and analysis related to customers and the marketplace.

The sales concept focuses on products and uses selling and promotion to achieve profits through sales volume. The underlying weakness is that the sales concept does not necessarily satisfy the consumer and may only culminate in short-term, rather than long-term, company success. The marketing concept focuses on customer needs and utilises integrated marketing to achieve profits through customer satisfaction (Figure 17.1).

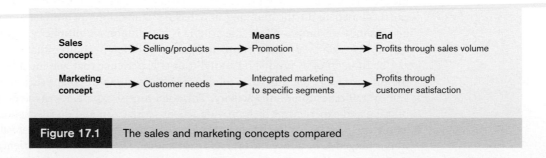

| Figure 17.1 | The sales and marketing concepts compared |

DIFFERENT BUSINESS PHILOSOPHIES

As we have seen, marketing is a business philosophy that places the consumer, and his or her needs, at the forefront of all activities. For example, it is known that business travellers want frequent and reliable transport systems with sensible timings of departure and arrival. They

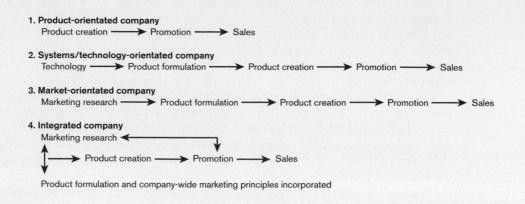

1. **Product-orientated company**
   Product creation ⟶ Promotion ⟶ Sales

2. **Systems/technology-orientated company**
   Technology ⟶ Product formulation ⟶ Product creation ⟶ Promotion ⟶ Sales

3. **Market-orientated company**
   Marketing research ⟶ Product formulation ⟶ Product creation ⟶ Promotion ⟶ Sales

4. **Integrated company**
   Marketing research ⟵
   ⟶ Product creation ⟶ Promotion ⟶ Sales

Product formulation and company-wide marketing principles incorporated

Figure 17.2	Four possible business philosophies

favour priority check-in and check-out facilities and efficient, good-quality staff. Business travellers need to feel they can make their trips and have their meetings without any worry of delay or discomfort. Therefore, knowledge of business travellers' needs occurs only when someone takes care to identify those needs.

While it is important to recognise the importance of structuring any organisation so that its focus is upon the customer, a number of alternative philosophies can be identified (see Figure 17.2). Each of these philosophies acts as a guiding orientation and system of approaching the market, and while a product-led company may be less effective, it is still possible to identify such companies within the tourism sector.

It is important to understand the initial starting place within the chains of the individual systems in Figure 17.2, since this is the first stage in the sequence of events which clearly demonstrates the focus of the organisation's approach to effecting exchange relationships. Examples (1) and (2) can be ineffective because of problems encountered in having the wrong product for the market and, as a consequence, having to waste more resources on promotion and selling in order to achieve a sale. In these examples it is normal to find that organisations believe their products are acceptable, and that all that is required for sales to occur is the identification of prime markets and methods of selling. Such an approach to the marketplace by a destination, hotel or airline marketing department is characterised by an emphasis on pictures of empty bedrooms, bleak-looking buildings or the exterior of an aircraft. An emphasis on the product rather than the benefits the consumer is seeking is still at the heart of a great deal of today's marketing. Quite often tourist promotional literature is devoid of scenes of tourists experiencing rest, enjoyment or good service. A product-focused philosophy is more acceptable when there is shortage or boom times, which are characterised by little competition. However, both the first two philosophies provide for inward-looking management, which concentrates on improvement within the company, rather than on outward-looking management, which concentrates on the consumer and emerging tourist needs.

Examples (3) and (4) in Figure 17.2 offer the ideal approach to organising business in the modern tourism marketplace. They are driven by research that creates an understanding of the consumer, the business and the marketplace. Research will be both secondary and primary. Information has to be collected from within and outside the company in order to establish a clear picture of the marketing environment. The integrated approach provides a sequence of events that commences with an understanding of the consumer, the competitors, the types of product that the company is capable of providing and a system that sensitises the whole organisation to a marketing orientation. The integrated system helps to ensure that methods of improving the satisfaction levels of the consumer are incorporated into each department's objectives.

Within the final two examples of company philosophy, it can be seen that the feedback process allows the marketing department to develop products as well as different forms of promotion that are right for the consumer. This establishes a more effective means of ensuring products are successful and that marketing budgets are used efficiently.

The tourism industry is spending vast sums of money on developing new attractions, improving products, building hotels and investing in technology. The only way for the risk level to be kept to a minimum is through the adoption of a marketing philosophy that provides products related to the needs of consumers.

However, all companies operate in a fiercely competitive environment that impinges upon the flexibility of management and company action. Marketing starts with the consumer and the market. This reflects the sovereignty of the consumer in the process. Such an approach has to be the correct strategy because it is the consumer who ultimately supports, through personal expenditure, tomorrow's tourism marketplace.

MARKETING ORIENTATION

The dynamic nature of business activity has led to many different sales and marketing opportunities in the tourism industry. The industry has thrown off many of its traditional attitudes toward the customer. This has come about through the realisation of the importance of a marketing orientation. As such, five main areas can be identified, as follows.

1. **It is a management orientation or philosophy.** The focus of the organisation's effort is placed on the consumer as a set of guiding values, and this then leads to the customer being the centre of attention. These ideals should lead to a proactive approach in ensuring marketing efforts optimise exchange transactions within which consumers feel they have been rewarded with value and satisfaction. When customers' needs are met they are more likely to return to the cruise line, tour operator, hotel or restaurant, and, more importantly, to let others know of their satisfaction. There is the recognition that the conduct of the organisation's business must revolve around the long-term interests and satisfactions of the customers it serves. This is an outward-looking orientation which requires responsive action in relation to external political, economic, social or technological events, and competitive actions.

2. **It encourages exchange to take place.** This involves the attitudes and decisions of consumers in relation to the willingness to buy from producers or distributors. As the marketplace becomes more competitive, strategies to strengthen an existing customer base have become increasingly important in tourism as it has been recognised that long-term relationships with existing customers are less expensive to maintain than forever attempting to attract new customers. If a close long-term relationship can be achieved, the possibility is that customers are more likely to provide higher purchase patterns and lower marketing costs per customer. While the objective of marketing is to achieve enduring relationships with the customer it should also be recognised that, in some situations, short-term sales (i.e. transaction marketing) may be just as important when there is little likelihood that the customer will be a repeat purchaser. As such marketers have to develop innovative methods to encourage both exchange transactions as well as retention.

There is the need to ensure the service offers value for money, which may mean there is a requirement for creating a range of benefits over time. This has led to loyalty schemes and what is known as 'relationship marketing' (RM). Relationship marketing is an approach whereby marketers attempt to retain the customer over longer periods of time through club or loyalty programmes such as hotel, car rental or airline frequent flyer programmes. This is based upon the organisation becoming more involved with the customer as part of relationship marketing as opposed to the idea of concentrating on only a single sale or transaction (Table 17.2).

Table 17.2	The difference between transaction and relationship marketing

Transaction marketing	Relationship marketing
Short-term orientation: sale as end result	Long-term orientation: the sale is only the beginning
'Me' orientated	'We' orientated
Focus on achieving a sale	Focus on retention and repeat sales
Emphasis on persuasion to buy	Stress on creating positive relationships
Need to win, manipulation	Providing trust and service
Stress of conflict of achieving a transaction	Partnership and cooperation to minimise defection and provide longer-term relationships (with customers or strategic alliances, joint ventures, vendor partnering, etc.)
Anonymous customer won by conquest in a carefully planned event	Individual profile of customer known so that a continuing process can emerge

As part of the analogy, the RM process is available to advance relationships to higher levels of loyalty until a status is achieved whereby the customer is not only loyal but also advocates the company, the employees and service to others. RM should not be confused with brand loyalty based upon simple commitment to the product, as RM is far more complex (see Gilbert, 1996, for a full discussion of relationship marketing and airlines). The rationale for RM is that it makes business sense to focus on long-term financial benefits that can accrue once a customer has been won for the first time. This is because it has been estimated to be five to ten times more expensive to recruit a new customer than to retain an existing one. Therefore, there is importance placed upon the retention of a customer with commercial consideration of the lifetime value of customers based upon quantity of repeat purchases. Such an approach enables the costs of acquisition and conversion of the prospect to be set against the revenues earned over the longer term. In an effective scheme sales and profits improve in direct proportion to the length of the relationship.

In relationship marketing customers will represent a diverse set of purchasing and spending patterns. However, it is important to be able to make marketing decisions which reflect the worth and potential of any one customer over a period of time. The analysis which allows this is known as **lifetime value** (LTV). Lifetime value, related to a frequent flyer programme or similar tourism loyalty scheme, allows for the measurement of the total worth to the organisation of its relationship with a particular identified customer over a period of time. This is based upon the time-related income and costs of that individual adjusted so that the future amounts are discounted in order to provide a net present value worth of the individual. Therefore, in order to make a calculation of LTV the company has to capture or estimate the costs and revenues of each relationship. The costs will be related to the acquisition, communication and any rewards or incentives given during any one year. The analysis of a frequent hotel guest or frequent flyer will reveal the profile of customers who provide high returns as well as those who are costly for the company to service. The LTV information will allow for improved decision-making regarding:

- The assigning of appropriate acquisition allowances to attract the higher-spending customers. The profile of these individuals is utilised to identify and segment the targeting strategy.

- Improving media strategies in order to acquire higher LTV individuals. Database analysis will provide information as to the optimal allocation of marketing communications budgets to alternative media in recruitment campaigns.

- Providing selection policies for customer marketing programmes. LTV analysis will allow a division of customers into graded levels of worth to the company. This allows for different rewards and privileges to be given to the different levels or categories of customer. It also allows for the cutback in communication for those individuals who represent only break-even or loss when marketing costs are taken into consideration.

- Which individuals to contact and reactivate from the lapsed category. The database can identify the timing and worth of purchases made by individuals. If a previously higher spending individual indicates lapsed behaviour a 'win-back' policy may be triggered. As such a reactivation allowance can be allocated based upon the likely return of the individual and their future revenue potential.

3. It involves long- and short-term planning. This requires the systematic organisation of strategic planning and tactical activity. In the short term an organisation does not normally have the flexibility to change rapidly even if the marketplace warrants this. The physical infrastructure of a hotel building, the skills of the workforce and other production capabilities can often only be changed marginally. Therefore, in the short term the constraints of earlier planning will restrict the choice a company or resort area may have. Because of the short-run constraints one aspect of planning which increases in importance to capacity risks is the control mechanisms for the monitoring of performance against targets. The long-term success of an organisation requires the efficient use of resources and assets, while tactical action will be required to keep plans on course. IT systems offer the opportunity to model demand and take tactical action at the earliest opportunity to sell unsold inventory or expand supply.

4. It requires efficient, cost-effective methods. Marketing's principal concern within any organisation has to be the delivery of maximum satisfaction and value to the customer at acceptable or minimum cost to the company so as to ensure long-term profit. The use of resources within marketing has to be both efficient and effective. The trend in the use of relationship marketing to build closer bonds and better retention with valued customers who provide repeat business is more effective than treating all customers as equal. However, in many organisations, the dilemma is that management is often judged by short-term success in relation to sales and profit performance.

5. It requires the development of an integrated company environment. The organisation's efforts and structure must be matched with the needs of the target customers. Everybody working for the organisation must participate in a total corporate, marketing environment with each division maximising the satisfaction level of consumers. Integration is not just a smile or politeness. Barriers to serving the customer well have to be destroyed. The onus is on the organisation to provide organisational structures that are responsive and able to undergo change to suit customer needs. Such an environment has to be based upon a culture of customer-focused adaptation.

TOURISM AS A SERVICE PRODUCT

With tourism, hospitality and leisure products we are dealing with a **service product** that has specific characteristics that set the product apart from the more general goods sold in the marketplace. An understanding of the complexity of the service product concept is an essential prerequisite for successful tourism marketing. This is because the emphasis is increasingly placed on the service provider to develop a deeper understanding of the linkages that correspond to consumer benefits sought and the nature of the service delivery system itself.

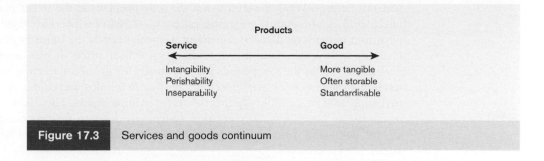

Figure 17.3 Services and goods continuum

A starting point is an examination of the dimensions and characteristics of the service product concept. Products can be placed along a continuum of services and goods, with most products being a combination of the two. A pure service would be consultancy or teaching whereas a pure good would be a can of beans or clothing. Some products will have more service content than others, and if they are able to be placed to the left-hand side of the continuum shown in Figure 17.3, they may be termed service products.

The characteristics of the service product

Intangibility

The service product has the characteristic of intangibility, which means it cannot be easily evaluated or demonstrated in advance of its purchase. For example, a travel agent cannot allow the testing or sampling of the tourism product and a sales representative for a hotel cannot take anything but secondary material to a sales call meeting. On the other hand, a car or computer game can be tested prior to purchase, and clothing can be tried on. Much of the selling of tourism and hospitality is related to the promise of safe and timely delivery of the individual by transport companies, or comfort and good service by accommodation companies. Only a ticket, voucher or Internet reservation number is exchanged at the time of purchase. The marketers of tourism and hospitality products, therefore, face greater difficulty. Because of fixed time and space constraints they cannot easily demonstrate the benefits of the products they are selling. The problem for the tourism service marketer is overcome by the production of a range of printed literature, videos or other means of providing cues as to the type of product on offer in an attempt to increase tangibility. In addition, there is a need to ensure marketing provides clear and well-managed branding of accommodation, transport and distribution organisations. This positions the brand name more tangibly in the mind of the consumer, in addition ensuring that the tangible aspects related to uniforms, decor and physical evidence give cues as to the quality of the service. These final points are important as marketers need to realise that there is a distinction which should be made between the degree of intangibility of the actual service and the intangibility, or lack of physical evidence, surrounding the process of service delivery. The airline industry is an example of this where the physical evidence represents a major component of the service because the performance characteristics are supported largely by means of tangible elements such as food and drink, the cabin configuration and comfort of the seat, in-flight entertainment system, etc.

Perishability

The characteristic of *perishability* means that service products such as tourism, unlike goods, cannot be stored for a sale on a future occasion. For example, a hotel bed or an airline seat unsold or a convention centre left empty is revenue that can never be recouped. This leads to the high-risk nature of the tourism industry. Perishability is also linked to the seasonality of demand whereby some companies or destinations have high and low periods of demand and in low periods the problem of perishability is exacerbated. Marketers in the tourism and hospitality sector have to devise complex pricing and promotion policies in an attempt to sell 'off-season' periods and create greater synchronisation of staffing levels and supply to match demand patterns. Weak demand is not the only problem as the sector is characterised by hotels, airlines, attractions, museums, galleries, etc., all of which have fixed capacity with a maximum upper level demand constraint. In peak periods the industry often has difficulty in coping with demand and therefore charges premium prices or uses queuing as a control mechanism, but in the low periods there is a need for greater marketing activity. The reaction to perishability is for marketers to try to smooth out demand curves by careful use of the marketing mix: for example, cheaper tickets for matinée shows. There is also a concentration on the use of computerised reservation systems in order to forecast the need for tactical action if demand is believed to be below expected levels, and of specialist web sites to sell off last minute availability.

Inseparability

Service products are often referred to as being **inseparable**, which means the product is often consumed and produced simultaneously. This means that both the service provider and customer are present when the service function occurs. Because there is less opportunity to manage and pre-check a tourism or hospitality product, it can vary in the standard of its service delivery. This is sometimes characterised by authors as *heterogeneity* or *variability*. The tourism sector offers an amalgam of services which make up the delivery of the product. This occurs in a fragmented system where different organisations may have responsibility for the level of service delivery. Even for a single service such as air travel there will be the travel agent, airport checking-in agent and staff, airline staff, catering company, baggage handling staff, cabin cleaning staff, all of whom provide the single continuous flight experience. Variance occurs because of the inseparable nature of the product's delivery when the customer is part of the production system. The simultaneous process of production and consumption can lead to situations where it is difficult to ensure the overall satisfaction of consumers. For example, peak demand load cannot always be forecast and may create dissatisfaction by way of secondary problems of lack of staffing. There is also the potential problem of having groups or types of clients with conflicting needs that may result in disharmony. A couple wanting a quiet romantic anniversary dinner in a restaurant could find the evening unacceptable if a group of the local football club supporters decide to eat at the same time. Whether on the aircraft, in the hotel, or in the restaurant there could be the clash of social values, noisiness, drunkenness, high spirits or a child crying. Staff may also have had personal problems or be feeling ill or tired, and this can affect their level of commitment to their performance of giving good service or resolving problems.

As the nature of the tourism service product is largely one of interpersonal relationships, where the performance level of staff is directly related to the satisfaction and overall experience of the consumer, there is a need for quality assurance programmes. Staff are emotional and changeable and if a high content of the product is based upon interpersonal relationships between 'strangers', as guest and service provider, it is important to ensure standardised service levels are adhered to. Quality assurance is important as a basis of planning for competitive advantage and controlling the standards of staff interactions. To reduce the problems that can be associated with inseparability there is a need for investment in company training programmes for all service staff.

Other aspects of tourism as a service product

1. **Shorter exposure to service delivery.** The customer's exposure to the delivery of the service is normally of short duration. This allows only a limited time during which company personnel can build a relationship and effect repeat business.

2. **More personal.** The self is very much involved emotionally in the service encounter and as such the personal feelings created by contact service personnel are an important determinant of future demand. Therefore, it is important to recruit staff for personal qualities and then train for skills.

3. **Growing use of self-service.** To reduce costs and provide more timely service companies are more likely to introduce self-service buffet meals, Internet reservation technology etc. rather than interpersonal service alternatives. This requires the customer to handle the self-service process or technology appropriately and for the service not to be so complicated that there is any danger of negative consequences. An important consideration for companies using self-service processes and technology is the potential lack of personal interaction between the service employee and the customer which allows the opportunity to exceed customer service expectations.

4. **Greater significance on managing evidence.** Due to the intangible nature of the tourism product it is important to plan to deliver cues as to the positioning and quality of the offer by means of cleanliness, decor, uniforms, signage, etc.

5. **Complementarity is greater.** The overall tourism product is often made up of an amalgam of many different services each of which has to add up to an overall positive experience. Destinations are aware that they have to control service quality to ensure a satisfactory experience and therefore attempt to regulate tourism providers.

6. **Easier copying of services.** Services can be easily benchmarked and copied by other organisations due to their visibility.

TOURISM PRODUCTS AND RISK

Tourism products are important in relation to the type of marketing they require. Tourism has developed rapidly over the past few decades, led by a marketing thrust which has created diversity of supply, focused on important consumer segments and stimulated high levels of demand. Within this development marketing has often concentrated more on improving the product than on understanding the consumer and the complexity of his or her decision processes. As uncertainty is part of the process of purchase and consumption this is often associated with personal reservations and a judgement of **perceived risk**.

A major aspect of consumer behaviour, linked to the purchase of tourism products, is the notion of risk and a consumer's judgement about the likelihood of a problem occurring. Tourism products often involve a complex decision-making process because the purchase is of relatively high risk and high involvement. However, the concept is complex given that throughout the population the threshold at which an individual perceives *economic, physical, performance* and *psychological* risk differs by age, income and experience. The concept is also related to individual feelings of uncertainty based upon the subjective possibility of any occurrence of the following types of risk.

Economic risk

Economic risk is associated with the decision for potential tourists as to whether the product offer is of good value or not. Given the range of prices offered for short-haul flights from both no-frills and scheduled carriers there is frequently some uncertainty as to which airline to book with and which price to pay. All consumers face economic or financial risk when they purchase tourism products given that they cannot be sure whether their choice will deliver the benefits they desire. Tourism often involves the purchase of an expensive product, such as the annual holiday, that cannot easily be seen or sampled prior to consumption. This type of risk is heightened for those with low levels of disposable income, for whom the purchase represents a major expenditure.

Physical risk

Some overseas destinations may be perceived as dangerous owing to disease or crime, and some transport companies such as ferry or airline operators are thought to be safer than others.

The fear of an illness such as SARS or travelling at the time of war or civil unrest is a clear indication of this concept. Some people fear flying no matter what airline they fly with, while others may reduce the perception of physical risks by selecting certain 'safer' airlines. A study by Lepp and Gibson (2003) based upon a random sample of US-born young adults found that there are seven important risk factors: health, political instability, terrorism, strange food, cultural barriers, a nation's political and religious dogma, and crime. Analysis revealed the more experienced tourist was less likely to be concerned about terrorism. It was also found that there is a difference by gender in that women perceived a greater degree of risk regarding health and food. However, tourist role was the most significant variable, with familiarity seekers being the most risk-averse.

Performance risk

The quality of different destinations or unknown hotel brands cannot be assessed in advance. This type of risk is associated with feelings that the product may not deliver the desired benefits. It is rarely possible for those who have had a bad holiday to make up for it by attempting to have another better holiday in the same year. Most consumers do not have the additional money or holiday entitlement to make good the holiday that went wrong. This heightens their awareness of the risk factors involved. One important performance risk for UK travellers is weather. The risk of poor weather while holidaying in the UK is one reason why many people travel abroad.

Psychological risk

Status can be lost through visiting the 'wrong' country because it has no status in the minds of others, or travelling with a company that has a poor image. This risk occurs when the potential customer feels the purchase may not reflect the self-image he or she wishes to portray. This may be connected to social risk, which suggests there could be a loss of social status due to the act of purchasing from a company that has a poor image.

From a marketing point of view, the above perceptions of risks need to be minimised through product and promotion strategies. Creating and delivering information in brochures and leaflets that helps to convince the potential traveller of the reliability of the company will lessen the perception of risk. However, it is important to realise that communications by word of mouth, whereby a friend reassures another about a purchase, is a more powerful source than company-controlled literature. By acquiring information the consumer builds up mental pictures and attitudes that create the expectation of positive benefits from the travel or destination experience.

It is also important for the quality of the product to be controlled especially in relation to the process of service delivery.

PLANNING THE SERVICE ENCOUNTER

If we examine a systems perspective that identifies the linkage between the consumer's needs and the service delivery, we can be more aware of the management principles associated with service products. This can also be utilised in the establishment of benchmark points against which the service can be positioned.

A well-positioned service enables the organisation to achieve the following two important objectives:

- to differentiate its position so as to distinguish itself from competitors; and
- to deliver service superior to that accepted as the norm.

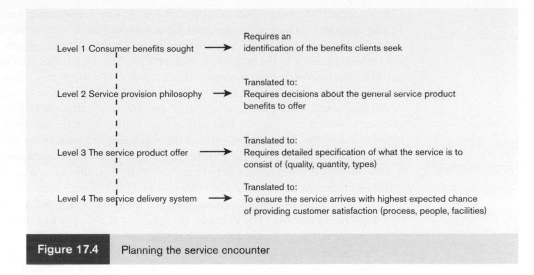

Level 1 Consumer benefits sought ⟶ Requires an identification of the benefits clients seek

Level 2 Service provision philosophy ⟶ Translated to: Requires decisions about the general service product benefits to offer

Level 3 The service product offer ⟶ Translated to: Requires detailed specification of what the service is to consist of (quality, quantity, types)

Level 4 The service delivery system ⟶ Translated to: To ensure the service arrives with highest expected chance of providing customer satisfaction (process, people, facilities)

Figure 17.4   Planning the service encounter

The above objectives allow the organisation to plan and build competitive advantage by establishing leadership principles of service standards and delivery. Once the standards are established there should be a policy to communicate and reinforce the service provision philosophy at every possible opportunity: meetings, training and internal marketing programmes, induction programmes and appraisal systems. The human resource function needs to be organised so as to ensure the different levels in Figure 17.3 are always clearly understood and reinforced through organisational culture and reward. Often services are managed on the subjective opinions of managers, when they should be based upon objective designs to ensure there is no confusion as to what needs to be achieved. Without good internal organisational procedures and relationships it is unlikely that even the best conceived of quality programmes will be successful.

The levels shown in Figure 17.4 illustrate the linkages for designing a successful service delivery process. For the model to be successful the implementation process must consider the need for the following:

- Leadership and commitment by senior management based upon clear goals and a policy on quality being established and communicated to employees. There is also the need to release the appropriate resources to create changes and achieve the required results.

- All changes and objectives to be defined by the customer. All the approaches related to quality delivery and standards have to be delineated in all of the dimensions of the service delivery with reference to what customers value. What customers expect and value should consequently be incorporated into the company induction and training programmes.

- The organisation having the flexibility to change and improve service. This requires a process and systems approach to match or exceed customer expectations. Such a system may incorporate a quality audit system which applies measurement and inspection to ensure defects are corrected and the system delivers optimum quality results.

- Effective human resource management to hire those with service competencies and inclinations and then to motivate, train and educate staff to deliver the concepts of quality. This is reinforced through teamwork values and a culture that champions quality product delivery as a prerequisite for competitive advantage.

- An assessment to be made of the added value and benefit of any change rather than there being a simple cost-cutting and price-leadership strategy. The long-term benefits of any change need to be the focus of service encounter decision-making.

- Quality audits and control to ensure the service meets or exceeds customer expectations.

It is crucial that an organisation creates its own quality management culture and does not simply attempt to clone a system used by a competitor. A successful service encounter approach requires honest two-way communication between management and staff which will build confidence in the implementation process. This means that staff have to be allowed to own up to weaknesses and problems of poor quality in a supportive atmosphere where the organisation attempts to learn from weaknesses rather than to punish staff. Such methods create teamwork, confidence and commitment. However, there is also the need for competence to deliver the changes. This may require further training and seminars for staff and follow-up sessions. The recognition that there is a need to treat other members of staff as internal customers will assist the transition to a **total quality management** (TQM) system.

It is obvious that organisations have customers from within as well as without. With this in mind, if employees visualise the relationships between each other based upon supplier and customer links as a quality chain, then the question is always, 'Am I meeting the full requirements of my role?' For example, the secretary is a supplier to the boss with the need to provide timely error-free work in order to aid him or her as supplier to his or her internal customer, who may be a director. An organisation, therefore, is a web of internal suppliers and customers. Such chains are easily weakened or broken by faulty equipment or by fallible people. The important issue is that an internal quality chain failure will ultimately have some effect on the external customer.

QUALITY MANAGEMENT

We cannot adequately describe the management of tourism without touching on the importance of the growing emphasis on quality management. There are four main reasons that can account for the growing relevance of quality management:

1. Organisations need to find ways of creating differential advantage by having better service levels than their competitors.
2. The increased level of consumerism and the greater media attention on quality has meant organisations have to be more responsive to quality issues. Consumers are far more aware of their rights and are less likely to suffer quietly from the results of poor quality.
3. There has been a growing sophistication of consumer markets with the non-price factors of image, product positioning and service delivery strategies becoming more important.
4. More recently technology is one of the new applications to quality enhancement. Technology can aid service by providing higher levels of convenience, for example automatic vending or ticketing machines or up-to-date information for products and services.

It is important for the quality of the product to be controlled, especially in relation to the process of service delivery. This is because relative quality between service providers or retailers has implications for market share and profitability. Quality is therefore one of the key components that contribute to a successful strategy. Quality has emerged as a major competitive component of a service organisation's strategy. However, when we examine the employment of the term 'quality', there is almost a superabundance of the use of this word in relation to the way management operates. There is a crusade for quality management and improvement within industry worldwide and the campaign for improved quality was rooted in the manufacturing industry prior to the expansion into the service industry. However, many individuals in the industry are still unaware of the theoretical grounding of quality management. Such management has to consider core and peripheral services which need to be developed and delivered after a careful diagnosis of customer expectations and perceptions.

What are the key terms for quality?

There are several key concepts related to quality. Quality is the totality of relationships between service providers (functional aspects) and the features of the product (technical aspects) which are related to the delivery of satisfaction. It is therefore important to create systems of **quality control** which are checks and monitoring to ensure measurement of service delivery is taking place. To this end TQM is a holistic organisational approach which systematically attempts to enhance customer satisfaction by focusing on continuous improvements without incurring unacceptable cost increases. These improvements are part of an unending quest for excellence in all aspects of quality service delivery. Therefore, TQM has to form the values and mindset for all employees, which leads to quality being an integrated element of corporate culture. For success, quality must be the concern of all employees and the culture, therefore, should not be based upon a departmental or technical understanding of quality. Instead, the notion of quality must be disseminated to employees throughout the organisational structure and implemented as a systematic process extending throughout the organisation. The focus of any change in quality must be based upon external customer expectations and not internal organisational ideas.

TQM is managed by **quality assurance** arrangements whereby a system is instituted to allocate responsibility for planned and systematic activities that will ensure the product will provide the right levels of satisfaction to all concerned. A service guarantee system can provide more quality control and data capture in an organisation.

This facilitates a better understanding of potential for improvement by capturing information on what is going wrong. Following this the information gathered on what goes wrong allows for a reaction in improvement of service. Some companies are now guaranteeing their service or paying out compensation with schemes such as flight delay insurance. A good service guarantee is identified as unconditional, easy to understand and communicate, meaningful, and easy to invoke in order to obtain recompense. But there is a need:

- not to promise something your customers already expect;
- not to shroud a guarantee in so many conditions that it is meaningless; or
- to offer a guarantee so mild that it is never invoked.

A guarantee can set clear standards and allow the company personnel to be clear about what the organisation stands for. If customers can complain easily, there is the benefit of collecting data on common problems that subsequently need to be addressed and eradicated. This is because a guarantee system forces the focus on why the failure occurred and what needs to be done about it to improve service quality. Moreover, a guarantee adds credibility and weight to the marketing effort of the organisation. It allows for a communication of the presence of the guarantee which may lead to a reduction in the perception of risk associated with purchase and can lead to higher levels of demand.

As a measure of whether the quality delivery complies with the planned delivery of the service a quality audit needs to take place to judge the effectiveness of the total service delivery arrangements. For a system to be audited correctly there is a need for a method of creating unbiased feedback. While a range of aspects of quality can be assessed, a number of categories exist. These may include the following, which are based upon various research that attempted to establish categories of service quality determinants:

- **Tangibles.** This will include physical evidence of the service, such as physical aspects of airline cabins, hotel bedrooms and facilities, or material the customer can see, touch, use etc., like equipment, merchandise, personnel, for example:
  - physical facilities such as extra legroom on the aircraft or size of hotel room;
  - appearance of personnel and condition of the surroundings;
  - technology or equipment used to provide the service;
  - physical representation of the service (e.g. airline loyalty card);
  - other customers in the service facility.

- **Reliability.** This involves consistency of performance and dependability. Gaining the customer's confidence is vital in service organisations. The ability of the service provider to establish a relationship of trust and faith greatly influences perceived service quality. A company should perform the service right the *first time* in order to achieve a good reputation. In many circumstances reliability is an expected dimension, as an airline should deliver this as a core service. It means the firm should honour its promises and have the ability to trust employees with the responsibility to deliver service consistently and accurately which meets policy standards, such as:
  - accuracy in a bill or charging;
  - collecting and keeping the correct records;
  - assuring confidentiality and security of any personal data held;
  - performing the service at designated time (e.g. delivery of opening or departure time promise).

- **Responsiveness.** This refers to the willingness or readiness of employees to provide service, their reaction and willingness to help customers and give timely service, such as:
  - providing complimentary drinks for a delayed flight;
  - mailing a transaction slip or sending an email immediately;
  - calling a customer back quickly after a query or problem;
  - giving prompt service (e.g. arranging a change of itinerary, or reacting to the hotel guest's request).

- **Competence.** This concerns knowledge and courtesy of employees as well as the peace of mind that the company is to be trusted. This then delivers the assurance that employees will have the knowledge, skills and courtesy to create trust and confidence in the customer base, for example:
  - knowledge and skill of the contact personnel;
  - explaining the actual and wider service available;
  - the reputation of the organisation;
  - personal characteristics of the contact personnel;
  - confidentiality, financial and personal security.

- **Empathy.** This relates to the individualised attention to customers, the caring, individual concern and attention for others and their emotions, such as:
  - recognising and relating to regular customers;
  - learning the customer-specific requirements;
  - providing individualised service (customisation or personalisation is regarded as an essential attribute of service offerings due to the ability to tailor offers to customer-specific requirements).

The elements that could be assessed in the above could also include availability of items the customer demands; after-sales service and contact; the way telephone orders and queries are handled by contact centres; the reliability and safety of the product being sold; availability of sales literature and brochures; the number and type of items that can be demonstrated; technical knowledge of staff; the way an employee deals with a complaint, etc. In addition the organisation can use the above list as a means to assess the way in which it could develop its positioning strategy in order to distinguish itself from its competitors.

Table 17.3 indicates some of the ways in which quality can be assessed. It is important to realise that whatever system is used to audit quality at the end of the day, that which is not measured cannot be controlled.

Given the nature of tourism as a people-based industry with employee performance and interaction being of paramount importance, then we are dealing with a human activity where

Table 17.3	Auditing systems	

Internal inspection	Auditing
• Statistical process control based upon quality failure information and objective measures	• Internal auditors of quality
	• External bodies
• Visual inspections to check against standards and consistency	• Consultants, regular users, non-user surveys and feedback
• Management by walking about	• Cross-department audits
• Quality control group feedback	• Mystery shoppers
• Inspection of competitors' offer and assessment of own company offer	• Content analysis of complaint and praise letters and documented problems
	• Free telephone line feedback

errors are inevitable. There is therefore a need to judge the benefit of increased usage and repeat business as opposed to the loss of custom. The moment of truth or impact on the bottom line of any organisation is therefore the judgement by customers of the quality of its service. Figure 17.5 is based upon Hart, Heskett and Sasser (1990) who argue for the linkages of service encounters as creating a self-reinforcing mechanism. It indicates the relationship between the customer on the left and the service provider on the right. This overcomes the notion that improvement in quality is associated with increased costs. The model indicates that in the long-term true quality improvement leads to an improved trading position.

The above proposition is that a continuous improvement in service is not a cost but an investment in a customer who will return more profit in the long term. The premise is based

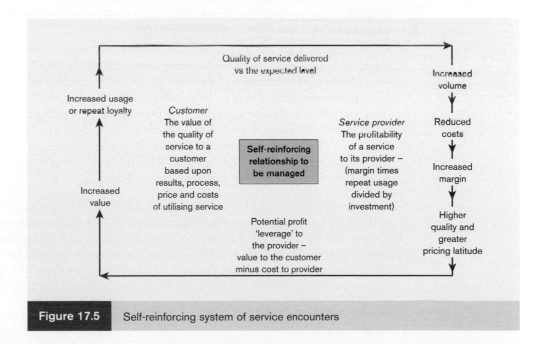

| Figure 17.5 | Self-reinforcing system of service encounters |

upon research which indicates that the cost of acquiring a new customer is five times as high as retaining an existing customer through providing quality service. Such argument is based upon non-traditional accounting practices which stress that satisfied customers will be willing to pay higher prices owing to the service quality they have experienced and liked; there is a free advertising benefit due to the positive word-of-mouth recommendation; and there is a different cost in acquiring new customers as opposed to the benefit of retaining existing customers over longer time periods. Thus, in general, following the ideas of relationship marketing, it is suggested that to keep a customer over the long term provides important savings. On a cost–benefit basis good service quality is thought to increase revenue and reduce long-term costs.

Given that the cost of finding a new customer is far greater than that of retaining an existing one, there is growing emphasis on customer retention and relationship marketing as discussed earlier in this chapter whereby long-term revenue can be enhanced by service recovery strategies. These include the following:

- **Training.** As service is an interpersonal performance activity then the provision of communication and customer relation skills will enhance the ability of staff to deal with the most difficult of situations. Perhaps, more importantly, training will allow staff to feel confident in the service encounter transaction and allow them to deal professionally with all situations.

- **Watching for sign language.** Allowing those customers who are reticent or mute when it comes to complaints to break their silence. Organisations need the opportunity to prove their commitment to the customer through service quality measures. However, the silent customer who is not satisfied will escape company notice but may tell many acquaintances of the problem. Some organisations provide free telephone lines for complainants or employee training to enable staff to test for the weak signals of a customer's dissatisfaction. Many organisations empower staff to provide remedial action if they suspect poor service has been experienced. Alternatively service may be tested with the use of mystery customers or staff listening to customers' reactions to the service provision.

- **Preplanning.** There is the need to analyse the service delivery process so as to anticipate those aspects of service that may exceed the tolerance level of customers. Times of peak demand or low levels of staffing may affect the judgement of the customer as to the overall level of service quality delivery. Staff can be asked to describe situations which if improved would lead to a more error-free service standard.

- **Empowerment.** A great deal of staff service delivery goes unsupervised. The front-line staff therefore need to react quickly to service problem situations without the input of supervisors. The policy of identifying problems quickly and correcting them at the local level is far more effective than relying on official complaint systems. A staff member who provides some extra means of satisfying a customer may allay a more difficult or serious situation. A long wait to be seated in a restaurant may be acknowledged by a reduction in the bill or free coffee. Empowerment provides an obligation to act in order to recover the situation which relies on trust of the front-line staff. This is in contrast to a system where the focus is on blame for a poor service encounter rather than resolution.

Good service recovery procedures allow a customer to refocus on the satisfactions received from the service delivery process rather than to question why corrective action was not taken. A problem tests the system and if a customer complaint is dealt with appropriately, the customer is likely to become more loyal. If a formal complaint is made it should be treated *individually* according to the *urgency* of the complaint and customer's *value* to the organisation.

A complaint system must be in place for prompt and personal customers' communication:

- to acknowledge the receipt of written/verbal complaints and to inform customers about the resolution;

Photograph 17.2   Service information is increasingly important as part of the product delivery.
Source: Getty Images / AFP

- to keep customers fully informed with progress reports;
- to encourage customers to appeal to a higher authority within the company in case of a unsatisfactory initial resolution;
- to assign and authorise one department to be accessible at reasonable hours for complaint processing and review;
- to have a complaint system which is both user and staff friendly.

We can classify the different approaches to quality management into two categories: the product-attribute approach and the consumer-orientated approach (Gilbert and Joshi, 1992).

The product-attribute approach

The product-attribute approach is based upon trying to match the product's conformance to standardised requirements which have been set by reference to what organisational managers think the failure point to be. Product-attribute approaches rely on trying to control the organisation's products using an internal product perspective. This relies on an inward-looking product-led approach.

The consumer-orientated approach

It is therefore more appropriate to adopt a consumer-orientated approach which recognises that the holistic process of service delivery has to be controlled by taking into consideration the expectations and attitudes of tourism and hospitality clients. In tourism, an assessment of quality is made during the process of service delivery and this can be treated as an encounter between the customer, the service provider and the physical aspects of the place of delivery. The customer will judge the outcome of this encounter in terms of levels of satisfaction. If the starting point for management is the understanding of how quality is judged by clients then the perception processes of this judgement, as to whether a service is good or bad, can be managed. Gronroos is a leading author who has clarified this concept.

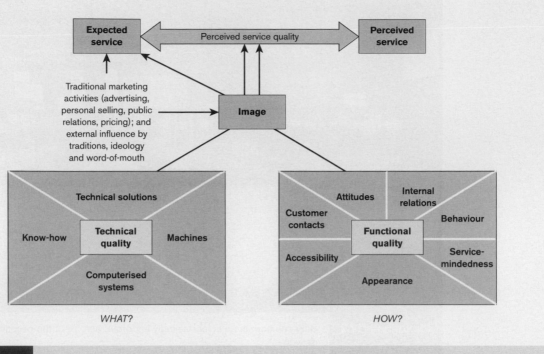

Figure 17.6	Managing the perceived service quality

Source: Gronroos, 1982

The Gronroos model

Gronroos (1982) developed a model to explain what he called the 'missing service quality concept'. The model shown in Figure 17.6 focuses mainly on the construct of image, which represents the point at which a gap can occur between expected service and perceived service. Gronroos makes us more aware of the ways image is created from the aggregation of different aspects of technical and functional variables. By following his model of different inputs, we are alerted to the fact that we should not reduce quality to a simplistic description, but should try to understand the full range of inputs. This is because to speak just of quality gives the manager no indication of what aspects of the product should be controlled.

Gronroos argued that the function and range of resources and activities include what customers are looking for, what they are evaluating, how service quality is perceived and in what way service quality is influenced. He defined the 'perceived quality' of the service as dependent on two variables. These are 'experienced service' and 'perceived service' which collectively provide the outcome of the evaluation.

As part of his analysis, Gronroos distinguished between 'technical quality' and 'functional quality' as the components of the service image delivery:

- Technical quality refers to what the customer is actually receiving from the service. This is capable of objective measurement, as with tangible goods.
- Functional quality refers to how the technical elements of the service are transferred. We know that a customer in a restaurant will not only evaluate the quality of the food consumed but also the way in which it was delivered (the style, manner and appearance of the staff, or the ambience of the place itself). Figure 17.6 shows that the attitudes, behaviour and general service-mindedness of personnel can be influenced by management.

MINI CASE STUDY 17.1
New Orleans report on tourism recovery progress

On April 12 in New York City, the New Orleans Metropolitan Convention & Visitors Bureau (NOMCVB) kicked off a 10-city International tour to spread the word about the city's renaissance. 'We're really bullish on the future,' said Stephen Perry, NOMCVB's president and CEO, who then gave reasons why.

In March, New Orleans welcomed 83,000 convention visitors, 10,000 more than in March 2005, showing that the all-important convention market is not only making its way back to pre-Katrina levels but in some cases surpassing it. 'We've had more renovations – from the convention center to hotels, restaurants and even streets,' Perry said, explaining that since February there has been a new sanitation service on Bourbon Street, leaving it constantly cleaner than any local could remember.

'The city is almost sold out right now for almost two solid weeks for Jazz Fest,' he continued. 'Homes are starting to be rebuilt, the economy is booming: the state's got the biggest surplus in history right now,' he reported.

And to really get to a New Yorker's heart, Perry spoke of what the two cities have in common. 'There are not many real, authentic places left – there's not much doubt where you are when you walk out the door in New York or New Orleans,' he said.

To draw attention to the city, the NOMCVB sprung a classic streetcar that ran on the Desire line (yes, a real streetcar named Desire) from a museum in Connecticut and positioned it in Times Square in front of the *Good Morning America* studios. The streetcar was to travel with them to Chicago, but not to other cities on this tour such as London, Paris and Dallas.

Source: Anastasia Mills, *Travel Agent*, 23 April 2007, pp. 12–13

DISCUSSION QUESTIONS

1. What would you have done to add to the marketing efforts to rebuild demand for the New Orleans area? Is PR enough or what else is required?

2. How important is a central convention and visitors' bureau in coordinating communications plans in overcoming the previous problems? Explain what they can do.

3. Look at The New Orleans web site and judge their communications campaigns.

The Parasuraman, Zeithaml and Berry model

Parasuraman, Zeithaml and Berry (1985) also developed a model of service quality which claimed the consumer evaluates the quality of a service experience as the outcome of the difference (gap) between expected and perceived service (Figure 17.7). The model highlighted the main requirements for a service provider delivering the expected service quality. By understanding the flow of this model we believe it is possible to provide greater management control over tourist service relationships. This should lead to an improved realisation of the key points of influence on the satisfactions of the consumer.

From the model we can identify five gaps that may lead to unsuccessful service delivery.

1. **Gap between consumer expectation and management perception.** This may result from a lack of understanding of what consumers expect from a service. An extensive study by Nightingale (1983) confirms this disparity, by revealing that what providers perceive as being important to consumers is often different from what consumers themselves actually expect.

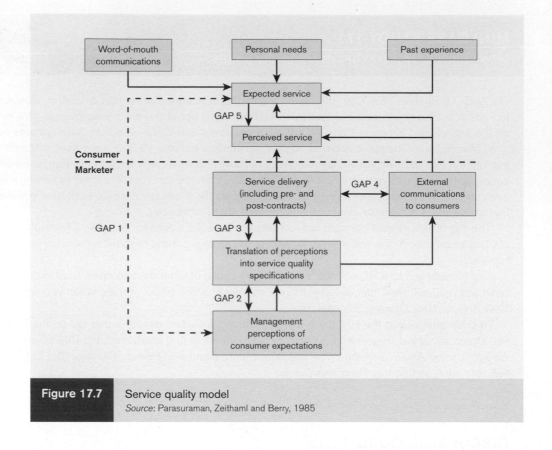

Figure 17.7 Service quality model
Source: Parasuraman, Zeithaml and Berry, 1985

2. **Gap between management perception and service quality specification.** This gap results when there is a discrepancy between what management perceives to be consumer expectations and the actual service quality specifications established. Management might not set quality standards or very clear ones, or they may be clear but unrealistic. Alternatively, the standards might be clear and realistic, but management may quite simply not be committed to enforcing them.

3. **Gap between service quality specifications and service delivery.** Even where guidelines exist for performing a service well, service delivery may not be of the appropriate quality owing to poor employee performance. Indeed, the employee plays a pivotal role in determining the quality of a service.

4. **Gap between service delivery and external communications.** Consumer expectations are affected by the promises made by the service provider's promotional message. Marketers must pay close attention to ensure consistency between the quality image portrayed in promotional activity and the actual quality offered.

5. **Gap between perceived service and delivered service.** This gap results when one or more of the previous gaps occur.

The focus on perceptions and expectations provides a guideline for quality management intervention strategies. To this end, on examining the model proposed by Parasuraman, Zeithaml and Berry, we believe that it has two main strengths to recommend it:

1. The model presents an entirely dyadic view of the marketing task of delivering service quality. The model alerts the marketer to consider the perceptions of both parties

(marketers and consumers) in the exchange process. This can lead to many insights, such as that the company may be providing the over-delivery as well as the under-delivery of service in different areas.

2. Addressing the gaps in the model can serve as a logical basis for formulating strategies and tactics to ensure consistent experiences and expectations.

Employee performance is crucial to improving the quality of service delivery and perceived service quality. Internal marketing is a means by which companies can influence the interpersonal performance of staff. Providing promotional communications that lead staff to achieve high levels of customer care and service quality is becoming increasingly important. One poster targeted to staff read, 'Good enough is not good enough' which sets the standards and aims of the company personnel above the average. This type of inward marketing provides a means to change the general attitudes of staff towards quality.

Zone of tolerance

The **zone of tolerance** concept assumes that customers do not have expectations of a service attribute on one given level. Rather, they can tolerate a variation in their experiences and still consider them acceptable or not according to their preconceived expectations. This concept implies that customers' expectations exist on two levels, a desired level and an adequate level. The desired level reflects what level the service could be, whereas the adequate level is what customers believe it should be. The latter level is the least acceptable level of the service experience. Expectations of service delivery will obviously alter on the basis of each customer as within the delivery of services consumers will have different levels of tolerance. There is a parameter for a service zone of tolerance whereby the majority of customers will fall within a zone between the upper and lower desired and adequate levels of performance. This is not fixed as the area of the zone of tolerance can increase or decrease for individual customers depending on other variables such as alternatives provided by the competition, how much was paid and whether it represented value for money, or other differences in the company's service. It is also important to realise that there are differences between individual customers' perceptions; similarly each customer may have different expectations of one brand in comparison with another. For example, if Airline A has delivered more consistent service over time than Airline B then the expectations for the Airline A brand are higher. If Airline A service were to decline to the level consistently offered by Airline B, the customer may be more disappointed by the service received from Airline A – even though the service standards are similar.

MANAGEMENT TASKS

A marketing orientation relies on a series of management responsibilities. To clarify the situation, marketing can be seen to provide for a business-to-customer or business-to-business interface with responsibility for specific management tasks. These tasks are more clearly explained in Chapter 19 on the marketing mix. However, it should be quite clear that tourism organisations without a proper commitment to a marketing orientation have little likelihood of effectively executing the marketing function.

The marketing function requires the combination of a number of related activities. Whether they are those involving staff, intermediaries or customers they are all focused on expediting transactions and relationships. The tasks itemised in Table 17.4 ensure that marketing will provide the functional inputs to deliver a sound basis for company activity. In addition this can be treated as a system which is designed to be an interface with the customer. This system is outlined in Figure 17.8.

Table 17.4	The business-to-customer interface

Task	Marketing function
1. Identifying the customers' needs for a tourism-related product	→ Marketing research and database analysis
2. Analysing marketing opportunities	→ Analysis and selection of target markets (segments) and understanding buyer/supplier relationships
3. Translating needs into products	→ Product planning and formulation
4. Determining the product's value to the customer at different seasonal periods	→ Pricing policy and creation of value delivery
5. Making the product available	→ Distribution policy
6. Informing and motivating the customer	→ Promotion (communicating, advertising, sales effort and relationship scheme)

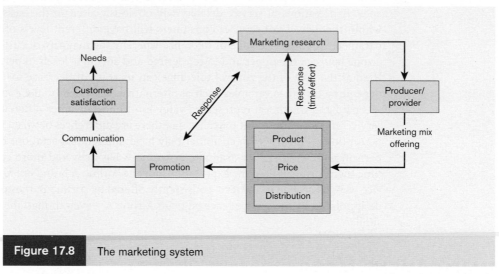

Figure 17.8	The marketing system

THE ADOPTION OF A MARKETING ORIENTATION

The tourist industry, owing to the high service-based content of the product, has been characterised by a history of custom and tradition. There has been a lack of vision in the industry which has meant the demise, merger and takeover of many organisations throughout the past 20 years. From the previous description of marketing and the examples presented, you should now be aware that tourism marketing involves a number of special characteristics:

- Marketing is a philosophy with the overriding value that the decision-making process of any organisation has to be led by the consumers' needs, the marketplace and the company's assets and resources.
- Successful marketing requires a special organisation structure that believes in integrating the principles of consumer orientation throughout the organisation.

- Marketing requires innovative methods of thinking and planning so that new ideas are generated to take advantage of opportunities or to improve existing methods of marketing.

However, it is important to remember that while the use of marketing is expanding, as a practice it is not without its critics.

CRITICISMS OF THE MARKETING CONCEPT

There is a growing concern for protection of the environment and the adoption of business policies that will enable the earth's resources to be sustained. The new values emerging are placing pressure on the underlying concepts of marketing. This is creating a great deal of debate regarding the ethical standpoint of marketing. Some of the most significant criticisms are considered in this section.

Environmental marketing impact

Tour operators/wholesalers have continuously developed new areas, expanded successful resorts and created promotional campaigns without due regard to the cost of impacts on the area and local population (see Part 2). Alongside this there is the over-abundance of different types of promotional material, which makes a home or overseas destination less attractive. There are roadside poster sites, advertisements on taxis, messages painted on buildings, and leaflets given away and then discarded, all of which create invasive pollution.

Overemphasis on profitable products

The marketing concept dictates that products can only be offered to the marketplace when they are profitable. This has culminated in the axing of bus and train transport routes and the disregard of low-spending individuals. Where a want exists and the marketing opportunity cannot deliver the required profit return, then the product is seldom developed. The market-based system is guided by self-interest and profit motivation. Therefore, consumer preferences are only accounted for if there is an ability to pay. These values are represented by a lack of concern for those who cannot afford a holiday, or for the supply of amenities to cater for those who are disadvantaged or handicapped. Facilities for blind, infirm and handicapped people are often of low priority in resort and accommodation planning.

Invasion of privacy

The power of IT allows organisations to capture a complete range of personal information for use in targeting direct mail campaigns. As organisations begin to spend more on research there is the problem of a greater use of telephone and high street interviews. If this is for a reputable survey there is no problem but a number of companies are simply collecting information under the disguise of research to be used in further sales efforts.

A personal computer is not that personal when emails can be sent which are unsolicited. It is estimated that hundreds of millions of emails are sent each day. Of these around 30% are unsolicited and form what is known as 'spam'. Spam emails are those which are not welcome and so should not have been sent. Therefore, companies should be considering permission marketing as a means to decide that a recipient is happy to receive information and messages. Good permission marketing is where the individual 'opts in' to receive the messages rather than has to tick an 'opt out' box in order not to get the mailings.

Waste of resources on tourism marketing

Marketing is perceived as wasteful owing to the high amounts of money spent on promoting products. The money given over to tourism promotion is often associated with enticing

MINI CASE STUDY 17.2
Tourism chiefs face guilt trip on green issues

The tourism industry has never had it so good, but its senior executives are feeling strangely guilty about their success and fearful of a green backlash. Expected to grow by 4.3 per cent a year over the next decade, the industry's bosses are fretting over climate change, worried that flying is seen as the most polluting activity, and falling over themselves to champion schemes that allow the travelling public to go on clocking up air miles.

'There is a real conundrum with how we grow in a way we feel good about,' said Andrew Cosslett, the chief executive of InterContinental Hotels Group. 'We need to find ways of making people feel very good about how they feel about these things.' Mr Cosslett was in Lisbon at the weekend, along with other hotel, airline and hospitality chief executives attending the annual global travel and tourism summit. Some wanted to rally governments to provide the infrastructure to meet the demand of the emerging middle classes of China, India and Mexico, who are readying themselves for global travel. Others were worried about fuel prices, security, visa problems, technological innovation and the armies of hospitality staff needed to cope with demand which, according to the World Travel and Tourism Council, will this year generate about $7bn of economic activity. But no one could escape the dark shadow of climate change, even though they wished it. 'We look at climate change as an image issue,' said Armin Meier, chief executive of Kuoni Travel, the luxury tour operator.

Maurice Flanagan, vice-chairman of Emirates Airline, was quite happy to share his trenchant view that global warming was 'an argument'. At the World Economic Forum in Davos earlier this year, he said he was taken aback at the way airlines were being 'demonised as the cause of all this'. Others were more philosophical. 'The debate is over,' said Sir Stelios Haji-Ioannou, founder of easyJet. Airlines had to replace their fleets with modern fuel-efficient engines, he said, 'but the replacement process is slow'. Airlines, hotels and other sectors in the industry will in the next couple of weeks pool resources in a public campaign in the UK to demonstrate that they are taking climate change seriously. They have given up trying to argue the technical niceties of aviation's contribution to carbon emissions. Whether it is 2, 3 or 5 per cent, it has to do something, they have concluded. 'At the end of the day, it is the developer, the capital-provider, who is going to be making the investment decision,' said Arthur de Haast, the chief executive of Jones Lang LaSalle Hotels. 'And the majority of them are still very focused on shareholder returns and maximising those returns,' he added.

For all the talk, practical meaningful solutions were little in evidence. It fell to James Russell of the Clinton Global Initiative to tell the industry what was expected of it. 'Don't be an Exxon,' he told the airlines, 'work out what you can do to drive down energy consumption. Travel agents should push hotels for carbon disclosure. The message to chief executives is that perceptions are changing and you have between 12 and 24 months to get on that route.'

Source: Roger Blitz, FT.com site, 13 May 2007

DISCUSSION QUESTIONS

1. Should the tourism industry become more proactive in relation to the environment by insisting suppliers are as green as possible, auditing and reporting on their own policies etc.? If you were responsible for a large hotel chain what measures could you employ to become truly green (without worrying about costs)?

2. Provide communication points for a campaign to convince people of the need for business travel, a deserved holiday rest for holidaymakers and benefits to the economy even though airports and flights produce environmental pollution.

3. Are politicians the people who are best suited to make decisions over the future environmental policies of air transport and the tourism industry? If not how should these decisions be made?

consumers to buy products that they may not want. In addition, competitive advertising is argued to be responsible for higher costs and subsequently higher prices. It is therefore argued that if advertising were reduced, or did not exist, there would be more competition based upon price and service. The consumerist standpoint is that it would be better to spend the money on informative advertising rather than competitive advertising. It is believed the most disadvantaged tourist consumers are the ones most likely to be influenced by high expenditure on tourism marketing. The levels of marketing expenditure are quite often blamed for changing consumer attitudes and bringing about a materialistic society where status is derived from the number and type of destinations we visit, or leisure and activities we undertake. There is little doubt that marketing panders to materialistic values. However, the question is does marketing create these values, or simply appeal to the values already embedded within society as even in the most simple of societies the drive towards accumulation of possessions is the norm?

A SOCIETAL MARKETING APPROACH

It has been argued that the pressures affecting the image of marketing need to be more carefully considered. This has culminated in the movement toward a societal concept of marketing which stresses the enhancement of the needs of society as well as the consumer. Some organisations such as brewers and distillers are creating campaigns to warn people of the excesses of drinking, but it is questionable whether they are worried as much about the customer as about the legislation that could affect their operations.

While some organisations may pay lip service to a societal concept for PR purposes, in a competitive situation many of the problems related to tourism, and its marketing, will continue. It is also important to recognise that consumers are now better educated and are competent to select products that are not creating undue problems to society. Moreover, if organisations or their products do create problems, there are articulate pressure groups and government legislation available for consumer and environmental protection.

There is growing recognition that companies need to discover approaches to the marketplace that will build a socially responsible and ethical company culture. There is a need to understand the following three basic issues:

- **Consumerism.** This is organised group pressure, by all consumers, to protect and benefit consumer groups and the environment. This means it is not solely those consumers buying from a company, it is a broad movement to bring about improved exchange relationships.

- **Corporate social responsibility.** This is the decision of a firm to conduct its business in the interest of society as a whole as well as its own interests.

- **Ethics.** This involves personal decisions on the moral principles of what would be the right or wrong activity for individual employees. These decisions will be linked to the values and culture of the organisation. Ethical values are the core beliefs and standards that will dictate the stance a company takes in relation to its marketing, such as honesty and fairness.

A truly societal marketing approach is problematic due to the need to resolve multifaceted decisions over profit, pollution, social and environmental impact concerns. However, some companies perform their marketing activities better than others and are judged in positive terms by the public. Some companies are quite good at giving something back to the industry that supports them. Since the early 1990s, United Airlines has donated some of its Boeing 727s and 737s to museums and universities in the USA. The universities turn the aircraft into hands-on classrooms for students pursuing careers in aircraft maintenance, flight or aviation administration. United's initiative on this will bring it longer-term benefits as the disposition of the public to a brand is an important aspect of contemporary marketing.

If managers are going to achieve change it is argued that they need to put themselves in the consumer's position with regard to how they or their family would feel others should treat them. The following points are relevant in this context:

1. Good business managers should be socially responsible to all stakeholders (customers, employees, suppliers, shareholders, society, etc.) related to the company or tourism offer so as to minimise social costs. They should also have regard for laws or regulations and be ethical in management decisions.

2. Managers should be honest in claims and promotions, not be deceptive or agree to misleading advertising. They should show fairness to third parties. In addition, there should not be any hidden costs – or they should identify extra costs which may be applicable. For example, hoteliers should display the prices of rooms and supplements in a prominent public position and always make their cancellation policy clear at the time of booking and have it written into their communication literature.

3. The products offered should not cause harm or unacceptable tourism impact and managers should communicate any risks which are known to be associated with any product.

4. Marketers should undertake not to adopt sales techniques under the guise of its being research (such as that associated with time-share selling). Also, it is unfair and unethical to use promotions as research when adequate stock is unavailable because the research is being used as a method of deciding on the supply requirements.

CONCLUSION

We have demonstrated that the concept of marketing and its practical application have evolved as a result of changing business and social conditions that have emerged throughout the last century. The differences between sales and marketing were covered so that the reader will be more aware of why marketing planning and understanding the consumer is an important component of tourism marketing. In the course of this chapter we have identified different business philosophies that currently exist, the benefits of a marketing orientation and the basis of the marketing concept – including that of building relationships and delivering superior value.

The tourism product is predominately a service product with the main characteristics of intangibility, perishability and inseparability. The tourism purchase involves complex decisions related to perceptions of risk and the expectation of high levels of quality. As such there is a need for a deeper understanding of the process of TQM and consumer's expectation of service delivery standards. Finally, the use of marketing should take into account the issues surrounding the criticism of its application and as such an understanding of consumerism, social responsibility and ethics is important.

SELF-CHECK QUESTIONS

1. Name up to three ways in which value can be added to the tourism product.

2. What are the economic benefits of adopting a relationship marketing approach to business?

3. Name three main aspects which characterises the service product.

4. Provide a list of the four main types of risk which a tourist may experience.

5. What are the reasons why quality management is now more important than in the past?

ESSAY QUESTIONS

1. Explain how more of an adherence to modern marketing concepts may bring about changes in small or medium-size coach or bus companies with which you are familiar.

2. List the aspects of value that were important to you the last time you went on a flight, including your time at the airport. Also, discuss how the service providers could have added more value to your experience.

3. Examine brochures for the older age market, airline web sites and tour operator brochures to identify the strategies that are used by the tourism industry to alleviate the perception of risk in the purchase of the tourism product.

4. Look at the risks associated with tourism for a journey to Africa, based upon a family holiday, and decide what ones need to be controlled for.

ANNOTATED FURTHER READING

Books

Kotler, P., Bowen, J. and Makens, J. (2006) *Marketing for Hospitality and Tourism*, 4th edn, Pearson, Upper Saddle River, NJ.
The book draws upon the marketing material of Philip Kotler's other books and as such is based upon his pedigree which has been developed over a number of years of writing marketing textbooks. However, the examples are often better in other texts and other specialist books need to be read in conjunction with this one. This latest edition now covers electronic marketing, has case studies and provides a broad understanding of the role of marketing in hospitality and tourism. Specialist areas covered are customer quality management and destination marketing.

Lovelock, C. and Wirtz, J. (2004) *Service Marketing: People, Technology and Strategy*, 5th edn, Pearson, Upper Saddle River, NJ.
This book offers insight into the challenges facing the service sector by providing a well-researched and, at the same time, practical text. Coverage is given to service processes and systems, service positioning and service management. The text questions other approaches and allows the reader to experience new material not to be found in other textbooks dealing with a similar subject area.

Martin, W. (2002) *Quality Service: What Every Hospitality Manager Needs to Know*, Prentice Hall, Harlow.
This book has many applications to the hospitality and tourism sector including not only tourism, hotels and restaurants but also theme parks and clubs. The book has a number of figures and clear explanation of some of the main concepts.

Middleton, V. and Clarke, J. (2001) *Marketing in Travel and Tourism*, 3rd edn, Butterworth Heinemann, Oxford.
Marketing in Travel and Tourism explains the basic principles and practice of marketing in the contemporary setting of the new pressures affecting tourism including areas not normally found in similar texts such as NTOs. In addition, international case studies are included.

Shaw, S. (2004) *Airline Marketing and Management*, 5th edn, Ashgate, Aldershot.
This fifth edition text offers a comprehensive overview of the needs of the current airline industry to utilise and formulate marketing approaches within their sector. It includes new material on terrorism, economic and regulatory pressures, as well as airline alliances. Its strength is that the book examines the structure of the airline marketplace against the major principles of marketing.

Web sites

www.britishairways.com/press/
http://www.easyjet.com/en/about/investorrelationsrfinancialnews.html
http://www.insights.org.uk/

References cited and bibliography

Ang, S.H., Leong, S.M. and Kotler, P. (2000) 'The Asian apocalypse: crisis marketing for consumers and businesses', *Long Range Planning* **33**(1), 97–119.

Baker, M. (1999) *The Marketing Book*, Butterworth Heinemann, Oxford.

Chartered Institute of Marketing (1984) Cookham, Berkshire.

Dann, G.M.S. (1981) 'Tourist motivation: an appraisal', *Annals of Tourism Research* **8**(2), 187–219.

Drucker, P. (1973) *Management Tasks, Responsibilities, Practices*, Harper & Row, New York.

Economist (2001) 'Ready for take off', *Economist* **361**(8247), 52.

Economist (2002) 'So many planes, so few passengers' and 'Signs of life', *Economist* **364**(8290), 51–52, 57.

Gilbert, D.C. (1989) 'Tourism marketing – its emergence and establishment', pp. 77–90 in Cooper, C. (ed.), *Progress in Tourism, Recreation and Hospitality Management*, Vol. 1, Belhaven Press, London.

Gilbert, D.C. (1991) 'An examination of the consumer behaviour process related to tourism', pp. 78–105 in Cooper, C. (ed.), *Progress in Tourism, Recreation and Hospitality Management*, Vol. 3, Belhaven Press, London.

Gilbert, D.C. (1996) 'Relationship marketing and airline loyalty schemes', *Tourism Management* **17**(8), 575–82.

Gilbert, D.C. and Bailey, N. (1990) 'The development of marketing – a compendium of historical approaches', *Quarterly Review of Marketing* **15**(2), 6–13.

Gilbert, D.C. and Joshi, I. (1992) 'Quality management and the tourism and hospitality industry', pp. 149–68 in Cooper, C. and Lockwood, A. (eds), *Progress in Tourism, Recreation and Hospitality Management*, Vol. 4, Belhaven Press, London.

Gronroos, C. (1982) *Strategic Management and Marketing in the Service Sector*, Swedish School of Economics and Business Administration, Helsinki.

Hart, C.W.L., Heskett, J.L. and Sasser, W.E. (1990) 'The profitable part of service recovery', *Harvard Business Review* July/August, 148–56.

Keith, R.J. (1981) 'The marketing revolution', pp. 44–9 in Enis, B.M. and Cox, K.K. (eds), *Marketing Classics*, 4th edn, Allyn & Bacon, London.

Kotler, P. and Keller, K. (2006) *Marketing Management*, Prentice Hall, Upper Saddle River, NJ.

Lepp, A. and Gibson, H. (2003) 'Tourist roles, perceived risk and international tourism', *Annals of Tourism Research* **30**(3), 606–24.

Levitt, T. (1960) 'Marketing myopia', *Harvard Business Review* July/August, 45–56.

Nightingale, M. (1983) Determination and control of quality standards in hospitality services, MPhil. thesis, University of Surrey.

Parasuraman, A., Zeithaml, V.A. and Berry, L.L. (1985) 'A conceptual model of service quality and its implications for future research', *Journal of Marketing* **49**(4), 41–50.

Yeoman, I. and Lederer, P. (2005) 'Scottish Tourism: Scenarios and Vision', *Journal of Vacation Marketing* **11**(1), 71–87.

Zeithaml, V.A. and Bitner, M.J. (2000) *Services Marketing*, 2nd edn, Irwin McGraw-Hill, New York.

MAJOR CASE STUDY 17.1
Scottish tourism: scenarios and vision

In order to understand the potential for tourism in Scotland, it is important to look beyond the near future. Four scenarios have been created that paint contrasting pictures of Scottish tourism in 2015 (see Figure 17.9).

SCENARIO 1 – DYNAMIC SCOTLAND

Scotland is a dynamic country which accepts a diversity of views. A contemporary culture drives tourism. Tourism is Scotland's number-one industry in terms of employment, recognition and GDP. Prosperity is fuelled by favourable exchange rates, lower income tax, a concern for the environment, less duty on fuel and investment in infrastructure. Scotland is an international destination with clearly segmented activities, such as festivals, culture, golf, conventions and well-being, targeting top-end AB socio-economic groups, young families and business tourists.

The key points of this scenario are:

- high disposable income
- favourable exchange rates
- leading international tourism destination
- growth from business and holiday tourism
- Scotland is a tourism economy
- 7 per cent growth in tourism expenditure.

Tourism is now a £10bn industry which has grown at a rate of 7 per cent per annum since 2003. The industry directly employs 350,000 people, making it Scotland's number-one industry in terms of employment and GDP. In the early part of the century, Scotland was losing its market share of international tourists. But all that changed around 2010, when international tourists wanted to come to Scotland for both holidays and business tourism. Tourism is now the chief revenue generator of the Scottish economy and Scotland is a leading international destination. The industry is embedded in everyday life.

It was the re-establishment of Scotland as an international tourism destination which made all the difference. Tourism in Scotland had for too long placed too much emphasis on domestic tourism, but with very favourable exchange rates, a first-class product and a desirable image, international tourists have flocked back, coming from both East and West. The American market, which traditionally had a high affinity with Scotland, grew even stronger. A realisation came across the world that everything Scottish and Celtic had cultural capital and acclaim – whether it was Sir Walter Scott's 'Lady of the Lake' or Billy Connolly's banter. VisitScotland's 110 per cent Scotland programme was important in uniting the partners and

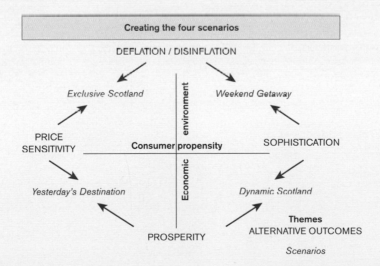

Figure 17.9   Creating the four scenarios

players in talking up a tourism economy in order to create and action change. The importance of tourism is now recognised in every sector of the Scottish economy, to the extent that every single person in Scotland now knows that the nation's prosperity is due to tourism.

Whereas in 2003 New Zealand was held up as the benchmark, now the tide has turned and Scotland is widely recognised as having the most efficient and welcoming tourism industry in the world. VisitScotland is now a public/private sector partnership, with the tourism industry driving strategy and marketing activity. VisitScotland is now benchmarked as being the best tourism agency in the world. It is envisaged that VisitScotland will be a wholly private company in 2020, because it is seen that the state no longer needs to intervene in tourism as the industry is strong, focused and successful.

Scotland's product portfolio is grouped into the following: playful Scotland; contemporary Scotland; body, mind and spirit; business tourism, city breaks; and touring and exploration. Each product integrates with VisitScotland's quality assurance scheme, which is like a club, is self-regulated and which all tourism providers want to join. The 'club' focuses on customer service and improvement – a sort of total-quality management approach.

Source: Abridged version of Yeoman and Lederer, 2005: 71

DISCUSSION QUESTIONS

1. Provide assessment of the case and indicate the strengths, weaknesses and missing opportunities it may reveal for the 'prosperous and sophisticated' segment identified.

2. Assess the product portfolio of Scotland by searching the Internet to see if the scenario in the case includes the right balance of product portfolio for a sophisticated international visitor.

3. Try to access the full paper to assess all the approaches in terms of their strengths and weaknesses.

CHAPTER 18
Marketing Planning

LEARNING OUTCOMES

Marketing planning is crucial to organisational survival in an environment that is increasingly unpredictable and volatile. In this chapter, therefore, we consider all aspects of marketing planning to ensure that, by the end of the chapter, the reader is able:

- to recognise the importance of marketing planning in respect of tourism and the implications of inefficient planning procedures;

- to understand the purposes of marketing planning in protecting the organisation and enhancing its market position;

- to appreciate the key stages of marketing planning and thus be in a better position to develop and implement a marketing plan successfully; and

- to identify the structure and content of an effective marketing plan.

Photograph: Stonehenge, Wiltshire, England

INTRODUCTION

In this chapter, we outline an approach to marketing planning in tourism and suggest that the marketing plan represents a structured guide to action. As such, it acts as a systematic method of data collection, logical analysis and objective setting of the most appropriate direction for an organisation, distributor or destination product. If a marketing plan is to be accepted by all concerned then the compilation of the plan has to involve all levels of personnel. This is because marketing plans require organisation-wide commitment if they are to be successful.

Giving the rate of change in tourism the plan must reflect the dynamic nature of the marketplace and as such the plan needs to be thought of as a loose-leaf binder rather than as a tablet of stone. This means the plan should act as a working document which can be updated or modified to take into account new opportunities, challenges or unanticipated problem situations.

WHAT IS MARKETING PLANNING?

We all need to plan to some extent if we are to make a success of our lives. Very few Olympic medallists could be successful without a planned programme of training and events leading up to their Olympic finals and achievements. Whether it is for examinations, sports events, going on holiday or organising a party, the use of planning leads to a greater certainty that the event will be a success. Without the right approach, and a sensible plan, alternative courses of action may not have been considered and, consequently, there is the likelihood that individuals, companies or organisations may not function to their maximum potential.

Planning is the most important activity of marketing management. It should provide a common structure and focus for all of the organisation's management activities. It is therefore essential for us to understand planning in its context as the key function of management.

The tourism sector provides a combination of different products and activities, which range from the small taxi firm and guest house to the largest airline or hotel group. The concepts of change and survival are as important to the small business as they are to a destination, major international hotel chain or airline. The fact that changes will occur, and with increasing speed, is the most predictable aspect of contemporary business life. It would therefore seem sensible to become familiar with the underlying trends and forces of change that impinge on tourism business activities. This enables the management of change towards desired objectives rather than being driven blindly before the tide of market forces.

The long-term survival of any organisation is dependent on how well the business relates to its environment. This relies on devising forward plans of where an organisation, destination or product would be best placed for the future. Some of the key points relating to marketing planning may be identified as follows:

- The plan requires control over the changes that have to be made.
- It needs to allow for the exploitation of any short-term advantages and improvement on weaknesses.
- It has to promote the use of analysis, reason and evaluation as an integral part of planning procedure.

A lack of marketing planning will result in a wide range of possible consequences. For a destination, this could involve one or more of the following:

- failure to take advantage of potential growth markets and new marketing opportunities – such as increasing use of the Internet;

- lack of maintenance of demand from a spread of markets and erosion of market share due to the actions of competitors;
- demand problems in low-season periods;
- low level of awareness of the destination's product offering;
- poor image of the destination;
- lack of support for cooperative marketing initiatives;
- poor or inadequate tourism information services;
- decline in quality levels below acceptable limits;
- difficulty in attracting intermediaries to market or package holidays;
- disillusionment and lack of motivation of tourism service employees.

Thus, the implementation of marketing planning procedures can be instrumental in alleviating many of the difficulties which tourism organisations may face. This is reflected in Major Case Study 18.1 which focuses on Disneyland® Resort Paris, and some of the weaknesses in the marketing planning procedures in respect of this venture.

However, although planning cannot guarantee success it can make the organisation less vulnerable to market forces and unpredictable events. Perhaps the first business casualties of tourism with the demise of Laker Airways, Braniff Airways, Courtline and ILG could have been avoided if more attention had been given to planning activities by their respective managements, especially in relation to cash flow, fixed cost and expansion attributes. The early lower price advantage of Sir Freddie Laker's operation or the image of Braniff with Gucci-designed uniforms and the cheap price policy of ILG provided excellent market positions for the products, yet the weakness of financial planning played a major part in each company's downfall.

Each organisation will adopt a different approach to the task of planning based upon the way senior executives see the purpose of a **marketing plan**. The values of any organisation fall along a continuum which begins at *wait and see*, moves through the next set of values to *prepare and predict* and finally ends with organisations that want to *make it happen*. An organisation will benefit more from a future that is made to happen because of the clear direction given, which provides fewer surprises for the workforce and less pressure on the requirements of company resources.

THE MARKETING ENVIRONMENT OF THE ORGANISATION

Each and every organisation has to operate within a market environment. This environment is made up of different levels of influence that will affect the opportunities and marketing decisions that need to be made. The historical conditions affecting competition and rivalry in company markets, the values of stakeholder groups and the political, economic, social and technological changes of the wider environment, all affect the likely performance of the organisation and its brands.

The organisational setting, or environment of operation, is related to the four levels identified in Table 18.1. It should be noted that the influences and pressures of the different levels shown are only taken into account by those organisations following a market-led business philosophy. At level 1 the organisation needs to be adequately resourced to be successful. As companies grow they have to be more aware of level 2 as the marketplace they operate in may become more difficult; and at level 3 there is the emphasis on creating a 'value chain' from the stakeholder participants whereby different relationships have to be fostered and reinforced in positive ways. The wider macro-environment (level 4) places pressures on management that are outside the control of the organisation. The broad categories of PESTEL (see the discussion on PESTEL further on in this chapter) involve a series of different levels

Table 18.1	Four levels of marketing environment affecting the organisation

Level 1	**The organisation**	Marketing sub-functions need to be well organised and integrated with other organisational functions. Marketing has to communicate the needs of the market environment as described in the subsequent levels and marketing thinking has to dominate any strategy formulation.
Level 2	**Company markets**	Identification of domestic and international consumer markets for products/services, or industrial, intermediary or institutional markets. The degree of rivalry and competitive activity as well as extent of consumer behaviour will affect market activity choice.
Level 3	**Organisational stakeholders**	Interest groups will affect the context of decision-making, e.g. shareholders, competitors, customers, employees, unions, government, suppliers, debtors, local community or banks, all of whom may have conflicting values but have some stake in the organisation.
Level 4	**The wider environment**	Analysis is required of political, economic, social, technological, environmental and legal aspects of the marketplace (PESTEL). Interrelations of the different forces and changes in the foregoing are powerful market environment determinants.

of aggregation: regional, national and international, which are related to business constraints as well as opportunities. We can examine these first.

THE PURPOSE OF THE MARKETING PLAN

The marketing plan is normally a short-term plan that will direct the organisation from one to three years. Typically, a five-year plan will be a strategic plan which is more general and less detailed than a marketing plan. Strategic planning involves developing and maintaining a fit between the environment, the competencies and resources of the organisation and its changing marketing opportunities. The strategic plan will concern itself more with external environmental influences and opportunities and less with the detail of the organisation's marketing activities. Strategic plans are normally either medium or long term and marketing plans are short or medium term.

The marketing plan and its compilation is able to provide a number of benefits for an organisation. The creation of a marketing plan will result in a wide range of management benefits as indicated in the following:

- To provide clear direction to the marketing operation based upon a systematic, written approach to planning and action. The planning system allows direction by virtue of requiring a written mission statement and set of objectives to be established, both of which can be transmitted to the workforce. This provides clear leadership principles and allows the workforce to know how their own efforts are essential to the achievement of desired results.

- To coordinate the resources of the organisation. This eliminates confusion and misunderstanding in order to achieve maximum cooperation. Tasks and responsibilities need to be set which clarify the direction and objectives of the organisation. To ensure there is a united effort, recommendations have to be presented in such a way that they can be fully understood at all organisational levels. The plan then acts as a master guide which will underpin all endeavours and decision-making. The plan should lead to greater employee cohesion and make everyone feel part of a team in which each individual believes he or she can make a valuable contribution.

- To set targets against which progress can be measured. Quantified targets for volume or revenue provide the focus for individual, departmental or company performance. Some organisations will set targets at achievable levels whereas others will set artificially high targets to encourage enhanced employee effort. The targets, once set, act as the benchmark against which all marketing programmes are monitored.

- To minimise risk through analysis of the internal and external environment. The planning procedure allows managers to identify areas of strength and weakness so that the first can be exploited and the second surmounted. In addition, threats and opportunities can be assessed.

- To examine the various ways of targeting to different market segments. This allows for different marketing mix strategies to be appraised prior to their implementation. As such estimates can be made of the likely impacts in relation to sales and revenue targets to the marketing budget. For example, targeting more segments could require an increase in sales literature which may increase cost rather than profit.

- To provide a record of the organisation's marketing policies and plans. This allows managers to check on what has been attempted in the past and to evaluate the effectiveness of previous programmes. It also provides continuity and a source of reference for new managers joining the organisation.

- To focus on longer-term business objectives. This allows the organisation to plan to be in the best position to achieve its longer-term future aims. This allows management to develop continuity of thought and action from one year to the next.

Given that you have understood the previous information on marketing then it will be agreed organisational objectives should be based upon relevant market-centred opportunities. It is the responsibility of tourism marketers to identify these opportunities and to devise a system of planning that may lead to their exploitation. However, planning can be fraught with problems as the next section explains.

MINI CASE STUDY 18.1
Tourism in a post-enchanted world

A paradox in tourism marketing is that while travel and adventure are inherently motivated by enchantment (the seeking of the unique or the fun of travel) and hunger for the romantic, tourism lives today in a world in which travel is anything but romantic and often not enjoyable. We still see beautiful advertisements in travel magazines and sense the allure of the romantic in the press, and the promise of an unforgettable experience. Most travellers, nevertheless, have experienced a different reality. Today's travel involves long lines, transportation hassles and poor service at many restaurants and hotels. The fact that tourism magazines now offer advice for surviving one's trip and that business people who travel a great deal are called 'road warriors' tells both the student and tourism professional that there is a wide gap between the promise and the reality of travel and tourism.

Too many in the industry still live in a time warp in which travel marketing still assumes an industrial version of mass travel that may soon no longer exist in the developed world. Indeed it can be hypothesised that as travel is sold on a more massive scale, its allure decreases and the enchantment of travel fades. While land tours of the 'if it's Monday, it must be . . .' variety, with the exception of bus tours, are now passé, the advent of the mass cruise industry and the all-inclusive is still very much a current tourism success story. As the post-enchanted age of tourism continues to dawn tourism specialists will need to consider new and innovative ways to recover something of tourism's past. An early example of the attempt to recreate enchantment in a post-enchanted age is the 'fly-drive' tour. These 'tours' permit travellers ways to personalise their trips and search for unique experiences rather than the common experience.

Despite tourism's claims to the contrary, our industry often develops its facilities, and uses the assumptions of mass marketing to judge itself. One only has to ask for some small variation at a convention meal to learn that kitchens are developed to sell a uniform product without addressing individual tastes, preferences, and/or health or religious needs. A simple survey of brochures provides us with an example of how much tourism is tied to a mass marketing design. A perusal of travel brochures demonstrates the uniformity of these brochures and it is not uncommon to see the same photo adorning the brochure of two different communities! In mass-produced tourism, the differentiated becomes undifferentiated, and reality merges with the imagination of the brochures' writers. This new world of travel has brought about all or some of the following factors which tourism professionals will need to consider:

- In a world in which no one is safe from the threat of terrorism or new illnesses such as SARS, the thrill of tourism has been tempered by the fear of travel.

- Destinations must become less dependent on brochures and other mass-produced and orientated forms of marketing. Instead, word-of-mouth advertising in which genuine emotions are displayed will act as the most effective market developer.

- Our resource of time is so limited that the pleasure traveller is now forced into a stressful search-for-fun vacation.

- Vacation groups are no longer stable. The industry must prepare itself and offer alternatives for cultural and social individualisation.

- Service is of greater importance in this post-enchanted high tech age: business people often no longer wish to travel.

- Originality is now essential. Locales that have truly original activities that can be protected and refined will have greater tourism pull than locales seeking to replicate that which already exists elsewhere.

- Being genuine is essential. No matter what the destination offers, the post-enchanted tourist will shun the ersatz for the genuine. Locations that are 'real' and touch our emotions will have the potential of becoming major destinations.

Source: Abridged version of Tarlow, 2003

DISCUSSION QUESTIONS

1. To what extent do you agree or disagree with Tarlow's assessment of current tourism and its marketing and are there other areas he could also have included?

2. How can marketing planning for tourism marketing have a positive impact on the future development of tourism given the points made by Tarlow?

3. Discuss what new forms of tourism are required for the new post-enchantment period and how your recommendations could become reality through a planning approach.

SUCCESSFUL PLANNING

Most textbooks suggest planning is simply the following of a series of simple steps. However, the true art of planning is to understand both the human aspects and procedural necessities involved. A poor planning experience may be a function of one or more of the following issues or problems:

- **Lack of senior management support.** A lack of support, from the chief executive and other senior people, is a major problem and one that is difficult to resolve. Any planning approach requires senior management support if it is to be treated seriously by employees.

- **Inappropriate planning procedures.** The system of planning which is adopted may not suit the organisation. There is often the separation of different planning functions from each other that leads to a lack of integration. Therefore, the planning system often has to be designed to match the organisation and to achieve a harmony of approach between employee groups.

- **Poor planning and management.** The system of planning is often blamed when the weakness is actually poor planning and management. Sometimes there is confusion over available data or even planning terms. The requirement is for a plan to be compiled which clarifies times and responsibilities for different actions and meetings which will lead to the appropriate information and people being utilised.

- **Unpredictable external events.** Unexpected environmental changes may create adverse affects on the organisation's performance. Planning is then often blamed for not having incorporated such a scenario. Plans need to be flexible and updated when necessary.

- **Organisational and managerial acceptance.** The values of the management team will imply different acceptance levels of the plan and may ultimately determine its success or failure. There is often hostility towards plans because of the feeling of a lack of involvement in the planning process. This often occurs when the planning is left solely to a planner or it becomes a once-a-year ritual.

- **Level of detail.** Problems occur when there is an over-abundance of information which has to be filtered for its relevance. Too much detail in the early stages can produce what is sometimes termed 'paralysis analysis' which means there is a need to decide what is important and what is not at an early stage of planning.

It is distressing that those travel companies that have recognised the need for a more structured approach to planning, and subsequently adopted the formalised procedures found in the literature, seldom enjoy the advantages claimed when embarking on planning. In fact, it is often planning itself which is brought into disrepute when it fails to bring about the desired changes within an organisation.

The problems faced in marketing planning have led to a growing body of literature which indicates that organisations should do what they are good at, rather than embarking upon higher level planning exercises. We believe this is a retrograde step because organisations should attempt to take the most logical direction and not be hampered by internal failings of the human resource aspects of implementation, lack of planning expertise or disregard of the involvement of others in the planning process. An understanding of the social aspects of the organisation is a prerequisite for successful planning. It is necessary for those involved in planning to recognise the need for involvement of all departments in the organisation in the formulation of the plan. This means that personnel are more likely to be motivated towards its successful implementation. Moreover, key personnel bring valuable knowledge and expertise to marketing plan formulation. It is also important to understand that most accomplishments in service industries, such as tourism, are made through people.

It is essential to ensure that plans are not prepared within the vacuum of one department or by a marketing team that believes it is an elite. Structured management meetings can offer a setting where deliberation, responsibility and authority are shared and taken by all. This precludes dogmatic assertions about the particular methods of preparing and organising marketing planning.

The marketing planning system offers a structured approach to organising and coordinating the efforts and activities of those involved in deciding on the future of an organisation. However, there is no one right system for any particular tourism organisation, since organisations differ in size and diversity of operations, the values of the senior management and the expertise of those involved in the planning exercise.

STRUCTURE OF THE MARKETING PLAN

The construction of the marketing plan is characterised by a range of headings developed by different theorists. Some authors offer a list of sections with the first headed 'SWOT issues' or 'situational analysis', the second headed 'statement of objectives and goals' or 'setting objectives', the third is 'strategy' or 'marketing programming' and the last is 'monitoring' or 'control'. We prefer to use different stages which are more easily understood by managers and students. The stages are:

1. What is it we want?
2. Where are we now?
3. Where do we want to go?
4. How do we get there?
5. Where did we get to?

These are represented in Figure 18.1. In reading the structure of the marketing planning model it is important to realise the system is not always the linear progression it appears. Quite often the process needs to involve an interplay between the various stages with the flexibility to move backwards as well as forwards. We should also understand that refinement of the plan takes place as understanding of the interconnections improves. We should not presume that perfection will be achieved until a number of drafts have been completed.

Linked to the simplistic stages above, the model of marketing planning can be described as involving:

1. Ensuring the consideration of human resources for successful planning.
2. Corporate mission and goals.
3. External and internal audit.
4. Business situation analysis.
5. Creating the objectives.
6. Providing an effective marketing mix strategy.
7. Monitoring the plan.

The consideration of human resources for successful planning

The involvement of different departments will help reduce resistance to future changes or tasks. Continuous concern about the human aspects of planning can provide a greater possibility of the plan's success. The planner or planning team should be aware that they are only a technical service to a wider team. However, we have to be careful not to make the system too open as to be in danger of creating anarchy and loss of focus. On the other hand, the system should not be too closed, as this leads to problems of bureaucracy and apathy.

Good planning is a combination of qualitative and quantitative factors based upon creative, as well as analytical and logical thinking. As Albert Einstein once remarked: 'When I examined myself, and my methods of thought, I came to the conclusion that the gift of fantasy has meant more to me than my talent for absorbing positive knowledge.' Creative thinkers are able to bring specific benefits to the planning process such as:

- challenges to norms and assumptions and the ability to question what others automatically accept as true;
- the focus on chance and the unexpected rather than safe answers;
- the development of new ways of thinking which transform familiar ideas into more unconventional approaches and so provide new ways and means of thinking of 'taken-for-granted' situations;

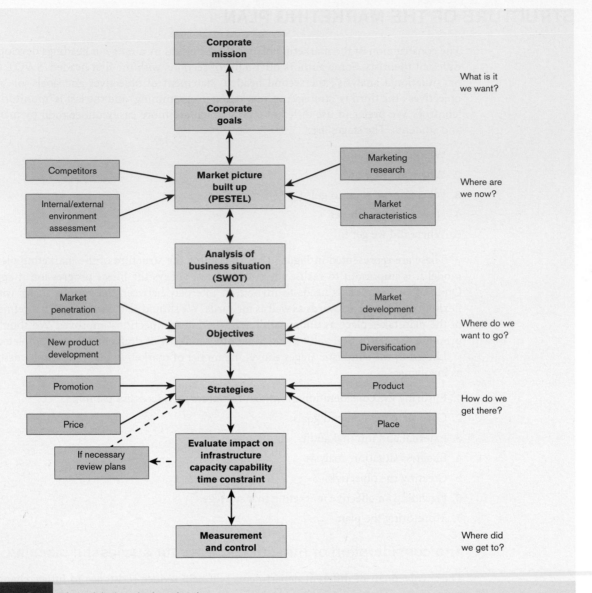

| **Figure 18.1** | A model of marketing planning |

- allowing individuals to make associations and so combine seemingly unrelated events, topics and ideas;
- allowing product, service and promotion ideas to be updated and revised; and
- keeping the planning function from becoming too boring and so retaining its excitement and innovation by bringing human resource values to the whole process.

One vital behavioural consideration of any plan which affects all aspects of the company is that it should not clash with the organisational culture. Such a clash can be overcome by ensuring staff values are incorporated into various stages of the planning cycle. The involvement of the full range of staff leads to a situation where the organisational culture values of staff are reflected in the 'bottom-up' comments. This helps to ensure that the plan is created as part of a process which makes it compatible with the corporate culture.

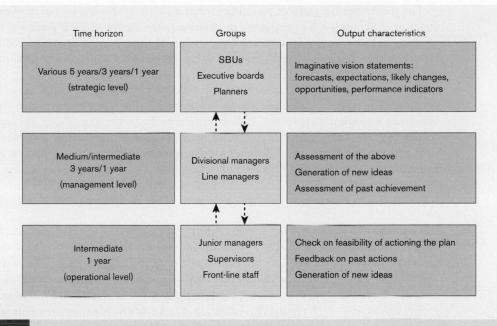

Time horizon	Groups	Output characteristics
Various 5 years/3 years/1 year (strategic level)	SBUs Executive boards Planners	Imaginative vision statements: forecasts, expectations, likely changes, opportunities, performance indicators
Medium/intermediate 3 years/1 year (management level)	Divisional managers Line managers	Assessment of the above Generation of new ideas Assessment of past achievement
Intermediate 1 year (operational level)	Junior managers Supervisors Front-line staff	Check on feasibility of actioning the plan Feedback on past actions Generation of new ideas

Figure 18.2   Involvement levels for marketing planning

Again, we stress that organisations have to plan for the involvement level of staff. This needs to be as seriously considered as planning for the company's markets. Figure 18.2 provides one approach in dealing with the need to have marketing planning involvement at all levels.

One other important aspect of influence when including a cross-section of people in planning is their ability to hinder or help the plan. Within any company or organisation, managers' competence to plan will be based upon how busy they are, their preoccupation with other business matters, their career goals, their experience and their ability to think analytically. These attributes are linked to other managers' values and the cultural climate within the organisation, which may be more or less responsive to change and adaptation through adherence to the planning system.

A plan when completed should be read by far more people than actually do read it. This is often due to the lack of time of busy executives and the complexity of the plan. To overcome the problem all plans require the addition of a good management summary, written in clear, concise language, which will ensure the dominant points and themes are communicated. The summary should concentrate on objectives, main target markets, opportunities and threats, key strategies and timings.

Corporate mission and goals

It is important to understand what is expected of the plan from the long-term goals set at corporate level. The goals may be based upon the values and objectives of the key shareholders, board directors or senior managers. In some situations goals are set only after the establishment and evaluation of the marketing programmes. This is a parochial, programme-led method of planning, where management does not attempt to meet higher level corporate goals within the planning process because managers are more prepared to settle for what they believe will work. An organisation with this approach will not investigate as broad a range of strategies as the organisation that is driven to ensure consistency with the overall corporate strategy and goals.

The most effective form of planning creates a balance between corporate direction and ensuring different levels of employee involvement (see Figure 18.2). If goals are dictated to employees, there is very little sense of ownership of the plan and a corresponding lack of motivation. Goals can be set in a functional, top-down approach or as a negotiation of goals through the combination of bottom-up and top-down processes.

The **mission statement** is a guide for employees to know what the purpose of the organisation is. The mission statement acts as a confirmation of what business the organisation is in from a consumer viewpoint. It then represents the overriding goal of the organisation. In the 1991/92 British Tourist Authority marketing plan the mission statement was: 'to strengthen the performance of Britain's tourist industry in international markets by encouraging the improvement and provision of tourist amenities and facilities in Britain'.

External and internal audit

It is necessary to gather enough relevant information about the external and internal organisational environment to be able to construct a business and market picture of current and future pressure and trends. One important part of marketing planning is knowing what to analyse. Executives have to be careful that they do not have too limited a view of the environment. Understanding the different needs of the tourist, as illustrated by Photograph 18.1, is only one aspect which requires investigation. Market knowledge requirements are so complex these days that having checklists of necessary information is one way to prevent organisations scanning the environment based upon what they intend to do, rather than in relation to what they could or should do.

The information collected should, at the very least, form the basis of a PESTEL investigation. PESTEL analysis is an examination of the conditions of Political, Economic, Social, Technological, Environmental and Legal changes that may affect the market, the organisation and ultimately the plan. Information-gathering is part of an internal and external audit which should collect a range of information, as detailed below. In addition to incorporating these factors in the marketing plan this information should be gathered on the basis of how it affects the organisation, especially in relation to its key competitors.

PESTEL analysis and market environment

The PESTEL analysis tool is a helpful framework approach for identifying those marketing activities that may impede or contribute to success in the macro (external) environment. It acts as an analysis for the various components of the macro environment. This includes the following:

- **Political:** taxation, duty, tourism policies, airport regulations.
- **Economic:** inflation, unemployment, fuel costs, exchange rates, average salaries, consumption patterns (see also the market environment list below).
- **Social:** demographics, cultural differences, language barriers, holiday/leisure time entitlement, values (consumerism), lifestyle, male/female role changes, delay of first child, education, workforce changes.
- **Technological:** innovations, new systems (reservations, yield management), Internet, better transference of data direct to customer, mobile technology such as 3G.
- **Environmental:** global warming and diminishing natural resources, pollution issues.
- **Legal:** regulation, constraints on companies and authorities.

Other important environmental factors

- **Total market:** size, growth, trends, value, industry structure, identify the competitors, barriers to entry, extent of under- or overcapacity of supply, marketing methods.

Photograph 18.1   Tourism marketing has to consider the different product needs of the tourist.

Source: Alamy Images/Vario Images GmbH & Co.KG (t); Alamy Images/Oote Boe Photography (b)

- **Companies:** level of investment, takeovers, promotional expenditure, redundancies, revenue, profits.
- **Product development:** trends, new product types, service enhancements, competitiveness of other companies' products.
- **Price:** levels, range, terms, practices.
- **Distribution:** patterns, trade structure, policies.
- **Promotion:** expenditure, types, communication messages, brand strengths, effectiveness of own current promotion methods.

Understanding competition – Porter's model

The plan has to be formulated in relation to those forces which impinge on the likelihood of success. Prime among such forces is competition. The plan cannot exist in isolation of other factors. As Porter has argued (1980), it is easy to view the competition too narrowly and too pessimistically. Porter views intense competition as natural, with the state of competition depending on the relationship between five basic forces (see Figure 18.3). Porter argues that it is the collective strength of these forces that determines the ultimate profit potential of any industry. The model has become widely known as the 'five forces' model of competition.

The focuses of rivalry among existing competitors are (1) the outcome of rivalry; (2) the bargaining power of suppliers; (3) the bargaining power of buyers; (4) the threat of new entrants; and (5) the threat of substitute products or services. Each of these forces, in turn, can be broken down into its constituent elements. The following discussion of these forces helps with our understanding of the tourism industry and clarifies the considerations we must take into account.

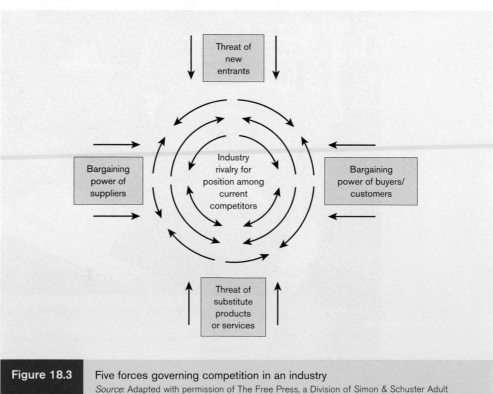

Figure 18.3	Five forces governing competition in an industry

Source: Adapted with permission of The Free Press, a Division of Simon & Schuster Adult Publishing Group, from *Competitive Strategy: Techniques for Analyzing Industries and Competitors*, by Michael E. Porter. Copyright © 1980, 1998 by The Free Press. All rights reserved

1. Rivalry among existing competitors

Factors which might affect the nature of competitiveness or 'the jockeying for position' by the use of tactics in the industry include the following:

- the degree of concentration in the industry and the number and relative size of the competitors;
- if industry growth is slow there will be increased struggle for market share;
- the extent and nature of product differentiation;
- when fixed costs are high or the product perishable as is the case with much of the tourism industry offerings;
- capacity in relation to demand and characteristics of demand;
- high exit barriers will keep companies competing even though they may be earning low or negative returns.

2. Bargaining power of suppliers

Factors relevant to the supply side of the industry will be similar to those mentioned on the customer side of the industry and, thus, include:

- the structure of the supplier side relative to the producer industry;
- the degree of product differentiation/substitutability;
- the potential for forward integration;
- the relative importance of the industry demand to suppliers;
- the feasibility and cost of producers switching suppliers.

3. Bargaining power of buyers

The bargaining power of the buyers (that is, demand for the products or services whether it is the company acting as buyer from suppliers or whether it is the final customer) is related to the following features:

- the degree of concentration relating to the relative importance of levels of demand on the customer side by comparison with that of the competing suppliers;
- the relative significance of the product or service to customers in terms of quality, expenditure and service;
- relative ease and cost of changing to new suppliers (switching costs);
- the amount of information possessed by buyers;
- the ability of buyers to integrate backwards;
- profit levels of buyers;
- the extent to which buyers want differentiated products.

4. Threat of new entrants

The ease, or difficulty, with which new producers may enter the industry affects the degree to which the structure of the industry can change due to the extra competition and the desire to gain market share. The seriousness of the threat is dependent on the type of barriers to entry and on the way existing competitors will react:

- the extent to which there are economies of scale (note that airline alliances such as Star or One World can provide these);
- the amount of capital required to capture customer loyalty and create brand identification;
- the capital required for inventories and absorbing start-up costs (for example, the cost of leasing new aircraft as a no-frills airline start-up);

- existing companies may have experienced learning curve benefits with lower costs (lower costs may be important to an airline when wanting to enter a new route on a large enough scale to compete with rivals);
- the level of customer switching costs (for example, for an airline are there frequent flyer benefits or loyalty considerations?);
- the existence of government regulation and legal limitations and barriers (for example, can an airline obtain desired take-off and landing slots or obtain an air operator's licence?).

5. *Threat of substitutes*

These include:

- the availability of substitutes and willingness of buyers to utilise substitute products which have the same functional capability (for example, video conferencing rather than business travel);
- the impact on profits of close substitutes;
- the impact of the comparative price and quality of substitutes.

The above approach to industry analysis can allow a company to understand the pressures on the industry and the likely effect on the prospects for short- and longer-term success. More specifically, a company is able to take into consideration its true competitive position with regard to its opponents and can identify the possible strengths and weaknesses due to the current state of rivalry in the industry. It may then proceed to consider what level of importance should be attached to the marketing planning process in order to provide a competitive advantage and a position from which to achieve its financial objectives.

Portfolio analysis

A portfolio approach allows for the analysis of an organisation's current position in relation to the marketplace, its own companies or products. A commonly used technique for consideration of the growth and share of an organisation is the Boston Consulting Group matrix (BCG). Portfolio analysis has been described as a family of techniques with BCG as the most famous (Abell and Hammond, 1979). The BCG approach has been used by a large number of planners in different marketing settings. This approach allows an organisation to classify the position of each of its strategic business units (SBUs) on one axis in terms of their market share relative to competitors and on the opposite axis to position annual industry growth. By creating a measurement based upon the scales of each of these axes, a spatial plot is derived which by the use of the creation of quadrants places each plot in a specific category. As part of the analysis, a company may identify which SBUs are dominant when compared to competitors, and whether the areas in which the company operates are growing, stable or declining. The two-by-two matrix (see Figure 18.4) describes four types of position labelled as star, question mark, cash cow and dog.

Stars

These are SBUs or products with a high market share in a fast growing market and, importantly, offering good prospects for growth. As such, the objective would be for an investment or protection for any SBU or product to be identified when it falls into this quadrant. The objective is to build on the strength of the position and/or to hold on to it in the face of any competition. If the organisation has a balanced portfolio, the transferring of money from a cash cow to the star SBU could be contemplated if this would create higher returns in the long run. This could be the airline route which offered the most return to the company or the destination to which a tour operator could obtain the highest demand.

Question marks

These are SBUs or products where there is some question about their position. Spatially, there is the potential for high market growth, but there is also low market share. The objectives would be to investigate further the possibility of any future movement in the market or from

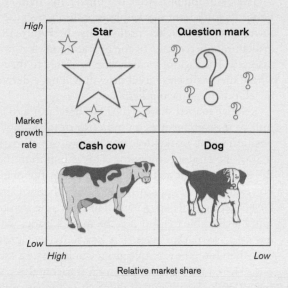

High

Star   **Question mark**

Market
growth
rate

Cash cow   **Dog**

Low

High   Low

Relative market share

Figure 18.4   Market growth – market share portfolio analysis matrix

the competition, creating a new position of either a star or a dog. If the question mark has the possibility of becoming a star and if the organisation has a cash cow then money should be transferred to build the question mark position with the objective of creating a star. Alternatively, a poor outcome for the analysis may mean the objective has to be one of becoming a niche operator – or even divestment. If the unit of consideration were an overseas destination for a tour operator and a certain destination such as Florida fell into this quadrant, there may need to be an expansion of brochure space for the area and the use of increased promotion to increase demand.

Cash cows

This category is where the SBU or product is enjoying the benefit of a high market share but in a low- or zero-growth market. The objective would be to exploit the strong, positive cash flow situation but not to devote any investment into the SBU or product apart from to ensure its maintenance. The objective is normally to hold the position and harvest money so that it can be used to grow other parts of the business. This can be the case in some seaside resort areas where a good hotel retains high-value business but the resort itself is in decline and there is no reason to expect any future increase in demand.

Dogs

These are SBUs or products with a low market share and static or no market growth. The inference is that any future earnings are bound to be low and little or no profit will be made. The objective would be either to create a niche area for activity or to withdraw from this area of business by selling out or planning closure. If the unit of consideration were items on a restaurant menu and certain items fell into this area, there would be an argument for reducing or removing the meal types from the menu. Another example is the withdrawal of British Airways from the Dublin route as it could not compete with other lower-cost carriers.

Each of the BCG model's spatial areas allows an identification of what strategies may be most appropriate. This allows objectives to be decided upon which are in the long-term interests of the organisation as a whole, so that a balanced approach is taken which considers all aspects of an operation.

The assumption is that the higher the market share of any strategic business unit the better its long-term marketplace position, because of the probability of economies of scale, lower costs and higher profitability. In Figure 18.4 the vertical axis identifies the annual growth rate percentage of the operating market for the SBUs, companies or products being assessed. The logic of its inclusion is related to the notion that any organisation in a situation where there is high market growth will have derived benefit from the situation of buoyant development in the marketplace.

Relative market share is the horizontal axis and is used because of its ability to provide the unit of measurement as an indicator of the ability to generate cash based upon the relative position to the market leader. The measure of market share is expressed as a comparison to that of the largest competitor. This is important because it reflects market share relative to the leader and shows the degree of power the market leader has over others in the market. For example, if company 'A' had 25% share of the market and its competitor 'B' also had 25%, there is little advantage. However, the market situation is dramatically different and more favourable to 'A' if it is the market leader with a 25% share and its closest competitor has a 12.5% market share. The horizontal axis provides a relative ratio to the market leader and, therefore, the example given would create a 1:1 ratio in the first case and 1:0.5 in the second. These ratios are plotted on the horizontal axis against the market leader's share to reflect the individual positions of dominance for different units of measurement. The axis can be divided on any scale which makes sense for the market being considered but should enable the relative positions, across the range of the axis, to be plotted. As there is the use of a market leader share figure, the left-hand end of the scale will be no larger than 1 as no other SBU, product or company can exceed the size of the leader's share.

A certain amount of caution has to be applied to the indiscriminate use of portfolio analysis. At the outset it should be realised that portfolio analysis has more dimensions than simply market and market growth. In fact, one of the difficulties is to decide upon the scales for the axes. Once these are agreed, it may be difficult to obtain competitive data. With a BCG approach the spatial positioning outcome of any analysis is not necessarily related to profitability, as a high market share could be based upon low profitability if prices are lower than the competition; or vice versa. In addition, a higher market share for a company or a product may reflect a disproportionate amount of promotional expenditure which in turn could be creating unacceptable cost implications. There are conceptual and practical problems in defining both products and markets when using the matrix. While international flights to America or Asia may be a star, the main business for the airline could be suffering due to the impact of no-frills operators on European routes. Finally, a market which is growing may not be a good environmental fit, or suit the business strengths of the SBU or company. None of these weaknesses indicates there is a major problem with the BCG matrix or its principles but simply that it has to be utilised with some degree of caution. Its strength is that it allows for a more detailed analysis of the business.

Competitive advantage

When tourism companies decide upon strategies that may offer them a higher likelihood of achieving market success they need to consider different generic routes to obtain competitive advantage. Porter (1980) describes the three generic strategies of *cost leadership* (a company that seeks, finds and exploits all sources of cost advantage – providing for a standard, no-frills package such as that successfully pioneered by Southwest Airlines in America and adopted a few years later by easyJet in the UK (see Figure 18.5)); *differentiation* (a company seeks something distinctive to set it apart from others that can bring in good profit returns – typically having attributes that are different to the competition such as the quality added value of the tour operator Kuoni); and a *focus* strategy (a company selects a segment of the market and targets that to the extent of excluding other segments whereby a tour company will specialise in a single type of product, such as walking holidays).

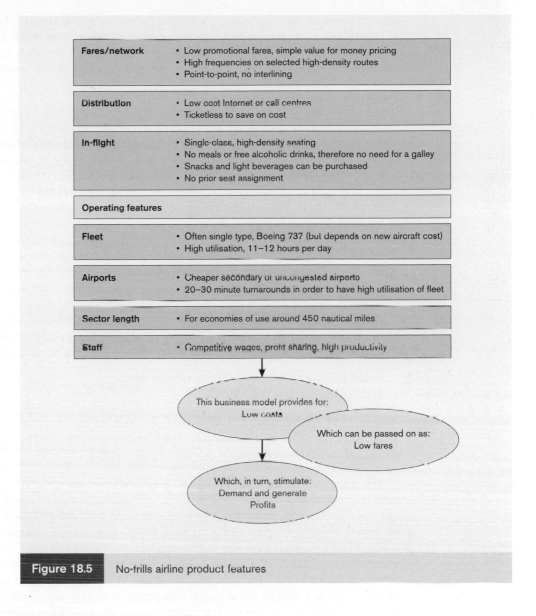

Fares/network	• Low promotional fares, simple value for money pricing • High frequencies on selected high-density routes • Point-to-point, no interlining
Distribution	• Low cost Internet or call centres • Ticketless to save on cost
In-flight	• Single-class, high-density seating • No meals or free alcoholic drinks, therefore no need for a galley • Snacks and light beverages can be purchased • No prior seat assignment
Operating features	
Fleet	• Often single type, Boeing 737 (but depends on new aircraft cost) • High utilisation, 11–12 hours per day
Airports	• Cheaper secondary or uncongested airports • 20–30 minute turnarounds in order to have high utilisation of fleet
Sector length	• For economies of use around 450 nautical miles
Staff	• Competitive wages, profit sharing, high productivity

This business model provides for:
Low costs

Which can be passed on as:
Low fares

Which, in turn, stimulate:
Demand and generate
Profits

Figure 18.5   No-frills airline product features

Business situation analysis

Once sufficient information has been collected, there is the need to carry out an analysis of the business situation and this is best done by identifying the major strengths, weaknesses, opportunities and threats facing an organisation. This is the so-called 'SWOT analysis'. There is also the need to check the results of the SWOT analysis against information provided from PESTEL analysis.

The systematic analysis carried out at this stage provides the formulation of a number of assumptions about the past performance, future conditions, product opportunities, resources and service priorities which all lead to the possibility of a range of strategic options for an organisation in the tourism sector.

At this stage of planning, it is possible to circulate the assumptions and forecasts to different company divisions. These should be offered as a range of alternatives. For example, if you have assumed the market will grow at x% and this will create £Y with a specific strategy, then it is also wise to create alternative scenarios. You should estimate sales at lower and higher rates than expected so that the impact on profits can be assessed. For example, a rate of growth of $x + 2\%$, given different relative cost implications, may create a profit of $1.3 \times £Y$, or alternatively $x - 2\%$ gives $0.7 \times £Y$. Managers can then involve their team in discussions about the relevance of the material created from the foregoing environmental scanning stage.

Creating the objectives

Objectives are a combination of what is expected of the organisation by its shareholders or directors, and an evaluation of the options emerging out of the first stages of the planning process. The objectives should emerge as the most logical course of action for the organisation to embark upon given the detailed analysis in the preceding stages.

We also have to ensure that the objectives are not only related to volume of sales and financial objectives, but also involve broader marketing objectives. One danger in planning is that large organisations often set financial objectives in terms of growth rate in earnings per share, return on equity or investment and so on, and ignore marketing objectives such as the selection of specific segments as target markets and the improvement of products, brand image or consumer awareness. Objectives should also include the expected market share achievements because this performance may only be realistic if certain budgets are made available.

Objectives need to be a balance of the aspirational and realistic so that the organisation attempts to improve its market position within acceptable risk limits. The basic criteria for setting objectives based upon the SMART acronym is that they need to be:

- **Specific**, by being focused on the results required.
- **Measurable** for each objective set.
- **Achievable**, set against trends and market position constraints and assessed fully.
- **Realistic**, given resource constraints of time and money, etc.; and set against
- **Time limits** of when the objective(s) should be reached.

The objective stage inputs of Figure 18.1 are based upon growth strategies whereby a company is attempting to expand. Organisations will normally want to attack the market share of others by penetrating the market to increase their own share of the market. This takes place in the current markets and is normally based upon a more aggressive use of the marketing mix. The organisation may attempt to increase existing customer usage rates or attract competitors' customers. For example, Visa combined with the Singapore Tourist Board and Singapore Airlines in 2004 to offer price discounts to platinum and gold card members; and the company has utilised promotional techniques such as being able to earn extra bonus points in relation to car hire in an attempt to get their cardholders to use their cards while on holiday in preference to competitors' cards. Larger organisations or companies will try to increase sales through market development by attempting to sell current products in new markets. This may involve the addition of new locations such as McDonald's opening outlets to compete at airports, at tourist attractions and even within office buildings. Market development may also be based upon convincing the customer to find new uses for existing products. Larger organisations or companies will try to develop markets by selling the benefits of, say, self-catering holidays to those who take hotel holidays. Organisations may also develop their markets by expanding internationally such as Holiday Inn and the Accor group.

Objectives may also include **new product development** or diversification. The Eurostar Channel Tunnel service in 2007 improved the service by changing the London-based terminus and reduced the travelling time to Paris. The objective for this investment required intensive product research and assessment as to the incremental business from northern cities. Tour operators/wholesalers develop new destinations and airlines embark upon new air routes. Diversification has occurred where companies such as Virgin developed a new business from its retail base into an airline operation in several different countries. Hotel organisations have developed contract catering operations and vice versa. There has also been the diversification of airlines into the hotel business.

Providing an effective marketing mix strategy

The success of the plan relies on creating the right marketing mix strategies for achieving the objectives (see Chapter 19 for a clear explanation of the different aspects of the marketing mix). The use of the marketing mix involves balancing the elements of the marketing mix to achieve the highest expected probability of meeting the plan's objectives. However, mix strategies have to be checked to ensure they are acceptable. For example, if the strategy is for expansion of a destination, say by means of price benefits, an impact or environmental analysis should be considered. Figure 18.6 shows a situation where there is no extra benefit in expanding tourist numbers since the social costs (due to extra arrivals) increase at the same rate as the benefits. Note that Q_1 and Q_2 are in exactly the same position in both parts (a) and (b) of Figure 18.6.

Figure 18.6(a) shows the relationship between demand and price for a tourism destination. If price is reduced from P_1 to P_2 then the resultant demand for the area increases from Q_1 to Q_2. Tourism destinations can reduce the average price of visits through government policies such as allowing more charter arrivals or reducing tourist taxes. If the positions of Figure 18.6(a) are examined against the social cost and benefit curves of Figure 18.6(b) it will be seen that position Q_2 is no better than position Q_1 as the social costs (such as those depicted in Photograph 18.2) have increased at a rate that cancels out the increase in social benefits. The result is that the destination is no better off socially from an increase in arrivals and may have to check other criteria and bring in policy changes before it agrees to expansion policies.

Market segmentation

Emanating out of the SWOT analysis will be the objective to target specific sub-markets or what are known as segments. Market segmentation is the process of dividing the total perceived market into subsets, in each of which the potential customers have characteristics in common, which lead to similar demand needs for a product or service. The marketer has to decide upon the coverage of the target market. This can be any one of a selection from a broad mass market, a selective market segment strategy or aiming at two or more multiple segments.

Mass tourism operators selling undifferentiated European and long-haul destinations will target a very broad subset of consumers. This is because their success lies in offering a wide

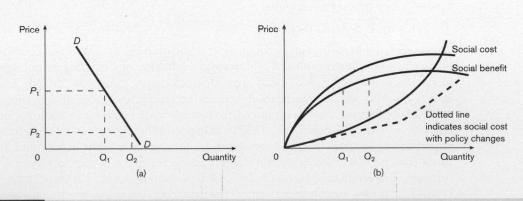

| **Figure 18.6** | Tourism demand problems |

Photograph 18.2 Every tourist destination should realise that social costs need to be managed.
Source: Alamy Images/Chuck Eckert

range of popular countries at value for money prices. In contrast, a specialist tour opera-tor/wholesaler can attempt to identify a new segment or adopt an upmarket or downmarket position. A current lifestyle change is towards being healthier. The medical profession and a number of magazines and newspapers have changed attitudes to both leisure pursuits and eating habits. Both of these will have repercussions on the provision of leisure centres in hotels and resorts, activity holiday supply and spa and health products as well as be an oppor-tunity for new product development.

Achieving strength of positioning

To be successful in positioning, a company or destination has to understand how to modify the perception of the consumer by improving, reinforcing or defending its position in the marketplace. Ries and Trout (1986) argue that positioning has to be correctly addressed, as it is the only way to counteract the confusion created by the communication jungle. Accordingly, Ries and Trout recommend 'the best approach in our over-communicated soci-ety is the over-simplified message'. This has to happen at the right time and as such the secret of positioning becomes the organised system for finding the window in the mind. Ries and Trout contend that: 'Positioning starts with a product. A piece of merchandise, a service, a company, an institution or even a person . . . But positioning is not what you do to a product. Positioning is what you do to the mind of the prospect. That is, you position the product in the mind of the prospect.' To achieve success at positioning the tourism product or brand there is a need to ensure the position has clarity, is credible, has consistency over time and

MINI CASE STUDY 18.2
Madeira: quality of service is key to region's appeal

The *Ventura do Mar*, a 50-foot, two-masted ketch built in the 1950s, cuts through the Atlantic en route from Funchal to the Desertas, three uninhabited islands 21 nautical miles to the south-east of Madeira. On board, a small group of birdwatchers from Norway, Britain and Portugal prepare their telescopes and binoculars to observe the seabirds found on the islands, including Zino's petrel, Cory's shearwater and the Madeiran storm petrel. The skipper, Luís Dias, a marine biologist, has already briefed the group on what they can expect to see on the four-hour trip, including dolphins, pilot whales and, occasionally, the monk seals that breed on the islands, a protected nature reserve.

Mr Dias, his wife Catarina, also a marine biologist, and a team of seven other guides and sailors also run trips to the more distant Selvagens islands, as well as sailing, diving, whale- and dolphin-watching tours and inland birdwatching, canoeing and trekking excursions. The *Ventura do Mar* represents a new aspect of tourism in Madeira, which wants to tap the full potential of the region, two-thirds of which is officially designated as a nature reserve. The aim is to extend the industry into new areas beyond the island's traditional market dominated by the big international tour operators. 'Nature tourism currently offers the best opportunities for growth,' says Dinarte Camacho, the island's regional director of tourism. 'Madeira has a rich natural heritage and a steadily increasing number of businesses, both small and large, offering a wide variety of outdoor activities for visitors.'

The island wants to diversify tourism products to attract new market segments, he says. 'But our aim will always be to provide quality services and to maximise the island's natural heritage as a key attraction.' Even if it were feasible, the idea of becoming a mass tourism market like the Canary Islands is anathema to Madeira. 'We cannot compete in quantity,' says Mr Camacho. 'We count instead on quality and supplying niche markets with differentiated products.' Tourism has nonetheless grown substantially over the past two decades. From just over 3m bed/nights and total revenue of about €150m in 1990, the industry had expanded to more than 5m bed/nights and revenue of about €270m in 2004. Tourist numbers were up by about 2.5 per cent in 2005 over the previous year. The growth the industry wants most is in room occupancy rates and average revenue per room. Occupancy averaged 54.7 per cent in 2005 and only 49 per cent for five-star hotels, levels unlikely to be profitable over the long term. Low occupancy rates are partly the result of a big increase in hotel beds in recent years, without a corresponding rise in demand. In addition, most flights to the island are run by charter airlines, which rely heavily on bookings by the big tour operators to fill seats.

Source: Peter Wise, FT.com site, 10 May 2006

DISCUSSION QUESTIONS

1. Search the web and marketing literature for alternative tourism holidays based upon sailing and assess the potential which is related to this market segment.

2. Provide arguments by use of a SWOT analysis for and against the emphasis on the development of alternative types of tourism such as that in the above article.

3. What main types of alternative holiday product such as that in the article above do you think could be successful for a small island economy?

will remain competitive in relation to the needs of the company's chosen target groups. This is explained as follows:

- **Clarity.** It is important to realise that positioning is about communicating a message to the consumer so as to spatially place the tourism service offered in their mind. This has to be based upon a clear message with no confusion. If the message is not clear the consumer will not understand what the brand or offer is about. A positioning strategy requires a clear message that most people will understand.

- **Credibility.** A positioning message has to be believable. If we claim that our travel agency offers better service than it delivers in reality, consumers may well utilise it a first time but never again. They may well feel cynical about the company claims if they find the delivery does not match the promise. This is particularly vital in the case of services where it is not possible for customers to sample an offering very easily. Also, customers have a preconceived set of relative positions already in their minds as expectations and therefore they have learnt what is possible in terms of any claim to a specific position.

- **Consistency.** It has been pointed out that positioning is all about creating an image in the mind of the consumer. Clearly for this to be achieved the message has to be consistent. If a company changes its communications policy there will be no clear messages and the public will not be able to visualise the positioning the company is attempting to occupy. Of course, it is possible to change positioning but this takes time to achieve.

- **Competitiveness.** In any decision over position there needs to be a strategic decision which positions the company relative to that of the competition (we are friendlier, larger, offer more value, have better service, more modern, safer etc.) and this has to be accepted by the customer. Positioning the brand with a set of attributes that the customer does not care about is never going to be effective.

Selecting the segments to target

The identification and selection of segments will require judgement based on the analysis of different data. The purpose of segmentation is to select a segment (target market) with the best potential on a range of criteria. The objective set is then to create product benefits, features and promotional messages which will appeal to the needs of the selected segment(s). A number of characteristics are examined when deciding upon target groups as shown in Table 18.2. (See Chapter 2 on consumer behaviour for further discussion of some of these characteristics.)

Table 18.2	Some general characteristics of segmentation strategies
Characteristic	**Typical classification**
Geographic	Region of world, country, area of country, urban, suburban, rural areas, city, town, post code, type of house or by climate type
Demographic	Age group, gender, education, family life cycle, ethnic group. Socio-economic classification of household based upon A, B, C1, C2, DE classifications
Psychographic	Lifestyle. Personality type – introvert, extrovert, high/low ego drive, independent, compulsive, gregarious, group worker
Usership	Non-user, current user, past user, potential user, loyalty type, heavy user, medium user, light user
Kind of purchase	Special occasion (honeymoon, anniversary), annual holiday trip, business travel, method of purchase (agent, direct, etc.)
Attitudes	Towards product area, towards brand, towards usership and use situations
Benefits sought	Status, convenience, luxury, economy, etc.

In order for segmentation to be successful there is a need to apply intellectual rigour to the segmentation procedure. When a target group is identified it is prudent to use a checklist to ensure the segment offers a viable opportunity for the organisation, such as:

- **Is the segment measurable?** Progress at various stages of the segmentation activity needs to be measured. Segment composition, size, purchasing power etc. in order for assessment need to be measurable.

- **Is the segment accessible?** The targeting decision requires that individual buyers can easily be contacted through promotional messages as well as be accessible to be offered a purchase opportunity or service.

- **Is the segment substantial?** The segment must be large enough to provide a viable level of business.

- **Is the segment sustainable?** The choice of segment has to take into account whether the demand will last. Fashion and 'lifestyle' market segments are prone to change and fall into demise.

- **Is the segment actionable?** Are there any impediments to putting together a marketing mix so that the target market can be reached with a clear product positioning strategy and message which will fit the needs, aspirational ideals and behaviour of the segment?

- **Is the segment defendable?** Can the target market be defended against competitor activity if they also select the same target group, and will rivalry cause any viability problems?

USA *market snapshot which helps in detecting segments and targeting them*

The USA market intelligence overview from the VisitBritain 2007 web site indicates:

- Population 298.4 million – growing and ageing (more Hispanics).
- IMF forecasts 2007: GDP (based on PPP per capita) USD$45,257. GDP Growth rate 2.9%. Unemployment 4.9%. Inflation 2.9%.
- No visa required.
- Only 27% of Americans have a valid passport (but this will grow to 2009 due to the need for local regional passport use, e.g. Canada).
- 25 Metropolitan areas of the USA have direct air links to the UK (this will grow with the new EU/US open skies policy).
- 64.6 million outbound in 2005. UK has 5.3% market share.
- UK ranked third outbound destination for American travellers (after Canada and Mexico).
- 3.4 million visits in 2005 (−5% on 2004).
- £2,384 million spent in 2005 (−1% on 2004). AEV £691; AED £90.
- In 2005 39% were holiday visitors; 25% VFR.
- 70% stay 1–7 nights
- 59% visit between April and September.
- Top towns: London, followed by Edinburgh, Glasgow, Manchester and Oxford.
- History, Heritage, Culture, Scenic Beauty, Ancestry and Sporting Events.
- Youth, DINKS/SINKS, Gay and Lesbian, Luxury Travellers, Seniors/Boomers.
- 45% aged 45+ (IPS, 2005).
- Internet access 69%.

Segmentation leads to positioning the service or product offer so that it is right for the target audience. This is reliant on adherence to the initial objectives and results in the final choice of the marketing mix. Once the segments have emerged from the consideration process the objectives need to be reconsidered. If it is found that there are no problems with the objectives, and the plan is to be adopted, there has to be some assessment of whether the objectives can be achieved within specific time constraints. Competitors may be able to develop more quickly or the organisation may find it too difficult to change in a short period of time. The ability to change is often related to the availability of resources. It is necessary to question whether the resources available are sufficient to achieve the objectives (budgets, personnel, technology, existing hotels, aircraft or built facilities). If, after evaluation, it is decided the strategy is unacceptable, there is a need to review and revise the plan's objectives.

Agreeing the marketing mix strategy has to be linked to laying down task-related programmes which allocate budgets and create responsibilities and timings for the plan's implementation. There is always a need to link planning with budgeting which will allow for the adoption and execution of an effective marketing mix strategy to achieve the objectives of the plan.

Monitoring the plan

There should be a means of monitoring the achievements of the plan so that tactical action can be taken either to get the plan back on course or to take advantage of new opportunities. There is therefore the need for the provision of assessment and measurement methods that will monitor progress towards the achievement of the plan's overall objectives. There is also the need to know what deviations from the initial objectives are acceptable. This will allow for the review and amendment of the plan on a continuous basis.

The tourism and hospitality industry has invested in reservation systems that allow a continuous flow of financial and booking pattern data. This has enabled the modelling of different performance indicators. These can include forecasts of probable load factors or occupancy levels as well as assessment of the effectiveness of regional or national sales promotion, price changes and sales representative campaigns. Nowadays, the airline and hotel sectors are applying these systems to yield management systems as a means to monitor demand and maximise the revenue from consumers.

CONCLUSION

Marketing planning is probably the most important activity for any tourism organisation. The long-term survival of an organisation is related to the way that it understands how to assess its environment, set sensible objectives and choose logical strategies for achieving success. Utilisation of different models such as SWOT, PESTEL, Porter's five force model and the BCG model all allow for a more informed approach to the planning analysis. The conditions for maximising the advantages from planning are based upon the need to understand the human aspects of the process as well as the formalised procedures of a structured approach.

SELF-CHECK QUESTIONS

1. Name the four levels of marketing environment affecting the company.
2. What do the acronyms PESTEL and SWOT stand for?
3. List the main sections you would expect to see in a marketing plan.
4. What do you understand the term 'portfolio analysis' to mean?
5. Explain the concept of positioning and its relationship to target groups.

ESSAY QUESTIONS

1. Provide a SWOT and PESTEL analysis indicating what may have led to the following changes that have taken place in the operation of cruise ships over the past years.

   Early cruise products
   - long distance; long duration; most of time at sea; larger liners used; departure from home-generating area ports

   Modern cruise products
   - short distance; shorter 7–14 night duration; majority of daytime in ports; specially designed for smaller ports and activity; fly–cruise arrangements or warm water port departures

2. One of the demographic trends in many countries is the increasing proportion of older adults. Is this important enough to warrant changes in approaches to the marketing of tourism products? Examine through a planning approach how either the hotel, cruise, airline or attractions markets may need to plan for such changes.

3. Describe the way you would assess the segments and targeting that may be possible from the information found in this chapter on the 2007 USA marketplace according to VisitBritain.

4. VisitBritain has identified the following dates and objectives to coincide with the Olympics in 2012. What marketing plan would you provide for the following objectives?

2009	Building Momentum
2010	Galvanising Britain
2011	Inviting the World
2012	Welcoming the World
2013 onwards	Delivering the Legacy

ANNOTATED FURTHER READING

Books

Evans, N., Campbell, D. and Stonehouse, G. (2003) *Strategic Management for Travel and Tourism*, Butterworth Heinemann, Oxford.
The text provides a comprehensive insight into strategic planning for tourism organisations. It offers approaches to the selection, evaluation and implementation of strategic planning. It is specifically written in relation to the travel and tourism industry with an explanation of strategic management applications and theory. In addition it has case studies from Southwest Airlines, Airtours, Marriott and Thomas Cook.

Kotler, P., Bowen, J. and Makens, J. (2006) *Marketing for Hospitality and Tourism*, 4th edn, Prentice Hall, Upper Saddle River, NJ.
The book draws upon the marketing material of Philip Kotler's other books and as such is based upon his pedigree which has been developed over a number of years of writing marketing textbooks. However, the examples are often better in other texts and other specialist books need to be read in conjunction with this one. This latest edition now covers electronic marketing, has case studies and provides a broad understanding of the role of marketing in hospitality and tourism. Specialist areas covered are customer quality management and destination marketing.

McDonald, M. and Keegan, W. (2001) *Marketing Plans That Work*, Butterworth Heinemann, Oxford.

This text provides the reader with a comprehensive coverage of all the aspects of producing a successful marketing plan. The book concentrates upon the logical development of a marketing plan and only deals with the marketing concepts in a perfunctory manner so is recommended solely for understanding the marketing planning process and approach.

References cited and bibliography

Abell, D.F. and Hammond, J.S. (1979) *Strategic Market Planning Problems and Analytical Approaches*, Prentice Hall, Englewood Cliffs, NJ.

Gilbert, C. (2003) *Retail Marketing Management*, 2nd edn, Financial Times/Prentice Hall, Harlow.

Gilbert, D., Child, D. and Bennett, M. (2001) 'A qualitative study of the current practice of "no-frills" airlines operating in the UK', *Journal of Vacation Marketing* 7(4), 302–15.

IPS (2005) *International Passenger Survey*, Office of National Statistics, Cardiff.

Kotler, P. (2000) *Marketing Management – The Millennium Edition*, Prentice Hall, Upper Saddle River, NJ.

McArdle, J. (1989) 'Product branding – the way forward', *Tourism Management* 10, 201.

McDonald, M. (1989) *Marketing Plans*, Heinemann, Oxford.

Mintel (2000) 'The gay holiday market', Mintel International Group, London.

Porter, M.E. (1980) *Competitive Strategy: Techniques for Analysing Industries and Competitors*, Free Press, New York.

Ries, A. and Trout, J. (1986) *Positioning: The Battle for Your Mind*, McGraw-Hill, London.

Tarlow, P. (2003) *e-Review of Tourism Research*, John Wiley & Sons, New York.

Urry, J. (1992) *The Tourist Gaze*, Sage, London.

MAJOR CASE STUDY 18.1
Disneyland® Resort Paris

When the Disney Corporation assessed the idea of a theme park in Europe initially a site with sufficient flat land and a good climate similar to Florida was thought to be in the Alicante area of Spain. However, the area also suffered from the notorious Mistral winds. The final decision was for the French location, at Marne-la-Vallee, due to its position which could attract European visitors and the benefit of close proximity to Paris. The location put the park within 4 hours' drive for around 68 million people, and 2 hours' flight or train journey for a further 300 million.

However, Disneyland® Resort Paris, formerly Euro Disney, became a huge embarrassment to the Walt Disney Corporation after it plunged into the red shortly after its opening in France in 1992. The initial cost of the theme park, at US$4.4 billion for the development of a 5,000-acre site, represented the largest single piece of construction in Europe's history apart from the Channel Tunnel project linking England and France.

Cumulative losses at the end of 1993 exceeded US$1 billion. The loss is all the more significant given that the then Euro Disney had only achieved target attendance objectives of 9 million rather than 11 million planned 'guests' in slightly over one year of operation. The situation did not improve in 1994 when Euro Disney reported a loss for the year to the end of September of US$317 million and attendance was 10% down on levels achieved in 1993. The Walt Disney company announced it would close the park unless the banks agreed to restructure the $1 billion debt that the park's construction and operation had accumulated. The banks could have been left with massive debt and therefore agreed to write off virtually all of the next two years' interest charges, and allowed a three year postponement of loan repayments. In return the Walt Disney company restructured its own share of the park and loan arrangements.

The question is what went wrong with the planning? The main problem for Euro Disney can be found to lie with the planning assumptions and forecasts which did not reflect the European economy or the willingness of consumers to pay high entrance fees. There was also a mistaken belief in a flatter seasonal demand curve, which characterises demand in the USA, as a result of mid-semester or off-peak visits by parents with their children. As a result, the levels and patterns of demand never reached those anticipated by planners.

An additional problem is related to the homogeneity of European markets. Disney planners in the USA initially treated Europe as a single country, underestimating the inherent differences between the existing markets in respect of demand and importing marketing methods which had succeeded in America but which did not successfully transplant to the European context. Consequently, the American parent company was forced to accept that tourists' habits vary a great deal throughout the European context and that its prices were too high for French visitors.

As an integral part of the financial subsidisation for the development of the park, the plan had assumed that well-appointed, high priced hotels and other property could be constructed and then sold on to entrepreneurs for considerable profits. Disney planners did not want to be faced with either the land-use problems they had experienced in the USA where extra land has had to be purchased for expansion or the financial limitations imposed in Tokyo where Japanese investors took huge profits while Disney earned 10% of gross earnings on rides and 5% on food and beverage. Consequently, the planners were concerned with attempting to maximise profit opportunities from the outset.

Disney planners overlooked the worsening economic conditions prevailing in Europe in the early 1990s which led to a severe slump in the property market for accommodation. Euro Disney had embarked on a vast property development – including hotels, shops, offices and residential housing – ignoring the severe handicap this posed of potentially unrealistic financial obligations to its American parent. The hotels were not sold as originally planned and, in addition, currency devaluation in Great Britain and Italy further depressed purchasing power, driving down demand for foreign travel.

Other planning problems materialised. The design of the hotel restaurants, for example, did not take into consideration the different tastes of the guests and were often too small, because of the belief that few Europeans would eat a full breakfast. Consequently, long waiting times and queuing problems ensued, culminating in guest dissatisfaction and complaints. The park's outlets were designed for snacking but the pattern was that at 1 o'clock there was a major demand for a reasonably substantial meal. Moreover, Disney outlets were restricted by a 'no alcohol' policy which meant the French custom of taking wine with a meal was not permissible.

The problems were further compounded by preopening reports by Disney that employees would have to comply with the written Disney code of dress which consisted, for women, of short fingernails, appropriate undergarments and strict policies on hairstyles. The global code was considered an insult by the French people who believed it attacked the underlying principles in French culture of individualism and privacy. Thus, unforeseen cultural issues emerged with newspapers, such as Le Figaro, stating: 'Euro Disney is the very symbol of the process by which people's cultural standards are lowered and money booomoo all conquering.'

French intellectuals accused Disney of stifling the imagination of young people, of turning children into consumers, even of creating a 'cultural Chernobyl'. In addition, Disney characters were attacked as likely to pollute the nation's culture. Euro Disney's image was further damaged by PR blunders by senior Disney officials who dismissed the criticism as fatuous. Nevertheless, concessions were made: emphasis was placed on European fairy-tale characters such as Snow White and Pinocchio rather than Bambi and Dumbo. Also, in order to echo French culture, the turret which the company's 'imagineers' built was modelled not on Neuschwanstein, the Bavarian castle reconstructed at Disney's other theme parks, but on a drawing from a fifteenth-century French manuscript.

RECENT CHANGES

Following the embarrassment of heavy losses and low levels of demand in 1993 and 1994, Disney brought in French senior management who orchestrated key developments at Euro Disney. The theme park was renamed Disneyland® Resort Paris and in 1994 a complete product reassessment and reduction programme was implemented. The number of souvenir lines was cut in half from 30,000 and restaurant menu items were also reduced from 5,400 to 2,000.

Marketing strategies were reappraised and advertising messages modified. The advertising was designed to make parents and grandparents sympathetic to their children's emotional pleasure while emphasising the adventure element for adults. Potential customers are targeted with special offers during off-peak winter months, a strategy which evolved in response to market research activity which demonstrated that levels of repeat visits were high. In addition, the promotional links with Eurostar have helped to increase the number of UK visitors.

Pricing policies were also adjusted to offer reduced entrance admission charges in the evening, for example. Job flexibility arrangements, customer care programmes and other efficiency drives were also instigated, leading to the first ever surplus for Disneyland® Resort Paris for 1995. This was related to improvements in hotel occupancy which rose steadily from 55% in 1993 to 68% in 1995, compared with an average of roughly 60% for hotels in and around the Paris area.

The current situation is linked closely to the need to pay off the park's debts and net loss in 2002 of 56 million euros, but this is not easy given the problems of lower tourist visitors to France. For example, the American visitor market in 2003 was down 30% on the previous year due to fear of travel and the negative image created by France's opposition to the Iraq war. In fact, in America there has been a general boycott of French products based upon the anger of Americans. The company blames its poor performance on a reduction in European travel and tourism, strikes in France and the poor economic conditions of its key markets. However, given that the vast majority of its visitors are French (40%), British (21%), and German (7%) then the theme park probably requires other changes. The hope was that the Walt Disney Studios, which was modelled on the success of Universal Studios in Florida, would attract higher numbers but this has not been the case.

Just 12.8 million visitors came in 2006 which is too low to provide profit and the result is that the company is just breaking even at the operating level. Furthermore, there are the repayments on outstanding debt of €1.9 billion, which produces a loss of nearly €90 million. The problems are not over and Disneyland® Paris's share dropped as low as €0.10 in 2007 despite its current assets of 2,000 hectares of land, a 27-hole golf course and seven hotels in addition to the park.

Therefore, it is crucial that financial and marketing planning are implemented professionally if the park is to maintain its profitability and prosper in the European marketplace. This is especially important given increasing competition from other European theme parks such as Port Aventura in Spain and Parc Asterix in France.

Source: Based on information from various newspaper articles including 'Tourist drought hits Disneyland Paris: Iraq fallout, strikes and forest fires have kept Americans and Europeans away', by Amelia Gentleman in Paris, *The Guardian*, August 2003. See also: http://www.telegraph.co.uk/arts/main. jhtml?xml=/arts/2003/08/25/ftdis25.xml&sSheet=/arts/2003 /08/25/ixartleft.html

DISCUSSION QUESTIONS

Provide some analysis and marketing solutions for Disneyland® Resort Paris. For example:

1. Is there a need to plan to attract different market segments by country and demographically, and if so how can this be achieved?

2. Look at and assess the PR activity for Disneyland Paris on the web. Does the park need to have an improved overall marketing communication strategy targeted to potential visitors and/or past visitors?

3. Is it important to focus on the heritage of the well-loved Disney characters and if so is the target group the under-tens or other segments?

CHAPTER 19
Marketing Mix Applications

LEARNING OUTCOMES

The marketing mix offers management a set of tools that may be manipulated to meet specific objectives and attract predefined target markets. The marketing mix is the focus of this chapter and, by the end of this chapter, you will be able to:

- identify the elements that make up the marketing mix and understand how this may be applied to a tourism product;

- recognise that the manipulation of the marketing mix generally, and the promotion and pricing in particular, will be beneficial in meeting specific predetermined objectives;

- appreciate that distribution and product formulation are linked to, and influenced by, technological and structural changes in the tourism industry; and

- understand the centrality of the concept of the target market to the marketing mix.

Photograph: View of Lake Tekapo, New Zealand © Hannah Cox

INTRODUCTION

Anyone who purchases a tourism product has probably been influenced by a promotional campaign, assessed the product offer, considered whether he or she is willing to pay the price and, finally, thought about how easy it would be to buy it. Each of these aspects of purchase is carefully planned by tourism marketers in an attempt to convince potential tourists to buy their products. They are the basic ingredients of the marketing mix, the aspect of marketing that we consider in detail in this chapter.

In actual fact a great deal of tourism management involves aspects of the marketing mix. Each of the areas that make up the marketing mix involves a complex set of management decisions which have to take into account not only the individual mix strategy but also the effect of such a mix on the target market groups. This chapter will therefore provide some of the most important considerations for the planning of the marketing mix.

WHAT IS THE MARKETING MIX?

It is customary to accept that the marketing mix (Figure 19.1) is within the control of management and refers to decisions made in relation to the four Ps. These may be defined as:

- Product.
- Price.
- Promotion.
- Place (distribution).

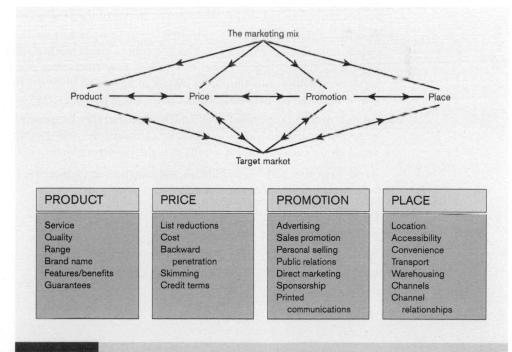

Figure 19.1   The marketing mix

There are, however, alternative approaches where authors stress the need for an expansion of these four. This is an interesting development because the four Ps were conceived by McCarthy (1978) as an abridged version of a much wider range of what were termed 'marketing ingredients'. McCarthy based the classification of his four Ps upon a whole collection of marketing ingredients offered much earlier by Borden (1965). We will discuss this later in this chapter.

Kotler and Armstrong (2005) indicate that the marketing mix is one of the key concepts in modern marketing theory. They define the marketing mix as 'the set of controllable, tactical marketing tools that the firm blends to produce the response it wants in the target market'.

Target market

The fundamental starting point for the creation of a successful marketing mix strategy is to ensure the target market is clearly defined. Although the target market is not part of the marketing mix, its role in dictating the different ways the mix is used makes it indistinguishable from the concept and of paramount importance. The target market is the focus for all marketing mix activity and is linked to the final selection of segments that we discussed in the previous chapter.

The market for a product is made up of actual and potential consumers. This total available group of consumers will be analysed and a decision will be made as to segments or subgroups to be targeted. The segments would probably have been identified as part of the marketing planning process (see Chapter 18 for an explanation of choosing segments) and would have emerged or been specified at the time of the setting of objectives. The specification of the target market has a number of important benefits which are discussed below.

Benefits of targeting

Targeting facilitates the following:

- A fuller understanding of the unique characteristics and needs of the group to be satisfied is reached. The target market acts as a reference point for marketing decisions, especially as to how the marketing mix should be planned. This should lead to greater effectiveness for the mix which in turn provides for the success of the programme.

- A better understanding of a company's competitors is gained because it is possible to detect those who have made a similar selection of target markets. If an organisation does not clarify the markets it wishes to target, it may treat every other organisation in its sector as an equal competitor. Once a main competitor is identified their marketing efforts can be more closely followed – or benchmarked and then reacted to.

- An improvement is possible in an understanding of the changes and developments in the needs of the target market. Awareness is heightened due to the scrutiny focused upon the target group's actions, and reactions to slightly different forms of the marketing mix.

As we have seen with the section on segmentation in Chapter 18, target markets can be based upon a number of factors such as:

- socio-economic groups;
- geographic location;
- age;
- sex;
- income levels;
- visitor type;
- benefits sought; and
- purchase behaviour and attitudes for both the international and domestic business, holiday visitor and recreationalist.

The target market acts as the focus for tailoring the mix so that target customers will judge the overall product to be superior to that of the competition. Segmentation and target marketing are central to efficient and effective marketing activity because they are instrumental in ensuring the marketing mix strategy is tailored to meet the specific needs of different customer groups.

PRODUCT

The effectiveness of planning the marketing mix depends as much on the ability to select the right target market as on the skill in devising a product offer which will generate high levels of satisfaction. We have to realise that the customer is looking for the right product to solve their problem of satisfying a need. Often this involves a portfolio approach. Club Mediterranée is treated as having a singular product to offer yet it has more than 80 different holiday villages in many different countries, as well as having expanded into other types of tour business. More recently Club Mediterranée utilised quality as a means to reduce its product range and improve its positioning. The service product (see Figure 19.2) is quite complex and can be thought of as being a combination of different levels with four important areas – *the core product; the facilitating product; the supporting product;* and *the augmented product.*

Core product

Every **product** is a package of problem-solving services and tangible attributes that will be successful if the package is valued enough to satisfy a need or want. A product includes everything that the customer receives and this includes the central level of the *core product* which is made up of the delivery of benefits and features. A holiday consumer in a travel agency is looking for the benefit of relaxing in the sun and having no hassle in the journey or stay. They leave the detail of how to arrange this to the travel agent. To put it another way, buyers 'do not buy quarter inch drills; they buy quarter inch holes'. Marketing staff have to uncover

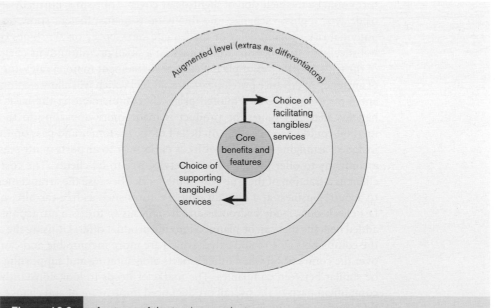

| **Figure 19.2** | Anatomy of the tourism product |

the subtle benefits that the consumer seeks when utilising a retail distribution channel or purchasing a product. We know that consumers buy products for the benefits they are expected to deliver. It therefore makes sense to incorporate different additions into the product that will help to differentiate it from the comparable product offered by competitors. Adding in the right features creates a higher probability that a purchase will occur. There are the different features which are added as the tangible aspects of the product which help to differentiate it from competitors. The tangible features may be the size of the hotel entrance, the physical aspects of a destination or the comfort of the airline seat. In order to understand a product it must be understood that service products are different and as such should not be confused with other general marketing literature concepts which are less complex in their approach.

Facilitating, supporting and augmented product

The *facilitating product* aspects must be present for the customer to utilise the services of the core product. This will be the service and goods such as lift service in a high-rise hotel, receptionist and telephone operator, credit card payment facilities, signage and easy access around the destination. *Core products* require *facilitating products* but do not necessarily have to include *supporting products* (see Figure 19.2). In fact the no-frills airlines need the facilitating products of check-in and baggage handling but only provide a minimum of supporting products in order to adhere to their cost-leadership strategy. The supporting product for a scheduled full service airline may include such extras as separate lounge area, higher employee numbers providing superior service, service to deal with children travelling, and so on as these are all supporting products which may be planned into the product offer.

The *augmented* product level is the added aspects of the product which form the extras and which can help the product compete more favourably in the marketplace. This could be achieved through sensory marketing such as creating a special atmosphere in an airline lounge area by creating garden setting spaces with birdsong and different lighting as well as having sanctuary areas of peace and quiet such as those areas and lounges at places such as Singapore's Changi airport. In fact, Changi also has a nature trail to follow. Companies should take the opportunity to consider factors such as the use of materials and the decor of public areas which will provide the atmosphere within which the customer interacts. A feature could be the inclusion of flight-delay cover. Tourism is normally associated with the risk of delayed flights, exchange rate fluctuations or insufficient snow on skiing holidays. The potential risk of flight delay or inadequate snow cover on ski slopes can be insured against holistically by the operator who passes on a small premium to its clients as part of the price of the trip. A further example is a contract agreement to hotel rates, the early buying forward of currency or advance purchase of aircraft fuel which will allow a company to offer the guarantee of no increase in a quoted price. By complementing the basic product with special benefits that add value, the product is made more appealing to the consumer. Another method could be to negotiate on behalf of the customer and pass on the added benefits. For instance, arranging a contract with car parks near to airports in off-season periods can allow a company to offer the car-parking service free to its clients. The cost is passed on to each client as a fraction of the true cost of the service because the arrangement allows the car park to acquire business at a difficult time. Features such as free car hire, pick up at the airport, fast check-outs, study bedrooms and free tickets to tourism attractions or the theatre are all added benefits that can be planned into the product offer. Utilising the augmented approach, the company is able to add extras which are more memorable and can act as differentiators over the competition when other aspects of facilitating and supporting products are likely to be similar between companies. The marketer needs to look constantly at how the different component parts of the overall product need improvement and change and this is sometimes referred to as the potential product in other contexts but here is seen as being within a development and renewal of existing levels, not a new level.

Service

This is concerned with creating the level of services to be offered. For a hotel, a tour operator/ wholesaler, a restaurant or an airline, this poses the questions of how much of the service should the client be expected to perform and how much should be provided by staff. For example, self-service buffet-style food operations or the personal carrying of hand luggage is now thought of as acceptable and, at times, desirable by clients. Similarly, tea- and coffee-making facilities in hotel bedrooms where the guest helps him/herself is now seen to be integral to the accommodation product offering, especially if the provision of room service is limited to certain hours. Service provision for air travellers now satisfies communication needs, as some airlines offer an improved business product with in-flight telephone provision, or access to power for a personal computer. These developments are indicative of the relentless quest for cost-effective improvements to the service content of the tourism product. Any tourism operation is predominately service-based and has to be able to deliver high levels of service.

Quality

Quality involves deciding on quality standards for the product and implementing a method of assurance on the performance level of staff and facilities. The management of quality is becoming an increasingly important management function (as discussed in Chapter 17) since it is crucial to create a good reputation for the quality of the product and service offered. This encourages a positive image for the company or organisation and a reputation for good quality is a major advantage in reducing the perception of risk in the minds of consumers. Tourism service providers are more likely to be successful if they can be depended upon to deliver higher quality service levels than their competitors. Success through quality is often associated with the outcome of the relationship between a customer's prior expectations of service delivery and the perception of the actual service. With this in mind, Swissair aims for at least 96% of its passengers to rate the quality of its service as good or superior, otherwise it will take remedial action.

Range

It is necessary to decide how different individual products will fit into the overall range of the organisation's products offered to the marketplace. A tour operator/wholesaler has to decide whether to include five-star or two-star hotels in their range of offering, or whether they should operate to traditional or newly emerging destinations. More recently the cruise market has expanded and many tour operators/wholesalers have altered their product range to include cruise ships to accommodate the resurgence in demand. In fact, the introduction of Cunard's *Queen Mary 2* as the longest, tallest and heaviest passenger ship ever, bears witness to the investment in this sector.

Tourism enterprises have to decide on the range of offers and how each product fits into the product mix. Such decisions will produce change over time, as illustrated by some of the milestones in the development and change of Thomas Cook in Table 19.1. The essence of the early success of Thomas Cook in providing unique experiences is reflected in the seeking out of new experiences, as shown in Photograph 19.1.

Brand name

A **brand** is a name, a symbol, term or design or a combination of these that marketers attempt to promote so that the brand is well known and provides added value to a product. This can lead to consumers insisting on the product by brand name and, as a consequence of the delivery of satisfaction, the achievement of brand loyalty or less price sensitivity.

The benefit of developing a strong brand is important as consumers are often prepared to pay a price premium for perceived added values related to buying well-marketed brands. The

Table 19.1	Examples of the historical aspects of Thomas Cook

1841	First excursion from Leicester to Loughborough
1845	Trip to Liverpool and excursions to Wales
1846	First tours to Scotland
1851	Trips for 165 000 people to the Great Exhibition
1855	First continental tours
1863	Tours organised to Switzerland
1866	First tours to North America
1869	First tours to the Holy Land
1872	Pioneers of round-the-world tours
1874	Traveller's cheques introduced
1902	First winter sports brochures and motor car tours
1919	The company advertises air tours
1927	First air charter, New York to Chicago for Dempsey fight
1939	First package tour to south of France
1972	Thomas Cook becomes part of the Midland Bank Group
1981	Agreement to launch euro traveller's cheques
1988	Cessation of operation in the short-haul market
1989	Reinvestment in retail outlets to upgrade them
1989	Direct sales operation set up
1992	Thomas Cook sold by Midland Bank to Westdeutsche Landesbank (WestLB) and the LTU Group
1992	21.6% shareholding acquired from Owners Abroad in order to form an alliance (now First Choice)
1994	Thomas Cook corporate travel business and USA franchised travel offices sold to American Express
1994	Travel Kiosks set up to sell direct by the use of advanced technology
1999	The company rationalises and reduces the number of its sub-brands and also launches the new JMC brand
2000	The company becomes wholly owned by Thomas Cook AG (formerly C&N Touristic AG – which itself was formed as a merger of Condor and Neckermann). The sale also took place of its Global and Financial Division to Travelex.
2001	Thomas Cook UK rationalised as part of a transformation programme to save costs and integrate the UK operation and JMC into the new parent group
2002	JMC brand abandoned three years after its introduction
2003	Thomscook.com adopt a customised system for customers to personalise their travel with a build-your-own (BYO) self-packaging technology linking flights, hotels, car hire and insurance
2003	Announcement of the merger of its two charter airlines, Condor Flugdienst and Condor Berlin, the sale of some of its hotels and other assets and a large reduction in staff, in order to reduce costs
2004	The integrated business model which Thomas Cook and larger German rival Tui operate of combining the elements of in-house airlines, tour operators and travel agents is not as sustainable given the level of independent travel driven by the success of low-cost airlines.
2005	Although Thomas Cook UK business generated record profits of £51 million ($98 million), the results were affected by losses elsewhere in the group. This led to cost-cutting and selling off 12 of its fleet of Boeing 757–200 aircraft.
2006	KarstadtQuelle, the German retailer, takes full control of Thomas Cook from partner Lufthansa, the German airline, for its half-share in Europe's second-largest travel group and charter airline Condor.
2007	MyTravel (formerly Airtours), the £1.1 billion UK holiday company, and Thomas Cook (owned by KarstadtQuelle, the German group), agree a merger with Thomas Cook owning 52% of the capital and MyTravel the remainder. The headquarters of the new business is planned for the UK.

Photograph 19.1   Consumers indicate a growing interest in new tourist experiences.
Source: Corbis/Arctic-Images

price premium, also known as *brand equity*, is the price customers are prepared to pay above the commodity value of a product or service. This being the case, well-respected brands – if well positioned and managed – can give a better return to the company. Brands with a strong personality are attractive to companies who own them and predator companies wishing to buy into their potency. A successful brand is a flag bearer as it provides visible signals of positional strength in the marketplace. There are also distribution benefits whereby a strong brand will obtain channel leverage due to customers wanting to purchase and travel agents or travel web sites wanting to have inventory. In this way successful brands provide their parent companies with a competitive advantage.

Figure 19.3 illustrates the benefit of creating a strong brand which is able to add value to the company offer. A differentiated position from that of the competition with a clear identity allows the brand to achieve higher prices and achieve higher levels of demand in periods of recession. A secondary consideration is that strong domestic brands provide a good base on which to build an international or global presence.

Brands, and ranges of brands, may fall into a number of different categories:

- **Family brands.** This is where each of the company's products adopts the same brand name. Examples include many of the leading hotel companies which have a family name. Accor as a leading international accommodation provider emphasises Accor as a single

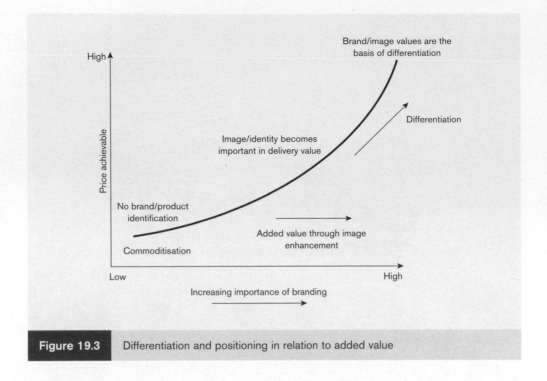

Figure 19.3   Differentiation and positioning in relation to added value

web page brand but offers Sofitel, Novotel, Ibis and Mercure under this group branding. Holiday Inn as part of the InterContinental hotels group offers Holiday Inn and Holiday Inn Express with different price and quality positioning so as to attract different market segments.

- **Individual brands.** Alternatively, products offered by the same company may be branded very differently. For example, a tour operator or airline can have individual brand names within its businesses, with its long-haul, medium and budget-priced product offerings each having individual brand names unrelated to the others. In America, Blackstone, the new owner of Hilton hotels, has also acquired with it the brands of Hampton Inn, Homewood Suites and Embassy Suite, which are individual brands.

- **Own-brands.** Finally, organisations can have own-brand products. For example, some travel agents will offer the leading tour operator products but may also have their own specialist brochures with the agency brand name which is used to sell their own product.

There are strengths and weaknesses associated with each strategy. The individual brand name approach, for example, allows a company to search for the most appropriate brand name. Its weakness is that the promotional budget for each brand has to be sufficiently large to support that brand. With family brands there is a spin-off effect for each of the brands from the expenditure on any one brand. Conversely, if one of the family brands obtains poor publicity, because of association there will be damage to the other brands. For family branding, careful attention has to be given to the quality control of the products. One other benefit of family branding is that each product brand performance (PBP) can be measured against the overall family brand performance (FBP). When FBP is divided by PBP and shows an increase over time, without good reason, it may mean that the product brand needs modification, revitalisation or a detailed review.

With individual branding an organisation is able to position brands and products at the cheaper (bottom) end of the market without the brand damaging the image of the rest of the company's brands. In addition, if there is bad publicity for one of the company's brands then the other company brands do not necessarily suffer.

Figure 19.4	The awareness pyramid

Brand awareness

People will often buy a familiar brand because they are comfortable with things familiar. There may be an assumption that the brand that is familiar is probably reliable, in business to stay, and of reasonable quality. A recognised brand will thus often be selected in preference to an unknown brand. The awareness factor is particularly important in contexts in which the brand must first enter the evoked set – it must be one of the brands that are evaluated. An unknown brand usually has little chance.

(Aaker, 1991: 19)

Creating awareness of a brand is one of the biggest challenges for marketers as they need to ensure their product/brand is thought of (enters the evoked set) by customers as one of any of the available brand options. In Figure 19.4 a customer's evoked set is shown by 'top of the mind' recall; this is the optimal awareness of a brand. This pyramid is only representative as there are no established scales or measurements connected with it, but it does serve as a conceptual framework.

Marketing strategy should take the 'evoked set' into consideration because the actual choices of individual customers depend crucially upon which brands are considered and evaluated by consumers and which are not. According to research it is found that consumers generally carry only a limited number of brands in their 'evoked set' – often no more than three to five brands. However, consumers do not necessarily select brands only from their 'evoked set' nor is their selection process logical, but if buyers recall a company's brand first the likelihood of their purchasing it increases. This concept accounts for the enormous amounts of money companies spend in buying out a well-branded competitor, to erase the visibility and reinforcement of alternative brands in the marketplace. Therefore, advertising is often aimed at facilitating the growth of brand awareness. Furthermore, it can develop an image and manipulate consumers' perception, which is fundamental to building values over and above the price–value relationship.

In addition, many consumers will also select a brand with which they are familiar and which, it has been proved, is capable of providing satisfaction and quality. A recognised destination will thus often be selected over an unknown destination: 'People will often buy a familiar brand because they are comfortable with the familiar' (Aaker, 1991: 19). The awareness factor here is particularly important so a destination featured in a recent film or the coverage of an Olympics will increase customer awareness. The establishment of a strong brand image makes it more likely that the destination will be remembered and evaluated against other brands. A weak destination brand usually has little chance of entering any assessment and consequently will not be as successful.

PRICE

The pricing policy selected for a tourism product is often directly related to the performance of its future demand. Setting the right **price** is also crucial to the profitability of the tourism enterprise. We believe that, of all the marketing mix, pricing decisions are the hardest to make. This is because prices for tourism products have to take into account the complexity created by seasonality of demand and the inherent perishability of the product. Also, within tourism there are major differences in segments such as business travellers and those taking a vacation. The relative elasticities of demand for these segments are dissimilar and price sensitivity is affected by different factors.

Figure 19.5 shows demand curves that indicate different market reactions to price change, i.e. where demand is highly responsive (or price elastic) and where demand is not price responsive (or price inelastic). Tourism industry products related to vacations are associated with an elastic demand curve, where a small increase in price creates a large fall in demand. Leisure travel is price elastic because of the following:

- The ratio of tourism prices to income is normally high. This is the case not only for overseas travel but also for leisure centres, cinemas and attractions, especially in times of recession. However, the different types of tourism demand from business travel to deciding on a secondary holiday will be associated with different elasticities. These may be as shown in Figure 19.6.

- The consumer can choose a substitute or forgo the purchase if the overall value is considered to be unacceptable.

- It is relatively easy to judge the offer of alternative brands and products, and therefore easy to switch demand to cheaper alternatives. Although price may be an indicator of quality, the consumer is able to choose between several offers, by referring, for example, to the type of aircraft they may fly on or the star rating or brand of accommodation.

Elasticity is a key element in the understanding of the demand process. It is defined as the ratio of the percentage response in the quantity sold to a percentage change in price or one of the other marketing mix elements, such as the expenditure on advertising. It therefore

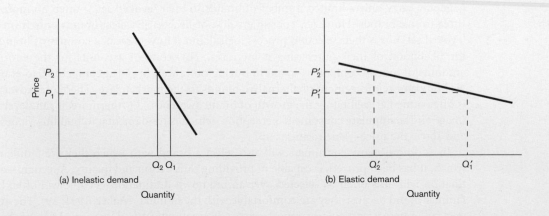

Figure 19.5   Price elasticity of demand

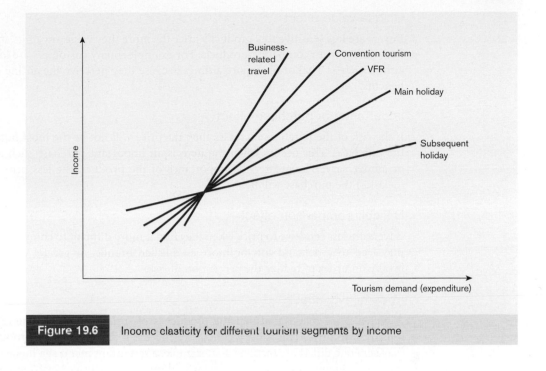

Figure 19.6   Income elasticity for different tourism segments by income

measures the sensitivity in quantity demanded to a change in the demand determinant. Mathematically, elasticity can be calculated as follows:

$$\text{Elasticity} = \frac{\text{Percentage change in quantity demanded}}{\text{Percentage change in any demand determinant}}$$

For price elasticity the denominator is simply changed to a percentage change in price. The coefficient of price elasticity is nearly always negative because the price and quantity are inversely related. This means that when the price falls, the quantity demanded tends to rise; and when price rises, the demand tends to fall. Thus the tourism marketer would be interested in the size of the coefficient as a coefficient of more than 1 indicates that demand is elastic (if price rises, demand falls significantly) and less than 1 that it is inelastic (if price rises, demand falls but only slightly).

From this it follows that the mark-up on highly competitive products such as package holidays to Spain tends to be low because the demand for such items is price elastic. In general, mark-ups should vary inversely with price elasticity of demand if profits are to be maximised.

Factors affecting price sensitivity

A number of factors will affect the price sensitivity of products. From a marketing viewpoint a deeper understanding of price sensitivity assists with an understanding of the different target segments and the development of strategic planning. The main factors to consider are listed under the following headings.

Perceived substitutes effect

Buyers are more sensitive the higher the product's price is in relation to another product or substitute they could purchase. Therefore, the consumer may choose a substitute or forgo the purchase if they believe the overall value is unacceptable. For example, local residents may avoid an area with higher priced shops frequented by tourists who are unaware of the alternatives.

Unique value effect

Buyers are less sensitive to a product's price the more they value any of its attributes that differentiate it from competing products. For example, many customers are loyal to a national airline such as Thai or Singapore airlines because they perceive the airline to offer superior benefits.

Importance of purchase effect

If the risk of the purchase increases then the price will not be the most important aspect of the purchase. This occurs when the item is an important purchase such as a honeymoon or anniversary. The greater the importance of the product, the less price sensitive (more inelastic) the purchase will be.

Difficult comparison effect

Buyers are less sensitive to price when they find it more difficult to compare alternatives. This may lead to a demand for the more established brands, or greater destination or brand loyalty, in order to reduce the perception of risk.

Price quality effect

A higher price may signal that the product is of superior quality. The result may be less sensitivity to price. This is not a conclusive effect as it applies to some products, while others may generate different reactions. For example, a restaurant menu at a higher price may signal improved quality but very few people would think higher priced fast-food items offered any real quality advantage.

Expenditure effect

Buyers become more price sensitive when the expenditure is larger, either in absolute money amounts or as a percentage of their income. This may curb demand for long-haul holidays and is most prevalent in low-income households in which all expenditure is carefully controlled. This effect is also stronger and more likely to occur in times of recession.

Fairness effect

If the buyer believes the price falls outside a band of what would be judged reasonable and fair then they become more price sensitive. With some types of products it is relatively easy to judge the offer of alternative brands and products and therefore easy to switch demand to cheaper alternatives. Consumers will perceive retailers, or the brands they stock, to be 'ripping off' customers if they exploit situations of shortage by being greedy. For example, street vendors are often seen to be selling drinks or ice creams at highly inflated prices when the temperature is extremely high.

Problems related to price cutting

The setting of price cannot be solely concerned with the consumer. Care and attention have to be given to both the reaction of the consumer as well as that of the competition. Owing to the high-risk nature of the tourism industry, a price advantage which takes market share from a competitor will often provoke a hostile repricing reaction. If Company A, in Figure 19.7(a), attempts to increase its market share by price cutting, it will need to take market share from Companies B and C. This is a situation in which C and B are likely to react by cutting their own prices. The outcome is that the market shares remain similar and can, as in the second example, lead the market to grow in volume, as in Figure 19.7(b), although not necessarily in overall revenue. The long-term result is that the market remains extremely unstable because smaller margins are being applied. In this situation an organisation has to ensure it has a high volume of business in order to exceed its break-even point. Price-cutting

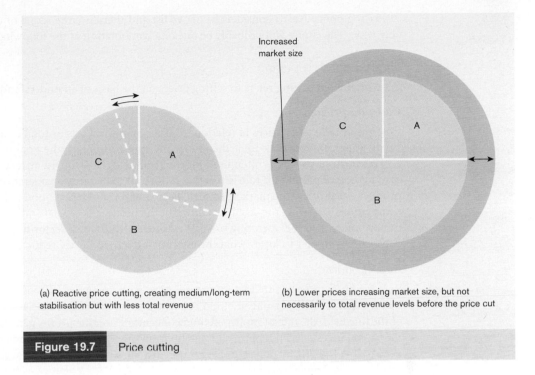

(a) Reactive price cutting, creating medium/long-term stabilisation but with less total revenue

(b) Lower prices increasing market size, but not necessarily to total revenue levels before the price cut

Figure 19.7   Price cutting

policies have been a feature of the tour-operating business in the UK and the example provided above helps us understand what has led to the collapse of a whole range of different companies. The following list shows the various influences on pricing in the tourism industry:

- The perishable nature of the product, which is unable to be stored until a future occasion, leads to various forms of last-minute tactical pricing.
- The high price elasticity of demand exhibited by holiday and leisure markets places emphasis on setting prices at the right levels.
- Increased price transparency due to the ease of access to price comparisons by use of the Internet.
- The volatility of the market due to short-run fluctuations in international costs, exchange rates, oil prices and political events requires sophisticated forward planning.
- Many companies are reliant on high volumes to break even and will forgo short-run profit in order to create acceptable load factor or occupancy levels.
- Cost control is an important part of pricing policy. Many tourism enterprises have high fixed costs and price near to break-even positions. This can make them vulnerable to financial collapse or takeover if costs are not controlled.
- Some regions and countries have price controls for airline travel and hotel accommodation.
- Seasonal demand leads to peak and low-season periods, which require demand management pricing to cope with the short-run capacity problems.
- Price is associated with the psychological aspects of both quality and status. It is therefore always important to gauge the way prices or their change will be perceived by the different target segments.
- Cash flow is high due to much of the payment for tourism products being made in advance of consumption. Many tourism companies make profit on the investment of this money.

Pricing policy has to consider the above list and therefore the scope of choice is remarkably wide. The choice will probably be one or a combination of the following types of pricing.

Cost-orientated pricing

Cost-orientated pricing refers to setting prices on the basis of an understanding of their costs.

Cost-plus pricing

Cost-plus pricing sets prices in relation to either marginal costs or total costs including overheads. A percentage mark-up is then normally applied to reach the final price.

This form of pricing is often used for the retail outlets of tourist attractions. Its weakness as a method of pricing for tourism is that it does not take into consideration demand for the product, what prices the marketplace will bear, and it is not based upon the price levels of the competitors. Knowing the cost breakdown of the product is crucial and it is often important to have calculated the operating price of a hotel bedroom or a sector flight airline seat. This allows the marketer to know what the effect of any tactical price reduction will be.

Rate of return

Rate of return pricing provides an organisation with an agreed rate of return on its investment. Whereas the cost-plus method concentrates on the costs associated with the running of the business, the rate of return method concentrates on the profits generated in relation to the capital invested. This approach is not appropriate for tourism enterprises as it ignores the need to link the pricing policy to the creation of a sales volume which is large enough to cover overheads and remains consistent over time.

To use either cost-plus or rate of return methods of pricing is generally not appropriate for tourism products that have to survive in a highly competitive marketplace because of the need to judge the contribution margin for different market segments so as to cover long run costs (see Chapter 11 on attractions).

Demand-orientated pricing

Demand-orientated pricing takes into consideration the factors of demand rather than the level of costs in order to set the price. A conference centre, for example, may charge one price for admission to a rock concert and only half that price for admission to a classical concert.

Discrimination pricing

This is sometimes called flexible pricing and is often used in tourism where products are sold at two or more different prices. Quite often students and older people are charged lower prices at attractions, or events, than other segments. Discrimination pricing is often time-related, with cheaper drink charges in 'happy hour' periods or cheaper meal prices in the early evening prior to high-demand periods. For price discrimination to be successful it is necessary to be able to identify those segments that, without the price differentials, would be unable to purchase the product.

To obtain a high flow of business, a hotel will have to discount for customers who offer significant volume. This means that, while business travellers may benefit from corporate rates, those on vacation may be staying on tour operator/wholesaler rates.

Discrimination can also be based upon increasing the price of products that have higher potential demand. For example, if rooms in a hotel are all the same but some have good scenic views of the countryside or sea, then those rooms could be sold for a higher price.

Backward pricing

This is a market-based method of pricing that focuses on what the consumer is willing to pay. The price is worked backwards. First, an acceptable margin is agreed upon. Next, the costs are closely monitored so that the estimated final price is deemed to be acceptable to the target segment. The objective is to set a price that matches consumer preference. If necessary an

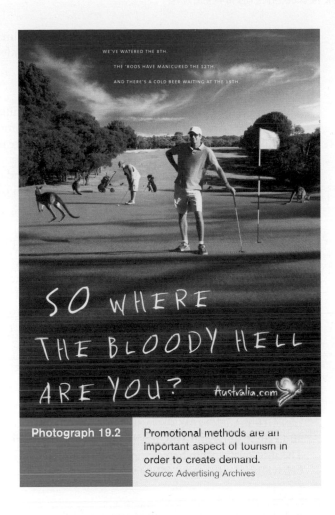

Photograph 19.2	Promotional methods are an important aspect of tourism in order to create demand.

Source: Advertising Archives

adjustment is made to the quality of the product offer or service to meet the cost led needs of this technique.

Tour operators/wholesalers selling on a price-led basis will often contract with hotels one or two blocks back from the seafront, if this lowers the room rates making up the final price. Other methods include lowering the flight content of a holiday price by organising cheaper night flights which may also save on the first night's accommodation cost. To be successful with this method of pricing it is important to understand the psychological effects of creating products that may appeal to the price conscious. However, the holiday may not give satisfaction if the holiday experience and company are considered to be of poor quality.

Market penetration pricing

Market penetration pricing is adopted when an organisation wants to establish itself quickly in a market. Prices are set below those of the competition in order to create high growth for the company's products. Tour operators/wholesalers, when setting up an operation to a new destination, will use market penetration pricing for that destination in the first couple of years and then, once that destination becomes better established, will slowly increase the prices.

Psychological pricing

Companies will often price products below a round figure. This could be the changing of a menu price from say £10 to £9.95 or £9.99 to foster the perception of the price as being below that threshold at which the customer is willing to buy. Just as £9.95 may appear to be significantly less than £10, so a holiday price of £488 may seem to be more on a £400 level than a £500 level. However, there is no conclusive evidence that such pricing policies make any significant difference to profits.

Skimming pricing

This term is used as if skimming off the cream from milk. The method is utilised when there is a shortage of supply of the product and where demand will not be dampened by charging a premium price. Luxury villas set in good locations are normally priced with higher margins than other accommodation products because of their relative shortage. Market skimming policies can only occur where there is a healthy demand or waiting lists, or to take advantage of a strong destination image such as that of the south of France.

Pricing and the relationship to value

Whatever pricing policy is adopted, a company has to take into consideration the potential consumer's perceptual assessment. In deciding to buy a product a consumer has to be willing to give up something in order to enjoy the satisfactions of the benefits the product will deliver. This concept is more complex than it seems. The majority of tourists are looking for value when they buy a product and value is derived from the functions of quality and price, as well as the added value of the image or brand. This may be expressed as:

$$\text{Value} = \frac{\text{Quality}}{\text{Price}} + \text{Image}$$

If a consumer believes the image and quality of a product is good, he or she will be willing to make greater sacrifices in order to purchase that product. This explains how first-class travel continues to be successful on different forms of transport such as trains, aircraft and cruise ships and why leading brands or destinations are able to attract higher prices. The interrelationship between price, quality and value plays a significant role in the buying behaviour of customers. Value was grouped into four categories by Zeithaml (1988):

- value as low price;
- value as whatever is wanted from a product;
- value as the quality one gets for the price paid;
- value as what one gets for what one gives.

Zeithaml describes value as a 'trade-off between salient benefit components and sacrifice components'. Benefit components according to Zeithaml include intrinsic attributes, extrinsic attributes, perceived quality and other relevant high abstractions. This means value is a judgement about superiority and benefits delivered. Therefore, having the lowest price may not be a sufficient strategy as the best route to marketplace success.

If prices change, this can affect the consumers' quality perception. A price reduction may be associated with a belief that the company is in financial trouble, that it will have to cut service and quality, or that prices are falling and, if one waits, a price will come down even more. The value of the product is thought to have decreased because quality, by association with the changes, is observed to have fallen by a greater ratio than prices.

Alternatively, a price increase may be interpreted as the way the company is going to pay to improve the quality and service of the offer. However, some consumers may simply think that the company is being greedy and that quality has not improved. This means the consumer may judge the value to have fallen. The outcome quite often depends on how the company explains the increase in price to the consumer.

To ensure the maximum chance of success for the pricing policy adopted there is a need to check each stage of the procedure, as in Figure 19.8. This figure identifies the important considerations required for the successful evolution of a pricing policy.

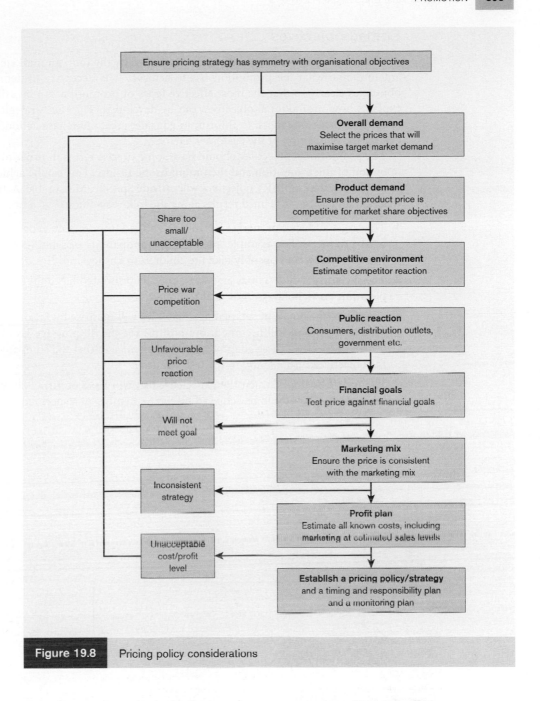

| **Figure 19.8** | Pricing policy considerations |

PROMOTION

Promotion is the descriptive term for the mix of communication activities that tourism organisations, or tourist boards, carry out in order to influence those publics on whom their sales depend. The important groups, which need to be influenced, are not simply the target market group of current and potential customers. There is the need also to influence trade contacts such as retail agents and suppliers, as well as opinion formers such as journalists and travel writers. Even local, national and international politicians and important professional groups may need to be influenced.

Setting objectives

A range of promotional methods can be employed by the tourism marketer, so it is important to define what the promotion has to achieve. It is necessary to define the marketing objectives clearly so that the most effective types of promotion can be utilised. Figure 19.9 explains how promotional objectives can be developed. The mix strategies could specify a need to achieve awareness; to inform; to educate; create purchase action; improve loyalty; change the perception of the customer, etc.

The promotional objectives should have some precise terms in order to clarify the entire intention of the promotion and then monitor the results. This can be achieved by means of SMART objectives. SMART objectives will provide Specific, Measurable, Actionable, Realistic/Relevant and Targeted/Timed results along the following lines:

1. The target audience or market has to be identified (by segment, geographical area, and for what products). For example, identifying grandparents of school-age children living in London who would possibly take the children to Disneyland® Resort Paris.

2. The specific product (goods and service) to be promoted has to be identified. For example, mini break holidays in or near to France.

3. Specific goals should be set, perhaps that sales will increase by £x, or that attitudes to the product or brand will become more positive for the 40-plus age group. To fit with the SMART objectives these goals have to be *achievable* in that the company has to deliver to the objectives; also *relevant* to the task required.

4. The time horizon of when the expected effect will have occurred should be stated. For example, targets should be achieved by end September of a specified year.

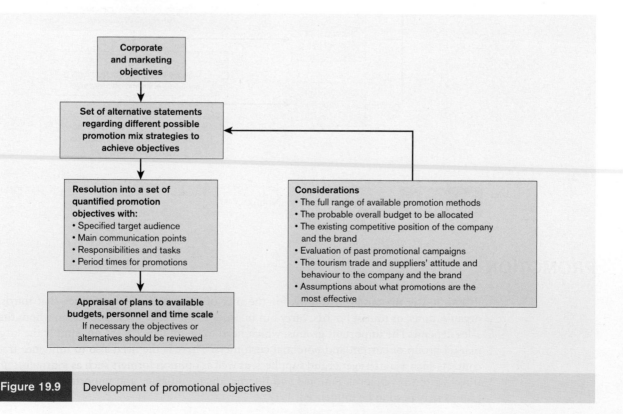

| Figure 19.9 | Development of promotional objectives |

Taking up the example used in the list above, a SMART objective would therefore be:

To ensure that the grandparents of children between the ages of 4 and 16, within the Greater London area, are communicated with and receive information on the France and Disneyland offers. Subsequently, sales for these products will increase by £150,000 over the previous year by 30 September.

Promotional budget approaches

The second important step in any promotional campaign is to agree the budget. There are different approaches to agreeing budgets that may be based upon a number of criteria. It is important to realise there is no one best method to set budgets. This is because promotional campaign measurement is not straightforward, given that there is often a time lag between the campaign and any resultant demand patterns. Also, other elements in the marketing mix will affect the demand.

Various factors determine the overall promotional budget but any decision has to take into account existing or potential sales of the company. The most common approaches are objective-and-task, affordable method, percentage of sales method, and competitive parity method:

- **Objective-and-task method** – whereby the budget is related to the communications objectives. If the company needs to create awareness, change attitudes and build a brand then these objectives become the necessary tasks against which the budget is determined.

- **Affordable method** – where the first step is to produce a budgeted period forecast of the expected sales and company costs, excluding the promotional expenditure. The difference between the surplus expected and the desired profit allows for a decision over the communications budget based upon what can be afforded. This approach treats the promotional budget as a cost of business and does not encourage marketers to spend against the likelihood of future problems or as an investment to increase sales.

- **Percentage of sales method** – is an approach where the communications budget is set on the basis of a predetermined percentage of the forecasted sales. The weakness is that the method assumes the historical percentage is still relevant for the current marketplace. It also relies on accurate forecasts which provide for the chance of unacceptable error. In addition, if a company wants to build preference for a new product launch then a system of budgeting based upon the percentage of sales method may not raise the necessary budget to achieve the short-term task of ensuring awareness and acceptability. The other problem is that the method will provide for lower budgets when there is a downturn in the market or due to loss of sales based upon increased competitor activity that takes away business. This may lead to further sales decline as less and less money is spent on the company's promotional effort.

- **Competitive parity method** – allows the setting of the budget based upon both the share of market of the product or company and also the estimated expenditure level of its competitors. This method does not allow for specific marketplace opportunities as the parity level of expenditure will be held and consequently a strategic penetration of the market may not be achieved.

Communication effects

There is always the need to plan to achieve the most effective response from the target market. An important part of the promotional effort is the building of brand and product awareness. Sometimes it will take a long time for the consumer to know about the brand and the type of products on offer.

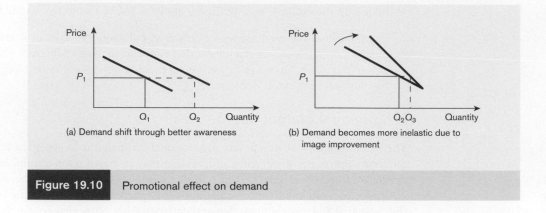

| Figure 19.10 | Promotional effect on demand |

A promotional campaign should aim to provide knowledge about the product, to ensure the consumer will feel favourable towards the product and build up preference for it. Any campaign has to sell the benefits that a customer would be seeking in a credible way so that the potential customer feels conviction and is more likely than not to make a purchase.

Figure 19.10 shows how a promotional campaign could be utilised by a destination or organisation to create awareness of the benefits of the product offer. The development of a positive image will create a more price-elastic demand curve, which means the product is more resilient to price rises and does not have to rely on having lower prices than the competition. In Figure 19.10(a) P_1Q_1 is existing demand before a campaign has been developed to create more awareness in the target audience. At P_1Q_2 demand has increased because, owing to a promotional effect, more people are now aware of the product benefits which the brand or destination can deliver. At P_1Q_3 in Figure 19.10(b) the campaign has improved the image of the organisation or destination so that more status is derived in travelling with the brand or to a destination. This changes the shape of the demand whereby it becomes more inelastic.

Advertising and sales promotion are the most widely used forms of promotion. Because of the intrusive characteristic of these forms of promotion, most consumers relate ideas of marketing to the use of advertising or sales promotion. The other major forms include personal selling and public relations.

Advertising

Advertising includes any paid form of non-personal communication through the media which details a product that has an identified sponsor. The media may include travel guides, newspapers, magazines, radio, television, direct mail, web pages and billboards.

Advertising is used to achieve a whole range of objectives which may include changing attitudes or building image, as well as achieving sales. Advertising is often described as 'above-the-line' promotion (due to the commission for the promotional activity being paid by the media company direct to the advertising agency) with all other forms of promotion, such as sales promotion or direct marketing, being termed 'below-the-line'. The difference between above and below the line is simply academic now as the emphasis is on integrating both areas, for example sales promotion and advertising working together to achieve the greatest impact. The approach is also to raise budgets for overall integrated campaigns so that expenditure accounting differences become non-existent. In addition, advertising has developed different ways of affecting the consumer. Direct mail is being used to build awareness and television is being used to sell products direct to the consumer, and therefore there is a great deal more flexibility in the use of different promotional media.

Communication theories

Communication theorists have proposed several models to explain the way advertising works and each have some similarity. The basic underlying approach is to theorise that the individual will first move to a *knowledge state* or *awareness state* on the basis of information gained through experience and methods of communication. *Attitudes* are then formed and the importance is to move the potential purchaser to a *behavioural action* phase of purchase through desire and *conviction*. One model known as the DAGMAR model (Defining Advertising Goals for Measured Advertising Results) describes the sequence of stages through which the prospective customer has to move:

- unawareness;
- awareness;
- comprehension of the offer;
- conviction;
- action or inaction.

Through advertising, the marketer will make the potential customer aware of the company or destination and its range of offers. As part of the advertising communication process, information has to be clearly transmitted so it can be decoded and comprehended properly. The process is then to make the offer credible so that the potential customer can be moved to a favourable attitude to the product. The act of purchase may then follow.

Advertising has the potential to affect a large number of people simultaneously with a single message. The secondary effect of advertising is personal communications among consumers. This is known as the *two-step flow of communication*. The first step in the process is the communications flow from media to opinion leaders – the individuals whose attitudes, opinions, preferences and actions affect others. The second step is word-of-mouth communications from opinion leaders to others (followers). This communication can occur through personal conversation between friends or with work colleagues based upon communication about the company or product. It can also occur through non-verbal communications when someone displays video or holiday photographs. One implication of the need to achieve as much benefit as possible from the two-step model is the requirement to reach and influence opinion leaders.

Sales promotion

Sales promotion involves any activity that offers an incentive to induce a desired result from potential customers, trade intermediaries or the sales force. Sales promotion campaigns will add value to the product because the incentives will ordinarily not accompany the product. For example, free wine or free accommodation offers are frequently used in sales promotion campaigns for hotel restaurants which need improved demand at certain periods. Most incentives are planned to be short term in nature.

An integral part of sales promotion is the aspect of merchandising. Merchandising includes materials used in travel agents or in-house locations to stimulate sales. For a hotel, these would include tent cards which may attempt to sell cocktails or deserts, menus, in-room material, posters and displays. Merchandising is important as a means of creating impulse purchase or reminding the consumer of what is on offer.

Sales promotion is often used in combination with other promotional tools in order to supplement the overall effort. However, it has to be remembered that it is sometimes difficult to terminate or change special promotions without causing adverse effects. Airline frequent flyer loyalty programmes are an example of this. Also, a sales promotion (or series of promotions) has to take account of the likely effect it may have on the image of the brand or outlet. For example, there may be an unanticipated surge of negative perception which may occur due to association with banal and frivolous promotions.

Evaluation of sales promotion

To evaluate a sales promotion there should be a consideration of:

- the cost of the promotion in employee time, as well as for the cost of any merchandise, giveaway items or promotional literature;
- the increase in sales and profit, or improvement in awareness, based upon the campaign;
- whether the campaign had secondary effects of switching demand from other company products which would have been sold;
- whether there were any additional sales outside of the promotion, due to customers being attracted to the company or tourism product offer.

It is not always easy to isolate the above effects from other marketing factors, but it is always important to make some assessment of the benefit of different types of promotion.

Personal selling

Personal selling is an attempt to gain benefit through face-to-face or telephone contact between the seller's representative and those people with whom the seller wants to communicate. This type of selling may be utilised by a non-profit-making tourist attraction as well as the conference manager of a large hotel.

A number of employees in travel agents or retail related to tourism are often viewed as order *takers* but they could possibly be order *procurers*. The intent of personal selling is:

- to obtain a sale – often customers enter the retail outlet after acquiring information and the salesperson needs to persuade potential customers to purchase;
- to stimulate sales of 'impulse buy' purchases by bringing attention to extra requirements such as travel insurance, car hire, excursions and airport transfers; or
- to complete a successful transaction with the customer utilising a range of sales skills.

This will leave the customer satisfied and well informed about the detail of the transaction.

The benefit of personal selling is that a salesperson can adapt the communication of benefits to be gained to the specific needs of the customer. The feedback process of listening to the customer's needs allows the salesperson to be flexible in his or her approach. This is made easier in a selling situation because the personal contact produces heightened awareness and attention by the customer. However, the sales functions of retailers have to be carefully handled because staff who lack empathy will be judged as 'pushy'.

If we take the example of a travel agency, the retail selling process is made up of a number of the steps outlined in Table 19.2: preparing, anticipating a prospective sale, approaching, presenting, dealing with concerns, gaining commitment and establishing relationships. All these are linked into the feedback process of active listening and response.

Public relations

Public relations (PR) is non-personal communication that changes opinion or achieves coverage in a mass medium and that is not paid for by the source. The coverage could include space given to a press release or favourable editorial comment. PR is important not only in obtaining editorial coverage, but also in suppressing potential bad coverage. An organisation that has good links with the media is more likely to have the opportunity to stop or moderate news that could be damaging to their organisation prior to its release.

The major benefit of PR is that it can provide and enhance an organisation's image. This is very important for service-based organisations which are reliant on a more tangible positive image in order to be successful. PR is a highly credible form of communication as people like to read 'news stories' and will believe them to be less biased than information provided in advertisements. However, editorial decisions over what is communicated will produce control over the message, its timing, placement and coverage.

Table 19.2	An approach to selling tourism products in a travel agents

1 Preparing through skills and knowledge (of the travel products available and systems)	Feedback and learning from prior listening and retail agency training
2 Anticipating and identifying a prospective sale based upon interaction with the customer	Having knowledge and an understanding of the needs of customers
3 Method of dealing with the potential customer in order to make a recommendation	Feedback and learning from prior listening plus asking appropriate questions
4 Presenting the features and benefits of the recommendation	Active selling skills and listening in order to check on acceptability of offer
5 Dealing with customer concerns	Active listening in order to revise the argument or recommendation to overcome objections
6 Building obligation and commitment and selling in other products (e.g. insurance)	Active listening in order to ensure the offer is acceptable and the sale can be concluded
7 Establishing affinity and relationship	Reinforcement of the relationship through creating a satisfied customer

Table 19.3 details the common activities undertaken as part of PR. The benefits of good PR effort and coverage emanating from this are:

- it is perceived to be impartial and acts as a neutral endorsement of the company;
- it is credible and believable as it is not identified as a paid form of promotion;
- it helps to build image of a brand and develop favourable opinions by the drip effect of the information provided;
- it can generate interest and increased sales;
- it allows for a cost-effective means to promote special offers and sales initiatives; and
- it can possibly limit or neutralise negative or hostile opinions.

Table 19.3	Activities of public relations

• Media information releases/contact/speeches	• Advertorials (which require PR copy along with an advertisement)
• Production of PR materials (videos, CDs, web information, press kits, corporate identity materials, etc.)	• In-house and customer magazines
• PR events, media conferences and newsworthy 'stunts'	• Facility visits to an overseas area (especially for travel writers), etc.
	• Sponsorship and donations
	• Lobbying

PR activity can be either planned or unplanned. Planned activity means the company attempts to retain control over the activity and news release. With unplanned activity, the company simply reacts in the most beneficial way to the chance of some publicity or to suppress a negative news item. Larger organisations will have a public relations agency or in-house department. These will attempt to influence the company's 'publics'. The 'publics' are made up of those important to the company – customers, shareholders, employees, suppliers, local community, the media and local and national government. Planned publicity will involve sending press releases and photographs to the media (trade papers, local and national press, radio and television), organising press conferences for more newsworthy events, sending letters to editors of journals or local newspapers, organising different creative 'stunts' to acquire the right tone of media coverage and making speeches (or writing articles) on informed tourism issues in order to be perceived as a well-informed company.

Other promotional activity

There is a growing use of **sponsorship** and **direct marketing**. These do not comfortably fit into the other four promotion categories. Sponsorship is the material or financial support of a specific activity, normally but not exclusively sport, education or the arts, which does not form part of the sponsor organisation's normal business. Direct marketing is direct communication with pre-selected target groups in order to obtain an immediate response or build closer relationships. Direct marketing is used extensively by direct-sell tour operators/wholesalers such as Saga Holidays and Portland. The main method is direct mail, which is postal communication by an identified sponsor. This is being expanded into database marketing based upon relationship marketing practices.

In addition, because tourism is an intangible product, a great deal of promotion includes the production of printed communications such as brochures or sales leaflets. The design, compilation and printing of tourism brochures is one of the most important promotional functions. Printed communications are often costly. In fact, the printing and distribution costs of brochures constitute the largest part of most marketing budgets within the tourism industry. This is a necessary expenditure as the brochure or leaflet is the major sales tool for tour operators/wholesalers and tourism organisations.

Characteristics of each promotional technique

Each of the above promotional elements has the capacity to achieve a different promotional objective. While personal selling has high potency for achieving communication objectives, only a relatively small number of people can be contacted. Therefore, advertising is a more effective method of reaching a high number of people at relatively low unit cost. Public relations is more credible than advertising but organisations lack the control they have over advertising messages which may also be repeated on a regular basis. Thus, when it is difficult to raise advertising budgets, public relations is a lower cost alternative, but it is difficult to control the timing and consistency of PR coverage. Sales promotion, such as leaflet drops that offer price discounts, may produce an initial trial for a product, such as the purchase of a leisure break in a hotel, but this type of promotion should only be used over a short-term period. Some promotions are permanent as they are related to known patterns of demand fluctuations and the 'happy hour' promotion is widely utilised in resorts to increase sales in early off-peak hours.

Each element of the promotions mix has its own strengths and weaknesses. While this may include the factors of cost, ability to target different groups and control, there are other important considerations. Figure 19.11 indicates the relative strengths of each of the four forms of promotion. They are compared on the basis of the level of awareness of the communication, its comprehension as well as whether it can build conviction and succeed in creating action.

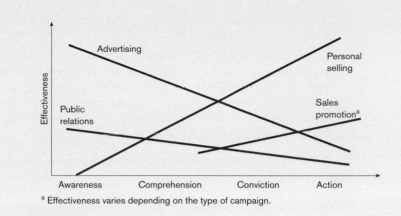

| **Figure 19.11** | Effectiveness of different promotion methods |

Integrated marketing communications

It should be obvious that many of the activities of tourism promotion will occur in different areas of the company and with different activities taking place based upon the predilections of the individuals in control. Therefore, while it is obvious that coordination is required it is often not carried out in a systematic way. If it were all elements of marketing communications could work in unison so as to create a whole that is greater than the sum of the parts. To ensure such impact is achieved there is a requirement for an **integrated marketing communications** (IMC) approach throughout the business. Integrated marketing communications is the process a company adopts in order to integrate and coordinate its messages and media to deliver clear reinforcing communication. However, this will only occur if the various components of the communication effort are coordinated. To achieve this the marketer has to provide policy planning guidelines which direct the efforts in every part of the organisation so that all aspects of communication will offer a reinforcement to each other.

PLACE (DISTRIBUTION)

The special characteristics of the tourism product have led to specific forms of distribution. The tourism product is one where no transfer of ownership takes place and service is simply rented or consumed. However, prior to consumption the tourism product has to be both available and accessible. This requires a distribution system – or choice of a marketing channel. A **distribution system** is the mix of channels used to gain access, or means by which a tourism service is made available to the potential buyers of the product.

The following aspects of tourism distribution should be noted:

- There is no actual product being distributed. There are only clues given through persuasive communication about the product.

- Tourism normally involves the episode of a purchase act related to decisions over travel to a destination, the stay and return. As such the nature of travel distribution is related to entering into the production as well as consumption of the product. Therefore, the method of selling and environment within which the purchase is made becomes part of the overall tourism experience.

- Major amounts of money are allocated by the industry to the production and printing of literature as well as to its delivery direct to the customer or to the retail travel agent.

Brochures and leaflets are produced in high quantity, and often the distribution cost involves an amount for warehousing and the planned despatch of packs of brochures via different modes of transport.

- Distribution of overseas holidays in the UK is now a balance of web-based services and travel agents who sell a homogeneous set of choices. These agents have important power and control over the companies that sell the products (principals). Agents decide on the brochures to display on their racks and the companies they will recommend to consumers. However, airline bookings are progressively being switched to Internet-based direct systems (see Chapter 20 for more information).

There is continuing development of CRSs (computer reservation systems) or GDSs (global distribution systems). These offer an agent instant access to airline bookings as well as the major hotel groups, car hire and cruise lines. Such systems, utilising the Internet, allow both agents to tailor holidays to suit individual client requirements as well as the consumer to make their own arrangements, and this may lead to increases in direct bookings. The CRSs are led by developments from the principal airlines, with Galileo dominating the UK and being strong in both Europe and the USA, Amadeus being predominately strong in Europe, Sabre dominating in the USA, and, finally, Worldspan, which has now merged with Galileo and has helped develop innovations for many reservation systems (see below).

- **Sabre** – founded in the 1960s by American Airlines, in 1996 Sabre became a separate legal entity of AMR (parent company of American Airlines). It has been involved in a lot of Internet-led development of booking sites (Sabre owns Travelocity.com, a major world wide online travel site) and is considered to be one of the most significant and competitive GDSs due to the fact that it anticipates and takes advantage of the changes in the information economy and develops innovative practices. The European equivalent of Orbitz, which is a US airline-led initiative to counteract the private reservation sites, called Opodo was founded in 2001 by nine European airlines as a competitor to start-up online travel agencies. Opodo was subsequently acquired by Sabre. It has faced tough competition in the UK, where it did not perform as well as ebookers.com, lastminute.com (subsequently acquired in 2005 by Sabre) and Expedia. In 2006 Sabre was sold to two private equity buyers, Silver Lake Holdings and Texas Pacific. The Sabre sale resulted in some of the world's most important travel distribution companies coming under private ownership.

- **Worldspan** – founded in 1990, and previously owned by affiliates of Delta, Northwest and American Airlines, Worldspan was purchased in 2006 by the private equity group Blackstone. Worldspan has successfully developed the strategies, solutions and services for web-based distribution. Worldspan provides electronic distribution of travel information, Internet products and connectivity and e-commerce capabilities for travel agencies, travel service providers and corporations. Worldspan helped launch the Orbitz site in 2001, which is now part of Blackstone and was previously a US airline alliance-led Internet site set up to counteract the successful trends in disintermediation by companies such as Travelocity, which was taking increasing revenue in commission charges and kept valuable customer data for its own purposes. Prior to this Worldspan agreed to provide the booking engines in 1995 for Microsoft's Expedia.com and in 1998 for Priceline.com. Worldspan currently serves over 20,000 travel agencies around the world.

- In 2006, **Galileo** and Worldspan, who are Sabre's main competitors in the US, agreed to merge in a $1.4 billion deal as part of the portfolio of Blackstone, the New York-based private equity group. The Galileo merger deal is based upon the historically important use of a system which was founded in 1993 by 11 major North American and European airlines: Aer Lingus, Air Canada, Alitalia, Austrian Airlines, British Airways, KLM Royal Dutch Airlines, Olympic Airlines, Swissair, TAP Air Portugal, United Airlines and US Airways. Galileo is still a major player in the GDS business throughout the world.

- Meanwhile, in Europe, the Amadeus group is also owned by buy-out groups. In addition, there are several minor GDSs, including SITA's Sahara, Infini (Japan), Axess (Japan), Tapas (Korea), Fantasia (South Pacific) and Abacus (Asia/Pacific) that serve smaller regional markets or countries.

The development of electronic distribution systems has strengthened the major players as the cost and adoption implications provide a barrier to entry. The current systems have standardised the channel for bookings to such an extent that small or medium-sized organisations will find it almost impossible to develop agency channel alternatives. This has implications for loss of control for smaller companies and therefore requires safeguards to ensure CRS owners do not manipulate the display or bookings procedure to favour their own brands.

Different tourism distribution needs

There are some forms of tourism such as museums, theme parks or physical attractions where no form of prior booking is required as there is almost always excess supply available and in peak periods queuing is the method of allocation. There are other types of tourism where excess demand and more complex product packaging and financial risk create the need for sophisticated advance booking systems. The booking system enables the organisation to spread demand as the consumer can often be persuaded to arrive or travel at a different time.

In order for a tourism organisation to sell in advance of consumption and to have a record of the reservation, the company has to sell its available capacity through an inventory system. Whether it is a small guest house or large hotel, a farmhouse or cruise ship, some method of allocating capacity and creating reservations without creating overbooking is important. The timing of these bookings may range from minutes prior to departure for an aircraft or a reserved place on a train service to several years for a major conference. For these reasons, the use of a database booking system (CRS/GDS) is common in tourism. These systems combine the memory capacity of computers (to update and store information constantly) with the communication facility of telecommunications, which rapidly inform travel agents of the current capacity remaining. Such systems can then be programmed to maximise the 'yield' of the capacity as it is sold to the customer.

The next consideration is related to the location of the business. A well-located hotel, theatre or attraction will be able to pick up passing demand. In this case the consumers will find the product easily and there may be less need for a separate distribution channel. This is because the product is easily available for purchase.

In an increasingly competitive world, however, it has been necessary for most organisations to consider different forms of direct distribution. Companies are able to sell direct either from their place of location or through direct marketing methods. Many hotels organise weekend-break programmes to improve the weekend occupancy levels. These weekend packages are often promoted directly in newspapers and are booked directly with the hotel.

Development of travel agency distribution

In the UK in 2005 there was the opportunity to have access to a wide network of around 4,727 distribution outlets controlled by the Association of British Travel Agents. The need for travel agents first arose in the 1950s due to the rapidly expanding operations of airline/ferry businesses. Transport providers required a means of distribution for their products that was more cost-effective than establishing individual networks of booking offices around the country. The subsequent development of travel agents was a direct result of the increasing consumer demand for inclusive tours from holidaymakers who were largely uneducated and unsophisticated, and therefore looked to 'experts' to facilitate the process. These agents charge commission on the sales they make and they need to hold a stock of the companies' brochures or sales literature. The travel retail agent sells a product that is both intangible and

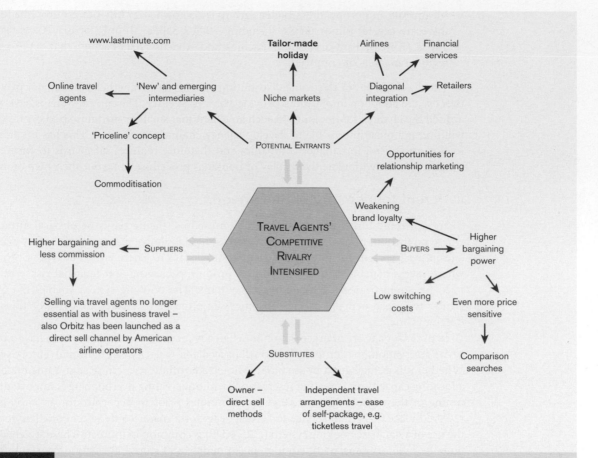

Figure 19.12	Application of Porter's five forces model to new distribution pressures for travel agents

Source: Adapted by D. Gilbert with the permission of The Free Press, a Division of Simon & Schuster Adult Publishing Group, from *Competitive Strategy: Techniques for Analyzing Industries and Competitors*, by Michael E. Porter. Copyright © 1980, 1998 by The Free Press. All rights reserved

perishable and this is very different from some of the more traditional types of retail business. The bookings made for travel abroad, from the UK, are often organised through either high street travel agents for holidays or by specialist business travel agents for business travel. For many travellers, a foreign holiday was an opportunity to emulate grand lifestyles through the services of a travel agent. However, changes in education, economic, social and experiential trends are leading to new ways of purchasing. Figure 19.12 indicates the trends emanating from new distribution pressures which are now taking place in this once traditional retail arena.

The Internet has many implications for all areas of business and every sector of society. Its effect can be seen already in the precarious balance of travel distribution. Disintermediation does not appear to be lessening the travel industry's complicated distribution network, if anything it is adding to it.

Electronic retailing

Electronic retailing to consumers (or B2C) was first developed in the 1980s. The area is advancing at a rapid rate with retail and tourism organisations realising the growing importance of the sale of products through these new distribution channels. Electronic delivery systems do not necessarily require direct human interaction and, as such, they offer specific advantages. In principle, quality can be assured, the costs are lower, there is consumer convenience of access and distribution can be wider than normal retail channels. The key underlying reasons behind electronic retailing are consumer time poverty, consumers wanting to have more control over time and place of transaction, the technology convergence allowing change to take place and growing experience of the benefits of the medium.

The companies that undertake electronic business can be classified in three main ways:

1. **Virtual distributors** – these have no shops or stores or physical presence in the high street, malls or out-of-town locations. They trade exclusively on the Internet or on television and have to find new ways of attracting custom and serving consumer needs. Examples of these are Travelocity.com and lastminute.com.

2. **Two-channel distributors** – these are established companies that have developed an electronic retailing capability as a major or minor aspect of their business. For example Thomas Cook has also set up the thomascook.com web site which it has promoted by offering special discounts or free insurance for a holiday booking.

3. **Multichannel distributors** – these are established companies which service customer needs in a number of ways, including shops, telephone ordering, the Internet, catalogues and television.

Although many observers originally felt that electronic retailing would be dominated by new *virtual* distributors, it now seems likely that the marketplace will be made up of all three categories. However, what is clear is that the Internet offers suppliers much more benefit than utilising a travel agent for their distribution. There are five main advantages associated with the Internet as a revenue channel, from which travel industry suppliers, such as hoteliers and airlines, stand to benefit if they develop more direct sales for their business. They are:

1. **Lower sales costs** – If a hotel were to sell its inventory via an online intermediary such as www.travelweb.com then the information need only be distributed via a switch to translate the data into a 'standard' language. However, selling with a travel agent involves a switch, a CRS and the travel agency booking fee, resulting in the hotel retaining substantially less revenue.

2. **Expanded market reach and presence** – The Internet does not recognise international borders, so tourism providers can potentially reach a world target audience. The site can be accessed 24 hours a day, which is also less restrictive. For example, an Asian customer in Hong Kong would be able to complete a transaction with an English company at a time that was convenient to them because the eight-hour time difference between the two destinations is immaterial. Also, many potential customers search the web site and then make an offline booking so it is important to have the web presence.

3. **Increased customer loyalty** – The decision by tourist providers to use travel agents to facilitate the sale of their products restricts the level of contact they have with the end customer, meaning that loyalty may be developed with the retailer rather than the actual provider. However, the Internet enables travel industry suppliers to address this and take a more active part in the transaction.

4. **Leverage for other sales channels** – Cost savings from this method of distribution can be used to have multichannel strategies as lower costs in one channel can subsidise the more expensive channels, such as travel agents.

5. **Collection of databases** – Any system which is owned by the company has the benefit of collecting data on customers which can be used as part of a future relationship marketing exercise.

Given the above benefits of increased direct sales it is important that travel agents should anticipate further competition from existing businesses diversifying their portfolios to exploit a potentially lucrative market opportunity. Figure 19.13 indicates the changes taking place and the complexity of the distribution of tourism products.

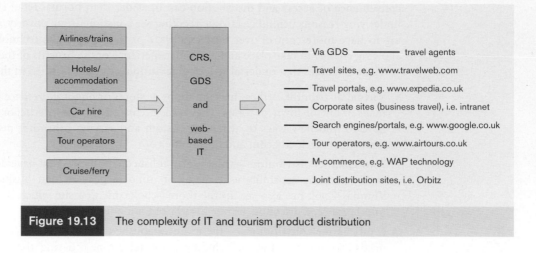

Airlines/trains		—— Via GDS —— travel agents
Hotels/accommodation	CRS,	—— Travel sites, e.g. www.travelweb.com
Car hire	GDS	—— Travel portals, e.g. www.expedia.co.uk
Tour operators	and	—— Corporate sites (business travel), i.e. intranet
Cruise/ferry	web-based IT	—— Search engines/portals, e.g. www.google.co.uk

Figure 19.13   The complexity of IT and tourism product distribution

Priceline.com

Priceline.com has positioned itself as offering the cheapest prices on the Internet. Priceline receives requests based upon the 'name-your-own-price' system for airline tickets, rental cars, hotel rooms, long-distance calls and even new cars. Priceline then attempts to match each individual request with a supplier who is willing to fulfil the order at an agreed transaction price. Priceline creates revenue using the spread between the prices at which airlines sell discounted tickets and consumers buy them. To achieve this Priceline monitors changing airline pricing and availability on a minute-by-minute basis. Consumers have the benefit of buying at a price which offers them value for money, while sellers may be able to move otherwise unsold capacity or to generate incremental revenue. The advantage of the Priceline e-commerce business model is they have no risk of inventory as they only facilitate transactions once they receive the customer's credit card details.

To date there is evidence that the sales of airline tickets are becoming more direct but not that the British package holidaymaker is buying direct in the same way. There is little doubt that for many, the convenience of using an agent to book the holiday is an important element in the buying process. This is because a travel agent may offer greater opportunities for advice on the parallel purchase of insurance, car hire, rail travel to the airport, traveller's cheques, and so on. As Table 19.4 outlines, the travel agent still offers a number of benefits, which may be the reason more travellers have not booked direct. (See also Chapters 13 and 20 on intermediaries and e-commerce.)

However, with Expedia and Travelocity now widely known and accepted, the use of more direct systems of booking are expected to make inroads into traditional forms of distribution.

THE MARKETING MIX REVISITED: ARE THE FOUR PS SUFFICIENT?

The adaptation of the marketing mix by authors such as Booms and Bitner (1981) has been based upon arguments that stress that the original marketing mix is more appropriate to manufacturing rather than service companies. For example, Booms and Bitner added three extra Ps (see Figure 19.14):

- people;
- physical evidence; and
- process.

Authors such as Booms and Bitner argue that the marketing mix of four Ps is not comprehensive enough for the tourism and hospitality industry. The major difference is said to

Table 19.4	Travel agent benefits

- **Easy accessibility**
  - to a full range and wide choice of brochures; to product components of visas, traveller's cheques, insurance, etc.;
  - to agent services in every main town and city, as well as to alternative agents, products and brands.

- **Convenience**
  - for obtaining independent information and advice (surfing the Web can be very time-consuming and may not provide for the best possible purchase; and the Internet often does not allow for further questions to be asked). Agents are more likely to take on an independent consultant's role, which is not offered through direct-sell operations;
  - for making the purchase and payment for the holiday (with less perceived risk than would be the case with payment by credit card to an Internet site);
  - for making complaints and being represented by a third party if things go wrong.

- **Habit**
  - People can get into a pattern of behaviour which becomes habit-forming. However, a major campaign by direct mail from Internet direct-sell tour operators/wholesalers could change this habit as could the greater familiarity of use of the Internet for booking air tickets.

- **Security/risk**
  - Consumers feel more secure when dealing with a reputable company or agent (Internet searches involve more personal individual responsibility of the outcome of payment and choice).

- **Environment/atmosphere**
  - Travel agents offer an environment that is part of the holiday experience. The travel agency environment is the perfect setting for personal selling methods which are a powerful means of generating bookings (the Internet is a much more impersonal medium).

- **Economic**
  - Because travel agents compete on price or added value, and tour operators/wholesalers have the smallest of margins, the price between travel agent's products and those available through direct-sell channels are not significantly different.

Source: Adapted from Gilbert, 1990a

Product	Price	Place	Promotion	People	Physical evidence	Process
Range	Level	Location	Advertising	Personnel:	Environment:	Policies
Quality	Discounts:	Accessibility	Personal selling	training	furnishings	Procedures
Level	allowances	Distribution	Sales promotion	discretion	colour	Mechanisation
Brand name	commissions	channels	Publicity	commitment	layout	Employee
Service line	Payment terms	Distribution	Public relations	incentives	noise level	discretion
Warranty	Customer's	coverage		appearance	Facilitating	Customer
After-sales	perceived			interpersonal	goods	involvement
service	value			behaviour	Tangible clues	Customer
	Quality/price			attitudes		direction
	Differentiation			Other customers:		Flow of activities
				behaviour		
				degree of		
				involvement		
				customer/		
				customer		
				contact		

Figure 19.14	The marketing mix for services
	Source: Reprinted by permission of the American Marketing Association from Booms and Bitner, 1981

MINI CASE STUDY 19.1
Is this journey's end for the travel agent?

With the agency business model facing increasing pressure from the growth of internet travel sites such as Expedia, lastminute.com and Travelocity, many tour operators are scaling back their investments in high street outlets. Indeed, with airlines such as British Airways, easyJet and Ryanair moving to sell a bigger proportion of their flights over the internet, travel agents face the grim prospect of being cut out of the industry altogether.

'There has been a 30 per cent decrease in the number of agents over the last three or four years,' says Chris Mottershead, chief executive of Travelzest, a company set up to acquire specialist travel businesses. 'The number is going to continue falling.' He points to the recent decision by MyTravel, one of Europe's largest tour operators, to close 100 of its high street outlets. 'The internet is the cause of this. More people can create their own holidays [using the internet] now and the fastest way to book is by doing it online rather than going to a travel agent.'

However, others say travel agents can prosper by using the internet, particularly if they sell niche products or specialise in areas such as business travel. 'The internet can be incredibly useful for traditional travel agencies,' says David Soskin, chief executive of Cheapflights.co.uk. 'This is particularly true if they have some speciality in terms of access to a particular part of the world or a good relationship with a particular airline.'

For many small travel agents, though, the internet has already proved a useful marketing tool. 'We always featured small independent travel agents on our site and they often have super prices because they can get discounts from airlines,' says Mr Soskin. 'These agents offer a very good way for airlines to shift inventory in a low key way.' The death of the travel agent has been exaggerated, he adds. 'The thing that is important to remember is that travel agents don't actually need to have shop premises. A lot of agents will have a call centre and specially trained staff who can sell a cheap flight or a higher margin product like car hire. And they can make money. It is simplistic to say that the internet is destroying the travel agency model. Travel agents just have to be wise to it and develop a speciality. They have to use the internet properly.'

Forming closer relationships with customers is becoming more important to travel agents under pressure from fast growing internet travel sites and more aggressive airlines. David Speakman, managing director of Travel Counsellors, which operates a network of people who specialise in particular destinations, says personal service is key. 'We have found there are a lot of people who are cash rich but time poor; and they want our advice. They want expertise, good advice and good service.'

But for companies that book business travel, agents still have an important role to play, says Keith Betton of the Association of British Travel Agents. Agents and specialist travel management companies are more suited to planning complex itineraries and reacting to changing schedules, he says. 'A traditional good quality travel agent will be excellent at handling business travel,' he says. 'If you book stuff online it's great if you only want to go from A to B. But a business traveller may want to add on extras and adjust the booking. The online world doesn't lend itself to someone with a complex booking. Business travel is about booking last minute, without feeling like you are going to have to travel on a budget deal. Most people wouldn't mind paying £100 extra to get the right deal rather than saving £100 to sit in a lounge for five more hours.'

But while bigger agents and travel management companies such as American Express have the capacity to respond to more complicated booking needs, smaller agents may suffer. This seems to be borne out by the decline in the number of registered travel agents. Five years ago there were 1,820 companies registered with the Association of British Travel Agents. These companies had an additional 5,234 outlets in the UK. However, by 2005 this had fallen to 1,397 companies with 4,727 outlets. However, while the number of agents has fallen, Sean Tipton, of the Association of British Travel Agents, says those that remain are expanding rapidly, with average turnover rising from £7.9 million in 2001 to £9.1 million this year. Challenges remain. But there may be life in travel agents yet.

Source: Matthew Garrahan, FT.com site, 14 November 2005

RUN AGROUND: HOW THE CLIMATE TURNED COMPETITIVE FOR ONLINE TRAVEL COMPANIES

The decline in the performances of lastminute.com and ebookers.com comes at a time when more traditional holiday companies are also under pressure. That model is under threat, partly because more people are choosing to build their own holidays using the internet. Why, then, are internet travel companies struggling? Online intermediaries make money by selling the products of other companies. Unlike traditional package tour operators, they allow consumers to decide how best to assemble the component parts of their holiday. But because they do not own the products they are selling, the online intermediaries will always be at risk if there is a change in their supply chain. Increased demand from travellers is now disrupting that supply chain.

Simon Champion, leisure analyst with Deutsche Bank, says that during the recent downturn many owners of travel 'products' – flights or hotels – found that online intermediaries were an excellent way of distributing unsold seats or rooms. 'In other words, you can distribute unsold inventory through online intermediaries when you have to. But when things pick up you don't have to sell so much distressed stock,' says Mr Champion.

'The underlying issue is that ownership of content has always been critical in the internet industry. If you are an internet travel company and you don't own the content you might be able to carve out a niche as a website that allows people to compare prices. But when things pick up, when hotels and cruise operators are trying to sell as much as they can, you are going to suffer.' In the US, for example, IAC earns some of its highest margins by selling unsold hotel room inventory. But there are fewer hotel rooms being made available by hotel operators because customer demand has increased. 'The likes of Hilton are still providing lastminute.com and the others with room stock,' says Rod Taylor, head of Barclays European hotels team. 'But they are insisting that this stock is sold at a minimum price. This is putting pressure on the online intermediaries because they can no longer promise that they are selling something cheaper than can be found anywhere else.' The online intermediaries are under pressure from other fronts. The low-cost airlines that have shaken up the aviation industry have sophisticated online sales operations that allow them to sell flights directly to customers. But they do not want to share their success with third-party internet operations such as ebookers.com or lastminute.com.

In the US, JetBlue and SouthWest, low-cost carriers, do not allow internet operations to sell their flights on their behalf. Ryanair and easyJet, Europe's largest low-cost carriers, have adopted a similar stance and use only their own websites to sell flights online. 'The only place you can buy Easyjet flights online is Easyjet.com,' says an easyJet spokesman. 'As a direct sales airline we want people to come to us. As soon as you start selling to Expedia customers will go there rather than come to us.'

In the US about 25 per cent of leisure and unmanaged business travel is booked online. 'We expect this to rise to about 65 per cent by 2010. In Europe, internet penetration for travel is not yet 10 per cent of [total travel bookings] but there's an expectation that half [of all trips] will eventually be booked online.'

Traditionally, GDS companies such as Sabre Holdings or Amadeus charged airlines and other suppliers a flat fee to publish their flight data on the computer terminals used by travel agents. The agents would then use the data to help holidaymakers choose the best deal. However, the growth of online travel and the low-cost airline market, where carriers sell direct to their customers, means holidaymakers are increasingly by-passing travel agencies. This has left GDS companies struggling to catch up.

Source: Matthew Garrahan, *Financial Times*, 16 August 2004

Consumers are the ultimate decision makers in the usage of distribution channel, and therefore, it is worth considering the positive and negative aspects of using the Internet (as seen by an end-user) over a 'bricks-and-mortar' travel agent. Also, of what benefit would it be for travel agents to develop Internet business? With these stakeholders specifically in mind Table 19.5 summarises the key strengths and weaknesses (as identified by the authors) associated with the Internet, which will then serve as the main basis of discussion. We now need to compare the above to the tabulation indicating the benefits of the Internet as a sales medium.

→

Table 19.5	The Internet as a sales medium

Travel agents

Strengths	Weaknesses
• Ability to create a global presence	• Opened up the competitive playing field – 'new' intermediaries are emerging
• Opportunities exist for relationship marketing	• Increased rivalry among travel intermediaries, which may worsen the competitive positions of some firms
• Capital investment required is much less	• Improves direct-sell opportunities among tourist providers
• Opportunity to maximise revenue-generating potential	• Wider choice may detrimentally affect brand loyalty
• Opportunity to create large databases for direct marketing purposes	• The cost of web site design and implementation
• Can allow own-brand product to be provided	

Consumers

Strengths	Weaknesses
• Lowers customers' search costs	• Successful surfing can be time-consuming
• Greater convenience	• A certain degree of inflexibility exists – what if consumers have further questions to ask?
• An opportunity to forge more effective supplier–customer relationships	• Can value really be won?
	• Security issues given perception of risk
	• Greater individual responsibility
	• Impersonality

DISCUSSION QUESTIONS

The preceding information should all be considered in conjunction with the other information in this chapter and then you are required to answer:

1. Do travel agents offer enough benefits to be able to survive the changes taking place with regard to alternative channels of distribution?

2. Provide a future scenario of what you expect to happen in travel distribution in the next 5, 10 and 20 years and justify your arguments.

3. Given the changes taking place with new web sites targeted to more affluent people such as selling wine and financial services what do you think will be the trends in travel industry web site strategies?

be the intangible element of human behaviour where quality and its control is of paramount importance.

We believe that there is a need for more research into the industry and its marketing before the four Ps require revision. For the present it is believed the four Ps offer an adequate framework into which the differences can be incorporated. The main task of marketers in tourism and hospitality is to understand the characteristics of the products they plan, control and manage. This will ensure that managers will attempt to control the aspects of the marketing mix which have most bearing on the satisfaction level of consumers. We provided the basis of this assessment in this chapter and Chapter 18 on marketing management.

While it is obvious that there are differences between manufactured and service products, the framework of the four Ps is sufficient for planning purposes as physical evidence, people or process are part of the category of product or its implementation. The four categories do not presuppose the relegation of service product considerations to secondary importance. On the contrary, the four categories should ensure that within product formulation greater focus will be placed on the integration of all the different service management considerations.

It should be apparent that marketing mix decisions must be geared to achieving the objectives of the company or organisation, and should be linked to acceptability throughout the organisation. While marketing departments often lead in setting the marketing mix strategy, they should not ignore input from others and should be sensitive to views on whether the strategy will be workable from an operational standpoint.

The marketing mix offers the range and spread of alternative strategies by which a marketer can influence demand. However, while the available range is very similar for all tourism marketers, the choice is not. For example, an NTO will not normally be involved in developing products or setting prices. The process of mix formulation and balancing is quite often unique to each organisation.

For an organisation to be successful with its marketing mix, it has to develop a differential advantage which will distinguish the organisation's product offering(s) from that of the competition. Only when an organisation has built an advantage will it find that customers seek it out, in which case it is easier to create higher profits. The advantage may be based upon quality, image, or product concept. Center Parcs in the UK has developed an advantage (through all-weather facilities, forest-like settings and many different activities) and the results can be seen in the high year-round demand for its product.

DESTINATION MARKETING

Destinations rely on tourism as a major tool in the creation of economic development and support for the indigenous population. In the current environment the marketing of destinations is of considerable importance as rivalry for the tourist grows and private and public sector marketing strategies become increasingly sophisticated. When we describe destinations they are of different types – see Chapter 16. Originally, destinations were thought of simply as geographical areas such as a country, an island or a town. In this way destinations can be local, regional or even national: we can speak of America, California or San Francisco with each, and all, capable of being a destination. However, Batchelor (1999) characterised destinations on a continuum with one end consisting of compact product entities such as theme parks. These may be product destinations which create differing lengths of visit or stay. At the other end of the continuum we would find countries or groups of countries which are marketed as a tourism destination. In between, there are many types of destination, defined by the tourist and/or administrative bodies that assume responsibility for them, and include: (1) self-contained resorts, country club hotels, holiday villages; (2) villages, towns, cities; (3) areas with cohesive identity such as national parks; and (4) a region as defined by administrative boundaries or brand names.

The understanding of destination image is important for any destination marketing plan. Destination image has two closely interrelated components: (1) the perceptive/cognitive evaluations, which refer to the individual's own knowledge and beliefs about the destination, and (2) affective appraisals, which refer to the individual's feelings towards the destination. The two components together form a compound image which an individual will draw upon to describe a destination to others, or in order to decide upon a visit. More specifically from a cognitive point of view, the tourist destination image comprises a set of attributes that match the physical, social and built resources that a tourist destination has at its disposal. A destination offers a number of elements which allow individuals a choice of activities, and which culminate in experiences to remember on return.

Tourists form an image of a tourist destination after undergoing a process which, according to Gunn (1988), involves the following stages:

1. accumulating mental images of the destination, thus forming an organic image;
2. modifying the initial image after more information, thus forming an induced image;
3. deciding to visit the destination;
4. visiting the destination;
5. sharing the destination;
6. returning home; and
7. modifying the image on the experience in the destination.

This led Gunn to distinguish between the two types of image – *organic* and *induced*. The organic image is based on non-commercial sources of information, such as news about the destination in the mass media, education at school, information received and opinions of friends and relatives. The induced image is based on commercial sources of information, such as different forms of advertising and information from travel agents and tour operators.

The marketing of destinations is complex as we are dealing not only with the tangible inventory of physical attributes such as the natural geography, built environment and attractions, accommodation and transport facilities, but also intangible social and cultural factors. Although the destination is often the focus for all the marketing effort, it does not follow that there will be a local, regional or national agency that will take responsibility for its marketing. It is also often the case that where there is an organisation charged with destination marketing, its responsibility is based upon a fairly narrow set of powers and limited resources. Traditionally the public sector has been involved in destination marketing through NTOs, regional boards such as DMOs or local authorities but, increasingly, a trend is emerging where marketing agencies or conference and visitor bureaux are established for cities. Such agencies are often funded by a mix of both private and public means.

The marketing of destinations

The marketing of destinations is a relatively new departure for many localities, particularly at the regional and local level. At these levels the lead agency tends to be the public sector and this, in turn, has a number of implications for the marketing process which are rooted in the inability of the public sector to control the product. In addition, there is an issue here in terms of whether we should transform places where people live, work and play into *products*. We are only beginning to understand how to translate generic marketing approaches to destinations. There are some key areas to consider here:

- The images of the destination which the marketing campaigns wish to communicate should take into account the views and sensitivities of local people.
- Public sector agencies have to be even-handed in their support for businesses at the destination – it is difficult politically for them to back 'product' winners.
- The public sector controls neither the business plans of private sector companies at the destination, nor the quality of service delivery.
- Public sector marketing organisations seldom *achieve the sale*, rather they are instrumental in attracting the consumer to the point of sale – usually a private sector company. It is therefore difficult to evaluate the effectiveness of destination marketing.
- Finally, the critical issue of resources is a constant problem for public sector marketing budgets, especially for activities which may be perceived as dispensable – such as market research – but which in reality are crucial to success in the tourism marketplace.

The traditional role of many of these approaches has been elementary. The emphasis has been confined to promotional strategies which aim to improve the destination image or to produce more positive 'mental concepts' in relation to both potential as well as actual tourists. This is often related to the selection of desirable market segments that are targeted through the use of advertising, direct mail, print or PR campaigns (as discussed earlier in this chapter). There is further emphasis on providing information at the destination through information posters or tourist information centres.

Destinations need to identify those product attributes that will appeal to different tourist segments and then to ensure that the promotional campaign delivers a cohesive message. There is also the need to produce a distinctive identity or 'brand' which forms the basis of the 'positioning' of a destination area, providing it with a personality and differentiating it from competitors.

De Chernatony and McDonald (1992) describe the necessary attributes of a successful brand and these may also be applied to tourism destinations:

> A successful brand is an identifiable product, service, person or place augmented in such a way that the buyer, or user, perceives relevant, unique added values which match their needs most closely. Its success results from being able to sustain these added values against competitors.

Such results may be achieved through the theming of an area by linking it to a famous personality who may have lived in the area, such as a painter (Constable country such as Dedham Vale, valley of the Stour river and East Bergholt), a writer or poet (Hemingway and Cuba or Wordsworth associated with the Lake District and Grasmere), a television series or film, a historical era (Pompeii) or seasonal beauty (New England in the autumn). There are many other themes, of course, but all need to be developed with a creative flair for the tastes of the potential visitor as well as the acceptability of the theme to the media.

The involvement of tourist boards at the national and regional level is often one of facilitation. Facilitation is made up of a series of assistance schemes which support the constituent service sectors of the tourist industry forming the accommodation, transport and attraction provision of a country, region or locality. This may take the form of a set of objectives related to:

- the development of specific tourism areas or products;
- the targeting of specific segments from generating areas;
- the level of expenditure available;
- a range of promotional activities (PR, advertising, exhibitions, literature production); or
- the need for cooperative private initiatives or expenditure.

The industry is diverse and fragmented, comprising many small companies which require help in areas such as:

- the collection and use of research data;
- the organisation of trade exhibitions and shows;
- representation through overseas offices;
- the production of trade manuals, catalogues and brochures (which can have space bought by smaller companies); and
- the development of global reservation systems which can provide local information on a global basis.

The facilitation process can help create an overall brand image of a destination through the total activity which takes place. However, the marketing, through all forms of promotion, will create a specific brand image. This is beneficial if a strong brand image is created.

An area that has a strong brand image is able:

- to achieve better margins and higher prices than commodity-positioned brands;
- to differentiate itself more easily from competitors;
- to provide a sense of added value and so more easily entice customers to purchase;
- to act as a sign and enticement to the potential traveller, which implies fulfilment of expectations;
- to build repeat visits and loyalty; and
- to improve the strength of its position as a status area rather than as a commodity.

A destination has an image of place associated with it. This can be based upon differences related to what is normal in both a tourist-generating area and in the culture of the destination. The differences may be real or imagined. Promotion of a destination is based on an image selected by the tourism marketer and communicated to the generating markets, often providing stereotypical images of an exotic, carefree host culture. In reality this may mask a whole set of socio-cultural realities of what life is like for the average inhabitant of a destination.

MINI CASE STUDY 19.2
Sitting pretty (airline lounges)

At Virgin Atlantic's new business lounge at London's Heathrow airport, passengers have been offered 'mind-gym' clinics, where they can be coached in mind-improving techniques; BlackBerry clinics, where they can get tips and information on how to use their portable handsets; and sunglasses styling clinics, where they are shown which sunglasses best suit their features. Virgin Atlantic's Heathrow offerings will look either gimmicky or useful, depending on your point of view, but they are also a sign that business lounges are having to do more than just provide a comfortable haven from the hustle and bustle of the terminals.

'There has been a huge shift in what people want from their travel experience,' says a British Airways spokeswoman. 'In the 1980s, business lounges were very much about the experience of getting there, but in the 1990s people started to really want the time they were spending travelling given back to them, so [business lounges] have become destinations in themselves.' This means that an increasing number of business lounges, in addition to providing the usual array of services: free buffet-style food, tea and coffee, comfortable seating, wi-fi and newspapers, are competing to offer an improved architectural and interior design experience, a range of themed bars, branded beauty and therapy centres, and swimming pools.

Malaysian Airlines's lounge in Kuala Lumpur, for example, has a glass-enclosed rainforest, with a river running through it, along with a gym, bedrooms, a computer-games corner and a nursery with babysitting services. BA's lounge at JFK offers a Molton Brown Travel Spa, with hydrotherapy showers, reflexology treatments and specially designed pre- and post-flight massages, while Cathay Pacific's lounge at Hong Kong International airport has private cubicles, complete with personal showers, beds and oversized tubs. 'Consumers are far more demanding. There is much greater awareness of the effects of jetlag and an understanding that travellers don't want to arrive at their destinations exhausted,' says BA.

In part, the changes have been driven by upgrades to airport facilities. With many terminals providing even economy-class flyers with comfortable seating, a choice of restaurants and an extensive range of shops, business lounges have had to do more to differentiate themselves from the mainstream. 'If you have wi-fi and a comfortable place to eat anyway, the value a lounge delivers starts to fall,' says Henry Harteveldt, vice-president and principal analyst of travel at Forrester, the research company. He says that many airlines in the US objected, for competitive reasons, to airports installing wi-fi in public spaces. 'Given that the argument was with their landlords,' he adds, 'there wasn't much they could do about it.'

The improvements have also been driven by the need to justify corporate expenditure on first class travel, traditionally the main users of business lounges. With companies cutting back on business and first class flights and encouraging staff to take both economy seats and use budget airlines, the high-end of the market has been forced to prove it is worth the expense. 'Travellers and corporations have to believe the premium they are paying for a first class or business class ticket is worth it,' says Mr Harteveldt. 'And if you are really a frequent flyer, what you care about are small courtesies. Airline travel is stressful and you want to be cushioned from its harsh realities.'

In some cases, companies are offering lounge access to compensate their staff for the economy class tickets bought for them. This has fuelled a proliferation in both independently run, pay-as-you-go lounges and schemes offering lounge access as a benefit. Thus, where once airport business lounges were restricted to the privileged few, travellers can now buy access for between £10 and £20 a person without the expense of a first class ticket. Companies such as Lounge Pass and PriorityPass offer lounge passes on a one-off or annual basis, as do many airlines and airline service companies, such as Servisair. Jennifer Archer, US director of marketing at PriorityPass, says: 'Corporations can save thousands of dollars by purchasing an unlimited access membership ticket to business lounges instead of buying a first class ticket. It's a no-brainer; a huge reward for almost no investment.' Although lounge services like this have been around since the early 1990s, they have grown in popularity as the extra waiting time associated with increased security over the past few years has grown. With passengers being asked to arrive at airports several hours early, even for domestic flights, business lounges are playing an even greater role in providing a place where passengers can get some work done or relax and enjoy time spent out of the office. 'It's an insurance scheme,' says Ms Archer. 'You never know when you might be at an airport longer than expected. With the increase in security, people are anticipating long lines, and now they can do something with any time left over. They can be productive and turn airport time into their time. And the increase in security demands isn't something that's going to go away today.' Some lounges are better than others. Not all offer day pass access, and for good reason. BA, for example, says that its business lounges are already busy, so it sees no need to open them up for casual use.

There are also differences between the US and Europe. Forrester's Mr Harteveldt says that US airlines in general tend to take a more mercantile approach to business lounges than European and Asian airlines, which tend to reserve them exclusively for their first class passengers, viewing them as a sanctuary and part of a paid-for privilege. 'American airlines tend to view lounges as just another product to be sold,' he says, 'and they're much better at up-selling to customers. So, it's just like when you go to McDonald's and they ask if you'd like fries with your Coke. They will ask if you'd like a business lounge pass with your economy ticket.' This trend is now spreading to Europe, with third parties selling airport lounge passes, including budget airlines such as easyJet. Business lounges have had to adapt to cultural trends. BA says an increasing number of men are using its spa treatment facilities, reflecting the overall rise in men using beauty products. Tailored services are also appreciated. Japanese travellers, for example, love spas, particularly foot treatments, the airline says. This suggests that business lounges, unlike their luxury-seeking clients, are being forced to undergo head-to-toe makeovers just to survive.

Source: Gill Plimmer, FT.com site, 24 October 2006

DISCUSSION QUESTIONS

1. If a lounge is to be redeveloped, what segments should be catered for and what exciting new services and environment do you think should be considered in the redevelopment programme?

2. What influence do you think a lounge has on the demand for an airline and an airport?

3. Provide a forecast scenario of ten years into the future as to what services there will be in major airports for the comfort of a passenger travelling on international flights.

The power to portray selective images of place relies on factors such as whether a tourist is a first-time visitor or a repeat visitor and also on the amount of information the tourist has gleaned from television, films, books or friends. A destination, once branded and having communicated a distinctive image, is in a far stronger position to influence demand if problems arise of price increases, excess demand and crowding or unfavourable currency exchange rates.

The Spanish Tourist Board, faced with the loss of a strong Spanish image for its resort areas, embarked upon an exercise to reposition and rebrand the country. The history, culture, traditions and inland areas had been under-promoted and weakly communicated. The campaign from 1992 emphasised the 'Spanishness' of the country within a campaign which stressed, 'Spain – Passion for life'. The painter, Miro, was commissioned to create a logo that would reflect the fundamental spirit of Spain. He created a vibrant logo reflecting the national flag colours of yellow and red and this was used on all communication messages.

Consumers' concept of 'self-image'

When consumers choose among brands, they rationally consider practical issues about the relative functional capabilities of all the brands on offer. At the same time, they evaluate different brand personalities, forming a view about the brand that most closely represents the image with which they wish to be associated.

Applying this to tourism, it is possible to suggest that when competing destinations are perceived as being equal and similar in terms of their physical capabilities, the brand that comes closest to enhancing the consumer's self-concept is more likely to be chosen. Consumers look to brands not only for what they can do, but also for the message they communicate about the purchaser to peer groups. Trips to Monte Carlo, for example, are chosen not just for their functional excellence, but also because they make an important statement about the traveller.

According to de Chernatony and McDonald (1992), the symbolic nature of brands increases the attraction for consumers as they:

- help set social scenes and enable people to mix with each other more easily;
- enable consumers to convey messages about themselves;
- provide a basis for a better understanding of the way people act; and
- help consumers say something to themselves.

In effect, consumers are transmitting subtle messages to others by purchasing and displaying the use of particular brands in the hope that their reference groups decode the messages in a positive and acceptable way. Consumers hold what is called their own 'self-image' and buy brands that conform to that image. Consumers, therefore, could be said to admit brands and their 'personalities' into their social circle, in much the same way as consumers enjoy having like-minded people around them. When friends or colleagues admire a holiday destination choice, the traveller feels pleased that the destination brand reinforces his or her self-image and may therefore repeat the purchase.

The economic and social situation in which consumers find themselves will dictate, to some extent, the type of image they wish to project. Through anticipating and subsequently evaluating the people that they will meet at a particular event or destination, consumers then seek brands to reflect the situational self-image that they wish to display.

CONCLUSION

The marketing mix cannot be effective without a full understanding of the target market and the needs of each of the segments. The marketing mix is formulated and implemented to satisfy the target market. We take the marketing mix to be made up of the four Ps of product, price, promotion and place (distribution), but there are alternative approaches where authors argue for an expansion owing to the service characteristics of tourism and hospitality products. However, the additional ingredients can be included in the existing headings associated with the four Ps and, as long as the characteristics of the tourism and hospitality product are emphasised, there is little benefit in pre-dating McCarthy's late 1970s' simplification of approach.

SELF-CHECK QUESTIONS

1. Name and describe the different product levels that may exist for a leading hotel.

2. Describe the benefits that a strong tourism brand may provide for the company.

3. Provide a list and understanding of at least five of the aspects which are related to price sensitivity.

4. Describe four ways of deciding upon the amount of money required when raising a promotion budget.

5. What are the five advantages related to use of the Internet as a channel?

ESSAY QUESTIONS

1. Provide a plan as to how travel agents can utilise the marketing mix to improve the service and value they provide for the holiday target market.

2. Identify the elements of the marketing mix and compare and contrast how they may be used by each of the following organisations: Ryanair and British Airways, the Savoy Hotel and Premier Inn.

3. Consider the role and importance of the target markets for a theme park such as Disneyland and the implications for the manipulation of the various elements of the marketing mix.

4. For each of the following choose and *justify* a brand name, product formulation, product positioning and target segments: new health and beauty clinic for men, a company offering adventure holidays in Africa. Also, discuss briefly what other marketing mix aspects you would adopt.

5. Visit the priceline.com web site and/or alternative travel-related web sites and discuss the trends and other impacts of the Internet on pricing policy for the tourism product.

ANNOTATED FURTHER READING

Books

Buhalis, D. (2003) *eTourism: Information Technologies for Strategic Tourism Management*, FT/Prentice Hall, London.
This book addresses the change to a digitisation of processes and value chains in the tourism industry. It offers insight into the new technological trends based upon the impacts of the information communication technology (ICT) revolution. The book adopts a strategic management and marketing perspective for tourism enterprises and destinations.

Kotler, P., Bowen J. and Makens, J. (2006) *Marketing for Hospitality and Tourism*, 4th edn, Pearson, Upper Saddle River, NJ.
The book draws upon the marketing material of Philip Kotler's other books and as such is based upon his pedigree which has been developed over a number of years of writing

marketing textbooks. However, the examples are often better in other texts and other specialist books need to be read in conjunction with this one. This latest edition now covers electronic marketing, has case studies and provides a broad understanding of the role of marketing in hospitality and tourism. Specialist areas covered are customer quality management and destination marketing.

Middleton, V. and Clarke. J. (2001) *Marketing in Travel and Tourism*, 3rd edn, Butterworth Heinemann, Oxford.
Marketing in Travel and Tourism explains the basic principles and practice of marketing in the contemporary setting of the new pressures affecting tourism including areas not normally covered in such texts such as NTOs. In addition, international case studies are included.

Morgan, N. and Pritchard, A. (1998) *Tourism Promotion and Power: Creating Images, Creating Identities*, John Wiley & Sons, Chichester.
The book is underpinned by marketing theory and does not simply deal with the more general concepts related to tourism promotion. The book offers a different approach by taking a sociological and cultural approach to tourism marketing. It focuses on contentious issues of tourism imagery by discussing issues such as gender, sexuality and race as key determinants of tourism power dimensions. The book is underpinned by good case studies which are thought-provoking.

Web sites

http://www.eyefortravel.com
http://world-tourism.org/
http://wttc.org/

References cited and bibliography

Aaker, D.A. (1991) *Managing Brand Equity: Capitalizing on the Value of a Brand Name*, Free Press, New York.
Aaker, D.A. and Biel, A.L. (1993) *Brand Equity and Advertising*, Lawrence Erlbaum Associates, Mahwah, NJ.
Batchelor, R. (1999) 'Strategic Marketing of Tourism Destinations', pp. 183–95 in Vellas, F. and Becherel, L. (eds), *The International Marketing of Travel and Tourism*, Macmillan Press, London.
Bierman, D. (2003) *Restoring Tourism Destinations in Crisis: A Strategic Marketing Approach*, CABI, Cambridge, MA.
Booms, B.H. and Bitner, M.J. (1981) 'Marketing strategies and organization structures for service firms', pp. 47–51 in Donnelly, J. and George, W.R. (eds), *Marketing of Services*, American Marketing Association, Chicago.
Borden, N.H. (1965) 'The concept of the marketing mix', pp. 386–97 in Schwartz, G., *Science in Marketing*, Wiley, Chichester.
CIMtIG (2004) D. Blastland (managing director, First Choice Holidays) 'Can tour operators and travel agents survive', Member minutes of meeting of Chartered Institute of Marketing Industry Group, January.
De Chernatony, L. and Daniels, K. (1994) 'Developing a more effective brand positioning', *Journal of Brand Management* 1(6), 373–9.
De Chernatony, L. and McDonald, M.H.B. (1992) *Creating Powerful Brands*, Butterworth Heinemann, Oxford.
De Chernatony, L. and McWilliam, G. (1989) 'The varying nature of brands as assets', *International Journal of Advertising* 8, 339–49.
Gilbert, D.C. (1990a) 'European product purchase methods and systems', *Service Industries Journal* 10(4), 664–79.

Gilbert, D.C. (1990b) 'Strategic marketing planning for national tourism', *Tourism Analysis* 1(90), 18–27.

Gunn, C. (1988) *Vacationscape: Designing Tourist Regions*, 2nd edn, Van Nostrand Reinhold, New York.

Hankinson, G. and Cowking, P. (1993) *Branding in Action: Cases and Strategies for Profitable Brand Management*, McGraw-Hill, London.

Kotler, P. and Armstrong, G. (2005) *Marketing: An Introduction*, Prentice Hall, Upper Saddle River, NJ.

McArdle, J. (1989) 'Product branding – the way forward', *Tourism Management* 10, 201.

McCarthy, E.J. (1978) *Basic Marketing: A Managerial Approach*, 6th edn, Irwin, Homewood, IL.

Zeithaml, V.A. (1988) 'Consumer perceptions of price, quality, and value: a means–end model and synthesis of evidence', *Journal of Marketing* 52, July, 2–22.

MAJOR CASE STUDY 19.1
Nisbet Plantation Beach Club and relationship marketing

Nisbet Plantation Beach Club in Nevis has won accolades for employing *Integrated 1-to-1 Marketing*. The hotel's approach was based upon three objectives:

1. Build strong, personal relationships with affluent customers, prospects and the travel agents serving them. Nisbet wanted to exploit the fact that the most effective marketing in leisure travel continues to be 'recommendations from friends and relatives'.

2. Maximise productive use of the Internet – expand Nisbet's customer database to include email addresses and an expansion of data related to those prospects similar to current customers; develop an effective, instantaneous and cost-effective dialogue with its best customers and prospects.

3. Increase both immediate and long-term sales.

To meet Nisbet's objectives the resort has employed the following five key strategies (the major improvement to achieve these was based upon Nisbet's integrated database system):

1. Build a new web site capable of supporting an *Integrated 1-to-1 Marketing* program – add new features to maximise the visitor experience and encourage multiple repeat visits; build a data-capture mechanism for site visitors including name, address, email and travel preferences for future digital re-marketing efforts; add an online booking engine.

2. Develop company-wide systems to capture names and addresses at *all* points of contact (i.e. at guest registration, email communications, non-customers visiting for lunch or dinner, visitors to resort's boutique, etc.).

3. Focus all communications on delivering a strong brand message and directing individuals to the web site for data capture and follow-up relationship building.

4. Develop a permission-based email-marketing newsletter. Reduce the use of paper communications.

5. Develop ways to maximise the effectiveness of a highly constrained budget.

BUILD A NEW WEB SITE CAPABLE OF SUPPORTING AN INTEGRATED 1-TO-1 MARKETING PROGRAM

Nisbet's previous web site consisted of only five pages categorised as typical first generation web brochure-ware. Immediate action included the development of a new site (http://www.NisbetPlantation.com) with significantly more content. Content throughout the site has been tailored to help ease visitors through the purchase process and to emphasise the resort's positioning as an *Unhurried, Unspoiled and Uncommon* vacation.

Online sweepstakes

To encourage visitors to enter personal information into the database a sweepstake was developed. A banner promoting the sweepstakes is prominently displayed throughout the site.

To further encourage sweepstakes sign-up (data capture), the resort's privacy policy is prominently displayed on the contest entry form, assuring registrants' personal information will be held in the strictest confidence. A contest winners' page was added to the site after the sweepstakes winners were announced.

Online booking engine

To facilitate the booking process for online consumers, Nisbet Plantation employed the ASP services of Synxix.

Photo contest

A photo contest was developed to serve three primary purposes:

- Generate more content for visitors.
- Get past visitors emotionally involved with the site and enhance the relationship.
- Have contest winners send friends and relatives to the site to see the photos and learn more about Nisbet and sign up for the sweepstakes (build the database).

Search engine marketing

Aware of the need for the web site to rank well in search engines, keywords and phrases were identified by examining server logs, customer comment cards, reservations staff and communications with customers. Emphasis was put on phrases customers used rather than words the hotel or marketing team would use to describe the resort. A plan was adopted for search engine marketing in order to achieve search engine optimisation; the linking of campaigns and to have paid placement.

STRATEGY TO DEVELOP SYSTEMS TO CAPTURE NAMES AND ADDRESSES AT ALL POINTS OF CONTACT

Consistent, high-quality brand messages are aligned to every form of communication, which wherever possible continue to direct individuals to the web site encouraging them to sign up for the sweepstakes and provide permission to receive more information from the resort. This strategy had its most significant impact on three areas:

1. Advertising.
2. Public relations.
3. Resort operations – training for effective email service/response.

Advertising

Several months before the new web site was operational an integrated marketing communications program designed to drive traffic to the site was developed. The communications included high-frequency schedules of small spaced advertising in a very few publications.

Targeted niche marketing Targeted niche marketing is concentrated in two areas: weddings and honeymoons and Sunday travel sections of major newspapers.

Sunday travel sections

Sunday travel sections of major metropolitan newspapers serve as the backbone of Nisbet's newspaper advertising. While size restrictions preclude the resort from promoting the sweepstakes, its web address is always featured prominently – continuing to address the primary marketing objective of driving traffic to the web site. Nisbet's headline includes the destination and web address while most other resorts feature the destination and the resort's name.

Public relations

Both the timing and message of public relations activity was coordinated with the advertising and promotional schedules to help maximise impact in the marketplace. Every press release included a mention of the resort's sweepstakes along with directions on where to go to sign up.

Resort operations – training

It was not long before the volume of email messages received by Nisbet began to increase dramatically – more than tripling daily volumes. Responding to enquiries and comments in the past was part of the daily routine. However, the increased volume began creating staffing problems and causing response time and quality issues. As a result, training sessions and a manual were developed and instituted. The staff at Nisbet Plantation has an excellent reputation for taking special care of its customers. What was needed was to take the same customer care that transpires naturally face to face and translate it to a computer-to-computer interaction. Exercises in visualising the individual at the other end were undertaken – trying to decipher based on their email who they are, what their major concerns are, and what information they would need to make Nisbet the resort of choice. Responses were regularly reviewed by management through a web interface and later used in exercises to analyse and improve responses to:

- build more dialogue and a deeper relationship with the individual (almost like having a pen pal);
- induce individuals to select Nisbet and/or recommend the resort to a friend or relative.

In addition to being used to improve email responses, the monitoring systems allowed the marketing department to view consumer requests/issues and adjust the web site and provide greater clarity.

Email messages could be separated into two main categories:

- requests for information; and
- comments.

'Requests for information' were designated as the highest priority and receive a complete and proper response within a few hours of receipt. Nisbet receives numerous 'comments' from individuals that are not really requests for information. The resort now looks upon all correspondence as an opportunity to create a dialogue and build a relationship.

Rather than sending out two paper newsletters each year as it had in the past the resort was now sending out 12 email newsletters. Nisbet's email database (including customers, prospects and travel agents) is now seven times larger that the resort's customer database. Nisbet can deliver email messages personalised to the reader: messages to customers are written recognising them as customers – travel agents as travel agents, etc. Tracking and follow-up – through the email program, the resort monitors individual click-through activity on specific promotions. This allows for follow-up targeted marketing activities, i.e. people who click on Nisbet's honeymoon package receive a package in the mail with a brochure and a personal invitation from the resort's general manager to honeymoon at Nisbet.

Direct mail

One of the most effective and efficient vehicles has been direct mail promotional postcard mailings. To ensure Nisbet stays in contact with all past guests the resort uses a series of postcard mailings. This allows Nisbet to increase the frequency of contact with past guests and to invite them back. In addition to providing a strong promotional message, the postcards also

encourage recipients to go to the web site and register for the sweepstakes.

RESULTS

This case study provides an overview of a few of the many different initiatives Nisbet took in order to develop its integrated relationship marketing program.

The following highlight the effectiveness of the program:

1. Occupancy – on a monthly basis, Nisbet consistently has either the highest or second highest occupancy of any resort in St Kitts and Nevis; well above average occupancy rates for all other island resorts and this occurs without discounting rates.

2. Relationship building – Nisbet's marketing program has generated a threefold increase in email communication between the resort and consumers and travel agents.

3. Database size – Nisbet has built a permission-based email database of customers, prospects and travel agents that is seven times larger than the total number of guests the resort has entertained over the past five years.

4. eNewsletter response – Nisbet's eNewsletter is a complete success with highly satisfactory (20%–40%) click-through rates and traffic driven to the web.

5. Online bookings – the online booking engine is now the number two producer for the resort.

6. Instantaneous dialogue capability – which can announce seat sales or other important news.

Source: Madigan Pratt & Associates, Inc.
www.MadiganPratt.com

DISCUSSION QUESTIONS

1. Identify the main reasons for the success of the changes made by Nisbet Plantation Hotel.

2. Create a model of the ways Nisbet have developed relationship marketing and compare this to the literature to find out if they have met or exceeded current theories.

3. Take a hotel that you know of and provide a plan of the project management implementation that would be required to develop its relationship marketing approaches.

CHAPTER 20

Information Technology in Tourism

LEARNING OUTCOMES

In this chapter we focus on the strategic and operational role of ICTs in tourism organisations. The chapter demonstrates a wide range of e-tourism concepts to provide you with:

● an understanding of the key ICT and e-tourism concepts;

● an appreciation of the generic ICTs applications in the tourism industry;

● a knowledge of the basic concepts of computer reservation systems and global distribution channels;

● an explanation of the key trends in Internet adoption around the world;

● a comprehension of the impact of the Internet and ICTs tools on the structure and components of the tourism system; and

● an appreciation of the strategic importance of ICTs and the Internet for the future of each stakeholder in the tourism industry.

INTRODUCTION

E-tourism, defined as the application of '**information communication technologies**' (ICTs) on the tourism industry, has dramatically affected the strategic and operational management of tourism organisations and destinations (Buhalis, 2003). ICT developments have changed the best operational and strategic practices for organisations on a global level and altered the competitiveness of enterprises and regions around the world. Innovative organisations, such as Marriott, Hilton, easyJet and British Airways, took advantage of the emerging technologies early in order to improve their operational processes and enhance their communication with consumers and stakeholders. The Internet provided the ability to expand the customer base to cover the global population cost-effectively. Large organisations, such as airlines and hotel chains, were able to access an international clientele and develop the tools to manage properties around the world at the touch of a button. Smaller companies could also for the first time develop their 'virtual size' and offer their services to global markets (Buhalis, 2003; O'Connor, 1999). Destinations could develop virtual representations and boost their image globally. However, several tourism organisations failed to meet the challenge that e-business introduced. Many of them failed to incorporate ICTs in their strategy and to appreciate the significant changes evident in the tourism industry structure caused by technology. Consequently they developed competitive disadvantages and found it increasingly difficult to maintain their position in the marketplace.

This chapter explores the main implications of the ICT developments in the tourism industry. It illuminates the complexity of the various types of systems and demonstrates how they fit together in the production, distribution and delivery of tourism products. The utilisation of ICTs and the Internet by different functions and sectors of the industry is examined and conclusions for the future impact of ICTs outlined.

INFORMATION COMMUNICATION TECHNOLOGIES AS A BUSINESS TOOL

Information communication technologies (ICTs) and the Internet introduced a second industrial revolution in the late 1990s. The development and application of computerised systems accelerated rapidly and enabled their use for a wider range of business functions and activities. The enhancements in ICT capabilities, in combination with the decrease of the size of equipment and ICT costs, improved the reliability, compatibility and inter-connectivity of numerous terminals and applications (Gupta, 2000). The emergence and mainstreaming of the Internet empowered the global networking of computers, enabling individuals and organisations to access a plethora of multimedia information and knowledge sources, regardless of their location or ownership, often free of charge. Thus, almost everybody with an Internet access (which, sadly, is still only about 16.6% of the global population in 2007) can effectively access unprecedented levels of information and knowledge. Interestingly worldwide Internet users reached 1.1 billion in 2007, with the USA leading with 210 million Internet users and a penetration level of 70% whilst China followed with 132 million users but only 10% penetration (www.internetworldstats.com).

E-business can be defined as: 'the use of digital tools for business functions and processes'. It is becoming increasingly evident that e-business is an essential prerequisite for successful organisations in the emerging, globally networked, Internet-empowered business environment. Many organisations had to go through a major business processes re-engineering to take advantage of the emerging technologies in order to transform their processes and data handling as well as their ability to operate and to compete in the emerging global marketplace (Laudon and Laudon, 2007). At the macro level, entire economies were empowered to communicate and trade through electronic tools, determining their ability to compete within the global economy. Consequently, economies and enterprises, regardless of their size, product and geographical coverage were affected and their competitiveness was dramatically altered.

The evolution of ICTs towards e-business

ICTs include not only the hardware and software required but also the groupware, netware and the intellectual capacity (humanware) to develop, program and maintain equipment (Table 20.1). Synergies emerging from the use of these systems effectively mean that information is widely available and accessible through a variety of media and locations. Users can use mobile devices such as portable computers, mobile phones as well as digital television and self-service terminals/kiosks to interact and perform several functions. This convergence of ICTs effectively integrates the entire range of hardware, software, groupware, netware and humanware and blurs the boundaries between equipment and software (Werthner and Klein, 1999).

The integration of information processing, multimedia and communications created the World Wide Web (WWW), a multimedia protocol which is using the Internet (the network of all networks) to enable the near instant distribution of media-rich documents (such as textual data, graphics, pictures, video and sounds) and to revolutionise the interactivity between computer users and servers. Perhaps one of the most interesting current developments is that of Web 2.0, a phrase coined by O'Reilly (2005) that refers to a second generation of web-based services based on citizen/consumer-generated content – such as social networking sites, blogs, wikis, communication tools and folksonomies – that emphasises online collaboration and sharing among users. A Web 2.0 web site may feature a number of the following techniques, including rich Internet application techniques, optionally Ajax-based; cascading style sheets (CSS); semantically valid XHTML mark-up and the use of microformats; syndication and aggregation of data in Really Simple Syndication (RSS/Atom); clean and meaningful URLs; extensive use of folksonomies (in the form of tags or tagclouds,

Table 20.1	Information Communication Technologies

Hardware: Physical equipment such as mechanical, magnetic, electrical, electronic or optical devices (as opposed to computer programs or method of use).

Software: Prewritten detailed instructions that control the operation of a computer system or of an electronic device. Software coordinates the work of hardware components in an information system. Software may incorporate standard software such as operating systems or applications, software processes, artificial intelligence and intelligent agents, and user interfaces.

Telecommunications: The transmission of signals over long distances, including not only data communications but also the transmission of images and voices using radio, television, telephony and other communication technologies.

Netware: Equipment and software required to develop and support a network or an interconnected system of computers, terminals and communication channels and devices.

Groupware: communication tools, such as email, voice mail, fax, video conferencing that foster electronic communication and collaboration among groups.

'Humanware': the intellect required for the development, programming, maintenance and operation of technological development. Humanware incorporates the knowledge and expertise pool of the society.

Adapted from: Gupta, 2000; O'Brien, 1996; Laudon and Laudon, 2007

Table 20.2	O'Reilly's examples formulating the sense of Web 2.0

Web 1.0		Web 2.0
DoubleClick	→	Google AdSense
Ofoto	→	Flickr
Akamai	→	BitTorrent
mp3.com	→	Napster
Britannica Online	→	Wikipedia
personal websites	→	blogging
evite	→	upcoming.org and EVDB
domain name speculation	→	search engine optimisation
page views	→	cost per click
screen scraping	→	web services
publishing	→	participation
multimap	→	Google Earth with content layers
content management systems	→	wikis
directories (taxonomy)	→	tagging ('folksonomy')
stickiness	→	syndication

Source: Based on O'Reilly Media, Inc, 2005

for example); use of wiki software; weblog publishing; Mashups and REST or XML Webservice APIs (see Table 20.2). Increasingly the Internet is becoming a platform of data/ views/knowledge creation and sharing which harness the network to get better information to all users.

As far as organisations are concerned the dynamic development of the Internet instituted an innovative platform for the efficient, live and timely exchange of ideas and products, whilst providing unprecedented and unforeseen opportunities for interactive marketing to all service providers. It also enabled the development of *intranets* ('closed', 'secured' or 'firewalled' networks) within organisations to harness the needs of internal business users, by using a single controlled, user-friendly interface to support all company data handling and processes. Increasingly enterprises need to formulate close partnerships with other members of the value chain for the production of goods and services. As a result, *extranets* utilise the same principle and computer networks to enhance the interactivity and transparency between organisations and their trusted partners. This facilitates the linking and sharing of data and processes between organisations to maximise the effectiveness of the entire network.

Buhalis (2003) concluded that ICTs include 'the entire range of electronic tools, which facilitate the operational and strategic management of organisations by enabling them to manage their information, functions and processes as well as to communicate interactively with their stakeholders for achieving their mission and objectives'. Thus, ICTs emerge as an integrated system of networked equipment and software, which enables effective data processing and communication for organisational benefit towards transforming organisations to e-businesses.

The pace of Internet adoption globally demonstrates clearly that ICTs and the Internet in particular restructure the way we live, work, shop and play. Millions of people worldwide rely on the Internet for home shopping, tele-entertainment, teleworking, tele-learning, telemedical support and telebanking. The electronic/interactive/intelligent/virtual home and enterprise has emerged gradually, facilitating the entire range of communications with the external world and supporting all functions of everyday personal and professional life through interactive computer networks. Increasingly, fast broadband connections and the rapid expansion of wireless connectivity through WiFi and WiMax enable both consumers and suppliers to be constantly connected and generate further opportunities and challenges.

ICTs, competitiveness and strategy

Since the beginning of the century the development of ICTs has had a major effect on the operation, structure and strategy of organisations. Not only do they reduce both communication and operational costs, but they also enhance flexibility, interactivity, efficiency, productivity and competitiveness. Although ICTs are not a panacea and cannot guarantee financial success on their own, ignoring and underutilising ICTs can generate significant competitive disadvantages. This is because ICTs are instrumental in ensuring efficient internal organisation, effective communication with partners and interactivity with consumers. Certain prerequisites are needed to be successful, namely:

- long-term planning and strategy;
- rational management and development of hardware and software;
- re-engineering of business processes;
- top management commitment; and
- training throughout the hierarchy.

These prerequisites facilitate the achievement of sustainable competitive advantage. Failure to address these issues can jeopardise the competitiveness, prosperity and even existence of tourism organisations (Buhalis, 1998).

Using ICTs as a stand-alone initiative is inadequate and has to be coupled with a redesign of processes, structures and management control systems. Provided that rational and innovative planning and management is exercised constantly and consistently, ICTs can support business success. As a consequence, 'business processes re-engineering' argues that yesterday's practices, traditional hierarchical and organisational structures, and habitual procedures are almost irrelevant. In contrast, corporations should be able to respond to current and future challenges, by having the resources and expertise to design new processes from scratch in a timely fashion. As a result of the rapid ICT developments corporations need to convert their operations from business functions to business processes, as well as reconceive their distribution channels strategy and, even more importantly, their corporate values and culture (Tapscott, 1996). Perhaps the greatest challenge organisations face is to identify and train managers who will be effective and innovative users of ICTs and would lead technology-based decision-making. *Intellect* therefore becomes a critical asset, while continuous education and training are instrumental for the innovative use of ICTs and the competitiveness of tourism organisations (Buhalis, 2003).

The ICT developments have introduced new best strategic and operational management practices that lead organisations to shift their orientation from product-orientation to a consumer-orientation that customises products and services and adopts flexible and responsive practices to the marketplace. Success will increasingly depend on sensing and responding to rapidly changing customer needs and using ICTs for delivering the right product, at the right time, at the right price, for the right customer. To the degree that ICTs can contribute to the value chain of products and services, by either improving their cost position or differentiation, they reshape competitiveness and thus have strategic implications for the prosperity of the organisation (Porter, 1985; 2001). The competitiveness of both tourism enterprises and destinations will increasingly therefore depend on the ability of those organisations to use ICTs strategically and tactically for improving their positioning.

E-TOURISM: TOURISM AND INFORMATION COMMUNICATION TECHNOLOGIES

The ICT revolution has already had profound implications for the tourism sector. Poon (1993) predicted that: 'a whole system of ICTs is being rapidly diffused throughout the tourism industry and no player will escape ICTs' impacts'. Buhalis (2003) suggests that e-tourism reflects the digitisation of all processes and value chains in the tourism, travel, hospitality and catering industries. At the tactical level, it includes e-commerce and applies ICTs for maximising the efficiency and effectiveness of the tourism organisation. At the strategic level, e-tourism revolutionises all business processes, the entire value chain as well as the strategic relationships of tourism organisations with all their stakeholders. E-tourism determines the competitiveness of the organisation by taking advantage of intranets for reorganising internal processes, extranets for developing transactions with trusted partners and the Internet for interacting with all its stakeholders. The e-tourism concept includes all business functions (e-commerce and e-marketing, e-finance and e-accounting, e-HRM, e-procurement, e-R&D, and e-production) as well as e-strategy, e-planning and e-management for all sectors of the tourism industry, including tourism, travel, transport, leisure, hospitality, principals, intermediaries and public sector organisations. Hence e-tourism bundles together three distinctive disciplines, namely, Business management, Information Systems and Management, and Tourism.

Information is the *lifeblood* of tourism and so technology is fundamental for the ability of the industry to operate. Unlike durable goods, intangible tourism services cannot be physically displayed or inspected at the point of sale before purchase. They are normally bought before the time of their use and away from the place of consumption. They therefore rely almost exclusively upon representations and descriptions by the travel trade and other intermediaries, for their ability to attract consumers. Timely and accurate information, relevant to consumers' needs is often the key to successful satisfaction of tourism demand. As few other activities require the generation, gathering, processing, application and communication of information for operations, ICTs are pivotal for tourism. Consequently the rapid development of both tourism supply and demand makes ICTs an imperative partner for the marketing, distribution, promotion and coordination of the tourism sector. ICTs have a dramatic impact on the travel industry because they force the sector as a whole to rethink the way in which it organises its business, values or norms of behaviour and the way in which it educates its workforce (Buhalis, 1998; Poon, 1993; Sheldon, 1997).

Hence, ICTs and the Internet enable tourism organisations to develop their processes and adapt their management to take advantage of the emerging digital tools and mechanisms to:

- increase their internal efficiency and manage their capacity and yields better. For example, an airline's reservations system allows the company to manage their inventory more efficiently and the managers to increase occupancy levels. Such systems also incorporate sophisticated yield management systems that enable organisations to adjust their pricing to demand fluctuations in order to maximise their profitability (Buhalis, 2004);

- interact effectively with consumers and personalise the product. For example, British Airways has launched the Customer Enabled BA (ceBA) strategy to enable passengers to undertake a number of processes, including booking, ticketing, check-in and seat and meal selection, from the convenience of their computer;

- revolutionise tourism intermediation and increase the points of sale. For example, Expedia, Travelocity, lastminute.com, Orbitz and Opodo have emerged as some of the most dominant global electronic travel agencies, offering a one-stop-shop for consumers;

- empower consumers to communicate with other consumers. For example, www.tripadvisor .com, www.virtualtourist.com or www.igoyougo.com support the exchange of destination information and tips, whilst www.untied.com or www.alitaliasacks.com enable dissatisfied customers to make their views available;

- provide location-based services by incorporating data, content and multimedia information on Google Maps and Google Earth;

- support efficient cooperation between partners in the value system. For example, Pegasus enables independent hotels to distribute their availability through their web sites and other partners online while an extranet allows hoteliers constantly to change availability and pricing;

- enhance the operational and geographic scope by offering strategic tools for global expansion.

E-tourism demand

The rapid growth of the volumes of travellers as well as the requirements for personalised, complex, specialised and quality products impose the need for ICT utilisation. Tourists have become increasingly demanding, requesting high quality products and value for their money. New/experienced/sophisticated/demanding travellers rely heavily on the Internet to seek information about destinations and experiences, such as price and availability, as well as to be able to communicate their needs and wishes to tourism suppliers rapidly.

The Internet enables travellers to access reliable and accurate information as well as to undertake reservations in a fraction of the time, cost and inconvenience required by conventional methods. Thus, they improve the service quality and contribute to a higher tourist satisfaction. The Internet provides access to transparent and easy-to-compare information on destinations, holiday packages, travel, lodging and leisure services, as well as about their real-time prices and availability. Increasingly consumers utilise commercial and non-commercial Internet sites for planning, searching, reserving, purchasing and amending their tourism products. They can also get immediate confirmation and speedy travel documents, enabling prospective travellers to book at the last minute. Experienced travellers are empowered by ICTs and use information and booking systems to improve their personal efficiency and competencies. A number of new organisations, such as Expedia, Travelocity and lastminute.com, emerged online in the late 1990s, empowering consumers to research their travel requirements. They gradually assumed a leading intermediation role on a global basis.

The Internet has enabled consumers to access this information rapidly and increasingly the development of domain specific search engines and meta-search engines such as Kelkoo and Kayak have introduced utter transparency in the marketplace (Wöber, 2006). In addition, consumer-generated content, through review portals such as Tripadvisor, multimedia sharing such as panoramio.com, and blogs also create accessible content that increase the level of information available on a global basis.

The use of ICTs is therefore driven by the development of complex demand requests, as well as by the rapid expansion and sophistication of new products, which tend to address niche market segments. There is evidence that e-tourism has already taken off in several countries. In Europe, the Internet is now more than twice as important as travel agents as an information source, although the travel trade is still very important in terms of travel distribution. According to IPK International's *European Travel Monitor* in 2006 and other sources, the information sources used by European outbound travellers were:

- Internet: 45%
- travel agency: 20%
- friends/relatives: 17%
- travel guide: 8%
- travel brochure: 7%
- newspaper: 3%
- tourist office: 2%
- television: 2%
- other: 5%

Marcussen (2006) demonstrates that the Internet European market has increased dramatically since 1998 and in 2006 accounted for 12.6% of the total market, as demonstrated in Table 20.3. The UK and Germany are the most mature travel markets and this is also demonstrated on the online markets where they represented 55% of the European expenditure in 2005, as demonstrated in Figure 20.1.

| Table 20.3 | Trends in overall online travel market size – Europe 1998–2007 |

Year	Market (€ billions)	Internet sales (€ billions)	Internet sales in % of market	Internet sales increase %
1998	200	0.2	0.1	NA
1999	212	0.8	0.4	257
2000	227	2.5	1.1	216
2001	223	5.0	2.3	99
2002	221	8.9	4.0	77
2003	215	13.9	6.5	56
2004	220	20.8	9.5	50
2005	235	30.2	12.9	45
2006	247	39.7	16.1	31
2007	254	49.4	19.4	24
2008	260	58.4	22.5	18
2009	266	69.9	25.2	15

Source: Marcussen, 2008

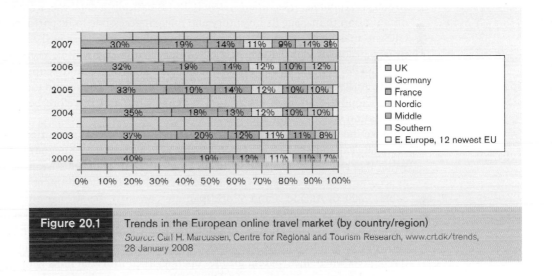

| Figure 20.1 | Trends in the European online travel market (by country/region) |

Source: Carl H. Marcussen, Centre for Regional and Tourism Research, www.crt.dk/trends, 28 January 2008

Looking forward, successful tourism organisations will increasingly need to identify consumer needs rapidly and to interact with prospective clients using comprehensive, personalised and up-to-date communication media for the design of products that satisfy tourism demand. Thus, destinations and principals need to utilise innovative communication methods in order to maintain and increase their competitiveness. They also increasingly need to engage in Web 2.0 activities and engage dynamically with all stakeholders that generate content for their regions and organisations.

ICTs in tourism supply: re-engineering the tourism industry distribution

On the tourism supply side, the impacts of ICTs are evident in the production, marketing, operational and distribution functions of both the private and public sectors. The development of computerised systems facilitated the production and management of tourism enterprises by enabling them to handle their inventory and perform their business functions effectively and productively. Understandably, larger organisations took advantage of the emergent technologies earlier than smaller ones, as they had the resources to do so, and ICTs facilitated their further expansion. The ability of tourism enterprises to communicate and cooperate efficiently with remote branches, destinations, principals and agencies, and to control their operational elements, enabled them to expand their activities while reducing costs and increasing their competitiveness. Both operational (schedule planning, pricing, inventory handling and reservations) and support (payroll, accounting, marketing) functions were improved considerably and enabled several tourism enterprises to establish their business worldwide. In the networking era, the development of intranets enable organisations to improve their management at all levels, by sharing media-rich data and processes internally. In addition, extranets empower the cooperation between partners, by enabling a certain degree of transparency and interactivity, and thus increasing efficiency and productivity without compromising on security and confidentiality. This will also improve the interactivity between tourism production and distribution partners, supporting a closer cooperation towards the provision of seamless products. The Internet has also enabled organisations to communicate directly with consumers, enforcing a certain degree of disintermediation in the marketplace.

ICTs and the Internet have pivotal implications for tourism distribution. Since the early 1970s computerised networks and electronic distribution have been leading dramatic structural changes within the tourism industry, and becoming central to the distribution mix and strategy. A *computer reservation system* (CRS) is basically a database, which enables a tourism organisation to manage its inventory and make it accessible to its partners. Principals utilise CRSs to manage their inventory and distribute their capacity as well as to manage the drastic expansion of global tourism. CRSs often charge competitive commission rates while enabling flexible pricing and capacity alterations, in order to adjust supply to demand fluctuations. Airlines pioneered this technology, although hotel chains and tour operators followed by developing centralised reservation systems. CRSs can therefore be characterised as the 'circulation system' of the tourism product.

Since the mid-1980s, airline CRSs developed into **global distribution systems** (GDSs) by gradually expanding their geographical coverage as well as by integrating both horizontally, with other airline systems, and vertically by incorporating the entire range of principals, such as accommodation, car rentals, train and ferry ticketing, entertainment and other provisions. Sabre, Galileo, Amadeus and Worldspan are currently the strongest GDSs in the marketplace. Suppliers therefore realised that the key success factor was in systems integration through GDSs and the creation of standards that enabled products to be displayed and purchased by consumers anywhere in the world. GDSs tend to have a stronger market share in the regions where their parent airlines operate, as commercial links with agencies have been exploited for the penetration of GDSs. GDSs concentrated primarily on business travel, as this was the most demanding and profitable part of the business. In the early 1990s GDSs emerged as the major driver of ICTs, as well as the backbone of the tourism industry, and the single most important facilitator of ICT globalisation (Sheldon, 1993). In essence, GDSs matured from their original development as airline CRSs to travel supermarkets. Since the late 1990s GDSs have emerged as businesses in their own right, specialising in travel distribution. Many airlines have chosen to sell their shares in GDSs to improve their financial position following the cash crisis after 9/11. Until their deregulation by the US Department of Transport in 2004, most GDSs represented the majority of principals, offering quite similar services. Their deregulation means that airlines and GDSs are free to negotiate individual deals, forcing both carriers and systems to change their relationships and their core business (Field and O'Toole, 2004). The four GDSs mentioned above have processed more than 1 billion air bookings each, and another 250 million for hotels, cruises and other non-air content, generating over US$6 billion in revenues. Sabre and Amadeus own the largest civilian data-processing centres in the USA and Europe respectively. The volume of global transactions through the GDSs has risen 4% year-on-year to 343 million. Worldwide, the GDSs reach some 230,000 points of sale (Alford, 2006).

However, the emergence of the Internet has also revolutionised GDSs. They are legacy systems that may have outlived their potential. The four major systems have enjoyed an oligopoly sustained by the high entry costs required to build the IT booking systems to link airlines, hotels and car rental operators with travel agents and consumers. The Internet challenged their position dramatically as both consumers and the travel trade had the opportunity to interact with airlines online without using GDS infrastructure. No-frills airlines totally bypassed GDSs and used the Internet to link with consumers and the trade. Scheduled airlines have also been trying to disintermediate GDSs especially for short-haul discounted tickets in order to reduce their distribution costs. In March 2007 British Airways' contracts with global distribution system providers expired without service interruption or BA immediately having to pursue a substantially new course, as some in the industry had feared. BA CEO Willie Walsh explained that the airline industry had struggled to generate levels of profitability that would be deemed acceptable. Other parts of the value chain, including the GDSs, have made operating margins in the double digits. BA has fares in their European operations that start at £29 and, after applying GDS fees (which can be as high as $7.50 or about £4) and taking out all taxes and charges, BA is left with a fare of about £2 (Bochmer and Cohen, 2007). The European eBusiness W@tch (2006) suggests that 'sales via internet platforms bear enormous cost savings for airlines compared to traditional channels via travel agencies, which usually run over GDS'. The report quotes Matthias van Leeuwen, Vice President Sales, EMEA, Lufthansa Systems Group as saying, 'Star Alliance member carriers currently spend an average of 12 US dollars per ticket in GDS fees. Global New Entrant (GNEs) such as G2 SwitchWorks, ITA and Farelogix have indicated to the group that they could offer the same product for 2–3 US dollars per ticket.' Therefore GDSs are forced to rethink their strategies and gradually relaunch themselves as technology platform providers for airlines and other members of the tourism industry.

The development of the Internet offered an unprecedented opportunity for distribution of multimedia information and interactivity between principals and consumers. The Web's interlinking structure enables the provision and packaging of similarly-themed information, products and services. Initially the information available on the Internet was chaotic and loosely structured, mainly due to the immaturity of ICTs and the lack of any type of standardisation. Several issues prevented the full potential of the Internet, namely:

- security of transmissions;
- credibility and accountability of information;
- intellectual property and copyrights;
- bandwidth and speed limitations;
- slow take-up of technology by potential customers;
- low speed of browsing especially on dial-up connections;
- user confusion and dissatisfaction;
- lack of adequately trained specialists;
- equal access for smaller and larger partners; and
- pricing structures for representation and distribution of information and reservations.

However, the Internet provided a globally distributed infrastructure for inexpensive delivery of multimedia information, promotion and distribution of tourism. It empowered the provision and marketing of tailor-made products to meet the needs of individual tourists and, hence, it bridged tourism demand and supply in a flexible and interactive way. By the year 2007, only 13 years after the general public used the first browser, there was a certain degree of maturity evident in the marketplace. This was particularly evident for organisations in well-developed economies, such as North America, Europe, Australia and North Asia. This was demonstrated by a number of indicators, namely:

- tourism was already one of the most successful areas of e-commerce and the sector that attracted the highest expenditure online;
- broadband was expanded in most developed countries and enabled users to browse at faster speeds and on more secure environments;
- most suppliers had established comprehensive and fully functional web sites;
- an estimate of almost 30% of all airline bookings were made on the Internet, often reaching more than 95% for no-frills carriers; almost 60% of the tickets issued were e-tickets (SITA, 2007);
- most hotel chains and international car rental firms were reporting a significant increase in their direct sales through their web sites;
- several key travel intermediaries emerged as global players with Expedia becoming the second largest travel agency in the world;
- a very large proportion of travellers search online before booking holidays; and
- most tourism destinations around the world had some sort of web site providing information for their region while advanced destinations had comprehensive systems supporting itinerary building and reservations. (See, for example, www.australia.com, www.amsterdam.nl or www.visiteurope.com).

Distribution is one of the few elements of the marketing mix that can still enable enterprises to improve their competitiveness and performance. ICTs enable the achievement of competitive advantage through product differentiation and/or cost advantage, by increasing both the unique characteristics of products, as well as efficiency throughout the production and distribution processes. ICTs increasingly transform distribution to an electronic marketplace, where access to information and ubiquity is achieved, while interactivity between principals and consumers provides major opportunities.

It is increasingly evident that many principals develop their business-to-consumer (B2C) offering. They invest heavily in customer acquisition through search engines optimisation and pay per click on portals such as Google and Yahoo. They also invest in sophisticated customer relationship management to ensure partnerships with their clientele and customer retention. A certain degree of disintermediation of the channel is inevitable, offering both opportunities and threats for all tourism stakeholders. In addition, we can also observe a trend towards the reintermediation of the tourism industry, as a plethora of online players emerge to bridge the gap between suppliers and customers, including hotel aggregators, electronic travel agencies and destination management organisations. In addition, meta search engines such as Kelkoo, Kayak and Sidestep enable consumers to search through a wide range of web sites of both suppliers and distributors simultaneously. Dynamic packaging also enables consumers to put together products and services that suit their individual tastes and to save money on the total price. The dramatic development of the Internet has instigated the re-engineering of the entire process of producing and delivering tourism products. It has also enabled the design of specialised products and promotions in order to maximise the value added provided to individual consumers.

A conceptual synthesis of ICTs in tourism

A conceptual synthesis of the emergent ICTs in tourism yields a multidimensional communication and operational framework, which will determine the future competitiveness of principals and destinations. This framework shows the paradigm shift and the business process re-engineering experienced, which has already started to reshape the tourism industry

MINI CASE STUDY 20.1

lastminute.com: from reservation system to lifestyle portal

In October 1998 Brent Hoberman and Martha Lane Fox launched lastminute.com in the UK. Using the Internet they match suppliers' distressed inventory with consumer last-minute demand. lastminute.com works with a range of suppliers in the travel, entertainment and gift industries and is dedicated to bringing its customers attractive products and services.

TOWARDS A LIFESTYLE PORTAL

Their mission statement suggests: 'lastminute.com encourages spontaneous, romantic and sometimes adventurous behaviour by offering people the chance to live their dreams at unbeatable prices!' This clearly defines their business as a lifestyle portal offering a wide range of products and services to people that purchase on impulse. Although tourism products dominate the site, several additional products are available including meals delivered at home, gifts including electronics and underwear, and insurance. The company has developed a distinctive brand, which communicates spontaneity and a sense of adventure, attracting a loyal community of registered subscribers that use the lastminute.com's web site and have submitted their email addresses and other data to receive weekly emails.

Between 2000 and 2004, lastminute.com purchased 14 businesses to gain scale and presence throughout Europe and also to expand its value chain backwards (by enhancing inventory and its value) and forwards (by accessing more consumers in Europe). lastminute.com now owns and operates online brands including holidayautos.com, travelprice.com, degriftour.com, travelselect.com, travel4less.co.uk, eXhilaration.co.uk, medhotels.com, first-option.co.uk, gemstonetravel.com, onlinetravel.com and lastminute.de.

GROWING TO A PAN-EUROPEAN BUSINESS

The growth of lastminute.com has been meteoric. lastminute.com had just three recorded customers in October 1998. In October 1999, lastminute.com was voted 'Best UK Internet start-up' by management consultants Bain & Company and *Management Today* magazine. Floated in March 2000, when company employees had grown to 165 and the business had moved to offices in Oxford Circus, lastminute.com became Europe's leading independent travel and leisure business which sells package holidays on behalf of 250 third party tour operators. It was the first company that offered customers the opportunity to dynamically package a unique holiday experience combining any flight with any hotel room and rental car. lastminute.com had a unique lifestyle proposition offering tickets to shows, gigs, festivals and theme parks, as well as leisure experiences, DVDs, restaurants and gifts. It operated in the core European markets of the UK, Germany, Italy and Spain.

lastminute.com has satellite offices in Ireland, Sweden, Australia and the Netherlands and joint ventures in Japan and UAE. It employed 2,000 people globally, with its head office in London housing 350 of them. In July 2004 a reservation was made on the Med Hotels web site every 2 minutes. lastminute.com is one of the top two most visited travel agency web sites in the UK, with an average of 6 million unique site visitors monthly, and receives most site hits on a Sunday, with almost 18% of overall visitors logging on on that day.

It has global deals with 100 airline partners and access to flight seats on around 600 carriers worldwide. Some 750,000 passengers flew in the six months between January and June 2005, enough to fill more than 2,500 Boeing 777 aircraft. It featured 80,000 hotels worldwide, with 25,000 merchant properties and sold close to 8 million hotel room nights each year. lastminute.com sold 150,000 tickets to the UK's leading theme parks in 2005.

Overall, it is evident that in order to consolidate its position in Europe lastminute.com grew rapidly through a number of acquisitions, making it one of the leading online players with a considerably diverse portfolio. The group as it stood in 2005 had sufficient inventory and excellent relationships with suppliers, while it had access to more than 10 million customers around Europe that regularly used the service for a variety of

→

leisure and business products. A number of trends in travel, technology and lifestyle are best supplied by the lastminute.com offering, demonstrating that the company has a promising future.

Given its market in Europe, lastminute.com became an attractive candidate for being purchased itself by a global company. In July 2005, the biggest acquisition in the dot.com industry was completed – Travelocity acquired lastminute.com PLC in order to expand and grow in the European market. The acquisition has been made by Travelocity Europe Ltd, an indirect subsidiary of Sabre Holdings. In a move aimed at creating Europe's largest online travel service company, Travelocity.com offered approximately £577 million (US$1.1 billion) paying 165p a share. The acquisition price for the shares in lastminute.com and the redemption price payable in respect of lastminute.com's bonds equates to an equity value of approximately £577 million and an enterprise value of approximately £584 million, including gross debt as at 20 July 2005 of approximately £79 million and estimated cash at bank in hand at 14 July 2005 of approximately £72 million. Hoberman, who remained as chief executive, received just over £26 million for his 15.8 million shares, while Lane Fox's stake of 8.2 million shares was worth around £13.5 million.

Source: Based on **http://www.lastminute.com/site/help/about_us/about-us.html**, and interviews conducted by the author

DISCUSSION QUESTIONS

1. What is the unique selling point of lastminute.com in comparison with other online intermediaries?
2. What do you think lastminute.com should do in order to achieve strategic competitive advantage?
3. What factors of the external environment can influence the development of lastminute.com?

radically. Table 20.4 illustrates several examples of the intra-and inter-organisational functions facilitated by ICTs. It also demonstrates how technologies advocate the multi-integration of the industry. Not only does this framework demonstrate the dependence of both demand and supply on ICTs, but it also illustrates that networking and interactivity will increasingly dominate the tourism production and consumption. This implies clearly that players who fail to participate in the electronic marketplace will be excluded from the production and consumption functions of the industry and jeopardise their future prosperity.

E-TOURISM AND THE TOURISM INDUSTRY SECTORS

The evolution of the Internet and ICTs has propelled a 'paradigm shift' where all practices and processes had to be changed dramatically, affecting the the industry structure. E-tourism provides opportunities for business expansion in all geographical, marketing and operational senses. Several major factors make ICTs an integral part of the strategy for all tourism organisations, namely:

- economic necessity, as fierce global competition requires maximum efficiency;
- rapid advancements in technology which provide new marketing opportunities;
- low barriers to entry allowing many new entrants to the market;
- improvements in ICT price/performance ratios which yield better productivity for capital employed in ICTs; and finally
- rising consumer expectations, as they become used to advanced products and expect better quality of presentation and service.

As a result of Internet developments a number of new players have come into the tourism marketplace. Perhaps the most significant change was the proliferation of no-frills airlines

Table 20.4	A multidimensional framework for tourism industry processes facilitated by ICTs

Intra-organisational communications and functions

- Within a tourism organisation
  - Management and marketing
    strategic planning
    competition analysis
    financial planning and control
    marketing research
    marketing strategy and implementation
    pricing decision and tactics
    middle-term planning and feedback
    management statistics/reports
    operational control
    management functions
  - Communication between departments
    networking and information exchange
    coordination of staff
    operational planning
    accounting/billing
    payroll
    supplies management
- Communication and function with remote branches
  coordination of operations
  availability/prices/information
  orders from headquarters/administration
  share of common resource databases for customer
  and operational information

Inter-organisational communications and functions

- Tourist product suppliers and intermediaries
  - Pre-travel arrangements
    direct marketing
    general information
    availability/prices enquiries
    negotiations and bargaining
    contracting
    reservations and confirmations
    ancillary services
  - Travel related documentation
    lists of groups/visitors
    receipts/documents
    vouchers and tickets production
  - Post-travel arrangements
    payments and commissions
    feedback and suggestions
    customer satisfaction survey
    complaint handling
    direct marketing

Consumer communication with tourism industry

- Travel advice/general information
- Request availability/prices/information
- Reservation & confirmation
- Amendments for a reservation
- Deposits and full settlements
- Electronic ticketing
- Special interest requests/inquiries
- Feedback/complaints
- Discussions groups/fun clubs

Tourism enterprise communication with non-tourism enterprises

- Other suppliers and ancillary services, vaccinations, travel formalities and visas
- Insurance companies and services
- Weather forecasting
- Banking/financial services/credit cards
- Remote Internet provision for travellers
- Other business services

that use the Internet as a main distribution mechanism for direct sales. This development educated consumers that they can only find cheap fares if they go direct to the carrier online, threatening both traditional/flag carriers as well as their entire distribution system (GDSs and travel agencies). Equally the development of major e-travel agencies such as Expedia, Travelocity, lastminute.com, Orbitz and Opodo has created powerful 'travel supermarkets' for consumers. They provide integrated travel solutions and a whole range of value-added services, such as destination guides, weather reports and insurance. By adopting dynamic packaging, i.e. the ability to package customised trips based on bundling individual components at a discounted total price, they effectively threaten the role of tour operators and other aggregators.

What follows is an analysis of ICT and the various sectors of the tourism industry. It demonstrates the key developments and the influence of ICTs and the Internet for their internal organisation, their relationships with partners and the interaction with consumers and stakeholders.

E-airlines

Airlines realised quite early the need for efficient, quick, inexpensive and accurate handling of their inventory and internal organisation, due to the complexity of their operations. Originally, reservations were made on manual display boards, where passengers were listed. Travel agencies had to locate the best routes and fares in manuals and then check availability and make a reservation by telephone, before issuing a ticket manually. In 1962, American Airlines introduced the Sabre CRS as an alternative in order to expand its Boeing 707 fleet by 50%. The growth of air traffic and air transportation deregulation stimulated the expansion of CRSs to gigantic computerised networks. As prices, schedules and routes were liberated, airlines could change them indefinitely, while new airlines entered the market. CRSs enabled airlines to compete by adapting their schedule and fares to demand. To increase competitiveness, airlines developed the 'hub-and-spoke' systems, while their pricing became very complex and flexible. Fare wars multiplied the fare structures and increased the computing and communication needs, while most major CRSs installed terminals in agencies to facilitate distribution. In addition, vendor airlines biased their CRS screens in order to give higher display priority to their flights rather than to their competitors. The remote printing of travel documents, such as tickets and boarding passes, itineraries and invoices, as well as the sale settlements between airlines and travel agencies, and the partnership marketing through frequent flyer programmes were invaluable benefits supported by the emerging ICTs. CRSs were developed to global distribution systems (GDSs) and re-engineered the entire marketing and distribution processes of airlines. They essentially became strategic business units (SBUs) in their own right due to their ability to generate income and to boost airlines' sales at the expense of their competitors. Many airlines sold their interests in GDSs' enabling them to operate as independent distribution companies.

Distribution is a crucial element of airlines' strategy and competitiveness, as it determines the cost and the ability to access consumers. The cost of distribution is increasing considerably and airlines find it difficult to control. Nowadays ICTs and internal CRSs are used heavily to support the Internet distribution of airline seats. These systems are at the heart of airline operational and strategic agendas (Buhalis, 2004). This is particularly the case for smaller and regional carriers as well as no-frills airlines which cannot afford the fees of GDSs and aim to sell their seats at competitive prices. This has forced even traditional/full-service/flag airlines, such as British Airways and Aer Lingus, to recognise the need for re-engineering the distribution processes, costs and pricing structures. Hence, they use the Internet for:

- enhancing interactivity and building relationships with consumers and partners;
- online reservations;
- electronic ticketing;
- yield management;
- electronic auctions for last minute available seats;
- disintermediation and redesign of agency commission schemes; and
- maximising the productivity of the new electronic distribution media (Buhalis, 2004).

The Airline IT Trends Survey 2007 – from Airline Business and SITA demonstrates that the vast majority of airlines have a 3-year IT strategy that aims to reduce costs and increase efficiency. Between 1999 and 2006 airlines spent on average between 2% and 3% of their revenue on ICT investment. As demonstrated in Table 20.5 on average 21.5% of airline bookings take place on an airline's own web site, and 29.7% on all online sales (SITA, 2007). Airlines are investing heavily in direct sales, which coupled with 'customer relations management' and 'revenue management systems', will enable them to better control their distribution and strategic marketing.

Table 20.5	Online sales and e-tickets for airlines

	Proportion of all tickets sold			
Percentage of total seat sales	Own airline website %	All online sales %	Call centres %	E-tickets issued %
None	1	6	3	6
2% or less	2	3	4	1
2%–10%	17	10	44	3
11%–20%	27	23	1	2
21%–30%	29	6	1	1
31%–40%	7	17	3	7
41%–50%	1	9	3	7
51% plus	20	30	3	80
Average 2007	26.6	35.2	13.4	71.5
Unweighted 2007	19.3	24.4	18.7	50.4
Average 2006	24.4	32.4	18.7	50.4
Average 2005	16.4	20.1	20.3	26.6
Average 2004	11.0	14.5	17.1	19.1
Average 2003	9.7	15.8	–	14.7

Source: Airline IT Trends Survey, SITA & Airline Business, 2007

E-hospitality

Hotels use ICTs in order to improve their operations, manage their inventory and maximise their profitability. Their systems facilitate both in-house management and distribution through electronic media. Property management systems (PMSs) coordinate front office, sales, planning and operational functions by administrating reservations and managing the hotel inventory. Moreover, PMSs integrate the 'back' and 'front' of the house management and improve general administration functions such as accounting and finance; marketing research and planning; forecasting and yield management; payroll and personnel; and pur chasing. Understandably, hotel chains gain more benefits from PMSs, as they can introduce a unified system for planning, budgeting, controlling and coordinating their properties centrally. Hotels also utilise ICTs and the Internet extensively for their distribution and marketing functions. Global presence is essential in order to enable both individual customers and the travel trade to access accurate information on availability and to provide easy, efficient, inexpensive and reliable ways of making and confirming reservations. Although central reservation offices (CROs) introduced central reservations in the 1970s, it was not until the expansion of airline CRSs and the recent ICT developments that hotels were forced to develop hotel CRSs in order to expand their distribution, improve efficiency, facilitate control, empower yield management, reduce labour costs and enable rapid response time to both customers and management requests. Following the development of hotel CRSs by most chains, the issue of interconnectivity with other CRSs and the Internet emerged. As a result, 'switch companies', such as Thisco and Wizcom, emerged to provide an interface between the various systems and enable a certain degree of transparency. This reduces both set-up and reservation costs, while facilitating reservations through several distribution channels (Emmer *et al.*, 1993; O'Connor, 2000).

One of the most promising developments in hospitality is application service providers (ASPs). ASPs will be increasingly more involved in hosting a number of business applications for hospitality organisations. Hotels will 'rent' the same software for a fee and will use it across the Internet. For example, some hotel firms may 'rent' their PMS software application from supplier Micros/Fidelio. ASPs are ideal for hotels, especially for smaller- to mid-sized ones that want to leverage the best vertical and enterprise support applications on the market without having to deal with the technology or pay for more functionality than needed. As they do not have extensive ICT departments and expertise, they can easily access up-to-date applications and benefit from the collective knowledge accumulated by ASP providers without having to invest extensively in technology or expertise building (Paraskevas and Buhalis, 2002).

The development of the Internet has provided more benefits as it reduces the capital and operational costs required for the representation and promotion of hotels. For example, the cost per individual booking can be reduced from US$10–15 for voice-based reservations, to US$7.50–3.50 for reservations through GDSs, to US$0.25 through the Web. Savings can also be achieved in printing, storing, administrating and posting promotional material.

Murphy *et al.* (2006) use diffusion of innovations and configurational theories to investigate how web-site features and email responses reflect evolving Internet adoption. The Internet adoption evolves from static to dynamic use, as organisations add web-site features and provide quality responses to customer emails. Chan and Law (2006) suggest that hotel web sites are a basic requirement to an increasing number of communication and business strategies. The usability of a web site, effectiveness of its interface, as well as the amount of information carried, ease of navigation and user-friendliness of its functions, are central to the success of these strategies and an automatic web-site evaluation system (AWES) can provide objective and quantitative guidance to web-site design.

However, many small and medium-sized, independent, seasonal and family hotels find it extremely difficult to utilise ICTs due to:

- lack of capital for purchasing hardware and software;
- lack of standardisation and professionalism;
- insufficient marketing and technology training and understanding;
- small size which multiplies the administration required by CRSs to deal with each property; and finally
- the unwillingness of proprietors to lose control over their property.

These properties are increasingly placed at a major disadvantage, as they cannot be represented in the electronic marketplace and so jeopardise their future existence. However, they cannot afford to ignore the rapid developments of ICTs and, therefore, should take advantage of the emergent ICT opportunities and decreasing costs to enhance their competitiveness. It is increasingly evident, however, that even the smallest accommodation establishments will have to take advantage of the Internet and promote themselves in the electronic marketplace. There are several solutions that can offer a cost-effective online presence. Small properties will find it difficult to continue trading unless they have an online presence as they will be invisible to consumers searching online. The establishment of destination-based collaboration ventures would perhaps enable small firms to pool resources in order to share development and operation costs. Distributing their products through the Internet would enable them to access their target markets at an affordable cost and gain benefits (Buhalis, 2003). Table 20.6 demonstrates the growth of online bookings and the online strategy for Hilton Hotels.

As it is estimated that one-third of bookings in hospitality in the USA will be generated from the Internet and another third will be directly influenced by online research, but booked offline, hoteliers gradually explore online marketing to increase their market awareness and to attract more guests and higher revenues. HeBS (2007) demonstrate that they use techniques like web-site design, search engine optimisation, paid search marketing and email blasts. In their benchmark survey of hospitality executives worldwide, including general managers, revenue managers, sales and marketing managers and other industry professionals, they found that:

Table 20.6	Hilton Hotels online bookings

Hilton Hotels Corporation expects more than $2.5 billion in revenues generated from bookings on its proprietary web sites for the full year 2006 compared to $709 million five years ago, in 2002. Bookings through its web sites have increased at a steady 30% year over year since 2002, and accelerated to a 39% increase in the third quarter of 2006 versus the third quarter of 2005. This represents a 60% increase in revenues and a 43% increase in room nights for third quarter 2006 versus prior year, according to the company. It further shared that web site bookings currently represent 17.2% of the company's overall distribution of bookings, compared with 9.1% in 2002, making it the most dominant central delivery channel for the company. In contrast, contribution of third-party online agencies has remained flat at 3% of reservations, and now represents just 15% of the company's Internet business.

The following online booking features have been introduced or enhanced within the past 18 months:

- e-Events is an industry first small group product that enables customers to go online and book anywhere from 5 to 25 guest rooms at any Hilton Family hotel.
- Calendaring is another first in the hotel industry, which enables customers with flexible travel dates to view at a glance a single hotel's best available rates and discounted advance purchase rates for their preferred length of stay across a 31-day span, and mix and match options that work best for their schedule.
- Compare/Travel Cart features allow customers the option to compare hotels side by side, without the hassle of jumping from one page to the other, and the ability to store hotels in a 'shopping cart' for future access.
- eCheck-in allows Gold and Diamond Hilton HHonors members the convenience of checking in on the Web from 2 to 36 hours prior to their arrival regardless of method of reservation.
- Travel Agent Portal where any travel agent planning a trip can easily find all the hotel information they need including images/virtual tours, access the full array of available Hilton Family products, as well as other convenient resources and agent services.
- Weddings Portal offers an easy and uniquely tailored experience for wedding planners and their guests, available on each of the Hilton Family of Hotels web sites.

Source: Adapted from Hilton Hotels Corporation News Release, 31 October 2006: http://www.eyefortravel.com/print.asp?news=53279

- in 2007, a remarkable 68% of hoteliers will be shifting their budgets from offline to online marketing activities, representing a huge shift from traditional methods;
- US properties rely more on direct to consumer bookings via their stand-alone web sites compared to intermediary sites as a percentage of their overall Internet business (20.7% and 16.6%, respectively) than do their international counterparts (15.3% and 17%, respectively) who are still receiving, on average, more of their Internet bookings from intermediaries;
- the top three Internet marketing formats hoteliers believe produce the highest Return on Investment (ROI) are web-site optimisation, Search Optimization + Organic Search, and web-site redesign;
- interestingly enough, more hoteliers believe new media formats such as consumer-generated media and blogs will generate better ROIs than traditional banner advertising;
- an average of 16.2% of Internet transactions occur through intermediary web sites;
- US hotels rely more heavily on keyword search marketing (PPC) and search engine optimisation (SEO) than their international counterparts who favour web-site redesign and optimisation and strategic linking;
- franchised hotels seem to rely more heavily on the chain web sites.

HeBS (2007) concludes that hoteliers have gradually matured and now understand that long-term, strategic objectives and formats such as web-site redesigns and optimisations, email marketing and strategic linking produce higher ROI than 'quick fix' solutions, such as search engine optimisation and pay-per-click strategies.

Finally, two main strategy issues emerged regarding online distribution for hospitality: price parity and brand integrity. Post 9/11, many hotels around the globe were having problems filling their rooms. This, in combination with the development of online intermediaries, such as Hotels.com and Expedia, that were using the merchant model of contracting at the time meant that many hotels effectively were unable to control their price on the various online outlets. This not only caused revenue loss, as prospective customers were shopping around, but also damaged their brands. Over a period of time major branded properties realised that control over pricing should be central to the marketing proposition and hence undertook a number of measures to address that. Key findings of O'Connor's (2002) study include that brands use multiple simultaneous routes to the marketplace, and that the rates offered over alternative routes have equalised.

E-tour operators

Leisure travellers often purchase 'packages', consisting of charter flights and accommodation, arranged by tour operators. Tour operators tend to pre-book these products and distribute them through brochures displayed in travel agencies. Hence, until recently in northern European countries, where tour operators dominate the leisure market, airline and hotel CRSs were rarely utilised for leisure travel. In the early 1980s, tour operators realised the benefits of ICTs in organising, promoting, distributing and coordinating their packages. The Thomson Open-line Programme (TOP) was the first real-time computer-based central reservation office in 1976. It introduced direct communication with travel agencies in 1982, and announced that reservations for Thomson Holidays would only be accepted through TOP in 1986. This move was the critical point for altering the communication processes between tour operators and travel agencies. Gradually, all major tour operators developed or acquired databases and established electronic links with travel agencies, aiming to reduce their information handling costs and increase the speed of information transfer and retrieval. This improved their productivity and capacity management while enhancing their services to agencies and consumers. Tour operators also utilised their CRSs for market intelligence, in order to adjust their supply to demand fluctuations, as well as to monitor the booking progress and productivity of travel agencies (Karcher, 1996).

Tour operators have been reluctant to focus on ICTs through their strategic planning. Few realise the major transformation of the marketplace, while the majority regard ICT exclusively as a facilitator of their current operations, and as a tool to reduce their costs. However, several tour operators in Germany, Scandinavia and the UK are moving towards electronic brochures and will begin to distribute their products electronically. Successful operators report up to 25% of their packages are booked directly by consumers online. This enables them to concentrate on niche markets by:

- offering customised packages;
- updating their brochures regularly;
- saving the 10–20% commission and reducing the costs of incentives, bonus and educational trips for travel agencies; and
- saving the cost of developing, printing, storing and distributing conventional brochures – estimated to be approximately £20 per booking.

Strategically Internet developments and dynamic packaging threatens the dominance of tour operators. Although a partial disintermediation seems inevitable, there will always be sufficient market share for tour operators who can add value to the tourism product and deliver innovative, personalised and competitive holiday packages. As ICTs will determine the future competitiveness of the industry, the distribution channel leadership and power of tour operators may be challenged, should other channel members or newcomers utilise ICTs effectively to package and distribute either unique or cheaper tourism products. However, many key players including TUI have started dis-integrating their packages and selling individual components directly to the consumers. In this sense they will be able to reintermediate, by offering their vast networks of suppliers through their channels. Innovative

MINI CASE STUDY 20.2
Hotel property management systems: Fidelio

Fidelio was founded in 1987 and it emerged as one of the leading and most innovative international property management systems provider for the hospitality industries. Their software is adaptable to changing business requirements and it integrates both the ongoing technological developments and the organisational change experienced. Fidelio allows hotels and chains of any size and type, restaurants, cruise ships and catering and conference operations to computerise their operations and to integrate major industry software products through analysing individual requirements and appreciating their uniqueness. Different hotel chains and managers require special information to accommodate the dissimilar legal requirements, accounting systems, tax reporting and guest statistics of each country they operate in. Fidelio aims to meet these challenges and satisfies every type of information requested.

Fidelio incorporates four sets of functions:

- **The front office function** which enables the management of reservations; guest histories and registration data; room itinerary management; pricing and yield management; billing per guest; group/allotment management; night auditing; cashiers function; maintenance; concierge programme; as well as production of operational and management reports.

- **The food and beverage management system** enables revenue and cost budget management; stock control; return on investment analysis for each menu; kitchen control systems; and bar management and control. A point of sales system integrates all revenue points with the central database, facilitating the accounting and cashiering functions.

- **The sales and marketing programme** supports the entire sales and marketing functions of the hotel, such as group event management and reservation; account management; activity management; contract generation; and follow-up activities.

- In addition, Fidelio provides several **support functions** such as word processing; mail manager; calendars; and daily schedules. The system interfaces with most telephone and call accounting; point of sales; door looking; mini bar; energy management; voice mail; video; and paging systems enabling a multi integrated management of all hotel processes. These functions are delivered through the development of a local area network, which coordinates all processes and enables hotel departments to share a data-rich and constantly updated data base.

Source: www.fidelio.com

DISCUSSION QUESTIONS

1. Explain the relationship between a property management system and the Internet distribution of a hotel chain.

2. How can Fidelio assist the strategic management of a hotel?

3. Discuss the suitability of Fidelio for a 20-room bed and breakfast operation and, if found unsuitable, design a system for their needs.

tour operators use the Internet extensively to promote their products and to attract direct customers. They also use the Internet to de-compose their packages and sell individual products. Thomson.co.uk, for example, has developed a comprehensive online strategy to provide media-rich information on its web site. The company supports podcasting, videocasting and also has integrated Google Earth geographical information data on its web site. It also distributes branded content on a wide range of Internet sites such as Youtube.com to attract consumers to its web site and to encourage them to book. In January 2007 a total of

5.5 million people visited the Thomson.co.uk web site demonstrating that the customer acquisition strategy used is effective. It is evident therefore that tour operators who use technology innovatively will be able to provide value to their clientele and safeguard their position in the marketplace.

E-travel agencies

ICTs are irreplaceable tools for travel agencies as they provide information and reservation facilities and support the intermediation between consumers and principals. Travel agencies operate various reservation systems, which mainly enable them to check availability and make reservations for tourism products. Until recently GDSs have been critical for business travel agencies to access information and make reservations on scheduled airlines, hotel chains, car rentals and a variety of ancillary services. GDSs help construct complicated itineraries, while they provide up-to-date schedules, prices and availability information, as well as an effective reservation method. In addition, they offer internal management modules integrating the back office (accounting, commission monitor, personnel) and front office (customers' history, itinerary construction, ticketing and communication with suppliers). Multiple travel agencies in particular experience more benefits by achieving better coordination and control between their remote branches and headquarters. Transactions can provide invaluable data for financial and operational control as well as for marketing research, which can analyse the market fluctuations and improve tactical decisions.

The vast majority of leisure travel agencies used 'videotext networks' to access tour operators and the reservation systems of other suppliers such as ferry operators, railways and insurance companies. On the plus side, videotext systems are relatively inexpensive to purchase and operate, require little training and expertise and are fairly reliable. However, on the minus side, they are slow: data has to be retyped for each individual database searched; they fail to integrate with the back office; cannot interface with multimedia applications; and are unable to take advantage of the emergent ICTs. Effectively, the type of agency and its clientele determine the type of ICTs utilised. Typically, business travel agencies are more GDS dependent, while leisure agencies and holiday shops are more likely to use videotext systems (Inkpen, 1998).

The Internet has revolutionised the travel agency industry as for the first time agencies had the ability to reach travel inventory directly without having to invest in time and costs for acquiring GDSs. They are able to search and book suppliers such as airlines and hotels online, increasing their bookable inventory. They also have the tools to sell their own services and to promote their organisations. However, until recently travel agencies have been reluctant to take full advantage of the ICTs, mainly due to:

- a limited strategic scope;
- deficient ICT expertise and understanding;
- low profit margins which prevents investments; and
- focus on human interaction with consumers.

This has resulted in a low level of integration of ICTs and capitalisation on the Internet's potential. Many agencies still do not have Internet access and are unable to access online information or suppliers. As a result many agencies lack access to the variety of information and reservation facilities readily available to consumers and therefore their credibility in the marketplace is severely reduced. This may jeopardise their ability to maintain their competitiveness and, consequently, they may be threatened by disintermediation. Several forces intensify this threat:

- consumers increasingly search information and make reservations online;
- principals aim to control distribution costs by communicating directly with consumers and by developing customer relationship management;

- commission cuts; and
- travel agencies have limited expertise as they employ inadequately trained personnel.

Gradually it is becoming evident that travel agencies around the world not only will have to utilise the Internet to access travel suppliers and information online but will also have to rely on the media to communicate with their clientele, to put the offerings forward to the marketplace and to attract business. Traditional travel agencies can use the Internet to provide extra value to their clientele by integrating additional products and services to their core products. In addition, they may use the Internet to specialise in particular niche markets and to offer specialised services to those markets.

In contrast, new players (such as Expedia, Travelocity, Orbitz, lastminute.com and Opodo) have already achieved a high penetration of the marketplace and grown spectacularly. Through a number of mergers and acquisitions there are effectively five major groups that have emerged in the marketplace as demonstrated in Table 20.7: Priceline that includes priceline.com, travelweb.com, active hotels and booking.com; the Cendant group that controls Orbitz, Ratestogo, HotelClub, eBookers and OctopusTravel.com while also owning Galileo; the Expedia group that includes Expedia.com, hotels.com, anyway.com, egencia, travelnow.com and tripadvisor; the Sabre group that includes Sabre, Travelocity, lastminute.com, Zuji and First Option; and finally, Amadeus that includes vacation.com and Opodo. It is estimated that these five groups are responsible for more than 75% of the total online revenue globally and it is becoming evident that the online travel agency market is increasingly centralised and concentrated.

Interestingly, even in areas with low Internet penetration, online travel agencies have taken off. The Chinese market is one of those markets that is growing rapidly (Li and Buhalis, 2006). For example, in early 2007 the Chinese online travel service provider Ctrip.com posted impressive results, demonstrating both the potential and the growth of the Chinese e-tourism market. Ctrip.com announced that for the full year ended 31 December 2006, total

Table 20.7	The five global brands of e-travel
Group	**Brand**
Priceline	Priceline.com
	Travelweb
	Active Hotels
	Booking.com
Cendant	Orbitz
	RatesToGo
	HotelClub.com
	OctopusTravel
Expedia	Expedia
	Hotels.com
	Tripadvisor
	Anyway.com
Sabre	Sabre
	Travelocity
	lastminute.com
Amadeus	Vacation.com
	Opodo
	Promovacances

Source: eTravel.org Limited

revenues were RMB834 million, representing a 49% increase from 2005. Hotel reservation revenues were RMB476 million, a 31% increase from 2005. The hotel reservation revenues accounted for 57% of the total revenues in 2006, compared to 65% in 2005. The total number of hotel room nights booked was approximately 6.84 million in 2006, compared to approximately 5.45 million booked in 2005. Air ticket booking revenues were RMB303 million, an 83% increase from 2005. The air ticket booking revenues accounted for 36% of the total revenues in 2006, compared to 30% in 2005. The total number of air tickets sold was approximately 6.39 million in 2006, compared to approximately 3.67 million in 2005. Packaged tour revenues were RMB42 million, an 83% increase from 2005. The packaged tour revenues accounted for 5% of the total revenues in 2006. For the full year ended December 31, 2006, net revenues were RMB780 million, a 49% increase from 2005, while gross margin was 80%, compared to 83% in 2005. For the full year 2007, Ctrip.com expects to continue the year-on-year net revenue growth at a rate of approximately 30%. Before share-based compensation charges, the company expects operating margin to be approximately 35%. This demonstrates clearly not only the size of the Chinese market and the huge potential but also the fact that even markets with low Internet penetration experience a dramatic growth of e-tourism (Ctrips.com, 2007).

As location becomes less significant electronic travel agents will dominate global travel retailing. Already in the USA more than 80% of online travel retailing is concentrated in the top five players. Therefore, the future of travel agencies will depend on their ability to utilise ICTs in order to increase the added value to the final tourism product and to serve their customer. Agencies that simply act as booking offices for tourism products will probably face severe financial difficulties in the future. In contrast, knowledgeable and innovative agencies, which utilise the entire range of technologies in order to provide suitable integrated tourism solutions, will add value to the tourist experience and increase their competitiveness. Traditional travel agencies will have to compete on both price and service with both suppliers and online travel agencies and will only be able to survive if they offer superior service.

E-destinations

Destinations are amalgams of tourism products, facilities and services which compose the total tourism expertise under one brand name. Traditionally the planning, management and coordination functions of destinations have been undertaken by either the public sector (at national, regional or local level) or by partnerships between stakeholders of the local tourism industry. They usually:

- provide information and undertake some marketing activities through mass media advertising;
- provide advisory service for consumers and the travel trade;
- design and distribute brochures, leaflets and guides; and
- coordinate local initiatives.

Although ICTs were never regarded as a critical instrument for the development and management of destinations, increasingly destination management organisations (DMOs) use ICTs in order to facilitate the tourist experience before, during and after the visit, as well as for coordinating all partners involved in the production and delivery of tourism. Thus, not only do DMOs attempt to provide information and accept reservations for local enterprises as well as coordinate their facilities, but they also utilise ICTs to promote their tourism policy, coordinate their operational functions, increase the expenditure of tourists, and boost the multiplier effects in the local economy.

Despite the fact that studies on destination-orientated CRSs have been traced back to as early as 1968, it was not until the early 1990s that the concept of destination management systems (DMSs) emerged. Even at this stage, however, most DMSs are mere facilitators of the conventional activities of tourism boards, such as information dissemination or local bookings. Several planned DMSs have failed in their development phase, mainly due to:

- inadequate financial support;
- lack of long-term vision of the developers;
- lack of understanding of industry mechanisms and the interest groups;
- expensive and inappropriate technological solutions; and
- IT leading rather following tourism marketing.

This has discouraged DMO managers from investing further in the development of suitable systems (Buhalis, 1997). However, by 2004 most destinations around the world had recognised the value of the DMS concept and had some type of system offering information about their region. In the last few years DMOs have realised that it is critical for their competitiveness to develop their online presence. To the degree that tourists increasingly research their holidays online, DMOs realise the need to have an inspirational web site that can encourage and facilitate tourist visitation. Most importantly, several DMS system providers – including Tiscover (see Photograph 20.1), World.net, Integra, and TouchVision – have emerged as the leading suppliers in the marketplace. Interesting destinations are coming together to 'coopete' – compete and collaborate at the same time. As shown in Photograph 20.2, the European portal visitEurope.com brings together 34 European destinations and creates a virtual window to the world where each destination both competes and collaborates online.

Using the emergent opportunities for multimedia distribution, DMSs increasingly utilise the Internet to provide interactive demonstrations of local amenities and attractions and to enable consumers to build their own itinerary based on their interests, requirements and constraints. In addition, DMSs are utilised to facilitate the management of DMOs, as well as the coordination of the local suppliers at the destination level. DMSs are particularly

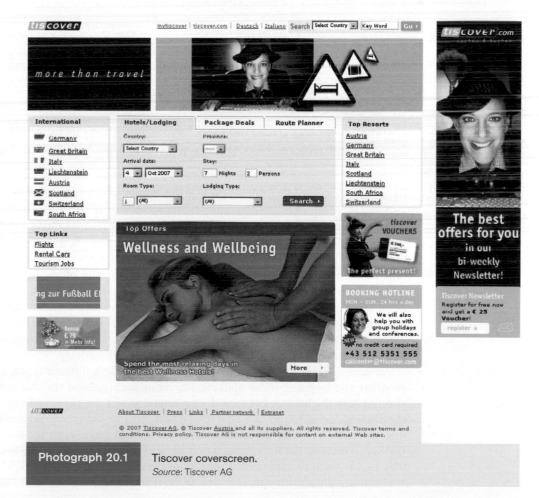

Photograph 20.1   Tiscover coverscreen.
Source: Tiscover AG

Photograph 20.2 The European Travel Commission portal: VisitEurope.com.
Source: European Travel Commission

significant for small and medium tourism enterprises which lack the capital and expertise to undertake a comprehensive marketing strategy and rely on destination authorities and inter-mediaries for the promotion and coordination of their products (Frew and O'Connor, 1999; WTO, 2001). Interestingly, it is not only DMOs that provide destination information online but a wide range of players (Buhalis and Deimezi, 2004). Govers and Go (2006) demonstrate how destination identity can be projected through the use of photographic imagery and narratives in an online environment in the context of marketing a fast-growing tourist destination such as Dubai. They conclude that private sector organisations, in particular hospitality and transport, are product-orientated and projected images relate primarily to the specific facilities and tourist activities on offer. In contrast, the destination marketing organ-isation focuses on the projection of cultural identity and heritage.

Advanced DMSs would enable destinations to achieve differentiation by theming their products and targeting niche markets. Providing accurate and realistic information would also improve the balance between the expectations and the perceived experiences for both tourists and locals, improving their interaction. This would enable destinations to integrate their offering and satisfy the needs of both the resident population and visitors. In addition, DMSs can increase the bargaining power of local enterprises with tourism intermediaries as they enable them to explore new and innovative distribution channels. The illustration of environmentally sensitive areas as well as the demonstration of socio-cultural rituals would enable a better understanding by locals and tourists and therefore would improve the tourism impacts in the area. DMOs should benefit by implementing advanced DMSs (or destination integrated computer information reservation management systems – DICIRMS) (Buhalis, 1993).

Gretzel and Fesenmaier (2003) suggest that the development of knowledge-based tourism business-to-business (B2B) communities requires the adoption of a multidimensional, multi-level perspective on system design that incorporates processes of knowledge creation and transformation and takes organisational stages of effective technology use into consideration. Integrating the management of information and knowledge flows can foster capacity-building among community members towards strengthening the collective competitiveness of destinations. DICIRMS can rationalise destination management and marketing by supporting their promotion, distribution and operations and also by offering innovative tools for strategic management and amelioration of tourism impacts (Buhalis and Spada, 2000; WTO, 2001; Buhalis, 2003).

CONCLUSION

E-tourism represents the *paradigm shift* experienced in the tourism industry as a result of the adoption of ICTs and the Internet. It is evident that all best business practices have been transformed as a result, and that each stakeholder in the marketplace is going through a redefinition of their role and scope. There are both challenges and opportunities emerging but the competitiveness of all tourism enterprises and destinations has been altered dramatically. It is evident that the 'only constant is change'. Organisations that 'compute' will be able to compete in the future. Although ICTs can introduce great benefits, especially in efficiency, coordination, differentiation and cost reduction, they are not a universal remedy and require a pervasive re-engineering of business processes, as well as strategic management vision and commitment in order to achieve their objectives.

Using Porter's five forces framework, Buhalis and Zoge (2007) illustrate that the emergence of the Internet altered the structure of the travel industry. Overall, consumers benefited the most as their bargaining power increased due to their ability to access accurate and relevant information instantly and to communicate directly with suppliers, while benefiting from lower switching costs. The Internet led to the intensification of rivalry among tourism suppliers as it introduced transparency, speed, convenience and a wide range of choice and flexibility in the marketplace. Transparency enabled buyers to increase their bargaining power by facilitating price comparisons and access to instant, inexpensive and accurate information but reduced the bargaining power of suppliers. Rivalry was further intensified because of lowered barriers to entry and because of the possibility of equal representation of small businesses. Innovative suppliers increasingly use advanced CRM to gather information on consumers' profiles and to offer tailored and value-added products while expanding their distribution mix widely to harness the marketplace. Suppliers should enhance their direct communications with end consumers and online intermediaries to save on costs, increase profitability and enhance their efficiency. Real-time representation facilitated instant distribution and led to bypassing the traditional distribution channels. This not only changed the structure of the tourism value system but also raised challenges for traditional intermediaries. The need for traditional intermediaries to shift their role to consumer advisers is becoming evident and unless TAs and TOs utilise Internet tools for building and delivering personalised tourism products they will be unable to compete in the future. Although the tourism industry structure has been altered dramatically it is evident that both tourism suppliers and online intermediaries should apply constant innovation, in terms of marketing techniques and technological advancements, in order to be able to offer differentiated, personalised, tailored and value-added products. The key point for sustaining their competitive advantage is to focus on their core competencies and to exploit the opportunities that technology offers to improve their strategic position in the tourism value system.

ICTs provide innovative strategic tools for tourism organisations and destinations to improve both their operations and positioning. Hence, the visibility and competitiveness of principals and destinations in the marketplace will increasingly be a function of the technologies and networks utilised to interact with individual and institutional customers. Unless the current tourism sector utilises the emergent ICTs, and develops a multichannel and multi-platform strategy, it will be unable to take full advantage of the emerging opportunities (Buhalis and Licata, 2001). It is safe to assume that only creative and innovative principals and destinations which continue to apply innovation in using intelligent e-tourism applications and adopt their processes accordingly will be able to achieve sustainable competitive advantages in the future.

SELF-CHECK QUESTIONS

1. How has the Internet changed the role of each player in the tourism industry?
2. What are the key factors that influence the adoption of ICTs in the tourism industry?
3. What is disintermediation and reintermediation in tourism?
4. How do airlines change their business functions as a result of the Internet?
5. How can tourism organisations maximise their online representation?
6. What are the Internet-related challenges for managing tourism brands?
7. How will the Web 2.0 influence the tourism industry?

ESSAY QUESTIONS

1. How has e-tourism changed the key strategic and operational functions for a tourism organisation of your choice?
2. Can small and medium-sized tourism enterprises benefit from e-tourism?
3. How can tourism organisations improve their strategic positioning by using e-tourism?
4. Can ICT-related competitive advantages be sustainable? And what are the main conditions for achieving that?
5. How can destinations use e-tourism to improve their competitiveness?

ANNOTATED FURTHER READING

Books

Buhalis, D. (2003) *eTourism: Information Technology for Strategic Tourism Management*, Financial Times/Prentice Hall, London.
Comprehensive coverage of e-tourism from a strategic perspective.

ENTER Conference Proceedings, Springer-Verlag, Vienna.
Wide range of papers on ICTs and tourism, published annually.

Mills, M. and Law, R. (eds) (2005) *Handbook of Consumer Behaviour, Tourism and the Internet*, Haworth Press, New York.
Focuses on consumer behaviour, the Internet and the emerging trends.

Nyheim, P., McFadden, F. and Connolly, D. (2005) *Technology Strategies for the Hospitality Industry*, Pearson-Prentice Hall, Upper Saddle River, NJ.
Focuses on technology, the Internet and the hospitality industry.

O'Connor, P. (1999) *Electronic Information Distribution in Tourism and Hospitality*, CAB International, Oxford.
Focuses on the Internet and the emerging trends.

O'Connor P. (2004) *Using Computers in Hospitality*, 3rd edn, Thomson Learning, London.
Focuses on technology, the Internet and the hospitality industry.

Poon, A. (1993) *Tourism, Technology and Competitive Strategies*, CAB International, Oxford.
Strategic thinking and vision towards the new tourism.

Sheldon, P. (1997) *Information Technologies for Tourism*, CAB International, Oxford.
Overview of systems used in the tourism industry.

Werthner, H. and Klein, S. (1999) *Information Technology and Tourism – A Challenging Relationship*, Springer, New York.
Comprehensive coverage of e-tourism from a technology and management techniques perspective.

WTO (1999) *Marketing Tourism Destinations Online: Strategies for the Information Age*, WTO, Madrid.
Focuses on technology, the Internet and destination management organisations.

WTO (2001) *eBusiness for Tourism: Practical Guidelines for Destinations and Businesses*, WTO, Madrid.
Focuses on technology, the Internet and destination management organisations.

Websites

Organisations	URL	Description
IFITT	http://www.ifitt.org/	IFITT's web site
Eye for Travel	http://www.eyefortravel.com/	Commercial web sites with news and white papers
Trends in European Internet Distribution	http://www.crt.dk/ uk/staff/chm/trends.htm	Carl H. Marcussen's statistics in European e-tourism
HotelMarketing.com	http://www.hotelmarketing.com	Monitoring e-tourism news
European Travel Commission	http://www.etcnewmedia.com/ review/default.asp?SectionID=10	New media group collecting statistics
Travel Daily News	http://www.traveldailynews.com	Newsletters and new developments
Travelmole	http://www.travelmole.com	Newsletters and new developments
TIA	http://www.tia.org/	Information on travel developments in the USA
Electronic Tourism	http://www.electronic-tourism.com	Newsletters and new developments and white papers
BTNonline	http://www.btnonline.com/	Newsletters and new developments
Hotel Online	http://www.hotel-online.com	Newsletters and new developments in e-hospitality
Internet World Statistics	www.internetworldstats.com	Internet Statistics
Jupiter	http://www.jup.com/	Internet Statistics
Forrester	http://www.forrester.com/	Internet Statistics
Genesys	http://www.genesys.net/	Information on tour operators and travel agencies
Phocuswright	http://www.phocuswright.com	Commercial web sites with news and white papers
Rene Waksburg's Wonderful Resources	http://www.waksberg.com/	Tourism research resources
World Tourism Organization	http://www.world-tourism.org/	World Tourism Organization
World Tourism Travel Council	http://www.wttc.org	World Tourism Travel Council
International Hotel Restaurant Associaton	http://www.ih-ra.com/	International Hotel Restaurant Associaton
StarUK	http://www.staruk.org.uk	Tourism Statistics in the UK

References cited and bibliography

Alford, P. (2006) 'Global Distribution Systems – International', *Mintel*, May.

Beekman, G. (2001) *Computer Confluence: Exploring Tomorrow's Technology*, 4th edn, Prentice Hall, Upper Saddle River, NJ.

Boehmer, J. and Cohen, A. (2007) BA, GDSs Still Talking: Business As Usual Despite Much-Hyped Contractual Expiration, *BTNonline magazine*, http://www.btnonline.com/businesstravelnews/headlines/frontpage_display.jsp?vnu_content_id=1003553031

Buhalis, D. (1993) 'Regional integrated computer information reservation management systems as a strategic tool for the small and medium tourism enterprises', *Tourism Management*, **14**(5), 366–78.

Buhalis, D. (1994) 'Information and telecommunications technologies as a strategic tool for small and medium tourism enterprises in the contemporary business environment', pp. 254–75 in Seaton, A. *et al.* (eds), *Tourism – The state of the art: the Strathclyde symposium*, Wiley, Chichester.

Buhalis, D. (1997) 'Information technologies as a strategic tool for economic, cultural and environmental benefits enhancement of tourism at destination regions', *Progress in Tourism and Hospitality Research* 3(1), 71–93.

Buhalis, D. (1998) 'Strategic use of information technologies in the tourism industry', *Tourism Management* 19(3), 409–23.

Buhalis, D. (2003) '*eTourism: Information technology for strategic tourism management*, Financial Times/Prentice Hall, London.

Buhalis, D. (2004) 'eAirlines: Strategic and tactical use of ICTs in the airline industry', *Information and Management* 41(7), 805–25.

Buhalis, D. and Deimezi R. (2004) 'eTourism developments in Greece', *International Journal of Tourism and Hospitality Research* 5(2), 103–30.

Buhalis, D. and Licata, C. (2002) 'The eTourism intermediaries', *Tourism Management* 23(3), 207–20.

Buhalis D. and O'Connor, P. (2005) 'Information communication technology – revolutionising tourism', *Tourism Recreation Research* 30(3), 7–16.

Buhalis, D. and Spada, A. (2000) 'Destination management systems: Criteria for success', *Information Technology and Tourism* 3(1), 41–58.

Buhalis, D. and Zoge, M. (2007) The Strategic Impact of the Internet on the Tourism Industry, pp. 481–92 in Sigala, M., Mich, L. and Murphy, J. (eds), ENTER 2007 Proceedings, Ljubljana, Springer-Verlag, Vienna.

Chan, S. and Law, R. (2006) 'Automatic website evaluations: The case of hotels in Hong Kong', *Journal of Information Technology and Tourism* 8(3–4), 255–69.

Clarke, R. (2004) 'Value proposition', *Airline Business*, March 44–5.

Connolly, D., Olsen, M. and Moore, R. (1998) 'The internet as a distribution channel', *Cornell Hotel and Restaurant Administration Quarterly* 39(4), 42–54.

Ctrip.com (2007) 'Ctrip.com posts impressive results', 12 February, http://www.chinatechnews.com/2007/02/12/4986-ctripcom-posts-impressive-results/print/

eBusiness W@tch (2006) 'ICT and e-business in the tourism industry', Sector Impact Study No. 08/2006, European Commission, http://www.ebusiness-watch.org/resources/tourism/SR08-2006_Tourism.pdf

Emmer, R., Tauck, C., Wilkinson, S. and Moore, R. (1993) 'Marketing hotels using global distribution systems', *Cornell Hotel Restaurant Administration Quarterly* 34(6), 80–9.

Feldman, J. (1988) 'CRS and fair airline competition', *Travel and Tourism Analyst* 2, 5–22.

Field, D. and O'Toole, K. (2004) 'Where next for the GDS?', *Airline Business*, March, 34–43.

Frew, A. and Horam, R. (1999) 'eCommerce in the UK hotel sector: a first look', *International Journal of Hospitality Information Technology* 1(1), 77–87.

Frew, A. and O'Connor, P. (1998) 'A comparative examination of the implementation of destination marketing system strategies: Scotland and Ireland', pp. 258–68 in Buhalis, D.,

Tjoa, A.M. and Jafari, J. (eds) *Information and Communications Technologies in Tourism*, ENTER 1998 Proceedings, Springer-Verlag, Vienna.

Frew, A. and O'Connor, P. (1999) 'Destination Marketing System Strategies: Refining and extending an assessment framework', pp. 398–407 in Buhalis, D. and Scherlter, W. (eds) *Information and Communications Technologies in Tourism*, ENTER 1999 Proceedings, Springer-Verlag, Vienna.

Govers, R. and Go, F. (2006) 'Projected destination image online: Website content analysis of pictures and text', *Journal of Information Technology and Tourism* 8(3–4), 73–89.

Gretzel, U. and Fesenmaier, D. (2003) 'Implementing a knowledge-based tourism marketing information system', *Illinois Tourism Network* 6(3), 245–55.

Gupta, U. (2000) *Information Systems: Success in the 21st Century*, Prentice Hall, Upper Saddle River, NJ.

Hammer, M. and Champy, J. (1993) *Re-engineering the Corporation: A manifesto for business revolution*, Nicholas Brealey, London.

HeBS (2007) 'Mastering Internet Marketing in 2007: A Benchmark Survey on Hotel Internet Marketing Budget Planning and Best Practices in Hospitality', http://www.hospitalityebusiness.com/hr/hr-Mar_05_2007_1520.html

Inkpen, G. (1998) *Information Technology for Travel and Tourism*, 2nd edn, Addison Wesley Longman, London.

Karcher, K. (1996) 'Re-engineering the package holiday business', pp. 221–33 in Klein, S. *et al.* (eds), *Information and Communication Technologies in Tourism*, ENTER 1996 Proceedings, Spinger-Verlag, Vienna.

Laudon, K. and Laudon, J. (2007) *Management Information Systems*, 10th edn, Prentice Hall, Upper Saddle River, NJ.

Li, L. and Buhalis, D. (2006) 'eCommerce in China: the case of travel', *International Journal of Information Management* 26(2), 153–66.

Marcussen, C. (2008) 'Internet Distribution of European Travel and Tourism Services', Research Centre of Bornholm, Denmark, http://www.crt.dk/uk/staff/chm/trends.htm

Murphy, J., Schegg, R. and Olaru, D. (2006) 'Investigating the evolution of hotel Internet adoption', *Journal of Information Technology and Tourism* 8(3–4), 161–77.

O'Brien, J. (1996) *Management Information Systems: Managing Information Technology in the Networked Enterprise*, Irwin, Chicago.

O'Connor, P. (1999) *Electronic Information Distribution in Tourism and Hospitality*, CABI, Oxford.

O'Connor, P. (2000) *Using computers in hospitality*, 2nd edn, Cassell, London.

O'Connor, P. (2002) 'An empirical analysis of hotel chain online pricing strategies', *Information Technology and Tourism*, 5(2), 65–72.

O'Connor, P. and Frew, A. (2000) 'Evaluating electronic channels of distribution in the hotel sector: A Delphi study', *Information Technology and Tourism* 3(3/4), 177–93.

O'Connor, P. and Horan, P. (1999) 'An analysis of web reservations facilities in the top 50 international hotel chains', *International Journal of Hospitality Information Technology* 1(1), 77–87.

O'Connor, P. and Rafferty J. (1997) 'Gulliver – distributing Irish tourism electronically', *Electronic Markets* 7(2), 40–5.

O'Reilly, T. (2005) 'What is Web 2.0: Design patterns and business models for the next generation of software', http://www.oreillynet.com/pub/a/oreilly/tim/news/2005/09/30/what-is-web-20.html

O'Toole, K. (2004) 'IT trends survey 2003', *Airline Business/SITA*, August.

Oz, E. (2000) *Management Information Systems*, 2nd edn, Thomson Learning, Boston.

Paraskevas, A. and Buhalis, D. (2002) 'Web-enabled ICT outsourcing for small hotels: Opportunities and challenges', *Cornell Hotel and Restaurant Administration Quarterly* 43(2), 27–39.

Peacock, M. (1995) *Information technology in hospitality*, Cassell, London.

Peppard, J. (ed.) (1993) *IT strategy for business*, Pitman, London.

Pollock, A. (1998) 'Creating intelligent destinations for wired customers', pp. 235–48 in Buhalis, D., Tjoa, A.M. and Jafari, J. (eds) *Information and Communications Technologies in Tourism*, ENTER 1998 Proceedings, Springer-Verlag, Vienna.

Poon, A. (1993) *Tourism, Technology and Competitive Strategies*, CAB International, Oxford.

Porter, M. (1985) *Competitive Advantage*, Free Press, New York.

Porter, M. (1989) 'Building competitive advantage by extending information systems', *Computerworld* 23(41), 19.

Porter, M. (2001) 'Strategy and the Internet', *Harvard Business Review*, March, 103D, 63–78.

Porter, M. and Millar, V. (1985) 'How information gives you competitive advantage', *Harvard Business Review*, July–August, **63**(4), 149–60.

Robson, W. (1994) *Strategic Management and Information Systems: An integrated approach*, Pitman, London.

Sheldon, P. (1993) 'Destination information systems', *Annals of Tourism Research* 20(4), 633–49.

Sheldon, P. (1997) *Information Technologies for Tourism*, CABI, Oxford.

SITA (2007) IT trends survey, *Airline Business*, Executive Summary, http://www.sita.aero/News_Centre/Industry_surveys_and_trends/Airport_IT_trends/default.htm

Smith, C. and Jenner, P. (1998) 'Tourism and the Internet', *Travel and Tourism Analyst* 1, 62–81.

Tapscott, D. (1996) *The Digital Economy: Promise and peril in the age of networked intelligence*, McGraw-Hill, New York.

Tapscott, D. and Caston, A. (1993) *Paradigm Shift: The new promise of information technology*, McGraw Hill, New York.

Truitt, L., Teye, V. and Farris, M. (1991) 'The role of computer reservation systems: International implications for the tourism industry', *Tourism Management* 12(1), 21–36.

Werthner, H. and Klein, S. (1999) *Information Technology and Tourism – A challenging relationship*, Springer, New York.

Wöber, K.W. (2006) 'Domain-specific Search Engines', pp. 205–26 in Fesenmaier, D.R., Werthner, H. and Wöber, K.W. (eds) *Destination Recommendation Systems: Behavioural Foundations and Applications*, CABI, Wallingford.

WTO (1995) *Global Distribution Systems in the Tourism Industry*, WTO, Madrid.

WTO (2001) *eBusiness for Tourism: Practical guidelines for destinations and businesses*, WTO, Madrid.

PART 5

TOURISM FUTURES

Photograph: Road through Monument Valley, Utah/Arizona, USA © Hannah Cox

INTRODUCTION

This final part of the book provides you with a comprehensive coverage of tourism futures. It aims to deliver three key knowledge areas:

1. A disciplined approach to analysing and viewing the future of the tourism system.
2. An understanding of the pace and scale of change in the world that impacts upon tourism.
3. An awareness of the importance of the linkage between products and markets in viewing future tourism scenarios.

Part 5 of this book comprises a major chapter focusing on tourism futures. Chapter 21 examines the dimensions of the changing world and analyses the impact upon the future of tourism. We believe that an understanding of future trends will allow the tourism sector to manage the future more effectively, and be prepared for the pace of change, which is now the rule not the exception.

We have been careful not to 'over-hype' this part with breathless accounts of flying cars and a world where robots replace hotel workers. Instead, we have provided a disciplined approach to examining the future of tourism that draws upon the approaches taken in 'futures research' such as scenario planning. We approach the future of tourism in two parts:

1. First, we provide a systematic analysis of the driving forces of change in the world. These include not only the recent upsurge in terrorism and concerns for the safety of travellers, but also demographic, social, political and technological influences.
2. We then set out a framework, based upon Leiper's tourism system, which links markets and products and so allows us to create future tourism scenarios.

Of course, throughout this part it must be remembered that, while we isolate these drivers of change for explanatory purposes, in reality they are closely linked, combining to create a world now termed the 'new normal' where 'rapid and unexpected change' impacts upon tourism. For example, a clear demographic trend is the influence of the baby boomer generation in Europe and North America. But we must be careful to recognise that it is this generation that has become the 'new tourist'; it is from this generation that opinion leaders have emerged to champion the causes of sustainability and ethical consumption of tourism; and it is from this generation that the leaders of the new political world order are found. So, the trends are intricately linked and interwoven, a fact that can be usefully drawn out in the classroom through the use of case studies.

In this part we provide a systematic review of the other drivers of change in the world, change which is often not under the control of the tourism sector and yet has major implications for how tourism will develop in the future. We then go on to assess the response of tourism to this world of change. Here the key is to take a long-term view of the future – for too long tourism has been concerned only with the short term. We know, for example, from forecasts, that volumes of international tourism will exceed 1 billion international tourist arrivals by 2010 and 1.5 billion by 2020. These are huge numbers and they will be accompanied by a change in the nature of the tourism market as other countries (such as China) emerge to dominate the world's travellers. This raises the question as to whether the tourism sector is prepared for these Chinese travellers: are the hotel rooms designed with the principles of feng shui in mind for example? Or do we really understand the motivations and preferences of the Chinese outbound market? Changes in the market will be also driven by demographic and social change in other generating markets. Not only will this be due to the ageing of some markets, but also new generations of consumers are emerging – generations X and Y – who are knowledgeable about technology and marketing and who will be experienced and empowered consumers of travel. To meet these challenges the tourism sector will need to recognise the importance of the 'new tourist' and develop new approaches to segmentation and deep qualitative research to understand and relate to them. Indeed, as we show in this part, it can be argued that we are moving away from a 'services' economy to an 'experience' economy where 'tourism experiences', whether natural or artificially generated, will be sought.

These driving forces are all linked to the 'generating region' of Leiper's tourism system. Factors in the 'destination region' are equally significant and include political and sustainability issues. Destinations are set within political administrations and systems, which are themselves changing with the rise of economic trading blocs, such as the EU, the strengthening of city-states where tourism and events play a major 'promotional' role and, of course, the pervasive influence of globalisation where both the private and the public sector are affected. It is these very political developments that have led to one of the most significant trends to impact upon tourism: that of terrorism – one of the 'wild cards' of futures research. Since the attacks on the USA of 11 September 2001, tourism has had to learn to live with terrorism. The cost has been increased safety and security for all travellers and the development of risk management and crisis management planning for the sector. Since the last edition of this book we have also been made increasingly aware of one factor that sits outside the tourism system and yet is proving to be very significant – that of climate change. Global warming in particular is having an impact upon consumer behaviour as beach resorts are shunned for fear of cancer and cataracts and upon the destinations themselves as coral reefs are damaged and low-lying islands put at risk (the Maldives, for example). The tourism industry is not immune here, and we are seeing a response in terms of carbon offsetting schemes as travellers recognise that their actions may impact upon the environment. In order to respond to these challenges, both destinations and the tourism sector are using concepts of sustainability as their organising framework. Notions of sustainability continue to evolve and now include community as well as environment. Here, destinations are involving their host communities in future planning as well as recognising the importance of being prepared for the demands of the new tourist through good visitor management and interpretation to satisfy the innate curiosity about these markets.

We conclude the chapter by looking at the shape of tourism products in the future in response to the combined demand- and supply-side trends identified above. Clearly, many tourism products of today will be around in the future, but there are emergent products – such as special interest tourism – which are catering for the increasingly fragmented market segments demanding niche products that range from gastronomic to 'dark' tourism. But for the more distant future it is technology that will take centre stage in delivering the tourist 'experience'. There is no doubt that there will be a winner in the 'space tourism race' and that space travel will become a reality for increasing numbers of tourists, while earthbound tourism may well become the preserve of virtual reality for a market 'cocooned' in their homes and safe from an increasingly dangerous world outside. But it is you, the readers of this book, who will be managing the tourism of the future and we hope that this part gives you the knowledge and approaches to succeed and shape the future.

CHAPTER 21

The Future of Tourism

LEARNING OUTCOMES

In this chapter we focus on the future of tourism, outlining trends and possible scenarios to provide you with:

- a disciplined approach to analysing and anticipating the future of the tourism system;
- an understanding of the scale of social and political change, including the need for security measures in tourism;
- an awareness of the key elements of changing tourism consumer behaviour;
- an approach to understanding future products in tourism; and
- an awareness of the significance of climate change for tourism futures.

Photograph: Yosemite National Park, California, USA © Kelly Miller

INTRODUCTION

Predicting the future of tourism is not an easy task. This is because tourism is increasingly faced with continuous, radical and unexpected change. Indeed, the United Nations World Tourism Organization (UNWTO) has termed this the 'new normal', suggesting that tourism will never return to the relatively stable conditions of the twentieth century. Futurists now accept that the one feature that will distinguish the new tourism from the old is the fact that not only will rapid change be evident, but also that it will be accepted as inevitable – and therefore will need to be managed. Disciplined management of tourism will be essential in ensuring that the sector responds appropriately to the changing environment and avoids 'strategic drift' away from the key issues. This chapter identifies a range of factors that will impact upon the future of tourism, some outside the control of the tourism sector, and others that can be managed. There is a danger, though, that in isolating one trend from another, their interrelationships will be overlooked. For example, consumer behaviour, political change and globalisation are all dynamic trends and changes in any one of these variables will impact upon the others. What is also clear is that, while it is possible to identify a range of key variables whose influence is already evident (such as the Internet), others are still emerging – such as climate change. Cutting across each of these trends is a range of other agents of change such as human resources, technology, sustainability and security. In combination, these will be instrumental in determining the future direction of tourism.

APPROACHING THE FUTURE

Although the history of tourism may be traced back to the Ancient Greeks and the Romans, it is only relatively recently, with the advent of mass tourism, that international activity has become so prevalent in the developed world. The rapid expansion of leisure travel from the 1960s onwards, precipitated by transportation developments such as the jet engine, continues to influence all aspects of the tourism system today, but it is the future of tourism to which we now turn our attention.

In this chapter we identify the variables that are the driving force of change in the tourism system. We know that in certain decades there have been predominant drivers of change. For example, in the mid-nineteenth century and the early decades of the twentieth century, transport developments were critical influences upon tourism. Since the 1980s it is both technological developments and the maturing of the tourism marketplace that have come to the fore, and in the early years of this century the sector is facing the challenges of climate change and security issues.

It is easy to 'hype up' the future of tourism and provide a sensationalist account of future scenarios from flying cars to virtual reality theme parks. However, this chapter takes a more disciplined approach to the issue by providing a framework within which to consider and analyse tourism futures. In the introduction to this book we introduced Leiper's (1990) tourism system as a way of thinking about tourism. It is possible to recast this model to take into account the ideas and issues involved in the future of tourism and use this to act as a framework for the chapter (Figure 21.1).

The reason we like Leiper's framework is that it is an all-encompassing approach to studying tourism. Tourism futurists commonly focus only on the tourism destination part of the system. But this fails to recognise the complexity of the tourism sector and the need to match up trends both on the demand side in terms of markets and consumer behaviour with trends in transportation and on the supply side, in terms of product developments and the destination. To consider any one of these in isolation would provide an unbalanced assessment of the future of tourism. The chapter therefore begins with an analysis of trends external to the

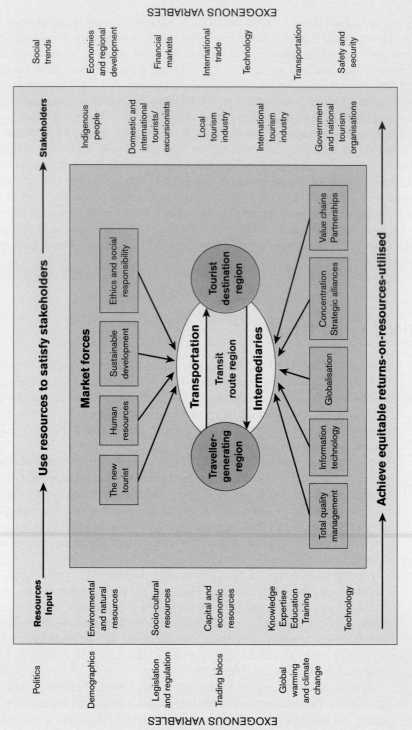

Figure 21.1 A framework for tourism trends analysis: exogenous variables

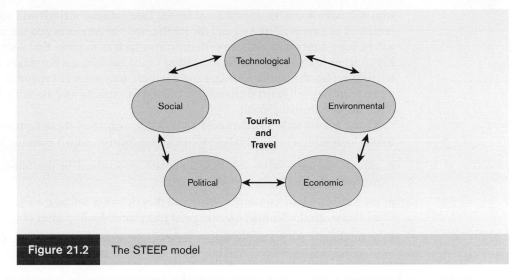

Figure 21.2   The STEEP model

tourism system but which will impact upon it, and finishes by examining trends associated with the components of the tourism system itself.

There are a number of important reports that cover both the demand and the supply sides of tourism futures. Nordin's (2005) report on *Tourism of Tomorrow* for the European Tourism Research Institute utilises techniques from futures research to analyse the driving forces of change for tourism. Her report is noteworthy for the adaptation of the STEEP methodology to understanding the environment within which tourism operates (Figure 21.2). STEEP characterises this environment as comprising social, technological, environmental, economic and political forces all of which work together. Nordin then draws in the idea of 'wild cards' – events that have a low probability of occurring, but which are devastating when they do so and often mark turning points in history. Of course, 9/11 is the defining 'wild card' for tourism. Still in Europe, the European Travel Commission have written (2006) a tight and comprehensive analysis of the future of tourism in Europe scanning both demand and supply side trends.

On the supply side, the World Travel and Tourism Council's (2003) *Blueprint for New Tourism* lays out an agenda for the future of the tourism sector. As the world's peak tourism industry body, the WTTC met in 2003 to discuss the state of tourism in the world. This meeting was held against the background of unprecedented security issues and economic uncertainties for the sector. Indeed, it is these very events that are changing the way that consumers behave, the way that the industry does business, and the way that the public sector views tourism. The WTTC's supply-side agenda for the 'new tourism' has three dimensions:

1. Governments must recognise travel and tourism as a top priority.

2. Tourism business must balance economics with environment, people and cultures.

3. Tourism must develop partnerships to share in the pursuit of long-term growth and prosperity.

A key issue here is the need for tourism to be viewed as an acceptable and responsible economic sector. We saw in the introductory chapter that tourism can make a positive contribution to poverty alleviation and sustainable development in the world. The Secretary-General of the UNWTO has used this as the focus for his 2007 strategic priorities for the future, see www.unwto.org.

On the demand side, the UNWTO has an honourable record of devising accurate forecasts of international tourism. These forecasts (WTO, 2001) suggest that, despite the setbacks of the early twenty-first century, tourism has grown from 456 million international arrivals in 1990 to 687 million in 2000 and will grow to 1 billion by 2010 and 1.56 billion by 2020. Yet, surprisingly, despite these huge numbers they represent only 7% of the world's population who will have access to international travel. International arrivals will continue to be concentrated in Europe, East Asia and the Pacific, and the Americas and the major growth areas will be long-haul travel and newer destinations such as those in East Asia and the Pacific. A key concern in this region is the forecast of China becoming a dominant force in outbound tourism across the world. Demand for domestic tourism will expand at a slower rate and some countries will reach demand-side ceilings of capacity and available leisure time which will constrain further growth.

At the micro scale VisitScotland (2005) has combined these demand and supply side trends to develop a series of future scenarios for tourism which examine issues such as:

- climate change – what will be the climate in Scotland in the future and how should tourism adapt;
- the future tourism consumer – who will they be, what will be their tastes and motivations and how can the Scottish tourism product be developed to meet their future needs; and
- technology – the impact of future technologies on consumer purchasing of the Scottish tourism product.

THE EXTERNAL ENVIRONMENT FOR TOURISM: FUTURE DRIVERS

There are a number of trends that are outside the control of tourism itself and yet will have an impact upon its development. In reality, most of these trends and variables are interlinked and mutually reinforcing. For example, while there is no doubt that the social trends that we identify will continue to encourage the growth of tourism, they will also act to change the nature of tourism with consequent implications for the management of destinations and development of products. And, of course, the very economic development that has fuelled tourism growth is contributing to the climate change that threatens to alter the nature of many destinations.

In other words, these trends, when combined, will have a fundamental impact upon future tourism scenarios and so cannot be ignored. While each of these trends will have a different impact upon different parts of the tourism system, no single trend will dominate. For example, demographic and social trends will be critical in shaping tourism demand in the twenty-first century and, clearly, these trends are closely linked. Demographic trends such as ageing populations in the major generating countries, for example the USA, Germany and Japan, allied to the declining numbers of young people as the post-1945 baby bulge works through the decades, are particularly important. Demographics are inextricably entangled with the social trends that are leading to later marriage, couples deferring having children, increased numbers of single and childless-couple households, and the enhanced role of women in travel activity. Interwoven with these trends are the changing values of the population which affect consumer behaviour, in particular the adoption of family values and the search for safety and security, all wrapped into cocooning behaviour where the home becomes the basis for leisure activities. In the developing world, a burgeoning workforce will lead to immigration to developed countries and the growth of knowledge and interest in other countries will mean we are likely to see a convergence of lifestyles across the world. With increased media attention and levels of education, these trends will give people more time, resources and inclination to travel, fuelled by the growth and spread of discretionary incomes and the liberalisation of trade on an international scale.

Social drivers of change

Demographic trends

For the majority of the traditional generators of both domestic and international tourism, population growth is either static or even negative. However, this is not the case for emerging

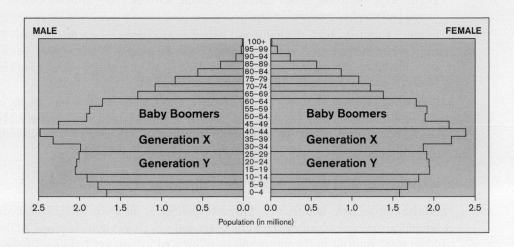

| **Figure 21.3** | UK population pyramid 2007, showing generations |

generators of international tourism such as China and India where populations continue to grow apace. In most generating countries, economies will keep growing, leading to higher per capita incomes and consumption of tourism products as discretionary income rises.

In the traditional generating markets for tourism, populations are ageing as birth rates fall and people live longer. Ageing populations tend to be associated with urbanisation and conservative politics and they are influencing patterns of public expenditure to reflect the needs of older people. Markets for the goods and services that older people need have clear implications for the tourism sector and it is the ageing baby boomer generations of the developed world that are one of the most important market segments. They will be fitter, healthier and more demanding consumers than the previous generations. Equally, the younger generations – X and Y – will remain in the youth market longer as they marry later, continue with their youth lifestyle and with it change the nature of the traditional nuclear family household. Generation Y is the largest population bulge since the baby boomers and will therefore influence future consumer behaviour as they will be technologically adept and more savvy and sceptical about marketing messages. The relationship between demographics and these generations is shown in Figure 21.3.

Social trends

Throughout much of society there is a move to more flexible working practices and a fluid balance between work and leisure. Also, there is an increasing and conflicting concern for the environment and an emphasis on hedonic conspicuous consumption – both trends demanding a response from the tourism sector, and in part boosted by the 9/11 attacks. In addition, tastes are polarising into either comfort or adventure-orientated activities. Family structures in the developed world are changing with a trend to later marriage, more one-parent families and having children at a later age. Each of these trends has implications for the consumer behaviour of tourists and the consequent development of tourism products. Summarising, there are three key social trends that have specific implications for tourism:

1. Worldwide, more people will choose to live in cities. Urbanisation skews public expenditure towards urban services and infrastructure and changes patterns of private consumption. This trend also has important policy implications in terms of the growth of city-states; the use of tourism to market cities; and the fact that tourist resources will be increasingly

located adjacent to the urban market, favouring artificial types of development such as theme parks as has occurred in Japan.

2. In many countries, both the status and influence of women are on the increase. Women will have an increasing say not only in purchasing decisions, but also in the types of products offered by the tourism sector. This is leading to companies such as Surflasolas, a Mexican women-only surf school (www.surflasolas.com).

3. Populations are becoming more culturally diverse as improved communications, increasing wealth and mobility stimulate people to try to understand other cultures. Tourism products and their marketing will increasingly have to embrace cultural diversity, and niche products – such as gay tourism – are emerging as a consequence.

International and political drivers of change

The future of tourism is intricately linked to politics at all levels. Initiatives at different geographical scales are changing the world order and will impact upon tourism. At the international level, tourism in the future will be influenced by two key trends – the forging of international trading blocs, and globalisation.

Trade blocs and regionalism

Opportunities for tourism will be enhanced by the formation of a number of trading blocs across the globe as country groupings come together in deregulated economic alliances. Notable here are the North American Free Trade Agreement (NAFTA), the creation and expansion of the European Union (EU) and the Association of South-East Asian Nations (ASEAN). In the EU, the adoption of the euro as a common currency has demonstrated the power of these blocs, as the currency encourages tourism across Europe, while the expansion of the EU itself will begin to change the balance of tourism flows within Europe.

A contradictory trend at the regional level is the rise of regionalism and a search for cultural identity – particularly among ethnic minorities. In the midst of this contradiction 'city-states' are emerging as major visitor destinations, where tourism plays a key role in 'boosting' the reputations, lifestyle and economies of cities. Examples here include the way that major events such as hosting the Olympic Games, F1 Grand Prix or the Football World Cup benefit the image of cities (compare the approach of Athens to hosting the Olympics to that of the 'green games' in Beijing for example, where Beijing is promoting the environmental measures being taken to minimise the impact of the games – see http://en.beijing2008.cn/12/12/greenolympics.shtml).

Globalisation

Underlying the changing world order is the globalisation of tourism businesses – a powerful force shaping national and regional economies which are linked and interdependent as never before. Globalisation is a product of combining the revolution in information technology, telecommunications and transport; a strengthening consensus among national governments in favour of free trade; and the democratisation of financial markets. The term applies to the increasing interdependence of markets and production in different countries. Key drivers of globalisation in tourism are:

- decreasing costs of international travel allowing access to most markets in the world;
- increasing income and wealth in the generating countries;
- newly emerging destinations and the increased demand for international travel;
- adoption of free trade agreements, removing barriers to international transactions;
- computer and communications technology encouraging 'e-business'; and
- worldwide acting suppliers utilising global distribution systems (GDSs).

Photograph 21.1	For the first time, symbols of tourism – aircraft – are used as weapons as the world order shifts.

Source: Corbis/Reuters

In the future the consequences of globalisation for the tourism sector will include increasingly standardised products, procedures and global brands such as Disney; pressure for alliances and mergers, increased concentration in the marketplace; and pressure on vulnerable businesses such as local SMEs.

It is the larger, international companies that can take advantage of these consequences. Indeed, globalisation goes hand in hand with increased concentration in the tourism industry as major companies gain market share and market influence. At the same time we are seeing the concentration of capital in the hands of a few major players in the tourism sector, a trend that also drives tourism towards the performance indicators and business practices demanded by the finance industry.

A particular problem associated with this trend is that most of the larger corporations do not have a relationship with a specific destination. They may therefore be less sensitive to the impact of their operations on host environments, economies and communities. In addition, small and medium-sized tourism enterprises and local destinations fear the 'neo-colonial' relationship which can emerge from dealing with large companies. This is an important consideration for tourism where, at the end of the day, the product is delivered locally; hence the conundrum of balancing the global forces upon an essentially 'local' product.

Safety, security and risk

Tourism is vulnerable to natural and man-made crises, unexpected events that affect traveller confidence in a destination. The events of the early years of the twenty-first century have tended to focus attention on security risks to travel associated with terrorism and acts of war. However, tourism is affected also by natural disasters such as pandemics, tsunamis, earthquakes, floods and avalanches. The UNWTO therefore defines a crisis as:

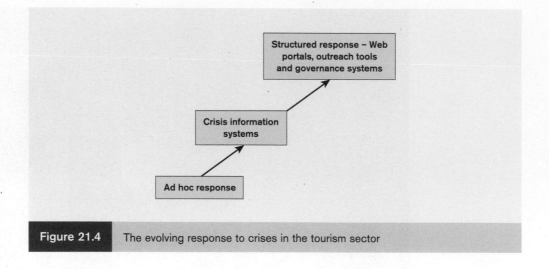

| Figure 21.4 | The evolving response to crises in the tourism sector |

Any unexpected event that affects traveler confidence in a destination and interferes with the ability to operate normally.

(WTO, 2003a)

These events have changed the way that we travel as acts of terrorism and war have brought both travellers and the tourism sector to the front line of the war against terrorism. Within a few weeks of the attacks of 9/11 the tourism sector had adopted a new vocabulary, including phrases such as 'risk management', 'destination recovery' and 'crisis management'. As the sector has become more resilient to and experienced in such events, the approach to their management has changed (Figure 21.4). Bierman (2002) has coined a new scale for tourism to describe the magnitude of crisis that can have an impact upon a destination. He calls this the DESTCON scale, with DESTCON 1 the most severe crisis that tourism can experience, down to DESTCON 5 when normality resumes.

From the industry's point of view, the WTTC recommends a twin-track approach to security:

1. Promoting the virtues of a coordinated strategy and operational measures across all parts of the tourism sector.

2. Convincing the public and industry employees that the reality of tourism must be to co-exist with terrorism, providing that the risk is mitigated.

The essence of the WTTC's approach is the forging of partnerships between the private sector and governments and the fact that security *cannot* be an area for commercial rivalry. Their approach is based upon four principles:

1. Coordinate policy actions and communications. Here, for example, there is an ongoing debate as to the role of 'travel advisories' – a travel advisory notifies potential travellers of the risks of travelling to an area. It is also important to use the media as a partner on these occasions.

2. Develop secure operating environments for travel, including both equipment and personnel. Of course, this will be an inconvenience for travellers as evidenced by the introduction of fingerprinting and photographs for all inbound travellers to the USA in 2004.

3. Access, share and work with the best intelligence to prevent future incidents and security breaches.

4. Deny terrorists freedom of action.

As a result largely of 9/11 tourism enterprises, destinations and governments have begun to develop and implement crisis and risk management strategies. These strategies recognise

Table 21.1	The UNWTO's crisis guidelines for the tourism industry
Before the crisis – be prepared	Prepare a crisis management plan Be prepared for promotional activity Review security systems Be research ready
During the crisis – minimise damage	Communicate from the front line Devise promotional messages Ensure security of the operation Do tactical research on the situation
After the crisis – recovering tourist confidence	Communicate confidence Use promotion imaginatively Evaluate security measures Use research effectively to build confidence

Source: WTO, 2003a

the timetable of a crisis and document appropriate responses, as can be seen from the UNWTO's crisis guidelines for the tourism industry (Table 21.1).

International travel can also be a bio-security threat as it facilitates the spread of infectious diseases. In the early years of the twenty-first century the threat of bird flu has prompted the UNWTO to establish a bio-security procedure. This procedure is advantaged by the fact that bird flu is a crisis that can be predicted, unlike terrorist attacks which are not predictable. The UNWTO have established the Tourism Emergency Response Network (TERN). TERN is a web-based portal for a network of linked organisations at all levels of government and the tourism sector that are primed to respond should a bird flu epidemic strike. Elsewhere, disease and decreasing levels of safety will constrain the uninhibited expansion of tourism. The spread of AIDS for example, may render some otherwise attractive destinations no-go areas while increasingly vociferous campaigns against sex tourism may also alter tourism flows and motivations. At the macro level, these factors are largely outside the control of tourism and their consequences may be severe, yet at the micro level, the tourism industry will increasingly have to manage issues such as safety and security, and unethical practices at the destination and ensure that security measures are implemented with a human touch. For the developing world there is a fine balance between reporting of such occurrences and protecting their income from tourism.

Climate change

Climate is altering the environment for tourism and has increasingly become a concerning focus for policy and management initiatives. The social, demographic and political drivers identified above have generally encouraged economic growth and tourism. Yet is this very growth over the last 150 years that has also begun to have far-reaching consequences for the earth's climate. There is no doubt that one of the most significant environmental influences upon the future of tourism will be global climate change. This includes long-term factors such as global warming and the erosion of the ozone layer. In order to analyse the impact of climate change on tourism we need to consider the total tourism system, including transport.

On the supply side, there is no doubt that the raising of the earth's temperature and the consequent rise in sea level will affect tourism destinations such as wetlands, islands and coastal areas. Much of tourism investment is found in locations that fringe the coast, and global warming will irrevocably alter vital tourism resources such as the flora and fauna of destinations, as well as ski resorts as the snowline recedes. On the demand side, fear of skin cancer and cataracts may reduce the demand for products such as beach tourism which, in turn will impact upon destination and product development. Finally, we have to recognise that some transport modes used for tourism contribute to climate change and will need to change. Growing recognition of the seriousness of the problem has prompted policy and management intervention. At the international level, in 2003 the UN World Tourism Organization issued *The Djerba Declaration on Tourism and Climate Change* (WTO, 2003b), urging governments to:

● adopt the Kyoto protocol and its approximations on greenhouse gas emissions;

● research and collaborate on climate change;

● move tourism up the agenda on climate change discussion;

● implement sustainable water use practices and the ecological management of sensitive areas; and

● raise consumer awareness of the issue.

MINI CASE STUDY 21.1
Carbon neutral travel?

Tourism is both a victim and vector of climate change. One of the ways in which tourism contributes to climate change is through carbon emissions from tourism-related activity such as transportation. These emissions are an example of a negative externality resulting from tourism. While approaches such as green taxes on carbon emitters, or carbon trading schemes, will undoubtedly target tourism in the future, carbon offsetting has emerged as an effective way to neutralise the greenhouse gases emitted by travel.

CARBON OFFSETTING: CHANGING TOURIST BEHAVIOUR

Carbon offsetting is an approach to neutralising the impact of an individual's greenhouse gas emissions. Effectively, travellers pay to balance out their emissions by funding projects that absorb, reduce or avoid an equivalent amount of greenhouse gases elsewhere. Concerned tourists can calculate the amount of carbon emission from their tourism activity – such as, say, an international flight – and offset that by driving a hybrid car, planting trees or paying a carbon offset company to act on their behalf. In the UK carbon offsetting companies include Climate Care, the Carbon Neutral Company, and Treeflights.com. This is a growing voluntary market, perhaps the vanguard before compulsory legislation or taxation schemes are introduced. Examples of carbon offsetting schemes include:

1. the Gold Coast City Council in Australia has calculated that for every tourist that stays on the Gold Coast, the Council needs to plant two trees to offset the tourist's carbon emissions during their stay;

2. tourism companies such as lastminute.com provide their customers with carbon offsetting schemes to help them be 'carbon neutral travellers'; and

3. Climate Care will use travellers' payments to fund energy renewal, energy efficiency and forest restoration. Examples of projects include providing energy-saving light bulbs in the developing world, funding clean cooking rather than open fires in Latin America and encouraging innovations such as the development of foot-operated pumps to replace diesel power in India.

While it is difficult to argue with the spirit of carbon offsetting it has, however, sparked controversy:

● Carbon offsetting schemes are often crude and open to abuse, particularly in terms of the accusation of 'greenwashing' as it is difficult for consumers to know whether they have made the promised carbon saving.

- Carbon offsetting does not reduce the emissions of carbon dioxide – indeed, while it may begin to change people's travel behaviour for the good, it also risks becoming an excuse for greater travel activity and not taking action for reducing carbon emissions.

- Particularly controversial is the notion that planting tress offsets carbon emissions from flying. The theory is that trees lock in stores of carbon, but the counter argument is that (i) the carbon in the trees can be released by, say, forest fires, and (ii) quite simply if tourism continues to grow at its current rate, the earth will run out of tree-planting space.

These objections to carbon offsetting are partly due to the fact that the market is unregulated and there are no standards. As a result, both the UK and the World Wildlife Fund are planning to introduce carbon offsetting standards to regulate the market.

REFERENCES

Article, information etc. from Global Policy Forum on energy tax: http://www.globalpolicy.org/socecon/glotax/carbon/index.htm

Economic effects in Australia, article: http://www.environment.gov.au/about/publications/economics/taxation/economic.html

The economics of carbon tax in Australia: http://www.cs.ntu.edu.au/homepages/jmitroy/sid101/uncc/fs230.html

A speech by the Australian Prime Minister giving the governing Labor Party's carbon tax plan: http://www.pm.gov.au/News/media_releases/media_Release2081.html

Gold Coast 2010 plan (PDF): http://www.goldcoast.qld.gov.au/attachment/environment/20020120_cpp.pdf

DISCUSSION QUESTIONS

1. High income travellers are responsible for high carbon emissions through air travel. Draft the outline of an 'awareness campaign' to persuade this group to reduce their leisure air travel.

2. Visit the Internet site of one of the major carbon offsetting companies and calculate the cost to offset your emissions from a flight of your choice. How realistic is this calculation?

3. Can carbon neutral travel ever be achieved?

COMPONENTS OF THE TOURISM SYSTEM: FUTURE DRIVERS

We now turn to the tourism elements of Leiper's (1990) system (Figure 21.1) and their future drivers. Leiper's system recognises the complexity of tourism and the need to match up trends both on the demand side in terms of markets and consumer behaviour, with trends on the supply side in terms of product developments and the destination. To consider any one of these in isolation would provide an unbalanced assessment of the future of tourism.

Future markets for tourism

When we consider Leiper's 'traveller generating region', the demographic and social trends identified above have combined to change both the scale and nature of tourism markets. Many tourism futurists have suggested that the maturing of the tourism market is creating a 'new tourist', or 'post-tourist', who can be characterised as experienced, sophisticated and demanding. This means that the traditional annual family holiday mostly spent in a beach resort may be gradually superseded by multi-interest travel and a range of creative and innovative travel experiences (such as activity, adventure, learning and nature-based tourism). These trends will see the relative importance of conventional packaged tours decline in favour of independently organised tourism, or at least a more bespoke form of tourism.

The new tourist

The new consumer of tourism is knowledgeable, discerning, seeks quality and participation and, in the developed world, is increasingly drawn from an older age group. Motivations for travel are moving away from passive sunlust towards educational and curiosity motives. At the same time, travel will be facilitated by flexible working practices. To an extent, the new sophisticated traveller has emerged as a result of experience. Tourists from the major generating regions of the world have become frequent travellers, are linguistically and technologically skilled and can function in multicultural and demanding environments overseas. Add to this media and Internet exposure of tourism destinations and the reduction of perceived distance to reach such places and the stage is set for a reappraisal of holiday formulae. Education too has played a part, together with enhanced communications, and has led to more sophisticated requirements from holidaymakers who are now looking for new experiences combined with rewarding activities to fill their leisure time and satisfy their cultural, intellectual and sporting interests. Here, the emergence of the knowledge-based society is significant for tourism as travel products are merged with education and entertainment. This creates 'info-tainment' or 'edu-tainment' at destinations and specifically at commercial attractions through interpretation and education programmes. Pine and Gilmore (1999) have taken this one step further by suggesting that in the future consumption will be driven by 'experiences'. Tourism is perfect for this approach as its consumers search for authenticity. For the new tourist travel is not just about *being at the destination*, but *experiencing being there* as travel becomes the medium for personal fulfilment and identity.

Of course, the sophistication of the customer will have an impact upon product development throughout the industry; not only will there be an increased requirement for high standards of product design, efficiency and safety, but also the tourist will be more critical of

MINI CASE STUDY 21.2
The experience economy

It is a well-known saying that tourism is an experience, and therefore differs from manufactured goods when we come to asses its value, or approach the marketing of tourism. As technology has constantly improved the quality of entertainment, visual images and sound in our own homes, so we have come to expect a similar level of quality in our tourism experience. Engineering tourism experiences is the way of the future and it also matches perfectly the expectation of the marketplace – particularly the 'new tourist'.

Pine and Gilmore's (1999) book, *The Experience Economy*, encapsulates this concept. They say that work is theatre and every business is a stage, a critical consideration for human resources in tourism where front-line workers in the restaurant, hotel reception or lobby shop are 'on stage'. The experience-based product is different from commodities, goods or services (Table 21.2), as the nature of the offering is memorable (the Disney parade for example is memorable for young children, it is personalised – the children can relate to their favourite characters; and it delivers sensations to the audience).

Pine and Gilmore argue that there are four types of experience that can be engineered by 'experience providers':

1. **Entertainment** – here entertainment can be added to existing products, such as the old-fashioned aquarium that now has dolphin and seal shows. This 'engages' the visitor, but does not normally 'involve' all but one or two visitors in the entertainment.

Table 21.2	From commodities to experiences			
	Commodities	**Goods**	**Services**	**Experiences**
Offering	Fungible	Tangible	Intangible	Memorable
Attribute	Natural	Standardised	Customised	Personal
Supply	Stored	Inventories after production	Delivered on demand	Revealed over a duration
Seller	Trader	Manufacturer	Provider	Stager
Buyer	Market	User	Client	Guest
Factor of demand	Characteristics	Features	Benefits	Sensations

Source: Pine and Gilmore, 1999, p. 6. Reprinted by permission of Harvard Business School Publishing. Copyright © 1999 by the Harvard Business School Publishing Corporation; all rights reserved

2. **Education** – again the visitor is the passive recipient of the experience, but is more actively engaged than with an entertaining experience, because the very nature of an educational experience will change their levels of knowledge or awareness about a topic. Here the concepts of info-tainment or edu-tainment have been used to describe the process. Examples here include the role of interpretation in bringing to life the indigenous landscapes of the Hualapai people on the rim of the Grand Canyon.

3. **Escapist** – this type of experience is much more about involving the visitor actively by immersing them in the experience. Here theme parks and virtual reality are examples.

4. **Aesthetic** – with this experience, the visitor is again immersed but does not impact upon the environment of the experience – gazing at the Taj Mahal or the Sphinx are examples here.

As we go down this list we find that the visitor is increasingly immersed in the experience and participates. Pine and Gilmore argue that the nature of the experience should be engineered to 'transform' the visitor. It is here that the ideas of the experience economy can be of great benefit for tourism. By transforming the nature of the visit to, say, sensitive natural sites, managers can change behaviour such that the visitor understands the nature of the site, and therefore is more inclined to protect it and behave in an appropriate way. Here marketing and visitor management come together to deliver the experiences that the 'new tourist' desires, while also beginning to change the way the visitors behave.

There is no doubt that the experience economy has many important insights for tourism, not only in how products are formulated and engineered into experiences, but also for the workforce that has to deliver these experiences, and for the next stage of the process – transformation – which may begin to change the behaviour of the 'new tourists' themselves.

DISCUSSION QUESTIONS

1. There are many critics of the experience approach who condemn it as an artificial and sterile world, where every worker is smiling. Do you agree with the critics or support Pine and Gilmore's view that the experience economy is the way of the future?

2. Taking each of Pine and Gilmore's types of experience (educational, aesthetic, etc.) draft a list of up to half a dozen tourism experiences for each category.

3. What are some of the issues that the workforce may face when creating 'experiences' for tourists?

the product and have the experience to compare offerings. At the same time, as the new tourist is conscious of value for money rather than simply price, other elements of the marketing mix will become important. In particular, this will mean that 'quality' will remain a key attribute in tourism product development and customer convenience in all its forms will be demanded by the new travellers, a trend fuelled by consumer legislation in tourism and the 'empowered' consumer. The issue of quality is increasingly important because the consumer is time poor and will increasingly demand that the products they purchase will be quality controlled and reliable. Determinants of quality will also link to their values of safeguarding the environment, authenticity and respecting communities at the destination.

Market segments

Every tourist is different, bringing a unique blend of experiences, motivations and desires. Tourism is increasingly following the trend of other industries towards customising. Here technology enables products to be tailored to meet individual tastes. The old tourism products did not adopt this approach. Instead they were general and unspecialised with very similar characteristics traded as commodities rather than services under the mass tourism philosophy. This philosophy said that tourism products should appeal to all tastes and be sold at a low price in order to attract as wide a range of customers as possible.

This discussion points to the need for effective segmentation of the tourism market. Traditionally, tourism marketers have been using geographic and demographic criteria in order to describe their markets, but psychographics and behavioural criteria will be increasingly used in order to:

1. provide detailed customer profiles;
2. identify motivations, needs and determinants; and
3. offer an appropriate marketing mix and service delivery strategy.

For the future, tourism market segments will be less stable and more fragmented. Tourism markets may be segmented in many different ways and there are no 'correct' segmentation criteria, only those that are more effective in differentiating between market segments and providing insights into the marketplace. Increasingly, segmentation approaches primarily based on product usage (comfort versus adventure) will be used, relying on the analysis of market research data. Indeed, one of the imperatives for understanding the tourist of the future will be deep and meaningful market research. The Roy Morgan Research Company, for example, has developed an effective market segmentation approach for tourism based upon research into consumer's values (www.roymorgan.com/products/values-segments/values-segments.cfn).

The destination

As the tourism system responds to the trends identified above, tourism flows will change as new generators of both domestic and international tourists, and new destinations, emerge. For Leiper's 'tourist destination region', there is no doubt that these destinations of the future will need to be better planned and managed and show more concern and respect for their environment and host community than did their earlier counterparts. Indeed, all tourism-visioning exercises suggest that everyone involved in tourism will have to take increased responsibility for social and environmental issues. In the future, the focus of tourism will be on the destination as new management techniques are adopted and the attention to volume will give way to concepts of visitor experience and value. These concerns will be addressed by enhanced tourism planning and visitor management techniques and a clear agenda to involve local communities in the futures of their destinations. In this way, the imperative will be for the sustainable management of tourism destinations and the conservation of their unique characteristics. Examples include the management of UNESCO world heritage sites such as Angkor Wat in Cambodia.

We can see that the central issue here is the gradual shift from short-term to longer-term thinking and planning in tourism. It is no longer acceptable for the industry to exploit and use up destinations and then move on; indeed we are already seeing the results of this in the demise of some of the mass-tourism resorts built in the 1960s and 1970s – Acapulco in Mexico, or Benidorm in Spain are examples here. The concepts of the tourism area life cycle and strategic planning provide a much needed long-term perspective in this respect. By this we mean that destinations can decide to remain at a particular point on the life cycle by using marketing and planning approaches, rather than being inexorably driven to grow – or decline. On the demand side there are also drivers of sustainability as consumers will place pressure upon the industry and destination managers to behave in a responsible manner; if they do not then their destination may be shunned as *environmentally unacceptable* to visit.

Future destinations: planning and management

Destinations are responding to these demands in a variety of ways. Resource-based destinations are adopting sophisticated planning, management and interpretative techniques to provide both a welcome and a rich experience for the tourist while at the same time ensuring protection of the resource itself. It is felt that once tourists understand why a destination is significant they will want to protect it. Good planning and management of the destination lies at the heart of providing the new tourist with a high-quality experience and it may be that tourists will have to accept increasingly restricted viewing times at popular sites, higher prices and even replicas of the real thing.

Future destinations: sustainable enterprises and destination value chains

Enterprises at the destination are also responding to the drive for sustainable destinations. This is occurring in two ways:

1. Increasingly the techniques and approaches for sustainable tourism practices are being operationalised and published as guidelines and manuals for sustainable enterprises (see, for example, the manuals produced by Australia's Sustainable Tourism Cooperative Research Centre at www.crctourism.com.au/CRCBookshop). The tourism industry is anxious to demonstrate that it is both responsible and acting to curb some of the excesses of past development. One approach is the certification and eco-labelling of products and companies. This serves to encourage tourism enterprises to 'raise their game' in terms of sustainability and allows the consumer to discern those enterprises that are attempting to be sustainable in their practices. Examples include the European 'Green Key' eco-label, awarded to accommodation units demonstrating high environmental standards (www.lacleverte.org)

The problem, of course, is that unless these systems are well policed, and therefore resourced, there is a danger that they will be abused by enterprises using them for 'greenwashing' purposes – in other words, they do not always practise what they preach. This is particularly the case if the systems are voluntary rather than mandatory. The other problem is that there is an increasing proliferation of these certification schemes and there is no common standard for the indicators used. There is also an element of self-preservation here as green products will become increasingly popular and a sector that is seen to be responsible will not attract regulation by government. It also raises the issue of the *ethical* consumption and development of tourism, where organisations recognise their long-term responsibilities and their relationship with a variety of stakeholders. This is becoming evident in the brochures of tour operators/wholesalers where the consumer is urged to 'respect, reuse, recycle *and* rescue' consumption.

2. Destinations will benefit from future trends in the tourism value chain. In the past, the tourism value chain was a combat zone with each member feeling they had to compete. For destinations this resulted in exploitation by tour operators who failed to recognise that the resort was, in fact, their product. In the future, tourism businesses will begin to recognise the importance of working with other members of the value chain and this will include tour operators investing in the destination.

TECHNOLOGY BOX 21.1
Virtual reality tourism

Technological innovations such as virtual reality (VR) may one day replace the authentic travel experience altogether; indeed the very nature of tourism as an 'experience' lends itself perfectly to VR. VR consists of three elements – visualisation of the destination through simulation; immersion in the destination; and interactivity with elements of the destination. In other words, VR is simply a further step along the road of 'engineering' tourist experiences and one that reinforces the trend of leisure activity based upon the home. Simply strapping on a body suit and plugging into the virtual reality program could transport you to the sights, sounds and sensations of, say, the Caribbean. The tourist experiences the destination but without any risk of skin cancer, AIDS or the other side-effects of travel; while for the destination, negative impacts are removed, but so also are the positive effects of income, jobs and regional development. The debate as to the real impact of VR is still ongoing:

- *Proponents* say that as cocooning behaviour increasingly places the home as a central and secure base for leisure activities, VR may depress demand for the real thing.

- *Opponents* contend that VR will simply whet the appetite for more travel through enhanced exposure to, and awareness of, the product, as VR is used simply as an advanced form of tourist brochure.

Networks or alliances of businesses and consumers along value chains will increase business efficiencies and improve communication. This trend is critical for the tourism sector and is leading to a shift in thinking away from management of individual sectors of the industry – such as transport, destinations, intermediaries and accommodation – to the concept of *integrated management*. For destinations, integrated management across all sectors of the tourism industry will be coordinated by NTOs or by strongly integrated companies. This allows the evolution of complementary products such as the merger of the business market with add-on leisure products. A further extension of the concept is that of destination-based marketing/cooperation. This is now recognised as a cooperative, effective way to increase visitation.

So what of the future for tourism destinations? We can discern two clear trends:

1. The first is the trend towards the use of artificially, technologically enhanced destinations such as theme parks, cruises and resorts. Examples here include Las Vegas, the Disney theme parks and Carnival Cruise Line. The product is unashamedly artificial, creating a fantasy world that will be increasingly part of the 'experience' economy.

2. The second trend is for authentic, well-managed contact with nature and indigenous communities. Here eco-tourism and heritage tourism are the obvious examples, with sympathetic encounters with wildlife (orangutan encounters in Rwanda) or native peoples (a Misaim campfire experience in Kenya). This type of destination demands a different type of management to the artificial fantasy destination as here it is the resource that is paramount in delivering the experience.

Transport

Historically, change in tourism has been closely linked to transport innovations in Leiper's 'transit route region'. In the future, the influence of transport will be diluted by the emergence of other new drivers of change. At the same time, transportation itself will benefit from technological change that will improve the speed, reduce the cost and improve the fuel efficiency of travel. Nonetheless, the influence of transport as a driver of tourism futures should not be underestimated. Tourism remains dependent upon transport technology and the consequent improvements in efficiency, range and safety of travel. This applies especially to new developments such as tourism in space. Equally, tourism may also be constrained by transportation in the future as old systems fail to accommodate increased levels of demand, or travellers perceive the security risks of travel as too great.

The inadequate capacity of transport infrastructure will act as a real constraint upon tourism growth in the future. The WTTC's (2002) infrastructure task force is concerned that this will particularly be the case in Europe and the USA.

The future will also see a change in the management and approach of transport enterprises with an emphasis on both marketing and the building of strategic alliances to gain market share. The airline sector, for example, was very heavily affected by the downturn in travel following 9/11, and has seriously rethought its response to future markets and patterns of travel. Here there are two schools of thought. Boeing sees the future in medium-sized aircraft that can operate flexibly between hubs and also secondary regional airports. Airbus, on the other hand, sees the future in larger aircraft, with a longer range that will dominantly ply long-haul routes. The key here will be to adjust the capacity and range of aircraft to 'match' market demand.

Environmental factors too will be a concern for all transport modes in the future, particularly as air transport emissions are unlikely to be reduced in the medium term. However, where the environmental factors may bite is in the consumer's concern for energy consumption and this may well lead to a gradual modal shift in transport away from air and towards surface modes. Here the response will be with high capacity, high-speed passenger vehicles. This competition between transport modes will increase in the future, characterised by improved rail services and products, the realisation of the environmental advantages of rail and continued technological developments in the area of high-speed train networks. A magnetically levitated (*maglev*) fast train service is already operating in Shanghai.

Forecasts of international transport predict that technological developments, increased airline efficiency and labour productivity savings will offset any rises in aviation fuel prices and thus, in real terms, fares will continue to fall. This is supported by the fact that on short-haul routes the low-cost carriers are gaining market share from the traditional 'scheduled' carriers. An important cost consideration is the escalating price of security at airports and in the air. While it can be said that security systems are much more effective than they used to be for air travel, the London and Madrid railway terrorist bombings have focused attention on securing surface transport networks from attack. This will be a much more difficult and expensive task.

HUMAN RESOURCES FOR TOURISM

Many of you reading this book will be looking towards the tourism industry for a career. Indeed, the challenges facing the tourism industry will only be met successfully by a well-educated, well-trained, bright, energetic, multilingual and entrepreneurial workforce who understand the nature of tourism and have a professional training. A high quality of professional human resources in tourism will allow enterprises to gain a competitive edge and deliver added value with their service. In this book, we have outlined a professional and analytical approach to tourism, an approach that demands high standards of professionalism and education. Achievement of many of the best practices that we outline will only be possible with a well-trained tourism workforce.

Tourism is a high-touch, high-tech, high-involvement industry where it is the people that make the difference. Yet, in a number of countries, an acute shortage of trained workers and skills are impacting upon the growth of tourism. There is no doubt that the tourism industry is under pressure. Changing markets, industry restructuring and more competitive domestic and international markets are placing great burdens on their expertise. The ability to succeed and the future performance of tourism and related activities will depend largely upon the skills, qualities and knowledge that managers will be able to bring to their business.

In the past, tourism has been characterised by a lack of sophistication in human resource policies and practices, imposed by outmoded styles of human resource management and approaches to operational circumstances. This leaves tourism vulnerable to ideas, takeovers and domination by management practices found in other economic sectors. Indeed, practices that are commonplace in other service industries – comprehensive induction, regular appraisal, effective employee communications – are underdeveloped in many tourism and leisure businesses. Educators and trainers have a role to play here by facilitating innovation, encouraging empowerment, motivating the workforce and, in partnership with industry, working to overcome the specific problems of tourism.

A high-quality tourism workforce can be achieved only through high standards of tourism education and training. Tourism education and training involves the communication of knowledge, concepts and techniques that are specific to the field of tourism, but which draw upon the core disciplines and themes of areas such as geography, finance and marketing. The future of tourism education will lie in changing modes of delivery of courses using technology such as the Internet, greater customisation of education to meet particular student groups, and a rethink of the content of tourism courses which currently have become mired in twentieth-century thinking.

CONCLUSION

The future of tourism is an exciting one with products being developed that are as diverse as adventures in space to sympathetic and managed encounters with endangered wildlife. Of course, tourism cannot control all the external forces that impact upon it. However, the message of this book has been that, whatever the tourism product and its delivery, the future will only be successful if we take a scientific and disciplined approach to understanding and managing tourism. This chapter, for example, has resisted the temptation to 'hype' the future of tourism and, instead, has taken an analytical approach to the future, taking into account impacts from outside the tourism system as well as inside. Of course, any book will be tested in a number of ways because tourism is faced with unexpected and rapid change in the modern world. However, we have tried to provide general principles and practices rather than specifics which will date. We offer you the challenges of tourism management and an exciting future – a future that we believe will become more legible if you follow the frameworks and approaches that we have provided. This will allow you all to become 'future makers'.

SELF-CHECK QUESTIONS

1. Draft a checklist of the factors that you think will be the most influential in shaping air travel in the next 20 years.

2. Outline your views on virtual reality tourism – hype or reality?

3. Can you find any examples of 'greenwashing' by tourism organisations in brochures or the media?

4. Draft a list of measurable characteristics that would allow a market researcher to identify a 'new tourist'.

5. Construct a list of the key dimensions of climate change and, for each, assess its potential impact on tourism.

ESSAY QUESTIONS

1. Critically review the contention that, in the developed world, tourists will begin to switch from air to surface transport in the future.

2. Identify and describe the major dimensions for market segmentation in tourism for future markets.

3. Review the challenges facing beach tourism destinations and their options to diversify their markets and change their products in the future.

4. Critically assess the impact of globalisation on a destination of your choice.

5. Is the future of tourism a secure one?

ANNOTATED FURTHER READING

Books

Bierman, D. (2002) *Restoring Tourism Destinations in Crisis: A Strategic Marketing Approach*, CAB, Wallingford.
An excellent framework for approaching crises and a useful set of case studies.

Hall, C. M. and Higham, J. (eds) (2005) *Tourism, Recreation and Climate Change*, Channelview Publications, Clevedon.
A thorough and wide-ranging introduction to climate change and its implications for tourism.

Nordin, S. (2005) *Tourism of Tomorrow – Travel Trends and Forces of Change*, European Tourism Research Institute, Östersund.
A wide-ranging and visionary report based upon the techniques of futures research.

Pine, J.B. and Gilmore, J.H. (1999) *The Experience Economy*, Harvard Business School Press, Boston.
A visionary book, casting glimpses into the way that tourism products will be engineered and themed as 'experiences' in the future.

Wahab, S. and Cooper, C. (2001) *Tourism in the Age of Globalisation*, Routledge, London.
A systematic review of the impact of globalisation on all sectors of tourism.

WTO (2001) *Tourism 2020 Vision*, WTO, Madrid.
A thorough analysis of future markets and products.

Web site

http://www.spacetourismsociety.org
A comprehensive web site covering all aspects of space tourism.

References cited

Bierman, D. (2002) *Restoring Tourism Destinations in Crisis: A Strategic Marketing Approach*, CAB, Wallingford.
European Travel Commission (2006) *Tourism Trends for Europe*, ETC, Brussels.
Leiper, N. (1990) *Tourism Systems*, Massey University Department of Management Systems Occasional Paper 2, Auckland, New Zealand.
Nordin, S. (2005) *Tourism of Tomorrow – Travel Trends and Forces of Change*, European Tourism Research Institute, Ostersund.
Pine, J.B. and Gilmore, J.H. (1999) *The Experience Economy*, Harvard Business School Press, Boston.

VisitScotland (2005) *Our Ambition for Scottish Tourism: A Journey to 2025*, VisitScotland, Edinburgh.

WTO (2001) *Tourism 2020 Vision*, WTO, Madrid.

WTO (2003a) *Crisis Guidelines for the Tourism Industry*, WTO Madrid.

WTO (2003b) *The Djerba Declaration on Tourism and Climate Change*, WTO, Madrid.

WTTC (2002) *Increasing Mobility, Expanding Infrastructure,* WTTC, London.

WTTC (2003) *Blueprint for New Tourism*, WTTC, London.

MAJOR CASE STUDY 21.1
The tourism space race

SPACE TOURISM

Although space tourism can be thought of as an activity in the distant future, it is estimated that by 2020 space technology will be applied to intercontinental travel. Already space tourists have gone into orbit and two companies govern the market – Space Adventures and Virgin Galactic. As if this were not evidence enough of the fact that space tourism is set to become a reality, the US House of Representatives passed a bill in 2004 regulating commercial space flights, and in 2007 the first international conference on space tourism was held.

Taking Leiper's system again, it is clear that space tourism should include not only the market for the product and the means of transport, but also the destination. For space tourism, the destination may indeed include the Moon, but it can also be thought of as present-day theme parks on Earth – such as the Kennedy Space Center at Cape Canaveral, Florida, or the simulated ride at Cape Canaveral – the 'Shuttle Launch Experience'. Other Earth-based simulations of weightlessness or driving Moon buggies could also come under the label of space tourism. In the future, options will not only include the ability to travel to destinations in space, but also activities such as orbital flight or the ability to stay in space-based hotels or space stations.

SPACE TOURISM PROVIDERS

This case study outlines the characteristics, positioning and products of one of the major space tourism providers. 'Space Adventures' is the longest standing company in the market.

Space Adventures

Space Adventures has a series of tourism products based upon space adventures and experiences. They also organise experiences that do not involve traveling into space (officially defined as 62 miles above the earth's atmosphere). The company was established in 1998 as a space tourism, entertainment and event production company that delivers and develops space experiences. It is based in Vienna, Virginia, USA and has a Russian office. To date they are the only company to have flown tourists into space. To quote their web site:

> Space Adventures will open space flight and the space frontier to private citizens. As the leading provider of space experiences to people on Earth, Space Adventures is in a unique position to . . . provide countless new opportunities for exploration and enterprise. Space Adventures will fly tens of thousands of people in space over the next 10–15 years and beyond, both orbital and suborbital, around the moon, and back, from spaceports both on Earth and in space, to and from private space stations, and aboard dozens of different vehicles; and by continually providing newly available space experiences.

Products   The company was the first to offer genuine space tourism products. Their products have been engineered to deliver real experiences – again the words of Space Adventures put it well:

> Our programs and products are not about travel and tourism; the experiences that we offer provide people with an insurmountable feeling, an intense sensation, and an awe-

Photograph 21.2 Designing economical launch vehicles is the biggest challenge faced by space tourism enterprises.

inspiring encounter that only the exploration of an unknown frontier incites.

This is achieved through working with the Russian space agency and accessing their facilities (such as the Gagarin Cosmonaut Training Centre) to deliver the 'excitement and fantasy of popular science fiction'.

Space Adventures has four basic 'experience' products:

1. **Orbital flights** – the company is the only one in the world to take clients into space to the International Space Station (ISS) using the Soyuz TMA spaceship.

2. **Sub-orbital flights** – a sub-orbital space program involving a flight into space with weightlessness 100 kilometres above the earth.

3. **Spaceflight training and spacewalks** – a range of training experiences which include products such as weightlessness training at Russian space centres and a spacewalk from the ISS.

4. **Steps to Space** – state-of-the-art training experiences for adventurers. Here, the company is clearly positioning its experiences at the very top of the market and targeting the corporate sector. For example, Space Adventures' 'reach for the stars' team-building programme is aimed at large corporate clients. This programme has been cleverly engineered to act as a memorable team-building exercise, provide unique 'space' experiences and deliver 'celebrity' status to the participants complete with DVD and certificate.

5. **Space-related flight adventures** – 'zero-gravity' parabolic flights.

Markets Space Adventures is positioned at the upper end of the tourism market. They cleverly straddle the events sector, and target three segments of 'adventurers' – not 'tourists'. In addition, all of the products use VIP airport lounges, VIP customs and immigration processing, limousine transfers, five-star accommodation, VIP guided tours of destinations, such as Moscow, and where relevant, contact with cosmonauts and those involved in the space business is arranged. Very much in tune with the 'experience product', all adventurers can join the 'spaceflight club' – the frequent flyer scheme of the future.

The company has three key target markets:

1. Individual and family adventurers – examples here include Dennis Tito, the first-ever space tourist in 2001.

2. Corporate buyers – corporate events, training days and team-building experiences have been designed to appeal to the corporate market. Clearly, this is the major market for the company's products.

3. Media and celebrity clients – the company works with the media to engineer experiences and with celebrities at their events.

SUMMARY

Space Adventures, along with Virgin Galactic, are the only two providers in the tourism space race. Both represent the future of tourism. They are professional, well-run organisations at the cutting edge of marketing, technology and tourism. They understand that they have to engineer experiences to create products and in so doing have become a hybrid of tourism, entertainment, event management and technology.

REFERENCES

http://www.spaceadventures.com
http://www.virgingalactic.com

Source: Space Adventures Ltd.

DISCUSSION QUESTIONS

1. Access the Space Adventures' web site (http://www.spaceadventures.com) and find the resellers' inquiry form. As an independent retail travel agent in your country, draft a response to the two questions on the form:

   ● which Space Adventures' offerings do you feel you will be able to sell well?; and

   ● describe how you intend to market Space Adventures' offerings.

2. Why do you think Space Adventures see themselves as being in the 'experience' business and not 'travel and tourism'?

GLOSSARY

9/11 The terrorist attacks in New York and Washington on 11 September 2001, *p. 3*.

A

Acidification The process of increasing acidity or becoming acidic, *p. 169*.

Additionality When new products or facilities are introduced if they add to the total value of tourist spend then they are said to provide additionality as opposed to displacement, *p. 461*.

Advanced passenger train Introduced in the UK in 1979 to provide fast intercity rail transport, *p. 410*.

Advanced purchase excursion fare Early booking of tickets often results in lower ticket prices; also known as APEX fares, *p. 419*.

Advertising Includes any paid form of non-personal communication through the media which details a product that is identifiable, *p. 596*.

Agenda 21 The programme action plan that came out of the 1992 Rio Summit. It was given the title Agenda 21 because of the 21 chapters dealing with a wide range of aspects relating to sustainable development, *p. 161*.

Agent A business that distributes the product of principals without alteration in the main, *p. 373*.

AIDS Acquired Immune Deficiency Syndrome, *p. 199*.

Air traffic control The system that directs the movement of aircraft in time and space, *p. 408*.

Air traffic movements Data on air traffic routes and runway utilisation, etc., *p. 409*.

Alternative tourism Has a wide variety of meanings and was put forward as a response to the excesses associated with mass tourism, *p. 232*.

Anthropology of tourism The study of tourism with respect to socio-cultural, linguistic and archaeological issues, *p. 188*.

Anti-trust legislation US legislation against controlling trusts or monopolies influencing market competition, *p. 399*.

Attraction 'icons' Those attractions that mark a destination in the mind of the tourist, giving instant association of the attraction with its location, *p. 309*.

Authenticity This term is generally used to show that something is original and honest, that it is what it appears to be, *p. 314*.

B

Balance of payments Refers to the balance between foreign exchange spent and received in an economy, *p. 151*.

Barriers to entry Devices designed to prevent new companies from entering an industry. The barriers may be through production secrets, scarcity of resources or through the high price of inputs, *p. 256*.

Biological diversity The number, range and abundance of species living within a common environment, *p. 165*.

Brand A name, a symbol, term or design or a combination of these, *p. 581*.

Brand extensions or stretching The extension of product range under a single brand, *p. 323*.

C

Cabotage This refers to where overseas airlines have been given the right to fly any routes they wish from particular airports, *p. 426*.

Capitalism A social system based on individual rights where goods and services are produced and exchanged with minimal government interference, *p. 247*.

Charter flights See charter services.

Charter services A system of conditions over a finite period that relates to levels of service and frequency of flights in order to secure capacity, *p. 423*.

Click-and-mortar agencies Established businesses with physical outlets engaging in e-commerce (Internet trade), *p. 383*.

Codesharing A procedure where different airlines, who are members of an alliance, agree to pool their different airline codes into one flight so as to use up spare capacity. It is particularly common with short-haul onward connections from main airport hubs, *p. 392*.

Commercialisation and bastardisation The change made to an event, skill, craft or ritual to make it more attractive to tourists, *p. 187*.

Commodification The transformation of non-commercial relationships into commercial relationships, *p. 439*.

Communism A society where the people are responsible for resource allocation, production and distribution. In theory, essentially classless and without a need for government, *p. 247*.

Comparative advantage Where the opportunity cost of producing a specific good or service is less than it is in another country then the former is considered to have a comparative advantage in the production of that good or service. Is used as a justification for international trade, *p. 135*.

Conservation Managing environmental resources in a way that optimises their contribution to the quality of life, *p. 162*.

Consortia A combination or group formed in order to undertake a venture that would be beyond the resources of a single individual/company, *p. 345*.

Consumer satisfaction The extent to which a company's business efforts matches or exceeds the expectations of the consumer, *p. 513*.

Contestable markets Those markets where firms' conduct is not determined by market structure, but rather the need to deter entry is the main influence on performance, *p. 399*.

Cost–benefit analysis Used in project appraisal to determine the monetary value of costs and benefits (to a community) relating to a project (such as an airport extension, highway, new sewage treatment plant) to see if it is worthwhile, *p. 137*.

Credence good A product or service bought on trust from the supplier since it is not possible to pre-test it prior to purchase, *p. 373*.

Customer needs Customer-felt state of deprivation, *p. 513*.

D

Delphi analysis An iterative panel method of analysis where the panel members do not meet, *p. 207*.

Demand determinants The factors that influence the scope and nature of travel, *p. 97*.

Demonstration effect Influencing the behaviour, dress and attitudes of people through demonstration/imitation and interaction, *p. 193*.

Destination image An individual's awareness of a destination made up of the cognitive evaluation of experiences, learning, emotions and perceptions, *p. 53*.

Destination management organisation A destination-based organisation tasked with the responsibility of coordinating and managing destination activity, including planning and promotion, *p. 483*.

Developing countries Countries that are defined as low- or middle-income countries by the World Bank, where living standards are thought to be low relative to high-income countries. Although there is no precise definition there are thought to be more than 125 countries with populations in excess of 1 million that have these characteristics, *pp. 129–30*.

Development strategies Approaches and plans designed to bring about the desired growth and development of tourism or an economy, *p. 162*.

Diagonal integration This refers to collaboration among different service providers (such as airlines, car hire companies, tour operators and financial services companies) designed to get closer to the consumer and reduce transaction costs through economies of scope, system gains and synergies, *p. 304*.

Direct marketing Direct communication with pre-selected target groups in order to obtain an immediate response or build closer relationships, *p. 600*.

Direct sell The absence of **intermediaries**. Therefore the product is sold directly from the supplier to the tourist, *p. 378*.

Disaggregation The degree to which the various productive sectors of the economy are broken down (e.g. the UN Standard Industrial Classification (SIC) 2, 3 or 4 digit levels of disaggregation), *p. 143*.

Discretionary incentives Incentives normally linked to conditions, such as job creation in depressed areas. Can also take the form of discretionary grants, *p. 462*.

Disintermediation A reduction in the amount or value of transactions that are distributed through intermediaries, *p. 379*.

Displacement Refers to the amount of current revenue that is displaced by a new development. For instance, if a new five-star hotel is built in Quebec and 50% of its business is attracted from existing five-star hotels in the city then there is a 50% displacement rate, *p. 136*.

Distribution system Mix of channels used to gain access or means by which a tourism service is made available to the potential buyers of the product, *p. 601*.

Distributive trade Refers to all companies involved in the distribution of goods and services. The UN Standard Industrial Classification (SIC) incorporates distributive trade under heading 6 (i.e. 6.1 wholesale trade, 6.2 retail trade, 6.3 hotels and catering), *p. 138*.

Diversification The broadening of the economic base by the development of different industries, and/or a strategy to achieve company growth by means of starting up or acquiring new businesses outside the existing company products or markets, *p. 131*.

Domestic tourism The activity of people visiting destinations within their own country's boundaries, *p. 4*.

E

Ecological system A collection of interconnected living beings (including humans) and the system in which they coexist such as the earth's surface, *p. 165*.

Economic dependence When the costs and revenues of one country, company or project depend upon that of another, *p. 133*.

Economic recession A decline in economic activity (GDP) that persists for at least two quarters, *p. 131*.

Eco-tourism Nature-based tourism that attempts to minimise its environmental impact, *p. 232*.

E-intermediaries E-intermediaries and emediaries are intermediaries that offer streamlined intermediation services across the Internet, *p. 385*.

Elasticities of demand and supply The responsiveness of supply and demand to changes in prices (price elasticity) or income (income elasticity), *p. 147*.

Empirical studies Studies that are based on experience, experiment or observation, *p. 162*.

Environmental Action Programmes Environmental policies and strategies, *p. 173*.

Environmental auditing A management system designed to mitigate environmental impacts, *p. 171*.

Eutrophication The process whereby water becomes enriched with plant nutrients and this replaces the oxygen, *p. 169*.

Exogenous change in demand A change in final demand brought about by changes outside the economy in question, *p. 141*.

Externalities The external economic effects that are not taken into account within the normal marketplace. Can be positive (benefits) or negative (costs) and are associated with the production or consumption of goods and services, *p. 414*.

F

Feudalism The social system that was prevalent in Europe from the eighth century onwards. Seen by some as control of a state by an entrenched minority for their own benefits, *p. 247*.

Fixed costs Those costs that do not vary with the volume of output, *p. 258*.

Flagship The chief or major one of a group, e.g. flagship attraction or hotel, *p. 309*.

Focus groups A method of undertaking collective interviews that explicitly uses the group's interaction to generate results, *p. 207*.

'Footloose' attractions Attractions that can be located almost anywhere where there is sufficient space, i.e. not dependent upon a specific natural resource or factor, *p. 321*.

G

GATS The General Agreement on Trade in Services. An attempt by the World Trade Organization to liberate the trade in services in the same way that the GATT did for trade in goods, *p. 131*.

GDP Gross domestic product. A key indicator of an economy's performance and is based on the total value of goods and services produced by a country within its economy, *p. 130*.

Global distribution system Computer databases used by intermediaries to book tourism products, *p. 630*.

Global warming The rise in the world's temperature due to the greenhouse effect, *p. 669*.

Globalisation A term that refers to the process of increasing economic and communication connectivity that has occurred over the past half century. Global markets replacing national and regional markets, e.g. capital markets, *p. 130*.

GNI Gross national income. The value of all income earned by residents of an economy whether it is earned within or outside the national boundary (see **GNP**), *p. 134*.

'Grand inspiration' attractions Attractions that are developed as a result of an individual's dream, *p. 321*.

H

Hallmark events Hallmark is generally a sign of quality, authenticity or distinguishing feature therefore a hallmark event is intended to make the destination distinctive in some way, *p. 313*

Hedging A strategy that is implemented to reduce risk. An example would be for a business to take up a position in a futures market that is opposite to that held in the cash market so that risks are reduced, *p. 393*.

Honey pots An expression used in tourism management whereby a viariety of attractions, shops, restaurants and accommodation are clustered at points where tourists want to visit to create a complex capable of absorbing a high population density, *p. 318*.

Horizontal integration The merging of two or more businesses that are operating at the same stage of the production process, *p. 304.*

I

Imagescape The medium or background in which people feel they live, *p. 320.*

Inclusive tours The package tour, *p. 376.*

Indigenous development Economic development that occurs as a result of changes within the country, *p. 441.*

Inflation A persistent increase in the general price level over time resulting in a decrease in the purchasing power of a unit of currency, e.g. dollar, *p. 134.*

Information communication technology (ICT) Digital tools used for business functions and processes, *p. 623.*

Infrastructural investment Investment in infrastructure such as roads, airports, water supply and communications, *p. 208.*

Input–output model A general equilibrium approach to measuring the effects of a change in final demand on the rest of the economy, *p. 135.*

Inseparability The service product is often produced and consumed simultaneously, *p. 522.*

Instant purchase fares Product is purchased at the time that the transaction takes place even though this may be well in advance of the dates of the trip, *p. 419.*

Institutionalised or mass tourism A constant stream of large numbers of tourists to destinations, *p. 190.*

Intangibility The tourism product cannot be easily demonstrated, assessed or tested prior to purchase, *p. 521.*

Integrated marketing communication The process a company adopts in order to integrate and coordinate its messages and media to deliver clear reinforcing communication, *p. 601.*

Integration The combination of businesses that are at the same or different stages of a process or distribution channel, *p. 379.*

Interlining This refers to where passengers transfer from one flight to another within the same company or alliance rather than switching to an alternative company or competing alliance, *p. 421.*

Intermediaries Companies or individuals that act as brokers or middlemen between the tourists and the suppliers (travel agents, tour operators), *p. 373.*

International tourism The activity of people visiting destinations outside their own country's boundaries, *p. 4.*

Intersectoral linkages The purchase and sale of goods and services between the various sectors of an economy – representing intermediate demand, *p. 130.*

Invisible export The export of a service as opposed to a visible export which would be a tangible good. International tourist receipts are exports, *p. 129.*

K

Key informants People able to provide collective and important viewpoints and opinions, *p. 207.*

L

Leakages Refers to money that drops out of circulation within the local economy, either by being saved or being spent on goods and services from outside the economy, *p. 136.*

Lifetime value The measurement of the total worth to the organisation of its relationship with a particular identified customer over a period of time, *p. 519.*

Limits of acceptable change The acceptable level of change that an environment can suffer without irreversible degradation, *p. 223.*

Linear homogeneity in production The assumption that all companies within a single sector are making the same product/service in the same way and that there are no economies of large-scale production so that the next unit of output will require exactly the same proportion of inputs as the previous unit of output, *p. 146.*

Load factor The measure of business and the indicator of efficiency for transport systems, generally expressed as the percentage of available seats that are occupied on the journey, *p. 423.*

Loss leader A good or service sold at less than market price in order to attract consumers, *p. 344.*

M

Marginal cost The incremental cost of producing one more unit of a good or service. Governments tend to intervene in the marketplace for market goods by providing subsidies or directly providing them so that the consumption of such goods and services is increased, *p. 329.*

Marginal propensity to consume The amount of each additional unit of income that an individual is likely to spend, *p. 143.*

Market failure The inability of a market system to truly reflect the social costs and/or benefits associated with transactions, an example being the over-consumption of non-priced elements in the production process, such as the environment. In such cases, the market fails to find an efficient solution to the distribution, *p. 316.*

Market or catchment area The area in which goods and services take place. Markets can also relate to the characteristics of potential purchasers and sellers such as specific segments of the population, *p. 310*.

Marketing concept The marketing management philosophy that places the satisfaction of the needs of the target market as a central guiding goal, *p. 514*.

Marketing mix The combination of product, price, place and promotion marketing tools that a company decides upon in order to affect consumer behaviour, *p. 506*.

Marketing plan A detailed company approach to the selection of target groups and the formulation of a marketing mix to achieve marketing objectives and financial targets, *p. 548*.

'Me too' attraction developments The development of an attraction on the basis of the evidence that it has worked before therefore it will work again, i.e. it ignores market saturation and displacement, *p. 321*.

Mega-events Mega is a prefix that means 1 million. A mega-event is generally considered to be a large-scale event that has global publicity and/or is associated with large-scale impacts, *p. 313*.

Merit goods Goods that are deemed to have a greater value to society than is reflected in their market price, *p. 326*.

Mission statement A short statement as to the main purpose or major goal of the organisation in relation to the wider environment, *p. 556*.

Monopolistic power The ability of a business to determine (to some extent) the price of the goods/services produced, *p. 257*.

Multinational agencies Agencies that operate across national boundaries, such as the United Nations Development Agency, *p. 439*.

Multiplier analysis An economic technique for estimating the impact of tourism on the local economy, *p. 129*.

N

National air carrier The airline that carries the national flag, the state airline, *p. 452*.

National tourist organisation The tourist authority for a state/country, *p. 439*.

New product development The introduction of a good, service or idea that is perceived by customers to be new, *p. 564*.

New tourist A tourist who is experienced, aware of opportunities and empowered, *p. 672*.

'New version' attractions Modern-day interpretations of classic attractions, e.g. from fairgrounds to theme parks, *p. 322*.

O

OECD Organisation for Economic Cooperation and Development. A collection of 30 member states that use the organisation as a discussion forum to further their aims for a free market system, *p. 161*.

Off-peak The periods when travel and tourist activities are in less demand. Often associated with discounts to attract business, *p. 406*.

Online travel The acquisition of information and the purchase of travel-related services from businesses selling on the Internet, *p. 382*.

Operating account An account for day-to-day operations of the business, *p. 387*.

Opportunity costs Costs a country, company or individual has to forego in order to have something, *p. 135*.

Overrides Extra commission paid by airlines, hotels and other suppliers for volume bookings, *p. 385*.

P

Paid holiday entitlement The practice of employers providing employees with time off with pay, *p. 98*.

Peak The prime period of demand, *p. 406*.

Perceived risk The interpretation of the seriousness of economic, physical, performance and pyschological aspects related to decision-making, *p. 523*.

Peripheral areas Areas away from the centre or the core, *p. 188*.

Perishability A characteristic of service products implies they cannot be easily stored for future sale, *p. 304*.

Personal selling An attempt to gain benefit through face-to-face or telephone contact between the seller's representative and those people with whom the seller wants to communicate, *p. 598*.

Polluter should pay Philosophy that supports the view that the costs of cleaning up pollution should be borne by those who create the pollution, *p. 333*.

Preservation Not using, or limiting the use of, resources so as to preserve them for future generations, *p. 162*.

Price The amount of money charged for a product or service based upon what a consumer is willing to give up in return for the benefits delivered, *p. 586*

Price competitive Where small changes in the price charged for a product may result in sales being won by a rival business, *p. 257*.

Primary data New data gathered by the researcher for the purpose of the study, *p. 262*.

Principal A trade term used to define the economic entity supplying the product, *p. 373*.

Product A package of problem-solving services and tangible attributes formulated to satisfy a need or want, *p. 579*.

Product differentiation Making the output of a business distinctly different from the output of competitors, *p. 256*.

Product life cycle A term borrowed from biological sciences that refers to the way in which a product evolves over time, *p. 379*.

Project appraisal Involves a collection of instruments (such as the internal rates of return) that can be used to determine the financial viability of a variety of projects, *p. 137*.

Promotion Descriptive term for the mix of communication activities that tourism organisations carry out in order to influence those publics on whom their sales depend, *p. 593*.

Property management system A computerised system for integrating all elements of hospitality information and management, *p. 637*.

Pro-poor tourism Tourism strategies designed to alleviate poverty, *p. 23*.

Protectionism The opposite to trade liberalisation – the imposition of tariffs or quotas to stop imports, *p. 257*.

Psychographic analysis A way of categorising tourists according to their attitudes, values, behaviour and beliefs, *p. 190*.

Public or collective good A public good is one that everyone feels the benefits of and from which no one can practically be excluded and is non-rival in consumption. Collective goods have similar qualities but exclusion is possible, e.g. television broadcasts started as collective goods but have largely moved into the private sector domain – this movement does not detract from the 'collective' qualities they possess and there is no suggestion that the private market achieves an efficient allocation, *p. 317*.

Public relations Non-personal communication that changes opinion or achieves coverage in a mass medium and that is not paid for by the source, *p. 598*.

Q

Quality assurance The system which assures the end customers receive a level of service with which they will be satisfied, *p. 527*.

Quality control The checks against standards set to ensure the organisation achieves its quality objectives, *p. 527*.

R

Regional disparities The differences between regions with respect to specified variables such as income, employment etc., *p. 441*.

Reintermediation A term used where traditional intermediaries in a transaction are redefined and re-employed in the distribution system, *p. 379*.

Repatriated income That income sent home (out of the economy) by foreign workers or companies, *p. 148*.

Resource allocation The way in which resources are allocated across different uses in an economy, *p. 151*.

Retention Retention of a customer is the ability to keep a customer over a period of time (by metric of at least a year) in order to maintain the company's customer base, *p. 519*.

Revenue management A term used to describe the manipulation of different market segments by suppliers so as to maximise sales in order to minimise unsold product at any one time, *p. 329*.

S

Sales promotion Involves any activity that offers an incentive to induce a desired result from potential customers, trade intermediaries or the sales force, *p. 597*.

Same-day visitor A person on a brief recreational trip, not exceeding 24 hours at the destination, *p. 12*.

Scheduled services Transport systems that operate according to strict conditions relating to frequency and scheduling, *p. 423*.

Seasonality The temporal fluctuations of tourism on a daily, weekly, monthly or annual basis, *p. 114*.

Sectoral linkages Refer to the transactions (sales and purchases) that take place between companies in a single economy, *p. 142*.

Segment A sub-market of consumers who have been chosen as a target group and are marketed to in a different way from other sub-groups, *p. 508*.

Segmentation The process of identifying the most appropriate sub-markets for the company's or destination's offer, *p. 513*.

Service industries Companies that produce output in the form of services rather than goods, *p. 187*.

Service product The formulation of an activity or benefit which is essentially intangible in nature and does not lead to the ownership of anything, *p. 520*.

Sex tourism Defines the specific motivation of tourists to go on holiday for the purpose of engaging in short-term sexual relations, *p. 199*.

Simultaneity of production Where the production of a service and its consumption occur at the same instant, *p. 254*.

SMEs Small and medium-sized enterprises. (Medium – no more than 250 employees; small – no more than 50 employees; and micro – no more than 10 employees.) Turnover or balance sheet restrictions also apply, *p. 175*.

Social cohesion The way in which society can work together as opposed to social divisions normally associated with gaps between the rich and the poor, *p. 441*.

Social net benefits The result of deducting social costs from social benefits. Adding the term social to benefits and costs means including a broader range of factors than purely financial ones, *p. 315*.

Socialism A system of social organisation whereby the state government takes responsibility for resource allocation, production and distribution, *p. 247*.

Socio-economic groups Categorising people into groups by resorting to demographics (age, sex, occupation etc.), *p. 192*.

Sponsorship Sponsorship is the material or financial support of a specific activity, normally but not exclusively sport, education or the arts, which does not form part of the sponsor organisation's normal business, *p. 600*.

Stagnation A time period in which there is either little or no economic growth, *p. 129*.

Stakeholders The groups of businesses, residents, governments and tourists who have a stake in the development of tourism, *p. 214*.

STEP analysis An analysis of the environment based upon factors of society, technology, economics and politics, *p. 104*.

Strategic planning A planning approach to ensure a fit between the environment, the competencies and resources of the organisation and its changing marketing opportunities, *p. 549*.

Structural adjustment Policy of increasing privatisation and trade liberalisation intended to help countries generate greater wealth and reduce poverty. Has been criticised for inducing economic decline and endangering the welfare of the economically vulnerable, *p. 439*.

Subsidiarity The assignment of political power to the smallest units of government, *p. 442*.

Supply constraints When one sector reaches or comes close to full productive capacity it will not be able to respond fully to a further increase in demand for its output, *p. 145*.

Sustainable development Development that meets the needs of the people today without compromising the ability of future generations to meet their own needs, *p. 215*.

Sustainable tourism development As sustainable development but relating specifically to the tourism industry, *p. 218*.

T

Target market A set of buyers selected as sharing similar needs or characteristics so that a company can organise a marketing mix to serve them, *p. 578*.

Tariff structure The nature of the tariffs associated with imports, *p. 263*.

Tied agency One who can deal only with the product or service of a single company, *p. 396*.

Tiger economies The term within this book is used to refer to the East Asian economies and includes Indonesia, Hong Kong, Malaysia, Singapore, South Korea, Taiwan and Thailand. The term 'tiger' relates to the aggressive policies of the countries towards achieving rapid growth, *p. 131*.

Total quality management An organisation-wide process and system of ensuring that all activities carried out adhere to pre-agreed quality standards, *p. 526*.

Total tourist experience The combined stages of pre-planning, the purchase, the journey, the visit and perhaps stay, the return journey and overall reflection on the activity, *p. 515*.

Tourism satellite accounts A set of accounts to show the total value to an economy of domestic and international tourism, *p. 129*.

Tourism system Leiper's (1979) description of a three-part system of tourist-generating region, transit region and tourism destination region set within social, economic and environmental contexts, *p. 7*.

Tourist satisfaction The rating that tourists give to their experience while on holiday, *p. 222*.

Tourist tax Taxes specifically levied on tourists generally through businesses that deal with tourists. Can be entry taxes, hotel taxes or other specific tourism industry-based tax, *p. 457*.

Trade deficit Occurs where a country's expenditures on imports of goods and services are greater (in value terms) than the receipts from the export of goods and services, *p. 134*.

Train à Grande Vitesse TGV (literally, *high-speed train*) holds the highest speed record for a train on any national railroad, *p. 410*.

Travel propensity The penetration of travel activity within a given population, *p. 34*.

Typologies Classifications, *p. 188*.

V

Value added The amount of monetary value added to a good or service by a company before it is offered for sale, *p. 136*.

Vertical integration When the same business owns establishments that are operating at more than one stage of the production, selling and delivery process, *p. 304*.

VFR Visiting friends and relatives (tourist motivation), *p. 15*.

W

'Wonder' attractions Attractions based upon some unique natural or artificial feature, *p. 322*.

Y

Yield management Management system that optimises the yield (returns) from a project, *p. 329*.

Z

Zone of tolerance A customer will tolerate a range of standards in an area between desired and adequate rather than have one set standard of assessment, *p. 535*.

INDEX